P9-EEE-988

DATE DUE

			PRINTED IN U.S.A.

FOR REFERENCE

Do Not Take From This Room

Literature Criticism from 1400 to 1800

Guide to Gale Literary Criticism Series

For criticism on	Consult these Gale series
Authors now living or who died after December 31, 1959	*CONTEMPORARY LITERARY CRITICISM (CLC)*
Authors who died between 1900 and 1959	*TWENTIETH-CENTURY LITERARY CRITICISM (TCLC)*
Authors who died between 1800 and 1899	*NINETEENTH-CENTURY LITERATURE CRITICISM (NCLC)*
Authors who died between 1400 and 1799	*LITERATURE CRITICISM FROM 1400 TO 1800 (LC)* *SHAKESPEAREAN CRITICISM (SC)*
Authors who died before 1400	*CLASSICAL AND MEDIEVAL LITERATURE CRITICISM (CMLC)*
Authors of books for children and young adults	*CHILDREN'S LITERATURE REVIEW (CLR)*
Dramatists	*DRAMA CRITICISM (DC)*
Poets	*POETRY CRITICISM (PC)*
Short story writers	*SHORT STORY CRITICISM (SSC)*
Black writers of the past two hundred years	*BLACK LITERATURE CRITICISM (BLC)*
Hispanic writers of the late nineteenth and twentieth centuries	*HISPANIC LITERATURE CRITICISM (HLC)*
Native North American writers and orators of the eighteenth, nineteenth, and twentieth centuries	*NATIVE NORTH AMERICAN LITERATURE (NNAL)*
Major authors from the Renaissance to the present	*WORLD LITERATURE CRITICISM, 1500 TO THE PRESENT (WLC)*

ISSN 0740-2880

Volume 53

Literature Criticism from 1400 to 1800

Critical Discussion of the Works of Fifteenth-, Sixteenth-, Seventeenth-, and Eighteenth-Century Novelists, Poets, Playwrights, Philosophers, and Other Creative Writers

Lawrence J. Trudeau
Marie Lazzari
Editors

GALE GROUP

Detroit
New York
San Francisco
London
Boston
Woodbridge, CT

Riverside Community College
Library
4800 Magnolia Avenue
Riverside, CA 92506

REFERENCE
PN86 .L56
Literature criticism from
1400 to 1800 : excerpts fro
criticism of the works of
fifteenth, sixteenth,
seventeenth, and eigh

STAFF

Marie Lazzari, Lawrence J. Trudeau, *Editors*

Lynn Spampinato, *Managing Editor*

Maria Franklin, *Permissions Manager*
Kimberly F. Smilay, *Permissions Specialist*
Kelly A. Quin, *Permissions Associate*
Sandra K. Gore, *Permissions Assistant*

Victoria B. Cariappa, *Research Manager*
Patricia T. Ballard, Tamara C. Nott, Tracie A. Richardson,
Corrine Stocker, Cheryl L. Warnock, *Research Associates*

Gary Leach, *Graphic Artist*
Randy Bassett, *Image Database Supervisor*
Mike Logusz, Robert Duncan, *Imaging Specialists*
Pamela A. Reed, *Imaging Coordinator*

This book is printed on acid-free paper that meets the minimum requirements of American National Standard for Information Sciences—Permanence Paper for Printed Library Materials, ANSI Z39.48-1984.

Library of Congress Catalog Card Number 94-29718

Since this page cannot legibly accommodate all copyright notices, the acknowledgments constitute an extension of the copyright notice.

While every effort has been made to secure permission to reprint material and to ensure the reliability of the information presented in this publication, The Gale Group neither guarantees the accuracy of the data contained herein nor assumes any responsibility for errors, omissions or discrepancies. Gale accepts no payment for listing; and inclusion in the publication of any organization, agency, institution, publication, service, or individual does not imply endorsement of the editors or publisher. Errors brought to the attention of the publisher and verified to the satisfaction of the publisher will be corrected in future editions.

This publication is a creative work fully protected by all applicable copyright laws, as well as by misappropriation, trade secret, unfair competition, and other applicable laws. The authors and editors of this work have added value to the underlying factual material herein through one or more of the following: unique and original selection, coordination, expression, arrangement, and classification of the information.

All rights to this publication will be vigorously defended.

Copyright © 2000 Gale Group, Inc.
27500 Drake Rd.
Farmington Hills, MI 48331-3535

Gale Group and Design is a trademark used herein under license.

ISBN 0-7876-3268-6
ISSN 0740-2880
Printed in the United States of America

10 9 8 7 6 5 4 3 2 1

Riverside Community College
Library
4800 Magnolia Avenue
Riverside, CA 92506

Contents

Preface vii

Acknowledgments xi

Special Volume Devoted to

Isaac Newton
1642-1727

Preface

*L*iterature Criticism from 1400 to 1800 (LC) presents critical discussion of world literature from the fifteenth through the eighteenth centuries. The literature of this period is especially vital: the years 1400 to 1800 saw the rise of modern European drama, the birth of the novel and personal essay forms, the emergence of newspapers and periodicals, and major achievements in poetry and philosophy. *LC* provides valuable insight into the art, life, thought, and cultural transformations that took place during these centuries.

Scope of the Series

LC provides an introduction to the great poets, dramatists, novelists, essayists, and philosophers of the fifteenth through eighteenth centuries, and to the most significant interpretations of these authors' works. Because criticism of this literature spans nearly six hundred years, an overwhelming amount of scholarship confronts the student. *LC* organizes this material concisely and logically. Every attempt is made to reprint the most noteworthy, relevant, and educationally valuable essays available.

A separate Gale reference series, *Shakespearean Criticism,* is devoted exclusively to Shakespearean studies. Although properly belonging to the period covered in *LC,* William Shakespeare has inspired such a tremendous and ever-growing body of secondary material that a separate series was deemed essential.

Each entry in *LC* presents a representative selection of critical response to an author, a literary topic, or to a single important work of literature. Early commentary is offered to indicate initial responses, later selections document changes in literary reputations, and retrospective analyses provide the reader with modern views. The size of each author entry is a relative reflection of the scope of criticism available in English. Every attempt has been made to identify and include the seminal essays on each author's work and to include recent commentary providing modern perspectives.

Volumes 1 through 12 of the series feature author entries arranged alphabetically by author. Volumes 13 through 47 of the series feature a thematic arrangement. Each volume includes an entry devoted to the general study of a specific literary or philosophical movement, writings surrounding important political and historical events, the philosophy and art associated with eras of cultural transformation, or the literature of specific social or ethnic groups. Each of these volumes also includes several author entries devoted to major representatives of the featured period, genre, or national literature. With Volume 48, the series returns to a standard author approach, with occasional entries devoted to a single important work of world literature. One volume annually is devoted wholly to literary topics.

Organization of the Book

Each entry consists of a heading, an introduction, a list of principal works, annotated works of criticism, each preceded by a bibliographical citation, and a bibliography of recommended further reading. Many of the entries include illustrations.

- The **Author Heading** consists of the most commonly used form of the author's name, followed by birth and death dates. Also located here are any name variations under which an author wrote, including transliterated forms for authors whose native languages use nonroman alphabets. Uncertain birth or death dates are indicated by question marks. Topic entries are preceded by a **Thematic Heading,** which simply states the subject of the entry. Single-work entries are preceded by the title of the work and its date of publication.

- The **Introduction** contains background information that concisely introduces the reader to the author, work, or topic that is the subject of the entry.

- The list of **Principal Works** is ordered chronologically by date of first publication. The genre and publication date of each work is given. In the case of foreign authors whose works have been translated into English, the title and date (if available) of the first English-language edition is given in brackets following the original title. Unless otherwise indicated, dramas are dated by first performance, not first publication. Lists of **Representative Works** by different authors appear with topic entries.

- Reprinted **Criticism** is arranged chronologically in each entry to provide a useful perspective on changes in critical evaluation over time. The critic's name and the date of composition or publication of the critical work are given at the beginning of each piece of criticism. Unsigned criticism is preceded by the title of the source in which it appeared. All titles by the author featured in the text are printed in boldface type. Footnotes are reprinted at the end of each essay or excerpt. In the case of excerpted criticism, only those footnotes that pertain to the excerpted text are included. Criticism in topic entries is arranged chronologically under a variety of subheadings to facilitate the study of different aspects of the topic.

- Critical essays are prefaced by brief **Annotations** explicating each piece.

- A complete **Bibliographical Citation** of the original essay or book precedes each piece of criticism.

- An annotated bibliography of **Further Reading** appears at the end of each entry and suggests resources for additional study. In some cases, significant essays for which the editors could not obtain reprint rights are included here.

Cumulative Indexes

Each volume of *LC* includes a series-specific cumulative **Nationality Index** in which author names are arranged alphabetically by nationality. The volume or volumes of *LC* in which each author appears are also listed.

Each volume of *LC* includes a cumulative **Author Index** listing all of the authors that appear in a wide variety of reference sources published by The Gale Group, including *LC*. A complete list of these sources is found facing the first page of the Author Index. The index also includes birth and death dates and cross references between pseudonyms and actual names.

LC includes a cumulative **Topic Index** that lists the literary themes and topics treated in the series as well as in *Nineteenth-Century Literature Criticism*, *Twentieth-Century Literary Criticism*, and the *Contemporary Literature Criticism* Yearbook.

Each volume of *LC* also includes a cumulative **Title Index,** an alphabetical listing of all the literary works discussed in the series. Each title listing includes the corresponding volume and page numbers where criticism may be located. Foreign-language titles that have been translated into English followed by the tiles of the translation—for example, *El ingenioso hidalgo Don Quixote de la Mancha (Don Quixote)*. Page numbers following these translated titles refer to all pages on which any form of the titles, either foreign-language or translated, appear. Titles of novels, dramas, nonfiction books, and poetry, short story, or essay collections are printed in italics, while individual poems, short stories, and essays are printed in roman type within quotation marks.

A Note to the Reader

When writing papers, students who quote directly from any volume in the Literary Criticism Series may use the following general format to footnote reprinted criticism. The first example pertains to material drawn from periodicals, the second to material reprinted from books.

Eileen Reeves, "Daniel 5 and the *Assayer*: Galileo Reads the Handwriting on the Wall," *The Journal of Medieval and Renaissance Studies,* Vol. 21, No. 1, Spring, 1991, pp. 1-27; reprinted in *Literature Criticism from 1400 to 1800,* Vol. 45, ed. Jelena O. Krstović and Marie Lazzari, Farmington Hills, Mich.: The Gale Group, 1999, pp. 297-310.

Margaret Anne Doody, *A Natural Passion: A Study of the Novels of Samuel Richardson*, Oxford University Press, 1974, pp. 17-22, 132-35, excerpted and reprinted in *Literature Criticism from 1400 to 1800,* Vol. 46, ed. Jelena O. Krstović and Marie Lazzari. Farmington Hills, Mich.: The Gale Group, 1999, pp. 20-2.

Suggestions Are Welcome

Readers who wish to suggest new features, topics, or authors to appear in future volumes, or who have other suggestions or comments are cordially invited to call, write, or fax the editor:

Editor, *Literature Criticism from 1400 to 1800*
The Gale Group
27500 Drake Road
Farmington Hills, MI 48133-3535
1-800-347-4253
fax: 248-699-8049

Acknowledgments

The editors wish to thank the copyright holders of the excerpted criticism included in this volume and the permissions managers of many book and magazine publishing companies for assisting us in securing reproduction rights. We are also grateful to the staffs of the Detroit Public Library, the Library of Congress, the University of Detroit Mercy Library, Wayne State University Purdy/Kresge Library Complex, and the University of Michigan Libraries for making their resources available to us. Following is a list of the copyright holders who have granted us permission to reproduce material in this volume of LC. Every effort has been made to trace copyright, but if omissions have been made, please let us know.

COPYRIGHTED MATERIAL IN *LC*, VOLUME 53, WERE REPRODUCED FROM THE FOLLOWING PERIODICALS:

Annals of Science, v. 22, December, 1966. Reproduced by permission of the publisher, Taylor & Francis, Ltd., http://www.tandf.co.uk/journals/asc.htm.—*CLIO,* v. 13, Summer, 1984 for "Hegel's Criticism of Newton" by M. J. Petry. © 1984 by Robert H. Canary and Henry Kozicki. Reproduced by permission of the author.—*Isis,* v. 51, June, 1960 for "Newton's Theory of Matter" by Rupert Hall and Marie Boas Hall. Copyright 1960, renewed 1988 by History of Science Society, Inc. Reproduced by permission of the authors.—*Journal of the History of Ideas,* v. XXXI, 1970; v. XLV, January-March, 1984. Copyright 1970, 1984, Journal of the History of Ideas, Inc. Both reproduced by permission of the Johns Hopkins University Press./ v. XII, January, 1951. Copyright 1951, renewed 1979, Journal of the History of Ideas, Inc. Reproduced by permission of the Johns Hopkins University Press.—*Manchester Guardian,* for "Isaac Newton" by Albert Einstein. Copyright © by Guardian Publications Ltd. Reproduced by permission of Guardian News Service, LTD.—*Notes and Records of the Royal Society of London,* v. 21, December, 1966 for "Newton and the 'Pipes of Pan'" by J. E. McGuire and P. M. Rattansi. Reproduced by permission of the publisher and the authors.—*Restoration: Studies in English Literary Culture, 1660-1700,* v. 13, Spring, 1989 for "Isaac Newton's Theological Writings: Problems and Prospects" by Robert Markley. Reproduced by permission of the publisher and the author.—*Studies in Eighteenth-Century Culture,* v. 10, 1981. Copyright © 1981 American Society for Eighteenth-Century Studies. All rights reserved. Reproduced by permission of The Johns Hopkins University Press.—*The Texas Quarterly,* v. X, Autumn, 1967. © 1967 by The University of Texas at Austin. Reproduced by permission.—*University of Toronto Quarterly,* v. 57, Summer, 1988. (c) University of Toronto Press 1988. Reproduced by permission of University of Toronto Press Incorporated.

COPYRIGHTED MATERIAL IN *LC,* VOLUME 53, WERE REPRODUCED FROM THE FOLLOWING BOOKS:

Cohen, I. Bernard. From a preface to *Opticks, or, a Treatise of the Reflections, Refractions, Inflections, and Colours of Light.* By Isaac Newton. Dover Publications, 1952. Copyright 1952, renewed 1980, by Dover Publications, Inc. Reproduced by permission.—Cohen, I. Bernard. From *Editing Texts in the History of Science and Medicine: Papers Given at the Seventeenth Annual Conference on Editorial Problems.* Garland Publishing, Inc., 1982. Reproduced by permission.—Cohen, I. Bernard. From *The Newtonian Revolution.* Cambridge University Press, 1980. © Cambridge University Press, 1980. Reproduced with the permission of Cambridge University Press and the author.—Dobbs, Betty Jo Teeter, and Margaret C. Jacob. From *Newton and the Culture of Newtonianism.* Humanities Press, 1995. Copyright © 1995 by Betty Jo Teeter Dobbs and Margaret C. Jacob. All rights reserved. Reproduced by permission.—Dobbs, Betty Jo Teeter. From *The Janus Faces of Genius: The Role of Alchemy in Newton's Thought.* Cambridge University Press, 1991. © Cambridge University Press 1991. Reproduced with the permission of Cambridge University Press and the Literary Estate of Betty Jo Teeter Dobbs.—Downs, Robert B. From *Books That Changed the World. Second Edition.* American Library Association, 1978. Reproduced by permission.—Ellis, Brian. From "The Origin and Nature of Newton's Laws of Motion" in *Beyond the Edge of Certainty: Essays in Contemporary Science and Philosophy.* Edited by Robert G. Colodny. Prentice Hall, 1965. © 1965 by Prentice-Hall, Inc. All rights reserved. Reproduced by permission of the author.—Force, James E. From "Newton's God of Dominion: The Unity of Newton's Theological Scientific, and Political Thought" in *Essays on the Context, Nature, and Influence of Isaac Newton's Theology.* By James E. Force and Richard H. Popkin. Kluwer Academic Publishers, 1990. © 1990 by Kluwer Academic Publishers. All Rights Reserved. Reproduced by permission with kind permission from Kluwer Academic Publishers.—Guerlac, Hugh. From *Newton on the*

Continent. Cornell University Press, 1981. © 1979 by Henry Guerlac, copyright© 1981 by Cornell University Press. All rights reserved. Used by permission of Cornell University Press.—Kuhn, Thomas S. From ***Newton's Papers & Letters on Natural Philosophy and Related Documents.*** Second Edition. Cambridge Mass.: Harvard University Press, 1978. © Copyright 1957, 1978 by the President and Fellows of Harvard College. Renewed 1985 by Thomas S. Kuhn. All rights reserved. Reproduced by permission Harvard University Press.—McGuire, J. E. From "Predicates of Pure Existence: Newton on God's Space and Time" in ***Philosophical Perspectives on Newtonian Science.*** Edited by Phillip Bricker and R. I. G. Hugues. MIT Press, 1990. © 1990 Massachusetts Institute of Technology. All rights reserved. Reproduced by permission of The MIT Press, Cambridge, MA.—Popkin, Richard H. From "Divine Causality: Newton, the Newtonians, and Hume" in ***Greene Centennial Studies: Essays Presented to Donald Greene in the Centennial Year of the University of Southern California.*** Edited by Paul J. Korshin and Robert R. Allen. University Press of Virginia, 1984. Copyright© 1984 by the Rector and Visitors of the University of Virginia. Reproduced by permission.—Popkin, Richard H. From "Newton as Bible Scholar" in ***Essays on the Context, Nature, and Influence of Isaac Newton's Theology.*** By James E. Force and Richard H. Popkin. Kluwer Academic Publishers, 1990. © 1990 by Kluwer Academic Publishers. All Rights Reserved. Reproduced by permission with kind permission from Kluwer Academic Publishers.—Rattansi, P. M. From "Newton's Alchemical Studies" in ***Science, Medicine, and Society in the Renaissance.*** Edited by Allen G. Debus. Science History Publications, 1972. © Science History Publications 1972. Reproduced by permission.—Rattansi, P. M. From "Voltaire and the Enlightenment Image of Newton" in ***History & Imagination: Essays in Honor of H. R. Trevor-Roper.*** Hugh Lloyd-Jones, Valerie Pearl, Blair Worden, eds. Holmes and Meier Publishers, 1981. Copyright© 1981 by Holmes and Meier Publishers. All rights reserved. Reproduced by permission.—Sepper, Dennis L. From "Goethe Against Newton: Towards Saving the Phenomenon" in ***Goethe and the Sciences: A Reappraisal.*** Frederick Amrine, Francis J. Zucker, Harvey Wheeler, eds. D. Reidel Publishing Company, 1987.© 1987 by D. Reidel Publishing Company. Reproduced by permission with kind permission from Kluwer Academic Publishers.—Winterbourne, A. T. From ***Archiv fur Geschichte de Philosophie.*** Walter de Gruyter, 1985. Reproduced by permission.

PHOTOGRAPHS AND ILLUSTRATIONS APPEARING IN *LC*, VOLUME 53, WERE RECEIVED FROM THE FOLLOWING SOURCES:

Sir Isaac Newton, engraving. Archive Photos, Inc. Reproduced by permission.—Newton's First Telescope and Death Mask, photograph. CORBIS/Jim Sugar Photography. Reproduced by permission.—Page from Isaac Newton's *The Method of Fluxions.* The Library of Congress.—Diagrams from Sir Isaac Newton's *Optics.* CORBIS/Archivo Iconografico, S. A. Reproduced by permission.—Title Page of Isaac Newton's *Philosopiae Naturalis Principia Mathematica.* CORBIS/Bettmann. Reproduced by permission.

Isaac Newton
1642-1727

English physicist and mathematician. For additional information on the life and works of Isaac Newton, see *Literature Criticism 1400 to 1800*, Volume 35.

INTRODUCTION

Inspired by the work of Galileo Galilei, Johannes Kepler, and Nicolaus Copernicus, among others, Newton developed experimental methods and theories in the areas of physics, optics, and mathematics. He is credited with determining the binomial theory and developing differential and integral calculus; his *Opticks* (1704) is the result of his exhaustive experimentation in light and color, work that led to his devising the reflecting telescope. Arguably Newton's most influential publication, *Philosophiae Naturalis Principia Mathematica* (or *Principia,* 1687), explains the movement of the planets through the establishment of three laws of motion and a theory of universal gravitation. Newton's work was influenced by theological as well as scientific principles, and he extensively wrote on theological issues and alchemy. While Newton viewed the universe as guided by mechanical, rational laws, he understood the first cause of such universal machinations to be God. His interest in nonscientific inquiry was long downplayed by critics, but many modern scholars have sought to understand the place and significance of such studies within the larger context of Newton's life and work.

Biographical Information

Newton was born in 1642 at Woolsthorpe, Lincolnshire, England, shortly after his father's death. He was educated at local schools before entering Trinity College, Cambridge, in 1661; he graduated in 1665. When the university subsequently closed for two years as a result of the plague, Newton returned home to Woolsthorpe and embarked upon a period of intense study and experimentation in the areas of astronomy, calculus, optics, and mechanics. In 1667 Newton returned to Cambridge to complete a master of arts degree. After Isaac Barrow, Lucasian chair in mathematics, championed Newton's privately circulated papers, Newton was appointed mathematics professor in 1669. In 1696 Newton was appointed master of the mint, and he left Cambridge for London. In his later years Newton spent his time writing on alchemy and theology. Although by this time he had ceased most of his scientific experimentation, he was regarded as the dean of English

science and was elected President of the Royal Society in 1703. Newton was knighted in 1705 and died in 1727.

Major Works

Newton's first published paper, "Of Colours" (1672), was based on a series of lectures he gave during his first three years of teaching. The treatise, which eventually became Book One of *Opticks,* explained Newton's theories on light and color. Book Two of *Opticks* was issued along with "Hypothesis Explaining the Properties of Light" (1675), a controversial essay outlining a new system of nature. The final section of the *Opticks* contains a series of "Queries" concerning light and color as well as other topics. A completed edition of *Opticks* was published in English in 1704; it wouldbecome the most widely read of Newton's books during his lifetime. While Newton's *Principia* was published in 1687, it contained theories Newton had worked through twenty years earlier, during the period he had retreated to

Woolsthorpe to avoid the plague. These theories concern the nature of motion and the orbit of the planets, as well as a revolutionary theory of universal gravitation. Astronomer Edmond Halley encouraged the development of Newton's theories and their corresponding calculations; Halley also served as the financial patron for the publication of *Principia*. The work was published in Latin, and Newton added a "General Scholium" to later editions in which he defended his methodologies. In terms of quantity of words, Newton's materials on theology and alchemy far surpass his writings on science; however, many of the notebooks on nonscientific matters contain passages Newton transcribed from other works he was studying. Of particular interest to Newton was the correct interpretation of Biblical prophecies, not to predict the future, but to identify divine activity in the world. His primary theological writings include the posthumously published *Chronology of Ancient Kingdoms Amended* (1728) and *Observations upon the Prophesies of Daniel and the Apocalypse of St. John* (1733).

Critical Reception

The contemporary reception of Newton's work was mixed. While his first published paper on light was generally well-received, a few scientists responded with skepticism, questioning his departure from the standard scientific method of establishing a hypothesis or exploring alternative theories. The *Principia* was slow to find acceptance, and Continental scholars were generally cooler in their responses than their English and Scottish counterparts. While early critics focused narrowly on Newton's scientific works, modern commentators have also examined his nonscientific writings, in an attempt to provide a fuller picture of Newton and his beliefs. I. Bernard Cohen has shown that manuscripts and other materials that became available only after Newton's death have made a much fuller analysis of Newton possible. He has argued that such documents reveal the significance of Newton's interest in theology and alchemy; the influence of René Descartes' thought on Newton's development; and the progression of Newton's views on the nature and significance of aether. Critics such as Christopher Hill, Betty Jo Teeter Dobbs, and Margaret C. Jacob have examined how personal and social issues influenced the development of Newton's work. Hill has suggested that Newton's Puritan upbringing, as well as his having lived in a post-revolutionary society (Newton was born the year in which the English civil war broke out), were both significant factors in the shaping of his thought. Dobbs and Jacob have maintained that an understanding and appreciation of Newton's efforts to "construct a unified system of God and nature," helps to explain his interest in alchemy and theology.

This developing picture, derived from readings of both his scientific and nonscientific work, offers a more complete understanding of Newton and his view of the world. Nevertheless, it is his achievements in the areas of physics and mathematics that have most greatly influenced later thought, affecting virtually all areas of Western culture. While some of Newton's principles have been supplanted by the theory of relativity and other advances in twentieth-century science, scholars agree that Newton's coherent and comprehensive description of the workings of the universe formed the necessary starting point for these modern developments, indeed, made such developments possible.

PRINCIPAL WORKS

Philosophiae Naturalis Principia Mathematica [*Mathematical Principles of Natural Philosophy*] (essay) 1687

Opticks: or, a Treatise of the Reflexions, Refractions, Inflexions and Colours of Light. Also Two Treatises of the species and Magnitude of curvilinear Figures (essays) 1704

Arithmetica Universalis [*Universal Arithmetic*] (essay) 1707

The Chronology of Ancient Kingdoms Amended (essay) 1728

Observations upon the Prophesies of Daniel and the Apocalypse of St. John (essay) 1733

The Correspondence of Isaac Newton. 7 vols. (letters) 1957-76

Isaac Newton's Papers and Letters on Natural Philosophy [Edited by I. Bernard Cohen] (essays and letters) 1958

Unpublished Scientific Papers of Isaac Newton (essays) 1962

The Mathematical Papers of Isaac Newton. 8 vols. (essays) 1984

The Optical Papers of Isaac Newton (essays) 1984

CRITICISM

Christopher Hill (essay date 1967)

SOURCE: "Newton and His Society," in *The Annus Mirabilis of Sir Isaac Newton, 1666-1966,* edited by Robert Palter, The M.I.T. Press, 1970, pp. 26-47.

[*In the following essay, Hill reviews the social and personal influences on Newton's life and work, suggesting that the most potent influences were Newton's Puritan upbringing and the post-revolutionary society in which he lived.*]

I

One way for me to approach the subject of Newton and his society would be to quote Professor Alexandre Koyré: "The social structure of England in the 17th century cannot explain Newton."[1] Then I could sit down. But of course we must gloss Koyré by emphasizing the word "explain." A complete explanation of Newton cannot be given in social terms. The historian, however, *qua* historian, is not interested in single causal explanations. The questions he asks are "Why here?", "Why now?" If science were a self-evolving chain of intellectual development, then it would be irrelevant that it was Newton, living in post-revolutionary England, who won international fame by following up Galileo, a persecuted Italian, and Descartes, a Frenchman living in exile in the Dutch republic. But for the historian the where, when, and why questions are vital. It is no more possible to treat the history of science as something uncontaminated by the world in which the scientists lived than it is to write the history of, say, philosophy or literature or the English constitution in isolation from the societies which gave birth to them.[2]

Often the important thing for scientific advance is asking new questions, approaching a given body of material from a fresh angle.[3] All the factors which precede and make possible such a breakthrough are therefore relevant. The real problem often is not How do men come to look at familiar facts in a fresh way? but How do they liberate themselves from looking at them in the old way? And here the history of the society in which the scientist lived, as well as the facts of his personal biography, may frequently be suggestive, if rarely conclusive. Newton shared much of the outlook of his scientific contemporaries, their limitations as well as their strengths. But I want to suggest that his Puritan upbringing, combined with the posttrevolutionary environment of Cambridge, and possibly certain psychological factors which are both personal and social, may have helped him to ask fresh questions and so to break through to his new synthesis.

II

Newton was born in 1642, the year in which the English civil war broke out. The first twenty-four years of his life saw a great revolution, culminating in the execution of Charles I and the proclamation of a republic. They saw the abolition of episcopacy, the execution of the Archbishop of Canterbury, and fifteen years of greater religious and political liberty than were to be seen again in England until the nineteenth century. The censorship broke down, church courts ceased to persecute. Hitherto proscribed sects preached and proselytized in public, and religious speculation ran riot, culminating in the democratic theories of the Levellers, the communism of Gerrard Winstanley and the Diggers, the scientific materialism of Hobbes and the economic determinism of Harrington. Books and pamphlets were published on a scale hitherto unprecedented on all subjects, including science, mathematics, and medicine; for the natural sciences, too, benefited from Parliament's victory. Oldenburg rightly said in 1659 that science got more encouragement in England than in France.[4] Bacon was popular among the Parliamentarians, and from 1640 onwards began that climb to fame which soon caused him to be hailed as "the dictator of philosophy"—an ascent which the Royal Society materially assisted.

The first two decades of Newton's life, then, saw a political revolution which was also a religious and intellectual revolution, the climax in England of a transformation in ways of thought which had been proceeding for a century and a half, and of which Renaissance, Reformation and the scientific revolution were all part. Protestantism, by its hostility to magic and ceremonial, its emphasis on experience against authority, on simplicity in theology, helped to prepare an intellectual climate receptive to science—not least in the covenant theology, so popular in Newton's Cambridge, with its rejection of arbitrary interference with law, its insistence that God normally works through second causes, not by miracles.[5] In England transubstantiation was publicly ridiculed from the pulpit; in Roman Catholic Europe the miracle of the mass was believed to be a daily event, to be treated with awe and reverence. In the sixteen sixties Sprat was arguing, in defence of the Royal Society, that it was only doing for philosophy what the Reformation had done for religion. Samuel Butler, an enemy of the Society, was arguing at the same time that Protestantism led to atheism.[6] Both saw connections between protestant and scientific revolutions.

But the years immediately before 1666 had seen a reaction. In 1660 Charles II, the House of Lords, and the bishops came back to England. An ecclesiastical censorship was restored. Oxford and Cambridge were purged again. The scientists regrouped in London around Gresham College, and succeeded in winning the patronage of Charles II. But it was not all plain sailing. In the early years of its existence the Royal Society had continually to defend itself against the accusation that science led to atheism and social subversion—the latter charge made plausible by the Parliamentarian past of the leading scientists. "The Act of Indemnity and Oblivion," the renegade Henry Stubbe sourly reminded his readers in 1670, had been "necessary to many of the Royal Society."[7] Next year Stubbe denounced Bacon's philosophy as the root cause of "contempt of the ancient ecclesiastical and civil jurisdiction and the old government, as well as the governors of the realm."[8] The fact that John Wilkins, the Society's secretary, conformed to the episcopal church in 1660 seemed less important to contemporaries than that he had been Oliver Cromwell's brother-in-law and that he had been intruded by the Parliamentary Commissioners as Warden of Wadham, where he gathered around him the group which later formed the nucleus of the Royal Society. In 1667 his fellow Secretary, Henry Oldenburg, was arrested on suspicion of treasonable correspondence. Conservatives and turncoats in the universities and among the bishops attacked both science and the Royal Society.

III

The mechanical philosophy suffered from its very name. The word *mechanic* was ambiguous. In one sense it meant "like a machine": the mechanic philosophy was what we should call the mechanistic philosophy. In this sense Oldenburg spoke of "the mechanical or Cartesian philosophy."[9] But not all Englishmen were Cartesians, and this meaning crystallized only in the later seventeenth century. When Dudley North in 1691 said "Knowledge in great measure is become mechanical" he thought it necessary to add a definition: "built upon clear and evident truths."[10] Long before Descartes wrote Bacon had been urging Englishmen to learn from mechanics, from artisans, and to draw a philosophy from their fumbling and unco-ordinated but successful practice. "The most acute and ingenious part of men being by custom and education engaged in empty speculations, the improvement of useful arts was left to the meaner sort of people, who had weaker parts and less opportunity to do it, and were therefore branded with the disgraceful name of mechanics." But chance or well-designed experiments led them on. (I quote not from Bacon but from Thomas Sydenham, who like Sprat learnt his Baconianism at Wadham in the sixteen fifties under Wilkins.[11])

Bacon too was only summing up a pre-existent ideology which held up to admiration "expert artisans, or any sensible industrious practitioners, howsoever unlectured in schools or unlettered in books" (Gabriel Harvey, 1593). John Dee referred to himself as "this mechanician." Marlowe expressed this ideology in heightened form in *Doctor Faustus*:

> O what a world of profit and delight,
> Of power, of honor and omnipotence,
> Is promised to the studious artisan!

Here the artisan was also a magician. But then so too was Dee; so, Lord Keynes would persuade us, was Newton.[12] We recall John Wilkins' *Mathematical Magick, or the Wonders that may be performed by Mechanical Geometry* (1648). Fulke Greville spoke of "the grace and disgrace of . . . arithmetic, geometry, astronomy" as resting "in the artisans' industry or vein." We recall also Wallis' reference to mathematics in the sixteen thirties as a "mechanical" study, meaning by that "the business of traders, merchants, seamen, carpenters, surveyors of lands and the like."

This ideology was shared by many of the early Fellows of the Royal Society, and expressed most forcibly by Boyle—no magician, but anxious to learn from alchemists. Boyle insisted that scientists must "converse with practitioners in their workhouses and shops," "carry philosophic materials from the shops to the schools"; it was "childish and unworthy of a philosopher" to refuse to learn from mechanics. Professor M. B. Hall is right to stress Boyle's good fortune in having not been subjected to the sort of academic education he would have got at a university before the Parliamentarian purges.[13] Hooke too consistently took counsel with skilled craftsmen. Cowley, in his *Ode to the Royal Society,* rejoiced that Bacon had directed our study "the mechanic way," to things not words. Newton himself was a skilled craftsman, who had already constructed a water clock, sundials, and a windmill while still a boy. Later he ground his own lenses, made his own grinding and polishing machines and his own telescopes, and conducted his own alchemical experiments. As late as the eighteenth century he was issuing specific and detailed instructions to Royal Society experimenters.

Yet the word "mechanic" was not neutral. It had other overtones. It conveyed the idea of social vulgarity, and also sometimes of atheism. The Copernican theory, said an archdeacon in 1618, "may go current in a mechanical tradesman's shop," but not with scholars and Christians. During the interregnum the word came into new prominence when applied as a pejorative adjective to "mechanic preachers," those doctrinally heretical and socially subversive laymen of the lower classes who took advantage of religious toleration to air their own disturbing views. Such men appealed to their own experience, and the experiences of their auditors, to confute authority, just as the scientists appealed to experiment. ("Faithfulness to experiment is not so different a discipline from faithfulness to experience," wrote Professor Longuet-Higgins recently.[14] "This I knew experimentally," said George Fox of his spiritual experiences in 1647.[15]) There is no need to labor the importance of the mechanic preachers, nor the consternation which they caused to their betters: this has been demonstrated in Professor Tyndall's admirable *John Bunyan, Mechanick Preacher,* analyzing both the genus and its supreme exemplar, who was safely in jail from 1660 to 1672, with many of his fellows. From 1641 onwards it had been a familiar royalist sneer that Parliament's supporters were "turbulent spirits, backed by rude and tumultuous mechanic persons," who "would have the total subversion of the government of the state"; "those whom many of our nation, in a contemptuous folly, term mechanics," wrote Marchamont Nedham defensively.[16] Many of the educational reforms proposed in the revolutionary decades were aimed at benefiting this class. Thus Petty proposed "colleges of tradesmen," where able mechanicians should be subsidized while performing experiments; William Dell wanted better educational opportunities for "towns-men's children."

So there were dangerous ambiguities in the word "mechanic," of which the Royal Society was painfully aware. (If its members ever forgot, Henry Stubbe was ready to remind them by denouncing them as "pitiful Mechanicks!")[17] Sprat in his *History,* in Baconian vein, spoke of "mechanics and artificers (for whom the true natural philosophy should be primarily intended)," and defined the Society's ideal of prose style as "the language of artisans, countrymen and merchants." But—consistently with his propagandist purpose—he was careful to insist that the technological problems of industry must be approached by "men of freer lives," gentlemen, unencumbered by "dull and unavoidable employments." "If mechanics alone were to make a philosophy, they would bring it all into their shops; and force it wholly to consist of springs and wheels and weights." This was part of a campaign to make the Royal Society respectable. The atheist Hobbes and the radical Parliamentarian Samuel Hartlib were kept out. Anyone of the rank of baron or over was automatically eligible for a Fellowship. A number of courtiers and gentlemen were made Fellows, some of whom were genuinely interested in science, but many of whom were not. The Society prepared pretty tricks for Charles II, Newton had to pretend that James II could be interested in the *Principia,* and that epoch-making work was issued over the imprimatur of Samuel Pepys as president of the Royal Society—an estimable man, but hardly Newton's peer.

In the long run, this had of course deplorable consequences for science. Despite Boyle's insistence, a gentleman dilettante like Evelyn could not lower himself to "conversing with mechanical, capricious persons."[18] Even Seth Ward, intruded professor of astronomy at Oxford during the interregnum, thought that "mechanic chemistry" was an unsuitable subject for the sons of the nobility and gentry to study at universities. But in the short run it was essential to free the scientists from the "mechanic atheism" which Cudworth scented in Cartesianism,[19] and from the stigma of sedition which clung around the word "mechanical." "Plebeians and mechanics," said a Restoration bishop, "have philosophized themselves into principles of impiety, and read their lectures of atheism in the streets and highways." Glanvill in his dedication to the Royal Society of *Scepsis Scientifica* in 1664 emphasized the Society's role in "securing the foundations of religion against all attempts of mechanical atheism"; "the mechanic philosophy yields no security to irreligion."

But there was a narrow tightrope here. Boyle, the "restorer of the mechanical philosophy," was opposed to occult qualities, wanted to expel mystery from the universe as far as was compatible with the retention of God. Wren had told a London audience in 1657: "Neither need we fear to diminish a miracle by explaining it."[20] "What cannot be understood is no object of belief," Newton said. "A man may imagine things that are false, but he can only understand things that are true."[21] But there were still many who held the view denounced by Bacon "in men of a devout policy"—"an inclination to have the people depend upon God the more, when they are less acquainted with second causes; and to have no stirring in philosophy, lest it may lead to an innovation in divinity, or else should discover matter of further contradiction to divinity." Experience of the interregnum had strengthened the prejudices of those who thought like that. And there were very real intellectual problems in combining scientific atomism with Christianity—problems which Boyle, the defenders of the Royal Society and Newton himself spent their lives trying to solve. Newton once referred, revealingly, to "this notion of bodies having as it were a complete, absolute and independent reality in themselves, such as almost all of us, through negligence, are accustomed to have in our minds from childhood." This was a main reason for atheism: we do not think of matter as created or dependent on the continuous action of the divine will.[22]

Professor Westfall has plausibly suggested that the violence of the scientists' attacks on atheism may spring from the fact that "the virtuosi nourished the atheists within their own minds."[23] Given the general social anxiety of the Restoration period, how were men to frame a theory of the universe which would accommodate both God and the new science? The problem was acute, "the vulgar opinion of the unity of the world being now exploded" (the words are those of Henry Oldenburg) "and that doctrine thought absurd which teacheth the sun and all the heavenly host, which are so many times bigger than our earth, to be made only to enlighten us."[24] Mechanic philosophy, purged of the atheism and enthusiasm of the rude mechanicals, offered the best hope. Newton ultimately supplied the acceptable answer; but he was only one of many trying to find it. The question would have been asked if Newton had never lived.

IV

We do not know how far Newton was aware of the great revolution which was going on while he was growing up, but it is difficult to think that it left him untouched. His country, Lincolnshire, was a center of strong pro-Parliamentarian feeling. His mother was an Ayscough, and Edward Ayscough was M. P. for Lincolnshire in the Long Parliament, a staunch Parliamentarian. Newton's maternal uncle became rector of Burton Coggles in 1642; the stepfather whom his mother married was rector of another Lincolnshire parish.[25] Both apparently remained on good terms with the Parliamentary ecclesiastical authorities. Newton lived for many years at Grantham while attending its grammar school. Until 1655 the leading ecclesiastical figure in Grantham was its lecturer, John Angell, a noted Puritan.[26] After his death, the tone was set by two more Puritans, both ejected for nonconformity at the Restoration, both praised by Richard Baxter. Over the church porch was a library given to the town fifty years earlier by Francis Trigge, another eminent Puritan, who wrote a treatise on the Apocalypse.[27] Newton almost certainly used this library; he may even have acquired his interest in the mysteries of the Book of Revelation from it.

I emphasize these points because there used to be a mistaken impression, based on a poem which he was believed to have written, that Newton was in some sense a royalist. Even L. T. More, Newton's best biographer, repeats this error. But this poem was not Newton's; he copied it from *Eikon Basilike* for his girl friend, Miss Storey. There is no evidence that Newton sympathized with the sentiments expressed in the poem. Even if he did regard Charles I as a martyr, this would not make him a royalist in any technical sense. Most of those who fought against Charles I in the civil war deplored his execution. The Army had first to purge the Presbyterians from Parliament. Indeed the author of *Eikon Basilike* was himself a Presbyterian divine, a popular preacher before Parliament during the civil war. It was only after the Restoration that he (like Wilkins and so many other Puritans) conformed to the episcopal church and took his reward in a bishopric.

Newton's whole education, then, was in the radical Protestant tradition, and we may assume that his outlook was Puritan when he went up to Cambridge in 1661. This helps to make sense of his later beliefs and interests; he did not take to theology after a mental breakdown in the sixteen nineties. Before 1661 he was learning Hebrew. In 1664-65, if not earlier, he was keeping notebooks on theology and on the ecclesiastical calendar.[28] He later argued that bishops and presbyters should be of equal status, and that elders should be elected by the people.[29] Newton conformed indeed to the restored episcopal church—as he had to do if he wanted an academic career. But he abandoned belief in the Trinity very early in life and resisted all pressure to be ordained. He seldom attended Trinity College chapel. He had a typically Puritan dislike of oaths, shared with Boyle and Ray. In Newton's scheme for tuition at Trinity he went out of his way to insist "No oaths of office to be imposed on the lecturers. I do not know a greater abuse of religion than that sort of oaths." In later life he was alleged to be "hearty for the Baptists."[30]

If Newton went up to Cambridge with Puritan inclinations, he can hardly have been happy in his first two years. John Wilkins had just been expelled from the mastership of Newton's College, despite the wishes of the fellows. We do not know how many fellows were ejected or forced to resign; the number may be of the order of twenty.[31] They included John Ray, who resigned in 1662, perhaps not before Newton had heard him preach sermons in the college chapel which were later written up as *The Wisdom of God manifested in the Works of the Creation* and *Miscellaneous Discourses concerning the Dissolution and Changes of the World*. (Those ejected also included John Davis, Fellow, Librarian and Hebrew Lecturer, and William Disney from Newton's county of Lincolnshire.) Ray had originally preached his sermons as a layman, but after 1660 ordination was insisted on for all fellows after their first seven years.[32]

As early as 1660 Ray had deplored the lack of interest in experimental philosophy and mathematics at Cambridge,[33] and the expulsion and withdrawal of men like himself and Wilkins did not help. By 1669, when the university entertained Cosimo de' Medici with a Latin disputation, the subject was "an examination of the experimental philosophy and a condemnation of the Copernican system." Newton can hardly have found this a congenial atmosphere.

Nevertheless, the interregnum left its mark on Cambridge. Isaac Barrow, who came up to Trinity in 1647, spoke of mathematics as then "neglected and all but unknown, even on the outward surface by most." A decade earlier Wallis and Seth Ward had both left Cambridge in order to learn mathematics from William Oughtred, a country parson. "The study of mathematics," Wallis said in an oft-quoted phrase, "was at that time more cultivated in London than in the universities." Wallis did not hear of the new philosophy till years after he went down. Barrow claimed to have introduced it to Cambridge, and in the sixteen fifties there was rapid progress there, as in Oxford. By 1654 or 1655 we find Barrow congratulating his university on escaping from traditional servility to scholasticism. "You have very recently begun to cultivate the mathematical sciences"; and natural philosophy (anatomy, medicine, chemistry) had lately started to be studied seriously. Barrow was one of the strongest early influences on Newton.[34]

Above all Cambridge had become interested in the Cartesian philosophy, and was the scene of the most elaborate attempt to adapt traditional Puritan covenant theology to accommodate the findings of the new science. This was the school misleadingly known as the Cambridge Platonists, which derived from Joseph Mede, whom we shall meet again when we discuss Newton's interest in the Apocalypse. Its members included Ralph Cudworth, Puritan and Parliamentarian, who had links with Newton; like Newton, he was accused of being unsound on the Trinity. The outstanding figure among the Cambridge Platonists when Newton came up to Trinity was Henry More, old boy of Newton's school at Grantham and tutor to two of his teachers there. More—later a Fellow of the Royal Society, like Cudworth—was strongly influenced by Descartes. But in 1659 More published *The Immortality of the Soul,* in which, he said, "I have demonstrated with evidence no less than mathematical, that there are substances incorporeal."[35] He hoped to become the Galileo of a new science of the spirit world. Newton was an intimate associate of More's, became an adherent of the atomic philosophy in his undergraduate days, and was influenced by Descartes. But in the sixties More came to reject the Cartesian mechanical philosophy because it led to atheism[36]; and Newton followed suit.

V

If we try to think ourselves back into the position of men living in this postrevolutionary world, we can see that there were various intellectual possibilities.

(1) The older generation of revolutionaries, who had seen their hopes of building God's kingdom betrayed, necessarily withdrew from politics. Most of them, like George Fox and the Quakers, decided that it had been a mistake to try to build God's kingdom on earth. They turned pacifist, their religion became a religion of personal morality, not of social reform. They accepted the position of minority sects, asking only for freedom from persecution. Bunyan, writing in jail, saw his pilgrim oppressed by the burden of sin, and concerned only to get rid of it; even wife and children are secondary to that consideration. The toughest of all the revolutionaries, Milton, still wrestled with God and history to justify God's ways to men. He completed *Paradise Lost* in 1665, published it in 1667; even he looked for "a Paradise within thee, happier far."

(2) The more intellectual among the returned royalists, their high hopes equally disappointed, found consolation in a cynical and mocking materialist atheism, which was probably only skin deep. Many, like Rochester, abandoned it when they believed they were on their deathbeds. But at court, and among the court dramatists, sceptical Hobbism was fashionable, if only to *épater* the bourgeois and the Puritans. "There is nothing," wrote Samuel Butler, whose *Hudibras* was a best seller in 1662-63, "that can prevail more to persuade a man to be an atheist as to see such unreasonable beasts pretend to religion."[37] His reference was probably to mechanic preachers. Oldham in 1682 wrote:

> There are, who disavow all Providence
> And think the world is only steered by
>   chance;
> Make God at best an idle looker-on,
> A lazy monarch lolling on his throne.[38]

(3) Others among the returned royalists found that their authoritarian leanings could best be expressed by a return to Catholicism. Laudianism was dead in Resto-

ration England, despite the apparent importance of some former Laudians in 1660. The revolution had made impossible any revival of the independent economic or political power of either church or crown. Henceforth both were subject to the ruling class in Parliament. Charles II and James II had to look for support from Catholic and absolutist France—or, still more desperately, from papist Ireland. Many men of authoritarian temperament were impressed by the achievements, military and cultural, of Louis XIV's France. Some ultimately were converted to Catholicism, like the former Trinity undergraduate Dryden; others, like Archbishop Sheldon, had abandoned the traditional Anglican doctrine that the Pope was Antichrist. Such men were in a dilemma in Restoration England, since most Englishmen regarded France as the national enemy. After 1688 this dilemma could be resolved by rallying to the Protestant William and Mary. But there was a time earlier when Catholicism was both intellectually and politically attractive, to the horror of traditional Protestant patriots. It was in this intellectual climate that Nell Gwyn claimed that, if she was a whore, at least she was a Protestant whore—unlike her French rival, the Duchess of Portsmouth. Newton would have applauded the theological part of her claim.

(4) The main group of middle of the road Parliamentarians adhered to a lay, secularized Puritanism. They accepted restored episcopacy in the Church, purged of Laudianism. They had no difficulty in joining hands with moderate and patriotic ex-Cavaliers. Both were enemies of enthusiasm (remembering the mechanic preachers) and of Hobbist atheism; but they were even more opposed to the much more real danger of popery. Atheism had no respectable support; it was a fashion, a whim. It was perhaps more important as a charge to hurl at the Royal Society and the scientists than in itself; and even here Henry Stubbe thought it necessary to accuse the Society of opening the door to popery as well as to atheism.[39]

Newton was of the postrevolutionary generation, and so had not known the former enthusiasm and present guilt of the revolutionaries. His Puritan upbringing ensured that by and large he shared the outlook of my last group—Puritans with the temperature reduced.

Caution was a natural result of the shock of the Restoration. Pepys was afraid someone might remember that after Charles I's execution in 1649 he had said that the right text to preach from would be "The memory of the wicked shall rot."[40] Men like Dryden, Waller, Cudworth, Henry More, no less than scientists like Wilkins, Wallis, Seth Ward, Goddard, and Petty, had complied with the revolutionary régimes far enough to be worried after 1660. Anyone with Puritan sympathies plus a reasonable desire to get on in the world would learn in the early sixties not to talk too much. Newton did want to get on, and he was cautious; yet there were limits beyond which he would not compromise. He refused to be ordained, and I think we must reasonably refer back to this period the very strong antipapist feelings which he always showed. On principle he was very tolerant, but he would never extend toleration to papists or atheists—any more than Milton or Locke would.

This is something which Newton's liberal biographers have found rather shocking and have tended to underestimate. I have already stressed the patriotic reasons for opposing popery. In view of the crypto-popery in high places under Charles and James II, Newton's attitude was also anti-court. In one of his manuscripts he declared that idolatry (i.e., popery) was even more dangerous than atheism "because apt by the authority of kings and under very specious pretences to insinuate itself into mankind." He added, prudently, that he referred to pre-Christian kings who enjoined ancestor worship, but the application to Charles and James was clear enough.[41] "Was it the interest of the people to cheat themselves into slavery . . . or was it not rather the business of the court to do it?" Newton asked in a passage about Assyria which Professor Manuel very properly relates to the conflict with James II.[42]

I should like to emphasize Newton's behavior in 1687, when in his first overt political action he led the antipapal party in Cambridge in opposition to James II's measures, at a time when such action needed a great deal of courage. It is in this light too I think that we should see his acceptance of public service after 1688. It need not have resulted merely from political or social ambition. Perhaps Newton really did think something important was at stake in the wars of the sixteen nineties. If England had been defeated, Catholicism and absolutism might have triumphed on a world scale. Newton believed that the Pope was Antichrist, for which he had sound Anglican backing; and all the best interpreters of the Biblical prophecies agreed that the sixteen nineties would be a climacteric decade: I return to this later. The Mint was not just a reward—or only in the sense that the reward of service is more service. We should think of Newton in the same terms as of Milton, sacrificing his eyes in the service of the English republic, or of Locke, going into exile with Shaftesbury—and also taking office after 1688; or of the gentle John Ray, who like Newton seldom referred to politics, which makes his paean on 1688 all the more noteworthy: "the yoke of slavery has been broken. . . . If only God grants us peace, we can rely upon prosperity and a real age of gold."[43] In 1714 Newton tried to get an act of Parliament passed declaring that Rome was a false church.[44] It must have been with considerable pleasure that in 1717 he used—to support a telescope—a maypole which had just been taken down from the Strand. For its erection in 1661 had been a symbol of the victory of those "popish elements" in church and state whose final defeat in 1714-15 must have delighted Newton.

VI

Nor was antipopery irrelevant to Newton's science. Copernicus' treatise was still on the papal Index; so were the writings of Descartes. Newton's dislike of mysteries and superstition is in the Protestant as well as the scientific tradition. And it also relates to his anti-Trinitarianism. In his **Quaeries regarding the word** ὁμοωσιος his object was just as much to draw attention to papal corruptions as to argue a positive case. Anti-Trinitarianism seemed to Newton the logical consequence of Protestantism. He referred to Luther, Bullinger, Grotius, and others when discussing papal corruptions of Scripture. But like so many others of Protestantism's logical consequences, this one had been drawn mainly by the most radical and socially subversive lower-class sects.[45] In England from 1583 to 1612 a number of anti-Trinitarians were burnt, including (1589) Francis Kett, grandson of the leader of the Norfolk rebels in 1549 and Christopher Marlowe's friend; and in 1612 Bartholomew Legate, cloth merchant, the last Englishman burnt for religious heresy.

Anti-Trinitarianism seems to have been endemic in England, despite this persecution. One of the abortive Laudian canons of 1640 was directed against its prevalence among the "younger or unsettled sort of people," and undergraduates were forbidden to own or read Socinian books. Like so many other heresies, anti-Trinitarianism flourished during the interregnum. In 1644 there was a Unitarian group in Coleman Street, that nest of heretics. In 1652 the first English translation of the Racovian catechism was published; next year a life of Socinus appeared in English translation.[46] The most notorious anti-Trinitarian was John Bidle, son of a Gloucestershire tailor, who was in prison more often than not from 1645 onwards, and was the cause of a storm in the Parliament of 1654-55. Bidle was saved from savage punishment only by Cromwell's sending him, quite illegally, to the Scilly Isles. Released in 1658, he was arrested again after the Restoration and in 1662 died in prison at the age of 46.[47]

One reason for the virulent persecution was the notorious fact that denial of the divinity of Christ had often been associated with social heresies. At the trial of Servetus in 1553 the subversive consequences of his heresy were strongly emphasized. The doctrines of Socinianism, thought an Oxford don in 1636, "are repugnant to our state and government"; he referred specifically to the pacifism and anarchism of its adherents.[48] "The fear of Socinianism," wrote Sir John Suckling in 1641, "renders every man that offers to give an account of religion by reason, suspected to have none at all."[49] In 1651 John Pordage was accused both of anti-Trinitarianism and of saying there would soon be no government in England; the saints would take over the property of the wicked. Pordage had connections with William Everard the Digger.[50] Socinus was a

Mortalist, Mede warned Hartlib; the chief English Mortalist was the Leveller leader, Richard Overton.[51]

Conservatives were alarmed by the spread of anti-Trinitarianism. Bishop Joseph Hall in 1648 thought that Socinians should be exempted from the toleration he was prepared to extend to all other Christians (now that he was no longer in a position to do so). Twelve years later the London Baptists were equally intolerant of Socinianism.[52] Nevertheless, anti-Trinitarians continued to exist, if only in small groups. But they were outlaws, specifically excluded from such toleration as was granted in 1689; in 1698 those who wrote or spoke against the Trinity were disabled from any office or employment. A Unitarian was executed in 1697, another imprisoned in 1703. In 1711 Newton's friend Whiston was expelled from Cambridge for Arianism. There was every reason for not proclaiming anti-Trinitarian sentiments. Milton and Locke shared Newton's caution in this respect.

VII

Newton's theology thus had radical associations. So had his studies of the Hebrew prophecies. Thanks to the work of Professor Manuel it is now recognized that this was a serious scholarly subject, occupying the best minds of the sixteenth and seventeenth centuries. Once grant, indeed, that the whole of the Bible is an inspired book and to be taken literally, it is difficult to see how a Christian could fail to be interested in trying to date the end of the world and the last judgment. Servetus had expected the end of the world to come soon. An official declaration of Elizabeth's government in 1589 spoke of "this declining age of the world."[53] Leading British mathematicians, from Napier through Oughtred to Newton, worked on the problem. (Napier's *Plaine Discovery of the Whole Revelation of St. John* ran to twenty-one editions between 1593 and 1700.)

The quest received especial stimulus and a new twist from the revolution of the sixteen forties: eighty tracts are said to have been published on the subject by 1649. "The Second Coming is each day and hour to be expected," said one published in 1647.[54] "Though men be of divers minds as to the precise time," claimed another of 1653, "yet all concur in the nighness and swiftness of its coming upon us."[55] The *raison d'être* of the sect of Muggletonians, the last witnesses, was that the end of the world was at hand. And many excited radicals thought it their duty to expedite the Second Coming of Christ by political action. "Men variously impoverished by the long troubles," observed the mathematician John Pell, "full of discontents and tried by long expectation of amendment, must needs have great propensions to hearken to those that proclaim times of refreshing—a golden age—at hand."[56] There were two not very significant military risings in London, in 1657 and 1661. Militant Fifth Monarchists

were an embarrassment to the scholarly interpreters of the prophecies, just as plebeian atheists were an embarrassment to mechanic philosophers; but the two activities were quite distinct in each case.

In England the best known scholarly interpreters were Thomas Brightman and Joseph Mede. Brightman, a supporter of the Presbyterian discipline, published his *Revelation of St. John Illustrated* in 1615; it was in its fourth English edition by 1644. He thought that the saints' reign of a thousand years had begun in 1300, that the Reformation had been a great turning point, and that now "truth doth get ground and strengthens every day more."[57] The abomination would be set up in 1650, and the year 1695 should see the utter destruction of Turkish power by the conversion of the Jews. "Then shall be indeed that golden age."[58]

Mede was a botanist, an anatomist, a mathematician, and an astronomer, as well as a precursor of the Cambridge Platonists.[59] He too saw the years since about 1300 as a continuous upward movement whose phases were (1) the Albigensian and Waldensian heresies; (2) the Lutheran Reformation; (3) the reign of Elizabeth; (4) the Thirty Years' War; (5) would be the destruction of Rome—the Pope being of course Antichrist; (6) the destruction of the Turkish Empire and the conversion of the Jews; (7) the final judgment and the millennium.[60] Mede was a Fellow of Christ's College, Cambridge, the college of the great Puritan William Perkins. At the time of his election (1602, the year of "our Mr. Perkins's" death) Mede was "thought to look too much to Geneva," and he was wary of publishing in the Laudian thirties; but he seems to have been a middle-of-the-road man.[61] In 1642 Mede's *Key of the Revelation* was published in English translation by order of the Long Parliament. The translator was Richard More, himself an M. P. and a Puritan writer, and the official character of the publication was enhanced by the inclusion of a preface by William Twisse, the Presbyterian divine who was Prolocutor of Parliament's Assembly of Divines gathered at Westminster, and who was so much of a Parliamentarian that in 1661 his remains were dug up from Westminster Abbey by royal command and thrown with others into a common pit. In 1635 William Twisse had said in a letter to his friend Mede "This old world of ours is almost at an end."[62] In his Preface Twisse, in Baconian vein, observed that the opening of the world by navigation and commerce met at one and the same time with an increase of scientific and Biblical knowledge.

So though the Long Parliament encouraged this belief for its own propagandist purposes, perfectly sane and respectable scholars were taking the prophecies very seriously, and were concluding that they would soon be fulfilled. Milton spoke of Christ as "shortly-expected king"; Henry More thought the ruin of Antichrist was near.[63] In 1651 a scholarly friend of Brian Duppa, future bishop, expected the end of the world within a year;[64] in 1655 the great mathematician William Oughtred, a royalist, had "strong apprehensions of some extraordinary event to happen the following year, from the calculation of coincidence with the diluvian period." Perhaps Jesus Christ would appear to judge the world.[65]

On dating testimony converged. Napier was believed to have predicted 1639 as the year of the destruction of the enemies of the church[66]—a prophecy which must have been noted when episcopacy was overthrown in his native Scotland in that year. Vavasor Powell thought "1650 . . . is to be the saints' year of jubilee."[67] In Sweden and Germany the downfall of the Beast was widely expected in 1654 or 1655.[68] Not only Brightman and Mede had foretold great events in the sixteen fifties; so too had Christopher Columbus, George Wither, Samuel Hartlib, Sir Henry Vane, and Lady Eleanor Davies (though this volatile lady had predicted catastrophe for many earlier dates).[69]

Once the sixteen fifties had passed, the next crucial period appeared likely to be the nineties. Brightman and Mede had both plumped for them. So did Nicholas of Cusa, Napier, Alsted, Henry Archer, Hanserd Knollys, Thomas Goodwin, Thomas Beverly the Behmenist, and John Mason.[70] The sixteen nineties saw Newton in the service of an English state now resolutely antipopish. The French Huguenot Jurieu thought that the destruction of Antichrist would occur between 1710 and 1715, following the defeat and protestantization of France.[71] Mede and Whiston expected the world to end in 1715.

It is thus not so odd as it used to be thought that Newton's theological manuscripts are as bulky as his mathematical and scientific writings. Perry Miller was perhaps a little bold to conclude positively that, from about 1693, Newton wanted to find out exactly how close he was to the end of the world.[72] Newton held, cautiously, that the prophecies would not be fully understood "before the last age of the world." But "amongst the interpreters of the last age," amongst whom he included Mede, "there is scarce one of note who hath not made some discovery worth knowing." "The great successes of late interpreters" suggested to Newton that "the last age, the age of opening these things," is "now approaching"; that God is about opening these mysteries." This gave him "more encouragement than ever to look into" them.[73] The point to emphasize is that this was an area of investigation which had traditionally attracted mathematical chronologists; Newton would have been in good company if he wished to throw light on the end of the world as well as on its beginning. And a number of serious scholars whom Newton respected, including Mede, had thought that great events might begin in the nineties. But again it was a subject which had radical associations and overtones; caution was needed.

VIII

By 1665-66 the Restoration honeymoon, such as it was, was over. Charles II's genuine attempt to continue Cromwell's policy of religious toleration had been defeated by Parliament. Between 1660 and 1662, 1760 ministers were driven out of the church. The Conventicle Act of 1664 and the Five Mile Act of 1665 expelled them from the towns which were the main centers of opposition. In 1665 England was involved in an aggressive commercial war with the Dutch ("What matters this or that reason? What we want is more of the trade the Dutch now have," said the Duke of Albermarle, with soldierly frankness[74]). This war was such a fiasco that men began to look back to the days when Oliver Cromwell had led England to victory. The city turned against Charles II as Dutch ships sailed up the Medway. Even Dryden, even in "Annus Mirabilis," said of the king

> He grieved the land he freed should be
>   oppressed,
> And he less for it than usurpers do.

(Dryden no doubt recalled his fulsome praise of Cromwell seven years earlier, in "Heroic Stanzas to the Glorious Memory of Cromwell.") Samuel Pepys, another former Cromwellian who now looked back nostalgically, recorded in February 1666 that his old patron the Earl of Sandwich feared there would be some very great revolutions in the coming months. Pepys himself was full of forebodings, and was getting money in against a foul day.[75] Fifteen years earlier the famous William Lilly had quoted a prophecy that "in 1666 there will be no king here or pretending to the crown of England." The Plague in 1665 and the Great Fire of London in 1666, together with the comets of 1664 and 1665, again made men think that the end of the world was at hand. Lilly was in trouble for having predicted the Fire.[76]

In these troubled years 1665-66, Newton, in his retirement at Woolsthorpe, was discovering the calculus, the nature of white light, and universal gravitation. He made another discovery when the Heralds visited Lincolnshire in 1666: that whereas his father had never claimed to be more than a yeoman, he, Isaac, was a gentleman.

I tread warily in discussing Newton's elusive personality. There are some aspects of genius which it is futile to try to explain. But if we recall that Shakespeare abandoned the theatre just as soon as he could afford to, and set himself up as a gentleman in his native Warwickshire, we shall perhaps be the less surprised by the young Newton's improvement on his illiterate father's social aspirations in 1666, or by Newton's apparent abandonment of science for more gentlemanly activities from the nineties.

By 1666, too, or soon afterwards, Newton had decided not to marry Miss Storey. Why? "Her portion being not considerable," Stukeley tells us, "and he being a fellow of a college, it was incompatible with his fortunes to marry."[77] The reasoning is ungallant and unromantic, but it makes sense. Marriage would either have necessitated ordination and taking a living (to which we know Newton's objections); or else would have condemned him to the kind of vagabond life, dependent on the charity of others, which a man like John Ray led for twenty years after 1660.

I feign no Freudian hypotheses. But the fact that Newton, a posthumous child, never had a father, is surely relevant. He saw little enough of his mother after he was two years old, living first with his grandmother and then with an apothecary at Grantham. Only for a couple of years between the ages of sixteen and eighteen did he live with his mother, now widowed for the second time. So the decision not to marry Miss Storey would seem finally to have cut love out of Newton's life. Newton's later complaisance to his niece's affair with Halifax, which so bothered nineteenth-century biographers, may have been simply due to his not noticing.

Newton's theology denied the sonship of Christ, and though the Father exists he is a *deus absconditus,* in no close personal relation with his creatures. He is the first cause of a universe lacking all secondary qualities, all warmth and light and color. The eternal silence of those infinite spaces seems never to have frightened Newton. Professor Manuel comments on his history: "Newton never wrote a history of men. . . . The individuals mentioned in his histories . . . have no distinctive human qualities. . . . Nations are . . . neutral as astronomical bodies; they invade and they are in their turn conquered . . . An interest in man's creations for their own sake, the aesthetic and the sensuous, is totally absent in his writings."[78]

It would be naïve to suppose that these things would have been different if Newton had married Miss Storey. But the decision not to, apparently so easily taken and accepted, on prudential economic grounds, fits in with all we know of Newton's personality—his careful and minute keeping of accounts from boyhood until he became a very rich man indeed. Fontenelle in his *Eloge* rightly singled out Newton's frugality and carefulness for very special mention.[79]

This leads on to consideration of Newton's caution. Again a little history dispels some of the legends that have grown up around it. Many men—like Pepys—had reason to be cautious in the Restoration period. Newton's reluctance to publish, moreover, was no more than was expected of someone who had aspirations to be thought a gentleman. The part played by Halley in getting the **Principia** published repeats almost verba-

tim Ent's description of his role in persuading Harvey to allow his *De Generatione Animalium* to be printed in 1651. One may suspect that both accounts are highly stylized, remembering how many seventeenth-century poets claimed to publish only under great pressure or after alleged attempts to pirate their poems. There were parallels among the scientists. Ralph Bathurst, physician, F.R.S., and president of Trinity College, Oxford, had a wife who "scorns that he should be in print."[80] Francis Willughby died reluctant to publish his *Ornithology,* which Ray issued posthumously.[81]

And of course in Newton's case there were very special reasons for caution. His anti-Trinitarian writings would have been dangerous to publish. For the same reason Milton, not normally averse to seeing himself in print, held back the *De Doctrina Christiana*; and Locke showed a similar reticence. Hobbes thought the bishops would like to burn him; Waller dared not praise Hobbes publicly. After 1688 Newton did once consider publishing his *Historical Account of Two Notable Corruptions of Scripture,* anonymously, in French, and on the continent; but he thought better even of that. His theological heresies had other consequences. Newton was firm enough in his convictions to refuse to be ordained; but not to risk leaving Cambridge. In 1675 the Royal Society induced Charles II to issue letters patent authorizing Newton to retain his fellowship although not a clergyman. By accepting this quite exceptional use of the dispensing power Newton gave hostages to fortune. Any scandal attaching to his name would certainly be made the occasion for drawing attention to his anomalous position, and might call the retention of his fellowship in question. This did not prevent Newton taking serious political risks in 1687, and all credit to him; but on that occasion his deepest convictions were stirred. On any lesser issue he would be likely to play safe. This, combined with a natural furtiveness of temperament, seems an entirely adequate explanation of his early reluctance to publish. By 1694 he was uninhibitedly discussing with David Gregory a whole range of projects for mathematical publications.[82]

IX

Many of Newton's attitudes can, I suggest, be related to the post-Restoration desire for order, an order which should be as uncomplicated as possible. Puritanism and Baconian science had for many years been preparing for this ordered simplicity which Newton triumphantly achieved in the **Principia,** where the watchmaker God, "very well skilled in mechanics and geometry," presided over an abstract mathematical universe.[83] Similarly, Newton thought, there is a natural religion, "one law for all nations, dictated . . . to all mankind by the light of reason."[84] The same simplification informs Newton's anti-Trinitarianism, with its denial of the mystery of the Incarnation. Newton thought he found in the writings of Joseph Mede a single key which would likewise dispel the apparent mystery of the Biblical prophecies. "The prophets," Newton believed, "wrote in a language as certain and definite in its significance as any vulgar language." The heavens, the sun and moon, signify kings and rulers; the earth signifies inferior people; hades or hell "the lowest and most miserable of the people."[85] ("In Newton's pragmatization of myth and reduction of prophecy to plain history," said Professor Manuel, we can see "a reflection of the new realities of middle-class society"—the society which triumphed in England after the revolution of the mid-century.)[86] Similarly Mr. Forbes and Mr. Sherwood Taylor have suggested that in Newton's alchemical experiments he may have hoped to find a key to the presumed common language of the alchemical writings, and a synthesis of the micro-structure of matter which would have been the counterpart to his celestial and terrestrial mechanics.87 In his concern with spelling reform, which goes back to his pre-Cambridge days, Newton wanted to find a "real character" which should replace Latin and be truly international because as abstract as mathematics. This was an interest he shared with Wallis, Evelyn, Wilkins, and many other Fellows of the Royal Society.[88] The quest for a simplified order in all intellectual spheres was very topical.

It is not unreasonable to compare Hobbes's simplification of the universe to matter and motion, of political science to individuals accepting sovereign power in the interests of order; or the literary classicism which was invented by the defeated royalists during the interregnum, yearning for decorum and order, and which became fashionable in the Restoration years of French influence, with the order-loving Dryden as its high priest.[89]

And yet—and yet. As has often been pointed out, Newton was not wholly a Newtonian. Though he stripped the universe of secondary qualities, his experiments with colors enabled eighteenth-century landscape painters and poets to paint far more brightly than before. Contradictions lurk in the heart of his universe. In his desire to refute the Cartesian mechanism, Newton, like Pascal, postulated an irrational God behind the irrational force of gravity, a *Deus absconditus* but very real. "A continual miracle is needed to prevent the sun and the fixed stars from rushing together through gravity."[90] "A Being eternal, infinite, all-wise and most perfect, *without dominion,* is not God but only Nature," Newton wrote.[91] Newton's God is as arbitrary as Hobbes's sovereign. Newton brought back into physics the notion of "attraction" which Boyle had devoted so much energy to expelling.[92] (It is ironical that the lectures in which Bentley used Newton's new "occult qualities" to confute atheism should have been endowed by Boyle; and not untypical of the difficulties in which seventeenth-century scientists found themselves in their determination to have both God and science.)

"Those things which men understand by improper and contradictious phrases," Newton assured the too impetuous Dr. Bentley, "may be sometimes really in nature without any contradiction at all."[93] Newton accepted, dogmatically, experimental science and Biblical revelation as equally self-validating. "Religion and philosophy are to be preserved distinct. We are not to introduce divine revelations into philosophy, nor philosophical opinions into religion."[94] Science deals with second causes. The experimental method itself assumes that there is an intelligible order in nature which is law-abiding, "simple and always consonant to itself."[95] The first cause is a matter of revelation. Perhaps one day, when the Baconian program has been completed, science and revelation can be linked. Newton never doubted that there was an ultimate mechanical cause of gravitation, though he could not discover it experimentally. But he had realized that this was a far longer-term program than Bacon had ever dreamed. "The great ocean of truth lay all undiscovered" before the "boy playing on the sea-shore . . . now and then finding a smoother pebble or a prettier shell than ordinary."[96] Newton may have worried lest the ocean itself might be annihilated before it was fully explored; but in fact the hope of linking science and revelation was abandoned before the explorers were out of sight of land.

Notes

[1] Ed. M. Claggett, *Critical Problems in the History of Science* (Madison, 1959), p. 855.

[2] For an example of the egregious misunderstanding into which ignorance of the historical context has led commentators on Thomas Hobbes, see Quentin Skinner, "The Ideological Context of Hobbes's Political Thought," *Historical Journal,* IX (1966), esp. pp. 313-17.

[3] A. R. Hall, "Merton Revisited," *History of Science,* II (1963), *passim.*

[4] Ed. A. R. and M. B. Hall, *The Correspondence of Henry Oldenburg* (University of Wisconsin Press, 1965-), I, p. 278.

[5] Perry Miller, "The Marrow of Puritan Divinity," *Publications of the Colonial Society of Massachusetts,* XXXII (1935), p. 266.

[6] T. Sprat, *History of the Royal Society* (1667), pp. 371-2; S. Butler, *Characters and Passages from Notebooks* (ed. A. R. Waller, Cambridge University Press, 1908), p. 458. Sprat's comparison was pretty trite by this date: see my *Intellectual Origins of the English Revolution* (Oxford University Press, 1965), pp. 25-6, which gives sources for quotations unidentified above.

[7] H. Stubbe, *Legends no Histories* (1670), Sig. +2.

[8] H. Stubbe, *The Lord Bacons Relation of the Sweating-sickness examined* (1671), Preface.

[9] Oldenburg, *Correspondence,* II, p. 630.

[10] North, *Discourses upon Trade* (1691), in J. R. McCulloch, *Early English Tracts on Commerce* (1952), p. 511.

[11] Sydenham, *De Arte Medica* (1669), in K. Dewhurst, *Dr. Thomas Sydenham* (Wellcome Historical Medical Library, 1966), p. 82.

[12] Lord Keynes, "Newton the Man," in the Royal Society's *Newton Tercentenary Celebrations* (Cambridge University Press, 1947), p. 27.

[13] M. Boas, "The Establishment of the Mechanical Philosophy," *Osiris,* X (1952), p. 418.

[14] The *Times Literary Supplement,* 25 October, 1963.

[15] G. Fox, *Journal* (1901), I, p. 11.

[16] Sir John Coniers, quoted by B. Manning, "The Nobles, the People and the Constitution," *Past and Present,* No. 9, p. 61; *Mercurius Britannicus,* No. 107, November 24-December 1, 1645. I owe this reference to the kindness of Mr. Ian McCalman.

[17] Stubbe, *Legends no Histories,* Sig. + Iv.

[18] R. Boyle, *Works* (1772), V, p. 397.

[19] J. Tulloch, *Rational Theology and Christian Philosophy in England in the 17th century* (1874), II, pp. 278-9.

[20] C. Wren, *Parentalia* (1700), p. 201.

[21] Ed. H. McLachlan, *Sir Isaac Newton's Theological Manuscripts* (Liverpool University Press, 1950), p. 17.

[22] Ed. A. R. and M. B. Hall, *Unpublished Scientific Papers of Isaac Newton* (Cambridge University Press, 1961), p. 197.

[23] R. S. Westfall, *Science and Religion in 17th century England* (Yale University Press, 1958), pp. 107-11, 205-6, 219-20.

[24] Oldenburg to Samuel Hartlib, in *The Correspondence of Henry Oldenburg,* I, p. 277.

[25] See C. W. Foster, "Sir Isaac Newton's Family," *Associated Architectural Societies' Reports and Papers,* XXXIX (1928), pp. 1-62.

[26] See Joan Simon, "The Two John Angels," *Transactions of the Leicestershire Archaeological and Historical Society,* XXXI (1955), pp. 38-41.

[27] H. McLachlan, *The Religious Opinions of Milton, Locke and Newton* (Manchester University Press, 1941), p. 119.

[28] Sir D. Brewster, *Memoirs of the Life, Writings and Discoveries of Sir Isaac Newton* (Edinburgh, 1855), II, p. 318; F. E. Manuel, *Isaac Newton, Historian* (Cambridge University Press, 1963), pp. 16, 268.

[29] H. McLachlan, *Sir Isaac Newton's Theological Manuscripts,* pp. 55, 137.

[30] W. W. Rouse Ball, *Cambridge Notes* (Cambridge, 1921), p. 258; Brewster, *op. cit.,* II, p. 338. The source for the last quotation (Whiston) is not of the most reliable.

[31] H. M. Innes, *Fellows of Trinity College* (Cambridge University Press, 1941).

[32] C. E. Raven, *John Ray* (2nd ed., 1950), pp. 57-8, 441, 461, 457. Ray reluctantly agreed to be ordained in December 1660, when he still hoped for a reasonable religious settlement.

[33] *Ibid.,* p. 28 and *passim.*

[34] I. Barrow, *Theological Works* (ed. A. Napier, 1859), IX, pp. 41-7; cf. R. H. Kargon, *Atomism in England from Hariot to Newton* (Oxford, 1966), pp. 78-9 and Chapter XI, *passim.*

[35] H. More, *The Immortality of the Soul* (1659), *passim;* *Collection of Several Philosophical Writings.* (1662), p. xv.

[36] Hall and Hall, *Unpublished Scientific Papers of Isaac Newton,* pp. 75, 187; A. R. Hall, "Sir Isaac Newton's Note-Book, 1661-5," *Cambridge Historical Journal,* IX (1948), pp. 243-4; Boas, "The Establishment of the Mechanical Philosophy," p. 505.

[37] Butler, *Characters and Passages from Notebooks,* p. 466.

[38] J. Oldham, *Poems* (Centaur Press, 1960), p. 178.

[39] Stubbe, *Legends no Histories,* Sig.*

[40] Pepys, *Diary* (ed. H. B. Wheatley, 1946), I, p. 253.

[41] McLachlan, *Sir Isaac Newton's Theological Manuscripts,* pp. 49-51, 131-2. Cf. Pepys's fear of Catholicism in the early sixties—all the more significant in a man who was later himself to be accused of papist leanings.

42 Manuel, *Isaac Newton, Historian,* p. 116.

43 Raven, *John Ray,* pp. 251-2.

44 Brewster, *op. cit.,* II, pp. 351-2.

45 E. M. Wilbur, *A History of Unitarianism* (Harvard University Press, 1946), chapter 2 and *passim.*

46 [Anon.], *The Life of that Incomparable man Faustus Socinus* (1653).

47 J. Bidle, *The Apostolical and True Opinion concerning the Holy Trinity* (1653), *passim.* I have used the 1691 edition, which contains a *Life of Bidle.*

48 Ed. F. S. Boas, *The Diary of Thomas Crosfield* (1935), pp. 85-6.

49 Sir J. Suckling, *An Account of Religion by Reason* (1641), The Preface. Cf. F. Osborn, *Advice to a Son* (1656): the Socinians are "looked upon as the most chemical and rational part of our many divisions" (in *Miscellaneous Works,* 11th ed., 1722, p. 91).

50 J. Pordage, *Innocence appearing through the dark Mists of Pretended Guilt* (1655), *passim;* cf. G. P. Gooch, *The History of English Democratic Ideas in the 17th century* (1927), p. 266. Pordage denied the accusations.

51 J. Mede, *Works* (ed. J. Worthington, 1664), II, p. 1082; [Richard Overton], *Mans Mortallitie* (Amsterdam, 1644), *passim.*

52 J. Hall, *Pax Terris* (1648); J. Waddington, *Congregational History, 1567-1700* (1874), p. 559.

53 H. S. Bennett, *English Books and Readers, 1558 to 1603* (Cambridge University Press, 1965), p. 225.

54 [Anon.], *Doomes-Day* (1647), p. 6.

55 J. Rogers, *Sagrir* (1653). By 1666 the Fifth Monarchy, Rogers predicted, "must be visible in all the earth."

56 John Pell to Secretary Thurloe, March 1655, in *The Protectorate of Oliver Cromwell* (ed. R. Vaughan, 1839), I, p. 156.

57 T. Brightman, *The Revelation of St. John Illustrated* (4th ed., 1644), pp. 378-81, 520, 824; cf. pp. 109-12, 124-5, 136-7, 157 and *passim.*

58 Brightman. *A most Comfortable Exposition of the last and most difficult pages of the Prophecies of Daniel* (1644), pp. 966-7; *A Commentary on Canticles* (1644), p. 1077 (pagination of these last two is continuous with Brightman's *Revelation,* with which they are bound).

59 Mede, *Works,* I, p. lxv.

60 Mede, *The Key of The Revelation* (2nd ed., 1656), pp. 114-25; *Works,* I, pp. xlviii-li.

61 Mede, *Works,* I, pp. lxv, xxxiv; II, pp. 978, 995.

62 Mede, *Works, II,* p. 979; cf. pp. 1006-7.

63 H. More, *Theological Works* (1708), p. 633.

64 Ed. Sir Gyles Isham, *The Correspondence of Bishop Brian Duppa and Sir Justinian Isham, 1650-60* (Northamptonshire Record Society, 1955), p. 37.

65 Ed. E. S. de Beer, *The Diary of John Evelyn* (Oxford University Press, 1955), III, p. 158.

66 [Anon.], *The Popes Spectacles* (1623), p. 1083.

67 V. Powell, *Saving Faith* (1651), p. 92.

68 M. Roberts, review in *Journal of Ecclesiastical History,* VIII (1957), pp. 112-15.

69 Brightman, *Daniel,* p. 967; Mede, *Remaines on some Passages in Revelation* (1650), p. 33; J. Merrien, *Christopher Columbus* (1958), p. 223; Wither, *Campo-Musae* (1643); Hartlib, *Clavis Apocalyptica* (1651); my *Puritanism and Revolution* (1958), p. 327; I owe Lady Eleanor Davies to the kindness of Professor Ivan Roots.

70 J. Trapp, *Commentary of the New Testament* (1958—first published 1647), pp. 250, 420; my *Puritanism and Revolution,* p. 329; G. F. Nuttall, *The Holy Spirit in Puritan Faith and Experience* (1946), p. 109; D. P. Walker, *The Decline of Hell* (Chicago University Press, 1964), p. 245.

71 G. H. Dodge, *The Political Theory of the Huguenots of the Dispersion* (Columbia University Press, 1947), pp. 35-8.

72 P. Miller, *Errand into the Wilderness* (Harvard University Press, 1956), p. 228.

73 Newton, *Opera Quae Exstant Omnia* (ed. S. Horsley, 1775), V. pp. 448, 450, 474.

74 A. T. Mahan, *The Influence of Sea Power upon History, 1660-1783* (1890), p. 107.

75 Pepys, *Diary,* IV, p. 366, V, pp. 218, 283-4, 328, VI, p. 113.

76 W. Lilly, *The Lord Merlins Prophecy Concerning the King of Scots* (1651), p. 4; *Monarchy or no Monarchy in England* (1651), *passim.*

[77] E. Turnor, *Collections for the History of the Town and Soke of Grantham* (1806), p. 179.

[78] Manuel, *op. cit.,* pp. 137-8, 193.

[79] *The Elogium of Sir Isaac Newton, by Monsieur Fontenelle* (1728), p. 32.

[80] A. Wood, *Athenae Oxonienses,* I, *Life of Wood* (Ecclesiastical History Society, Oxford, 1848), p. 188.

[81] *Op. cit.,* Preface.

[82] Ed. H. W. Turnbull, *Correspondence of Sir Isaac Newton,* (1959-), III, pp. 335-6, 338.

[83] *Opera Quae Exstant Omnia,* V, p. 432.

[84] McLachlan, *Sir Isaac Newton's Theological Manuscripts,* p. 52. Wilkins has been described as "the English godfather of natural or moral religion" (G. McColley, "The Ross Wilkins Controversy," *Annals of Science,* III, pp. 155, 186).

[85] McLachlan, *Sir Isaac Newton's Theological Manuscripts,* pp. 119-21; Newton, *Opera Quae Exstant Omnia.* V, pp. 306-10; cf. T. Brightman, *The Revelation of St. John Illustrated,* pp. 232-3, 273-92; J. Mede, *Works,* I, Sig.* xxx 4; J. Mede, *The Key of the Revelation* (1656), Sig. A4.

[86] Manuel, *op. cit.,* p. 121.

[87] R. J. Forbes, "Was Newton an Alchemist?," *Chymia,* II (1949), pp. 35-6; F. Sherwood Taylor, "An Alchemical Work of Sir Isaac Newton," *Ambix,* V (1956), p. 64; cf. I. B. Cohen, "Newton in the Light of Recent Scholarship," *Isis,* LI (1960), pp. 503-4.

[88] R. W. V. Elliott, "Isaac Newton's 'Of an Universall Language,'" *Modern Language Review,* LII (1957), pp. 1-18; cf. Elliott, "Isaac Newton as Phonetician," *ibid.,* XLIX (1954), pp. 5-12.

[89] P. W. Thomas, "John Berkenhead in Literature and Politics, 1640-1663" (unpublished Oxford D.Phil. Thesis, 1962), *passim.*

[90] *Correspondence of Sir Isaac Newton,* III, pp. 334, 336, 355; cf. A. J. Snow, *Matter and Gravity in Newton's Physical Philosophy* (Oxford University Press, 1926), *passim.*

[91] Hall and Hall, *Unpublished Scientific Papers of Isaac Newton,* p. 363 (my italics).

[92] Boas, "The Establishment of the Mechanical Philosophy," pp. 420-2, 479, 489 and *passim;* cf. Turnor, *Collections for the History of the Town and Soke of Grantham,* pp. 172-3.

[93] *Opera Quae Exstant Omnia,* IV, p. 439.

[94] McLachlan, *Sir Isaac Newton's Theological Manuscripts,* p. 58.

[95] Newton, *Mathematical Principles of Natural Philosophy* (transl. A. Motte, ed. F. Cajori, University of California Press, 1934), pp. 398-9.

[96] L. T. More, *Isaac Newton: A Biography* (New York, 1962), p. 664. The famous phrase curiously recalls one of Donne's sermons: "Divers men may walk by the sea-side and, the same beams of the sun giving light to them all, one gathereth by the benefit of that light pebbles or speckled shells for curious vanity, and another gathers precious pearl or medicinal amber by the same light. So the common light of reason illumines us all; but one employs this light upon the searching of impertinent vanities, another by a better use of the same light finds out the mysteries of religion; and when he hath found them, loves them not for the light's sake, but for the natural and true worth of the thing itself. . . . But . . . if thou attend the light of natural reason, and cherish that and exalt that, so that that bring thee to a love of the Scriptures, and that love to a belief of the truth thereof . . . thou shalt see that thou by thy small light hast gathered pearl and amber, and they [worldly men] by their great lights nothing but shells and pebbles; they have determined the light of nature upon the book of nature, this world; and thou hast carried the light of nature higher" (ed. G. R. Potter and E. M. Simpson, *The Sermons of John Donne,* California University Press, III, 1957, pp. 359, 361). It is too dreadful to think of Newton reading Donne, even Donne's sermons; but the passage was so relevant to the problems of the scientists that it was no doubt borrowed by many preachers in the Cambridge of Newton's youth.

I. Bernard Cohen (lecture date 1981)

SOURCE: "The Thrice-Revealed Newton," in *Editing Texts in the History of Science and Medicine: Papers Given at the Seventeenth Annual Conference on Editorial Problems,* Garland Publishing, Inc., 1982, pp. 117-84.

[In the following, which was first delivered as a lecture in 1981, Cohen shows how Newton's interests and works have been revealed in three stages: in the material Newton himself chose to publish; in the manuscripts that were discovered and published after his death; and in the remaining manuscripts, correspondence, notebooks, and annotated texts that were sold at auc-

tion in 1936 by Newton's family. Furthermore, Cohen discusses the relevance of such findings, arguing that they demonstrate, among other things, the importance of Descartes' work in the development of Newton's own thought.]

The First Revelation

I have entitled my presentation "the thrice-revealed Newton" because we have learned about Isaac Newton in a succession of three revelations. First of all, there was the Newton revealed by his own choice of material to be published. For Newton, "published" has the sense of being made public, that is, it includes distribution of long-hand copies and is not limited to works put into print. In Newton's lifetime, this revelation was made through the **Principles,** the **Opticks,** his famous letter on the production of prismatic colors and the nature of white light, certain tracts on mathematics, and his study of **The Chronology of Ancient Kingdoms Amended.**[1] Newton thus showed himself to the world as a mathematician and mathematical physicist and astronomer, a master of experiment, and a careful reasoner about questions of chronology and succession related to Scripture. There was also circulated a paper entitled **"De natura acidorum,"** which revealed some of Newton's chemical (and possibly alchemical) interests and speculations.[2] But the major image that Newton showed to the world was that of the prince of reason in an age in which reason was highly esteemed.

The major revelation of Newton the scientist was made in his celebrated **Mathematical Principles of Natural Philosophy.** Here was a cold, formal, logical presentation, in which—apparently—a rational system of the world was deduced by logic and mathematics from a series of first principles or "axioms" which Newton designated as "Axioms, or Laws of Motion," following upon a series of Definitions.[3] Second to the **Principles** was the **Opticks,** a non-mathematical treatise on "The Reflections, Refractions, Inflections, and Colours of Light."[4] For about a century and a half, with a few exceptions,[5] the image of Newton that dominated the thinking of men and women was that of a mathematician and physicist who was the highest representative of the Augustan Age, the Age of Reason.

This image of Newton was celebrated in verse, in sculpture, in painting. Newton was seen in the role of lawgiver of nature, or at least the agent who, by the exercise of his reason, had revealed nature's laws.[6] This was expressed succinctly in Alexander Pope's couplet:

> Nature and Nature's laws lay hid in night;
> God said, Let Newton be, and all was light.

For many people of that Augustan Age, the twin luminaries of reason were Isaac Newton and the philosopher of common sense, John Locke.[7] These were two heroes to Thomas Jefferson, who ordered portraits of them, along with a portrait of a third great Englishman, Francis Bacon, so that the three could adorn the walls of his study, as they do to this day.[8]

In order to present such an image of himself to the world, Newton had to make a very careful selection from among his writings or among the subjects of his interest, putting aside his explorations of theology, including interpretations of the prophecies in the Book of Revelation.[9] He had equally to conceal a long-abiding passion for alchemy[10] and his belief in priscan knowledge, a belief that much of the science that we know today was but a rediscovery of the wisdom known to ancient sages and seers.[11] On Newton's death, in 1727, the executors of his estate bundled up the manuscripts on these strange or esoteric subjects and marked them with the words that still remain for all to see who study Newton's manuscripts in the University Library at Cambridge or in the library of King's College,[12] "Not fit to be printed."[13]

This side of Newton, however, could not be totally hidden. Although later generations of scientists and philosophers hailed Newton as a positivies,[14] as a hard-headed scientist, there are traces to be found in the writings that Newton allowed to be published of the "other" Newton, even though our complete knowledge of the "other" Newton had to await a second and even a third revelation. For instance, the so-called positivist Newton says plainly in the General Scholium, which he wrote for the second edition of the **Principles** (1713),[15]

> Hitherto I have explained the phenomena of the heavens and of our sea by the force of gravity, but I have not yet assigned a cause to gravity. . . . It is enough that gravity really exists and acts according to the laws set forth by us and can produce all the motions of the heavenly bodies and of our sea.

But the non-positivist[16] Newton says in that very same General Scholium that to discuss God "on the basis of phenomena belongs to experimental philosophy," a sentence somewhat toned down in the third edition (1726) to read that a discussion of God on the basis of phenomena belongs to "natural philosophy." And in the **Opticks,** in the queries added to the Latin edition of 1706 and printed in the second English edition of 1717/18,[17] Newton twice called space the sensorium of God, which—after the book had been printed—he slightly toned down in one place (but not in the other) by adding the Latin word "tanquam"—meaning "as it were."[18]

That Newton was concerned with theological questions, and that he was concerned with them in direct relation to his science, was also made apparent by other portions of the **Principles** and the **Opticks.** For example, in the first edition of the **Principles,** Newton refers to God's wisdom in creating the planets of such relative masses and densities that those which are nearest to the sun could best withstand the sun's heat.[19] And in the second edition of the **Principles** the concluding General Scholium (to which I have just referred) begins with a somewhat similar argument: that the solar system, with the planets all encircling the sun in approximately a single plane, all moving in the same direction, and with their satellites similarly arranged, could not come into being without the active intervention of a divine being.[20] Although we tend to concentrate on the penultimate paragraph of the General Scholium, in which Newton seems almost to argue like a positivist and where we find his famous slogan, *Hypotheses non fingo* ("I feign [or frame][21] no hypotheses"), most of that General Scholium, some 80% or so, is devoted to the being, attributes, and name of God.

In the **Opticks,** in the later versions, in both the Latin edition of 1706 and the English edition of 1717/18, Newton not only talks about the way in which God created the world in terms of indivisible, non-wearing, everlasting atomic particles, but discusses the relation of science and morality, the corruptions of the sons of Noah, and other questions of a theological nature—not all of which are directly related to science.[22] For the cognoscenti, there were also references in the **Opticks** to nature's delight in making transmutations,[23] which may possibly have been read as a hint concerning the great man's interest in alchemy, the science of transmutation. It must be admitted, however, that Newton also uses the word transmutation for the changes that occur constantly around us by natural processes, and even for certain changes that occur in projective geometry, i.e., the "transmutation" of geometric figures.[24] The third and final book of Newton's **Principles** (1687) opens with a series of "Hypotheses," which in the later editions were largely divided into "Phenomena" and "Rules for Natural Philosophy";[25] the third "Hypothesis"[26] stated that "all matter can be transformed into matter of any other kind and successively undergo all the intermediate stages of qualities."[27] It must be said at once, however, that this particular statement was given by Newton without explanation; it was not really used in the rest of Book Three of the **Principles,** of which it was part of the introductory section.[28] Furthermore, it was labcled "Hypothesis III," which could have indicated that it was introduced for discussion as a hypothesis and was not necessarily a firm statement of Newton's own belief.[29]

We now know, however, that during the 1690's Newton planned to add certain additional scholiums to the third book of his **Principles,** in which he would give rein to some of his extravagant and certainly non-positivistic ideas. In part, he would include here some extracts from the *De rerum natura* of the Roman poet Lucretius and would also explain his idea that the ancient sages had a knowledge of nature which included even the law of universal gravity.[30] But apparently he thought better of this idea, and that revelation was made only about 300 years later, when his manuscript annotations in preparation for a new edition of the *Principles* were discovered and published.[31]

Newton's **Chronology of Ancient Kingdoms Amended** was circulated by Newton, but not intended to be printed.[32] Yet soon this work was in general circulation and did get into print.[33] It is not a very daring book for a rationalist or positivist. In developing his subject, Newton did assume that—among other things—the voyage of the "good ship Argo" was a real event and that one could believe all the accounts of the Argonauts and their search for the Golden Fleece, as reported by Apollonius of Rhodes, and similar kinds of events of the past. On this basis Newton essentially attempted to make a rational reconstruction of past events. He assumed that the precession of the equinoxes has been constant over the ages; he found in the literature of the past certain statements which he took as evidence of the appearance (visibility and position) of constellations and consequently as a basis for computing the dates of those alleged celestial observations. This is, in short, to some degree, a "scientific chronology" based on clearly stated hypotheses or assumptions. The point is that this endeavor is based on rational procedures.[34] The only part of such an analysis which would make us question its being worthy of the author of the great **Principles** or the **Opticks** would be the degree of Newton's credulity about what he assumes to have been actual historical events. Furthermore, we might be a little astonished that the prince of rationalism and the greatest scientist of his age should have devoted so much of his time and energy to the study of biblical history and the annals of ancient history, which—by comparison—would seem to us to have been a somewhat trivial occupation.

Newton's anti-Trinitarian views, on the other hand, were more carefully kept private.[35] The nearest to a "public" work relating to interpretation of Scripture, as opposed to purely chronological aspects of Scripture, was his study of the Book of Revelation, published shortly after his death.[36] It may be pointed out, however, that in Newton's day it would not have seemed unusual for a mathematical scientist to occupy himself with this subject. There was, in fact, that prior example of John Napier, Laird of Merchiston, known to us as the inventor of logarithms, who also produced a lengthy treatise on the Book of Revelation.[37]

In this work, Newton's aim was to interpret the prophecies to find out what they meant, but—as Frank Manuel has shown[38]—stopping short of actually making predictions of the future.[39] In evaluating this work, we must remember that in those days in Britain there was produced an enormous mass of literature concerning prophecy.[40] In the fourth decade of the 17th century, a Cambridge man, Joseph Mede of Christ's, had invented a rather new way of reading the prophetic literature, producing an innovation in method that Manuel has likened to a Copernican revolution[41] and that his contemporary "admirers glorified as equal in importance to Aristotle's syllogistic reasoning."[42] Newton's method of studying prophecy depended greatly on the work of Mede. I shall not go into the details of the method,[43] but it should be noted that Newton did not proceed by attempting a mystical union with the authors of the prophetic texts. For the most part his method was based on rational procedures and had the appearance of a "scientific" inquiry. Manuel has noted[44] that some Cambridge drafts of this work "used formal scientific" headings like 'Propositiones' and 'Lemmata'." This "scientific" aspect of Newton's work is plainly displayed in a general introduction to one of the Keynes manuscripts in King's College, Cambridge, entitled **"The First Book Concerning the Language of the Prophets"** (complete in itself in 152 pages; 50,000 words). Here Newton explains his method.

> He that would understand a book written in a strange language must first learn the language, and if he would understand it well must learn the language perfectly. Such a language was that wherein the Prophets wrote, and the want of sufficient skill in that language is the main reason why they are so little understood. John did not write in one language, Daniel in another, Isaiah in a third, and the rest in others peculiar to themselves, but they all write in one and the same mystical language . . . [which], so far as I can find, was as certain and definite in its signification as is the vulgar language of any nation. . . .[45]

This is the basic premise of the work. Next Newton explains that "it is only through want of skill therein that Interpreters so frequently turn the Prophetic types and phrases to signify whatever their fancies and hypotheses lead them to." As with Cartesian philosophical romances, it was owing to ignorance that hypotheses took the place of correct explanations based on fact. The main procedural principle was stated as follows:

> The Rule I have followed has been to compare the several mystical places of scripture where the same prophetic phrase or type is used, and to fix such a signification to that phrase as agrees best with all the places: . . . and, when I had found the necessary significations, to reject all others as the offspring of luxuriant fancy, for no more significations are to be admitted for true ones than can be proved.

This statement sounds so much like the Rules at the beginning of Book Three of the *Principles* that it may well serve to illustrate the essential oneness of Newton's thought. It embodies the proper approach of a man who believes in the experimental (empirical) philosophy, and we shall see that a similar point of view may be found in Newton's studies of alchemy.

The published book of *Observations upon the Prophecies of Daniel and the Apocalypse of St. John*[46] deals with this same problem of "the Prophetic Language"—a "figurative language" used by the Prophets and "taken from the analogy between the world natural, and an empire or kingdom considered as a world politic." Essentially the whole matter turns on Daniel's prophecy concerning the Messiah, and the preliminary prophetic statements about an "Image composed of four Metals" and a stone which broke "the four Metals to pieces." These are the four nations successively ruling the earth (*viz* the people of Babylonia, the Persians, the Greeks, and the Romans). The four nations are represented again in the "four Beasts." Reading through Newton's text is an exercise in history and a rather dull one. Here is no ecstasy of a mystic St Teresa or St John of the Cross, but a seemingly endless parade of dated events, lists of kings, battles, and successions, and an attempt to place all of them into a chronological frame that is more reminiscent of Newton's own *Chronology of Ancient Kingdoms Amended* than of the mystical writings of a Boehme. "The folly of Interpreters," says Newton, has been "to foretel times and things by this Prophecy, as if God designed to make them Prophets." This was, however, far from God's intent, according to Newton, for the prophecies were meant by God "not to gratify men's curiosities by enabling them to foreknow things" but rather to stand as witnesses to God's providence when "after they were fulfilled they might be interpreted by the event." Surely, he said, "the event of things predicted many ages before, will then be a convincing argument that the world is governed by providence." Nor is the *Observations* free from reference to Newton's favorite themes of the corruption of scripture and the corruption of Christianity.[47]

Newton died intestate in March 1727. Since he never married and had no children there inevitably arose a quarrel among his surviving relatives over the division of his estate—which we know amounted to "a considerable fortune."[48] Newton's papers were inventoried and evaluated for the heirs, and it was agreed that "only the *Chronology & Prophecies* [were] fit to be appraised"—the value of £250 was set for the *Chronology* "& no value upon the *Prophecies* they being imperfect."[49] Thomas Pellet, a Fellow of the Royal Society, gave his own examination, and most of Newton's manuscripts to this day bear his annotation, to which I have referred earlier, "Not fit to be printed." Very likely—as Whiteside reminds us—this remark has nothing to do with what we would consider the scholarly or intrinsic intellectual value of Newton's manuscripts, papers, or notebooks, but rather relates strictly to their "fitness" as complete works ready for printing and accordingly having monetary value.

A description of the evaluation of Newton's papers was written by John Conduitt, the husband of Newton's niece and Newton's successor at the Mint. Conduitt hoped to preserve as intact as possible all the remaining writings of the great man into whose family he had married. He relates that, according to Dr Pellet, there were only five works which were possibly in a state "fitt to be printed."[50] These included the ***Chronology of Ancient Kingdoms Amended,*** sold for £350 and printed for J. Tonson, the Strand bookseller; what was described as "A Mathematical tract De Motu Corporum," sold to Tonson for £31-10 and printed under the editorship of John Conduitt with the confusing title *De mundi systemate;*[51] Newton's work on the prophecies, published under the title ***Observations upon the Prophecies of Daniel and the Apocalypse of St. John*** (printed in 1733 by" J. Darby and T. Browne in Bartholomew Close"); a set of "Paradoxical Questions concerning Athanasius" which remains unpublished to this day, although extracts were published by David Brewster in his two-volume biography of Newton in 1855,[52] further extracts published by H. McLachlan in 1950,[53] and further extracts by F. E. Manuel in 1963;[54] and, finally, what is described as "an Imperfect Mathematical tract," probably—according to Whiteside[55]—a combination of "the unfinished 1666 English and 1671 Latin fluxional tracts . . . which Horsley was to find packaged together in 1777."

Conduitt attempted to prepare a biography of Newton, of which we have many fragmentary drafts, containing extracts from letters and biographical accounts which Conduitt solicited from many of those who knew Newton; these are precious documents for any biographer.[56] But Conduitt never took care to order, to catalogue in detail, or even to find a proper repository for the unpublished manuscripts, notebooks, correspondence, and other documents belonging to Newton.[57] His wife Catherine, Newton's niece,[58] was especially anxious to publish the papers of her famous uncle dealing with problems of religion and chronology; her will contains a codicil in which her executor is directed to "lay all the Tracts relating to Divinity before Dr. Sykes . . . in hopes he will prepare them for the press. . . ." Further, "I ordain" that "all of them . . . shall be printed and published, so as they be done with care and exactness." She noted that in relation to "whatever proffit may arise from the same, my dear Mr. Conduitt has given a bond of £2000 to be responsible to the seven nearest of kin to Sir Is. Newton." Therefore, she declared, "the papers must be carefully kept" and "no copys may be taken and printed." Additionally, "Dr. Sykes [is] desired to peruse them here, otherways if any accident comes to them the penalty of the Bond will be levy'd."[59] Apparently, "no new work of Isaac Newton's appeared in the stationers' catalogues"[60] until the Latin version of the 1671 fluxional tract was published fifty years later as part of the five-volume edition of Newton's ***Opera*** edited by Samuel Horsley.

John Conduitt died in May 1737, his wife Catherine in January 1739. Then Newton's papers passed to their daughter, who married John Wallop, who became Viscount Lymington when his father was created the first Earl of Portsmouth in 1743. These precious documents[61] remained in the Portsmouth family until, as we shall see, the "scientific portion" came to the University of Cambridge in the late 1880's and the rest were dispersed at public auction in the 1930's.

For various reasons, Horsley's five-volume edition of Newton's ***Opera*** does not contain any considerable new manuscript material, an exception being the selections from Newton's correspondence with Oldenburg which appear in Volume Four.[62] Horsley apparently was allowed to see the family collection too late to make any extensive use of it, for "his first volume [was] already in press in London and anxiously awaited by his subscribers."[63] Accordingly, in the mathematical field he only "suitably improved certain texts already scheduled for publication by collating them with the manuscript (notably emending the text of the "Geometria analytica,") which he had previously derived from two inferior copies, one indeed derivative from the other. . . ." A creative editor by the standards of his time, Horsley did make divisions, for example into chapters and paragraphs, and he provided valuable annotations for his edition of the ***Opticks,*** in which he indicated important changes in the queries from edition to edition, which have stood until our own times as the only major attempt to delineate the development of Isaac Newton's ideas on the nature of light, atoms, aether, particulate forces, and chemistry, as expressed in the queries.

The Second Revelation

The works in print by the end of the decade following Newton's death provided the world with an image of Newton and a knowledge of his mathematical and scientific acheivements that remained essentially unaltered for a century or more. The second revelation really began in about the middle of the 19th century, with the publication in 1855 of the two volumes of David Brewster's massive biography of Newton, with its extensive appendixes containing new texts published from manuscript sources.

Brewster's biography was only one of four important works published in the middle of the 19th century, each containing new material based upon manuscripts relating to Isaac Newton. The first was a collection by S. P. Rigaud (1838) containing documents chiefly relating to Newton's ***Principles*** with an important introduction. Rigaud published for the first time the text of the tract ***De motu*** which Newton wrote out after Halley's famous visit in 1684 and which is the first organized and complete statement of his analysis of elliptical orbital motion and his proof that if elliptical orbits result from the action of a central force on a body, the force must vary inversely as the square of the distance.[64] Rigaud also began a two-volume collection of correspondence in the possession of the Earl of Macclesfield, which contains valuable correspondence by and to Isaac Newton and the correspondence of others which is related to Newton. This collection, begun and organized by Rigaud, was finally published by his son in 1841, but an index was added by Augustus De Morgan only a number of years later (1862). A third work, one of the most valuable contributions to Newtonian scholarship ever produced, was the edition in 1850 of the letters which passed between Newton and Cotes (who prepared the second edition of the *Principles* under Newton's direction) and which are preserved in a large volume in the Trinity College Library. This exemplary work, with very illuminating and important notes by the editor, Joseph Edleston, is preceded by an extremely valuable detailed chronology of Newton's life, filled in with important documentary materials, such as Newton's entrances and exits from Trinity College according to the Register Book.

These three works filled out many details concerning Newton's scientific thought, but they do not really constitute a major revelation about Newton. That was reserved for David Brewster's two-volume biography (1855) with extensive documentary appendices.[65] It has been assumed, as L. T. More (a later biographer of Newton) asserted, that Brewster "made a very considerable use of Conduitt's manuscripts and of abstracts from Newton's correspondence, and some use of the mathematical notes and papers [but] used his discretion in extracting and in omitting many important documents which seemed to him not advantageous to Newton's reputation.[66] But Whiteside has shown that "Brewster was apparently never allowed unrestricted access to the Portsmouth manuscripts but limited almost wholly to the selection of biographically pertinent material, letters and papers selected for him by [Henry] Fellowes."[67] Brewster himself, as Whiteside has noted, is rather explicit on this matter:

> In this examination [of "the large mass of papers which Sir Isaac had left behind him"] our attention was particularly directed to such letters and papers as were calculated to throw light upon his early and academical life, and, with the assistance of Mr. Fellowes, who copied for me several important documents, I was enabled to collect many valuable materials unknown to preceding biographers. . . .

> The materials . . . are of great value; and in so far as Mr. H. A. Fellowes and I could make an abstract of these and other manuscripts during a week's visit at [Hurstbourne] Park, I have availed myself of them in composing the first volume of this work, which was printed before the papers themselves came into my hands.[68]

For the second volume, Brewster says that "I had the good fortune to obtain from the Earl of Portsmouth the collection of manuscripts and correspondence which the late Mr. H. A. Fellowes had examined and arranged as peculiarly fitted to throw light on the Life and Discoveries of Sir Isaac."[69]

Brewster has often been castigated for the fact that he so adulated his hero that he referred to Newton even in his school days as "young Sir Isaac," even though Newton was not knighted until old age. He was also criticized for having again and again called Newton the "High Priest of Science." Yet it must be kept in mind that the phrase "High Priest of Science" was not of Brewster's own invention but was merely taken over by him from what is perhaps the first true biography of Newton, by William Stukeley,[70] who wrote a short version to be used by Conduitt in preparing his own biography of Newton. Stukeley did a considerable amount of research, it should be noted, and he even submitted Newton to an oral-history interview, thereby inaugurating that practice in the history of science. Stukeley relates that when he asked Newton how he came to think of the law of universal gravity, Newton replied that it was while sitting in a garden, much as he was while having tea with Stukeley.[71] Apparently, therefore, Newton himself was the originator of the apple story.[72] I have long considered that Stukeley's actions may serve as an object lesson to all historians of science. He had a unique opportunity to ask Newton: And what were the circumstances? How did the falling of an apple bring this idea into your mind? In what year did this occur? What had you been thinking about at that time? But Stukeley merely went on to the next subject.[73]

What is probably of the greatest significance in Brewster's two-volume life is the fact that for the first time in print some real indication was given of Newton's actual manuscript writings on theology and alchemy. With regard to the latter, Brewster was quite shocked to find that the "High Priest of Science" not only had been a devotee of alchemy, but had copied out (in his own hand) works that Brewster could only describe as foul and characterized by charlatanry.[74] He also wanted it believed that one of Newton's major aims in studying alchemy was to discredit the pretensions of that subject. Yet, for all that, Brewster had to admit: "There is no problem of more difficult solution than that which relates to the belief in alchemy, and to the practice of its arts, by men of high character and lofty attainments."[75] Brewster pointed out that there are remarkable changes in nature, such as that gold and silver and other metals "may be extracted from transparent crystals, which scarcely differ in their appearance from a piece of common salt or a bit of sugar-candy."[76] He also said that it is astonishing that aluminum "can be extracted from clay," or that "lights of the most dazzling colours can be obtained from the combustion of colourless salts," or that "gas, giving the most brilliant light, resides in a lump of coal or a block of wood." Need we then wonder, says Brewster, "that the most extravagant expectations were entertained of procuring from the basest materials the precious metals and the noblest gems."[77]

But how really could men of such rational character and scientific soundness—Newton, Boyle, and Locke—give their time and intellectual energy to the study of alchemy? Of course, said Brewster, the "ambition neither of wealth nor of praise prompted their studies." He pompously declared: "We may safely say that a love of truth alone, a desire to make new discoveries in chemistry, and a wish to test the extraordinary pretensions of their predecessors and their contemporaries, were the only motives by which they were actuated."[78] Thus, he continued, "insofar as Newton's inquiries were limited to the transmutation and multiplication of metals, and even to the discovery of the universal tincture, we may find some apology for his researches."[79] But Brewster quite frankly admitted his own complete inability to "understand how a mind of such power, and so nobly occupied with the abstractions of geometry, and the study of the material world, could stoop to be even the copyist of the most contemptible alchemical poetry, and the annotator of a work, the obvious production of a fool and a knave." Yet he was forced to explain: "Such, however, was the taste of the century in which Newton lived, and, when we denounce the mental epidemics of the past age, we may find some palliation of them in those of our own times."[80] Brewster sadly admitted the fact and there was nothing he could do about it, but he did conclude with the expression of a pious belief that "there is reason to believe" that Newton "had learned to have but little confidence even in the humbler department of the multiplication of metals." Forsooth!

Brewster was honest enough to admit that he had seen in Newton's own handwriting *The Metamorphoses of the Planets* by John De Monte Snyders together with a key to it, plus "numerous pages of alchemist poetry," chiefly from Norton's *Ordinal* and Basil Valentine's *Mystery of the Microcosm*. He also had seen a copy of *Secrets Revealed, Or an Open Entrance to the Shut Palace of the King,* "covered with notes in Sir Isaac's hand, in which great changes are made upon the language and meaning of the thirty-five chapters of which it consists."[81] And so on. Brewster did not hide from the world the fact that Newton made "copious extracts from the writings of the alchemists of all ages," and that he produced a "very large *Index Chemicus* and *Supplementum Indicis Chemici,* with minute references to the different subjects to which they relate."[82] Who could doubt that Newton had been a serious student of alchemy, even making alchemical experiments during his most creative period of life, the 1680's, while writing the **Principles**?

With regard to theology, the problem was somewhat different for Brewster. He had earlier published a one-volume work in which he asserted that Newton was certainly a believer in the Trinity and orthodox.[83] But now, having had access to the manuscripts, from which he quoted at length, he had to tone down his earlier assertion. Painful as it must have been for him, Brewster did print a number of texts and extracts from the manuscripts which make it obvious that Newton had strong Unitarian or Arian leanings.[84]

On the more positive side, Brewster assembled sound evidence to prove that Biot had made an error in assuming that Newton's interest in theology arose in his old age, when he was in his dotage and unable to do any more creative work in mathematics and the sciences. And Brewster made available an enormous amount of new documentary information concerning Newton's creative scientific career, the development and reception of his ideas and their philosophical implications, and the facts of Newton's life. But although Brewster did show that there was substance in the rumors concerning Newton's pursuit of alchemy and interest in theology, this second revelation did not inspire scholars to attempt to make a further study of Newton's manuscripts (which might have proved impossible in any event). Thus Brewster's biography remained the standard source for knowledge of Newton's religious beliefs until the third revelation, which has only occurred in the last decades.

Between the Second and Third Revelations

A number of significant events occurred between the second and third revelations. In July 1872, two eminent Cambridge mathematicians, Professor John Couch Adams and Professor Sir George G. Stokes, went to Hurstbourne Park "to look over the Newton papers"[85] and to report back to the university concerning them. When Adams and Stokes saw the vast size and variety of the collection, they quickly realized that they could not study these manuscripts in the time of a brief visit. Lord Portsmouth graciously agreed to send all of the papers, including "two *copies* of the Principia 1st & 2nd Editions corrected by Newton" and "a Number of Fragments relating to Mathematics," plus "some very interesting letters from Eminent Men to Newton" and "memoranda Books &c relating to personal matters."[86] Lord Portsmouth made it clear, however, that he was only "willing to *lend*" most of these items. It was his "wish," he said, "to advance the interests of science by placing these Papers at the service of the University, but [he concluded] I would rather cut my hand off than sever my connection with Newton which is the proudest Boast of my Family."[87]

It was evidently the wish of the Earl of Portsmouth "to make . . . over to the University" the papers and correspondence relating to science, since he believed "that these would find a more appropriate home in the Library of Newton's own University than in that of a private individual."[87a]

Newton's manuscripts, correspondence, and papers were studied in Cambridge over the next 16 years by a syndicate composed of Adams and Stokes plus the Reverend Henry Richards Luard (Registry of the University and Perpetual Curate of Great St Mary's) and George Downing Liveing (of St John's College, professor of chemistry). This syndicate produced a catalogue of the collection[88] after they had made a laborious examination and classification. They divided the collection into two parts, half of which was given by the Earl of Portsmouth to the University Library, where it is usually referred to as the Portsmouth Collection,[89] and the remainder returned to the Earl. The syndicate noted that the job "has proved a lengthy and laborious business, as many of the papers were found to be in great confusion—mathematical notes being often inserted in the middle of theological treatises, and even numbered leaves of MSS. having got out of order. Moreover a large portion of the collection has been grievously damaged by fire and damp. The correspondence, however, is in a very fair condition throughout, and had been arranged in an orderly manner."[90]

It should be noted that the catalogue covers the whole collection of Newton's books and papers, not merely the portion given to the University. The preface of 20 pages begins with a two-page summary of the history of the manuscripts and an account of the committee's activities, then devotes two pages to Newton's work on the lunar theory, two pages to Newton's work on refraction, half a page to the determination of "the form of the solid of least resistance," and two pages to the extensive manuscript materials relating to Newton's quarrel with Leibniz over priority in the invention of the calculus.[91] A whole page is devoted to an autobiographical statement about how Newton made his discoveries, and then there are brief notes concerning the manuscripts on alchemy and on historical and theological subjects, plus an appendix giving a sample of the riches of the collection.[92] While studying the collection, Adams and Luard made careful long-hand transcripts of many letters and documents which were intended to be returned to the Earl of Portsmouth.[93]

It might be supposed that the availability to scholars of this rich treasure of historical materials, the nature of which was made evident by the published catalogue, would have attracted a certain amount of scholarly attention. But for about half a century this great collection remained virtually unused in the University Library at Cambridge. We may agree with Whiteside that "inexplicably its contemporary impact was almost nil."[94] Perhaps the reason is that "no member of the cataloguing syndicate implemented the official report with an enlightening secondary study, historical or

biographical, of any of the documents he had pondered over so long."

The literature of the history of science shows that during this period of a half-century, only one major use was made of the collection, by the historian of mathematics Walter William Rouse Ball. He published the results of a careful examination of Newton's unpublished manuscript (in the Portsmouth Collection) on the classification of cubic curves (1891) and also a brief but important critique of a manuscript of Newton on central forces (1892). He also published, from the manuscripts, an essay of Newton's on the role of mathematics in university education.[95] Additionally, he drew on the Newtonian manuscript corpus in preparing his important essay on the "genesis of the *Principia.*"[96] Here, among other things, Rouse Ball included the text of Newton's tract *De motu,* which—as I have mentioned—had been published some 50 years earlier by Rigaud, from the version in the Royal Society.

Whiteside found only two other serious users of the Portsmouth Collection prior to the 1930's.[97] Duncan C. Fraser published and analyzed some of Newton's papers on interpolation,[98] and a German scholar, Alexander Witting, "studied the fluxional manuscripts in Cambridge and prepared a preliminary report."[99] The latter undertook this work a few years before the 1914 war and, when the war was over, never returned to it.

In the 30's, Louis Trenchard More examined the papers in the Portsmouth Collection in the University Library and also had access to the papers still in the possession of the family. In the preface to his biography (1934), he expressed his gratitude "to Blanche, Lady Portsmouth, and to her nephew, Viscount Lymington, who, although I was then a stranger to them, sent their priceless collection in Hurstbourne Park to the British Museum in order that I might examine and use it at my leisure." Although More quoted some extracts from Newton's MS documents and notebooks, he apparently did not bother much with the large body of material assembled by Newton relating to alchemy. In his discussion of this subject, in fact, the only extracts he quoted are a letter from Newton to Oldenburg about Boyle's experiments (previously published in the works of Boyle and in Rigaud's two volumes of selections from the Macclesfield Collection) and a little over a page extracted from the published Query 31 of the *Opticks.* But More did state, unequivocally, "The fact of the matter is, Newton was an alchemist, and his major interest in chemistry, in his earlier years, centred in the possibility of transmuting metals." And he added that there was "a mystical strain" in Newton's "character which had been quite overlooked. It showed itself not only in his persistent reading of the esoteric formulae of the alchemists, but also in his sympathy for the philosophy of the Cambridge Platonists and in his extended interpretations of the prophecies of the

Books of Daniel and of the Revelation."[100] More argued that "there can be no doubt that [Newton] not only seriously sought the transmutation of metals into gold and the universal panacea for disease and old age, but also believed them to be the chief goal of the chemist."[101] But More gave no idea of the vast extent of Newton's alchemical manuscripts, including his lengthy transcripts of writings on this subject, his attempt to catalogue the authors and to find out which were the best, and his efforts to find identities in language and expression among the many writers on the subject.

In a lengthy footnote occupying half a page, More[102] attacked the statement of Brewster that Newton's alchemy, as well as Boyle's and Locke's, was not of the kind "commencing in fraud and terminating in mysticism." And he indicated that Brewster had erred in stating that it had been "a love of truth alone" and "a wish to test the *extraordinary pretensions* of their predecessors and their contemporaries" that had provided "the only motives by which [Boyle, Newton, and Locke] were actuated."

More, however, did better with Newton's theology. In fact, More stated expressly:

> What we can learn from the published theological works of Newton is obscured by his caution, a caution which must have been increased by the misfortunes of Whiston. When I was generously given permission to examine, and to make extracts from, the *Portsmouth Collection* I was particularly anxious to see whether the vexed question of his religious opinions could not be answered from the documents which Horsley and Brewster did not feel it wise to publish. And I think the answer can now be given.[103]

More concluded that Newton "was wholly committed, as was Milton, to the Protestant doctrine against the authority of the Church Councils." And he emphasized the fact that "personally, Newton was an Arian since he states definitely that the Father and the Son are not one substance; that the Son was created and therefore of a different substance for, if they were of one substance then, the Father having created the substance of the Son, He must have created His own substance."[104] According to More, "Newton goes much farther than merely to deny the doctrine of consubstantiation. He had rationally adopted the Unitarian position that Jesus was sent by the Father into the world as a Prophet who differed from the other Prophets only in the immediacy of the message delivered to him." Yet, "like so may other Unitarians of the day, such as Locke, he . . . makes a break between reason and practice, since he maintained his affiliation with the Church of England."[105] Clearly, save for an aspect of Newton's theological beliefs, More's biography did not substantially change our view of Newton. The third revelation had not yet occurred by the 1930's, despite a half-century of availability of the Portsmouth Collection.[105a]

The Third Revelation

The first date in the third revelation is 1936. In that year, in order to pay the death duties, the family turned over the remaining mass of Newtonian manuscripts, annotated books, correspondence, notebooks, and personal memorabilia, including portraits and busts (but not the major portraits in oil) for public auction at Sotheby's. There were in the material put up for auction some three million words in Newton's autograph, according to the estimate of the cataloguer, and—shocking as it seems to us today—the total realized by this sale was a mere £9030-10s-0d, less than $30,000. The late A.N.L. Munby remarked that the sale did have at least one beneficial effect: the sale catalogue assembled by John Taylor.[106] This catalogue is a learned document, giving extensive extracts from many of the most important documents, and reproducing pages from a number of the major texts in facsimile. Here, for example, was startling and dramatic proof of the extent of Newton's involvement in alchemy.

As a result of the sale, Newton's manuscripts were literally scattered to the four corners of the earth and some have—one hopes only temporarily—disappeared from sight altogether. Thanks to the foresight of Lord Keynes (the economist John Maynard Keynes),[107] a large number of Newton's major alchemical manuscripts and the materials assembled by John Conduitt for preparing a biography of Newton were put together in a single collection and returned to the University of Cambridge, permanently this time, in King's College Library. Also, thanks to the activities of a variety of interested parties, some of these important documents ended up in Trinity, which had already been given a major part of the books from Newton's personal library, some of them annotated in Newton's hand and others dog-eared—as was Newton's fashion—so that the corner of the page would point toward a place of interest.[108]

One of the effects of this sale was to call attention to the extent of Newton's still unpublished papers, but it must be confessed that there was not an immediate flurry of Newton scholarship. The reason is that many of Newton's papers had been purchased by dealers in books and manuscripts and were not available for study. Only gradually did they become concentrated in a few private collections and find their way into libraries where they could be studied. No doubt, interest in Newton and in his manuscripts would have been stimulated by the tercentenary of his birth (1942), but even that could not be properly celebrated until after the war.[109]

As everyone knows, since the 1950's, Newton scholarship has grown into what has become called a "Newton industry," although there has been no concerted effort to produce a standard and uniform edition of Newton's writings like the editions of Galileo, of Huygens, and (in progress) of Kepler. The Royal Society did undertake to produce an edition of Newton's correspondence, now complete in seven volumes, begun under the editorship of H. W. Turnbull, continued by J. F. Scott, and completed by A. Rupert Hall and Laura Tilling. Not only does this edition include letters written by Newton and received by him, but there is also a generous selection of manuscript documents relating to scientific and other questions by Newton and—in particular—by David Gregory, who made many memoranda after visiting Newton and seeing his manuscripts and work in progress. The most notable work of editing in Newtonian scholarship has been the magisterial *Mathematical Papers of Isaac Newton,* produced under the able editorship of D.T. Whiteside of Cambridge University, just completed in eight tremendous volumes. Here are assembled, ordered, and classified all of Newton's writings on—or related to—mathematics, together with historical, analytical, and interpretive commentaries and introductions that by themselves constitute one of the major contributions to the history of mathematics, the history of 17th-century science, and our understanding of Newton's development, Alexandre Koyré, Anne Whitman, and I assembled an edition of Newton's *Principles* that was based on a collation of the printer's MS, the three printed editions (1687, 1713, 1726), and two examples of the second and of the first editions containing Newton's MS revisions. This work is currently being supplemented by a new English version of Newton's *Principles* and of the *Essay on the System of the Universe.*[110] Two major jobs of editing Newton's writings are Henry Guerlac's forthcoming edition of the *Opticks* and Alan Shapiro's edition of the *Optical Lectures.* In 1962, A. Rupert and Marie Boas Hall brought out a major collection of *Unpublished Scientific Papers of Isaac Newton,* followed in 1965 by John Herivel's *The Background to Newton's "Principia,"* a substantial part of which was an edited anthology of MS writings of Isaac Newton. Newton's published *Papers & Letters on Natural Philosophy* were edited for publication in 1958 (second edition, 1978) by I. B. Cohen, assisted by R. E. Schofield. A large company of scholars have studied, edited, or published important manuscript material in books and articles. They include A. Rupert Hall and Marie Boas Hall, John W. Herivel, Frank Manuel, Henry Guerlac, J. E. McGuire, P.M. Rattansi, Alexandre Koyré, R. S. Westfall, Betty Jo Teeter Dobbs, Karin Figala, I. B. Cohen, Alan Shapiro, J. P. Lohne, and others. The effect of their writings cumulatively is to produce the third revelation of Newton.[110a]

The esoteric side of this thrice-revealed Newton was heralded in a famous lecture written by Lord Keynes and read by his brother, Sir Geoffrey, at the Newton Tercentenary Meetings at the Royal Society. A some-what startled audience heard that Keynes—who had studied deeply the manuscripts that he had collected after the sale of the Portsmouth Papers—no longer believed in the traditional image of Newton but held that there was an altogether different Newton revealed by his secret papers. This now thrice-revealed Newton was described by Keynes as follows:

> In the eighteenth century and since, Newton came to be thought of as the first and greatest of the modern age of scientists, a rationalist, one who taught us to think on the lines of cold and untinctured reason.
>
> I do not see him in this light. I do not think that any one who has pored over the contents of that box which he packed up when he finally left Cambridge in 1696 and which, though partly dispersed, have come down to us, can see him like that. Newton was not the first of the age of reason. He was the last of the magicians, the last of the Babylonians and Sumerians, the last great mind which looked out on the visible and intellectual world with the same eyes as those who began to build our intellectual inheritance rather less than 10,000 years ago. Isaac Newton, a posthumous child born with no father on Christmas Day, 1642, was the last wonderchild to whom the Magi could do sincere and appropriate homage.

Then Keynes went on to say:

> Why do I call him a magician? Because he looked on the whole universe and all that is in it *as a riddle,* as a secret which could be read by applying pure thought to certain evidence, certain mystic clues which God had laid about the world to allow a sort of philosopher's treasure hunt to the esoteric brotherhood. He believed that these clues were to be found partly in the evidence of the heavens and in the constitution of elements (and that is what gives the false suggestion of his being an experimental natural philosopher), but also partly in certain papers and traditions handed down by the brethren in an unbroken chain back to the original cryptic revelation in Babylonia. He regarded the universe as a cryptogram set by the Almighty—just as he himself wrapt the discovery of the calculus in a cryptogram when he communicated with Leibnitz. By pure thought, by concentration of mind, the riddle, he believed, would be revealed to the initiate.[111]

This was strong medicine and hard to take, for Keynes was suggesting that Newton was to be understood through alchemy, mystic philosophy, and the Hermetic tradition and not through mathematics, physics, and astronomy, as had been customary for three centuries.

Keynes's paper was written for a private group in Trinity College, and there was no way of telling whether or not he might have rewritten it for a public lecture to an international company of scientists at the Royal Society's celebrations of the tercentenary of Newton's birth. He died before the celebrations, and the original text—unrevised—was read by his brother in 1946 and published as part of the proceedings in 1947. One year later, in 1948, A. Rupert Hall published what may now be considered a landmark article on "Sir Isaac Newton's Note-Book," the first scholarly article of the third revelation to be based on the manuscripts.[112]

As far as I can tell, the next work to use Newton's unpublished MSS was the edition of Newton's *Theological Manuscripts* in 1950 by Herbert McLachlan, who drew upon the riches of the Keynes Collection. In that same year, there was published *A Descriptive Catalogue of the Grace K. Babson Collection of the Works of Isaac Newton,* with an account of the great manuscripts acquired from the Portsmouth sale. Here were full descriptions of alchemical MSS, Newton's treatise in MS on Solomon's Temple, notes on the Athanasian creed, and other theological documents. But there was no further new revelation from the MSS until Hall's second paper, in 1955, on "Further Optical Experiments of Newton." My own *Franklin and Newton* of 1956 did not draw on MSS at all, since its aim was to trace the public tradition of Newtonian science during the 18th century.[113] In 1953, however, Professor Turnbull revealed some aspects of Newton's calculations of lunar gravity of 1665-66, but he did so not in a scholarly journal but in the *Manchester Guardian.*[114]

I find that the next use of MSS, in 1957, was again by Rupert Hall, on Newton's early calculation of central forces. And in the following year, 1958, there was the first of a series of papers by A. Rupert Hall and Marie Boas Hall, drawing on Newton's MSS—this one on Newton's chemical experiments. It was in this same year that I brought out my edition of Newton's published *Papers & Letters on Natural Philosophy.*

In 1959, the first volume of the long-awaited edition of Newton's correspondence heralded a new wealth of available source materials for understanding the life and thought of Isaac Newton, and in 1962, A.R. Hall and Marie Boas Hall continued the pioneer work of the third revelation of Newton with their volume of *Unpublished Scientific Papers of Isaac Newton.* The Halls listed the major scholars known to them who had used or quoted from Newton's manuscripts. Among the names in their list were D. Geoghegan, who in 1957 had published a few extracts from "the alchemical papers in King's College;" F. Sherwood Taylor, who in that same year printed "a composite of quotations from alchemical authors put together by Newton;" and Sir John Craig, who had used "the papers sold in 1936, though printing none *in extenso.*"[115] The Halls also referred to David Eugene Smith, who in 1927 had published two documents; Alexandre Koyré,

who in 1961 had published the MS texts of Newton's "Rules"; J. W. Herivel, who in 1960 and 1961 had published his first extracts from Newton's early studies of dynamics; and R. S. Westfall, who in 1958 had discussed "Newton's theology with some reference to the King's College papers." It was not a very impressive list, and it gave no hint of the "Newton industry" just coming into being.

I shall not attempt to summarize the contents of the Halls' seminal volume. But there are at least four extraordinary revelations about Newton in it. One is an essay which the Halls entitled "De gravitatione et aequipondio fluidorum," a general discussion of the principles of physics based upon young Newton's reading in Descartes' *Principles of Philosophy* and published scientific correspondence. Here was an indication of the profound influence of Descartes' science and philosophy upon Newton. Another was the revelation of Newton's intended but incomplete" Conclusio" written for his *Principles,* in which Newton expressed his aim of producing a science of particulate matter equivalent to his science of gross bodies. A third was the analysis of the stages of composition of the "General Scholium" with its mysterious reference to "subtle spirit," which turned out to be Hauksbee's electrical effluvia. Finally, the Halls showed how Newton was tending toward a philosophy of nature in which he added the concept of particulate forces (attraction and repulsion) to the received categories or principles of the "mechanical philosophy"—matter and motion.

What Has Been Revealed

I shall not attempt here to make a complete review of all of the new revelations brought about by the study of the manuscripts. To do so would be tantamount to making a critical inventory of the whole corpus of Newton scholarship during the last 20 years or so. But I shall indicate some of the highlights of the scholarly work that constitutes the third and final revelation.[116] To me, one of the most interesting parts of the revelation has been the demonstration of the true importance of Descartes in the development of Newton's scientific and mathematical thought. It is generally known that in his *Principles* Newton refers to Descartes only indirectly, in a proof at the end of Book Two that the system of vortices is inconsistent with the astronomical phenomena, namely, Kepler's laws of planetary motion.[117] Mathematicians and historians, going back at least to Clairaut and Lagrange,[118] have even suggested that the whole purpose of Book Two was to demolish the Cartesian theory of vortices. Not only was Newton's dynamical astronomy thus supposed to be a frontal attack on the Cartesian scientific system, but this was the case also in mathematics. Newton's relation to Descartes was charaterized by the remarks quoted by Brewster that Newton's copy of Descartes' *Geometry* bore the comments in Newton's hand, again and again, "Error" or "non est Geom."[119] Accordingly, it came as a considerable surprise—as first shown, with full documentary detail, by Rupert and Marie Hall[120] that Newton had made a careful study of Descartes' writings and that many of his own scientific ideas—for instance, those about dynamics and inertia—were developed as he contemplated the writings of Descartes. The relation between Descartes' physical concepts and Newton's was clarified by the writings of Alexandre Koyré, who traced the relationship between Newton's definition and statement of the law of inertia and Descartes' statement,[121] a study which I myself helped to complete by showing the steps of transmission and transformation by which Newton attained his own first law of motion from Descartes' law of nature.[122] It even turns out that the title of Newton's "Mathematical Principles of Natural Philosophy" is only a transformation of Descartes' title "Principles of Philosophy." The very phrase used by Newton, "Axiomata, sive Leges Motus,"[123] was a transformation of what he found in Descartes' *Principles,* "Regulae quaedem sive leges naturae."[124] Not only did Newton write in terms of the new idea of a "state" of motion (which, as Koyré showed, was obtained directly from Descartes),[125] but I found that even such a phrase as "quantum in se est" which Newton used for inertia was taken directly from Descartes in this context; it came originally from Lucretius. Thus I found a dramatic illustration of how Newton's concepts were born by transformation of Descartes' ideas.[126] At the same time, Whiteside showed in the first volume of his monumental edition of *The Mathematical Papers of Isaac Newton* that Newton's fundamental ideas of the calculus were first forged and developed in his study of Descartes' *Geometry,* in a Latin edition by Schooten with tracts by other mathematicians. Thus there could no longer be any doubt whatever of the supreme importance of Descartes for Newton's dynamics and eventually celestial mechanics, as well as his invention of the calculus. And, as it finally turned out, the volume of Descartes' *Geometry* in which Newton had written "Error, Error" did not contain this word as a characterization of Cartesian mathematics as a whole, but indicated where Descartes had made errors; and "non est Geom." appeared in certain places where Newton indicated that the discussion by Descartes was not from a narrow and strict point of view to be considered "geometry."[127]

Another aspect of Newton's thought revealed by the manuscripts has been studied primarily by Henry Guerlac,[128] who has traced the vagaries or variations in Newton's concept of the aether and the degree of his adherence to a belief in the aether. Thus, while Newton early believed in an aether that had a kind of substance, he then went through a period in which he thought that the aether—if it existed at all—had to be so tenuous that it could not produce most of the effects that he wished to attribute to it. Then later on he became excited by the work of Hauksbee and adopted a

different kind of aether or "aetherial medium" in the final queries of the *Opticks.*[129] R. S. Westfall has traced the relations between Newton's changing views about the aether and his concept of force.[130] Meanwhile, J. E. McGuire, working alone and also with P. M. Rattansi, showed how Newton believed in a priscan wisdom and thus thought that the scientific knowledge attained by Newton himself had largely been known to ancient seers or sages in Greece or Asia Minor.[131] Newton considered that many of the great advances in science in his day (including his own discovery of universal gravity) were to a large degree only rediscoveries of what had been known long before. McGuire has also used the manuscripts to show the development of Newton's ideas about transmutation and transformation of matter and has elucidated Newton's conception of "passive" and "active" forces in matter.[132] This has been a very valuable part of our understanding of Newton's concept of force in general and of the properties of matter, which are of course basic to his physics. At the same time, Frank Manuel has made a very fundamental contribution to our understanding of Newton's historical studies, notably his chronologies, and the stages of development of his religious ideas.[133] He has also drawn heavily on the corpus of Newtonian MSS for his *Portrait of Isaac Newton* (1968). The Halls and R. S. Westfall have written about Newton's ideas concerning matter and force. In particular, Westfall has used the manuscripts of Newton not only to trace the development of Newton's idea of force, but to elucidate what he calls Newton's radical revision of the "mechanical philosophy" of Descartes to which he generally adhered, according to which all phenomena were to be explained by matter and motion.[134] Westfall sees Newton as having added to that received philosophy the concept of force.[135] Westfall has also studied the optical manuscripts of Newton, another aspect of tracing the development of Newton's ideas concerning the aether.[136] It should be added that J. A. Lohne and Alan Shapiro have also worked fruitfully with the optical manuscripts.[137] Among other interesting revelations here is the fact that Newton's great paper on the nature of light and colors (1672) turns out to be something of a "scenario," because the way in which he describes the events of his exploration of dispersion and his description of his own reaction to his observations of prismatic spectra cannot be squared with the evidence of his prior knowledge as provided by the manuscript notebooks.[138] It should be noted that Zev Bechler has made an interesting set of studies of Newton's attempts to formulate a mathematical model for optical theory, in a style somewhat like that adopted for dynamics and celestial mechanics in Newton's *Principles.*[139] Westfall has also made a thorough study of Newton's early theological manuscripts and has shown among other things that Newton's concern for theology arose when it became necessary for him to contemplate holy orders in order to keep his Trinity College Fellowship.

In this, Westfall has drawn heavily on the Yahuda manuscripts, now in the University of Jerusalem and acquired by A. S. Yahuda from the Portsmouth sale at Sotheby's.[140] This subject has also been explored in an illuminating manner by Frank Manuel in his volume on Newton's religion, based upon this same collection of Newtonian manuscripts in Jerusalem.[141]

One of the long-standing puzzles about Newton's scientific work was how he could have claimed to have used the law for centrifugal force (v^2/r) in the 1660's in order to derive the inverse-square law of force for uniform circular motion.[142] The problem was one of dates, since Huygens did not publish the law until 1673 in his *Horologium oscillatorium.* The MSS contain the answer, as J. W. Herivel discovered.[143] He found that Newton had come upon this law independently about a decade or so before the publication of Huygens's book. Newton's derivation and the form in which he presented the law differ greatly from what is found in Huygens's book (which contains no derivatives or proof, but only a bare statement of the law in words). Since Newton is apt to be not wholly trustworthy on questions of dates and discoveries, it is pleasant to be able to record that in this case the MSS show that he had discovered this law just as he said he had done.

There is one further aspect of this third revelation which I have reserved until last, because it is in many ways the most striking and the most controversial. I refer here to Newton and hermeticism in general, and Newton's relation to alchemy in particular.

Today we look on Newton's alchemy in a way that is totally different from that of the 19th-century commentators on Newton, of whom Brewster is a striking example. Part of the third revelation concerning Newton has been the result of carefully reading his papers on alchemy and finding that during the most creative period of his life Newton was a serious student of alchemy, as in fact Brewster reluctantly had to admit. But we do not necessarily approach the subject today by considering it contemptible. After all, modern atomic and nuclear physics has shown that Newton was distressingly right when he said that Nature delights in transmutations.[144] We have learned in our own century that transmutations of the elements are constantly going on naturally all around us as one atom dies and gives birth to another in all the radioactive elements and that these transformations have been going on since the beginning of matter.

In this area we are indebted to F. Sherwood Taylor and D. Geoghegan[145] for brave beginnings and to A. Rupert and Marie Boas Hall[146] for serious inquiries, carried on by Richard S. Westfall.[147] But of greatest consequence are two full-length works of major importance on Newton's alchemical manuscripts and their meaning by Betty Jo Teeter Dobbs[148] and by Karin Figala. As a result of these studies, it is now, as the lawyers say, "open and notorious" that Newton was so deeply steeped in his alchemical studies and researches that—to use a kind of alchemical term—much of his scientific thinking must obviously have been "tinctured" with alchemical ideas, imagery, and theories.[149] For example, Newton's concept of the aether was clearly related to his alchemical thinking.[150] And there can be, it seems to me, no doubt whatsoever (a conclusion which is so obvious that it would seem almost supererogatory to say it, save that no one did say it until fairly recently) that Newton's extensive reflections on the "theory of matter," and especially on the composition of matter and the particulate forces in matter, must be closely related to and possibly even to some degree derived from the realm of alchemy.

And so the study and the editing of Newton's manuscripts show that Keynes was to a degree correct. There is revealed to us a man who, during the three decades of his residence in Cambridge, most of it as Lucasian Professor of Mathematics, was devoting intense creative energies to studying the literature of alchemy—both esoteric and exoteric—and making alchemical experiments, working out the meaning of the prophetic books of the Bible (Daniel and Revelation), trying to find the wisdom of ancient sages and seers, solving (to his own satisfaction) problems of biblical and historical chronology, studying church history, and wrestling with problems of pure theology. Is this the same Newton who is revered as the founder of modern rational science? In the extreme it has been suggested that we have "perhaps mistaken the thrust of Newton's career," that whereas "to us, the *Principia* inevitably appears as [the] . . . climax [of that career], in Newton's perspective it may have seemed more like an interruption of his primary labor."[151]

Betty Jo Teeter Dobbs, who has produced exemplary studies of the principles and practices of alchemy as revealed in Newton's MSS, comes to the general conclusion that it was "the *wedding* of the Hermetic tradition with the mechanical philosophy which produced modern science as its offspring." Part of the reason is that "Newton's concept of forces between particles derived initially from terrestrial phenomena, especially chemical ones," and that "it was the concept of gravitation, that fundamental tenet of Newton's law of universal gravitation, which was so derived." She would thus suggest that "the 'active Principles' of the Hermetic tradition" were "incorporated into the attractive force of gravity."[152]

I believe we must be extremely careful about this third revelation, for there is a temptation to assume that because Newton had such deep interests in alchemy and prophecy and ancient wisdom he produced his positive science out of these elements. But I believe the documents do not support this position. Newton, it seems to me, was not unusual because of his concern with prophecy, alchemy, and ancient wisdom. Indeed, when we think of the similar interests of Boyle and Locke, we find that it would have been unusual if Newton had *not* been so concerned.[153] To me, it is not significant that the founder of our rational mathematics and physical science should have been so steeped in esoteric subjects, but that he could have under those conditions, or in spite of those conditions, produced his masterpiece of modern hard science and established or inaugurated the first clearly recognized revolution in modern physical science. But, as Frances Yates wisely remarked to me when I discussed this extraordinary aspect of Newton's career with her, "We must remember that Newton was a genius."[153a]

The Documents of the Third Revelation

Let me now turn to the documents that have enabled us to make this third revelation. The mass of documentary materials that comprise the corpus of Newtonian MSS is staggering in its extent. A literal pack rat, he saved scraps of paper from his college days and his early notebooks as a student. There remain thousands of MS pages relating to optics, astronomy, mechanics, mathematics, chronology, theology, alchemy, and the Mint, and a huge stack devoted to the controversy with Leibniz on priority in the matter of the calculus. There are books from his library with extensive MS annotations. The result is that we can trace the development of Newton's ideas in agonizing detail in many domains of his intellectual interest. But there is one major exception. We do not have the working papers in which he made the rough drafts and notes for the *Mathematical Principles of Natural Philosophy.* There are contemporaneous stories about Newton having burned some of his papers, and perhaps these were among the ones thrown into the flames. We can trace the alterations—proposed and actual—to the *Principles* once it was cast in all but final form, but we do not know how he discovered and proved his theorems.[154] I myself am convinced that the path of Newton's intellectual invention proceeded more or less in the order and form in which he presented his results in the *Principles.* Newton, however, alleged that the theorems in large part had been "invented by [the method of] Analysis." But, as he said, "considering that the Ancients . . . admitted nothing into Geometry before it was demonstrated by Composition [or Synthesis], I composed what I invented by Analysis to make it more Geometrically authentic & fit for the publick."[155] This was part of Newton's campaign to make it appear that he had actually used the newly invented calculus in the first stages of the *Principles* and then rewritten his work "in words at length after the manner of the Ancients without Analytical calculations." Such was his answer to the charge raised by the Leibnizians: If the really had invented the fluxional calculus, how could he possibly have written the *Principles* without using fluxions? Could it

be that he destroyed this particular set of papers so as to be able to defend an invented scenario of discovery without having material evidence at hand to disturb his conscience?[156]

When the first edition of the **Principles** was published in 1687, Newton prepared at least two special copies to record emendations for a future edition—one was interleaved and specially bound for this purpose. And he did the same for the second edition in preparation for an eventual third edition.[157] I know of no author at this time who made such specially annotated and interleaved copies of his works. And so when Alexandre Koyré, Anne Whitman, and I came to edit the **Principles,** we were able to collate the three printed versions, the printer's MS, an annotated and an interleaved first edition, and an annotated and an interleaved second edition—eight in all.

Some of the differences are minor, some of great significance. In the first edition, "The System of the Universe" (Book 3) opens with a set of hypotheses. In the second edition, some of them become phenomena.[157a] While writing out the concluding General Scholium for the second edition (1713), with its famous slogan *Hypotheses non fingo* ("I frame [or feign] no hypotheses"), Newton said that whatever is neither a phenomenon nor deduced from phenomena is a hypothesis. This statement occurs plainly in the published version. Had he changed his mind? In any event, there are still three plainly labeled hypotheses in the final **Principles,** despite *Hypotheses non fingo.*[157b]

Of the major changes in successive editions, attention may be called to the following. In Book One of the **Principles,** in the first edition, prop. 16 proves the falsity of the rule of planetary motions in which it is supposed that the orbital speed in an ellipse is inversely proportional to the planet's distance from the sun. This result is of more than ordinary interest, since Hooke had asserted in a letter to Newton (6 January 1680) that if the solar force varies inversely as the square of the distance, the speed will be "as Kepler Supposes Reciprocall to the Distance."[158] Hooke evidently was not aware that this speed law had been rejected by Kepler and is in fact inconsistent with an inverse-square law of force. Hooke cited this letter to bolster his claim that he had anticipated Newton in the matter of the inverse-square law of force, and Newton replied by sending on to Halley a new scholium for prop. 4, giving a youthful demonstration of the law of centrifugal/centripetal force for uniform circular motion, which leads by the simplest algebra to the inverse-square law. For the second edition of the **Principles,** Newton shifted to prop. 2 the corollaries originally following prop. 1 of Book One, and he inserted a new set of corollaries following prop. 1. The first of these contains the statement of the true law of speed (that it is proportional, not inversely to the distance from the sun to the planet's position, but to the perpendicular distance from the sun to the tangent drawn through that position). Newton's effective reply to Hooke was thus advanced from prop. 16 to the extremely prominent place of the first corollary to the first proposition in the first book of the **Principles**.[159]

Another important change was to correct the proof of prop. 10 of Book Two. A significant error in the proof had been brought to Newton's attention by Nikolaus Bernoulli after the pages containing this proof had been printed off for the second edition. For the new proof it was thus necessary to reprint the whole sheet of signature "Hh" and the leaf containing pages 233-34, which is a cancel pasted onto the stub of the original leaf in every copy of the **Principles** with which I am familiar.[160] In the second edition, most of Section 7 of Book Two, on the resistance of fluids and on the motion of a fluid flowing out of a vessel, was completely recast.[161] As mentioned above, there were significant alterations in the opening of Book Three, the original "Hypotheses" being converted largely into "Phaenomena" and "Regulae Philosophandi." And Newton also completely rewrote and expanded the scholium following prop. 35 of Book Three, in which he claimed to have derived the theory of the moon's motion entirely from mathematical considerations of the action of gravitational forces of the sun and the earth on the moon.[162]

The title pages of each of Newton's major treatises offer puzzles to the prospective editor. For example, there exist two different forms of the title page of the **Principles** in the first edition (1687). One bears the name of the printer Joseph Streater and says: "Prostat apud plures Bibliopolas." The other (sometimes called "a reissue of the first edition") differs only in that the imprint declares: "Prostant Venales apud *Sam. Smith* ad insignia Principis *Walliae* in Coemiterio D. *Pauli,* aliosq; nonnullos Bibliopolas." It has been conjectured that the copies without *"Sam. Smith"* in the imprint may have been intended for sale abroad and those with *"Sam. Smith"* for home consumption.[163] What is perhaps of even greater interest is the fact that Samuel Pepys's name appears more prominently than Newton's. In Newton's annotated copy of the first edition, the name of the learned diarist has been cancelled and the form of Newton's name has been revised and his rank and position (*Sir* Isaac Newton, President of the Royal Society) have been brought up to date—by Richard Bentley.[163a]

The title page of the **Opticks** (1704) is even more puzzling, for it does not contain the name of the author. This was hardly an oversight, but rather intentional, since there exists at least one special copy ("of record"?) in which the lines of type of the title page have been slightly rearranged to accommodate the additional line, placed between two rules, "By ISAAC NEWTON."[164] We do not know why Newton did not want his name on the title page (the preface is signed "I. N."), but there are two possible reasons for this action. The first is that the **Opticks** is written in the vernacular. We may recall that Christiaan Huygens's *Traité de la lumière* (also written in the vernacular) was similarly published without the author's name on the title page, which bears only the initials, "Par C.H.D.Z." But there exist at least two copies in which—as with the one example of Newton's **Opticks**—the author's name is given in full: "Par Monsieur Christian Huygens, Seigneur de Zeelhem."[164a] Newton's **Opticks** was written up in words, with quantitative results of experiments and some calculations, but not with proofs of propositions by mathematical methods (i.e., geometry, algebra or ratios, fluxions, infinite series, etc.) from first principles. The propositions tend to have a "Proof by Experiments." The reason is not that Newton did not want to develop physical optics mathematically in what I have called "the Newtonian style." Rather, his attempts to do so in terms of various proposed mathematico-physical models proved to be failures. In this sense, the form of the **Opticks** was a kind of confession of failure, suggesting it to be an imperfect work suitable only for publication in a vernacular language and presumably not fully worthy of bearing the author's name.[164b]

At the height of the controversy with Leibniz, the Royal Society—at Leibniz's request—mounted an investigation. They appointed a so-called international committee which produced their famous report, the *Commercium epistolicum,* in which it is claimed that Newton was the sole and primary inventor of the calculus.[165] Leibniz was judged to have been a plagiarist. Looking at the composition of the committee, no one ever could have supposed it impartial. But what we now know from the study of Newton's MSS is that Newton actually drafted the report, for there exist a large number of drafts and versions of the report written out in his own hand.[166] We can watch Newton ask himself whether he would have the committee say, "We are satisfied that Mr. Newton invented the method of fluxions before 1669," or whether it might sound more convincing to say simply, "We find that he invented the method of fluxions before 1669." Perhaps it would be even better to put it, "We are satisfied that Mr. Newton was the first author of the method." He liked that, but decided it was not strong enough, so he added some evidence to back it up and concluded, ". . . for which reason we reckon Mr. Newton the first inventor." When the anonymous *Commercium* was eventually published, there appeared a lengthy book review of it in the *Philosophical Transactions of the Royal Society of London.* It was long suspected that Newton must have helped write this review, but the MSS show dozens of versions of it in his own hand. He was the sole author. Finally, when the *Commercium* was reprinted in 1722 in a second edition, this review was added as an introduction, still anonymous, but translated into Latin. But now there was added a new anonymous preface commending the review and emphasizing its major points. Who wrote it? Isaac Newton—as is shown by the many MS versions of it in his own hand.[166a]

Since I have mentioned the number of different versions of the same text in Newton's MSS, it is appropriate to call attention to one of the major problems in editing Newton's unpublished writings. Not only are there successive versions or drafts, but Newton had the maddening habit of making multiple copies of the same document, sometimes with only minor variations. He even copied out whole sections of books from his own library. I have referred (in section 2 *supra*) to Brewster's astonishment on finding that Newton had copied out texts (in part or in full) of alchemical treatises, some of them appearing twice in identical versions. A theological MS in the Keynes Collection called "Irenicum, or Ecclesiastical Polity Tending to Peace" exists in seven almost identical autograph drafts. Whiston recorded that Newton wrote out "eighteen copies of the first and principal chapter of the Chronology with his own hand but little different from one another." The small tract **De motu corporum,** preliminary to the **Principles,** exists (as I have mentioned earlier) in at least five (and possibly six) variant versions with different titles.[167] There are four separate commentaries on Daniel and the Apocalypse. The only saving grace for an editor is that Newton's handwriting is generally clear and easy to read. It has even been conjectured that Newton may have delighted in copying out extracts from printed works as well as his own compositions because he was overly enamored of his own handwriting. Here is yet another textual mystery.

There is no plan or program for producing a uniform series of all of Newton's writings. A somewhat similar format has been adopted by Cambridge University Press for the seven-volume set of Newton's Correspondence, the eight volumes of D. T. Whiteside's edition of **The Mathematical Papers of Isaac Newton,** and the three volumes of our edition of Newton's **Philosophiae naturalis principia mathematica** with variant readings. But the same publisher used a different format for the Halls' **Unpublished Scientific Papers of Isaac Newton,** and it is doubtful whether the grand style and format can withstand the pressures of inflation.

Whoever laments the lack of a great edition of all of Newton's writings should be aware of the paradox that there is not a one-to-one correspondence between the existence of a great scholarly edition of a scientist's works and a body of significant scholarly writings concerning that figure. A notable example is Christiaan Huygens, one of the major mathematicians and scientists of the second half of the 17th century—easily the greatest scientist of his time but for Newton. In fact, Huygens is the only scientist of Newton's day to whom Newton applied the appellation *summus.* The

edition of Huygens's writings is a tremendous monument to scholarship, unrivalled in the annals of science. Published by the Dutch Society of Sciences, the edition eventually filled 22 magnificent volumes, the first appearing in 1888 and the last in 1950. Words cannot convey the quality of this edition. The volumes are in a large quarto size, beautifully printed in large type. The paper is of an extravagant quality, handmade specially for this edition and watermarked "Christiaan Huygens." Each subject and each major paper is introduced by a historical essay, and there are extensive scholarly annotations. Furthermore, each volume has three long and complete indexes: one of books and articles mentioned in the text or in the notes and introductions, another of persons mentioned, and a third of subjects. It is an edition that puts to shame all others. And yet it must be reported that the last quarter century has produced very little in the way of scholarly articles on Huygens and his work. There are no major studies of importance on his contributions to astronomy (his telescopes, his resolution of Saturn's ring, his discovery of a satellite of Saturn), nor of his work in geometry and analysis (including his work on the cycloid), his discovery of the laws of impact, his great study of circular motion and his finding of the laws of "centrifugal" force, nor is there even an adequate critical and scholarly analysis of his discovery of the isochronism of the epicycloidal pendulum and the invention of the clock escapement. There is not even a true biography of Huygens worthy of the man and on a par with the great edition of his *Oeuvres.*

By contrast, the Newton industry—like the Darwin industry—goes on apace. One can scarcely keep up with all the books and articles in these fields. In both cases, radical new interpretations have been emerging—based on extensive use of the manuscripts. Yet in the case of both Newton and Darwin there is no real edition of their works, although an edition of Darwin's correspondence is in progress.

Will there be a fourth revelation of Isaac Newton, or have we reached the final stages of knowledge with the completion of the trinity? I very much doubt that there will be a new revelation as far-reaching and as profound as the third has been. But in this regard historians would be wise to follow the advice given to young chemists by Harvard's Professor E. P. Kohler. A lecture-demonstration had ended in an explosion that destroyed the lecture table and the front of the lecture room, instead of merely producing the change in color and substance that he had announced to his class in organic chemistry. In these matters, he said, a chemist should be a historian and not a prophet.

Notes

[1] The original publications of Isaac Newton are listed in Babson (1950), Gray (1907), and Wallis (1977); the

work by Wallis contains also references to the secondary literature. A good guide to the main scholarly works concerning Newton is to be found in Cohen (1974). The current literature is listed in the annual Critical Bibliography published in *Isis,* the official quarterly journal of the History of Science Society. The advance of Newton scholarship can be followed year by year during a half-century in Pighetti (1960).

[2] On the circulation and printing of this paper in Newton's day, see the introduction to the facsimile reprint of it in Newton (1958). An admirable discussion of the publication of Newton's writings is to be found in the introduction to the first volume of D.T. Whiteside's edition of Newton's *Mathematical papers.*

[3] These appear at the beginning of the volume. See Cohen (1971). An edition of Newton's *Principles,* with variant readings, was published in 1972. A new English translation by Anne Whitman and the writer is currently being completed for publication.

[4] The *Opticks* is available in a paperback reprint (1952). A scholarly edition of this work, with an analysis of the difference between the several editions, has been completed for publication by Henry Guerlac.

[5] Of course, Newton's publications on chronology and the interpretation of the prophetic books of Scripture were available to all, and there were hints aplenty concerning Newton's interest in alchemy. A major text of Newton's, giving a clue to the fact that Newton's interests were not limited to mathematical physics and experiment, was published by Gregory in 1832.

[6] Of course, during the 18th century the Cartesians and various other groups did not accept the Newtonian principles and so did not look upon Newton as the lawgiver. For representations of Newton in art, see the article by Haskell in Palter (1970); also Cohen (1979).

[7] See Buchdahl (1961).

[8] Malone (1948), 101.

[9] See Westfall (1980), Manuel (1959, 1963, 1974).

[10] See Dobbs (1975), Figala (1977, 1977*a*).

[11] See McGuire & Rattansi (1966).

[12] See Munby (1952*b*).

[13] The fullest account of the history of Newton's manuscripts is to be found in D.T. Whiteside's introduction to the first volume of his edition of Newton's *Mathematical papers.*

[14] E.g., Mach (1960), 236-7.

[15] See Cohen (1971), ch 9, section 7.

[16] *Ibid,* 242.

[17] See Koyré (1960); the changes in the queries are indicated in Horsley's edition (1779-85). See Guerlac's edition (referred to in note 4 *supra*).

[18] Koyré & Cohen (1961, 1962); see in Priestley (1970).

[19] This is discussed in Cohen (1969).

[20] In a letter to Bentley (10 Dec. 1692), Newton said: "When I wrote my treatise about our Systeme I had an eye upon such Principles as might work wth considering men for the beleife of a Deity & nothing can rejoyce me more then to find it usefull for that purpose." See *Correspondence, 3,* 233.

[21] The translation "I feign" for "fingo" was suggested by Alexandre Koyré; see Cohen (1962). See query 31 in the second and later English editions.

[22] The discussions of these questions occur in the second part of the last paragraph of the concluding query 31 in the second and later editions.

[23] This occurs in query 30: "Nature . . . seems delighted with Transmutations."

[24] See the edition of Newton's *Principles* (1972) with variant readings, p 87 (line 9), p 89 (lines 1, 3, 6, 7, 12, 16, 29), p 90 (line 32), p 402 (line 20).

[25] See Cohen (1966), Koyré (1965).

[26] This hypothesis was eliminated in the second edition.

[27] See Cohen (1966), and especially McGuire (1967).

[28] On the way in which it was used, see Cohen (1966). See also McMullin (1978).

[29] I have indicated, in Cohen (1966), that this was a hypothesis of the Aristotelians and Cartesians, rather than Newton's own belief.

[30] Cohen (1964).

[31] *Ibid.*

[32] See Manuel (1963).

[33] *Ibid.*

[34] *Ibid.*

[35] See Westfall (1980).

[36] See Manuel (1974).

[37] A catalogue of Napier's works by W. R. MacDonald is given in the latter's English translation of Napier's *Canon* (1889).

[38] Manuel (1974), 99.

[39] *Ibid,* 99-100. See Hill (1965).

[40] Cf, e.g., Hill (1965), 7.

[41] Manuel (1974), 90-1.

[42] *Ibid,* 92.

[43] For an account of Newton's method, see Manuel (1963, 1974).

[44] Manuel (1974), 93.

[45] Quoting from McLachlan (1950), 119.

[46] See Cohen (1960), 500-1.

[47] Newton (1733).

[48] Quoted from D.T. Whiteside (1967), introduction to *Math. Papers, 1,* xviii.

[49] *Ibid,* xix.

[50] *Ibid,* xix-xx.

[51] *Ibid,* xx, n 12.

[52] Brewster (1855), 2, 342-6.

[53] McLachlan published only a selection, in which the texts were chosen to illustrate a particular point of view. It would be a great desideratum to bring out a rather fuller selection of Newton's theological writings, including texts from the Yahuda MSS now in Jerusalem.

[54] Manuel (1963); also see Manuel (1974).

[55] *Op cit,* xx, n 15.

[56] These are now largely to be found in the Keynes MSS in the library of King's College in Cambridge.

[57] For an account of Conduitt's activities in relation to these Newtonian documents, see Whiteside, *op cit.*

[58] See DeMorgan (1885).

[59] Whiteside, *op cit* xxii-xxiii.

[60] *Ibid.*

[61] See the complete catalogue, Portsmouth Collection (1888).

[62] Newton (1779-85).

[63] See Whiteside, *op cit.,* xxvii.

[64] This tract was published by Rigaud (1838), app 1, 1-19, from the text in the Royal Society. Versions based on the MSS in the University Library, Cambridge, have been published in Ball (1893), 51-6; Hall & Hall (1962), 243-67; Herivel (1965), 257-74; and Whiteside (*Math. Papers, 6,* 30-80). On the background to the composition of *De motu,* see Cohen (1970), ch 3, 47-81 (esp. 54-62); on its significance, see Cohen (1980), ch 5 (esp. sections 5.5, 5.6).

[65] There are two states of the first edition, one having Edinburgh and London on the title page, the other Edinburgh and Boston, both 1855; the second edition (1860) has only Edinburgh. A facsimile reprint (1965) of the first edition includes an introduction by R. S. Westfall.

[66] More (1934), vi.

[67] Introduction (1967) to *Math. Papers, 1,* xxix.

[68] Brewster (1855), *1,* vii-viii, x.

[69] *Ibid,* x.

[70] See Stukeley (1936), *passim.*

[71] *Ibid,* 20; see Cohen (1946).

[72] See McKie & DeBeer (1952).

[73] Actually, Stukeley's example can serve as a "cautionary tale" to all practicing historians of science. In fact, it was on contemplating Stukeley's example that I began a program of oral history in relation to certain crucial developments in the history of contemporary physics and in the rise of the computer.

[74] Brewster (1855), *2,* 371-6.

[75] *Ibid,* 372.

[76] *Ibid.*

[77] *Ibid,* 372-3.

[78] *Ibid,* 374.

[79] *Ibid.*

[80] *Ibid,* 374-6.

[81] *Ibid,* 371-2.

[82] *Ibid,* 372, n 1.

[83] See note 65 *supra.*

[84] These occur primarily in vol 2, ch 24; also in appendixes 29-30.

[85] Letter from Lord Portsmouth to the Vice Chancellor of Cambridge University, 23 July 1872; quoted in Whiteside's "General Introduction" to vol 1 of his edition of Newton's *Math. Papers,* p xxxi.

[86] From a note by Lord Portsmouth, 2 Aug. 1872 (ULC MS Add 2588, ff 494-5), quoted by Whiteside, *op cit,* xxxi.

[87] *Ibid,* f 496

[87a] *Ibid;* also, preface to Portsmouth Collection (1888), ix.

[88] Portsmouth Collection (1888).

[89] The collection is not officially known as "The Portsmouth Collection," and it is catalogued as a series of separate or individual entries, one for each group of manuscripts or each book. Since the catalogue (1888) is officially entitled *A catalogue of the Portsmouth Collection of small books and papers . . . ,* the portion given to the University Library is generally (but only informally) known as the Portsmouth Collection.

[90] Portsmouth Collection (1888), ix-x.

[91] The catalogue as printed would give the user no idea that the papers relating to the questions of priority in the invention of the calculus (ULC MS Add 3968) occupy some thousand manuscript pages. For a report on these, with critical comments and extracts, see vol 8 of D.T. Whiteside's edition of Newton's *Math. Papers;* also, Hall (1980).

[92] The three appendixes deal with "The form of the Solid of Least Resistance" (see schol. to prop. 35 of book 2 of Newton's *Principles*), "A List of Propositions in the Lunar Theory intended to be inserted in a second edition of the *Principia,*" and "The motion of the Apogee in an elliptic orbit of very small eccentricity, caused by given disturbing forces." Often reprinted and quoted is an autobiographical statement of Newton's about the stages of his discovery of his main ideas on celestial dynamics (p xviii); a complete version of this document, with critical comments, has been published in Cohen (1971), supp 1.

[93] These are largely collected together in ULC MS Add. 4007.

[94] *Op cit,* xxxiii.

[95] This is reprinted, together with other essays, in Ball (1918).

[96] Ball (1893).

[97] *Op cit,* xxxiv.

[98] Fraser's publications are listed in Wallis & Wallis (1977). See especially, Fraser (1927).

[99] Witting (1911-12); see Whiteside, *op cit,* xxxiv.

[100] More (1934), 158.

[101] *Ibid,* 159.

[102] *Ibid,* 159, n 6.

[103] *Ibid,* 641.

[104] *Ibid,* 644.

[105] *Ibid.*

[105a] In the preface to his biography (p vi), More castigated Brewster for having adopted "the rôle of advocate to 'The High Priest of Science' as he calls Newton" and for portraying his hero "without blemish intellectually and morally." More noted that Brewster had said that "where he found evidence which confirmed facts known to reflect adversely on Newton's character, he published it; but if the facts were not previously known, he felt bound in honour to respect the privacy of his discovery." But in the end More himself admitted (p vii): "There is absolutely nothing in his life so serious that it should have been suppressed." I have always found this a curious statement, since it seems to imply that if there had been something "serious" in Newton's life, then "it should have been suppressed." And it is to be noted that although More thought that Brewster had gone to extremes in defending his hero, the critical reader today cannot help but observe how More did the same. More (p 333) found it necessary to attack "Professor Einstein's Generalised Theory of Relativity" for apparently daring to diminish the greatness or permanence of the system of dynamics of Newton's *Principles.* He would have Einstein's work be "merely a logical exercise of the active mind," which "ignores the world of brute facts." It "may be interesting, but it ultimately evaporates into a scholasticism. And if it persists, it will cause the decadence of science as surely as the mediaeval scholasticism preceded the decadence of religion." So much, then, for the popular belief that "modern criticism has at last broken down the classical mechanics."

Indeed, More felt the need of defending not only Newton against the onslaught of the physics of the 20th century, but also Aristotle. He said (p 332): "It is a notable fact that these two works [Newton's *Principles* and Aristotle's *Organon*], probably the two most stupendous creations of the scientific brain, are now under attack—the *Organon* by modern symbolists in logic, and the *Principia* by the relativists in physics." It was More's judgement that "Aristotle and Newton will be honoured and *used* when the modernists are long forgotten."

[106] Munby (1952); see Sotheby (1936).

[107] See Munby (1952).

[108] See Harrison (1978).

[109] See Royal Society (1947).

[110] This new version, prepared by Anne Whitman and me, will be published by Harvard University Press and Cambridge University Press.

[110a] Others, whose work is referred to below, who have contributed to this third revelation are Zev Bechler, Joan L. Hawes, and Peter Heimann. See also the important researches on Newton's prism experiments and telescope by A.A. Mills.

[111] Keynes's essay was published in Royal Society (1947) and has been since reprinted with other essays of his.

[112] Hall (1948).

[113] Indeed, despite some obvious faults and its limitations, the presentation of Newton in this volume has a special value today, since it indicates the "public" or "semi-public" view of Newton available in the two centuries following Newton's death before our attention was riveted to some of the more startling aspects of Newton's private life, which have been brought to light by recent studies of his manuscripts.

[114] Turnbull (1953).

[115] See Craig (1946), *Newton at the Mint*. An interesting use of the Mint MSS has been made by Manuel in ch 11 of his *Portrait* (1968).

[116] The limitations of space prevent my giving here even an approximation to what could be considered *all* of the major revelations brought about by the study of the Newtonian MSS. Accordingly, the examples that follow should not be considered as constituting in any sense a definitive set of what I consider to be the first-rate works of Newtonian scholarship of the last three decades or so. In other words, the omission of the name of any particular scholar should certainly *not* be taken to imply that I do not esteem his or her work as

highly as those that I mention or discuss. In fact, some of the particular choices and omissions have resulted from an attempt to give an indication of the different kinds of scholarship, rather than to make a selection of the highest forms of scholarship to be recommended to any student of Newton. A rather complete bibliography of Newton scholarship, divided into convenient categories, is printed as part of my *DSB* article (1974). Two other bibliographies of major recent Newtonian scholarship, chiefly in relation to my own research, are to be found in my *Introduction* (1971) and my *Newtonian revolution* (1980). A volume currently in press, edited by Zev Bechler and being published by Reidel, containing articles by Whiteside, Westfall, Dobbs, myself, and others, will certainly serve as a good review of current Newtonian scholarship in a variety of fields (with bibliographical guides). Two earlier surveys of the state of Newtonian scholarship are Cohen (1960) and Whiteside (1962). See also the important collection of Newtonian studies edited by Robert Palter (1970).

[117] The penultimate sentence of the final scholium of Book Two of Newton's *Principles* reads: "Therefore the hypothesis of vortices can in no way be reconciled with astronomical phenomena and serves less to clarify the celestial motions than to obscure them."

[118] In the commentary to the French translation of Newton's *Principles* (1759), vol 2, second part, p 9, it is said: "This second Book, which contains a very profound theory of fluids and the motions of bodies in fluids, seems to have been intended to destroy the system of vortices, although it is only in the scholium to the last Proposition that M. Newton overtly attacks Descartes and shows that the celestial motions cannot be carried out by his vortices."

[119] Brewster (1855), vol 1, 22, n 1, states: "Newton's copy of Descartes' Geometry I have seen among the family papers. It is marked in many places with his own hand, *Error, Error, non est Geom.*" Since this volume did not appear among either the books given by Lord Portsmouth to the University Library, Cambridge, nor in the auction sale, it came to be believed that Brewster had been wholly in error and that no copy with these annotations existed. See, further, note 127 *infra*.

[120] This is the untitled essay which the Halls called "De gravitatione et aequipondio fluidorum" and which they published in their 1962 volume (pp 89-156), with translation and commentary.

[121] See especially the long essay on Newton and Descartes in Koyré (1965), which, together with its appendixes, makes up half of the volume.

[122] Cohen (1964).

123 See Cohen (1980), 186-7.

124 For the texts of Descartes compared and contrasted to the texts of Newton, see Cohen (1980), 183-4.

125 Koyré (1965), 66-70.

126 Cohen (1964).

127 The copy of Descartes' *Géométrie* in Latin in which Newton made his annotations was found a few years ago among some books that had at one time been destined to be discarded from the Trinity College Library.

128 Guerlac has developed these ideas in a number of publications, some of which are published in Guerlac (1977*a*); his ideas have been revised and summarized in his biography of Hauksbee in the *DSB*.

129 See note 128 *supra*; see also Koyré (1960). The final queries of the second (1717-18) English edition of the *Opticks* first appeared in the Latin *Opticae* (1706). The rise and fall of Newton's ideas concerning the aether and the experiments of Newton relating to this topic have been studied by R. S. Westfall and others, most recently in Cohen (1980) and in a long essay contributed to the volume (in press) being edited by Zev Bechler (see note 116 *supra*). Important studies of Newton's ideas of the aether, chiefly in relation to electricity, have been made by the Halls and by Joan L. Hawes. Zev Bechler has made a number of studies of Newton's optical ideas, based upon the manuscripts, and in particular has explored Newton's attempt to explain various optical phenomena by means of mathematical-physical models. Other important studies of Newton's optical experiments and ideas have been made by J. A. Lohne, who has in particular made an extensive study of the experimental conditions of Newton's prism experiments. Alan Shapiro has published several studies on aspects of Newton's work in optics and is currently preparing an edition of Newton's *Lectiones opticae*. Valuable insights into the topic of Newton's views of the aether have been provided by Peter Heimann.

130 See Westfall (1971).

131 McGuire & Rattansi (1966).

132 McGuire (1967, 1968).

133 See the various writings of Manuel listed in the bibliography.

134 The mechanical philosophy associated with the name of Descartes gained wide adherence in the days of Newton. There can be no doubt that Newton was strongly influenced by the mechanical philosophy and sought indeed to explain all natural occurrences by means of matter and motion; when Newton disagreed with the Cartesian point of view, it was because he was a convinced atomist and thus believed in the existence of the vacuum or void space, which Descartes could not imagine to exist.

135 Westfall (1971), 377: "The significance of the redirection of his philosophy of nature undertaken by Newton about 1679 can scarcely be overstated." Newton's addition of the concept of force to the traditional concepts of the Cartesian mechanical philosophy had been suggested earlier by the Halls (1962). For a somewhat contrasting view of Newton's philosophy and the possible redirection of it, see my *Newtonian revolution* (1980) and the essay in the volume edited by Bechler (cited in note 116 *supra*).

136 See Westfall (1970).

137 See Lohne (1961, 1965, 1967, 1968); also Lohne & Sticker (1969). Shapiro's edition of the *Lectiones opticae* has not yet appeared. He has recently given a general summary of his ideas concerning optical problems of Newton in an article in *Isis* (1980).

138 This has been particularly brought out in Lohne (1965).

139 See Bechler's articles in the bibliography.

140 Westfall's ideas are most readily available in his recent biography (1980).

141 Manuel (1974).

142 Newton's early derivation is adumbrated in the last paragraph of the scholium to prop. 4, book 1, of his *Principles*. This paragraph was not part of the original MS, but was added while Halley was editing Newton's MS for publication. See the edition of Newton's *Principles* with variant readings (1972).

143 Herivel (1960, 1965).

144 In query 30 of the *Opticks,* Newton says: "The changing of Bodies into Light, and Light into Bodies, is very conformable to the Course of Nature, which seems delighted with Transmutations."

145 See the bibliography. An excellent bibliographical essay for this area is to be found in Dobbs (1975).

146 See, in particular, Boas & Hall (1958), M.B. Hall (1975).

147 Westfall (1972, 1975).

148 Dobbs (1975), Figala (1977, 1977*a*).

[149] See, for example, Whiteside's review of Dobbs (1975) in *Isis* (1977), vol 68, pp 116-21.

[150] On this subject, see Rattansi (1972); this whole area of the relation of Newton's interests in alchemy to the development of his thought in mechanics is treated in my article, forthcoming in the volume edited by Bechler (see note 116 *supra*).

[151] Westfall (1975), p 196.

[152] Dobbs (1975), pp 211, 221.

[153] On this subject, see Hill (1965), p 7.

[153a] Although studies of alchemy are important for opening up an examination of a major aspect of Newton's intellectual concerns, and although it is clear that alchemical questions are directly related to the nature of aether and Newton's conceptions of matter, a Scottish verdict of "nonproven" must be given to the assertions now being made that Newton's hermetic or alchemical concerns and thinking led him to universal gravity. Here, it seems to me, a gross error is made in not distinguishing between an understanding of terrestrial gravity (or weight) and the concept of universal gravity or the force produced by universal gravitation. In one case, that of weight, all that is required is some kind of process that draws bodies toward the earth. For instance, Newton himself advanced explanations of this phenomenon in terms of a shower of aetherial particles and later on in terms of an aether of varying degrees of density. I see no reason why the kind of "forces" that are related to or involved in alchemical processes could not be a source of an explanation of this kind of weight—in which, be it noted, there is no need of specifying whether a body is pushed toward the earth, pulled toward the earth, or gets acted on so as to be moved toward the earth by a mutual interaction between it and the earth.

In the case of universal gravity, however, the situation is entirely different. Here it is necessary not only to have a process that impels an object (such as a rock, an apple, or the moon) toward the earth, but one that at the same time impels the earth toward the object (whether a rock or an apple or a moon). There is nothing that I am familiar with in Newton's considerations of an alchemical kind that would have led to such a mutual interaction.

Furthermore, the steps that led Newton toward universal gravity were conditioned by considerations that began with the idea of a force directed toward a center where there was no body. This was related to the question proposed by Hooke to Newton in their correspondence in 1679-80, which set Newton going on the path that led him to universal gravity and finally to the *Principles*. This notion came to Newton not from considerations of alchemy, but rather directly from a question put to him by Robert Hooke. Newton's early solution was to begin by considering the orbital motion of a particle about an abstract center of force—a situation for which there is no analogue whatsoever in alchemy. It was only after Newton had developed such a system (not really a system, since there is only one body in it), that he recognized that in nature (as in the solar system) there is never a single body, but always a pair of bodies. For instance, the sun is at the center of the motion of the earth, the earth at the center of the motion of its moon; the sun is at the center of the motion of Jupiter, and Jupiter at the center of the motion of its moons. In any such system of two bodies, as Newton was quick to realize, the law of action and reaction (Newton's "third law") requires that the action be mutual, that if the sun is pulling on the earth, then the earth must be pulling on the sun with a force equal in magnitude but opposite in direction. And it is the same for the earth and its moon and even for the earth and an apple. Eventually, by a series of arguments of this kind, Newton was led to a principle of mutual interacting forces and to universal gravity—a process in which alchemical considerations are conspicuously absent. These topics are further developed in my *Newtonian revolution* (1980), my article on this topic in *Scientific American* (1981), and the article in the forthcoming volume edited by Bechler (cited in note 116 *supra*).

[154] For details, see my *Introduction* (1971, ch 3, section 7).

[155] Newton (1715), 206.

[156] For instance, Newton said specifically that by "the inverse Method of Fluxions I found in the year 1677 [should be 1679/80] the demonstration of Kepler's Astronomical Proposition viz. that the Planets move in Ellipses, which is the eleventh Proposition of the first book of the Principles." See my *Introduction* (1971), 80, 289-98.

[157] See Newton (1972), ix; see also my *Introduction* (1971). For further information concerning these volumes, see Harrison (1978).

[157a] See Newton (1972), 550-63. "Hypothesis 1" and "Hypothesis 2" of the first edition became "Rule 1" and "Rule 2" in the second edition. "Hypothesis 3" of the first edition was omitted in the second edition, where a wholly new "Rule 3" was introduced. A "Rule 4" appears for the first time in the third edition.

"Hypothesis 4" of the first edition became "Hypothesis 1" in the second and third editions and was removed to a later part of Book 3.

"Hypothesis 5" became "Phenomenon 1" in the second edition, where a wholly new "Phenomenon 2" was introduced. "Hypothesis 6 . . . Hypothesis 9" became in the second edition "Phenomenon 3 . . . Phenomenon 6." For the significance of these changes, see Cohen (1966).

[157b] One of the three "hypotheses" in the second and third editions of Newton's *Principles* was the original "Hypothesis 4," for which see n. 157a. Another, appearing also in Book 3 in the second and third editions (and there labeled "Hypothesis 2"), following prop. 38, was originally a "Lemma 4." Newton was unable to prove this lemma and so changed it to a hypothesis. According to Ball (1893), 110, "Laplace was the first writer to prove it." The third hypothesis in the second and third editions occurs at the beginning of section 9 of Book 2: "Hypothesis: The resistance which arises from the friction [*lit.,* lack of lubricity, i.e., slipperiness] of the parts of a fluid is, other things being equal, proportional to the velocity with which the parts of the fluid are separated from one another." This hypothesis appeared identically in the first edition as well.

[158] Newton, *Correspondence,* vol 2, p 309. This letter was part of the epistolary exchanges between Hooke and Newton during 1679 and 1680, in the course of which Hooke taught Newton that the proper way to analyze orbital motion was in terms of two components: a linear inertial component along the tangent to the curve and an accelerated motion directed toward the sun or center of force. See further my *Newtonian revolution* (1980), ch 5, sections 4-5.

[159] See my *Newtonian revolution* (1980), 244-5; my *Introduction* (1971), 236-8; and Newton (1972). This alteration is summarized in Ball (1893), 100.

[160] See my *Introduction* (1971), ch 9, section 4.

[161] See Newton (1972), vol 2, app 1.

[162] On this topic see the introduction to Newton (1975).

[163] See Munby (1952).

[163a] See my *Introduction* (1971), pl. 13.

[164] The copy with the author's name on the title page is in the library at the British Optical Society, London; see Sutcliffe (1932), where this title page is reproduced.

[164a] One of these belonged to Prof E. N. da C. Andrade and is described in Sotheby (1965), where the title page is reproduced on p 65; for the other, see Horblit (1964), section 54, with reproduction (in colour) of both forms of the title page.

[164b] This theme is developed in full in my *Newtonian revolution* (1980).

[165] The best edition is that of F. Lefort and J.-B. Biot, i.e., Collins (1856); see Hall (1980) and vol 8 of Whiteside's edition of Newton's *Math. Papers.*

[166] U.L.C. ms Add. 3968.

[166a] See Hoskin (1961).

[167] In addition to the one in the Royal Society and the three in the University Library, Cambridge, there is presumably one in the Macclesfield collection.

Bibliography

Editor's note: Where the bibliography contains more than one publication by the same author in a given year, these are distinguished, for brevity in notes and in cross-references, by a lower case letter following the date. See, e.g., Guerlac (1963) & (1963a)

Aiton, E. J. (1962). "The celestial mechanics of Leibniz in the light of Newtonian criticism." *Annals of Science, 18,* 31-41;

———1964. "The celestial mechanics of Leibniz: a new interpretation." *Annals of Science, 20,* 111-23.

———1964a. "The inverse problem of central forces." *Annals of Science, 20,* 81-99.

———1965 [1966]. "An imaginary error in the celestial mechanics of Leibniz." *Annals of Science, 21,* 169-73.

———1969. "Kepler's second law of planetary motion." *Isis, 60,* 75-90.

———1972. *The vortex theory of planetary motions.* London: Macdonald; New York: American Elsevier.

———1975a. "The elliptical orbit and the area law." *Vistas in Astronomy, 18,* 573-83.

Andrade, E. N. Da C. 1935. "Newton's early notebook." *Nature, 135,* 360.

———1950. "Wilkins lecture, Robert Hooke." *Proceedings of the Royal Society, 201A,* 439-73.

———1953b. "A Newton collection." *Endeavour, 12,* 68-75.

———*See also* Sotheby. 1965.

Axtell, James, L. 1965. "Locke, Newton, and the elements of natural philosophy." *Paedagogica Europaea, 1,* 235-44.

————1965a. "Locke's review of the *Principia*." *Notes and Records of the Royal Society of London, 20,* 152-61.

Babson Collection. 1950. *A descriptive catalogue of the Grace K. Babson collection of the works of Sir Isaac Newton, and the material relating to him in the Babson Institute Library, Babson Park, Mass.* Intro. Roger Babson Webber. New York: Herbert Reichner. Supplement compiled by Henry P. Macomber, Babson Institute, 1955.

Ball, W. W. Rouse. 1891. "On Newton's classification of cubic curves." *Proceedings of the London Mathematical Society, 22,* 104-43.

————1892. "A Newtonian fragment relating to centripetal forces." *Proceedings of the London Mathematical Society, 23,* 226-31.

————1893. *An essay on Newton's "Principia".* London, New York: Macmillan. Photo-reprint, introd. I. B. Cohen. New York, London: Johnson, 1972.

————1893a. *A short account of the history of mathematics.* 2nd ed. London, New York: Macmillan. Contains an excellent chapter (16, pp 319-58), "The life and works of Newton."

————1918. *Cambridge papers.* London: Macmillan.

Bechler, Zev. 1978. "Newton's search for a mechanistic model of colour dispersion: a suggested interpretation." *Archive for History of Exact Sciences, 11,* 1-37.

————1974. "Newton's law of forces which are inversely as the mass: a suggested interpretation of his later efforts to normalise a mechanistic model of optical dispersion." *Centaurus, 18,* 184-222.

————1974a. "Newton's 1672 optical controversies: a study in the grammar of scientic dissent." In *Elkana.* ed. 1974. pp 115-42.

————1975. "'A less agreeable matter': the disagreeable case of Newton and achromatic refraction." *British Journal for the History of Science, 8,* 101-26.

Biot, J.-B., and F. Lefort. *See* Collins et al., 1856.

Boas, Marie. 1958. "Newton's chemical papers." In *Newton,* 1958, 241-8.

————*See also* Hall, Marie Boas.

Boas, Marie, and A. Rupert Hall. 1958. "Newton's chemical experiments." *Archives Internationales d'Histoire des Sciences, 11,* 113-52.

————*See also* Hall and Hall.

Brewster, Sir David. 1855. *Memoirs of the life, writings, and discoveries of Sir Isaac Newton.* 2 vols. Edinburgh: Thomas Constable. Photoreprint, intro. Richard S. Westfall. New York, London: Johnston, 1965.

Brougham, Henry, Lord, and E. J. Routh. 1855. *Analytical view of Sir Isaac Newton's "Principia".* London: Longman, Brown, Green, and Longmans, [&] C. Knight; Edinburgh: A. and C. Black; Glasgow: R. Griffin. Reprinted New York, London: Johnson, 1972.

Brunet, Pierre. 1929. *Maupertuis.* [1] Etude biographique. [2] L'oeuvre et sa place dans la pensée scientifique et philosophique du XVIIIe siècle. Paris: Librairie Scientifique Albert Blanchard.

————1931. *L'introduction des théories de Newton en France au XVIIIe siècle.* Vol. I, avant 1738. Paris: Librairie Scientifique Albert Blanchard.

Buchdahl, Gerd. 1961. *The image of Newton and Locke in the age of reason.* London, New York: Sheed and Ward.

————1973. "Explanation and gravity." In Teich and Young. 1973. pp 167-203.

Chandler, Philip P., II. 1975. Newton and Clairaut on the motion of the lunar apse. Diss. San Diego: University of California.

Cohen, I. Bernard. 1946. "Authenticity of scientific anecdotes." *Nature, 157,* 196-7.

————1956. *Franklin and Newton: an inquiry into speculative Newtonian experimental science and Franklin's work in electricity as an example thereof.* Philadelphia: American Philosophical Society. Reprint Cambridge [Mass.]: Harvard University Press, 1966.

————1960. "Newton in the light of recent scholarship." *Isis, 51,* 489-514.

————1962. "The first English version of Newton's 'Hypotheses non fingo'." *Isis, 53,* 379-88.

————1963. "Pemberton's translation of Newton's *Principia,* with notes on Motte's translation." *Isis, 54,* 319-51.

————1964. "Isaac Newton, Hans Sloane, and the Académie Royale des Sciences." In Cohen and Taton, eds., 1964, pp 61-116.

————1964a. "'Quantum in se est': Newton's concept of inertia in relation to Descartes and Lucretius." *Notes and Records of the Royal Society of London, 19,* 131-55.

————1966. "Hypotheses in Newton's philosophy." *Physis, 8,* 163-84.

————1967. "Dynamics: the key to the 'new science' of the seventeenth century." *Acta Historiae Rerum Naturalium necnon Technicarum.* Czechoslovak Studies in the History of Science. Prague, Special Issue 3, 79-114.

————1967a. "Galileo, Newton, and the divine order of the solar system." In *Galileo, man of science.* Edited by E. McMullin. New York, London: Basic Books, 1967, pp 207-31.

————1967b. "Newton's attribution of the first two laws of motion to Galileo." *Atti del Symposium Internazionale di Storia, Metodologia, Logica e Filosofia della Scienza, "Galileo nella Storia e nella Filosofia della Scienza,"* xxv-xliv. Collection des Travaux de l'Académie Internationale d'Histoire des Sciences, No. 16. Vinci (Florence): Gruppo Italiano di Storia della Scienza.

————1969. Introduction to Newton. 1969. pp vii-xxii.

————1969a. "Isaac Newton's *Principia,* the scriptures and the divine providence." In *Essays in honor of Ernest Nagel: philosophy, science and method.* Edited by Morgenbesser, Suppes, and White. New York, St. Martin's Press, pp 523-48.

————1969b. "The French translation of Isaac Newton's *Philosophiae naturalis principia mathematica* (1756, 1759, 1966)." *Archives Internationales d'Histoire des Sciences, 72,* 37-67.

————1969c. "Newton's *System of the world:* some textual and bibliographical notes." *Physis, 11,*152-66.

————1970. "Newton's second law and the concept of force in the *Principia.*" In Palter, ed. 1970. pp 143-85. A considerably revised and corrected version of a preliminary text published in *Texas Quarterly, 10,* No. 3 (1967).

————1971. *Introduction to Newton's "Principia".* Cambridge [Mass.]; Harvard University Press; Cambridge [England]: Cambridge University Press.

————1972. "Newton and Keplerian inertia: an echo of Newton's controversy with Leibniz." In Debus, ed. 1972, 2, 199-211.

————1974. "Newton, Isaac." *Dictionary of Scientific Biography, 10,* 42-103. Rev. and enl. ed. forthcoming, New York: Scribner's.

————1974a. "Isaac Newton, the calculus of variations, and the design of ships: an example of pure mathematics in Newton's *Principia,* allegedly developed for the sake of practical applications." In R. S. Cohen et al., eds. 1974. pp 169-87.

————1974b. "Newton's theory vs. Kepler's theory and Galileo's theory: an example of a difference between a philosophical and a historical analysis of science." In Elkana, ed. 1974. pp 299-338.

————1975. Bibliographical and historical introduction, in Newton. 1975. pp 1-87.

————1979. "Notes on Newton in the art and architecture of the Enlightenment." *Vistas in Astronomy, 22* (pt. 4), 523-37.

————1980. *The Newtonian revolution, with illustrations of the transformation of scientific ideas.* Cambridge [England]; London, New York, New Rochelle: Cambridge University Press.

————1981. "Newton's discovery of gravity." *Scientific American, 244,* No. 3 (March), 166-79.

Cohen, I. Bernard and Robert E. Schofield. *See* Newton. 1958.

Cohen, I. Bernard and René Taton, eds. 1964. *Mélanges Alexandre Koyré.* Vol. 1, *L'aventure de la science*; Vol. 2, *L'aventure de l'esprit.* Paris: Hermann, Histoire de la Pensée, Nos. 12 and 13.

————*See also* Koyré and Cohen. 1960, 1961, 1962.

Cohen, R. S., J. J. Stachel, and M. W. Wartofsky, eds. 1974. *For Dirk Struik. Scientific, historical and political essays in honor of Dirk J. Struik.* Boston Studies in the Philosophy of Science, Vol. 15, Dordrecht, Boston: D. Reidel Publishing Company.

Collins, John, et al. 1856. *Commercium epistolicum J. Collins et aliorum de analysi promota, etc., ou, Correspondance de J. Collins et d'autres savants célèbres du XVIIe siècle, relative à l'analyse supérieure, réimprimée sur l'édition originale de 1712 avec l'indication des variantes de l'édition de 1722, complétée par une collection de pièces justificatives et de documents, et publiée par J.-B. Biot et F. Lefort.* Paris: Mallet-Bachelier.

Cotes, Roger. *See* Edleston, 1850.

Craig, Sir John. 1946. *Newton at the Mint.* Cambridge [England]: Cambridge University Press.

De Beer, G. R. *See* McKie and De Beer. 1952.

De Morgan, Augustus. 1848. "On the additions made

to the second edition of the Commercium epistolicum." *Philosophical Magazine, 32,* 446-56.

————1852. "On the authorship of the account of the Commercium epistolicum, published in the Philosophical Transactions." *Philosophical Magazine, 3,* 440-4.

————1885. *Newton: his friend: and his niece.* London: Elliot Stock.

————1914. *Essays on the life and work of Newton.* Edited, with notes and appendices, by Philip E. B. Jourdain. Chicago, London: Open Court Publishing Company.

De Villamil, R. 1931. *Newton: the man.* London: Gordon D. Knox.

Debus, Allen G., ed. 1972. *Science, medicine and society: essays to honor Walter Pagel.* 2 vols. New York: Science History Publications, Vol. 1 contains an appreciation of Pagel by Debus (pp 1-9); vol. 2 contains a bibliography of the writings of Pagel by Marianne Winder (pp 289-326).

Dobbs, Betty Jo Teeter. 1975. *The foundations of Newton's alchemy, or "The hunting of the greene lyon".* Cambridge [England], London, New York, Melbourne: Cambridge University Press.

Domson, Charles Andrew. 1972. "Nicolas Fatio de Duillier and the prophets of London: an essay in the historical interaction of natural philosophy and millennial belief in the age of Newton." Diss. New Haven: Yale University.

Dreyer, J. L. E. 1924. "Address delivered by the President, Dr. J. L. E. Dreyer, on the desirability of publishing a new edition of Isaac Newton's collected works." *Monthly Notices of the Royal Astronomical Society, 84,* 298-304.

Edleston, J. 1850. *Correspondence of Sir Isaac Newton and Professor Cotes, including letters of other eminent men, now first published from the originals in the Library of Trinity College, Cambridge; together with an appendix, containing other unpublished letters and papers by Newton.* London: John W. Parker; Cambridge [England]: John Deighton.

Elkana, Yehuda, ed. 1974. *The interaction between science and philosophy.* Atlantic Highlands, N.J.: Humanities Press.

Figala, Karin. 1977. *Die "Kompositionshierarchie" der Materie—Newtons quantitative Theorie und Interpretation der qualitativen Alchemie.* Munich: unpublished Habilitationsschrift in the Technische Universität.

————1977a "Newton as alchemist." *History of Science, 15,* 102-37. Essay based on Dobbs. 1975.

Fraser, Duncan C. 1919. *Newton's interpolation formulas.* London: C. dE. Layton. Identical in content to Fraser's articles in *The Journal of the Institute of Actuaries, 51* (Oct. 1918), 77-106, (Apr. 1919), 211-32. Supplementary material from Newton's *MSS* was published in *58* (Mar. 1927), 53-95, and was then included in a reprint of the earlier work under the same title in 1927 (London: C. dE. Layton).

Gabbey, Alan [W. Allan]. 1971. "Force and inertia in seventeenth-century dynamics." *Studies in History and Philosophy of Science, 2,* 1-67.

————1976. "Essay review of Newton. 1972." *Historia Mathematica, 3,* 237-43.

Geoghegan, D. 1957. "Some indications of Newton's attitude towards alchemy." *Ambix, 6,* 102-6.

Gray, George J. 1907. *A bibliography of the works of Sir Isaac Newton, together with a list of books illustrating his works.* 2d. ed. rev. and enl. Cambridge [England]: Bowes and Bowes.

Greenstreet, W. J., ed. 1927. *Isaac Newton, 1642-1727. A memorial volume edited for the Mathematical Association.* London: G. Bell and Sons.

Gregory, David. 1937. *David Gregory, Isaac Newton and their circle, extracts from David Gregory's memoranda 1677-1708.* Edited by W. G. Hiscock. Oxford: printed for the editor.

Gregory, James Craufurd. 1832. "Notice concerning an autograph manuscript by Sir Isaac Newton, containing some notes upon the third book of the *Principia,* and found among the papers of Dr David Gregory, formerly Savilian Professor of Astronomy in the University of Oxford." *Transactions of the Royal Society of Edinburgh, 12,* 64-76.

Guerlac, Henry. 1963. "Francis Hauksbee: Expérimentateur au profit de Newton." *Archives Internationales d'Histoire des Sciences, 16,* 113-28.

————1963a. *Newton et Epicure.* Paris: Palais de la Découverte [Histoire des Sciences: D-91].

————1964. "Sir Isaac and the ingenious Mr. Hauksbee." In Cohen and Taton, eds. 1964. 1. 228-53.

————1967. "Newton's optical aether. His draft of a proposed addition to his *Opticks.*" *Notes and Records of the Royal Society of London, 22,* 45-57.

————1972. "Hales, Stephen." *Dictionary of Scientific Biography, 6,* 35-48.

————1972a. "Hauksbee, Francis." *Dictionary of Scientific Biography, 6,* 169-75.

————1973. "Newton and the method of analysis." In *Dictionary of the history of ideas, 3.* Edited by Philip P. Wiener. New York: Scribner's, 378-91.

————1977. "The Newtonianism of Dortous de Mairan." In *Essays on the age of enlightenment in honor of Ira O. Wade.* Edited by Jean Macary, Geneva: Librairie Droz, 131-41.

————1977a. *Essays and papers in the history of science.* Baltimore, London: Johns Hopkins University Press. Contains most of Guerlac's early papers on Newton and the aether, on the *Opticks,* and on Hauksbee and Newton, but not (alas!) Guerlac (1972).

————1981. *Newton on the continent.* Ithaca: Cornell University Press.

Hall, A. Rupert. 1948. "Sir Isaac Newton's note-book, 1661-1665." *Cambridge Historical Journal, 9,* 239-50.

————1957. "Newton on the calculation of central forces." *Annals of Science, 13,* 62-71.

————1980. *Philosophers at war: the quarrel between Newton and Leibniz.* Cambridge [England], London, New York, New Rochelle: Cambridge University Press.

Hall, A. Rupert and Marie Boas Hall. 1959. "Newton's electric spirit: four oddities." *Isis, 50,* 473-76.

————1959a. "Newton's 'mechanical principles'." *Journal of the History of Ideas, 20,* 167-78.

————1960. "Newton's theory of matter." *Isis, 51,* 131-44.

————1961. "Clarke and Newton." *Isis, 52,* 583-5.

————eds. 1962. *Unpublished scientific papers of Isaac Newton. A selection from the Portsmouth Collection in the University Library, Cambridge.* Cambridge [England]: Cambridge University Press.

Hall, Marie Boas. 1975. "Newton's voyage in the strange seas of alchemy." In Righini Bonelli and Shea, eds. 1975. 239-46.

————*See also* Boas, Marie.

Harrison, John. 1978. *The library of Isaac Newton.* Cambridge [England], London, New York, Melbourne: Cambridge University Press.

Hawes, Joan L. 1968. "Newton and the 'electrical attraction unexcited'." *Annals of Science, 24,* 121-30.

Heimann, Peter M. 1973. "'Nature is a perpetual worker': Newton's aether and 18th-century natural philosophy." *Ambix, 20,* 1-25.

Herivel, J. W. 1960. "Newton's discovery of the law of centrifugal force." *Isis, 51,* 546-53.

————1960a. "Suggested identification of the missing original of a celebrated communication of Newton's to the Royal Society." *Archives Internationales d'Histoire des Sciences, 13,* 71-8.

————1961. "Interpretation of an early Newton manuscript." *Isis, 52,* 410-16.

————1961a. "The originals of the two propositions discovered by Newton in December 1679?" *Archives Internationales d'Histoire des Sciences, 14,* 23-33.

————1962. "Early Newtonian dynamical *MSS.*" *Archives Internationales d'Histoire des Sciences, 15,* 149-50.

————1965. *The background to Newton's "Principia." A Study of Newton's dynamical researches in the years 1664-84.* Oxford: Clarendon Press.

————1965a. "Newton's first solution to the problem of Kepler motion." *British Journal for the History of Science, 2,* 350-4.

Hill, Christopher. 1965. *Intellectual origins of the English revolution.* Oxford: Clarendon Press.

Horblit, Harrison D. 1964. *One hundred books famous in science.* Based on an exhibition held at the Grolier Club. New York: Grolier Club.

Horsley, Samuel. *See* Newton. 1779-.

Hoskin, Michael. 1961. "The mind of Newton." *The Listener, 66* (19 October), 597-9.

Huxley, G. L. 1959. "Two Newtonian studies, I—Newton's boyhood interests; II—Newton and Greek geometry." *Harvard Library Bulletin, 13,* 348-61.

Huygens, Christiaan. 1888-. *Oeuvres complètes de Christiaan Huygens.* Publiées par la Société Hollandaise des Sciences. The Hague: Martinus Nijhoff. Vol. 22: Supplément á la correspondance, varia, biographie de Chr. Huygens . . . , published in 1950.

Koyré, Alexandre. 1939. *Etudes galiléennes.* Paris: Hermann & Cie. Reprinted 1966.

————1950. "The significance of the Newtonian synthesis." *Archives Internationales d'Histoire des Sciences, 3* [29], 291-311.

————1952. "An unpublished letter of Robert Hooke to Isaac Newton." *Isis, 43,* 312-37.

————1955. "Pour une édition critique des oeuvres de Newton." *Revue d'Histoire des Sciences, 8,* 19-37.

————1956. "L'hypothèse et l'expérience chez Newton." *Bulletin de la Société francais de Philosophie, 50,* 59-79.

————1960. "Newton, Galileo, and Plato." *Actes du IXe Congrès International d'Histoire des Sciences,* Barcelona-Madrid, 1959, 165-97. Reprinted in *Annales: Economies, Sociétés, Civilisations,* Vol. 6, 1041-59, and in Koyré. 1965. pp 201-20.

————1960a. "Les queries de l'Optique." *Archives Internationales d'Histoire des Sciences, 13,* 15-29.

————b. "Les Regulae philosophandi." *Archives Internationales d'Histoire des Sciences, 13,* 3-14.

————1965. *Newtonian studies.* Cambridge [Mass.]: Harvard University Press; London: Chapman & Hall. More than half the volume consists of a previously unpublished study, "Newton and Descartes," pp 53-200.

————1966. *Etudes d'histoire de la pensée scientifique.* Paris: Presses Universitaries de France.

Koyré, Alexandre and I. Bernard Cohen. 1960. "Newton's 'electric & elastic spirit'." *Isis, 51,* 337.

————1961. "The case of the missing *tanquam*: Leibniz, Newton and Clarke." *Isis, 52,* 555-66.

————1962. "Newton & the Leibniz-Clarke correspondence, with notes on Newton, Conti, and Des Maizeaux." *Archives Internationales d'Histoire des Sciences, 15,* 63-126.

Lagrange, Joseph Louis. 1788. *Méchanique analytique.* Paris: chez la veuve Desaint, Librairie.

————1797. *Théorie des fonctions analytiques, contenant les principes du calcul différentiel, dégagés de toute considération d'infiniment petits ou d'évanouissans, de limites ou de fluxions, et réduits à l'analyse algébrique des quantités finies.* Paris: Impr. de la République [prairial an V].

Larmor, Joseph. 1924. "On editing Newton." *Nature, 113,* 744.

Lefort, F., and J.-B. Biot. *See* Collins et al. 1856.

Lohne, Johannes A. 1960. "Hooke versus Newton. An analysis of the documents in the case of free fall and planetary motion." *Centaurus, 7,* 6-52.

————1961. "Newton's 'proof' of the sine law." *Archive for History of Exact Sciences, 1,* 389-405.

————1965. "Isaac Newton: the rise of a scientist 1661-1671." *Notes and Records of the Royal Society of London, 20,* 125-39.

————1967. "The increasing corruption of Newton's diagrams." *History of Science, 6,* 69-89.

————1968. "Experimentum crucis." *Notes and Records of the Royal Society of London, 23,* 169-99.

Lohne, Johannes A., and Bernhard Sticker. 1969. *Newtons Theorie der Prismenfarben mit Ubersetzung und Erläuterung der Abhandlung von 1672.* Munich: Werner Fritsch.

Mach, Ernst. 1926. *The principles of physical optics, an historical and philosophical treatment.* Trans. John S. Anderson and A. F. A. Young. London: Methuen. Reprinted New York: Dover, 1953.

————1960. *The science of mechanics: a critical and historical account of its development.* Trans. Thomas J. McCormack, new introduction by Karl Menger, 6th ed., with revisions through 9th German ed. La Salle, [Ill.]: Open Court Publishing Co.

Malone, Dumas. 1948. *Jefferson the Virginian.* Boston: Little, Brown.

Manuel, Frank E. 1959. *The eighteenth century confronts the gods.* Cambridge [Mass.]: Harvard University Press.

————1963. *Isaac Newton, historian.* Cambridge [Mass.]: Harvard University Press, Belknap Press.

————1968. *A portrait of Isaac Newton.* Cambridge [Mass.]: Harvard University Press, Belknap Press.

————1974. *The religion of Isaac Newton.* Oxford: Clarendon Press.

McGuire, J. E. 1966. "Body and void and Newton's *De mundi systemate*: some new sources." *Archive for History of Exact Sciences, 3,* 206-48.

————1967. "Transmutation and immutability: Newton's doctrine of physical qualities." *Ambix, 14,* 69-95.

————1968. "The origin of Newton's doctrine of essential qualities." *Centaurus, 12,* 233-60.

McGuire, J. E. and P. M. Rattansi. 1966. "Newton and the 'pipes of Pan'." *Notes and Records of the Royal Society of London, 21,* 108-43.

————*See also* Westman and McGuire, 1977.

McKie, Douglas, and G. R. De Beer. 1952. "Newton's apple." *Notes and Records of the Royal Society of London, 9,* 46-54, 333-5.

McLachlan, Herbert, ed. *See* Newton. 1950.

McMullin, Ernan. 1978. *Newton on matter and activity.* Notre Dame [Indiana], London: University of Notre Dame Press.

Miller, Perry. 1958. "Bentley and Newton." In Newton. 1958. pp 271-8.

Mills, A. A. 1981. "Newton's prisms and his experiments on the spectrum." *Notes and Records of the Royal Society of London, 36,.* 13-36.

Mills, A. A. and P. J. Turvey. 1979. "Newton's Telescope." *Notes and Records of the Royal Society of London, 33,* 133-55.

More, L. T. 1934. *Isaac Newton: a biography.* New York, London: Scribner's. Reprinted. New York: Dover.

Motte, Andrew. *See* Newton. 1729. 1934.

Munby, A. N. L. 1951, 1952. "The two title-pages of the *Principia.*" *Times Literary Supplement, 50* (21 December), 2603; *51* (28 March), 228.

————*1952a.* "The distribution of the first edition of Newton's *Principia.*" *Notes and Records of the Royal Society of London, 10,* 28-39.

————*1952b.* "The Keynes Collection of the works of Sir Isaac Newton at King's College, Cambridge." *Notes and Records of the Royal Society of London, 10,* 40-50.

Napier, John. 1889. *The construction of the wonderful canon of logarithms.* Translated from Latin into English, with notes and a catalogue of the various editions of Napier's works, by William Rae MacDonald. Edinburgh, London: William Blackwood and Sons.

Newton, Isaac. 1672. "A letter of Mr. Isaac Newton . . . containing his new theory about light and colors." *Philosophical Transactions, 6,* 3075-87.

————1702. *A new and most accurate theory of the moon's motion; whereby all her irregularities may be solved, and her place truly calculated to two minutes.* Written by the incomparable mathematician Mr. Isaac Newton, and published in Latin by Mr. David Gregory in his excellent astronomy. London: printed and sold by A. Baldwin. Reprinted in Newton. 1975.

————1715. "[Recensio Libri=] An account of the book entituled *Commercium epistolicum Collinii & aliorum, de analysi promota,* published by order of the Royal-Society, in relation to the dispute between Mr. Leibnits and Dr. Keill, about the right of invention of the new method of fluxions, by some call'd the differential method." *Philosophical Transactions, 29,* 173-224. The title of the book given in the *Philosophical Transactions* is not the exact title of the *Commercium epistolicum* [first edition] itself. A French translation appeared in the *Journal Littéraire,* Nov./Dec. 1715, vol. 6, pp 13 ff, 345 ff.

————1728. *A treatise of the system of the world.* Translated into English. London: printed for F. Fayram.

————*1728a. De mundi systemate liber.* London: impensis J. Tonson, J. Osborn, & T. Longman.

————*1728b. Optical lectures read in the publick schools of the University of Cambridge, anno Domini, 1669.* By the late Sir Isaac Newton, then Lucasian Professor of the Mathematicks. Never before printed. Translated into English out of the original Latin. London: printed for Francis Fayram.

————1729. *The mathematical principles of natural philosophy.* Translated into English by Andrew Motte. *To which are added, The laws of the moon's motion, according to gravity.* By John Machin. In two volumes. London: printed for Benjamin Motte. Facsimile reprint, intro. I. Bernard Cohen. London: Dawsons of Pall Mall, 1968.

————1733. *Observations upon the prophecies of Daniel and the Apocalypse of St. John.* London: printed by J. Darby and T. Browne.

————1759. *Principes mathématiques de la philosophie naturelle.* Translated "par feue Madame la Marquise du Chastellet." 2 vols. Paris: chez Desaint & Saillant [& chez] Lambert.

————1779—. *Opera quae exstant omnia.* Commentariis illustrabat Samuel Horsley. 5 vols. London: John Nichols. Volume 5 was published in 1785. 5 vol. reprinted in 1964. Stuttgart-Bad Cannstatt. Friedrich Verlag (Günther-Holzboog).

————1931. *Opticks or a treatise of the reflections, refractions, inflections & colours of light.* Reprinted from the fourth edition [London, 1730]. Foreword by Prof. Albert Einstein, Nobel Laureate. Introduction by Prof. E. T. Whittaker, F. R. S. London: G. Bell & Sons.

————1934. *Sir Isaac Newton's Mathematical principles of natural philosophy and his System of the world.* Translated into English by Andrew Motte in 1729. The translations revised, and supplied with an historical and explanatory appendix, by Florian Cajori. Berkeley: University of California Press.

————1950. *Theological manuscripts.* Edited by H. McLachlan. Liverpool: University Press.

————1952. *Opticks or a treatise of the reflections, refractions, inflections & colours of light.* Based on the fourth edition: London, 1730. With foreword by Albert Einstein; Introduction by Sir Edmund Whittaker; Preface by I. Bernard Cohen; Analytical table of contents prepared by Duane H. D. Roller. New York: Dover Publications.

————1958. *Isaac Newton's papers & letters on natural philosophy and related documents.* Edited, with a general introduction, by I. Bernard Cohen assisted by Robert E. Schofield. Cambridge [Mass.] Harvard University Press. 2d ed., rev. and enl. Harvard University Press, 1978.

————1959-1977. *The correspondence of Isaac Newton.* Vol 1, 1661-1675 (1959), vol 2,1676-1687 (1960), vol 3, 1688-1694 (1961), Edited by H. W. Turnbull; vol 4, 1694-1709 (1967), Edited by J. F. Scott; vol 5, 1709-1713 (1975), vol 6, 1713-1718 (1976), vol 7, 1718-1727 (1977), Edited by A. Rupert Hall and Laura Tilling. Published for the Royal Society. Cambridge [England]: Cambridge University Press.

————1964-1967. *The mathematical works of Isaac Newton.* Assembled with an introduction by Dr. Derek T. Whiteside. 2 vols. New York, London: Johnson Reprints [The Sources of Science].

————1967-. *The mathematical papers of Isaac Newton.* Vol 1, 1664-1666 (1967); vol 2, 1667-1670 (1968); vol 3, 1670-1673 (1969); vol 4, 1674-1684 (1971); vol 5, 1683-1684 (1972); vol 6, 1684-1691 (1974); vol 7, 1691-1695 (1976); Edited by D. T. Whiteside, with the assistance in publication of M. A. Hoskin and A. Prag. Cambridge: Cambridge University Press. To be complete in 8 vols.

————1969. *A treatise of the system of the world.* Translated into English. With an introduction by I. B. Cohen. London: Dawsons of Pall Mall. Photo-reprint of the 2d ed. (1731), plus the front matter of the 1st ed. (1728).

————1972. *Isaac Newton's Philosophiae naturalis principia mathematica.* the third edition (1726) with variant readings assembled by Alexandre Koyré, I. Bernard Cohen, & Anne Whitman. 2 vols. Cambridge [England]: Cambridge University Press; Cambridge [Mass.]: Harvard University Press.

————1973. *The unpublished first version of Isaac Newton's Cambridge lectures on optics 1670-1672.* A facsimile of the autograph, now Cambridge University Library *MS.* Add. 4002, with an introduction by D. T. ide. Cambridge [England]: The University Library.

————1975. *Isaac Newton's "Theory of the moon's motion" (1702).* With a bibliographical and historical introduction by I. Bernard Cohen. London: Dawson.

Palter, Robert. 1970. "Newton and the inductive method." In Palter, ed. 1970. pp 244-57.

————ed. 1970. *The annus mirabilis of Sir Isaac Newton 1666-1966.* Cambridge [Mass.], London: M.I.T. Press.

Patterson, Louise Diehl. 1949, 1950. "Hooke's gravitation theory and its influence on Newton. I: Hooke's gravitation theory. II: The insufficiency of the traditional estimate." *Isis, 40,* 327-41; *41,* 32-45.

Pighetti, Clelia. 1960. "Cinquant'anni di studi newtoniani (1908-1959)." *Rivista Critica di Storia della Filosofia,* fascicoli 2-3, 181-203, 295-318.

Portsmouth Collection. 1888. *A catalogue of the Portsmouth Collection of books and papers written by or belonging to Sir Isaac Newton, the scientific portion of which has been presented by the Earl of Portsmouth to the University of Cambridge.* Prepared by H. R. Luard, G. G. Stokes, J. C. Adams, and G. D. Liveing. Cambridge [England]: Cambridge University Press.

Priestley, F. E. L. 1970. "The Clarke-Leibniz controversy." In *The methodological heritage of Newton.* Edited by Robert E. Butts and John W. Davis. Oxford: Basil Blackwell, pp 34-56.

Rattansi, P. M. 1972. "Newton's alchemical studies." In Debus, ed. 1972. Vol. 2, pp 167-82.

————1973. "Some evaluations of reason in sixteenth- and seventeenth-century natural philosophy." In Teich and Young, eds. 1973. pp 148-66.

Rigaud, Stephen Peter. 1838. *Historical essay on the first publication of Sir Isaac Newton's "Principia".* Oxford: Oxford University Press. Reprinted, New York, London: Johnson 1972.

————ed. 1841. *Correspondence of scientific men of the seventeenth century . . . in the collection of . . . the Earl of Macclesfield.* 2 vols. Oxford: Oxford University Press.

Righini Bonelli, M. L. and William R. Shea, eds. 1975. *Reason, experiment, and mysticism in the scientific revolution.* New York: Science History Publications.

Royal Society. 1947. *Newton tercentenary celebrations.* Cambridge [England]: Cambridge University

Press. Contains E. N. da C. Andrade, "Newton"; Lord Keynes, "Newton, the man"; J. Hadamard, "Newton and the infinitesimal calculus"; S. I. Vavilov, "Newton and the atomic theory"; N. Bohr, "Newton's principles and modern atomic mechanics"; H. W. Turnbull, "Newton: the algebraist and geometer"; W. Adams, "Newton's contributions to observational astronomy"; J. C. Hunsaker, "Newton and fluid mechanics."

Ruffner, James Alan. 1966. "The background and early development of Newton's theory of comets." Diss. Bloomington: Indiana University.

————1971. "The curved and the straight: cometary theory from Kepler to Hevelius." *Journal for the History of Astronomy, 2,* 178-95.

Sabra, A. I. 1967. *Theories of light from Descartes to Newton.* London: Oldbourne.

Sampson, R. A. 1924. "On editing Newton." *Monthly Notices of the Royal Astronomical Society, 84,* 378-83.

Schofield, Robert E. 1958. "Halley and the *Principia.*" In Newton. 1958. pp 397-404.

Scott, J. F. *See* Newton. 1959-1977.

Shapiro, Alan E. 1980. "The evolving structure of Newton's theory of white light and color." *Isis, 71,* 211-35.

Smith, David Eugene. 1927. "Two unpublished documents of Sir Isaac Newton." In *Isaac Newton, 1942-1727.* Edited by W. J. Greenstreet. London: G. Bell and Sons, pp 16-34.

Sotheby & Co. 1936. *Catalogue of the Newton papers, sold by order of the Viscount Lymington to whom they have descended from Catherine Conduitt, Viscountess Lymington, great-niece of Sir Isaac Newton.* London: Sotheby & Co.

————1965. *Catalogue of the fine collection of scientific books, the property of Professor E. N. da C. Andrade, F.R.S.* London: Sotheby & Co.

Stukeley, William. 1936. *Memoirs of Sir Isaac Newton's life, 1752: being some account of his family and chiefly of the junior part of his life.* Edited by A. Hastings White. London: Taylor and Francis.

Sutcliffe, John H., comp. and ed. 1932. *British Optical Association Library and Museum catalogue.* London: Council of the British Optical Association.

Taylor, F. Sherwood. 1956. "An alchemical work of Sir Isaac Newton." *Ambix, 5,* 59-84.

Teich, Mikulas and Robert Young, eds. 1973. *Changing perspectives in the history of science: essays in honour of Joseph Needham.* London: Heinemann.

Turnbull, Herbert Western, ed. 1939. *James Gregory: tercentenary memorial volume. Containing his correspondence with John Collins and his hitherto unpublished mathematical manuscripts, together with addresses and essays communicated to the Royal Society of Edinburgh, July 4, 1938.* Published for the Royal Society of Edinburgh. London: G. Bell and Sons.

————1951. "The discovery of the infinitesimal calculus." *Nature, 167,* 1048-50.

————1953. "Isaac Newton's letters: some discoveries." *Manchester Guardian,* 3 October, p 4. Reprinted, *Manchester Guardian Weekly,* 8 October, p 11.

————*See also* Newton. 1959-1977.

Turnor, Edmund. 1806. *Collections for the history of the twon and soke of Grantham, containing authentic memoirs of Sir Isaac Newton, now first published from the original MSS, in the possession of the Earl of Portsmouth.* London: William Miller.

Waff, Craig. 1975. *Universal gravitation and the motion of the moon's apogee: the establishment and reception of Newton's inverse square law, 1687-1749.* Diss. Baltimore: Johns Hopkins University.

————1967. "Isaac Newton, the motion of the lunar apogee, and the establishment of the inverse square law." *Vistas in Astronomy, 20,* 99-103.

Wallis, Peter and Ruth Wallis. 1977. *Newton and Newtoniana, a bibliography.* Folkestone [Kent, England]: Dawson.

Westfall, Richard S. 1962. "The foundations of Newton's philosophy of nature." *British Journal for the History of Science, 1,* 171-82.

————1963. "Newton's reply to Hooke and the theory of colors." *Isis, 54,* 82-96.

————1963a. "Short-writing and the state of Newton's conscience, 1662." *Notes and Records of the Royal Society of London, 18,* 10-16.

————1967. "Uneasily fitful reflections on fits of easy transmission." *Texas Quarterly, 10,* No. 3 (Autumn), 86-102.

————1967a. "Hooke and the law of universal gravitation." *The British Journal for the History of Science, 3,* 245-61.

————1970. "Uneasily fitful reflections on fits of easy transmission." In Palter, ed. 1970. 88-104.

————1971. *Force in Newton's physics: the science of dynamics in the seventeenth century.* London: Macdonald; New York: American Elsevier.

————1972. "Newton and the hermetic tradition." In Debus, ed. 1972. 2, 183-98.

————1973. "Newton and the fudge factor." *Science, 179,* 751-8.

————1975. "The role of alchemy in Newton's career." In Righini Bonelli and Shea, eds. 1975. pp 189-232.

————1980. *Never at rest, a biography of Isaac Newton.* Cambridge [England], London, New York, New Rochelle: Cambridge University Press.

Westman, Robert S., and J. E. McGuire. 1977. *Hermeticism and the scientific revolution.* Los Angeles: University of California, William Andrews Clark Memorial Library.

Whiteside, Derek T. 1961. "Newton's discovery of the general binomial theorem." *Mathematical Gazette, 45,* 175-80.

————1961*a.* "Patterns of mathematical thought in the later seventeenth century." *Archive for History of Exact Sciences, 1,* 179-388.

————1962. "The expanding world of Newtonian research." *History of Science, 1,* 16-29.

————1964. "Isaac Newton: birth of a mathematician." *Notes and Records of the Royal Society of London, 19,* 53-62.

————1964*a.* "Newton's early thoughts on planetary motion: a fresh look." *British Journal for the History of Science, 2,* 117-37.

————1966. "Newtonian dynamics." *History of Science, 5,* 104-17. Review article on Herivel. 1965.

————1966*a.* "Newton's marvellous year: 1666 and all that." *Notes and Records of the Royal Society of London, 21,* 32-41.

————1970. "Before the *Principia:* the maturing of Newton's thoughts on dynamical astronomy, 1664-84." *Journal for the History of Astronomy, 1,* 5-19.

————1970*a.* "The mathematical principles underlying Newton's *Principia.*" *Journal for the History of Astronomy, 1,* 116-38.

————1976. "Newton's lunar theory: from high hope to disenchantment." *Vistas in Astronomy, 19,* 317-28.

————1977. "From his claw the greene lyon." *Isis, 68,* 116-21. Essay-review of Dobbs. 1975.

————*See also* Newton. 1964-1967, 1967-.

Wightman, W. P. D. 1953. "Gregory's 'Notae in Isaaci Newtoni Principia Philosophiae'." *Nature, 172,* 690.

Wilson, Curtis. 1970. "From Kepler's laws, so-called, to universal gravitation: empirical factors." *Archive for History of Exact Sciences, 6,* 89-170.

————1974. "Newton and some philosophers on Kepler's 'laws'." *Journal of the History of Ideas, 35,* 231-58.

Writting, Alexander. 1911-12. "Zur Frage der Erfindung des Algorithmus der Newtonschen Fluxionsrechnung." *Bibliotheca Mathematica,* series 3, Vol. 12, 56-60.

Zeitlinger, H. 1927. "A Newton bibliography." In Greenstreet. ed. 1927. pp 148-70.

Milton Wilson (essay date 1988)

SOURCE: "Reading Locke and Newton as Literature," in *University of Toronto Quarterly,* Vol. 57, No. 4, Summer 1988, pp. 472-82.

[*In the following essay, Wilson argues that such literary topics as narration, point of view, diction, image patterns, and "creative myth making or imaginative range" may be found in the works of both Locke and Newton. Wilson explores Newton's use of first-person narration, the settings and props used in discussion of experiments, and the use of negative interrogative syntax.*]

What does one expect from a title like 'Reading Locke and Newton as Literature'? Maybe some account of their prose style, or, more broadly, of their rhetoric, as it contributes to the persuasive quality of what they are arguing for. Well, it would certainly be possible to include my particular concerns, plus plenty of other matters, under the broad umbrella of rhetoric. But what I really want to do is discuss Locke and Newton in terms which would not seem out of place in a course on poetry or drama or, more especially, fiction. I am thinking of such long-standing critical topics as narration, point of view, characteristic diction, patterns of images or exempla, quality of mimetic detail, even creative myth-making or imaginative range. And I am interested not so much in how these things contribute to the arguments of Locke and Newton as in how they don't: that is to say, in how the excesses and unpredictabilities of these authors' literary invention go beyond the philosophy (or natural philosophy in Newton's case) in ways that, while not always subversive of the philosophic purpose, manage to seem somehow self-sustaining. Obviously my two authors are not among those philosophical changelings whom poets are fond of claiming as their brethren, like Plato or Nietzsche. No librarian has ever had second thoughts about shelving Locke's *Essay concerning Human Understanding* or Newton's **Opticks.** What follows is, I suppose, an attempt to provide grounds for such an idiosyncratic librarian. I should add that, although this paper contains few specific debts to them, I nevertheless feel hovering over its pages the presence of three former teachers in Toronto's English department: I am thinking of Kenneth MacLean and Rosalie Colie on Locke and F. E. L. Priestley on Newton.

As is often pointed out, much of the effect of a philosophical argument comes from the skill with which instances are chosen and applied. But whereas the philosophic reader needs to be convinced by their relevance to the author's argument and somehow kept from regarding them as an unrepresentative batch, the literary reader may easily be more concerned with their place in the author's self-presentation. Locke's autobiographical tone is pervasive and, unlike that of Descartes in the *Meditations,* it is casual and informal, and, unlike that of Montaigne, it extends over an essay of nearly a thousand pages. His instances seem drawn from a lifetime of experience and imply thousands more.

I needn't spend much time on staple phrases in the texture of Locke's *Essay* such as 'I once knew a man . . . who told me he had never dreamed in his life . . .' or 'I once saw a creature that was the issue of a cat and a rat' or 'I was once in a meeting of very learned and ingenious physicians' or 'a sort of birds I lately saw in St. James's park'; these have the essay flavour of things in Bacon like 'I knew two who were competitors for the secretary's place in Queen Elizabeth's time.' But we get more than Locke ransacking his store of past episodes, we also get the present essayist writing in the here and now. Whereas philosophical commentators, when they discuss his account of identity, are understandably concerned with such useful instances as 'the soul of a prince . . . enter[ing] and inform[ing] the body of a cobbler' or Socrates awake and Socrates asleep, a literary reader might be more struck by the reflexive moments when Locke at work on his *Essay* is the instance at hand. After all, the famous tabula rasa image isn't just an image for the mind; it faces Locke literally from his desk. He says,

> Had I the same consciousness that I saw the ark and Noah's flood, as that I saw an overflowing of the Thames last winter, or as that I write now, I could

no more doubt that I who write this now, that saw the Thames overflowed last winter, and that viewed the flood at the general deluge, was the same *self* . . . than that I who write this am the same *myself* now whilst I write . . .that I was yesterday. (II, xxvii, 16)[1]

In a particular discussion of the grounds for supposing that our sensations come from things outside us, he keeps looking at the white paper before him and the marks he is making on it, and the phrase 'whilst I write this' keeps recurring. But such reflexive moments invite expansion beyond the narrative present. For example, he looks up from the paper at what he regards as the undoubted existence of a stretch of water in front of him right then (he's in Rotterdam; maybe his desk overlooks a canal); then he asserts that his today's experience of its existence will not disappear; after all, his memory of seeing the water yesterday is still with him today. Here is how Locke puts it:

> Thus, seeing water at this instant, it is an unquestionable truth to me that water doth exist: and remembering that I saw it yesterday, it will also be always true, and as long as my memory retains it always an undoubted proposition to me that water did exist the 10th of July, 1688. (IV, xi, 11)

Then having moved from present to past and back to present, he goes on to speculate about the water's continued existence in the future when it is no longer before him. Such narrative self-consciousness, which takes to an extreme the natural introspection of empiricism, can focus, however, not just on a single instance but on the process of writing the *Essay* as a whole. It was, of course, a work that grew and, as the commentators keep pointing out, every addition or revision faced the problem of precursors that refused to be superseded. Locke has no hesitation about telling us that the whole of Book III is an afterthought. 'I must confess,' he writes, 'that, when I first began this Discourse of the Understanding, and a good while after, I had not the least thought that any consideration of words was at all necessary to it' (III, ix, 21). The brief chapter on the association of ideas appended to Book II was a very late insertion, and what it does not talk about is as striking as what it does. It clearly implies the need for a new look at the terminology with which complex ideas are discussed earlier, but in fact it sticks to the pathology of association; associating ideas turns out to be merely a prescription for madness. All the topic's positive potential has to wait for Hume and Hartley in the following century. Locke's *Essay* is both a perpetually half-revised and an increasingly open-ended book. It belongs among those big, impossible-to-complete, self-conscious and self-creative process-works which include *The Anatomy of Melancholy, A Tale of a Tub, Tristram Shandy,* and the *Biographia Literaria,* not to mention poems like *The Prelude* and *Don Juan.*

Is there anything in what I have so far said about Locke applicable to Newton? In contrasting the *Principia* with the *Opticks,* Bernard Cohen has emphasized how much the former depends on other people's observations accumulated over a considerable historical sweep, from Aristotle to Flamsteed, whereas the latter is firmly grounded on Newton's own experience.[2] The current scholarly interest in the first-person narration of scientific experiment has certainly something to contribute to our appreciation of Newton. I think of the ways in which information and events are ordered (logically and chronologically), in which alternatives are rejected and chosen ('I might have drawn black Lines with a Pen, but the Threds were smaller and better defined' [23]), in which peripheral narrative contexts are provided ('an Artist in *London* undertook to imitate it; but using another way of polishing them than I did, he fell much short . . . as I afterwards understood by discoursing the Under-workman he had employed' [104]). But, instead of discussing the narration, let me just draw your attention to the setting and props through which the story is told. Of course, the antiseptic world of the twentieth-century lab is missing. Seventeenth-century experimenting rarely existed in any specialized space, but rather as an addendum to, or in the midst of, an everyday world of places and objects. This is, to be sure, as true for, say, Boyle and Hooke as for Newton. I recommend a literary reading of Hooke's *Micrographia.* Still, Newton's *Opticks,* with its experiments apparently carried out in the little country house of his birth at Woolthorpe (to which he returned during the plague years) and in his rooms at Cambridge, has its own distinctive flavour of cottage industry, or of a first-person domestic novel before its time. One of the pleasures of reading it is the feeling that anyone anywhere could do what is going on. The equipment just seems like odds and ends around the house. The prisms and lenses are the only specialized goods and there is plenty of discussion of their inadequacies: bubbles and waves and veins and curls and smoky streaks. For the rest all he needs is a sunny window, some boards with holes in them, black thread, red and blue paint, sheets of black paper, a candle, any old book, a hair from someone's head (presumably Newton's own), some pieces of a broken mirror, a smooth white ruler, soap froth, a sort of oversize comb with sixteen teeth (made by himself), even some flies (house flies I take it, not butterflies). Needless to say, this is not an exhaustive, just a characteristic list. All of these ingredients are deployed within that chamber which he darkens or admits light into at will. If a casual visitor appears, he can be coopted into the experiment too, as with one on degrees of whiteness. 'When I was trying this,' says Newton, 'a Friend coming to visit me, I stopp'd him at the Door, and before I told him what the Colours were, or what I was doing; I asked him, Which of the two Whites were the best, and wherein they differed' (153). The friend finds them equally white, the observation for which Newton is hoping.

It is also hard not to see the *Opticks* as a kind of process-work like Locke's *Essay.* Book III (the final one) is concerned with experiments which show how bodies seem to act on light rays passing them at a distance. But after twenty pages of experiments and calculations he writes:

> When I made the foregoing Observations, I design'd to repeat most of them with more care and exactness, and to make some new ones. . . . But I was then interrupted, and cannot now think of taking these things into farther Consideration. And since I have not finish'd this part of my Design, I shall conclude with proposing only some Queries, in order to a farther search to be made by others. (338-9)

So the last sixty pages or so (added in 1717) consist of those famous thirty-one queries, in whose negative interrogative syntax Newton is able to express and repress his most far-out speculations and bring together optical problems from his present book and gravitational ones from the *Principia.* 'Have not,' he asks at the beginning of the culminating query, 'the small Particles of Bodies certain Powers, Virtues, or Forces, by which they act at a distance, not only upon the Rays of Light, . . . but also upon one another . . . ?' (375-6). The whole final division of the *Opticks* has the cliff-hanging title Book III, Part 1 and in the last paragraph of this Johnsonian 'conclusion in which nothing is concluded,' Newton says: 'I have only begun the Analysis . . . hinting several things.' Of course we are not far from the commonplace that science is long but life is short (or from the famous Newton-on-the-beach image); yet we are also (structurally speaking) not that far from Byron in Canto XII of *Don Juan,* whatever the difference in tone:

> But now I will begin my poem. 'Tis
>   Perhaps a little strange, if not quite new,
> That from the first of Cantos up to this
>   I've not begun what we have to go
>   through.
> These first twelve books are merely flourishes,
>   *Preludios,* trying just a string or two
> Upon my lyre, or making the pegs sure;
> And when so, you shall have the overture.

But let us not overemphasize this Lockian and Newtonian self-consciousness. In Locke what exceeds the philosophic desire for convincing instances is not just the first person and its point of view. There is also an inventive excess in the instances themselves. For example, Locke is not content with some straightforward tales about how children learn things; he has to pursue his instances into the womb itself. Even the status of the foetus becomes an issue (its baptizability for example), as he tries to understand what we can learn before, at, or immediately after birth. In a particularly memorable instance of the sort, he imagines the limited operations of one sense after another in that pre-natal scene, where, in his words, 'there is little or no variety, or change of objects, to move the senses' (II, i, 24). He also has a vivid vignette of 'children new-born; who always turn their eyes to that part from whence the light comes, lay them how you please' (II, ix, 7). It sounds like Wordsworth's *Immortality Ode,* though the purpose is very different.

Mentioning Wordsworth makes me think of *Tintern Abbey's* 'landscape to a blind man's eye,' which his commentators like to trace to Locke. It might be easy to suppose (judging from eighteenth-century references in Hume and Fielding and Burke) that Locke's only blind-man story is the one about the man who thought the idea of scarlet was like the sound of a trumpet. Far from it. There's the man 'who lost his sight by small-pox when he was a child, and had no more notion of colours than one born blind.' There's the blind man imagined in a quoted letter of Molyneux who could distinguish a cube from a sphere by touch. If he regained sight could his eye immediately know which was which? Molyneux thought not, and Locke agreed (II, ix, 8). Locke also tells us an elaborate judgment-of-Midas-like anecdote of the painter and the sculptor competing before the blind man, and how he prefers the painter, whose figures he can neither see nor touch (III, iv, 12). Then there's the problem of how a blind man derives his sense of time. This selection of examples is perhaps enough to show the exhaustive multiplicity with which some kinds of instance are used. But I can't resist taking one short step from the blind man who recovers his sight to Locke's Adam naming what he encounters for the first time. Of course this Adam doesn't just have to name complex ideas of substance (like 'every beast of the field and every fowl of the air' in Genesis); there are also complex ideas of mixed modes. Locke's story (III, vi, 44) of how fallen Adam produces the words adultery and jealousy spontaneously in conversation with Eve after jumping to mistaken conclusions about the cause of his married son's melancholy is certainly enterprising, although no doubt it needed the talents of a Richardson to really work. And it goes far beyond the need to show how nominal essences can exist before their real essences do.

I give you one final piece of Lockian narrative excess. His invented occurrence is intended to define an instant as a succession of events in which our sense of succession is lost. Locke imagines a man standing in a room. A cannon is fired and its bullet passes through the room entering via one wall and exiting via its opposite. Locke's point is that the man in the room cannot separate the two sounds: hitting one wall and hitting the other. They both form one instant. So far, so good. But his hyperactive invention cannot resist inserting another step. Suppose the bullet also goes through the man. Can he distinguish between the pains of the successive bodily impacts? I shall quote the whole example, in which Locke makes his two different, but combined, versions of a single instant more remarkable, if a lot less convincing, than one might have been.

> Let a cannon-bullet pass through a room, and in its way take with it any limb, or fleshy parts of man, it is as clear as any demonstration can be, that it must strike successively the two sides of the room: it is also evident, that it must touch one part of the flesh first, and another after, and so in succession: and yet, I believe, nobody who ever felt the pain of such a shot, or heard the blow against the two distant walls, could perceive any succession either in the pain or sound of so swift a stroke. Such a part of duration as this, wherein we perceive no succession, is that which we call an *instant.* (II, xiv, 10)

We must not suppose that the sort of unpredictable and self-sustaining narrative invention which I have been illustrating can be found with the same abundance in, say, comparable philosophic works by Hobbes or Berkeley or even Hume. The instances in Hobbes and Berkeley are far more conventional (drawn from a well-worn traditional stock), as well as straightforwardly functional. Berkeley has no interest in stories as stories, but only as a means of making a point, and when, in the *Dialogues* for example, he does go out on a limb and try to relate his argument to the narrative of creation in Genesis, he in fact disregards the order of events and what the story actually includes.[3] And the vast majority of Hume's instances in the *Treatise* are brief, uninventive, and functional, although of course often very wittily handled, and he saves his literary invention for peripheral places like the comic conclusion to Book I, where he compares his philosophic self to an almost shipwrecked sailor in one paragraph and to an uncouth monster in another. Hume's *Enquiries* are, of course, a different matter, with their multitude of instances from other texts. In half a dozen characteristic pages from Section VII of the morals *Enquiry,* he refers to, and sometimes quotes, Horace, Shakespeare, St Evremond, Homer, Longinus, a play of Seneca, Boileau, Plutarch, Demosthenes, Tacitus, Herodotus, Fénelon, Thucydides, and even Spenser (although his prose not his poetry). While Locke benefits from being read as literature, he is not literary in the vulgar sense of perpetually referring to works of literature, whereas Hume, in some works, certainly is. Indeed, you can find little evidence in Locke's *Essay* that he read modern vernacular literature at all, outside of books of travel. The only such writer he mentions is Cervantes, who provides him with an analogy to the blind man (and his trumpet-tongued scarlet) in Sancho Panza, 'who had the faculty to see Dulcinea by hearsay' (III, iv, 11).

But I want to turn from instances with some element of narrative to lists of items. The rhetoric of lists has interested readers of poets as diverse as Alexander Pope and Leonard Cohen, the most notorious lists being those with anomalous items, like Pope's 'Puffs, Powders, Patches, Bibles, Billet-doux,' or Dryden's 'chemist, fiddler, statesman and buffoon,' to which one might add cluttered lists like Locke's 'Seth, Ismael, Socrates, Pilate, St. Austin and Caesar Borgia' or even his 'to slide, roll, tumble, walk, creep, run, dance, leap, skip.' I begin, however, with Newton this time. Scientists since Bacon have had an understandable urge towards evidential overkill, and for the virtuosos in and out of the Royal Society the collection of items could be almost an end in itself. Newton, despite the centrality of mathematical abstraction in his natural philosophy, includes as many instances as possible. In Query 8, after a negative interrogative on the vibrations that cause some bodies to 'emit Light and shine,' he continues:

> As for instance; Sea-Water in a raging storm; Quicksilver agitated in *vacuo;* the Back of a Cat, or Neck of a Horse, obliquely struck or rubbed in a dark place; Wood, Fish and Flesh while they putrefy; Vapours arising from putrefy'd Waters, usually call'd *Ignes Fatui;* Stacks of moist Hay or Corn growing hot by fermentation; Glow-worms and the Eyes of some Animals by vital Motions; the vulgar *Phosphorus* agitated by the attrition of any Body, or by the acid Particles of the Air; Amber and some Diamonds by striking, pressing or rubbing them; Scrapings of Steel struck off by a Flint; Iron hammer'd very nimbly till it become so hot as to kindle Sulphur thrown upon it; the Axletrees of Chariots taking fire by the rapid rotation of the Wheels. (340-1).

Plus a few more.

But on Locke my concern is not going to be with such richly various and vivid lists but with a feature also to be found in the parallels and antitheses characteristic of the heroic-couplet poetry of his time. I am thinking of witty, suggestive, and sometimes paradoxical pairings. Here are a few out of context. 'It is as significant to ask whether his sleep be swift or his virtue square'; 'neither having the notion of God nor being cast into sleep by opium'; 'it will be impossible to know what things are or ought to be called a horse, or antimony.' Even when they seem less arbitrary, and alliteration or some other common feature establishes connections, the obsessive search for twos stimulates Locke's invention in lively ways: 'whether this be a tiger or that tea,' 'the croaking of their bellies and the cries of their children,' 'let him put a flint or a football between his hands.' Maybe it is only *my* taste buds that get an odd *frisson* from a juxtaposition like 'he that from his childhood never tasted an oyster, or a pineapple.' My final example is not intended to be a striking, just a characteristic, sequence of Lockian pairings.

> Vulgar notions suit vulgar discourses: and both, though confused enough, yet serve pretty well the

market and the wake. Merchants and lovers, cooks and tailors, have words wherewithal to dispatch their ordinary affairs: and so, I think, might philosophers and disputants too, if they had a mind to understand, and to be clearly understood. (III, xi, 10)

That quotation would provide a good occasion for discussing Locke's manipulation of levels of usage, how he suggests replacing substance with 'underpropping' and accident with 'sticking on,' how he explains that, in turning simple ideas into complex ones, we just 'bind them into bundles and rank them . . . into sorts,' how he sees the association of ideas as 'the whole gang show[ing] themselves together.' Hume follows in Locke's verbal footsteps when he defines the mind as 'nothing but a heap . . . of different perceptions,' although he dilutes the word a bit by adding 'or collection.' But more significant (no doubt) than the level of usage are the basic images themselves by which Locke depicts the processes of mind. How, for example, does he cope with the inadequacies of that inherited commonplace image of the mind as 'white paper'? Those inadequacies are most obvious when the subjects of memory and continuing identity appear. What can seem more fragile than a paper mind and less likely to last than what is written on it? And there is no use quoting Shakespeare's *Sonnets* to the contrary. One way in which Locke tries to handle that paper mind is by adulterating it with plenty of other images, some of them less obviously transient, like an empty cabinet in which ideas are lodged. There is an interesting passage, rather in the manner of Spenser's allegory of the Castle of Alma, which depicts the body as if it were a kind of royal palace, with different senses as the gates where particular perceptions 'have admittance' and with nerve conduits to 'convey them . . . to their audience in the brain,' which Locke calls 'the mind's presence room.' There is, we are told, 'no postern to be admitted by' (III, i, 1). When memory is being emphasized we get a host of images now inherited by computers: storehouses and repositories and registers. Locke is as attracted by the idea of total recall as Coleridge was repelled by it (calling it 'the dread book of judgment' in the *Biographia*) or as Swift, with his 'Secretary of the Universe' indexing everything ever known, was amused by it (in *A Tale of a Tub*). The closest Locke can get to computers who forget nothing is in his conception of those 'superior created intellectual beings' (presumably angels) who are 'able to retain together, and constantly set before them, as in one picture, all their past knowledge at once' (II, x, 9).

But, whatever the importance of the imprinted white paper (or alternative images) to Locke's conception of permanent identity as self-memory, his imagination operates more inventively when the theme is the transience of selfhood and the images tell of 'characters drawn on dust' or 'impressions made on a heap of atoms.' Then the memory fails and its ideas fade, 'leaving,' in his words, 'no more footsteps or remaining characters of themselves than shadows do flying over fields of corn.' 'Thus,' he writes a page later,

> the ideas, as well as the children of our youth, often die before us: and our minds represent to us those tombs to which we are approaching; where, though the brass and marble remain, yet the inscriptions are effaced by time, and the imagery moulders away. (II, x, 5)

Indeed, if one considers the whole range of Locke's images, it is the negative or privative ones that might justify calling him a literary myth-maker of some scope and power. I have already referred to his most obvious image of disability: the blind man and the idea of colours in the dark. But darkness itself obsesses Locke. He considers how much of our daytime life is unconsciously spent in the dark through the repeated blinking of our eyes (II, ix, 10). In another place he tells us that in order not 'to launch out . . . into that abyss of darkness' beyond the extent of human knowledge we must 'look a little into the dark side' (IV, iii, 22). He merges Plato and Newton in calling the mind a dark room with just a few little openings to the light (what Blake will call 'chinks')—a good image, Locke thinks, if 'the pictures coming into such a dark room [would] but stay there' (II, xi, 17). He appeals to our experience, whether 'the shadow of a man . . . does not, when a man looks at it, cause as clear and positive an idea in his mind, as a man himself though covered over with clear sunshine.' 'The picture of a shadow,' he says, 'is a positive thing. . . . And thus one may truly be said to see darkness' (II, viii, 5, 6). It is easy to understand why this passage makes Kenneth MacLean invoke Milton's 'darkness visible.'[4] Elsewhere Locke notes that whereas excess of cold pains us as notably as excess of heat, the eye can take excess of darkness without 'disease' but not excess of light (II, vii, 4). Most striking of all, perhaps, after he speaks of seeing darkness and supposes the figure of a hole perfectly dark, he turns to the pen and paper before him and asks 'whether the ink I write with makes any other idea' than darkness (II, viii, 6).

Parallel to what I've said about darkness, I could produce a portrait of 'the undistinguishable inane' in Locke, that vacuum or void which he prefers to the Descartian plenum for more than scientific reasons. I could even juxtapose what Milton's Belial says about 'those thoughts that wander through eternity' with what Locke says about how the mind 'extends its thoughts often beyond the utmost expansion of Matter and makes excursions into that incomprehensible Inane' (II, vii, 10). But enough is enough. My clutter of exempla is in danger of justifying a characteristic sceptical pun uttered (so I have been told) by A. S. P. Woodhouse on the Lockian tradition: 'Locke, stock and barrel.'

Let me end with a few remarks on the mythmaking implications of Newton. At the 1987 ACUTE Conference I heard a fine paper by Gerald Prince called 'Disnarrated' on how things are not told or untold or distold in stories. In the discussion that followed he suggested, just in passing, that his topic could be extended to cover the techniques of negative narration in scientific description. It occurs to me that one of the most compelling of these negative narrative strands in the history of the literature of scientists is their concern with what might happen if what they are describing were not true. Book I of the *De Rerum Natura* of Lucretius ends with a great example of that 'might': the famous account of the cosmological chaos that would occur if a desire *for* the middle were defeated by a flight *from* the middle. I quote it in somewhat revised Loeb-Classics prose:

> lest the walls of the world suddenly flee apart, dissolved through the vast inane like flying flames, and the rest follow in the same manner, and lest the thundering regions of the sky rush upwards, the earth rapidly slip from under our feet, and amidst the commingled ruin of earth and sky, all things dissolving their bodies vanish through the deep inane, so that in one point of time nothing is left behind except desert space and the invisible atoms.[5]

The fact that this passage begins with a subordinate clause hanging in space following a lacuna in the text makes it even more memorable and terrifying a piece of poetry. What gives it a new lease on life in the seventeenth and eighteenth centuries (apart from the atomic revival in general) is the identification of the Lucretian desire *for* the middle with Newtonian gravity and atomic cohesion, and the Lucretian flight *from* the middle with Newtonian tangential motion. Pope's vision of chaos in the *Essay on Man*, F. E. L. Priestley insists,[6] is not primarily an ontological vision of the dissolution of the Great Chain of Being, but a Newtonian physico-theological vision of the withdrawal of the divine gravitational Will:

> Let Earth unbalanced from her orbit fly,
> Planets and Suns run lawless through the Sky.

But let us look at the natural philosophers not the poets. Here is William Whiston, Newton's successor as Lucasian Professor of Mathematics at Cambridge:

> If that Power of Gravity were suspended, all the whole System would immediately dissolve; and each of the Heavenly Bodies would be crumbled into Dust; the single Atoms commencing their several Motions in such several strait Lines, according to which the projectile Motion chanc'd to be at the Instant when that Influence was suspended or withdrawn.[7]

Of course, the non-occurring event in such a scientific narrative could be the projectile motion itself; so Newton's popularizer, John Clarke, decides to 'suppose the Moon's Motion to be stopped and that the Moon be let fall in such a manner, as to descend toward the Earth with all the Force with which it is retained in its Orb.'[8] When I read that supposition I wish for a moment that Blake had been sufficiently Newtonian in *Auguries of Innocence* to write: 'If the Sun and Moon should stop, / Then immediately they'd drop.' Clarke also creates what I can only call a Newtonian gravitational descent to the underworld.

> If there were a Hole bored in any part of the Earth's Surface quite through the Centre to the opposite Surface, and any Number of Bodies let fall at the same time at different Distances, some very near the Centre, and some very near the Surface; they would all arrive at the Centre together, and then separate, and get as far from the Centre on the other side, as they were when first let fall; after which they would all at the same time begin to come back to the Centre again, and arrive at it all of them together, and thus they would uniformly vibrate backward and forward continually.[9]

Clarke's intention, of course, is just to support the uniformity of square-of-the-distance-from-the-centre acceleration, but these bodies, uniting and separating in alternation forever, at the mercy of unstoppable gravity and inertia, these Ixions and Tantaluses of physics, exist in a hypothetical underworld where, as Virgil might have told us, it is easy to descend—but equally easy to rise, except that it becomes hard to tell which is which.

If you accept my extreme literary reading of that passage, you may still be wondering where Newton himself comes in, and not just his imaginative disciples. The most commonly quoted pieces of Newtonian mythmaking come from the General Scholium of the **Principia,** and there are some tempting passages in it elsewhere, especially in the sections on comets. But I want to provide Newton's own English words and not Andrew Motte's Englishing of the **Principia**'s Latin; so I shall stick to the vernacular **Opticks.** For a negation in the Lucretian atomic tradition, I offer his speculation about what would happen if nature's basic particles failed to retain their essential impenetrability. 'God in the beginning,' says Newton in the last query, 'form'd Matter in solid, massy, hard, impenetrable, movable Particles.' They are 'so very hard,' he goes on to tell us, 'as never to wear or break in pieces' unless some Power beyond the ordinary were (and now the language is close to echoing the marriage service) 'able to divide what God himself made one in the first Creation.' He hovers on the verge of speculation about such a changed world, 'composed,' as he phrases it, 'of old worn Particles and Fragments of Particles' (400). But for me Newton's most striking visionary passage is not an end-of-the-world speculation or even a descent to the underworld, but one of those mountain-top

views that mythmaking is full of. Let me end this paper by quoting what I think of as a kind of revised hundred-year-later version of a passage from the *Mutabilitie Cantos,* not alas in the Spenserian stanza. Newton is telling us of the perpetual tremors of the earth's atmosphere through which we gaze at the heavens; about how large-lensed telescopes can, out of a mixture of heterogeneous tremors, create an illusion of pure lucidity; about how long telescopes cannot control the tremors at all; and, finally, about how only from a mountain-top can a true remedy for trembling vision be found.

> For the Air through which we look upon the Stars, is in a perpetual Tremor; as may be seen by the tremulous Motion of Shadows cast from high Towers, and by the twinkling of the fix'd Stars. But these Stars do not twinkle when viewed through Telescopes which have large apertures. For the Rays of Light which pass through divers parts of the aperture, tremble each of them apart, and by means of their various and sometimes contrary Tremors, fall at one and the same time upon different points in the bottom of the Eye, and their trembling Motions are too quick and confused to be perceived severally. And all these illuminated Points constitute one broad lucid Point, composed of those many trembling Points confusedly and insensibly mixed with one another by very short and swift Tremors, and thereby cause the Star to appear broader than it is, and without any trembling of the whole. Long Telescopes may cause Objects to appear brighter and larger than short ones can do, but they cannot be so formed as to take away that confusion of the Rays which arises from the Tremors of the Atmosphere. The only Remedy is a most serene and quiet Air, such as may perhaps be found on the tops of the highest Mountains above the grosser Clouds. (110-11)

Notes

[1] I take my Locke quotations (identified by book, chapter, and section numbers) from *An Essay concerning Human Understanding,* ed A. C. Fraser (New York: Dover 1959).

[2] See his Preface to Newton's *Opticks* (New York: Dover 1952; repr 1979), xxxv. My quotations from the *Opticks* (identified by page numbers) will also be taken from this edition.

[3] *Berkeley's Philosophical Writings,* ed David M. Armstrong (New York: Collier 1965), 214-15.

[4] *John Locke and English Literature of the Eighteenth Century* (New Haven: Yale University Press 1936), 12.

[5] *De Rerum Natura,* ed M. F. Smith with English translation by W. H. D. Rouse (Cambridge, Mass: Harvard University Press 1975), 90-3.

[6] See 'Pope and the Great Chain of Being,' *Essays in English Literature . . . Presented to A. S. P. Woodhouse,* ed Millar MacLure and F. W. Watt (Toronto: University of Toronto Press 1964), 213-28.

[7] *Astronomical Principles of Religion* (London: J. Senex, W. and J. Innys, J. Osborne and T. Longman 1725), 82.

[8] *A Demonstration of Some of the Principal Sections of Sir Isaac Newton's Principles of Natural Philosophy* (1730; repr. New York: Johnson Reprint 1972), 142.

[9] Ibid, 226.

Betty Jo Teeter Dobbs and Margaret C. Jacob (essay date 1995)

SOURCE: "Isaac Newton (1642-1727)," in *Newton and the Culture of Newtonianism,* Humanities Press, 1995, pp. 3-31.

[*In the following excerpt, Dobbs and Jacob survey Newton's life and works, highlighting Newton's primary beliefs, influences, and discoveries up to his writing of the* Principia.]

Newton's Youth

Isaac Newton was born on Christmas Day 1642, the premature, posthumous, and only child of an illiterate yeoman farmer of Lincolnshire in England. Not really expected at first to live—he was later to remark that at his birth he was so small that he might have been put into a quart mug—he survived war, revolution, plague, and the seventeenth-century pharmacopoeia to the age of 84, to be buried in Westminster Abbey (the traditional place of interment for the queens and kings of England), idolized by many of his countrymen and admired by much of the Western world.

His genius appeared more mechanical than intellectual at first: as a boy he constructed water clocks, windmills, kites, and sundials and cleverly used the force of the wind to enable himself to outjump the other boys. But, nurtured by neighboring village schools and the King's School at Grantham, his intellectual prowess and his enormous powers of concentration slowly became apparent. Recalled from school by his mother to learn the art of farming, he spent his time under the hedges with his books and his calculations, to the utter neglect of the life of his ancestors. Eventually a maternal uncle, a Cambridge man himself, intervened to have him returned to the school at Grantham to be prepared for Cambridge University, and Isaac went up to that venerable seat of learning in 1661, entering Trinity College. He was aged 18, a little older than most entering students and probably less well prepared than many, but evidently with all his faculties ready to flower. [9; 13; 17; 66; 101]

Early University Studies

Since the great period of the translation of Greek and Arabic scientific literature into Latin in the eleventh, twelfth, and thirteenth centuries, core curricula in the universities of western Europe had been based on the work of Aristotle (384-322 B.C.). And even though one may see in retrospect that a number of challenges to it had developed both within and without the university world in the sixteenth and seventeenth centuries, when Newton entered Cambridge in 1661 the core curriculum was still based on the Latin or Greek texts of Aristotle and on medieval and Renaissance commentators on and expositors of Aristotelian doctrines. For about two years the young Newton applied himself to learning Aristotelian logic, ethics, rhetoric, metaphysics, and natural philosophy. [55; 98:23-44]

In natural philosophy, that would have meant that he learned that the cosmos (the entire created world) was organized around the earth at the center and was made up of nesting spheres. The first set of spheres comprised the four Aristotelian elements: earth at the center, then the spheres of water, air, and fire, filling all the volume up to the sphere of the Moon; there were no empty spaces in the Aristotelian cosmos.

The sphere of the moon was a great dividing line, with change limited to the world below the moon where motions of various sorts brought about changes of several kinds. Aristotle designated four types of change: (1) generation/corruption, as in the birth and death of a living creature; (2) qualitative, like changes in such qualities as heat, cold, dryness, and wetness; (3) quantitative, as in the enlargement of something that has the ability to expand (Aristotle's example would perhaps have been inflating a sheep's bladder; a more modern example might be blowing up a balloon); (4) change of place or "local motion"—from which our word *locomotion* is derived—as a car traveling down a highway, or in Aristotle's case more likely a man walking from his home to Aristotle's school in the center of Athens.

Above the sphere of the moon, on the other hand, were the eternal and changeless spheres of the other planets, those that (including the moon) comprised the anciently known planets for which the days of the week are named: Moon, Venus, Sun, Mars, Jupiter, and Saturn. Finally, at the edge of the closed system was the sphere of the "fixed stars" that appeared not to change at all in relation to each other, only to whirl around the earth once every 24 hours. The planets (the word means "wanderers") do appear to move in relation to each other, as well as in relation to the earth and to the fixed background of stars. But the only motion allowed to those celestial objects was a circular one, a movement always returning to its beginning point and hence eternal. No real change occurred on the moon or above, and, again, there were no empty spaces; the heavens were perhaps filled with an invisible celestial "quintessence" or fifth element, or perhaps the planets and stars were embedded in crystalline (invisible) spheres that fitted neatly together. Aristotle, like many other Greek thinkers, seems to have thought of the cosmos as all fitted together like a living creature, an organism, that was alive in its own self and that human beings could understand by rational and logical thought processes. [45; 55]

Nevertheless, even though Aristotle was still being taught in the universities, western Europe was by the seventeenth century saturated with machines and labor-saving devices that went far beyond the purview of Aristotelian patterns of thought: mechanical clocks that utilized the force of gravity; windmills and water mills that similarly exploited the motive forces of wind and water. The early mechanical genius of Newton's childhood constructions shows him aligned in significant ways with the mechanistic aspects of Western culture, so it comes as no surprise to find him adopting the new mechanical natural philosophies of the seventeenth century about halfway through his undergraduate career.

Mechanism and Other Influences on Newton

The appearance of mechanistic philosophies of nature in the seventeenth century was a broad-based phenomenon but one that was in sharp contrast to Aristotelianism, for the mechanical philosophies held that nature acts like a machine rather than like a living organism. No doubt encouraged by the prevalence of mechanical devices developed in Christian Europe, mechanical philosophies also had ancient roots in the works of Lucretius, a Roman poet of the first century B.C., and in the work of Epicurus, a Hellenistic Greek philosopher of the fourth and third centuries B.C. Revived by humanistic scholarship, interest in these ancient systems of thought, antithetical as they were to Aristotelian doctrines as well as Christian ones, had spread across national boundaries from Italy to northern Europe to England.

In general, the seventeenth-century philosophies that were at least partially based on ancient mechanism argued for the existence of very small—indeed imperceptible—particles that were all made of the same sort of matter and had only mathematical properties such as extension, size, shape, and perhaps weight. The particles could combine with each other to form larger material masses, or they could dissociate from each other and be re-formed in other ways. Such corporeal associations and dissociations accounted for much change in the natural world; the analogy frequently invoked was that of the alphabet: the letters can be associated in various ways to form words, and the words in turn dissociated to yield the basic letters that can then be re-formed into different words. But if the imperceptible particles of matter were thought to be like letters of the alphabet, similar to the movable type used in contemporary printing presses, the world as a whole was thought to be organized like an intricate machine designed and ordered by the Creator God of Judeo-Christian tradition. Just as human artisans designed and ordered the intricate mechanical clocks, printing presses, and wind and water mills that were common in western Europe, so the Deity had created a world-machine and set it in motion in ways that human beings could learn to understand. [19; 45]

Of the many varieties of mechanical philosophy available in the 1660s, those of the French philosophers René Descartes (1596-1650) and Pierre Gassendi (1592-1655) were important to Newton, as were those of the English philosophers Walter Charleton (1619-1707), Robert Boyle (1627-91), Thomas Hobbes (1588-1679), Kenelm Digby (1603-65), and Henry More (1614-87). Descartes had created the first total world system since that of Aristotle: his system was a plenum (completely full of matter) like that of Aristotle, but indefinite in extent rather than limited and bounded by the sphere of the fixed stars as Aristotle's had been. The matter in Descartes's system could be ground down into ever finer pieces. Gassendi, on the other hand, paid more attention to the ancient version of Epicurus, and so argued that the particles of matter were really atoms and therefore "uncuttable," which is what the Greek word *atomos* means. Uncuttable atoms moving in void (empty) space made Gassendi's system quite different from that of Descartes, and Gassendi's work was made widely known in England by an English version of it published by Charleton. Boyle had studied both Descartes's and Gassendi's systems but, declining to choose between them, utilized elements from each. Hobbes's version was much too materialistic in the eyes of most English natural philosophers, because Hobbes did not make sufficient room in his system for spirit, soul, and the Deity, and Henry More thought there were similar materialistic tendencies even in Descartes's version. Digby, who was not a very systematic thinker, was much influenced by Descartes but kept so many elements of Aristotelian thought also that his version of the mechanical philosophy was marked by severe inconsistencies. Although there indeed were many problems with these various mechanical philosophies, problems both scientific and theological, they were the cutting edge of natural philosophical thought in the seventeenth century, and after Newton absorbed their basic principles he seldom utilized Aristotelian doctrines again, though he was later to supplement mechanistic thought with other ancient systems in good humanistic fashion. [14; 17; 18; 27; 45; 47; 50; 51; 62; 79; 80; 81; 101; 104]

Newton's later fame could hardly have been predicted during his student years, but he was soon to tackle—and solve—many of the physical and mathematical questions that engaged his contemporaries. In January 1665 he took his Bachelor of Arts degree, but in the summer of 1665 he was forced to retire to his home at Woolsthorpe because the university was closed from an outbreak of bubonic plague (endemic in Europe since the first great pandemic in 1348-49 known as the Black Death). The university remained closed most of the time until the spring of 1667, and Newton's enforced sojourn at Woolsthorpe has come to be known as his *annus mirabilis,* the marvelous year in which he invented his "fluxions" (the calculus), discovered white light to be compounded of all the distinctly colored rays of the spectrum, and found a mathematical law of gravity, at least in alternative form. [9; 40; 73; 101; 104]

The gradual development and unfolding to the world throughout subsequent years of the productions of that brief period were to establish his reputation upon the granite foundation it still enjoys. We will return to a consideration of each of these major achievements, which are still recognized and admired by the modern world, but we must also give due consideration to the fact that physical and mathematical problems were not the issues of greatest concern to most people in the seventeenth century, nor were they the issues of greatest concern to Newton himself. He lavished much more of his time on alchemy, church history, theology, prophecy, ancient philosophy, and "the chronology of ancient kingdoms."

Newton was born into the crucible of civil war in England, and the religious and political struggles of the period were to affect him deeply. The Reformation of the sixteenth century had shattered Christendom irrevocably, and, as religious sects had proliferated, especially in northern Europe, the intensity of political issues had grown as well, for church and state had formerly been perceived as a unity, like the two sides of a single coin. With such an understanding of the relationship of religious belief and political power, the notion of religious toleration was at first virtually inconceivable: divisions in creed and dogma were thus fought out on physical as well as intellectual battlefields. The full force of the tumult that had already torn Continental Europe for over a century arrived in England just at the time of Newton's birth. So even though Newton's long life carried him well into the eighteenth century and he came to be perceived as one of the principal founders of eighteenth-century Enlightenment thought, his own concerns remained centered to a great extent on the political and religious problems of the mid-seventeenth century, and he himself

desired above all else to restore religion to the pristine purity, power, and centrality it had once enjoyed in human life. [6; 9; 18; 45; 50; 65; 66; 67; 99; 101]

In looking backward to the pure original religion he supposed humanity to have known and practiced at the beginning of time, Newton reflected the reverence for antiquity that had been the hallmark of Renaissance humanism. In many ways, indeed, Newton's intellectual development is best understood as a product of the late Renaissance, a time when the revival of antiquity had conditioned the thinkers of western Europe to look backward for Truth. The Renaissance humanists of the fourteenth century had rediscovered the glories of Roman poetry and prose, while in the fifteenth century a newly restored proficiency in the Greek language had revealed the awesome philosophical power and beauty of the works of Plato (427?-347 B.C.) and the Neoplatonists, as well as the mysterious doctrines of the Hermetic Corpus. Hermes Trismegistus (his surname meant "Thrice Greatest"), the supposed author of the Hermetic Corpus, was not a real person, although the thinkers of the Renaissance believed him to be not only real but also very ancient, perhaps even more ancient than Moses (who had composed several of the first books of the Judeo-Christian Bible). His supposed antiquity gave Hermes great authority in the eyes of Renaissance scholars, and Hermetic doctrines supported all sorts of magical, astrological, and alchemical enterprises in the sixteenth and seventeenth centuries. [18; 21; 52; 58; 69; 94; 99]

Humanist scholars revived innumerable other treatises from antiquity as well: treatises on medicine, mathematics, natural philosophy, astronomy, magic, alchemy, astrology, and cosmology, including the works of Lucretius and Epicurus mentioned above. Such materials were previously unknown in western Europe or known before only through inadequate translations. What an intellectual ferment they created! And as the new printing presses of western Europe spread the new editions of ancient works, and as the Renaissance spread north from its original Italian base, materials from Jewish, Egyptian, and Christian antiquity were added to the heady mixture, where they contributed to Reformation scholarship, to an interest in the Hebrew language and the cabala, and to early attempts to decipher Egyptian hieroglyphics. [5; 6; 21; 65; 69; 99]

Newton's Way of Thinking and Working

Thanks to this great revival of ancient thought, to humanist scholarship, to the quarrels of the Reformation, and to new developments in medicine, science, mathematics, and natural philosophy prior to or contemporary with his most intense period of study, Newton clearly had access to an unusually large number of systems of thought. Each system had its own set of guiding assumptions, so in that particular historical milieu some comparative judgment between and among competing systems was perhaps inevitable. One could hardly accept them all as equally valid. But such judgments were difficult to make without a culturally conditioned consensus on standards of evaluation. By the mid-seventeenth century the old verities in both religion and natural philosophy had been subverted but no new ones agreed upon.

A standard of evaluation was precisely what was lacking, a situation that led many people to adopt a skeptical attitude and to doubt that any true knowledge about the world or God could ever be attained. The formalized skepticism of Pyrrhonism had been revived along with other aspects of antiquity, but one may trace an increase in a less formal but rather generalized skepticism at least from the beginning of the sixteenth century, as competing systems laid claim to Truth and denied the claims of their rivals. As a consequence, western Europe underwent something of an intellectual crisis in the sixteenth and seventeenth centuries. What, indeed, was it possible for one to know without lingering and bewildering doubts? Among so many competing systems, how was one to achieve certainty? Could the human being attain Truth? [18; 69; 83; 84; 99]

Newton was not a skeptic. On the contrary, he seems to have adopted a contemporary response to questions of valid knowledge called the doctrine of "the unity of Truth," a position that was in face one answer to the problem of skepticism. Not only did Newton respect the idea that Truth was accessible to the human mind, but also he was very much inclined to accord to several systems of thought the right to claim access to some aspect of the Truth. For those who adopted this point of view, the many different systems they encountered tended to appear complementary rather than competitive. The assumption they made was that Truth did indeed exist somewhere beyond the apparently conflicting representations of it currently available. True knowledge was unitary, and its unity was guaranteed by the unity of the Deity, He being the source of all Truth. As a practical matter, those who followed this doctrine of the unity of Truth became quite eclectic, which is to say that each thinker selected parts of different systems and welded them into a new synthetic whole that seemed to him (or her) to be closer to Truth. That was certainly Newton's method, and in the course of his long life he marshaled the evidence from every source of knowledge available to him: mathematics, experiment, observation, reason, the divine revelations in biblical texts, historical records, mythology, contemporary scientific texts, the tattered remnants of ancient philosophical wisdom, and the literature and practice of alchemy. [18; 84; 85]

One must realize, however, that in making selections from the various sources of knowledge available to

him Newton utilized a sophisticated balancing procedure that enabled him to make critical judgments about the relative validity of each. Perhaps the most important element in Newton's contribution to scientific method as it developed in subsequent centuries was the element of balance, for no *single* approach to knowledge ever proved to be effective in settling the knowledge crisis of the Renaissance and early modern periods. Human senses are subject to error; so is human reason. So is the interpretation of revelation; so is the mathematico-deductive scientific method put forward by Descartes earlier in the century. Since every single approach to knowledge was subject to error, a more certain knowledge was to be obtained by utilizing each approach to correct the other: the senses to be rectified by reason, reason to be rectified by revelation, and so forth. [18]

The self-correcting character of Newton's procedure constitutes the superiority of Newton's method over that of earlier natural philosophers, for others had certainly used the separate elements of inductive reasoning, deductive reasoning, mathematics, experiment, and observation before him, and often in some combination. But Newton's method was not limited to the balancing of those approaches to knowledge that still constitute the elements of modern scientific methodology, nor has one any reason to assume that he would deliberately have limited himself to those familiar approaches even if he had been prescient enough to realize that those were all the future would consider important. Newton's goal was much broader than the goal of modern science. Modern science focuses on a knowledge of nature and only on that. In contrast, Newton's goal was a Truth that encompassed natural principles but also divine ones as well. He had a deep religious concern to establish the relationship between God and His creation (nature), and so he constantly searched for the boundaries between God and nature where divine and natural principles met and fused. As a result, Newton's balancing procedure included also the knowledge he had garnered from theology, revelation, alchemy, history, and the wise ancients. [18]

Blinded by the brilliance of the laws of motion, the laws of optics, the calculus, the concept of universal gravitation, the rigorous experimentation, and the methodological success, subsequent generations have seldom wondered whether the discovery of the laws of nature was all Newton had in mind. Scholars have often missed the religious foundation of his quest and taken the stunningly successful by-products for his primary goal. But Newton wished to look through nature to see God, and it was not false modesty when in old age he said he had been only like a boy at the seashore picking up now and again a smoother pebble or a prettier shell than usual while the great ocean of Truth lay all undiscovered before him. [18]

Eighteenth-, nineteenth-, and early twentieth-century views of Newton were developed almost entirely on the basis of his principal published works: ***Philosophiae naturalis principia mathematica*** (1687, 1713, 1726); ***Opticks: or, a Treatise of the Reflexions, Refractions, Inflexions and Colours of Light. Also Two Treatises of the species and Magnitude of curvilinear Figures*** (1704, 1706, 1721, and the posthumous edition of 1730); ***Arithmetica universalis*** (1707); ***De analysi*** and ***Methodus differentialis*** (1711). The Newtonian world-view, developed almost wholly on the basis of his successes in mathematics and physical science, so subtly and deeply colored the outlook of succeeding generations that the fuller seventeenth-century context in which Newton's thought had developed was lost to view. Thus it became a curious anomaly—and one to be explained away—that Newton's studies in astronomy, optics, and mathematics only occupied a small portion of his time. In fact most of his great powers were poured out quite otherwise.

The fact might never have been recognized, however, except for the survival of great quantities of manuscripts in Newton's hand. When Newton died in 1727 without leaving a will, his possessions passed to his niece, Catherine Barton Conduitt, and afterward to her descendants. The papers were examined with a view to possible publication later in 1727, and a few were published shortly afterward, but many of them were marked "not fit to be printed," and almost all of them were put back in their boxes. In the nineteenth century the family offered them to Cambridge University. The university appointed a group of men, mostly eminent scientists of the period, to examine the papers, and they selected for retention those focused on mathematics and physical science. These now comprise the Portsmouth Collection, University Library, Cambridge. The rest were returned to the family as being of no interest to the university and so remained largely unknown until they were sold at auction in 1936. The auction scattered them all over the world; although a number of them are still in the hands of private collectors, most of them are now held by research libraries and so are available for study. It is from detailed studies of these manuscripts of Newton's that our new and historically more accurate portrait of him has emerged. [7; 8; 11; 18; 23; 40; 61; 63; 65; 66; 67; 73; 76; 78; 87; 91; 98; 100; 101; 102; 103; 104]

Once one grasps the immensity of Newton's goal, many otherwise inexplicable aspects of his career fall into place. Now it is no longer necessary to explain away his fierce interest in alchemy or his dogged attempts at the correct interpretation of biblical prophecies, as many earlier biographers and scientists tried to do. If Newton's purpose was to construct a unified system of God and nature, as indeed it was, then it becomes possible to see all of his various fields of study as potential contributors to his overarching goal. It also becomes

possible from this point of view to recognize that Newton's belief in the unity of Truth contributed greatly to his remarkable scientific creativity. For in the course of his long search for Truth he constructed many different partial systems and changed from one to another in ways that have often appeared erratic and inconsistent to later scholars. One may now see, however, that the pattern of change resulted from his slow fusion and selective disentanglement of essentially antithetical systems: Neoplatonism, mechanical philosophy, Stoicism; chemistry, alchemy, atomism; biblical, patristic, and pagan religions. It was precisely where his many different lines of investigation met, where he tried to synthesize their discrepancies into a more fundamental unity, when he attempted to fit partial Truth to partial Truth, that he achieved his greatest insights.

Newton's Early Mechanism: Cohesion and Gravity

With this broad view of Newton's work in hand, one may now begin to explore the intricate and marvelous development of the views that ultimately brought him so much acclaim.

Sometime during his student years Newton began to study the mechanical philosophers, as noted above, and he became a "corpuscularian." In the seventeenth century the term "corpuscularian" referred to anyone who believed that matter was comprised of small material particles or "corpuscles," whether the particles were understood to be infinitely divisible or whether there was supposed to be a limit to divisibility as in atomism, *atom* simply meaning "uncuttable," as we saw above. Newton chose elements of matter theory from Descartes, Gassendi (via Charleton), Boyle, Hobbes, Digby, and More and left a record of his thoughts in his student notebook. He seems to have acceptable the notion that matter had least parts or atoms that were not further divisible. [18; 62]

At first Newton, like other mechanical philosophers of his time, placed considerable faith in the existence of an all-pervasive material medium that served as an agent of change in the natural world. By postulating a subtle aether, a medium imperceptible to the senses but capable of transmitting effects by pressure and impact, mechanical philosophers had devised a convention that rid natural philosophy of incomprehensible occult influences acting at a distance (e.g., magnetic attraction and lunar effects). For Newton just such a mechanical aether, pervading and filling the whole world, became an unquestioned assumption. By it he explained gravity and, to a certain extent, the cohesion of particles of matter. But because of the general passivity of matter in the mechanical philosophy, certain problems arose for many contemporary philosophers regarding cohesion and life, and eventually, for Newton, regarding gravity also. [18; 62]

The question of cohesion—that is, the problem of what makes the tiny corpuscles stick together—had always plagued theories of discrete particles, atomism having been criticized even in antiquity on this point. The cohesion of living forms seems intuitively to be qualitatively different from anything that the random, mechanical motion of small particles of matter might produce. Nor does atomism explain even mechanical cohesion in nonliving materials very well (such as, for example, the regular patterns in crystals of salts or gemstones), for any explanation of such regularity seems to require unverifiable hypotheses about the geometric configurations of the atoms or else speculation about their quiescence (or rest) under certain circumstances. [18; 51; 62; 105]

In the various forms in which corpuscularianism was revived in the seventeenth century, the problems remained and variants of ancient answers were redeployed. Descartes, for example, held that an external pressure from surrounding subtle matter (the aether) just balanced the internal pressure of the coarser particles that constituted the cohesive body. Thus no special explanation for cohesion was required, he claimed: the parts cohered simply because they were at rest close to each other in an equilibrated system. Gassendi's atoms, on the other hand, stuck together through the interlacing of antlers or hooks and claws, much as the atoms of Lucretius had before them, in what one might call a sort of primitive Velcro system. Charleton found not only hooks and claws but also the pressure of neighboring atoms and the absence of disturbing atoms necessary to account for cohesion. Francis Bacon (1561-1626) introduced certain spirits or "pneumaticals" into his speculations. In a system reminiscent of the Stoics, who were ancient critics of atomism, Bacon concluded that gross matter must be associated with active, shaping, material spirits, the spirits being responsible for the forms and qualities of tangible bodies, producing organized shapes and effecting digestion, assimilation, and so forth. For Newton during his student years, with his mechanical aether ready at hand as an explanatory device, a pressure mechanism seemed sufficient to explain cohesion. He did not think that the simple resting (quiescence) of the particles close to each other could account for cohesion, but he did think that the "crowding" or pressure of the aethereal matter that filled all space might account for it. He noted the occasional geometric approach of Descartes but did not himself develop it. Newton was later to offer a radically different explanation of cohesion, one based on alchemical and Stoic considerations, but not while he was still an undergraduate. [18; 62; 68]

At first, in the 1660s, Newton considered gravity to be a mechanical mode of action. What is gravity, and what causes it? Modern science has still not found all the answers to these fundamental questions, but we know from common everyday experience that some-thing makes bodies like ripe apples fall to the ground when they are detached from their trees, and that something will surely make us do likewise if we lean too far out an open window. Newton began to ponder the problem of gravity about 1664, and his first mechanical theory was derivative and nonmathematical, influenced by the theories of Descartes, Digby, and Boyle. Though the precise form was Newton's own, his theory was a restatement of impact physics, a conventional, orthodox (at that time) variety of mechanical philosophy: in short, an aether theory of gravitation. Bodies descend to earth, he said, through the impulsion of fine material particles; it is a mechanical stream of aethereal matter causing gravity, just as a flowing stream of water will carry wood chips downstream. [18; 62]

No hint exists in Newton's earliest statement of what gravity is later to become for him: an active principle (not mechanical) directly or indirectly dependent upon the activity of the Deity, the Creator God Who had made the world-machine and Who kept it in motion. Newton seems never to have focused solely on the material part of the natural world, as modern scientists usually do, but he always remained conscious of the presence of the Deity. Even in his undergraduate student notebook there is a recognition of God's omnipresence, the literally "being present everywhere" of the Deity that is later to subsume universal gravity in Newton's system of the world. When bodies are in motion in a world full of the aether, Newton said in this early notebook, some of the matter has to be crowded out of the way, so the motion meets with resistance. But in a vacuum that would not be the case. Even though God is present in the vacuum, God is a spirit and penetrates all matter, Newton added. God's presence causes no resistance, however, just as if nothing were in the way. Newton was to repeat much later his conviction that God is present where there is no body, as well as present where body is also present. There, as in the student notebook, God penetrates all matter. But whereas later the omnipresence of God and His ability to penetrate matter have the utmost significance with respect to gravity, that was not the case in the student notebook, where gravity was caused by the mechanical motion of small particles of matter to which God's presence simply constituted no obstacle. [18; 41; 62]

Newton's Early Mathematics: The Binomial Theorem and the "Fluxions"

At about the same time, in 1664, Newton began seriously to study mathematics. His preuniversity training had probably been limited to the basic rules of arithmetic, an elementary knowledge of weights and measure, and simple accounting techniques. Then he bought a book at a fair; he later called it a book on astrology, but it might equally well have been a book on astronomy, for the two terms were often used interchangeably in the seventeenth century. He could not understand it, however, not then being acquainted with trigonometry, so he bought a book on trigonometry only to discover that he was deficient in the background to that topic, never having studied the great fundamental work on plane geometry from antiquity, the *Elements* of Euclid. So he began to read Euclid. At first he found the propositions so easy to understand that he wondered why anyone would bother to write demonstrations of them, but he soon found propositions that were not intuitively obvious to him and then studied them with greater care. [104]

Once he had come to appreciate the logical power of Euclid's demonstrations, Newton turned to more modern mathematicians, reading the *Clavis mathematicae* of William Oughtred (1575-1660) and the *Geometry* of Descartes, both of which at first gave him some difficulty. By degrees he mastered them and soon moved on to the mathematical miscellanies of Franz van Schooten (1615-60) and the *Arithmetica infinitorum* of John Wallis (1616-1703). A few additional works apparently completed Newton's self-directed apprenticeship, and he began to discover and formulate new theorems of his own. [2; 3; 20; 73; 101; 103; 104]

The first of these of lasting significance was his discovery of the general binomial expansion in the winter of 1664-65, inspired by his reading of Wallis's work. A binomial is a mathematical expression with two terms in it, such as an x and a y. If the terms are added together, or if one is subtracted from the other, as in the expressions "$x + y$" or "$x - y$," the expression with the two terms in it is called a binomial. Suppose, then, that one wishes to multiply the term "$x + y$" by itself (or square it). The procedure may be expressed in mathematical notation as $(x + y)^2$, where the 2 is known as the power or exponent to which the binomial is to be raised. The exponent might be 2 or any higher positive number (integer). If the designated multiplication is actually carried out, one obtains an expansion of the binomial, which in this case would be $x^2 + 2xy + y^2$, where the coefficients of the three terms are 1, 2, 1. Mathematicians prior to Newton's time had discovered rules for finding the coefficients for other positive powers to which the binomial could be raised, and such general rules were of great value in obtaining binomial expansions, for they made it unnecessary actually to carry out the lengthy process of multiplication. But whereas binomial coefficients for such positive integral powers had been known for some time, Newton's method was much more general, for it allowed the use of negative or fractional exponents also. [2; 20; 73; 104]

When the exponent is neither a positive integer nor zero, some binomial expansions constitute series with infinitely many terms. Newton was able to demonstrate that when such binomial expansions form infinite series the results do not just yield approximations (as mathematicians had previously supposed) but are subject to general definite laws, just as the algebra of finite quantities is. Infinite series expansions soon came to play a central role in his development of the calculus. [20; 73; 104]

His work on the fluxional calculus began in the autumn of 1664, and by the spring of 1665 Newton had resolved his several approaches into a general procedure for differentiation. Inspired in this case by Descartes's *Geometry,* in which algebra and geometry were combined to yield analytic geometry, Newton had focused on problems of finding tangents to curves, as well as normals and the radius of curvature at a general point. Newton regarded the curve as the locus of a moving point in a suitable coordinate system, the point itself being the intersection of two moving lines, one vertical and the other horizontal. The vertical and horizontal components changed with the "flux" or flow of time, and the "fluxions" of the variables were their derivatives with respect to time, indefinitely small and ultimately vanishing increments of the variables. By October of 1666 Newton had also mastered a general method for the reverse procedure, integration, to compute the area under the curve. Although various limited procedures for finding areas and tangents had been in use by the early seventeenth century, Newton's methods yielded general and systematic techniques and demonstrated the inverse relation between area problems and tangent problems. For a young man not yet 24, and apparently completely self-taught in this area, that was quite a dramatic achievement, and he himself said much later that he was then in the prime of his life for invention. But of course there was more to come. [20; 33; 73; 103; 104]

As Newton sat in the garden at Woolsthorpe one day during his *annus mirabilis,* some apples fell to the ground close to him. The event prompted him to consider the power of gravity that had brought the apples down and to speculate that the power of gravity might extend as high as the moon and help keep the moon in its orbit around the earth. The story of the apples is so well known now that in a recent set of British postage stamps commemorating the life and work of Isaac Newton one stamp had no design on it but an apple, the symbol of Newton's solution to the problem of gravity. [21; 100]

But the exact significance of the episode in Newton's developing thought on the subject of gravity has been less well understood. For a long time it was supposed that his creative genius allowed Newton at that time to formulate the law of universal gravity, so there was much scholarly speculation regarding the 20-year "delay" before he published his new discovery. Now the predominant interpretation of the episode of the falling apples is quite different: at most Newton then worked through an inconclusive comparison of the fall of an apple with the fall of the moon that yielded an approximation of the so-called inverse-square relationship, that is, the mathematical law that indicates that the power of gravity diminishes as the square of the distance between two gravitating bodies increases. It was only much later that the full generality and universality of the law emerged, for it required from Newton some major conceptual revisions. [12; 18; 40; 71; 73; 77; 78; 102]

In 1666, when the apples fell and he was prompted to consider also the fall of the moon, Newton had accepted the doctrine of a mechanical aether as the cause of gravity, as noted above. In particular, he had accepted Descartes's version of the aether, a version in which the aether swirled around the earth in a vortex pattern, a sort of imperceptible whirlpool that carried the moon in its orbit around the earth and accounted for the fall of objects like apples to the surface of the earth. Other planets had their own vortices also in Descartes's system, and around the sun there was supposed to be a giant whirlpool that carried the planets, including earth, around the sun in their regular cycles. Newton held to that general belief until about 1684. Indeed, in 1666 the manuscript evidence shows him thinking only about gravity with respect to the earth and the earth-moon system; he apparently did not generalize the system even to include the sun and other planets until 1675. So it seems that in 1666 his concept of gravity was far from the universal one that appeared in the *Principia* in 1687. [12; 18]

Acting against the downward pressure of the gravitational aether in Newton's early mechanics was the opposing endeavor to recede from the center, a centrifugal (center-fleeing) force. The term "centrifugal" was coined by Christiaan Huygens (1629-95), a Dutch natural philosopher and mathematician who was also a follower of Descartes. The centrifugal force accounted for the tendency of objects in circular motion to fly away from the center of motion, as in the case of a stone whirled at the end of a sling. Treated by physicists now as an illusory force, in the 1660s, 1670s, and early 1680s Newton accepted it as a real force that balanced and was balanced by the pressure of the vortex, the balance of the two forces being what kept the moon in its orbit. The same sort of analysis of forces appeared also in his early work on terrestrial mechanics during this period. But in the 1680s, when writing the *Principia,* Newton recognized the illusory nature of the centrifugal force and of the aethereal vortex as well. At that time he changed his analytic framework to two other opposing forces: inertia (the tendency of a body to continue in straight-line motion or at rest unless a force is applied to it) and a centripetal (center-seeking) force, a term he coined himself and one that reflects his new understanding of the

center-seeking force as the mirror image of Huygens's center-fleeing force. We will return later to the insights of the 1680s that allowed Newton to revise his understanding of celestial mechanics, to generalize and universalize the force of gravity, and to construct a system of the world that would last virtually unchallenged for three centuries. [12; 18; 40; 71; 73; 77; 78; 102]

Newton's Early Optics: Particles and Prisms

Still in a white heat of creativity, what he later called his prime time of invention, Newton also began about 1666 to revise and reform contemporary views on the nature of light and color. Descartes had argued that the light from the sun that we see is simply a pressure in the aether. On the analogy of a blind person's walking stick, the pressure on the end of which is transmitted instantaneously to the hand, the sun's light sets up a chain of pressure from sun to eye that one then experiences as the sensation of light. That theory really would not do at all, Newton observed, because if light is just pressure on the eyeball, then one should be able to see perfectly well at night by running forward, since the forward motion of the runner would generate pressure of air and aether against the eye. [62]

Newton opted for a particulate definition of light, that is, the emission by the sun and other luminous bodies of extrafine corpuscles that we experience as light. Newton's theory of particulate emission implies that the transmission of light is not instantaneous but, on the contrary, must have a definite velocity. Early measurements of the speed of light later in the seventeenth century seemed to justify Newton's views, and light was then treated as particulate until the early nineteenth century. At that time a wave theory of light came to dominate scientific thought on the subject. Newton had recognized certain wavelike phenomena associated with light but had supposed them to be explained by motions in the all-pervading aether as the light corpuscles passed through it; he had denied that light itself might be a wave. It did not appear to him to spread out into the shadow of obstacles it passed (as water waves, for example, will do). More precise measurements in the nineteenth century having demonstrated conclusively that light does have the wave properties Newton had denied, his theory was thoroughly rejected for about a century—one of the very few cases of a total rejection of Newton's theories by later scientists. But modern quantum theory has at least partially reinstated Newton's views in the twentieth century, for it is now recognized that light does sometimes appear as quanta (tiny particulate packets of energy) while under other circumstances its continuous wave properties predominate. [75; 101]

As for colors, Newton tackled that issue with prisms. Robert Hooke (1635-1702) had published his *Micro-*

graphia in 1665, a book rightly famous for its wonderful illustrations of observations made with the then new microscope. Hooke was an English natural philosopher, sometime employed as an experimental operator by Robert Boyle and later Curator of Experiments for the Royal Society of London for Improving of Natural Knowledge. In his book *Micrographia* Hooke argued for a theory of colors as oblique and confused pulses of light. The color blue was for Hooke such a pulse in which the weakest part comes first with the strongest following; the color red had its parts in reverse order. In general, according to Hooke, the colors formed a scale of strength between lightness and darkness, with red closest to pure white light and blue the last step before darkness. Newton attacked Hooke's theory at the root by analyzing white light into the spectrum of colors with the prism and showing how the different colors were refracted at different angles thereby. Refraction is the change of direction of a ray (of light, in this case) when it passes from one medium into another, from air into and out of the glass prism in Newton's experiment.

If the ray of white light passes into the glass at an oblique angle, it is split into all the colors of the rainbow, because each color acts as an independent ray and has its own precise and specific angle of changed direction. An oblong rainbow of separate colors thus becomes visible as the rays leave the prism. The colored rays kept their unique angles of refraction when passed through a second prism, Newton demonstrated, and they also could be recombined to constitute white light. So, Newton argued, the colored rays are the fundamental individuals, and white light is a confused mixture of them. With respect to the colors of bodies, he continued, it is clear that most of the colored rays are absorbed by the body while one is reflected back to our eyes, such as green, for example, in the case of most living plants. [75; 101]

Utilizing both experimental and mathematical analyses, Newton developed his insights into light and color over several years. When he was appointed to the Lucasian Chair of Mathematics at Cambridge in 1669 he gave his first set of lectures on his optical discoveries. He sent papers on optics to the Royal Society in the 1670s also, but the strong opposition his papers encountered from Hooke and others discouraged him from further publication to such an extent that he never published the full text of **Opticks** until 1704, by which time Hooke had died and so could no longer attack Newton's views. The laws of optics reported there were, however, virtually all established while Newton was less than 30 years of age. [71; 75; 101]

But light had significance for Newton that went far beyond the laws of optics, for in both Christian and Neoplatonic traditions light carried with it the aura of divinity. Light was God's first created creature in the Genesis account of creation, and it was both symbol and agent of divinity in Neoplatonism. The metaphysics of light had a long and distinguished career in Christian Europe; as Newton was soon to discover, it was also closely associated with divine creativity in the literature of alchemy. [15; 18; 42; 56; 63]

Newton's Early Alchemy: Life, Cohesion, and Divine Guidance

Newton turned to a study of alchemy about 1668. It is possible that he had already learned some of the rudiments of chemistry before he entered Cambridge, when he lodged with a local apothecary (or druggist) in Grantham while attending the King's School there. But Newton certainly made himself the master of contemporary chemistry shortly after his return to Cambridge after the plague years, in 1667 or 1668, the date of the chemical dictionary he compiled then. Newton's turn to alchemy, however, was altogether a different enterprise from learning basic chemistry. [17]

Even though in the seventeenth century there was some overlap between chemistry and alchemy, and of course both fields shared some mutual interest in the manipulation and transformation of the different forms of matter by chemical techniques, chemistry and alchemy had quite distinct goals. Alchemy never was, and never was intended to be, solely a study of matter for its own sake. Nor was it, strictly speaking, a branch of natural philosophy, for there was a spiritual dimension to alchemy—a search for spiritual perfection for the alchemist himself or herself, or a search for an agent of perfection (the "philosopher's stone") that could transform base metals into silver or gold or perhaps could even redeem the world. It was in fact the spiritual dimension to alchemy that led Newton to study it, but his goal was not exactly one of the traditional ones. He perceived alchemy as an arena in which natural and divine principles met and fused, and he understood that through alchemy it might be possible for him to correct the theological and scientific problems of the seventeenth-century mechanical philosophies. [15; 16; 17; 18; 58]

Since sometime earlier in the 1660s Newton had been troubled by a theological problem, and he hoped alchemy could provide a solution. He was, as were his older contemporaries Isaac Barrow (1630-77), Henry More, and Ralph Cudworth (1617-88), alarmed at the atheistic potentialities of the revived corpuscularianism of their century, particularly of Cartesianism (the mechanical philosophy of Descartes). Although the ancient atomists had not really been atheists in any precise modern sense, they had frequently been so labeled because their atoms in random mechanical motion received no guidance from the gods. Descartes, Gassendi, and Charleton had been at pains to allay the fear that the revived corpuscular philosophy would carry the stigma of atheism adhering to ancient atomism. They had solved the problem, they thought, by having God endow the particles of matter with motion at the moment of creation. All that resulted then was due not to random corpuscular action but to the initial intention of the Deity. [6; 17; 18; 30; 79; 80; 81]

Later writers, going further, had carefully instated a Christian Providence among the atoms (where the ancients, of course, had never had it). Only Providence could account for the obviously designed concatenations (or organization) of the particles, and so, via Christianity, a fundamental Stoic critique of the ancient atomists actually came to be incorporated into seventeenth-century atomism. This development was all to the good in the eyes of most Christian philosophers: atomism now supported religion, because without the providential action of God the atoms could never have assumed the lovely forms of plants and animals so perfectly fitted to their habitats. This was called "the argument from design" for the existence of a Deity: the presence of design (planned organization) in the natural world implied the existence of a Designer, a Deity Who had done the planning and organizing of the so obviously designed creatures in the natural world. The "argument from design" had quite ancient roots and had been present in Christianity from a very early period, but it assumed unparalleled importance in the seventeenth century. For if the new heliocentric astronomy, having moved the earth out of its central location in the cosmos, raised doubts about the focus of Providence upon such an obscure minor planet as earth now seemed, the new atomism seemed to relieve such doubts and reassure human beings that indeed divine Providence still cared for the world. [18; 57; 64; 96; 97]

The difficulty came when one began to wonder *how* Providence operated in the law-bound universe that was emerging from the new science, and that difficulty was especially severe in the Cartesian system, where only matter and motion were acceptable explanations. Even though Descartes had argued that God constantly and actively supported the universe with His will, it seemed to Henry More and others that Descartes's Deity was in danger of becoming a sort of absentee landlord, a Deity Who had set matter in motion in the beginning but Who then had no way of exercising His providential care. [18]

Newton faced this theological difficulty squarely and directly. The mechanical action of matter in motion was not enough. Granted that such mechanical action existed among the particles and could account for large classes of phenomena, yet it could not account for all. It could not account for the processes of life, where cohesive and guiding principles were clearly operative. It could not account even for the manifold riches of the phenomenal world. All forms of matter, never

mind how various they appeared, could be reduced back to a common primordial matter according to the mechanical philosophers, but how had they been produced in the first place? From the particles of a universal matter with only primary mathematical properties, there seemed no sufficient reason for the forms and qualities of the phenomenal world to emerge at all. But emerge they did, and in such incredible and well-crafted plenitude that causal explanations based on mechanical interactions seemed totally insufficient. As Newton was finally to say in the General Scholium to the *Principia,* mechanical action (what he called "blind metaphysical necessity") could not produce variety because it is always and everywhere the same. Variety requires some further cause, a divine agent, and that is what he began to search for in his alchemical studies. [18; 30; 77]

In addition to learning contemporary chemistry and beginning his study of alchemy when he returned to Cambridge, Newton proceeded to Master of Arts and was elected a Fellow of Trinity College, a position that assured him an income and position in academic life—assured, that is, if he complied with the Fellowship regulation that he become an ordained Anglican priest within the next seven years. As we shall see, the prospect of ordination in the Church of England eventually became a source of deep anxiety to him.

Newton also polished some of his mathematical work from the Woolsthorpe period and showed portions of it to Isaac Barrow, who was then Lucasian Professor of Mathematics at Cambridge; he immediately put Newton's work into circulation (in manuscript form) among interested English mathematicians. The mathematical professorship had recently been created and endowed by Henry Lucas, and Barrow was its first incumbent. But Barrow soon resigned to return to his preferred life of theological study and preaching, and Newton was elected to replace him in 1669. His age was not yet quite 27 years. Already he could add the luster of his new optics and his new calculus to the Chair; in 1687 he would also add the *Principia.*

But the truth of the matter was that, for all the honor the Lucasian Professorship brought to Newton and for all the honor he brought to it, he had already immersed himself in the study of alchemy, and that was to be his most consuming passion for many years. Probably he had begun to read alchemical literature in 1668; in 1669 he purchased chemicals, chemical glassware, materials for furnaces, and the six massive folio volumes of *Theatrum chemicum,* a compilation of alchemical treatises. He established a laboratory of his own at Trinity College, and the records of his subsequent laboratory experimentation still exist in manuscript. Each brief, and often cryptic, laboratory report hides behind itself untold hours with hand-built furnaces of brick, with crucibles, with mortar and pestle, with the apparatus of distillation, and with charcoal fires; experimental sequences sometimes ran for weeks, months, or even years. He combed the literature of alchemy also, compiling voluminous notes and even transcribing entire treatises in his own hand. Eventually he drafted treatises of his own, filled with references to the older literature. The manuscript legacy of his scholarly endeavor is very large and represents a huge commitment of his time, but to it one must add the record of that extensive experimentation, a record that involves an amount of time impossible to estimate but surely equally huge. He seems to have continued his serious work on alchemy from about 1668 until 1696, when he left Cambridge for London and the Royal Mint, and even after 1696 he continued to study alchemical texts and to rework his own alchemical papers. [17; 18]

The focus of Newton's work in alchemy was already apparent in one of his very earliest independent alchemical papers; easily distinguishable from his reading notes and transcriptions, it is a short paper of alchemical propositions, in which he argued for the existence of a vital agent diffused through all things. This paper was probably written in 1669 (though Newton left it undated, as he did most of his papers), and it represents one of his earliest attempts to order the chaotic alchemical literature he was encountering.

The vital agent Newton described in that paper was universal in its operations. It had a general method of operating in all things but accommodated itself to the particular nature of particular subjects, and it assumed the particular form of each subject so as to be indistinguishable from the subject. In this manuscript Newton called the vital agent "the mercurial spirit": later he was to call it a "fermental virtue" or the "vegetable spirit" and eventually, in the *Opticks,* the "force of fermentation." It was responsible for organizing particles of matter into all the various forms of the phenomenal world; it was also responsible for disorganizing them, for reducing organized forms back to the primordial particles. It was the natural agent God used to organize matter and put His will into effect in the natural world. [18]

Alchemy and the mechanical philosophies of the seventeenth century seem to have shared the doctrine of the unity of matter, the idea that ultimately all forms of matter were capable of being reduced back to a primordial condition in which all matter was alike and without form. In the philosophy of Aristotle, upon which much alchemical thought was predicated, such formless material would have been called "prime matter" and would not have been treated as particulate, as it was in the mechanical philosophies. Nevertheless, the notion that the material substances of ordinary, everyday experience could all be reduced to something more primal, something without the ordinary properties of color, taste, odor, texture, and so forth, was not foreign to either sort of matter theory. So there was nothing antimechanistic about the idea Newton expressed in his alchemical propositions paper: that something might act upon a substance to break down the formed aggregate and reduce it to a chaotic condition in which it had no ordinary properties.

On the other hand, it seems impossible to find a mechanistic counterpart to the agent itself, for it was indeed profoundly antimechanistic. It did not act by pressure or impact, as mechanistic particles did, but instead acted in a way that suggested design and willed or planned activity, for example, in the beautifully regular patterns that form in mineral crystallization, or in the changes that occur in fermentation as grape juice is transformed into wine, or in the marvelous transmutation of an acorn into an oak or an egg into a chick. There was no distinction made in seventeenth-century alchemical thought between what we would call the chemical and the biological realms. [15; 18]

Newton had become preoccupied with a process of disorganization and reorganization by which developed species of matter might be radically reduced, revivified, and led to generate new forms. The alchemical agent was able to cause death and putrefaction, returning matter to an unformed condition; but it was equally able to infuse the unformed matter with new life and to lead it to new forms of organization. For as he himself said later, all matter duly formed is attended by signs of life. The implication of that statement of Newton's is, of course, that matter in a formed condition is quite different from the passive ultimate particles of unformed matter. Formed matter has somehow acquired the quality of being alive, a quality conveyed to it by the active, vital alchemical agent that acts in the formation of everything. [18; 30]

From what sources has Newton derived his ideas on the universal vital agent that he is here busily attaching to seventeenth-century mechanism? Quite possibly only from alchemy at this early stage in his development, though his vitalistic ideas were soon reinforced by other sources, especially the Stoic philosophers. [18]

Vitalism seems to belong to the very origins of alchemy. In the early Christian centuries, when alchemical ideas were taking shape, metals had not been well characterized as distinct species. They were sometimes thought to have variable properties, like modern alloys. More frequently, they were thought to be like a mix of dough, in which the introduction of a leaven might produce desired changes by a process of fermentation, or even similar to a material matrix of unformed matter, in which the injection of an active male sperm or seed might lead to a process of generation. By analogy, alchemists referred to this critical phase of the alchemical process as fermentation or generation, and the search for the vital metallic ferment or seed became a fundamental part of their quest. Similar ideas occur in Aristotle and were commonplace in Newton's time.

Inspired by his interest in a vital agent, Newton had begun to grope his way toward mending the deficiencies of ancient atomism and contemporary corpuscularianism. He had concerned himself with life and cohesion. He now sought the source of all the apparently spontaneous processes of fermentation, putrefaction, generation, and vegetation—that is, everything associated with normal life and growth, such as digestion and assimilation, *vegetation* being originally from the Latin *vegetare*, "to animate, enliven." These processes produced the endless variety of living forms and could not be relegated to the mechanical actions of gross corpuscles, a point he emphasized in the 1670s and to which we will return later. Mechanical action could never account for the process of assimilation, in which foodstuffs were turned into the bodies of animals, vegetables, and minerals. Nor could it account for the sheer variety of forms in this world, all of which had somehow sprung from the common matter. [18]

Newton's Discovery of Stoic Philosophy and His Later Alchemy

The most comprehensive answer to such problems of life and cohesion in antiquity had been given by the Stoics. The Stoics postulated a continuous material medium, the tension and activity of which molded the cosmos into a living whole and the various parts of the cosmic animal into coherent bodies as well. Compounded of air and a creative fire, this medium was the Stoic *pneuma* (a Greek work meaning "breath" or "an airy matter") and was related to the concept of the "breath of life" that escapes from a living body at the time of death and allows the formerly coherent body in which it had resided to disintegrate into its disparate parts. Although always material, the *pneuma* becomes finer and more active as one ascends the scale of being, and the (more corporeal) air decreases as the (less corporeal) fire increases. The Stoic Deity, literally omnipresent in the universe, is the hottest, most tense and creative form of the cosmic *pneuma* or aether, pure fire or nearly so. The cosmos permeated and shaped by the *pneuma* is not only living, it is rational and orderly and under the benevolent, providential care of the Deity. Though the Stoics were determinists, their Deity was immanent and active in the cosmos, and one of their most telling arguments against the atomists was that the order, beauty, symmetry, and purpose to be seen in the world could never have come from random, mechanical action. Only a providential God could produce and maintain such lovely, meaningful forms, and this "argument from design" for the existence of a Deity was later adopted by Christian thinkers, as we saw above. The universe, as a living body, was born

when the creative fire generated the four elements of earth, water, air, and fire; it lived out its life span, permeated by vital heat and breath, cycling back to final conflagration in the divine active principle, and always regenerated itself in a perpetual circle of life and death. [17; 32; 46; 54; 86; 88; 94; 96]

The original writings of the Stoics were mostly lost, but not before ideas of *pneuma* and *spiritus* (a Latin word with a similar meaning) came to pervade medical doctrine, alchemical theory, and indeed the general culture with form-giving spirits, souls, and vital principles, for Stoicism was one of the dominant philosophies of late antiquity. Spiritualized forms of the *pneuma* entered early Christian theology in discussions of the immanence and transcendence of God and of the Holy Ghost, just as the Stoic arguments that order and beauty demonstrate the existence of God and of Providence entered Christianity as the argument from design for the existence of a Deity. The creative emanations of Stoic fire melded with the creative emanations of light in Neoplatonism. In addition to this broad spectrum of at least vaguely Stoic ideas, excellent, though not always sympathetic, summaries of philosophical Stoicism were available in many of the learned authors of late antiquity: Cicero, Seneca, Plutarch, Diogenes Laertius, Sextus Empiricus, and others. By the seventeenth century ideas compatible with Stoicism were very widely diffused, and latter-day Stoics, Pythagoreans, Platonists, medical men, chemists, alchemists, and even the followers of Aristotle vied with each other in celebrating the occult (hidden, secret) virtues of a cosmic aether that was the vehicle of a pure, hidden, creative fire.

Nonetheless, such a vital aether or *pneuma* was to be found in its most developed form in philosophical Stoicism. It is probable, as Newton's concern for the processes of life and cohesion grew apace in the early 1670s, that he amplified his mechanical philosophy further by a close reading of the available literature on the Stoics. Virtually all of the scanty fragments of ancient Stoicism known today had already been recovered by western Europe during the Renaissance, and Newton had most of them. Newton could surely have reconstructed for himself a reasonably sophisticated and comprehensive knowledge of Stoic thought from books in his own library. [18; 34]

Such reading would have affected Newton's alchemy only in reinforcing certain critical ideas, for most of his early alchemical sources were distinctly Neoplatonic in tone, and in them the universal spirit or soul of the world already permeated the cosmos with its fermental virtue. But Stoic ideas would have affected his views on the mechanical aether of his student years. It seems one may conclude that if Newton had not read the Stoics, then he must independently have reached answers similar to theirs when confronted with similar problems, for by about 1672 the original mechanical aether of his student notebook had assumed a strongly Stoic cast.

Newton described his new vitalistic aether in an alchemical treatise of about 1672, **"Of Natures obvious laws & processes in vegetation."** There he described the earth as a great animal or vegetable that inhales an aethereal breath for its vital processes and exhales again with a grosser breath. He called the aethereal breath a subtle spirit, nature's universal agent, her secret fire, and the material soul of all matter. The similarity between this particular Newtonian aether and the Stoic *pneuma* is unmistakable: they are both material, and both somehow inspire the forms of bodies and give to bodies the continuity and coherence of form that is associated with life. Furthermore, Newton was quite explicit in this treatise that the processes of life, what he called vegetation, were similar in all three kingdoms of nature: the animal, the vegetable, and the mineral. In this treatise Newton made a sharp distinction between mechanism and the life processes of vegetation: "Nature's actions are either vegetable or purely mechanical," he said. As purely mechanical he listed two items of special interest, gravity (to which we will return later) and what he called vulgar or common chemistry. [15; 18:30]

In common chemistry, of course, nature (or the chemist) may effect many changes in textures, and so forth, but, Newton argued, that sort of change occurs just by rearranging the corpuscles. On the other hand, vegetative or growth processes require some further cause, and the difference between the two sorts of chemistry (mechanical and vegetable) is "vast and fundamental." [18:30] Vegetable chemistry in the mineral kingdom is what we usually call alchemy, for the alchemists believed that metals grow in the earth just as plants grow on the surface of the earth. Newton was convinced that metals were the only part of the mineral kingdom that vegetate, other mineral substances being formed mechanically. Vegetation in metals, of which the alchemists wrote, was thus the simplest case for study, the vegetation of the animals and vegetables in the other kingdoms of nature being obviously more complex. So in the vegetation of metals (alchemy) lay the most accessible key to the problem of nonmechanical action, the kind of divinely guided activity in nature that Newton thought was necessary to correct the overly mechanized system of Descartes. [15; 18]

Newton's distinction between mechanical and vegetable chemistry thus emerges as crucial to his solution of the theological problem posed by his Cartesian inheritance. Mechanical chemistry may be accounted for simply by the mechanical coalitions and separations of the particles and requires no further explanation. But for all that great class of beings that nature produces by vegetation, we must have recourse to some further cause. Ultimately the cause is God, and within the realm of vegetable chemistry one may find an area of continuing divine guidance of the world and of matter, an area of providential care. It is God's will that directs the motion of the particles of matter and guides them into their designed arrangements. The vital Stoic and alchemical agent, the subtle spirit of life, the secret fire in the earth's aethereal breath is thus simply the natural agent God uses in directing the motion of the passive particles of matter.

One may now see that Newton was concerned from the first in his alchemical work to find evidence for the existence of a vegetative principle operating in the natural world, a principle that he understood to be the secret, universal, animating spirit of which the alchemists spoke. His early conviction was amplified by Stoic doctrines on the breath of life, the Stoic *pneuma* or *spiritus* or vital aether. He later came to see analogies between the vegetable principle and light, drawing on the Christian and Neoplatonic metaphysics of light, and he also came to see analogies between the alchemical process and the work of the Deity at the time of the creation of the world, when matter was first guided into organized forms. But above all Newton thought, and continued to think for the rest of his life, that by the use of this active vegetative principle God constantly molded the universe to His providential design, producing all manner of generations, resurrections, fermentations, and vegetation.

In short, the action of the secret animating spirit of alchemy kept the universe from being the sort of closed mechanical system for which Descartes had argued. Left to run by itself without provision for divine providential care, the Cartesian universe threatened traditional Christian values. Newton thought that belief in the Cartesian mechanical system, where matter filled all space and there was little or no room for spirit, and where no divine guidance seemed to be required on a daily basis, could lead to a materialist philosophy, to deism, or even to atheism. [18; 50; 62]

A materialist would emphasize matter to the exclusion of spirit; a deist might still believe that a Deity created the world and set it in motion but then left it to run by itself; an atheist would deny the existence of the Deity completely. Newton had a horror of all those philosophico-religious positions and was determined to do everything he could to counteract them. He thought that an irrefutable scientific demonstration of divine providential guidance of the small particles of matter would provide the needed evidence for the existence and activity of the Deity and would restore to humanity the true religion that had been lost. Given the importance of what he hoped to gain from his alchemical studies, it is easy enough to understand why he experimented and studied in that field with such persistence, year after year after year.

None of Newton's convictions in this area of his work ever suffered substantial change, and though later he revised his terms "vegetable" and "mechanical" to the terminology of "active" and "passive" (terms he had learned from Stoic philosophy), the new terminology served exactly the same metaphysical purpose as the old. The foundational thinking about "active" (divine) and "passive" (material) principles that Newton first developed in his alchemical work later supported his basic patterns of thought in both the ***Principia*** and the ***Opticks,*** but let us next see how his other religious studies developed. [18]

Newton's Work in Other Religious Subjects

We have just seen that Newton's work in alchemy had a religious motivation, for he was convinced that a demonstration of divine activity in the guidance of the passive particles of matter was possible through alchemy. Other areas of his interests were even more directly and obviously focused on religion, but the ultimate goal of one of them at least was virtually identical to his goal in studying alchemy. That was the correct interpretation of biblical prophecy and its correlation with the recorded events of history, for such a correlation would also demonstrate divine activity in the world. Newton began work on the prophecies in the 1670s if not earlier, and he is thought to have still been working on his last version of their interpretation the night before he died in 1727. [18; 24; 101]

As alchemy was the story of God's ongoing activity in the world of matter for Newton, so history was the story of God's ongoing activity in the moral world, and as such it was a key for the interpretation of prophecy. Prophecy in the Bible was divinely inspired, and Newton spent untold hours on the writings of Daniel and the Apocalypse of St. John. But human beings could fully understand prophecy only after it had been fulfilled, for it was written in "mystical" language that was not readily accessible. In any event, Newton argued, a person was not to presume to interpret it with an eye for concrete prediction of the future. Only after the prophesied events had occurred could one see that they had been the fulfillment of prophecy. Then God's action in the world was demonstrated. [18; 24; 67; 71; 74; 76; 101]

> The folly of Interpreters has been, to foretel times and things by this Prophecy [John's], as if God had designed to make them prophets. By this rashness they have not only exposed themselves, but brought the Prophecy also into contempt. The design of God was much otherwise. He gave this and the Prophecies of the Old Testament, not to gratify men's curiosities by enabling them to foreknow things, but that after they were fulfilled they might be interpreted by the event, and his own Providence, not the Interpreters, be then manifested thereby to

the world. For the event of things predicted many ages before, will then be a convincing argument that the world is governed by providence. [74:251]

Newton's methodology in prophetic interpretation was undoubtedly influenced by the methods of others, particularly of recent Protestant interpreters including Joseph Mede (1586-1638) and Henry More, both of Cambridge University. Yet there was in addition something peculiarly Newtonian about it. In Newton's mind history seemed to bear a direct correspondence with experimental or even mathematical demonstration. Just as an experiment might enable the investigator to decide between alternative theories of natural phenomena, so historical facts might enable the interpreter to choose between possible interpretations of prophecy. For Newton only the firm correspondence of fact with correctly interpreted prophecy provided an adequate demonstration of God's providential action. What had been adumbrated or prophesied by divine agency in the prophecy had then been fulfilled by divine agency. What God had said He would do, He had done. That, and only that, provided for Newton a "convincing argument" for God's providential governance of the moral world. When actual historical developments exactly matched predicted ones in "the event of things predicted many ages before," one hears an echo of that universally satisfying geometrical conclusion, *quod erat demonstrandum:* QED. [74:251-52] That was exactly what Newton wanted to demonstrate with his prophetic and historical studies—God's providential action in the moral world—just as he desired by his alchemical studies to demonstrate God's providential action in the natural world. [18; 24; 74; 99]

Probably Newton labored over prophetical interpretations for fifty years, if not more, but in another part of his religious work he labored intensively for only a few years. After that relatively brief time, he was convinced that the entire Christian tradition since the fourth century had been in error and that he, Newton, had come closer to the Truth of primitive Christianity. Afterwards he adhered to his new convictions in spite of the problems they caused him in his own society. The issue was a doctrinal or theological one having to do with the nature of the Deity. Orthodox Christian doctrine in the seventeenth century was trinitarian; that is to say, the accepted belief was that God was "Three-in-One" or "One-in-Three," one God in Three Persons (God the Father, God the Son, and God the Holy Ghost) all coequal and coeternal and ultimately One. Newton disagreed. [22; 23; 76; 101]

The problem arose initially because Newton's Fellowship at his Cambridge college required that he accept ordination as a member of the clergy of the Church of England after seven years, or else resign his Fellowship, as we saw above. During the years preceding that deadline, Newton understandably immersed himself in theological studies, and in so doing read exhaustively in the patristic literature, that is, the treatises written by the fathers of the church in the early centuries of Christianity. Among those documents he found traces of the views of Arius, a theologian of the third and fourth centuries, and of the debates on the nature of Christ (God the Son) that culminated in the decision of a church council, the Council of Nicaea in 325, that Christ, God's Son, was of the same substance as God the Father and was "begotten, not made, being of one substance with the Father," in the words of the Nicaean Creed issued by the council. Arius, who lost the argument, had believed that the Son was created, not begotten, and was *not* of the same substance as the Father. Newton decided, on the basis of the documents in the case, that Arius was right and that all of Christendom had been in error since 325. In the eyes of his contemporaries, however, had they but known of Newton's decision for Arius, Newton would have been the heretic and in mortal danger of losing not only his college Fellowship but also his Lucasian Chair of Mathematics. [28; 82; 101]

The viewpoint of Arius that Newton accepted was not trinitarian and thus was not orthodox, for in Arian theology the Son was created by the Supreme Deity and so was not coeternal with the Almighty God. Newton did think for a while that he would lose his Fellowship, but he cautiously let it be known that he preferred not to be ordained even while maintaining a discreet silence on the reason for that preference. The outcome was favorable for Newton: a permanent dispensation from the Fellowship requirement for ordination was obtained from the crown for the Lucasian Professor. Thus Newton was saved: he neither had to perjure himself by claiming to believe the trinitarian doctrine that he no longer believed, nor did he lose his university and college positions. [101]

Newton was so discreet about the whole matter that hardly anyone knew until the twentieth century that Newton had become an Arian in the early 1670s. Religious heterodoxy is not always a burning issue in the modern world, but getting at the Truth was a burning issue for Newton, and he was clearly prepared to relinquish his academic honors for the sake of his convictions. He remained a convinced Arian to the end of his days, and late in life he formulated an Arian creed that he presumably hoped would replace the Nicaean Creed for all believers. His Arian theology had an interesting impact on his natural philosophy also, for, as we have seen, Newton believed that Truth from any area of his studies should coalesce with Truth from any other area. We will return to a discussion of Arianism in connection with Newton's changing ideas on the cause of gravity, and in Part II we will see that a number of Newton's followers also became Arians in theology. [18; 22]

Newton's Mechanistic Theories of Gravity

As we have seen, when Newton first learned about the new mechanical philosophies of nature in his undergraduate years, he adopted a mechanistic explanation of gravity, relying on a shower of imperceptible aethereal particles that pressed bodies down toward earth. In his student notebook he even sketched two bits of machinery that might be built to take advantage of the shower of fine particles to produce perpetual motion, one machine constructed like a water wheel, the other with vanes somewhat like those of a windmill. Each was designed to operate from the impacts of the mechanical stream of aethereal matter causing gravity. [62]

A similar but more developed mechanistic explanation of gravity appeared a few years later in another of Newton's private papers, the alchemical treatise **"Of Natures obvious laws & processes in vegetation,"** probably written about 1672. That may seem a very odd place for Newton to offer a speculative scenario about gravity, but that treatise is one of the prime exemplars of a small group of papers in which Newton was trying to fit partial Truth to partial Truth from some of his different lines of investigation. So although the mechanical aether for gravity and the vitalistic aether that carried the secret vivifying fire of the alchemists had originated in quite different studies in his early work, in this alchemical treatise Newton had combined them. The complex aether Newton then described followed a great circulatory path, not unlike that of the Cartesian vortices. It swept down to earth, making bodies heavy, but its finer and more active parts also provided the vivifying alchemical spirit. When it reached the earth, it continued into the earth's interior where it helped to generate air. The air in turn ascended from the interior to constitute the atmosphere, vapors, clouds, and so forth, until it reached the aethereal regions above. There the air pressed on the aether, forcing it to descend again toward the earth. [15; 18]

In 1675 Newton sent a paper to the Royal Society in London that contained a very similar system, but one in which the gravitational and vegetative functions of the aether were even more thoroughly combined. The movement up of air and the movement down of aether continued, with the air being "attenuated into its first principle" of aether when it reached the great aethereal spaces above. "For nature is a perpetuall circulatory worker . . . , Some things to ascend & make the upper terrestrial juices, Rivers and the Atmosphere; & by consequence others to descend for a Requittal to the former." [18:103; 71]

But in the 1675 paper there is one striking difference, and that is that the whole speculative system has moved toward universality. Appearing almost as an afterthought at the end of his description of the earthbound circulatory pattern, the operations of the gravitational-vegetative aether expanded to include the solar system. [18; 71]

> And as the Earth, so perhaps may the Sun imbibe this Spirit copiously to conserve his Shineing, & keep the Planets from recedeing further from him. And they that will, may also suppose, that this Spirit affords or carrys with it thither the solary fewell [fuel] & materiall Principle of Light; And that the vast aethereall Spaces between us, & the stars are for a sufficient repository for this food of the Sunn & Planets. [71]

Newton's speculative aethereal system was enormously expanded in its scale of application when he thus extended it to the sun and other planets, but in no way did that expansion affect the mode of operation of the system, for both gravitational and vegetative functions were still attributed to the "Spirit." The "Spirit" had the stated gravitational function of keeping the planets in their orbits: the sun imbibed the "Spirit" to "keep the Planets from recedeing further from him." The vegetative function of the "Spirit," on the other hand, is readily apparent in other phrases: this spirit provided "food" and "fewell." It furthermore carried with it the "materiall Principle of Light," a sharp and unmistakable echo of Newton's identification of the vegetable spirit with "the body of light" in an earlier alchemical paper. [15; 18:104]

This combination of functions, both gravitational and vegetative, in Newton's speculative aethers was not to last, however. By 1679, in a letter to Robert Boyle, Newton had completely separated them and had formulated two new mechanistic scenarios to explain gravity. The new systems did not rely on a stream of aethereal particles as the old ones had done. Instead of a stream of particles flowing like a stream of water, Newton used in 1679 a nonmoving aether that was more dense in some places than in others. In both systems described to Boyle, however, gravity was again fully mechanized and detached from the vital alchemical agent.

Newton told Boyle that one of the gravitational conjectures in his letter came into his mind only as he was writing the letter, and, though we will meet a variant of that particular aethereal system again, it did not have a very long life in its original form. For a few months later, toward the end of 1679, Robert Hooke's challenges to Newton regarding the motion of bodies set Newton on a course of development that changed forever the conditions for aethereal speculation. [18; 71]

The correspondence with Hooke provided the stimulus for Newton's first solution to the problem of celestial dynamics in the terms later to appear in the *Principia.* As we have seen, Newton's earlier analysis of celestial motion had been cast in terms of a center-fleeing (cen-

trifugal) force counterbalanced by the pressure of the aethereal vortex that carried the moon around the earth or the planets around the sun. In 1679 Hooke argued for a different way of approaching the problem: an attractive force *toward* the center of the orbit (what Newton later called the centripetal or center-seeking force), counterbalanced by the tendency of the planet or moon to move away from its orbit in a tangent (a straight line only touching the orbit in one place), due to its inertia. Having been very busy with his alchemical and theological studies during the 1670s, Newton had barely considered celestial dynamics quantitatively and had done no original work in that area since the 1660s. Hooke diverted him from his other studies and irritated him by correcting some errors Newton had made and by what Newton called Hooke's "dogmaticalnes," so Newton was "inclined" to try Hooke's mode of analysis using the centripetal force and inertia and then found the theorem by which he "afterward examined ye Ellipsis." It is possible that Newton made his trial of the new method late in 1679 or early in 1680, but even if so he once more quickly put his calculations aside for other studies, primarily alchemical and theological ones. [18:119; 71; 101]

Newton's conceptualization of gravity remained unsettled for several years following his interchange with Hooke. In an exchange of letters with Thomas Burnet (1635-1715) late in 1680 and early in the following year, Newton suggested a mechanism of vortical pressure for gravity, discussed the centrifugal force of the planets (a component of his pre-Hookian dynamical analysis), and mentioned "gravitation towards a center" without offering any mechanism for it. When conferring with John Flamsteed (1646-1719), Astronomer-Royal of England, about the comet of 1680, Newton mentioned the "attraction of ye earth by its gravity" but also mentioned the "motion of a Vortex." He was willing to "allow an attractive power" in the sun "whereby the Planets are kept in their courses about him from going away in tangent lines," which seems to presuppose Hooke's analysis, but, in refuting Flamsteed's notion that such an attraction might be magnetic, Newton utilized both the idea of the sun's vortex and the concept of the centrifugal force. About 1682 he referred to the material fluid of the heavens that gyrates around the center of the cosmic system according to the course of the planets. Not until 1684 do Newton's papers reflect the clarity of thought on dynamical principles that enabled him to launch the writing of the *Principia,* and only in the course of writing that work did Newton confront the problems that inhered in all his various early aethereal gravitational systems. [18:126; 71; 101; 102] . . .

Bibliography

Excellent reference works for students of intellectual history and the history of science are the multivolume sets *The Dictionary of the History of Ideas* and *The Dictionary of Scientific Biography*. Both will provide not only information but also additional bibliography to guide further research. For Newton himself *The Newton Handbook* by Derek Gjertsen (item [26] below) is perhaps the best starting place. All of the works listed below will also guide the student toward additional sources for research.

[1] H. G. Alexander, ed. *The Leibniz-Clarke Correspondence, Together with Extracts from Newton's "Principia" and "Opticks."* Introduction and notes by H. G. Alexander. Philosophical Classics, general ed., Peter G. Lucas. Manchester: Manchester University Press, 1956.

[2] Carl B. Boyer. *A History of Mathematics.* New York, London, and Sydney: John Wiley and Sons, 1968.

[3] Carl B. Boyer. *The History of the Calculus and Its Conceptual Development (The Concepts of the Calculus).* Foreword by Richard Courant. 1949; rpt. New York: Dover, 1959.

[4] Edwin Arthur Burtt. *The Metaphysical Foundations of Modern Science.* 2d rev. ed. Rpt. Garden City, NY: Doubleday, 1954.

[5] Max Caspar. *Kepler.* Trans. and ed. C. Doris Hellman. London: Abelard-Schuman, 1959.

[6] Ernst Cassirer. *The Platonic Renaissance in England.* Trans. James P. Pettegrove. Austin: University of Texas Press, 1953.

[7] *Catalogue of the Newton Papers Sold by Order of the Viscount Lymington to Whom They Have Descended from Catherine Conduitt, Viscountess Lymington, Great-Niece of Sir Isaac Newton.* London: Sotheby, 1936.

[8] *A Catalogue of the Portsmouth Collection of Books and Papers written by or belonging to Sir Isaac Newton, the scientific portion of which has been presented by the Earl of Portsmouth to the University of Cambridge. Drawn up by the Syndicate appointed the 6th November, 1872.* Cambridge: Cambridge University Press, 1888.

[9] Gale E. Christianson. *In the Presence of the Creator: Isaac Newton and His Times.* New York: Free Press; London: Collier Macmillan, 1984.

[10] I. Bernard. Cohen. *The Birth of a New Physics.* Rev. and updated. New York and London: Norton, 1985.

[11] I. Bernard Cohen. *Introduction to Newton's "Principia."* Cambridge: Harvard University Press; Cambridge: Cambridge University Press, 1971.

[12] I. Bernard Cohen. *The Newtonian Revolution: With Illustrations of the Transformation of Scientific Ideas.* Cambridge and New York: Cambridge University Press, 1980.

[13] John Conduitt. "Memoirs of Sir Isaac Newton, sent by Mr. Conduitt to Monsieur Fontenelle, in 1727." In Edmund Turnor, *Collections for the History of the Town and Soke of Grantham. Containing Authentic Memoirs of Sir Isaac Newton, Now First Published From the Original MSS. in the Possession of the Earl of Portsmouth.* London: Printed for William Miller, Albemarle-Street, by W. Bulmer and Co., Cleveland-Row, St. James's, 1806.

[14] René Descartes. *Oeuvres de Descartes publiées par Charles Adam et Paul Tannery.* 11 vols. Paris: Librairie Philosophique J. Vrin, 1964-74.

[15] B. J. T. Dobbs. *Alchemical Death and Resurrection: The Significance of Alchemy in the Age of Newton. A lecture sponsored by the Smithsonian Institution Libraries in conjunction with the Washington Collegium for the Humanities Lecture Series: Death and the Afterlife in Art and Literature. Presented at the Smithsonian Institution, February 16, 1988.* Washington, DC: Smithsonian Institution Libraries, 1990.

[16] B. J. T. Dobbs. "From the Secrecy of Alchemy to the Openness of Chemistry." In Tore Frängsmyr, ed., *Solomon's House Revisited: The Organization and Institutionalization of Science. Nobel Symposium 75.* Canton, MA.: Science History Publications, 1990.

[17] B. J. T. Dobbs. *The Foundations of Newton's Alchemy, or "The Hunting of the Greene Lyon."* Cambridge and New York: Cambridge University Press, 1975.

[18] B. J. T. Dobbs. *The Janus Faces of Genius: The Role of Alchemy in Newton's Thought.* Cambridge and New York: Cambridge University Press, 1991.

[19] Samuel Y. Edgerton, Jr. *The Heritage of Giotto's Geometry: Art and Science on the Eve of the Scientific Revolution.* Ithaca and London: Cornell University Press, 1991.

[20] C. H. Edwards, Jr. *The Historical Development of the Calculus.* New York, Heidelberg, and Berlin: Springer-Verlag, 1979.

[21] John Fauvel, Raymond Flood, Michael Shortland, and Robin Wilson, eds. *Let Newton Be!* Oxford: Oxford University Press, 1988.

[22] James E. Force. *William Whiston: Honest Newtonian.* Cambridge and New York: Cambridge University Press, 1985.

[23] James E. Force and Richard H. Popkin. *Essays on the Context, Nature, and Influence of Isaac Newton's Theology.* International Archives of the History of Ideas, no. 129. Dordrecht: Kluwer Academic Publishers, 1990.

[24] LeRoy Edwin Froom. *The Prophetic Faith of Our Fathers: The Historical Development of Prophetic Interpretation.* 4 vols. Washington, DC: Review and Herald, 1946-54.

[25] Sara Schechner Genuth. "Comets, Teleology, and the Relationship of Chemistry to Cosmology in Newton's Thought." *Annali dell' Instituto e Museo di Storia della Scienza di Firenze* 10 (1985): 31-65.

[26] Derek Gjertsen. *The Newton Handbook.* London and New York: Routledge and Kegan Paul, 1986.

[27] Edward Grant. *Much Ado about Nothing: Theories of Space and Vacuum from the Middle Ages to the Scientific Revolution.* Cambridge and New York: Cambridge University Press, 1981.

[28] Robert C. Gregg and Dennis E. Groh. *Early Arianism: A View of Salvation.* Philadelphia: Fortress Press, 1981.

[29] Henry Guerlac. *Essays and Papers in the History of Modern Science.* Baltimore: Johns Hopkins University Press, 1977.

[30] Henry Guerlac. "Theological Voluntarism and Biological Analogies in Newton's Physical Thought." *Journal of the History of Ideas* 44 (1983): 219-29.

[31] Henry Guerlac and M. C. Jacob. "Bentley, Newton, and Providence (The Boyle Lectures Once More)." *Journal of the History of Ideas* 30 (1969): 307-18.

[32] David E. Hahm. *The Origins of Stoic Cosmology.* Columbus: Ohio State University Press, 1977.

[33] A. Rupert Hall. *Philosophers at War: The Quarrel between Newton and Leibniz.* Cambridge and London: Cambridge University Press, 1980.

[34] John Harrison. *The Library of Isaac Newton.* Cambridge and London: Cambridge University Press, 1978.

[35] Joan L. Hawes. "Newton and the 'Electrical Attraction Unexcited.'" *Annals of Science* 24 (1968): 121-30.

[36] Joan L. Hawes. "Newton's Revival of the Aether Hypothesis and the Explanation of Gravitational Attraction." *Notes and Records of the Royal Society of London* 23 (1968): 200-212.

[37] Joan L. Hawes. "Newton's Two Electricities." *Annals of Science* 27 (1971): 95-103.

[38] J. L. Heilbron. *Electricity in the Seventeenth and Eighteenth Centuries: A Study of Early Modern Physics.* Berkeley and Los Angeles: University of California Press, 1979.

[39] J. L. Heilbron. *Physics at the Royal Society during Newton's Presidency.* Los Angeles: William Andrews Clark Memorial Library, UCLA, 1983.

[40] John Herivel. *The Background to Newton's "Principia": A Study of Newton's Dynamical Researches in the Years 1664-84.* Oxford: Clarendon Press, 1965.

[41] W. G. Hiscock, ed. *David Gregory, Isaac Newton, and Their Circle: Extracts from David Gregory's Memoranda, 1677-1708.* Oxford: Printed for the Editor, 1937.

[42] *The Holy Bible containing the Old and New Testaments. Authorized King James Version.* Oxford: Oxford University Press, n.d.

[43] R. W. Home. "Force, Electricity, and the Powers of Living Matter in Newton's Mature Philosophy of Nature." In Margaret J. Osler and Paul Lawrence Farber, eds., *Religion, Science, and Worldview: Essays in Honor of Richard S. Westfall.* Cambridge and New York: Cambridge University Press, 1985.

[44] R. W. Home. "Newton on Electricity and the Aether." In Zev Bechler, ed., *Contemporary Newtonian Research.* Studies in the History of Modern Science, no. 9. Dordrecht: D. Reidel, 1982.

[45] Reijer Hooykaas. *Religion and the Rise of Modern Science.* Edinburgh: Scottish Academic Press, 1973.

[46] H. A. K. Hunt. *A Physical Interpretation of the Universe: The Doctrines of Zeno the Stoic.* Melbourne: Melbourne University Press, 1976.

[47] Keith Hutchinson. "Supernaturalism and the Mechanical Philosophy." *History of Science* 21 (1983): 297-333.

[48] Margaret C. Jacob. "Newton and the French Prophets: New Evidence." *History of Science* 16 (1978): 134-42.

[49] Margaret C. Jacob. *The Newtonians and the English Revolution, 1689-1720.* 1976; rpt. New York: Gordon and Breach, 1991.

[50] Margaret C. Jacob. *The Cultural Meaning of the Scientific Revolution.* 1988; new ed. New York: Oxford University Press, 1995.

[51] Robert Hugh Kargon. *Atomism in England from Hariot to Newton.* Oxford: Clarendon Press, 1966.

[52] Alexandre Koyré. *From the Closed World to the Infinite Universe.* 1957; rpt. New York: Harper and Brothers, 1958.

[53] Alexandre Koyré. *Newtonian Studies.* Cambridge: Harvard University Press, 1965.

[54] David Charles Kubrin. "Newton and the Cyclical Cosmos: Providence and the Mechanical Philosophy." *Journal of the History of Ideas* 28 (1967): 325-46.

[55] David C. Lindberg. *The Beginnings of Western Science: The European Scientific Tradition in Philosophical, Religious, and Institutional Context, 600* B.C. *to* A.D. *1450.* Chicago and London: University of Chicago Press, 1992.

[56] David C. Lindberg. "The Genesis of Kepler's Theory of Light: Light Metaphysics from Plotinusto Kepler." *Osiris,* 2d ser. 2 (1986): 5-42.

[57] David C. Lindberg and Ronald L. Numbers, eds. *God and Nature: Historical Essays on the Encounter between Christianity and Science.* Berkeley and Los Angeles: University of California Press, 1986.

[58] Jack Lindsay. *The Origins of Alchemy in Graeco-Roman Egypt.* New York: Barnes and Noble, 1970.

[59] A. A. Long. *Hellenistic Philosophy: Stoics, Epicureans, Sceptics.* London: Duckworth, 1974.

[60] J. E. McGuire and P. M. Heimann. "The Rejection of Newton's Concept of Matter in the Eighteenth Century." In Ernan McMullin, ed., *The Concept of Matter in Modern Philosophy.* Notre Dame and London: University of Notre Dame Press, 1978.

[61] J. E. McGuire and P. M. Rattansi. "Newton and the 'Pipes of Pan.'" *Notes and Records of the Royal Society of London* 21 (1966): 108-43.

[62] J. E. McGuire and Martin Tammy. *Certain Philosophical Questions: Newton's Trinity Notebook.* Cambridge and London: Cambridge: University Press, 1983.

[63] Ernan McMullin. *Newton on Matter and Activity.* Notre Dame: University of Notre Dame Press, 1978.

[64] Elizabeth Mackenzie. "The Growth of Plants: A Seventeenth-Century Metaphor." In *English Renaissance Studies Presented to Dame Helen Gardner in Honour of Her Seventieth Birthday.* Oxford: Clarendon Press, 1980.

[65] Frank E. Manuel. *Isaac Newton, Historian.* Cambridge: Belknap Press of Harvard University Press, 1963.

[66] Frank E. Manuel. *A Portrait of Isaac Newton.* Cambridge: Belknap Press of Harvard University Press, 1968.

[67] Frank E. Manuel. *The Religion of Isaac Newton: The Fremantle Lectures 1973.* Oxford: Clarendon Press, 1974.

[68] E. C. Millington. "Theories of Cohesion in the Seventeenth Century." *Annals of Science* 5 (1941-47): 253-69.

[69] Charles G. Nauert, Jr. *Agrippa and the Crisis of Renaissance Thought.* Illinois Studies in the Social Sciences, no. 55. Urbana: University of Illinois Press, 1965.

[70] Isaac Newton. *The Chronology of Ancient Kingdoms Amended. To which is Prefix'd, A Short Chronicle from the First Memory of Things in Europe, to the Conquest of Persia by Alexander the Great.* London: Printed for J. Tonson in the Strand, and J. Osborn and T. Longman in Paternoster Row, 1728.

[71] Isaac Newton. *The Correspondence of Isaac Newton.* Ed. H. W. Turnbull, J. P. Scott, A. R. Hall, and Laura Tilling. 7 vols. Cambridge: Published for the Royal Society at the University Press, 1959-77.

[72] Isaac Newton. *Manuscripts and Papers Collected and Published on Microfilm by Chawyck-Healey.* Ed. Peter Jones. Cambridge: Chadwyck-Healey, 1991.

[73] Isaac Newton. *The Mathematical Papers of Isaac Newton.* Ed. Derek T. Whiteside with the assistance in publication of M. A. Hoskin. 8 vols. Cambridge: Cambridge University Press, 1967-80.

[74] Isaac Newton. *Observations upon the Prophecies of Daniel, and the Apocalypse of St. John. In Two Parts.* London: Printed by J. Darby and T. Browne in Bartholomew-Close. And sold by J. Roberts in Warwick-lane, J. Tonson in the Strand, W. Innys and R. Manby at the West End of St. Paul's Church-Yard, J. Osborn and T. Longman in Pater-Noster-Row, J. Noon near Mercers Chapel in Cheapside, T. Hatchett at the Royal Exchange, S. Harding in St. Martin's lane, J. Stagg in Westminster-Hall, J. Parker in Pall-mall, and J. Brindley in New Bond-street, 1733.

[75] Isaac Newton. *Opticks, or A Treatise of the Reflections, Refractions, Inflections & Colours of Light.* Foreword by Albert Einstein, introduction by Sir Edmund Whittaker, preface by I. Bernard Cohen, analytical table of contents by Duane H. D. Roller. Based on the 4th London ed. of 1730. New York: Dover, 1952.

[76] Isaac Newton. *Sir Isaac Newton: Theological Manuscripts.* Selected and ed. with an introduction by

H. McLachlan. Liverpool: At the University Press, 1950.

[77] Isaac Newton. *Sir Isaac Newton's Mathematical Principles of Natural Philosophy and His System of the World.* Trans. Andrew Motte, 1729. Ed. Florian Cajori. 2 vols. 1934; rpt. Berkeley and Los Angeles: University of California Press, 1962.

[78] Isaac Newton. *Unpublished Scientific Papers of Isaac Newton: A Selection from the Portsmouth Collection in the University Library, Cambridge. Chosen, edited, and translated by A. Rupert Hall and Marie Boas Hall.* Cambridge: Cambridge University Press, 1962.

[79] Margaret J. Osler. "Descartes and Charleton on Nature and God." *Journal of the History of Ideas* 40 (1979): 445-56.

[80] Margaret J. Osler. "Eternal Truths and the Laws of Nature: The Theological Foundations of Descartes' Philosophy of Nature." *Journal of the History of Ideas* 46 (1985): 349-62.

[81] Margaret J. Osler. "Providence and Divine Will in Gassendi's Views on Scientific Knowledge." *Journal of the History of Ideas* 44 (1983): 549-60.

[82] Edward Peters, ed. *Heresy and Authority in Medieval Europe: Documents in Translation.* Introduction by Edward Peters. Philadelphia: University of Pennsylvania Press, 1980.

[83] Richard H. Popkin. *The History of Scepticism from Erasmus to Spinoza.* Berkeley and Los Angeles: University of California Press, 1979.

[84] Richard H. Popkin, ed. *Millenarianism and Messianism in English Literature and Thought, 1650-1800. Clark Library Lectures, 1981-82.* Publications from the Clark Library Professorship, UCLA, no. 10. Leiden: E. J. Brill, 1988.

[85] Arthur Quinn. *The Confidence of British Philosophers: An Essay in Historical Narrative.* Studies in the History of Christian Thought, vol. 17. Ed. Heiko A. Oberman, in cooperation with Henry Chadwick, Edward A. Dowey, Jaroslav Pelikan, and E. David Willis. Leiden: E. J. Brill, 1977.

[86] John Rist, ed. *The Stoics.* Berkeley and Los Angeles: University of California Press, 1978.

[87] Danton B. Sailor. "Newton's Debt to Cudworth." *Journal of the History of Ideas* 49 (1988): 511-18.

[88] Samuel Sambursky. *Physics of the Stoics.* 1959; rpt. London: Hutchinson, 1971.

[89] Samuel Sandmel. *Philo of Alexandria: An Introduction.* New York: Oxford University Press, 1979.

[90] Jason Lewis Saunders. *Justus Lipsius: The Philosophy of Renaissance Stoicism.* New York: Liberal Arts Press, 1955.

[91] Simon Schaffer. "Newton's Comets and the Transformation of Astrology." In Patrick Curry, ed., *Astrology, Science and Society. Historical Essays.* Woodbridge, Suffolk: Boydell Press, 1987.

[92] P. B. Scheuer and G. Debrock, eds. *Newton's Scientific and Philosophical Legacy.* International Archives of the History of Ideas, no. 123. Dordrecht: Kluwer Academic Publishers, 1988.

[93] Hillel Schwartz. *The French Prophets: The History of a Millenarian Group in Eighteenth-Century England.* Berkeley and Los Angeles: University of California Press, 1980.

[94] Taylor, Frank Sherwood. "The Idea of the Quintessence." In E. Ashworth Underwood, ed., *Science, Medicine, and History: Essays on the Evolution of Scientific Thought and Medical Practice Written in Honour of Charles Singer,* vol. 1. London: Oxford University Press, Geoffrey Cumberlege, 1953.

[95] Arnold Thackray. *Atoms and Powers: An Essay on Newtonian Matter-Theory and the Development of Chemistry.* Cambridge: Harvard University Press, 1970.

[96] G. Verbeke. *L'Evolution de la doctrine du pneuma du stoicism à S. Augustin: Etude Philosophique.* Bibliothèque de l'Institut Supérieur de Philosophie Université de Louvain. Paris: Desclée De Brouwer; Louvain: Editions de l'Institut Supérieur de Philosophie, 1945.

[97] Jacob Viner. *The Role of Providence in the Social Order: An Essay in Intellectual History. Jayne Lectures for 1966.* Foreword by Joseph R. Strayer. Memoirs of the American Philosophical Society Held at Philadelphia for Promoting Useful Knowledge, vol. 90. Philadelphia: American Philosophical Society, 1972.

[98] W. A. Wallace. "Newton's Early Writings: Beginning of a New Direction." In G. V. Coyne, M. Heller, and J. Zyci ski, eds., *Newton and the New Direction in Science: Proceedings of the Cracow Conference 25 to 28 May 1987.* Vatican City: Specola Vaticana, 1988.

[99] Charles Webster *From Paracelsus to Newton: Magic and the Making of Modern Science. The Eddington Memorial Lectures Delivered at Cambridge, November 1980.* Cambridge: Cambridge University Press, 1982.

[100] Richard S. Westfall. "Isaac Newton's *Theologiae Gentilis Origines Philosophicae.*" In W. Warren Wa-

gar, ed., *The Secular Mind: Transformations of Faith in Modern Europe. Essays Presented to Franklin L. Baumer, Randolph W. Townsend Professor of History, Yale University.* New York: Holmes and Meier, 1982.

[101] Richard S. Westfall. *Never at Rest: A Biography of Isaac Newton.* Cambridge and New York: Cambridge University Press, 1980.

[102] Derek T. Whiteside. "Before the *Principia:* The Maturing of Newton's Thoughts on Dynamical Astronomy, 1664-1684." *Journal for the History of Astronomy* 1 (1970): 5-19.

[103] Derek T. Whiteside. "Isaac Newton: Birth of a Mathematician." *Notes and Records of the Royal Society of London* 19 (1964): 53-62.

[104] Derek T. Whiteside. "Sources and Strengths of Newton's Early Mathematical Thought." In *The Annus Mirabilis of Sir Isaac Newton Tricentennial Celebration. Texas Quarterly* 10, no. 3 (Autumn 1967): 69-85.

[105] Lancelot Law Whyte. *Essay on Atomism: From Democritus to 1960.* 1961; rpt. New York: Harper and Row, 1963.

[106] Curtis Wilson. "How Did Kepler Discover His First Two Laws?" *Scientific American* 226, no. 3 (1972): 93-106.

[107] Curtis Wilson. "Kepler's Derivation of the Elliptical Path." *Isis* 59 (1968): 5-25.

FURTHER READING

Bibliography

Wallis, Peter and Ruth Wallis. *Newton and Newtoniana, 1672-1975: A Bibliography.* Folkestone, England: Dawson, 1977, 362 p.

An exhaustive bibliography of works by and about Newton.

Biography

Westfall, Richard S. *Never at Rest: A Biography of Isaac Newton.* Cambridge: Cambridge University Press, 1980, 960 p.

A definitive biography using recent scholarship. Contains an extensive bibliographic essay.

Criticism

Cohen, I. Bernard. "Newton in the Light of Recent Scholarship." *Isis* 51, Part 4, No. 166 (December 1960): 489-514.

Reviews the reasons for extensive Newtonian historical scholarship, and discusses the variety and revelations of such study.

Markley, Robert. "Representing Order: Natural Philosophy, Mathematics, and Theology in the Newtonian Revolution." In *Chaos and Order: Complex Dynamics in Literature and Science,* edited by N. Katherine Hayles, pp. 125-48. Chicago: University of Chicago Press, 1991.

Challenges historical scientists who assert that Newton and his peers "reflexively identified order with mathematics" and argues that "the discourses of 'order' before and during the Newtonian revolution are the sites of complex attempts both to describe accurately and to idealize the natural world."

Scheurer, P. B. and G. Debrock, eds. *Newton's Scientific and Philosophical Legacy.* Dordrecht: Kluwer Academic Publishers, 1988, 382 p.

Collection of essays dealing with Newtonian science, as Newton himself understood the term "science"; the influence of Newton on later science; the methodological influence of Newton; and the philosophical legacy of Newton.

Early Reception and Influence

INTRODUCTION

Newton had a profound impact on the realms of mathematics and science through his discoveries, methods, and conclusions. Although some of his principles have been replaced by modern theories and twentieth-century advancements, his work remains the foundation of many aspects of modern science. Not only have his achievements influenced later scientific developments, but his principles and discoveries also deeply penetrated the seventeenth-, eighteenth-, and nineteenth-century philosophical and literary arenas as well.

Critical Reception

Critics such as Henry Guerlac and P. M. Rattansi have analyzed the reception Newton received in the late seventeenth and early eighteenth centuries. While many scholars have held that the *Principia* was ignored on the European continent, Guerlac asserts that this was not the case. Prior to the publication of *Principia,* Newton was hailed as a mathematical genius; his work in mathematics was held in higher regard than his theories of light and color and his invention of the reflecting telescope. Publication of *Principia* served to further bolster Newton's status as a mathematician. Guerlac does concede that German philosopher and mathematician Gottfried Wilhelm Leibniz (1646-1716) and Dutch mathematician, physicist, and astronomer Christian Huygens (1629-95) were "competent, sophisticated, and persistent critics of Newton's theory of celestial motions." Leibniz's criticisms and his later conflict with Newton over who had discovered calculus (among other areas of debate) notwithstanding, Leibniz greatly admired Newton's work, Guerlac insists. Rattansi also takes note of Huygens' and Leibniz's critiques of Newton's theories, contrasting their negative appraisals with English astronomer Edmond Halley's (1656-1742) "awe" of Newton's thinking. Rattansi goes on to trace the influence of Voltaire (1694-1778) in familiarizing an educated public with Newton's scientific ideas. In his crusade to promote Newton, Rattansi argues, Voltaire had to "dethrone" René Descartes and his purely mechanistic conception of the universe.

In the nineteenth century, poet and philosopher Samuel Taylor Coleridge (1772-1834) commented on Newton in a number of letters and notes, noting the debt Newton owed to Johannes Kepler. Remarking on the limitations of Newton's way of thinking, Coleridge observed that Kepler, John Milton, and William Shakespeare were all "greater" individuals than Newton. In addition to criticizing Newton's *Opticks,* Coleridge contended that *Observations upon the Prophecies of Daniel and the Apocalypse of St. John* seems to be "little less than mere raving." Other nineteenth-century writers and thinkers, including Georg Wilhelm Friedrich Hegel (1770-1831), Johann Wolfgang von Goethe (1749-1832), and William Blake (1757-1827), also took issue with Newton's work. M. J. Petry analyzes Hegel's opposition to Newton and Newtonianism, demonstrating that Hegel criticized "the scientific procedures on which Newtonianism was based." Petry stresses, however, that Hegel's arguments were focused more on the way Newton was being interpreted and used by Hegel's nineteenth-century contemporaries than on Newton himself. Both Newton and Hegel, Petry explains, believed that "all valid knowledge concerning the natural world must be based upon observation and experiment." Petry also notes that Hegel attempted to demonstrate that Goethe's theory of colors was superior to Newton's. Dennis L. Sepper investigates Goethe's arguments against Newton's theory of white light and colors. While acknowledging the limitations of Goethe's polemic against Newton's theory, Sepper maintains that Goethe's critique was justified on several grounds. One of Goethe's primary difficulties with Newton's theory, Sepper explains, was that Newton's methodology "misconceived" the proper relationship between theory and phenomenon. Like his German counterparts, Blake lodged a complaint against Newton's science as well, objecting to what he viewed as Newton's spiritless, mechanical conception of the universe. Stuart Peterfreund analyzes Blake's objection to Newtonian physics as evidenced by his *Milton.* Unlike Hegel and Goethe, who focused their attention on Newton's *Opticks,* Blake's anti-Newtonianism stemmed from his reading of *Principia.* Peterfreund demonstrates that Blake viewed "the painful and oppressive conditions of human existence . . . as being in part descended from the 'reasonable' assumptions of Newtonian physics, translated into Newtonian metaphysics and implemented as social policy."

Blake was not the only poet influenced in some manner by Newton and Newtonianism. Julia L. Epstein and Mark L. Greenburg trace the changing image of the rainbow in literature, maintaining that, following the publication of Newton's *Opticks* and the absorption of its ideas into both scientific and popular culture, the image of the rainbow was dramatically transformed. Prior to Newton, the rainbow image in science, religion, and literature served primarily as a symbol for the relationship between God and humankind. In post-Newtonian poetry, "biblical authority" has been replaced by "human genius, acting to discover the workings of the wondrous image." In the poetry of James Thomson (1700-48), Epstein and Greenburg state, the relationship between Newton and the physical world is sexualized, with a feminized nature yields herself to the masculine scientist. Thomson's depiction of a rainbow, they observe, "personifies a natural phenomenon in intimate embrace with Newton in a richly-evocative scene that . . . concerns light, the scientist's participatory eye, and the power of Newton's mind to 'transpierce' a willing lover's outer garments in order to delight in her inner form." Richard Glover (1712-85) followed Thomson's lead in his own poetry, portraying Newton's investigations of light as "a charming encounter between lovers." Coleridge, John Keats (1795-1821) and other nineteenth-century Romantic poets took a different view of Newton, nature, and the rainbow, however; these writers protested that the image of rainbow was diminished by Newton's analysis of it. In Blake's poetry, however, the rainbow was invigorated with new life. According to Epstein and Greenburg, Newton's probings embodied for Blake "the potential for a commingling, not between God and his creation, or between the poet and God, or even between the poet and Newton, but instead a commingling between artist and audience."

CRITICISM

Samuel Taylor Coleridge (essay date 1834?)

SOURCE: "Isaac Newton," in *Coleridge on the Seventeenth Century,* edited by Roberta Florence Brinkley, Duke University Press, 1955, pp. 399-408.

[*In the following excerpts, which are taken from various published and unpublished sources, including letters and notes written in the margins of books, Coleridge comments on Newton's debt to Johannes Kepler, criticizes Newton's* Opticks, *and notes that Newton's* Observations *on the biblical books of Daniel and Revelations are "little less than mere raving." Given the variety of sources from which these observations are drawn, the date assigned is based on the year of Coleridge's death.*]

Galileo was a great genius, and so was Newton; but it would take two or three Galileos and Newtons to make one Kepler. It is in the order of Providence, that the inventive, generative, constitutive mind—the Kepler—should come first; and then that the patient and collective mind—the Newton—should follow, and elaborate the pregnant queries and illumining guesses of the former. The laws of the planetary system are, in fact,

due to Kepler. There is not a more glorious achievement of scientific genius upon record, than Kepler's guesses, prophecies, and ultimate apprehension of the law of the mean distances of the planets as connected with the periods of their revolutions round the sun. Gravitation, too, he had fully conceived; but, because it seemed inconsistent with some received observations on light, he gave it up, in allegiance, as he says, to Nature. Yet the idea vexed and haunted his mind; *"Vexat me et lacessit,"* are his words, I believe.[7]

* * *

When, however, after a short interval, the Genius of Kepler, expanded and organized in the soul of Newton, and there (if I may hazard so bold an expression) refining itself into an almost celestial Clearness, had expelled the Cartesian Vortices, then the necessity of an active power, of positive forces present in the Material Universe, forced itself on the conviction. For as a Law without a Law-giver is a mere abstraction; so a *Law* without an Agent to realize it, a *Constitution* without an abiding Executive, is, in fact, not a Law but *an Idea!*[8]

* * *

In the system of gravity, Newton only developed the idea of Kepler. He advanced a step, and there he fixed his followers. Kepler would have progressed, or have been stationary in act at least.[9]

* * *

What a thing, what a living thing is not Shakespeare—and in point of real utility I look on Sir Isaac Newton as a very puny agent compared with Milton—and I have taken some pains with the comparison and disputed with transient conviction for hours together in favour of the former.[10]

* * *

Newton *was* a great man, but you must excuse me if I think that it would take many Newtons to make one Milton.[11]

* * *

My opinion is this—that deep Thinking is attainable only by a man of deep Feeling, and that all Truth is a species of Revelation. The more I understand of Sir Isaac Newton's works, the more boldly I dare utter to my own mind, & therefore to *you,* that I believe the Souls of 500 Sir Isaac Newtons would go to the making up of a Shakespere or a Milton. But if it please the Almighty to grant me health, hope, and a steady mind, (always the 3 clauses of my hourly prayers) before my 30th year I will thoroughly understand the whole of Newton's Works—at present, I must content myself with endeavouring to make myself entire master of his easier work, that on Optics. I am exceedingly delighted with the beauty and newness of his experiments, & with the accuracy of his *immediate* Deductions from them—but the opinions founded on these Deductions, and indeed his whole Theory is, I am persuaded, so exceedingly superficial as without impropriety to be deemed false. Newton was a mere materialist—*mind,* in his system is always passive,—a lazy Looker-on on an external World. If the mind be not *passive,* if it be indeed made in God's Image, & that too in the sublimest sense—the Image of the *Creator*—there is ground for suspicion, that any system built on the passiveness of the mind must be false, as a system.[12]

* * *

Even where, as in the **Optics** of Sir I. Newton, or rather in that part of the Newtonian optics which relates to colour, the premises are derived from experiment, the facts must have been proved before the scientific reasoning begins. In reference both to the process and to the result or product of science and as far as the knowledge is scientific, there is no difference in the character of the premises. Whether self evident, or the evident result of some other science grounded on self evident truths, or prepared for the occasion by observation, or experiment, the premises occupy the same place & exercise the same function as premises of a science. For if they were not (*expostulata* and *præconcessa*) demanded on the one side & preconceded on the other, the science could not have commenced; it would have perished in birth.[13]

* * *

Sir Isaac Newton at the end of the last edition of his **Optics,** supposes that a very subtile & elastic fluid, which he calls æther, is diffused thro' the pores of gross bodies, as well as thro' the open spaces that are void of gross matter; he supposes it to pierce all bodies, and to touch their least particles, acting on them with a force proportional to their number or to the matter of the body on which it acts. He supposes likewise, that it is rarer in the pores of bodies than in open spaces, & even rarer in small pores and dense bodies, than in large pores and rare bodies; & also that its density increases in receding from gross matter; so for instance as to be greater at the 1/100 of an inch from the surface of any body, than at its surface; & so on. To the action of this æther he ascribes the attractions of gravitation & cohæsion, the attraction & repulsion of electrical bodies, the mutual influences of bodies & light upon each other, the effects & communication of heat, & the performance of animal sensation & motion. David Hartley from whom this account of æther is chiefly borrowed, makes it the instrument of propagating those vibrations or confygurative motions which are ideas. As it appears to me, no hypothesis ever in-

volved so many contradictions: for how can the same fluid be both dense & rare in the same body at one time? yet in the Earth as gravitating to the Moon, it must be very rare; & in the Earth as gravitating to the Sun, it must be very dense. For, as Andrew Baxter well observes, it doth not appear sufficient to account how this fluid may act with a force proportional to the body to which another is impelled, to assert that it is rarer in great bodies than in small ones: it must be farther asserted that this fluid is rarer or denser in the same body, whether small or great, according as the body to which that is impelled is itself small or great. But whatever may be the solidity of this objection, the following seems unanswerable.

If every particle thro' the whole solidity of a heavy body, receive its impulse from the particles of this fluid, it should seem that the fluid itself must be as dense as the very densest heavy body, gold for instance; there being as many impinging particles in the one, as there are gravitating particles in the other which receive their gravitation by being impinged upon: so that, throwing gold or any heavy body upward, against the impulse of this fluid, would be like throwing gold *thro'* gold; and as this æther must be equally diffused over the whole sphere of its activity, it must be as dense when it impels cork as when it impels gold: so that to throw a piece of cork upward, would be as if we endeavoured to make cork penetrate a medium as dense as gold: & tho' we were to adopt the extravagant opinions which have been advanced concerning the progressions of pores, yet however porous we suppose a body, if it be not all pore, the argument holds equally; the fluid must be *as* dense as the body in order to give every particle its impulse.

It has been asserted that Sir Isaac Newtons philosophy leads in its consequences to Atheism; perhaps not without reason, for if matter by any powers or properties *given* to it, can produce the order of the visible world, & even generate thought; why may it not have possessed such properties by *inherent* right? & where is the necessity of a God? Matter is, according to the mechanic philosophy, capable of acting most wisely & most beneficently without consciousness of Wisdom or Benevolence; & what more does the Atheist assert? if matter could possess these properties, why might it not possess them from all eternity? Sir Isaac Newtons Deity seems to be alternately operose & indolent, to have delegated so much power as to make it inconceivable what he can have reserved. He is dethroned by Vice-regent second causes.

We seem placed here to acquire a knowledge of *effects.* Whenever we would pierce into the *Adyta* of Causation, we bewilder ourselves—and all, that laborious Conjecture can do, is to fill up the gaps of Imagination. We are restless, because *invisible* things are not the objects of vision—and philosophical Systems, for the most part, are received not for their Truth, but in proportion as they give to Causes a susceptibility of being *seen,* whenever our visual organs shall have become sufficiently powerful.[14]

* * *

I am anxious to leave the specific objections of the Mathematicians to Goethe's Farbenlehre as far as it is an attack on the *assumptions* of Newton. To me, I confess, Newton's assumptions, first, of a *Ray* of Light, as a physical synodical *Individuum,* secondly that 7 specific individua are co-existent (by what copula?) in this complex yet divisible Ray; thirdly, that the Prism is a mere mechanic Dissector of this Ray; and lastly, that Light, as the common result, is = confusion; have always, and years before I ever heard of Goethe, appeared monstrous *Fictions!*[15]

* * *

Oken, L., Erste Ideen zur Theorie des Lichtes *(Jena: 1808), p. 14.*

> Es ist nichts leichter, als *Newtons* Optik zu widerlegen, ohne allen Apparat, mit einigen Prismen von ganz gemeinen Glase, mit Linsen, gefärbtem Papier nebst einem finstern Zimmer ist alles abgethan; mehr aber wird erfodert, um die wahre Theorie des Lichtes durch Versuche zu beweisen, weil das Licht nicht in einem bloss mechanischen Brechen, Ablenken, Zerstreuen der Stralen besteht, sondern in einem chemischen Act, der bis ins Innerste der Materie wirkt und sie verändert, nicht etwas bloss durch Erwärmung, also Ausdehnung; sondern durch geistige Action durch Polarisirungen, aus denen chemische Änderungen hervorgehen. Ich spreche hier stark und hart aber nicht ungerecht gegen *Newton,* nur um die Gelehrten mit Ernst auf die bisher gänze Theorie des Lichtes aufmerksam zu machen. In der Folge werde ich *Newtons* Lehre ganz ruhig widerlegen.

Good heavens! how much more good would Oken have done, how much more both wit and wisdom would have been displayed, if instead of this rough Railing and *d—n-your-eyes-you-lie* Ipsedixits, he had *begun* with this "quite quiet confutation of the Newtonian Doctrine," especially it being so very easy a task! Goethe (not indeed *"ganz ruhig"*) had attempted it in detail both by impeachment of Newton's Experiments, and by Counter-experiments of his own. And yet G. himself confesses, that he had not succeeded in convincing or converting a single Mathematician, not even among his own friends and Intimates! That a clear and sober Confutation of Newton's Theory of Colors is practicable, the exceeding unsatisfied state, in which Sir I. Newton's first Book of *Optics* leaves my mind— strongly persuades me. And it is Oken's mountebank Boasting and Threatening that alone makes me sceptical as to his own ability to perform the promise, here

given by him. S. T. C. P. s. I readily admit, that the full exhibition of another Theory adequate to the Sum of the Phænomena, and grounded on more safe and solid principles, would virtually be the best confutation— but no one who knows [left unfinished].

Oken, Erste Ideen, *p. 40.*

Goethe, & then Schelling & Steffens, had opposed to the Newtonian Optics the ancient doctrine of Light and Shadow on the grand principle of Polarity—Yellow being the positive, Blue the negative, Pole, Red the Culmination and Green, the Indifference. Oken follows them—but stop! He waits till they are out of sight—Hangs out a new Banner (i. e. metaphors) and becomes a Leader himself.[16]

* * *

de Boyer, Kabbalistische Briefe, *IV, 114-15.*

> In truth sage and wise Abukibak, the greatest Geometricians have been obliged to abandon in Physics their principal demonstration. We see for instance one example in Newton: although Geometry showed him the infinite divisibility of matter, as a Physicist he dared not acknowledge it; he felt what a repugnance he had to the divisibility of matter not stopping at a certain point. He admitted the atoms of Epicurus; and sustained that it was impossible to divide into several parts what had originally been made one by the disposition of God himself.

What philosophic mathematician ever supposed Geometry to be anything else, than a system of the conceivable and inconceivable in the mind's constructive Intuitions? It is *wholly* ideal. Newton's solid atoms are utter aliens from Geometry, in which the mind exclusively contemplates it's own energies; and *applies* them not otherwise, than hypothetically. Newton erred by introducing *Dogmatic Realism* into the *Ideal World.* Solid atoms are not an *hypothesis,* as Gravity is; but a mere *Hypopoësis.*[17]

* * *

Various are the difficulties that oppose themselves to my comprehension of the Newtonian Theory of Comets. Some of these admit seemingly of a more natural solution on the Helvetian Hypothesis (= the old Aristotelian idea rectified and expanded by it's adaptation to the Copernican System) that the substance of Comets is meteoric and their curve of motion a parabola. For the moment, therefore, they throw some weight into the Helvetian Scale: tho' I have not the smallest doubt that all against all, the latter would kick the beam. Some of these difficulties relate to the facts of the disturbances of the cometary path by the attraction of the orbs, nearest which it must have passed, having been often *assumed,* but never *proved*—and vice versâ that the Comet, which passed so close to Jupiter and to one of the Jovial Satellites, had a *nucleus* calculated as equal in magnitude to Jupiter itself. The same Comet had an alarming Perihelium to our Moon. And yet neither the Jovial nor the Tellurial Satellite suffered the slightest perturbation. But this is of little comparative weight with me, being conscious that I have not enough mathematico-astronomical science to appreciate rightly the force or weakness of the Objection. I turn therefore to the physical phænomena, and here I cannot hesitate a moment in assigning the preference to your view of the Cauda, as a circumambient atmosphere of prodigious expansion, deriving it's apparent form and direction from it's relative position to the Sun and the solar radiance. But here too it is that I am puzzled—and namely by the following argument. If the vapor be self-luminous, and analogous to electric matter, the solution, in the form above stated at least, will no longer apply. The Solar Rays can in this case be causative of the direction, size and increased Splendor of the Tail &c., by *chemical excitement,* of which we have no proof or tenable analogy. On the other hand, that the phænomenon does somehow or other depend on the proximity of the Sun is a matter *of fact*—but if self-luminous, the very contrary *ought to* be the fact: and this will remain a most weighty objection to the *self-luminous* hypothesis, till some valid proof shall be given of an *evocative* action: the solar light not *constituting,* but *exciting* and *evolving,* the varying luminosity of the cometary atmosphere. And on this supposition the apparent position of the Tail must be the *real* one. If then to avoid this complex difficulty, I deny it's self-luminous nature and adhere to your scheme, I am encountered by another objection—and it is of this that I crave a solution from your sounder and more extended knowledge of these subjects. The reflective power of æriform matter is *inversely* as the rarity—the rarity on the other hand in a direct ratio to the expansion, and of a continuous increase (i. e. diminution of density) so stupendous that according to the Newtonian Calculus a cubic Inch of Air at the surface of our Earth would at the distance of a thousand miles suffice to fill the whole Area within the orbit of Saturn. Yet what is this to an expansion of 50, nay according to Schröter of more than 100,000,000 of miles, as affirmed of the luminous Tails of certain Comets? How is it conceivable, that a vapor of such rarity (an arithmetical denomination of which would require an x = 0 as the quotient of the density at the end of the first hundred Leagues—so that long before we had reached half-way thro' the Fan-tail we should have in secula seculorum)—how is it possible, I say, that a vapor of such rarity should *reflect* light or even perceptibly obey the projectile or the gravitating force?

I cherish, I must confess, a *pet* system, a bye blow of my own Philosophizing, but it is so unlike to all the opinions and modes of reasoning grounded on the Atoms, Corpuscular and mechanic Philosophy, which is alone tolerated in the present day, and which since the

time of Newton has been universally taken as synonimous with Philosophy itself—that I must content myself with caressing the heretical Brat in private under the name of Zoödynamic method—or the doctrine of *Life.*[18]

* * *

But the patient wisdom of the experimental philosophy teaches its disciples that investigation is in all cases a sacred duty: and the conviction of this truth actuated the two great masters of this philosophy in a manner most apposite to our argument. Sir Isaac confessed that he had once seriously studied astrology, and Boyle did not conceal that he had formerly been attached to alchemy and natural magic.[19]

* * *

The immortal Newton, to whom more than to any other human being Europe owes the purification of its general notions concerning the heavenly bodies, studied Astrology with much earnestness, and did not reject it till he had demonstrated the falsehood of all its pretended grounds and principles.[20]

* * *

To invent was different from to discover. A watchmaker invented a time-piece; but a profound thinker only could discover. Sir Isaac Newton, when he thought upon the apple falling from the tree, discovered but did not invent the law of gravitation; others, following this grand idea, carried elementary principles into particles, and elucidated chemistry. Sir Isaac Newton, having once found that a body fell to the centre, knew that all other appearances of nature would receive a consequence, agreeably to the law of cause and effect; for it was a criterion of science, that when causes were determined, effects could be stated with the accuracy of prophecy.[21]

* * *

We praise Newton's clearness and steadiness. He *was* clear and steady, no doubt, while working out, by the help of an admirable geometry, the idea brought forth by another. Newton had his ether and could not rest in—he could not conceive—the idea of a law. He thought it a physical thing after all. As for his chronology, I believe, those who are most competent to judge, rely on it less and less every day. His lucubrations on Daniel and the Revelations seem to me little less than mere raving.[22]

* * *

In the Hebrew poets each thing has a life of its own, and yet they are all our life. In God they move and live and *have* their being; not *had,* as the cold system of Newtonian Theology represents, but *have.*[23]

* * *

Robinson, Works, *IV, 17.*[24]

First: this donation implies, that in the opinion of the donors, the Bible is a *plain,* easy book . . .

!! What if I were to call Newton's **Principia** a *plain,* easy Book, because certain passages were axiomatic, & because the results were evident to common-sense? What? The Pentateuch? the Solomon's Song! The Prophets in general, & Ezekiel in particular! What? the Ecclesiastes? The praise of Jael? of Ehud? of David? What? St. John's Gospel, & his Revelations? the *apparent* Discordances of the Evangelists in the most important affirmation, that of the Resurrection? What? St. Paul's Epistles, declared by a contemporary Apostle, dark and hard? are these parts of a plain & easy Book? . . .

Robinson, Works, *IV, 19.*

Secondly: the donation of a Bible only, implies, that each reader hath *a right of private judgment.* This is another just notion, truly scriptural, and entirely protestant. To give a man a book to read, and to deny him the right of judging its meaning, seems the summit of absurdity.

Doubtless!—but may there not be folly in giving a child (and an ignorant man is a child in knowledge) a book, he cannot understand, without any assistance to enable him so to do? To an ignorant man I would not give Newton at all: for not only he cannot understand it, but he may do very well without it. To the same man I would give the Bible, though a very large part would be worse than unintelligible, for it would be misintelligible—yet as it does concern him, I would give it, only with "all the means & appliances to boot," that would preclude a dangerous misinterpretation.

* * *

The commercial spirit, and the ascendency of the experimental philosophy which took place at the close of the seventeenth century, though both good and beneficial in their own kinds, combined to foster its corruption. Flattered and dazzled by the real or supposed discoveries which it had made, the more the understanding was enriched, the more did it become debased; till science itself put on a selfish and sensual character, and *immediate utility,* in exclusive reference to the gratification of the wants and appetites of the animal, the vanities and caprices of the social, and the ambition of the political, man was imposed as the test of all intellectual powers and pursuits. *Worth*

was degraded into a lazy synonyme of *value*; and the value was exclusively attached to the interest of the senses.[25]

Notes

[7] Oct. 8, 1830. *Table Talk S,* VI, 350-51.

[8] *Aids,* pp. 393-94. Cf. Shedd, I, 360-61.

[9] Allsop, *Letters,* I, 127.

[10] To Southey, Aug. 11, 1801. Griggs, *Unp. Letters,* I, 180.

[11] July 4, 1833. *Table Talk S,* VI, 469.

[12] To Thomas Poole, March 23, 1801. British Museum, Add. MSS, 35,343, fol. 265 verso-266. Printed in *Letters,* I, 351-52.

[13] Coleridge, *On the Divine Ideas,* pp. 219-21. Printed for the first time by the kind permission of the Huntington Library from HM 8195.

[14] This comment appears in the first edition of Southey's *Joan of Arc* but is transcribed from British Museum Add. MSS, 28,016, fol. 26 verso-29. Only the last paragraph is in Coleridge's hand; the remainder is in Southey's hand. The note is to *Joan of Arc,* II, 1. 34: "Their subtle fluids, impacts, essences."

[15] To Ludwig Tieck, July 4, 1817. Griggs, *Unp. Letters,* II, 201.

[16] Comments printed for the first time from volume in the British Museum, *c.* 44. g. 4.(1).

[17] Jean Baptiste de Boyer, Marquis D'Argens, *Kabbalistische Briefe* (8 vols. in 2; Danzig: 1773). British Museum, C. 43. a. 2. Part IV, pp. 114-15. Comment is printed for the first time.

[18] To the editor of *Blackwood's,* Add. MSS, 34,225, fol. 187.

[19] To the author of "A Letter to Edward Long Fox, M. D.," *Athenæum,* May 2, 1908, p. 542.

[20] *Statesman's Manual,* Appendix C, p. xxiii.

[21] Lecture VIII of Surrey Institute Lectures, 1812-13. Reported in the *Gazette.* Printed by Raysor, *Shakes. Crit.,* II, 289.

[22] Oct. 8, 1830. *Table Talk S,* VI, 351.

[23] To W. Sotheby, Sept. 10, 1802. Coleridge, E. H., *Letters,* I, 406.

[24] Robert Robinson, *Miscellaneous Works* (4 vols.; Harlow: 1807) with Coleridge's notes is in the Huntington Library, which has given me permission to excerpt the two notes here printed for the first time.

[25] *Statesman's Manual,* Appendix C, p. xvi.

M. J. Petry (lecture date 1981)

SOURCE: "Hegel's Criticism of Newton," in *CLIO,* Vol. 13, No. 4, Summer 1984, pp. 331-48.

[*In the following essay, originally delivered as a lecture in 1981, the critic surveys Georg Wilhelm Friedrich Hegel's criticism of the scientific procedures that formed the basis of Newtonianism. Petry argues that Hegel opposed the conclusions drawn by nineteenth-century Newtonians, including physicists and philosophers, more than he opposed Newton himself.*]

Introduction

Even now, when we look back upon Newton's **Principia** and **Opticks** over a period of nearly three hundred years, it is difficult to imagine what modern physics would have been like had these books never been written. The experimental procedures on which they are based, their manner of exposition, the discoveries they made known, are so indispensable a part of the modern physicist's stock in trade, that he would be at a loss to define his discipline at all clearly were they to be brought into fundamental discredit. Nor is it easy to make out a convincing case for regarding Newton's accomplishment as nothing more than the embodiment of his intellectual presuppositions, his world-view, his conception of scientific method. Although it cannot be denied that his works bear the marks of their time and of the conditions under which they were written, one can hardly help admitting that they also communicate a body of universal scientific knowledge. Is it at all reasonable to assume that if Newton had not announced that "every particle of matter in the universe attracts every other particle with a force that varies inversely as the squares of the distances between them and directly as the products of their masses," no one else would have done so? If he had not demonstrated that "the whiteness of the sun's light is compounded of all the primary colours mixed in due proportion," is it at all likely that we should still be ignorant of the fact?[1] Any modern physicist who takes the trouble to consult Newton's texts soon discovers, moreover, that he was able to make such discoveries because he was informed and clearsighted enough to devise programs of research which would still do credit to the great majority of his modern counterparts. By present-day standards Newton's scientific procedures are limited and cumbersome, but no modern physicist will have any difficulty in realizing that as a fundamental discipline they still constitute the broad tradition within which he lives and moves and has his being.

It is of paramount importance, therefore, that anyone attempting to evaluate the present-day significance of Hegel's manner of philosophizing should take into consideration his attitude to Newtonian physics. If any attempt is to be made to establish the contemporary relevance of Hegelianism, it is essential not to overlook the fact that its originator was highly critical not only of the scientific procedures on which Newtonianism was based, but also of the conclusions being drawn from them by early nineteenth-century physicists and philosophers. What is more, this criticism was by no means a mere sideline, a fortuitous consequence of a broader strategy, something incidental to Hegel's central philosophical convictions, for he made no bones about proclaiming that he was prepared to stake his whole reputation on it. He inaugurated his career as a university teacher with a critical analysis of Newtonian mechanics, and over a period of almost thirty years made a point of publicly announcing the results of experimental work, the main object of which was to demonstrate the superiority of Goethe's theory of colors over its Newtonian counterpart.[2] To the historian of philosophy, this assessment of Newtonian science is therefore a matter of no little importance. To the contemporary thinker, to anyone aware of the directions given to modern philosophy by dialectical materialism and the Vienna Circle, to anyone attempting to convince anyone worth convincing that Hegelian methodology still warrants serious attention, it should surely be a matter of absolutely central concern.

It is worth noting, therefore, that of the fifteen thousand five hundred main courses in philosophy given in the universities of the German Federal Republic between 1945 and 1970, only two were concerned exclusively with Hegel's treatment of the natural sciences. The neglect of the subject in other countries during this period was even more complete, and one finds no reason to revise one's general assessment of it if one takes the trouble to check on the books and articles that were published. How is one to account for this almost incredible lack of intellectual curiosity? To some extent it was probably due to nothing more than the structure forced upon our university education by the need for specialists, to the widely recognized lack of communication between natural scientists, historians, and philosophers. But it seems also to have been the result of bad history, of inadequate research, of the successful propagation of the simplistic idea that in Newton "the study of nature saw a goal placed before it which, over the following two hundred years, it was to regard as the only thinkable one."[3] Such history is never entirely harmless, but in this particular case it has contributed to the establishment of a wholly unacceptable prejudice.

Newton

To say that Newton's scientific accomplishment was more than simply the embodiment of his intellectual presuppositions, is not to say that these presuppositions are irrelevant to the understanding of the intrinsic significance and reception of this accomplishment. The great bulk of his private papers remained unknown to the eighteenth century, but even then it was common knowledge that he was not simply a mathematician and a physicist, that powerful personal convictions had driven him to his scientific work. It was no secret, for example, that he held unorthodox views concerning the nature of the Christian Trinity. The neo-Platonism of his Cambridge colleagues, especially Henry More, had had a great influence upon him, and it was evidently within the framework of this manner of thinking that he conceived of the ontological status of causation. It was William Law who first claimed that Newton had "ploughed with Behmen's heifer when he brought forth the discovery of the three great laws of matter and motion."[4] Of recent years, many of his private papers have been examined and published, and modern scholarship has, if anything, tended to overemphasize the importance of his private philosophy. His most recent biographers, for example, have brought out the significance of his psychology and his alchemical interests to such an extent, that there would appear to be the danger of overlooking the fact that his mathematics and physics can also be grasped and appreciated without knowing anything at all about the personal peculiarities of their author.[5]

It is not often realized that although Newton influenced nearly every branch of the physical and human sciences throughout the eighteenth century, the scientific scope of his published work is fairly limited. Although he concerned himself with nearly every branch of pure and applied mathematics, for example, he paid very little attention to the logical foundations of the science, and his contemporaries were not slow in calling attention to this neglect. Nieuwentijt, in *Gronden van Zekerheid* (1720), showed how essential it is to draw a sharp distinction between the philosophical or logical foundations of pure and of applied mathematics. Berkeley, in *The Analyst* (1734), while not calling in question the utility of the calculus or the validity of the results obtained by means of it, demonstrated clearly the difficulties implicit in its theoretical foundations. Newton was able to deal successfully with the motion of bodies in the first book of the **Principia** because he had proved that the force of attraction between two homogeneously layered spheres is directed along the line of their centers and is independent of their diameters. In his study of the miscellaneous problems of fluid mechanics in the second book he was much less successful, however, and it was left to the Bernoullis and Euler to attempt to master the highly complex questions he raised concerning the mechanics of rigid and flexible and fluid and elastic bodies. Since the conclusions he reached concerning the motion of bodies in resisting mediums were so varied and hypothetical, he made no attempt to apply them to the solar system in the third book of the **Principia,** although it had been his original intention to do so.[6] In his **Opticks** he was highly successful in laying the foundations of the modern physical theory of light and colors, but he barely touched upon the complicated problems of color perception. When Edmund Halley, for example, called his attention to the curious phenomena of colored shadows, he attempted to explain them as a purely objective or physical matter, whereas it was soon to become increasingly apparent, especially to De Godart and Rumford later in the eighteenth century, that a satisfactory explanation of them would also have to involve a consideration of subjective or physiological factors.[7]

If we are to account for Newton's reputation throughout the eighteenth century, it is therefore essential that we should not confine ourselves to a consideration of his personal convictions and the obviously successful aspects of his physics. Some may have been persuaded to put his "philosophy" into practice because they approved of his Unitarianism or Behmenism or because they had grasped the significance of his contributions to mechanics and optics, but the great majority did so because they saw him as the most distinguished exponent of the new Baconian brand of experimentalism, of applied philosophy, of the wholly universal scientific methodology which was in the process of proving the practical effectiveness of philosophy by laying the foundations of modern technology and so improving the material condition of the human lot. As President of the Royal Society of London Newton was the institutionalized head of this movement, the embodiment of the widespread conviction that natural philosophy is not merely an individual preoccupation but essentially an intersubjective or social activity. In the eyes of the general public of Europe, he was the foremost representative of the most progressive and effective intellectual movement of the time, the most distinguished proponent of the idea that nature was to be mastered in the practical interests of man through the application of the Baconian inductive method, through the testing, exchanging, and co-ordinating of information by means of scientific societies and their journals.

It is worth considering rather closely the precise nature of this methodology. As against Cartesianism, it involved the rigorous exclusion of all ideas or hypotheses concerning the natural world which could not be tested against observations and verified by experiment. It shared important ground with Aristotelian physics, with Zabarella, and with the highly successful non-Baconian methods of Galileo and Hobbes in that it took the analytical and synthetic procedures of resolution and composition to be central to all scientific work.

The first task of the scientist was to classify and define his sphere of inquiry. The second was to resolve this sphere, by inductive analysis, into a series of sub-spheres or subordinate fields of inquiry, into increasingly basic or general causes or presuppositions. The third was to carry out, in the light of this analysis, a systematic reconstruction of the original field of research which would enable it to be seen in the scientific light of the basic analytical work. In Newton's *Principia,* for example, the solar system was the main sphere of inquiry, the motions of bodies in resisting and nonresisting mediums were the two major subordinate fields, and the layout of the work gave expression to Newton's conception of the interrelationship between the sub-spheres brought to light by his analytical investigations.

The ideal in Cartesian physics had been the resolution of physical investigations into mathematics, or, more precisely, into algebraic formulae. The physicist carried out his empirical investigations with the ultimate objective of discovering clear and distinct conceptions which could be expressed in mathematical terms. The purpose of Spinoza's *Algebraic Calculation of the Rainbow,* for example, was to translate the physical complexity of the phenomenon itself into a series of algebraic equations.[8] In Cartesianism, therefore, mathematics was the ultimate standard by which the success or final validity of empirical inquiry was to be judged. In Newtonianism it was not a standard but a tool which was to be used for calculating on the basis of data. Newton knew, for example, that he could make no progress with his mathematical theory concerning the motions of the Moon without the observations of the astronomer Flamsteed.[9] He was fully aware that as an intersubjective discipline mathematics was no more than the language which enables us to communicate the nature of the regularities we have discovered in nature. Although he was not always as consistent on the point as he should have been, he therefore insisted on drawing a clear distinction between the material realities being investigated and the mathematical formulation of the results of the research. In his famous letters to Richard Bentley on the religious implications of Newtonianism, for example, he censures him for losing sight of this distinction: "You some times speak of gravity as essential and inherent to matter. Pray, do not ascribe that notion to me; for the cause of gravity is what I do not pretend to know, and therefore would take more time to consider of it."[10]

Newtonianism

Since Hegel concerned himself not only with Newton's own writings but also with those of his followers, it is essential, when dealing with the significance of his criticism of eighteenth-century physics and metaphysics, that one should distinguish between the expert Newtonianism of the mathematicians and physi-cists who were aware of both the importance and the limitations of Newton's accomplishment, and the uncritical popularization of his ideas. We have already noticed that although no one who knew anything at all about mathematics and physics could possibly have doubted the usefulness of the calculus, many of the experts were puzzled and perplexed concerning its logical foundations and the ontological status of the computations that could be made by means of it. The prevailing conception of physical reality was that it was basically atomistic. In thinking about the occurrence of motion within this reality, eighteenth-century mathematicians and physicists were therefore obliged to wrestle with the ancient paradoxes of space, time, and motion put forward by Zeno, which had been restated with admirable clarity and sharpness and brought to the attention of the general public by means of Bayle's *Dictionary.* Since it was not yet general practice to distinguish between the purely formal or mathematical aspect of the calculus and its ontological significance, Zeno's paradoxes concerning physical reality gave rise to mathematical perplexities. Berkeley criticized Newton's fluxions as being "the ghosts of departed quantities," and argued that the idea of supposing a finite ratio to exist between two absolutely evanescent terms was absurd and unintelligible. Newton's views on the existence of variables which reach their limits were therefore brought into general discussion, and his followers were obliged to reject the idea of the existence of infinitely small quantities. One of the best modern histories of the development of the calculus therefore characterizes the eighteenth century as "the period of indecision."[11] It was only toward the end of it, and during the early decades of the nineteenth century, that such mathematicians as Lagrange, Lacroix, and Cauchy began to lay the foundations of a rigorous formulation of the calculus by distinguishing with increasing sharpness between its formal and its applied aspects.

Newton's cosmology was also the subject of constant questioning and revision among the experts during the eighteenth century. Buffon attempted to explain the origin of the centrifugal force within the solar system by postulating a collision between the Sun and a comet as a result of which a jet of matter had been torn away from the Sun's surface and had condensed into the planets at various distances from the central body. Laplace suggested that the solar system had originated from an immense incandescent nebula, rotating from west to east, which had eventually broken up into the rotating masses of the solar bodies. The observation of irregularities in the movements of Mercury and of the new planet Uranus discovered in 1781, made it a matter of general knowledge that Newton's law of gravitation could not easily account for all planetary motions.[12]

Apart from the discovery of the importance of physiological factors in the perception of color, the scientists of the eighteenth century also found it necessary to supplement and revise Newton's ideas on the physics of light. Newton had argued, for example, that since all refracting substances disperse the prismatic colors in a constant proportion to their mean refraction, refraction could not be produced without color, and no improvement could therefore be expected from the refracting telescope. As early as 1733, however, a telescope exhibiting objects free from color had been constructed, and by 1758 John Dollond had made the invention public. In 1800 Thomas Young published a paper in which he criticized Newton's rejection of Huyghens's undulatory theory of light, and after calling attention to similarities between the phenomena of sound and light, suggested that a wave theory of light would be an improvement upon Newton's corpuscular theory in providing the basis for progressive research in the field.[13]

While the experts were engaged in developing and revising Newton's contributions to the three main fields in which he had published, and while the technologists were reaping the benefits of a well-founded experimentalism, various popular philosophers were engaged in puffing Newtonianism up into a dogma, a worldview. These popularizers had little interest in Newton's private philosophy, his Unitarianism, neo-Platonism or Behmenism, and the last thing they were capable of doing was to appreciate the significance of his methodology, an attempt to exclude hypothetical theorizing by means of rigorous experimentalism, the practical and theoretical implications of the methods of resolution and composition, the conception of mathematics as a tool and not as a standard, the distinction between material reality and the mathematical formulation of the results of research. Their object was to enlist their interpretation of the scientific advances being made in the service of their conception of enlightenment, and they were not prepared to confine enlightenment to the sober and carefully formulated objectives of Baconianism. The social ideal put forward in Bacon's *New Atlantis* is a Christian monarchy in which institutions cultivating the natural sciences are encouraged by the government as part of a broad policy of furthering social harmony and welfare. Voltaire's book on Newton was part of his general program of opposition to the church and monarchical absolutism. Enlightenment was to be exhibited as incompatible with clericalism and monarchism, and as involving the application of an attitude of mind which had proved its effectiveness in revolutionizing man's conception of the natural world, to the solution of social and cultural problems.[14]

This Newtonian world-view tended to draw its inspiration not from Newton himself, or from the experts who were engaged in the apparently dry and short-sighted business of developing the rather specialized fields of scientific research he had opened up, but from those engaged in popularizing natural science—the schoolteachers, the itinerant lecturers, the ordinary run of university professors, the writers of textbooks and encyclopedias. It is important to remember that the eighteenth century, no less than the nineteenth, was the great age of popularized and potted natural science. It was still possible for the layman to get a fairly good grasp of fairly comprehensive fields of inquiry by applying himself to a textbook or attending a series of lectures. As we have seen from the extract from his letter to Bentley, Newton was well aware that when he used the concept of force in order to bring various qualitatively distinct fields of research in relation to the law of gravitation and hence within the scope of quantitative computation, a distinction had to be drawn between the mathematical and physical significance of his expositions. Those who popularized his work were often entirely unaware of the necessity of this distinction, and proceeded without inhibition to treat all branches of natural science as nothing more than quantitative procedures, exploration of the whole extent of which was simply a matter of computation. As Koyré has pointed out, one of the most pernicious results of this methodological confusion was that "the eighteenth century, with very few exceptions, became reconciled to the ununderstandable."[15] When considering the intrinsic significance of Hegel's criticism of Newton it is certainly worth noting, therefore, that he had in his private library not only Newton's own works, but also several of the most popular and influential expositions of them.[16]

What seems to have fascinated the popular scientists of the eighteenth century more than anything else was Newton's postulation of the two mutually opposed forces inherent within planetary motion. Just as the opposition between the centripetal and the centrifugal forces was used to enlighten the interested layman as to the true nature of elliptical orbits, of a planet's radius vector always describing equal areas in equal times, of the cubes of the mean distances of the planets from the Sun being proportional to the squares of their times of revolution, so similarly opposed forces were postulated in order to account for the most diverse phenomena. Everything was to be made philosophical by being exhibited as arising out of the interaction of opposites, and hence as an illustration and confirmation of the central Newtonian insight. It seems unlikely that the universality with which the idea was accepted was entirely unrelated to the ease with which it may be comprehended. What is more, the grasping of this simple triadicity had the inestimable advantage of opening up the most diverse fields of inquiry to philosophical interpretation without requiring that the philosopher should be too deeply acquainted with the perplexing intricacies of empirical research. The Yugoslavian Jesuit Roger Boscovich extended the theory of gravitation to the nature of the atom, which he took to be the non-spatial point-center of the opposed forces of attraction and repulsion. The Scottish chemist Joseph Black, though by no means averse to exact empirical research, attempted to base the whole of physics and chemistry upon the Newtonian conception of opposing forces. The English Roman Catholic John Needham, as the result of his use of the microscope in examining organisms, attempted to prove that animals are brought to life from putridity, that they are formed by an expansive and a resistant force, and that they degenerate into vegetables. The Dutch civil servant Frans Hemsterhuis imported the Newtonian forces into psychology, and made use of mathematical analogies in explicating the nature of human desires and abnegations. The Irish statesman Edmund Burke, in a work on aesthetics which anticipates romanticism, related the twin emotions toward the sublime and the beautiful to the expansion and contraction of the nerves. The German polymath Johann von Herder even attempted to define God as the supreme unification of opposed forces.[17]

This eighteenth-century obsession with the uncritical postulation of opposed forces in the most diverse and heterogeneous contexts could be dismissed as nothing more than a harmless academic eccentricity were it not for the catastrophic effect it had upon peoples' lives through the way in which it influenced medical practice. During the seventeenth century Lorenzo Bellini had put forward the not entirely improbable idea that virtually all pathological states were the result of aberrations in the circulation of the blood. Taking this interesting suggestion to be a verified truth, Archibald Pitcairne set about transforming the medical sciences into a branch of Newtonian mathematics. What Pitcairne lacked in common sense he made up for in self-assurance. In his inaugural oration at the University of Leiden (1691) he maintained that empirical investigation, the search for physical causes, was "entirely useless and unnecessary to physicians," and that it was "not allowable to advance anything into a principle either in the theory or practice of medicine, which is called in question by the mathematicians." This general approach was inflated into a comprehensive Newtonian "philosophy" of the medical sciences by Richard Mead, who displayed a certain genius for dressing up even the most fantastic hypotheses in the form of mathematical truths. The movement reached its climax in the continental influence exercised by the medical writings of the Scotsman John Brown. According to Brown, the health of an organism depends upon its maintaining a due equilibrium between its inherent "excitability" and various stimuli. Consequently, disease is the result of either over- or under-stimulation. All the doctor has to do, therefore, is to prescribe the right means for correcting the equilibrium. Although the beautiful simplicity of this totally quantified and mathematicizable medicine failed to impress Brown's countrymen, it was taken up with great enthusiasm all over the continent. It stimulated academic passions to such an extent that in Göttingen in 1802, for example,

a troop of Hanoverian cavalry had to be used to put down the rioting which broke out between Brown's disciples and their opponents. It is interesting to note, moreover, that Brown managed to kill more people by means of his medicine than Napoleon did by means of his wars.[18]

It could be argued with some justification that by resolving such concepts as atoms, chemical compounds, organisms, etc., into two components, and then reconstructing the original unity from out of these "opposites," the eighteenth-century popularizers of Newtonianism were doing something not so very different from Newton himself when he applied the method of resolution and composition. It should be noted, however, that Newton and those who made genuine advances upon his work would never have dreamed of deciding beforehand that the analysis of a complex field of inquiry can only bring to light two significant sub-fields and that these have always to be regarded as "opposites." The truth of the matter is that those who dealt in these triads were nearly always guilty of not having considered the significance of Newton's distinction between pure and applied mathematics. They were in fact foisting an entirely arbitrary formalistic interpretation upon fields of research in which genuine experimental work, a valid inductive search for causes or presuppositions, would have yielded not tidy triads but a whole multitude of distinctly untidy and certainly perplexing sub-disciplines. It was, of course, easier to accept Pitcairne's advice and plump for the facility of a mathematical solution, disregarding the distinction between its pure and applied aspects. In doing so, however, they were rendering themselves incapable of making any authentic contribution to scientific knowledge, and therefore disqualifying themselves as genuine natural philosophers.

Although the methodological confusions out of which this manner of thinking arose were essentially those of the natural sciences, toward the end of the eighteenth century they began to be used in the development of a new brand of historicism. A monstrous misrepresentation of physical reality began to give birth to an even more monstrous philosophy of history. Kant, in his review of Herder's main work on the subject, gave forthright expression to the apprehension with which he regarded this new development: "What is one to think of the hypothesis of invisible forces producing organization, and the device of attempting to explain what one does not understand by means of what one understands even less? To assume an affinity among them, whereby either one genus would have arisen from the other and all from one original genus, or possibly from one generative mother womb, would give rise to ideas so monstrous that reason recoils from them."[19]

In one instance, and in one instance only, did this naive faith in the relevance of purely a priori mathematical or triadic reasoning to the organization of empirical research give rise to a significant scientific discovery. As early as 1724 Christian Wolff observed that "If one divides the distance of the Earth from the Sun into 10 parts, the distance of Mercury consists of 4 of them, that of Venus 7, that of Mars 15, that of Jupiter 52, and that of Saturn 95." Even before the discovery of Uranus in 1781, the distance of which was found to consist of 196 parts, Heinrich Lambert put forward the idea that it might be worthwhile to look for a planet moving in the gap between Mars and Jupiter. Johann Titius opined that the "Lord Architect" of the universe would never have violated the regularity of the arithmetical series by leaving the gap empty. The Berlin astronomer Johann Bode suggested that it was unlikely that the "Founder of the Universe" would have tolerated such untidiness. Piety and a faith in the a priori validity of mathematics, in a tidy universe, motivated the search for a planetary body to complete the series, and on January 1, 1801, they were rewarded when an Italian astronomer discovered the largest asteroid.[20]

Hegel

In a few lines at the end of his inaugural dissertation on the planetary orbits, which he defended at the University of Jena at the end of August 1801, Hegel criticizes Bode's uncritical projection of an a priori mathematical pattern onto the empirical facts provided by observation, and suggests, evidently not without some irony, that the sequence attributed to the demiurge by Plato might provide a better guide to research, since it not only accounts for the known planetary sequence, but also simplifies consideration of the satellites of Jupiter and Saturn. Hegel should have known that the empirical facts had been altered by the observation of January 1, 1801, but it is, perhaps, worth remembering that no theoretical justification for Bode's Law has yet been found, and that the discovery of Neptune in 1846 disproved it to some extent.[21]

Just prior to Hegel's arrival at Jena, his friend Schelling had developed a new form of natural philosophy which drew its inspiration from the popular triadic Newtonianism of Herder and the teleological thinking analyzed and advocated by Kant in his *Critique of Judgement*. According to Schelling, the analytical work carried out by the various branches of the natural sciences is to be used as the basis for viewing the whole of nature from the telos of consciousness. Consciousness is to comprehend nature as a hierarchy or sequence of levels approximating with increasing degrees of adequacy to that which is comprehending them. Hegel accepted the broad outlines of Schelling's conception, but criticized him severely for relying too heavily upon Herder and the popularizers, for not paying enough attention to the empiricists and the scientific professionals, and for failing to apply the methods of resolution and composition to their findings with the requisite rigor.[22]

It would be no exaggeration to say that until very recently the only outcome of research into Hegel's philosophy of the natural sciences has been an almost universal miscomprehension of is criticism of Bode's Law and a totally undifferentiated assessment of his indebtedness to Schelling.

In his inaugural dissertation, as in all the systematic works he published after 1801, Hegel's methodology involves a radical and comprehensive application of the methods of resolution and composition to the general state of knowledge and research in the empirical sciences. With regard to the problem of motion, for example, he accepts Kant's conclusion that space and time, without which there could be no motion, are the a priori elements, the presuppositions of our knowledge of the natural world. He also points out, however, that not only our knowledge, but also the natural world itself, presupposes space, time, and motion. What is more, space, time, and simple mechanical motions can be systematically considered without also considering their specific involvement in planetary, plant, or animal movements, whereas these movements cannot be considered without presupposing the more universal factors of space, time, and mechanics. It is therefore essential to a clear and consistent natural philosophy, and indeed to any other branch of philosophy, that such asymmetrical relationships should be borne in mind when dealing with the multifarious details and the metaphysical pretensions of the empirical sciences.[23]

Kant had shown that not only space and time, but also certain universal logical categories have to be regarded as the systematic presuppositions of human knowledge. In this respect also, Hegel extends the presuppositional structure of Kant's conception to include the natural world, and treats the working out of the systematic interrelationships between logical categories by means of the methods of resolution and composition as a philosophical science antecedent to natural philosophy. It is within this fundamental or purely abstract science that he works out the asymmetrical relationships subsisting between the logical categories employed in mathematics. Taking the unit to be the most basic category of pure mathematics, he develops a survey of the logical structure of the various branches of the science by indicating the way in which measure, ratio, infinity, intensive and extensive magnitude, number, quantity, etc., are systematically interrelated. He is, therefore, in full agreement with the mathematicians of his time—Lagrange, Lacroix, Cauchy, etc.—who were attempting to establish a logical foundation for the calculus by drawing a sharp distinction between its formal and its applied aspects. Although the methodological basis of his distinction between pure and applied mathematics is not identical with theirs, it certainly justifies his joining them in their criticism of the uncritical Newtonianism of those who were unaware of the necessity of distinguishing between mathematics and physics. He first published his critical analysis of the logical and categorial structure of mathematics in 1812, and he revised it with detailed reference to current developments at the end of his life. It is, therefore, high time that someone attempted to place it in the general context of ideas on the logical foundations of mathematics.[24]

Since Hegel pays so much attention to the categorial structure of pure mathematics, it cannot be said that he regards the science simply as a tool in the hands of the physicist. He is ready to admit, however, that the physicist can make valid use of it in communicating the formal structure of the regularities he has discovered in nature. He himself makes good use of mathematics in his expositions of celestial mechanics and musical sounds, for example, and he praises J. B. Richter for having followed up Kant's suggestion and developed stoichiometry, the calculation of the ratios in which chemical substances have an effect upon one another, as a branch of applied mathematics.[25] What he never fails to object to is the failure to realize that such calculations are quite distinct from empirical research, and the metaphysical theorizing that can arise out of this confusion: "The import of this reflection is simply this, that the distinctions and determinations employed by mathematical analysis, and the course to which its methods commit it, should be sharply distinguished from whatever is supposed to have a physical reality. It is not the assumptions, procedures, and results which analysis requires and affords which are questioned here, but the physical worth and the physical significance of its determinations and procedure. It is here that attention should be concentrated, in order to explain why physical mechanics has been flooded by a monstrous metaphysic, which, contrary to both experience and the Notion, has its sole source in these mathematical determinations."[26]

What Hegel proposes as the alternative to the confusions of popular Newtonianism is a systematic treatment of the mechanical sciences very similar to that of the ***Principia.*** Just as Newton's use of the analytical and synthetic procedures of resolution and composition had led him to break down the solar system, his major sphere of inquiry, into the two subordinate fields of the motions of bodies in resisting and non-resisting mediums, so Hegel's use of these procedures led him to break down the same major sphere into the subordinate fields of Kepler's laws, universal gravitation, fall, impact, inertia, matter, motion, etc. He works out the subordinate asymmetrical relationships between these fields with greater precision than Newton, and the details of his exposition reflect the empirical advances made during the intervening period. Evidently building upon the work of the Bernoullis and Euler, for example, he treats the subject-matter of Newton's second book, the mechanics of rigid and flexible and fluid and elastic bodies, as having its systematic context in physics rather than mechanics, that is to say, as presupposing the simpler motions of classical mechanics.[27] In thus revising the general complexity relationships of eighteenth-century mechanics and physics, he evidently relied fairly heavily upon the work of the French mathematician and physicist L. B. Francoeur. Once again, one can only hope that the precise nature of his assessment of this basic work will eventually be submitted to a thorough investigation.[28]

To a great extent, Hegel's criticism of Newton's ***Opticks*** was determined by his acceptance of the general validity of the theory put forward in Goethe's *Theory of Colours.* Both Hegel and Goethe performed a large number of experiments involving the passage of light through various mediums—gases, liquids, crystals, etc. From them they drew the conclusion that colored light is not, as Newton had maintained, the result of the resolution of the composite nature of white light into its constituents, but that it arises from the homogeneous nature of white light being dimmed or darkened by a medium. The colors which appear when white light is passed through a prism, for example, are not the result of its being resolved into its constituents, but of its being dimmed in a series of gradations resulting from the various degrees of refraction brought about by the physical structure of the prism.

Although a modern scientist has to regard Goethe's theory of the physics of light and colors as essentially erroneous, it was a plausible hypothesis at the time, and it was backed up with some first-rate experimental work and a critical analysis of Newton's experiments and the conclusions he drew from them which is still worth taking seriously and examining in detail. The most valuable part of Goethe's *Theory of Colours* is not its physics, however, but the contribution it makes to our understanding of the perception of color. Goethe explored the implications of the discoveries made by Halley, De Godart, and Rumford, and showed conclusively that the explanation of phenomena such as colored shadows involved consideration of physiological as well as physical factors. Heisenberg has therefore pointed out that Newton's and Goethe's contributions to our understanding of color are in fact complementary.[29]

Hegel's handling of the Newton-Goethe controversy is by no means as satisfactory as it would have been had he made proper use of his own philosophical principles. He could easily have provided a systematic assessment of Newton's ***Opticks*** in his *Physics* and a corresponding assessment of Goethe's theory in his *Physiology* and *Psychology,* and so brought out the complementary nature of the two apparently rival approaches. He decided instead to treat the physiological and psychological aspects of color perception in an extremely cursory manner, and to concentrate upon defending Goethe and refuting Newton in respect of the physics of light. Although he accepted Goethe's postulate of the essential homogeneity of white light, he also regarded it as involving a complexity of motions which required that it should be classified as a physical rather than a merely mechanical phenomenon. As a field of inquiry, he therefore took white light to be the initiation of the sphere of physics, in the sense that its motions constitute the absolute presupposition of physical phenomena. He also regarded color as an essentially physical phenomenon, but since he took it to involve not only white light but also the darkening of white light, he could only deal with it within a rational or systematic physics once the factors in this darkening had also been given their systematic exposition. In his *Physics,* therefore, the treatment of light is followed by the treatment of specific gravity, cohesion, shape, magnetism, crystallography, transparency, refraction, etc. Only once refraction has been given its systematic exposition, does he present his theory of colors, his criticism of Newton, and his defense of Goethe. The implication of this procedure is not, of course, that white light and colors do not occur together in the physical world, but simply that a systematic or philosophical exposition of color involves such an analytical and synthetic survey of its presuppositions, of the factors in its occurrence which have been brought to light by empirical physics.[30]

Conclusion

Despite the limitedness of the fields in which he published, Newton's contribution to natural science is still an integral part of modern physics, largely on account of the excellence of his experimental work and his realistic assessment of the significance of mathematics. When attempting to gauge the significance of Hegel's criticism of this contribution, it is therefore essential that a distinction should be drawn between Newton's own work and the way in which it was interpreted and exploited throughout the eighteenth century. As we have shown, the main thrust of Hegel's arguments is directed against the Newtonians of his own time rather than Newton himself. Even the very limited research carried out so far has made it clear that in such fields as the logical foundations of mathematics, the basic methodology of the science of mechanics, even the perception of color, Hegel's work has to be regarded as complementing rather than refuting Newton's. What is more, both Newton and Hegel insisted that all valid knowledge concerning the natural world must be based upon observation and experiment, both made good use of the methods of resolution and composition, and both objected forthrightly to the metaphysics of those intent upon popularizing empirical knowledge for non-scientific purposes.

If there is a fundamental difference between them, it is that between the natural scientist, wholly preoccupied with the empirical precision and the pragmatic significance of his discoveries, and the philosopher, primarily concerned with the wider implications of the methodology of the sciences. These are, however, not mutually exclusive but complementary interests, and even a cursory reading of Hegel's writings on the natural sciences will soon show that he was well aware of the fact.

Notes

[1] Newton, *Mathematical Principles,* ed. F. Cajori and tr. A. Motte (1687; Berkeley, 1934), bk. I, prop. 76, cor. 3 and 4; *Opticks,* ed. I. B. Cohen (1704; New York, 1952), bk. I. pt. 2 (prop. 5, theorem 4).

[2] Hegel, *De orbitis planetarum,* ed. and tr. F. De Gandt (1801; Paris, 1979); *Philosophy of Nature,* ed. and tr. M. J. Petry, 3 vols. (1842; London, 1970), II:135-60 (320).

[3] E. J. Dijksterhuis, *De Mechanisering van het Wereldbeeld* (Amsterdam, 1977), 543.

[4] *Notes and Records of the Royal Society of London* (1966), XXI:124-25; Stephen Hobhouse, *Isaac Newton and Jacob Boehme* (Belgrade, 1937).

[5] F. E. Manuel, *A Portrait of Isaac Newton* (London, 1980); R. S. Westfall, *Never at Rest. A Biography of Isaac Newton* (Cambridge, 1980), emphasizes the importance of Newton's *unpublished* alchemical notes.

[6] C. Truesdell, "Reactions of Late Baroque Mechanics to Success, Conjecture, Error, and Failure in Newton's *Principia,*" in R. Palter, *The Annus Mirabilis of Sir Isaac Newton* (Cambridge, Mass., 1967), 192-234.

[7] *Opticks,* bk. I, prop. X, Prob. V, p. 183; *Journal de Physique de Rozier* (1776), VIII: 270; *Philosophical Transactions of the Royal Society* (1794), pt. I, p. 107.

[8] *Spinoza. Kernmomenten in zijn denken* (Baarn, 1977), 31-43.

[9] *The Correspondence of Isaac Newton 1694-1709,* ed. J. F. Scott (Cambridge, 1967), IV:87-303.

[10] *Correspondence,* III:233-43

[11] C. B. Boyer, *The History of the Calculus and its Conceptual Development* (Dover Books, 1959), ch. vi.

[12] G. L. L. Buffon, *Histoire Naturelle* (Paris, 1749-1804), supplement vol. V; P. S. Laplace, *Exposition du Système du Monde* (Paris, 1796); N. R. Hanson, *Leverrier: The Zenith and Nadir of Newtonian Mechanics, Isis* 53 (1962): 359-78.

[13] *Opticks,* bk. I, pt. i, prop. 7, theor. 6; *Philosophical Transactions of the Royal Society* (1758), 733-43; vol.

90 (1800), 106; H. J. Steffens, *The Development of Newtonian Optics in England* (New York, 1977); K. F. Weinmann, *Die Natur des Lichts* (Darmstadt, 1980), 83-135.

[14] *Elemens de la Philosophie de Neuton, mis à la portée de tout le monde* (Amsterdam, 1738).

[15] Alexandre Koyré, *Newtonian Studies* (London, 1965), 163.

[16] *Verzeichniss der von dem Professor . . . Hegel . . . hinterlassenen Bücher-Sammlung* (Berlin, 1832), nos. 1277-1515; Colin Maclaurin, *An Account of Sir Isaac Newton's Philosophical Discoveries,* 1748; French tr. 1749; Latin tr. from French, Vienna, 1761); Benjamin Martin, *A Plain and Familiar Introduction to the Newtonian Philosophy,* tr. German Berlin (1778).

[17] L. L. Whyte, *Roger Joseph Boscovich* (New York, 1964); A. L. Donovan, *Philosophical Chemistry in the Scottish Enlightenment* (Edinburgh, 1975); J. T. Needham, *Nouvelles Observations Microsopiques* (Paris, 1750); F. Hemsterhuis, *Lettre sur les Désirs in Oeuvres philosophiques* (Paris, 1809), I:61-90; E. Burke, *On the Sublime and the Beautiful,* ed. I. T. Bulton (1757; London, 1958); J. G. Herder, *Gott, einige Gespräche,* ed. F. H. Burkhardt (1787; New York, 1940).

[18] *The Works of Dr. Archibald Pitcairne* (London, 1704), 10; *Authentic Memoirs of the Life of Richard Mead* (London, 1755); W. Coleman, "Mechanical Philosophy and Hypothetical Physiology" in R. Palter, pp. 322-32; Hegel, *Philosophy of Nature,* III:378-80.

[19] Kant, *Werke* (Akademie Ausgabe, 1784/5), VIII:43-58.

[20] H. A. M. Snelders, "Numerology in German Romanticism," *Janus* 60 (1973): 25-40.

[21] B. Beaumont, *Hegel and the Seven Planets, Mind* 63 (1954): 246-48; Hegel, *Les Orbites des Planètes* (note 2).

[22] *Philosophy of Nature,* I:46-48, 179-93.

[23] *Philosophy of Nature,* I:223-44, 260-83; III:49, 102-107.

[24] *Wissenschaft der Logik,* ed. G. Lasson, 2 pts. (Hamburg, 1975), 154-387; *Philosophy of Nature,* I:336-38.

[25] *Philosophy of Nature,* I:263-81; II:73-81, 210-13.

[26] *Philosophy of Nature,* I:265.

[27] *Philosophy of Nature,* II:42-69.

[28] *Philosophy of Nature,* I:264, 332; L. B. Francoeur, *Traité elémentaire de Mécanique* (Paris, 1801).

[29] *Die Goethesche und die Newtonsche Farbenlehre im Lichte der modernen Physik* in *Wandlungen in den Grundlagen der Naturwissenschaft* (1941; Hamburg, 1967).

[30] *Philosophy of Nature,* II:9-160.

Stuart Peterfreund   (essay date 1981)

SOURCE: "Blake and Newton: Argument as Art, Argument as Science," in *Studies in Eighteenth-Century Culture,* Vol. 10, 1981, pp. 205-26.

[*In the following essay, Peterfreund examines the direct relationship of William Blake's* Milton *to the* Principia, *demonstrating that Blake's work reveals the poet's opposition to Newton's physics and his conception of the universe.*]

There has been a good deal of discussion recently, by George S. Rousseau and others, about the status of the relationship between literature and science as modes of discourse.[1] Interestingly enough, much of what has been written about literature and science has been focused on the relationship of the two modes as viewed in the context of the eighteenth century, when the relationship of the two, clearly defined or otherwise, seems to have been the strongest. Problems with defining the status of the relationship seem to have arisen from the variety of its "surface" manifestations. These range from the implicit relationship of Book III of *Gulliver's Travels* to *Philosophical Transactions of the Royal Society,* so astutely perceived and documented by Marjorie Hope Nicolson,[2] to the highly explicit relationship of Blake's *Milton* to Newton's **Principia,** with which this essay will be principally concerned. But before entering into the substance of the discussion, it would seem proper to raise a question begged by the preceding remarks: on what basis or common ground may literature and science be discussed, with the purpose of understanding their relationship?

One answer to this question is that literature and science may be viewed as artifacts of rhetoric—as arguments, in other words. One who begins from such a view proceeds in the study of the relationship between literature and science with the understanding that, when any argument, either literary or scientific, speaks to the issues raised by another argument with the goal of overturning that other argument, the critical argument in question proceeds from a rhetorical position no less well defined and interested than that of the argument it seeks to overturn. Seen in this perspective, the General Scholium of the **Principia** differs from the "conversation" of the "Visionary forms dramatic" that takes place at the end of Blake's *Jerusalem*[3] not so much in terms of what it argues for as in terms of its refusal to acknowledge its status as argument—with the corollary refusal to acknowledge that what is being said, or argued for, must ultimately be reflexive to the interested position of the person mounting the discussion. Newton, for example, having disposed of the Cartesian model of vortical planetary motion, is not content to rest on his calculations, nor is he content to regard those calculations as evidence brought forth in support of his argument. Instead, by disclaiming any personal interest in elaborating the model of the solar system based on the principle of elliptical rotation, Newton is able to deny that there is any argument on his part in the first place, averring instead that "this most beautiful system of the sun, planets, and comets, could only proceed from the counsel and dominion of an intelligent and powerful Being."[4] This "Being," happily enough for Newton, is also the source of the language and rhetoric that Newton "discovers" for the purpose of propagating his (His?) celestial mechanics, just as Newton "discovers" the system of mechanics itself. Blake's Four Zoas, by way of contrast, do not discover, in their use of language, the space and time that are the parameters of Newton's system. Rather, the Zoas are seen "Creating Space, Creating Time according to the wonders Divine / Of Human Imagination." The consequence, which would be an abhorrence to Newton, with his allied conceptions of absolute time and absolute space, is the "variation of Time & Space / Which vary according as the Organs of Perception vary."[5]

To be sure, many of the eighteenth-century writers active before the 1790's, when Blake came to intellectual and artistic maturity, recognized the rhetorical and ontological status of Newtonian argument, *as argument,* and they evinced a shared concern about the full significance of that argument and the limits to which it might be made, by analogy, to serve in other fields of inquiry. Writers as far apart in politics as Addison and Pope and as far apart in temperament as Desaguliers and Doctor Johnson all had something to say about the impact of Newtonian mechanics and optics and the implications to be derived therefrom. These responses have already been dealt with in several fine studies, including book-length treatments by Nicolson, Richard B. Schwartz, and Margaret C. Jacob,[6] and need only be mentioned here in passing to emphasize the crucial difference between Blake's response to Newton and the responses of English writers before him. Addison, Pope, Desaguliers, Johnson, *et al.* may have disagreed over the extent to which Newtonian physics could, by argument from analogy, be used to help see the "subjective" aspects of the universe in an orderly manner. But these and other writers of the eighteenth century were of one mind concerning the "objective" truth of Newtonian physics *per se.* Pope may have taken issue

with Addison over how far Newtonian argument might be extended in the areas of perceptual psychology and political economy, but both writers agreed on the paramount importance of the physics itself to Western thought. And although Johnson may have placed less emphasis on the discovery of physical truths than on the discovery of moral and religious ones, he still considered Newton a model of scientific thought and conduct.[7] Up to Blake's time, the response of eighteenth-century literature to Newtonian science is unanimous in its belief that Newton's mathematics and physics are fully disinterested, inductive, impartial, and authoritative. It is only in the question of how far Newtonian thought might be extended into other spheres of inquiry that there is any real debate.

For Blake, however, the painful and oppressive conditions of human existence, which he viewed as being in part descended from the "reasonable" assumptions of Newtonian physics, translated into Newtonian metaphysics and implemented as social policy, meant that there was something wrong with the physics itself. Blake seems to have understood, as we now do, that the metaphysics might precede the physics as well as follow from it. Accordingly, Blake undertook the critique and demonstration, whose record is to be found throughout the Prophetic Books, especially in *Milton,* a critique and demonstration anticipatory, in the essentials, of the insights set forth by relativity physics concerning the space-time continuum and other matters in the latter physics' correction of the Newtonian model of the universe.[8]

Lest it be objected, however, that the present strategy is to turn Blake into an *ur*-Einstein, the point should be made that Blake's insights about, and critique of Newtonian physics—indeed, his critical responses to many of the language-bound activities of the age— owe a good deal to his grasp of the nature and function of language, as well as of the way in which one reads that language. Blake's senses of language and reading depend upon his understanding that all texts, as the artifacts of specific individuals writing in specific contexts of time and place, are rhetorical, or argumentative, and that the situation could not be otherwise, since all language is produced by individuals speaking from positions more or less clearly defined, but always definite.[9] Accordingly, there is no such thing as disinterestedness, only concealed or dissembled interest; no such thing as pure induction, only induction with a concealed or impure hypothesis, usually disguised as an "axiom" or "truth"; no impartiality, only imperfectly revealed partiality; and no authority, only usurped freedom.

Blake's idea of language has been discussed at some length previously by Robert F. Gleckner and this writer. These discussions emphasize that fallen humanity uses a fallen language that is at best partial in its grasp of phenomena and at worst tyrannous in its insistence on the authority of that partial grasp.[10] But neither of the discussions deals with the relationship between language and reading, or with the role of reading as an instrument of language reform. Blake has a vision of how language functions when properly used, and that vision is closely tied to his idea of how one should read. Before turning to the way in which Blake reads and responds to Newtonian language specifically, it might be helpful to develop an understanding, in general terms, of the relationship between language properly spoken and reading properly practiced.

Blake's most complete account of language properly spoken is found at the end of *Jerusalem,* in his rendering of the "conversation" dealt with briefly above. The Four Zoas

> conversed together in Visionary forms
>   dramatic which bright
> Redounded from their Tongues in thunderous
>   majesty, in Visions
> In new Expanses, creating exemplars of
>   Memory and of Intellect
> Creating Space, Creating Time according to
>   the wonders Divine
> Of Human Imagination, throughout all Three
>   Regions immense
> Of Childhood, Manhood & Old Age [;] & the
>   all tremendous unfathomable Non Ens
> Of Death was seen in regenerations terrific or
>   complacent varying
> According to the subject of discourse & every
>   Word & every Character
> Was Human according to the Expansion or
>   Contraction, the Translucence or
> Opakeness of Nervous fibres such was the
>   variation of Time & Space
> Which vary according as the Organs of
>   Perception vary.
>
>   (98.28-38)

The language spoken by the Four Zoas creates what it refers to rather than merely describing something thought to have been created previously. "Exemplars of Memory and of Intellect," up to and including space and time themselves, are created in the course of such speech. But the overall qualities of any given "Exemplar" are entirely reflexive to the qualities of the speaker in question: "Human Imagination," the speaker's age, "the subject of discourse," and the variables having to do with differences in "the Organs of Perception" from speaker to speaker. In a "conversation" of the sort described by Blake, no one speaker lays claim to, or is accorded, the authority that would make that speaker's position the only "right" or "reasonable" one among other "wrong" or "unreasonable" alternatives. Authoritative meaning under such circumstances is comprehensive meaning, which takes the form of a living body

of utterance, augmented by each additional utterance but never completed by it. Thus the sense of the verb *redounded,* as Blake uses it, meaning in the context of *Jerusalem,* pl. 98, "to add, yield, cause to accrue" (*OED,* VIII.309).[11]

In order to use language as the Four Zoas do at the end of *Jerusalem,* it is necessary to relinquish the coercive authority implicit in point of view and usually identified in Blake's lexicon as *selfhood.* Selfhood is Blake's cardinal sin, replacing the more usual pride and posing a threat to the individual far greater than might be posed by pride alone, since selfhood is an amalgam of pride and of deceit that denies the existence of that very pride, a powerful amalgam indeed. As Albion faces the prospect of putting off his selfhood, for example, he comments on the powerful bond between pride and deceit, a bond which gives the resultant selfhood the power of a mighty army.

> O Lord what can I do! My Selfhood cruel
> Marches against thee deceitful from Sinai &
>   from Edom
> Into the Wilderness of Judah to meet thee in
>   his pride.
>
>   (96.8-10)

Albion must put off selfhood in order to be united with the paragon of selfless energy, Jesus. The goal of doing so is one proposed by Blake for all of creation in the Greek epigraph to *Jerusalem,* μονος ο Ιεςνς (one in Jesus), and describes as occurring at the end of the epic, when the triumphant "All Human Forms identified" is pronounced and those forms are described as "Awaking in his [i.e. Jesus's] Bosom in the Life of Immortality" (99.1, 4).

As Enitharmon notes slightly earlier in the poem, the putting off of selfhood must necessarily entail the repudiation of Bacon, Newton, Locke, and others like them—those who worship a "natural" order they both have created and have refused to take responsibility for creating.

> We shall not die! we shall be united in
>   Jesus.
> Will you suffer this Satan this Body of Doubt
>   that Seems but is Not
> To occupy the very threshold of Eternal Life.
>   If Bacon, Newton, Locke,
> Deny a Conscience in Man & the Communion
>   of Saints & Angels
> Contemning the Divine Vision & Fruition,
>   Worshiping the Deus
> Of the Heathen, the God of This World, & the
>   Goddess Nature
> Mystery Babylon the Great, the Druid Dragon
>   & hidden Harlot[,]
> Is it not the Signal of the Morning which was

told us in the Beginning?

(93.19-26)

How does one go about repudiating those who champion the empirical mode of observation and the argument by induction, while at the same time worshiping the horrible Antichrist under its several names and guises? Blake's answer is that one reads the texts produced by these and other usurpers—all texts, for that matter—in what he calls the "infernal or diabolical sense." This reading strategy is described in *The Marriage of Heaven and Hell.*

The speaker of Blake's mixed media polemic has just shown an "Angel" that the Gospels, although written by men of genius about a man of genius,[12] have been misread consistently because of the interpositions of the priesthood in the reading process. These interpositions have perverted Christianity, until it has become an organized religion along typically tradition-bound lines.

> . . . a system was formed, which some took advantage of & enslav'd the vulgar by attempting to realize or abstract mental deities from their objects; thus began Priesthood.
>
>   Choosing forms of worship from poetic tales.
>   And at length they pronouncd that the Gods had orderd such things.
>   Thus men forgot that All deities reside in the human breast.

(pl. 11)

In the sense that both are attempts to exercise spiritual sovereignty in the name of an absent, originary "other," priesthood and selfhood are synonymous. Both are interested points of view that pretend to disinterestedness, calling on "Jehovah," "Nature," or suchlike to bear witness to the impartiality with which they hold sway. Both priesthood and selfhood are in fact argumentative positions that deny the existence of any argument whatsoever, in light of their self-image of authoritativeness and permanence.

Priesthood and selfhood have their antithesis in the authentic voice of religious vision, that of the prophet. The nature of the antithesis is made clear in Blake's account of a "dinner conversation" with Isaiah and Ezekiel, in which Blake asks the two Prophets why they should not be charged with the same crime of selfhood attributed to the priests. Isaiah answers that he "was then perswaded, & remain[s] confirm'd; that the voice of honest indignation is the voice of God, I cared not for the consequences but wrote" (pl. 12). Thus emerges the doctrine of "firm perswasion," which furnishes a useful gloss on Blake's statement, also in *The Marriage,* "that all deities reside in the human breast" (pl. 11). As a state of mind, "firm perswasion"

is characteristic not only of Isaiah and Ezekiel, but of the Four Zoas at the end of *Jerusalem* as well. In such a state, the fact that language is always argument, always coming from an interested position, is openly acknowledged, and the creative, verbal energy liberated by that very acknowledgement is of a magnitude comparable to that of the Zoas as they create and recreate space and time in their respective images. Blake inquires as to the potential for such energy through the acknowledgement of one's interested position, and Isaiah tells him that there is no reality without that acknowledgement.

> Then I asked: does a firm perswasion that a thing is so, make it so?
> He replied. All poets believe that it does, & in ages of imagination this firm perswasion removed mountains; but many are not capable of a firm perswasion of any thing.

(pl. 12)

Reading in "the infernal or diabolical sense" proceeds on the understanding that the primary difference between prophecy (inspired poetry) and the literature of doubt ("philosophy," "rational discourse," "dogma," etc.) is that the former affirms, even celebrates, its "perswasion," or interested position, while the latter denies the very existence of such a position. Blake's venture in reading, then, is to "converse" with the text in order to locate and identify the human form responsible for producing it and its point of view. This venture is made clear in *The Marriage* and even clearer in Blake's Annotations of various authors, where his designedly *ad hominem* stance is aimed at producing from behind his words the writer who has refused to take full responsibility for the substance and implications of his text. "Conversing" in this context is Blake's reading strategy for prophecy and the literature of doubt alike, for the locus of rhetorical interest in each is alike in its need for elaboration and clarification. Blake therefore reads prophecy and the literature of doubt in precisely the same way, and in each case he fully acknowledges the status of his own discourse in the process of doing so. With specific reference to Blake's reading of Newton, it should be noted that Blake's adversary position is not held with the hope of "destroying" Newton. Blake acknowledges the power of the scientist's intellect; moreover, he wishes to "save" the intellect in much the same way that he wishes to "save" Milton's creative genius: by having both Newton and Milton acknowledge that their texts are the creations of a self-interested position, then having them cast off the selfhood that ordains and disguises the self-interest inherent in the position.

Blake does indeed "save" Newton in much the same way that he "saves" Milton. In the case of the latter, the process of this "salvation" is clearly chronicled in the brief epic that bears his name. In the case of Newton, however, the process is less clear, being carried forward by means of what might be termed "Christian association": the use of Christlike, visionary avatars, whose putting off of selfhood is done both for their own good and, by example, for the good of others. Milton functions as one such avatar for Newton, as does Albion, who functions in this capacity for Milton and Newton alike. Near the end of *Jerusalem,* shortly after Albion has confronted Jesus and participated in the "Mysterious / Offering of Self for Another" (96.20-21), the time of the fallen world ends, and all those immured in that time reappear in their eternal forms. "The innumerable Chariots of the Almighty appeard in Heaven / and Bacon & Newton & Locke, & Milton & Shakspear & Chaucer" (98.8-9).

Salvation of the sort Blake practices and preaches depends upon criticism, the sort of "Opposition" that "is true Friendship" (*MHH,* pl. 20). Blake's criticism of Newtonian physics is one instance among many of Blake's friendly opposition to what he conceives of as being deluded thinking. At this point it is time to turn to an examination of Blake's criticism of Newton, in order to see how well the former understands the latter's physics and metaphysics. If Blake's criticism is to be considered cogent, it may only be so if his understanding is equal to Newton's, in much the same way that the unceasing "Mental Fight" that Blake announces in *Milton,* 1.13, must occur between equally matched antagonists if it is to be successful in redeeming them from error.

The evidence for Blake's having read widely and deeply in Newtonian literature is extensive, both in Blake's own writing and in discussions of it by Donald D. Ault and F. B. Curtis, among others.[13] There is accordingly no need to reargue the issue of Blake's degree of familiarity with Newtonian thought. What does need to be argued, however, is that Blake's reading of Newton led him to focus on the *Principia* as much if not more so than on the *Optics,* the primary source of Newtonian thought for Blake, according to Ault and Nicolson before him.[14] The importance of Blake's knowledge of the *Principia* for the creation of *Milton* will be demonstrated in the discussion below. A general reason for such having been the case may be ventured at this point, however. The reason "that the English poets who wrote about science in the eighteenth century put greater emphasis on the *Principia* than on the *Optics,*" according to William Powell Jones, is that "the poets knew . . . that Newton had mathematically demonstrated the order of the universe. . . . They used this idea over and over in numerous variations, not only when they mentioned Newton by name but when, in their illustrations of various branches of science they devoted more space to celestial order . . . than to the physics of light and color."[15] It is precisely on this issue of celestial order—where ideas of it come from and what force they ought and do have—that Blake confronts

Newton. Blake's understanding is that such "celestial order" is in fact the order of Newton's mind, projected outward and argued for subtly but powerfully for the purpose of compelling the very consensus of opinion commented on by Jones above.

As Blake assesses it, the net effect of the Newtonian argument in the *Principia* is to create the universe in Newton's image, an act of creation for which Newton refuses to take responsibility, assigning it instead to a God with whom Newton and no one else is able to communicate on an intimate, father-son basis.[16] It is in response to this Newtonian move and all the implications to be derived from it that Blake frames the narrative of *Milton,* in which the poem's namesake must fight off not only the implications of the Newtonian model of the universe, but also the implications of the continuing cast of mind that is always ready to fabricate such models. That cast of mind may be viewed in the context of a tradition that embodies it, a tradition known as the *prisca sapientia,* or *prisca theologia,* and recently discussed by Ault in relation to Blake.[17] This tradition of ancient, or pristine wisdom, or theology is what Blake has in mind when he derides "The Stolen and Perverted Writings of Homer & Ovid: of Plato & Cicero. Which all Men ought to contemn" (pl. 1). Milton's goal in condemning this ancient tradition, as all ought to, according to Blake, is to be reunited with his "emanation," Ololon, who represents space just as Milton represents time. Ololon, for example, is described as being "Sixfold" (2.19), a multiple unique to her in all of Blake's number symbolism, at least in part because Blake associates her spatialized being with Newton's conception of the "six primary planets."[18] Seen in a larger frame, the reuniting of Ololon with Milton is but one in a series of similar reunions, including those of Enitharmon with Los, Vala with Luvah, and Jerusalem with Albion, the overall purpose being to reunite fallen time, which Blake sees as being male, with fallen space, which Blake sees as being female and somehow being "generated" by time. Out of this multiple reconstitution of the space-time continuum Blake hopes to see established conditions under which space and time, energy and matter, approach identity at the speed of light itself.[19]

But any such reconstitution must begin with a taking stock of what conditions are like in the fallen world and how they have come to pass. Blake does so in *Milton* by retelling the story of the Creation, which he had told several times previously, for example in *The Book of Urizen* and *The Four Zoas* (1794, 1797). Implicit in such a retelling is the awareness that the Creation and Fall have been as fully multiple as the reconstitution that corrects them must be. For Blake, the story of the Creation is the story of a fall into finitude, brought about by the sort of God Newton talks about in the General Scholium of the *Principia.* Creation in *Milton* begins when Los, Blake's avatar for all poets and prophets, is unable to "identify" Urizen, whom Ault associates with Newton,[20] such "identification" being a matter of giving Urizen an eternal form or an eternal name.

> Los siezd his Hammer & Tongs; he labourd at his resolute Anvil
> Among indefinite Druid rocks & snows of doubt & reasoning.
> Refusing all Definite Form, the Abstract Horror roofd. stony hard
> And a first Age passed over & a State of dismal woe!
>
> (3.7-10)

Urizen's "Refusing all Definite Form" cuts at least two ways, given the Newtonian background of *Milton.* On the more obvious level, Urizen is Newton's God, "utterly void of all body and bodily figure" (p. 545). But on a subtler level, Blake's description—or non-description—goes right to the core of the Newtonian argument. Blake senses the relationship between the attributes of Newton's God and the habits of Newton's thought. "Refusing all Definite Form" is also a gibing reference to Newton's claim to "frame no hypotheses" (p. 545). Blake, who by his own account knew how to read Latin tolerably well by 1803,[21] seems to have in mind a pun on the Latin original of Newton's statement about framing hypotheses: *"hypothese non fingo."*[22] "I frame no hypotheses" is an adequate translation of the Latin, but it is by no means the only adequate one. *Fingo,* which may mean *to form* or *to frame* in the sense usually understood of Newton, may also have other meanings of interest in light of the present discussion. Two other translations of the verb are possible on the basis of the definitions of the Latin root, which discuss it in terms" of the plastic art, *to form* or *fashion by art . . . to mould or model,* as a statuary," and "with the access. notion of untruth, *to alter, change,* for the purpose of dissembling."[23]

The net effect of such a pun is to show that Newton's God and Newton are one and the same, and that a God who refuses definite form is the creation of a man who dissembles about the fact that he has created God in his own image and refuses to acknowledge the responsibility for exercising the creative initiative that would lead him to do so, since by the standards of such a mind being found out would mean being caught lying, not caught in the act of creating art. This particular set of circumstances accounts for Urizen's continual disavowal, here and elsewhere throughout the Prophetic Books, of form. It also accounts for the confrontation that occurs later in Milton proper, in which Milton marches against Urizen at the River Arnon and attempts to give him form through the sculptorly act of moulding to his formless bones the red clay of Succoth (pls. 19-20). Urizen must realize his own full presence, of body as well as of mind, before he can experience

the full presence of the God he creates—and realize that such a God is only as powerful and good as its creator. The applicable text, from Blake's "The Everlasting Gospel," is "Thou art a Man God is no more / thy own humanity learn to adore" (pp. 52-54, ll. 75-76).

A far cry from the Four Zoas who, at the end of *Jerusalem,* freely create space and time in their own images with dazzling rapidity, Urizen/Newton denies responsibility for creating what is "out there," much as Newton before him had denied responsibility for the hypothesis that placed God, invisible, at the center of a universe composed of very visible, very dead, atomistic matter. Somehow, even though he wishes to disavow any knowledge of, or responsibility for it, creation—or anti-creation—of a universe of dead matter centered by a materialistic sun possessed of invisible force(s) is a direct result of Urizen's refusal to assume form. After the "first Age," in which Urizen is characterized as "Refusing all Definite Form,"

> Down sunk with fright a red round Globe hot burning. Deep
> Deep down into the Abyss. Panting: conglobing: trembling
> And a second Age passed over & a State of dismal woe.
>
> (3.11-13)

Because he disavows any responsibility for voluntarily creating a centered, materialistic universe, Urizen suffers the fate of all Blake's self-denying artificers who refuse to take responsibility for their creations: the process appears to be reversed, and the created appears to have created the creator. Nor will the creator correct this misapprehension, owing to his ulterior motives. Thus Urizen/Newton postulates a universe that is centered by "a round red Globe hot burning," denies responsibility for doing so, and instead appears to become what he beholds, his organs of vision appearing to have been formed by the sun at the center of that postulated universe, when that sun in fact has been looked into place by eyes that do the bidding of a will. And that will exercises a *fiat* every bit as powerful, within its own sphere, as the first such *fiat: fiat lux.*

> Rolling around into two little Orbs & closed in two little Caves
> The Eyes beheld the Abyss: lest bones of solidness freeze over all
> And a third Age passed over & a State of dismal woe.
>
> (3.14-16)

The "creation," which is in fact a fall into a state of fragmented materialism, continues apace. Urizen/Newton's failure to assume responsibility for framing the first hypothesis causes the division of the creative consciousness into a fragmented, materialistic world "out there" and five contracted senses with which to perceive it. Stunned momentarily by doubt, Los believes that the "creation" taking place "out there" has a spiritual as well as a material reality. His doubt leads to Los's recapitulation, willy-nilly, of the fall of Urizen into generation. With no sense, momentarily, of his own creative energy, no sense that voids and absolute space exist only for those who do not fill them with plenitude by perceiving *through* them to the infinite, Los becomes fearful. As Blake elsewhere notes, "One thought fills immensity" (*MHH,* pl. 8.36). But when fear leads the individual to cease thinking creatively, the process reverses and immensity fills the thinker. In this particular case, instead of Los filling the void, the void fills Los, fragmenting him into the fallen categories of Newtonian space and time.

> Terrified Los stood in the Abyss & his
>   immortal limbs
> Grew deadly pale: he became what he beheld:
>   for a red
> Round Globe sunk down from his Bosom into
>   the Deep in pangs
> He hoverd over it trembling & weeping.
>   Suspended it shook
> The nether Abyss in tremblings. He wept over
>   it, he cherish'd it
> In deadly sickening pain: till separated into a
>   Female pale
> As the cloud that brings the snow: all the
>   while from his Back
> A blue fluid exuded into Sinews hardening in
>   the Abyss
> Till it separated into a Male Form howling in
>   Jealousy.
>
>   (3.28-36)

The "Female pale" is of course Enitharmon. She is "pale," as is Los, because of an act of self-deception fundamental to the process of "creation" in which both are involved. When the void fills and fragments Los, it causes him to fragment into his likeness. Paleness in Blake usually connotes desire restrained or repressed.[24] In restraining his creative energies, Los does not totally abdicate his role as a creator—not any more than Urizen/Newton does, in fact. Instead, Los creates Enitharmon in the image of his restrained desire—pale creator, pale creation. His "trembling & weeping" are also symptomatic of the creative drive sublimated, and these symptoms are likewise passed along in the creation of a female who shakes "the nether Abyss in tremblings."

The creation/fragmentation that occurs leads Los to believe that he and Enitharmon are separated by some insurmountable obstacle, a "Male Form howling in Jealousy." Like Enitharmon, however, this male form is the creation of Los's own mind and body, and is separated from Los when, because of fear, he refuses to do anything to halt or control the fragmentation. In this particular case, the spectre that is created bears a striking resemblance to Newtonian absolute space, a resemblance that is hardly accidental. The idea of "A blue fluid . . . hardening in the Abyss" is derived from at least two of Newton's concealed axioms concerning the nature of space. The first of these states *"That the centre of the system of the world is immovable"* (p. 419),[25] that is, that absolute space is rigid. The second of these states that "the matter of the heavens is fluid" (p. 549). The fact that the *locus maledictus* of Los's activity is described alternately as an abyss or a void has to do with Newton's description of absolute space as being *"void of resistance"* (p. 68). Space, absolute or otherwise, of course appears to be blue to the earthbound observer.

Los assumes, as Newton seems to assume, that all the materialistic fragmentation he encounters is "really" going on "out there," that is, that it arises because of an external, "natural" cause that is responsible for all instances of fragmentation, perceived as external, "natural" effect. In doing so, Los is only being "reasonable," in the sense of following the line of logic laid down by Newton in the "Rules of Reasoning in Philosophy" that preface the third book of the ***Principia.***[26] The result of Los's being "reasonable" on the basis of his assumptions is bitterly humorous. Believing the cause to be external and doubting his ability to stem the fragmentation, the deluded Los makes fragmentation the law of the universe, using a distinctly Newtonian style of inductive reasoning to do so. And in his longing and lusting after Enitharmon as a discrete being forever fragmented and apart from him, Los participates in the further fragmentation of the universe, by begetting on Enitharmon children who add to the force of the "selfhood explosion," by means of which the universe is populated with discrete little bodies, which are, at least in this context, Blake's visionary rendering of what is implied by Newton's corpuscular theory of matter. A corpuscle is, in the root sense of the Latin, a little body. The irony underlying the whole of Los's project is that he causes additional fragmentation in the very attempt, albeit a deluded one, to end the process by somehow transcending and comprehending what is already deployed in the depths of spectral, rigid, absolute space.

> Within labouring, beholding Without: from
>   Particulars to Generals
> Subduing his Spectre, they built the Looms
>   of Generation
> They Builded Great Golgonooza Times on
>   Times Ages on Ages
> First Orc was Born then the Shadowy Female:
>   then all of Los's Family
> At last Enitharmon brought Forth Satan
>   Refusing Form, in vain

The Miller of Eternity made subservient to the
  Great Harvest
That he may go to his own Place Prince of
  the Starry Wheels

                                    (3.37-43)

The reference to the idea of moving "from Particulars to Generals" is Blake's gibing allusion to Newtonian inductive method and summary of it as it, for example, *generalizes,* in the "Rules of Reasoning in Philosophy," about the *particular,* or particle-like nature of matter. The third of the rules would seem to be the one Blake has explicitly in mind. By the use of inductive method, Newton concludes, in the third Rule of Reasoning dealing with matter, that "the hardness of the whole arises from the hardness of the parts, we therefore justly infer the hardness of the undivided particles not only of the bodies we feel but of all others" (p. 399).

Satan's refusal of form is a trait that helps the reader trace his lineage back to Urizen/Newton, as indeed Los and Enitharmon do later in *Milton,* when they discover that "Satan is Urizen / Drawn down by Orc & the Shadowy Female into Generation" (10.1-2). The fact that Satan is the last-born of Los and Enitharmon's children is significant, in the sense that his birth indicates that the limits of "particularization," of fragmentation, have been reached. As the "Miller of Eternity," Satan, who is also the most finely-ground grist of his "mill," has witnessed, both in the creation of his own body and that of the world as the body-image he sees from it, the matter of the fallen world divided as finely as it can be divided. Henceforth, in Blake's theatre of visionary action, the forces of particularization and fragmentation are to be made "subservient to the Great Harvest," made to look inward into living, visionary space, rather than outward into dead, Newtonian space. In so doing, all "human forms" will be "identified" and will therefore be able to put off that corpuscular identity which is selfhood. Under such circumstances, seemingly dead corpuscles will be perceived as actually being living seeds, which throw off their dead husks to become grapes and grain, which in turn throw off their individual identities, in the winepress and the mill, to become wine and bread, which in turn give up their identities in a massive and progressive Eucharist. Ultimately, all of creation becomes the flesh and blood of one body, the one seen at the end of *Jerusalem* walking "To & fro in Eternity as One Man reflecting each in each & clearly seen / And seeing . . ." (98.39-40). The task of bringing this Eucharist to pass is the task of all of Blake's visionary avatar-heroes, Milton, Los, and Albion among them.

Until such a putting off of selfhood is made to occur, however, Satan presides over all that is to be annihilated, known as the world of the Ulro, an "*ul*timate *ratio*" of dead particles acted upon by blind forces, both particles and forces in fact being reflexive to the wills of their self-effacing, self-deceiving creators. Satan's "own place," the very phrase commenting on the solipsistic nature of such a place by echoing Satan's speech in *Paradise Lost,*[27] is that of the presiding spirit, "Prince of the Starry Wheels." This title is yet another gibing reference to the Newtonian model of the universe, in which planets, moons, and comets revolve around "fixed stars" in circular or elliptical orbits, making their motion seem wheel-like. The proprietary role connoted by the phrase "own Place" should also serve to indicate that Satan, rather than being merely the superintendent of these "Starry Wheels," is their creator as well.

The particularization and fragmentation of the universe will never be more complete in any of Blake's other poems than it is at the end of the third plate of *Milton.* It is at this point that affairs begin to reverse, with the recognition, by Los, of Satan's true identity: the latter is the Supreme Being Newton refers to in the General Scholium, the God Newton creates in his own image through the use of concealed hypotheses and assumptions, all the while denying the existence of these hypotheses and assumptions and asserting that the will has no role in promulgating his view of the matter. In a flash of *insight,* Los identifies his multifaceted, yet unitary enemy as Satan/Newton/the God of Natural Religion/Locke's God revealed by Reason/Urizen.

O Satan my youngest born, art thou not
  Prince of the Starry Hosts
And of the Wheels of Heaven, to turn the
  Mills day & night?
Art thou not Newtons Pantocrator weaving the
  Woof of Locke[?]

                                    (4.9-11)

The identification of Satan as "Newtons Pantocrator" is a direct reference to the General Scholium, in which Newton has occasion to talk of a "Being" who "governs all things, not as the soul of the world, but as Lord over all; and on account of his dominion he is wont to be called *Lord God* παντοκράτωρ, or *Universal Ruler*; for *God* is a relative word, and has a respect to servants; and *Deity* is the dominion of God not over his own body, as those imagine who fancy God to be the soul of the world, but over servants" (p. 544). The relevance of the idea of "Newtons Pantocrator" in a poem about Milton has to do with Blake's critique of Milton's allegiances in *Paradise Lost,* given in full in *The Marriage of Heaven and Hell,* pl. 5. In that critique, Blake argues that Milton mistook the real Satan, in all of his dissembling humility, for God, who was actually immanent not in Heaven but in the energy of the fallen angels and in the realm of art they created by dint of that energy. The reason that Milton, Los, and Blake himself are all walking about in the "Eternity" (1.16) that frames *Milton* is to begin the task that culminates in the announcement of "All Human Forms identified" at the end of *Jerusalem.* The first step of that task seems to entail calling a pantocrator a pantocrator, thus identifying covert selfhood.

In one important sense, though Milton may have initially been deluded in his allegiances, he saw clearly enough that the Fall was fortunate. For it did lead Adam to turn his gaze from the outer world, which begins to fragment at the very moment that the angels fall, to the inner world, which may be retained as a paradise inviolate, notwithstanding the vicissitudes of "natural," external change. Adam and Eve do have to experience the selfhood that comes from the eating of forbidden fruit in order to realize the limits one faces in attempting to look outward for coherence. The outer world is a realm of fragmentation and particularization; it is the Hell depicted by Milton in Book II of *Paradise Lost.*

> . . . many a Frozen, many a Fiery Alp,
> Rocks, Caves, Lakes, Fens, Bogs, Dens, and
>   shades of death,
> A Universe of death. . . .[28]

Outward lies a "Universe of death"; inward lies something else entirely. Surrounded by that universe as the result of eating the forbidden fruit, Adam, at the behest of Michael, looks inward and sees the deeds of all time spread out before him. As the result of this perception, Adam realizes the delusory nature of fallen time and fragmentation, and he heeds Michael's injunctions in the hope of possessing "A Paradise within . . . happier farr"[29] than the materialist Paradise he is about to leave.

Insight plays the crucial role in Adam's realization, as it does in the realizations of Milton, Los, and Blake. Jehovah the tempter must get *into* Adam and Eve, be ingested as the apple in what is essentially an "anti-Eucharist," in order to force them to look *outward* with his point of view and see the fragmentation that he sees. Similarly, Urizen must get *into* Milton, Satan must get *into* Los, and Newton must get *into* Blake, the last of these, at least, by means of reading, which is but another form of ingestion, witness Blake's reading of dining with Isaiah and Ezekiel in *The Marriage.* But whereas Isaiah and Ezekiel are "wholesome," in the sense that their "firm perswasion" on issues vouchsafes against the possibility of any deception on their part, Urizen, Satan, and Newton are not "wholesome," in the sense that they do practice deception in the name of reason. One of Blake's "Proverbs of Hell" is to the point: "All wholsom food is caught without a net or a trap" (*MHH,* pl. 7.13). The nature of the "poisonous" reason in question is to impose, with few or no symptoms, an alien point of view on the victim, under the guise of being "natural," thus substituting the selfhood of the "poisoner" for that of the "poisoned" and "killing" the "poisoned" individual, as is the case in "A Poison Tree."[30]

Accordingly, when Los "identifies" Satan, or when Milton and Blake do the same thing to Urizen and Newton, respectively, two steps are involved. The first of these has to do with the recognition that the figure "identified" is only seen to be *outside* because he has "poisoned," or gotten *inside,* his victim. Los sees Satan as "Newton's Pantocrator" because Satan has managed to put that "Pantocrator" *inside* Los by "poisoning" him, either with food for the body or food for the mind, if in fact a distinction can be made between the two in the world of symbolic action of Blake's poetry.

The second step involved in "identifying" Satan has to do with replacing the "poison" of another selfhood imposing its views on its victim with the healthy food of self-nurture. Only by this means can one freely create the world in one's own image and then merge in full plenitude and likeness with that image.

Thus it is, at the point when fragmentation has reached its utmost limit and Satan is "identified" by Los that Blake, by means of a marvelous transposition, is able to turn the dead and potentially "poisonous" Newtonian corpuscles into living seeds of the life of humanity to come. At a later point in *Milton,* Los will be able to proclaim the plenitude of those seeds, harvested as grain and grape, the stuff of bread and wine, flesh and blood. "Fellow Labourers! The Great Vintage & Harvest is now upon Earth / The whole extent of the Globe is explored" (25.17-18). But at the outset of the struggle in *Milton,* the outcome seems very much in doubt. The seeds of the humanity to come must be made to grow, which means that they must be regarded and responded to as though there were a life force within their apparently lifeless exteriors, a life force in need of liberation and nurture. Only in such a manner can the collective power of the life force within be revealed, and only in such a manner can that collective life force merge so as to liberate its full apocalyptic energy, "To go forth," as Milton does at the end of the poem bearing his name, "to the Great Harvest & Vintage of the Nations" (43.1).

Notes

[1] The present essay grows out of a discussion and dialogue begun with George S. Rousseau in the meeting of the Literature and Science section of the 1978 MLA convention, where I delivered a paper entitled "Visionary Semantics: Blake, Newton, and the Language of Scientific Authority," currently in circulation. Rousseau himself delivered "Literature and Science: Decoding the State of the Field" in a special session convened to discuss the implications of his paper and the papers of those presenting in the section for new and future directions in literature and science. Rousseau's paper, slightly reworked, appears as "Literature and Science: The State of the Field," *Isis,* 9 (1978), 583-91. In it, he claims that the current vogue

of structuralist and post-structuralist approaches to the history of ideas have rendered traditional approaches to literature and science moribund, if not obsolete. For example, the rise to prominence of Michel Foucault, "all of whose books inherently deal with literature and science," had the result of repelling "most serious students then [i.e., in the sixties] . . . and had the further effect of transforming old categories, in a sense rendering them obsolete. The question for someone writing about science and literature changed from 'what type of critic are you?' to 'how much self-consciousness do you have about your methodology?'" (p. 589). This essay constitutes a response to Rousseau's gloomy portrayal of the field and, it is hoped, one conceptual approach to the field that can arrogate to itself the close analysis of rhetoric that is at the heart of the structuralist and post-structuralist methodologies, while at the same time dealing with recognizable scientific and literary texts in a manner that is plausible, if not wholly conventional. In its original form, the essay was presented at a seminar chaired by John Neubauer and entitled "Conceptual Approaches to Literature and Science in the Eighteenth Century." The seminar was convened at the 1979 meeting of ASECS, held in Atlanta.

[2] See *Science and Imagination* (Ithaca, N.Y.: Cornell University Press, 1956), ch. V, "The Scientific Background of Swift's *Voyage to Laputa*," pp. 110-54.

[3] *The Poetry and Prose of William Blake,* ed. David V. Erdman, commentator Harold Bloom (Garden City, N.Y.: Doubleday, 1965), pl. 98, ll. 27 ff. Subsequent references to Blake will be to this text, and will appear in the text of the essay, cited by plate, plate and line, or page and line, as appropriate.

[4] Newton's conception of absolute space is made clear in Book I, Section II, of the *Principia*. The passage quoted in the text of the essay may be found in *Sir Isaac Newton, Principia,* trans. Andrew Motte, rev. Florian Cajori, 2 vols. (Berkeley and Los Angeles: University of California Press, 1934), p. 549. Subsequent references to the *Principia* will be to this edition and will be made by page number only in the text of the essay. The rationale for omitting the volume number is that the Cajori edition uses running pagination, even though it is printed in two volumes. Newton's conception of absolute time, i.e., a framed, six-thousand-year Biblical chronology, is made clear elsewhere, in *Observations on the Prophecies of Daniel and the Apocalypse of St. John in Two Parts,* 2 vols. (London: J. Roberts, 1733).

[5] See note 4 for Newton on absolute space and time.

[6] See Nicolson's *Newton Demands the Muse: Newton's "Opticks" and the Eighteenth Century Poets* (Princeton: Princeton University Press, 1946); Schwartz's *Samuel Johnson and the New Science* (Madison: University of Wisconsin Press, 1971); and Jacob's *The Newtonians and the English Revolution, 1689-1720* (Ithaca, N.Y.: Cornell University Press, 1976).

[7] On Pope and Addison, see *Newton Demands the Muse,* pp. 123-64. On Johnson, see *Samuel Johnson . . . Science,* pp. 59-93.

[8] A fuller elaboration than can be made here has been made in my "Blake on Space and Time," forthcoming in *Science/Technology and the Humanities*. Briefly, it might be noted that the Four Zoas, as they approach the condition of instantaneous change at the end of *Jerusalem,* also approach the condition of light, under circumstances in which the newly merged categories of space and time become one and the same, existing in a continuum. The energy exhibited by the Four Zoas, which appears as consuming fire to the fallen and as delight to the redeemed, is derived from the ability of the "matter" of the Zoas to change instantaneously—with the speed of light, in fact. The space-time continuum Blake is describing in his visionary way, a continuum in which energy is liberated by matter moving at the speed of light, is, in its essentials, very close to the continuum described by Einstein in his world-shaking equation $e=mc^2$.

[9] For a good and pithy restatement of this position for a modern critical audience, see Stanley E. Fish, "Normal Circumstances, Literal Language, Direct Speech Acts, the Ordinary, the Everyday, the Obvious, What Goes without Saying, and Other Special Cases," *Critical Inquiry,* 4 (1978), 625-44.

[10] For Gleckner's discussion, see "Most Holy Forms of Thought: Some Observations on Blake and Language," *ELH,* 41 (1974), 555-77. My "Visionary Semantics" is discussed in note 1.

[11] The sense is that of a corpus, the term used by linguists to describe a body of utterances made and recorded diachronically, as opposed to the total number of possible utterances in the language deployed synchronically. See Claude Lévi-Strauss, *Le cru et le cuit* (Paris: Plon, 1964), especially the conclusion. See also Jonathan Culler, *Structuralist Poetics* (Ithaca, N.Y.: Cornell University Press, 1975), pp. 43 ff.

[12] *The Marriage of Heaven and Hell,* pls. 22-23, makes as much clear. According to Blake, "The Worship of God is. Honouring his gifts in other men, each according to his genius." And "if Jesus is the Greatest man, you ought to love him in the greatest degree." The Gospels were written by those who loved such a "man of genius," and thus the Gospels exhibited the genius of those who wrote them.

[13] See Ault's *Visionary Physics: Blake's Response to Newton* (Chicago: University of Chicago Press, 1974);

his "Incommensurability and Interconnection in Blake's Anti-Newtonian Text," *Studies in Romanticism,* 16 (1977), 277-303; and Curtis's "Blake and the 'Moment of Time': An Eighteenth-Century Controversy in Mathematics," *Philological Quarterly,* 51 (1972), 460-70.

[14] See *Visionary Physics* and *Newton Demands the Muse.*

[15] *The Rhetoric of Science: A Study of Scientific Imagery and Ideas in Eighteenth-Century English Poetry* (Berkeley and Los Angeles: University of California Press, 1966), p. 97.

[16] For a full discussion of this "father-son" relationship, see Frank E. Manuel, *A Portrait of Isaac Newton* (Cambridge, Mass.: Harvard University Press, 1968), pp. 23-35, 51-67.

[17] See "Incommensurability and Interconnection," cited above. See also J. E. McGuire and P. M. Rattansi, "Newton and the 'Pipes of Pan,'" *Notes and Records of the Royal Society of London,* 21 (1966), 108-43, also cited by Ault, p. 277n.

[18] Newton begins by talking of the *"five primary planets, Mercury, Venus, Mars, Jupiter, and Saturn"* (p. 403), then proves that the earth exhibits similar properties of motion, talking finally of the six in the General Scholium, p. 543.

[19] See note 8.

[20] *Visionary Physics,* pp. 96-140.

[21] In a letter to his brother James, dated January 30, 1803, Blake writes that he goes "on Merrily with my Greek & Latin . . . as I find it very Easy . . ." (in *Blake,* ed. Erdman, p. 696).

[22] For a fuller discussion of Newton's meaning and his dilemma, see Colin Murray Turbayne, *The Myth of Metaphor* (1962; rpt. Columbia, S.C.: University of South Carolina Press, 1970), pp. 44-45.

[23] *Harper's Latin Dictionary,* eds. Charlton T. Lewis and Charles Short, rev. ed. (1879; rpt. New York: Harper Brothers, 1907), p. 750.

[24] The connotation is consistent and of long standing, going all the way back to Blake's earliest preserved writings. See, for example, the Ossianic fragment "then She bore Pale desire," contemporaneous with *Poetical Sketches* (1783), in *Blake,* ed. Erdman, pp. 437-39.

[25] For Ault's comments, see *Visionary Physics,* pp. 155-56.

[26] These rules, found on pp. 398-400, attempt to standardize the causes of apparently similar phenomena, the covert motivation being to move toward a view of the universe in which formal cause and efficient cause proceed from one and the same source—God.

[27] "The mind is its own place, and in it self / Can make a Heav'n of Hell, a Hell of Heav'n" (II.254-55).

[28] Ll. 620-22.

[29] XII.587.

[30] The speaker of that poem puts his selfhood into the seemingly selfless task of tending a tree, rather than confronting the friend who angers him. As the result of his choice of strategies, the tree produces an apple which, like the apple in the Garden, is a deceptive form of selfhood.

> And I waterd it in fears,
> Night & morning with my tears:
> And I sunned it with my smiles,
> And with soft deceitful wiles
>
> (ll. 5-8)

When the speaker's friend steals, and presumably eats, the apple, he is seen to be "outstretched beneath the tree" (l. 16)—"dead," in the sense of having been deprived of his free and autonomous selfhood. For the speaker, now "inside" his erstwhile friend, has taken over that selfhood. Without the full Gothic trappings, the concept seems very much like that of the vampire, interest in which grew and evolved during the late eighteenth and nineteenth centuries. On the other hand, Blake may be viewed as being caught up in the same currents of thought that led Sade to write of the utter possession of one individual by another. See Michel Foucault, "Language to Infinity," in *Language, Counter-Memory, Practice: Selected Essays and Interviews,* trans. Donald F. Bouchard and Sherry Simon (Ithaca, N.Y.: Cornell University Press, 1977), pp. 53-67, esp. 60-63, 65-66.

P. M. Rattansi   (essay date 1981)

SOURCE: "Voltaire and the Enlightenment Image of Newton," in *History & Imagination: Essays in Honor of H. R. Trevor-Roper,* Hugh Lloyd-Jones, Valerie Pearl, Blair Worden, eds., Holmes and Meier Publishers, 1981, pp. 218-32.

[*In the following essay, Rattansi analyzes Voltaire's interest in Newton and his scientific writings, tracing the impact Voltaire had on the public's acceptance of Newton's conception of the universe, as opposed to that of René Descartes.*]

While the publication of the ***Principia Mathematica*** in 1687 secured almost universal admiration for the scientific and mathematical genius of Sir Isaac Newton, his contemporaries differed widely in their assessments of what he had achieved in his masterpiece. Edmond Halley placed Newton's genius nearest to the gods in the ode he prefixed to that work. One of Newton's greatest scientific contemporaries, Christian Huygens, was astonished, however, that Newton should have chosen to rear his magnificent structure on such a 'manifest absurdity' as the idea of an universal attraction.[1] Leibniz was to accuse Newton of having turned all the operations of nature into a perpetual miracle.[2] Brought up on Cartesian rationalism, Huygens and Leibniz saw in the acceptance of 'unintelligible' attraction a reversion to the 'occult' qualities of the despised scholastics and an abandonment of that luminous clarity the Cartesian revolution had brought into physical thought. It was the combination of 'rational' (a rigorous mathematical-mechanical method) and 'irrational' (the use of a notion of force not reducible to mechanical impact) that they found dismaying and disconcerting in Newton. The first review of the **Principia** in the *Journal des Savants* set the tone for the dominant continental response. The reviewer recognised that Newton had laid claim to the creation of a new 'system of the world'. What he had created, in fact, was a system of mechanics, more perfect than anyone could have dared to imagine, but based on assumptions that were arbitrary and unprovable. Newton wrote as a geometer, not as a physicist. Only when he substituted true motions in place of the ones he had imagined would he succeed in founding a new physics.[3]

Nearly half a century was to pass before Newton found worthy champions in the land of Descartes. Recalling that time, the physicist Maupertuis wrote of the timidity, fear and caution with which, in his earliest work of 1732, he had pleaded with his countrymen not to dismiss Newton's concept of 'attraction' out of hand. According to Maupertuis, the notion remained almost wholly confined to its island home. If it ever chanced to cross the Channel, it was feared as a monstrous apparition. So charmed were those on the Continent with having given a semblance of the mechanical to their explanations of nature, 'that they rejected without hearing true mechanism when it offered itself.[4] But Maupertuis was not alone. He was soon joined by a populariser of genius, Voltaire. Once he had been reassured by Maupertuis of the scientific worth of Newton's work, Voltaire used all his propagandist skills to familiarise an educated public with Newton's ideas and to persuade it to adopt them. He succeeded in achieving Newton's apotheosis as the founding father of a new age of reason.

Long familiarity has dulled the surprise we ought to feel at Voltaire's taking it upon himself to dethrone Descartes and install Newton as a pioneer of the Enlightenment. To have made the Cartesian mode of explaining nature appear no more than 'a semblance of

mechanism', while conferring the status of *la méchanisme veritable* on a system based on attraction, was no mean achievement. Why did that cause enlist Voltaire's passionate interest and how did he help to carry it to victory? Those questions deserve a serious answer since it is Descartes who, at first glance, would seem to be a much more fitting symbol for an age of reason.

Descartes had supplied a philosophical basis for the ancient dream that the lucidity and rigour which seemed uniquely characteristic of mathematical reasoning could be extended to all human knowledge. Aristotle had traced the power of mathematical demonstration to the patterns of reasoning it employed. By formalising it in his logic, he believed he had laid the way open for the attainment of a comparable degree of certainty in other fields of knowledge. For Aristotle such an enterprise by no means demanded that the richness of the sensible world be reduced to the pale abstractions of mathematics, as Plato had attempted in his *Timaeus*. By the sixteenth century, the scholastic-Aristotelian edifice of knowledge aroused in some innovators the same revulsion as the Gothic cathedral. They reverted to the classical ideal of mathematical harmony as articulated by Pythagoreans and Platonists. That ideal inspired and provided the justification for Copernicus' overthrow of ancient cosmology and substitution of a more 'harmonious' system of the world. The appeal of his reform remained largely confined to those who, like Kepler and Galileo, accepted the mathematical ideal. It was Descartes who grasped that their piecemeal attempts to amend the old structure were futile.

In his *Discourse* (1637), Descartes had compared received knowledge to a ruined building, now beyond repair. It must be razed to the ground. A new one was to rise in its place, on new foundations and according to the design of a single architect, Descartes himself. It was to be a classical edifice, not the Gothic monstrosity with which his teachers had familiarised him at La Flèche. Mathematics was again to supply the supreme model for all human knowledge. By accepting that ideal, Descartes was rejecting Aristotle's view of the power and fascination of mathematics.

For Aristotle the conviction carried by mathematical demonstration lay in the patterns of reasoning it embodied, not in its use of such specifically mathematical concepts as points, lines, surfaces and solids. Each science had its own appropriate basic concepts and entities, and in each it was possible to arrive at secure knowledge by valid reasoning. The immobile and insensible served the science of the immobile and insensible, that is, of mathematics. It would be quite inappropriate to build up a science of the changing and the sensible realm of physics by using Plato's geometrical atoms. Aristotle's four elements, themselves sensible and changeable, could explain changes in that realm far more adequately.[5]

Descartes insisted that the power of mathematics resided in its indubitable starting-points. Nothing short of the certainty available in arithmetic and geometry was to be aimed at in all human knowledge. That could be attained only by confining attention to questions of order and measure. Our ideas would then carry the hallmarks of truth: clarity and distinctness. Sense experience was delusive and confused, and sensed qualities were utterly dependent on the more basic mathematical features of matter as it impinged on the senses. The simplest basic concepts for physics were matter and motion.

Voltaire did not deny Descartes' importance as a destroyer of old ideas. He had given sight to the blind.[6] But he had expelled ancient reveries only to introduce novel chimeras.[7] 'A man who disdained experience, never cited Galileo, and ventured to construct without materials, could not but erect an imaginary edifice.'[8] Descartes' system had turned for Voltaire into 'an enchanted castle'.[9] Descartes had achieved results quite contrary to those he had intended because, although one of the greatest geometers of his age, he had soon abandoned geometry and the 'geometric spirit' for the *esprit de système*. His philosophy was an ingenious romance, his physics a tissue of errors. Galileo was greater than Descartes, since he had not tried to create an imaginary universe, but was content to examine that which existed.[10]

Voltaire recognised in Descartes the pioneer of the conception that the *esprit géométrique* need not remain confined to mathematical sciences but could be extended to all knowledge. He had blazed the trail for the *philosophes* by addressing his reform not to the academies but to the educated layman. One of Descartes' early works affirmed that his interest did not lie in 'scholastic type' distinctions but in devising rules to serve the contingencies of decision in everyday life.[11] He had not embellished his work with the names of past thinkers, and he emphasised the distinction between erudition and the search for truth. He thought those who were best acquainted with the thinkers of the past were likely to be most infected with their errors and least fitted to receive his novel ideas.[12]

According to Voltaire Newton was superior to Descartes because his discoveries had been made by experience and then confirmed by geometry. In his early 'Philosophical Letters' (1734), Voltaire attempted a lengthy Plutarchian comparison of the two thinkers. He portrayed a Newton who had quickly detected the falsity of the vortices which Descartes had imagined to explain the motion of the planets round the sun and gravitation on the earth. Newton had exploded the notion of such vortices, to his own satisfaction, by rigorous calculation—that guide which had ceased to keep in check the extravagancies of Descartes' lively imagination. Newton had then despaired of any other way of explaining those phenomena. The sight of a falling apple in the solitude of a garden during the Plague year of 1666 had plunged him into a profound meditation, carefully guided by mathematical reasoning. How scrupulous Newton was in not mistaking conjecture for truth was shown by the fact that he rejected the results of those meditations because they did not accord with the faulty measure of the earth then available. Only the revision of that measure prompted him to take up his former calculations again.

Newton's approach, so different from Descartes', was equally evident in his optics, where he had 'anatomised' a single ray of light with more dexterity than the most skilled dissector of a human body. By 'the bare assistance of a prism'[13] he had demonstrated that light consisted of a mixture of coloured rays. Descartes had gained immortal fame by mathematically explaining the rainbow, but had then committed himself to a fundamentally erroneous conception of the nature of light.

Voltaire was aware that his comparison would shock his countrymen. They had recognised numerous defects in Descartes' philosophical and scientific ideas. They believed those defects could be remedied. Certainly, they were not generally disposed to replace them with Newton's doctrines. Voltaire dated the beginnings of the decline of the 'Chimerical philosophy' of Descartes in France to 1730.[14] His own conversion to Newton's doctrines had begun during his self-imposed exile in England after his second confinement in the Bastille. The fruits of his sojourn were the *Lettres philosophiques* (1734), four of which were devoted to Newton. Voltaire depicted a land where the spirit of toleration, reason and good sense prevailed in every sphere of life. He believed that the same spirit of sanity and modesty was evident in the greatest of English thinkers: Bacon, Locke and Newton.

Voltaire said he had found nothing in English thought comparable to the corroding scepticism of Montaigne, La Rochefoucauld's biting satires on human nature, Pascal's tragic pessimism, Malebranche's 'sublime illusions', or the deeply flawed teaching of Descartes. Instead, the English had given the world Bacon's experimental philosophy, Locke's anatomy of the human mind and Newton's great system of the world. In the four letters on Newton, Voltaire described his optical discoveries, explained his ideas of gravitational attraction, assigned to Newton priority in the discovery of the infinitesimal calculus, and had praise even for his Biblical chronology.

The thorniest part of Voltaire's endeavour was the defence of Newtonian attraction. It was precisely in the name of reason that continental thinkers had denounced it. They complained that when Newton and his followers were asked to explain how parts of matter could act on other parts without any material intermediary, they resorted to obscure ideas which involved a continuous divine intervention. 'In the time of Mr. Boyle, nobody would have ventured to publish such chimerical notions,' Leibniz complained to Samuel Clarke in 1716. 'But it is men's misfortune to grow, at last, out of conceit with reason itself, and to be weary of light . . . What has happened in poetry, happens also in the philosophical world. People are grown weary of rational romances . . . and they are become fond again of tales of fairies.'[15]

Voltaire defended Newton against the charge of reviving 'occult' qualities by using arguments that implied a revision of the notion of what constituted a rational explanation. The man who had first traced the ascent of water in a force pump to the pressure of the atmosphere, or of the movement of the arm to muscular contraction, had discovered something new and useful, even if the causes of the elasticity of the air or muscular contraction remained unknown. Newton had shown that the reason why heavy bodies fell towards earth and the planets were retained in their orbits around the sun was a gravitational attraction, and that no subtle matter nor any other force could possibly be involved. It was not necessary for him to have furnished 'the cause of this cause', one of the secrets of God. Voltaire hinted that those who were dissatisfied with Newton's explanations demanded that a rational explanation must be anchored not only in a systematic, but in a *complete* account of nature, and were falling prey, like Descartes, to the *esprit de système*.[16]

One unexpected feature of the *Elémens* is the extent to which Voltaire commended the Newtonian system of thought for its decisive *theological* superiority over those of two other leading thinkers, Descartes and Leibniz—unexpected since the 'rational' God of the continental thinkers may, at first sight, appear more congenial to a champion of Enlightenment rationalism. Voltaire did not doubt Descartes' piety, but pointed out how often Cartesians tended to succumb to atheism. 'Give me matter and motion and I shall build you a universe.' How easily could Descartes' proud boast turn into a denial of God's role in creation, as Spinoza's had done! Newton placed no such confidence in the power of puny human reason to reconstruct even a 'likely story' about the way in which God had put together the universe. He had regarded the universe as expressing not rational necessity or a principle of 'sufficient reason', but God's unfettered and sovereign voluntary choice. Fallen man had access only to the results of that choice, as revealed in the arrangement of the world, in the structure and organisation of living things, and in the motions and processes ruling natural phenomena.

Underlying the contrasting ways in which Descartes and Newton studied nature were, thus, to Voltaire's mind, two different ways of conceiving the relation between God and his creation, emphasising either the 'Hellenic' or 'Hebraic' elements in the Christian conception of God. If the stress was on divine reason, then, as Descartes had affirmed, human reason could be said to participate in it whenever it conceived clear and distinct ideas which could then serve as the first principles of an essentially deductive account of nature. Experience would need to be called upon only to decide between alternate ways in which a particular effect mechanically resulted.[17] On the other hand, if the stress was on the divine will, we would be content to study phenomena through experience and experiment, and trace its causes in so far as we could mathematically prove them. It would lead us to renounce the hope of ever attaining the knowledge of ultimate causes or a complete system of knowledge like that envisaged by Descartes or Leibniz.

It was true that the voluntaristic conception of God had been declared unworthy and favourable to atheism. Was not a God who made planets orbit the sun from west to east, and decided upon a particular number of animal species, planets and stars in His universe, like a capricious artisan? Just before the Hanoverian succession, Leibniz had accused Newton of promoting the decay of religion in England by holding such a view of God. God, surely, always chose the best. When Samuel Clarke, who defended Newton's opinions, replied that there were indifferent states of affairs which offered no 'rational' basis for a choice, Leibniz insisted that nowhere in nature was it possible to find two exactly similar things. If God had made things between which differences were 'indiscernible', He would be deprived of 'sufficient reason' for placing one rather than another in a particular place. Clarke retorted that it was exact similarity which made it possible for two individual rays of light to produce the sensation of redness.[18] For Leibniz 'indiscernibleness' detracted from the rationality of God, while for Clarke it served best to express the power and majesty of God.

Voltaire accepted and repeated Clarke's arguments. His preference for a will-theology was also evident in his defence of Newtonian ideas of space and time. Rationalist thinkers had traditionally rejected the conception of space as a featureless void. Descartes, stripping matter to its bare essence, had finally arrived at the clear and distinct idea of 'extension'. Since extension could hardly be the extension of nothing, he had then proceeded to identify space and matter making the universe a plenum. Leibniz said space was nothing but an order of co-existence among things, as time was an order of succession among events. Newton, by contrast, conceived space and time not merely as states of relations but as absolutes. According to Voltaire, Newton's conception served far better to establish the existence and true attributes of God. If the world was finite and contained a void or empty space, then the existence of matter was not a necessity but a result of divine choice. Once matter existed, it had to be extended. There was no such necessity in its possession of powers such as those of gravitational attraction. It had been endowed with them by God's free choice. Newton's world was radically contingent on the divine will. Descartes' world could easily be imagined as self-sufficient. It was 'indefinitely' extended and wholly material, and never ran down because the total quantity of motion in it always remained constant. Newton's conception was therefore far more favourable to establishing the necessity of a divine creator and the utterly dependent nature of matter, and offered the greatest protection against pantheism or materialism.

Why was the Newtonian idea of God as a *dominus* and the absolute disparity between the divine and human intellects more congenial to Voltaire than the rational supreme architect of Descartes and Leibniz? His bitter experience of persecution for his opinions in France and his reflections on the tolerant atmosphere he had breathed in England had led Voltaire to trace the roots of intolerance to the conviction of being in absolute possession of the truth. Descartes and Leibniz overturned the old dogmatism of the schools, only to fall prey to the *esprit de système*. A moderately sceptical view of the limits of human knowledge, such as the one precisely delineated by Locke, was the best guarantee of freedom of thought.

Voltaire was justified in his belief that Newton attached great value to the theological superiority of his own ideas of space and time over those of Descartes and Leibniz. During his years of exile in England, Voltaire had been close to Samuel Clarke. His testimony is an accurate reflection of the indivisibility of scientific and religious concerns in Newton's circle. 'When I wrote my treatise about our Systeme,' Newton had written to Richard Bentley in 1692, 'I had my eye on such Principles as might work with considering men for the beliefe of a Deity . . .'[19] The religious ideas appended to the second edition of the **Principia** were not pious afterthoughts tacked on to a scientific treatise to deflect the criticisms of religious zealots. The union of science and religion is evident in Newton's earliest manuscript remains. It determined his initial response to the teachings of Descartes. In a manuscript dating from the 1670s, Newton rejected Cartesian ideas of matter, of motion and of mind or soul.[20]

Newton believed that at the heart of Cartesian philosophy lay a radically defective notion of extension, which offered 'a path to atheism'. It was necessary to 'overthrow' it, for only then would it be possible to lay 'truer foundations of the mechanical sciences'.[21] Descartes had identified extension with matter. But a clear idea of extension revealed it as infinite, uncreated and existing eternally. It was an absolute idea involving no reference to God, and no contradiction was involved when the idea of the existence of matter was combined with that of the non-existence of God. Such an idea of matter paved the way to atheism. The idea of motion which Descartes had adopted (in part to circumvent the Catholic ban on Copernicanism) was purely relative, and took no account of the fact that *real* forces were involved in true, as distinct from merely relative, motion. It was necessary to refer motion to 'some motionless thing such as extension alone or space in so far as it is seen to be truly distinct from bodies'. Moreover, by his absolute distinction between thinking and extended body, Descartes had rendered the union of mind and body 'unintelligible'.[22]

All these grave disadvantages could be avoided by sharply distinguishing space from matter. Extension could be 'clearly conceived', as outside of the world and empty of body. The idea was not one of nothing, but rather an 'excessively clear' one.[23] 'Nothing' had no properties, while extension was uniform and unlimited in length, breadth and depth. It could not be imagined, but could certainly be understood. Once space and matter were distinguished, the idea of matter became indissolubly united with that of God. Space was an 'emanent effect of God' and in that sense necessary. 'If ever space had not existed God at that time would have been nowhere.' Matter existed only because God had so willed: God had 'created the world solely by an act of will'.[24]

So intensely did Newton wish to downgrade matter that he suggested that it would be possible entirely to do away with the concept of matter or body. Imagine that God had made a portion of space tangible, impenetrable and mobile. It would then have all the properties of body as known to us. It would excite perceptions in created minds and be capable of being moved by them. Even our own power to move what we took to be our bodies could be conceived as a much weaker analogue of the divine power to make empty space impenetrable. Just as God was not space, but contained it 'eminently', so created mind could then also be said 'eminently' to contain body. Newton believed that such a conception of body or matter would explain and confirm 'the chief truths of metaphysics': that God existed, that He had created the world from nothing, and that bodies differ from minds but can combine with them.[25]

Already in the 1670s Newton was elaborating the array of concepts that he would deploy in the **Principia** and in the 'General Scholium' added to its second edition: the ideas of absolute space and time, of forces as real entities, and of an analogy between God's creative and sustaining activity and the power of human beings to move their bodies by the exercise of the will.

Voltaire believed that a will-theology served to cut down human pretensions to absolute knowledge. By providing the basis for the empirical and experimental approach of Newton and Locke, it had contributed to the spirit of toleration characteristic of English life. The virtues of a distinct English 'experimental philosophy', free from the opposing dogmatisms attributed to scholasticism and Cartesianism, had already been emphasised by the founders and publicists of the Royal Society soon after the Restoration in 1660. They praised it as the best preservative against the 'enthusiasm' or fanaticism which they condemned as the root cause of civil war and regicide in England. By undermining excessive confidence in opinions, the 'experimental philosophy' would make men more obedient to authority. Bishop Sprat, the Royal Society's first historian, remarked that '. . . the doubtful, the scrupulous, the diligent Observer of Nature, is nearer to make a modest, a severe, a meek, an humble Christian . . .'. The Fellows of the Society met every week to witness experiments. They did not speculate prematurely on the causes involved in them beforehand, since they knew how easy it was to fit experiments to preconceptions. When their interpretations of the experiments diverged, no quarrels arose, since they recognised that 'there may be several Methods of Nature, in producing the same Thing, and all equally good'.[26] Robert Hooke, who as first Curator of the Society was entrusted with presenting a weekly experiment before the Fellows, agreed that scientific knowledge was likely to grow very slowly. Besides the obscurity of things, there was the added difficulty that 'even the forces of our own minds conspire to betray us'. The only safeguard was in 'the real, the mechanical, the experimental Philosophy . . .'.[27]

The myth of an 'experimental philosophy', free from all speculative commitments and presuppositions, deriving theories solely from experiments, was already taking shape in the mid-seventeenth century. It was expressed in a popular and influential form by Sprat. He berated the founders of 'new dogmatisms' who had rejected the ancient varieties of that same distemper, but had then imposed their own theories on men's reason. It reinforced for him the lesson of the English civil war: 'For we also have beheld the Pretenders to publick Liberty, turn the greatest *Tyrants* themselves.' Sprat obviously included the Cartesians among the new 'dogmatists'. He sharply contrasted the approach of the Royal Society with that of Descartes, who had rejected all he could learn from the senses 'and wholly gave himself over to a reflexion on the naked *Ideas* of his own mind'. The result was narrow and obscure apprehensions and a wilful ignorance. Very different was the method of the members of the Society, meeting to view experiments, and only then taking it upon themselves to '*judge* and resolve upon the matters of fact'. They venerated 'the inartificial process of the *Experiment,* and not the Acuteness of any Commentary upon it . . .'. If disputes arose, they were never such as to divide them into factions, since they would

be based 'not on matters of speculation or opinion, but onely of sence . . .'.[28]

Sprat wished to present the 'experimental philosophy' purely as a method. Like any method claiming to lead to truth, it was really anchored in a metaphysic—a set of assumptions about what the world is like and what constitutes a satisfactory and adequate explanation of change. The myth of the 'experiment' as a quasi-religious act, which permitted the true nature of things to be reflected in the cleansed and polished 'mirror of the human mind', occasionally broke down in Sprat's treatise. That is evident in Sprat's discussion of the merits of Sir Christopher Wren, whom he chose as exemplifying the Society's ideal. Sprat gave Wren's reformulation of the Cartesian laws of motion precedence above all his other achievements. Descartes had based them only on 'gross Trials' of tennis and billiard balls, while Wren had devised a special instrument for the purpose and had confirmed his conclusions by hundreds of experiments. Why was so much importance to be attached to the laws of motion and why were they to be regarded as the 'Principles of all Demonstrations in Natural Philosophy'? Sprat's answer is revealing: because '. . . Generation, Corruption, Alteration, and all the Vicissitudes of Nature, are nothing else but the effects arising from the meeting of little Bodies, of differing Figures, Magnitudes, and Velocities'.[29]

Such a conception of what nature is like and how all changes in it are to be explained could scarcely have been derived from experiment. Rather, it provided the *framework* for the interpretation of experiments and, at least in the 'exact sciences' of that time, governed the choice and design of the experiments themselves. The 'mechanical-mathematical' conception of nature which Sprat described had only recently been clearly articulated and no one had contributed more to it than Descartes. It was misleading, therefore, to set up a contrast between a Descartes who began with presuppositions about nature and proceeded to build up a deductive account of natural phenomena, and the English experimental philosophers who were said to have begun with the results of observation and experiment which they then generalised by induction. When discussing the errors of Descartes, Voltaire singled out his laws of motion, his vortices of subtle matter, and his ideas about the nature of light and colour, magnetism and the motion of the heart. It would be difficult to attribute these to a tendency to devise *a priori* explanations in preference to induction from phenomena. Historians today attribute them, rather, to failures of conceptualisation, or mathematisation, or experimental testing of hypotheses.[30] Descartes himself was conscious of many of these deficiencies, but had aimed above all at persuading others that it was possible, in principle, to construct mechanical explanations for all natural phenomena.[31]

The contrast between the English 'experimental philosophy' and the Cartesian philosophy, as propagated by the Royal Society, was accepted fully by Newton in his earliest published work. His paper on light and colours, read before the Society in 1672, seemed like a classic vindication of the 'experimental philosophy'. Wishing to investigate colours, Newton had darkened his chamber and made experiments with a prism. Conclusions 'rigidly' drawn from experimental results were subjected to further experimental tests which culminated in a single 'crucial experiment'. From these experiments, which appeared to have been carried out in a single session, emerged a new theory of colours, overturning all previous ones. Newton had found that each beam of coloured light, as it emerged from the prism on to a screen, had a characteristic index of refraction. He had not been able to change the colour or the degree of refraction by reflection, refraction or other optical means. That was proof, to Newton, that visible 'white' light was a mixture of rays of different colours. A prism separated out the colours, but did not create them by mixing light and shade, as ancient and even contemporary theories held.

Newton's attempt to tailor his account to fit the methodological prescriptions of the dominant 'experimental philosophy' was not entirely successful. Hooke conceded that Newton's discovery of an invariant relation between colour and refrangibility was an important experimental discovery. However, Newton's conclusion that white light was a mixture of colours depended on the hypothesis that light consisted of material particles. Hooke suggested that the experimental results were equally compatible with his own pressure-wave theory. In his reply Newton insisted that he did not need 'to explicate my Doctrine by an *Hypothesis*' at all, and that what he had asserted was 'most rigid consequence', drawn from 'experiments concluding positively and directly'.[32]

Recent historical studies have established that a far longer period of preparation, reflection and trials lay behind the idealised 'historical narration' Newton presented in the paper read before the Society. Only an experimenter with great mathematical competence would have been puzzled, as he said he was, by the fact that an oblong spectrum emerged from the prism instead of the round image of the sun. His experiments were by no means as independent of theories about the nature of light and colours as he maintained.[33] Indeed, theory, experiment and interpretation were so intertwined in his work—as in that of his other great scientific contemporaries—that they could not adequately be restated in terms of either of the two major conceptions of legitimate scientific method which then prevailed.

By Voltaire's time, Newton's redefinition had given a much greater mathematical tone to the 'experimental philosophy'. Newton's disciple, Colin Maclaurin, wrote that experiments and observations alone could not have enabled Newton to explain causes from effects and then effects from those causes: 'a sublime geometry was his guide in this nice and difficult enquiry.'[34] Newton believed that our knowledge is confined to gathering the properties of things from the phenomena, but that we must always seek quantitative laws linking the variations in those properties, because scientific knowledge must assume the form of the most secure knowledge that, besides revelation, we are acquainted with, that of mathematics. The mathematical link between colour and refrangibility of a light ray was an example of such a relationship. 'Hypotheses', to explain why that was so, had an inferior degree of certainty. Similarly, mathematical laws subjecting the motions of gross bodies of the whole *machina mundi* to precise calculation could be formulated on the assumption that bodies behave as if they attract each other, with a force varying in accordance with a universal law, although the nature of the 'attraction' remained a matter for conjecture. Newton had also relaxed the requirement, prominent in the 'experimental philosophy' of the early Royal Society, that any forces involved in natural phenomena must ultimately be reducible to contact of one body with another, since that was the only kind of action that was intelligible. That criterion led the continental *savants* to condemn Newtonian attraction. Newton assigned the assertion that 'all the Phaenomena of Nature are purely mechanical' to the class of 'Hypotheses that can never be established by experiments'.[35]

Newton's modification of the 'experimental philosophy' was grounded in a voluntaristic theology. In the 'General Scholium' added to the **Principia** he rejected the view that the diversity of things in the world was to be attributed to 'Blind metaphysical necessity'; thus he pointedly dissented from Leibniz's views. That diversity depended, rather, on the 'ideas and will of a Being necessarily existing', a 'living, intelligent, and powerful Being'.[36] It is unnecessary to assume that Newton came to favour a voluntaristic conception of God only as the chorus of continental criticisms grew louder. The conception was an important component not only of the 'context of justification' of his gravitational theory, but equally of the 'context of discovery' in which it was formulated. It helped to loosen the tyranny of picturable or 'intelligible' mechanisms upon his conceptual imagination.

What has been said so far may seem to vindicate the historical accuracy of the image of Newton that Voltaire presented in his *Elémens*. There was, nevertheless, a difference of nuance in Voltaire's enthusiastic adoption and advocacy of Newton's 'experimental philosophy' and its associated theological stance. Newton's attitude had been fashioned in the religious and political atmosphere of mid-seventeenth-century England. Like the Cambridge Platonist thinkers whose arguments found many echoes in his early manuscript writing, **'De gravitatione'**, Newton regarded it as urgently necessary to revise Cartesian conceptions of matter and motion because they unwittingly lent strong support to the menacing forces of materialism and atheism. His God was the God of Abraham and Isaac, not the cold rationalist principle of Deism.[37] In exalting the conception of God as 'pantokrator' in the 'General Scholium' in 1713, he set his face against the temper of a time when the Church of England was relaxing the requirements of belief it demanded from its flock.

Voltaire, on the other hand, was not really aiming to overwhelm the individual consciousness with an image of God of will and power continually and most intimately involved in the universe He had created. Voltaire chose to emphasise human insignificance in the vastness of the universe rather than divine immensity.[38] His fervent promotion of the Newtonian God of will and power was not aimed primarily at countering materialism and atheism. Voltaire regarded the greatest threat to freedom of thought as originating in grandiose systems of thought, made binding by authority on pain of persecution. Cartesianism was the latest example of that menace. A repressive church had first unsuccessfully tried to stifle its influence in France, but later came to embrace it as the basis for a new theology. Malebranche had reconciled Descartes with orthodox faith. Arnauld and Bossuet came to see Cartesianism as a new version of the *philosophia perennis* of Plato and St. Augustine. It was the same Bossuet, tutor to the Dauphin, who had condemned scepticism and toleration as twin monsters bred by the Reformation.[39] Traditionally, a will-theology had served to demolish the pretensions of a rational theology. In Voltaire's hands, it was turned against *all* grand systems of thought. The *esprit de système,* most recently expressed by Descartes and Leibniz, must itself be extirpated. The 'experimental philosophy' would make it impossible to set up any new dogma and would fatally weaken the power of authority to suppress free thought and to bar the way to human progress and happiness. Voltaire would enthusiastically have approved Maclaurin's verdict on the Cartesian philosophy: '. . . the foundation is so faulty, and the whole superstructure so erroneous, that it were much better to abandon the fabrick, and suffer the ruins to remain a memorial, in all time to come, of the folly of philosophical presumption and pride.'[40]

Voltaire had fully recognised the intimate link binding Newton's view of God and his conception of 'experimental philosophy', but he would have found uncongenial some other implications which flowed from Newton's will-theology. Newton believed that God's hidden will was revealed to fallen man not only in the structure and workings of nature, but in the unfolding course of history. By comparing historical events with Biblical prophecy, it was possible to demonstrate that the future had been foretold in minute detail. Newton devoted a great deal of his energy to such an enterprise, with the aims of confuting those who scoffed at religion and of securing the Protestant reliance on the Bible against the Catholic Counter-Reformation onslaught.[41] Knowledge about history was hidden in the Bible but could be seen to be there only retrospectively. So, too, truths about nature were concealed in ancient bodies of wisdom, but their full meaning would become clear only when they had been 'inductively' rediscovered. The Pythagorean 'harmony of the spheres' was really an enigmatic representation of Newton's law of universal gravitation; the literature of alchemy contained hints of the active principles which operated in nature.[42]

With the growing influence of Voltaire's image of Newton as the founder of a new kind of rationalism, which had supposedly broken free of theology and metaphysics and required nothing but the immediate testimony of the senses to build up its picture of the world, the integration of the religious and the scientific in Newton's thought became increasingly incomprehensible to succeeding generations. To Biot and Laplace, Newton's monumental labours in Biblical prophecy appeared so eccentric that they were tempted to regard them as proof that Newton's famous mental collapse of 1693 had left his intellect gravely impaired. Those charges were refuted by Sir David Brewster, who published the first comprehensive life of Newton in 1855 when the Darwinian storm lay in the future, and the alliance between science and religion in England through natural theology remained intact. But work on Newton's manuscripts shocked Brewster by revealing an aspect of Newton's thought that he, too, found irrational: the study of alchemy to which he had found Newton had devoted a great portion of his most creative years.[43]

The 'Newton industry' of the last few decades has given us much deeper knowledge of many diverse facets of Newton's life and work on the basis of his great manuscript remains, but without fully reconciling what seems 'rational' and 'irrational' to us in Newton's thought.[44] It is only by going beyond Voltaire's image to that seventeenth-century *milieu* in which Newton's intellectual formation took place that we can hope to bring together all that recent scholarship has discovered in a truer likeness of Isaac Newton.

Notes

[1] Huygens, *Oeuvres Complètes* (The Hague 1888-1950), IX, 538.

[2] H. G. Alexander (ed.), *The Leibniz-Clarke Correspondence* (Manchester 1956), 11-12.

[3] *Journal* (1688), cited in P. Mouy, *La Devéloppement de la Physique Cartésienne* (Paris 1934), 256.

[4] Cited by P. Burnet, *L'Introduction des Théories de Newton en France au XVIIe siècle* (Paris 1931), 9.

[5] A. Mansion, *Introduction à la Physique Aristotelienne* (Louvain-Paris 1945), 134-8.

[6] 'Lettres philosophiques', in *Oeuvres Complètes* (Paris 1879), XXII, 132.

[7] Letter to Comte des Alleurs, 1736, in ibid., XXXV, 51.

[8] 'Siècle de Louis XIV', in ibid., XIV, 534.

[9] Ibid., XXXV, 51.

[10] Ibid., XXXV, 52.

[11] Descartes, *Philosophical Works*, tr. Haldane & Ross (Cambridge 1931), 'Regulae', 1, 2.

[12] 'Principia philosophiae', in ibid., I, 209.

[13] Letter XVI, in *Oeuvres Complètes,* XXII, 141.

[14] Ecrivains français du siècle de Louis XIV', in ibid., XIV, 63.

[15] Alexander, *Leibniz-Clarke Correspondence,* 92.

[16] *Oeuvres Complètes,* XXII, 131.

[17] G. Buchdahl, *Metaphysics and the Philosophy of Science* (Oxford 1969), 79-180.

[18] Alexander, op. cit., esp. 97-101.

[19] Newton, *Correspondence* (Cambridge 1959), III, 233.

[20] 'De gravitatione', in A. R. and M. B. Hall (eds & trs), *Unpublished Scientific Papers of Isaac Newton* (Cambridge 1962), 89-156.

[21] Ibid., 131.

[22] Ibid., 143.

[23] Ibid., 132.

[24] Ibid., 141.

[25] Ibid., 142.

[26] Sprat, *The History of the Royal Society of London* (London 1702 edn), 92.

[27] Hooke, *Micrographia* (London 1665), Preface.

[28] Sprat, op. cit., 95-7, 91-2.

[29] Ibid., 312.

[30] P. Mouy, op. cit., 1-71; R. S. Westfall, *Force in Newton's Physics* (London-New York, 1971), 56-98; Buchdahl, op. cit., 79-180.

[31] Mouy, *La Développement de la Physique Cartésienne,* 142.

[32] I. Bernard Cohen (ed.), *Isaac Newton's Papers and Letters on Natural Philosophy,* second ed. (Cambridge, Mass.-London 1978), 123.

[33] Recent studies are listed in ibid., 499-501.

[34] C. Maclaurin, *An Account of Sir Isaac Newton's Philosophical Discoveries,* second ed. (London 1750), 8.

[35] A. Koyré and I. B. Cohen, 'Newton and the Leibniz-Clarke correspondence', *Arch. inter. d'Hist. des Sc.,* XV (1962), 114.

[36] A. Motte and F. Cajori (eds & trs), *Mathematical Principles of Natural Philosophy* (New York 1969), II, 546.

[37] Frank E. Manuel, *The Religion of Isaac Newton* (Oxford 1974).

[38] P. Pomeau, *La Religion de Voltaire* (Paris 1969), 215; J. Erhard, *L'Idée de Nature en France dans la Première Moitié du XVIIe Siècle* (Paris 1963), 133ff.

[39] Bossuet, 'Défense de l'Histoire', in *Oeuvres Choisies* (Nimes 1785), III, 425.

[40] Maclaurin, op. cit., 82.

[41] Frank E. Manuel, *Isaac Newton, Historian* (Cambridge 1963).

[42] J. E. McGuire and P. M. Rattansi, 'Newton and the "Pipes of Pan" ', *Notes & Records Roy. Soc. Lond.,* XXI (1966), 108-43; B. J. T. Dobbs, *The Foundations of Newton's Alchemy (Cambridge 1975).*

[43] Brewster, *Memoirs of the Life, Writings and Discoveries of Sir Isaac Newton* (Edinburgh 1855), II, 374-5.

[44] R. S. Westfall, 'The changing world of the Newtonian industry', *Journ. Hist. Ideas,* XXXVII (1976), 175-86; Cohen, *Papers,* 498-504.

Newton's death mask and the reflecting telescope he invented.

Henry Guerlac (essay date 1981)

SOURCE: "Newton on the Continent: The Early Reception of His Physical Thought," in *Newton on the Continent,* Cornell University Press, 1981, pp. 41-73.

[*In the following essay, Guerlac investigates the nature of Newton's reputation in France prior to 1699 and reassesses the view held by some critics that, prior to 1738, there was great opposition between individuals who advocated Newton's physical theories and those who propounded the theories of René Descartes.*]

Besides the technical study of Newton's achievements in mathematics, optics, and dynamics, there is a phase of Newtonian scholarship which has attracted renewed interest and which we may call the "influence," the "reception," or the "legacy" of Newton. This is ambiguous, of course, for there are at least two ways in which the subject can be viewed: we can consider

Newton's reception by his learned contemporaries or his influence upon his scientific successors (by any definition of what the history of science is about, surely this is of major importance); or, on the other hand, we can deal with the influence he exerted through his natural philosophy and his advocacy of the experimental approach—that is, those aspects of his achievement comprehensible to the intelligent layman—upon the *Weltanschauung* of his age or later times. Clearly, this is a legitimate part of cultural or intellectual history, as scholars like Daniel Mornet and Preserved Smith (to name only two) long ago perceived.[1] And within our ranks of historians of science, Hélène Metzger, with her book on what she called the Newtonian "commentators," was surely an outstanding pioneer.[2]

I hasten to add that this second aspect of Newton's "legacy" has little or nothing to do with the so-called "externalist" approach to the history of science. It projects outwardly from science, or a branch of science, to observe its reception by society, instead of pointing inwardly to seek social, economic, and intellectual influences upon a scientist's work, influences which I happen to believe we cannot, in many cases, safely ignore. The current externalist—internalist debate—like many "either-or" disputes—seems utterly contrived and fatuous.[3]

Mme Metzger's book is a classic; yet she did not seriously raise, or try to answer, the question why the Boyle lecturers, the popularizers like John Keill and Henry Pemberton, or mavericks like John Toland, felt it important to interpret Newton's new system of the world for their contemporaries. The problem has recently been tackled by Margaret Jacob in various articles and in her rather audacious book, where she has argued that the popular exposition of Newton's world view by these "commentators" served ideological, religious, and sociopolitical ends.[4]

As to the reception of Newton in France, we are left—despite the books of Pierre Brunet, Ira Wade, and others—with considerable murkiness and oversimplification; and for the early period, say from 1672 to 1699, we have only tantalizing allusions, and scattered nuggets, in books written with other purposes in mind. In this paper I should like to single out two areas, two aspects of Newton's reception in France, that seem to call for more systematic investigation, and in the second area, for some reassessment.

The first has to do with Newton's reputation on the Continent before 1699, the year in which he was made a foreign associate of the Royal Academy of Sciences in Paris. The second, which I shall treat in some detail, is the reassessment of the conventional picture—of Cartesians arrayed against Newtonians—which Pierre Brunet sets forth in his study of the introduction of Newton's physical theories in France before 1738, that is, before Maupertuis, Clairaut, and Voltaire hoisted the banner of Newtonian physics in France.[5]

When did scientists on the Continent first hear of Newton? By what stages did his reputation grow until, for his recognized accomplishments, he was honored by the Academy of Sciences in 1699? We can, I think, pass over the flattering reference to him by name, as early as 1669, in the preface of Isaac Barrow's lectures on optics, or the appearance of the edition of Varenius's *Geographia generalis* Newton published in Cambridge in 1672. Neither could have aroused much interest abroad in this obscure, if obviously very gifted, young Englishman.

The chief events that brought Newton's name before the European scientific public were doubtless: (1) the publication in February 1672 of his now-famous first letter on light and color;[6] (2) his invention of the reflecting telescope, which brought about his election as F.R.S. in January 1672; and (3) Henry Oldenburg's orchestrated propaganda on Newton's behalf.

It was Newton's stubby little telescope, which promised to eliminate the chromatic aberration—the colored fringes—invariably encountered in the refracting telescopes of that day, that excited Christiaan Huygens (and others) when Oldenburg wrote him about Newton's discoveries.[7] In the new theory of the origin of color, Huygens evinced little interest, although Oldenburg repeatedly importuned him for his opinion.[8]

The first French savant to give serious attention to Newton's early paper on light and color was the Jesuit scientist, Father Ignace Gaston Pardies (1636-1673). This has always struck me as curious. Pardies was not a member of the Academy of Sciences, nor had he any longstanding contact with the Royal Society.[9] But he was a friend of Huygens, and a frequent participant at the meetings of the so-called Academy of the Abbé Bourdelot, an informal society, antedating the creation of the Academy.[10] After 1666, the membership of Bourdelot's group consisted chiefly of persons whom the Academy, for one reason or another (such as being, like Pardies, a Jesuit) did not admit; but members of the Academy, Huygens among them, were sometimes seen *chez* Boudelot.[11] Huygens, in any case, was aware that Pardies had a keen interest in optics, indeed was at work on a treatise that made use of a wave or pulse theory of the nature of light.[12] Perhaps Huygens, preoccupied with other matters (he had not begun to work out the theory he developed in his *Traité de la lumière* of 1690) brought Newton's paper to the attention of Pardies, with the suggestion that he evaluate it. All this, of course, is conjectural, but it may explain why Pardies's unsolicited paper, a letter to Oldenburg dated 9 April 1672, was the first response any French scientist made to Newton's new theory of color.[13]

Except for one element of confusion, the story of the cool reception of Newton's challenging new theory is all too familiar, and need not be repeated here. This element deserves at least a passing mention, otherwise it would be hard to understand the lack of interest in Newton's theory of color during these early years. Pardies never claimed to have repeated successfully Newton's famous two-prism experiment, the so-called *experimentum crucis.* Yet English or American readers could readily believe that this is so, if they confine their attention to the English version of the concessive phrases of Pardies's letter of 9 July 1672. The mistranslation of these important sentences appeared in the *Philosophical Transactions Abridged* (1809), which I. Bernard Cohen chose to use in his ***Isaac Newton's Papers and Letters on Natural Philosophy.***[14] This English version reads, with reference to the *experimentum crucis,* "When the experiment was performed after this manner, *everything succeeded,* and I have nothing further to desire."[15] Pardies, in fact, having finally understood the experiment, with the help of a sketch supplied by Newton, had simply written: "L'expérience ayant esté faite de cette façon je n'ay rien à dire." There is no reference to an experiment "succeeding."

At all events it was Newton's optical work, together with the reflecting telescope, that first made his name familiar in French scientific circles.[16] The experimental results he claimed, and the ingenuity of his theory, made it impossible to neglect his results for long. About 1679 France's leading experimental scientist, Edme Mariotte, determined to confirm or refute the Newtonian doctrine of color. He successfully repeated a number of Newton's experiments, but when he tried the *experimentum crucis* he concluded that the rays separated by the first prism did not appear to be monochromatic; on the contrary, they seemed to be further modified by the action of the second prism, yielding fringes of different colors.[17] Newton's theory, he concluded, could not be accepted. For more than a generation, this was gospel in France, and Newton's theory of color remained in disfavor.[18]

It is generally agreed, although the supporting evidence has not been fully marshalled, that Newton's reputation in these years as a meteoric mathematical genius outshone his work on light and color or even the invention of his reflecting telescope. Although he had published none of his mathematical discoveries before the appearance of his ***Principia,*** his repute as a mathematician of extraordinary ability was clearly established.

As historians of ideas we are happiest when we can navigate from the firm ground of one document to the next, and we are prone to forget how great a part travel, gossip, and word-of-mouth have played in the diffusion of scientific knowledge, indeed of knowledge of all sorts. We are truly fortunate when surviving letters or memoranda give us some hint of these informal exchanges.

In 1669, the self-educated London mathematician, John Collins, that "clearing house for mathematical gossip," as D. T. Whiteside has called him, learned from Isaac Barrow of Newton's *De analysi,* the earliest of Newton's mathematical papers to be circulated.[19] It contained an outline of his discoveries concerning infinite series and various applications of series expansion, but only a hint of the fluxional calculus. Collins, with his extensive contacts on the Continent, communicated Newton's results, but apparently not the precise methods used, to Slusius in Holland, to Jean Bertet and Francis Vernon in Paris, and to the venerable Giovanni Borelli in Italy. In May 1672, soon after he had learned about Newton's optical investigations, Christiaan Huygens heard from Henry Oldenburg that Newton had in hand an enlargement and corrected version of Mercator's Latin translation of Kinckhuysen's *Algebra,* a work for which Newton, it turned out, never found a publisher.[20]

It was not long before Leibniz—diplomat, philosopher, and polyhistor, and soon to emerge as Europe's most brilliant mathematician—learned about Newton. We are so accustomed to thinking of these two great men in terms of their later dispute over the invention of the calculus or of their philosophical differences set forth in the letters of the Clarke-Leibniz correspondence, that we overlook their earlier relations, or at least the occasions on which Leibniz spoke of Newton with admiration.

In 1672 Leibniz came to Paris on a diplomatic mission, chiefly designed to dangle before Louis XIV the proposal that he embark on the conquest of Egypt to satisfy the French monarch's martial ambitions and to wean him away from invading the Low Countries and Germany. The plan was offered too late—although, long after, it appealed to Napoleon Bonaparte—for the troops of the Sun King were already on the march. During this visit, however, Leibniz formed a close tie with Christian Huygens, met other members of the Academy of Sciences, and must have learned something about Newton's reflecting telescope and the new theory of color.[21]

Early the following year Leibniz was in London where he surely heard echoes of Newton's mathematical prowess, for he came to know various English scientists (among them Oldenburg, Robert Boyle, and the mathematician John Pell) and attended a meeting of the Royal Society.[22] Perhaps he met John Collins who, despite a lack of university training, had been made F.R.S. in 1667; but he certainly did not see Newton, comfortably immured in Trinity College, Cambridge. Leibniz's second English visit, in 1676, was in many respects more rewarding. At Collins's urging, Newton wrote for Leibniz his *Epistola prior* (13 June) describing his generalized binomial theorem. When Leibniz asked for more information, Newton replied with his *Epistola posterior* (24 October) expounding in more detail his binomial theorem, but also giving the key to his calculus—to the general method of drawing tangents, solving problems of maxima and minima, and so on—but only by means of his famous cipher, a seemingly meaningless jumble of letters and numbers.[23] Leibniz was suitably impressed; and referring to Newton's work on series he wrote: "That remarkable man is one of the few who have advanced the frontiers of the sciences."[24]

Whatever else it may have done—and it did not produce a crop of instant Newtonians across the Channel—the publication of the *Principia* greatly enhanced Newton's stature as a mathematician. As early as 1686, European scientists heard rumors about a forthcoming book by Newton. The source was, not surprisingly, Edmond Halley, who had not only cajoled Newton into writing and publishing it, and advanced the sum for printing it, but announced it in the *Philosophical Transactions* in 1686 and by personal letter. Huygens, for his part, learned of it in June 1687 through his young friend, Fatio de Duillier,[25] and wrote that he was eager to see the book.[26] His copy seems to have arrived sometime in 1688 and he read it carefully enough to comment on it that year, in what Westfall calls "a cryptic note": "Vortices destroyed by Newton. Vortices of spherical motion in their place."[27] Huygens's reference is to a theory he had defended as early as 1669 in a debate at the Academy in which Frénicle, Roberval, and others took part. While unhappy with the Cartesian vortex theory, he could not suffer Roberval's willingness to invoke an attractive power as the cause of gravity.[28] For an explanation to be intelligible Huygens argued, like the mechanical philosopher he essentially was, nothing should be invoked but matter in motion. He proposed a radical departure from the Cartesian *tourbillons,* suggesting that the circulatory motion of an aether or subtle matter took place in all planes about the earth; its tendency is everywhere centrifugal, thrusting heavy bodies toward the center.[29]

Only the advent of Newton's *Principia,* with its references, albeit cautiously phrased, to an attractive force, caused Huygens to resurrect his early theory. Evidently he talked the matter over with Fatio de Duillier, for in July of 1688 Fatio was in England and described to the Royal Society the theory that Huygens had advanced to explain gravity. He promised "with Mr. Huygens's leave" to provide the Society with a copy "thereof in writing."[30] Whether this was done I do not know. In any case Huygens published his "Discours de la cause de la pesanteur" in 1690 as an appendage to his *Traité de la lumière.* Since the body of this little treatise, the "Discourse," had been written before the appearance of Newton's *Principia,* Huygens concluded with an "Addition" making mention of some of its contributions. It was impossible, he wrote, to withhold assent from the mathematical demonstration of Kepler's laws. Newton must be correct that gravity acts throughout the solar system and that it decreases in strength in proportion to the square of the distance. But the idea of an attractive force was unacceptable; gravity must be explained in some manner by motion.[31]

In 1688 reviews in European journals began to appear: in the *Bibliothèque universelle et historique,* in the Leipzig *Acta eruditorum,* and a well-known one in the *Journal des sçavans.*[32] All attempted a summary of this complex book. But the reviewer in the *Journal des sçavans* judged the *Principia* to be the work of a mathematician (*un géomètre*) rather than that of a natural philosopher (*un physicien*). Its abstract, mathematical character was that of a work in mechanics (in the seventeenth century a recognized branch of the so-called mixed mathematics) rather than of a work of physics. To create a physics as perfect as his mechanics, so said the reviewer, the author must substitute real motions for those he has imagined.[33]

Leibniz first read a summary of the *Principia* during a diplomatic mission to Italy in 1688, when a friend gave him some recent monthly issues of the *Acta eruditorum.* In the June issue he read "eagerly and with much enjoyment" (*avide et magna cum delectatione legi*) an account of the celebrated Isaac Newton's Mathematical Principles of Nature.[34] The book itself, which had been given Fatio de Duillier to be sent to Leibniz, reached him in Rome, where he arrived on 14 April 1689.[35]

After reading the summary of the *Principia* in the *Acta,* Leibniz—like Huygens—was inspired to put down his own views. His treatise attempting to explain the motions of the heavenly bodies (the *Tentamen de motuum coelestium causis*) was dispatched to the *Acta* from Vienna and published in the issue for February 1689.[36]

The *Principia* was not as ignored on the European continent as is sometimes believed, yet Huygens and Leibniz were the only competent, sophisticated, and persistent critics of Newton's theory of celestial motions. They studied each other's attempts to devise a theory more compatible with their adherence to the mechanical philosophy, yet not at odds with Newton's manifest discoveries. From 1690 until Huygens's death in 1695 their points of agreement and disagreement, with each other and with Newton, frequently arose in their correspondence.[37] Both men were convinced that the *tourbillons* of Descartes had to be abandoned if Kepler's empirical laws were to be explained by a "deferent matter" carrying the planets around.[38] Neither accepted Newton's use of attractive forces, or was at all certain what Newton meant by his use of the

word "attraction." On certain fundamental matters the two men differed. In April of 1692 Leibniz wrote: "In rereading your explanation of gravity recently, I noticed that you are in favor of a vacuum and of atoms. . . . I do not see the necessity which compels you to return to such extraordinary entities."[39]

It should be noted that neither man attacked Newton in print, despite their differences with him. Both held him in high regard. Leibniz's position was not greatly different from the views set forth in the addition Huygens made to his "Discourse." It is true, Leibniz wrote Huygens in September 1689, that according to Newton's explanation planets "move as if there were only one motion of trajection or of proper direction, combined with gravity," yet they also move "as if they were carried along smoothly by a matter whose circulation is harmonious."[40] And he adds that he cannot abandon his deferent matter because he can find no other explanation for the fact (true as far as astronomical knowledge went in the seventeenth century) "that all the planets move somewhat in the same direction and in a single region." In a letter to Newton, written in March 1693, Leibniz is generous, and I think sincere, in his praise, yet candid as to the nature of his disagreement:

> How great I think the debt owed to you, by our knowledge of mathematics and of all nature, I have acknowledged in public also when occasion offered. . . . You have made the astonishing discovery that Kepler's ellipses result simply from the conception of attraction or gravitation and passage [*trajectio*] in a planet. And yet I would incline to believe that all these are caused or regulated by the motion of a fluid medium, on the analogy of gravity and magnetism as we know it here. Yet this solution would not detract from the value and truth of your discovery.[41]

Leibniz's last sentence is especially interesting, for it echoes the widely held position that Newton's brilliant explanation is a mathematical "hypothesis" that saves the phenomena, but does not provide a valid "physical" account.

Whatever their reluctance to follow Newton into the mysterious realm of an attractionist dynamics, the readers of the *Principia* were provided with the best illustration of his mathematical brilliance, with tantalizing glimpses of his new calculus, veiled though it was by a geometrical, rather than an analytical, presentation. What both Huygens and Leibniz saw in the *Principia* aroused their curiosity and their interest in the rumor that the expected Latin version of John Wallis's *Algebra* was to contain something by Newton himself about his new methods. Both Leibniz and the Marquis de l'Hospital (of whom more shortly) asked Huygens, as soon as a copy should reach him, to transcribe the Newtonian passages for them. When Leibniz finally received his copy of the extract, he thanked Huygens, but expressed his disappointment; much that he found there, he wrote, was already familiar to him.[42]

I should like to turn my attention to the second area of this proto-investigation: the need for a reassessment of the so-called Cartesian-Newtonian debates in France before 1738. I doubt that we can accept, without modification, the highly polarized—indeed oversimplified—image that Pierre Brunet has handed on to us. To this end I wish first to discuss briefly the central figure of this reinterpretation: the French philosopher, Father Nicolas Malebranche (1638-1715). Malebranche has aroused a mild amount of interest on the part of English and American historians of philosophy for the influence he exerted upon the thought of John Norris and Bishop Berkeley, on Hume's dismemberment of the notion of causation, and at one remove upon the American Samuel Johnson (1696-1772). For most modern writers, however, Malebranche simply appears as a relic of a religious age, a metaphysician whose goal, unlike that of Descartes to whom he owed so much, was to put the master's New Philosophy at the service of religion, not for ensuring man's dominance over nature. While it is not difficult to describe Malebranche's philosophical position—it has been done many times—it is less easy to categorize him and determine at what points, and how far, he departed from Descartes.[43] His Christian metaphysics can be described as more voluntarist than (in the theological sense) rationalist, and his epistemology is often summed up in the phrase that "we see all things in God." The influence of Saint Augustine was acknowledged by Malebranche himself,[44] but his Platonism is also evident: ideas are not innate in the human mind (in the Cartesian sense); they are imperfect reflections of ideas *in* God. Indeed, it is not too much to say that Malebranche anchored Plato's archetypal ideas in the divine mind. His doctrine of occasionalism, by no means original with Malebranche, is always stressed when his philosophy is summarized: events in the physical world are not *caused,* but provide the *occasion* for God, constantly conserving his creation,[45] to set in motion laws of nature which we perceive as *rapports,* or relations, between the objects of our experience.

Malebranche came to philosophy, to Descartes, and to mathematics, fairly late in his career. Frail as a child—indeed appearing so all his long life—he was educated at home until 1754-1756 when he studied at the Collège de la Marche under a Peripatetic master. After three years of theological study at the Sorbonne, he began his novitiate in 1660 in the Congregation of the Oratory, a priestly order founded by Pierre Bérulle during the Catholic religious revival in early seventeenth-century France, and which soon was famed as a liberal teaching order. He was ordained in 1664, having devoted himself to Church history, biblical scholarship, and the study of Hebrew. From that time on until his death he lived in the Paris house of the Ora-

torians on the rue St. Honoré, across the street from the Louvre where the Academy of Sciences, to which he was admitted in his later years, held its biweekly meetings.

As is well known, Malebranche's intellectual inspiration—what has been called his conversion—came from his reading of Descartes's posthumously published *Traité de l'homme* (1664), which aroused his interest not only in physiology and psychology, but in other branches of science and the great scheme of Cartesian philosophy.[46] He cast aside his historical and linguistic inquiries and set out to master all the writings of Descartes. From these, notably the *Géométrie,* stemmed his preoccupation with mathematics, and his urge to keep abreast of developments in the sciences. These interests are clearly evident in the first edition (1675) of his most important work: the *Recherche de la vérité.* This work shows his familiarity with discoveries in embryology, microscopy, and the psychology and physiology of perception.[47] He admired Mariotte's work, as exemplifying the role of experiment, and cited Von Guericke's famous experiments. The books in his library tell us still more: on his shelves were the writings of Steno, Bartholinus, Malpighi, Pecquet, Redi, and Swammerdam among other physicians and naturalists. Chemistry, where we note the books of Béguin, Robert Boyle, and Christopher Glaser, played only a small part. But he owned, among physical and astronomical works, Kepler's *Epitome astronomiae Copernicanae,* Huygen's *Horologium,* and La Hire's *Traité de mécanique.*[48]

Of the scientific disciplines, the centrally important one for Malebranche was mathematics. His library was rich in mathematical works: besides the classical authors (Euclid, Apollonius, and the rest) and of course, the *Géométrie* of Descartes, he owned the books of Herigone and Slusius, Oughtred's famous *Clavis,* Franz van Schooten's *Exercitationes* (the chief work that made Descartes's analytical geometry comprehensible) and Isaac Barrow's *Mathematical Lectures.*[49] And Malebranche once described mathematics as "the foremost and fundamental discipline of all the human sciences," excluding, that is, theology, which is a divine, not a human, subject.

At the Oratory, always the teacher, Malebranche brought together a group of mathematicians and physicists who are fairly credited with introducing the Leibnizian calculus into France,[50] and this in turn opened the way to the fuller understanding of Newton's accomplishments. With one of his early disciples, Jean Prestet (1648-1690), Malebranche supervised, or at least collaborated in the writing of, an *Elémens des mathématiques* (1675) that was published under Prestet's name. Malebranche was later to disavow this conservative treatise, for it supported the Cartesian position that mathematics has no business dealing with the infinite, whether large or small. Later this group came to include a fellow Oratorian, Father Charles-René Reyneau (1656-1728), Louis Carré (1663-1711), Pierre Rémond de Montmort (1678-1720), and the man whom André Robinet has called the leader, the "chef de file," of the Malebranchistes: the Marquis de l'Hospital (1661-1704). These men not only introduced the Leibnizian calculus into France, but defended it against its conservative detractors, like Pierre Rolle (1652-1749). On the fringes of this group, all of whom sooner or later became members of the Academy of Sciences, stood the figure of Pierre Varignon (1654-1722), something of a late convert to the new mathematics.

The steps by which the calculus came to France have often been retraced, and a brief summary here should suffice. Leibniz's first publication of 1684 on the calculus was a compressed memoir of six pages published in the *Acta eruditorum.* Cryptic, tightly constructed, and further obscured by numerous misprints, it made no immediate impact upon the scientific world. Nevertheless, without instruction or elucidations from Leibniz, Jacob (James) Bernoulli, a professor of mathematics at Basel, fought his way through it, and taught it to his younger brother Johann (John or Jean I). Johann, on a visit to Paris in 1691-1692, came into contact with Malebranche and his circle and lectured on the Leibnizian calculus. His lessons, as well as notes taken by Malebranche, have survived.[51] Here Johann met the Marquis de l'Hospital, who became his most assiduous convert, studying with him in Paris and engaging him to continue his teaching at l'Hospital's country seat at Oucques, a village in the Orléanais. In 1696 appeared the first French textbook of the calculus, l'Hospital's *Analyse des infiniment petits pour l'intelligence des lignes courbes.*[52]

Before going further, we should perhaps stop to ask what made the Malebranche circle, and Malebranche himself, so receptive to the Leibnizian "infinitesimal calculus," as it soon came to be called. How, to paraphrase André Robinet, can one explain the transformation of Malebranche-Prestet, opposed to infinites, into Malebranche-l'Hospital, so readily persuaded to adopt this radical new posture?

Various scholars have pointed out the fact that Malebranche's metaphysical principles dovetailed admirably with his mathematical interests. In particular, it has been suggested that the philosophy of mathematics Malebranche evolved in his later years—which tied in closely with his epistemology, and which can be traced as it evolved in later editions of the *Recherche de la vérité*—was a powerful force leading him to depart from the strictly Cartesian mathematics with which he had begun.[53]

Malebranche's theory of mathematics is intimately tied to his metaphysical postulate that the only truth open to man's finite intellect is the perception of the relations, the *rapports,* between things; knowledge can only be knowledge of such relations. Furthermore, the clearest and most distinct relations we can determine are those of equality and inequality: relations of magnitude. Consequently, since mathematics is precisely the science of these relations, it is the most exact and unimpeachable form of knowledge we can attain. The emphasis here, as in Malebranche's epistemology, must be placed on formal relations, relations of relations, and so on, *instead of on conceivability.* These basic assumptions led to important consequences: (1) doubts were set aside as to the logical foundations of the calculus, widely recognized as dubious, so the way was opened to accept infinitesimals, the inconceivable "infinitely small"; and (2) a premium was placed upon enriching and developing the mathematically expressed laws increasingly used to describe the observed relations of the natural world; (3) finally those, or at least some of those, who accepted these assumptions, were disposed to look with a degree of understanding upon Newton's mathematical world picture.

It would be interesting to know with some exactitude when Malebranche, or members of his group, first came to know Newton's *Principia.* What Paul Mouy calls the "diatribe" against the idea of attraction in the first edition of the *Recherche de la vérité* (1675) could not, from the date alone, have been directed against Newton who, in any case, was invoking the aether in his "Hypothesis explaining the properties of light," and was not (as Mouy has claimed) already an attractionist. We are told that Malebranche first came into direct contact with Newton's writings sometime between 1700 (when the fifth edition of the *Recherche* appeared) and the year 1712, when the sixth edition of that work was published.[54] This may be so, for Malebranche read Newton's *Opticks* soon after its appearance and became at least a partial convert to Newton's discoveries about color. Yet he certainly knew about the *Principia,* and heard it discussed, at a much earlier date. A letter from Malebranche's friend Jacquemet to Charles-René Reyneau, written on 9 April 1690, contains the remark—if indeed it was not a boast—that he, Jacquemet, had completed his reading of Newton's book earlier that year.[55] Yet, although there is no mention of the *Principia* in Malebranche's *Recherche,* there is a passage in the sixth edition of that work (the edition where his approval of Newton's optical experiments is announced) which suggests that he had grasped Newton's essential discovery concerning planetary motion. For what the evidence is worth, we know that a copy of the first edition of the *Principia* is listed as having had a place on Malebranche's bookshelves.

It was soon evident to the men of Malebranche's circle that Newton's celestial dynamics—his mathematical approach to physical nature—had to be taken seriously, despite his attack on Descartes's vortex theory of planetary motion, from which they could not free themselves completely. There was much in the **Principia** with which they were intellectually attuned: newly discovered relations or *rapports,* laws of the physical world, the mathematical approach to nature. It struck a number of them that this Newtonian mathematization of nature could be clarified and enriched if it could be translated into Leibnizian analytical methods and symbolism.

Both Johann Bernoulli and the Marquis de l'Hospital began cautiously to treat central forces analytically. But it was Varignon, Professor of Mathematics at the newly founded Collège Mazarin (a post he later combined with a chair at the Collège Royal), who took up these questions as matters of real importance. Earlier he had remained faithful to Descartes and had difficulty in moving beyond a mathematics of finitude to an acceptance of the Leibnizian calculus. But at last, reassured by Malebranche's position on mathematical intelligibility (as distinguished from conceivability), he became a convert to the new mathematics and turned to applying the calculus of Leibniz to Newtonian dynamics.[56] In a series of papers contributed to the *Mémoires* of the Academy of Sciences during the early years of the eighteenth century he treated such problems as: (1) given the law of force, to find the path of a moving body; or (2) conversely, given the path, to find the implied law of force. He was able to show, for example, that a logarithmic or hyperbolic spiral path implied a central force proportional to the cube of the distance.

Earlier in this paper I questioned the sharp polarity between Cartesians and Newtonians that Voltaire taught us and which, in our century, Pierre Brunet set forth in his book on the acceptance of the Newtonian physics in France. I shall now suggest that the followers of Malebranche—indeed the aging philosopher himself—occupied a midway position, and conceded enough to Newton to pave the way for the full-fledged Newtonianism of the later eighteenth century. These men, far from merely tinkering with Descartes's *tourbillon* model (which they continued to do as had Huygens and Leibniz), abandoned at least the outworks of the Cartesian fortress. These Malebranchistes in the Royal Academy of Sciences brought into the Age of Enlightenment not only Malebranche's doctrine that knowledge of nature is a knowledge of mathematical relationships, but carried too the Master's respect for evidence, his willingness to recast, or depart from, the specific doctrines of Descartes. In so doing they weakened the opposition to Newton and prepared the way for the more militant Newtonianism of Maupertuis, Clairaut, and Voltaire in the late 1730s. Let me offer the following general propositions to be examined *à fond* by others:

(1) These Malebranchistes (and in this they were not alone) recognized Newton as a major figure to reckon with, not only in mathematics, but in the mathematizing of nature.

(2) On the basis of what they regarded as Newton's experimental brilliance, they were the first in France to deem Newton's optical experiments a model of proper procedure to follow, and an essential part of his doctrine of the origin of color, albeit with certain theoretical deviations.

(3) They were won over to Newton's laws, the inverse square principle of "universal" gravitation, and the successful application of his mathematical rules of nature to Kepler's empirical description of planetary motion.

All this they accepted without being obliged to adopt the notion of a void, and the apparently absurd notion of bodies attracting one another through the emptiness of space. Although all adhered to some sort of doctrine of an aetherial vortex, the concessions, the departures from Descartes, paved the way for an overt acceptance of Newtonian doctrine, root and branch.

The first steps were taken by Malebranche himself when in several respects he departed from Cartesian physical thought. Most thoroughly studied are the changes he made in the Cartesian laws of impact—probably influenced by the experiments of John Wallis and of Mariotte—but he further denied that cohesion and solidity were simply caused by matter at rest. Indeed, in suggesting that rest is a mere privation of motion, he came close to the Newtonian position that rest and motion are merely "states" of matter. More fundamental, perhaps, was his modification of Descartes's theory of matter.[57] Descartes constructed his universe of three elements: his first element is composed of exceedingly fine particles that make up the luminous matter of the sun and fixed stars, and are so fine, and of such varied shapes, that they can fill all the spaces between the other elements. The second element is the key to Descartes's physical model; it consists of rounded, hard, and inflexible particles through which the light of the sun is instantaneously transmitted to illumine the larger masses of the terrestrial bodies: the earth, moon, the planets and their satellites, that make up the third element.

Malebranche, even before encountering Newton, had fundamentally revised this picture of the second element. Instead of being hard spheres, the particles are compressed fluid matter, tiny vortices. Nor did he precisely follow the Cartesian theory of the nature of light. For example, Olaus Roemer's discovery convinced him that light was not transmitted instantaneously, but required time for its passage through the second element.

Soon after his election to the Academy of Sciences in 1699, Malebranche communicated a theory of light and color that departed from Descartes. Here he attempted to supply a mechanical model, a plausible hypothesis, to account for the origin of color. Light, to Malebranche as to Pardies, Huygens, and others, is a pulse or vibratory motion of the aether or second element. But for Malebranche, colors result from the different frequencies of these pulses. Not all the hues of the spectrum are produced by this mechanism, but only the *primaries* (red, yellow, and blue). The sensation of white is produced when the original vibrations from a luminous source are unaltered in their transmission.[58] This is a version of what historians call a *modification* theory of prismatic color.

At the time his paper was presented, Malebranche seems to have been wholly ignorant of, or indifferent to, Newton's famous early paper of 1672.[59] In 1706, it seems, the Latin edition of Newton's **Opticks** came into his hands, and he was soon converted. Thus when he prepared the last edition of his *Recherche de la vérité,* the sixth (1712), he profoundly altered that appendix or "éclaircissement" he had added in 1700 and which was, in effect, his 1699 paper. In his revision he accepted Newton's notion that there existed in white light an infinite range of properties producing the different colors. The colors corresponded to various frequencies which the prism sorted out. Each color, he wrote, citing the "excellent work of M. Newton," has its characteristic refrangibility. He even adopts Newton's terminology, at least up to a point. The "primitive colours" of his earlier paper he now refers to, as Newton does, as "simple" or "homogeneous." White solar light ("the most composite of all") is described according to his own adaptation of Newton as "composed of an assemblage of different vibrations." Owing in part to Malebranche's great influence, Newton's **Opticks** was accepted, early in the eighteenth century in France, as a model of scientific inquiry.[60] One of Malebranche's disciples, Pierre Varignon, was a key figure in seeing through the press the Paris edition (1722) of Pierre Coste's French translation of the **Opticks.**[61] But it should be emphasized that there is no evidence that Malebranche, an elderly cleric, repeated any of Newton's optical experiments. He seems simply to have been persuaded by Newton's testimony as presented in the **Optice.** This last edition of the *Recherche* shows that Malebranche was led on to the **Principia,** for he added a sort of appendix to his theory of little vortices to alter the Cartesian explanation of gravity and adjust his thought so far as possible to Newton's findings.

To illustrate my point that we can no longer justly speak of an academic world divided between Cartesians and Newtonians (or, if you will, dominated by strict Cartesians struggling to fend off a Newtonian invasion) I should like to say something about three of Malebranche's disciples and admirers: the Oratorian father, Charles René Reyneau, Jean-Baptiste Dortous

de Mairan (1678-1771), and Joseph Privat de Molières (1676-1742).

In 1708 Father Reyneau, a professor of mathematics at Angers, published his *Analyse démontrée* which continued and brought up to date Descartes's work on the theory of equations and introduced the reader to the calculus. Modern analysis, he wrote, had its beginnings in Descartes's *Géométrie.* But Descartes lacked a mathematics that could precisely represent nature; for nature produces curves by continuous motion, and nature's curves are made up of "parties insensibles," parts smaller than we can determine, and of instants of time swifter than we can imagine. What was needed was a new form of mathematical expression, and this was devised "at the same time in Germany by M. Leibniz and in England by M. Newton." Further on the mentions the "savant ouvrage" (the learned work) of Newton, the **Principia.**[62]

Dortous de Mairan, a young provincial of the country gentry, was born in Béziers. He was sent to Paris to attend a sort of finishing school, where horsemanship, fencing, dancing, and other proper accomplishments were taught to young noblemen. In Paris, he came under the spell of Malebranche who taught him to understand the Marquis de l'Hospital's *Analyse des infiniment petits,* and gave him other lessons in mathematics and physics.[63]

Mairan returned to his native Languedoc. Uncertain of his future course, he toyed with the philosophical and theological difficulties encountered in reading Spinoza, and wrote his old teacher, the aging Malebranche, for guidance.

In their correspondence, Malebranche not only rescued Dortous from the pitfall of Spinozistic pantheism, but incidentally informed his young friend that he had abandoned his earlier views about light and color after reading Newton's **Opticks.** He went on to tell Mairan (in August 1714) that his version of Newton's theory could be found in the last edition of his *Recherche.* Mairan promptly acquired Malebranche's book, and probably soon afterward the Latin **Optice** as well, for Pierre Coste, the translator of the **Opticks** into French (1720 and 1722), tells us that Mairan in 1716-1717 was the first in France to repeat successfully Newton's optical experiments. The influence of Newton's work soon became apparent in Mairan's memoirs. In his earliest scientific contribution, his *Dissertation sur les variations du baromètre* (Bordeaux, 1715), he mentioned Richer's discovery that a pendulum, whose period of oscillation in Paris is a second, has to be shortened near the equator. And he remarked that "certain celebrated mathematicians" had concluded that the earth was a globe flattened at the poles. A note cites Huygens's *Discours de la cause de la pesanteur* and Newton's *Principia.*[64] The following year (1716) in his

Dissertation sur la glace Mairan showed himself quite at home with the **Optice,** for he wrote about the relation of color to refrangibility, the transparency of bodies, and other matters discussed by Newton.

The most explicit of Mairan's early references to Newton's work on light and color appears in a short essay on phosphorescence published in 1717.[65] Here he summarized Newton's discovery that each colored ray has its characteristic refrangibility, and recounted the "ingenious experiments" which had led Newton to this discovery "in order to acquaint those who have not seen the **Opticks** of Mr. Newton with what I shall have to say on this matter."

Not so long after, we find Mairan in Paris, for in 1718 he became *associé géomètre* in the Academy of Sciences, taking the place of Guisnée, a member of Malebranche's circle who died in that year. His earliest contributions as an academician show the profound influence the **Opticks** had on him. In one, he draws upon Newton's analogy between the colors of the spectrum and the intervals of the octave and suggests that, just as Malebranche believed colors to be caused by differently vibrating globules of the *matière subtile,* so air must transmit sound by means of distinct particles having different rates of vibration.[66] In another paper he argued against Descartes's theory that colors are derived from the differential rotation of kinds of globules, by showing that spheres rotating differently and striking a surface obliquely would reflect at different angles. Thus, contrary to the established law of equiangular reflection, rays of different colors would then have characteristic reflectivities.[67] Mairan, more explicitly than Newton, held an emission theory in which light rays consist of trains of corpuscles, of *corps lumineux.* Moreover, he believed that reflection does not occur at the point of actual contact of rays of light with a solid surface, but when the corpuscles encounter a "fluide subtile répandu dans leurs pores," a view he recognized as similar to that held by Newton in the **Opticks.**[68]

There can be little doubt that Mairan was reluctant to abandon the mechanism of subtle fluids, nor that he felt increasingly allured by Newton's views and by his own respect for experimental evidence. Often he was troubled by contradictions in empirical data and he tried to reconcile them. For example he found Jacques Cassini's geodetic measurements, leading to the inference of an elongated earth, in conflict with Huygens's and Newton's inference from Richer's pendulum observations at Cayenne that the earth should have the shape of an oblate spheroid. He attempted to show that both observations led to a *sphéroïde oblong,* if one denied the primitive sphericity of the earth which Huygens had assumed as a postulate.[69]

Mairan's reluctance to give up the vortex theory led him to some extraordinary mental gymnastics. A much-cited argument against Descartes's *tourbillons* was the existence of retrograde comets, comets whose motion is opposite to that of the planets. Mairan pointed out that planets at portions of their orbits appear to stop and reverse their "direct" motion from west to east, but he pointed out that this is merely an optical effect produced by a combination of the earth's revolution and the direct planetary path. Could not retrograde comets be planets that are only visible during the retrograde portion of their path?

Unlike some of his contemporaries who favored the existence of a deferent subtle fluid, Mairan had—even more than Malebranche—a keen respect for observed fact. Certain Cartesians, like Villemont, argued that comets did not enter the solar system below Saturn. Mairan knew that in fact, on occasion, they did. But if they come close, yet do not penetrate our solar vortex, then our vortex, Mairan argued, cannot be spherical but must sometimes be depressed. Comets, he suggested, are planets of nearby vortices, moving about their own suns; their vortices can act upon others, including ours, engaging one another, as Fontenelle put it—like gears of a clock—but altering their shape. The flattening of our vortex allows comets to approach closely yet without penetrating it.[70]

We can detect, I believe, a growing familiarity with, and acceptance of, much that we associate with Newton. In a memoir of 1724 he sought to explain short-range forces of attraction and repulsion, in particular the behavior of water and mercury in capillary tubes. Assuming that around all bodies—not only magnets—there is an atmosphere of *matière subtile,* he sought to explain why bodies attract or repel. Water wets glass because the atmospheres are in some manner compatible, whereas in the case of mercury its surrounding atmosphere is opposed by that of the glass, thus accounting for the convex meniscus. Here, as Fontenelle perceived, Mairan was toying dangerously with those attractive forces which a good Cartesian held in abhorrence.[71]

Another problem brought the Cartesian scheme into court, that of the diurnal rotation of the earth. The Newtonian world view simply took the spin of the earth for granted: once established, inertia would keep the planets rotating. But there was no way that the Newtonian attractionist system could start a planet spinning. A Cartesian vortex by itself was little help: indeed it would seem to demand a rotation opposite to that which actually takes place. Mairan believed the key was the assumption that the two hemispheres of a spherical planet must "weigh" differently towards the sun, according to the inverse square law of gravity, and respond oppositely to the deferent fluid of the vortex. Brunet found it ironic that a Cartesian should find it necessary to go to Newton for principles with which to defend Cartesianism.[72]

There is clear evidence that Mairan was moved to study the *Principia.* From Newton's gravitational data, he estimated the relative weight of an identical mass on the surface of the sun and on the earth, noting that the numbers Newton cited differed in the three editions, because—he pointed out—Newton used different values for the solar parallax. By 1733 Mairan had not only made use of points here and there in the *Principia* but had gone a long way toward accepting Newton's celestial dynamics, and the Newtonian principle that central forces in the solar system operate according to the inverse square law. These laws of the solar system, he wrote, are well known and fit modern observations. And he continues:

> We therefore admit these principles in conformity with what one finds about them in the *Mathematical principles* of Newton . . . without claiming to enter . . . into the discussion of causes.

> The heavens better understood, the laws of motion better developed, gave to this great man [Newton] an advantage over Descartes and the early Cartesians which cannot deprive them of the glory they have justly gained . . . or forbid them the use of knowledge that time has brought forth, on the pretext that this knowledge did not emanate from their school.[73]

My third specimen, Joseph Privat de Molières (1677-1742), was, like Dortous deMairan, a man from the Midi. Born in Provence of a distinguished family he was educated in various nearby Oratorian schools (at Aix-en-Provence, Arles, and Marseilles), eventually ending up at Angers, where he studied mathematics and natural philosophy with Charles René Reyneau in 1698-1699. This relationship influenced his future. Against the wishes of his family, he became a priest of the Congregation of the Oratory, and in 1704, determined to devote his life to science, he came to Paris to sit at the feet of Malebranche and absorb his wisdom.[74] To Malebranche's influence we can safely attribute his central concern: the elaboration of a modified Cartesian physics in which, while remaining faithful to the notion of a *plenum* and to strictly mechanical explanations, he attempted to account mathematically for the inverse square law of gravitation and Newton's demonstration of Kepler's laws, by means of a modified vortex model.

In 1721 Privat de Molières entered the Academy of Sciences as *adjoint mécanicien,* and two years later he succeeded Varignon as professor of philosophy at the Collège Royal. In memoirs read to the Academy in 1728 and 1729, and at greater length in the four volumes of his *Leçons de physique*—lectures delivered at the Collège Royal and published between 1734 and 1739—he concentrated upon what Mme du Châtelet called the "curious business" of trying to reconcile Newton and Descartes. The result was what Robinet

has called a "monument malebranchiste," in which—while opposing the doctrines of empty space and the hypothesis of attraction—he freed himself from the narrow Cartesians and took the position of the "cartésiens malebranchistes réformateurs."[75]

In 1728, taking his cue from Varignon's work on central forces, he launched his effort to shore up the theory of *tourbillons* by a mathematical analysis of the centrifugal forces at work in a cylindrical vortex whose axis is equal to the diameter of its base. He found that if the various layers into which one imagines the cylindrical mass to be composed revolve in times proportional to the distance from the axis, no part or globule will approach or recede from the axis. On the other hand, in a *spherical* vortex the condition of equilibrium is different: there will be stability of all layers if the central forces are inversely as the square of the distance from the center.[76] Privat de Molières claimed to show, also, that in a spherical vortex the distances from the center of points moving in the concentric shells are as the cube roots of the squares of the periodic times. This, he pointed out, was "la fameuse règle de Képler."[77] Unfortunately, as he recognized, this held only for points moving in the plane of the equator, and his law lacked the generality it had with Kepler and Newton.

In 1729 he tackled the problem of deriving Kepler's First Law, i.e., the elliptical path of planets, from vortex theory.[78] It was clear that the problem was insoluble if the vortex was made up of the hard globules of Descartes. In consequence, he adapted Malebranche's theory of *petits tourbillons,* of small, elastic vortices, composed in their turn of still smaller vortices (*tourbillons du second genre*).[79] In effect he assumed the infinite divisibility of matter, imagining as many levels as were necessary to account for particular phenomena, and applying to matter the *infiniment petits* so useful to the "mathematicians of our age." His model envisaged a planet moving in a vortex "distorted into an elliptical shape by the unequal pressures of the neighbouring vortices."[80]

In the *Leçons de physique* his theory of mini-vortices was elaborated and applied not only to celestial mechanics, but also to chemistry and electricity. The successive volumes of the *Leçons* received the official approval of committees of the Academy of Sciences, on each of which sat his Malebranchiste colleague, Dortous de Mairan.[81] From the first, Privat de Molières set out to demonstrate, as he put it, that "the chief doctrines of the two most celebrated philosophers of our time, Descartes and Newton," which appear so incompatible, can in fact be reconciled. In a series of closely articulated propositions, the reader, he predicted, will find "perhaps with surprise that, although the two men followed what seem to be completely opposing paths, these paths nevertheless led to the same goal." And Privat goes on confidently:

You will see emerging out of the plenist system
that Descartes followed, even Newton's void, that
non-resisting space of which this philosopher has
irrefutably established the existence.

And from impulse or impact he will find derived that
attraction of gravity

> which increases and decreases inversely as the squares
> of the distances, from which Newton, without how-
> ever being able to discover the mechanical cause,
> has drawn so many splendid consequences, based
> on a calculus . . . of which this great man is the first
> inventor.[82]

Dortous de Mairan and Privat de Molières have both
been described as leading eighteenth-century Cartesians.
Pierre Brunet gives special treatment to both men in
his chapter entitled "L'effort des grands cartésiens."
Quite recently Martin Fichman wrote in his article in
the *Dictionary of Scientific Biography* that Dortous de
Mairan was a "major figure in the protracted struggle
against the importation of Newtonian science in France,"
and "devoted his career to developing and improving
Cartesian physics."

Yet both writers—Brunet and Fichman—have had to
emphasize that the two men in question were by no
means rigidly Cartesian. At one point, Brunet remarked
that while Dortous remained attached to Cartesianism
on most fundamental questions (whatever that may
mean) he was nevertheless enticed—his word is *sé-
duit*—by Newton's ideas, chiefly because of his admiration, like Fontenelle's, for Newton's experimental
skill. And Martin Fichman conceded in another *Dictionary* article that Privat de Molières, while persuaded
of the correctness of Descartes's ideal of a purely
mechanical science (that is, of a mechanics of impact)
was nevertheless "cognizant of the superiority of Newtonian precision in comparison with Cartesian vague-
ness in its explication of natural phenomena." Vague-
ness is hardly a word I should use in connection with
Descartes. I was glad to discover that my friend John
Heilbron of Berkeley, in his book on the early history
of electricity, quite bluntly and accurately calls Privat
de Molières "a devout Malebranchiste."

I can only repeat the main theme of this part of my
paper: that Malebranche and his followers broke down
the initial barriers of the Cartesian fortress, and made
the way easier for radical Newtonians like Maupertuis,
Clairaut, and Voltaire.[83] Paul Mouy did not exaggerate
when he wrote that around 1730 an eclectic fusion of
Malebranchiste and Newtonian ideas was very much *à
la mode* in French science. As Voltaire's Minerva of
France, his "immortelle Emilie," wrote of Cartesianism to Cisternay Dufay: "It is a house collapsing into
ruins, propped up on every side . . . I think it would
be prudent to leave."[84]

Notes

From *History of Science,* 17 (1979). Originally entitled
"Some Areas for Further Newtonian Studies," this paper
was presented at a Colloquium held at Churchill College, Cambridge, in August 1977 and devoted to this
subject. The problems raised here were first gone over
in my graduate seminar at Cornell in 1962, and I am
indebted to the stimulus of my students.

[1] Daniel Mornet, *Les sciences de la nature en France
au XVIIIᵉ siècle* (Paris, 1911); Preserved Smith, *A
History of Modern Culture,* II (New York, 1934), esp.
chaps. 2-4.

[2] Hélène Metzger, *Attraction universelle et religion
naturelle chez quelques commentateurs anglais de Newton* (Paris, 1938).

[3] The distinction between "internal" and "external"
influences upon science is older than the present-day
methodologists of the history of science may realize.
The distinction—obvious enough in itself—and even
the precise terminology appeared as early as 1948 in a
paper presented by Jean Pelseneer to the Comité Belge
d'Histoire des Sciences, and published as "Les influences dans l'histoire des sciences," in the *Archives
internationales d'histoire des sciences,* 1 (1947-48),
347-353.

[4] Margaret C. Jacob, *The Newtonians and the English
Revolution, 1689—1720* (Ithaca, N.Y., 1976).

[5] Pierre Brunet, *L'introduction des théories de Newton
en France au XVIIIᵉ siècle,* I: Avant 1738 (Paris, 1931).
This one volume carrying the story to 1738 was all
that was published.

[6] *Phil. Trans.,* 6 (1671-72), No. 80, 3075-3087. Newton's "Accompt of a New Catadioptrical Telescope"
was published later in the same volume, 4004-4010.
These optical papers may be conveniently consulted in
Newton's Papers, pp. 47-67.

[7] Oldenburg first informed Huygens of Newton's new
kind of telescope by letters of 1 and 15 January 1671/
72. See *Oeuvres de Huygens,* VII (1897), 124-125,
and 128; also Newton *Correspondence,* I (1959), 72-
76, and 81-82; and Oldenburg *Correspondence,* VIII
(1971), 443-445, and 468-473. Greatly impressed, Huygens sent a description of Newton's telescope, with a
letter giving his opinion of it, to Jean Gallois, editor of
the *Journal des sçavans.* Gallois published both in the
issue of 29 February 1672. Other French savants, among
them Adrien Auzout, Jean-Baptiste Denis, and of course
Cassegrain, were interested in Newton's invention.

[8] In March 1672 Oldenburg sent Huygens the number
of the *Transactions* containing Newton's pioneer pa-

per on light and color, asking for his opinion of the new theory. See *Oeuvres de Huygens,* VII, 156; Newton *Correspondence,* I, 117; and Oldenburg *Correspondence,* VIII, 584-585. Huygens contented himself with replying: "Pour ce qui est de sa nouvelle Théorie des couleurs, elle me paroit fort ingenieuse, mais il faudra veoir si elle est compatible avec toutes les expéiences" (*Oeuvres de Huygens,* VII, 165). With slight variations this passage was quoted in a letter of Oldenburg to Newton (19 April 1672), in Newton *Correspondence,* I, 135.

9 Pardies's *Discours du mouvement local* (Paris, 1670), published anonymously, had been translated by Oldenburg and published in London that same year. Pardies's first formal communication was a flattering letter to Oldenburg, dated 18 July 1671, remarking that he had just been shown parts of the *Philosophical Transactions* and learned that Oldenburg had translated his *Discours* into English (Oldenburg *Correspondence,* VIII, 143-145).

10 The Academy of the Abbé Bourdelot has been described in Harcourt Brown, *Scientific Organisations in Seventeenth Century France (1620-1680)* (Baltimore, 1934), chap. 11.

11 Huygens made an early reference to the Bourdelot group in a letter written from Paris on 26 April 1664 to his brother Lodewijk. See Brown, p. 233.

12 Pardies did not live to complete his book on optics; but material from his draft was used, with full acknowledgment, by Father Pierre Ango, a fellow Jesuit, in his *L'optique divisée en trois livres* (Paris, 1682), unpaginated dedicatory preface and p. 14. If Pardies had accepted Newton's theory of color, there is no trace of it in Father Ango's book, where all the colors are explained according to the old theory of a mixing of black and white.

13 For Pardies's first letter see Newton *Correspondence* I, 130-133.

14 *Philosophical Transactions Abridged* (London, 1809), VII, 743, and *Newton's Papers,* p. 109. The three-volume abridgement of the early *Transactions* by John Lowthorpe (London, 1705), gives Pardies's statement of concession only in Latin (I, 144).

15 The italics in the quotation are my own.

16 For the French original of this passage see Newton *Correspondence,* I, 205-206. The error is not attributable to Oldenburg's translating the French into Latin, the language in which it appears in the original *Transactions,* for what we read is a good rendering of the French: "Experimentum peractum cùm fuerit isto modo, nil habeo quod in eo desiderem ampliùs (*Phil. Trans.,*

7 [1672-75], 5018, reproduced in *Newton's Papers,* p. 103).

17 Edme Mariotte, *De la nature des couleurs* (Paris, 1681), p. 211. This paper was reprinted in the *Oeuvres de Mariotte,* 2 vols. (Leiden, 1717), I, 227-228, and in a later edition of the *Oeuvres,* 2 vols-in-one (The Hague, 1740), consecutively paginated. The supposed refutation of Newton's experiment appears on pp. 227-228 of this edition.

18 For new material on the later stages of the penetration of Newtonian optics into France see A. Rupert Hall, "Newton in France: A New View," *History of Science,* 13 (1975), 233-250.

19 Derek T. Whiteside, *The Mathematical Works of Isaac Newton* (New York and London, 1964), p. xii. Whiteside reprints in facsimile John Stewart's 1745 English translation of the *De analysi.* For the original Latin version, a new translation, and illuminating notes, see Whiteside, *Newton's Mathematical Papers,* II (1968), 206-247.

20 Newton *Correspondence,* I, 155-156. For Newton's work on the Kinckhuysen *Algebra,* see Whiteside, *Newton's Mathematical Papers,* II, 277-291.

21 Henri L. Brugmans, *Le séjour de Christian Huygens à Paris* (Paris, 1935), pp. 72-73. In August 1676 Leibniz wrote to Oldenburg: "Inventa Neutoni ejus ingenio digna sunt, quod ex Optices experimentis et Tubo Catadioptrico abunde eluxit" (Newton *Correspondence,* II (1960), 57). Oldenburg had earlier drawn Huygens's attention to Leibniz, mentioning in a letter of late March 1671 Leibniz's *Hypothesis physica nova,* his earliest study of motion, dedicated to the Royal Society. See Oldenburg *Correspondence,* VII (1977), 573-579. For this work see the article "Leibniz: Physics, Logic, Metaphysics" by Jürgen Mittelstrass and Eric J. Aiton in DSB, VIII (1973), 150-160.

22 For Leibniz's participation in the meeting of 22 January 1672/73, see Birch, *History of the Royal Society,* III, 73. Leibniz demonstrated an early version of his calculating machine. He was elected F.R.S. on 9 April 1673.

23 For these Latin letters to Leibniz, with English translations, see Newton *Correspondence,* II, 20-47, and 110-161.

24 Newton *Correspondence,* III (1961), 3-5.

25 *Oeuvres de Huygens,* IX (1901), 167. Cf. I. Bernard Cohen, *Introduction to Newton's "Principia"* (Cambridge, Mass., 1971), p. 138, n. 9. For Fatio's aspirations as editor of a second edition of the *Principia,* see ibid., pp. 177-187.

[26] "Je souhaitte de voir le livre de Newton. Je veux bien qu'il ne soit pas Cartesien pourveu qu'il ne nous fasse pas de suppositions comme celle de l'attraction" (Huygens to Fatio [11 July 1687], *Oeuvres de Huygens*, IX, 190). Cf. Richard S. Westfall, *Force in Newton's Physics* (London and New York, 1971), p. 184.

[27] *Oeuvres de Huygens*, XXI, 437. See Westfall, 186. Turnbull, in Newton *Correspondence*, III, 2, n. 1, avers that Huygens "had recently" received his copy of the *Principia* from his brother Constantyn. Turnbull's reference is to a letter of Christiaan to Constantyn dated 30 December 1688 (*Oeuvres de Huygens,* IX, 304-305) which merely tells us that Huygens had read the book before that date. But a letter of Constantyn to Christiaan, dated from Loo in Western Flanders on 13 October 1687, includes the sentence: "Dr. Stanley est allé en Angleterre et me portera encore des livres curieux. Il ne revient que vers le temps que nous irons a la Haye c'est a dire dans un mois d'icy" (*Oeuvres de Huygens*, IX, 234). This supports the notion that Constantyn was the intermediary, but suggests that Christiaan may have received his copy of the *Principia* either late in 1687 or early in 1688. William Stanley (1647-1731), Dean of St. Asaph, was chaplain to the future Queen Mary and after the accession of William III was made clerk of the closet.

[28] For Roberval's gravitational theory, similar to that advanced by Copernicus and Galileo, see "Un débat à l'Académie des sciences sur la pesanteur," in Léon Auger, *Gilles Personne de Roberval (1602-1675)* (Paris, 1962), esp. p. 179. See also Westfall, pp. 184-186.

[29] Westfall, p. 187.

[30] Royal Society Journal Book for 18 January 1687/88 and 4 July 1688. Fatio had been elected F.R.S. in 1687. In May 1688 he described at a meeting of the Society the pendulum clock that Huygens had devised, and which had been "sent to the Cape of Good Hope by a person skilled in Astronomy, with design to trie what might be done in the matter of Longitude by that method of clocks" (Journal Book, 9 May 1688). When Huygens met Newton for the first time in 1689 it was on a trip to England in the company of Fatio. For the meeting at Gresham College on 12 June 1689, where Huygens "gave an account" of his forthcoming "Treatise concerning the Cause of Gravity" and had an exchange with Newton about the double refraction of Iceland spar, see Royal Society Journal Book, 12 June 1689, cited by Turnbull, Newton *Correspondence*, III, 31, n. 1.

[31] *Traité de la lumiere . . . par C.H.D.Z. Avec un discours de la cause de la pesanteur* (Leiden, 1690). The *Traité,* the *Discours,* and the Newtonian "Addition" are consecutively paginated. The *Discours* is reprinted separately in *Oeuvres de Huygens*, XXI, 451-499.

[32] Edmond Halley's laudatory review, an unabashed and rhetorical bit of promotional material, can hardly have persuaded any Continental critic of Newton. See *Phil. Trans.,* 16, No. 186 (1687), 291-297.

[33] *Journal des sçavans*, 2 August 1688 (Amsterdam, 1689), 237-238. A similar view was set forth by Malebranche who wrote in 1707: "Quoique Mr. Newton ne soit point physicien, son livre [the *Optice*] est tres curieux et tres utile a ceux qui ont de bons principes de physique, il est d'ailleurs excellent geometre . . ." (*Oeuvres complètes de Malebranche* [Bibliothèque des textes philosophiques: Directeur, Henri Gouhier], XIX [1961], 771-772). This edition will be the one cited henceforth, except in n. 47.

[34] Leibniz to Mencke, in Newton *Correspondence*, III, 3-4.

[35] In October 1690 Leibniz wrote to Huygens remarking on the "quantité de belles choses" the book contained (Newton *Correspondence,* III, 80). Leibniz's own copy of the first edition of the *Principia* was discovered in 1969 by E. A. Fellmann of Basel. Leibniz's marginal annotations have been reproduced in facsimile, together with transcriptions of the marginalia and a commentary, in *Marginalia in Newtoni Principia Mathematica,* ed. E. A. Fellmann (Paris, 1973).

[36] E. J. Aiton, *The Vortex Theory of Planetary Motion* (London and New York, 1972), p. 127.

[37] Early in 1690 Leibniz received a copy of Huygens's *Traité de la lumière,* containing the Dutch scientist's *Discours de la cause de la pesanteur.* In an accompanying letter, Huygens asked Leibniz if he had modified his planetary theory after reading Newton's *Principia,* proof incidentally that Huygens had already digested the "Tentamen."

[38] For Huygens's "spherical vortex" see Westfall, p. 187. Leibniz's "harmonic circulation" of a deferent aether is described by Aiton, *Vortex Theory,* pp. 125-151, and by Westfall, *Force,* pp. 303-310.

[39] Leibniz, *Philosophical Papers and Letters,* ed. L. E. Loemker, 2 vols. (Chicago, 1956), II, 679. Huygens saw no incompatibility between his aether and the concepts of atoms and the void. He conceived of his aether as rare because each particle is porous, its component subparticles being separated by many empty spaces.

[40] Leibniz, *Philosophical Papers and Letters,* II, 681.

[41] Newton *Correspondence*, III, 257-258. "Trajection" or "projection" would be preferable translations of *trajectio.*

[42] For this correspondence, see *Oeuvres de Huygens,* IX, letters nos. 2777, 2785, 2815, 2839, 2854, 2866, 2873, 2876. On 4 October 1694 the Marquis de l'Hospital remarked in a letter to Huygens (letter no. 2879): "Je n'ai plus de curiosité de voir ce qu'il y a de Mr. Neuton dans le livre de Vallis apres ce que vous me mandez."

[43] The extent to which Malebranche departed from Descartes in his fundamental doctrines has been much debated. Compare, for example, M. Geroult's article "Métaphysique et physique de la force chez Descartes et chez Malebranche," in the *Revue de métaphysique et de morale,* 54 (1954), 113-134, with the account of Malebranche by Willis Doney in the *Encyclopedia of Philosophy,* V (New York, 1967), 140-144. In physics Malebranche differed from Descartes on the cause of the solidity of bodies, on the laws of impact, the nature of light, and many other points. He emphasized that Descartes's *Principes de la philosophie* must be read with caution, "sans rien recevoir de ce qu'il dit, que lorsque la force et l'evidence de ses raisons ne nous permettront point d'en douter." Cited by Paul Mouy, *Le développement de la physique cartésienne* (Paris, 1934), p. 279.

[44] See Ferdinant Alquié, *Le Cartésianisme de Malebranche* (Paris, 1974), p. 25 and n. 9.

[45] The originator of the doctrine of occasionalism is often said to be Geulincx of Antwerp (1625-1669), but other followers of Descartes adopted a similar position. Malebranche, in any case, greatly extended Geulincx's doctrine, giving it a central role in his epistemology and his religious philosophy.

[46] Henri Gouhier, *La vocation de Malebranche* (Paris, 1926) is a fine study of this aspect of Malebranche's career. Gouhier (pp. 56-62) pointed out that it was not the *Traité de l'homme* alone that introduced Malebranche to Descartes. The edition of 1664 which Malebranche purchased was that of Clerselier, and included Descartes's *Description du corps humain,* with its unfinished preface stressing the dualistic doctrine of mind and body, as well as writings of Clerselier and other Cartesians which gave malebranche a conspectus of Descartes's philosophy in all its breadth. Cf. Alquié, *Cartésianisme,* p. 25.

[47] For a compact view of Malebranche as mathematician and savant, see the article by Pierre Costabel in the DSB, IX (1974), 47-53. A good introduction to Malebranche's interest in the progress of the life sciences is the single volume of the abortive *Oeuvres complètes de Malebranche,* ed. Désiré Roustan with the collaboration of Paul Schrecker, of which only the one volume (Paris, 1938) appeared before the outbreak of World War II and Schrecker's emigration to the United States. See especially the "Notes des éditeurs," pp. 399-447. Of interest too is Schrecker's "Malebranche et le préformisme biologique," *Revue internationale de philosophie,* 1 (1938), 77-97.

[48] *Oeuvres de Malebranche,* XX ("Malebranche vivant," ed. André Robinet, 1967), chap. 6, "La bibliothèque de Malebranche."

[49] Ibid.

[50] *Oeuvres de Malebranche,* XX, chap. 3, "Le groupe malebranchiste de l'Oratoire," 137-170; André Robinet, "Le groupe malebranchiste introducteur du calcul infinitésimal en France," *Revue d'histoire des sciences,* 13 (1960), 287-308; André Robinet, *Malebranche de l'Académie des sciences* (Paris, 1970).

[51] *Oeuvres de Malebranche,* XVII-2 (*Mathematica,* ed. Pierre Costabel, 1968), 131-294.

[52] Only in the fifth edition of the *Recherche de la vérité* does Malebranche mention the Marquis de l'Hospital and his book, and introduce the names of two new mathematical sciences, the differential and the integral calculus. The former, he writes, has been carefully treated by l'Hospital; the letter still awaits a comparable book, although "plusieurs savants géomètres" are working on the subject. For the moment one must be content with the "petit ouvrage de M. Carré," his *Méthode pour la mesure des surfaces,* etc. Cited by Mouy, *Développement de la physique cartésienne,* p. 269.

[53] See Paul Schrecker, "Malebranche et les mathématiques," *Travaux du IXe congrès international de philosophie—Congrès Descartes* (Paris, 1937), pp. 33-40, and his "Leparallélisme théologico-mathématique chez Malebranche," *Revue philosophique,* 63 (1938), 215-252. Also André Robinet, "La philosophie malebranchiste des mathématiques," *Revue d'histoire des sciences,* 14 (1961), 205-254.

[54] See Paul Mouy, "Malebranche et Newton," *Revue de métaphysique et de morale,* 45 (1938), 411-435.

[55] *Oeuvres de Malebranche,* XVII-2 (*Mathematica,* ed. Pierre Costabel, 1968), 62. See also the later letter in which Jacquemet thanks Reyneau for information on Barrow's method, remarking that "dans le fond" it is the same as that of the Marquis de l'Hospital and Newton, except that the latter applied it to incommensurables "qu'on prétend être une des plus belles et des plus utiles inventions de ce siècle dont Messieurs Leibniz et Newton ont tout l'honneur" (ibid., p. 61).

[56] For Varignon, see the article by Pierre Costabel in DSB, XIII (1976), 584-587, and his *Pierre Varignon et la diffusion en France du calcul différentiel et intégral* (Paris, 1965). An important article is J. O. Fleck-

enstein, "Pierre Varignon und die mathematischen Wissenschaften im Zeitalter der Cartesianismus," *Archives internationales d'histoire des sciences,* 2 (1945), 76-138.

[57] Mouy, *Développement de la physique cartésienne,* pp. 282-290.

[58] Pierre Duhem, "L'optique de Malebranche," *Revue de métaphysique et de morale,* 43 (1916), 37-91.

[59] Ibid.

[60] As, for example, Fontenelle's *éloge* of Newton. For the early English version (London, 1728) see *Newton's Papers,* pp. 444-474.

[61] Hall, "Newton in France," p. 244.

[62] Mouy, "Malebranche et Newton," p. 421.

[63] See my "Newtonianism of Dortous de Mairan," reprinted in my *Essays and Papers in the History of Modern Science* (Baltimore and London, 1977), pp. 479-490. Originally published in the Festschrift for Ira Wade, it suffered from some typographical legerdemain on the part of the printer. This has been corrected, and the article somewhat expanded.

[64] Mairan had doubtless read Huygens's "Discours de la cause de la pesanteur" appended to his *Traité de la lumière.* Whether at this time he had seen Newton's *Principia* is less certain, although he refers to it, for he could have learned of Newton's views on the shape of the earth from the remarks in Huygens's "Addition." See above, n. 31.

[65] *Dissertation sur la cause de la lumière des phosphores et des noctiluques* (Bordeaux, 1717), p. 48.

[66] Fontenelle, *His. Acad. Sci.,* 1720 (1722), pp. 11-12 (cited by Brunet, pp. 84-85). See also the article on Mairan (by Sigalia Dostrovsky) in DSB XIII, 33.

[67] *Mém. Acad. Sci.,* 1722 (1724), pp. 6-51.

[68] Ibid., pp. 50-51. Cited by Brunet, pp. 115-116.

[69] Recherches géométriques sur la diminution des degrès terrestres, en allant de l'équateur vers les pôles," *Mém. Acad. Sci.,* 1720 (1722), pp. 231-277.

[70] Brunet, pp. 134-135.

[71] Brunet writes: "Cette explication par la physique tourbillonnaire est d'autant plus caractéristique ici des préférences cartésiennes de Dortous de Mairan que, puisqu'il faisait appel à une sorte d'extension du magnétisme, il pouvait encore trouver là une occasion de se rallier, plus ou moins directement et explicitement, à la théorie de l'attraction" (ibid., p. 121).

[72] Ibid., p. 170. For a detailed analysis of Mairan's theory of planetary notation, see Aiton, *Vortex Theory,* pp. 182-187.

[73] *Traité physique et historique de l'aurore boréale* (Paris, 1733), p. 88. In the expanded edition of his *Dissertation sur la glace* (Paris, 1749), Dortous de Mairan expressed his pleasure that Newton's letter to Boyle of February 1678/79, recently published by Thomas Birch in his *Life of the Honourable Robert Boyle* (1744), showed Newton an advocate of the sort of *matière subtile* that he, Mairan, used to explain various phenomena. See the "Preface," pp. xviii-xxii.

[74] The primary source for biographical information on Privat de Molières is the *éloge* pronounced by his friend Dortous de Mairan in *Hist. Acad. Sci.,* 1742 (1745), pp. 195-205, reprinted in Jean-Jacques Dortous de Mairan, *Eloges des académiciens de l'Académie royale des Sciences, morts dans les années 1741, 1742, 1743* (Paris, 1747), pp. 201-234. There is a brief summary by Martin Fichman in his article on Privat de Molières in DSB, XI (1975), 157-158.

[75] *Oeuvres de Malebranche,* XX, 170-171.

[76] "Lois générales du mouvement dans le tourbillon sphérique," in *Mem. Acad. Sci.,* 1728 (1730), 245-267.

[77] Cited by Brunet, p. 159.

[78] "Problème physico-mathématique, dont la solution tend à servir de réponse à une des objections de M. Newton contre la possibilité des tourbillons célestes," in *Mém. Acad. Sci.,* 1729 (1731), pp. 235-244.

[79] Privat de Molières was not alone in being influenced by Malebranche's theory of *petits tourbillons.* In 1726 Pierre Mazière offered a mechanical explanation of elastic collision in terms of such tiny aetherial vortices. See Carolyn Iltis, "The Decline of Cartesianism in Mechanics: The Leibnizian-Cartesian Debates," *Isis,* 64 (1973), 360-363. Cf. Brunet, *L'introduction,* pp. 140-144.

[80] Aiton, *Vortex Theory,* p. 209.

[81] For vol. I (1734) the committee was composed of Mairan and Louis Godin; for the subsequent three volumes of 1735, 1737, and 1739, the committee consisted of Mairan and the Abbé de Bragelongne, the latter also a disciple of Malebranche. See Robinet in *Oeuvres de Malebranche,* XX, 152-153, 170, 359.

[82] Joseph Privat de Molières, *Leçons de physique,* 4 vols. (Paris, 1734-39), I, vii-x. His vortices, he writes (I, 307), provide "une cause mécanique de la pesan-

teur, ou de la force centripète, telle que M. Newton la demande, qui croît & décroît en raison inverse des quarrés des distances au centre, & qu'il avoüe n'avoir pû déduire de ses suppositions." Newton, he adds (I, 308), was obliged to regard gravity as a universal principle "& un effet sans cause."

83 For the persistent influence of Malebranche, especially his criticism of the concept of force, on these later Newtonians, notably Maupertuis, see the excellent article of Thomas L. Hankins, "The Influence of Malebranche on the Science of Mechanics during the Eighteenth Century," *Journal of the History of Ideas,* 28 (1967), 193-210.

84 *Les lettres de la marquise du Châtelet,* ed. T. Besterman, 2 vols. (Geneva, 1958), I, 261. Cited by J. L. Heilbron in his *Electricity in the 17th and 18th Centuries: A Study of Early Modern Physics* (Berkeley and Los Angeles, 1979), p. 278.

Julia L. Epstein and Mark L. Greenburg (essay date 1984)

SOURCE: "Decomposing Newton's Rainbow," in *Journal of the History of Ideas,* Vol. XLV, No. 1, January-March 1984, pp. 115-40.

[*In the following essay, Epstein and Greenburg examine how the image of the rainbow was affected by Newton's* Opticks. *The critics focus particularly on how the literary representation of the rainbow changed and developed during and after Newton's life.*]

Sir Isaac Newton has intrigued philosophers, poets, artists, and critics alike as the scientist "with his prism and silent face," a "mind forever voyaging through strange seas of thought alone."[1] The deified figure of Newton, images and metaphors drawn from Newtonian science, and poetic versions of Newtonian cosmology all appear repeatedly in the poetry written after Newton's death, and these phenomena have been extensively studied.[2] Such studies as identify Newton's presence in eighteenth-century literature generally interpret particular poems or movements in poetry insofar as Newton's imagery or cosmology affected them. Most literary scholars have looked at Newtonianism as a key for understanding individual poems. But the pervasive presence of Sir Isaac Newton in the poetry written during the hundred years following his death suggests some larger questions about the impact of science on the production and reception of literature. We shall examine Newtonian reverberations in Neoclassical and Romantic poetry as a problem in the history of ideas: How are images from early science transmitted to literature, translated into poetry, and transformed by the poetic process? To approach these questions, we shall focus on a particular optical and poetic image and its history in physics and in literature: the image of the rainbow.

I.

To offer a coherent, comprehensive scientific explanation of rainbows had long been a standard problem of physics before Sir Isaac Newton began his optical experiments.[3] Ptolemy had tried to formulate the law of refraction in his *Optica,* and both Aristotle and Seneca worked toward definitions of the rainbow and its relation to the properties of light. The rainbow phenomenon, indeed, was a central concern in the early history of optics, a science which, until around 1600, investigated two things: the nature and propagation of light; and the process of visual perception. Indeed, the facts on which Newton's theory of color was built had already been discovered by others. Newton's achievement in optics was to recognize the significance of these facts as others before him had not, and to explain, finally and unequivocally, the colors of the rainbow in terms of the refraction (and internal reflection) in rain drops. The language Newton used to present that achievement altered the way nonscientists looked at rainbows.

When Newton published his treatise on *Opticks* in 1704, he presented it to the public in a straightforward expository style addressed not only to natural philosophers but to the *general* English reader. Unlike the 1687 *Principia,* which was written in dry mathematical prose and published in Latin, Newton deliberately made the *Opticks* accessible to the nonscientist, communicating to his culture the discoveries of his singular mental voyage.[4] In fact, it was one of the first major modern scientific works to engage a wide audience. The shift from erudite Latin to vernacular English in Newton's writings marks a crucial moment in the history of scientific literature, and explains in part why so many eighteenth-century popularizers of science produced texts that purported to broadcast Newton's clear English language descriptions to a wide lay audience.[5] With the *Opticks,* the imagery and language of a major discovery in science became available to lay readers and "scientific amateurs" conceived and addressed as such.

One of Newton's central concerns in thus broadly addressing the *Opticks* to a nonspecialist public was to use scientific language in a way adequate to convey the complexity of natural laws simply and clearly. He attempts to free his language of metaphor and conceit and, indeed, Newton's prose in the *Opticks* approaches the ideal fiction that the language of science is a purified discourse untinged with emotion, bias, or ideology, free from poetic imagery—a neutral discourse.[6] Since this is so, why did Newton's discoveries reverberate so powerfully in lyric poetry? Clearly, Newton investigated natural phenomena—light, vision, color—that had for centuries been invested with symbolic mystical and religious significance, and had also attracted serious scientific investigators from antiquity on. Yet a key answer to this question lies in understanding that, although Newton's exposition of light's properties, for example, was not itself figurative or laden with rhetorical *inventio,* a great part of its appeal to poets lay in its power to evoke images and metaphors. Newton's enterprise, after all, involves the unraveling of invisible structure, and that task, we shall see, is itself a poetic—or image-laden—undertaking.

To illustrate this enterprise, the diagram Newton provides and its accompanying discussion indicate the participatory relationship between perceiver's eye and rainbow. The diagram graphically illustrates that no two perceivers see the same rainbow, nor does any one perceiver see the identical rainbow from moment to moment.[7] Newton's insistence upon the crucial completing role of the viewer in achieving the rainbow image appealed especially to writers and readers during the eighteenth century and to their romantic heirs. For in that age, deliberately unfinished or unelaborated verse, painting, and music depended for their completion upon the reader's, spectator's, or listener's imaginative engagement and active artistic complicity. And readers expected to encounter this condition (known as the *non finito* and as "ideal presence") in the greatest art.[8] Such aesthetic expectation and the mental attitudes it engendered also functioned to pave the way for the smooth transition of the rainbow from cultural icon to object of scientific inquiry to poetic image.

The clarity of Newton's explanation of the rainbow in the **Opticks** invited participation and appropriation by readers. After discussing the refraction of light, Newton wrote in a letter to Oldenburg, "Why the Colours of the *Rainbow* appear in falling drops of Rain, is also from hence evident."[9] He devoted a proposition of the **Opticks** to explaining the colors of the rainbow by the properties of light he had discovered: differently colored rays of the spectrum have differing refrangibilities. In that chapter, he discusses the ancient view of rainbows, repeats the experiments Antonius de Dominis and Descartes had performed with a glass globe filled with water, presents diagrams to explain the angles and measurements of rainbows, and extends his analysis to candlelight and to spherical hailstones. But the crux of the matter occurs in just the few short opening sentences:

> This Bow never appears, but where it rains in the Sun-shine, and may be made artificially by spouting up Water which may break aloft, and scatter into Drops, and fall down like Rain. For the Sun shining upon these Drops certainly causes the Bow to appear to a Spectator standing in a due Position to the Rain and Sun. And hence it is now agreed upon, that this Bow is made by refraction of the Sun's Light in drops of falling Rain.[10]

The explanation of this mystical symbol in scientific terms thus turns out to be surprisingly simple.

Almost in proportion to its simplicity and clarity, Newton's explanation of the rainbow and its colors evoked a vast outpouring of imaginative responses, particularly from the period following his death through the High Romantic age. At the beginning of this period, the concepts of "art" and "science" had not yet split apart, as they were later to do. Writers and painters would not yet have conceded Ruskin's injunction that "the ordinary powers of human perception are almost certain to be disturbed by the knowledge of the real nature of what they draw: and, until you are quite fearless of your faithfulness to the appearances of things, the less you know of their reality the better."[11] In fact, artists actively sought scientific explanations for the natural objects that intrigued them. Their renderings of the rainbow present specific examples of early scientific discourse reaching beyond its immediate context and utterly transforming culturally-laden terms which it opens to fresh aesthetic interpretation. For succeeding imaginations, Newton had altered the rainbow, charging an ancient cultural icon with new significance.

II.

The concern to simplify, clarify, and communicate scientific language led to a spate of popular works that attempted to educate the general public about Newton's discoveries and his world view. The avalanche of popular interpretations began with religious books like William Whiston's *A New Theory of the Earth* (1696), George Cheyne's *Philosophical Principles of Natural Religion* (1705), William Derham's *Astro-Theology* (1715) and William Wollaston's *The Religion of Nature Delineated* (1722). More serious books about science—such as J. T. Desaguliers' *Physicomechanical Lectures* (1717) and Maupertuis' *Discours sur les differentes figures des astres avec une exposition des systèmes de MM. Descartes et Newton* (1732), Voltaire's *Eléments de la philosophie de Newton* (1738), and Colin MacLaurin's *An Account of Sir Isaac Newton's Philosophy* (1748) followed. Two biographical works also quickly appeared: Henry Pemberton's *A View of Sir Isaac Newton's Philosophy* (1728) and William Stukeley's *Memoirs of Sir Isaac Newton's Life* (1752). Some of the compositions inspired by Newton's writings were intended for women and children.[12] The most successful of this group included Francesco Algarotti's *Sir Isaac Newton's Philosophy Explain'd for the Use of the Ladies,* translated from the Italian by Elizabeth Carter in 1739, and Benjamin Martin's *Tom Telescope: The Newtonian System of Philosophy, Explained by Familiar Objects, In an Entertaining Manner, For the Use of Young Persons* and *A Plain and Familiar Introduction to the Newtonian Experimental Philosophy* (1754).

These works reflect shifting views about science writing during the eighteenth century, a period characterized by a need to come to terms with the impact of new scientific discoveries on traditional philosophy, cosmology, and the emerging institution of "literature."[13] In the late seventeenth century, new scientific prose standards were elaborated so that a plain style for science writing could be established. Scientists sought a way to represent their discoveries in adequate language: language that would be congruent to what it referred, as is the symbolic language of mathematics. Francis Bacon had initiated a distrust of the euphuistic, metaphorical, precious style then current, and scientists tried to locate an appropriate language not just to describe nature, but to *indicate* the thing described.[14] The most famous statement of this ideal of scientific discourse appears in Thomas Sprat's *History of the Royal Society.* Sprat attacks what he calls "this vicious Abundance of *Phrase,* this Trick of *Metaphors,* this Volubility of Tongue, which makes so great a noise in the World." He concludes that "the only Remedy that can be found for this Extravagance . . . has been a constant Resolution, to reject all the Amplifications, Digressions, and Swellings of Style; to return back to the Primitive Purity and Shortness, when Men deliver'd so many *Things,* almost in an equal Number of Words." The Royal Society, in Sprat's exposition, "extracted from all their Members, a close, naked, natural way of Speaking; positive Expressions, clear Senses; a native Easiness; bringing all Things as near the mathematical Plainness as they can; and preferring the Language of Artizans, Countrymen, and Merchants, before that of Wits, or Scholars."[15] Scientific discourse, then, aimed at becoming "demonstrative" and "referential" beginning in the seventeenth century, and scientific description tried to be mimetic.

This attempt to forge a language in which words are equivalent to things, of course, represented a linguistic ideal. Language was to annihilate metaphorical modes of expression, according to these new standards, through reduction to a pure sign system in which metaphor would be literalized. The universal language philosophers of the period sought for a symbolic representation of discoveries in natural philosophy that would be wholly adequate to the processes of the material world. Guidebooks and theories about such a purified language were published: Samuel Hartlib's *Common Writing* in 1647, Cave Beck's *Universal Character* in 1657, Henry Edmunson's *Lingua Linguarum* in 1658 and, most importantly because sponsored by the Royal Society itself, John Wilkins' *An Essay Towards a Real Character and a Philosophical Language* in 1668.[16] Indeed, the young Newton sketched a universal language system of his own in 1661.[17]

From the perspective of these linguistic philosophers, one recent critic asserts, "scientific language set out programmatically to subordinate and even to swallow poetic discourse"; and he argues that the "most persistent post-Baconian tendency was the pseudo-scientific curbing of all language out of suspicion about its insidious powers. . . ."[18] In practice, however, complex changes in *both* science and poetry were wrought: poetic language absorbed the images of science, and scientific descriptions retained many of their metaphors.

In part as a result of the aggressive stance taken by some language reformers, poets' concepts of themselves were shaped in reaction to what they perceived as attacks on the imagination and its expression in figuratively rich language; and at the end of the eighteenth century Wordsworth, for example, argued for a spare poetic discourse. The importance of personified abstractions in eighteenth-century writing argues for the extra-rational myth-making faculty of the age's poets pressing back against the rational claims and achievements of science even as the poets turned the scientists themselves into myths.[19]

Writers of scientific treatises could not, of course, control the interpretations to which their writing was subject. Newton's discovery of the elements that constitute a rainbow, for example, shifts the meaning of an already-existing word, a word laden with manifold meanings in the west over thousands of years. In Newton's study of the rainbow, in fact, the scientist transvalues language. In decomposing the rainbow phenomenon, he recasts the very word "rainbow" by re-observing its object and re-interpreting its significance. David Hume later pointed out in his *History of England* the central irony of Newton's philosophical activity: "While Newton seemed to draw off the veil from some of the mysteries of nature, he showed at the same time the imperfections of the mechanical philosophy; and thereby restored her ultimate secrets to that obscurity in which they ever did and ever will remain."[20]

The legacy of Newton's writings, as a consequence, profoundly influenced aesthetic theory in the eighteenth century. Aesthetic experience came to be understood, not as a property of objects (in nature or in art) themselves, but as a subjective event, a capacity of the perceiving mind, a way of looking at objects in the world.[21] The work of eighteenth-century theorists—Burke, Diderot, Schiller, Goethe—reflects this interest in locating aesthetic experience *inside* the mind, and the concept of the sublime—aesthetics as psychology—derived from this interest. Simultaneously, by explaining natural phenomena, Newton at once affirmed his reputation as a genius and was seen by eighteenth-century poets to have demystified nature. Newton himself never conceived of his work in this way, of course, but for those who followed him and whose writings reflect his legacy, what had once been invested with mythic significance became worldly. Such profound shifts argue for the interconnectedness of early scientific discourse, aesthetics, psychology, cosmology, and the signifying power of language—indeed for their inseparability.

III.

If we isolate one image from the **Opticks**—the image of the rainbow—and trace its subsequent history, we can understand how the demystifying power of poetic versions of Newtonianism worked, and how it in turn generated new myths. Studying poetic appropriations of Newton's rainbow diachronically reveals the historical importance of a deeply engrained interconnection between science issues, scientific discourse, and aesthetic values. Examining this particular moment—Newton's straight-forward explanation of how light diffracted to form a rainbow, and the complex poetic responses it engendered—in the context of poetry written prior to and following the eighteenth century reveals that poets transformed science for their readers just as science, modulating its significance by interpretation and rendering, influenced the context and form of poetry.

The rainbow image came to Newton laden with over two thousand years' burden of interpretations. When Newton definitively explained the phenomenon in his **Opticks,** nonscientists thought he had decomposed and reintegrated a symbol of great power, displacing a large portion of its meaning forever from the sacred realm into the profane. His explanation, to judge by responses to it, reached beyond optics; it implied, for Newton's audience, a cosmology and a psychology. Before the philosophers' rainbow, there was God's. As a written image, the rainbow originates in the Bible, where it heralds the end of the Flood, though interpretations of it predate the Scriptures. Ancient peoples "imagined the rainbow as God's weapon," or bow, "from which the lightnings of his arrows were shot."[22] But following the great flood, according to the Bible, God inverts the rainbow in the sky as a sign to human beings and a reminder to himself of his covenant with humankind.

> I do set my bow in the cloud, and it shall be for a token of the covenant between me and the earth. And it shall come to pass, when I bring a cloud over the earth, that the bow shall be seen in the cloud: And I will remember my covenant, which is between me and you and every living creature of all flesh; and the waters shall no more become a flood to destroy all flesh. And the bow shall be in the cloud; and I will look upon it, that I may remember the everlasting covenant between God and every living creature of all flesh that *is* upon the earth. And God said unto Noah, This *is* the token of the covenant, which I have established between me and all flesh that *is* upon the earth. (*Genesis* 9: 13-17)

This rainbow achieves what seventeenth-century language philosophers sought and what Coleridge later describes as symbol: that which is what it describes.

In this context of object and symbol, a natural phenomenon—the rainbow—mediates between God and all living creatures, between heaven and earth; it signifies a relationship between God and humankind, and symbolizes the peace achieved through divine providence and law; and it endures, occurring periodically as a visual sign to its creator of his promise. As such, the rainbow functions as a natural event which comes to be interpreted as a divinely instituted sign in a sacramental universe. The voice of God establishes this pattern: His law becomes, for Him as for us, a "token." The natural phenomenon is itself a signifier; its meanings shift dramatically over time, the result of scientific discovery, expressed in language, which is immediately interpreted cosmologically. Until the symbol becomes revalued in the eighteenth century, it remains for pre-Newtonian culture a symbol of God's relationship with human beings. After Newton, as we shall demonstrate, the symbol signifies humankind's relationship with nature figured intimately, even sexually. Ultimately, eighteenth-century poets imply a congruence between the adverting mind and humanized, receptive nature.

Like much Old Testament writing, the significance of the rainbow was revalued by exegetes. Interpreted typologically, it became a symbol of Christ's new covenant of mercy. Such interpretations occur particularly in the English poetry written before the age of Newton. Sixteenth and seventeenth century English poets—for our purposes, pre-Newtonian poets—invoke the rainbow to signify several of the meanings we have suggested. It appears as a wondrous image of complex colors and natural beauty and bounty; more often, as a visual symbol of God's covenant with humankind; or, typologically, as a visual reminder overlaying Christ's covenant of forgiveness upon the earlier covenant. Many poets exploit it deliberately as a complex symbol that blends these general meanings: it illuminates for them a sacramental universe in which nature bodies forth the divine assurance of peace. Before Newton, poets could confidently rely upon their audience's foreknowledge of its symbolic religious significance.

Before Newton, however, the rainbow was not associated closely and consistently with a mortal. The relationship it described existed between God—or Christ—and humankind. Poetic responses to Newton's explanation of the rainbow introduce new participants in a fresh relationship. For post-Newtonian poets, Biblical authority has been displaced by human genius acting to discover the workings of the wondrous image, and the relationship engendered exists between nature (often figured as a woman) yielding herself to Sir Isaac Newton, or the force of Newton's intellect figuratively ravishing nature. The terms and agency of the rainbow's significance, of the relationships it signifies, become altered forever, for now the mind becomes congruent with nature. For the Romantic and Victorian poets—and their modern heirs—the rainbow loses its ability to designate singly once Newton's discoveries, interpreted by the poets, displaced from the rainbow its earlier meanings. The history of responses to the rainbow, then, the history of this important image's meaning, becomes inseparable from the progress of ideas and their rendition and interpretation in language.

IV. The rainbow image begins to appear frequently and prominently in the English poetry of the Renaissance.[23] The image derives its power from the physical size, beauty, and range of colors of the natural phenomenon, from its biblical associations with covenant and peace, or from both together. Spencer's Cuddie in the "February" eclogue of *The Shepheardes Calender* (1579) calls forth the natural image's breadth to describe a "Bullocke": "His hornes bene as broade, as Rainebowe bent."[24] Similarly, in "The Ruines of Time" (1591), Spenser figures a "Bridge, made all of golde" as "like the coulored Rainbowe arched wide" (lines 547, 550). And as one of a series of alternative metaphors for "Cynthiaes . . . glorie" in "Colin Clouts Come Home Againe" (1595), Spenser likens that goddess to the "circlet of a Turtle true, / In which all colours of the rainbow bee" (lines 340-341). Shakespeare extends the image's meaning while avoiding its strictly biblical associations. Falstaff, a master of hyperbole, complains to Mistress Quickly that "I was beaten myself into all the colours of the rainbow."[25] In *King John* (1595) (IV, ii, 13-16) adding "another hue / Unto the rainbow," like gilding the lily, expresses "wasteful and ridiculous excess." Yet in *The Rape of Lucrece* (1594) the rainbow represents the heroine's psychological trauma: Lucrece appears "clad in mourning black: / And round about her tear-distained eye / Blue circles stream'd, like rainbows in the sky: / These water-galls in her dim element / Foretell new storms to these already spent" (lines 1585-89). Shakespeare draws upon the naturally-occurring "water-galls," or "secondary or imperfectly-formed rainbows" (*OED*), and the traditional belief that, because imperfect, they portend evil, to extend the rainbow's metaphoric significance here.

John Milton draws upon ancient mythologies of the rainbow to evoke its range of colors while also offering biblical and specifically Christian interpretations of it. He links the visual image with its rich history of associations. In *A Mask Presented at Ludlow-Castle, 1634*, Comus describes a scene which he takes for a

> faëry vision
> Of som gay creatures of the element
> That in the colors of the Rainbow live
> And play i'th plighted clouds.[26]

Later in the *Mask* a Spirit sings of the rainbow goddess with her scarf "purfl'd"—fringed with color:

> *Iris* there with humid bow,
> Waters the odorous banks that blow

> Flowers of more mingled hew
> Than her purfl'd scarf can shew.

> > (lines 992-95)

The peacock in *Paradise Lost* (1667) (VII, 445-6) appears "colourd with the Florid hue / Of rainbows," God's ground-based creation mirroring the heavenly image. The rainbow of Milton also presages apocalypse: in 1673 he figures the coming of "Truth, and Justice . . . Orb'd in a Rain-bow" ("On the Morning of Christ's Nativity," lines 141, 143). In another passage in *Paradise Lost*, the image both describes the dazzling appearance of God's "Saphir Throne, inlaid with pure / Amber, and colours of the showrie Arch" and is itself prefigured in the "Bow / And Quiver" hanging beside the throne (VI, 758-59; 763). And in Book XI (lines 865-67, 896-98), in its best known appearance, the rainbow betokens the Covenant.

Devotional poets of the sixteenth and seventeenth centuries revalue the rainbow typologically, as for them it signals the new covenant between Christ and humankind. "Gascoigne's Good Morrow" (1573) typifies this rendering. Here, the rainbow both symbolizes God and forecasts salvation through Christ:

> The rainbow bending in the sky,
> Bedecked with sundry hues,
> Is like the seat of God on high
> And seems to tell these news:
> That, as thereby he promisëd
> To drown the world no more,
> So by the blood which Christ hath shed
> He will our health restore.[27]

Henry Vaughan entitles one of *Silex Scintillans, or Sacred Poems* (1650, 1655) "The Rain-bow."[28] Vaughan there also traces the image's symbolic history from its Old Testament appearance: "How bright wert thou, when *Shems* admiring eye / Thy burnisht, flaming *Arch* did first descry!" (lines 3-4). Even now, the poet cries,

> When I behold thee, though my light be dim,
> Distant and low, I can in thine see him,
> Who looks upon thee from his glorious throne
> And mindes the Covenant 'twixt *All* and *One*.

> > (lines 15-18)

Yet in a world still sinful after the flood, Vaughan's rainbow ultimately augurs another coming which will also consume the rainbow itself:

> For though some think, thou shin'st but to restrain
> Bold storms, and simply dost attend on rain,
> Yet I know well, and so our sins require,
> Thou dost but Court cold rain, till *Rain* turns *Fire*.

> > (lines 39-42)

The image itself, however, remains static: Unlike later, eighteenth-century poetic treatments of the rainbow, this image does not itself act or change, nor is it acted upon.

For Andrew Marvell (1621-78) and John Dryden (1631-1700), the rainbow also remains a static vehicle in a metaphor, though these poets redirect its meaning. Drawing upon the rainbow's rich cultural and religious burden, they invoke the image not to glorify God or Christ or to foretell apocalypse but rather, relying upon the reader's awareness of those associations, these poets redirect its meaning in order to compliment mortals. In a sense, Dryden and Marvell forecast a specific and rather wide-ranging shift in the treatment of the rainbow which occurs in eighteenth-century deifications of Newton. They respond, too, to what is by the mid-seventeenth century a clear diminution of the rainbow's power to signify. Advances in science, skepticism engendered by Baconian method, and the popularity of the image, worked together to empty much of the rainbow's force as a literary sign referring to the original or the typological covenant. But transfigured further, it could illuminate great people. Thus Marvell concludes "A Poem Upon the Death of O. C." with a vision of the peaceful succession of power from Oliver to Richard Cromwell.[29] Richard is crowned with the sign of peace, and the rainbow then also figures the social transition from turmoil to calm:

> Heav'n to this choice prepar'd a diadem,
> Richer than any eastern silk, or gemme;
> A pearly rainbow, where the sun inchas'd
> His brows, like an imperial jewel grac'd.
> . . . . .
> Cease now our griefs, calme peace succeeds a
>   war,
> Rainbows to storms, Richard to Oliver.
>   (lines 315-18, 321-322)

In the dedicatory "To Her Grace the Duchess of Ormond," John Dryden also figures this noble's return to power following the "Waste of Civil Wars" in grand terms   a second coming:

> So when You came, with loud repeated Cries,
> The Nation took an Omen from your Eyes,
> And God advanc'd his Rainbow in the Skies,
> To sign inviolable Peace restor'd.[30]

The eyes of the Duchess signal peace on earth and also seem to spur God's advancement of the rainbow. Dryden reminds us that in rare instances the rainbow refers to the iris of the eye (*OED*), and that Iris is goddess of the rainbow, a messenger, like the rainbow image, which links sky and earth. The passage signals this noble woman's ascent with the rainbow which she causes: Dryden, like Marvell, shifts the rainbow's past association to the present and to a particular person. The image's power to signify has been redirected. In

a sense, the ground has been prepared for the astonishing relationships figured by Newton's rainbow in eighteenth-century poetry. Yet the symbol itself remains static, whole, of a piece once it appears, its rather circumscribed meanings deriving principally from Genesis. For Marvell and Dryden, the image never interacts with the mortals it adorns or symbolizes. And once these poets invoke the rainbow, quickly they move on, secure in the cultural associations it engenders.

V. For post-Newtonian poets, the rainbow begins to emerge as process, rather than fixed though divine product, as nature's loveliest secret revealing itself to the adverting mind of the scientist. The remarkable figurations that we describe below animate a heretofore static image, personifying the rainbow almost in direct proportion to the scientific spirit's distrust of such rhetorical figures. Poets assert themselves as creators of new relationships precisely in the face of the scientific distrust of metaphors and other poetic figures. The poets propound new unities, emphasizing vision over sight, even as they describe Newton's rational analysis of the rainbow into its constituent colors. Earl Wasserman has maintained that "it was not Wordsworth [objecting to hollow personifications] who dealt the death-blow to Prosopopoeia, but the metaphysics that Coleridge ushered in"; and, recently, Hans Eichner has also declared more generally that "Romanticism is perhaps predominantly, a desperate rearguard action against the spirit and the implications of modern science. . . ."[31] Yet we believe that even before Romanticism, eighteenth-century poets sensed the enormous power of scientific method to explain physical phenomena and to produce tangible benefits and material progress, even as advocates of science appeared to reject poetry. Poets, consequently, chose to depict scientific power in their own terms.

Critics have located the widening gulf between literature and science in High Romanticism. Raymond Williams, in his *Culture and Society 1780-1950,* holds that Romanticism elaborated an aesthetics of opposition to the culture as a way of defending "certain human values, capacities, energies, which the development of society towards an industrial civilization was felt to be threatening or even destroying."[32] Recently, Alvin B. Kernan has argued that the "institution of literature as it developed in the late eighteenth and nineteenth centuries . . . was built up not *ex nihilo,* but in close interaction with certain profound social changes." Foremost among these changes, Kernan cites industrialism and technology emerging as dominant institutions: "The literary world-view and values—imagination, mystery, creativity, tradition, interaction of man and nature," which, Kernan asserts, we associate with Romanticism and its aftermath in Modern art and literature, "grew not purely out of the mind of man but out of a complex process of social adjustments in an attempt to assert and maintain an endangered way of thinking and feeling about man's nature and relation-ship to the world."[33] In poets' struggle to render science in metaphoric language, we find evidence of this assertion. While the scientific poets of the eighteenth century have been interpreted traditionally as glorifiers of the new science and deifiers of Newton, its greatest mind, some of their methods reveal them also to be uneasy outsiders insinuating their way of seeing the world (through metaphors, of which personification is the chief example) into a world which increasingly rejects such metaphorical vision. They are thus more nearly precursors to Romantic attitudes and aesthetics than the Romantics themselves would admit.

While Newton was alive, poets longed to join him in his lofty imaginings, to wander through unexplained worlds with him. In *The Ecstacy* (1720), for example, John Hughes' soul floats above humankind where it encounters Newton's soul in its diurnal voyage of discovery:

> The Great Columbus of the skies I know!
> 'Tis Newton's soul, that daily travels here
> In search of knowledge for Mankind below[34]

This scene of recognition, voiced by the poet from an imaginatively exalted position, elevates the poet to the figurative high plane occupied by the scientist's mind. Simultaneously it exalts poetry, with its ability to communicate this visionary experience and to approach an accurate description of the grand Newton in the only way conceivable to Hughes, through metaphor.

Newton's deification in poetry after his death in 1727 is well known, as are the many poetic passages from that period which represent the rainbow.[35] Marjorie Hope Nicholson, M. H. Abrams, and William Powell Jones have each examined these passages to study Newton's general impact on poetry. But poetic transformations of Newton figured through his relationship with rainbows can also tell us about poetry and language and the power of figuration. Poets deify Newton partially to bask in self-reflected glory: rather than Newton demanding the muse, Newton becomes the primal force poets seize, shape, represent, and ultimately appropriate in tropes. Only such visionary rendering, these passages implicitly declare, can approach the lofty reaches of Newton's mind. Moreover, poets create for themselves a participatory role in their verse: they figure themselves present at Newton's moments of discovery. They adopt this role in response to two mutually-intensifying problems which result from deifying Newton: how does one fashion a language adequate to figure forth a god (especially in light of the attack upon figurative language)?; and what is the poet's place in a culture dominated by a scientist whom the poet himself is mythologizing? The responses to these questions, expressed at least partially in the following passages, show that even as poets glo-

rify Newton, invoking their most powerful methaphors to do so, their poetry embodies anxiety about the adequacy of poetic language—and also about the place of poetry in the culture. Perhaps the remarkable out-pouring of poems on Newton's rainbow (as, of course, on Newton) reveals poets' desire to appropriate Newton for themselves, capturing his power, in effect, for poetry.[36]

James Thomson, the most important eighteenth-century poet to install his vision of Newton's intellect and imagery in the natural world, pictures the scientist's mind in action while centering his own poetic perspective at the point of intercourse between mind and nature.[37] In his elegy, "To the Memory of Sir Isaac Newton" (1727), Thomson personifies the relationship between Newton and the physical world, transfiguring sexually an intellectual interchange:

> Nature herself
> Stood all subdued by him, and open laid
> Her every latent glory to his view
>
> (lines 36-38)

Newton dominates Nature; Nature, feminized, yields herself to Newton. Thomson extends the metaphoric sexual relationship between Newton and nature as the scientist, "beloved / Of Heaven!" (lines 72-3), perceives visually Nature's "frame"—at once the physical form of the created world and that world figured as a body in motion. The poet, imaginatively present at the scene, animates a remarkably palpable encounter in which Newton's

> well purged penetrating eye
> The mystic veil transpiercing, inly scanned
> The rising, moving, wide-established frame.
>
> (lines 73-75)

The subject of this passage for eighteenth-century readers would have been as much Thomson's heightened consciousness as Newton's penetrating vision: As Earl Wasserman demonstrated, eighteenth-century critics assumed that "only great boldness and intense emotional force could create effective personification . . . the artistic use of this figure effectively conveyed to the reader the passionate transport of the author."[38]

The rainbow offers Thomson the opportunity to figure Newton's eye unfolding one of nature's loveliest visions in his "beauteous . . . refractive law" (line 124). Thomson locates his famous passage on light and the rainbow at the center of his poem. Again he personifies a natural phenomenon in intimate embrace with Newton in a richly-evocative scene that here concerns light, the scientist's participatory eye, and the power of Newton's mind to "transpierce" a willing lover's outer garments in order to delight in her inner form:

Even Light itself, which every thing displays,
Shone undiscovered, till his brighter mind
Untwisted all the shining robe of day;
And, from the whitening undistinguished
   blaze,
Collecting every ray into his kind,
To the charmed eye educed the gorgeous train
Of parent colours.

(lines 96-102)

The scene renders Newton's refraction of light as a mental action envisioned by the poet. Wasserman again illuminates the significance of such poetic description for contemporary readers, as the eighteenth-century mind, he observes, almost consistently associated "personification with vision," out of the "conviction that personification is the consequence of vehement feeling and an imagination flying to the farthest reaches its sensory nature will allow."[39] The subject, then, becomes not only Newton's mental action, but also that of the poet. Moreover, in this scene of unrobing, the poet stands as observer, first as voyeur and then as reporter. The poet is at once creator of the vision and consequently coeval with Newton's own visionary intellect, and privileged participant in the deliciously sensual undressing of a willing nature.

But as reporter, the poet also strives to dazzle, educate, and identify his readers with the overt subject of his poem, with Newton's refraction of light, though he does so, significantly, in terms of the rainbow as beautiful "vision." Hence, after elaborating each color perceived by Newton's "charmed eye," Thomson locates his perspective on the ground, inviting his readers to recall Newton's analysis of light each time they see a rainbow, yet to perceive the bow whole, as infinitely variable and inexhaustably beautiful. The rainbow's colors

when the clouds distil the rosy shower,
Shine out distinct adown the watery bow;
While o'er our heads the dewy vision bends
Delightful, melting on the fields beneath.
Myriads of mingling dyes from these result,
And myriads still remain—infinite source
Of beauty, ever flushing, ever new.

(lines 112-119)

The poet now stands among us, picturing the personified rainbow "o'er our heads," shifting his perspective from Newton's mental plane to the plane of human sight and vision. And he does so in rich poetic language—regular cadences, variegated texture, emotionally-charged words, evocative sounds—which emphasizes the poet's mythmaking power by calling attention to the forms in which Thomson renders Newton and Newton's relation to the world. In a single verse paragraph, then, Thomson translates metaphorically an essentially intellectual, scientifically methodical discovery—refraction of light into its constituent colors—into an apotheosis of the poet and poetry. Perhaps the poem's greatest irony emerges from Thomson's anxious questions following the rainbow passage, concerning poetry's power to deliver Newton: "But who can number up his labours? who / His high discoveries sing? . . . How shall the muse then grasp the mighty theme?" (lines 132-33, 136). Certainly, these interrogatives express the conventional self-effacement of poets; but more important, they also voice this post-Newtonian poet's particular sense of his diminished social importance as he struggles with inadequate language to embrace Newton's knowledge, a knowledge which Thomson himself has just mythologized.

The social function of personification and point of view becomes crucial for a poet in an age of scientific ascendency and concomitant diminution of the writer's authority. Clifford Siskin has recently described the advantages of personification for the *poet* in terms that underscore our discussion: "In personification . . . the procrustean poet desires to fit all things to human form. The result is a transformation of potential chaos into uniform human community, for the 'real' world has been troped to actualize myth within the poem. That community then reflects back upon the speaker as an expression of how he wants to be. As the maker of the trope, the speaker constitutes himself as the center of the community—the abiding presence who is its Spokesperson."[40] The clear advantages to be gained for the poet himself and for his art by appropriating the scientist's power through personification, and his undeclared though privileged presence at the personified scene, accounts for the poetic outpourings devoted to Newton's rainbow. In fact, the anxieties induced in writers by the dramatically increasing social recognition of science, pure reason and, by association, prose discourse, accounts in part for a poetry which is overtly declared to be homage but which is also—perhaps principally—transfiguration and appropriation. Walter Jackson Bate has described the force of accumulated literary greatness upon the eighteenth-century poet in *The Burden of the Past and the English Poet.* Before the "rich and intimidating legacy of the past," Bate writes, poets since the late seventeenth century self-consciously brood, wondering *"What is there left to do?"*[41] The burden of the present, in the form of science generally and embodied in Newton particularly, also presses hard upon poets who see themselves displaced from the center of society to its circumference. This process begins during the age of Newton and continues to this day.

The range of eighteenth-century poetic evocations of Newton's rainbow exemplifies the quiet battle we have described, fought with language weapons on a remarkably circumscribed field. Poets figure Newton's dominance over nature in overtly sexual scenes which they witness and narrate. In Thomson's "Spring" (1728), from *The Seasons,* Newton possesses the prismatic agency of the rain (having explained the phenomenon), though the subject of the passage becomes the action of the poet's mind:

> Meantime refracted from yon eastern Cloud,
> Bestriding Earth, the grand Ethereal Bow
> Shoots up immense.
>
> (lines 203-205)

Thomson invests the rainbow with orgasmic power, while he also appropriates scientific language—"refracted"—for his poetry. Rather than the natural phenomenon reflecting this power, the poet's mythologizing bestows it. His eyes alone have followed the rainbow from the ground to its apex, so that it appears only to *him* as if the bow "Shoots up." The real subject of these lines becomes the emotion engendered by the speaker's visual process which he confers upon the essentially static image of the rainbow. This passage from "Spring" continues with an apostrophe to the late scientist. Thomson's trope displays the power of language to call into existence one not present:

> Here, awful NEWTON, the dissolving Clouds
> Form, fronting of the Sun, thy showery Prism;
> And to the sage-instructed Eye unfold
> The various twine of Light, by thee disclos'd
> From the white mingling Maze.
>
> (lines 208-212)

Again, with quasi-scientific descriptive precision, Thomson's vision centers upon his reception of the rainbow. The "showery prism" may be "Newton's," now a mythologized presence, but the participatory "sage-instructed eye" belongs to the poem's speaker whose visionary reception of refracted light constitutes the subject of this passage.

Richard Glover joins Thomson in sexualizing Newton's patriarchal dominion over nature. Glover's "A Poem on Newton," which prefaced Pemberton's *A View of Sir Isaac Newton's Philosophy* (London, 1728), intensifies the overtly sexual figuration of Newton's relationship with light which we first witnessed in Thomson's elegy to Newton. Glover conceives alternative intimate scenarios to account for the moment of Newton's understanding of refraction as he asks the sun

> How Newton dar'd advent'rous to unbraid
> The yellow tresses of thy shining hair.
> Or didst thou gracious leave thy radiant
>   sphere,
> And to his hand thy lucid splendours give,
> T'unweave the light-diffusing wreath, and part
> The blended glories of thy golden plumes?

Overtly, Glover has imagined the moment of Newton's discovery in explicitly feminine sexual terms of braiding, weaving, and parting. Glover dramatizes an essentially intellectual process in terms of two possible sexual encounters. The poet seeks to determine from the sun whether Newton, emboldened, was the aggressor daring to "unbraid" light's tresses or whether light presented herself as Newton's suppliant lover, giving herself over for him "T'unweave." The description becomes palpable as light "to his hand" yields her "splendours" and refraction becomes the scientist parting his beloved's hair. Glover thus assumes an exalted position as light's inquisitor. The poet quests after the mysterious moment of creation (and creative discovery) in terms of procreation. He imaginatively expands Newton's interior discovery in space and in time. And by inquiring about the nature of the creative process itself in detail, Glover shifts focus from science to metaphor. Newton may have unwoven the rainbow, but the particular way his mind operated upon nature becomes here the poet's text (as "text" also means something "woven"). Newton deconstructs nature by stripping her of her mystifying garments; the poet deconstructs the moment of deconstruction and then reintegrates it in human form, as a charming encounter between lovers.

To judge from poetic treatments of the rainbow, by mid-eighteenth century the intense imaginative activity we have witnessed—almost a competitive anxiety to capture for poetry Newton's powerful intimacy with nature—gives way to a number of poems featuring a rainbow forever altered by Newton's explanation of refraction which the poet celebrates. In picturing the rainbow, for example, Mark Akenside composes a scientific treatise in verse. A portion of his *Pleasures of the Imagination* (1744), this passage merely translates into poetic diction and cadence the language of science; it appears more a product of fancy than of imagination (in Coleridge's terms):

> Nor ever yet
> The melting rainbow's vernal-tinctur'd hues
> To me have shown so pleasing, as when first
> The hand of science pointed out the path
> In which the sun-beams gleaming from the
>   west
> Fall on the watry cloud, . . .
>   and that trickling show'r
> Piercing thro' every crystalline convex
> Of clust'ring dew-drops to their flight
>   oppos'd,
> Recoil at length where concave all behind
> Th' internal surface of each glassy orb
> Repells their forward passage into air.
>
> (II, lines 103-114)

This mildly personified passage recapitulates in ornamental language Newton's own description of light reflected and refracted within droplets of mist or rain. The poet stands upon the earth now, unlike the lofty Thomson or Glover, and claims to behold a process he really can only imagine. In a sense, Akenside too mythologizes Newton: seeing the rainbow he imagines the "path" indicated by the "hand of science." Despite the response to the rainbow, Newton's simple and clear prose explanation has altered human perception, an alteration evident in the prominence and dynamic shifts in meaning of the rainbow.

VI. While Akenside could glory simply in his new knowledge, for the English romantic poets Newton's rainbow becomes more problematic. As we have shown, the symbol has undergone several revaluations. The image continues to fascinate the romantic poets, although they extend its range of meanings: No longer is the rainbow God's or Christ's or Newton's, but rather it becomes more fully appropriated by each poet to his own purposes. Instead of relying upon past meanings of the rainbow, romantic poets create their own meanings for it. Principally through context, the Romantics revalue the image once more, typically as a projection of mind or mental state. The range of its romantic appearances suggests the image's flexibility and also the lack of a unified romantic response to a symbol closely associated in their time with Newton. Although Keats, Lamb, and Campbell agree that Newton had "destroyed all the poetry of the rainbow by reducing it to the prismatic colors"[42], Blake, Wordsworth, Shelley, and Byron invoke rainbows sometimes naturalistically, sometimes to reject its biblical meaning, and sometimes also as analogs of mental process.[43] Poets in the nineteenth century, however, no longer figure Newton's intimate knowledge of the rainbow. They fix instead upon the product of Newton's discovery, or reinvent a process which the rainbow figures.

The best known romantic appearances of the rainbow are a passage in Keats' "Lamia" and Campbell's "To the Rainbow," although each of the High Romantics invokes the image independently. For Keats and Campbell, Newton had emptied the rainbow of its poetry, and Newton's rather simple explanation of refraction, moreover, implied a metaphysics which threatened mind's vital relationship with nature. These familiar topoi provide a sharp contrast to less well known but revelatory appearances of the rainbow in other romantic poems. In his famous lines, Keats asks

> Do not all charms fly
> At the mere touch of cold philosophy?
> There was an awful rainbow once in heaven:
> We know her woof, her texture; she is given
> In the dull catalogue of common things.
> Philosophy will clip an Angel's wings,
> Conquer all mysteries by rule and line,
> Empty the haunted air, and gnomed mine—
> Unweave a rainbow.[44]

Keats distances himself from Thomson: where the eighteenth-century poet figures "awful Newton" unweav-

ing the rainbow, to discover its intimate essence figured sexually, Keats uses the same language to decry the reduction of the image's power as a result of Newton's "cold" analysis. We agree with M. H. Abrams that "Keats accedes to the fallacy . . . that, when a perceptual phenomenon is explained by correlating it with something more elementary than itself, the explanation discredits and replaces the perception."[45] But regardless of the consistency of Keats' thinking, his depiction of the rainbow again as "text"—"her woof, her texture . . . unweave a rainbow"—and his point of view with respect to it, signifies another shift in the revaluations of the rainbow. No longer is the poet part of the scene; now he is alienated by the very existence of Newton's text. Campbell's attempt to resuscitate the biblical and typological significance through poetry, indeed, seems belated as he declares

> I ask not proud Philosophy
> To teach me what thou art.[46]

He longs for the rainbow to accord with childhood visions of it, yet his poetry fails to actualize that departed vision:

> Still seem as to my childhood's sight
> . . . . .
> Can all that optics teach, unfold
> Thy form to please me so,
> As when I dreamt of gems and gold
> Hid in thy radiant bow?
> When Science from Creation's face
> Enchantment's veil withdraws,
> What lovely visions yield their place
> To cold material laws!
>
> (lines 5, 9-16)

Campbell attempts to recapture the rainbow for poetry by asking the image itself to revive its own primordial power and create itself anew as poetic subject. Campbell requests from the depleted image an agency his verse seems powerless to enact; "Theme of primeval prophecy, / Be still the poet's theme" (lines 37-38). But Campbell has arrived too late to recapture that rainbow, and he fails to find a new context for the image: the sound is forced here, the notes are few.

For Blake, a poet whose complex imaginative struggle with Newton engages him more deeply than the other Romantics with the scientist, the rainbow takes on new life. It embodies the potential for a commingling, not between God and his creation, or between the poet and God, or even between the poet and Newton, but instead a commingling between artist and audience. Blake uses the rainbow in one instance as Image which he asks us to "enter into" with him in order to trigger our own mental apocalypse. Referring to his painting of the Last Judgment, Blake encourages a new union:

If the Spectator could Enter into these
    Images in
his Imagination approaching them on the Fiery
    Chariot
of his Contemplative Thought if he could
    Enter into
Noahs Rainbow or into his bosom or could
    make a
Friend & Companion of one of these Images
    of wonder . . .
then would he arise from his grave then
    would he meet
the Lord in the Air & then would he be
    happy.[47]

Blake displaces the overtly biblical reference—"Noahs Rainbow"—from the mystical realm to psychology-and-aesthetics (for Blake, inseparable). He creates of the image for artist and perceiver, a mental space which he asks us to occupy with him.

Wordsworth and Coleridge also project mental states in terms of the rainbow, or use it naturalistically, as an image of color. It appears rarely in their verse and never itself as elaborated focus. No longer principal subject, it becomes principally metaphor.[48] For them, the image has been drained of the significant biblical associations, its intimate connection with Newton exhausted by the Newtonian poets and the counterresponse issued by Keats and Campbell. For Wordsworth, the rainbow embodies Marmaduke's passion in *The Borderers* as he figures the celestial image in opposition to earthly reality:

> Rainbow arches,
> Highways of dreaming passion, have too long
> . . . diverted wish and hope
> From the unpretending ground we mortals
>   tread.
>
> (II, lines 930-33)

In the 1802 untitled "My heart leaps up," Wordsworth attributes that emotional leap to beholding "A rainbow in the sky" which for him remains serenely untouched by cold philosophy. The "Rainbow" also represents a kind of natural constancy-in-change which unceremoniously "comes and goes," diminished now for Wordsworth, and fit emblem of how much he has lost from the days of his leaping heart. The subject here is not the demythologized rainbow but rather Wordsworth's inability to be stirred deeply by it, to commune with it.

Coleridge's antipathy to Newtonian mechanism and, specifically, to Newton's optical theories has received fresh and detailed treatment recently. Coleridge perceived light as a dynamic force which also resonates with symbolic significances, according to Trevor H. Levere, who remarks that Coleridge "saw Newton's fragmentation of sunlight into the colors of the spec-trum as totally false to the integral harmony and dynamism of light."[49] Coleridge was attracted to Goethe's theory of color as emerging from the interaction of light and darkness, and he focused like Goethe upon the *perceiver* of color rather than upon the natural phenomenon. Coleridge expressed significantly his belief in the harmony between the mind, religion, and nature by alluding to the rainbow: "a scheme of the Christian faith which does not arise out of, and shoot its beams downward into, the scheme of nature, but stands aloof . . . must be false or distorted in all its particulars."[50] Much as Coleridge figures the "silent icicles, / Quietly shining to the quiet Moon" in "Frost at Midnight," he concludes his poem "The Gentle Look" by depicting the "bright Rainbow" metaphorically reflected "on a willowy stream." Coleridge was fond enough of this reflected rainbow, in fact, to repeat it as the "imag'd Rainbow" in "To Robert Southey." Coleridge's rainbow thus linked heaven and earth with the perceiver of its reflection.

Although Shelley also studied natural phenomena and knew at least as much about science as many of the Newtonian poets, the rainbow does not figure importantly in his work.[51] He treats the image in a number of poems, most tellingly in what George Landow rightly terms a mockery of the "conventional association of rainbow and covenant," a "blasphemous parody" of this association in *Queen Mab* (1813; VII, 225-34).[52] In its other appearances, however, the rainbow mostly signifies transitoriness, or adjectivally, having variegated colors. So it appears, for example, in Shelley's *Alastor* (lines 334 and 431). It also appears in a metaphor for the servant child standing by her kin in *The Revolt of Islam*: "she stood beside him like a rainbow braided / within some storm" (V, xxiv, 1-2). The rainbow here is humanized, almost deflated in power as it becomes reduced by the poet to figure two people together.

Byron accepts and glories in Newton's purely physical rainbow, a vision created on earth by a natural process over which neither human beings nor God exerts control. His attitudes toward the image adumbrate the future "problematic" appearances of the rainbow in Victorian and modern literature and art which George Landow has studied. Specifically, the image no longer has the ability to assure us of divine peace or Christ's promise for salvation or even to matter as the emblem of Newton's intercourse with nature. The narrator of *Don Juan* sings, "'tis sweet to view on high / The rainbow, based on ocean, span the sky."[53] The lovely paradox centers the rainbow upon the earth where it is viewed from below. Similarly, a rainbow appears to the shipwrecked men in *Don Juan,* changed its shape, and then "Forsook the dim eyes of these shipwrecked men." (II, xci). Byron refuses to accord the rainbow its traditional religious significance, to believe in its signifying anything beyond its physical appearance and mutability, accepting the image as only a fleeting visual event: "It changed, of course; a heavenly chameleon, / The airy child of vapour and the sun" (II, xcii). For Byron, nature acts capriciously and the rainbow means only a band of colored light. Shelley and Byron deliberately reduce the image as a way of mocking religious iconography. Simultaneously, they also deflate the rainbow, and reach a limit in the emblem's decomposition.

VII. The permutations that characterize the history of the rainbow as natural object, as object of scientific study, and as poetic image suggest that nature imitates science as well as art. To perceive scientific discourse as simply self-referring and self-enclosed is to forget the impact of Newton's rainbow on the imagination, and the figurations that the rainbow stimulated in the century after Newton's death (1727). Regardless of the varied response, these poets' imaginations illustrate the resonances, the emotional appeal, of seemingly cold, rigorous scientific discourse. The variety of responses also attests to poetry's absorption, appropriation, and aesthetic transfiguration of the language and imagery of science, as science had similarly transvalued sensory nature and earlier nature myths. Enlightenment and romantic writers inherited the language of natural philosophers, and decomposed and reintegrated that language into poetry, thereby canonizing images from experimental science and rendering them in complex ways that humanized scientific language.

These writers would not, as we noted earlier, have believed Ruskin when he suggested that too much technical understanding of the stars clouds an artist's vision. But they would subscribe to Ruskin's "optical" view of the artist's function:

> The whole function of the artist in the world is to be a seeing and feeling creature; to be an instrument of such tenderness and sensitiveness, that no shadow, no hue, no line, no instantaneous and evanescent expression of the visible thing around him, nor any of the emotions which they are capable of conveying to the spirit which has been given him, shall either be left unrecorded, or fade from the book of record.[54]

To record the evanescent, to translate light and color into language, to portray the arc and texture of a rainbow: these were goals shared by both Newton and the poets whose imaginations were fascinated by "his prism and silent face." Our examination of the literary history and implications of Newton's rainbow as both an optical phenomenon and a richly-suggestive aesthetic image reinforces the view that scientific treatises do more than use language to represent the way the qualities of natural objects can be organized, classified, predicted, and understood. The reception of early scientific language reflects a complicated intersection of discovery, invention, and aesthetic interpretation of the natural world, and its transfiguration by scientists. The poetic metamorphoses of Newton's rainbow merely extend a process of the imagination already implicit in Newton's optics.

Notes

1 *The Prelude or Growth of a Poet's Mind,* ed. Ernest De Selincourt, 2nd ed. rev. by Helen Darbishire (Oxford, 1959), III, lines 61-63, 75.

2 See Marjorie Hope Nicolson's classic study of Newton's *Opticks* and eighteenth-century poetry and poetics, *Newton Demands the Muse: Newton's "Opticks" and the Eighteenth-Century Poets* (Princeton, 1946). For other important studies of the impact of early science on poetry, see Chap. 11 of M. H. Abrams, *The Mirror and the Lamp: Romantic Theory and the Critical Tradition* (New York, 1953) and William Powell Jones, *The Rhetoric of Science: A Study of Scientific Ideas and Imagery in Eighteenth-Century English Poetry* (London, Paul, 1966).

3 For historical background see Alistair C. Crombie's *Robert Grosseteste and the Origins of Experimental Science, 1100-1700* (Oxford and New York, 1953), a comprehensive survey of optical experimentation from Ptolemy to Grosseteste. David C. Lindberg has contributed a systematic analysis of optical theories in his *Theories of Vision from AlKindi to Kepler* (Chicago, 1976); and A. I. Sabra discusses the history of rainbow explanations in *Theories of Light from Descartes to Newton* (Cambridge, England, 1981), 61-68.

4 G. S. Rousseau has argued that both the *Principia* and the *Opticks* are essentially mathematical treatises, capable of translation into words but fundamentally quantifications of phenomena ("Science," *The Eighteenth Century,* ed. Pat Rogers [New York, 1978], 165). We disagree. Newton's concern throughout his life with language, representation, and the scientific communication process is illustrated by his early interest in universal language systems and his work on the calculus as a mathematical language.

5 Although Newton domesticated science and its language in the *Opticks,* Robert Boyle, a generation before Newton's *Opticks* appeared, had already published scientific works in English, as well as simultaneously in Latin and English editions. Boyle, however, did not conceive of the "scientific amateur" (as opposed to the mathematician) as his audience.

6 James L. Kinneavy in his *A Theory of Discourse* (Englewood Cliffs, N.J., 1971) presents a twentieth-century Machian view of the idea that scientific language is a neutral discourse; For a commentary on early views about the differences between the languages of science and of poetry, see Joseph Anthony Mazzeo, *Renaissance and Revolution: The Remaking of*

European Thought (New York, 1965), 325-28. J. M. Coetzee has recently discussed Newton's efforts to curb metaphor, to translate his scientific observations seamlessly into language: "Newton and the Ideal of a Transparent Scientific Language," *Journal of Literary Semantics,* 11 (April 1982), 3-13.

[7] See *Opticks, or A Treatise of* the *Reflections, Inflections, & Colours of Light,* based on the Fourth London Edition, 1730 (New York, 1952), 173, Figure 15.

[8] For a discussion of these concepts, see Eric Rothstein, "'Ideal Presence' and the 'Non Finito' in Eighteenth-Century Aesthetics," *Eighteenth-Century Studies,* 9 (1976), 307-32.

[9] *The Correspondence of Isaac Newton,* Vol. I (1661-1675), ed. H. W. Turnbull (Cambridge: Published for the Royal Society, 1959), 99.

[10] *Opticks,* 168-69.

[11] *The Art Criticism of John Ruskin,* ed. Robert L. Herbert (Garden City, N.Y., 1964), 25.

[12] See Gerald Dennis Meyer, *The Scientific Lady in England 1650-1760: An Account of Her Rise, with Emphasis on the Major Roles of the Telescope and Microscope* (Berkeley, 1955) for an account of the role of women in popularized science.

[13] According to René Wellek, "What Is Literature?" in *What Is Literature?* ed. Paul Hernadi (Bloomington, Indiana, 1978), 20-21. See also Paul Oskar Kristeller, "The Modern System of the Arts," reprinted most recently in his *Renaissance Thought and the Arts: Collected Essays* (Princeton, 1980), 163-227.

[14] See James Stephens, *Francis Bacon and the Style of Science* (Chicago, 1975).

[15] Thomas Sprat, Bishop of Rochester, *The History of the Royal Society of London, for the Improving of Natural Knowledge* (1667), 3rd edition corrected, (London, 1722), 112-13. Jonathan Swift satirizes this equivalency of "words" and "things" in Book III of *Gulliver's Travels.* Ambrose Philips also wrote of this equivalency in *The Free-Thinker,* where he discusses the linguistic activity of great poets: "Words, in His Disposal, are Things: And, the Deception proves so strong, that the Reader forgets he is perusing a Piece of Writing" (Vol. II, 51 [No. 63], cited by Rothstein, 311).

[16] For the best comprehensive discussion of seventeenth and eighteenth-century language theories and their cultural importance, see Murray Cohen, *Sensible Words: Linguistic Practice in England, 1640-1785* (Baltimore, 1977). Other related works on seventeenth-century scientific language include three articles by Richard Foster Jones, "Science and Language in England of the Mid-Seventeenth Century," in *The Seventeenth Century: Studies in the History of English Thought and Literature from Bacon to Pope,* ed. Marjorie Hope Nicolson *et al.* (Palo Alto, 1951), 143-160; "Science and English Prose Style in the Third Quarter of the Seventeenth Century," *ibid.,* 75-110; and "The Rhetoric of Science in England of the Mid-Seventeenth Century," in *Restoration and Eighteenth-Century Literature Essays in Honor of Alan Dugald McKillop* (Chicago: University of Chicago Press, 1963), 5-24. See also Hans Aarsleff, *The Study of Language in England, 1780-1860* (Princeton, 1967).

[17] For a discussion of this little-known early Newton manuscript, see Ralph W. V. Elliott, "Isaac Newton's 'Of an Universal Language,'" *Modern Language Review,* 52 (1957), 1-17. Elliott reprints portions of Newton's experimental linguistic scheme.

[18] Gerald Gillespie, "Scientific Discourse and Postmodernity: Francis Bacon and the Empirical Birth of 'Revision'," *Boundary 2,* VII (1979), 124; 125. We believe quite the opposite: poetic language, unsquashable, insinuated itself into scientific language.

[19] Earl Wasserman, in fact, has argued convincingly that for the eighteenth century poet "there is to be found the last significant vestige of the myth of an analogically ordered universe, but greatly weakened by the rhetorical tradition, associationism, and science . . ." ("Nature Moralized: The Divine Analogy in the Eighteenth Century," *ELH,* 20 [1953], 67). Furthermore, in "The Inherent Values of Eighteenth-Century Personification," *PMLA,* 65 (1950), 435-63, Wasserman holds that "prosopopoeia is precisely" the rhetorical figure "that best corresponds to the true nature of human abstraction, for it presents a universal in the corporeal substance by which alone it has existence for man and can be comprehended by him" (450). Most recently, Hans Eichner, in "The Rise of Modern Science and the Genesis of Romanticism," *PMLA,* 97 (January 1982), 8-30, has discussed the eighteenth-century belief in the congruence between the mind and the created world as the age's justification for projecting human drives and desire onto nature: see esp. 9-11.

[20] (Oxford, 1826), Vol. 8, p. 294.

[21] See John Dixon Hunt's study, *The Figure in the Landscape: Poetry, Painting, and Gardening during the Eighteenth Century* (Baltimore, 1976); and also John W. Yolton "As in a Looking-Glass: Perceptual Acquaintance in Eighteenth-Century Britain," *Journal of the History of Ideas* 40 (1979), 207-234. Yolton points out that comparisons of the eye to a *camera obscura* was a standard practice in writings on optics in the eighteenth century (211).

[22] *The New Oxford Annotated Bible with the Apocrypha* (Revised Standard Version) (New York and Oxford, 1977), 11. Carl R. Boyer in *The Rainbow: From Myth to Mathematics* (New York, 1959) traces recorded ideas on the subject from antiquity to the mid-twentieth century.

[23] The following brief survey suggests the range of the rainbow's poetic significations; we do not intend to exhaust its occurrences.

[24] All references to Spenser derive from Ernest De Selincourt, ed., *Spenser's Minor Poems* (Oxford and New York, 1910). This citation, line 73.

[25] Citations from Shakespeare derive from Hardin Craig, ed., *The Complete Works of Shakespeare* (Glenview, Ill.: Scott, Foresman and Co., 1951). This reference: *Merry Wives of Windsor* (1597), IV, v, 117.

[26] *Milton's Poetical Works,* ed. Helen Darbishire, 2 vols. (Oxford: Clarendon Press, 1952-55), lines 298-301. We take subsequent citations from this text.

[27] From *A Hundreth Sundrie Flowers* in *The Complete Works of George Gascoigne,* ed. J. W. Cunliffe (Cambridge, England, 1907-1910), lines 41-48.

[28] Our text for Vaughan is *Works,* ed. L. C. Martin, 2nd ed. Oxford: Clarendon Press, 1957).

[29] Richard (1626-1712) was proclaimed Protector upon his father's death, 3 September 1658, but resigned the title in April 1659. The following lines derive from *The Poems and Letters of Andrew Marvell,* ed. H. M. Margoliouth, 3rd ed. rev. by Pierre Legouis and E. E. Duncan-Jones, 2 vols. (Oxford and New York, 1971).

[30] Our text for Dryden is the 4-vol. edition of *Poems,* ed. James Kinsley (Oxford, 1958). We cite lines 75-78.

[31] Wasserman, "Inherent Values," 437; Eichner, "Rise of Modern Science," 8 (both cited in note 20 above).

[32] (New York, 1958), 36.

[33] *The Imaginary Library: An Essay on Literature and Society* (Princeton, 1982), 28. Kernan also argues that the "Shift from neoclassic to romantic literature appears as a sharp revolutionary change . . . not so much because of internal contradictions in the system . . . but because of radical changes in society outside the literary institution which called its fundamental values, its world-view, into question and forced the poets and critics to explain their art in different ways . . ." (30). We perceive the beginnings of this "revolution" distinctly in the poets' specific reactions to Newton's

explanation of the rainbow, focused expressions of the larger response of writers to science and industrialism. As Marilyn Butler asserts, writing from a different perspective, romanticism emerged from "Social and economic pressures . . . building up from the 1760s, if not earlier." *Romantics, Rebels, and Reactionaries: English Literature and Its Background, 1760-1830* (Oxford, 1982), 11.

[34] *The Ecstacy* (London, 1735), II, 307.

[35] For commentary on the status of the scientist at the end of the seventeenth century, see John M. Steadman, "Beyond Hercules: Bacon and the Scientist as Hero," *Studies in the Literary Imagination,* 4 (1971), 3-47. For commentaries on eighteenth-century responses to Newton generally, see Henry Guerlac, "Where the Statue Stood: Divergent Loyalties to Newton in the Eighteenth Century," in *Aspects of the Eighteenth Century,* ed. Earl R. Wasserman (Baltimore, 1965), 317-34; Gerd Buchdahl, *The Image of Newton and Locke in the Age of Reason* (London, 1961); A. J. Kuhn, "Nature Spiritualized: Aspects of Anti-Newtonianism," in *ELH Essays for Earl R. Wasserman,* ed. Ronald Paulson and Arnold Stein (Baltimore, 1974), 110-22; and Robert Shackleton, "Newtonianism and Literature," in *Literature and Science: Proceedings of the Sixth Triennial Congress of the International Federation for Modern Languages and Literatures* (Oxford, 1955), 157-64. There is, of course, an important skeptical and satirical literary reaction to the New Science. Works like Swift's *Tale of a Tub* and *Gulliver's Travels,* Pope's *Dunciad,* Shadwell's *Virtuoso,* and a host of other Restoration and Augustan satires on science by Butler, Aphra Behn, Shenstone, Arbuthnot, and Gay primarily attacked abstract "projectors" and boorish pedants; the skeptical reaction to science, however, is not central to the argument we are advancing here.

[36] M. H. Abrams, *The Mirror and the Lamp,* 305-306, addresses the anxious state of some poets; but Abrams does not detail poets' active struggle to wrest the rainbow from Newton while appearing to glorify him.

[37] We take all references to Thomson's elegy from Alan Dugald McKillop, eds., *The Catle of Indolence and Other Poems* (Lawrence, 1961). For references from *The Seasons,* we cite *The Seasons,* ed. James Sambrook (Oxford, 1981).

[38] "Inherent Values," 441.

[39] *Ibid.,* 446

[40] "Personification and Community: Literary Change in the Mid- and Late-Eighteenth Century," *Eighteenth-Century Studies,* 15 (1982), 378-79.

[41] (New York, 1972), 4, 3. Harold Bloom describes this condition as misprision, in psychoanalytic terms first voiced in *The Anxiety of Influence* (New York and Oxford, 1973) and reasserted subsequently in a spate of books on poetic influence.

[42] *The Autobiography and Memoirs of Benjamin Haydon,* ed. Tom Taylor, new ed. (London, 1926), I, 269.

[43] The Romantics' complex responses to Newtonian science and to scientific progress generally have received a great deal of attention lately. On this large topic see Hans Eichner, "The Rise of Modern Science," (cited above in note 20) with its extensive bibliography; and M. H. Abrams, *Natural Supernaturalism* (New York, 1971). *Studies in Romanticism* devoted its summer 1977 issue (vol. 16) to "Romanticism and Science." See also D. M. Knight, "The Physical Sciences and the Romantic Movement," *History of Science,* 9 (1970), 54-75.

[44] Jack Stillinger, ed., *The Poems of John Keats* (Cambridge, Mass., 1978), part II, 229-37.

[45] *Mirror and the Lamp,* 307.

[46] "To the Rainbow," lines 3-4, from *The Complete Poetical Works of Thomas Campbell,* ed. J. Logie Robertson (Oxford, 1907). All references to the poem derive from this text.

[47] *The Complete Poetry and Prose of William Blake,* ed. David V. Erdman, commentary by Harold Bloom, newly rev. ed. (Berkeley and Los Angeles, 1982), 560. For Blake's aesthetic theories, see Morris Eaves, *William Blake's Theory of Art* (Princeton, 1982), esp. 180-95. A great deal has been written on Blake's relationship to science and particularly to Newton; for relevant bibliography and Blake's protean response to changes in "science," see Mark L. Greenberg, "Blake's 'Science'," *Studies in Eighteenth-Century Culture,* 12 (Madison, Wisconsin, 1983), 115-30. The fullest study of Blake's response to Newton is Donald Ault's *Visionary Physics* (Chicago, 1974).

[48] The image appears only thirteen times in all of Wordsworth's poetry and only eight times in Coleridge's verse. Our texts for these poets are *The Poetical Works of William Wordsworth,* ed. Ernest De Selincourt and Helen Darbishire (Oxford, 1940-59); and *The Complete Poetical Works of Samuel Taylor Coleridge,* 2 vols., ed. E. H. Coleridge (Oxford, 1912).

[49] *Poetry Realized in Nature: Samuel Taylor Coleridge and Early Nineteenth-Century Science* (Cambridge: Cambridge University Press, 1981), p. 149. See especially "Light and Colors," pp. 149-156.

[50] "Notes on Henry More," cited in Levere, pp. 7-8.

[51] On Shelley and science, see Harry White, "Shelley's Defence of Science," *Studies in Romanticism* 16 (1977), 319-330.

[52] "The Rainbow: A Problematic Image," in U. C. Knoepflmacher and G. B. Tennyson, eds., *Nature and the Victorian Imagination* (Berkeley and Los Angeles: University of California Press, 1977), p. 356. Landow discusses a range of nineteenth-century pictorial and literary responses, principally to the rainbow as biblical emblem. We cite Shelley's verse from Thomas Hutchinson, ed., *Shelley: Poetical Works,* new ed. corr. by G. M. Mathews (London: Oxford University Press, 1970).

[53] We cite Byron's poetry from Frederick Page (ed.), *Byron: Poetical Works,* new ed. corr. by John Jump (London and Oxford, 1970). These lines appear in I, cxxii.

[54] *The Art Criticism of John Ruskin,* 17.

Dennis L. Sepper (essay date 1987)

SOURCE: "Goethe against Newton: Towards Saving the Phenomenon," in *Goethe and the Sciences: A Reappraisal,* Frederick Amrine, Francis J. Zucker, Harvey Wheeler, eds., D. Reidel Publishing Company, 1987, pp. 175-93.

[*In the following essay, Sepper studies Johann Wolfgang von Goethe's attack on Newton's theory of white light and colors, maintaining that while Goethe's critique is sometimes flawed by "excessive vehemence" and an "all-encompassing condemnation" of Newton's theory, Goethe nevertheless presents a justified opposition to Newton's methods.*]

> Wer ein Phänomen vor Augen hat, denkt
> schon oft drüber hinaus; wer nur davon
> erzählen hört, denkt gar nicht.
> (Goethe, *Maximen,* No. 1227)

In all the scientific work of Johann Wolfgang von Goethe nothing is more notorious than his polemic against Isaac Newton's theory of white light and colors.[1] This "great error" has been a constant source of embarrassment to reverers of Goethe that seemingly can be explained only by analyzing his psyche or his poetic metaphysics. Not a few, including Hermann von Helmholtz, thought that precisely Goethe's poetic talent prevented him from understanding modern natural science. His advocacy of direct and immediate experience, it is said, made possible his contributions to descriptive sciences like plant and animal morphology but also kept him from real insight into the abstract techniques and power of mathematico-physical science (1971, pp. 21-44). His polemics against Newton are taken to be the clearest testimony of Goethe's one-sidedness; the most one can say in his defense, it seems, is that in the struggle to assert the rights of the world of appearances he sinned against a truth that can only be uncovered by methods that go behind and beyond the phenomena. Of course in the twentieth century there has been a partial rehabilitation of the *Farbenlehre,* especially in its treatment of physiological and psychological aspects of color, and a greater readiness to acknowledge its virtues (e.g. concreteness) *vis-à-vis* modern theoretical physics. Yet we still tend by and large to construe Goethe's undertaking as directed *against* modern physics, not least because of the polemic against Newton.

Is Goethe an opponent of modern physics? He opposed Newton's optics; but few realize that he spoke approvingly of the wave-theory of light, which was formulated in a much more sophisticated mathematics than was Newton's.[2] I do not propose to give an unambiguous yes or no to the question of Goethe's attitude towards modern physics here; rather, I wish to reopen it by arguing that Goethe's theory of color and in particular his polemic against Newton's theory have been largely misconceived, even by Goetheans, as the result of ahistorical presuppositions about the character and extent of Newton's achievement and the principal aims of Goethe's science. To put things as succinctly as possible: Goethe was not a poet who blundered into the alien territory of physics, but rather someone who actually *looked* at the phenomena and compared them with what the prevailing theory said; someone who knew Newton's writings on optics and colors far better than anyone except perhaps Newton himself; someone who knew the history of chromatics and not just the history of optics; someone who gave prolonged thought to the methodological and philosophical problems implicit in experimental science, especially those of claiming factuality, of proving theory by experiment, and of mathematizing phenomenal description. Goethe made his initial foray into the sciences of optics and color because he noted a condition that had been overlooked in most eighteenth-century statements of the theory and that led to certain inconsistencies between what was expected and what actually happened. He went about this work with the intention of creating a rigorously and comprehensively inductive science that kept facts or phenomena strictly separated from hypotheses. Through research that was historical as well as experimental, he become ever more aware how theory and fact are intertwined, how every attentive look at the world already involves theorizing.[3] Yet he did not abandon the distinction between theory and phenomenon as a result, for especially from the example of Newton's theory he realized that the more one puts hypotheses and abstractly theoretical statements (and their proof) at the focal point of sci-

ence the harder it becomes to look at the phenomena with an unprejudiced eye; indeed, abstractly theoretical seeing distorts actual seeing. In opposition to the theory-centered approach of Newtonian chromatics Goethe proposed to make phenomena and their ways of appearing the heart of science. Concomitantly he explored and tried to incorporate into science the variety of ways in which phenomena can be experienced and conceived (what he called the *Vorstellungsarten*—'modes of conceptualization'). Accordingly the major aim of natural science could no longer be to establish the truth of an hypothesis, e.g. by showing there is an (approximately) exact fit between prediction and experimental result in a few "crucial" cases, but rather to strive for overall fidelity in one's way of seeing (*theoria*) to the variety of phenomena conceived as comprehensively as possible. Far from repudiating quantity and exactitude, this approach rather locates them within the network of which they are a part: the array of knowledge, praxis, and experience that ranges from the circumstances of everyday life to the sophisticated and highly-instrumentalized inquiries of the abstract theorist. Goethe feared that by neglecting this context the natural sciences risked becoming deracinated and irrational, and that in cultivating hypotheses more intently than phenomena they exposed themselves to the vagaries of undisciplined imagination.[4]

The *Farbenlehre* is thus far more than an alternative 'theory' or 'doctrine' of color; it is in fact a reconstitution of chromatics, the science of color as distinguished from optics, and a refounding of the principles and methods of the empirical natural sciences. It embraces experimental science, history of science, and philosophy of science, understood not as independent undertakings but as the three major aspects of the single human project of encountering and comprehending nature.

Elsewhere[5] I have substantiated the preceding claims and have narrated how and why phenomenality became for Goethe the chief foundational principle for the empirical natural sciences and their historical continuity. Here I can indicate only in a *general* way the origins of Goethe's confrontation with Newton and the historical horizon of the *Farbenlehre*—and therefore run the risk of oversimplification, a problem endemic to accounts of Goethe's science, both pro and contra.

What was Goethe opposing when he criticized Newton's theory? First and foremost, a theory that misrepresented the phenomena; second, a method that misconceived the proper relationship between theory and phenomenon; third, a community of science that for more than a century had failed to examine critically work esteemed as much for the sake of the man who wrote it as for its content.

Newton's optical work of course is considered today the foundation of modern color science, and from his experimental techniques a fundamental tool of modern physics, spectroscopy, grew. Moreover, if we consider the history of the natural sciences in the eighteenth century we recognize that the method Newton employed in presenting his theory became that century's major paradigm of how experimental science should be conducted and what it can achieve. With so much in Newton's favor, both then and now, Goethe's critique was bound to provoke incredulity. Nevertheless it was by and large justified, even though it is marred by passages of excessive vehemence and a sometimes too all-encompassing condemnation of Newton's theory in every aspect.

Newton's theory indeed has many aspects, and one cannot understand the major thrusts of Goethe's critique unless one has a fairly clear sense of at least a few of them. A bit of history can perhaps explain some of the issues. Before Newton, optics and the science of color were only tenuously connected; it would probably be an exaggeration to say that before him there *was* a full-fledged science of color. But Newton joined the two into a unified science by combining the mathematical approach of geometrical optics with the approach of empirical physics and thereby made the study of light and color a mathematico-physical, empirical science. The chief tool of the new approach was the *experimentum crucis,* or crucial experiment, the paradigm case of which is to be found under that name in a letter of Newton's to the Royal Society of London from February 1672 (1959, vol. 1, pp. 92-102). Into a darkened room he admitted a beam of sunlight through a narrow opening; this beam was refracted by a glass prism (with a large refracting angle, approximately 60°); it was almost immediately intercepted by a board with a small circular aperture; the light that passed through this aperture proceeded to a second board, about 12 feet from the first and also provided with a small circular hole; the light that passed through this was immediately refracted by a second prism similar to the first and cast on the wall. By rotating the first prism in this set-up Newton was able to make the spectrum that appeared on the second board move up or down, so that any small segment of the spectrum desired might be made to fall on the hole; in this way different rays could be isolated and refracted by the second prism. With this apparatus and technique he was able to show that the light most refracted the first time (i.e. the light appearing at the violet end of the spectrum cast on the second board) is also the most refracted the second time—with both prisms arranged to refract upwards it will appear highest on the wall—and as you proceed through the spectrum towards the opposite end you find that the second refraction is progressively less, and at a minimum with red. Newton concluded that ordinary light is composite, i.e. that different kinds of rays with different degrees of refrangibility exist already in the original white light (the doctrine of diverse refrangibility). Moreover, the same experiment

shows that there is a close correlation between refrangibility and color (note that the crucial experiment seems to depend only on position, not on color, though for the sake of easy reference it is convenient to mention the colors), and Newton proceeded immediately to elaborate a corollary theory of color, according to which there was a "very precise and strict" proportion between degree of refrangibility and color. He claimed that he had put the properties of diverse refrangibility and color beyond suspicion of doubt, indeed that he had made the science of colors mathematical.[6]

Although Newton later went on to explore other phenomena of color and light, he retained this basic theory with only slight modifications. The first book of the *Opticks* presents it in a quasi-Euclidean format, where the proof no longer depends on a single crucial experiment but rather proceeds through series of them, each of which is meant to prove theorems and confirm or refute propositions.[7]

Scientists of the eighteenth century were greatly impressed and influenced by this theory and its presentation. They accepted the basic theory as proven fact, as clearly and indubitably true, just as Newton had intended. Yet they seem also to have accepted that the science of color was essentially complete—apart from leaving unexplained the exact workings of the eye and the 'sensorium,' Newton certainly cultivated this impression—and were thus discouraged from doing further color research. After Newton the eighteenth century has relatively little to show in the science of color and even in optics; and we must always keep in mind when considering Goethe's polemics, which savaged the inertia of Newton's successors even more than the errors of the master, that the century he looked back upon had added virtually nothing to the original doctrine and in many cases had corrupted it. We who look back on the rich progress of chromatics since the middle of the nineteenth century and who therefore know that a great deal remained to be done tend to forget this. We also easily overlook that after Goethe's lifetime the notion of what kind of certainty and durability scientific theories can have started to change. A scientist today could not responsibly make the kinds of truth-claims that Newton did. Furthermore, historians in this century have revealed that Newton's arguments are neither perfectly cogent nor free of underlying hypotheses—Newton's assertions to the contrary notwithstanding—and that he sometimes described phenomena tendentiously and even occasionally misrepresented them.[8] If we ignore these things we will have overlooked some of the major foci of Goethe's attacks, in particular the fetish of exactitude and absolutely certain and exhaustive proof that was integral to Newton's theory and that became an ideal *manqué* of eighteenth-century experimental science.

Thus, although there is no doubt that Newton introduced important tools and concepts and that many of his insights eventually proved immensely fruitful, the immediate effect was not so fortunate. Besides the dogmatism and the excessive claims about the theory's validity and scope already noted, Newton created certain conceptual tensions in the science of color. For example, today we commonly distinguish between the physics of color and the perception of color, and we know that the former, which corresponds to the bulk of Newton's work, cannot in itself explain the latter.[9] Although Newton occasionally drew this same kind of distinction, the entire tendency of his work was to reduce color to a simple function of refrangibility and to endow the colors of spectral light with ontological primacy. The theory of (real!) colors was to be a corollary of the theory of diverse refrangibility. Even as his later work compelled him to make concessions to the difference between physics and perception (e.g. with his color circle), he tried to assimilate the results to diverse refrangibility. Indeed he had to, if he was to preserve the latter doctrine's aura of certainty intact, for its proof requires the closest connection between refrangibility and color.[10]

One does not need the sophisticated color research since Helmholtz and Grassmann to discover a certain incommensurability between color and the physical composition of light. For example, the phenomena of colored shadows, which Goethe explored thoroughly already in the early 1790s, demonstrate that light falling on the retina which is physically the same can produce radically different colors under different circumstances of ambient illumination. But one needn't go so far afield: Newton's spectrum itself is a witness against the strong version of his basic theory (i.e. that there is a strict proportionality or equivalence between refrangibility and color in the spectrum). Refrangibility is measured on an indifferent numerical or linear continuum; the visible solar spectrum produced by Newton on the other hand is continuous in the sense that it displays no gaps (with circular rather than linear apertures absorption lines do not appear), but its chromatic qualities are anything but indifferent. Arithmetically, 1.50 is equidistant from 1.49 and 1.51, but the spectral color corresponding to a given physical index (e.g. wavelength or refractive index) is very likely not to be equidistant in perceptual terms from two colors whose corresponding physical indexes are equally far from one another. Rather than showing an 'infinite' number of gradations of color, Newton's spectrum appears to display a limited number arrayed in broad, fairly distinct segments, with hardly any obvious variation in hue across each segment. Even if we isolate very narrow spectral bands and do a side-by-side comparison, the number of discriminable hues will be small compared to the several thousand we could enumerate in, say, wholenumbers of Ångstroms.[11]

It is interesting in this connection that Newton typically described the spectrum as consisting of red, yellow, green, blue, and violet (and added sometimes orange and indigo) *and,* as he would go on to say, all intermediate gradations. That is, despite the quantitative indifference there are good perceptual reasons for emphasizing certain hues rather than others, though on quantitative grounds all would have claim to equal status. He also spent much energy in vain trying to show that the proportions between the segments of color in the spectrum corresponded to the ratios of the diatonic musical scale—which once again reveals that there are relationships in the perceived spectrum that do not simply reduce themselves to refrangibility. These phenomena may not be as striking as the crucial experiment, but they intimate that some other kind of approach is needed to extend the science of color and make it more complete.

It is also highly significant that most subsequent eighteenth-century accounts of the theory overlooked the infinite gradations and sometimes even asserted the existence of just seven kinds of rays.[12] Newton cannot be held accountable for all the mistakes of his followers, but surely the consistent misinterpretation points to some dimly-felt need to resolve the tension between the continuous and the discrete, between the phenomenon according to theory and the phenomenon that is seen.

Goethe was chiefly interested in exploring precisely those properties and relationships of color that escape the rather elementary mathematics of the Newtonian theory. He tirelessly explored phenomena and aspects of them that lay beyond the standard theory's ken, and he was made all the more tenacious by the repeated insistence of his physicist acquaintances that Newton had already "perfectly explained" (*HA* 14, p. 260) the phenomena of color. He was, as it were, forced into a critical attitude towards Newton and the Newtonians. At any rate, the inertia of his contemporaries compelled him to undertake the effortful work of reperforming and analyzing Newton's experiments and proofs, of uncovering their misrepresentations of the phenomena, of elaborating their hidden assumptions and tendencies, and of bringing to light the logic and rhetoric of Newton's presentation. The result was the polemical part of the *Farbenlehre,* which is less a philippic than an exegesis (of the first book of the **Opticks**), less a venting of spleen on his great nemesis than an indictment of those who had come after and instead of setting about the work of reexamination, correction, and extension had fallen down in adulation. Goethe believed that it was necessary to refound chromatics, not as an appendage to optics but as a science in its own right, and to lay a foundation of phenomena rather than of theory. His efforts at elaborating from this foundation a positive doctrine were tentative and sometimes defective, and they were greatly weakened both by his failure to investigate light with the same thoroughness he had employed in his analyses of color—the *Farbenlehre* explicitly excludes a closer study of light from its scope, or rather presumes the existence of such a study (*HA* 13, pp. 315 and 323)—and by his unwillingness to take advantage in any way of the economy and precision that mathematical formulations and measurements can lend when appropriately applied to the study of nature. Although he did concede that number and measure could be applied to his work and urged others to undertake the task, he greatly damaged his cause by not showing from the beginning how they might be fruitfully employed in the *Farbenlehre*.

It would be misleading, however, to leave the impression that Goethe opposed Newton's theory for forty years and even resorted to polemics simply because Newton had gotten a few things wrong and Goethe wanted to supplant him with his own chromatics. That may be a viewpoint adequate for understanding his earliest studies but not their continuation. More than anything else Goethe was combatting a defective conception of *science and scientific method* that had helped bring about the dogmatic entrenchment of diverse refrangibility. The methodological focus of Goethe's critique, explained hardly at all in his earliest publications on color, the two *Beiträge zur Optik* of 1791 and 1792, but at length in an essay written almost contemporaneously with them (unfortunately not published until three decades later), 'The Experiment as Mediator between Object and Subject,'[13] is the question of how one keeps one's *experience* of phenomena and experiments separate from what one *thinks* and *hypothesizes* about them. According to Goethe, the great danger of any science that aims at proving—and, we might add, disproving—hypotheses and theories is that it stirs up all the lurking enemies of truth in the human spirit, which longs to be able to claim the whole truth when it possesses just part, to have certainty when it can produce only plausibility. This kind of approach puts a premium on making the theory appear true: strong points are placed most favorably in view, while weak points are minimized or concealed. Science thus becomes rhetorical rather than rigorous and logical. As alternative Goethe proposed a method, painstakingly comprehensive, of experimentally producing the phenomena and enumerating and describing their essential circumstances as a foundation for the rest of the scientist's work. The best scientist, reflected Goethe, in the first instance stays close to his initial insight into the truth by studying intensively the phenomenon that first caught his attention. He does this by *Vermannigfaltigung* ('variegating'), which works gradually and systematically outward from the initial phenomenon (or the experiment that replicates it) by augmenting and ramifying it. He must articulate the experimental phenomenon, analyze it into its basic conditions, and then vary these. His first intention is not to isolate a cause, the study of which demands of the scientist considerable philosophical acumen, but to establish the correlations between changes in the conditions of the experiments and changes in the phenomenon, with the fullest possible elaboration of the relevant conditions. Indeed, this kind of work is essential even in trying to prove hypotheses, and it points up a major lacuna in Newton's procedure. Consider: Why did Newton choose the particular circumstances described in his experiments? The only possible answers are either that the circumstances are arbitrary, and thus not consonant with scientific discourse, or that precisely these circumstances produce some notable effect pre-eminently. The latter alternative shows that a choice has been made by comparing one instance with many others and thereby deriving criteria that dictate its use in preference to others. That is, Newton's choice can be justified only by a more complete acquaintance with the phenomena of refraction than his few specimens give.

The Goethean method might urge us to proceed somewhat as follows: Begin with the simpler rather than the more complex, for example with a single refraction as opposed to multiple refractions. For each of the particular circumstances of the experiment let us then introduce variation. In some cases we can vary a circumstance continuously; e.g. we can move the prism closer to or farther from the screen, we can change the distance of the prism from the aperture, we can (with an adjustable diaphragm) alter the aperture's size. In other cases we must be satisfied with discrete changes, though continuity may be more or less approximated: we can substitute glass prisms with larger and smaller refracting angles (with a hinged water-prism, however, we could again perform a continuous variation). Of course we shall also encounter conditions that may simply not lend themselves to continuous variation, e.g. the material of the prism; but by resorting to sequential or side-by-side comparisons, for instance by substituting identical refracting angles in different substances, we may, by persistent labor, analysis, and ingenuity, find some other principle of order. By varying all these circumstances we can actually watch and describe the phenomenon in evolution and thereby gain a fuller notion of how the initial experiment fits into the totality of phenomena of the same type. We should note that this technique really does circumscribe a range of phenomena which constitute a natural family (and which, taken discretely, would be infinite), and that it calls attention to what happens as one approaches limits which in actual practice may be unreachable (e.g. when the aperture has null diameter or the screen is at extreme distances).

By following this method of amplification and complication Goethe hoped, ca. 1792, to produce a completely unhypothetical presentation of virtually all the phenomena of color, and correspondingly unhypothetical but absolutely sure descriptions and low-level generalizations, that would serve as a certain and unshakable foundation for future researchers and their attempts at yet higher levels of generalization. The *Beiträge zur Optik* were to be continued until, as Goethe said, they should have traversed the entire circle of color. From this basis science would ascend by a process of rigorous induction. This vision of science, in its theoretical reticence and its strict induction, is Baconian. Goethe was less worried by the possible baneful influences of hypotheses, theories, and imagination at the higher levels, however; they did not need to be suppressed but only restrained until the researcher should have had the chance to gain an overview, precise and comprehensive, of all the phenomena that pertain to the science and that thus needed to be embraced by future work.

If Goethe had stopped at this point he would deserve nothing more than a footnote in histories of the natural sciences as one of the last and most rigorous inductivists. But he did not stop here, he went on to elaborate a philosophical and historical vision of natural science that rivals even the best 20th-century philosophy and history of science (a vision which Friedrich Schiller christened rational empiricism).[14] At some point in the decade of the 1790s Goethe came to recognize that there could be no single, comprehensive, and authoritative way of conceiving and presenting the phenomena of color. There were many factors at work in this development, including his attempts to continue the series of the *Beiträge zur Optik* (which led to his discovery of the fundamental importance of the so-called physiological colors), his reading of Kant and his conversations with the Kantian Schiller, the deepening of his historical studies, and his growing awareness that the resistance to his work was motivated not simply by blockheadedness or ill-will but by a different way of seeing and explaining the world that had become inveterate in physicists and even in the educated public. In response he began to note with avidity and assiduity the variety of ways of (re)presenting the world, the *Vorstellungsarten,* for which the history of the natural sciences is the richest source. These *Vorstellungsarten,* at least in first approximation, appear to be ideal types of consciousness that are historically rare in unalloyed form but that nevertheless are fundamentally at work in science, in experience, in language. The historical part of the *Farbenlehre,* though it does not offer a formalized schema of the *Vorstellungsarten,* is suffused with their presence. As we read through it we see the continual emergence, interplay, adaptation, ebb, and reemergence of—to name some of the chief ones—the genetic and the atomistic, the dynamic and the mechanical, the concrete and the abstract, the mathematical and the physical, the material and the spiritual ways of thinking and conceiving things. One concrete example: Newton's intelligence Goethe describes as atomistic, mechanical, and above all mathematical; he himself inclines more to the genetic, the dynamic, and the concrete. He understood these characteristic traits as influencing all of one's cognitive life, right down to

apparently innocuous attempts at describing and organizing simple phenomena.

Ironic as it may be, the man who found himself compelled to polemicize against the Newtonian theory of white light and color because of the undue limitations and distortions it had imposed on scientific seeing was really a scientific pluralist who believed that proof and refutation can have only limited scope and thus can not be the essential activity of science. The truth, to be comprehended, must be approached from all its many sides. *A priori* there is no single, authoritative way to approach a given phenomenon; and a single human being, plagued by many kinds of one-sidedness, would scarcely be able to produce a science on his own. Thus pluralism is not just one among many desiderata but an absolute prerequisite for a constructive and progressive science, whose goal is less to produce a set of true propositions and indoctrinate scientists into their intention than to amplify the human experience of nature—which includes amplifying the store of technical means—and to enrich our comprehension of it by cultivating our ability to see natural wholes (e.g. the unity of a potentially infinite class of prismatic experiments) and to recognize the *complex* of their interrelationships to which 'nature' refers. One consequence is that mathematical exactitude is to be sought where it is truly exacting, i.e. faithful to the disciplined scientific seeing that arises from the comprehensive rehearsal of the phenomena; yet it cannot be allowed to supplant actual scientific experience (in the way that Newton's theory supplanted and obscured the phenomena of color so that ultimately his followers either merely repeated his formulations or used his experiments to reconfirm what he had said). The education of scientists, the methods of research, the role of serendipity, the standards of rationality, the civilized conduct of debate: these and a whole spectrum of other activities, entities, and relationships concomitant with and sometimes essential to science can never be adequately quantified or systematized. All these things are the scientist's concern; let us then treat them as such, says Goethe, and not as secondary or peripheral because our measuring stick won't work.

In twentieth-century philosophy of science the theory-ladenness of facts has led to the paradoxes of apparently self-validating theories (the theory shapes the fact, the fact in turn is used to confirm the theory) and the incommensurability of competing theories, with the result that science and its changes take place on ground that is constantly in danger of shifting. If there are no independent facts, and if no two theories are strictly comparable with one another or about the same things, then science and scientific change appear to suffer from a fundamental irrationality that makes them subject to the preferences and prejudices of individuals and institutions, to the winds of philosophical fashion, to the vagaries of political interests, in fact to a whole host of extraneous factors. The conclusion is of course alarming to those who, like Goethe, see natural science as one of the noblest ventures that human beings have undertaken; yet it appears that once we grant the theory-ladenness of facts we lose the last foothold on a slippery slope, where nostalgia for the certainties of positivism and the invocation of a new realism will be of little help. It seems to me that Goethe already faced this twentieth-century perplexity more than 150 years ago without succumbing to irrationalism, apathetic skepticism, or a new variety of dogmatism. The key to his perseverance and whatever success he achieved lies in the phenomenality of his science: nature and nature's phenomena, not theories about the phenomena, are its center and its center of gravity. For Goethe the phenomena are not the totality of science, but they are where it commences and the place to which it must constantly recur—often enough with previously unnoticed phenomena, sometimes with a new way of looking at them, sometimes even with hypotheses that help us to see with new, more alert eyes. Even under the regime of theory-ladenness the phenomena are not infinitely malleable, and the more one aims at comprehensiveness, the more one works to elaborate intrinsic relationships among them, the greater becomes the specific resistance that they offer to arbitrary interpretations. The great danger in the kind of science that cultivates hypotheses and theories as the real core of science is that it encourages one to care about the phenomena only insofar as they seem relevant to the theory (and then to see and describe them in the *theory's* terms) and to treat what is remotest from sense, what is experienceable only by hypothesis, as though it were indistinguishable from (sometimes even more reliable than) what is nearer to sense. Whatever may be said in defense of these induced beliefs in sciences like particle physics, it is absurd to think that they can lead unproblematically to a genuine science of color.[15]

If phenomena are laden with theory, if every attentive look at the world is the beginning of theoretical activity, there still remains the possibility that some phenomena are less theoretical than others, and that there exists in the human being a non-apodictic capacity to note this difference and to start the work of sorting out the consequences. If this possibility is authentic, it can be realized only by acts of comparison, which in turn require something better than a randomly-assembled group of phenomena. A comprehensive survey, or at the very least the intention of comprehensiveness and the ethic it imposes,[16] is the only basis for the adequate comparison of the less with more. And a survey conducted in awareness of implicit theory is less likely to be tendentious than one undertaken in the spirit of unproblematic factuality. Thus even though it is never possible in science to claim with certainty that one has overcome all inappropriate preconceptions, it may well be possible to present the phenomena in a way that, though it reflects certain *Vorstellungsarten,* neverthe-

less will be useful even to those who do not share these ways of conceiving things. Despite his knowledge that the *Farbenlehre* was only a new beginning for chromatic science and was inevitably marked by characteristic *Vorstellungsarten,* then, Goethe could still argue that the didactic part of the work had general utility. The mere existence of such a compendium of phenomena, systematically arranged and more exhaustive than any that had preceded, would help recall color scientists to the matter of their subject and its proper forms, and might prevent overanxious theorists from disregarding entire groups of phenomena or dismissing them as unimportant or anomalous. It could serve the pedagogical function of orienting beginners in the science, who otherwise would know the phenomena only in the terms of theories. Even the circumstance that it reflected certain *Vorstellungsarten* and not others could be a virtue: for only when scientists confront other *Vorstellungsarten* can they well assess the strengths and limitations of their own, and by seeing the truth—even if partial—of other ways they may be able to amplify and enrich their experience and conceptions of things.[17]

Goethe frequently pointed out to friends that his scientific work had made him many-sided by compelling him to entertain different points of view, some of which he was able to incorporate into his own; and by practicing sciences he gradually developed "organs" for experiencing and understanding that originally he had not possessed (see, for example, *LA* I.3, pp. 303 and 305). He had learned even to appreciate the attractions and merits of notions that were not compatible with his own way of seeing. By giving up the insistence that there is one and only one truth, expressible in a set of propositions on which all could agree and towards which all researchers would converge, yet retaining the imperative of comprehensiveness in experience, he bade farewell to the absoluteness of certainty in favor of a rich, many-sided scientific culture, which in turn is embraced by the human culture in which science takes place. For him, the rationality of science was grounded in a human openness to the world that is always going beyond itself as it seeks a way back to its origins.

We must not edify ourselves into thinking that this Goethean rationality is easy; certainly the limited success of his *Farbenlehre* should make us wonder. Perhaps it was Goethe himself who best recognized the difficulties, as can be seen from the scientific essays of the last decades of his life and even more in works like *Wahlverwandtschaften, Wilhelm Meisters Wanderjahre,* and the second part of *Faust.* The difficulties are perhaps starkest in the contrast near the end of *Faust* between the contemplative, all-seeing watchman Lynkeus and the dynamic but blind and dying Faust. To understand nature and the world we must achieve a perspective from which we can perceive everything as it has been and is: the situation of Lynkeus. In the struggle to experience and understand, however, we must act; action is always particular, and dealing with things particularly ordinarily cannot reveal them in their wholeness, in fact it may alter them. The interests, including self-interests, that our actions serve may even blind us to tensions and contradictions we have fostered. This is the dilemma of the mighty Faust, who has transformed the world in his quest to come face to face with nature, simply, as a man alone. He has acted as though truth is fundamentally remote and hidden (albeit manipulable once it is discovered) and tried to force it to appear. In seeking what is furthest, however, he has ravaged the object of his hope and pursuit. Even in blindness, however, he seems to share in the truth; prepared as he is to continue devastating earth and sea for the sake of his constructions, he sees in imagination a world where he might find it possible and desirable to live and abide. Is the conclusion that human erring is inevitable but still oriented towards truth, if only partial truth, and that even in the depths of errancy we in some sense anticipate it? This could be reason for perseverant hope, if not optimism. The hope would be that the passion for revealing a world in naked truth does not destroy what is near and true but inconspicuous because of its constant proximity; and that the light in our inward eye is not the blinding fireball searing everything near and far. To realize this hope we would need to remember that in trying to understand nature we likewise reveal our own nature. Unless we are constantly attentive to both, we shall surely, albeit darkly, live out the consequences of our science, in all its magnificence, in all its partiality.

Notes

[1] Earlier versions of portions of this essay appeared in papers delivered at the 1982 meeting of the Claremont Institute in Denver and the 1983 History of Science Society meeting in Norwalk, Connecticut. I wish to express special thanks to Drs. John Cornell and Neil Ribe, who have been unstinting in their conversations, comments, and encouragement, and to F. J. Zucker for his critique of the penultimate version of this essay.

[2] For example *LA* I.8, p. 276 and *LA* I.11, pp. 289-294. Goethe's unhappiness with the application of mathematics in the natural sciences may have been directed chiefly against the reduction of these sciences to what he called *Rechenkunst* and *Meßkunst* (the arts of reckoning and measuring, viz. elementary arithmetic and geometry). We must recall, too, that Newton's presentations of his theory, apart from the posthumously-published *Lectiones opticae,* hardly require anything more advanced than arithmetic and elementary plane geometry. Goethe's comments about *higher* mathematics were typically generous, and he even conceded that symbols "taken from mathematics, because intuitions [*Anschauungen*] likewise lie at their foundation [i.e.

just as with other kinds of symbol], can become in the highest sense identical with the appearances" (*LA* I.3, p. 418).

[3] *HA* 13, p. 317. Cf. Goethe, *Maximen,* no. 575: "Das Höchste wäre zu begreifen, daß alles Factische schon Theorie ist."

[4] Goethe's polemics against Newton's theory display some remarkable parallels to his critique of Romanticism: in both he sees the danger of imagination twisting reality to its own purposes. See Schrimpf.

[5] In *Seeing and Knowing: Goethe against Newton on the Theory of Colors,* forthcoming, and in the author's doctoral dissertation, "Goethe, Newton, and Color: The Background and Rationale of an Unrealized Scientific Controversy" (University of Chicago, 1981).

[6] See, for instance, Newton, 1959-1976, Vol. 1, pp. 96-97 and 187-188. Zev Bechler (1974) has shown that Newton's early critics disagreed more with the extravagance of his truth-claims than with the substance of his theory, and points to Newton's apparent incomprehension of their epistemological arguments as beginning the era of the "blind spot" for such matters. Below we shall deal with the issue of the correlation of refrangibility and color; here it should be mentioned that the proof of the pre-existence of diverse rays in the original light is defective. In *Seeing and Knowing,* part 3, I have argued that the proof depends on a subtle question-begging implicit in Newton's geometrical interpretation. But its invalidity can also be shown by counterexample. Newton believed that his proof would remain valid whatever light turned out to be in its fine structure, in particular whether light turned out to consist of tiny corpuscles or of waves. When the wave-theory of light displaced the particle-theory in the first half of the nineteenth-century physicists saw no reason to disagree. But in the last decades of the century the French physicist Louis-Georges Gouy showed on mathematical and empirical grounds that the wave theory was compatible with the notion that the prism actually manufactures the differentiated rays out of an originally simple pulse rather than sorts out rays already present in the original beam. But this was the leading principle of modification theories of light, which were the chief competitors of Newton's theory in the seventeenth century and which have affinities with Goethe's positive doctrine of color. See Wood (1911), pp. 648-666.

[7] On the modifications, see Shapiro (1980), pp. 211-235. I believe that most historians of optics would now agree that the mathematical format of the *Opticks* is more rhetoric than substance. This format, plus the greater number of experiments, often described in minute detail, bolstered the appearance of certainty but did not respond to the epistemological and material criticisms advanced earlier (1672-1677). It is interesting to

note that the last of the original critics died the year before the *Opticks* was published.

[8] Besides Shapiro (1980), one might also consult such works as Lohne (1968), Sabra (1967), and Laymon (1978). Among recent philosophers and historians of science, only Feyerabend (1970) has realized that this very type of critique had already been carried out by Goethe.

[9] The interested reader can find out more about the history of modern color science and differences between physical and perceptual approaches from, for example, Wasserman (1978). Though Ronchi (1957) deals chiefly with optics rather than color theory, he is highly instructive about confusions between physics and perception. Ronchi shows in astonishing detail how the relative successes of geometrical and physical optics have led scientists to overlook even gross discrepancies between theory and what is seen in actuality. Ronchi's desire to establish a science of optics (of the seeing eye) independent of the science of radiation parallels Goethe's wish to set up a chromatics independent of optics. We must not forget, however, that our articulation of the sciences, and in particular our mathematico-physical science of radiation, has (and probably always will have) roots going back into the phenomena and thus will not be independent of the more phenomenally-oriented science.

[10] In asserting this I take issue with the standard claim that Newton proved diverse refrangibility without needing any reference to color. In order to see this, one must first realize that the *experimentum crucis* depends very much on its context, a context that relies heavily on the essential equivalence in the spectrum of refrangibility and coloration. The proof benefits from the ambiguity created by what precedes it. I argue this at length in *Seeing and Knowing,* part 3.

[11] C. V. Raman (1968), pp. 22-28, discusses the appearance of the spectrum under various conditions and theoretical and empirical considerations concerning the human ability to discriminate the colors at wavelengths close to one another. The spectrum, when viewed as a whole, has an almost eerie beauty, attributable in part to its seeming to change almost imperceptibly as one observes it. Exactly what hue one sees at any particular point depends on a wide range of circumstances, e.g. the duration, intensity, direction, and distance of viewing. Other changes are quite determinate. For example, as pointed out by Goethe, when the screen is placed at a great distance from the prism some of the colors begin to disappear, until a tricolored spectrum is obtained. Apparently this phenomenon is intended to raise a question that is difficult to resolve in a purely physical framework: what has happened to all those unchangeable indigo-, blue-, yellow-, and orange-producing rays that were supposed to have been separated? These kinds of changes, and even more the differ-

ent dispersive power of various refracting materials, make any notion of 'the' spectrum fallacious.

[12] On the number of spectral colors in Newton and later eighteenth-century accounts see Hargreave (1973), esp. pp. 477-495. It is likely that when ca. 1790 Goethe consulted a scientific text to find out about the theory of Newton he read that with a small aperture it was possible to get a "spectrum" consisting of seven *separate,* differently-colored circles aligned in a row; see *Seeing and Knowing,* Part 2. If initially he had some misconceptions about the theory, he may not have been at fault.

[13] *HA* 13, pp. 10-20. A superb analysis of this essay and of the structure of Goethe's method is Gögelein (1972).

[14] A christening highlighted already by Matthaei in *LA* I.3, pp. 302-314, which reproduces letters exchanged by Goethe and Schiller in early 1798 and represents *in nuce* the philosophical rationale of the *Farbenlehre* as well as an important stage in Goethe's understanding of the *Vorstellungsarten.*

[15] I have glossed over the question of whether modern discussions of the theory-ladenness of *facts* really penetrates the problem of the theorizing that is implicit in observing *phenomena.* One issue that is in need of reflection is possible distinctions between *fact* and *phenomenon:* e.g. energy conservation can be a fact but probably not a phenomenon, whereas this rainbow I am looking at is a phenomenon but perhaps not a fact (though clearly I can make statements of fact about it). Much of the recent philosophical discussion about the theory-ladenness of facts concerns sciences already constituted at a highly abstract level, where most of the evidence is mediated by complex instrumentation, so that the kind of phenomenality that can be claimed for the evidence is a *question.* Of course there is the more directly accessible issue whether a pre-Copernican and a post-Copernican see the sun rise or the horizon sink below the sun (the complications of which are too great to be disposed of in a note). However, that it is possible (in thought, at least) to have both look to the East one morning, that they could discuss the event and agree to disagree, indicates the central field to which questions about the differences must be addressed. For a discussion of the changing use of the term 'fact' over the last three centuries, see Sepper, *Seeing and Knowing,* Part 4.

[16] The undertaking of any science already presupposes an ethics and politics of science, i.e. an understanding of science's place in the being of human beings (in the economy of their faculties) and in their community. All important philosophies of science recognize this, at least implicitly (e.g. the positivistic conception of the historical emergence of reason)—and for Goethe it

is an explicit concern, both in his scientific and his literary works. For a discussion see Sepper, *Seeing and Knowing,* Parts 1 and 5.

[17] The parallels between Goethe's method and twentieth-century phenomenology are interesting and significant but run into difficulties on the matter of apodicticity—though the themes of the life-world and the historicity of science in the late Husserl provide a point of contact again. But if one is looking for parallels with recent philosophy there is also the fundamentally hermeneutic character of Goethe's science, which makes the history of science (or rather the history of knowing) part of science itself, and which through the doctrine of the *Vorstellungsarten* is thematically concerned with the horizons within which all knowing is appropriated. For Goethe science is intrinsically historical, so that it can never be adequately grasped if it is understood as essentially a result, e.g. by ignoring its ethical and political character (see note 16).

Bibliography

Bechler, Z.: 'Newton's 1672 Optical Controversies: A Study in the Grammar of Scientific Dissent', in *The Interaction between Science and Philosophy* (ed. by Y. Elkana), Humanities Press, Atlantic Highlands, N. J., 1974.

Feyerabend, P. K.: 'Classical Empiricism', in *The Methodological Heritage of Newton* (ed. by R. E. Butts and J. W. Davis), Univ. of Toronto Press, Toronto, 1970. Gögelein, C.: *Zu Goethes Begriff von Wissenschaft auf dem Wege der Methodik seiner Farbstudien,* Hanser, Munich, 1972.

Goethe, J. W. von: *Maximen und Reflexionen* (ed. by M. Hecker), *Schriften der Goethe-Gesellschaft,* Vol. 21, Goethe-Gesellschaft, Weimar, 1907.

Hargreave, D.: 'Thomas Young's Theory of Color Vision: Its Roots, Development, and Acceptance by the British Scientific Community', Diss. Univ. of Wisconsin, 1973.

Helmholtz, H. von: 'Ueber Goethes naturwissenschaftliche Arbeiten', *Philosophische Vorträge und Aufsätze* (ed. by H. Hörz and S. Wollgast), Akademie-Verlag, Berlin, 1971.

Laymon, R.: 'Newton's *Experimentum Crucis* and the Logic of Idealization and Theory Refutation', *Studies in History and Philosophy of Science* 9 (1978) 51-77.

Lohne, J.: 'Experimentum Crucis', *Notes and Records of the Royal Society of London* 23 (1968) 169-199.

Newton, I.: *The Correspondence of Isaac Newton* (ed. by H. W. Turnbull *et al.*), 7 vols., Cambridge Univ. Press for the Royal Society, Cambridge, 1959-1976.

Raman, C. V.: *The Physiology of Vision,* Indian Academy of Sciences, Bangalore, 1968.

Ronchi, V.: *Optics, the Science of Vision* (trans. by E. Rosen), New York Univ. Press, New York, 1957.

Sabra, A. I.: *Theories of Light from Descartes to Newton,* Oldbourne, London, 1967.

Schrimpf, H.-J.: 'Ueber die geschichtliche Bedeutung von Goethes Newton-Polemik und Romantik-Kritik', in *Gratulatio: Festschrift für Christian Wegner zum 70. Geburtstag am 9. September 1963* (ed. by M. Honeit and M. Wegner), Wegner, Hamburg, 1963.

Shapiro, A. I.: 'The Evolving Structure of Newton's Theory of White Light and Color', *Isis* 70 (1980) 211-235.

Wood, R. W.: *Physical Optics,* 2nd ed., Macmillan, New York, 1911.

FURTHER READING

Balakier, Ann Stewart and James J. Balakier. "The Addisonian Connection between James Thomson's *The Seasons* and Sir Isaac Newton's *Principia*." *University of Dayton Review* 19, No. 2 (Summer 1988): 69-77.

> Examines the relationship between Newton's mechanics of nature, Joseph Addison's formulation of the concept of "a natural sublime," and James Thomson's *The Seasons,* which, the critics argue, is influenced by the work of both Newton and Addison.

John, David G. "Newton's *Opticks* and Brockes' Early Poetry." *Orbis Litterarum* 38, No. 3 (1983): 205-14.

> Studies the influence of Newton's theory of light on the German poet Barthold Heinrich Brockes, demonstrating how Brockes' work reflects his general fascination with light as a scientific phenomenon and includes direct references to *Opticks.*

Ketcham, Michael G. "Scientific and Poetic Imagination in James Thomson's 'Poem Sacred to the Memory of Sir Isaac Newton'." *Philological Quarterly* 61, No. 1 (Winter 1992): 33-50.

> A detailed analysis of Thomson's poem, focusing on how the form, content, and imagery used in the poem are informed by Newton's achievements.

Peterfreund, Stuart. "Power Tropes: 'The Tyger' As Enacted Critique of Newtonian Metonymic Logic and Natural Theology." *New Orleans Review* 18, No. 1 (Spring 1991): 27-35.

> Analyzes the relationship between the logic of William Blake's "The Tyger" and that of Book III of Newton's *Principia,* which contains his "Rules of Reasoning in Philosophy."

Natural Philosophy
Including Mathematics, Optics, and Alchemy

INTRODUCTION

In Newton's day, the term "natural philosophy" referred to the physical sciences, and Newton's work in this area was informed by his belief in a universe which operated on mechanical principles and which was set into motion by God. His scientific study focused on identifying the nature of these mechanical principles. In the course of this study, Newton discovered, developed, and elucidated the mathematical rules by which motion is governed; the fruits of this labor are presented in *Philosophiae Naturalis Principia Mathematica* (1687). Newton also sought to examine through extensive experimentation the properties of light and color, and his findings are published in *Opticks* (1704). Modern critics analyze and debate Newton's scientific and mathematical achievements as evidenced by these two works as well as by several of Newton's unpublished papers. Another area of critical discussion focuses on the historical sources that may have influenced Newton's work. Newton's interest in alchemy has proved to be a topic of controversy among critics, as many students and scholars of Newton find it difficult to reconcile his rational, scientific work with a subject deemed occult and false.

Major Works

Many of the calculations found in *Principia* were worked out by Newton many years earlier, after he had returned to his home in Woolsthorpe, when Trinity College closed due to the plague in 1665. In 1684 astronomer Edmund Halley approached Newton, asking him to describe the orbit of the planets. Newton responded that he had mathematically determined the orbit to be elliptical. Halley urged Newton to send him the calculations, which Newton did. With Halley's encouragement and patronage, Newton elaborated and expanded the work, which became the *Principia*. In this work, Newton explains the laws of the motion of the planets, moons, comets, the tides, and the earth. He also presents his theory of universal gravitation. The differential calculus Newton had earlier developed became a tool used for the calculations in *Principia*. In *Opticks,* Newton presents the results of his experiments with prisms, in which he had broken down white light into a spectrum of primary colors. This led to his theory that light was comprised of individual particles, or corpuscles. Also described in *Opticks* are Newton's experiments with colors of thin films. These experiments led to his theory that light could be both reflected and refracted. Additionally, *Opticks* contained a list of "Queries," in which Newton speculates not only about light and color, but other subjects of physics and philosophy as well.

Critical Reception

Modern critics have continued to assess the relevance and significance of Newton's mathematical and scientific achievements. After noting the influence of Johannes Kepler and Galileo on Newton, Albert Einstein examined Newton's approach to the problem of motion and comments on the importance of Newton's findings. Einstein noted that while the theories of electromagnetic fields and relativity have limited the significance of some of Newton's work, Newton's mechanics nevertheless paved the way in other areas, making a theory of fields possible. Unlike Einstein, Brian Ellis has argued that Newton's laws of motion are more historically related to Cartesian physics than to Galileo's work in kinematics. In addition to demonstrating Newton's debt to René Descartes, Ellis also emphasizes the conceptual nature of Newton's laws of motion, arguing that they are not deduced from or supported by observation or experimentation. Rupert Hall and Marie Boas Hall center their study on Newton's theory of matter, maintaining that his unpublished manuscripts on this subject help to demonstrate the development of his theory. The critics discussed Newton's exploration of the role of aether in the movement of particles and commented on the influence of Newton's theological beliefs on his theory of matter. Critics such as Robert B. Downs and I. Bernard Cohen focus on the subject matter and significance of the *Principia*. Downs surveys the content of the three books of the *Principia* and emphasizes Newton's application of mathematics to the movement of bodies. Likewise, Cohen states that "Newton's outstanding achievement was to show how to introduce mathematical analysis into the study of nature in a new and particularly fruitful way." Cohen goes on to identify the aspects of *Principia* which may be deemed "revolutionary."

Given that Newton's achievements in mathematics made his scientific discoveries possible, it is not surprising that much criticism has been devoted to the discussion of Newton's mathematical studies and accomplishments. E. W. Strong explores the procedure Newton identified as a method for "mathematically determining all kinds of phenomena." In particular, Strong underscores the importance to Newton of measurement, experimental investigation, and demonstration from principles. In evaluating Newton's contributions to mathematics, D. T. Whiteside states that Newton "transmuted the received theoretical bases of infinitesimal calculus, dynamics, and optics into their classical forms." Whiteside also discusses Newton's discovery of the general binomial expansion and maintains that fluxional calculus is Newton's "undivided glory."

Just as aspects of Newton's thinking on matter and motion have been supplanted by twentieth-century developments in science, so has his corpuscular theory of light. Nevertheless, his work in the area of light and color laid the foundation for future study. I. Bernard Cohen, in his examination of the content, textual history, and contemporary reception of Newton's *Opticks,* demonstrates that while the work was an exposition of the corpuscular theory of light, it also contained many basic principles of "undulation," or wave theory. The fact that Newton adopted two competing theories in one essay, Cohen explains, accounts for the negative reception the work received in the nineteenth century. In the eighteenth century, *Opticks* had gained much more popular appeal than *Principia.* Cohen compares the two works and argues that while *Principia* is "forbidding" to the nonspecialist, *Opticks* is more able to capture and retain the interest of the layperson. Additionally, Cohen observes, *Opticks* was published in English and written in an intimate style, whereas *Principia* was written in Latin, which was characteristic of its emphasis on mathematical principles. Thomas S. Kuhn analyzes the content of the papers on optical theory that Newton published in scientific journals. While Kuhn identifies the significance of Newton's findings in these papers, he also identifies problem areas in Newton's experimental procedures and presentation, such as Newton's habit of failing to fully explain the intellectual extrapolations he makes.

Critics who study Newton's interest in alchemy, evidenced by his many notebooks on the subject, write against a tradition that downplays or ignores Newton's alchemical studies. P. M. Rattansi states that many critics find Newton's interest in a subject such as alchemy completely inconsistent with his rational, scientific studies. The relationship between these two areas of study may be better understood, Rattansi contends, if Newton's interest in both biblical studies and ancient natural philosophy are further examined. Rattansi explains that the underlying assumptions of Newton's study of biblical prophesy and ancient natural philosophy was that truth about the "true system of the world," among other things, was given to man in ancient times but in a veiled and mysterious way, as in Scripture. It is Rattansi's suggestion that Newton's alchemical studies represented, like the rest of Newton's interest, his search for truth. Similarly, Betty Jo Teeter Dobbs argues that for Newton and his search for truth, no singular approach to knowledge was sufficient. For Newton, Dobbs maintains, the search for the "alchemical spirit" was one way of identifying God's action in the world. Additionally, Dobbs stress-

es that Newton's work in alchemy influenced his scientific thought. As Dobbs and other critics have argued, Newton sought a unified system of God and nature, and his work in mathematics, optics, motion, matter, and alchemy all supported this goal.

CRITICISM

Albert Einstein   (essay date 1927)

SOURCE: "Isaac Newton," in *Smithsonian Treasury of Science,* edited by Webster P. True, Simon and Schuster, Inc., 1960, pp. 278-86.

[*In the following essay, originally published in 1927, Einstein examines the methods by which Newton approached scientific inquiry and comments on the significance of Newton's achievement.*]

The two-hundredth anniversary of the death of Newton falls at this time. One's thoughts cannot but turn to this shining spirit, who pointed out, as none before or after him did, the path of Western thought and research and practical construction. He was not only an inventor of genius in respect of particular guiding methods; he also showed a unique mastery of the empirical material known in his time, and he was marvelously inventive in special mathematical and physical demonstrations. For all these reasons he deserves our deep veneration. He is, however, a yet more significant figure than his own mastery makes him, since he was placed by fate at a turning point in the world's intellectual development. This is brought home vividly to us when we recall that before Newton there was no comprehensive system of physical causality which could in any way render the deeper characters of the world of concrete experience.

The great materialists of ancient Greek civilization had indeed postulated the reference of all material phenomena to a process of atomic movements controlled by rigid laws, without appealing to the will of living creatures as an independent cause. Descartes, in his own fashion, had revived this ultimate conception. But it remained a bold postulate, the problematic ideal of a school of philosophy. In the way of actual justification of our confidence in the existence of an entirely physical causality, virtually nothing had been achieved before Newton.

Newton's Aim

Newton's aim was to find an answer to the question: Does there exist a simple rule by which the motion of the heavenly bodies of our planetary system can be completely calculated, if the state of motion of all these bodies at a single moment is known? Kepler's empirical laws of the motion of the planets, based on Tycho Brahe's observations, were already enunciated, and demanded an interpretation. [Everyone knows today what gigantic efforts were needed to discover these laws from the empirically ascertained orbits of the planets. But few reflect on the genius of the method by which Kepler ascertained the true orbits from the apparent ones; i.e., their directions as observed from the earth.] These laws gave a complete answer to the question how the planets moved round the sun (elliptical orbit, equal areas described by the radius vector in equal periods, relation between semi-major axis and period of revolution). But these rules do not satisfy the requirement of causality. The three rules are logically independent of one another, and show no sign of any interconnection. The third law cannot be extended numerically as it stands, from the sun to another central body; there is, for instance, no relation between a planet's period of revolution round the sun and the period of revolution of a moon round its planet.

But the principal thing is that these laws have reference to motion as a whole, and not to the question how there is developed from one condition of motion of a system that which immediately follows it in time. They are, in our phraseology of today, integral laws and not differential laws.

The differential law is the form which alone entirely satisfies the modern physicist's requirement of causality. The clear conception of the differential law is one of the greatest of Newton's intellectual achievements. What was needed was not only the idea but a formal mathematical method which was, indeed, extant in rudiment but had still to gain a systematic shape. This also Newton found in the differential and integral calculus. It is unnecessary to consider whether Leibnitz arrived at these same mathematical methods independently of Newton or not; in any case, their development was a necessity for Newton, as they were required in order to give Newton the means of expressing his thought.

The Step from Galileo to Newton

Galileo had already made a significant first step in the recognition of the law of motion. He discovered the law of inertia and the law of free falling in the earth's field of gravitation: A mass (or, more accurately, a material point) uninfluenced by other masses moves uniformly in a straight line; the vertical velocity of a free body increases in the field of gravity in proportion to the time. It may seem to us today to be only a small step from Galileo's observations to Newton's laws of motion. But it has to be observed that the two propositions above, in the form in which they are given, relate to motion as a whole, while Newton's law of

motion gives an answer to the question: How does the condition of motion of a point-mass change in an infinitely small period under the influence of an external force? Only after proceeding to consider the phenomenon during an infinitely short period (differential law) does Newton arrive at a formula which is applicable to all motions. He takes the conception of force from the already highly developed theory of statics. He is only able to connect force with acceleration by introducing the new conception of mass, which, indeed, is supported curiously enough by an apparent definition. Today we are so accustomed to forming conceptions which correspond to differential quotients that we can hardly realize any longer how great a capacity for abstraction was needed to pass across a double barrier to the general differential laws of motion, with the further need to evolve the conception of mass.

But this was still a long way from the causal comprehension of the phenomena of motion. For the motion was only determined by the equation of motion if the force was given. Newton had the idea, to which he was probably led by the laws of the planetary motions, that the force acting on a mass is determined by the position of all masses at a sufficiently small distance from the mass in question. Not until this connection was realized was a completely causal comprehension of the phenomena of motion obtained. How Newton, proceeding from Kepler's laws of the motion of planets, solved this problem for gravitation and so discovered the identity of the nature of gravity with the motive forces acting on the stars is common knowledge. It is only the combination of—

(Law of motion) + (Law of attraction)

through which is constituted that wonderful thought-structure which enables the earlier and later conditions of a system to be calculated from the conditions ruling at one particular time, in so far as the phenomena occur under the sole influence of the forces of gravitation. The logical completeness of Newton's system of ideas lay in the fact that the sole causes of the acceleration of the masses of a system prove to be the masses themselves.

On the basis sketched Newton succeeded in explaining the motions of the planets, moons, comets, down to fine details, as well as the ebb and flow of the tides and the precessional movement of the earth—this last a deductive achievement of peculiar brilliance. It was, no doubt, especially impressive to learn that the cause of the movements of the heavenly bodies is identical with the force of gravity, so familiar to us from everyday experience.

Significance of Newton's Achievement

The significance, however, of Newton's achievement lay not only in its provision of a serviceable and logically satisfactory basis for mechanics proper; up to the end of the nineteenth century it formed the program of all theoretical physical research. All physical phenomena were to be referred to masses subject to Newton's law of motion. Only the law of force had to be amplified and adapted to the type of phenomena which was being considered. Newton himself tried to apply this program in optics, on the hypothesis that light consisted of inert corpuscles. The optics of the undulatory theory also made use of Newton's law of motion, the law being applied to continuously diffused masses. The kinetic theory of heat rested solely on Newton's formulae of motion; and this theory not only prepared people's minds for the recognition of the law of the conservation of energy, but also supplied a theory of gases confirmed in its smallest details, and a deepened conception of the nature of the second law of thermodynamics. The theory of electricity and magnetism also developed down to modern times entirely under the guidance of Newton's basic ideas (electric and magnetic substance, forces at a distance). Even Faraday and Maxwell's revolution in electrodynamics and optics, which was the first great advance in the fundamental principles of theoretical physics since Newton, was still achieved entirely under the guidance of Newton's ideas. Maxwell, Boltzmann, and Lord Kelvin never tired of trying again and again to reduce electromagnetic fields and their dynamical reciprocal action to mechanical processes occurring in continuously distributed hypothetical masses. But owing to the barrenness, or at least unfruitfulness, of these efforts there gradually occurred, after the end of the nineteenth century, a revulsion in fundamental conceptions; theoretical physics outgrew Newton's framework, which had for nearly two centuries provided fixity and intellectual guidance for science.

Newton on Its Limitations

Newton's basic principles were so satisfying from a logical standpoint that the impulse to fresh departures could only come from the pressure of the facts of experience. Before I enter into this I must emphasize that Newton himself was better aware of the weak sides of his thought-structure than the succeeding generations of students. This fact has always excited my reverent admiration; I should like, therefore, to dwell a little on it.

1. Although everyone has remarked how Newton strove to represent his thought-system as necessarily subject to the confirmation of experience, and to introduce the minimum of conceptions not directly referable to matters of experience, he makes use of the conceptions of absolute space and absolute time. In our own day he has often been criticized for this. But it is in this very point that Newton is particularly consistent. He had recognized that the observable geometrical magnitudes (distances of material points from one another) and their change in process of time do not completely

determine movements in a physical sense. He shows this in the famous bucket experiment. There is, therefore, in addition to masses and their distances, varying with time, something else, which determines what happens; this "something" he conceives as the relation to "absolute space." He recognizes that space must possess a sort of physical reality if his laws of motion are to have a meaning, a reality of the same sort as the material points and their distances.

This clear recognition shows both Newton's wisdom and a weak side of his theory. For a logical construction of the theory would certainly be more satisfactory without this shadowy conception; only those objects (point-masses, distances) would then come into the laws whose relation to our perceptions is perfectly clear.

2. The introduction of direct, instantaneously acting forces at a distance into the exposition of the effects of gravitation does not correspond to the character of most of the phenomena which are familiar to us in our daily experience. Newton meets this objection by pointing out that his law of reciprocal gravitation is not to be taken as an ultimate explanation, but as a rule induced from experience.

3. Newton's theory offered no explanation of the very remarkable fact that the weight and inertia of a body are determined by the same magnitude (the mass). The remarkable nature of this fact struck Newton also.

None of these three points can rank as a logical objection against the theory. They form, as it were, merely unsatisfied needs of the scientific spirit in its effort to penetrate the processes of nature by a complete and unified set of ideas.

The Theory of the Electromagnetic Field

Newton's theory of motion, considered as a program for the whole field of theoretical physics, suffered its first shock from Maxwell's theory of electricity. It was found that the reciprocal action between bodies through electrical and magnetic bodies does not take place through instantaneously acting forces at a distance, but through processes which are transmitted with finite velocity through space. Alongside the point-mass and its movements there arose, in Faraday's conception, a new sort of physically real thing, the "field." It was first sought to conceive this, with the aid of mechanical modes of thought, as a mechanical condition (of movement or strain) of a hypothetical space-filling medium (the ether). When, however, in spite of the most obstinate efforts, this mechanical interpretation refused to work, students slowly accustomed themselves to the conception of the "electromagnetic field" as the ultimate irreducible foundation stone of physical reality. We owe to H. Hertz the deliberate liberation of the conception of the field from all the scaffolding of the conceptions of mechanics, and to H. A. Lorentz the liberation of the conception of the field from a material bearer; according to Lorentz the physical empty space (or ether) alone figured as bearer of the field; in Newton's mechanics, indeed, space had not been devoid of all physical functions. When this development had been completed, no one any longer believed in directly acting instantaneous forces at a distance, even in connection with gravitation, though a field theory for gravitation, for lack of sufficient known facts, was not unmistakably indicated. The development of the theory of the electromagnetic field also led, after Newton's hypothesis of action at a distance had been abandoned, to the attempt to find an electromagnetic explanation for Newton's law of motion, or to replace that law by a more accurate law based on the field theory. These efforts were not crowned with full success, but the mechanical basic conceptions ceased to be regarded as foundation stones of the physical conception of the universe.

The Maxwell-Lorentz theory led inevitably to the special theory of relativity, which, by destroying the conception of absolute simultaneity, negatived the existence of forces at a distance. Under this theory mass is not an unalterable magnitude, but a magnitude dependent on (and, indeed, identical with) the amount of energy. The theory also showed that Newton's law of motion can only be considered as a limiting law valid only for small velocities, and substituted for it a new law of motion, in which the velocity of light in a vacuum appears as the limiting velocity.

The General Theory of Relativity

The last step in the development of the program of the field theory was the general theory of relativity. Quantitatively it made little modification in Newton's theory, but qualitatively a deep-seated one. Inertia, gravitation, and the metrical behavior of bodies and clocks were reduced to the single quality of a field, and this field in turn was made dependent on the bodies (generalization of Newton's law of gravitation or of the corresponding field law, as formulated by Poisson). Space and time were so divested, not of their reality, but of their causal absoluteness (absoluteness—influencing, that is, not influenced), which Newton was compelled to attribute to them in order to be able to give expression to the laws then known. The generalized law of inertia takes over the role of Newton's law of motion. From this short characterization it will be clear how the elements of Newton's theory passed over into the general theory of relativity, the three defects above mentioned being at the same time overcome. It appears that within the framework of the general theory of relativity the law of motion can be deduced from the law of the field, which corresponds to Newton's law of force. Only when this aim has been fully attained can we speak of a pure theory of fields.

Newton's mechanics prepared the way for the theory of fields in a yet more formal sense. The application of Newton's mechanics to continuously distributed masses led necessarily to the discovery and application of partial differential equations, which in turn supplied the language in which alone the laws of the theory of fields could be expressed. In this formal connection also Newton's conception of the differential law forms the first decisive step to the subsequent development.

The whole development of our ideas concerning natural phenomena, which has been described above, may be conceived as an organic development of Newton's thought. But while the construction of the theory of fields was still actively in progress, the facts of heat radiation, spectra, radioactivity, and so on, revealed a limit to the employment of the whole system of thought, which, in spite of gigantic successes in detail, seems to us today completely insurmountable. Many physicists maintain, not without weighty arguments, that in face of these facts not only the differential law but the law of causality itself—hitherto the ultimate basic postulate of all natural science—fails.

The very possibility of a spatio-temporal construction which can be clearly brought into consonance with physical experience is denied. That a mechanical system should permanently admit only discrete values of energy or discrete states—as experience, so to say, directly shows—seems at first hardly deducible from a theory of fields working with differential equations. The method of De Broglie and Schrödinger, which has, in a certain sense, the character of a theory of fields, does deduce, on the basis of differential equations, from a sort of considerations of resonance the existence of purely discrete states and their transition into one another in amazing agreement with the facts of experience; but it has to dispense with a localization of the mass-particles and with strictly causal laws. Who would be so venturesome as to decide today the question whether causal law and differential law, these ultimate premises of Newton's treatment of nature must be definitely abandoned?

E. W. Strong (essay date 1951)

SOURCE: "Newton's Mathematical Way," in *Journal of the History of Ideas,* Vol. XII, No. 1, January 1951, pp. 90-110.

[In the following essay, Strong analyzes Newton's method for "mathematically determining" natural phenomena. Aspects of this mathematical procedure, Strong states, include experimental investigation, demonstration from principles, and an emphasis on measurement.]

The task of this historical essay is to make out the procedure which Newton designates as a "mathematical way" to be followed in physical science—a way of "mathematically determining all kinds of phenomena."[1] This procedure with respect to the role of measurement in experimental inquiry can be called mathematical experimentalism and, with respect to reasoning from principles, mathematical demonstration. Pemberton, the editor of the third edition of the **Principia** and an expositor of Newton's science, reiterates a position taken by Newton when he states. "The proofs in natural philosophy cannot be so absolutely conclusive, as in the mathematics. For the subjects of that science are purely the ideas of our own minds. They may be represented to our senses by material objects, but they are themselves the arbitrary productions of our own thoughts; so that as the mind can have a full and adequate knowledge of its own ideas, the reasoning in geometry can be rendered perfect. But in natural knowledge the subject of our contemplation is without us, and not so completely to be known." Pemberton concludes by saying. "It is only here required to steer a just course between the conjectural method of proceeding . . . and demanding so rigorous a proof, as will reduce all philosophy to mere scepticism, and exclude all prospect of making any progress in the knowledge of nature."[2]

E. A. Burtt[3] and J. H. Randall, Jr.,[4] have argued that there is an unreconciled conflict in Newton's thought between his mathematical rationalism, on the one hand, and his empiricism, on the other. Neither critic, however, has done justice to Newton's statements about measurement and its role in the formulation of principles.[5] Newton's "mathematical way" encompasses both experimental investigation and demonstration from principles, that is, from laws or theorems established through investigation. Measurements and rules of measure are crucial to mechanics and optics, for they provide the quantitative data and formulas upon which mathematical demonstrations in these physical sciences depend. When one sees how "measure" prepares for demonstration, there is good ground for modifying the assertion made by Randall, *viz., "Newton*'s actual mathematical procedure made it necessary for him to assume much that his empiricism could not justify; and in his ideas of 'the real world' his scientific procedure and his empirical theory collide violently."

It is true that there has been an opposition of theories with regard to the status of concepts and principles in physical science as these are mathematically formulated. The opposition is reminiscent of the lines from Gilbert:

> Every man that's born alive
> Is either a little lib-er-al
> Or else a little con-ser-va-tive.

Reworded to fit the clash of theories:

> Every philosopher in his twist
> Is either boldly rational
> Or else a cautious empiricist.

Considering the long-standing disputes between rationalists and empiricists concerning the status of mathematical ideas and of how mathematical demonstration holds good for physical phenomena, it is not surprising that discussions of Newton's scientific thought have tried to characterize it by seeking to ascertain to which camp Newton belonged. On the one hand. Newton appears to be a mathematical realist when he asserts that space, time and motion are to be conceived as "absolute, true, and mathematical." On the other hand. Newton was positivistically-minded in his experimental work and in his statements about method in science. If Newton, then, resists classification under one or the other type of thought but is in both camps at once, what is more natural than to argue that there is a fundamental conflict of two theories within his thinking? Yet since Newton's mathematical-physical science could not, without neglect of essential matters, slight either the need for data provided by experimental analysis or the proofs provided by mathematical demonstration, it is pertinent to ask how, on *methodological* grounds, Newton connects investigation and demonstration. What he has to say about "principles' is of central importance here. Once we have made out Newton's position concerning the mathematical way to be employed in physical science, we will then take up a second question, namely, that of the status of strictly mathematical ideas in Newton's method of analysis as set forth in the **Principia** and in his **Quadrature of Curves**. A. J. Snow[6] asserts that Newton assumes or supposes a one-to-one correspondence between elements and relations of his mathematical analysis and those of a physical analysis of nature. Had Newton maintained this, he would indeed have been a rationalist comparable to Kant who maintained that Euclidean geometry was an *a priori* necessary schematism of spatial extension.

The problem characteristic of rationalistic theory is one of descent from pure mathematics to mathematical demonstration in physical science. The problem characteristic of empirical theory is one of ascent from mechanics in an attempt to account for mathematics *per se* in terms of abstractions from experienced objects and physical operations. Hobbes, for example, sought to mount an empirical ladder in providing a physicalist explanation of geometry, and had the ladder pulled out from under him by Wallis. Bishop Berkeley, in his criticism of Newton, was not so easily routed. He capitalized upon the defense which British mathematicians had made of Newton's method of fluxions in proclaiming it to be superior to Leibniz's differential calculus. The defenders of Newton maintained that the indivisibles of Leibniz were not to be admitted into mathematics because, they said, "they have no

Being either in Geometry or in Nature." They argued the legitimacy of mathematical ideas by resting their case upon what is actually or really generated in the physical world. Berkeley was himself a champion of this argument, but turned it against the Newtonians by challenging the logic of their reasoning by which, for example, a physical division *in infinitum* was asserted by Keill and Halley. Like Ernst Mach after him, Berkeley contended that geometry is an abstracted physical science, and that where the abstracting from experienced things could not be established for a mathematical idea, the mathematicians did not know what they were reasoning about. By 1750, the controversies centering around Leibniz and Berkeley had produced admirable clarifications of disputed questions in the writings of Robins, Simpson, and Maclaurin; but the matters to be clarified in Newton's method of fluxions were not so much confounded by Newton as by his followers.

I. *Newton's Mathematical Way in Physical Science*

"In mathematics," Newton writes, "we are to investigate the quantities of forces with their proportions consequent upon any conditions supposed; then, when we enter upon physics, we compare those proportions with the phenomena of nature, that we may know what conditions of those forces answer to the several kinds of attractive bodies. And this preparation being made, we argue more safely concerning the physical species, causes, and proportions of the forces."[7]

In this statement, Newton may be said to differentiate the work in theory of a mathematical physicist from the work of the experimentalist. The former consists in discoveries and demonstrations "upon any conditions supposed" in an inquiry dealing with "quantities of forces with their proportions." How these quantities are furnished to the calculator involves Newton's general statement of method set forth in his **"Rules of Reasoning in Philosophy"** and his account of the role of measurement in experimental investigation. The rules of reasoning, as Pemberton[8] points out, are the "concessions" of induction required in natural philosophy but not needed in purely mathematical reasoning. These concessions are the following:

> 1. "that more causes are not to be received in philosophy, than are sufficient to explain the appearances of nature;"

> 2. "that to like effects are to be ascribed the same causes;" and

> 3. "That those qualities, which in the same body can neither be lessened or increased, and which belong to all bodies that are in our power to make trial upon, ought to be accounted the universal properties of all bodies whatever."

A fourth rule is designed by Pemberton as an "additional precept" by which Newton enforces the "method of induction" in Rule 3, "whereupon all philosophy is founded." Newton states this general precept in these words: "In experimental philosophy we are to look upon propositions inferred by general induction from phenomena as accurately or very nearly true, notwithstanding any contrary hypotheses that may be imagined, till such time as other phenomena occur, by which they may either be made more accurate, or liable to exceptions. This rule we must follow, that the argument of induction may not be evaded by hypotheses." Pemberton remarks, "In this precept is founded that method of arguing by induction, without which no progress could be made in natural philosophy. For as the qualities of bodies become known to us by experiments only; we have no other way of finding the properties of such bodies, as are out of our reach to experiment upon, but by drawing conclusions from those which fall under our examination."

To follow Newton in his statement of the fourth rule of reasoning in philosophy and in other statements in which the terms "hypothesis," "principle," and "theory" occur we need first to make clear how he uses these terms. A "natural philosopher" is one who investigates phenomena, for example, the motions and paths of bodies, and engages in theory in the calculation of forces. Forces are not observed but computed in their actions. From the composition of forces in accordance with mathematical-physical or "mechanical principles," phenomena of nature are demonstrated. A supposed force, medium, substance, or structure of nature presented as an unverified causal assumption is called a "physical hypothesis." A physical hypothesis is also a mechanical hypothesis when assumed properties are conceived to be subject to the same kind of quantitative analysis that holds for measured bodies and motions—what Newton calls their "sensible measures." Qualities that are not in principle measurable are excluded from "mechanical philosophy." Hypothesis is differentiated not only from principles but also from theory. A theory is inductively inferred and abstracted from the results of observations and experiments. The soundness of theory is regarded as independent of the truth or falsity of "hypotheses," where by this term is meant explanation by an assumed cause not empirically verified. Newton uses "query" or "question" for suppositions that lead to further experiment (*i.e.,* for hypothesis in our modern sense as a supposition which is a candidate for verification). What Newton has to say about not making hypotheses refers only to explanations by assumed causes, and not to leading questions to be decided by experiments. Such queries may be corroborated or corrected, whereas mechanical hypotheses, unless brought to experiment and in this converted into queries, remain unconfirmed explanations.

Newton himself advances a mechanical hypothesis in his supposition that light is composed of corporeal particles, and that it is transmitted through an "etherial medium." He vigorously insists, however, upon the differentiation between the corpuscular hypothesis as a "conjecture" about light and his theory concluded from experiments. A strong empiricistic temper is exhibited throughout in his replies to objections brought against his theory.[9]

Having defined Newton's terms as he employs them, we can now restate the questions pertaining to Newton's scientific thought in the light of his description of his method of inquiry.

> As in Mathematicks, so in Natural Philosophy, the investigation of difficult Things by the Method of Analysis, ought ever to precede the Method of Composition. This Analysis consists in making Experiments and Observations, and in drawing general Conclusions from them by Induction, and admitting of no Objections against the Conclusions, but such as are taken from Experiments or other certain Truths. For Hypotheses are not to be regarded in experimental Philosophy. And although the arguing from Experiments and Observations be no Demonstration of general Conclusions, yet it is the best way of arguing which the Nature of Things admits of, and may be looked upon as so much the stronger, by how much the Induction is more general. And if no Exception occurs from Phaenomena, the Conclusions may be pronounced generally. But if at any time afterwards any Exception shall occur from Experiments, it may then begin to be pronounced with such Exceptions as occur. By this way of Analysis we may proceed from. Compounds to Ingredients, and from Motions to the Forces producing them; and in general, from the Effects to their Causes, and from particular Causes to more General ones, till the Argument end in the most general. This is the method of Analysis: and the Synthesis consists in assuming the Causes discover'd and establish'd as Principles, and by them explaining the Phenomena proceeding from them and proving the Explanations.[10]

The questions to be examined in turn are the following: (1) How is an inductive generalization constituted as a mechanical principle from which a scientist is to proceed mathematically to "estimate effects" and to explain phenomena? (2) What does Newton designate as "analysis" in mathematics and what does the analogy between the terms of this analysis and those of experimental inquiry amount to?

Newton states in the Preface to his ***Principia*** that the "whole burden of philosophy seems to consist in this—from the phenomena of motions to investigate the forces of nature, and then from these forces to demonstrate the other phenomena." Quantity is only traced out if there are measures, for it is measurement alone which provides quantified data for calculation. A principle in physics is "mathematical" if its enunciation states a ratio or proportion, or, as we would now say, a formula or functional relationship. The rôle of geometry in the science of mechanics is defined by Newton as "that part of universal mechanics which accurately proposes and demonstrates the art of measuring. In this sense," Newton continues, "rational mechanics will be the science of motions resulting from any forces whatsoever, and of the forces required to produce any motions, accurately proposed and demonstrated." There are, then, no laws of mechanics which are supplied solely by reasoning in mathematics. Demonstration, of course, is a procedure of mathematical reasoning, but such reasoning, as Newton states, is from "the laws and *measures* of gravity and other forces."

One example will serve to show how Newton proceeds from the method of experimental analysis to the method of composition. Having discovered invariable refractive indices of a prism for rays of differently colored light and having stated his discoveries as "the Laws of Refraction made out of Glass into Air" and "out of Air into Glass," Newton derives two "Theorems." He comments as follows:

> By the first Theorem the Refractions of the Rays of every sort made out of any Medium into Air are known by having the Refraction of the Rays of any one sort. . . . By the latter Theorem the Refraction out of one Medium into another is gathered as often as you have the Refractions out of them both into any third Medium.[11]

The two theorems state laws of refrangibility, and have the status of axioms or principles in the demonstration of optical phenomena. Newton adds the following highly significant comment. "And these Theorems being admitted into Opticks, there would be scope enough of handling that Science voluminously after a new manner; not only by teaching those things which tend to the perfection of Vision [*i.e.*, theory of telescopes], but also by determining mathematically all kinds of Phaenomena of Colours which could be produced by Refractions."[12] Methodologically, there is a "determining mathematically" in observation and experiment in making measurements; but such measurements do not of themselves yield laws. To compute a ratio or proportion of quantified data is to institute a *rule of measure*: and such a rule of measure is the comprehension of the scientist of the relevance of what he has measured. Measurements alone of angles, distances, periodicities, and the like yield quantified data. When correlated in some ratio or proportionality, the numbers which read off the measures are now handled by calculations and computations. In some cases, the arraying of measurements may be intuitively grasped by the scientist as exhibiting a rule of measure. In others, the making of computations may disclose some function which can be formulated as a general theorem. The investigator has then discovered a rule of measure and, with respect to what has been measured, he may now consider that he has discovered a physical law.

How had it happened, Newton asks, that, although previous experimenters had measured refractions, they had not discovered the refrangibility of several rays of light, and hence had not arrived at these new theorems for "determining mathematically all kinds of Phaenomena of Colours which could be produced by refractions?" One must know not only how to measure but what to measure.

> The late Writers in Opticks teach, that the Sines of Incidence are in a given Proportion to the Sines of Refraction, as was explained in the fifth Axiom; and some by Instruments fitted for measuring of Refractions, or otherwise experimentally examining this Proportion, do acquaint us that they have found it accurate. But whilst they, not understanding the different Refrangibility of several Rays, conceived them all to be refracted according to one and the same Proportion, 'tis to be presumed that they adapted their Measures only to the middle of the refracted Light; so that from their Measures we may conclude only that the Rays which have a mean Degree of Refrangibility (that is, those which when separated from the rest appear green), are refracted according to a given Proportion of their Sines. And therefore we are now to shew, that the like given Proportions obtain in all the rest.[13]

Newton proceeds to a mathematical demonstration of the proposition, concluding, "So, then, if the *ratio* of the Sines of Incidence and Refraction of any sorts of Rays be found in any one case, 'tis given in all cases." Finally, he presents the method used and results obtained experimentally which confirm the conclusion.

In working through Book I of Newton's *Opticks,* I had supplied the expression "rule of measure" suitable to the sense in which Newton uses the word "measure" as meaning a ratio or proportion of numbers supplied by measurements. That this accorded with Newton's reasoning was confirmed in *Opticks,* Book II, Part I. Newton, in this part dealing with "rings of Colour" produced by thin transparent bodies, presents a table of measurements.[14]

"And from these Measures," Newton concludes, "I seem to gather this Rule: That the Thickness of the Air is proportional to the Secant of an Angle, whose sine is a certain mean Proportional between the Sines of Incidence and Refraction."

Newton then states this mean proportional so far as he can determine it from the measures he has made. From the measurements in knowing what to measure, the rule is formulated which is now a principle from which

to demonstrate phenomena. Towards the end of the *Opticks* Newton remarks upon the method of composition in these words: "Now as all these things follow from the properties of light by a mathematical way of reasoning, so the truth of them may be manifested by experiments." In a communication to Oldenburg, July 11, 1672, Newton makes what is perhaps the best summarization about "principles" to be found anywhere in his writings:

> In the last place, I should take notice of a casual expression, which intimates a greater certainty in these things, than I ever promised, *viz, the certainty of Mathematical Demonstrations.* I said, indeed, that the science of colours was mathematical, and as certain as any other part of *Opticks*; but who knows not that Optics, and many other mathematical sciences, depend as well on physical sciences, as on mathematical demonstrations? And the absolute certainty of a science cannot exceed the certainty of its principles. Now the evidence, by which I asserted the propositions of colours, is in the next words expressed to be from experiments, and so but physical: whence the Propositions themselves can be esteemed no more than physical principles of a science. And if those principles be such, that on them a mathematician may determine all the phaenomena of colours, that can be caused by refractions, and by disputing or demonstrating after what manner and how much, those refractions do separate or mingle the rays, in which the several colours are originally inherent; I suppose the science of colours will be granted mathematical, and as certain as any part of Optics. And that this may be done, I have good reason to believe, because ever since I became first acquainted with these principles, I have, with constant success in the events, made use of them for this purpose.

Newton's mathematical way, then, requires measures for the formulation of principles in optics and mechanics—principles that incorporate a rule of measure. Were there not mathematical determination in the experiment, there would be no subsequent determination in the demonstration. The quantities with which rational mechanics are concerned are measures expressed in a rule. This is clear in Newton's definitions of mass and momentum in the *Principia*:

Def. I. The Quantity of matter is the measure of the same, arising from its density and bulk conjointly

Def. II. The quantity of motion is the measure of the same, arising from the velocity and quantity of matter conjointly. The bearing of Definitions I and II upon Newton's idea of *Force* is pointed out by Cajori.

> By Newton's second Definition, "quantity of motion" (momentum) arises "from the velocity and quantity of matter conjointly," that is, from mv. By Newton's second Law of Motion, "change of motion," that is,

change in the quantity of motion, "is proportional to the motive force impressed." Thus we have "change of motion" as the measure of the force which produces it. Thus arose the measurement of force by the product of mass and acceleration.

In view of Newton's position with regard to principles to be admitted into mathematical-physical science, what is one to make of his definitions of absolute, true, and mathematical time and space and motion? Newton writes that parts of an absolute space, like parts of an absolute time, are not

> distinguished from one another by our senses, therefore in their stead we use sensible measures of them. For from the positions and distances of things from any body considered as immovable, we define all places; and then with respect to such places, we estimate all motions, considering bodies as transferred from some of those places into others. And so, instead of absolute places and motions, we use relative ones; and that without any inconvenience in common affairs; but in philosophical disquisitions, we ought to abstract from our senses, and consider things themselves, distinct from what are only sensible measures of theme. For it may be that there is no body really at rest, to which the places and motions of others may be referred.

Similarly, Newton states, "It may be, that there is no such thing as an equable motion whereby time may be accurately measured. All motions may be accelerated and retarded, but the flowing of absolute time is not liable to any change."

The abstracting "from the senses" here recommended, in view of Newton's own admission that there may be no equable motion and no body absolutely at rest strongly suggests that absolute space, time, and motion are being proposed as postulates and hence as a possible or presupposed system. Undoubtedly Newton believed that the "absolutes" he postulated were not conventional constructs but were a real order of nature, yet lack of empirical confirmation restrained him from asserting this as a matter of knowledge. ". . . there may be some body absolutely at rest," Newton writes, "but impossible to know, from the position of bodies to one another in our regions, whether any of these do keep the same position to that remote body." It follows "that absolute rest cannot be determined from the position of bodies in our regions." Newton thought that the matter was not "altogether desperate" empirically with regard to absolute motion if one considered the evidence in determining angular velocity from the rotation of vessels filled with water. The experiment, however, does not provide empirical warrant for absolute rectilinear motion implied in the first Law: "every body continues in its state of rest, or of uniform motion in a right line, unless it is compelled to change that state by forces impressed upon it."

There is no conflict or confusion in Newton's reasoning regarding an absolute, true, and mathematical system provided he does not employ the asserted "absolutes" as more than postulates. Newton does assume absolute coordinates from which to compute sensible measures of bodies and motions, but in so doing the expressions are unexceptionable if asserted not as *physical* but only as *mathematical.* A careful reading of Newton supports the following conclusions concerning abstracting from the senses. In effect, Newton distinguishes three levels. In a first level of abstracting, propositions are said to be inferred or deduced from phenomena. In a second level, the propositions are "rendered general by induction," for example, the two theorems in optics previously discussed. As derived from mathematical experimentation, these principles are *mechanical* principles, or mathematical-physical formulas. When Newton postulates absolute, true, and mathematical space, time, and motion, he introduces principles which are not evinced by experiments. Such principles, so far as Newton believes they express a real order of nature, are thereby metaphysical in the sense of being unverified assumptions. They are constructs introduced on the second level of abstracting, but not themselves inductively derived and thereby empirically grounded. So far as Newton's scientific purpose is concerned in his mechanics, nothing more need be asserted or assumed. Yet a third level appears in Newton's views expressed in the General Scholium at the end of the *Principia* and in the conclusion of the *Opticks* where Newton attributes the order of nature to God as the first Cause.

Where interpreters of Newton have gone astray is in supposing that Newton held that Space and Time constitute the "sensorium of God" in order to preserve empiricism in principle for the atomic ingredients and absolute structure of his system. Yet Newton *added* the General Scholium in the second edition of the *Principia* in 1713, twenty-six years after the first edition; and the theological views expressed in the *Opticks,* Queries 28 and 31, did not appear in the first edition of 1704. Had Newton supposed these discussions to be fundamental to his science, he would hardly have omitted them originally. Newton, of course, believed that his system of the world was not incompatible with a traditional conception of God which he never questioned. He wrote the general scholium at the urging of Cotes, who became alarmed by the criticism of Leibniz to the prejudice of a work in which God had not been employed. Newton, however, did not suppose that his scientific theorems either proved the theological doctrine or needed to assume it. His famous statement, "Hypotheses non fingo," is his judgment upon the pertinence of the theological discussion which immediately precedes it. The philosophers who take this third level to be a subscription on Newton's part to theological foundations of his physical science have not followed Newton in his own disavowal. Science proper is limited, by Newton, to the first two levels of abstracting.

Some main points emerging from the preceding discussion can now be summarized:

1. In mathematical computation and demonstration, Newton introduced mathematical postulates which are not mechanical principles but mathematical only. He believed in the reality of these mathematical absolutes, but does not argue that this reality is known from observation and experiment.

2. Success in demonstration tended to confirm Newton's belief in the reality of an absolute system. In Rule III of his **"Rules of Reasoning in Philosophy,"** Newton held that "since the qualities of bodies are known to us only by experiments, we are to hold for universal all such as universally agree with experiments." By extension of this rule, a system of demonstration which holds for phenomena is likewise to be held for universal, not here because the mathematical postulates introduced are derived from experiments but because predictions are verified. Such verification with no known exceptions is a strong impulsion to believe that non-empirical postulates are to be accepted as real in the nature of things.

3. Mechanical principles established from sensible measures have the status of inductive generalizations, or empirically established laws. Definitions of mass and momentum incorporate rules of measure as the meaning of these concepts.

4. Mechanical principles conjoined with mathematical postulates constitute the premises of Newton's theoretical physics. As stated by Roberts and Thomas,[15] "Given clear notions of the method of measuring time and distance, it is possible to define velocity and acceleration relative to some fixed framework. . . . Add to these a satisfactory definition of 'mass' and you have the foundation of Newtonian science: the laws of nature are uniform throughout space, and all observations can be expressed, for scientific purposes, in terms of space, time, and mass."

II. *Mathematical Analysis and Mathematical Ideas*

An assumption of Newton's physical analysis is that "the least particles of all bodies" are "extended and hard and impenetrable and movable, and endowed with their proper inertia." Such particles are ingredients of composite, molar bodies. Newton warns against confusing a mathematical analysis of division of quantity *in infinitum* with an actual, physical separation: ". . . that the divided but contiguous particles of bodies may be separated from one another, is a matter of observation; and in the particles that remain undivided, our *minds* are able to distinguish yet lesser parts, as is *mathemat-*

ically demonstrated. But whether the parts *so* distinguished, and not yet divided, may, by the powers of Nature, be *actually* divided and separated from one another, we cannot certainly determine."

What our minds are able to distinguish as mathematically demonstrated with regard to infinitesimals has here no empirical determination. Infinitesimals, nascent and evanescent quantities, and the like are mathematical only. As De Morgan[16] has shown, Newton used infinitesimally small quantities, or fixed infinitesimals in his algebraical calculus up to the year 1704; and, according to Cajori, even later. In the first edition of the **Principia,** Newton warns against looking upon "moments" as finite particles comprising magnitudes by apposition, for this, he says, is "contrary to their continuous increase or decrease." Rather, they are to be regarded as "the just nascent principles of finite magnitudes." In 1704, in his **Quadrature of Curves,** Newton tried to avoid use of infinitely small constants. He designates a fluxion as a velocity or time-derivative of a fluent or flowing quantity, and states that fluxions are "in the *first ratio* of the nascent augments," or "in the *ultimate ratio* of the evanescent part." Cajori[17] remarks that

> Unless the fully developed theory of limits is read into these phrases, they will involve either infinitely little parts or other quantities no less mysterious. At any rate, the history of fluxions shows that these expressions did not meet the demands for clearness and freedom from mysticism. Newton himself knew full well the logical difficulties involved in the words 'prime and ultimate ratios'; for in 1687 he said, 'it is objected, that there was no ultimate proportion of evanescent quantities; because the proportion before the quantities have vanished, is not ultimate; and, when they have vanished, is none.'

The problem of quadratures (integration) consisted in how to find the total amount of change in a given time, given a formula expressing the rate of change at all moments. The problem of tangents (differentiation) consisted in how to find the rate of change at any moment given a formula which expresses the total of all moments. These problems were "equivalent to finding the area enclosed by a curve of any given form, and finding the slope of the tangent to a given curve at a given point."[18] Newton's analysis in dealing with these problems did involve elements which were difficult to define clearly and rigorously within the method itself. For example, an "ultimate velocity" is said to be that velocity "with which the body is moved, neither before it arrives at its last place and the motion ceases, nor after, but at the very instant it arrives; that is, that velocity with which the body arrives at its last place, and with which the motion ceases." Again, "the ratio of evanescent quantities" is said to be that "with which they vanish" and not the ratio just before or just afterwards. If by "prime and ultimate ratios" a theory of limits is intended, then the language of "nascent augments" and "evanescent decrements" is a circumlocution more apt to bewilder than to clarify the logic of reasoning. Yet Newton quite early is at least flirting with the idea of limits; for in defending the intelligibility of an "ultimate proportion of evanescent quantities" in the *Principia* (39), he writes:

> There is a limit which the velocity at the end of the motion may attain, but not exceed. This is the ultimate velocity. And there is the like limit in all quantities and proportions that begin and cease to be. And since such limits are certain and definite, to determine the same is a problem strictly geometrical. But whatever is geometrical we may use in determining and demonstrating any other thing that is also geometrical.

Newton insists throughout that the conception of "quantities as least, or evanescent, or ultimate," is not of quantities of any determinate magnitude, "but such as are conceived as always diminished without end." From Newton's own comment about quantities so conceived, it is clear that he regards them as strictly mathematical, and that their assertion in mathematical analysis posits no identity with physical particles and magnitudes.

Newton's use of the term *Analysis* for infinite processes dates, according to H. W. Turnbull,[19] from Newton's comment about the method of series in his *De Analysi* (1669).

> Neither do I know anything of this kind to which this method does not extend, and that in various ways. Yea, tangents may be drawn to mechanical curves by it, when it happens that it can be done by no other means. And whatever the common Analysis performs by means of equations of a finite number of terms (provided that can be done) this can always perform the same by means of infinite equations. So I have not made any question of giving this the name Analysis likewise. For the reasonings in this are no less certain than in the other; nor are the equations less exact.

As Turnbull points out, it was the contribution of this modern analysis to show that ideas of number, variable, and functionality were more fundamental than those of geometrical points, curves, and tangents which gave rise to them. It is to be noted that in *The Method of Fluxions* Newton first states the problems to be solved geometrically and then restates them in the terms of his new analysis. Was this done to lend weight to a statement which had disastrous consequences when British mathematicians referred to it in arguing the superiority of Newton's calculus? The statement occurs in the "Introduction" to the *Quadrature of Curves.* In asserting that the mathematical quantities treated in the analysis to follow are described by continuous motion. Newton added, "These geneses really take place in the nature of

things and are daily seen in the motion of bodies." By Newton's own differentiation of elements that are strictly mathematical from those that are physical and known by observation, as well as from his assertion that analysis by means of infinite equations is no less certain and exact than that of the common analysis, he would appear to be asserting only that we do see bodies passing from motion to rest and from rest to motion.

Yet the notion that geometrical concepts are fundamental in mathematics because of their close "analogy" to nature had prevailed in Barrow who was Newton's teacher. There is no significant departure from Barrow in Newton's work in mathematics up to 1665, which consisted in working over what he had learned from his teacher and from Descartes and Wallis, combined with some original contributions upon methods of infinite series and reversions of series. In the plague years of 1665-1667, he left Cambridge and entered upon a highly fruitful period of mathematical discoveries. J. M. Child[20] points out that "Within a few months, by November 13, 1665, he had so far perfected the method of fluxions that he was able to find the radius of the curvature of any curve at any point, and within another year was applying the method to problems on the theory of equations." The labors formed the groundwork of the *De Analysi* which he communicated to Barrow in July, 1669. Child asks, "Where then does the marvellous development of the later years come from? I suggest, as the source, Barrow's *Lectiones Geometricae*; as the opportunity, Newton's help in preparing them for press; as the occasion, *the removal of the hampering geometrical influence of Barrow*; as the spur, the problems of gravitation and the preparation of the *Principia.*"

In the *Quadrature of Curves,* Newton declares that it is the mind which contributes in the reasoning of his analysis "a method of determining quantities from the velocities of the motions of increments, with which they are generated, denominating the increments by the name of *fluxions* and the generated quantities *fluents.*" The ideas of space and time are designated as mathematical terms and not as physical concepts.

> Since we have no estimation of time except in so far as it is expounded and measured by equable spatial motion, and further, since we may compare quantities of the same kind and also the increments and decrements of their mutual velocities, for that reason I shall not be mindful of time formally in what follows, but from the proposed quantities which are of the same kind I shall conceive another to be increased by an equable motion, to which the rest shall be referred to as the time, and so to which the name of time may be deservedly attributed by analogy.

In conceiving time as a fundamental variable, what's in the name attributed by analogy? Is some dependence upon geometry or upon nature being argued as conferring legitimacy upon the method in its elements and terms?

After defining *Fluents* and *Fluxions* with their notations, Newton states the two problems to be solved: Problem I: "The Length of the Space described being continually (that is, at all Times) given, to find the Velocity of the Motion at the Time proposed." Problem II: "The Velocity of the Motion being continually given; to find the Length of the Space described at any Time proposed." Restated, Problem I reads: "The Relation of Flowing quantities to one another being given, to determine the Relation of their Fluxions." And Problem II: "An Equation being proposed, including the Fluxion of Quantities, to find the Relation of the Quantities to one another." The idea of quantity infinitely increased or diminished is a logical tool in the solution of physical problems, and is nowhere considered to be more than that by Newton. Although concern for the use of mathematics as an instrument of investigation and demonstration can legitimately have regard for an analogy with nature, the notion that mathematical ideas must correspond to empirically grounded concepts is not championed by him. In physical science, Newton states, we have to do with "such principles as have been received by mathematicians, and are confirmed by abundance of experiments." Newton's mathematical way in physical science, as I have tried to show, requires mathematical experimentalism in which measurements and rules of measure prepare the mechanical principles from which demonstrative reasoning proceeds. Mathematical analysis *per se* is a logic of reasoning advancing concepts requiring no appeal to geometry or to nature. At the same time, as developed by Newton, it was a tool devised to assist in the solution of physical problems.

What was the source of the difficulties in which British mathematicians were caught in their defense of Newton's method of fluxions, first, against Leibniz, and secondly, against Berkeley? The argument presented in the *Commercium Epistolicum* was trapped in a dilemma. Holding that Newton was the original inventor of the calculus and Leibniz the borrower, it was essential to argue that there was nothing to be found in the Leibnizian method that was not in Newton's. Thus Article IV states that "The differential method is one and the same with the method of fluxions, excepting the name and mode of notation." The same argument appears in Humphry Ditton[21] in the statement that the two methods "agree perfectly in all their Operations as to the Point of Practice." Yet the defenders felt it incumbent upon them to maintain the *superiority* and not merely the priority of the fluxional method. The legitimate arguments would have been, first, that of the simplicity and efficiency of the Newtonian method in respect to principles, notation, and operations, could this have been made out; and, second, that of the pow-

er to solve problems presented, *e.g.,* the problem of the curve of quickest descent proposed by John Bernoulli in 1696. But Hayes,[22] Raphson,[23] and Keill[24] in putting Leibniz under (and subsequently James Jurin[25] and Colson[26] in reply to Berkeley's attack in *The Analyst*) argued, with Ditton, that "The Fundamental Principles which the **Method of Fluxions** is built upon, and proceeds (in all its Operations) from; appear to be more accurate, clear, and convincing, than those of the differential calculus."

In seeking to establish an asserted "great difference" between the two methods, two extra-mathematical arguments were introduced. The first was a theory of knowledge which insisted that mathematical ideas framed in the mind or imagination had legitimacy only so far as abstraction from physical objects and processes, or analogy with them, could be shown. The second was a metaphysical contention that only that which has a being in geometry and nature is eligible to be asserted as an element in mathematics. Conceivability upon an empirical basis and reference to physical reality were the two criteria. Both arguments were employed to repudiate the infinitesimals of the Leibnizian calculus. Newton's rejection of infinitely small quantities in the **Quadrature of Curves** was affirmed by the defenders of Newton, who ignored or tried to rationalize away Newton's use in the **Principia** of moments as infinitely little parts.

A typical argument is one appearing in Volume 29, No. 342 of the *Philosophical Transactions* attributed to Keill.

> We have no Ideas of infinitely little Quantities, and therefore Mr. Newton introduced Fluxions into his Method, that it might proceed with finite Quantities as much as possible. It is more Natural and Geometrical, because founded on the prime ratios of nascent quantities, which have a being in Geometry, while Indivisibles, upon which the Differential Method is founded, have no Being either in Geometry or in Nature.

Having committed themselves to the argument that "the idea of the generation of quantities" is to be admitted into mathematics, but not Leibniz's infinitesimals, because the latter are both inconceivable and have no being in nature, the British mathematicians became vulnerable to precisely the objections advanced by Berkeley. If it be held that mathematical ideas must have this double warrant of empirical conceivability and existential reality, where in our knowledge of nature are we entitled to assert, Berkeley asks, "quantities infinitely less than the least discernible Quantity; and other infinitely less than the preceding infinitesimals, and so on without end or limit?" Discernible quantity and assignable number, says Berkeley, are intelligible and proper notions; but the infinites of the modern analysis are such that "we shall discover much Emptiness, Darkness, and confusion; nay, if I mistake not, direct Impossibilities and Contradictions."

Neither Berkeley nor his opponents differentiated the meaning of terms assigned within a mathematical system in its procedures from ideas about existence which are subject to an empirical criterion of meaning.

> Now as our Sense is strained and puzzled with the perception of Objects extremely minute, even so the Imagination, which Faculty derives from Sense, is very much strained and puzzled to frame clear Ideas of the least Particles of time, or the least Increments generated therein: and much more so to comprehend the Moments, or those Increments of the flowing Quantities in *statu nascenti,* in their very first origin or beginning to exist, before they become finite Particles. And it seems still more difficult, to conceive the abstracted Velocities of such nascent imperfect Entities. But the Velocities of the Velocities, the second, third, fourth, and fifth Velocities, &c. exceed, if I mistake not, all Humane Understanding. The further the Mind analyseth and pursueth these fugitive Ideas, the more it is lost and bewildered; the Objects, at first fleeting and minute, and soon vanishing out of sight. Certainly in any Sense, a second or a third Fluxion seems an obscure Mystery.[27]

Berkeley had a lot of fun in deriding "shadowy entities" and the "ghosts of departed quantities." If the defenders of Newton had acknowledged that Newton used infinitely small quantities in his calculus up to 1704 but had then changed his system, the contradictions pointed out by Berkeley in comparing the **Quadrature of Curves** with statements about *moments* in the **Principia** would not have proved so embarrassing. In any event, Berkeley prodded Robins[28] and Maclaurin[29] to an examination of the foundations of the calculus. Both responded by rejecting the extra-mathematical arguments which their predecessors had advanced in supporting the superiority of the fluxional method and each contributed clarification of the idea of limits. Newton himself had a hand in his defense in claims made of priority and superiority, and so cannot be exempted from criticism brought against the arguments of his friends. Yet he does not assert, as they did, that the foundations of mathematics are to be sought in correspondence of mathematical terms with physical properties. Such a supposition, either on rationalistic or empiricistic theorizing, is offered to account for the success of mathematical reasoning in solving physical problems. Newton rejects both Descartes' *a priori* rationalism in mathematics and the notion that abstraction from experienced objects needs to be argued in support of mathematical ideas. The mathematical way of proceeding in physical science requires no bond beyond itself to connect physical phenomena with mathematical determinations; for the very procedures

of quantifying data by measurement and of instituting rules of measure results in the mathematical-physical principles upon which demonstration depends. The devising of mathematical concepts and instruments for the solution of problems presented is the mind's work. The development of an analytical principle is itself a passage from problems presented in geometry and mechanics to universal methods of expansion, differentiation, and integration.

Notes

[1] The title of this essay is taken from a passage in Newton's *System of the World*: ". . . our purpose is only to trace out the quantity and properties of this force from the phenomena, and to apply what we discover in some simple cases as principles, by which, in a mathematical way, we may estimate the effects thereof in more involved cases, for it would be endless and impossible to bring every particular to direct and immediate observation. We said, *in a mathematical way,* to avoid all questions about the nature or quality of this force, which we would not be understood to determine by any hypothesis; . . ."

[2] *A View of Sir Isaac Newton's Philosophy* (London, 1728), Introduction, 23.

[3] *The Metaphysical Foundations of Modern Physical Science* (New York, 1927).

[4] "Newton's Natural Philosophy: Its Problems and Consequences," in *Philosophical Essays in Honor of Edgar Arthur Singer, Jr.,* ed. by Clarke and Nahm (Philadelphia, 1942).

[5] Burtt devotes four pages to "The Mathematical Aspect" of Newton's method (*op. cit., 204-207*). He refers to the passage in the *Opticks* where Newton speaks of "determining mathematically all kinds of phenomena of colours which could be produced by refractions." From this "determination" and the theorems established, Newton concludes that "the science of colours becomes a speculation as truly mathematical as any other part of optics." Burtt is quite right in saying that the science of colors was esteemed to be "truly mathematical" by Newton "as a result of his precise experimental determination of the qualities of refrangibility and reflexibility." But what, then, is this "precise experimental determination" (measurement) and what do Newton's actual procedures, as well as his statements, reveal as its place and importance methodologically? Burtt does not explore the question but stops short in saying only that "Newton's eagerness thus to reduce another group of phenomena to mathematical formulae illustrates again the fundamental place of mathematics in his work; but as regards the method by which he accomplished that reduction his statements are too brief to be of much aid."

Randall's account of Newton's "mathematical experi-mentalism" presents no discussion of "measure" as this term is used in Newton, nor makes mention of what might be the significance of statements in Newton about measurement.

[6] *Matter and Gravity in Newton's Physical Philosophy* (London, 1926), 233. "Newton, however, employing mathematics as a method of procedure, presupposed . . . that each step in a mathematical demonstration is true of the physical world."

[7] *Sir Isaac Newton's Mathematical Principles of Natural Philosophy,* tr. by Florian Cajori (Berkeley, 1934), 192.

[8] *Op. cit.,* 24-25.

[9] *Phil. Tr.* Vol. VII, No. 85, pp. 5004-5005. The following quotation is typical. "You know, the proper Method for *inquiring* after the properties of things is to deduce them from Experiments. . . . Therefore I could wish all objections suspended taken from Hypothesis or any other heads than these two: of shewing the insufficiency of Experiments to determine these Quaeries or prove any other parts of the Theory, by assigning the flaws and defects in my conclusion drawn from them; or of producing other Experiments which directly contradict me, if any such may seem to occur."

[10] *Opticks* (London, 1730), 380.

[11] *Opticks,* 113, 114.

[12] *Ibid.,* 114.

[13] *Opticks,* 65.

[14] *Opticks,* 180. "In the first two Columns are express'd the Obliquities of the incident and emergent Rays to the Plate of the Air, that is, their Angles of Incidence and Refraction. In the third Column the Diameter of any colour'd Ring at those Obliquities is expressed in Parts, of which ten constitute the Diameter when the Rays are perpendicular. And in the fourth Column the Thickness of the Air at the Circumference of that Ring is expressed in Parts, of which also ten constitute its Thickness when the Rays are perpendicular."

[15] *Newton and the Origin of Colours* (London, 1934), 42.

[16] *Philosophical Magazine* (Nov. 1852), 321-330, "On the Early History of Infinitesimals in England." Also, *Essays in the Life and Work of Newton* (Chicago and London, 1914), II, "A Short Account of Some Recent Discoveries Relative to the Controversy on the Invention of Fluxions," 67-101.

[17] *A History of the Conceptions of Limits and Fluxions in Great Britain from Newton to Woodhouse* (Chicago and London, 1919), 36.

[18] *Newton and the Origin of Colours,* 31.

[19] *The Mathematical Discoveries of Newton* (London and Glasgow, 1945).

[20] "Newton and the Art of Discovery," in *Isaac Newton, 1642—1727, A Memorial Volume,* ed. by W. J. Greenstreet (London, 1927), 122-124.

[21] *An Institution of Fluxions* (London, 1726; 2nd edition).

[22] *A Treatise of Fluxions* (London, 1704).

[23] *The History of Fluxions* (London, 1715).

[24] *Phil. Trans.,* Vol. 29, No. 342, pp. 205-206. "An Account of a Book entitled Commercium Epistolicum. . . ."

[25] *Geometry, No Friend to Infidelity;* or a Defense of Sir Isaac Newton and the British Mathematicians in a Letter Addressed to the Author of the Analyst (London, 1734). Written under the pseudonym of Philalethes Cantabrigiensis; *The Minute Mathematician* (London, 1735).

[26] *The History of Fluxions* (London, 1736).

[27] *The Analyst: or a Discourse Addressed to an Infidel Mathematician* (London, 1734), 8-9.

[28] *A Discourse Concerning the Nature and Certainty of Sir Isaac Newton's Methods of Fluxions, and of Prime and Ultimate Ratios* (London, 1735).

[29] *A Treatise of Fluxions,* 2 vols. (Edinburgh, 1742).

I. Bernard Cohen (essay date 1952)

SOURCE: A preface to *Opticks, or, a Treatise of the Reflections, Refractions, Inflections, and Colours of Light,* by Isaac Newton, Dover Publications, 1952, pp. ix-lxxvii.

[*In the following essay, Cohen reviews the content, textual history, and contemporary and later reception of Newton's* Opticks.]

Great creations—whether of science or of art—can never be viewed dispassionately. The **Opticks,** like any other scientific masterpiece, is a difficult book to view objectively; first, because of the unique place of its author, Isaac Newton, in the history of science, and, second, because of the doctrine it contains. One of the most readable of all the great books in the history of physical science, the **Opticks** remained out of print for a century and a half, until about two decades ago, while the **Principia** was constantly being reprinted. One of the reasons for this neglect was that the **Opticks** was out of harmony with the ideas of 19th-century physics. The burden of this book was an exposition of the "wrong" (i.e., corpuscular) theory of light,—even though it also contained many of the basic principles of the "correct" (i.e., wave) theory. Not only had Newton erred in his choice of the corpuscular theory, but also he apparently had found no insuperable difficulty in simultaneously embracing features of two opposing theories. It was not just that Newton couldn't make up his mind between them; that could be easily forgiven. Rather, by adopting a combination of the two theories at once, he had violated one of the major canons of 19th-century physics, which held that whenever there are two conflicting theories, a crucial experiment must always decide uniquely in favor of one or the other.

Every age finds a particular sympathy for certain masterpieces of science and of art. Our present age lends a particularly appreciative eye and ear to the paintings of Lucas Cranach the elder and Jheronimus Bosch, and the poetry of John Donne and William Blake. Since our reading in the past great works of science is conditioned by the science of our own time, our interpretations and evaluations are as different from those of the last century as our tastes in poetry and art. We esteem the **Principia** as much as the Victorians did, but we know its limitations and cannot help but read it in the light of the theory of relativity. Today our point of view is influenced by the theory of photons and matter waves, or the more general principle of complementarity of Niels Bohr; and we may read with a new interest Newton's ideas on the interaction of light and matter or his explanation of the corpuscular and undulatory aspects of light. It is not surprising, therefore, that the last decades have witnessed a revival of Newton's **Opticks,** finally reprinted in 1931 by Messrs. G. Bell and Sons of London with a foreword by Albert Einstein and introduction by E. T. (now Sir Edmund) Whittaker, a new printing of which now makes this work again available thanks to the enterprise of Mr. Hayward Cirker of the Dover Publications. Sir Edmund's introduction delineates the effect on the reputation of the **Opticks** of the vicissitudes of the corpuscular theory of light which Newton espoused, and the general feeling during the latter 19th century that since the wave theory of light was the only true explanation of optical processes, the **Opticks** was a work of interest chiefly to the historian rather than the scientist, exhibiting, despite its brilliant exposition, an unhappy example of how wrong a great man might be.

So great, however, was Newton's fame among men of science that a number of writers on optics, especially among the British, took care to inform their readers that Newton's corpuscular theory, while clearly incorrect, was nevertheless a very ingenious creation and had been fully able to explain all of the facts about light known in Newton's day. In other words, this theory was not wholly relegated to the realms of the antique and the curious but was rather presented to the reader with an apology and a discussion of the 17th-century situation in physics. The book itself makes plain that Newton's theory was in fact adequate to the phenomena it attempted to explain, and it was in many respects better than the rival theory of Huygens. Yet the sympathetic explanation of Newton's approach to optics, in terms of the physics of his day, is conspicuous in such books because the authors of scientific treatises in the 19th century were not usually quite so generous to their predecessors when it came to "erroneous" theories of the past. Their attitude is all the more remarkable when we see that they usually felt bound to add that Newton's choice of the "wrong" theory of light had been a serious impediment to the search for the "correct" theory.

Thus, in a book on optics oft reprinted during the 19th century, Dionysius Lardner wrote of the corpuscular theory of light: ". . . probably, from veneration of his [Newton's] authority, English philosophers, until recently, have very generally given the preference to that theory."[1] And as late as 1909 Sir Arthur Schuster, in a general treatise on optics, still felt it incumbent upon him to apologise for the apparent failure of the greatest of British men of science and wrote: "While there is no doubt that Newton's great authority kept back the progress of the undulatory theory for more than a century, this is more than compensated by the fact that the science of Optics owes the scientific foundation of its experimental investigation in great part to him."[2]

The revival of the wave theory of light, in opposition to the corpuscular theory advocated by Newton, was due largely to the labors of Dr. Thomas Young who, in a series of three papers published in 1802-04 in the *Philosophical Transactions* of the Royal Society[3], added a new fundamental principle, the so-called principle of interference, and established the wave theory on a basis that has from then until now remained unassailable[4]. Despite Young's insistence in all his papers that his own work derived from the experiments and suppositions of Newton, and his introduction of many quotations from Newton to show that he was modifying rather than destroying the Newtonian doctrine, Young was attacked mercilessly. The most important antagonist appears to have been Lord Brougham, in all probability the author of two anonymous discussions of Young's work in the *Edinburgh Review*. Brougham was particularly incensed at the suggestion of Newton's fallibility and he accused Young of having insinuated "that Sir Isaac Newton was but a sorry philosopher."[5] Had not Fresnel and Arago in France become interested in the work of Young, it seems probable that the influence of the great name of Newton would effectively have blocked any pursuit of Young's ideas—at least in England—and any further development of the wave theory of light. This situation is not unlike that in mathematics during the 18th century, when a blind adherence to the Newtonian algorithm and a complete rejection of the Leibnizian or Continental methods seem to have deadened the sensibilities of British mathematicians and to have produced an era of almost complete sterility with regard to progress in the calculus.[6]

The comparison of works of science and works of art is especially relevant to our understanding of the history of the reputation of the *Opticks.* Having known Picasso and Dali, Cranach and Bosch do not seem as strange to us as they would have to a Victorian spectator. Similarly, having known Planck, Einstein, Bohr, de Broglie, Schrödinger and Heisenberg, Newton's suggestions concerning the interaction of particles of light and particles of matter, and his adumbration of a corpuscular theory of light that also embraced undulatory behaviour, are not to us—as they were to the Victorian physicists—a puzzling set of ideas, seemingly devoid of any physical meaning and, therefore, outside the limits of comprehensibility. One of the great classic treatises on light of the late 19th century was written by Thomas Preston, Professor of Natural Philosophy in University College, Dublin. First printed in 1890, it still served as a principal textbook for this subject in the '30's (in the fifth edition published in 1928). It was notable for its magnificent expository style and the clarity of its explanations, and also for the valuable historical discussions and long extracts from Newton's *Opticks;* indeed, many students of physics, including the writer, learned of Newton's *Opticks* for the first time through reading the selections printed in Preston's *Theory of Light.* One group of extracts was intended to present Newton's "theory in his own words" and to "show how much more closely than is generally supposed it resembles the undulatory theory now accepted." Preston wanted his readers to understand that Newton's position was, if not exactly that of the late 19th century, at least very much like it. By "suitably framing his fundamental postulates," Preston wrote, "an ingenious exponent of the emission [or corpuscular] theory . . . might fairly meet all the objections that have been raised against it." Yet, when these "necessary postulates" are introduced, the corpuscles become endowed "with the periodic characteristics of a wave motion, and . . . the corpuscles themselves may be eliminated. . . ."[7] Thus Preston's attitude was to "save the theory" by eliminating its fundamental corpuscular character. Writing long before the rise of quantum mechanics, Preston could not find any virtue in a theory of light which simultaneously em-

braced corpuscular and undulatory aspects and he therefore destroyed the former in order to preserve the latter.

Yet if Newton's *Opticks* appears to contain ideas that seem like anticipations of our present concepts, we must be very careful not to make too much of it. For, if we were to praise Newton today, simply because his statements about the dual properties of light—corpuscular and undulatory—and the interaction of light and matter are in some ways like those of the 20th century, we are in a sense adopting a procedure of as little worth as did those who disparaged Newton 75 years ago because his optical theory did not quite meet the requirements of late 19th-century physics. However great Newton's insight may have been—and it was almost incredibly penetrating—it was hardly sufficient to give him a prevision of quantum theory; nor to enable him to see two centuries ahead to the science of spectroscopy built upon the foundation of his investigations of the prismatic spectrum of the sun; nor to allow him a guess as to what would be the problems of black-body radiation and the failure of the theorem of the equipartition of energy, the very data for which were not to be discovered until more than 150 years after his death. Nor could Newton have had even the faintest glimmering of the photo-electric effect and the theory of electrons, since in Newton's day the subject of electricity had not yet attained the status of a separate branch of science. Even the distinction between conductors and non-conductors had not yet been made; nor had the two kinds of electric charge (vitreous and resinous) been yet discovered; and Franklin, who produced in middle age the first unitary theory of electrical action, was not born until two years after the *Opticks* had been published.

We may find an appeal in the *Opticks* because we know the theory of photons and quantum mechanics, but we must also keep in mind that the physics of the 20th century was developed from the brute facts of experiment of the late 19th century and the early 20th, and in reaction to the inadequacy of the then-current theories which could not account for the incontrovertible observed data. The physics of the 20th century derives directly from the physics of the 19th century, not from a conscious return to the physics of the 18th century and Newton's *Opticks.* But the physics of the 20th century does in a definite sense derive from that of the 18th, since the latter produced the physics of the 19th century just as the physics of the 19th century, in turn, produced that of the 20th. In terms of the physics of our own time, then, the importance of the *Opticks* does not lie in any possible kind of prevision of the theory of photons, but rather in the effect it had on the physicists in its own day and on the generations immediately following its publication. In making an evaluation of the *Opticks,* therefore, we must choose between (1) the historical or (2) the antiquarian approach to the development of science—between the historian's evaluation of Newton's achievement in terms of the living creation and its influence on the scientists in the century following the publication of his results, or the antiquarian's sifting of the *disjecta membra* of the *Opticks* (often out of context) for an occasional "precursorship" of one or another 20th-century physical concept.

My own interest in the *Opticks* was aroused in the course of extended research into the theories of electricity as developed in the 18th century, as a part of a larger study on the growth in the 18th century of concepts crucial in 19th-century physics, such as charge, field, potential, force, action-at-a distance, atom, energy, etc.[8] I soon found that of the many references to Newton in 18th-century electrical writings only a very small number were to the *Principia,* the greater part by far were to the *Opticks.* This was true not alone of the electrical writings but also in other fields of experimental enquiry.

As an example of the influence of the *Opticks,* we may look at the *Vegetable Staticks* of Stephen Hales, a work of the highest rank among experimental treatises, and one that has earned for its author the title of father of plant physiology. This book provides a splendid example of the application of quantitative methods to biology in its account of precise measurements of leaf growth, root pressure, and kindred subjects, and its quantitative studies on air and gases, just as in the companion volume, *Haemostaticks,* Hales initiated measurements of the blood pressure in animals. The *Vegetable Staticks* bears on the verso of the title page Newton's imprimatur as President of the Royal Society: "Feb. 16, 1726/7. *Imprimatur* Isaac Newton. *Pr. Reg. Soc.*" The first mention of Newton occurs in the preface, where Hales notes how "it appears by many chymico-statical Experiments, that there is diffused thro' all natural, mutually attracting bodies, a large proportion of particles, which, as the first Author of this important discovery, Sir Isaac Newton, observes, are capable of being thrown off from dense bodies by heat or fermentation into a vigorously elastick and repelling state . . .", a reference to the *Opticks* (see, below, Qu. 30 and Qu. 31). In addition to a discussion of "attraction: that universal principle which is so operative in all the very different works of nature,"[9] without mentioning Newton's name, there are by actual count 17 places in the book where Newton's name occurs. Of these, 15 are either quotations from the *Opticks* or references to the *Opticks,* and neither of the remaining two are concerned with the *Principia*: one discusses Newton's mode of calibrating thermometers (described in the *Phil. Trans. Roy. Soc.*[10]) and the other is a quotation containing Newton's theory about the dissolution of metals arising from the attractive force exerted by the "particles of acids" (taken from the introduction to vol. 2 of John Harris' *Lexicon Technicum*[11]).

In order to understand the extraordinary appeal that the *Opticks* had in the 18th century, we must compare it to the *Principia*[12]—in scientific, philosophic, and speculative content; literary style; and the approach of the author to the subject. On such a comparison, an important difference between the two books is immediately apparent. The *Opticks* invites and holds the attention of the non-specialist reader while the other, the *Principia,* is as austere and forbidding to the non-specialist as it can possibly be. Of course, the general reader of the *Opticks* would be more interested in the final section of "Queries" than in the rest of the work, just as the general reader of the *Principia* would be drawn to the General Scholium at the end of Book Three; but whereas in the *Opticks* such a reader could enjoy almost 70 pages, in the *Principia* there would be but four. The latter would discuss for him the mechanism of universal gravitation and give him a hint of the direction of Newton's thinking about this important problem; but the former would allow the reader to roam, with great Newton as his guide, through the major unresolved problems of science and even the relation of the whole world of nature to Him who had created it.

Wholly apart from the general reader, the scientist who was not well trained in mathematics could make little headway in the *Principia.* Not only was this masterpiece written in an austere mathematical style, consisting largely of definitions, theorems, lemmas, scholia, and demonstrations, but it was in a definite sense written in an archaic mathematical language. Newton did not consistently apply his own discovery of the calculus, but preferred to use the geometrical style of Apollonios and Euclid—whose works he recommended, along with others, to the theologian William Bentley who wished to present the work of Newton in a popular way as proof of the wisdom of the Creator of the universe. Bentley had first written to the Scotch mathematician John Craigie[13] and appears to have been so alarmed by the number of mathematical authors recommended by Craigie as being necessary to understand the *Principia,* that he then applied to Newton himself for advice. The latter's list is formidable enough; a non-mathematician would have to be in earnest indeed to undertake the preparation which Newton deemed necessary for reading the *Principia* even with the limited objective of a "first perusal," for which Newton advised that "it's enough if you understand the Propositions with some of the Demonstrations which are easier than the rest."[14]

The famous philosopher John Locke was more sensible than Bentley and freely admitted that his mathematics would never be equal to reading the great book. He was satisfied with an examination of the reasoning behind the propositions and corollaries to be drawn from them. To be sure that all was well, he inquired of the Dutch physicist Christiaan Huygens whether the mathematics were sound, and once assured that this was the case he was content with the physical principles, the doctrine the book expounded, without bothering about the proofs and details of the text itself. We have an account of Locke's procedure written by Newton's disciple and friend, the Rev. J. T. Desaguliers, who informs us that he was told the story "several times by Sir *Isaac Newton* himself":

> But to return to the *Newtonian Philosophy:* Tho' its Truth is supported by Mathematicks, yet its Physical Discoveries may be communicated without. The great Mr. *Locke* was the first who became a *Newtonian Philosopher* without the help of Geometry; for having asked Mr. *Huygens,* whether all the mathematical *Propositions* in Sir *Isaac's* **Principia** were true, and being told he might depend upon their Certainty; he took them for granted, and carefully examined the Reasonings and *Corollaries* drawn from them, became Master of all the Physics, and was fully convinc'd of the great Discoveries contained in that Book.[15]

Newton himself had given a warrant for Locke's procedure in the opening lines of the third book of the *Principia,* where he wrote that in the two preceding books he had "laid down the principles of philosophy; principles not philosophical but mathematical," that these "principles are the laws and conditions of certain motions, and powers of forces"; lest they "should have appeared of themselves dry and barren, I have illustrated them here and there with some philosophical scholiums. . . ."

Desaguliers contrasts Locke's reading of the *Principia* with the way in which "he read the *Opticks* with pleasure, acquainting himself with every thing in them that was not merely mathematical."[16] The merely mathematical section consisted of "Two Treatises of the Species and Magnitude of Curvilinear Figures," which Newton omitted after the first edition, since they were in no way connected with the text of the *Opticks.*

Another distinction between the *Opticks* and the *Principia,* apart from the mathematical difficulty of the latter, is that the *Opticks* was written in English while the *Principia* was written in Latin. While this did not make as much difference in the 17th century as it would today, there is no question but what the austere Latin of the *Principia* was as characteristic of its essentially mathematical form as the gentle English of the *Opticks* was characteristic of the intimate style of that work[17]. For in the *Opticks* Newton did not adopt the motto to be found in the *Principia*—*Hypotheses non fingo*; I frame no hypotheses—but, so to speak, let himself go, allowing his imagination full reign and by far exceeding the bounds of experimental evidence.

It should, of course, be borne in mind that Newton's phrase *Hypotheses non fingo* was applied by him to the nature of the gravitational attraction and was never a guiding principle in his work. It is equally clear, however, that many of the readers of the *Principia* tended to think of this motto as characteristic of the book. Thus Roger Cotes, who superintended the preparation of the second edition of the *Principia* under Newton's direction and who wrote a preface to it, begged Newton to revise "the last Sheet of your Book which is not yet printed off," since he felt he could not "undertake to answer any one who should assert that You do *Hypothesim fingere,* [since] I think You seem tacitly to make this supposition that the Attractive force resides in the Central Body."[18] In a letter written in 1672 by Newton to Henry Oldenberg, Secretary of the Royal Society, in response to an objection that had been raised to his first publication on optics, Newton discussed the function of hypotheses at length:

> For the best and safest method of philosophizing seems to be, first diligently to investigate the properties of things and establish them by experiment, and then to seek hypotheses to explain them. For hypotheses ought to be fitted merely to explain the properties of things and not attempt to predetermine them except in so far as they can be an aid to experiments. If any one offers conjectures about the truth of things from the mere possibility of hypotheses, I do not see how anything certain can be determined in any science; for it is always possible to contrive hypotheses, one after another, which are found rich in new tribulations. Wherefore I judged that one should abstain from considering hypotheses as from a fallacious argument, and that the force of their opposition must be removed, that one may arrive at a maturer and more general explanation.[19]

The first book of the *Opticks* deals with the reflection and refraction of light, the formation of images, the production of spectra by prisms, the properties of colored light and the composition of white light and its dispersion. Based on definitions and axioms, and embodying a wealth of experimental data, this first book had, according to Newton, the "Design . . . not to explain the Properties of Light by Hypotheses, but to propose and prove them by Reason and Experiments." The second book, devoted largely to the production of colors in what we would call interference phenomena, contains no such declaration, and it is here that Newton introduces the notion of "fits" of easy transmission and easy reflection, and kindred concepts not derived by induction from experiments. And although Newton points out (p. 280) that on the score of fits of easy transmission and easy reflection: "What kind of action or disposition this is; Whether it consists in a circulating or a vibrating motion of the Ray, or of the Medium, or something else, I do not here enquire," he adds:

> Those that are averse from assenting to any new Discoveries, but such as they can explain by an Hypothesis, may for the present suppose, that as

Stones by falling upon Water put the Water into an undulating Motion, and all Bodies by percussion excite vibrations in the Air; so the Rays of Light, by impinging on any refracting or reflecting Surface, excite vibrations in the refracting or reflecting Medium or Substance, and by exciting them agitate the solid parts of the refracting or reflecting Body, and by agitating them cause the Body to grow warm or hot; that the vibrations thus excited . . . move faster than the Rays so as to overtake them; . . . and, by consequence, that every Ray is successively disposed to be easily reflected, or easily transmitted, by every vibration which overtakes it. But whether this Hypothesis be true or false I do not here consider. I content my self with the bare Discovery, that the Rays of Light are by some cause or other alternately disposed to be reflected or refracted for many vicissitudes.

The second book thus admits hypotheses, although without any consideration of their truth or falsity. In the third (and last) book, the opening section deals with Newton's experiments on diffraction, followed by the famous Queries in which, as we shall see, Newton introduced a variety of "hypotheses"—not alone on light, but on a great many subjects of physics and philosophy, as if in his final work he had emptied his mind of the conjectures he had accumulated in a life-time of scientific activity. Clearly, *Hypotheses non fingo* could not be applied to the *Opticks.* And it is, in a very real sense, the progressively conjectural character of this book that makes it so interesting to read. As Albert Einstein saw so clearly when he wrote his admirable Foreword, this book "alone can afford us the enjoyment of a look at the personal activity of this unique man."

In its own day, the *Opticks* aroused interest in a way that was directly related to the *Principia.* Not only did the reputation of the *Principia* create a ready market for a more readable book by its author, but in the *Principia* Newton had raised important philosophical questions which he discussed at greater length in the *Opticks,* in the Queries at the end of Book Three, and which Newton mentioned—but only in passing—in the famous General Scholium to the third book of the *Principia,* addressed to the nature of the gravitational attraction between bodies, and in which the phrase *Hypotheses non fingo* appeared.

Newton had shown that celestial and terrestrial motions were in accordance with a law of universal gravitation in which the attraction between any two bodies in the universe depends only on their masses and (inversely) on the square of the distance between them. This led to an attribution to Newton of ideas that he abhorred. One was that since the gravitational attraction is a function of the masses of bodies irrespective of any other properties save their separation in space, this attraction arises simply from the existence of matter.

This materialist position was castigated by Newton in a letter to Bentley in which he said: "You sometimes speak of gravity as essential and inherent to matter. Pray, do not ascribe that notion to me; for the cause of gravity is what I do not pretend to know. . . ." And in another letter to Bentley, he amplified his position: "It is inconceivable, that inanimate brute matter should, without the mediation of something else, which is not material, operate upon and affect other matter without mutual contact. . . ."[20]

Another point of argument arose in a letter written by Leibniz which had been published in an English translation. Cotes wrote to Newton of "some prejudices which have been industriously laid against" the *Principia,* "As that it deserts Mechanical causes, is built upon Miracles, & recurrs to Occult qualitys." Newton would find "a very extraordinary Letter of Mr Leibnitz to Mr Hartsoeker which will confirm what I have said," Cotes continued, in "a Weekly Paper called *Memoires of Literature* & sold by Ann Baldwin in Warwick-Lane."[21]

In the preface which he wrote to the second edition of the *Principia,* Cotes replied to Leibniz—although without mentioning his name; ". . . twere better to neglect him," he had written to Newton.[22] Cotes also discussed the general nature of gravitation and forces acting at a distance. For this second edition, Newton wrote the famous General Scholium to Book Three, in which he attacked the vortex theory of Descartes, declared that the "most beautiful system of the sun, planets, and comets, could only proceed from the counsel and dominion of an intelligent and powerful Being," and discussed the nature of God, concluding: "And thus much concerning God; to discourse of whom from the appearance of things, does certainly belong to Natural Philosophy."[23] Newton then addressed himself to the problem of what gravitation is and how it might work, admitting that no assignment had been made of "the cause of this power" whose action explains the phenomena of the heavens and the tides of the seas. This is followed by the famous penultimate paragraph which reads:

> But hitherto I have not been able to discover the cause of those properties of gravity from phenomena, and I frame no hypotheses; for whatever is not deduced from the phenomena is to be called an hypothesis; and hypotheses, whether metaphysical or physical, whether of occult qualities or mechanical, have no place in experimental philosophy. . . . And to us it is enough that gravity does really exist, and act according to the laws which we have explained, and abundantly serves to account for all the motions of the celestial bodies, and of our sea.

It was apparently the purpose of the General Scholium to prevent any misunderstanding of Newton's position such as had been made by Bentley and Leibniz after reading the first edition of the *Principia* in which this General Scholium did not appear. Yet the cautious wording prevented the reader from gaining any insight into Newton's actual beliefs on this subject, as contained, for example, in a letter to Boyle written on 28 February 1678/9, prior to the publication of the *Principia* and not published until the mid-18th century. In this letter Newton wrote out his speculations concerning the "cause of gravity" and attempted to explain gravitational attraction by the operation of an all-pervading "aether" consisting of "parts differing from one another in subtility by indefinite degrees."[24] Some hint, but not more, of Newton's view was contained in the final paragraph of the above General Scholium, in which Newton wrote:

> And now we might add something concerning a certain most subtle spirit which pervades and lies hid in all gross bodies; by the force and action of which spirit the particles of bodies attract one another at near distances, and cohere, if contiguous; and electric bodies operate to greater distances as well repelling as attracting the neighboring corpuscles; and light is emitted, reflected, refracted, inflected, and heats bodies; and all sensation is excited, and the members of animal bodies move at the command of the will, namely, by the vibrations of this spirit, mutually propagated along the solid filaments of the nerves, from the outward organs of sense to the brain, and from the brain into the muscles. But these are things that cannot be explained in few words, nor are we furnished with that sufficiency of experiments which is required to an accurate determination and demonstration of the laws by which this electric and elastic spirit operates.

Thus the 18th-century reader who had become convinced that the system of Newton's *Principia* accounted for the workings of the universe and then naturally enough wondered what the cause of gravity might be, was tantalized by the final statement that Newton might have elucidated this topic but had decided not to do so. Hungry for a further discussion of the nature of "this electric and elastic spirit," or "aether," so intimately associated with the behaviour of material bodies and the communication of animal sensation, such a reader would devour anything else that Newton wrote on the subject.

Since Newton devoted a considerable portion of the *Opticks* to this question, neatly avoided in the *Principia,* we can understand at once why the *Opticks* must have exerted so strong a fascination on men like John Locke and on all the others who wanted to know the cause of gravity and the fundamental principle of the universe. Indeed, in the 1717 edition of the *Opticks* Newton inserted an "Advertisement" . . . explicitly declaring that he did "not take Gravity for an Essential Property of Bodies," and nothing that among the new Queries or Questions added to the new edition was

"one Question concerning its Cause," Newton "chusing to propose it by way of a Question" since he was "not yet satisfied about it for want of experiments."

The first edition of the *Opticks* was published in English in 1704 and contained only the first 16 queries. The Latin version, prepared at Newton's suggestion by Samuel Clarke, was issued two years later in 1706; to it were added Queries 17-23 in which Newton discussed the nature of the aether.[25] Here he compared the production of water waves by a stone to the vibrations excited in the refracting or reflecting medium by particles of light (Qu. 17), and proposed the theory that the vibrations so excited "overtake the Rays of Light, and by overtaking them successively, put them into the fits of easy Reflexion and easy Transmission. . . ." He also suggested that the aether is a "much subtiler Medium than Air" and that its vibrations convey heat, both radiant heat which may pass through a vacuum and the heat communicated by hot bodies "to contiguous cold ones" (Qu. 18); it is also "more elastick and active" than air. This aether (Qu. 19, 20) is responsible for refraction and, because of its unequal density, also produces "Inflexions of the Rays of Light" or diffraction of the sort recorded by Grimaldi. Newton indicated (Qu. 21) his belief that the variations in density of the aether are the cause of gravitation; and he pointed out that this aether must be highly elastic to support the enormous speed of light, but that the aether does not (Qu. 22) interfere with the motions of planets and comets; and he compared the gravitational action of the aether to the action of electrified and magnetic bodies in attracting, respectively, "leaf Copper, or Leaf Gold, at . . . [a] distance . . . from the electrick Body. . . . And . . . through a Plate of Glass . . . to turn a magnetick Needle. . . ." The last of these new Queries (Qu. 23) relates the vibrations of the aether to vision and possibly to hearing.

One of the most interesting aspects of this group of Queries is that it follows in outline the letter written to Boyle some 20 years earlier, and which had not yet been published. While Newton was apparently willing to print his conjectures on the aether and gravitation in the Queries of the *Opticks,* when he came to revise the *Principia* for the second edition of 1713, seven years after the appearance of the Latin version of the *Opticks,* he was much more cautious. He refused, as we saw above, to discuss the cause of gravitation, begging off with the phrase *Hypotheses non fingo;*[26] and he actually declared that all one needs to know is that gravity exists, that it follows the law of the inverse square, and that it serves to describe the motions of the celestial bodies and the tides. Newton concluded the General Scholium with the statement that he might discuss the aether but refrained from doing so. While it can never be proved, it is possible that Newton's procedure in this matter may indicate an appreciation of the fundamentally differing character of his two books—the *Principia* with its mathematical demonstrations and general avoidance of speculation, and the *Opticks* with its large speculative content.

To be sure, the speculations of the *Opticks* were not hypotheses, at least to the extent that they were framed in questions. Yet if we use Newton's own definition, that "whatever is not deduced from the phenomena is to be called an hypothesis," they are hypotheses indeed. The question form may have been adopted in order to allay criticism, but it does not hide the extent of Newton's belief. For every one of the Queries is phrased in the negative! Thus Newton does not ask in a truly interrogatory way (Qu. I): "Do Bodies act upon Light at a distance . . . ?"—as if he did not know the answer. Rather, he puts it: "Do not Bodies act upon Light at a distance . . . ?"—as if he knew the answer well—"Why, of course they do!" But if the addition of the question mark made it possible for Newton to free himself from the restrictions imposed by that "sufficiency of experiments which is required to an accurate determination and demonstration of the laws," we can only be grateful for the opportunity to see the mind of Newton at work, and to share his profound inspiration. As it was said in the 18th century, any of the fine accounts of the Newtonian system of celestial mechanics—such as those of Pemberton, Maclaurin, and Voltaire—could afford the reader a sufficient understanding of the *Principia* which, therefore, need not be read in Newton's original; but when it came to the *Opticks,* no *abrégé* or *vulgarization* could take the place of Newton's own words.

A glance at the analytical table of contents will show the range of subjects covered by Newton in the *Opticks* and especially in the Queries. For the latter not only took up questions of light as such, and gravitation, but also chemistry, pneumatics, physiology, the circulation of the blood, metabolism and digestion, animal sensation, the Creation, the flood, the true nature of scientific inquiry, how to make experiments and how to draw the proper conclusions from them by induction, the relation of cause and effect, and natural philosophy in relation to moral philosophy. Here, then, was a rich intellectual feast for philosophers as well as scientists, for poets as well as experimenters, for theologians as well as painters, and for all amateurs of the products of the human imagination at its highest degree of refinement. Not only, therefore, did the *Opticks* come to enjoy a special place in 18th-century science, but also it had an appeal wholly its own for the British poets of the 18th century. Miss Marjorie Nicolson, in the course of her investigations of science and the literary imagination, arrived independently at the same conclusion concerning the *Opticks* and the 18th-century literary writers that I had found to be true of the *Opticks* and the 18th-century experimenters. "While reading widely in eighteenth-century poetry for other purposes," she writes, "I found myself constantly

teased by dozens of references to Newton which had nothing to do with the *Principia,* until I became persuaded that, among the poets, the *Opticks* was even more familiar than the more famous work."[27]

One reason why the *Opticks* should enjoy a greater vogue among experimenters than the *Principia* is plain: the *Opticks* was, in great part, an account of experiments performed by Newton and the conclusions drawn by him from the experimental results; but in the *Principia* Newton described only two or three important experiments that he actually had made[28] and, for the rest, merely cited data obtained by contemporaries and predecessors. We must remember, furthermore, that throughout the history of science there have been two types of investigator: the theoretician and experimenter, characterized in modern times by such basic figures as Einstein and Rutherford. It is rare that the two are combined within one individual as they were in Newton. Newton the mathematical physicist of the *Principia* did not in general appeal to those who, by the application of the imagination and the experimental art, were exploring new fields depending on empirical investigation for their future progress: such as plant physiology, chemical reactions, heat, and electricity. The mentor and guide of those who explored these new fields was Newton the heroic experimenter of the *Opticks* and the author of the Queries; and many of them, such as Franklin, who read and re-read the *Opticks,* did not even have the mathematical training to attempt to read the *Principia,* had they wanted to do so.

From the point of view of the 18th century, as indeed from that of the 19th, Newton's *Principia* with its law of universal gravitation had apparently, but for certain minor revisions and emendations, settled the problem of heavenly motions once and for all. Certain situations were not soluble; for example, the famous three-body problem does not admit of a general analytic solution. Yet the law of universal gravitation was unquestionably true, something to be believed even when all else failed. This faith is mirrored for us in a letter which the naturalist Thomas H. Huxley wrote, in 1860, after the death of his son, "I know what I mean when I say I believe in the law of the inverse squares, and I will not rest my life and my hopes upon weaker convictions."[29]

But while the *Principia* seemed the terminal point of an ancient line of inquiry, the *Opticks,* with its newly discovered phenomena concerning colors and diffraction, clearly marked the beginning of a new direction in physical inquiry. Whereas Newton could end the *Principia* with a General Scholium and supplement it with *The System of the World,* he closed the *Opticks* on a note of uncertainty, on a set of Queries—of which some, but by no means all, might be resolved by the work of future generations.

The point was made earlier that Newton's optical researches are related to our present views, not by a conscious return of 20th-century physicists to the Newtonian ideas, but rather through a chain that extends from one end of the 19th century to the other. The 19th century produced a succession of brilliant research, of which the crowning achievement was Clerk Maxwell's electromagnetic theory of light. In the end, it was the partial failure of this theory that led to the quantum theory of Planck and the photon theory of Einstein. The electromagnetic theory derives in part from the extension by Clerk Maxwell of Faraday's notions concerning the propagation of electric and magnetic effects through space,[30] and it brought to a superlative conclusion the wave theory of light, revived by Thomas Young in the opening years of the century.

Young's initial contributions were made as a result of studying a class of optical phenomena which we call today effects of interference and diffraction, but which Newton called the "inflection" of light. The first major account of such phenomena was that published by F. M. Grimaldi in his *Physico-Mathesis de Lumine Coloribus et Iride* (Bologna 1665). Further studies of diffraction were made by Boyle and Hooke as well as Newton, but the most significant and quantitative results were those obtained by Newton while studying the interference rings produced when the curved surface of a plano-convex lens was pressed against a flat optical surface. Newton's magnificent experiments, described in the text in Book Two, provided conclusive evidence that some kind of periodicity is associated with the several colors into which he divided visible light. Such periodicity can in no way be accounted for by the mechanical action of corpuscles moving in right lines and Newton was, therefore, forced into the position of having to postulate some kind of waves accompanying the corpuscles; these were the famous aether waves. Newton had to account for the successive refraction and reflection that he supposed must occur at the glass-air interfaces between a convex and a flat optical surface when the interference rings are produced. He suggested that the alternate "fits of easy reflection" and "fits of easy refraction" arise from the action of the aether waves which overtake the particles of light and put them into one or the other state.

Newton's measurements of the separation of these rings and his computations of the thickness of the thin film of air between the two glass surfaces were of the highest order of accuracy. After Young had explained the production of "Newton's rings" by the application of his new principle of interference to the wave theory of light, he used Newton's data to compute the wave-length of different colors in the visible spectrum and also the wave-numbers (in "Number of Undulations in an Inch"); Young's computations,[31] based on Newton's measurements, yielded a wave-length for the "Extreme red" of 0.000, 026, 6 inches, or a wave-number of 37640 "un-dulations in an inch" and a frequency of 436×10^6 "undulations for a second"; and for the "extreme violet" the same quantities had values 0.000, 016, 7 inches, 59750 per inch, and 735×10^6 per sec, respectively, in close agreement with present-day accepted values.[32]

Young was indebted to Newton for more than the data for computing wave-lengths, wave-numbers, and frequencies; the whole wave theory of light was developed by him from the suggestions in Newton's *Opticks,* with several important additions, chiefly (1) considering the waves in the aether to be transverse, (2) supplementing the wave theory by the principle of interference. It was from Young's work that the 19th-century developments leading to the electromagnetic theory may be said to have begun; and since Young's work was inspired by Newton's, we have an historical chain leading from Newton to Young, and from Young to Fresnel and Arago, and from them to Clerk Maxwell and eventually to Planck and Einstein.

Young was extremely explicit about his debt to Newton. Thus, in the first of the three foundational papers in the *Philosophical Transactions,* Young stated:

> The optical observations of Newton are yet unrivalled; and, excepting some casual inaccuracies, they only rise in our estimation as we compare them with later attempts to improve on them. A further consideration of the colours of thin plates, as they are described in the second book of Newton's Optics, has converted the prepossession which I before entertained for the undulatory system of light, into a very strong conviction of its truth and sufficiency; a conviction which has been since most strikingly confirmed by an analysis of the colours of striated substances. . . .

> A more extensive examination of Newton's various writings has shown me that he was in reality the first that suggested such a theory as I shall endeavour to maintain. . . .

Young even pointed out that the wave theory of light should be given a hearty welcome because it originated with Newton who was universally venerated.

> Those who are attached, as they may be with the greatest justice, to every doctrine which is stamped with the Newtonian approbation, will probably be disposed to bestow on these considerations so much the more of their attention, as they appear to coincide more nearly with Newton's own opinions. For this reason, after having stated each particular position of my theory, I shall collect, from Newton's various writings, such passages as seem to me the most favourable to its admission. . . .

In conformity with this plan, almost half of the article is made up of quotations from Newton.

In his "Reply to the Edinburgh Reviewers,"[33] Young described the history of his ideas concerning light, once again expressing the degree to which they derived from Newton's writings. Even the principle of interference, he insists, was discovered by him in May 1801 "by reflecting on the beautiful experiments of Newton . . . ," and although "there was nothing that could have led to it in any author with whom I am acquainted," Young noted how Newton had used a similar conception in explaining "the combinations of tides in the Port of Batsha."[34] Although there is, therefore, no question of the influence of Newton on Young, one suspects that Young, like the Player Queen in Hamlet, doth protest too much. The *Edinburgh Review,* in its condemnation of Young, was of course grossly unfair when it used against him the phrase that a person may, "with the greatest justice, be attached to every doctrine which is stamped with the Newtonian approbation," but without quotation marks (as if this were a position *contra*-Young on the part of a *pro*-Newton reviewer rather than a statement by Young himself); but Young should not really have been as astonished as he would have us believe he was; after all, in the minds of everyone at that time, Newton stood for the corpuscular theory of light and against the theory of light waves.

This raises for us the very real question of whether we can, with Young and Preston, strip Newton's theory of the corpuscles and leave only the waves as the essential components. And this question rapidly leads us into another, which is, why did Newton build his theory on corpuscles, or, why did he reject the wave theory that others in the 19th century in vain tried to attribute to him?

I shall not attempt to trace here the complete history of Newton's ideas concerning the theory of light, nor even to collate all the evidence relating to this subject that may be found in his various published works and letters, but shall rather limit myself to the information provided in the **Opticks** itself. Foremost among the reasons why Newton insisted upon the corpuscularity of light was the general atomism of the age; indeed, the very hallmark of the "New Science" in the 17th century, among such men as Bacon, Galileo, Boyle, and others, was a belief in atomism, in what Boyle called the "corpuscular philosophy." Whereas the scholastic doctrine had placed light and the phenomena of colors in the category of "forms and qualities," men such as Newton opposed to this traditional view an explanation of the phenomena of nature in terms of the mechanical action of atoms, or of matter and motion. Summing up the many reasons for a general belief in atoms in the final Query, Newton wrote:

> All these things being consider'd, it seems probable to me, that God in the Beginning form'd Matter in solid, massy, hard, impenetrable, moveable Particles, of such Sizes and Figures, and with such other Properties, and in such Proportion to Space, as most conduced to the End for which he form'd them. . . .

> Now by the help of these Principles, all material Things seem to have been composed of the hard and solid Particles above-mention'd, variously associated in the first Creation by the Counsel of an intelligent Agent. For it became him who created them to set them in order. And if he did so, it's unphilosophical to seek for any other Origin of the World. . . .

Then, too, it was well known that waves of whatever sort would spread out in all directions in any homogeneous medium, rather than travel in straight lines as light is observed to do when it produces a sharply defined shadow. Thus, says Newton (Qu. 29): "Are not the Rays of Light very small Bodies emitted from shining Substances? For such Bodies will pass through uniform Mediums in right Lines without bending into the Shadow, which is the Nature of the Rays of Light." Furthermore, that material bodies moving in a straight line oblique to a surface will be reflected so as to obey the law of reflection, i.e. that the angle of incidence equals the angle of refraction, had been well known since classical antiquity. Refraction might easily be explained on the basis of the corpuscular theory since the attraction exerted by the particles of glass, say, on the corpuscles of light incident upon the glass from air would produce an increase in the vertical component of the velocity of the particles and, therefore, would result in a bending toward the normal which is always observed to be the case.[35]

Of course, a rival theory to Newton's, the wave theory of Christiaan Huygens, had offered a geometrical construction for reflection and refraction in wholly different terms. And this theory led to an exactly opposite conclusion to that of Newton's theory in respect to the relative speeds of light in air and in glass or water. Whereas Newton's corpuscular theory demands a speed of light greater in glass or water than in air, the theory of Huygens requires a speed of light in air that must be greater than the speed of light in water or in glass. Unfortunately, the possibility of putting these opposing conclusions to the test of experiment did not occur until well into the 19th century, when the labors of Young and Fresnel had already established the wave theory of light, so that this test, favoring the conclusions of the wave theory rather than the corpuscular, was but an additional argument, rather than the primary one, for the wave theory of light.

Newton's rejection of Huygens' theory was based, in part, on his own cherished belief in atomicity and also on the fact that Huygens' theory was geometrical rather than mechanical, and contradicted physical principles. Although Huygens had provided a brilliant meth-

od for constructing the wave front in the case of refraction or reflection, the waves he postulated were
without the primary characteristic of a physical wave
motion, i.e., periodicity. In fact, Huygens' denial of
periodicity in his postulated light waves was an attempt to account for the possibility of a number of
waves crossing each other without in any way interfer-
ing one with another. But without the property of periodicity, such waves could not account for color, nor
any of the other periodic properties of light which
Newton had observed in the various types of interference and diffraction phenomena he had studied so
carefully in the *Opticks.* Nor could Huygens, without
the principle of destructive interference invented by
Young a little more than a hundred years later, adequately account for the simplest of all optical phenomena, rectilinear propagation.

Finally, the most brilliant of all the portions of Huygens' *Treatise on Light*[36] provided Newton with an
argument against Huygens' theory. For, by extending
the geometric construction of wave fronts from isotro-
pic to anisotropic media, Huygens had been able to
account for the phenomenon of double refraction in
calcite, or Iceland spar, by two different wave forms.
Newton (Qu. 28) considered this to be an important
weapon against Huygens' "Hypothesis." Newton grasped
the salient aspect of Huygens' investigation, which was
that "the Rays of Light have different Properties in
their different Sides," and he quoted from the original
French of Huygens to prove how baffling this phenomenon was to the author of the wave theory himself; plainly, "Pressions . . . propagated . . . through an
uniform Medium, must be on all sides alike." It never
apparently occurred to Huygens, who thought in terms
of a geometric scheme, nor to Newton, that the undulations might be perpendicular to the direction of propagation. When, eventually, it was suggested by Young
and Fresnel that light waves must be transverse rather
than longitudinal, then for the first time was it possible
to explain the polarization of light, or the way in which
light—to use Newton's phrase—has "sides." The study
of the interference of polarized beams of light provided in the 19th century one of the chief arguments for
the advocates of the wave theory. But in Newton's day
and for a hundred years thereafter, the only way to
account for the "sides" of light was to suppose that the
corpuscles were not perfectly spherical and would
present, therefore, different sides depending on their
orientation to the axis of motion.

It is one of the ironies of history that the *Opticks,*
based on Newton's secure belief that light rays consist
of streams of corpuscles, should have provided, a century later, as great a contribution to the wave theory as
the *Traité de la lumière* of his rival Huygens. And it
is just this feature which makes the *Opticks* such an
attractive work for anyone to read who is interested in
that stage of creation when the greatest and clearest of

minds is baffled by the observed data and cannot reduce them to a simple, clear, straightforward conceptual scheme. As we watch Newton wrestle with the
problems of the nature of light, we get in the following
pages some measure of the extraordinary difficulty of
scientific research applied to the most fundamental
problems. And if Newton's elegant conceptions do not
always permit us to follow his argument in every detail, we can at any rate be grateful for the opportunity
to observe in action one of the greatest minds that
science has ever produced, so beautifully described by
Wordsworth's "Newton with his prism and silent face,"
his "mind forever voyaging through strange seas of
thought alone."[37]

Notes

[1] From the version edited by T. Oliver Harding: *Handbook of Natural Philosophy: Optics,* sixth thousand,
London, James Walton, 1869, p. 164.

[2] Arthur Schuster: *An Introduction to the Theory of
Optics,* second edition, revised, London, Edward Arnold, 1909, p. 86.

[3] These three memoirs, together with other writings on
the subject by Young, may be found in George Peacock, editor, *Miscellaneous Works of the Late Thomas
Young,* London, John Murray, 1855. "On the Theory
of Light and Colours" was a Bakerian Lecture read at
the Royal Society on 12 Nov. 1801 and was published
in the *Phil. Trans.* for 1802, pp. 12 ff. (reprinted in
Misc. Works, vol. 1, pp. 140 ff.), "An Account of some
Cases of the Production of Colours not hitherto described," was read at the Royal Society on 1 July 1802
and was published in the *Phil. Trans.* for 1802, pp.
387 ff. (reprinted in *Misc. Works,* vol. 1, pp. 170 ff.),
and "Experiments and Calculations relative to Physical
Optics" was a Bakerian Lecture read at the Royal
Society on 24 Nov. 1803 and was printed in the *Phil.
Trans.* for 1804, pp. 1 ff. (reprinted in *Misc. Works,*
vol. 1, pp. 179 ff.).

[4] By "unassailable," I do not of course mean that the
wave theory, as an exclusive explanation of optical
phenomena, has remained unassailable; but rather that
the application of the principle of interference to diffraction phenomena has remained the major basis for
our belief in waves, whether these be matter waves,
probability waves, electro-magnetic waves, or old-fash-
ioned aether waves. Thus, when Louis de Broglie predicted the existence of matter waves having a wave-
length $\lambda = h/mv$, evidence for their existence in the case
of electrons was provided by the diffraction pattern produced by a crystalline metal on a beam of thermal electrons—in accordance with the application of the principle of interference in much the same manner as it had
been applied to visible light in Young's pin-hole experiment and to X-rays in Laue's crystal experiments.

5 The attack on Young's three memoirs was published in the *Edinburgh Review,* nos. II and IX. The authorship of the attack is discussed by Peacock in the note added to the reprint of Young's reply (*Misc. Works,* vol. 1, pp. 192 ff.).

6 Cf. Florian Cajori, *A History of the Conceptions of Limits and Fluxions in Great Britain from Newton to Woodhouse,* Chicago, Open Court Pub. Co., 1919.

7 Thomas Preston, *Theory of Light,* fifth edition, edited by Alfred W. Porter, London, Macmillan, 1928, p. 21; the preface to the first edition is dated July 1890.

8 This research has been sponsored by a generous grant in aid from the American Philosophical Society. A preliminary report has been published in *The American Philosophical Society Year Book 1949,* Philadelphia, 1950, pp. 240-243. It is hoped that a long memoir, embodying the results of research on the nature of physical theory in the 18th century and its effect on that of the 19th, stressing the role of Newton's *Opticks* and Franklin's unitary theory of electrical action, will be published by the American Philosophical Society late in 1952.

9 "Vegetable Staticks," vol. 1 of *Statical Essays,* ed. 2, London, W. Innys et al., 1731. An important study of Hales, clearly indicating the indebtedness of Hales to the Queries in the *Opticks,* is Henry Guerlac: "The Continental Reputation of Stephen Hales," *Archives Internationales d'Histoire des Sciences,* 1951, No. 15, pp. 393-404.

10 Hales refers to Motte's abridgment of the *Phil. Trans.,* vol. 2, p. 1.

11 This may also be found in Qu. 31 of the *Opticks*; see pp. 380-381 below.

12 The *Principia* is available in Florian Cajori's version of Andrew Motte's English trans. of 1729, Berkeley, Univ. of Calif. Press, 1934.

13 Craigie's letter to Bentley, dated 24 June 1691, may be found in Sir David Brewster, *Memoirs of the Life, Writings, and Discoveries of Sir Isaac Newton,* Edinburgh, Thomas Constable, 1855, vol. 1, p. 465.

14 *Ibid,* p. 464.

15 Cf. preface to Jean-Théophile Desaguliers, *Course of Experimental Philosophy,* ed. 3, vol. 1, London, A. Millar, 1763, p. viii.

16 *Ibid.*

17 A Latin edition of the *Opticks* was later prepared at Newton's request by Samuel Clarke and published in London in 1706, two years after the English edition.

18 J. Edleston, ed., *Correspondence of Sir Isaac Newton and Professor Cotes . . . ,* London, John W. Parker, 1850, p. 153.

19 This letter, in the original Latin, may be found in Newton's *Opera,* ed. by Samuel Horsley, vol. 4, London, John Nichols, 1782, pp. 314 ff. The English translation is quoted from Cajori's notes to his edition of the *Principia,* ed. cit., p. 673. Horsley printed the entire letter; when originally published in the *Phil. Trans.,* this part of the letter had been omitted.

20 The Newton-Bentley correspondence may be found in Newton's *Opera,* ed. by Horsley, vol. 4, pp. 427 ff.

21 *Correspondence of Sir Isaac Newton and Professor Cotes,* p. 153. [Cotes told Newton that the Leibniz letter appeared in "the 18th Number of the second Volume" of the *Memoirs of Literature.* In the second edition of the *Memoirs of Literature,* "revised and corrected," Leibniz's letter appears in vol. 4 (London, R. Knaplock, 1722), art. LXXV, pp. 452 ff.]

22 *Ibid.*

23 All quotations from the *Principia* are taken from Cajori's edition (note 12).

24 Newton's letter to Boyle, dated 28 Feb. 1678/9 was first printed in Boyle's *Works,* edited by Thomas Birch, vol. 1, London, A. Millar, 1744, Life, pp. 70 ff. The aether, in respect of its rarity and density, not only was supposed to produce gravitation but also the diffraction phenomena described by Grimaldi. This letter is reprinted in Sir David Brewster, *Memoirs,* ed. cit. (note 13).

25 These Queries, 17-23, next appeared in the second English edition, first issued in 1717, together with new Queries 24-31.

26 An important discussion of Newton's use of hypotheses, and the meaning of the phrase *Hypotheses non fingo,* by Cajori may be found in his edition of the *Principia,* p. 671.

27 Marjorie Hope Nicolson, *Newton demands the Muse: Newton's "Opticks" and the Eighteenth Century Poets,* Princeton, Princeton Univ. Press, 1946, p. vii.

28 Three major experiments performed by Newton and described at length in the *Principia* are (1) the production of interference fringes by the diffraction of light produced by the "edges of gold, silver, and brass coins, or of knives, or broken pieces of stone o[r] glass," as "lately discovered by Grimaldi," Scholium following prop. XCVI, th. L, bk. 1 (pp. 229 ff., Cajori's ed.); this Scholium occurs in a group of theorems in which is shown "the analogy there is between the propagation

of the rays of light and the motion of bodies," but "not at all considering the nature of the rays of light, or inquiring whether they are bodies or not"; (2) a study of the "resistance of mediums by pendulums oscillating therein," General Scholium following prop. XXXI, th. XXV, bk. II (pp. 316 ff.); (3) an investigation of "the resistances of fluids from experiments," consisting of measurements of the time of descent of spheres made of (or filled with) various substances, when allowed to fall through water and air, Scholium following prop. XL, prob. IX, bk. 2 (pp. 355 ff.).

[29] The letter, written to Charles Kingsley, may be found in *Life and Letters of Thomas Henry Huxley,* edited by Leonard Huxley, vol. 1, London, Macmillan, 1900, p. 218.

[30] Faraday used to quote Newton's letter to Bentley as inspiration for his own concern over the role of the medium in the action of one body upon another at a distance from it. Cf. John Tyndall: *Faraday as a Discoverer,* new ed., London, Longmans, Green, 1870, p. 81.

[31] "On the Theory of Light and Colours" (see footnote 3 above) in *Misc. Works,* vol. 1, p. 161.

[32] Newton never computed wave-lengths, but on many occasions noted that the vibrations of the "aether" corresponding to the several colors might be likened to the vibrations of air which, according to their several "bignesses, makes several Tones in Sound." One may conclude from the analogy of sound to light (Qu. 28) that Newton's aether waves would be longitudinal pulses; yet Newton also referred to the mode of production of water waves by a stone thrown into a stagnant water (Qu. 17) as an analogy to the "aether" waves arising from the motion of light-particles, and in this case the disturbance would be transverse.

[33] Reprinted in *Misc. Works,* vol. 1, pp. 192 ff.

[34] This example is discussed more fully in I. B. Cohen, "The First Explanation of Interference," *Am. J. Physics* (1940), vol. 8, pp. 99 ff.

[35] In one of his earliest publications in optics, Newton had already indicated that rectilinear propagation was contrary to the suppositions of a wave theory: "For, to me, the Fundamental Supposition it self seems impossible; namely, That the *Waves* or Vibrations of any Fluid, can, like the Rays of Light, be propagated in *Streight* lines, without a Continual and very extravagant spreading and bending every way into the Quiescent Medium, where they are terminated by it. I mistake, if there be not both Experiment and Demonstration to the contrary." (*Phil. Trans.,* no. 88, p. 5089). In the *Principia,* Prop. XLII, th. XXXIII, bk. II, there is a demonstration that "All motion propagated through a

fluid diverges from a rectilinear progress into the unmoved spaces." The scholium to Prop. L, Problem XII, bk. II, deals with the determination of the wave-number of a sound-vibration, but begins with a declaration that the rectilinear propagation of light proves that light cannot consist of waves alone.

In Query 28, Newton indicated by examples that "Waves, Pulsations or Vibrations of the Air, wherein Sound consists, bend manifestly, though not so much as the Waves of Water." Does not the evidence of the bending of light in diffraction experiments, as described in the beginning of Book Three, indicate the wave nature of light? Although Newton referred to such experiments (p. 388) as examples of "how the Rays of Light are bent in their passage by Bodies," they were interpreted as illustrating not wave motion or "pression" so much as the way (Qu. 1) "Bodies act upon Light at a distance, and by their action bend its Rays." In Query 28, the difference between the bending of light and of waves is discussed; we find, "The Rays which pass very near to the edges of any Body, are bent a little by the action of the Body, as we shew'd above; but this bending is not towards but from the Shadow, and is perform'd only in the passage of the Ray by the Body, and at a very small distance from it."

[36] Huygens' work is available in an English version by S. P. Thompson as *Treatise on Light,* London, Macmillan, 1912; reprinted by the University of Chicago Press.

[37] In addition to the works mentioned in the footnotes, a few others may be cited for those who may wish to pursue some aspect of this subject further. An excellent bibliographical study of the major publications of Newton and important commentaries may be found in *A Descriptive Catalogue of the Grace K. Babson Collection of the Works of Isaac Newton and the Material relating to him in the Babson Institute Library,* New York, Herbert Reichner, 1950, which supplements but does not entirely supersede George K. Gray: *A Bibliography of the Works of Sir Isaac Newton, together with a List of Books illustrating his Works,* second ed., Cambridge, Bowes and Bowes, 1907. A number of important and stimulating essays may be found in The Royal Society: *Newton Tercentenary Celebrations, 15-19 July 1946,* Cambridge, Cambridge Univ. Press, 1947, especially those by E. N. da C. Andrade, Lord Keynes, and S. I. Vavilov. George F. Shirras is writing a new biography which will have, among other merits, the benefit of study of many unpublished manuscript documents, a considerable portion of which were collected by his teacher, the late Lord Keynes. Alexandre Koyré is preparing a series of Newtonian Studies to match his *Etudes Galiléennes;* he has provided an earnest of this great work in "The Significance of the Newtonian Synthesis," *Archives Internationales d'Histoire des Sciences,* 1950, vol. 29, pp. 291-311. An

admirable exposition of Newton's early work on color and the prismatic spectrum is Michael Roberts and E. R. Thomas, *Newton and the Origin of Colours,* London, G. Bell & Sons, 1934.

Rupert Hall and Marie Boas Hall   (essay date 1960)

SOURCE: "Newton's Theory of Matter," in *Isis,* Vol. 51, No. 164, June 1960, pp. 131-44.

[*In the following essay, Hall and Hall examine several of Newton's unpublished manuscripts in order to better understand the development of his theory of matter.*]

A clear understanding of Newton's real thoughts about the nature of matter and of the forces associated with material particles has always been (to borrow his own phrase) "pressed with difficulties." That a corpuscular or particulate theory was unreservedly adopted by him has long been abundantly evident from many passages in the *Principia,* and from the *Quaeries* in *Opticks,* to mention only discussions fully approved for publication by Newton himself. So far, then, Newton was undoubtedly a "mechanical philosopher" in the spirit of his age, the spirit otherwise expressed, for example, by Boyle and Locke. But of the exact content and form of his mechanical philosophy it is less easy to be certain. In the *Principia* it is set in a strictly mathematical mould, and Newton for the most part restricts his statements to what is necessary for the development of a mathematical theory of gravitational force: only phenomena of motion are considered. In the *Quaeries,* on the other hand, Newton treats the mechanical philosophy qualitatively, and, having deliberately given to his thoughts a speculative dress, in order not to seem utterly committed to them, he roams widely over the phenomena of optics, heat, surface tension, chemistry, and so on, rarely being definite and on occasion being inconsistent. As Newton intended, the *Quaeries* tantalize: we are never sure whether he really means what he says or not.

Interpretations of the *Quaeries,* and of certain passages in the *Principia,* have been further complicated by overemphasis of the positivist element in Newton's scientific method. When the philosopher who declared "Hypotheses non fingo" is found to be framing hypotheses and formulating conjectures, should these be taken seriously or not? Even if we recognize that Newton did not—for he could not—avoid or mercilessly condemn any entertainment of a hypothesis, it is often tempting to distinguish between Newton the mathematical theorist, and Newton the author of philosophical speculations.

Similar doubts obscure other discussions, especially the *Hypothesis of Light*[1] and the *Letter to Boyle*:[2] again, when touching on fundamental explanations, Newton seems to don a cloak of elusiveness. Of the former he wrote almost in terms of impatience. Considering, he said, that a hypothesis would illustrate his optical papers, or at least that they were felt to need such an explanation by some great virtuosos in the Royal Society whose heads ran much upon hypotheses: "I have not scrupled to describe one, as I could on a sudden recollect my thoughts about it; not concerning myself whether it shall be thought probable or improbable, so it do but render the papers I send you, and others I sent formerly, more intelligible." And he made it clear that he was not to be supposed to accept this hypothesis himself, or to be seeking adherents for it. This is as much as to say: if the virtuosos must amuse themselves with hypotheses, I will supply one, as good as any other.[3] As for the *Letter to Boyle,* it begins with an apology for reproducing notions so ill digested "that I am not well satisfied my self in them; and what I am not satisfied in, I can scarce esteem fit to be communicated to others; especially in natural philosophy, where there is no end of fancying." And the letter ends yet more discouragingly: "For my own part, I have so little fancy to things of this nature, that, had not your encouragement moved me to it, I should never, I think, have thus far set pen to paper about them."[4]

These pieces, together with *De natura acidorum,*[5] are so brief and so *ad hoc* in their composition, and so little related to the main stream of Newton's mathematical and experimental enquiry, that they have defied accurate assessment. Historians have been inclined to take Newton at his word and dismiss them as occasional pieces not truly representative of his permanent convictions. Although Newton was thirty-three in 1675 and had by this time performed original work of outstanding quality—indeed, no truly creative thought entered his mind after this date—it has been tempting to suppose that these papers were juvenilia, products of a state of mind which the author of the *Principia* has outgrown. That Newton only renounced almost total public silence in 1717 with the final group of *Quaeries* seemed to indicate that his thoughts were uncertain until that time. Even after going into print (with all the safeguards of the *Quaery* form) Newton was still undecided, apt to plan further discussion and then draw back. For he informed Roger Cotes, editor of the second edition of the *Principia,* that "I intended to have said much more about the attraction of the small particles of bodies, but upon second thoughts I have chose rather to add but one short Paragraph about that part of Philosophy."[6] This was with reference to the final passage of the *General Scholium,* which Newton ultimately re-wrote so mysteriously that its meaning has escaped commentators ever since.[7] Once more Newton could not speak his mind openly and plainly; once more his compulsion to utter only unchallengeable truths or perplexing generalities prevailed over his sense of the importance of explaining his theory of matter.

We can extend our understanding of Newton's intention by consideration of unpublished manuscript sources, papers which Newton wrote at various periods of his life, which cover a wide variety of subjects. These include the following, given here in the order of their composition, as far as that can be determined:

(1) Notes on Hooke's *Micrographia* (ca. 1665).[8]

(2) *De Gravitatione et aequipondio fluidorum*[9] (before 1670); an elaborately written though unfinished work, violently anti-Cartesian, and hence containing a long disquisition on the nature of matter.

(3) *De Aere et Aethere,*[10] an unfinished and much corrected work, in two short chapters (about 1674).

(4) *Conclusio,*[11] the original ending to the *Principia.*

(5) Draft of the Preface to the *Principia,* much longer than the printed version.[12]

(6) Drafts of the *General Scholium*[13] (for the second edition of 1713).

These documents clearly prove that it was not lack of continuity in his ideas, nor want of an impulse to publish them that caused Newton to hover between silence and oracular utterance. Newton planned and drafted more versions of his theory of matter both before writing the *Principia* and in conjunction with it than have been known hitherto. The various versions with their similar phrases and identical examples form a continuous chain over the years 1675-1713 to show that the basic fabric of Newton's theory of matter remained always the same. Moreover, despite all his overt professions, Newton was genuinely anxious to discuss his theory of matter in detail and publicly. Three times he tried to find a place for it in the *Principia*: in the *Conclusio,* in the *Preface* and in the *General Scholium*; and three times he rejected it. Somewhere, he seems to have felt, some notice should be given of the microscopic architecture of nature side by side with the majestic system of celestial motions unfolded by mathematical analysis. But all that at length emerged after painful reflection was a cautious hint in the printed version of the Preface to the first edition, to be followed years later by the oracular but confusing conclusion to the *General Scholium* in the second edition. No one can be sure of knowing the reasons for the ultimate suppression of his cherished ideas. The most plausible is Newton's persistent fear of committing himself to some position which might be made to seem foolish. It may also have struck him that the juxtaposition of the mathematical positivism of the *Principia* (where he was so careful to deny that when he spoke

of gravitational *attraction* he meant attraction at all) and speculations about half-a-dozen other attractive forces (even less well known than gravity) would be particularly strange. Especially since the *Principia* was the work which Newton was the most anxious to make immune from attack. His second thoughts were no doubt tactically wise, and helped avoid bitter controversy; yet, as we shall try to show, the annexing of an essay in the mechanical philosophy to the *Principia mathematica* would have been by no means so paradoxical as it might seem.

Newton's adherence to the mechanical philosophy was a very early development. In his student days he had read with care the *Principia Philosophiae* of Descartes, the *Origin of Forms and Qualities* among many works of Boyle, and the writings of Henry More and Robert Hooke, with others of the generation somewhat senior to his own.[14] His annotations portray him as thoroughly imbued with the mechanical philosophy, and among his earliest original notes there occur, for example, speculations "Of Attomes." A very little later—perhaps about 1665—there is a sketch of an attempt to trace colour to the reflection and absorption of light in the pores of solid bodies.[15] Probably to this same period—it can hardly be very much later—belongs *De gravitatione et aequipondio fluidorum* which also indicates the mechanical outlook, and which contains some traces of the later Newtonian theory of matter. The first surviving document fully devoted to this theory we believe to be *De aere et aethere,* in which it emerges in a tolerably complete form. The existence of this document, in fact, belies Newton's own statement to Boyle that his ideas would never have been committed to paper but for the latter's persuasion, or the earlier claim to Oldenburg, that it was only to gratify the virtuosos that he had written a hypothesis of light. The well-organized though summary treatment in two chapters suggests that it was intended as a synopsis of a more ambitious work. From internal evidence it seems to have been written between 1673, when Boyle's calcination experiments which it mentions were described in his *New Experiments to Make Fire and Flame Stable and Ponderable,*[16] and 1675 when Newton wrote the *Hypothesis of Light.* Comparison of *De aere et aethere* with parallel passages in the *Hypothesis* and in the *Letter to Boyle* indicates that while the same observations and examples were used in all three, as they were to be used many times more until Newton's ideas crystallized in print in the *Quaeries,* the explanations offered of the observed phenomena represents a less mature stage of development than those of the *Hypothesis.*

The feature of *De aere et aethere* that immediately distinguishes it from Newton's other discussions of phenomena of attraction and repulsion (the examples here are capillary attraction, the lack of cohesion in a dry powder, the difficulty of pressing two surfaces together, the walking of flies on water—all to be used repeatedly again) is that he here finds the cause of the effect in the repulsive force of air particles. In later works (the **Hypothesis of Light** and the **Letter to Boyle**) these forces were transferred to an aether. Thus, in **De aere et aethere** the particles of air are, so to speak, active agents in phenomena by virtue of their intrinsic repulsive force. In the **Letter to Boyle** this is no longer the case: particles of air or of other matter, even light-rays, are passively subjected to the force exerted by aether particles, to which the intrinsic repulsive force has now been transferred. Some economy of explanation is gained by the change. For instead of supposing that material particles are endowed with a variety of forces, gravitational, chemical, electrical and so forth, it may be possible to reduce all these to one force in the aether—but unfortunately for economy, Newton did not succeed in this. On the other hand, there has necessarily been a multiplication of entities in a fashion to invite the slash of Ockham's razor. Besides, the aether cannot be inferred from the phenomena; it can only be imagined.

This was a perpetual problem in Newton's philosophy of matter. He could adopt either of two kinds of language. He could speak of forces between the material particles (of whose existence he was confident) as being the cause of phenomena; or he could speak of the forces between the aetherial particles, which in turn acted on the material particles, as being the true causes of phenomena. Sometimes, but not always, he could translate from one language to the other. It would be tempting, perhaps, to consider that when Newton attributed forces to material particles, he always meant that these forces were produced by an aether. But this, as we shall show, was not the case; and in any event the aether-version of the particulate theory of matter as Newton developed it cannot be considered as a profounder theory underlying the force-version, for it takes a totally different view of the ultimate properties of material particles.

Using this criterion, Newton's writings on the theory of matter fall into two groups. He used aether-language in the **Hypothesis** of 1675, the **Letter to Boyle,** and certain of the *Quaeries*. He attributed forces directly to material particles, without the interposition of an aether, in **De aere et aethere,** the whole text and printed preface of the **Principia,** the suppressed *Conclusio* and draft preface, and certain other *Quaeries*. It is significant that when dealing with some of the most obscure—because not directly observable—phenomena of attraction and repulsion, in chemical reaction, Newton never introduced the aether at all, but always spoke of forces between the reactive particles.[17] On the other hand, Newton was particularly careful not to commit himself to the aetherial hypotheses of 1675 and 1678; the aether-language is always qualified by a cautionary note, whereas when he spoke of forces

exerted by material particles he felt no such disclaimer to be necessary.

One should hesitate, therefore, before thinking that Newton's theory of matter consisted of nothing but a series of hypotheses about the aether and its importance in phenomena. Rather, the solid part of this theory consisted of the view that phenomena result from the motions of material particles, and that these motions are the result of the interplay of forces between the particles. This he suggests again and again, both in print and in previously unpublished drafts. Nothing could be more emphatic than the statement of *Quaery* 31, free from conjectural disguises and disclaimers about hypotheses:

> It seems probable to me that God in the beginning formed matter in solid, massy, hard, impenetrable, moveable particles . . . it seems to me farther that these particles have not only a *vis inertiae,* accompanied with such passive laws of motion as naturally result from that force, but also that they are moved by certain active principles, such as is that of gravity, and that which causes fermentation, and the cohesion of bodies.

Nothing that Newton wrote furnishes authority for going beyond this, nor for fathering upon him the opinion that aether was the ultimate cause of everything, as was mistakenly and ridiculously done by Bryan Robinson in the eighteenth century.[18] It is true that Newton, going beyond the bounds of his theory, would speculate on the hypothesis that all the forces of Nature might originate in the properties of an aether, but this speculation is no more essential to the theory proper (as described in so many passages where there is no mention of an aether) than Darwin's hypothesis of pangenesis is to the theory of evolution, or (for that matter) Maxwell's aether is to Maxwell's equations.

Without seeking to cramp Newton's thought into a Procrustean bed of positivism, to which indeed his theory of matter is ill adapted, it seems unnecessary to run to the opposite extreme and (with Lord Keynes) make Newton a *magus* whose scientific thinking was at the mercy of inexplicable whims and mediaeval fancies. Nor can we agree with Professor Cohen, who has suggested that, although "Newton presented his thoughts on the aether with some degree of tentativeness, he did so over so long a period of time that the conclusion is inescapable that a belief in an aetherial medium, penetrating all bodies and filling empty space, was a central pillar of his system of nature."[19] For, since Newton always presented his aetherial hypotheses tentatively, even at the height of his scientific prestige, there is no reason to suppose that he regarded them as other than tentative; he was certainly not equally coy about his theory of particulate motions and forces, which in a far more real and effective sense he looked upon as offering a key to the understanding of the inner mysteries of nature. It may be that in a sense Newton pointed the way up a blind alley. The very fact that he speculated at all on the aether as a mechanism to account for the forces attributed to material particles gratified the prejudice of an age that, lacking any concept of field-theory, loathed the notion of action at a distance and saw in the push-and-pull mechanism of an aether the only escape from it. Faced with a choice between a universe of Cartesian, billiard-ball mechanism rewritten in Newtonian terms and a universe requiring the inconceivable concept of action at a distance, the seventeenth, eighteenth and nineteenth centuries preferred the former. But, because this was so, and because Newton himself shared the general contempt for the notion of action at a distance, we should not suppose that Newton was unaware of the distinction between a hypothesis and a theory; nor should we conclude that his speculations on the aether were the foundation of his theory of matter, when in fact they were at most no more than hypothetical ancillaries to it.

If, then, the existence of forces in an ultimate fact of nature, one that despite Newton's own aetherial hypotheses cannot in the last resort be explained away by a simple Cartesian type of mechanism, what does the word "force," or, as he otherwise termed it, power, virtue, or active principle mean for Newton? Unfortunately, he gives no specific answer. The forces between particles are certainly of the same nature as those between macroscopic bodies;[20] they can be qualified as gravitational, magnetic, electric, "and there may be more attractive powers than these;" they are identifiable from experimental phenomena. But precisely what their nature is Newton never did declare, because he could not discover it. Confronting this difficulty, Professor Alexandre Koyré takes the view that, as Newton knew that forces could not be explained in terms of aetherial mechanisms, he held "them to be non-mechanical, immaterial and even 'spiritual' energy extraneous to matter."[21] As Newton wrote to Bentley, "It is inconceivable, that inanimate brute Matter should, without the Mediation of something else, *which is not material,* operate upon, and affect other Matter, without mutual contact. . . ."[22] Forces would thus require, for Newton, "in the last analysis, the constant action in the world of the Omnipresent and All-powerful God."[23] Professor Koyré's position appears to be this: Newton was much too intelligent not to perceive that the mechanical hypotheses of forces lead to infinite regress, therefore he must on the contrary have believed that forces are non-mechanical, quasi-spiritual.

Undoubtedly Newton was a teleologist for whom the celestial system was the product of divine design, who believed that God had created particles with such properties, and moved by such forces, as were necessary to create the phenomena intended in the divine plan. Just as Newton rejected Descartes' contention that God could not create extension without matter, so he would have denied that God could not create matter without forces. Therefore forces were certainly not innate in matter. If asked why the planetary orbits have certain parameters and not others, or why particles have certain forces and not others, Newton would reply: Because God made them so. God could have made our world differently if he wished.[24] So, to discourse of God "from the appearances of things, does certainly belong to Natural Philosophy" for natural philosophy teaches "what is the first Cause, what power he has over us, and what benefits we receive from him."[25] Moreover, Newton seemed to require God's activity not in the first creation alone, but continually. Why should not the matter in the universe congregate together, unless a divine power prevented it?[26] How could the action of comets and planets upon each other avoid a disturbance of the celestial harmony, unless the same power preserved it?[27] And how could the quantity of motion in the universe be hindered from decreasing?[28]

For attributing such a ceaseless activity to God Newton was criticized by Leibniz and in turn defended by Samuel Clarke who, nevertheless, did not challenge the accuracy of Leibniz's understanding of Newton's views.[29] Professor Koyré believes that the metaphysical opinions of Newton's champion accurately represent those of Newton himself, as seems indeed probable.[30] Clarke maintains that there is no true distinction between "natural" and "miraculous" things, both being the work of God; the former are regular and common, the latter irregular and rare.[31] Nothing, even a miracle, (allowed by both Clarke and Leibniz) is more the result of divine intervention than anything else, since everything that is depends always on God's actual government of the world.[32]

As Clarke wrote,

> The notion of the world's being a great machine, going on without the interposition of God, as a clock continues to go without the assistance of a clockmaker; is the notion of materialism and fate; and tends, (under pretence of making God a *supramundane* intelligence) to exclude providence and God's government in reality out of the world.[33]

Clarke here argues that the Newtonian conception of forces involves nothing extraordinary when God's relation to the world is properly understood; forces are divinely produced because the whole of nature is divinely maintained; they are not mechanically produced because the universe is not a machine.

There is no more spiritual quality to forces, than to matter itself; and matter, Newton had long believed, depends immediately on God for its very existence. This had, in fact, long been his prime argument against the Cartesian notion of matter as extension; he had written in the early *De gravitatione et aequipondio fluidorum*: "If we say with Descartes that extension is body, do we not offer a path to Atheism, both because extension is not created but has existed eternally, and because we have an absolute idea of it without any relationship to God?" Extension only became matter when endowed by God with attributes; and that there was a moment of creation by divine will does not mean that matter is now independent of God. On the contrary, matter exists by a continued act of God's will; equally the properties of matter—the result of particles acting on one another through forces defined by God—must exist because of a continued exertion of God's will. Natural forces are certainly immaterial, equally they are physical, subject to law and open to experimental investigation in a way that miracles and spiritual powers are not.

This is a difficult, perhaps an impossible, metaphysic. Clarke, accepting it, was nevertheless forced by Leibniz into seeking for a middle position where there seemed to be none. Neither he nor his mentor Newton (who said nothing about the question openly) was able to give a clear idea of forces that, although within the natural order of things, were at the same time neither material and mechanical, nor miraculous and spiritual. Leibniz presented the nature of forces as a metaphysical problem, in which Clarke (and Newton) were invited to say that they were *either* spiritual *or* mechanical, one or the other. Clarke wanted a *tertium quid,* which he could not define, because Newton could not solve the problem of force in physical terms. Leibniz was right: Newton's conception of force could not be justified by his metaphysic; it could only be justified by its empirical usefulness in physics.

The content of this theory, discernible in published work such as the *Quaeries,* is made still clearer in the suppressed *Conclusio* to the **Principia.** Here the motions of the particles in hot, fermenting and growing bodies (such, in other words, as exhibit the principal phenomena of change) are said to be strictly analogous to "the greater motions that can easily be detected," and these motions offer the chief clue to "the whole nature of bodies as far as the mechanical causes of things are concerned." The same reasoning applies to the lesser motions as to the greater one, and just as the latter "depend upon the greater attractive forces of larger bodies," so do the former upon "the lesser forces, as yet unobserved, of insensible particles." In chemical phenomena the rapid motion of particles is made especially evident, but Newton suggests that the attractive force actively involved in chemical reaction is the same as that responsible for the static cohesion of particles; and the interplay of cohesive force with particulate shape yields the varying characteristics of fluidity, hardness, elasticity, and so on, that different bodies exhibit. Particles both repel and attract: the repulsive

force acts more strongly at greater distances while the attractive force, diminishing more rapidly with distance, preponderates when particles are in close proximity. For this reason contiguous particles in a solid cohere; but as soon as the particles are separated, whatever the means, they fly further apart, forming an air or vapour whose particles are mutually repellent. If the particles were sufficiently heavy and dense, as Newton had explained in **De aere et aethere,** they would constitute permanent air, and in fact he expressly stated that metals were the most apt to do this.

Many other phenomena are discussed, and then Newton pauses a moment to consider his purpose in entering into so much detail:

> I have briefly set these matters out, not in order to make a rash assertion that there are attractive and repulsive forces in bodies, but so that I can give an opportunity to imagine further experiments by which it can be ascertained more certainly whether they exist or not. For if it shall be settled that they are true [forces] it will remain for us to investigate their causes and properties diligently, as being the true principles from which, according to geometrical reasoning, all the more secret motions of the least particles are no less brought into being than are the motions of greater bodies which as we saw in the foregoing [books] derived from the laws of gravity.

After this he turns to a problem that often excites his interest, that of order and pattern in the arrangement of particles. They are not, he says, thrown together like a heap of stones, for "they coalesce into the form of highly regular structures almost like those made by art, as happens in the formation of snow and salts." This occurs, he suggests, because the individual particles join up into long elastic rods, the rods in turn forming retiform corpuscles, and so on until visible bodies take shape. Bodies assembled in this regular way will transmit light and the vibrations of heat, and permit variation of density through chemical change. "Thus," writes Newton, "almost all the phenomena of nature will depend upon the forces of particles if only it be possible to prove that forces of this kind do exist."

The theory of matter in the *Conclusio* could, indeed, almost be reconstructed from scattered passages in the published writings. It is presented in compressed form in the well-known sentence of the printed Preface:

> I wish we could derive the rest of the phenomena of Nature by the same kind of reasoning from mechanical principles, for I am induced by many reasons to suspect that they may all depend upon certain forces by which the particles of bodies, by some causes hitherto unknown, are either mutually impelled towards one another, and cohere in regular figures, or are repelled and recede from one another,

which is a perfect summary of Newton's thinking on the subject. And a fuller account of this theory as a part of the **Principia** itself would hardly have been inappropriate. The **Principia** is, for the most part, a treatise on the one force of nature, the gravitating force which ultimately resides in the particles of matter and whose laws Newton was able to determine. Having determined these laws, and believing that real theoretical physics was mathematical physics and not a parlour game of hypotheses, Newton went on to work out mathematically the consequences of the laws of gravity and to show that these correspond with observable phenomena.[34] This was Newton's second great advance in the mechanical philosophy, arising from his conception of particulate forces—that which rendered it mathematical. None of his predecessors had succeeded in this, or even attempted it, though many had seen its desirability. But the "mechanical principles" of the **Principia** require that the forces acting on particles and the motions produced by them be exactly calculated. In the **Principia** dynamics and the mechanical philosophy are united—but only with respect to the force of gravity. This, as Newton conceived it, was to be the general pattern of theoretical physics; if only it were possible to extend this union of dynamics and the mechanical philosophy until it embraced the operation of other forces, such as those of electricity or chemical reaction, and thereby effected a precise correspondence between theory and phenomena such as he had achieved for the force of gravity, then indeed these phenomena of nature would be rationally understood.[35] This extension of a philosophy that was at once mathematical and mechanical Newton did not expect to accomplish himself, and the suggestions he made in **Opticks** and elsewhere were intended for the guidance of others. Yet perhaps the best guide he could have provided, in some such explanation of his widest conception of matter and its forces as he drafted in the *Conclusio,* he denied them. This remains inexplicable. The sentence in the *Preface* already quoted survived as an indication of his hopes; was he afraid of influencing posterity too much by offering more explicit directions?

Before the final version of the *Preface* went to the printer, Newton again contemplated a more open statement. In this draft he proposed

> the inquiry whether or not there be many forces of this kind never yet perceived, by which the particles of bodies agitate one another and coalesce into various structures. For if Nature be simple and pretty conformable to herself, causes will operate in the same kind of way in all phenomena, so that the motions of smaller bodies depend upon certain smaller forces just as the motions of larger bodies are ruled by the greater force of gravity.

As before, particles are said to exhibit both repulsive and attractive forces, the former having a longer range,

and in general the discussion is much like that of the *Conclusio,* with the same examples, though of course on a smaller scale. Once more, however, Newton changed his mind and omitted all but the simple statement of his hopes already quoted.

There the matter rested until Newton composed the *Quaeries* in **Opticks,** nearly twenty years later, demonstrating both the continuity of his thought by the essential similarity between the *Quaeries* and the earlier drafts, and the liveliness of his interest in these oft-considered problems by the vigour of this fresh attempt to express his mind.

The *Quaeries* show, however, that Newton's theory of matter had made no progress since 1687, or even earlier, for its roots are visible in the chapter **De aere** written before 1675. His conception of the production of natural phenomena from the motion of material corpuscles caused by action of a variety of forces, illustrated by many observations and experiments, had not been given greater definition. He was not even sure whether there was one basic force, or a pair of repulsive and attractive forces, or as many forces as there were classes of phenomena—gravitational, magnetic, electrical, optical, chemical and physiological—involving such forces. For the further development of this theory three requirements had to be met. It was necessary to be able to analyse the motions of particles mathematically; some of the methods of doing this had been established in the **Principia.** Secondly, it was necessary to know more, from experiments, of the nature of the force or forces; in comparison, the discovery of the laws of gravitation and of the way in which these explained the phenomena of astronomy and tidal motion had been a relatively straight-forward task. Newton recognized that the experimental insight available to him was far too shallow to carry a theoretical superstructure. "I have least of all undertaken the improvement of this part of philosophy," he wrote in the *Conclusio.* Too much, indeed, was founded on his reiterated assumption (found in the Third Rule of Reasoning in the **Principia**) that "Nature is always simple and conformable to herself." That this principle could be relied on in the study of particulate forces had never been experimentally (or mathematically) proved, though it seemed to be confirmed in the case of gravity. And thirdly, it was necessary to resolve the philosophic doubt concerning action at a distance, always lurking in the attribution of forces to material particles. In the **Principia,** when speaking of gravity as an attractive force, Newton several times asserted that he used such terms as attraction only in a loose or popular sense, not considering how the motion so described was produced. "Attraction" at this level was a description of an observable effect, seen when an apple falls or iron is drawn to a magnet, without causative implications. By extension Newton applied the same word "attraction" to, for example, chemical phenomena where the motions of invisible particles could not, like those of the iron or the apple, be actually seen but were inferred. It now described an unobservable effect and in such cases again, when revealing his theory of matter, Newton was careful to assert that his language was not to have implications fastened upon it; he was not considering the cause of the particle's motion, though he could call this cause a force because forces are the causes of motions.[36]

This last presented him with a supreme conceptual difficulty. In the **Principia** Newton had penetrated as deeply into the nature of the gravitational force as science seemed to permit; he had a far more complete understanding of this force and its effects than he could hope to attain of any other. Yet he had failed to discover the cause of gravity or any approach to such a discovery; he could say only that it existed, in proportion to the quantity of matter. Far less, therefore, could he hope to elucidate the cause or origins of the forces that seemed to operate in optics and chemistry, whose laws and phenomena were quite unknown. When pressed —or soliciting himself—to declare the cause of gravity and the manner of its action between material bodies (to avoid the charge of countenancing action at a distance) Newton could only fall back on speculative hypotheses, as Descartes and Huygens had done before him. Yet such hypotheses are far from central to Newton's theory of gravitation; indeed he always maintained that this theory had no need of them. He did, indeed, frame aetherial hypotheses of light and gravity; he never even attempted to do this for magnetism and electricity, or cohesion, or chemical combination. Whatever mechanism he describes, it is quite clear that Newton thought of his aether neither in Cartesian terms nor in terms of a "field," for it was invariably particulate and mechanical.

Without doubt the most puzzling of Newton's declarations of his aetherial hypothesis is that concluding the *Scholium Generale* of the second edition of the **Principia.** We have described in *Isis* a fuller version of the *Scholium Generale,* which permits explanation of the words in the printed version.[37] This unpublished version contains Newton's last private thoughts upon the origin of the natural forces by which particles are moved and visible phenomena occasioned, and they are very hard to interpret. The electric spirit there spoken of is the cause of cohesion, for it causes a strong attraction between contiguous particles; at the same time it causes repulsion at greater distances. It permeates all bodies, emits and bends light, and when vibrating rapidly causes the sensation of heat. Physiologically, it is the vehicle by which sensation is transmitted to the brain, and by which that organ commands the muscles; it also effects nutrition. This is virtually to allege that the electric spirit effects all the phenomena of nature; yet Newton's propositions do not say what it really is, nor how it operates. The statement that the electric spirit

emits light reminds one of the experiment with the frictional machine described in *Quaery* 8, where the glass globe becomes luminous when rubbed, and it suggests that Newton understands "electric" in the normal sense. Seemingly, the electric spirit was the "fluid" (as the eighteenth century would have said) collected by friction on glass and sulphureous materials. Newton appears to suggest that whereas in experiments in electricity large forces give rise to conspicuous effects of attraction, repulsion and luminous discharge, in the minute world of material particles electric forces might exist normally without excitation, though such "attraction without friction extends only to small distances."[38] This undetectable electric force might cause the invisible motions of the particles that are sensed as heat, light or chemical change. But it is hard to understand how Newton could imagine that the electric force between particles which is a force of attraction at microscopic distances could become a force of repulsion between bodies at macroscopic distances, if that is what he means. And although it is easy to see how electrification could be associated with attraction and repulsion, and light and hence heat, its connection with animal physiology seems obscure. Nor does this hypothesis really solve his difficulties in giving a true explanation of natural forces, for to convert the aether or earlier writings into an electric spirit may avoid the implications of the word "aether," so inevitably associated with Cartesian and plenist speculations, and it may offer an analogy. But it leaves the cause of these forces no less mysterious than before, and no less removed from any experimental verification.

However hard he struggled, Newton could not devise a theory which would overcome the supreme deficiency which he always recognized: lack of experimental information. His aetherial hypotheses, early or late, could do nothing to remedy this. As a mechanical philosopher Newton knew that no theory of matter could be firmly established until the forces effecting phenomena were thoroughly understood from experimental investigation of the phenomena themselves, while as a mathematical physicist, he required such a theory to have mathematical rigour. When Newton wrote adversely of hypotheses he was (though condemning himself) methodologically correct in the sense he meant, for the theory of matter could not be advanced by framing hypotheses that were neither verifiable nor falsifiable, especially at a time when even an elementary theory of the transmission of light, the strength of bodies, and the formation of chemical compounds was still totally lacking. He was aware that his own theory of interparticulate forces was defective and incomplete, except perhaps in the case of gravity. It could not even explain adequately how water was variously a solid, a liquid and a vapour, yet this was apparently a relatively easy problem for the mechanical philosophy to solve. As for fundamental mechanical causes—the true cause of the forces of gravity, cohesion, optical refraction, chemical attachment and so on—insight into these was almost impossibly remote. Hence Newton's remark:

> To tell us that every species of things is endow'd with an occult specifick quality by which it acts and produces manifest effects, is to tell us nothing; But to derive two or three general principles of motion from phaenomena, and afterward to tell us how the properties and actions of all corporeal things follow from those manifest principles, would be a very great step in philosophy, though the causes of those principles were not yet discover'd. And therefore I scruple not to propose the principles of motion above mention'd, they being of very great Extent, and leave their causes to be found out.[39]

This is primarily Newton's justification for using the words "attraction" and "repulsion": they were not occult qualities to him. One may translate his statement: if a few more phenomena could be verifiably accounted for in terms of attractive and repulsive forces, as I have accounted for gravity, that would be a great deal; let the elucidation of the causes of those forces come afterward, when it may. Hypotheses about the causes—which could only be finally discovered *after* the first objective was attained—were of merit in the meantime only insofar as they suggested new experimental enquiries; otherwise they were as useless as Hooke's hypothesis of colour or Descartes' of gravity, which were formulated before the basic theories of colour and gravity were known.

And yet—after all this, and after allowing Clarke to underline his metaphysical opinions, Newton still continued to face both ways. The *Quaeries* of 1717 confuse his role as the mechanical philosopher who wrote the **Principia** with his role as a maker of mechanical hypotheses. One is left with an enigma. Newton appears to have been in some part of his mind a Cartesian *malgré lui*: conscious of the folly of aetherial speculations (which, for him, had neither physical basis nor metaphysical justification) he could not wholly resist playing that beguiling game, even if it meant inventing an aether 49×10^{10} times more elastic than air in proportion to its density.[40] Leibniz seemed to show that the heads of the virtuosos still ran upon mechanical explanations, as they had forty years before. In response Newton could devise plausible mechanical explanations, though he knew that they could not contain the ultimate cause of natural forces. One remembers his *cri de coeur* to Bentley: "You sometimes speak of Gravity as essential and inherent to Matter. Pray do not ascribe that Notion to me. . . ." From this peril the aetherial hypothesis, the concept of force as mass multiplied by acceleration, a shock-wave in a line of billiard-balls, offered an escape—or at least a reprieve.

"I have not yet disclosed the cause of gravity, nor have I undertaken to explain it, since I could not understand it from the phenomena," he said in one draft of the *General Scholium*. In one obvious sense this is true, and that sense knocks the bottom out of aetherial hypothesis. In another sense it is false: Newton knew that God was the cause of gravity, as he was the cause of all natural forces, of everything that exists and happens. That his statement could be both true and false was Newton's dilemma; in spite of his confident expectations, physics and metaphysics (or rather theology) did not smoothly combine. In the end, mechanism and Newton's conception of God could not be reconciled. The *tertium quid* demanded by Clarke's arguments was not really available. Newton's mind must make the enormous leap from particles and forces (the proximate causes of phenomena) to the First Cause—as though leaping a chasm were a proof of its nonexistence. Forced to choose, Newton preferred God to Leibniz.

Notes

[1] Published in T. Birch, *History of the Royal Society* (London, 1756-7), III, 247-269, 296-305. (Reprinted in I. B. Cohen, ed., *Isaac Newton's Papers and Letters on Natural Philosophy* [Cambridge, Mass., 1958], pp. 178-235).

[2] First published in Birch, *The Life and Works of the Honourable Robert Boyle* (London, 1744), I, 74 (1772, cxvii-cxviii and *Papers and Letters,* 254).

[3] T. Birch, *History of the Royal Society,* III, 248-249.

[4] Birch, *Boyle,* 1744, I, 70, 73.

[5] John Harris, *Lexicon Technicum,* II, 1710, introduction (*Papers and Letters,* 256-258).

[6] 2nd March 1712/13. Letter LXXV in Joseph Edleston, *Correspondence of Sir Isaac Newton and Professor Cotes* (London, 1850), p. 147.

[7] See below p. 142.

[8] Cambridge University Library, MS. Add. 3958, fols. 1-2.

[9] C.U.L. MS Add. 4003.

[10] C.U.L. MS Add. 3970, fols. 652-653.

[11] C.U.L. MS Add. 4005, fols. 25-28, 30-32.

[12] C.U.L. MS Add. 3965, fol. 620.

[13] C.U.L. MS Add. 3965, fols. 357-365.

[14] A. R. Hall, "Sir Isaac Newton's Note-Book, 1661-1665," *Cambridge Historical Journal,* 1948, 9: 239-250.

[15] *Ibid.,* pp. 243, 248.

[16] Birch, *Boyle,* 1772, III, 706 ff.

[17] There would appear to be an exception in the discussion of solution in the *Letter to Boyle*; but in the hypothetical explanation offered there, any reference to the role of the aether is quite superfluous.

[18] *A Dissertation on the Aether of Sir Isaac Newton,* 1743; *Sir Isaac Newton's Account of the Aether, with some additions by way of an appendix,* 1745. The latter was occasioned by the first appearance in print of the *Letter to Boyle.*

[19] *Papers & Letters,* General Introduction, p. 7.

[20] *Quaery* 31, *Opticks,* 5th edition (London, 1931), p. 376.

[21] *From the Closed World to the Infinite Universe* (Baltimore, 1957), p. 209.

[22] *Four Letters from Sir Isaac Newton to Doctor Bentley* (London, 1756), p. 25; *Papers & Letters,* 302. Italics added.

[23] Koyré, *op. cit.,* p. 217.

[24] *Quaery* 31, pp. 403-404.

[25] *General Scholium,* F. Cajori, *Sir Isaac Newton's Mathematical Principles of Natural Philosophy* (Berkeley, 1946), p. 546; *Quaery* 31, p. 405.

[26] *Quaery* 28, p. 369. *Four Letters,* p. 29; *Papers & Letters,* p. 306. However, in a draft of the *Scholium Generale* Newton supposes that the stars are too remote from each other to experience a centripetal tendency.

[27] *Quaery* 31, p. 402.

[28] *Quaery* 31, p. 397-399.

[29] H. G. Alexander, *The Leibniz-Clarke Correspondence* (Manchester, 1956).

[30] Koyré, *op. cit.,* p. 301.

[31] Alexander, *op. cit.,* pp. 23-24, 35.

[32] Alexander, p. 117.

[33] Alexander, p. 14.

[34] This is, of course, a summary of the intellectual architecture of the book; how Newton formed his ideas and developed his theory of gravitation would be a very different story.

[35] We have discussed this view of the *Principia* more amply in our article on "Newton's Mechanical Principles," *Journal of the History of Ideas,* 1959, *20:* 167-178.

[36] *Conclusio:* "The force of whatever kind by which distant particles rush towards one another is usually, in popular speech, called an attraction. For with common folk I call every force by which distant particles are impelled mutually towards one another, or come together by any means and cohere, an attraction."

[37] *Isis,* 1959, *50:* 473-476.

[38] Cf. *Quaery* 31: ". . . and perhaps electrical attraction may reach to such small distances, even without being excited by friction."

[39] *Quaery* 31, p. 401-402.

[40] *Quaeries* 21 and 22.

Brian Ellis (essay date 1965)

SOURCE: "The Origin and Nature of Newton's Laws of Motion," in *Beyond the Edge of Certainty: Essays in Contemporary Science and Philosophy,* edited by Robert G. Colodny, Prentice Hall, 1965, pp. 29-68.

[*In the following essay, Ellis studies the historical origins of Newton's laws of motion and argues that contrary to popular belief the laws are more derivative of the physics of Descartes than the theories of Galileo. Ellis further emphasizes the conceptual nature of the laws, maintaining that they are not derived from or supported by observation or experimentation.*]

Are the laws of acceleration and of the composition of forces only arbitrary conventions? Conventions, yes; arbitrary, no—they would be so if we lost sight of the experiments which led the founders of the science to adopt them, and which, imperfect as they were, were sufficient to justify their adoption. It is well from time to time to let our attention dwell on the experimental origin of these conventions.

—Henri Poincaré, *Science and Hypothesis*

When we speak of a law of motion, we do not speak of the way in which bodies actually move. Rather we speak of the way in which they *would* move, given that they are subject to the action of certain forces. Laws of motion, therefore, whether they be Newtonian, Aristotelian, or relativistic are laws of *dynamics* rather than kinematics.

The study of the nature of a law of motion is the study of the role that it has within the body of science, of the reasons for its acceptance, and of the conditions under which it might be rejected. In making such a study, we should first want to know how the law in question initially came to be accepted—not because its present role in science is thereby determined, or because the reasons why it is now accepted are necessarily the same as the original ones, but rather because doubts and misconceptions about the origin of a law may spill over into doubts and misconceptions as to its present status. If, for example, we read that Newton claimed that his laws were directly confirmed experimentally, then all arguments as to the impossibility of this may fail to carry conviction, for in the absence of an historical investigation, doubt may remain that Newton had in fact done what our arguments seemed to show was impossible. The historical investigation should clear the air of possible doubts and misconceptions arising from such sources.

Next, we should want to known on what grounds or what conditions a law of motion *might* be accepted or rejected. And this is now a philosophical question rather than an historical one, for in answering it, we are free to imagine whatever sort of world and whatever sorts of experimental outcomes we please. We are not constrained by the feasibility of there being such a world, of conducting such experiments, or of their having the outcomes that we suppose. The problem here is to describe *generally* the sorts of grounds on which laws of motion might be accepted or rejected.

The study of this problem will naturally involve a study of the concept of force, for the laws of motion are laws of dynamics, and force is obviously the central concept. We should want to know what sort of thing a force is, under what conditions a force may be said to be acting upon a body, and under what conditions a body may be said to be free from the action of the forces. If possible, we should try to state these conditions generally. Our discussion should not be limited to the criteria for the existence or nonexistence of *particular kinds* of forces, for the problem is a very general one. Laws of motion do not distinguish between different kinds of forces.

Although Newton's laws of motion are the immediate subject of this essay, the arguments that will be produced are not intended to apply only to Newton's laws. Rather they are intended to apply to *any* law of motion, i.e., to any law that says how bodies would move given that they are subject to the action of certain forces (or given that they are not subject to the action of any forces). Newton's laws feature only by way of example. For the purposes of this essay, therefore, it is not necessary to consider the relativistic corrections that must be made to Newton's laws, for this would serve no purpose other than to complicate the example. In the following sections of this essay, it will simply be assumed that no such corrections are necessary.

Section I will be concerned with the historical origins of Newton's laws of motion. It will be argued that no detailed experimental evidence existed that would have warranted the acceptance of Newton's laws of motion in the seventeenth century. It is often supposed that the experimental foundation for Newton's laws is to be found in the kinematics of Galileo. But quite apart from the question of whether any study of kinematics could serve as the experimental foundation for a system of dynamics, it will be shown that it is extremely doubtful whether there is even any close *historical* connection between the kinematics of Galileo and Newton's laws of motion. Rather it is much more plausible to suppose that Newton's laws of motion were derived directly from Cartesian physics, and that the only experimental evidence that was in any way directly relevant to the truth of Newton's laws was the evidence upon which Descartes and Huyghens supported their law of conservation of momentum.

The problem of assessing the weight of the evidence upon which Newton's laws were historically founded thus reduces to that of assessing the historical evidence for the law of conservation of momentum. The historical origin of this law beginning with Descartes' crude formulation of it (*c.* 1629) will therefore be discussed.

Section II will deal with the law of inertia and the concept of force, and the attempt will be made to formulate general criteria for arguing that a body is or is not subject to the action of a force. It will be seen that there is a general class of concepts in science that might legitimately be called force concepts, and that our concept of motive or dynamical force is only one member of this more general class. The distinguishing feature of forces generally is that in some sense their existence *entails and is entailed by* the existence of the effects they are supposed to produce. This being the case, the ontological status of forces within science is a very peculiar one, since, it will be argued, there is always an element of convention in deciding what we should regard as an effect, and hence, to the extent to which there is this element of convention, the existence of forces is also conventional.

But to this very extent, the laws of dynamics must also be conventional. And to illustrate this, a system of dynamics, at least as powerful as Newton's but which contains a different law of inertia, will be constructed.

Section III will be a discussion for the logical status of Newton's second law of motion—with particular emphasis on the relationship between the concepts of force and mass. Section IV will deal with the principle of action and reaction.

I. *The Origin of Newton's Laws of Motion*

The argument in this section will be mainly concerned with the relationship between Galileian kinematics, Cartesian physics, and Newtonian dynamics. It will be shown that, contrary to popular belief, all three of Newton's laws were probably derived from Cartesian physics, and not, as is often supposed, from Galileo's kinematics. But the main object will be to reinforce the view of Butterfield[1] that Newton's laws were primarily *conceptual* in origin, in that they represented a new way of conceiving dynamical problems. It will be shown that they were not originally supported by any evidence which need in any way have upset the views of anyone who accepted certain medieval postulates concerning force and motion. If any one factor can be said to be primarily responsible for bringing about the conceptual change, it was the anachronism of a homocentric system of dynamics in a world that was no longer believed to be earth-centered.

Galileian Kinematics. The *Two New Sciences*[2] of Galileo is often said to have laid the foundations of strength of materials and dynamics. But as I understand the term, it is inappropriate to describe the science discussed in the third and fourth "Days" of this great dialogue as dynamics, for dynamics is the science that deals specifically with causes of motion or changes of state of motion. It attempts to lay down the principles from which the motion of a body can be inferred from a knowledge of the forces acting upon it, or conversely, principles from which the forces acting upon a body can be inferred from a knowledge of its motion. Kinematics, on the other hand, is the study of the motions that bodies actually have in certain circumstances, and it seeks merely to represent these motions and to describe them without inquiring into the causes of their production. And since Galileo specifically rejected this latter inquiry as lying outside the scope of his essay,[3] his system can hardly be described as a system of dynamics.

The relevant parts of Galileo's *Two New Sciences* dealt mainly with the problem of describing free fall and projectile motion, and of stating the principles that govern these phenomena. His achievement in dealing successfully with this problem is certainly of first-rank importance in the history of science. Nevertheless, it is apt to be overestimated. Galileo did not state the law of inertia, as is sometimes supposed, and his *Two New Sciences* makes no commitment to any particular system of dynamics. He did, it is true, say that if a body is set in motion along a perfectly smooth horizontal plane, it will continue to move "with a motion which is uniform and perpetual provided that the plane has no limits."[4] But when (in the dialogue) he was questioned about this plane, and asked whether he meant a plane tangential to the earth's surface, he withdrew and said that his statement was

at least as good an approximation to the truth as Archimedes' assumption that the scale pans of a beam balance hang parallel to each other.[5] In any case, Galileo said nothing whatever here about forces. He simply said that in such and such circumstances (described without reference to forces) a body would move in such and such a way. His law is therefore a purely kinematic law.

Moreover, it is extremely doubtful whether Galileo would have considered that a body in the state described would not be subject to the action of any forces, for at the time of writing he was evidently sympathetic to Buridan's impetus theory, according to which every change of *position* requires the action of some force.[6] Added to this, in the one place where Galileo did discuss dynamical questions—in his *Two Chief World Systems*[7]—he clearly and emphatically rejected uniform straight line motion as natural motion, and maintained equally emphatically that uniform circular motion was the only motion suitable to the preservation of order in the universe.[8] Consequently, when Galileo's statement about the motion of an object along a smooth horizontal plane is viewed in the light of his general dynamical views (expressed only a few years previously), it is hard to read it as a statement of the law of inertia.

It is, of course, possible that Newton read Galileo's statement and saw it as a statement of the law of inertia. But one who rejected the law of inertia or accepted another system of dynamics would be unlikely to give it this interpretation—although he might well accept it as true, since it is a purely kinematical law. It seems likely then that Newton already accepted the law of inertia and merely found in Galileo an historical anticipation of it.

Cartesian Physics. Descartes was in many ways the antithesis of Galileo. Philosophically he was a rationalist, that is, he believed that the various principles which govern the behavior of things in the world are derivable from certain a priori truths—propositions whose truth is immediately, clearly, and certainly apprehended by anyone who sufficiently understands the terms in which they are expressed.

Descartes took the geometry of Euclid as his model of science. To him this represented the ultimate in scientific achievement, for as he viewed the matter, it is a system of knowledge every element of which is known with certainty to be true. The axioms and postulates were considered to be a priori truths. The theorems are derived from the axioms by simple logical transitions, and are thus invested with the same order of certainty as the initial axioms themselves. Descartes believed that all scientific knowledge should be similarly derivable, provided only that the correct axioms from which to proceed could be found.[9]

As a rationalist, Descartes believed that he could demonstrate the existence of God—an immutable God—and from this immutability could demonstrate certain propositions concerning matter and motion, for according to Descartes' ontology, the universe consists simply of matter and motion. But God is immutable, hence He must preserve in the universe as much matter and motion as He originally included. Consequently, the total quantity of matter in the universe must be conserved. Changes in the quantity of matter in any individual object may indeed occur, but all such changes must be accompanied by equal and opposite changes in the total quantity of matter in the rest of the universe. Likewise, he argued, the total quantity of *motion* in the universe must be conserved. Changes of motion may occur—indeed all changes in the universe were considered to be mere changes of motion—but every change of motion must be accompanied by an equal and opposite change in the motion of something else, the total being thus conserved.[10]

The principle of *conservation of motion,* which represents the first crude statement of the law of conservation of momentum, was one of the central doctrines of Cartesian physics. No one who is even vaguely familiar with Cartesian natural philosophy could be unfamiliar with this principle. Motion was defined by Descartes as the product of velocity and quantity of matter; hence his statement comes very near to the modern principle. The only essential difference concerns Descartes' concept of velocity. Descartes did not conceive of velocity as a fully vector quantity, for he had no rules for adding or subtracting velocities when those were not similarly directed. It is better, therefore, to call Descartes' principle "conservation of motion" and to reserve the phrase "conservation of momentum" for use in connection with the modern law.

Descartes first expressed these ideas in his *Le Monde, ou traité de la lumière,*[11] which he wrote in 1629-1633, that is, nearly sixty years before the publication of Newton's **Principia.** The manuscript was not published at the time but was revised and published posthumously in *Principles of Philosophy,* Part II (1644).[12] In this original manuscript, Descartes set out the law of conservation of momentum in the crude form in which I have just expressed it. But more than this, he also gave us the law of inertia—and gave it to us in its complete and modern form.

Descartes presented his law of inertia in two parts, dealing separately with speed and direction. (We shall here consider these two parts together.) He argued in the following way. At any given moment a body has a definite state of motion—a definite speed and direction of motion. But every body remains in the state in which it is unless it is caused by some external agency to change that state. Thus at any given moment a body has a definite shape, size, color, texture, and so on,

and it will retain these specific properties unless it is acted upon by some external agency. Consequently, Descartes argued, a body must retain its speed and direction of motion unless it is acted upon by some external agency. Or, in more modern language, every body must continue in its state of rest or uniform motion in a straight line unless it is caused by some external force to change that state.

The argument would, of course, be quite unconvincing to anyone who did not already accept the law of inertia. In the first place, what reason had Descartes to describe the speed and direction of a body as a *state* of that body? Could we not equally well argue that at any given moment a body has a definite *position,* and that consequently it must remain in the *place* in which it is unless it is acted upon by some external agency? In other words, could we not use this argument to support a dynamics of rest? In the second place, why should we accept the general premise that every body remains in the state in which it is unless it is caused by some external agency to change that state? After all, we believe that things do change in shape and temperature, for example, without the influence of any external agencies. A vibrating rod changes in shape without any such external influence, and a hot body will cool down unless there is some source of heat to maintain its temperature above that of its surroundings. Finally, why *external* agency? If one accepts the impetus theory of Jean Buridan and Nicolas of Orêsme, then one would surely reject the thesis that every body remains in the state in which it is unless acted upon by some external agency, for this is precisely what the impetus theory denied.

The argument is therefore little more than an absurd piece of sophistry, and it is hard to believe that it was this argument which led Descartes to accept the law of inertia. It seems far more likely that he arrived at it via his general metaphysical position and his principle of conservation of motion. He does, it is true, offer some empirical support for this law. But in the absence of criteria for the existence (or absence) of forces independent of the law of inertia, this, too, is little better than a piece of sophistry.

The experiment he describes is that of whirling a stone in a sling, releasing it, and noting the speed and direction of its subsequent motion.[13] He remarks that the speed of the stone will be the same as its orbital speed, and that its direction will be tangential to its orbital path at the point of release. And we are invited to conclude that when the constraining force is removed, the body continues in the state of motion which it had at that instant. Neither of these contentions could be said to be experimentally established by Descartes, but even if we grant that they were, the law of inertia most certainly does not follow. It lends not even the slightest inductive support for the law of inertia.

The law of inertia states that every body not subject to the action of forces continues in its state of rest or uniform motion in a straight line. But a follower of Buridan and Nicolas of Orêsme would immediately object that the stone is subject to a force after it leaves the sling—an *internal* force, or impetus. He would therefore reject Descartes' experiment as quite irrelevant to the issue of whether or not a body would continue to move with uniform motion when it was not subject to the action of a force.

But more than this, even if we suppose that Descartes had criteria for the absence of internal forces such as Buridan postulated, the experiment would still be irrelevant on other grounds, for it is patently false that the stone continues to move uniformly in a straight line after it leaves the sling. It describes a roughly parabolic path. True, we should say that this is due to gravity. But in the first place this is simply an admission that the experiment is irrelevant. One cannot prove one's ability to run a four-minute mile before lunch by demonstrating one's inability to run a four-minute mile after lunch. Likewise, Descartes cannot prove that a body would continue to move with uniform motion in a straight line without gravity by showing that it does not move in a straight line with gravity.

Finally, what reason has Descartes for saying (if he does) that there is a force of gravity at all apart from the evident fact that projectiles do not move in straight lines? What independent criteria does he have for the existence of such a force? He might point to the fact that bodies have weight. But at best this only shows that a force is required to retain a body in a state of rest above the surface of the earth—a conclusion that *prima facie* at least *contradicts* the law of inertia.

The last point raises a very important issue, namely, what are the criteria for the existence of forces? The whole question of the logical status of Newton's laws of motion hinges upon it. But it is mentioned here only in passing; it will be considered in detail in Part II.

Following Descartes, Huyghens continued with investigations relevant to the law of conservation of momentum. Descartes had merely stated that the total quantity of motion in the universe must be conserved. By "motion" he meant "product of quantity of matter and velocity." Hence "motion" may be roughly translated by our modern term "momentum." But Descartes was not clear about momentum as a *vector* quantity, and hence cannot be said to have stated the law in its complete and modern form. As a result of a number of collision experiments, the necessary corrections were made by Huyghens in the 1650's, and his results were eventually published in the *Journal des Savants* in March, 1669.

Newtonian Dynamics. The key to the origin of Newton's laws of motion is to be found in the wording of the second law. The original Latin reads:

MUTATIONEM MOTUS *PROPORTIONALEM ESSE VI MOTRICI IMPRESSAE, ET FIERI SECUNDUM LINEAM RECTAM QUA VIS ILLA IMPRIMITUR.*[14]

This is correctly translated by Cajori to read:

THE CHANGE OF MOTION IS PROPORTIONAL TO THE MOTIVE FORCE IMPRESSED; AND IS MADE IN THE DIRECTION OF THE RIGHT LINE IN WHICH THAT FORCE IS IMPRESSED.[15]

The important words are *mutationem motus*.[15] Nearly everyone has assumed that when Newton said "change of motion" he really meant "rate of change of motion." Jammer, for example, remarks that ". . . what Newton meant by saying *mutatio motus* should be rendered in modern English as 'rate of change of momentum.'"[16] There is, of course, no reason to quarrel with the translation of *motus* as "momentum," for Newton himself explicitly defines *motus* as the product of mass and velocity. But why translate *mutatio* as "rate of change"? What justification is there, linguistic or contextual, for this translation? It will be argued here that there is no justification for this translation—*either* linguistic *or* contextual. Moreover, it will be shown that this translation is inconsistent with several passages in the immediate context.

This being the case, several important consequences follow. First, Newton's concept of motive force is very different from our modern concept. Second, the concept of motive force that Newton actually employed is not the kind that would naturally be used to explain the phenomena of free fall or projectile motion. Rather it is the kind of concept that is naturally suited to the explanation of impact phenomena. Consequently, it is reasonable to suppose that there is a close historical connection between the laws of motion and the laws of impact (e.g., conservation of momentum), a supposition that becomes greatly reinforced when it is seen that Newton's laws, correctly interpreted, can be derived very easily from the law of conservation of momentum. Thus there is good reason to believe that all three of Newton's laws of motion were derived directly from Cartesian physics.

There is, to begin with, no justification in classical or medieval Latin for translating *mutatio* as "rate of change," and no one has ever argued that there is such a justification. If the translation is to be justified, therefore, it must be on contextual grounds.

What, then, is the immediate context? The sentence that expresses Newton's second law of motion is immediately followed by the words: "If any force generates a motion, a double force will generate double the motion, a triple force, triple the motion, *whether that force be impressed altogether and at once or gradually and successively.*"[17] Now clearly, this does not provide any positive support for the translation of *mutatio* as "rate of change." On the contrary, to make this translation is to make nonsense of Newton's second law, for according to this translation we must suppose Newton to be saying that the *rate of change* of momentum is proportional to the motive force impressed "whether that force be impressed altogether and at once or gradually and successively." Clearly, Newton meant to say that the change of momentum is proportional to the (total) motive force impressed "whether that force be impressed altogether and at once or gradually and successively," that is, exactly what he did say.

Next, consider the First Corollary, which occurs immediately after the statement of the three laws of motion. It concerns the composition of forces. The proof begins with the words: "If a body in a given time, by the force *M* impressed apart in the place *A,* should with an *uniform* motion be carried from *A* to *B* . . ."[18] Now if the magnitude of the force *M* is proportional to the *change* of motion that it produces, then this sentence is intelligible, and *M* is the measure of what we would call "impulse." But if *M* is proportional to the *rate of change* of momentum, then the sentence should read: "If a body, initially in the place *A,* should be subject to a force *M* which carries it with *uniformly accelerated* motion to the place *B.*" Consequently, the argument of the First Corollary is also inconsistent with the translation of *mutatio* as "rate of change."

Looking further afield, we see that throughout the whole section on "Axioms, or Laws of Motion" in Newton's **Principia** there is not a single phrase that would suggest the usual interpretation of Newton's second law. It is therefore quite incontrovertible that Newton meant what he said. When he said "change of motion," he meant "change of motion." It would, in any case, be rather extraordinary if Newton did not exercise a little more than his usual care in formulating the basic principles upon which his whole system of dynamics depends.

Given, then, that Newton meant "change of motion" when he said "change of motion," it becomes immediately clear that Newton's concept of "motive force impressed" is radically different from our modern one. It corresponds far more closely to the primitive concept of a push or a kick than it does to the strength of a push at any given instant.

Consider once again Corollary I. Quite clearly, Newton thought of the motive force *M* impressed apart at the place *A* as a push or a kick given to the object at this point that carries it along with *uniform* speed to the place *B* in the given time. And by his second law

of motion, he considered the magnitude of this kick to be proportional to the *total* change of momentum that the body undergoes. Hence Newton's concept of motive force is much nearer to our present-day concept of impulse—the only essential difference being that, whereas Newton regarded motive force as a *primitive* concept, we define impulse in terms of instantaneous force.

To reinforce the interpretation, consider the following passage from the Scholium at the end of the section on "Axioms, or Laws of Motion":

> When a body is falling, the uniform force of its gravity acting equally, impresses, *in equal intervals of time,* equal forces upon that body, and therefore generates equal velocities; *and in the whole time, impresses a whole force, and generates a whole velocity proportional to the time.*[19]

What could be more explicit? The force impressed upon a body (by gravity) is a function of the time. The longer a body is allowed to fall, the greater the impressed force that acts upon it. There is simply no other interpretation that can be put upon this statement. It is quite absurd, therefore, to maintain that by "motive force impressed" Newton meant anything like "instantaneous force." And it is quite beyond any reasonable doubt that "motive force impressed" meant something like "impulse."

From the point of view of the mathematical development of Newtonian dynamics, there is little to choose between the two interpretations under discussion. Newton's law is correctly formulated:

$$\Delta I = \Delta(MV) \tag{1}$$

where ΔI is the impressed force imparted to a body in a time Δt, and $\Delta(MV)$ is the change of momentum that the body undergoes in the time Δt, hence:

$$\Delta I / \Delta t = \Delta(MV) / \Delta t \tag{2}$$

Then if f (instantaneous force) is defined by:

$$f = \lim / \Delta t \quad 0 \rightarrow \Delta I / \Delta t \tag{3}$$

we have at once that:

$$f = d \, (MV) / dt \tag{4}$$

Nevertheless, there is an important conceptual difference between the two formulations (1) and (4). And if we are interested in finding the origin of Newton's laws, it is important to consider the conceptual scheme that Newton actually used.

If, as has been maintained, impulse was the primitive force concept in Newtonian dynamics, then the first conclusion to be drawn is that Newtonian dynamics was historically more closely linked to the theory of impact than to the theory of free fall or projectile motion, for in the latter connection, impulse is necessarily a derivative notion. Gravitational forces do not come into being or cease to operate. Hence to define the impulse given to a body in free fall, an arbitrary time interval has to be specified. The primitive force concept in this connection is obviously *weight*. However, the situation is reversed when we turn to the phenomena of impact. Here it is the modern concept of instantaneous force that is necessarily derivative and the concept of impulse that is primitive, for we naturally conceive the action of one body on another in a collision as a simple phenomenon—a whole temporally extended event. Thus we have terms in ordinary language like "a push," "a kick," and "a thrust" to refer to such events. It is reasonable to suppose, therefore, that Newton's laws of motion were closely tied to the laws of impact—if not actually derived from them. And certainly the suggestion that they were derived from Galileo's work on free fall seems highly implausible.

Now in fact there was only one law of impact that was widely accepted in the 1660's when Newton was working out his main ideas on dynamics. This was the Cartesian law (as refined by Huyghens) of conservation of momentum. If, therefore, Newton's laws of motion were derived from the laws of impact, they must have been derived from conservation of momentum. And when we examine the matter, we see that this is very plausible indeed, for all three laws of motion (as here interpreted) are direct consequences of the law of conservation of momentum (L.C.M.), provided only that we are prepared to assume: (1) that a force is the cause of a change of motion, and (2) that a cause is proportional to (or equal to) its effect. And since (1) is simply a paraphrase of Newton's own definition of motive force impressed (Definition IV),[20] and since (2) was a universally received doctrine in the seventeenth century,[21] it is not unreasonable to suppose that Newton would have accepted both of these assumptions.

The derivation is very simple. The law of inertia follows immediately from L.C.M. when we apply this law to a system consisting of a single body. The second law of motion follows immediately from assumptions (1) and (2). The change of momentum (the effect) is proportional to the motive force impressed (the cause) and takes place in the direction of the right line in which that force is impressed (additional stipulation). The third law of motion follows in two steps. If momentum is conserved, then every change of momentum must be accompanied by an equal and opposite change of momentum. Hence every cause of change of momentum that comes into being (i.e., every action) must be accompanied by an equal and opposite cause of change of momentum (a reaction). Hence action and reaction must be equal and opposite.

There is no denying the plausibility of this derivation. Of course it is impossible to be certain that it accurately reflects Newton's own reasoning on the matter. Nevertheless, it seems far more plausible than any other alternative, and we may be reasonably confident that it is not too far from the truth.

Conclusion. If the thesis that has been presented here is substantially correct, then there can be no doubt that Newton's laws were primarily conceptual in origin. They were neither derived from nor supported by careful observations or detailed experiments. Rather they were the delayed products of Descartes' wondering what sorts of laws would obtain in a world presided over by an immutable God. They were the product of asking how things *ought* to be, rather than how things actually are. That this was Descartes' procedure there can be no doubt whatever. In *Le Monde* he remarks:

> But even if all that our senses have ever experienced in the actual world would seem manifestly to be contrary to what is contained in these two rules, the reasoning which has led me to them seems so strong that I am quite certain that I would have to make the same supposition in any new world of which I have been given an account.[22]

A more specific rejection of empiricism is hard to find anywhere in the literature of science. That Newton's laws were derived from Cartesian physics in the way suggested may be somewhat more doubtful, but the account is the best that we have. If it is true, then Newton's laws can hardly claim a stronger empirical foundation than Descartes'.

Of course it is true that empirical considerations had an important if not decisive role in bringing this conceptual revolution about. The planetary theory of Kepler, and thus, ultimately, the astronomical observations of Tycho de Brahé, had created the need for a nonhomocentric system of dynamics. When it became no longer possible to accept that the earth was the center of the universe, a system of dynamics that was not earth-centered was clearly needed. The homocentric dynamics of Aristotle were an anachronism in the heliocentric universe of Kepler.

It is also true that considerable research work was needed to convert Descartes' crude law of conservation of motion into Huyghens' law of conservation of momentum. But even when these qualifications are made, it remains a sound historical judgment to say that Newton's laws of motion were not primarily the expression of new empirical findings unknown to the ancient world. Rather, to paraphrase Butterfield, they expressed the result of putting on a new conceptual thinking cap.

II. *The Logical Status of Newton's Law of Inertia*

It has been argued that Newton's laws of motion were primarily conceptual in origin. The question now arises: What is their status today? Could they in fact, or even in principle, be shown experimentally to be true?

In one way, the answer to this question is obvious. Laws of motion have *in fact* been replaced by other laws of motion—the Aristotelian and medieval laws by the Newtonian, and the Newtonian by the relativistic. But this answer fails to distinguish between conceptual adequacy and empirical truth. The fact that Newton's laws have been replaced by other laws does not tell us much about their logical status. An empirical proposition may be rejected and (in a sense) replaced by some other empirical proposition. But a conceptual schema can also be replaced by a more adequate conceptual schema. Hence the fact that Newton's laws have been superseded does not tell us whether they are empirical propositions or merely conceptual truths. The logical status of these propositions is still an open question.

Let us suppose, then, that Newton's laws had never been superseded, and that no reason had ever been found for thinking Newtonian dynamics to be an inadequate or anachronous system. We could still ask, could we not, whether these laws could in fact or in principle be shown experimentally to be true. It will be argued here that it is in principle impossible to do this, since the existence of forces is always to some extent conventional. And to illustrate this thesis, the conventionality of the law of inertia will be established by the construction of a system of dynamics in every way as adequate as Newton's, but using a different principle of natural motion.

The Existence of Gravity (Preliminary Remarks). In Part I of this essay, Descartes' example of releasing a stone from a sling was discussed. The example was supposed to provide at least some empirical support for the law of inertia. It was argued that in the absence of independent criteria for the existence of forces, it does nothing at all to support this law. The final point raised turned on the question of the existence of gravity. What reason have we, independent of the law of inertia, for saying that gravitational forces exist? It was remarked that to say that we know there is a gravitational field because projectiles do not move with uniform motion in a straight line is obviously to beg the question. It is simply to assume the truth of the law whose truth we wish to establish. It was also remarked that to say that we know there is a gravitational field because bodies have weight is equally absurd. For at best this shows only that a force is required to *maintain* a body in a state of rest or uniform motion in a straight line—a conclusion that *prima facie* contradicts the law of inertia.

Of course it may be objected that a force is required only to maintain a body in a state of rest or uniform motion in a straight line just because of the existence of a gravitational field. But this is clearly circular, for it presupposes the existence of the very entity whose existence is in question.

Again, it may be argued that the existence of a gravitational force equal and opposite to the sustaining force exerted (e.g., by a spring balance) follows from Newton's principle of action and reaction. This raises the question of why we should accept Newton's third law. But for the moment let us accept it. Even then the existence of a gravitational force does not follow. For the principle of action and reaction merely tells us that to every action there is an equal and opposite reaction. And the reaction in this case is located in whatever supports the spring balance. The upward force exerted by the spring balance on the suspended body finds its reaction in the downward force exerted by the spring balance on its support.

Now it may be said: "Surely the *body suspended* must be acted upon by a force equal and opposite to the force exerted by the spring balance." But why? What reason have we, independent of the law of inertia, for saying such a thing? If we accept the law of inertia (and the principle of composition of forces), then we must accept that the body suspended is acted upon by a force equal and opposite to the sustaining force, for otherwise we must say that the body would be accelerated upward. But if we do not accept the law of inertia, then no such conclusion follows. We may, for example, be prepared to say that the suspending force exerted by the spring balance is an *unbalanced* force. The argument seems to have force only because we naturally think of a state of suspension as being a state of equilibrium. But our tendency to think in this way is a *consequence* of our accepting the law of inertia, and hence we cannot use this fact to *support* the law.

Some of the persuasiveness of this argument arises from the fact that the word "equilibrium" is ambiguous. There is one sense in which we may all agree that the suspended body is in equilibrium—whatever dynamic principles we accept. This is the sense of "kinematic equilibrium," where "equilibrium" simply means "does not move." But kinematic equilibrium does not entail *dynamic* equilibrium unless we hold the dynamic principle that a body which does not move is not subject to the action of any unbalanced forces. And since this is part of the law of inertia, it follows that we cannot argue to the existence of a gravitational force equal and opposite to the suspending force without presupposing the relevant part of the law of inertia. The argument from the kinematic equilibrium of suspended bodies to the existence of gravitational forces is therefore invalid.

The Existence of Forces. It is evident that if we are to see our way out of this maze, we must make the attempt to formulate criteria for the existence of forces, for the question of the logical status of the law of inertia obviously depends upon whether we have any criteria that are independent of this law.

What, then, are our criteria for the existence of forces? There are, it seems, two completely general criteria. We may say that a system is subject to the action of a force if and only if (1) the system persists in what we regard as an *unnatural state,* or (2) the system is changing in what we consider to be an *unnatural way.* The concepts of natural state and natural change must, of course, be explicated. But there will be some advantage in clarity gained by postponing this for the present. Here we shall say merely that a system is thought to be an unnatural state if and only if we consider that its persistence in that state *requires causal explanation,* and a system is considered to be changing in an unnatural way if and only if we think that its changing in that way requires causal explanation. The conditions under which we should say that the behavior of a system does or does not require causal explanation will be discussed later. For the moment we shall proceed intuitively, and show the application of these criteria by means of examples.

Example 1. In Aristotelian dynamics it was considered natural for a body to return to its proper place by the shortest path. A freely falling body was therefore not considered to be subject to the action of any forces. A force was required only to *arrest* this natural motion. In mediaeval dynamics the uniform motion of an object along a horizontal plane (e.g., a rolling wheel) required the action of a force (impetus) for its maintenance. Any change of position of an object that did not result from its motion directly to its natural place was regarded as an unnatural change, and hence required a force for its explanation.

Example 2. In Cartesian and later in Newtonian dynamics, the Aristotelian-mediaeval concepts of natural place and natural motion were replaced by new concepts. The concept of natural place was abandoned, and uniform straight line motion was considered to be natural motion. Of course this does not mean that every case of uniform straight line motion would be counted as a case of natural motion, for in many cases the continuance of a body in such a state would require causal explanation. The point is simply that while there are no circumstances in which we should consider nonuniform motion to be natural motion, there may be circumstances in which the continuance of a body in a state of rest or uniform motion would not require causal explanation. This is what is meant by describing uniform straight line motion as natural motion.

Example 3. Every solid object that can be said to be deformed or in a state of *strain* must be conceived as having a natural shape and size against which this deformation can be gauged, i.e., it must be conceived as having a shape and size, continuance in which would not necessarily require causal explanation. The natural shape of a body is that shape which a body has in circumstances in which: (a) its shape is stable (i.e., not a function of time), (b) its shape is independent of its orientation, and (c) the change in shape that the body undergoes when it is given a positive or negative rotation about any given axis is independent of the *sense* of its rotation about that axis. Thus a body sitting on a horizontal table is deformed, since under these circumstances, we believe, its shape is a function of its orientation. Of course in one sense its shape need not depend on its orientation under these circumstances, for it may assume the *same geometrical figure* whatever its orientation. But that is not what is meant here by *sameness of shape.* An object retains its shape (in the required sense) if and only if the distance between every pair of points in its surface remains the same. Thus even a ball sitting on a horizontal table, whose geometrical figure (some kind of oblate spheroid) may be independent of its orientation, may nevertheless be in a state of strain.

The application of (a) is obvious. Every vibrating object is at least sometimes in a state of strain. By (c) it is intended to rule out strains produced by spin, for if an object is spinning about a given axis, criteria (a) and (b) may well be satisfied. Nevertheless, we may wish to say that it is in a state of strain. But if now the object is given an *additional* rotation (positive or negative) about that axis, then the change of shape that the body undergoes will depend upon the sense of this additional rotation. Hence by criterion (c) the body can be concluded to be in a state of strain.

Every solid object that by any of these criteria is deformed requires the existence of some force or forces to explain its deformation.

Example 4. Suppose that a body initially at the same temperature as its surroundings begins to increase in temperature. Such a body would be conceived by us to be changing in an unnatural way, and a causal explanation of its changing in that way would be demanded. We should say that it must have some source of supply of *energy.*

Now it will be said that energy is not a force concept. But as force concepts are here understood, energy is a force, and supplying energy to a body is a way of acting upon that body by a force. There is, in fact, historical precedence for this. Until the mid-nineteenth century, the quantities we now call forms of energy were always described as forces.

Example 5. Suppose that a body undergoes a change of mass. Then such a change may be conceived by us to be an unnatural change, and hence to require the existence of a force to produce it. Such changes do not in fact occur in isolation from other changes. Relativistic changes of mass are regarded as *side effects* of acceleration-producing forces. The reason for this is not obvious. Why a change of state of motion should be regarded as a *central* effect of a force and a change of mass as a *side* effect needs to be explained. The reasons may be partly historical and partly a matter of the obviousness of the changes that occur. But whatever the reasons, if changes of mass were to occur in the absence of changes of state of motion (and other obvious changes), such changes would no doubt be regarded as unnatural (i.e., as requiring causal explanation) and purely mass-changing forces would be needed to account for them.

In general, then, we may say that a system is acted upon by a force (or forces) if and only if we consider that the system persists in an unnatural state or that it is changing in an unnatural way.

We have remarked that a system is considered to be in an unnatural state if and only if we consider that its continuance in that state requires what has been called "causal explanation." But under what conditions should we say that we consider (some aspect of) the behavior of a given system to require causal explanation? In answering this, we do not propose to offer any analysis of causality or to give any positive characterization of causal explanations. For the purposes of this essay, we shall simply *say* that the behavior of a given system is considered to require causal explanation if and only if we feel that this behavior is not sufficiently explained by its subsumption under a law of *succession*.

A law of succession is any law that enables us to predict the future states of any system (or given class of systems) simply from a knowledge of its present state, assuming that the conditions under which it exists do not change. The law of radioactive decay is such a law. From a knowledge of the number of atoms contained in a given sample of a radioactive element, the number of atoms of that element contained in that sample at any future time can be predicted (provided that the decay constant is known). The law of free fall is another such law. From a knowledge of the present position and state of motion of a freely falling body, the future positions and states of motion can be predicted (provided that *g* is known). Kepler's laws of planetary motion provide yet other examples of laws of succession. From a knowledge of the present position and state of motion of a given planet, the future positions and states of motion of that planet can be predicted.

Now it is maintained that provided that subsumption under such a law is considered to give a *final explana-*

tion of the behavior of a given system, then the system is considered to be in a natural state or to be changing in a natural way. That subsumption under such a law is considered to be a final explanation is shown by the fact that we would reject any request for an explanation of why systems behave in that way or remain in that state as *inappropriate* in the context of the given inquiry.

The law of inertia is a law of succession according to the above criteria. But this law, unlike the others cited, has a special role within our conceptual scheme, for if the behavior of a given object could be explained simply by subsumption under this law, then we should reject the question of why that object remains in that state. Normally, however, matters are more complicated than this, and the law of inertia is not used in such a straightforward way. Nevertheless, essentially the same point can be made. Consider the problem of explaining projectile motion. The motion is divided (conceptually) into two components—a uniform straight line and a uniformly accelerated motion. The first component is explained by subsumption under the law of inertia and the second by subsumption under the law of free fall. The two laws of succession are then used to predict the future velocity components of the projectile. But the two laws have very different status, for while it is thought legitimate to ask why the projectile accelerates toward the center of the earth, it is not thought legitimate to ask why it has a *constant velocity* component as well.

Corresponding to the law of inertia, there is an analogous law in the fields of statics and strength of materials—a law that has similar logical status. This is the law (L^1) that *"every solid object remains undistorted unless it becomes subject to stress."* The close analogy between this law and the law of inertia is worth pursuing. In the first place, if the behavior of a solid object could be explained simply by subsumption under this law, the question of why the object remains undistorted would be rejected as inappropriate. Second, even if the object changes its shape, or remains in a state of strain, we should divide (conceptually) the actual shape of the body into two components—a natural shape and a distortion—and we should attempt to explain only the magnitude and (possibly) variation of the latter component. But we should not postulate the existence of any forces to explain the magnitude or invariance of the former component. To this extent, then, there is a close analogy between L^1 and the law of inertia.

The existence of L^1 raises some interesting possibilities, for might it not be possible to base a criterion for the existence of forces on L^1 (a criterion that would be independent of the law of inertia) and hence to establish the law of inertia inductively? The examination of this suggestion will be the main subject matter of the next section.

Before we proceed with this, however, it is necessary to make some general remarks about the ontological status of forces. According to the proposed criteria for the existence of forces, there is clearly some truth in the idea that the forces we say exist in nature have a kind of *conventional existence,* for a force exists only because we *choose to regard* some succession of states as an unnatural succession. But there appears to be no objective criterion for distinguishing between natural and unnatural successions of states. The fact that a given succession is lawlike (i.e., can be explained by subsumption under a law of succession) clearly does not mean that we should regard this as a natural succession. We have, in fact, drawn certain lines and come to regard certain successions of states as natural and others as unnatural. But in the absence of any clear and objective reasons for drawing these lines as we do, we may wonder whether other lines could be drawn, or whether, indeed, it is necessary to draw any lines at all. Why shouldn't all successions of states be regarded as natural? Or, if that is too radical, why shouldn't all *lawlike* successions be regarded as natural?

Forces are peculiar scientific entities for other reasons, for while the action of a force is supposed to explain (causally) certain patterns of behavior, the occurrence of these patterns is considered a *sufficient* condition for the existence of the precise force required to produce them. If a body accelerates, then it must be acted upon by a force sufficient to produce this acceleration. If a body is distorted, then it must be subject to a stress sufficient to produce this distortion. The nature of this entailment (whether it is physical or logical) will concern us later. But that there *is* such an entailment already marks forces off from other scientific entities, for it is agreed by all that the existence of molecules, genes, and electrons is not entailed by the existence of the effects they are designed to explain.

The Conventionality of the Law of Inertia. It was suggested in the previous section that it may be possible to provide inductive support for the law of inertia, using the law that every body remains undistorted unless it becomes subject to stress to provide us with independent criteria for the existence of forces. Let us now take up this suggestion.

Consider first the case of a solid object sliding on a rough horizontal surface. Such an object will possess a certain shear strain ϕ and a certain deceleration $d,$ and by plotting ϕ against $d,$ for different surfaces it should in principle be possible to determine d for $\phi = 0$. Let us then assume that $d = 0$. But even so, the object is still subject to strain, since its shape will still be a function of its orientation. The object will be compressed in the direction perpendicular to the earth's surface.

Let us now put this object in orbit in such a way that it is not spinning relative to the fixed stars. Under these conditions we should find that its shape is very nearly independent of its orientation. We may be tempted to conclude from this that some kind of accelerated motion must be the natural motion for any physical object. Even under these conditions, however, the object should exhibit tidal distortions. And again, it should be possible (in principle) to plot the distortion ö against the acceleration a for similar objects placed in different orbits. Conceivably, we might discover that when $\phi = 0$, $a = 0$, i.e., we might find that every body that is not subject to stress continues in its state of rest or uniform motion in a straight line relative to the fixed stars. Then if finally we are prepared to accept the principle that a body is subject to stress if and only if it is subject to the action of a force, then it follows that if a body is *not* subject to the action of a force it will continue in its state of rest or uniform motion in a straight line relative to the fixed stars.

The argument is certainly tempting—although it is open to a number of criticisms. In the first place, if our present theories are correct, then the observed tidal distortions would not only be a function of the acceleration. They would also be a function of the *convergence* of the gravitational field in which the object is placed, so that if in any small region of space there existed a *uniform* gravitational field, natural motion in this field would turn out to be a uniformly accelerated motion. But it is very doubtful whether we should reject the law of inertia on the evidence of such a discovery—especially if the phenomena described could be explained on the basis of Newtonian theories.

Second, it is not evident that our concept of *uniform straight line* motion is sufficiently precise for these considerations to have any weight at all—even supposing that the measurements of tidal distortion could be made. Moreover, what of our concept of *remaining the same in shape?* Is this a sufficiently precise concept for the purposes of such an investigation?

All of these difficulties need to be discussed. But there is one objection that is fatal to the whole program, for even supposing that these questions can be answered satisfactorily, the demonstration could not completely remove the conventional element from the law of inertia. At best it could only show that our concept of natural motion is cognate with our concept of natural shape. They would be seen to depend upon each other, so that if a new concept of natural motion were introduced, a new concept of natural shape would also be required and vice versa. And there seems to be no reason, in principle, why such new concepts should not be introduced.

To establish that this element of conventionality does indeed exist, let us see how we might proceed to construct a system of dynamics, at least as powerful as Newton's, but using a different principle of natural motion. We begin with the observation that if Newton's law of gravitation is correct, and A and B are any two isolated bodies of mass M_A and M_B, respectively, then:

$$f = G \quad M_A \cdot M_B \, / \, r^2_{AB}$$

where f is the force of attraction, and r_{AB} is the distance between A and B. From this it follows (by Newton's second law) that the absolute acceleration of A and B must be given by:

$$a_A = G \quad M_B \, / \, r^2_{AB} \quad \text{and} \quad a_B = G \quad M_A \, / \, r^2_{AB}$$

In other words, it is a direct consequence of Newtonian mechanics that every body accelerates toward every other body in the universe with a *relative* acceleration directly proportional to the *sum* of their masses and inversely proportional to the square of the distance between them.

It is important to understand exactly what this means. It does not mean that if measurements of relative accelerations, masses, and distances could be made we should always obtain results exactly in accordance with this formula, for relative accelerations may be compounded. It means only that in working out relative accelerations we should assume that there are relative acceleration *components* that accord with this law.[23] The relative acceleration of the earth and the moon, for example, may be very nearly in accordance with this formula, and so too may be the relative acceleration between the earth and the sun. But the relative acceleration between the moon and the sun would not be even roughly in accordance with this formula.

Now the law derived from Newtonian mechanics is a law of succession. And there appears to be no reason why we should not consider any changes that accord with this law as natural changes. The first law of motion in our new system of mechanics will therefore be that "every body has a component of relative acceleration toward every other body in the universe directly proportional to the sum of their masses and inversely proportional to the square of the distance between them—*unless it is acted upon by a force.*"

For simplicity we shall take the other laws of motion to be identical with Newton's.[24]

To see that this achieves the desired result, let us follow out some of the consequences of accepting this new principle of natural motion. In the first place, it follows that if we have a number of objects of finite mass, randomly distributed and sufficiently removed from each other, then their relative accelerations tend to zero. And assuming our galaxy to be such a system, it follows that any body sufficiently far removed from other bodies in the galaxy will continue in its state of rest or uniform motion in a straight line relative to the various stars in the galaxy unless it is acted upon by a force. The fixed stars may therefore serve as an *absolute* frame of reference in Newtonian mechanics. Adopting this principle of natural motion thus leads to the consequence that it is unnecessary to make any prior distinction between absolute and relative motion in formulating our dynamical principles.

Next, assuming that the system of fixed stars constitutes an absolute frame of reference, and that the sum is sufficiently far removed from other stars in this system, it follows that the center of mass of the solar system must continue in its state of rest or uniform motion in a straight line relative to the fixed stars. Taken individually, the planets must accelerate toward each other, toward the sun, and toward the frame of reference of the fixed stars. But this acceleration would be regarded as a natural acceleration. No force would be required to explain it. Similarly, the parabolic motion of a projectile (as modified by Coriolis's deflection) must be regarded as natural motion, for a body that is accelerating toward the center of the earth with an acceleration g would not be regarded as subject to the action of a force. A force would be required only to arrest this acceleration, e.g., to impart to it an acceleration equal and opposite to its natural acceleration. The measure of this force would be simply the weight of the body.

It follows that in this new system of dynamics, kinematic equilibrium cannot be taken to imply dynamic equilibrium. The fact that a body remains at rest does imply that it is not subject to the action of any *unbalanced* forces. It also follows that in this new system of dynamics no distinction can be drawn between *gravitational* and *inertial* mass, for weighing a body is simply a special way of determining the inertial mass. The weight of a body is only a measure of the force required to impart an acceleration to it equal and opposite to its natural acceleration. The puzzle of the identity of gravitational and inertial mass is therefore simply a puzzle generated by our choosing to regard a certain kind of motion as natural, and it may be resolved without making any assumptions inconsistent with the predictions of Newtonian physics.

On the negative side it must be said that the adoption of this principle of natural motion might force us to revise our concept of natural shape, for tidal effects must either be regarded as *natural effects* produced by the differential natural accelerations of the different parts of orbited bodies, or else they must be regarded as *distortions* set up in these bodies by the action of some stress. If the former alternative were taken (as undoubtedly it would be) then our concept of natural shape would need to be modified. If the latter alternative were adopted, we could retain our concept of natural shape, but we should need to postulate the existence of a kind of inverse square "stress field" surrounding massive bodies.

The adoption of this principle of natural motion would have other ramifications. It would mean, for example, that the law of conservation of momentum would have to be rejected and that a new law relating the *variation* of momentum with the disposition of other massive objects in the universe would come to replace it. But conservation of energy would not be affected, for work would still need to be done to raise a heavy weight.

There is no need, however, to trace through all of the ramifications of adopting the new principle, for since the law of succession upon which this principle is founded is a simple consequence of Newtonian dynamics, the new system is internally consistent and applicable to the world if and only if Newtonian dynamics is. The only difference between the two systems of dynamics is a conceptual one. But it is important that such an alternative system of dynamics can be constructed, for it is proof positive that the law of inertia is not an empirical proposition. It is the sort of proposition that an international gathering of scientists could declare to be false even though they produced not a single fact contradicting it. The possibility of such an alternative dynamic is therefore proof positive of the conventionality of the law of inertia.

The Arbitrariness of the Law of Inertia. The conventionality of the law of inertia has been demonstrated, but its arbitrariness is another matter. We have shown that there is an area of choice, but we have not shown that it is a matter of indifference which choice we make. We shall proceed by making some general remarks concerning the problem of choosing between kinematically equivalent descriptions.

Suppose that the meter rod in Paris were suddenly to burst through the ends (both ends) of its glass case. There are at least two kinematically equivalent ways in which we may describe what has happened. We may say that the universe and everything in it (except the meter rod) has shrunk in size; or we may say that the rod has expanded and the rest of the universe remained the same. Now according to certain positivists, these two descriptions are identical, and it is a matter of complete indifference which we use. But given that we hold the dynamical views which we do—viz., that a body remains the same in size unless it is acted upon by a (compressive or expansive) force—the two descriptions are not dynamically equivalent, and it makes a great deal of difference how we choose to describe what has happened. If the first description were really accepted, then we should want to know what had insulated the rod against this otherwise universal compressive force. Accordingly, we should examine the rod's *present surroundings,* hoping to find some relevant peculiarity. If, on the other hand, the second description were accepted, then we should examine the rod's *past history,* hoping to find some special conditions that might have produced the expansion—although such an inquiry would obviously be *irrelevant* if we believed that the rod had not changed.

Far from its being a matter of indifference which of two kinematically equivalent descriptions we choose, it is a matter of the utmost importance, for the different descriptions make different *theoretical commitments.*

Now this same problem might have arisen in another way. Let us suppose that two scientists, A and B, view the phenomenon of the meter rod, that A holds the principle that every body expands unless it is acted upon by a force, while B holds that every body remains the same in size unless it is acted upon by a force. Let us further suppose that A and B agree on the kinematic description of the phenomenon in question. Let us say that both agree that the rod has expanded, and that the rest of the universe has remained the same. Nevertheless, the two scientists will make different investigations. A will examine the rod's present surroundings, hoping to find what has insulated the rod against the otherwise universal compressive force, while B will examine the rod's past history, hoping to find the cause of its expansion.

Our choices between different dynamical principles should therefore be governed by the same sorts of considerations as those that govern our choices between kinematically equivalent descriptions, and these choices will depend on what theoretical commitments we wish to make.

The whole course of scientific inquiry is guided by just such choices. Consider, for example, the changeover from the homocentric to the heliocentric universe. *Kinematically,* the heliocentric system of Copernicus is virtually equivalent to the homocentric system of Tycho de Brahé. With slight modifications, the homocentric system of Tycho can be obtained from the heliocentric one of Copernicus by a simple coordinate transformation. But *dynamically,* these two systems are far from equivalent, for they raise very different problems of explanation. So long as a homocentric cosmology is accepted, a homocentric dynamic such as Aristotle's is tenable. But once a heliocentric cosmology is accepted, we must, if we adhere to Aristotelian dynamics, be prepared to say that although the planets move around the sun, they *would* move around the earth if it weren't for the action of certain forces. Hence we must be prepared to explain uniform circular motion about the sun as a *deviation* from uniform circular motion about the earth.

It cannot be maintained therefore that the choice of dynamic principles is arbitrary. To borrow a phrase from Poincaré, they are "conventional, yes; but arbitrary, no."

III. *Newton's Second Law of Motion*

The essential conventionality of Newton's first law of motion has been established. By similar arguments it should be possible to establish the conventionality of any law whose role in science is to provide us with criteria for the absence of forces, for forces exist only because we choose to regard certain changes or states as natural and others as unnatural. While criteria of simplicity (regarding the format of our laws of distribution and succession of forces) and coherence (between, for example, our concepts of natural motion and natural shape) may guide us in making those choices, it seems that in general there will always remain some area of choice. Consequently, the arguments of the previous section should have general significance and should apply to any law, whether dynamical or otherwise, that attempts to state the conditions under which a system is free from the action of forces.

But what of Newton's second law of motion? What is the logical status of this law? Is it a definition of force? Of mass? Or is it an empirical proposition relating force, mass, and acceleration? In the tradition that has succeeded Mach, Newton's second law of motion has been widely regarded as a definition of force—mass being defined independently via Newton's third law of motion. But is this account correct? By what criteria should we judge it to be correct?

It will be seen that the answers to these questions must depend on the purpose of our discussion. If we are attempting a rational reconstruction of mechanics, then the received account may be satisfactory. But if we are attempting to describe the actual role of Newton's second law in physical science, then it will be seen that this account is highly misleading. And our purpose here is the latter, for a description of the logical status of a law is here understood to be simply a generalized description of its role in physical science. It will therefore be argued that the received account of the logical status of Newton's second law of motion is unsatisfactory. The attempt will then be made to replace this account by a more satisfactory one.

Is Newton's Second Law a Definition of Force? In its original formulation, Newton's second law of motion simply asserted that the motive force acting on a body in (a given time) is proportional to the change of momentum that it undergoes (in that time) and is similarly directed. Thus if a football is kicked, then the magnitude of the kick is proportional to the change of momentum that the football undergoes from the initial to the final moments of contact with the boot. In this form, then, the law was obviously definitional. It was simply a definition erected according to the precept

that a cause is proportional to its effect, for certainly Newton had no independent criteria for determining the magnitude and direction of a kick.

But nowadays we have a different conceptual scheme. Instantaneous force is our fundamental dynamical force concept, and impulse is a defined concept. This historical argument therefore says little about the present status of Newton's second law. Nevertheless, the connection between the historical and the modern law is suggestive. Let $I(t)$ be the Newtonian motive force impressed upon a body in time t, and let $M(t)$ be the change of momentum which the body undergoes in that time. Then we have:

$$I(t) = M(t) \text{ (by definition)}$$

Now, provided that $M(t)$ is differentiable with respect to time, we may define the instantaneous force $f(t)$ as:

$$f(t) = dI(t) / dt = dM(t)$$

Hence the modern law is immediately derivable from the original, and it is tempting to argue that it can hardly be any less conventional.

However, the situation is not quite so simple. In the first place, we do not always *in fact* decide what magnitude of resultant force is acting on a given system by measuring its mass and acceleration. And it is seldom if ever true that we *must* use this procedure to determine the magnitude of such a force. Consequently, if the definitional status of (1) is to be maintained, then it must be shown that in the case of conflicting results concerning the magnitude of resultant forces, those results obtained using Newton's second law would always be preferred.

Second, a force is usually thought to be a *cause* of change of momentum, for if a change of momentum ΔM occurs in a time Δt, then we should say that this change must be produced by a force whose average value is $\Delta M / \Delta t$. But since causes and effects are always conceived to be independent existences, we should be reluctant to say that the existence of the effect (ΔM) *logically entails* the existence of a resultant force whose average measure is $\Delta M / \Delta t$. If a force of this magnitude does indeed exist, then this ought to be something that, according to our ordinary conception of force, is independently discoverable.

Of course it may be that our ordinary conception of resultant force is at fault, and that what we say about such forces is at variance with what we do. But if so— if (1) is true by definition—then our concept of resultant force must be entirely lacking in explanatory power, for we obviously cannot explain the existence of an effect by postulating the existence of something whose sole raison d'être is that it produces the given effect.

In fact, there is a variety of ways of determining the magnitude of the resultant force acting on a given system—ways based on a variety of different force laws. Never mind, for the moment, how these laws themselves are established. The fact is that we can determine the magnitude of the resultant force acting on a given system without *explicitly* relying upon Newton's second law of motion. Thus *prima facie* at least, our concept of resultant force is not lacking in explanatory power, and our ordinary conception of resultant force is not at fault. And if this is the case, then Newton's second law of motion can be held to be true by definition only if we are prepared, if necessary, to divest our concept of resultant force of all explanatory power.

Third, there appears to be a simple category mistake in saying that force is the product of mass and acceleration, for although we may distinguish different kinds of forces, it does not seem that we can also distinguish different kinds of products of mass and acceleration. We might say that the product of the mass and acceleration of a given object defines a scale for the measurement of the resultant force acting on that object. But then the question arises: Why should this scale be taken to be a scale of *force*? Is this an analytic connection? Or is this something that is empirically discoverable? If it is agreed that forces are not to be identified with rates of change of momentum, then how can the measure of the resultant force acting on a given system be identified with the measure of the rate of change of momentum? What kind of connection relates these two quantities? To answer these questions, it is necessary to clarify our ideas concerning scales and quantities.

Scales and Quantities. The existence of a quantity depends upon the existence of an objective linear order, for if the objects (systems, events, states, etc.) A_1, $A_2, A_3 \ldots A_n$ possess a given quantity q, it must always be possible to arrange those things in order of q by some objective ordering procedure-an objective ordering procedure being any that, if perfectly executed, would always lead to the same ordering among the same particulars under the same conditions, independent of who does the ordering. Moreover, if two or more logically independent and objective ordering procedures would always in fact generate the same order among the same particulars under the same conditions, then we should say that they are procedures for ordering those particulars in respect of a quantity q. Neither of these conditions is *both* necessary and sufficient for the existence of a quantity, but the first is necessary, and the second is sufficient.

Of course these conditions are somewhat idealized. Independent procedures for ordering things in respect of the same quantity (e.g., temperature) may differ in both range and definement. But *significant inversions* of order could not be tolerated. If two or more logical-ly independent and objective ordering procedures led to significantly different orders among the same things under the same conditions, then we should say that they were procedures for ordering things in respect of the *different* quantities.

Now, in general, there may be many logically independent procedures for ordering things in respect of the same quantity. In the case of temperature, for example, there are literally dozens of such procedures. Consequently, the criteria for the identity of quantities cannot be tied to the ordering procedures. We cannot, without destroying the whole structure of our science, say that every independent ordering procedure defines a different quantity. Rather we must say that it is the *order,* and not the ordering relationships, which provides us with criteria for the identity of quantities. The order may in fact be *identified* by any of a number of logically independent ordering procedures (just as a man may be identified by any of a number of independent descriptions). But it does not follow from this that any *particular* ordering procedure is essential to the concept of any given quantity (any more than it follows that any particular identifying descriptions belong essentially to the man they identify). Consequently, *it can be an empirical question* whether any given ordering procedure is a procedure for ordering things in respect of a given quantity. For our quantity concepts are, in Gasking's terminology, generally *cluster* concepts.[25]

An ordering procedure does not, of course, define a *scale.* To have a scale we must have some objective procedure for assigning numbers to things. And to have a *scale for the measurement of a given quantity* q, we must have an objective procedure for assigning numbers to things such that if those things are arranged in the order of numbers assigned, they will in fact be arranged in the order of *q*. Consequently, it is also usually an *empirical* question whether a given scale is a scale for the measurement of some given quantity. To discover, for example, whether a given scale is one for measuring temperature, we should usually have to discover whether or not the above criterion is in fact satisfied, i.e., whether the numerical order corresponds to the temperature order.

Consequently, if force is a quantity, it cannot be absurd in principle to ask whether any particular procedure for assigning numbers to things is a way of measuring the force acting upon them. True enough, to assign the number $dM(t)/dt$ to a given object at a given time is to make a measurement. But is this necessarily a way of measuring the resultant force acting on that body at that time?

To answer this question, we must consider how in fact we are able to order things in respect of the resultant forces acting upon them. One procedure, of course, is to place them in order of the rates at which their momenta are changing. But if this were the *only* procedure, then although the answer to our question would be obvious, it would mean that our concept of resultant force is utterly empty of explanatory power. There are, however, other procedures, for we can often *calculate* the measure of the resultant force acting upon a given system from a knowledge of the measures of the independent forces to which it is subject (assuming the principle of composition of forces). Hence it may yet be a legitimate question to ask whether $f(t) = dM(t)/dt$ necessarily defines a scale for the measurement of resultant forces.

Now there are, in fact, many and various procedures by which the magnitudes of the individual forces acting on a given system may be determined—electrostatic forces by charge and distance measurements, elastic forces by measurement of strain, magnetic forces by current and distance determinations, gravitational forces by mass and distance measurements, and so on. And it is an empirical fact that when all such force measurements are made and the magnitude of the resultant force determined, then the rate of change of momentum of the system under consideration is found to be proportional to the magnitude of this resultant force. It is this fact that justifies us in taking $f(t) = dM(t)/dt$ to define a scale for the measurement of *resultant force.*

Of course if the *calculated* measure of the resultant force did not agree even approximately with the *direct* measure of resultant force, we should not automatically cease to regard $dM(t)/dt$ as defining a scale for the measurement of resultant force. There are many other possible alternatives. We might, for example, question the accuracy of the measurements upon which our calculations were based. We might doubt the validity of applying some law (e.g., Hooke's law) to the particular case in question. We might even doubt the general validity of the principle of composition of forces. Or finally, we might doubt whether we had taken all of the active component forces into consideration. But all such doubts can be reduced. Doubts about the accuracy of our measurements may be reduced by careful repetition. Doubts about the validity of applying, say, Hooke's law could be diminished if the material in question could be shown to be elastic. The principle of composition of forces could be checked statically. And finally, if no side effects were discoverable that were uniquely correlated with the additional component forces required to yield the identity of the calculated and directly measured resultant forces, then we should have no *independent* reason for believing in the existence of any such forces.

However, although we may in this way become more and more doubtful about the legitimacy of taking $dM(t)/dt$ to define a scale for the measurement of resultant force, the rejection of this definition would seem to create an enormous conceptual problem. Many of the primary measurements that must be made to determine the resultant force acting on a given system and many of the principles that must be used in carrying out the necessary calculations will themselves be seen to be justified only on the assumption of the general validity of taking $dM(t)/dt$ to define a scale of resultant force. This does not mean, however, that there is any vicious circularity in the procedure by which we justify our considering $dM(t)/dt$ to be a measure of the resultant force acting upon a system, for it is by no means necessary that the whole complex of inference patterns which we have set up should cohere. On the contrary, it is a truly remarkable fact that they cohere as well as they do. But it is just this fact that would seem to create the enormous conceptual problem of ever rejecting the second law of motion and adopting an entirely different law.

There are some minor adjustments that might be made to Newton's second law without doing great violence to our conceptual framework. Thus we would adopt a scale of force that is nonlinear with respect to our ordinary scales of force without any but the most trivial changes. We could, for example, consider $dM(t)/dt$ to be proportional to the *square* of the resultant force. And then, to retain the coherence of our system of physics, we should merely have to substitute f^2 for f in all physical equations. But such a change would be a mere mathematical manipulation; its possibility tells us very little about the logical status of Newton's second law, for the form of the mathematical expression of *any* law is a function of the kinds of scales on which the related quantities are measured. The really fundamental change, which would demand some kind of conceptual revolution, would result if $dM(t)/dt$ were not considered to define *any* kind of scale for the measurement of resultant force.

If significant differences between the calculated and directly measured resultant forces did in fact exist in a sufficient number and variety of cases, and if, furthermore, there appeared to be no way of explaining these differences without resort to *ad hoc* devices, then no doubt such a fundamental change in our conceptual scheme would be forced upon us. Thus we may say that it is an empirical fact that we are able to maintain Newton's second law in a way that is *methodologically satisfactory.* And we may *express* this point by saying that Newton's second law is empirical. Nevertheless, we may question whether, even in the face of this fact, it would be *irrational* or *methodologically unsound* to accept any other law in its place. If not, then there is a clear sense in saying that it is only conventional that we accept $dM(t)/dt$ as defining a scale of resultant force. And we may express this fact by saying that Newton's second law of motion is only *conventionally* true.

Now in fact, *without* assuming that the results of our calculations and direct measurements of resultant force ever differ significantly or inexplicably, we could cease to consider that the rate of change of momentum of a body provides us with a measure of the resultant force that acts upon it, for if the principle of natural motion described in Part II were adopted, then we should consider that a body may change in momentum even though no forces were acting upon it. The reason is simply that any concept of naturally accelerated motion involves a concept of natural changes of momentum. In place of Newton's second law, therefore, we may postulate that the magnitude of the resultant force acting upon a body is proportional to the *difference* between its natural and its actual rate of change of momentum. This conceptual scheme will then be no less applicable to the physical world than is Newton's.

Consequently, although there is good and sound sense in describing Newton's second law as empirical, there is also good and sound sense in describing it as conventional.

Force and Mass. The problem most usually discussed in connection with Newton's second law is that of the relationship between force and mass, for it is obvious that unless a scale of mass can be set up independently of Newton's second law, we cannot use this law to define a scale of force. Consequently, if Newton's second law is to have any claim to any kind of empirical status, it must be possible to define a scale of mass independently.

But before we proceed to see whether this is possible, let us be more specific about what is required. According to our analysis in the previous section, we have a scale of mass if and only if we have a procedure for assigning numbers to things such that if these things are arranged in order of the numerical assignments, they are thereby arranged in order of mass. What, then, is the order of mass? There are a number of different ordering relationships that serve to identify this order. For ordinary terrestrial objects the order may be identified in any of a number of different ways, e.g., by substitution experiments on a beam balance, by noting velocity changes in collision experiments, or by noting mutually induced accelerations. For microscopic and submicroscopic objects, the first and last of these methods are generally inapplicable and the second is the most useful. But other methods, of varying degrees of directness ranging from mass spectograph readings to quite complex calculations based upon electronic charge measurements, equivalent weights, combining weights, and combining volumes, are also available. And it is hard to say that any one procedure for ordering such things in respect of mass is any more fundamental than any other. They are all regarded as mass ordering (or measuring) procedures because they yield similar results wherever their ranges of applicability overlap.

For macroscopic objects, such as the earth or the sun, the primary criterion is undoubtedly dependent upon the noting of mutually induced accelerations, although even here there are other relevant considerations.

Now it is evident that there is no single, universally applicable procedure for determining the mass order. And it is surely questionable whether we should expect to find such a procedure. At least it seems that we cannot assume a priori that there must be such a procedure, unless we are also prepared to accept a Lockean doctrine of real essences. But most philosophers nowadays would reject this doctrine for the very good reason that they have now become clear as to the "cluster" nature of many of our concepts. Consider once again the concept of temperature. As in the case of mass, there are a number of different temperature-ordering procedures. But no one of these is in fact applicable over the whole temperature range to all types and varieties of substances. Nevertheless, we do not feel that there must be a universally applicable temperature-ordering procedure that we could use once and for all to define the temperature order. We are content to allow the unity of the concept of temperature to rest upon the fact that the various temperature-ordering procedures yield similar results wherever their ranges of applicability overlap.

Why, then, should we make other demands of our concept of mass? Yet this demand is constantly made. Time and again, throughout the literature on Newton's second law of motion, the question is asked: what is the definition of mass? And this is almost invariably a request for a unique, universally applicable procedure for assigning numbers to things that will serve the dual purpose of defining the mass order and defining a scale for the measurement of mass. Of course there would be a certain satisfaction in discovering such a definition, for it might well pave the way to a *theoretical* interpretation of mass (just as the discovery of the thermodynamic scale of temperature paved the way for the kinetic theory of temperature). But this has nothing whatever to do with the logical status of Newton's second law of motion. It would only be relevant if the mass order could not be identified in any part of its range except via Newton's second law of motion. And in that case, our concept of mass would be akin to our concept of refractive index—a mere constant of proportionality. But since it is patently false that the various parts of the mass order can be identified only in this way, the quest for a unique, universally applicable procedure for measuring mass, however revealing it may otherwise be, is simply irrelevant to the logical status of Newton's second law.

However, there is some point, relevant to our purposes, in making another kind of investigation, viz., in trying to find a way of defining a scale of mass on which the masses of *macroscopic* objects (such as the sun and the planets) might be determined independently of Newton's second law. It may be held that the cosmologist is justified in regarding the concept of mass that he uses as having something like the status of a constant of proportionality, while the engineer and the chemist are not justified in regarding their concepts as having a similar logical status. It is not clear on what grounds such a view may be held, but presumably they would have to do with the different relevance of empirical considerations to the truth of statements concerning mass relationships in the different fields.

Whether such a view is tenable or not, there is a way of defining a scale of mass on which the masses of macroscopic objects may be determined, and which is independent of Newton's second law of motion. It is easily proved that if A_1, A_2, A_3 . . . A_n is any set of bodies moving only under the influence of mutually induced gravitational forces, then, assuming that the absolute accelerations $\bar{a}_1$, $\bar{a}_2$, $\bar{a}_3$, . . . $\bar{a}_n$ of A_1, A_2, A_3 . . . A_n are determinable, and that the mutual distances and angular displacements are known, the relative masses of these various bodies can be determined on the basis of this information alone.

Let the absolute accelerations $\bar{a}_1$, $\bar{a}_2$, $\bar{a}_3$, . . . $\bar{a}_n$ of A_1, A_2, A_3 . . . A_n, respectively, be resolved into components such that:

$$\bar{a}_i = C_{i1} I_{i1} + C_{i2} I_{i2} + \ldots + C_{i,\ i-i} I_{i,\ i-1} \ldots + C_{i,\ i+1} I_{i,\ i+1} \ldots + C_{in} I_{in} \ (i = 1, 2, \ldots n) \qquad (1)$$

where I_{ij} is a unit acceleration vector directed from A_i to A_j, and where C_{ij} is the magnitude of the component acceleration directed from A_i to A_j. Now in general it will be possible to achieve such a resolution in a variety of different ways, since the n equations (1) contain $2C^n_2$ unknown magnitudes (the C_{ij}'s). However, if we make the additional restrictions that:

$$M_i C_{ij} = M_j C_{ji} \quad (i, j = 1, 2, \ldots n, \ i \neq j) \quad (2)$$

M_i and M_j being the masses of A_i and A_j, respectively (this restriction being made in accordance with the kinematic principle of action and reaction—to be discussed in Part IV) and that:

$$C_{ij} + C_{ji} = G \quad M_i + M_j / r_{ij}^2 \quad (i, j = 1, 2, \ldots n, \ i \neq j) \qquad (3)$$

r_{ij} being the distance separating A_i and A_j (this restriction being in accordance with the law of distribution and succession which we have seen is derivable from Newton's law of gravitation), then, if the value of G is arbitrarily fixed, we have, in the sets of equations (1), (2), and (3), $C^n_2 + n$ independent equations involving $2C^n_2 + n$ unknowns. There are $2C^n_2$ unknown component acceleration magnitudes (the C_{ij}'s) and n unknown masses, and n equations (1), C^n_2 equations (2), C^n_2

equations (3). Hence the masses of the various objects moving only under the influence of mutually induced gravitational forces may all be determined.[26]

It may never be necessary, in any field, to rely on Newton's second law to define a scale of mass, for the argument shows that, even in the field of cosmology, it may be possible to set up a mass scale, suitable for determining the masses of macroscopic objects (such as those that comprise the solar system), on the basis of the assumed law that every body accelerates toward every other body in the universe with a component of relative acceleration that is directly proportional to the sum of their masses and inversely proportional to the square of the distance between them, unless they are acted upon by some (nongravitational) forces.

The Logical Status of Newton's Second Law. How, then, should we answer our question concerning the logical status of Newton's second law? Once the cluster nature of our concepts of force and mass becomes evident, it also becomes clear that no short answer is possible. Consider how Newton's second law is actually used. In some fields it is unquestionably true that Newton's second law is used to define a scale of force. How else, for example, can we measure interplanetary gravitational forces? But it is also unquestionably true that Newton's second law is sometimes used to define a scale of mass. Consider, for example, the use of the mass spectrograph. And in yet other fields, where force, mass, and acceleration are all easily and independently measurable, Newton's second law of motion functions as an empirical correlation between these three quantities. Consider, for example, the application of Newton's second law in ballistics and rocketry.

Newton's second law of motion thus has a variety of different roles. Sometimes it is used in one role, sometimes in another. To suppose that Newton's second law of motion, or *any* law for that matter, must have a unique role that we can describe generally and call the logical status is an unfounded and unjustifiable supposition. Many laws simply do not have such a unique function. Even a cursory inspection of the way in which we actually use many of our laws reveals this. Whether in fact we can *ascribe* unique roles to each of our various physical laws and still have a useful conceptual scheme is another and important question. But it is not the question of logical status. It is the question of whether it is possible to achieve a rational reconstruction of physics in which each law has a simple and easily characterizable logical status.

But how can a law be *both* an empirical proposition relating force, mass, and acceleration and, say, a definition of a scale of force? Isn't it self-contradictory to say such a thing? In one way, yes. The one law cannot play two such different roles in a single occurrence within a piece of scientific discourse. But in another way, no. The one law can play two quite different roles in two different pieces of scientific discourse. A contradiction can therefore be derived only if we assume that the one law can have only one role and that this role must be independent of the context of its use. But this is precisely what is being denied. It seems, then, quite evident that we use our laws to do a large variety of different jobs.

Consider an analogy. What is the logical status of the proposition that the angle between a tangent and a chord is equal to the angle in the alternate segment? Well, consider how the sentence can be used. It can be used to express the conclusion that might be drawn from a series of well-executed measurements made on certain kinds of pencil-drawn figures. It can also be used to express the conclusion of a Euclidean geometrical proof. Is the sentence ambiguous? That is certainly one way of thinking about it. But it is not the only way, for we could also say that different sorts of considerations are relevant to the truth of one and the same proposition—the formal considerations of Euclidean geometry as well as the empirical considerations of empirical geometry. And this way of thinking about it is no less natural or more forced than any other.

Now this is roughly the situation with regard to Newton's second law of motion. We have one formula that we use in a variety of different ways. But we do not say that the formula is ambiguous, or expresses a different proposition in each different context of use. Instead, we allow that it expresses one and the same proposition (i.e., Newton's second law) and also plays a variety of different roles. Sometimes it is used to define a scale of force, at other times to define a scale of mass, and at yet other times it expresses an empirical correlation between the results of force, mass, and acceleration measurements.

IV. *The Principle of Action and Reaction*

If any one of Newton's laws of motion can lay claim to being an empirical law, it is the principle of action and reaction. Let A and B be any two bodies. Then if we define the *free* motion of A without B as the motion that A would have in the absence of the body B, and the *free* motion of the body B without A as the motion that B would have in the absence of A, then it is an empirical fact the change of momentum (gauged relative to the free motion of A) that the body A undergoes in any given time is equal and opposite to the change of momentum (gauged relative to the free motion of B) which the body B undergoes in that same time. Thus if two bodies A and B collide in free fall, then the change of momentum of A (gauged relative to the free motion of A) is equal and opposite to the change of momentum of B (gauged relative to the free motion of B).

Let us call this law the *kinematic principle of action and reaction*. Now this appears to be an empirical law. It appears to be something that could be discovered, using the sorts of techniques that Huyghens used in connection with the law of conservation of momentum. It does not depend upon the adoption of any concept of *natural* motion. Hence it does not derive any element of conventionality from the same source as the first two laws. It is true that we need a concept of free motion for the body A without B, and a concept of the free motion of B without A. But then these concepts are operationally definable, for we may define the free motion of the body A without B as the motion that A would have when the body B was removed to a place infinitely distant from A. In fact, infinite removal is not a possibility. But in many cases (sufficiently many, it seems, to justify the universal generalization), infinite removal is not necessary, for as the body B is removed, it is seen that the motion of the body A (in the given circumstances) is independent of the position of the body B.

Consequently (provided only that changes of momentum can be gauged independently), there is a law that is at least a very close relative of the principle of action and reaction and that may well be described as empirical. The law cannot, of course, be tested in all cases. We cannot remove a planet from the solar system in order to gauge the free motions of the remaining planets (in the absence of the given planet). Nevertheless, this hardly counts against its being an empirical law. No law is everywhere testable. The important point is that it *can* be tested for a wide variety of terrestrial objects, composed of a wide variety of different substances, and moving in any of a wide variety of circumstances. And this point seems sufficient to establish the empirical character of the law.

What remains, then, is to see what relationship there is between this law and the principle of action and reaction, and to examine whether changes of momentum can be gauged independently of this law.

Mass, Action, and Reaction. The concepts of free and natural motion are clearly related concepts. Nevertheless, they are not identical, for we may have precisely the same concept of free motion whatever our concept of natural motion. The former is a purely kinematic concept. It is entirely noncommittal about forces. The free motion of A without B in a given situation can be found simply by removing B from that situation to such a position that further removal makes no difference. Whether or not we should say that A is then subject to the action of forces is irrelevant. The concept of natural motion, on the other hand, is a dynamic concept, for a body is moving naturally if and only if it is not subject to the action of forces. It would be absurd, therefore, to equate these two concepts, or to maintain that our concept of free motion is in any way dependent on our concept of natural motion.

Yet the principle of action and reaction, as it is usually understood, is a dynamic principle. Hence, since the law we have stated is purely kinematic and depends only on kinematic concepts, it cannot be maintained that the principle of action and reaction is identical with this law. Nevertheless, the connection is very close, for if it is assumed that the Newtonian "motive force" exerted by the body B on the body A is proportional to the change of momentum that A undergoes (gauged relative to the free motion of A without B) and vice versa, then we have at once that the motive forces exerted by A on B and B on A are equal and opposite. This is precisely Newton's third law of motion. Hence Newton's third law is derivable from this kinematic law (provided only that his second law is taken as an additional premise), and consequently, if the kinematic law may be said to be empirical, the principle of action and reaction may also be said to be an empirical law.

The only thing, then, that appears to stand in the way of an unqualified claim that the principle of action and reaction is an empirical law is the question of whether changes of momentum (relative to the free motions of the bodies concerned) can be gauged independently of this law. And since relative velocities are clearly measurable independently of the law, this comes down to the question of whether a scale of mass can be defined independently of the third law of motion.

For ordinary terrestrial objects, like cricket balls and tennis racquets, the answer to this question is obvious. A scale suitable for determining the masses of such things can be set up by the straightforward procedures of fundamental measurement (e.g., by substitution on a beam balance). Hence in the only range in which the law in question might be directly tested empirically, an independent scale of mass can undoubtedly be defined. The empirical character of the principle of action and reaction therefore appears to be established.

Of course it is much less clear that scales of mass suitable for determining the masses of macroscopic objects (such as planets) or microscopic objects (such as electrons and protons) can be set up independently of this principle. Even the scale proposed on p. 58 presupposes at least the kinematic principle of action and reaction. But then since no spatially and temporally unrestricted generalization is empirically testable over the whole of its range, this point does not tell against the empirical claim.

Yet even now the status of Newton's third law of motion is not clear, for how do we know that the mass of an object is independent of its state of motion or its situation? We could never tell this by making experiments with beam balances—unless the masses of different substances were affected differently by changes of situation or motion. Of course if no differential effects of this kind are known to exist, we may as a matter of convention adopt the principle of invariance of mass and then use this principle to test empirically the principle of action and reaction. But then it is doubtful whether we should in fact prefer the principle of invariance of mass to the principle of action and reaction. In other words, if our measurements of mass and velocity change were to conflict with the kinematic principle of action and reaction, we might prefer to reject the principle of invariance of mass and retain the principle of action and reaction. That is, we might prefer to define a scale for the mass of a moving object via the principle of action and reaction, and to reject, if necessary, the principle of invariance of mass.

Thus we may argue that although Newton's third law of motion was initially an empirical discovery, its status today is not that of an empirical proposition, but rather that of a definition, since the mass ratio MA/MB may be held to be equal to—$()V_B/)V_A)$ by definition [where $)V_A$ and $)V_B$ are the changes of velocity that A and B undergo (determined with respect to their free velocities) when A and B interact]. Of course it is an empirical fact that a scale of *mass* can be defined in this fashion, for it is an empirical fact that $)V_A$ and $)V_B$ are always oppositely directed and that M_A/M_B thus defined accords well with other independent determinations of mass ratios.

However, it seems that neither characterization of Newton's third law is entirely satisfactory. In many cases, in ballistics and rocketry, for example, its role is that of an empirical principle which enables us to predict velocity changes from a knowledge of certain masses and certain other velocity changes. In other cases, however, especially in microphysics, its role is more like that of a definition, for it provides us with one of our principal criteria for comparing the masses of microparticles.

V. Conclusion

It has been argued that Newton's laws of motion were primarily conceptual in origin and that all three of these laws were probably derived directly from Cartesian physics. It cannot, therefore, be claimed that these laws were originally supported by or derived inductively from detailed experimental work. It has also been shown that this lack of empirical support, at least in the case of the law of inertia, was not just an accidental feature, for no amount of experimental work could ever establish a principle of natural motion, or even provide inductive support for such a principle. The reason for this, it was argued, derives from our concept of a force. Forces exist only to explain effects. Since we are at liberty to choose to regard whatever changes or states we please as natural (i.e., as *not* being effects), it follows that the forces which we should say are operative in nature depend upon the choices we actually make.

For this reason, then, a principle of natural motion, such as the law of inertia, cannot be an empirical principle. Of course it does not follow that our choice of principle of natural motion is arbitrary. On the contrary, it has been shown that it is just such choices which govern the whole course of physical inquiry. The choices we actually make are always theory committed. Nevertheless, it has been seen that there still remains some area of choice. And, in fact, it is possible to construct a system of dynamics that appears to be the equal of Newton's, but that employs an entirely different principle of natural motion.

Newton's second law of motion was seen to present different problems. Is it an empirical principle relating force, mass, and acceleration? Does it define a scale for the measurement of resultant force? Or does it, perhaps, define a scale for the measurement of mass?

It has been argued that no clear affirmative or negative answers can be given to any of these questions. Any answer we give will misrepresent the role that the second law of motion actually has within the body of science. Does the engineer ever predict the acceleration of a given body from a knowledge of its mass and of the forces acting upon it? Of course. Does the chemist ever measure the mass of an atom by measuring its acceleration in a given field of force? Yes. Does the physicist ever determine the strength of a field by measuring the acceleration of a known mass in that field? Certainly. Why then, should any one of these roles be singled out as the role of Newton's second law of motion? The fact is that it has a variety of different roles. In some fields, where mass is particularly difficult to measure, Newton's second law may provide us with a scale for the measurement of mass. In other fields, where force measurement is otherwise difficult or impossible, Newton's second law may provide us with a suitable scale for the measurement of force. And in yet other fields, where force, mass, and acceleration are all easily and independently measurable, Newton's second law appears as an empirical principle relating these three quantities. To suppose that there must be a *central* role is an unwarranted metaphysical postulate. The important question is: "How is the law in question actually used in science?"

Similar considerations were seen to apply to Newton's third law of motion. Is it an empirical proposition relating momentum changes? Or is it a proposition whose role in science is to define a scale of mass? The most appropriate answer is "both." Consider its role in science. Clearly, it sometimes has the role of an empirical proposition, for momentum changes are often determinable independently of this law. But also clearly, its role is sometimes to define a scale of mass. To maintain that its role *must* be one or the other is an unwarranted and unjustifiable assumption.

In discussing the three laws of motion, the framework of Newtonian physics has been assumed throughout. No questions concerning *absolute* motion, *uniform* motion, or *straight line* motion have been asked or considered. This is indeed a serious omission. But in that most discussions of Newtonian dynamics have concentrated on these questions to the neglect of those concerning the concepts of force and mass, it is hoped that this essay may serve as a useful complement. To embark now on a discussion of these other concepts would require an essay at least as long as the present one.

Notes

[1] H. Butterfield, *The Origins of Modern Science, 1300-1800* (London: G. Bell & Sons, Ltd., 1949).

[2] Galileo Galilei, *Dialogues Concerning Two New Sciences,* H. Crew and A. de Salvio, trans. (New York: Dover Publications, Inc., 1914).

[3] *Ibid.,* p. 166.

[4] *Ibid.,* p. 244.

[5] *Ibid.,* p. 251.

[6] *Ibid.,* pp. 165-166.

[7] Galileo Galilei, *Dialogue Concerning the Two Chief World Systems—Ptolemaic and Copernican,* Stillman Drake, trans. (Berkeley: University of California Press, 1953).

[8] *Ibid.,* pp. 19, 31.

[9] René Descartes, *A Discourse on Method, etc.,* John Veitch, trans. (London: J. M. Dent & Sons, Ltd., 1912), p. 16.

[10] René Descartes, *Philosophical Writings,* E. Anscombe and P. Geach, trans. and eds. (London: Thomas Nelson & Sons, 1954), p. 215.

[11] *Oeuvres de Descartes,* Charles Adam and Paul Tannery, eds., Vol. XI (Paris: Cerf, 1909).

[12] For an English translation of most of the relevant sections, see *Philosophical Writings, op. cit.,* pp. 199-228.

[13] *Ibid.,* p. 217.

[14] Sir Isaac Newton, *Philosophiae Naturalis Principia Mathematica,* 2nd ed. (1713), p. 12. Emphasis added.

[15] Sir Isaac Newton, *Mathematical Principles of Natural Philosophy,* Andrew Motte, trans., rev. by F. Cajori (London: Cambridge University Press, 1934). Emphasis added.

[16] M. Jammer, *Concepts of Force* (Cambridge: Harvard University Press, 1957), p. 124.

[17] *Principia,* p. 13. Emphasis added.

[18] *Ibid.,* p. 14. Emphasis added.

[19] *Ibid.,* p. 21. Emphasis added.

[20] *Ibid.,* p. 2.

[21] It was a universally received doctrine that forces are conserved, and hence that they are in some sense equal to the effects they produce. The only point of disagreement concerned the true measure of force. The Cartesians measured force by the product of mass and velocity, the Leibnizians by the product of mass and velocity squared (*vis viva*). But all were agreed that forces are conserved. For an account of this dispute, see W. F. Magie, *A Sourcebook in Physics* (McGraw-Hill Book Company, 1935).

In any case, the doctrine, *causa aequat effectam,* must be supposed to lie behind Newton's second law of motion however it is interpreted. *Cf.* d'Alembert's comment on Newton's second law of motion that it is "a principle based on that single, vague and obscure axiom that the effect is proportional to its cause."

[22] *Oeuvres de Descartes, op. cit.,* Vol. XI, p. 43.

[23] The precise meaning of this law is explained more fully in Section III, where it is applied to show that an analytic solution of the *n*-body problem is in principle possible—a conclusion that incidentally demonstrates the possibility of setting up a purely *kinematic* definition of mass.

[24] Identical in formulation—although not identical in application, for "acceleration" must here be taken to mean "acceleration relative to the natural acceleration" rather than "acceleration relative to the natural *unaccelerated* motion."

[25] D. A. T. Gasking, "Clusters," *Australasian Journal of Philosophy,* Vol. XXXVIII, No. 1 (May, 1960).

[26] Some comments on this demonstration are in order. First, the resolution of the absolute accelerations into component accelerations of *finite* magnitude may not always be possible. If, for example, the n bodies A_1, A_2, A_3 . . . A_n are all coplanar, but the absolute acceleration $\bar{a}_1$, $\bar{a}_2$, $\bar{a}_3$, . . . $\bar{a}_n$ are not similarly coplanar, then the resolution will not be possible. Hence a necessary condition for the general applicability of this procedure to determine a set of M's is that there should exist in the set A_1, A_2, A_3 . . . A_n at least four bodies that are not coplanar. Second, the M's determined by this procedure may not all be positive. They must all be real, since all of the constants must be real, and all of the equations are linear in each variable. But the equations themselves give no guarantee that the M's will be > 0, or that they will remain invariant, in time. Nevertheless, if the equations of Newtonian mechanics accurately describe the motions of a set of objects that move only under the influence of mutually induced gravitational forces, then such results should not *in fact* be obtained. And if, in isolated cases, such results were obtained, then we may suspect either that the chosen frame of reference (for the determination of absolute accelerations) was not an inertial frame, or that some forces other than gravitational forces were operative.

D. T. Whiteside (essay date 1967)

SOURCE: "Sources and Strengths of Newton's Early Mathematical Thought," in *The Texas Quarterly,* Vol. X, No. 3, Autumn 1967, pp. 69-85.

[*In the following excerpt, Whiteside traces the development of Newton's mathematical thought and comments on his achievements in calculus.*]

In this tercentenary year we celebrate, in spirit if perhaps not with full historical accuracy, the first maturing of Newton the exact scientist. Persuaded by a wealth of pleasant traditional anecdote and autobiographical reminiscence, our thoughts go back three hundred years to a young Cambridge student, at twenty-three scarcely on the brink of manhood, working away undisturbed in a cramped, roughhewn study set in a sunny corner of the small stone house where he was born, amidst the lazy, undulating fields of his native Lincolnshire countryside. The busy intellectual stir of the university at which he recently graduated and the daily excitements of student life at Trinity College are eighty miles distant to the south and a world away in mood. We are a little awed at the explosion of mental energy in a man in the prime of his age for invention, who in little more than a year transmuted the received theoretical bases of infinitesimal calculus, dynamics, and optics into their classical forms. But we live in a skeptical, hardheaded age and all this is for us uncomfortably close to heroic myth, if not to wonderland. What we praise and commemorate we now require to have had a real past existence and we seek the historical truth which underlies the tradition of Newton's *annus mirabilis.* What did happen in 1666? Where and how did it happen? What was its significance? What formative pattern did it create for the future development of Newton's scientific thought? The detailed illumination

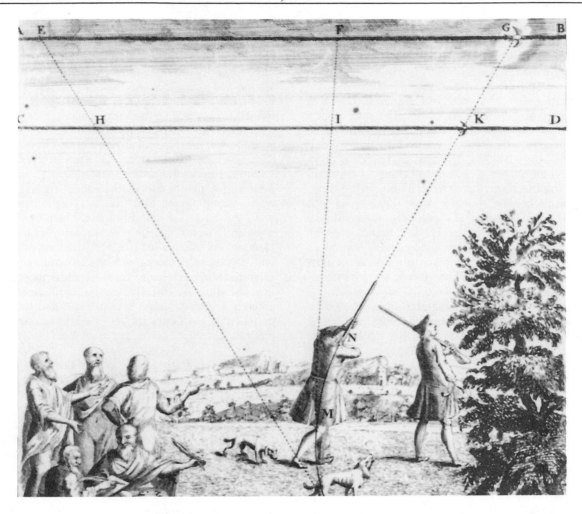

An Illustration from The Method of Fluxions *(1671).*

of the sequence and import of his discoveries in natural philosophy at a time when he minded it "more then at any time since" I leave in the capable hands of my colleagues. For almost ten years now I have been myself preoccupied with the study of Newton's mathematical achievement per se. Let me then, for my own part, discuss his preliminary researches in that field up to the end of his magical year of discovery and try to assess their role in the creation of Newton's mature mathematical method.

When we talk conventionally of Newton's mathematical achievement we refer, directly or obliquely, to the content of six small tracts of his authorship—precisely, the *De Analysi per Æquationes Numero Terminorum Infinitas* of 1669, the so-called *Methodus Fluxionum et Serierum Infinitarum* of 1671, the *Arithmetica Universalis* of 1683, the *De Quadratura Curvarum* of 1693, the *Enumeratio Linearum Tertij Ordinis* of 1695, and the *Methodus Differentialis,* which went into its final form as late as 1710.[1] We have also,

perhaps, one eye on the relevant portions of his *Lectiones Opticæ* of 1672 and especially of his *Principia Mathematica* of 1686. (These dates, I would hasten to say, are rough terminal dates of composition, not those of their first publication.) In fact, however, a stream of mathematical researches poured forth from Newton's pen with scarcely a break between early 1664, when he was in his last undergraduate year, and the spring of 1696, when he forwent the sheltered, routine existence of a university mathematics professor with a bare minimum of teaching obligations for the demanding, sophisticated whirl of public life in London. Even thereafter his creative flame was not quenched but flared up again from time to time—not least, indeed, in his eightieth year when he personally edited the second edition of his *Universal Arithmetic* in correction of Whiston's unauthorized version of fifteen years before. In bulk, the extant record of the totality of that achievement covers something of the order of five thousand quarto and folio sheets crowded with Newton's small, distinctive writing and ranging in subject from elementary mensuration to sophisticated projective geometry, from analysis of fundamental algebraic operations and introductory number theory to finite differences and abstruse theory of equations, from the first principles of coordinate geometry and the tracing of curves to the detailed subclassification of cubics and the general theory of lines of higher order, from the finding *ad hoc* of tangents to simple curves and the "squaring" of their area to the complex ramifications of a mighty fluxional calculus which, in application, clarified geometrical dioptrics and revolutionized the study of celestial mechanics. In the first installment of what, I hope, will eventually be a comprehensive selection from this huge corpus of unpublished manuscript[2] I have recently, with the able secretaryship of Dr. Michael Hoskin, gathered within the confines of a single volume that portion composed during the period 1664-66 whose terminal year we now celebrate. In what follows let me use it as my bible.

For anyone who attempts to understand Newton's first mathematical years one question immediately arises: How and where did Newton receive his mathematical education and what was its content?[3]

Out of necessity, for our knowledge of Newton's pre-university education we rely heavily on William Stukeley and John Conduitt,[4] only the latter of whom personally knew him well. We learn that he passed a couple of years at local dame schools as a child and then spent his boyhood and youth, except for a period in his late teens when his mother recalled him to manage the Woolsthorpe farm, at grammar school in the nearby market town of Grantham. At the first he would receive a bare introduction to the elements of reading, writing and reckoning, while we know enough of the latter's headmaster, John Stokes, to realize that he was progressive and would take pains to inculcate into his pupils something more than Ben Jonson's despised "small Latine and lesse Greeke." But we should be careful not to overestimate the mathematical content of the curriculum even of a go-ahead English school at this period. The comparison, tempting though it is to make, with that of a modern grammar or high school course in mathematics is wholly invalid and we should remember that the study of Euclid was at this time a university discipline while algebra and trigonometry were not even there taught formally—indeed, in contemporary English academic circles they were widely held to be essentially practical subjects which did not adequately exercise the mind and were therefore better left to the working mathematical practitioners of London and the main provincial centers of business and trade. Perhaps the content of a small notebook, dated 1654, which is now in Grantham Public Library[5] affords a truer glimpse into Newton's preuniversity mathematical studies. If its worked examples are typical of those which he himself went through at school in Grantham he would there have acquired a passable facility with the basic arithmetical rules and a ready acquaintance with elementary

weight and mensuration problems and the casting of accounts—otherwise, little. The few details we have of Newton's early life in effect confirm this impression, though we would very much like to know what he read among the miscellany of books parcelled up in the garret of the town apothecary, Mr. Clark, with whom he lodged for several years. From Stukeley we hear tales of an interest in constructing sundials and of a developed aptitude for mechanical invention and that the walls of the same Grantham garret "were full of the drawings he had made upon them, with charcole: . . . birds, beasts, men, ships, plants and mathematical figures as he took them, being circles and triangles"—perhaps these last were similar to the roughly incised sets of "intersecting lines and circles" scribbled, we presume, by the young Newton on the walls of his Woolsthorpe home.[6] Nowhere is there evidence of real mathematical (or indeed scientific) precociousness and we must accept that up to the time, June of 1661, when, in his nineteenth year, he entered Trinity College Newton had had no proper experience of mathematics as a deductive, structural discipline.

With Newton's admission to Cambridge we pass from loose hearsay knowledge backed with but little direct information to a factual world firmly defined by extant documentation. The content of an undergraduate notebook[7] which annotates texts by Aristotle and several contemporary standard commentaries upon him stresses the sound disciplining in the trivium of logic, ethics, and rhetoric which Newton received in his early university years under a system still essentially scholastic in structure, one laying emphasis both in formal lecture and informal disputation on the teaching of Aristotle and with its classical bias reinforced in Newton's own case by the interests of his tutor, Benjamin Pulleyn, soon to become Regius Professor of Greek. To his hard training at this time in the intricacies of syllogistic argument Newton's later vigorous clarity of logical exposition certainly owed much, but the mathematical content of such a medieval program of study was low, consisting almost entirely in the analysis of elementary portions of Euclid's *Elements* from a logical viewpoint. When Newton sought to evaluate the technical content which underlay the complicated formal logic by which Euclid's propositions were deduced he was, if we may trust Conduitt,[8] disillusioned, finding it so easy and self-evident that he wondered anybody would be at the pains of writing a demonstration of them and laid Euclid aside as a trifling book. Whether or not he paid for his early neglect of Euclid when later he was thwarted in his aspiration to be a Scholar of his college—a setback redeemed, we are told, only after he had satisfied Barrow of his knowledge of the *Elements*[9]—need not concern us, though we should remember that the many crowded margins of Newton's copy of Barrow's 1655 edition, now in his old college, Trinity,[10] reveal that no later than early 1664 he had made a close study of the more "arithmetical" books, V, VII, and X. In his later years, of course, he referred back frequently to a variety of Euclidean theorems in support of stages in his own mathematical arguments. Nonetheless we will not find in Euclid, or indeed any of the Greek masters, notably Archimedes, whom he later studied, the source of his first creative researches. Indeed, the true mathematical fount of the fertile discoveries of Newton's *annus mirabilis* is not to be located in anything he learned formally from his teachers during his undergraduate years in Cambridge, but rather may we trace it to the books he then read without official guidance or approval, whose content he mastered and then transmuted by his own unaided genius. Newton was an autodidact genius, not a gifted pupil.

The year 1664 I just now mentioned is a crucial period in Newton's development both as scientist and mathematician. Then it was he began to extend his reading beyond such conventional Aristotelian texts as Magirus' *Physiologia Peripatetica* to the modern mechanical philosophy expounded by Gassendi, Charleton, and Boyle and to the "new" Keplerian astronomy promoted by Ward and Streete.[11] In the same notebook in which he made his jottings on Magirus he began a new section of his own *Quæstiones quædam philosophicæ* whose tone, at first conventionally scholastic, changed rapidly to accommodate the bons mots of the new philosophers. Above all, Newton was one of Roger North's "brisk part of the university"[12] who in that year began to be stirred by the Cartesian ideas which, propagated by Rohault, were to dominate the Cambridge scene for over thirty years and to encourage such theses for disputation as that defended by Wharton in 1682: "Cartesiana Cometarum explicatio nec Physicis nec Astronomicis repugnat Principiis."[13] Within a few months it would appear that Newton read everything of Descartes's available in print, and certainly the *Dioptrique, Geometrie,* and *Principia Philosophiæ* whose themes recur again and again in his mature work. It was inevitable that to advance in these demanding scientific studies Newton would have to acquire a competency in existing mathematical techniques—without it whole stretches not only of Kepler, Descartes and Galileo but even of Streete's modest *Astronomia Carolina* were denied to him. In the event, according to De Moivre, the expatriate French intimate of Newton in his last years, the immediate impulse to begin a course of mathematical self-education was that, in skimming through a "book of Astrology" (perhaps Streete's *Astronomia*?) bought at Stourbridge fair, he was halted by "a figure of the heavens which he could not understand for want of being acquainted with Trigonometry," and when he bought an unnamed work on that topic he was at a loss for want of knowledge of Euclid's *Elements*. He therefore

> Got Euclid to fit himself for understanding the ground of Trigonometry. Read only the titles of the propositions, which he found so easy to understand

that he wondered how any body would amuse themselves to write any demonstrations of them. Began to change his mind when he read that Parallelograms upon the same base and between the same Parallels are equal, and that other proposition that in a right angled Triangle the square of the Hypothenuse is equal to the squares of the two other sides. Began again to read Euclid with more attention than he had done before and went through it.

> Read Oughtreds [*Clavis*] which he understood tho not entirely, he having some difficulties about what the Author called Scala secundi & tertii gradus, relating to the solution of quadratick [&] Cubick Equations. Took Descartes's *Geometry* in hand, tho he had been told it would be very difficult, read some ten pages in it, then stopt, began again, went a little further than the first time, stopt again, went back again to the beginning, read on till by degrees he made himself master of the whole, to that degree that he understood Descartes's Geometry better than he had done Euclid.

> Read Euclid again & then Descartes's Geometry for a second time. Read next Dr Wallis's *Arithmetica Infinitorum,* & on the occasion of a certain interpolation for the quadrature of the circle, found that admirable Theorem for raising a Binomial to a power given. But before that time, a little after reading Descartes's Geometry, [he] wrote many things concerning the vertices Axes [&] diameters of curves, which afterwards gave rise to that excellent tract de Curvis secundi generis. . . .[14]

This has the ring of authenticity and is surely at least an accurate recounting of Newton's own version of his mathematical baptism. The order in which he read Oughtred and Descartes we cannot confirm but the former's *Clavis Mathematicæ,* especially in its latest 1652 edition (a copy of which Newton bought),[15] was widely studied as an introductory text in higher mathematics, while Descartes's *Geometrie* was in every sense an advanced monograph, made indeed, by its author's own testimony, deliberately obscure. Newton's unpublished investigations of the properties of curves by transforming their Cartesian equations to new axes, dated between September and December of 1664, still exist[16] and certainly precede by several months his researches in generalization of Wallis into the binomial expansion, which invariably in later life he delegated to the following winter. What we miss in De Moivre's account is a detailed list of Newton's early reading. Newton himself long afterward went some way towards widening our knowledge of this aspect, adding in parenthesis to his still extant early notes on Wallis' *Arithmetica* and Schooten's *Miscellanea*[17] that "By consulting an accompt of my expenses at Cambridge in the years 1663 & 1664 I find that in ye year 1664 a little before Christmas . . . I bought Schooten's Miscellanies & Cartes's Geometry (having read this Geometry & Oughtred's Clavis above half a year before) & borrowed Wallis's works and by consequence made these annotations out of Schooten & Wallis in winter between the years 1664 & 1665."[18] If we add a few other names, especially those of Viète, Hudde, and Heuraet, we will have a tolerably complete list of the external sources of Newton's mathematical achievement during the two years preceding his *annus mirabilis*. These names we encounter time and again when we read through the extant record of his mathematical researches during those two golden years of invention, investigations whose detailed elaboration was to occupy him with but brief intermission the remainder of his active life.

What I have tried to suggest is that up to the beginning of 1664 Newton's grounding in basic mathematics was not deep, that, though adequately competent in the techniques of arithmetic and elementary mensuration, he had but a sketchy knowledge of the fundaments of algebra and trigonometry, and that his appreciation of geometrical structure went little further than the opening propositions of the *Elements*. In a very real sense Oughtred's *Clavis Mathematicæ* was a mathematical key which unlocked for Newton the door to a realization of the potentialities of the algebraic free ("specious") variable in codifying not merely arithmetic but also geometry. It further directed him to the more profound investigations of Viète, conveniently collected in Schooten's 1646 Leyden edition.[19] In the opening pages of a small pocket book, now in the Fitzwilliam Museum in Cambridge, we may see Newton noting the Pythagorean theorem which relates the sides of right triangles—that which had halted him in his first progress through the *Elements*—stating it in algebraic form but hesitating between a reference to Caput XVIII (the "Penus analytica") of the *Clavis* and to Euclid I, 47, then ultimately settling for the latter. In a second notebook, now in Cambridge University Library, we find him shortly afterward annotating Viète's method for resolving numerical equations but making wide use of the simplified notation introduced by Oughtred in his appended *De Æquationum Affectarum Resolutione in numeris* in so doing.[20] From the two thick volumes of Wallis' *Opera Mathematica*[21] which he borrowed at the close of 1664 he gained his first insight into the naïve calculus of indivisibles, learning how to compound and interpolate integrals in mathematically significant ways and sharpening Wallis' methods of so doing. Out of his annotations of "Dr. Wallis his Arithmetica infinitorum,"[22] exactly as he told Leibniz twelve years later in his *epistola posterior*,[23] there of course developed his series expansion of the general binomial. But Schooten's bulky second Latin edition of Descartes's *Geometrie* was the work which, with some complements from Schooten's own fat *Exercitationes Mathematicæ* of 1657,[24] was overwhelmingly to direct the future course of Newton's mathematical development. The concept of the defining equation of a locus with respect to suitable coordinate line lengths, not

necessarily "Cartesian" but perhaps bipolar (an alternative suggested by Descartes) or one of the variants proposed by Newton in a paper of October 1664, as the algebraic mirror of the geometrical curve which the locus represented was the essential idea which the *Geometrie* explored, though inexpertly and incoherently—to appreciate it fully, indeed, it was necessary to cut away much of the dross with which Descartes loaded his tract, not least his approach to curves by paired degrees. In his elaboration[25] Newton was for the first time to make the algebraic concept of degree fundamental in the subclassification of curves and to systematize the linear transformations of coordinates by which they are reduced to canonical forms (as Descartes had reduced the conic locus to its three nondegenerate species). At a differential level the Cartesian algorithm for constructing the "subnormal" at a point on a curve was to be of fundamental importance in clarifying his thoughts on differentiation and in suggesting to him that it is an exact converse to integration.[26] When in May 1665 Newton became interested in the geometrical construction of equations[27] the *Geometrie* was once more his inspiration. It was, lastly, in tracts appended to the Latin *Geometrie* that Newton encountered the others I have mentioned: Hudde, whose algorithmic improvement of Descartes's subnormal method[28] was highly cherished by Newton, and Heuraet, whose rectification procedure[29] suggested to him a geometrical proof of the inverse nature of the methods of tangents and of quadratures.

In all this a strong bias to the analytical away from the purely geometrical is noticeable and that emphasis is clearly borne out by a reading of the documentary record of Newton's early researches. What little of "Greek" geometry there is, mostly derivative from Viète or Schooten, is usually approached in Cartesian fashion by reduction to an algebraic equivalent. We are, too, perhaps a little disappointed that Newton read so little of standard contemporary mathematical works, or if he did has left no hint—nowhere in his early autograph papers do we find the names of Napier, Briggs, Desargues, Fermat, Pascal, Kepler, Torricelli, or even Archimedes and Barrow. Nevertheless, we will readily admit that from his reading Newton fashioned all that a creative mathematician needs: a usable, flexible set of notations, a competent expertise with basic mathematical structures, an excellent technical grasp of the hard core of contemporary knowledge in his subject and, not least, some sense of promising avenues for research. Nor should we think of the period of Newton's annotations as a defined first stage in his mathematical development which can be set off as a period of submissive apprenticeship to his chosen discipline. Already in his first notes on Schooten, Descartes and Wallis it is difficult to separate mere annotation from creative reaction: a few months later, by the spring of 1665, they had outlived their usefulness for him and it was time for Newton to pursue his own independent researches.

Leaving aside further discussion of the sequence of external historical event, let me now try and suggest to you something of the creative power and excitement which a reading of the still extant manuscript record of those researches evokes. At the same time let me attempt to draw certain inferences which I believe to be true of Newton's mathematical development generally.

Not unexpectedly, his first researches in a mathematical field stemmed directly, in the early autumn of 1664, from the *Geometrie* and its appended tracts. In the Fitzwilliam notebook we see him slowly mastering the intricacies of the geometrical and analytical theory of conics and also, not always correctly, essaying certain improvements of his own. He there shows himself to be fascinated by the mechanical descriptions of those curves which he found in Schooten and De Witt[30]—an interest which a few years later was to lead him to consider their unified "organic" construction and then develop their projective theory.[31] Elsewhere at this time, on the verso of the first page of his Waste Book, he was hard at work seeking to perfect his understanding of the ovals which Descartes had, in his second book, introduced for their refractive property of transmitting all rays of white light emergent from one point through a second.[32] A few weeks later Newton approached one of the most difficult problems of elementary analytical geometry: given a coordinate system and some defining equation, to draw the "crooked Line" which that equation represents and evaluate its "propertys." The particular properties he chose to concentrate his attention upon were all generalizations of ones significant in a conic, namely "axes, vertices, diamiters, centers or asymptotes . . . supposeing it have them."[33] His technique was beautifully simple: try to reduce the given defining equation by permissible transformation to a form which evidently represents a curve possessed of the required property. In example, his criterion for a curve to have a diameter was that its equation be reducible by linear transform to a second in which odd powers of one of the coordinate variables were not present. The technical implementation of this insight was, of course, less easy. In reducing the second degree equation to its three nondegenerate canonical species Descartes had made use, but only implicitly, of a simple change of coordinates: the general theory of such transformations from one oblique pair to another had nowhere yet been worked out. Over the three months October to December of 1664 Newton did just that, developing the theory of such transforms in complete generality and indeed, for easier manipulation in their practical application, constructing lengthy, complicated tables of coefficients. . . .

These researches into curve properties and coordinate transformation were not, however, to receive their true reward till some years later when he first attacked—and brilliantly if not quite completely resolved—the problem of subclassifying the general cubic on the analogy of the three subspecies of conic. After applying a general linear transform to the ten terms of the cubic's defining equation he was faced with simplifying a derived equation of eighty-four terms. It is a tribute to his mental stamina and concentration no less than to his genius that he did so, and then proceeded to enumerate almost all of the seventy-eight species into which the cubic subdivides on Newton's terms. The complexity bothered him somewhat, so he thereupon gave the more manageable Eulerian division into sixteen species differentiated only by the nature of their infinite branches![35]

But what above all we celebrate in this tercentenary year is Newton's creation of his calculus of fluxions and his first insights into infinite series. From his own autobiographical reminiscence in old age and from certain other documents published, or at least circulated, at the time of his priority dispute with the Leibnizians, it has long been known that his early researches in these topics were considerable.[36] No one, however, who has not worked through the still extant manuscript of those researches can begin to appreciate their massive complexity. In my edition of those papers, indeed, I have found it helpful to incorporate a guide map to the ramifications of their highways and byways.[37] I do not need to say that I cannot here begin to summarize their detail.

On Newton's celebrated discovery of the general binomial expansion in the winter of 1664/5 let me be brief.[38] Exactly as he later admitted, Newton's inspiration derived from his careful study of Wallis' interpolation of the "circle" integral $1/\int_0^1 (1 - x^2)^p.dx$, $p = \frac{1}{2}$, in the integral sequence defined as p varies between zero and infinity. (This fruitful integral, may I interject, was the source both of Wallis' infinite-product and Brouncker's continued-fraction development of $4/\pi$.)[39] In hindsight it will be obvious that the numerical upper bound, unity, to Wallis' integral sequence was the main reason why he himself failed to detect the crucial binomial pattern of coefficients implicit in its expansion, but we will at the same time appreciate the brilliance which led Newton to make it algebraically free and consider the binomial pattern as it emerges from a suitable spectrum of values of p. The remaining generalization,

$$\int_0^x (1 - x^2)^p.dx = X - \binom{P}{1} . 1/3X^3 + \binom{P}{2} . 1/5X^5 - \dots .$$

and its more usual derivative form, is all but trivial to formulate. (Its proof is, of course, something else and Newton nowhere attempted it.[40]) I should not forget to recall that he was for a period highly delighted with his result, from the expansion for $p = \frac{1}{2}$ deriving the inverse sine series in various ways and from that for $p = -1$ computing the logarithmic series with which, at Boothby in the summer of 1665, he spent many a happy hour calculating natural logarithms to "two and fifty" and more places—numerically correct, however, to scarcely half that number.[41] Nor that within a few years of Newton's discovery, which he did not circulate, infinite series (such as Mercator's for the logarithm and Leibniz' for the inverse tangent) which made implicit use of particular binomial expansions were common. It is hard to resist the impression that the binomial expansion was going to be discovered, come what may, and that Newton was chosen to do so by historical accident. I have myself, indeed, elsewhere shown that the expansion for index ½ is implicit in Chapter 8 of Briggs's preface to his 1624 *Arithmetica Logarithmica,* while since 1939 we know that James Gregory rediscovered the general expansion in 1670 as a corollary to his finite-difference researches.[42] Even more startling perhaps, as J. A. Lohne will no doubt soon show us, are the anticipations to be found in the still unpublished manuscripts of Thomas Harriot, penned around 1605.

The fluxional calculus, however, is Newton's undivided glory. Beginning in the early autumn of 1664 with Descartes's double-root algorithm for constructing the subnormal to an algebraic curve—the projection of the normal at any point upon the curve's base—Newton swiftly appreciated the computational facility of Hudde's multipliers for finding maxima and minima (expounded in a tract of his[43] appended by Schooten to the Latin *Geometrie*) and straightaway applied it to the construction of the subtangent—the similar projection of the tangent—and circle of curvature at a general point on a curve. Within a few months, by the spring of 1665, he had unified his several methods of resolving normal, tangent, and curvature problems into a general differentiation procedure founded upon the concept of an indefinitely small and ultimately vanishing increment of a variable, whether algebraic or a general geometrical line-segment.[44]

Essentially, Newton found the derivative of the function $y = f(x)$ (and so, in geometrical terms, the slope at a point on the curve represented by that equation in some oblique Cartesian co-ordinate system) by positing the small increment o of its base variable x and then considering the limit of $z = f(x+o)$ as o tends to zero. (This "little zero" notation for an increment, an unconscious echo of Beaugrand's usage of thirty years before,[45] first appears in Newton's rough notes, in September 1664 or a little after, on the Cartesian-inspired problem of two refractions[46] but was at once taken over into his more narrowly mathematical researches.) . . .

Over his other early achievements in calculus I must, for want of time, pass quickly. Making the Cartesian subnormal $v = y \, dy/dx$ his derivative basis (and using a superscript double-dot homogenized notation) Newton was able, about the same time or soon after, to state[53] the standard differential algorithms in full generality a decade before Leibniz (and nineteen years

before they were published by him). A parallel stream of researches in integration, founded on Wallis' "arithmetick of infinites" and on Heuraet's rectification procedure, led to a firm grasp on Newton's part of the problem of quadrature and the geometrical insight that it is an exact inverse to that of tangents.[54] In the summer and early autumn of 1665, away in Lincolnshire with ample time for unhurried reassessment, he recast the theoretical basis of his newly acquired calculus techniques, making the change from the fundamental concept of the indefinitely small, discrete increment of a variable to that of its "moment," the product of its fluxion and the unit increment of the conventional variable of "time."[55] Whatever the logical satisfaction of the new basis, from a technical viewpoint, of course, the transition was without effect: in modern terms, it involved merely the replacing of each increment dx of a variable x by its equal ox, where o is the increment of time variable t and $\dot{x} = dx/dt$ is the "fluxion" of x. Also at this time he made a first attack on simple fluxional equations but with very limited success[56]—but it is startling that he should attempt their systematic resolution at all in 1665. Later, in the autumn of that year, Newton returned to the tangent problem, attacking it for a curve defined in an arbitrary co-ordinate system by evaluating and suitably compounding the limit-motions at a given point. After a crisis on October 29,[57] when he attempted to apply the parallelogram of "forces" to the construction of the tangent to the quadratrix of Dinostratus (the meet of a uniformly translating line with a uniformly rotating radius vector), he discovered his howler and wrote up the correct construction in a paper on tangents to "mechanichall" curves ten days later.[58] The next May (1666), between the fourteenth and the sixteenth, he formulated a comprehensive general analysis of such limit-motions, extending its application in a novel way to the finding of a curve's points of inflexion.[59] (Hitherto his method had been to define such points as those at which the curvature was zero.) A few months later in the following October, in a grand finale to two crowded years of mathematical discovery Newton reworked his calculus discoveries and, together with a long list of integrals, began to enter them in condensed form in a small tract on fluxions and series methods.[60] Unfortunately, probably diverted by the growing demands of his optical researches, he never finished it and it was five years later to be merged into his 1671 fluxional treatise. Even so, the thirty crowded pages he did write—published in full for the first time only four years ago[61]—are irrefutable documentary proof of his achievement in mathematics by the close of his *annus mirabilis.*

Together, Newton's fluxional algorithms and infinite series expansions, successively unfolded in his *De Analysi* of 1669, the 1671 calculus tract, and the several versions of his *De Quadratura Curvarum,* were to be the keystone of his mature mathematical method, and his development of Descartes's "analytical" geometry was to be the means of applying it universally. In his ***Lectiones Opticæ*** he was to apply it to theoretical optics, making use of the first derivative in elementary refraction problems and progressing to the second in his consideration of diacaustics. Above all, in his ***Principia Mathematica*** he was to employ it time and again in expounding his quantitative theory of universal gravitation (whose action he defined to be second-order differential impulses of "force" and whose composition therefore, in orbital problems, required a double integration). But I will leave my colleagues the pleasure of listing the splendors of that mathematical treasure house, with its general solution of the two-body problem (and approximate resolution of that of three) and variety of sophisticated mathematical procedures and results.

Let me conclude. On looking back I see that I have said a great deal concerning the two preparatory years, 1664 and 1665, but only too little of the *annus mirabilis* we now celebrate. From a mathematical viewpoint the emphasis has, I think, not been misplaced. In calculus, particularly, the great creative period of discovery was the year and a half from mid-1664 on. The only two significant 1666 papers, that of May 14-16, and the uncompleted October 1666 tract, were essentially the securing of ground already won. The extensive researches into the theory of equations and the location of their real and complex roots,[62] his introduction of finite-difference techniques into the study of the factorization of polynomials,[63] his findings in the general theory of angle sections,[64] all belong to the spring and summer of 1665, while his codification of plane and spherical trigonometry,[65] contemporaneous with his investigations into the division of the musical octave,[66] belongs firmly to the following autumn. What we may rightly conclude is that by the end of 1666, having matured rapidly over two richly crowded years, Newton's genius was fully formed and had begun to express itself on the frontiers of current mathematical advance. Henceforth, in mathematics at least, a pattern for future discovery existed. Remembering, then, his parallel achievements at this time in optics and dynamics—however difficult it may now be for us to document them with precision—and allowing for his good fortune in being born at the right time and place to take full advantage of the work of his predecessors, we may justly celebrate, three hundred years on, if not one single magical year at least a *biennium mirabilissimum*.

Notes

(Unless otherwise stated the manuscripts listed are in Cambridge University Library.)

[1] These six tracts have recently been reissued, in contemporary English versions, as *The Mathematical Works of Isaac Newton*, New York, 2 vols. 1964-7: in my editorial introductions I seek to place them in the totality of Newton's mathematical experience.

[2] *The Mathematical Papers of Isaac Newton, Volume I: 1664-1666,* Cambridge, 1967. Seven more volumes will complete the set.

[3] See also my articles, "Isaac Newton: birth of a mathematician" and "Newton's marvellous year: 1666 and all that," *Notes and Records of the Royal Society of London 19,* 1964, 53-62; *21,* 1966,

[4] Especially we are heavily in debt to Stukeley's letter to Richard Mead (King's College, Keynes MS 136, partially printed in Edmund Turnor's *Collections for the History of the Town and Soke of Grantham,* London, 1806, 174-80), which was the common basis for the early portions of Stukeley's own *Memoirs of Sir Isaac Newton (1752)* (ed. A. Hastings White), London, 1936 and of Conduitt's several accounts (especially King's College, Keynes MS 130.4).

[5] Grantham Public Library D/N 2267 (Hill 31).

[6] Stukeley's *Memoirs* (note 4), 42; H. W. Robinson, "Note on some recently discovered geometrical drawings in the stonework of Woolsthorpe Manor House," *Notes and Records of the Royal Society of London 5,* 1947/8, 35-6.

[7] Add 3996.

[8] King's College, Keynes MS 130.4, 5.

[9] This story, an interpolation by Conduitt in his composite of the accounts of Stukeley and De Moivre, seems highly disputable.

[10] *Euclidis Elementorum Libri XV. breviter demonstrati . . . Euclidis Data succinctè demonstrata,* Cambridge, 1655: Newton's copy is Trinity College, NQ.16.201.

[11] The main portion of his notes on these "philosophers" was entered in Add 3996: the following *Quæstiones* are ff.88^r-135^r of the same notebook.

[12] MS Baker 163^r: see M. H. Curtis, *Oxford and Cambridge in Transition, 1558-1642,* Oxford, 1959, 257-8.

[13] Lambeth Palace (London), MS 592 (Cod. H. Wharton 592), 8 pp. (unpaginated).

[14] Add 4007, 706^r-707^r (Luard's nineteenth century copy of the "Memorandum relating to Sr Isaac Newton given me by Mr Demoivre in Novr 1727," the original of which was sold at Sotheby's in 1936).

[15] Trinity College, NQ.8.59 (partly manuscript copy).

[16] Add 4004, 6^v-27^v.

[17] Add 4000, 82^r-84^r/15^r-24^v; 12^r-14^r/90^r-92^r.

[18] Add 4000, 14^v.

[19] *Francisci Vietae Opera Mathematica, In unum Volumen congesta, ac recognita . . .*, Leyden, 1646. Newton seems never to have had a personal copy.

[20] Add 4000, 2^r-6^r/8^r-11^v.

[21] *Operum Mathematicorum Pars Prima/Altera*, Oxford, 1657/1656. The *Arithmetica Infinitorum, sive Nova Methodus Inquirendi in Curvilineorum Quadraturam . . .* appears in the latter volume (published first).

[22] Add 4000, 15^r-18^v.

[23] Newton to Oldenburg for Leibniz, 24 October 1676 (*The Correspondence of Isaac Newton 2*, Cambridge, 1960, 11off).

[24] *Exercitationum Mathematicarum Libri Quinque*, Leyden, 1657, the fifth book of which contains "Sectiones trigintas Miscellaneas." Newton's lightly annotated copy is now in Trinity College (NQ.16.184).

[25] Especially Add 4004, 15^vff.

[26] Add 4000, 93^v-116^r.

[27] Add 4004, 67^v-69^r.

[28] *Johannis Huddenii Epistola Secunda, de Maximis et Minimis* (*Geometria*, 1659, 507-16).

[29] *Henrici van Heuraet Epistola de Transmutatione Curvarum Linearum in Rectas* (*Geometria*, 1659, 517-20).

[30] *Johannis De Witt Elementa Curvarum Linearum* (*Geometria*, Tom.2, 1661, 153-340).

[31] The autograph manuscript of these projective researches (in the decade from *ca.* 1667), mostly in private possession, will be reproduced in the second and fourth volumes of my edition of Newton's *Mathematical Papers* (note 2).

[32] Add 4004, 1^v-4^v.

[33] Add 4004, 15^v-16^r.

[34] Add 4004, 24^r.

[35] Add 3961.1, *passim*: these researches will be reproduced in the second volume of my edition of his *Mathematical Papers* (note 2).

[36] See especially his anonymous review, "An Account of the Book entituled *Commercium Epistolicum . . .*" (*Philosophical Transactions 29*. No. 342 [for January/February 1714/15], 173-224) of his own *Commercium Epistolicum D. Johannis Collins, et Aliorum de Analysi Promota*, London, 1712; and his equally anonymous appendix (pp. 97-123) to Joseph Raphson's *Historia Fluxionum*, London, 1715 [-16].

[37] *Mathematical Papers* (note 2) I, 154.

[38] I have discussed this topic in "Newton's Discovery of the General Binomial Theorem," *Mathematical Gazette 45*, 1961, 175-80.

[39] See my "Patterns of Mathematical Thought in the later Seventeenth Century," *Archive for History of Exact Sciences 1*, 1961, 179-388, especially 210-13, 236-41.

[40] Roger Cotes, in still unpublished researches of about 1709 (Trinity College, R.16.38, 362^rff), was, I believe, the first to attempt any proof.

[41] Compare Add 4000, 14^v and 19^rff.

[42] See my "Henry Briggs: The Binomial Theorem Anticipated," *Mathematical Gazette 45*, 1961, 9-12; and H. W. Turnbull, *James Gregory Tercentenary Memorial Volume*, London, 1939, 132ff,370ff.

[43] See note 28.

[44] Add 4004, 30^v-33^v, 47^r-50^r.

[45] *De la Manière de trouver les Tangentes des Lignes Courbes par l'Algebre . . .* (first published by C. de Waard in his *Supplement* to the *Œuvres de Fermat*, Paris, 1922, 98-114, especially 106ff).

[46] Add 4004, 2^r.

[47] Add 4004, 8^v (revised on 47^r).

[48] Add 4004, 6^r and 30^vff.

[49] See his *Œuvres complètes 14*, The Hague, 1920, 387-406, especially 391-6.

[50] Add 4004, 47^r-50^r.

[51] See their correspondence in late 1694 and March 1695 in (ed.) C. I. Gerhardt, *Leibnizens Mathematische Schriften 2*, Berlin, 1850, 261ff.

[52] Newton's curvature algorithm is developed implicitly by Hayes on p. 190 (239) of his *A Treatise of Fluxions: Or, An Introduction to Mathematical Philosophy*, London, 1704. This book was the first English work to make systematic use of the Leibnizian "S" sign for integration.

[53] Add 4000, 120^{r}ff; Add 3960.12, 206 and 199-202.

[54] Add 4000, 120^r-122^r/134^v-136^r.

[55] Add 4000, 152^r; Add 4004, 57^r/57^v.

[56] Add 3958.2, 30^r/30^v.

[57] Add 3958.2, 34^r/37^v.

[58] Add 4004, 50^v/51^r (dated 8 November 1665).

[59] Add 4004, 51^r/51^v.

[60] Add 3958.3, 48^v-63^v.

[61] In A. Rupert Hall and Marie Boas Hall, *Unpublished Scientific Papers of Isaac Newton,* Cambridge, 1962, 15-64 (though substantial excerpts from it appeared in James Wilson's edition of the *Mathematical Tracts of the late Benjamin Robins,* London, 1761, *2,* Appendix: 351-6).

[62] Add 4004, 55^r-56^v and 85^r-86^v.

[63] Add 4004, 87^r-89^r.

[64] Add 4000, 80^v-82^v.

[65] Add 3958.2, 31^r/31^v (revised as ff 23^r-25^v of a notebook now in the Pierpont Morgan Library, New York).

[66] Add 3958.2, 34^v/35^r/37^r; Add 4000, 104^r-113^r and 137^v-143^r.

Dudley Shapere (essay date 1967)

SOURCE: "The Philosophical Significance of Newton's Science," in *The Texas Quarterly,* Vol. X, No. 3, Autumn 1967, pp. 201-15.

[*In the following essay, Shapere explores the relationship of philosophy and science in Newton's thought, suggesting that Newton approached scientific study in a philosophical manner.*]

In a famous passage in the preface to the first edition of his **Principia,** Newton declared that:

> I offer this work as the mathematical principles of philosophy, for the whole burden of philosophy seems to consist in this—from the phenomena of motions to investigate the forces of nature, and then from these forces to demonstrate the other phenomena. . . . I wish we could derive the rest of the phenomena of Nature [besides those dealt with in this work] by the same kind of reasoning from mechanical principles, for I am induced by many reasons to suspect that they may all depend upon

certain forces by which the particles of bodies, by some causes hitherto unknown, are either mutually impelled towards one another, and cohere in regular figures, or are repelled and recede from one another.[1]

Newton's statement is characteristically cautious: the "burden of philosophy" is not described categorically; it only "*seems* to be. . . ." Again, he only *suspects,* on the basis of "many reasons," that his view is correct—phenomena "*may* all depend upon certain forces," etc. And finally, at the end of the paragraph from which the quoted passage is taken, he notes the possibility that there may be "some truer method of philosophy." In spite of these qualifications, however, and in spite of some more specific uneasiness which, as we shall see later, Newton himself (to say nothing of his contemporaries) felt about the adequacy of this statement as a description of the whole, ultimate burden of philosophy—despite all this, the passage is important for understanding the logic behind the greater part of Newton's own scientific (or "philosophical") reasoning, as well as the problems and approaches of a whole tradition of succeeding thinkers. For in many ways, this passage defines those problems and approaches—that tradition. Besides prefacing a monumental example of "philosophy," reaching specific conclusions, in terms of the motions and forces of particles, about a vast body of "phenomena of Nature," and thus providing "many reasons" for suspecting that the approach may prove successful in other domains, this statement of "the whole burden of philosophy" lays down a program for further work. It establishes at once an ideal or goal of scientific investigation—a picture of what a completed science would look like—and a set of categories in terms of which the attempt to reach that goal should be made. It provides, that is, a statement of the terms in which proper possible ultimate explanations are to be formulated. The phenomena of nature—all of them—are to be approached and explained in terms of "forces" directed radially toward or away from "particles" which (to add a gloss to the passage) are at rest or in motion in an infinite space. And a completed science would be one which explained all the phenomena of nature in terms of the interactions, through such forces, of such particles moving in space. And, finally, the principles of explanation of nature are to be expressed in the language of mathematics, the symbols of which are to be interpreted as standing for the forces, particles, and motions which exist in nature.

More detailed examination of the body of Newton's writings brings out further features of this picture of the aims, language, and subject-matter of science. At the end of the *Opticks,* Newton suggests, after having presented a number of reasons, that

> All these things being consider'd, it seems probable to me, that God in the Beginning form'd Matter in

solid, massy, hard, impenetrable, moveable Particles, of such Sizes and Figures, and with such other Properties, and in such Proportion to Space, as most conduced to the End for which he form'd them; and that these primitive Particles being Solids, are incomparably harder than any porous Bodies compounded of them; even so very hard, as never to wear or break in pieces; no ordinary Power being able to divide what God himself made one in the first Creation. While the Particles continue entire, they may compose Bodies of one and the same Nature and Texture in all Ages: But should they wear away, or break in pieces, the Nature of Things depending on them, would be changed. . . . And therefore, that Nature may be lasting, the Changes of corporeal Things are to be placed only in the various Separations and new Associations and Motions of these permanent Particles.[2]

Stripped of their theological trappings, these remarks stand out both as a sketch of the "particles" of Nature and as a sketch of units to be appealed to in proper ultimate explanations. For to say that "God in the Beginning form'd Matter" in such a manner is, in part, one way of saying that no further explanation need be sought for the particles and their properties: they are explanatory, not in need of explanation. The assertion of their indestructibility has the same logical force. And, finally, the location of all "Changes of corporeal Things . . . only in the various Separations and new Associations and Motions of these permanent Particles" tells us what it is that needs to be explained: changes, under which heading must be included qualitative changes, e.g., of color, sound, etc., which are to be explained in terms of the motions (and forces) of particles. (It should also be added that *differences* of such qualities, e.g., of colors, as well as *changes* thereof, are to be explained thusly.) Further, as we shall see, the "changes" which are to be explained also include, for Newton, certain types of motions of the particles themselves, while other such types do not (at least in the same sense) require such explanation.[3]

The "other Properties" with which the particles are endowed are forces; one, a *vis inertiae,* which Newton equates (Definition III, ***Principia***) with the *vis insita*:

> The *vis insita,* or innate force of matter, is a power of resisting, by which every Body, as much as in it lies, continues in its present state, whether it be of rest, or of moving uniformly forwards in a right line . . . this *vis insita* may, by a most significant name, be called inertia (*vis inertiae*) or force of inactivity.

This "innate force of matter," as has often been noted,[4] is akin to the "impetus" of the fourteenth-century Parisian school of Buridan, Oresme, and others; but the differences between the two concepts must not be passed over lightly. In the first place, Newton's *vis*

insita opposes change of state of rest as well as of motion; impetus was definitely only a moving force, fully in the Aristotelian tradition of *omne quod movetur ab alio movetur* (everything that moves must be moved by something). A body at rest had no impetus. Secondly, Newton's force is "innate" and invariable; for most of the impetus theorists, on the other hand, impetus was something which could be added to or taken away from a body.[5] Thirdly, the *vis insita* or *vis inertiae* acts to keep a moving body moving in a specific way: rectilinearly, and at a uniform velocity; but there was rarely, among the fourteenth-century impetus theorists, a clear statement of precisely how impetus would affect the velocity of the body, and much confusion existed as to the kind of curve in which the body would move under the influence of impetus.[6] And finally, impetus was a force which *kept* the body (particle) going in motion, which drove it as a mover, in the old Aristotelian sense, the only difference being that impetus was an internal mover. Newton's *vis inertiae,* on the other hand, does not act to *keep* the body moving, but manifests itself *only* when its response is called up to resist some external agency which is trying to alter the state of motion or rest of the body.[7]

In addition to the *vis inertiae,* there are other sorts of forces also:

> It seems to me farther, that these Particles have not only a *Vis inertiae,* accompanied with such passive Laws of Motion as naturally result from that Force, but also that they are moved by certain active Principles, such as is that of Gravity, and that which causes Fermentation, and the Cohesion of Bodies.[8]

These "active forces" also originate in particles, but it is they that act to change the state of motion or rest of other particles. They are thus, in the language of ***Principia,*** "impressed forces" (or, perhaps better, the causes of impressed forces).

> Definition IV. An impressed force is an action exerted upon a body, in order to change its state, either of rest, or of uniform motion in a right line.

> This force consists in the action only, and remains no longer in the body when the action is over. For a body maintains every new state it acquires, by its inertia only. But impressed forces are of different origins, as from percussion, from pressure, from centripetal force.

Indeed, Newton maintained an open mind as to the kinds of such "active forces" there might be:

> . . . it's well known, that Bodies act one upon the other by the Attractions of Gravity, Magnetism, and Electricity; and these Instances shew the Tenor and Course of Nature, and make it not improbable but

that there may be more attractive Powers than these. For Nature is very consonant and conformable to her self.[9]

There are some crucial differences between the concepts of *vis inertiae* and *vis impressa*. The *vis inertiae* of a body, as was remarked above, does not (as the concept of impetus did) explain the continuance of a body in its state of rest or uniform rectilinear motion, in the sense of being an internal pushing agent causing that body to be or continue in that state. Let us examine this point further; for one might suppose that, even though Newton's own definition is (or should be) perfectly clear on this point, it would at least have been consistent for the concept of inertia to be interpreted as referring to an internal force causing a body to continue at rest or with uniform velocity. That this is not even' a *possible* interpretation—that to treat *vis inertiae* as a cause *in the same sense* as impressed force (the only difference being that the former is internal, the latter external) would lead to contradiction— is shown by the following considerations. First, if it were such a force, then, as Jammer points out,[10] the third law of motion would be violated: for what would be the equal and opposite reaction? And if there were, in this exceptional sort of case, no equal and opposite reaction, then the unresisted force constantly acting on the body (from within) should, on other sound Newtonian principles, produce a constant acceleration instead of a constant velocity. Furthermore, inertia is a constant, unvarying property of a body, while the uniform rectilinear velocity which the body possesses can take on any of an infinite number of values. But it is a logical property of the notion of "cause" (or "causal explanation"), or at least of the most usual usage of that expression, that a variation in an effect requires a corresponding variation in the cause.[11] Thus it is no accident that inertia—the inertial mass—enters into calculations in Newtonian physics not as a "force" causing or explaining the rest or uniform rectilinear motion of a body; rather, it enters into other sorts of calculations entirely: fundamentally,[12] into calculations of the *impressed* forces acting *on* the body (or, when the forces are known, into calculations of the body's response thereto); or, when inertia acts as "impulse," when "the body, by not easily giving way to the impressed forces of another, endeavors to change the state of that other" (Definition III), it enters into calculation of the *impressed* forces which the body exerts on *other* bodies. Inertia, like other characteristics of bodies (particles), manifests itself in interactions with other bodies—in its effects on and responses to other bodies— not as an internal driving *vis* maintaining the body in its "inertial" state.

The differences between *vis inertiae* and *vis impressa* may be characterized in either of two alternative ways. On the one hand, we may rest content with Newton's use of the term "*vis*" in connection with inertia, and, concomitantly, we may describe the role of the *vis inertiae* as being that of a cause (or as providing a causal explanation) of a body's maintaining an inertial state. But if we do so speak, we must remember that the terms "*vis*" and "cause" are being used in a sense very different from that in which they are used in connection with impressed forces. It is clearly the latter that, in Newton's physics, play the role of "causes" *in the sense that* they are (or, more precisely, originate in) independent agencies in terms of which variable effects are to be explained. And in this sense, the *vis inertiae* is not an internal pushing-agent counterpart of the *vis impressa*— a distinct agent causing a certain kind and degree of effect; it is essential to particles, definitory (or at least forming part of the definition) of them.

There are undoubtedly historical precedents for Newton's use of the word "*vis*" in connection with inertia, and for our describing the role of inertia as that of a "cause" of a body's maintaining its state of rest or uniform rectilinear motion: Aristotle himself, after all, spoke of "nature" as "a source or *cause* (aitia) of being moved and of being at rest . . ." etc.[13] But on the other hand, it must also be recalled that it was against just such sorts of "explanations," among others, that sixteenth- and seventeenth-century philosophical revolutionaries were objecting when they protested all appeals to internal, invisible, "occult" causes as not being *truly* explanatory.

For this reason, as well as because of the potential confusion resulting from the use of the same term for two very different ideas, it is therefore tempting to make the distinction between *vis inertiae* and *vis impressa* explicit by saying that the fact that a body is at rest, or is in uniform rectilinear motion, is not to be explained (causally) in terms of the *vis inertiae*—or, for that matter, for Newton, in terms of any other sort of "force." (That is, in this sense of the word "cause," and in the sense in which a "force" is a "cause" of the behavior of particles, *vis inertiae* is not a force.) Being in an inertial state is, indeed, on this use of the term "cause," not to be explained causally in terms of *anything*: bodies (particles) simply *do* continue in a state of rest or uniform rectilinear motion unless compelled to change that state by external (impressed) forces. Inertial motion (or rest) is thus *uncaused*; and it is further tempting to put this point positively by saying that the inertial state is "natural" to bodies, what requires causal explanation being any deviation from such a state.

Characterization of the inertial state as "natural" is not uncommon. One of the most recent descriptions in this vein is that given by Margula Perl, who also quotes a very early similar description:

> The first [law of motion, the] "Law of Inertia," is probably the least problematic, and Maclaurin's

comment that "From this law it appears why we inquire not in philosophy concerning the cause of the continuation of the rest of bodies, or of their uniform motion in a right line" is still probably the best comment on the law.[14]

In spite of the frequency of this way of characterizing the inertial state, and of contrasting it with accelerated motion, however, calling the inertial state of a body "natural" has its dangers too. As with all such technical terms, one must be wary here of being misled. For example, the notion of "natural" applied as above to inertial motion (or rest) is not in every way the same as the notion of "natural" in Aristotle. For bodies in Newton's science to respond to impressed forces by accelerating in specific ways can in one sense be characterized as being just as "natural" as for them to continue in uniform rectilinear motion in the absence of such forces. Thus the word "natural" applied to the inertial state must not be taken as the opposite of "unnatural"—a contrast that is easy to make in connection with Aristotle's usage. But if we understand the term "natural" as meaning simply "not in need of explanation in terms of external agencies," we shall see shortly that Newton's science may be viewed in an illuminating way in terms of this distinction: in a way which, in taking account of the differences between *vis inertiae* and *vis impressa* in Newton's science, does not do violence to the actual intent of those concepts, and in a way which, further, brings out important features of his science as compared and contrasted with other scientific traditions.[15]

The preceding discussion enables us to see, behind the Newtonian views outlined above, a deep background framework of ideas concerning the nature of explanation and related notions. For there is, lying behind Newton's approach, a family of concepts or terms which, in at least some important uses, are strongly interlocked with one another—so much so that the applicability of one such concept or term may (in those uses or senses) be said to "imply" something about the applicability of the others. Whether such relationships should be referred to as "logical," or, with Wittgenstein, as "grammatical" (suggesting that they are relationships between linguistic terms or usages), or simply as "conceptual," and whether (and in precisely what way) anything would be gained by referring to them as "non-empirical," are real and important issues. But I will not consider these issues at present, but will simply use the terms "logical," "conceptual," "grammatical," and "non-empirical" indiscriminately.[16] In any case, the family of thus interrelated terms (concepts) relevant to the present discussion includes "explanation," "change," and "cause."[17] And the relevant relationship between these concepts is expressed adequately enough for present purposes in the philosophical dictum, "Every change (or every event) must have a cause (or, requires a causal explanation)."

In many uses—the uses which are of primary relevance to the discussion of Newton's science—these terms are also linked "logically" to another class of terms which includes the terms "entity" and "behavior (of entities)," in such a way that implications hold between the concepts of "change," "cause," and "explanation" on the one hand, and "entity" and "behavior (of entities)" on the other. Thus it is a logical truth—not an "empirical" one, in any clear sense of that difficult term—that, in the senses relevant here, "The cause of any change must lie in the behavior of an entity." Further, a very important point, for our purposes, is that the "entity" whose "behavior" causes a "change" must—and this "must" is, again, a sign that the point is a logical (conceptual, grammatical) one, not an "empirical" one—lie "outside of," or be "external to" or "independent of" the change (changing event, changing entity) itself.[18]

But all this network of interconnected concepts is not sufficient for the purpose of application: for that, it must be made specific. For, though the interrelationships outlined do hold for those uses of these terms which are relevant here, they leave open a number of questions. What, precisely, is to count as an "entity"—something capable of behaving, of causing (and, it may be added, of being affected)? What is to count as the behavior of an entity? As a change? As something happening "outside of" or "independent of" an event or change? And how, specifically, is the behavior of an entity linked to the causing (the causal explanation) of some change or event?

The principle of inertia as contrasted with the Aristotelian view of motion provides a well-known example of how such specification can, and needs to be, made, and of how it can be made differently by different thinkers (and, indeed, of how the specifications can be *characteristic* of the theories and their differences from one another). For the Aristotelian tradition, rest—at least of an element in its natural place—was "natural" (in our sense, even if in others also) to a body: it did not constitute a change requiring a causal explanation in the sense outlined above (the "nature" of the body was the "cause" of that behavior[19]). Motion, on the other hand—or at least violent motion[20]—did count as such a change, and required an external cause constantly applied in contact with the moving body. Upon removal of the cause, the body would (if in its natural place) come to rest immediately or (if not in its natural place) immediately assume its natural motion toward its natural place of rest.

The concept of inertia constituted a shift as to what it is about motion that needs to be explained in terms of an external cause, and what does not. Certain sorts of motions—uniform rectilinear ones—are now put into the same category as rest had been in for the Aristotelian tradition. For whereas uniform rectilinear motion (at least when "violent") required, in Aristotelian physics, a constantly applied external cause, it no longer does so in Newtonian physics. To put the point in terms of the preceding discussion, inertial motion no longer counts as the *kind* of "change" that requires a causal explanation: accelerations are such "changes." Care must be exercised here: for though it is true that, in one sense, even inertial motion can be called a "change"—it is change of position—nevertheless the mere fact that a body changes position is not, for Newton, sufficient ground for asking for a causal explanation—an explanation in terms of an external agency responsible for the behavior. What *counts* as the kind of "change" requiring a "cause" has, in Newtonian science, shifted from its Aristotelian meaning; in the sense of the term "change" in which "every change requires a cause," not all kinds of motion are "changes."[21]

The whole of Newton's conception of the subject-matter of science can, in fact, be profitably viewed as a set of such specifications of the general network of concepts involving "change," "explanation," "cause," "externality," "entity," and "behavior." The kind of "change" that requires explanation in terms of a "cause" is, as we have seen, acceleration—and, it must be added, all "qualities," such as colors and sounds and their differences and changes. What does not require such explanation is the state of uniform rectilinear motion, of which rest is a special case. This is in opposition to the Aristotelian specification, according to which rest and motion (at least when violent) are not on a par, uniform rectilinear motion (at least when violent) being included in the class of changes requiring explanation in terms of a cause.

Further, the notion of "mass" is a specification, in Newton's physics, of what counts as an entity (or at least as an ultimately real or fundamental entity, all other so-called entities being associations of mass-particles, and all their properties and behavior being ultimately explainable in terms of the motions of masses and the forces centered therein). The notion of mass-centered, centrally-directed forces is a determinate expression of what counts as a cause, along with the motions of bodies which alter the strength of those forces with respect to other bodies within their range. The motions of particles, and their impression of forces on other bodies (including the variation of those impressed forces with the changes of relative position of the particles concerned) specifies what counts as the "behavior" of entities. And, finally, the notion that a cause must be "external" to its effect is reflected, and specified, in the fundamental explanatory role played in Newtonian physics by impressed forces.

These specifications are summarized in part, though implicitly, in the laws of motion, particularly in the first two. For we can look on those laws as making, in effect, the distinction made above between "natural"

and "deviant" behavior—between behavior that does not require explanation in terms of a cause (an "external" cause) and behavior that does. The laws distinguish, that is, between "behavior" that is "uniform," and which therefore (logically) does not require a causal explanation, and "behavior" that is not "uniform"—behavior that counts as "change" in the sense in which it is a "logical" truth that "every change requires a cause (causal explanation)." The first law of motion ("Every body perseveres in its state of rest, or of uniform motion in a right line, unless it is compelled to change that state by forces impressed thereon") has, among other jobs, the function of telling us that it is only deviations from uniform straight-line motion (or rest) that need to be accounted for in terms of a cause (in the form of an external agency)—ordinarily, at least[22]—and that such deviations are to be accounted for (causally) in terms of "impressed forces." The second law ("The alteration of motion is ever proportional to the motive force impressed; and is made in the direction of the right line in which that force is impressed") spells out in more detail the precise characteristics (the direction and amount) of the forces required to produce a given amount of deviation. And elsewhere in Newton's writings we learn that such forces acting on any particle must ultimately originate in other centers of mass.[23]

In this paper, we have distinguished between two levels in Newton's view of the subject-matter which science is to investigate: first, a general conceptual framework consisting of "logically" related concepts like "change," "cause," and "entity"; and second, a set of specifications of that background framework in terms of such notions as "accelerated motion," "force," and "mass." What seems peculiarly Newtonian is the way the general framework has been specified; for Aristotelian science specified some of the same (or, more precisely, a closely related) background framework differently.[24] A number of questions arise concerning these different specifications. What warrant is there, ultimately, for selecting one set of specifications of a general background framework rather than another? Are there really "many reasons" which support the Newtonian specification of what counts, e.g., as a "change" requiring a "cause," and which cannot be taken account of in terms of the Aristotelian specification? Or is the difference merely a matter of "handling the same bundle of data as before, but placing them in a new system of relations with one another by giving them a different framework, all of which virtually means putting on a different kind of thinking-cap"[25]? Is it a matter of adopting a different "paradigm"[26] with which to approach nature, in the sense that a radically new set of problems to meet, definitions of facts, and standards of acceptability, replaces an old one with which it is not only incompatible but even "incommensurable," and such that no good reasons can *really* be given for its acceptability?

These are important questions, to be sure; but there are also questions that need to be asked about the background framework itself. Is there—*can* there be—only one such framework, which lies (or even which *must* lie) behind all science, past, present, and future? Need there always be one, or is the reliance on such backgrounds something that science outgrows with maturity? (Or, alternatively, does the development of science make it more and more impossible for philosophers to abstract from concrete scientific theories any such "background framework"?) And if there is more than one background, are there any good reasons for employing, in science, one rather than another, or for abandoning one in favor of another? Is the background framework (whatever may be said about its set of specifications) described adequately as a set of "*a priori* assumptions," as "metaphysical presuppositions," or at least as containing a strong element thereof? Again, we may ask whether the background framework is described adequately as a set of "metascientific concepts," the special concern of philosophers, who are supposed to deal (according to some views) not with the actual content of science, but rather with the analysis of those terms which are used in talking *about* science ("metascientific" ones, including such terms as "explanation," "cause," "entity").

Not all of these questions can be answered here, of course; but some light can be thrown on the issues concerned by contrasting the view presented here with certain traditional philosophical doctrines. For, after all, such concepts as "cause," "change," and "entity," which form part of the background of Newton's science as interpreted here, have traditionally been discussed or employed in writings referred to as "metaphysical." The latter word covers so many different ideas as to be almost useless; but there are a few reasonably clear allegations which have been made as to the role of such concepts with regard to science. And none of these roles is played by the background framework as conceived here. Thus, if that framework is characterized as "metaphysical," it is not metaphysical in the most usual or clear senses of classical philosophy. It does not consist of a set of propositions from which the substantive propositions of science can (allegedly) be deduced; nor does it consist of a set of propositions which (allegedly) must be added as premises to some or any scientific propositions in order to deduce further consequences; nor does it consist of a set of "presuppositions" guaranteeing that scientific method will work as a tool of discovery or of induction. On the contrary, the background framework as conceived here consists of a set of concepts (and propositions relating those concepts) which are made specific and applicable by a particular scientific theory.[27]

Nor, again, is there any implication, in the view presented in this paper, that the background framework of Newtonian science consists of a set of concepts which cannot be avoided—which must be employed in *any* attempt, past, present, or future, to characterize the scientific endeavor. Indeed, I have suggested elsewhere, "There is in the range of scientific theories a spectrum of departures from such everyday-life concepts as 'entity' and 'behavior' that makes those terms inadequate to a lesser or greater degree for talking about those theories."[28] Unless we stretch the meanings of the words beyond utility, the concepts of (for example) "entity" and "behavior of entities," which are so naturally applied in discussion of Newtonian physics, become harder to apply to theories which talk, e.g., about electromagnetic fields and variations in field intensities. Thus the framework in terms of which Newtonian science has been discussed here does not consist of a set of necessary, *a priori* propositions (and concepts) in terms of which *any* scientific system must be specified. Nor, correlatively, does it consist of a set of "metascientific" concepts, *at least* in the sense of a set of category-terms for characterizing any scientific theory.

The interpretations given in this paper must not be considered as being concerned with *all* aspects of Newton's work, but only with that facet, illustrated by the passages referred to earlier, which was most influential on the subsequent history of thought: which provided a conception of the aims, methods, and subject-matter of science, and the clarification and extension of which set the problems for a whole tradition of succeeding philosophers and scientists. There are, however, other sides of Newton. Two of these stand out most prominently, though not as facets completely independent of that outlined here, but rather as attempts to answer criticisms, levelled chiefly by continental thinkers, against views connected with those discussed here. On the one side, we find him attempting to answer such objections by giving an account of gravitation in terms of an "Aethereal Medium."[29] And on the other side, we see him answering the same objections by maintaining that, in speaking of attraction, he is not attempting to give an explanation at all, but only a description. The present interpretation is not meant to apply to those views, but rather to provide an account of a central body of Newtonian doctrine in terms of which his adoption of those other views can be understood.

Notes

[1] I. Newton, *Philosophiae Naturalis Principia Mathematica,* Berkeley, University of California Press, 1946, pp. xvii-xviii.

[2] Newton, *Opticks,* New York, Dover, 1952, p. 400. Another list of properties of particles, somewhat, though not fundamentally, different from the account in the *Opticks,* occurs in *Principia:* "The extension, hardness, impenetrability, mobility, and inertia of the whole, result

from the extension, hardness, impenetrability, mobility, and inertia of the parts; and hence we conclude the least particles of all bodies to be also all extended, and hard and impenetrable, and movable, and endowed with their proper inertia. And this is the foundation of all philosophy." (*Principia,* p. 399) The basis of this inference from "macroscopic" to "microscopic" characteristics is Rule III of the Rules of Reasoning in Philosophy: "The qualities of bodies, which admit neither intensification nor remission of degrees, and which are found to belong to all bodies within reach of our experiments, are to be esteemed the universal qualities of all bodies whatsoever." (p. 398) In the light of contemporary quantum theory, such a principle of inference appears naïve and erroneous.

Note the absence of gravity from Newton's lists of the properties of particles. For though gravity, like inertia, is universally found in the bodies we experience, and admits of "neither intensification nor remission of degrees," Newton refuses to draw the conclusion that it is *essential* to matter, a primary property of particles, like inertia: "we must . . . universally allow that all bodies whatsoever are endowed with a principle of mutual gravitation. . . . Not that I affirm gravity to be essential to bodies: by their *vis insita* I mean nothing but their inertia." (*Principia,* pp. 399-400) Action at a distance proved embarrassing enough to Newton to lead him here to make an exception in the application of Rule III, and to distinguish, in this case, between what is essential and what is merely universal in matter.

³ The concept of explanation has traditionally exerted more or less definite types of intuitive appeals, directing analyses of that concept, and, correlatively, of nature and of science, along certain general paths. Such tendencies of analysis have, however, usually been left tacit, and, furthermore, are not necessarily consistent with one another. Among the historically and philosophically more important of these tendencies (together with some sketch of the kind of tacit line of argument accompanying them) are the following. "What require explanation are *changes*; and therefore what does not require explanation, *i.e.,* the fundamental explanatory factors themselves, must be absolutely unchanging. For if they changed (or even, perhaps, if they could change), then those changes (or the possibility thereof) would have to be subject to explanation, and so those factors would not be fundamental explanatory factors at all. And thus if explanation—or at least ultimate explanation—is to be possible at all, there must be explanatory factors which are not subject to change." What require explanation are *differences*; therefore what does not require explanation, the fundamental explanatory factors themselves, must be factors which are 'alike.'" (The remainder of the accompanying argument in this and the succeeding cases is similar to that in the first example.) "What requires explanation is *diversity*; hence what is used to explain must

be a 'unity'." "What requires explanation is *complexity*; therefore what is appealed to for the sake of explaining must be 'simple.'" The rationale behind various interpretations of the aims and subject-matter of scientific investigation—e.g., those interpretations associated with atomistic "theories"—have thus not always been purely empirical, but have often rested on such *a priori* considerations as these. There have been a multitude of other such "tendencies," some associated with conflicts between continuum and discrete theories of matter, others connected with controversies as to the respective roles of the concepts of space ("geometry") and matter in scientific explanation, and still others with the tension between traditional "metaphysical" and "empiricist" approaches to explanation. These forces in the development of science have received little or no attention from philosophers of science: yet a thorough analysis of them, and of their precise logical role in the scientific endeavor, seems very much needed.

⁴ For example, by Dijksterhuis: "Newton still shares Aristotle's view that every motion requires a *motor,* in the modified form of it given by the Paris Terminists, who assumed that this motor resides in the body. The *Vis Inertiae* apparently is identical with the *Impetus* of this school and the *Vis Impressa* of Galileo." (E. J. Dijksterhuis, *The Mechanization of the World Picture,* Oxford, Clarendon, 1961, p. 466.) Dijksterhuis does not discuss any differences between Newton's conception and these earlier ones, but apparently simply equates them.

⁵ With regard to this point (as in many other respects), the closest parallel to Newton's view among the impetus theorists, at least until the sixteenth century, was the view of John Buridan. Buridan did look upon impetus as something which was not *self*-expending (as his chief predecessor, Franciscus of Marchia, and his chief immediate successor, Nicole Oresme, maintained); in the absence of counterforces, the impetus will be conserved, according to Buridan, and in this sense is "permanent." It will, however, be destroyed by contrary agencies, if any are present—as Newton's inertia cannot be. For Newton, the measure of inertia is the (inertial) mass of the body, and this is invariant: a body at rest still has it. For Buridan, however, presumably when the impetus is used up in combating external resisting or otherwise corruptive influences, the body comes to rest *and is left with no further impetus.* Buridan's view that the impetus of the celestial spheres, at least, is incorruptible is, of course, no argument against this interpretation; for those impetuses are incorruptible as a matter of *fact* rather than of *logic.* (". . . these impetuses which [God] impressed in the celestial bodies were not decreased or corrupted afterwards because there was no inclination of the celestial bodies for other movements. Nor was there resistance which would be corruptive or repressive of that impetus." (M. Clagett, *The Science of Mechanics*

in the Middle Ages, Madison, University of Wisconsin Press, 1959, p. 525)) For such impetuses *would* be corrupted if as a matter of fact there *were* any contrary agencies present. In other words, Buridan's celestial impetus is something imposed by God, inessential to the heavenly bodies. Newton's inertia *cannot* be corrupted; it is constitutive, indeed definitive (at least partially) of particles. A body may be brought to rest (for example) by contrary forces; but it still has the same amount of inertia.

[6] As Clagett (*op. cit.,* p. 520) notes, the successors of Buridan (at least until the sixteenth century) were generally confused as to whether impetus tends to produce uniform motion or accelerated motion; further, "One serious defect of this medieval theory is that there was no sure distinction between rectilinear and circular impetus. It was equally possible to impose rectilinear or circular impetus. We must await the sixteenth century for a clarification of the directional aspects of impetus." (Clagett, *op. cit.,* p. 525) Buridan did, in a "quasi-quantitative" way, according to Clagett, hold that impetus is proportional to the velocity of the projectile (as well as to the quantity of matter—but note that this makes the concept analogous not to inertia, but rather to momentum). (Clagett, pp. 522-23) The impetus theory, in its various manifestations (especially with Buridan) was certainly an important step on the way to the Newtonian conception of inertia, and shows many vital similarities to the Newtonian idea, as I have tried to point out elsewhere (D. Shapere, "Meaning and Scientific Change," in R. Colodny (ed.), *Mind and Cosmos,* Pittsburgh, University of Pittsburgh Press, 1966, pp. 41-85; see especially pp. 71-81). But the differences noted here must not be ignored. It is also true that, with the sixteenth century, particularly with Benedetti, the impetus theory tended more and more clearly toward the Newtonian conception. Even there, however, many of the differences noted here remained.

[7] We must not be deceived here by Newton's remark that inertia "is resistance so far as the body, for maintaining its present state, opposes the force impressed; it is impulse so far as the body, by not easily giving way to the impressed force of another, endeavors to change the state of that other." (Def. III) For this passage does not imply that inertia, like impetus, is the cause of the motion of the body itself.

[8] Newton, *Opticks,* p. 401.

[9] *Ibid.,* p. 376. In this connection, the Halls have noted that Newton "was not even sure whether there was one basic force, or a pair of repulsive and attractive forces, or as many forces as there were classes of phenomena—gravitational, magnetic, electrical, optical, chemical, and physiological—involving such forces." (A. R. Hall and M. B. Hall (eds.), *Unpublished Scientific Papers of Isaac Newton,* Cambridge, Cambridge University Press, 1962, p. 203.)

Newton also considered forces to be *effects* of (accelerated) motions as well as causes thereof; this aspect of his work will not, however, be considered in this paper.

[10] M. Jammer, *Concepts of Mass,* Cambridge, Harvard University Press, 1961, p. 71.

[11] Mill's "Method of Concomitant Variation," when filtered of its many errors and misleading features, reduces essentially to this logical point.

The aspect of the notion of "cause" which will be central in the following discussion is that of "cause of a change"; such notions as "cause of existence" and "cause of difference" will not be discussed, despite the fact that the latter notion, in particular, is important in Newton's science. For in his theory of light, differences of color in a spectrum are explained (causally) by differences in the component rays of white light and their different degrees of refrangibility.

[12] I.e., except when the notion of (inertial) mass (which turns out in calculational practice to be the heart of the notion of "quantity of matter") enters into the *definition* of a quantity, as it does in the definition of "quantity of motion" (Def. II).

Jammer (*Concepts of Mass,* p. 72) argues that "for Newton, in contrast to 'Newtonian mechanics,' 'inertial mass' is a reducible property of physical bodies, depending on their 'quantity of matter.'" It is not easy to see what Jammer means by "reducible" in this connection; as he himself points out, "It is, of course, always rather difficult to state exactly whether two concepts are involved or only one, once a general proportionality between the concepts has been established." (This remark is not entirely correct, for inertial and gravitational mass are, despite their necessary proportionality, clearly distinct in Newtonian physics due to their independent mode of introduction.) Apparently the reasoning behind Jammer's view is that *quantitas materiae* has other properties than inertial mass; he cites gravitational mass. (". . . it is fairly obvious that 'quantity of matter' is still a notion for itself. A careful examination of the text of Book III of the *Principia,* for instance, shows clearly that it is *quantitas materiae* in the original sense of the word which determines the magnitude of gravitational attraction.") Jammer's appeal to gravitation, however, is unfortunate; for, as was pointed out above, gravitational mass is not an essential characteristic of matter, while inertia is. ("Not that I affirm gravity to be essential to bodies: by their *vis insita* I mean nothing but their inertia.") On the other hand, it is true that, for Newton, there are characteristics besides inertia which *are* essential to matter—e.g., solidity, hardness, impenetrability. And in this sense, inertia (inertial mass) constitutes only *part* of the notion (definition, essence) of matter; and—still in this sense—inertia can be said, somewhat confusingly, to be "reducible" to *quantitas materiae.* Jammer's view, when properly interpreted, is thus defensible, although it is rather more innocuous than it might at first seem: for inertial mass is certainly not to be *understood in terms of quantitas materiae;* nor is it caused by the latter, and so is not "reducible" to the latter in either of these interesting senses.

[13] Aristotle, *Physics,* Bk. II, 192b 22.

[14] M. Perl, "Newton's Justification of the Laws of Motion," *Journal of the History of Ideas,* Vol. XXVII (1966), p. 585.

[15] I do not, of course, wish to suggest that this distinction between "natural" and "deviant," as employed here in connection with Newton, is an essential feature of explanation, or of scientific explanation in particular. Specifically, I do not mean to imply that there must be, within any scientific theory, a distinction between two classes of events, one of which includes events always requiring causal explanation, and the other of which includes events not doing so.

[16] Indeed, one must suspect that the distinction between "empirical" and "non-empirical," at least, is highly misleading when applied to the sorts of relationships being discussed here: for many of the same sorts of considerations that count for or against what are usually referred to as "empirical" propositions in science have also counted for or against ideas and interconnections in this "non-empirical" framework of ideas.

[17] Not *all* types or facets of the uses of these terms exhibit the connections here noted, however; thus the term "explanation" has wider uses than those in which it is linked to the notions of "cause" and "change." For example, in such statements as, "Explain how to play chess," "Explain the theory of relativity to me," and "Einstein's theory explains the advance of the perihelion of Mercury," the sense of "explanation" is not that of what has been referred to here as "causal explanation." Again, it is not true that all "explanations" which are appropriately called "causal" are explanations of what may appropriately be called "changes": some causal explanations (e.g., explanations of difference of color in optics) are explanations of differences rather than of changes. (See Footnote 3, above.) And not all "changes" require "causes" either—as the present argument attempts to show, changes of position do not, for Newton, always require causes. There are similar exceptions in the cases of the other terms discussed here. Nevertheless, there do exist uses (senses) of these expressions in which the "logical" connections asserted do hold.

[18] One sort of objection (there were others also) made in the seventeenth century against "occult causes" rested essentially on this point: that the supposed "causes" were really not explanatory at all, but rather were identical with the object or event to be explained. The requirement that the cause be "distinct from," "external to," or "independent of" the effect thus involves not merely an objection against appealing to causes which cannot be discovered or observed; it involves a "logical" point as to what can *count* as an explanation—as to what can properly be called "an explanation."

[19] See Aristotle's definition of "nature," quoted above.

[20] The Aristotelian and Newtonian conceptions of the relation between force and motion are often distinguished by saying that, for the former, force is the cause of motion, whereas for the latter, force is the cause of change of motion. This way of stating the difference, however, is misleading. For example, apart from reading the notion of force into Aristotelian physics, where it does not unambiguously belong, the view that, for that tradition, all motion requires a "force" applies primarily to violent motion. For while natural motion requires a mover, that mover is, for most of the tradition, the "nature" of the thing moved, and not an external (or, if internal, at least independent) agency.

[21] This is presumably the point behind referring to uniform rectilinear motions (and rest) as *states:* "*Status* of motion: by using this expression Newton implies or asserts that motion is not, as had been believed for about two thousand years—since Aristotle—a process of change, in contradistinction to *rest,* which is truly a *status,* but is also a *state,* that is, something that no more implies change than does rest. . . . Nothing changes without a cause . . . as Newton expressly states. Thus, so long as motion was a process, it could not continue without a mover. It is only motion as *state* that does not need a cause or mover. Now, not all motion is such a *state,* but only that which proceeds uniformly and in a right line . . ." (A. Koyré, *Newtonian Studies,* Cambridge, Harvard University Press, 1965, pp. 66-67).

Later on page 67, Koyré makes an erroneous claim, which he and others have also made elsewhere, that "the law of inertia implies an infinite world." There is no logical reason, based on the law of inertia, why a body should not have its uniform rectilinear motion interfered with by impact against the "walls" of a finite universe.

[22] It is, of course, possible to ask, within Newtonian physics, why a certain particular body continues to move in a straight line with uniform velocity. But though the answer to such a question is to be given in terms of the balance of forces originating in other

masses, nevertheless a body would continue in its state of uniform rectilinear motion even if there were no other masses in the universe. Uniform rectilinear motion does not *require* explanatory appeal to the existence of other masses—as accelerated motion always does.

Reformulations of classical mechanics have been constructed which would make illegitimate (or even "meaningless") any talk of the motion of a body in a universe devoid of other bodies. Such a reformulation has the effect of restoring a complete symmetry between the kinds of questions that can be raised concerning uniform rectilinear and accelerated motion. This symmetry is purchased, however, only at the expense of creating another asymmetry—namely, between universes in which there is only one object (particle) and universes in which there is more than one object (particle). (Often the illegitimacy is not limited to universes of only one object, but is extended to those of as many as four or five, on the ground that a "reference-frame" is necessary in order to be able to speak meaningfully of the motion of a particle.)

[23] In this connection, a particularly revealing remark occurs in the context of an argument, in *The System of the World,* to the effect that the stars cannot really go around the earth. If that view were correct, he says, then those stars which do not lie on the celestial equator would describe, in their daily rotations around the earth, circles whose centers would be, not the center of mass of the earth, but rather points on the earth's axis or on extensions of that axis into empty space. But, he declares in refutation of such a possibility, "That forces should be directed to no body on which they physically depend, but to innumerable imaginary points in the axis of the earth, is an hypothesis too incongruous." (Newton, *The System of the World,* included in the California edition of *Principia,* p. 553.) "An hypothesis too incongruous": there must be a center of mass at the focus of the curve (or, if not, then the force centered there must be the resultant of forces which *are* centered in masses). Only an entity can cause an effect in another entity; and this, too, is a "logical" point.

[24] In what sense can the general background framework be said to be (or to have been) "presupposed"? In the case of Newton, it is certainly not suggested that he explicitly formulated such a "background framework," whether in advance of "specifying" it, or at any other period of his career. Nor, however—at the opposite extreme—would it be reasonable to contend that the set of background concepts outlined above constitutes merely a "reconstruction" of his scientific work, and one which, moreover, would have been fundamentally foreign to him and irrelevant to his own thought. There is abundant evidence throughout his writings that he thought of masses as entities acting on one another, causing them to behave in the ways they do (except for that "inertial" behavior which was "natu-

ral," requiring no such causal explanation). It is thus plausible to consider the present interpretation as lying between radical description and extreme reconstruction: although the background framework outlined here is not purely descriptive of Newton's most conscious, articulated thought, nevertheless it is an interpretation which has a solid grounding in his writings.

[25] H. Butterfield, *The Origins of Modern Science,* New York, Macmillan, 1958, p. I. The word "framework" in this passage, of course, does not correspond closely to the meaning of "background framework" in our usage.

[26] T. S. Kuhn, *The Structure of Scientific Revolutions,* Chicago, University of Chicago Press, 1962. For a discussion of Kuhn's views, see my "The Structure of Scientific Revolutions," *Philosophical Review,* LXXIII (1964), 383-394. The present essay may be looked upon, partly, as showing (with reference to a particular historical case) what elements of Kuhn's view (and that of Paul Feyerabend) are correct, while at the same time avoiding crucial objections against their views. In this connection, the present paper should be read as a continuation of the review of Kuhn and of my article, "Meaning and Scientific Change," referred to above in Note 6. The latter paper ends with a discussion of similarities and continuities between late medieval and Newtonian mechanics, as the present paper begins with a discussion of differences between those theories.

[27] The "specification" that has been spoken of in this paper cannot be looked upon as consisting simply of the statement of a premise (e.g., "Deviations from uniform rectilinear motion or rest are changes") which, when conjoined with a "background premise" (e.g., "Every change requires a cause") implies the scientific law (e.g., "Deviations from uniform rectilinear motion require a cause"—though here further specification is necessary to convert "cause" into "force"). For such a way of interpreting the relationship evades the crucial connections between the *terms* involved.

It is almost ironic that the "background concepts" *might* be looked upon as a set of purely "theoretical concepts," defined "implicitly" by their relations to one another, and given an "empirical interpretation" in terms of a set of "correspondence rules" (their specifications). Surely the positivistic tradition would have blanched at the possibility of thus letting "metaphysics" in through the "back door" of science! (This possible "positivistic" way of looking at our "background framework" was suggested to me by Peter Achinstein.)

[28] D. Shapere, "The Causal Efficacy of Space," *Philosophy of Science,* XXXI (1964), p. 115.

[29] E.g., in Book Three of the *Opticks.*

P. M. Rattansi (essay date 1972)

SOURCE: "Newton's Alchemical Studies," in *Science, Medicine, and Society in the Renaissance,* edited by Allen G. Debus, Science History Publications, 1972, pp. 167-82.

[*In the following essay, Rattansi emphasizes that examination of Newton's work in alchemy should not be divorced from the remainder of his scientific work, nor should such examination attempt to divide Newton into "irreconcilable 'scientific' and 'mystical' selves."*]

Newton's alchemical studies first came to public notice when Brewster published his magisterial biography of Newton in 1855. Brewster was troubled by Newton's obsessive interest in the subject, and confessed that:

> we cannot understand how a mind of such power, and nobly occupied with the abstractions of geometry, and the study of the material world, could stoop to be even the copyist of the most contemptible alchemical poetry, and the annotator of a work, the obvious product of a fool and a knave.[1]

But the full extent of Newton's interest in the subject became clear only when the Cambridge University committee which examined the Portsmouth Manuscripts published their report in 1888, and even more fully when the alchemical manuscripts were described in detail in the catalogue of the Sotheby sale of 1936 which was to scatter them all over the world.[2] It was now revealed that, besides the 1,300,000 words on the theological and Biblical topics, there were extant about 650,000 words on alchemy, almost wholly in Newton's own hand.[3]

It seems fair to say that historians who have discussed Newton's alchemical studies since Brewster have tended to adopt diametrically opposed views about their significance. L. T. More, in his 1934 biography of Newton, claimed:

> The fact of the matter is, Newton was an alchemist, and his major interest in chemistry, in his earlier years, centered on the possibility of transmuting metals.

Lord Keynes, who helped to save a great many of the alchemical manuscripts from dispersion at the 1936 sale, commented in 1947 (in what has been called "an unfortunately memorable phrase")[5] that Newton, who had left behind him an enormous mass of alchemical material that was "wholly magical and wholly devoid of scientific value," was to be seen as "not the first of the age of reason," but "the last of the magicians."[6] After a more searching and careful survey, the historian of alchemy and early chemistry, F. Sherwood Taylor, reaffirmed More's judgement in 1956:

He conducted alchemical experiments, he read widely and universally in alchemical treatises of all types, and he wrote alchemy, not like Newton, but like an alchemist.

There are obvious difficulties in accepting such a verdict. Not only does it radically challenge our image of Newton as the greatest of the early modern scientists who broke the spell both of scholasticism and of the Renaissance pseudo-sciences in the study of nature. It also raises in an acute form the problem of reconciling his supposedly alchemical commitments with his published views on chemical topics. However strange Newton's views on Biblical prophecy may now appear, they presumably have little relevance for understanding his scientific work; but it seems inconceivable that there should be no connection between his alchemical studies and the reasonably coherent chemical philosophy which can be reconstructed from his printed works. The historians who have described Newton as an "alchemist" have done little to link that belief with his "official" science. L. T. More suggested that Newton was searching for some unifying principle that would connect all chemical actions. Sherwood Taylor pointed to Newton's attempts to explain gravitation, electrical and magnetic actions, and animal motion in terms of an aethereal medium, and saw here a connection with alchemy, since "a great part of alchemy is concerned with that universal medium, the philosopher's mercury."

Such suggestions have seemed to others to raise more problems than they set out to solve. Professor and Mrs. Rupert Hall have commented that to identify the aether of the "General Scholium" with the "Philosophical Mercury" of the alchemists, instead of making Newton's thinking more comprehensible, makes it less so.[8] Since that view prefaces their own valuable and pioneering study (1958) of the neglected notebook of Newton in which he had actually recorded many of his chemical (or alchemical?) experiments, it is surprising that their conclusions do not, at first sight, seem to conflict with L. T. More's and Sherwood Taylor's assessment. They state that most of Newton's experiments on metals aimed at discovering ways in which metals could be made more volatile, as well as at preparing alloys of low melting and boiling points. Sal Ammoniac was a key ingredient in both sorts of experiments. The Halls admit that the alchemists of the time shared these aims. The art of changing volatile to fixed had "an alchemical significance." Though Newton never explained his interest in alloys of a low melting point, it was probably connected with the alchemical search for the "philosopher's mercury." Again, Newton's preference for using indeterminate ores rather than smelted metal was perhaps connected with the alchemical idea that the metallic mineral was alive and fertile, while smelted metal was dead and inert.

But the Halls insist that these striking similarities must not be taken to mean that Newton aimed at the same result—the Stone and the Elixir—as the alchemists. They point to his careful techniques, keen attention to measurement, and "rational" interpretation of alchemical terms and symbols as proof of Newton's "rational" approach to alchemy. Newton's work on *speculum* metals for his reflecting telescope perhaps provoked questions in his mind about the structure of metals and alloys. Besides this accidental stimulus, he may have found metals extremely suitable subjects for the study of structural composition. And when one studied metallurgical chemistry in the seventeenth century, where else would one turn to than the alchemist. The notebook itself provides no clues about Newton's purpose. But (the Halls contend) except as a repository of certain valuable facts, alchemy had nothing to offer Newton: it was not a variant natural philosophy, but merely a theory of metals plus the operations necessary for its realisation, with a lump of gold as the end-product.[9]

However much such a view of Newton's alchemical studies may seem to fit the Newton we know from the **Principia** and the **Opticks,** it is not free from many difficulties. First of all, the alchemical excerpts, considered both in respect to the choice of authors and of topics, do not really support the idea that Newton was merely looking for chemical and metallurgical information. A large number of extracts are descriptions of alchemical processes; others relate to such alchemical topics as the different sorts of stones created by the alchemists and the fantastic powers they conferred on the possessor; and a whole class of extracts (mostly from the alchemist Michael Maier) is an elaborate discussion of the alchemical significance of pagan mythology. Moreover, in a number of his own manuscript compositions, Newton employs alchemical beliefs in a matter of fact way in his discussion of the problem of generation in the animal, vegetable, and mineral kingdoms: for example, in a manuscript now in the Burndy Library, which discusses the properties of the "two Elixirs" and of the Alkahest.[10]

Secondly, Newton himself, to judge from an early indication of his opinion, did not regard alchemy merely as an *Goldmachenkunst.* A rare occasion, when (to use his own words) he "shot his bolt" about alchemy, was in a letter to Henry Oldenberg (then Secretary of the Royal Society) on 26th April 1676, commenting on a paper by Robert Boyle in the *Philosophical Transactions* on the "incalescence" of gold and mercury. Boyle had offered a corpuscular explanation of the process, and Newton offered an alternative one, in terms of the size and mechanical actions of the particles. But he went on to commend Boyle for concealing some parts of the process, since it was

> possibly an inlet to something more noble, and not to be communicated without immense dammage to

ye world if there be any verity in ye Hermetick writers . . ."[11]

To discover its true significance, Boyle should hold his "high silence" and reflect on his true experiment or consult someone who really understood what Boyle had talked about,

> that is, of a true Hermetic Philosopher, whose judgmt (if there be any such) would be more to be regarded in this point then that of all ye world beside to ye contrary, there being other things beside ye transmutation of metalls (if those great pretenders bragg not) wch none but they understand.

The letter is laced with caution about the claims of the alchemists, but the hint that Boyle did not really comprehend what manner of things he was meddling with, recurs in Newton's later correspondence. These remarks, together with the evidence of the manuscripts, reinforce a feeling that it is far easier to attribute Boyle's interest in alchemical authors to a search for valuable information than Newton's.

Newton's comment that the wide dissemination of alchemical secrets could result in "immense dammage to ye world" may refer merely to the monetary and social consequences of easy transmutation; but he hinted that more was involved than transmutation. In the alchemical works he himself studied, success in alchemy was said to open the gates to knowledge of all the secrets of the universe. His contemporary, Elias Ashmole, introducing the collection which Newton constantly studied, said that making gold was

> scarce any intent of the ancient Philosophers, and lowest use the Adepti made of the Materia. For they being lovers of Wisdom more than worldly Wealth, drove at higher and more Excellent Operations: And certainly He to whom the whole Course of Nature lyes open, rejoyceth not so much that he can make Gold and Silver, or the Divells to become subject to him, as that he sees the Heavens open, the Angells of God Ascending and Descending, and that his own Name is fairely written in the Book of Life . . .

> In briefe, by the true and various uses of the Philosopher's Prima Materia . . . the perfection of Liberall Sciences are made known, the whole Wisdome of Nature may be grasped: And . . .There are yet hid greater things than these, for we have seen but few of his Workes.[12]

In pointing out the difficulties of what its expositors see as a more rational interpretation of Newton's alchemical studies, I may seem to have slid back to viewing him as a convinced alchemist. But it is to be noted that even in the letter to Oldenburg in which he extols the knowledge of the Hermetic philosophers, Newton couches his explanation of Boyle's process in strictly corpuscular and mechanical terms. We seem to be impaled here on the horns of a dilemma: how could the rational and scientific Newton, who obviously interpreted alchemical processes not in mystical or traditional alchemical terms, but within a mechanical framework, have placed any credence in their larger and wilder claims?

I should like to suggest that the relation between Newton's alchemical studies and his "official" science becomes clearer if we examine the assumptions guiding two other sorts of studies which absorbed a great deal of his attention. These are, first, his Biblical studies,[13] especially of the prophetic books of the Bible; and second, his studies of ancient natural philosophy, undertaken in the 1690's in connection with the revised second edition of the *Principia.* Underlying both sorts of studies, for Newton, was the assumption that truth—whether about the unfolding course of history or the true system of the world—was anciently given, but in a veiled and enigmatic form to conceal it from the vulgar. The prefiguring of future events in Scripture would become clear only when those events had come to pass, for their sole function was to *demonstrate* the Providence which guided the course of history; that was the task which Newton attempted in his study of ancient history. Similarly, the fact that the ancients had possessed knowledge of the true physical system of the world could only be seen when that system had been recovered, on the basis of a rigorous inductive and experimental method. So convinced was Newton that this was so, that he intended at the time to add classical annotations in the second edition to show that the key propositions of the *Principia* were well known to some of the ancients; indeed, he argues in elaborate detail that Pythagoras must have known the law of universal gravitation. What Newton was employing was a characteristic Renaissance tactic, the idea of a *prisca sapientia* which had served to legitimize the concern of the Florentine Platonists with the Hermetic magical works, and later, from the end of the sixteenth century, to remove the tinge of atheism from atomic doctrines by attributing them to a certain Moschus, who, many classical scholars held, was none other than Moses himself; and Newton's contemporaries at Cambridge, the Platonists Henry More and Ralph Cudworth, used the same tactic to present the Mechanical Philosophy as no more than the restoration of an ancient Mosaic theology-cum-natural philosophy which had become separated after Pythagoras.

Now the idea of a pristine knowledge of nature, delivered in a mysterious text—the "Tabula Smaragdina"—and to be unravelled by the practical "work of the fire", aided by the works of the succession of masters through the ages who had penetrated the secret, is central to alchemy. Expanding earlier hints and influenced by a Renaissance mythographic tradition, the

17th century German alchemist, Michael Maier, had greatly extended the range of alchemically "relevant" materials by arguing that the whole of Greek and Roman mythology was a veiled representation of alchemical secrets.

In view of his later attitude, it is probably significant that even during his last year at school at Grantham, Newton owned and annotated a work expounding the ethical, historical, and scientific significance of the fables narrated by Ovid in his *Metamorphoses.*[14] When he came to Cambridge he imbibed the mechanical philosophy during his undergraduate years, not only from the works of Descartes and other continental masters, but also from those of Henry More, where it was presented as the rediscovery of a most ancient philosophy. The earliest known indication of Newton's alchemical interest is the letter he wrote to his friend Francis Aston in 1669, and the manuscript evidence makes it certain that the transmutations he asked Aston to investigate during his travels are derived from the works of Michael Maier. Newton's continuous fascination with Maier's works is evident from the long extracts he made from them, and from the many citations in the various alchemical indices which Newton compiled. Newton's own chemical experiments began probably at this time, and continued at least until 1696.[15]

As his letter to Oldenburg in 1676 hinted, Newton did not regard alchemy merely as the search for transmutation; much deeper things were involved in it. The symbolic and enigmatic from in which alchemists had expressed themselves was essential to the nature of the art. His views on alchemy have, in fact, a much less modern ring than those of Robert Boyle. Boyle probably influenced Newton profoundly in his belief that the mechanical philosophers should concern themselves much more closely with chemical phenomena, in part by studying the experiments reported by the best of the chemical authors. Boyle did not wish to dismiss the possibility that some alchemical "adepts" may have been in possession of the secret of transmutation, for the corpuscular philosophy implied the transmutability of matter.[16] But he was emphatic in asserting that these valuable results were only an accidental byproduct of the fact that the alchemists had sought the Stone and the Elixir by practical laboratory operations. Certainly, their confused and false theories had nothing to offer to the mechanical philosopher, and were based on competing element-theories which had all now been refuted. Most of the authors whom Boyle himself discussed in this connection were those who had renounced the search for transmutation in favour of the search for *arcana* and "Quintessences" useful in medicine: Paracelsus and followers of his *tria prima* like Duchesne and Beguin; Sala; Sennert; Libavius; and especially Helmont.

None of these particular authors appear in the lists of the best chemical authors compiled at various times by

Newton. His interest was in the great masters of the alchemical succession, from the Hermes Trismegistus whom he took to have lived in the time of the Patriarchs down to contemporaries like the Theodorus Mundanus, whose alchemical views were published by Edmund Dickinson in 1686.[17] More than half of the authors he most frequently consulted were then believed to have lived between the time of Moses and the thirteenth century. Those in whom Boyle was especially interested do not appear in Newton's lists, presumably because they did not concern themselves primarily with the "Great Work" (although Helmont is studied for his "Alkahest"). The extant Newtonian alchemical manuscripts consist almost wholly of extracts from alchemical works, and there can be no doubt that most of them deal with the processes involved in making the Stone. However, these works insisted at the same time that the Stone was valued by the true *adepti* not because it would transmute metals and cure all diseases, but because it would make it possible to understand the greatest secret of nature: the subtle spirit or the "Philosopher's Mercury" which was the source of all activity in the universe. To quote Ashmole again:

> . . . the Power and Vertue is not in Plants, Stones, Minerals &c. (though we sensibly perceive the Effects from them) but 'tis that universal and All-piercing Spirit, the One operative vertue and immortall Seede of Worldly things, that God in the beginning infused into the Chaos, which is every where Active and still flows through the world in all kindes of things by universall extension, and manifests itself by the aforesaid Productions. Which Spirit a true Artist knowes how-so to handle (though its activity be as it were dul'd and streightly bound up, in the close Prison of Grosse and Earthie bodies) as to take it from Corporeity, free it from Captivity, and let it loose that it may freely worke as it doth in the AEtheriall Bodies.[18]

The Hermetic Tablet, the basic text of alchemy, described the operations of this Spirit, and many of Newton's extracts deal with the numerous different forms of activity in the universe in which it was involved.[19] It is difficult to understand how, without a conviction that deep truths were concealed in alchemy, Newton should have attached much significance to such ideas, or to have believed (as the Halls contend) that

> the profoundly esoteric terminology of alchemy was only an extension of the superficially esoteric language of ordinary chemistry; and similarly that the more recondite experimentation of the former was but an extension of the better-known and clearer experimentation of the latter.[20]

Boyle, in various places, referred to "the Universal spirit, asserted by some Chymists", as a substitute for or in combination with the *tria prima* of elements, but implied that it was superfluous, since it would have to

be understood in corpuscular terms before it could satisfactorily explain any thing in nature.[21] Newton's assumptions, on the other hand, imply some sort of dialectic between new inductively- and experimentally- based scientific knowledge and the ancient texts: the rise of the mechanical philosophy made a deeper penetration into the meaning of those texts possible, but did not invalidate the truths they embodied.[22] The Aristotelian element-theory was employed, in most part, in the alchemical texts to characterise the various phases of matter, and Newton took over that phraseology in many of his own works; and he characteristically read a deeper meaning into the sulphur-mercury theory, arguing in an early draft of his **"De natura acidorum"**:

> Note that what is said by chemists, that everything is made from sulphur and mercury is true, because by sulphur they mean acid, and by mercury they mean earth.[23]

If the interpretation that has been offered of the enormous amount of time and labour devoted by Newton to the study of an astonishing variety of alchemical writings and to experiments over several decades is correct, then we must seriously re-examine Sherwood Taylor's suggestion that there is some connection between Newton's various aethereal speculations and the "philosopher's mercury" sought by the alchemists. The alchemical flavour of the aethereal hypotheses presented by Newton in his 1675 letter to Oldenburg and 1679 letter to Boyle has been noted by a number of authors.[24] The letter to Oldenburg is primarily concerned with describing an optical hypothesis, but is prefaced by a long section outlining a wide range of phenomena (including electrical and magnetic actions, chemical phenomena, animal motion, and gravitation) which are explained in terms of an aethereal medium. There can be no doubt that Newton's account offers variations on the Cartesian vortical aether and is strongly influenced by Boyle's model of the "ocean of air".[25] But at least three of the themes of these speculations bear a striking resemblance to those he was studying at that time in the alchemical authors. These are: firstly, the creation of all things from aether by condensation, and the idea of a particular spirit within that aether which is contained within the pores of matter as a principle of activity "for the continual uses of nature"; secondly, the continual condensation of that particular spirit by the earth, while the exchange of 'as much matter" sent out in an aerial form from the bowels of the earth sets up a circulation; thirdly, the existence of "sociability" and "unsociability" between various substances through "a secret principle" and action of intermediaries in resolving it.

The first two themes are directly related to the *Tabula* and its interpretation by alchemical authors. A manuscript commentary on the *Tabula* in Newton's hand describes how all things were generated from the alchemical chaos or aether, and how that aether ascends into the heavens by sublimations and in time by reiterated sublimations descends to earth—a process which the alchemist must emulate in his own operations. The third theme, that of the secret sympathies and antipathies between various chemical substances, was a basic one in alchemical discussions.[26]

Newton sought to explain a much wider range of phenomena by his "Spirit" than was usual in alchemical discussions;[27] and, of course, there is no analogue in the alchemical writings for his explanation of many of these phenomena in terms of the "mechanical" properties of the aether. But that he was equating the alchemical *spiritus* with a quasi-Cartesian ether can now be shown much more convincingly by recourse to the Burndy Library manuscript already cited. In that document Newton considered a favourite alchemical theme, the analogy between generation and maturation in each of the three kingdoms of nature, for the light it cast upon the "vegetation of metals", and, presumably, upon the processes by which the Great Work might be accomplished.

Newton sharply distinguished nature's "vegetable" actions from the "purely mechanical" ones. The former included generation and corruption, the latter gravitation, the tides, "meteors" and "vulgar Chymistry". The reactions of ordinary chemistry may at times seem to human senses "as strange transmutations as those of nature", but they really involved merely the "mechanical coalitions or separations of particles". If vegetation involved something more, then "this difference is vast and fundamental because nothing could ever yet be made without vegetation which nature useth to produce by it", and he significantly included the supposed transmutation of iron into copper as an example.[28] What distinguished vegetation from mechanism was the fact that it consisted of an interaction between the aether as an activating principle and the "rudements" or seeds of things, that is "that substance in them that is attained to the fullest degree of maturity that is in that thing". The descent of the aether from the heavens could itself be explained mechanically. Enormous quantities of vapours and airs ascended continually from the earth by "mineral dissolutions and fermentation" and they compressed the aether and finally forced it to descend, illustrating once more that it was "very agreeable to nature's proceedings to make a circulation of all things": "Thus this earth resembles a great animal or rather inanimate vegetable, and draws in aethereal breath for its daily refreshment & vital ferment & transpires again with gross exhalations . . . And thus a great pt if not all the moles of sensible matter is nothing but AEther congealed & interwoven into various textures whose life depends on that pt of it wch is in a middle state, not wholly distinct & loose from it like ye AEther in wch it swims as in a fluid nor wholly joined & compacted together with it under one form but in some

degree condensed [&] united to it & yet remaining of a much more rare texture & subtle disposition & so this seems to be the principle of its acting."

On further reflection Newton concluded that "'tis more probable ye aether is but a vehicle to some more active spt & yᵉ bodies may be concreted of both together, they may imbibe aether well as air in generation & in yᵉ aether yᵉ spt is entangled. This spt is yᵉ body of light because both have a prodigious active principle, both are prodigious workers . . ."

These remarks do much to clarify Newton's view of alchemy at the time. In the course of developing his thoughts on the "vegetation of metals," he cited the Elixir and the Alkahest, the initially green colour of the Stone and the generation of much air in the Stone's "first solution" as part of his evidence. His identification of the most active part of the aether with light is particularly interesting. The *spiritus* was regarded by the alchemists as present in all bodies, constituting the principle of their activity. When extracted from substances and concentrated within the Stone, it was often described as being most like light. The *spiritus* must necessarily be a substance of the finest subtlety since it entered the smallest parts of gross matter and separated them in the processes of generation and maturation, but (in Newton's own words) "not after yᵉ way of common menstruums by rending them violently asunder &c.", but by "a more subtle sweet & noble way of working . . ." Newton's reflections seem, then, to indicate that Newton may, at least at that time, have conceived the goal of the alchemical quest as the recovery of the body of light itself through practical laboratory operations. Newton had not ceased to speculate on these lines even when he published his **Opticks** in its second English edition of 1717, and in Query 30 he asked: "Are not gross Bodies and Light convertible into one another, and may not Bodies receive much of their Activity from Particles of Light which enter their Composition? . . . The changing of Bodies into Light, and Light into Bodies, is very comfortable to the Course of Nature, which seems delighted with Transmutations."[29]

Newton's thoughts on the aether and the *spiritus* are made more intelligible when they are viewed against the vicissitudes of the idea of *spiritus* through the 16th and 17th centuries, and its place in one particular variant of the mechanical philosophy in England. The alchemical *spiritus* was invoked in natural-philosophical discussions by authors of very different philosophical allegiances. It provided a *rationale* for non-demonic "natural magic" to the Florentine Platonists and their successors;[30] furnished an explanation of the Aristotelian "occult" qualities for Jean Fernel;[31] and served as an explanatory principle in the works of such innovators as Telesio, Basso, Campanella, and Francis Bacon.[32] The "Spagyrick" authors who wished to turn chemical studies away from traditional alchemy and towards medicine often identified the *spiritus* with particular substances; for example Glauber and the Paracelsians equated it with the "nitro-aerial spirit," unintentionally aiding its identification with familiar substances.[33] So various were the functions assigned to the *spiritus,* which was itself increasingly regarded as a material fluid, that William Harvey condemned it as the *deus ex machina* of inferior writers.[34]

More immediately relevant for studying Newton's ideas is the tactic adopted in 1657 by Henry More, the Cambridge Platonist, in his amalgam of Cartesianism and Neo-Platonism. He identified the First and Second Matters of Descartes with the *spiritus* of the Renaissance Platonists—the *spiritus* which Ficino had said was the same as the alchemical Fifth Element or Quintessence—in order to avoid the Cartesian dualism of mind and matter.[35] A simple identification of the alchemical *spiritus* and the Cartesian ether will be found, again, with citations to Henry More, in the professedly Cartesian work, *Experimental Philosophy,* published by Newton's contemporary, Henry Power in 1664. Power called it "the main (though invisible) Agent in all Natures three Kingdoms Mineral, Vegetal, and Animal."[36] They were responsible for fermentation in minerals, vegetation and maturation in plants, and life, sense, and motion in animals; they explained the conjunction of soul and body in man through the mediation of the animal spirits.

Henry More's view of the mechanical philosophy as the restoration of the lost "Mosaic" system of the world seems to have generally influenced Newton, and it is likely that he was equally impressed by More's pointing to the basic similarities between the Neo-Platonic *spiritus* and the Cartesian aether. Given these assumptions, the alchemical texts would enormously extend the range of materials in which that aether had been discussed and described, and even open the possibility of being able to recover that extremely active substance through laboratory operations. That was not incompatible with devising "mechanically" intelligible explanations of the myriad phenomena which ultimately depended on the action of the aether.

This paper has attempted to outline an approach to Newton's alchemical studies that would avoid the opposing dangers of either isolating them from his total scientific and intellectual labours, or of splitting Newton into irreconcilable "scientific" and "mystical" selves. The changes in Newton's attitude to alchemy, and their bearing on, say, the "cometary spirit" of the **Principia,** and the "Active Principles" of the **Opticks,** are problems for future research to clarify. But we cannot even begin to grapple with them unless we take account of a legacy of Renaissance ideas which had not lost their force during Newton's lifetime.

What is particularly impressive, and perhaps vital for understanding the complexities of Newton's own worldview, is the influence of the Renaissance "pristine" concept in Newton's attempts to unify some of the major ideas enshrined in the very different sorts of literature he studied intensively at various periods of his life: the vast labyrinth of alchemy; the theology of the early Church Fathers, especially the Alexandrian Fathers; and the scientific views of the ancients. Historians of ideas have recently begun to explore the recurrence and transformation of such ideas as those of the *pneuma,* or the teachings of the mysterious Hermes Trismegistus, in these different sorts of works.[37] The Newtonian manuscripts show that Newton was well aware of these resemblances, and regarded them as proof of the consonance between the truths he had discovered by rigorous scientific procedures and the clues scattered in enigmatic form in very disparate realms of ancient and late-antique thought.

It is true that the approach advocated here demands a significant modification of the conventional view of Newton. Certainly, the labels of "Rationalist," "empiricist," or "mystic" which have been variously applied in this context fail to do justice to the complexities of Newton's thought. In common with the other great natural philosophers of his age, like Descartes, or even more, like Leibniz, Newton strove for a unified solution that would encompass not only the mysteries of celestial and terrestrial physics, but also the perennial religious problems of the relation between the Creator and his universe. These wider endeavours of Newton may appear naively fundamentalist and philosophically unsophisticated when compared, say, with the coherence and majesty of the system of Leibniz. But any total account of Newton's thought must fully consider them. Otherwise, we shall remain wedded to a simplistic view of the rich, strange, complex world of Newton's thought, and harried by problems of interpretation which have usually been met by desperate expedients which recent achievements in the historiography of science, particularly the outstanding work of Walter Pagel,[37] should make us extremely wary of adopting.

The "strange seas of thought" over which Isaac Newton voyaged may now seem even stranger than we had suspected. Charting their extent and plumbing their depths will demand a sensitivity and a breadth of contextual knowledge for which Pagel's work has set up almost impossibly high standards.

References

[1] Brewster, Sir David, *"Memoirs of the Life, Writings, & Discoveries of Sir Isaac Newton",* Edinburg & London, 1855, II, 374-5.

[2] *"A Catalogue of the Portsmouth Collection of Books and Papers Written by or belonging to Sir Isaac New-*

ton . . . Drawn up by the Syndicate appointed the 6th November 1872", Cambridge, 1888. *Catalogue of the Newton Papers,* Sotheby's, London, 1936.

[3] Estimate by F. Sherwood Taylor, "An Alchemical Work of Sir Isaac Newton", *Ambix,* V (1956), 60.

[4] More, L. T., *Isaac Newton, A Biography,* New York & London, 1934, 158 and 52.

[5] Boas, Marie, and Hall, A. Rupert, "Newton's Chemical Experiments," *Archives internationales d'Histoire des sciences, XI* (1958), 113.

[6] The Royal Society, *Newton Tercentenary Celebrations* (15-19 July 1946), Cambridge, 1947, J. M. Keynes, "Newton, the Man," 32 & 27.

[7] Taylor, *op. cit.,* 63.

[8] Halls, 118.

[9] *Ibid.,* 133-152.

[10] The item was listed in the Sotheby Sale Catalogue as No. 516, and begins: "Of natures obvious laws & processes in vegetation."

[11] Turnbull, H. W., (ed.), *The Correspondence of Isaac Newton,* II, Cambridge, 1960, 1-3; Boyle's paper appeared in *Phil. Trans., X* (1675/6), 515-33.

[12] *Theatrum Chemicum Britannicum,* London, 1652, Prolegomena, [A4^v] & B2^r.

[13] Discussed in McGuire, J. E. & Rattansi, P. M., "Newton and the 'Pipes of Pan,'" *Notes & Records of the Royal Society of London, XXI* (1966), 108-143. Cf. Newton on *Daniel and the Apocalypse,* (ed.) White, W., London, 1922, 305-6.

[14] *A Descriptive Catalogue of the Grace K. Babson Collection of the Works of Sir Isaac Newton,* New York, 1950, 187-6, records: "Sabinus, Georgius . . . Ovidii / Metamorphoses, / sev Fabvlae Poeticae: / Earemque Interpretatio / Ethica, Physica et Historica / . . . ultima editio, 1593, Frankfurt," and on the flyleaf: "Isaci Newtoni / Liber / Octobris 15 / 1659. / praetium -0-1-6," and various marginal notes.

[15] On Newton's interest in alchemy, consult Brewster, More, the Halls, Sherwood Taylor, in works cited *supra.*; also Forbes, R. J., "Was Newton an alchemist?," *Chymia, II* (1949), 27-36, and Geoghegan, D., "Some Indications of Newton's attitude towards Alchemy," *Ambix, VI* (1957), 102-106. Keynes Manuscript 32 at King's College, Cambridge, contains 88 pages of notes in Newton's hands from four works by Maier, totalling about 50,000 words; Maier continued

to be cited in the indices Newton compiled in the late 17th century.

[16] See e.g. Boyle, *Works,* (ed.) Birch, T., 1744, III, 621; cf. the appendix on "the Producibleness of Chymicall Principles" added to the 1680 ed. of the *Sceptical Chymist,* where Boyle affirms his strong belief in adepts with "among other rare things some *Alkahestical* or other extraordinarily potent Menstruum," p. [*7^{rv}].

[17] The shortest list among the Keynes MSS. reads: "Best authors: Hermes, Turba, Morien, Artephius, Abraham the Jew and Flammel, Scala, Ripley, Maier, the great Rosary, Charnock, Trevisan, Philalethea, D'espagnet." The longest list, among those grouped in Keynes, M. S. 13, contains 63 works, including Edmund Dickinson's of 1684.

[18] Ashmole, *op. cit.,* 446-7.

[19] An English translation of the *Tabula* in Newton's hand, as well the Latin text with a commentary, are in Keynes, M. S. 28; cf. in the Burndy Library MS.: "That vegetation is ye sole effect of a latent spt & that this spt is ye same in all things only discriminated by degrees of maturity . . ."

[20] Halls, *op. cit.,* 151-2.

[21] Boyle, *Works,* III, 453.

[22] McGuire & Rattansi, *op. cit.;* in the manuscript discussed there, Newton said that by the fiction of a lion falling out of the moon and stones out of the sun Anaxagoras indicated the gravity of the sun and moon towards the earth, and the force of rotation against gravity, respectively, for "the mystical philosophers by this kind of fiction were wont to adumbrate the doctrines in mystical language." Cf. Newton's note in Keynes MS. 32: "Pythagoras fuit adeptus, (fit ejus metampsychosis cum tinctura lapidis in imperfecta metalla transfertur. fflata (i.e. lapis Philos) non est conedena.)"

[23] Newton, *Correspondence,* III, 206 and 210.

[24] E.G. Löhne, J., in *Archive for the History of Exact Sciences, I* (1961), 401.

[25] Guerlac, Henry, *Newton et Epicure,* Paris, 1963, 9.

[26] Festugière, P., *La revelation d'Hermès Trismégiste,* Paris, 1944, I, 233-237.

[27] Cf. (ed.) Turnbull, H. W., *The Correspondence of Isaac Newton,* I, Cambridge, 1959, 11 and note 6, 13.

[28] Cited from the Dover ed., New York, 1952, 374. In *ibid.,* 405, Newton said that in the observations and

queries of the Third Book, he had "only begun the Analysis of what remains to be discovere'd about Light and its Effects upon the Frame of Nature, hinting several things about it, and leaving the Hints to be examin'd and improv'd by the further Experiments and Observations of such as are inquisitive."

[29] Walker, D. P., *Spiritual and demonic Magic from Ficino to Campanella,* London, 1958.

[30] Walker, "The Astral Body in Renaissance Medicine," *Journal of the Warburg & Courtauld Institutes, XXI* (1958).

[31] Siebeck, H., "Neue beiträge zur entwicklungsgeschichte des Geist-Begriffs," *Archiv für Geschichte der Philosophie, XX* (1914), 1-16.

[32] Sherwood Taylor, F., "The Idea of the Quintessence," in (ed.) Underwood, E. Ashworth, *Science, Medicine and History,* London, 1953, I, 247-265.

[33] In the "Excert. alt. ad J. Riolan," 1649, and again in the *De generatione* (1651), Harvey rejected any attempt to explain vital phenomena by a material cause, and adduced empirical evidence against the presence of the *spiritus* in physiological cavities. On the sun, the spirit, and the aerial niter in the seventeenth century chemical literature see Allen G. Debus, "The Sun in the Universe of Robert Fludd," *Le Soleil à la Renaissance-Sciences et Mythes,* Travaux de l'Institut pour l'étude de la Renaissance et de l'Humanisme, Brussels, 1965, 259-278; "The Paracelsian Aerial Niter," *Isis,* LV (1964), 43-61.

[34] More, Henry, *The Immortality of the Soul* (1659), B. 2, ch. iv.

[35] Power, Henry, *Experimental Philosophy in Three Books,* London, 1664, "A Digression on Animal Spirits," 61-71; also C. Webster, "Henry Power's Experimental Philosophy," *Ambix XIV* (1967), 150-78 and Rattansi, *Ambix XVI* (1969), 173-5.

[36] Verbeke, G., *L'Evolution de la doctrine du pneuma,* Paris & Louvain, 1945; Festugière, *op. cit.* (note 26).

[37] See Pagel's remarks in *Das Medizinische Weltbild des Paracelsus, seine zussamenhänge mit Neuplatonismus und Gnosis,* Wiesbaden, 1962, 14-16.

Robert B. Downs   (essay date 1978)

SOURCE: "System of the World," in *Books That Changed the World,* Second Edition, American Library Association, 1978, pp. 334-74.

[*In the following essay, Downs surveys the content, scope, and reception of Newton's* Principia.]

Sir Isaac Newton: Principia Mathematica

Of all the books which have profoundly influenced human affairs, few have been more celebrated and none read by fewer people than Sir Isaac Newton's *Philosophiae Naturalis Principia Mathematica* ("Mathematical Principles of Natural Philosophy"). Deliberately written in the most abstruse and technical Latin, profusely illustrated by complex geometrical diagrams, the work's direct audience has been limited to highly erudite astronomers, mathematicians, and physicists.

One of Newton's chief biographers has stated that when the *Principia* was published in the last quarter of the seventeenth century there were not more than three or four men living who could comprehend it; another generously stretched the number to ten or a dozen. The author himself admitted that it was "a hard book," but he had no apologies, for he planned it that way, making no concessions to the mathematically illiterate.

Yet, notable men of science hold Newton to be one of the great intellectual figures of all time. Laplace, a brilliant French astronomer, termed the *Principia* "preeminent above any other production of human genius." Lagrange, famous mathematician, asserted that Newton was the greatest genius who ever lived. Boltzmann, a pioneer of modern mathematical physics, called the *Principia* the first and greatest work ever written on theoretical physics. An eminent American astronomer, W. W. Campbell, remarked, "To me it is clear that Sir Isaac Newton, easily the greatest man of physical science in historic time, was uniquely the great pioneer of astro-physics." Comments from other leading scientists over the past two-and-a-half centuries have been phrased in like superlatives. The layman must necessarily accept these judgments on faith, and on the basis of results.

Newton was born almost exactly a century after the death of Copernicus, and in the same year as Galileo's death. These giants in the world of astronomy, together with Johannes Kepler, furnished the foundations upon which Newton continued to build.

Newton was a mathematical wizard in an age of gifted mathematicians. As Marvin pointed out, "the seventeenth century was the flowering age of mathematics, as the eighteenth was of chemistry and the nineteenth of biology, and the last four decades of the seventeenth saw more forward steps taken than any other period in history." Newton combined in himself the major physical sciences—mathematics, chemistry, physics, and astronomy—for in the seventeenth century, before the era of extreme specialization, a scientist could encompass all fields.

Newton, born on Christmas Day, 1642, in his early years saw the rise and fall of Oliver Cromwell's Commonwealth Government, the Great Fire which practically destroyed London, and the Great Plague which wiped out a third of the city's population. After eighteen years spent in the little hamlet of Woolsthorpe, Newton was sent to Cambridge University. There he was fortunate to come under the guidance of an able and inspiring teacher, Isaac Barrow, professor of mathematics, who has been called Newton's "intellectual father." Barrow recognized, encouraged, and stimulated the growing genius of young Newton. While still in college, Newton discovered the binomial theorem.

Because of the plague, Cambridge was closed in 1665, and Newton returned to the country. For the next two years, largely cut off from the world, he devoted himself to scientific experimentation and meditation. The consequences were astounding. Before he had reached the age of twenty-five, Newton had made three discoveries that entitle him to be ranked among the supreme scientific minds of all time. First was the invention of the differential calculus, termed "fluxions" by Newton, because it deals with variable or "flowing" quantities. The calculus is involved in all problems of flow, movement of bodies, and waves, and is essential to the solution of physical problems concerned with any kind of movement. "It seemed to unlock the gates guarding the storehouse of mathematical treasures; to lay the mathematical world at the feet of Newton and his followers," according to one commentator.

Newton's second major discovery was the law of composition of light, from which he proceeded to analyze the nature of color and of white light. It was shown that the white light of the sun is compounded of rays of light of all the colors of the rainbow. Color is therefore a characteristic of light, and the appearance of white light—as Newton's experiments with a prism demonstrated—comes from mixing the colors of the spectrum. Through knowledge gained from this discovery, Newton was able to construct the first satisfactory reflecting telescope.

Even more noteworthy was Newton's third revelation: the law of universal gravitation, which is said to have stirred the imaginations of scientists more than any theoretical discovery of modern times. According to a well-known anecdote, the flash of intuition which came to Newton when he observed the fall of an apple led to formulation of the law. There was nothing particularly new in the idea of the earth's attraction for bodies near its surface. Newton's great contribution was in conceiving the gravitation law to be universal in application—a force no less powerful in relation to celestial bodies than to the earth—and then producing mathematical proof of his theory.

Curiously enough, Newton published nothing at the time on these three highly significant discoveries on the calculus, color, and gravitation. Possessed of an extremely reticent, even secretive nature, he had an almost morbid dislike of public attention and controversy. Consequently, he was inclined to suppress the results of his experiments. Whatever he published later was done under pressure from friends, and afterward he nearly always regretted surrendering to their entreaties. Publication led to criticism and discussion of his work by fellow-scientists, something which Newton, with his sensitive nature, completely detested and resented.

Following the enforced isolation and leisure of the plague years, Newton returned to Cambridge, received a master's degree, and was appointed a fellow of Trinity College. Shortly thereafter his old teacher, Barrow, withdrew, and Newton, at the age of twenty-seven, became professor of mathematics, a position which he held for the next twenty-seven years. For the next decade or two little was heard of Newton. It is known that he continued his investigations of light, and published a paper on his discovery of the composite nature of white light. Immediately he became involved in controversy, first because his conclusions on the subject of light were in opposition to those then prevailing; and, second, because he had included in the paper a statement on his philosophy of science. In the latter, he had expressed the point of view that the chief function of science is to carry out carefully planned experiments, to record observations of the experiments, and lastly to prepare mathematical laws based on the results. As Newton stated it, the "proper method for enquiring after the properties of things is to deduce them from experiments." While these principles are in complete accord with modern scientific research, they were by no means fully accepted in Newton's day. Beliefs founded on imagination, reason, and the appearance of things, usually inherited from ancient philosophers, were preferred to experimental evidence.

Attacks on his paper by such established scientists as Huygens and Hooke so angered Newton that he resolved to escape future irritations by doing no more publishing. "I was so persecuted," he said, "with discussions arising from the publication of my theory of light, that I blamed my own imprudence for parting with so substantial a blessing as my quiet to run after a shadow." He even expressed an acute distaste for science itself, insisting that he had lost his former "affection" for it. Later, he had to be "spurred, cajoled and importuned" into writing his greatest work, the *Principia.* In fact, creation of the *Principia* appears to have come about more or less by chance.

In 1684, through computations by Picard, the earth's exact circumference was determined for the first time. Using the French astronomer's data, Newton applied the principle of gravitation to prove that the power which guides the moon around the earth and the planets around the sun is the force of gravity. The force varies directly with the mass of the attracted bodies and inversely as the square of their distances. Newton went on to show that this accounts for the elliptical orbits of the planets. The pull of gravity kept the moon and the planets in their paths, balancing the centrifugal forces of their motions.

Again, Newton failed to reveal his phenomenal discovery of nature's greatest secret. As it happened, however, other scientists were engaged in a search for a solution of the same problem. Several astronomers had suggested that the planets were bound to the sun by the force of gravity. Among these was Robert Hooke, Newton's severest and most persistent critic. But none of the theorists had been able to offer mathematical proof. By now Newton had won considerable reputation as a mathematician, and he was visited at Cambridge by the astronomer Edmund Halley who requested his help. When Halley stated the problem, he learned that it had been solved two years before by Newton. Further, Newton had worked out the principal laws of motion of bodies moving under the force of gravity. Characteristically, though, Newton had no intention of publishing his findings.

Halley at once recognized the significance of Newton's accomplishment, and used all his powers of persuasion to convince the stubborn Newton that his discovery should be developed and exploited. Moved by Halley's enthusiasm and with his own interest rekindled, Newton began the writing of his masterpiece, the *Principia,* termed by Langer "a veritable reservoir of mechanistic philosophy, one of the most original works ever produced."

Not the least remarkable feature of the *Principia* was that its composition was completed in eighteen months, during which, it is said, Newton was so engrossed that he often went without food and took little time to sleep. Only the most intense and prolonged concentration could have brought forth such a monumental intellectual achievement in so brief a period. It left Newton mentally and physically exhausted.

Furthermore, during the time of writing, Newton's peace of mind was intensely disturbed by the usual controversies, particularly with Hooke, who maintained he should receive credit for originating the theory that the motion of the planets could be explained by an inverse square law of attraction. Newton, who had finished two-thirds of the *Principia,* was so incensed by what he considered an unjustified claim, that he threatened to omit the third and most important section of his treatise. Again Halley used his influence and prevailed on Newton to complete the work as first planned.

The role played by Edmund Halley in the whole history of the *Principia* deserves the highest commendation. Not only was he responsible for inducing Newton to undertake the work in the first place, but he obtained an agreement with the Royal Society to publish it, and unselfishly dropped everything he was doing to supervise the final printing. Finally, when the Royal Society reneged on its promise to finance the publication, Halley stepped in and paid the entire expense out of his own pocket, though he was a man of moderate means, with a family to support.

Surmounting all obstacles, the *Principia* came from the press in 1687, in a small edition, selling for ten or twelve shillings a copy. The title page bore the imprimatur of Samuel Pepys, then President of the Royal Society, "although it is to be doubted," remarked one commentator, "whether the learned diarist could have understood so much as a single sentence of it."

Any brief summary of the *Principia* in nontechnical language is a difficult, if not impossible, undertaking, but some highlights may be indicated. The work as a whole deals with the motions of bodies treated mathematically, in particular, the application of dynamics and universal gravitation to the solar system. It begins with an explanation of the differential calculus or "fluxions," invented by Newton and used as a tool for calculations throughout the *Principia.* There follow definitions of the meaning of space and time, and a statement of the laws of motion, as formulated by Newton, with illustrations of their application. The fundamental principle is stated that every particle of matter is attracted by every other particle of matter with a force inversely proportional to the square of their distances apart. Also given are the laws governing the problem of bodies colliding with each other. Everything is expressed in classical geometrical forms.

The first book of the *Principia* is concerned with the motion of bodies in free space, while the second treats of "motion in a resisting medium," such as water. In the latter section, the complex problems of the motion of fluids are considered and solved, methods discussed for determining the velocity of sound, and wave motions described mathematically. Herein is laid the groundwork for the modern science of mathematical physics, hydrostatics, and hydrodynamics.

In the second book Newton effectively demolished the world system of Descartes, then in popular vogue. According to Descartes' theory, the motions of the heavenly bodies were due to vortexes. All space is filled with a thin fluid, and at certain points the fluid matter forms vortexes. For example, the solar system has fourteen vortexes, the largest of them containing the sun. The planets are carried around like chips in an eddy. These whirlpools were Descartes' explanation for the phenomena of gravitation. Newton proceeded to demonstrate experimentally and mathematically that "the Vortex Theory is in complete conflict with astronomical facts, and so far from explaining celestial motions would tend to upset them."

In the third book, entitled "The System of the World," Newton was at his greatest as he dealt with the astronomical consequences of the law of gravitation.

> In the preceding books I have laid down the principles of philosophy [science]; principles not philosophical but mathematical. . . . These principles are the laws and conditions of certain motions, and powers or forces. . . . I have illustrated them here and there . . . with . . . an account of such things as are of more general nature . . . such as the density and the resistance of bodies, spaces void of all bodies, and the motion of light and sound. It remains that, from the same principles, I now demonstrate the frame of the System of the World.

Explaining why he had not popularized his work, Newton revealed that—

> Upon this subject I had, indeed, composed the third Book in a popular method, that it might be read by many, but afterwards, considering that such as had not sufficiently entered into the principles could not easily discern the strength of the consequences, nor lay aside the prejudices to which they had been many years accustomed, therefore, to prevent the disputes which might be raised upon such accounts, I chose to reduce the substance of this Book in the form of Propositions (in the mathematical way), which should be read by those only who had first made themselves masters of the principles established in the preceding Books; not that I would advise anyone to the previous study of every Proposition of those Books; for they abound with such as might cost too much time, even to readers of good mathematical learning.

For this reason, the style of the ***Principia*** has been described as "glacial remoteness, written in the aloof manner of a high priest."

At the outset, Newton makes a fundamental break with the past by insisting that there is no difference between earthly and celestial phenomena. "Like effects in nature are produc'd by like causes," he asserted, "as breathing in man and in beast, the fall of stones in Europe and in America, the light of the kitchen fire and of the sun, the reflection of light on the earth and on the planets." Thus was discarded the ancient belief that other worlds are perfect and only the earth is imperfect. Now all were governed by the same rational laws, "bringing order and system," as John MacMurray said, "where chaos and mystery had reigned before."

A mere listing of the principal topics covered in the third book is impressive. The motions of the planets and of the satellites around the planets are established; methods for measuring the masses of the sun and planets are shown; and the density of the earth, the precession of the equinoxes, theory of tides, orbits of the comets, the moon's motion, and related matters discussed and resolved.

By his theory of "perturbations" Newton proved that the moon is attracted by both the earth and the sun, and therefore the moon's orbit is disturbed by the sun's pull, though the earth provides the stronger attraction. Likewise, the planets are subject to perturbations. The sun is not the stationary center of the universe, contrary to previous beliefs, but is attracted by the planets, just as they are attracted to it, and moves in the same way. In later centuries, application of the perturbations theory led to the discovery of the planets Neptune and Pluto.

The masses of different planets and the masses of the sun Newton determined by relating them to the earth's mass. He estimated that the earth's density is between five and six times that of water (the figure used by scientists today is 5.5), and on this basis Newton calculated the masses of the sun and of the planets with satellites, an achievement which Adam Smith called "above the reach of human reason and experience."

Next, the fact that the earth is not an exact sphere, but is flattened at the poles because of rotation, was explained, and the amount of flattening was calculated. Because of the flattening at the poles and the slight bulge at the equator, Newton deducted that the force of gravity must be less at the poles than at the equator—a phenomenon that accounts for the precession of the equinoxes, the conical motion of the earth's axis, resembling a gyroscope. By studying the shape of the planet, furthermore, the possibility of estimating the length of day and night on the planet was shown.

Another application of the law of universal gravitation was Newton's exploration of the tides. When the moon is fullest, the earth's waters experience their maximum attraction, and high tide results. The sun also affects the tides, and when the sun and moon are in line, the tide is highest.

Still another subject of popular interest on which Newton shed light was comets. His theory was that comets, moving under the sun's attraction, travel elliptical paths of incredible magnitude, requiring many years to complete. Henceforth, comets, which were once regarded by the superstitious as evil omens, took their proper place as beautiful and harmless celestial phenomena. By using Newton's theories of comets, Edmund Halley was able to identify and to predict accurately the reappearance about every seventy-five years of the famous Halley's Comet. Once a comet has been observed, its future path can be accurately determined.

One of the most amazing discoveries made by Newton was his method for estimating the distance of a fixed star, based on the amount of light received by reflection of the sun's light from a planet.

The *Principia* made no attempt to explain the *why* but only the *how* of the universe. Later, in response to charges that his was a completely mechanistic scheme, making no provision for ultimate causes or for a Supreme Creator, Newton added a confession of faith to the second edition of his work.

> This most beautiful system of the sun, planets, and comets could only proceed from the counsel and dominion of an intelligent and powerful Being. . . . As a blind man has no idea of colours, so have we no idea of the manner by which the all-wise God perceives and understands all things.

The function of science, he believed, was to go on building knowledge, and the more complete our knowledge is, the nearer are we brought to an understanding of the Cause, though man might never discover the true and exact scientific laws of nature.

Brilliant achievement that the *Principia* was, it was not written in a vacuum as Newton's most ardent admirers concede. I. Bernard Cohen stated:

> The great Newtonian synthesis was based on the work of predecessors. The immediate past had produced the analytical geometry of Descartes and Fermat, the algebra of Oughtred, Harriot and Wallis, Kepler's law of motion, Galileo's law of falling bodies. It had also produced Galileo's law of the composition of velocities—a law stating that a motion may be divided into component parts, each independent of the other (for example the motion of a projectile is composed of a uniform forward velocity and a downward accelerated velocity like that of a freely falling body). The afore-mentioned are but a few of the ingredients present and waiting for the grand Newtonian synthesis. But it remained for the genius of Newton to add the master touch; to show finally, and once and for all, in just what manner the ordered universe is regulated by mathematical law.

It was evident that the world needed, as Sir James Jeans described Newton, "a man who could systematize, synthesize and extend the whole, and it found him in superlative excellence in Newton."

Newton himself recognized that his "System of the World," his mechanics of the universe, was built upon the work begun by Copernicus and so notably carried forward by Tycho Brahe, Kepler, and Galileo. "If I have seen farther than other men," Newton said, "it is by standing on the shoulders of giants."

In fact, the probable cause of the controversies that dogged Newton's life was the intellectual ferment prevailing in his time. The air was full of new theories, and many able scientists were exploring them. It is not surprising that two men would make the same discovery almost simultaneously and quite independently. Precisely this appears to have happened in Newton's two principal controversies, those with Leibniz and Hooke. Leibniz invented the differential calculus, and Hooke advanced a theory of universal gravitation, both somewhat later than Newton's, but announced to the world first, because Newton had neglected to publish his work.

The contemporary reception of the *Principia* was more cordial in England and Scotland than on the Continent, but everywhere slow. As Newton had foreseen, an understanding of it required great mathematical ability. The extraordinary nature of the performance was acknowledged, however, even by those who had only a dim conception of Newton's contribution. Gradually, scientists everywhere accepted the Newtonian system, and by the eighteenth century it was firmly established in the world of science.

After the *Principia,* Newton appears to have lost any active interest in scientific research, though he lived for forty years after its publication. During this period he was the recipient of many honors: he was appointed Master of the Mint, knighted by Queen Anne, elected President of the Royal Society from 1703 until his death in 1727, saw publication of the second and third editions of the *Principia,* and, in general, was held in the highest respect and esteem.

Scientific discoveries in the twentieth century have modified or shown inadequacies in Newton's work, especially in relation to astronomy. Einstein's theory of relativity, for example, maintains that space and time are not absolute, as Newton had taught. Nevertheless, as various authorities in science and technology have pointed out, the structure of a skyscraper, the safety of a railroad bridge, the motion of a motor car, the flight of an airplane, the navigation of a ship across the ocean, the measure of time, and other evidences of our contemporary civilization still depend fundamentally on Newton's laws. As Sir James Jean wrote, the Newtonian principles are "inadequate only with reference to the ultra-refinements of modern science. When the astronomer wishes to prepare his 'Nautical Almanac,' or to discuss the motions of the planets, he uses the Newtonian scheme almost exclusively. The engineer who is building a bridge or a ship or a locomotive does precisely what he would have done had Newton's scheme never been proved inadequate. The same is true of the electrical engineer, whether he is mending a telephone or designing a power station. The science of everyday life is still wholly Newtonian; and it is impossible to estimate how much this science owes to

Newton's clear and penetrating mind having set it on the right road, and this so firmly and convincingly that none who understood his methods could doubt their rightness."

The tribute paid Newton by Einstein should remove any question of rival philosophies: "Nature to him was an open book, whose letters he could read without effort. In one person he combined the experimenter, the theorist, the mechanic and, not least, the artist in expression."

Newton's own estimate of his career, made near the end of a long life, was characteristic of his modesty: "I do not know what I may appear to the world, but to myself I seem to have been only like a boy on the seashore, and diverting myself in now and then finding a smoother pebble or a prettier shell than ordinary, while the great ocean of truth lay all undiscovered before me."

Thomas S. Kuhn (essay date 1978)

SOURCE: "Newton's Optical Papers," in *Newton's Papers & Letters on Natural Philosophy and Related Documents,* Second Edition, Harvard University Press, 1978, pp. 3-24, 27-45.

[*In the following essay, Kuhn examines Newton's optical experiments and publications, commenting on the significance of his findings as well as the limitations of his experimental procedures and his presentation of results.*]

The original publication of the optical papers of Isaac Newton marked the beginning of an era in the development of the physical sciences. These papers, reprinted below, were the first public pronouncements by the man who has been to all subsequent generations the archetype of preëminent scientific creativity, and their appearance in early volumes of the *Philosophical Transactions of the Royal Society of London* constituted the first major contribution to science made through a technical journal, the medium that rapidly became the standard mode of communication among scientists.

Until the last third of the seventeenth century most original contributions to the sciences appeared in books, usually in large books: Copernicus' *De Revolutionibus* (1543), Kepler's *Astronomia Nova* (1609), Galileo's *Dialogo* (1632), Descartes's *Dioptrique* (1637), or Boyle's *Experiments and Considerations Touching Colours* (1664). In such books the author's original contributions were usually lost within a systematic exposition of a larger subject matter, so that constructive interchange of scientific experiment and hypothesis was hampered by premature systematization or, as

in the case of Boyle, by the mere bulk of the experimental compilation.[1] Each scientist tended to erect his own system upon his own experiments; those experiments that could not support an entire system were frequently lost to the embryonic profession.

The first important breaches of this traditional mode of presentation occurred in the decade of 1660. The chartering of the Royal Society in 1662 and of the Académie Royale des Sciences in 1666, the first publication of the *Journal des Sçavans* and of the *Philosophical Transactions* in 1665, gave institutional expression and sanction to the new conception of science as a coöperative enterprise with utilitarian goals. The immediate objective of the individual scientist became the experimental contribution to an ultimate reconstruction of a system of nature rather than the construction of the system itself, and the journal article—an immediate report on technical experimentation or a preliminary interpretation of experiments—began to replace the book as the unit communiqué of the scientist.

Newton was the first to advance through this new medium an experimentally based proposal for the radical reform of a scientific theory, and his proposal was the first to arouse international discussion and debate within the columns of a scientific journal. Through the discussion, in which all the participants modified their positions, a consensus of scientific opinion was obtained. Within this novel pattern of public announcement, discussion, and ultimate achievement of professional consensus science has advanced ever since.

Newton's optical papers have a further importance to the student of the development of scientific thought. These brief and occasionally hasty communications to the editor of the *Philosophical Transactions* yield an insight into the personality and mental processes of their author that is obscured by the more usual approach to Newton through his **Principia** (1687) and **Opticks** (1704). In these later monumental creations, from which has emerged our picture of Newton the Olympian father of modern science, the creative role of the author is deliberately hidden by the superfluity of documentation and illustration and by the formality and impersonality of the organization.[2] It is primarily in his early papers, as in his letters, his notes, and his largely unpublished manuscripts, that Newton the creative scientist is to be discovered. And the shock of the discovery may be considerable, for this Newton does not always fit our ideal image.

Newton's first paper, the **"New Theory about Light and Colors,"** is almost autobiographical in its development, and so it facilitates, more than any of Newton's other published scientific works, the search for the sources of the novel optical concepts that he drew from the "celebrated phaenomena of colours."[3] The prismatic colors to which Newton referred had been well known for centuries: white objects viewed through a triangular glass prism are seen with rainbow fringes at their edges; a beam of sunlight refracted by a prism produces all the colors of the rainbow at the screen upon which it falls. Seneca recorded the observations, which must be as old as shattered glass; Witelo, in the 13th century, employed a water-filled globe to generate rainbow colors; by the 17th century prisms, because of their striking colors, were an important item in the negotiations of the Jesuits in China.[4] Before Newton began his experiments at least four natural philosophers, Descartes, Marcus Marci, Boyle, and Grimaldi, had discussed in optical treatises the colored iris produced by a prism, and Hooke had based much of his theory of light upon the colors generated by a single refraction of sunlight at an air-water interface.[5] The "phaenomena" were indeed "celebrated." Newton, when he repeated them for his own edification, can have had no reason to anticipate a result that he would later describe as "the oddest, if not the most considerable detection, which hath hitherto been made in the operations of nature."[6]

But Newton's version of the experiment differed in an essential respect from that employed by most of his predecessors; furthermore, as we shall see, Newton's optical education and experience were not those of the earlier experimentalists who had employed the prism. Previously, when white light had been passed through a prism, the image of the refracted beam had normally been observed on a screen placed close to the prism.[7] With such an arrangement of the apparatus, the diverging beams of "pure" colors had little opportunity to separate before striking the screen, and the shape of the image cast on the screen was therefore identical with that produced by the unrefracted beam. But in passing through the prism the beam had acquired a red-orange fringe along one edge and a blue-violet fringe along the other.

The colored fringes on an otherwise unaltered beam of white light seemed to bear out an ancient theory of the nature of the rainbow's colors, a theory which held that a succession of modifications of sunlight by the droplets of a rain cloud produced the colors of the bow. In the century and a half preceding Newton's work such a theory was repeatedly and variously reformulated and applied to the colored iris generated by the prism. In all theories the colors were viewed as a minor perturbation restricted primarily to the edges of the homogeneous beam of sunlight. They were due to a mixture of light and shade at the region of contact between the refracted beam and the dark (Descartes); or they were a consequence of the varying "condensation" and "rarefaction" produced at the edges of the beam by the variation in the angle at which rays from the finite sun were incident upon the prism (Grimaldi); or they were generated by some other mechanical modification (Hooke and the later Cartesians).

There was no consensus as to the nature of the particular modification that tinted white light, but there was agreement that there was only one such modification and that its positive or negative application (for example, condensation *or* rarefaction) to white light could produce only two *primary* colors. These two colors, usually red and blue, represented the extreme applications of the modification, so that their mixture in appropriate proportions would generate any other color by producing the corresponding intermediate degree of modification. More recent experiments have, of course, shown that two primary colors will not suffice, but color-mixing experiments performed with crude equipment are extremely deceptive, a fact that may also account for Newton's initially surprising assertion that spectral yellow and blue combine to produce a green.[8]

All of the modification theories of prismatic colors fail ultimately because of their inability to account quantitatively for the elongation of the spectrum observed when, as in Newton's version of the experiment, the screen is placed a long distance from the prism. But even with the equipment so arranged, it is not immediately apparent that the elongation of the spectrum is incompatible with the modification theories. For since the sun has a finite breadth, rays from different portions of its disk are incident upon the prism at different angles, and even in the absence of dispersion this difference in angle of incidence will normally produce an elongation of the refracted beam qualitatively similar to that observed by Newton. Those of Newton's predecessors who, like Grimaldi, had noted the elongation of the spectrum had employed this device to account for it, and this was the explanation given by the Jesuit Ignatius Pardies, in his first letter objecting to Newton's theory.[9] To destroy the modification theory it was necessary to notice a *quantitative* discrepancy between the elongation predicted by that theory and the elongation actually observed, and this required an experimenter with a knowledge of the mathematical law governing refraction (not announced until 1637) and with considerable experience in applying the law to optical problems. In 1666 these qualifications were uniquely Newton's. Descartes, who shared Newton's mathematical interests, had performed the experiment with the screen close to the prism, and had noted no elongation. Boyle and Hooke, whose apparatus probably generated an elongated spectrum, shared with Grimaldi a prevalent indifference to the power of mathematics in physics.

It was, then, the large elongation produced in the Newtonian version of the experiment plus the recognition that the size of the spectrum was not that predicted by Snel's new law of refraction that transformed a routine repetition of a common experiment into the "oddest . . . detection, which hath hitherto been made in the operations of nature." The oddity was not the spectrum itself, but the discrepancy between the observed length of the spectrum and the length predicted by existing theory. And this discrepancy, emphasized and investigated with far more mathematical detail in Newton's earlier oral presentations of the experiment, forced Newton to search for a new theory.[10]

Newton found the clue to the new theory in the geometrical idealization that he reported as the shape of the spectrum rather than in the elongation that had caused the search. His beam of sunlight was a cylinder ¼ inch in diameter, formed by allowing sunlight to enter his chamber through a circular hole in his "window shuts." After refraction the beam fell upon the opposite wall of the room, distant 22 feet from the prism, where, according to Newton, it produced an elongated spectrum, 13¼ inches in length, bounded by parallel sides 2 inches apart, and capped by semicircular ends. The shape suggested its own interpretation. For the semicircular "caps" could be viewed as the residua of the shape imposed by the circular hole in the shutter, and the spectrum could then be analyzed into an infinite series of differently colored overlapping circles whose centers lay on a straight line perpendicular to the axis of the prism. In his early lectures, as in the later *Opticks,* Newton frequently sketched the spectrum in this way, one end formed by a pure blue circular image of the original hole, the other formed by a pure red image, and the intermediate region composed of a number of variously colored circles displaced along the axis of the spectrum. By this device the existing laws of refraction, which for Newton's arrangement of the prism predicted a circular image, could be preserved. But the law now had to be applied, not to the incident beam as a whole, but to every one of the colored beams contained in the original beam. Sunlight was a mixture of all the colors of the rainbow; each of the incident colored beams obeyed the laws of optics; but each was refracted through a different angle in its passage through the prism. This was the essence of Newton's new theory, derived primarily from the reported shape of the spectrum.[11]

The reported shape leaves a puzzle illustrative of the nature of Newton's genius. Though the spectrum described cries aloud for the interpretation that Newton provided, it is very doubtful that he saw any such shape. Only the central 2-inch strip of his 2 -inch-wide spectrum was illuminated uniformly by light from the disk of the sun. The balance of the width of the spectrum consisted of a penumbral region in which the various colors gradually shaded off into the black. Since the eye can distinguish red much farther into the penumbral region than it can distinguish blue, Newton probably saw a figure appreciably narrower and more pointed at the blue end than at the red.[12] This is the shape that Newton's bitterest and least intelligent critic, Franciscus Linus, described, and this is the only one of Linus's criticisms to which Newton never responded.[13] Newton combined a precise and detailed description of

his experimental apparatus with an imaginative idealization of his experimental results.

Newton's leap from the full and unintelligible complexity of the observable phenomenon to the geometrical idealization underlying it is symptomatic of the intellectual extrapolations that mark his contributions to science. And he was apparently aware of and concerned with the extrapolation, though he made it explicit in none of his communications to the Royal Society. In the optical lectures, which he delivered in Cambridge prior to the composition of his first published paper, Newton included a description of two experiments that he had designed to investigate the shape of the spectrum produced without a penumbral region. In one of these he used a lens, placed one focal length in front of the screen, to refocus the colored circular sun images of which the spectrum was composed. In a second he utilized the planet Venus, effectively a point source, instead of the sun in order to generate his spectrum. He had justified his extrapolation to himself, but, except for implicit references to the problem in his correspondence with Moray and in the *Opticks,* he did not tell his readers how to follow him.

Newton's announcement in 1672 of the discoveries made six to eight years earlier induced a great controversy within the columns of the *Philosophical Transactions.*[14] The prismatic colors that he discussed were well known, at least qualitatively, and there was widespread conviction among 17th-century opticians that they could be adequately treated by existing optical theories. No wonder there was resentment of a newcomer who claimed that precise analysis of a well-known effect necessitated discarding established theories. Opponents could easily find grounds for rejecting the proposals. They could, for example, deny the existence of the experimental effect. The sun is an unreliable and a moving source of light; the prism generates a number of emergent beams, only one of which satisfies Newton's description; quantitative results vary with the sort of glass employed in the prism. Alternatively, they could accept Newton's experimental results, but deny the necessity or even the validity of his interpretation.

The nature and psychological sources of the controversy were typical, but the reaction was less severe than that usually produced by so radical a proposal. Newton's predecessors had all employed some form of modification theory, but, having reached no consensus on the nature of the modification, they lacked a stable base for a counterattack. And Newton's experimental documentation of his theory is a classic in its simplicity and its incisiveness. The modification theorists might finally have explained the elongation of the spectrum, but how could they have evaded the implications of the *experimentum crucis?* An innovator in the sciences has never stood on surer ground.

As a result the controversy that followed the original announcement is of particular interest today for the light it sheds upon Newton's character.[15] In particular the controversial literature illuminates the genesis of Newton's relation with the Royal Society's curator, Robert Hooke, with whom he later engaged in a priority battle over the inverse-square law of gravitation.[16] Hooke's claim to the authorship of the inverse-square law almost caused Newton to omit the Third Book of the *Principia,* and it was apparently Hooke's continuing opposition to Newton's optical theories that caused Newton to delay publication of the *Opticks* until long after his own active research in the field had ended. Hooke died in 1703, and the *Opticks,* much of which had existed in manuscript for years, first appeared in the following year.

Newton's first paper was read to the assembled members of the Royal Society on February 8, 1671/2. On February 15 Hooke delivered, at the request of the Society's members, a report on and evaluation of Newton's work. Coming from a senior member of the profession, a man already established as the most original optical experimentalist of the day, the report was most judicious, though it contained important errors and displayed Hooke's typically Baconian indifference to quantitative mathematical formulations. Hooke praised and confirmed Newton's experimental results, and he conceded that the theory which Newton had derived from them was entirely adequate to explain the effects. His only major criticism (excepting the remarks on telescopes, for which see below) is that Newton's interpretation was not a *necessary* consequence of the experiments. Hooke felt that Newton had performed too few experiments to justify the theory, that another theory (his own) could equally well explain Newton's experiments, and that other experiments (particularly his own on the colors of thin films) could not be explained by Newton's theory.

Hooke's Baconian criticism is an index of the prevalent methodological emphasis upon experimentation, an emphasis that made the "experimental history" a typical scientific product of the day. Most members of the Royal Society would have concurred. But Hooke was quite wrong in thinking that his own version of the modification theory could explain Newton's results; at least he never gave a satisfactory explanation of the production of colors.[17] On the other hand, Hooke was right that Newton's theory could not explain some of the experiments upon which Hooke had based his own theory. In particular, Newton's theory, as of 1672, would not explain either diffraction or the colors of thin sheets of mica, both of which Hooke had described in his *Micrographia* (1665). Nor would Newton's theory explain the colors produced by confining air between sheets of glass, an observation that Hooke reported to the Society on April 4 and June 19 in his further examination of Newton's doctrine.[18] The latter

communication, incidentally, included a clear description of the phenomenon usually known as "Newton's rings," and it seems probable that Newton borrowed it from Hooke and employed it to develop a revised theory adequate to handle Hooke's experiments. For Newton, in his long letters of December and January 1675/6, did succeed in solving Hooke's problems to his own satisfaction and to that of most of his contemporaries. But to do so he had to modify his original theory by the introduction of an explicit Æthereal medium which could transmit impulses as pressure waves, and this was an immense step toward Hooke's theory. Hooke, of course, did not accept even this later modification. He always felt that Newton's use of *both* corpuscles and Æther impulses violated Occam's injunction against the needless multiplication of conceptual entities.[19]

In the final analysis Hooke was wrong. As Newton clearly showed in his belated reply, Hooke's pulse theory of light was incapable of accounting for linear propagation; nor could Hooke's modification theory of color account either for the *experimentum crucis* or for any of the novel color-mixing experiments that Newton apparently designed specifically to meet Hooke's objections. This much of the reply was effective, and Newton might better have begun and ended with the elaboration of these arguments, for Hooke had challenged neither Newton's experiments nor the adequacy of his theory to resolve the experiments. But this is not what Newton did. In his lengthy and gratuitously caustic response, whose incongruity with Hooke's critique has escaped attention since the two have not before been printed together,[20] Newton attacked Hooke on three apparently incompatible grounds: Hooke had attributed to Newton a corpuscular theory that Newton had not developed; Hooke's impulse theory was not basically incompatible with the corpuscular theory (which Newton had disowned); and Hooke's impulse theory was incapable of accounting for the phenomena. Newton might have employed any of these three lines of attack alone—though only the third seems both relevant and accurate—but it is difficult to see how anything but consuming passion could have led him to employ them concurrently.

Newton was a man of passions. It is difficult to read many of his responses to criticism without concurring in a recent judgment of Newton's personality by the late Lord Keynes. After a lengthy examination of Newton's manuscripts Keynes wrote:

> For in vulgar modern terms Newton was profoundly neurotic of a not unfamiliar type, but—I should say from the records—a most extreme example. His deepest instincts were occult, esoteric, semantic—with profound shrinking from the world, a paralyzing fear of exposing his thoughts, his beliefs, his discoveries in all nakedness to the inspection and criticism of the world. "Of the most fearful, cautious and suspicious temper that I ever knew," said Whis-

ton, his successor in the Lucasian Chair. The too well-known conflicts and ignoble quarrels with Hooke, Flamsteed, Leibnitz are only too clear an evidence of this. Like all his type he was wholly aloof from women. He parted with and published nothing except under the extreme pressure of friends.[21]

Newton's fear of exposure and the correlated compulsion to be invariably and entirely immune to criticism show throughout the controversial writings. They are apparent in both the tone and the substance of his reply to Hooke, where they are also combined with the beginning of that tendency to deny the apparent implications of earlier writings (rather than either defending them or admitting to a change of mind) which has so consistently misled subsequent students of his work. Did Hooke really misinterpret the intent of Newton's remarks on the difficulties of constructing refracting telescopes? Is Newton honest in rejecting the corpuscular hypothesis that Hooke ascribes to him? Or, to take a later and far clearer example, is not Newton convicted of an irrationally motivated lie in his reply to Huygens's remarks about the composition of the color white? In his first paper Newton had said, in discussing colors:

> But the most . . . wonderful composition is that of *Whiteness* . . . 'Tis ever compounded, and to its composition are requisite all the aforesaid primary Colours, mixed in a due proportion . . . Hence therefore it comes to pass, that *Whiteness* is the usual colour of *Light*; for Light is a confused aggregate of Rays indued with all sorts of Colours . . . if any one predominate, the Light must incline to that colour.

Yet when Huygens suggested that the combination of yellow and blue might generate white, Newton admitted the possibility but claimed that he had never meant anything else. The apparent contradiction he reconciled by saying that Huygens's white would be different from his own by virtue of its composition. Newton's position was correct in the reply, but surely he had changed his mind in reaching it.

The same defensiveness had more serious consequences in Newton's writings on telescopes. Here Newton's influence appears to have been predominantly negative. His own work on telescopes was of little practical importance, and his remarks on design were frequently wrong. Although he built the first working reflector, he was never able to perfect the model sufficiently to enable it to compete with existing refractors, and so his position was not very different from that of the contemporary and independent designers, James Gregory and Guillaume Cassegrain.[22] The reflecting telescope remained a curious toy on the shelves of the Royal Society until, in 1722, James Hadley succeeded

in grinding a parabolic mirror. But as soon as the reflector could compete with the refractor, Newton's design was discarded in favor of the designs by Gregory and Cassegrain that Newton had so vehemently criticized for essentially irrelevant reasons.[23]

Far more important in the development of telescopes were Newton's mistakes in the evaluation of optical aberrations. Having been led to the reflecting telescope by the discovery of the chromatic aberration caused by the variation of refractive index with color, Newton always insisted that chromatic rather than spherical aberration imposed the major limitation upon the power of refracting telescopes. Newton's theoretical comparisons of the two were both mathematically and optically correct, but, as Huygens pointed out in his comment, Newton's interpretation of the calculations was incompatible with the observed performance of spherical lenses. Newton explained the discrepancy correctly as due to the small effect on the eye of the widely dispersed red and blue rays, but he failed to notice that in practice this made chromatic aberrations little or no more important than spherical. So Newton continued to insist upon the practical superiority of reflectors.[24] Subsequent history bore out the judgment expressed by Huygens in his last letter of the optics controversy that until it became possible to grind nonspherical mirrors the future of practical telescopic observations would be associated with refractors of long focal length and consequently low aberrations.[25]

But among the aspects of Newton's thought that are illuminated by recognition of his dread of controversy, the most important is his attitude toward "hypotheses." Like most of his contemporaries, Newton was guided throughout his scientific career by the conception of the universe as a gigantic machine whose components are microscopic corpuscles moving and interacting in accordance with immutable laws.[26] Most of Newton's work in physics can be viewed appropriately as a part of a consistent campaign to discover the mathematical laws governing the aggregation and motion of the corpuscles of a mechanical "clock-work universe," and many of his specifically optical, chemical, or dynamical writings are difficult to comprehend without reference to the corpuscular metaphysic which played an active role in their creation.[27] Yet from most of his published writings Newton tried, never completely successfully, to eliminate just these hypothetical and therefore controversial elements.

In the notebook in which he recorded the progress of his early optical research Newton continually referred to light rays as composed of "globules," traveling with finite velocities and interacting in accordance with the known laws of impact.[28] But in his first published paper Newton omitted all explicit reference to particular corpuscular mechanisms which determine the behavior of light. He substituted geometrical entities ("rays") for physical entities (corpuscles moving in definite paths); and he contented himself with a retrospective argument showing that the experimentally determined properties of the rays must make light a substance rather than a quality. In his controversy with Hooke, who seems to have known more about the hypotheses than Newton had allowed to enter in his published discussion, he reneged on even this argument, and thus continued a retreat that had begun in his first paper and developed further in his letters to Pardies.

That this is a genuine retreat from the defense of metaphysical hypotheses which Newton believed and employed creatively is amply, if incompletely, attested by the inconsistencies in his discussions and use of hypotheses throughout the optical papers printed below. In the first paper light was a substance. In the letters to Pardies light was either a substance or a quality, but the definition of light rays in terms of "indefinitely small . . . independent" parts made light again corporeal. In the same letter Newton proclaimed that his observations and *theories* could be reconciled with the pressure *hypotheses* of either Hooke or Descartes, but in the letter to Hooke he forcefully demonstrated the inadequacy of all pressure hypotheses to explain the phenomena of light and colors. Newton denied his adherence to the corpuscular hypothesis, and he stated that his credence was restricted to laws that could be proved by experiment, but he returned to the pattern of his notebook by employing implicitly the hypothetical scatterings of corpuscles at points of focus to prove the disadvantages of the Gregorian telescope.[29] In 1672 he denied the utility of hypotheses when presenting a theory which he believed could be made independent of them, but in dealing with the colors of thin films in the important letters of 1675/6 he employed explicit hypotheses, presumably because the new subject matter of these letters could not otherwise be elaborated. Significantly, it was just these later letters, from which large segments of Books II and III of the **Opticks** were transcribed, that Newton refused to publish until after Hooke's death. Of all his optical writings, these letters best reflect the procedures of Newton at work.[30]

Much of modern science inherits from Newton the admirable pragmatic aim, never completely realized, of eliminating from the final reports of scientific discovery all reference to the more speculative hypotheses that played a role in the process of discovery. The desirability of this Newtonian mode of presenting theories is well illustrated by the subsequent history of Newton's own hypotheses. The next great step in optics, the development of an adequate wave theory, was retarded by the grip of Newton's corpuscular hypotheses upon the scientific mind. But Newton's remarks about the role of hypotheses in science were dictated by personal idiosyncrasy as often as by philosophical acumen; repeatedly he renounces hypotheses simply to avoid debate. And so he has seemed to support the further assertion that scientific research can and should be confined to the experimental pursuit of mathematical regularity—that hypotheses which transcend the immediate evidence of experiment have no place in science. Careful examination of Newton's less systematic published writings provides no evidence that Newton imposed upon himself so drastic a restriction upon scientific imagination.

The achievements initiated by Newton's own imagination are unsurpassed, and it is primarily the magnitude of his achievements that directs attention to the man. If the resulting study displays error and idiosyncrasy in Newton's complex and difficult personality, it cannot lessen his unparalleled accomplishments. It can alter only our image of the requisites for preëminent scientific achievement. But this alteration is a goal worth pursuing: a true image of the successful scientist is a first condition for understanding science.

Notes

[1] For example, Experiments IV and V in Part III of Boyle's *Colours* are almost identical with the first and last of the three experiments that Newton employed in his first published presentation of the new theory of light and color. In Experiment IV Boyle generates a spectrum and in V he uses a lens to invert the order of the colors. But in Boyle's Baconian compilation these are but two among hundreds of experimental items. There is no evidence that they had the slightest effect on Boyle's contemporaries or successors. See *The Works of the Honourable Robert Boyle,* ed. Thomas Birch (London, 1744), vol. 2, p. 42.

[2] The "Queries" that Newton appended to the *Opticks* are the one portion of his later published scientific works in which he allowed the fecundity of his creative imagination to appear. These speculative postscripts to his last technical work do provide a more intimate view of their author. Of course even the *Opticks* proper is a less impersonal work than the *Principia,* but, despite the frequent informality of literary style, the contents and organization are those of a treatise.

[3] The phrase is Newton's. See the beginning of the first optical paper, below.

[4] Joseph Priestley, *The History and Present State of Discoveries Relating to Vision, Light, and Colours* (London, 1722), pp. 7, 21, 169.

[5] Descartes's discussion of the prism occurs in Discours VIII of *Les météores* (1637). For Boyle's experiments see note 1, above. Marci's experiments are described in his *Thaumantias liber de arcu coelesti . . .* (Prague, 1648) and are discussed by L. Rosenfeld in *Isis 17,* 325-330 (1932). Grimaldi's *Physico-mathesis*

de lumine . . . (Bologna, 1665) includes many discussions of prism experiments. Hooke's theory and experiments appear in his *Micrographia* (1665), reprinted by R. T. Gunther as vol. XIII of *Early Science in Oxford* (Oxford, 1938), pp. 47-67. There is no reason to suppose that Newton in 1672 knew of the work of either Marci or Grimaldi, but it is an index of the state of optical experimentation in the 17th century that Grimaldi, Marci, and Boyle had, among them, performed all three of the experiments that Newton employed in his first optical paper.

[6] Letter from Newton to Oldenburg, the secretary of the Royal Society, dated Cambridge, 18 January, 1671/2. Thomas Birch, *The History of the Royal Society of London* (London, 1757), vol. 3, p. 5.

[7] See particularly Descartes's diagrams and discussion, cited in note 5, above.

[8] In modern terminology, blue and yellow *light* are complementary; that is, they mix to give white. The green produced when blue and yellow *pigments* are mixed is the result of subtractive color mixing, a process different from the mixing of spectral colors. But in fact a long-wavelength spectral blue and a short-wave-length spectral red can be combined to produce a light-green tint. By combining in different proportions a blue near the green region of the spectrum with a red near the yellow it is actually possible to produce a number of shades of blue, green, red, yellow, and intermediate colors. The two-color theories were not so foreign to experience as has been imagined.

[9] Ignace Gaston Pardies, S.J. (1636-1673), was born at Pau in Southern France. At the time of his dispute with Newton he was the professor of rhetoric at the Collège Louis-le-grand in Paris.

[10] Newton first presented his new theory in a series of lectures delivered at Cambridge during 1669. The lectures were not printed until 1728, after his death, when they appeared in an English translation from the Latin manuscript. A Latin edition, containing lectures for the years 1669, 1670, and 1671, appeared in 1729. Certain of the features emphasized in the present discussion emerge with even greater clarity from the lectures than from the first optical paper. The two may profitably be read together.

[11] The preceding reconstruction of Newton's research follows the essentially autobiographical narrative provided by Newton himself in the first of the optical papers. It may require important modification as a result of a recent study of Newton's manuscripts by A. R. Hall, "Sir Isaac Newton's Note-Book, 1661-1665," *Cambridge Historical Journal 9*, 239-250 (1948). On this topic, see the references to further studies in the Supplement.

Hall believes that Newton discovered the variation of refractive index with color by observing a two-colored thread through a prism, and he suggests that the experiment in which a beam of sunlight is passed through a prism was not performed until a later date. For a variety of reasons I find this portion of Hall's reconstruction implausible. The textual and historical evidence available, though not decisive, persuades me that Newton had already passed a beam of sunlight through a prism when he performed the experiments that Hall has discovered in the "Note-Book."

If so, Newton's account of the development of the new theory remains autobiographical in the sense that the prism experiment did provide the initial impetus as well as an important clue for the new theory, as discussed above. But, as Hall does conclusively show, the implication of Newton's account is wrong in that Newton did not proceed so directly or so immediately from the first prism experiment to the final version of the theory as the first paper would imply. When he made the entries in his college notebook, Newton had not arrived at the final form of the new theory. So far as I can tell from the fragments reproduced by Hall, Newton then believed that different colors were refracted through different angles, but he still held that the individual colors were generated within the prism by modifications of the initially homogeneous white light. This intermediate stage of Newton's thought provides a fascinating field for further study.

[12] It is impossible to be precise about the actual shape of the spectrum viewed by Newton. The sensitivity of the human eye to short-wavelength blue varies from one individual to another, and the relative intensity of the blue in the spectrum is also a function of atmospheric conditions.

[13] Linus's description occurs midway through the first paragraph of his second letter of criticism. Although the position of Linus's prism was different from that of Newton's, the "sharp cone or pyramis" described by Linus is due to the same penumbral effects that must have caused the sides of Newton's spectrum to deviate from parallelism.

Franciscus Linus (Francis Hall or Line), S.J., was born in London in 1595. During his controversy with Newton he was a teacher of mathematics and Hebrew at the English college of Liège. He spent much of his later life attempting to reconcile the results of 17th-century experimentation with Aristotelian physics. Linus was the author of the "funiculus" hypothesis by which he claimed to explain the results of Boyle's barometer experiments without recourse to the vacuum or atmospheric pressure, and experiments designed to refute him led to the discovery of Boyle's Law. Linus died in 1675, midway through the dispute with Newton, but his cause was taken up by two of his students, Gascoigne and Lucas.

Anthony Lucas (1633-1693), another British Jesuit, appears to have been a meticulous experimenter. His inability to obtain the large dispersion reported by Newton must have been due to his use of a different sort of glass. Lucas's experimental "proofs" of the inadequacy of Newton's theory are a fascinating index of the difficulties in designing unequivocal dispersion experiments. In most experiments the effects are so small that they can be fitted to any theory, so incisive documentation of a particular theory requires careful selection from the multiplicity of available phenomena. At first glance Newton's failure to answer any of Lucas's experimental criticism seems strange, particularly since Newton did respond at such length to the one remark by Lucas that did not reflect at all upon the validity of Newton's conclusions. But see the discussion, below, of Newton's attitude toward controversy.

[14] A. R. Hall, "Sir Isaac Newton's Note-Book," has pointed out that Newton probably intended to write "1665" rather than "1666" for the date of the prism experiment which opens his first paper. He also argues that Newton's work with the prism may have begun as early as 1664.

[15] There are, however, many points of technical interest in the debate. These are discussed more fully in L. Rosenfeld, "La théorie des couleurs de Newton et ses adversaires," *Isis 9,* 44-65 (1927). A stimulating elementary account of some of the same material has been provided by M. Roberts and E. R. Thomas, *Newton and the Origin of Colours* (London: G. Bell & Sons, 1934).

[16] For bibliography and a definitive account of the gravitation controversy, see A. Koyré, "An Unpublished Letter of Robert Hooke to Isaac Newton," *Isis 43,* 312-337 (1952).

[17] The difficulty in adapting a pressure-wave theory of light like Hooke's to the various color phenomena explored by Newton is well illustrated by the experience of Huygens, who brought these theories to their most perfect 17th-century form in his *Traité de la lumière* (1690). Huygens wrote Leibniz that he had "said nothing respecting colours in my *Traité de la lumière,* finding this subject very difficult, and particularly from the great number of different ways in which colours are produced." Sir David Brewster, *Memoirs of the Life, Writings, and Discoveries of Sir Isaac Newton* (Edinburgh, 1855), vol. 1, p. 95 n.

[18] Birch, *History of the Royal Society,* vol. 3, pp. 41 & 54.

[19] *Ibid.,* p. 295.

[20] Oldenburg, the secretary of the Royal Society and editor of the *Philosophical Transactions,* is known to have hated Hooke. This may well explain his failure to print Hooke's critique with Newton's reply. The omission must have seemed a gratuitous insult to Hooke, particularly in view of the tone and substance of Newton's comments.

[21] J. M. Keynes, "Newton the Man," in the Royal Society's *Newton Tercentenary Celebrations* (Cambridge, 1947), p. 28. These documents can be put to other uses, however. Examine, for an opinion of the Hooke-Newton exchange directly opposed to the one given above, the analysis provided by Brewster, *Memoirs,* vol. 1, pp. 86-92. But Brewster cannot avoid providing repeated illustrations of Newton's efforts to escape from controversy (for example, pp. 95-99).

[22] James Gregory (1638-1675), a Scottish mathematician, described a reflecting telescope in his *Optica Promota* (1633), and Newton had studied Gregory's design when he started his own. Sieur Guillaume Cassegrain was a modeler and founder of statues in the employ of Louis XIV. His design was surely independent of Newton's and may have been independent of Gregory's. Both Gregory and Cassegrain tried to build reflectors but were unable to polish adequate mirrors.

[23] On Newton's contributions to the development of telescopes see Louis Bell, *The Telescope* (New York, 1922).

[24] The study of Newton's most important and damaging error in his writings on the telescope is complicated rather than clarified by the papers reprinted below. In his *Opticks* (Book I, Part II, Experiment 8) Newton "proved" that it was impossible to build an achromatic lens, that is, a lens compounded from two or more materials so differing in dispersive power that they will refract a ray of white light without separating the colors in it. Newton claimed to have found by experiment that when a beam of light was passed through a succession of prisms of glass and water a spectrum was invariably generated unless the emergent and incident beams were parallel. He concluded that any combination of materials which could correct dispersion would also nullify refraction, so that no achromatic lens was possible. The error may well have hindered the development of achromatic lenses.

To get the experimental result Newton must either have shut his eyes, used sugar to raise the refractive index of his water, or employed a variety of glass with unusually low dispersive power. All three of these explanations have been advanced by subsequent historians, most of whom have also expressed surprise at Newton's readiness to draw so general a conclusion from such slight experimental evidence. For a full account of the development of achromatic lenses see N. V. E. Nordenmark and J. Nordstrom, "Om uppfinningen av den akromatiska och aplanatiska linsen," *Lychnos 4,* 1-

52 (1938); *5,* 313-384 (1939). The second portion of the article includes some appendices and an abstract in English.

It is apparent from the optical papers below that Newton's theorem concerning the relation of dispersion and refractive index was the best possible refutation for three of his early critics. It nullified the objections of Hooke and Huygens, who had urged that more attention be given to the perfection of refracting telescopes, and it made it certain that Lucas had erred in reporting the small dispersion of his prism. For this reason most historians have argued that the theorem developed in the *Opticks* was in Newton's mind, at least implicitly, from the beginning of his optical researches and that this is why he failed to consider more seriously the merits of his opponents' positions. But—and this is where the new complication enters—I can find no way of interpreting the text of Newton's response to Hooke without supposing that Newton is there proposing an achromatic lens made by compounding a water lens with two convexo-concave lenses of glass.

On this topic, see the works by D. T. Whiteside and Zev Bechler, referred to in the Supplement.

[25] The letters to and from Huygens reprinted below are only a part of a larger correspondence, most of which was not published until recently. L. T. More discusses the complete correspondence more fully in his biography, *Isaac Newton* (New York, 1934). The letters themselves will be found in volume VII of the *Oeuvres complètes de Christiaan Huygens* (The Hague, 1888-1944).

[26] M. Boas, "The Establishment of the Mechanical Philosophy," *Osiris 10,* 412-541 (1952).

[27] For the role of the metaphysic in Newton's chemistry see the next section of this book. For its role in Newton's dynamics, see A. Koyré, "The Significance of the Newtonian Synthesis," *Archives internationales d'histoires des sciences 29,* 291-311 (1950), and T. S. Kuhn, *The Copernican Revolution* (Cambridge, Mass., 1957), chap. 7.

[28] For example: "Though 2 rays be equally swift yet if one ray be lesse y^n ye other that ray shall have so much lesse effect on y^e sensorium as it has lesse motion y^n y^e others &c.

"Whence supposing y^t there are loose particles in y^e pores of a body bearing proportion to y^e greater rays, as 9:12 & y^e less globulus is in proportion to y^e greater as 2:9, y^e greater globulus by impinging on such a particle will loose $6/_7$ parts of its motion y^e less glob. will loose $2/_7$ parts of its motion & y^e remaining motion of y^e glob. will have almost such a proportion to one another as their quantity have viz. $5/_7 : 1/_7 :: 9/_7 : 1 4/_5$ w^{ch}

is almost 2 y^e lesse glob. & such a body may produce blews and purples. But if y^e particles on wch y^e globuli reflect are equal to y^e lesse globulus it shall loose its motion & y^e greater glob. shall loose $2/_{11}$ parts of its motion and such a body may be red or yellow." Hall, "Sir Isaac Newton's Note-Book," p. 248.

[29] Brewster, *Memoirs,* p. 50 n.

[30] These critically important letters, reprinted below, deserve far more study and discussion than they here receive. But such discussion necessarily assumes the proportion of a critical analysis of the second and third books of the *Opticks* for which these letters provided a draft, and the space for such an analysis is not here available. For a discussion of the central ideas in these later letters, as they emerge in the *Opticks,* see I. B. Cohen's introduction to the recent reissue of the *Opticks* (New York, 1952).

Space limitations also prevent my discussing Newton's posthumously published design of "An instrument for observing the Moon's Distance from the fixed Stars at Sea." When written this paper contained important novelties of design, but before it was published these new features had been independently incorporated in practical navigational instruments by several designers. On these instruments see Lloyd Brown, *The Story of Maps* (Boston, 1949), pp. 191 ff.

I. Bernard Cohen   (essay date 1980)

SOURCE: "The Newtonian Revolution in Science," in *The Newtonian Revolution,* Cambridge University Press, 1980, pp. 1-37, 290-99.

[*In the following essay, Cohen offers an overview of the developments in the scientific community during Newton's time. Cohen then identifies the qualities of Newton's* Principia *that made the work so revolutionary.*]

1.1 *Some basic features of the Scientific Revolution*

A study of the Newtonian revolution in science rests on the fundamental assumption that revolutions actually occur in science. A correlative assumption must be that the achievements of Isaac Newton were of such a kind or magnitude as to constitute a revolution that may be set apart from other scientific revolutions of the sixteenth and seventeenth centuries. At once we are apt to be plunged deep into controversy. Although few expressions are more commonly used in writing about science than "scientific revolution", there is a continuing debate as to the propriety of applying the concept and term "revolution" to scientific change.[1] There is, furthermore, a wide difference of opinion as to what may constitute a revolution. And although almost all historians would agree that a genuine alteration of an exceptionally radical nature (*the* Scientific Revolution[2]) occurred in the sciences at some time between the late fifteenth (or early sixteenth) century and the end of the seventeenth century, the question of exactly when this revolution occurred arouses as much scholarly disagreement as the cognate question of precisely what it was. Some scholars would place its origins in 1543, the year of publication of both Vesalius's great work on the fabric of the human body and Copernicus's treatise on the revolutions of the celestial spheres (Copernicus, 1543; Vesalius, 1543). Others would have the revolution be inaugurated by Galileo, possibly in concert with Kepler, while yet others would see Descartes as the true prime revolutionary. Contrariwise, a whole school of historians declare that many of the most significant features of the so-called Galilean revolution had emerged during the late Middle Ages.[3]

A historical analysis of the Newtonian revolution in science does not, however, require participation in the current philosophical and sociological debates on these issues. For the fact of the matter is that the concept of revolution in science—in the sense in which we would understand this term nowadays—arose during Newton's day and was applied (see §2.2) first to a part of mathematics in which he made his greatest contribution, the calculus, and then to his work in celestial mechanics. Accordingly, the historian's task may legitimately be restricted to determining what features of Newton's science seemed so extraordinary in the age of Newton as to earn the designation of revolution. There is no necessity to inquire here into the various meanings of the term "revolution" and to adjudge on the basis of each such meaning the correctness of referring to a Newtonian revolution in the sciences.

The new science that took form during the seventeenth century may be distinguished by both external and internal criteria from the science and the philosophical study or contemplation of nature of the antecedent periods. Such an external criterion is the emergence in the seventeenth century of a scientific "community": individuals linked together by more or less common aims and methods, and dedicated to the finding of new knowledge about the external world of nature and of man that would be consonant with—and, accordingly, testable by—experience in the form of direct experiment and controlled observation. The existence of such a scientific community was characterized by the organization of scientific men into permanent formal societies, chiefly along national lines, with some degree of patronage or support by the state.[4] The primary goal of such societies was the improvement of "natural knowledge".[5] One way by which they sought to gain that end was through communication; thus the seventeenth century witnessed the establishment of scientific and learned journals, often the organs of scientific societies, including the *Philosophical Transactions* of the Royal Society of London, the *Journal des Sçavans,* and the *Acta eruditorum* of Leipzig.[6] Another visible sign of the existence of a "new science" was the founding of research institutions, such as the Royal Greenwich Observatory, which celebrated its three-hundredth birthday in 1975. Newton's scientific career exhibits aspects of these several manifestations of the new science and the scientific community. He depended on the Astronomer Royal, John Flamsteed, for observational evidence that Jupiter might perturb the orbital motion of Saturn near conjunction and later needed lunar positions from Flamsteed at the Greenwich Observatory in order to test and to advance his lunar theory, especially in the 1690s. His first scientific publication was his famous article on light and colors, which appeared in the pages of the *Philosophical Transactions*; his **Principia** was officially published by the Royal Society, of which he became president in 1703 (an office he kept until his death in 1727). While the Royal Society was thus of great importance in Newton's scientific life, it cannot be said that his activities in relation to that organization or its journal were in any way revolutionary.

The signs of the revolution can also be seen in internal aspects of science: aims, methods, results. Bacon and Descartes agreed on one aim of the new science, that the fruits of scientific investigation would be the improvement of man's condition here on earth:[7] agriculture, medicine, navigation and transportation, communication, warfare, manufacturing, mining.[8] Many scientists of the seventeenth century held to an older point of view, that the pursuit of scientific understanding of nature was practical insofar as it might advance man's comprehension of the divine wisdom and power. Science was traditionally practical in serving the cause of religion; but a revolutionary feature of the new science was the additional pragmatic goal of bettering everyday life here and now through applied science. The conviction that had been developing in the sixteenth and seventeenth centuries, that a true goal of the search for scientific truth must be to affect the material conditions of life, was then strong and widely shared, and constituted a novel and even a characteristic feature of the new science.

Newton often declared his conviction as to the older of these practicalities, as when he wrote to Bentley about his satisfaction in having advanced the cause of true religion by his scientific discoveries. Five years after the publication of his **Principia,** he wrote to Bentley that while composing the **Principia** ('my Treatise about our system'), 'I had an eye upon such Principles as might work with considering Men, for the Belief of a Deity' (Newton, 1958, p. 280; 1959-1977, vol. 3, p. 233). About two decades later, in 1713, he declared in the concluding general scholium to the **Principia** that the system of the world 'could not have arisen without the design and dominion of an intelligent and powerful being'. Newton was probably committed to some degree to the new practicality; at least he served as advisor to the official group concerned with the problem of finding methods of determining the longitude at sea. Yet it was not Newton himself, but other scientists such as Halley, who attempted to link the Newtonian lunar theory with the needs of navigators, and the only major practical innovation that he produced was an instrument for science (the reflecting telescope) rather than inventions for man's more mundane needs.[9]

Another feature of the revolution was the attention to method. The attempts to codify method—by such diverse figures as Descartes, Bacon, Huygens, Hooke, Boyle, and Newton—signify that discoveries were to be made by applying a new tool of inquiry (a *novum organum,* as Bacon put it) that would direct the mind unerringly to the uncovering of nature's secrets. The new method was largely experimental, and has been said to have been based on induction; it also was quantitative and not merely observational and so could lead to mathematical laws and principles. I believe that the seventeenth-century evaluation of the importance of method was directly related to the role of experience (experiment and observation) in the new science. For it seems to have been a tacit postulate that any reasonably skilled man or woman should be able to reproduce an experiment or observation, provided that the report of that experiment or observation was given honestly and in sufficient detail. A consequence of this postulate was that anyone who understood the true methods of scientific enquiry and had acquired the necessary skill to make experiments and observations could have made the discovery in the first instance-provided, of course, that he had been gifted with the wit and insight to ask the right questions.[10]

This experimental or experiential feature of the new science shows itself also in the habit that arose of beginning an enquiry by repeating or reproducing an experiment or observation that had come to one's attention through a rumor or an oral or written report. When Galileo heard of a Dutch optical invention that enabled an observer to see distant objects as clearly as if they were close at hand, he at once set himself to reconstructing such an instrument.[11] Newton relates how he had bought a prism 'to try therewith the celebrated Phaenomena of Colours'.[12] From that day to this, woe betide any investigator whose experiments and observations could not be reproduced, or which were reported falsely; this attitude was based upon a fundamental conviction that nature's occurrences are constant and reproducible, thus subject to universal laws. This twin requirement of performability and reproducibility imposed a code of honesty and integrity upon the scientific community that is itself yet another distinguishing feature of the new science.

The empirical aspect of the new science was just as significant with respect to the result achieved as with respect to the aims and methods. The law of falling bodies, put forth by Galileo, describes how real bodies actually fall on this earth—due consideration being given to the difference between the ideal case of a vacuum and the realities of an air-filled world, with winds, air resistance, and the effects of spin. Some of the laws of uniform and accelerated motion announced by Galileo can be found in the writings of certain late medieval philosopher-scientists, but the latter (with a single known exception of no real importance[13]) never even asked whether these laws might possibly correspond to any real or observable motions in the external world. In the new science, laws which do not apply to the world of observation and experiment could have no real significance, save as mathematical exercises. This point of view is clearly enunciated by Galileo in the introduction of the subject of 'naturally accelerated motion', in his *Two New Sciences* (1638). Galileo states the aim of his research to have been 'to seek out and clarify the definition that best agrees with that [accelerated motion] which nature employs' (Galileo, 1974, p. 153; 1890-1909, vol. 8, p. 197). From his point of view, there is nothing 'wrong with inventing at pleasure some kind of motion and theorizing about its consequent properties, in the way that some men have derived spiral and conchoidal lines from certain motions, though nature makes no use of these [paths]'. But this is different from studying motion in nature, for in exploring phenomena of the real external world, a definition is to be sought that accords with nature as revealed by experience:

> But since nature does employ a certain kind of acceleration for descending heavy things, we decided to look into their properties so that we might be sure that the definition of accelerated motion which we are about to adduce agrees with the essence of naturally accelerated motion. And at length, after continual agitation of mind, we are confident that this has been found, chiefly for the very powerful reason that the essentials successively demonstrated by us correspond to, and are seen to be in agreement with, that which physical experiments [*naturalia experimenta*] show forth to the senses [ibid.].

Galileo's procedure is likened by him to having 'been led by the hand to the investigation of naturally accelerated motion by consideration of the custom and procedure of nature herself'.

Like Galileo, Newton the physicist saw the primary importance of concepts and rules or laws that relate to (or arise directly from) experience. But Newton the mathematician could not help but be interested in other possibilities. Recognizing that certain relations are of physical significance (as that 'the periodic times are as the 3/2 power of the radii', or Kepler's third law), his mind leaped at once to the more universal condition (as that 'the periodic time is as any power R^n of the radius R').[14] Though Newton was willing to explore the mathematical consequences of attractions of spheres according to any rational function of the distance, he concentrated on the powers of index 1 and -2 since they are the ones that occur in nature: the power of index 1 of the distance from the center applies to a particle within a solid sphere and the power of index -2 to a particle outside either a hollow or solid sphere.[15] It was his aim, in the **Principia,** to show that the abstract or 'mathematical principles' of the first two books could be applied to the phenomenologically revealed world, an assignment which he undertook in the third book. To do so, after Galileo, Kepler, Descartes, and Huygens, was not in itself revolutionary, although the scope of the **Principia** and the degree of confirmed application could well be so designated and thus be integral to the Newtonian revolution in science.

An excessive insistence on an out-and-out empirical foundation of seventeenth-century science has often led scholars to exaggerations.[16] The scientists of that age did not demand that each and every statement be put to the test of experiment or observation, or even have such a capability, a condition that would effectively have blocked the production of scientific knowledge as we know it. But there was an insistence that the goal of science was to understand the real external world, and that this required the possibility of predicting testable results and retrodicting the data of actual experience: the accumulated results of experiment and controlled observation. This continual growth of factual knowledge garnered from the researches and observations made all over the world, paralleled by an equal and continual advance of understanding, was another major aspect of the new science, and has been a distinguishing characteristic of the whole scientific enterprise ever since. Newton certainly made great additions to the stock of knowledge. In the variety and fundamental quality of these contributions we may see the distinguishing mark of his great creative genius, but this is something distinct from having created a revolution.

1.2 *A Newtonian revolution in science: the varieties of Newtonian science*

In the sciences, Newton is known for his contributions to pure and applied mathematics, his work in the general area of optics, his experiments and speculations relating to theory of matter and chemistry (including alchemy), and his systematization of rational mechanics (dynamics) and his celestial dynamics (including the Newtonian "system of the world"). Even a modest portion of these achievements would have sufficed to earn him an unquestioned place among the scientific immortals. In his own day (as we shall see below in Ch. 2), the word "revolution" began to be applied to the sciences in the sense of a radical change; one of

the first areas in which such a revolution was seen to have occurred was in the discovery or invention of the calculus: a revolution in mathematics.[1] There is also evidence aplenty that in the age of Newton and afterwards, his **Principia** was conceived to have ushered in a revolution in the physical sciences. And it is precisely this revolution whose characteristic features I aim to elucidate.

Newton's studies of chemistry and theory of matter yielded certain useful results[2] and numerous speculations. The latter were chiefly revealed in the queries at the end of the **Opticks,** especially the later ones,[3] and in such a tract as the **De natura acidorum.**[4] The significance of these writings and their influence have been aggrandized (from Newton's day to ours) by the extraordinary place in science held by their author. At best, they are incomplete and programmatic and—in a sense—they chart out a possible revolution, but a revolution never achieved by Newton nor ever realized along the lines that he set down. Newton's program and suggestions had a notable influence on the science of the eighteenth century, particularly the development of theories of heat and electricity (with their subtle elastic fluids) (cf. Cohen, 1956, Ch. 7, 8). Newton had a number of brilliant insights into the structure of matter and the process of chemical reaction, but the true revolution in chemistry did not come into being until the work of Lavoisier, which was not directly Newtonian (see Guerlac, 1975).

The main thrust of Newton's views on matter was the hope of deriving 'the rest of the phenomena of nature by the same kind of reasoning from mechanical principles' that had served in deducing 'the motions of the planets, the comets, the moon, and the sea'. He was convinced that all such phenomena, as he said in the preface (1686) to the first edition of the **Principia,** 'may depend upon certain forces by which the particles of bodies . . . are either mutually impelled [attracted] toward one another so as to cohere in regular figures' or 'are repelled and recede from one another'.[5] In this way, as he put it on another occasion, the analogy of nature would be complete: 'Whatever reasoning holds for greater motions, should hold for lesser ones as well. The former depend upon the greater attractive forces of larger bodies, and I suspect that the latter depend upon the lesser forces, as yet unobserved, of insensible particles'. In short, Newton would have nature be thus 'exceedingly simple and conformable to herself'.[6] This particular program was a conspicuous failure. Yet it was novel and can even be said to have had revolutionary features, so that it may at best represent a failed (or at least a never-achieved) revolution. But since we are concerned here with a positive Newtonian revolution, Newton's hope to develop a micro-mechanics analogous to his successful macro-mechanics is not our main concern. We cannot wholly neglect this topic, however, since it has been alleged that Newton's mode of attack on the physics of gross bodies and his supreme success in celestial mechanics was the product of his investigations of short-range forces, despite the fact that Newton himself said (and said repeatedly) that it was his success in the area of gravitation that led him to believe that the forces of particles could be developed in the same style. R. S. Westfall (1972, 1975) would not even stop there, but would have the 'forces of attraction between particles of matter', and also 'gravitational attraction which was probably the last one [of such forces] to appear', be 'primarily the offspring of alchemical active principles'. This particular thesis is intriguing in that it would give a unity to Newton's intellectual endeavor; but I do not believe it can be established by direct evidence (see Whiteside, 1977). In any event, Newton's unpublished papers on alchemy and his published (and unpublished) papers on chemistry and theory of matter hardly merit the appellation of "revolution", in the sense of the radical influence on the advance of science that was exerted by the *Principia.*

In optics, the science of light and colors, Newton's contributions were outstanding. But his published work on 'The Reflections, Refractions, Inflexions [i.e., diffraction] & Colours of Light', as the *Opticks* was subtitled, was not revolutionary in the sense that the *Principia* was. Perhaps this was a result of the fact that the papers and book on optics published by Newton in his lifetime do not boldly display the mathematical properties of forces acting (as he thought) in the production of dispersion and other optical phenomena, although a hint of a mathematical model in the Newtonian style is given in passing in the *Opticks* (see §3.11) and a model is developed more fully in sect. 14 of bk. one of the *Principia.* Newton's first published paper was on optics, specifically on his prismatic experiments relating to dispersion and the composition of sunlight and the nature of color. These results were expanded in his *Opticks* (1704; Latin ed. 1706; second English ed. 1717/1718), which also contains his experiments and conclusions on other aspects of optics, including a large variety of what are known today as diffraction and interference phenomena (some of which Newton called the "inflexion" of light). By quantitative experiment and measurement he explored the cause of the rainbow, the formation of "Newton's rings" in sunlight and in monochromatic light, the colors and other phenomena produced by thin and thick "plates", and a host of other optical effects.[7] He explained how bodies exhibit colors in relation to the type of illumination and their selective powers of absorption and transmission or reflection of different colors. The *Opticks,* even apart from the queries, is a brilliant display of the experimenter's art, where (as Andrade, 1947, p. 12, put it so well) we may see Newton's 'pleasure in shaping'. Some of his measurements were so precise that a century later they yielded to Thomas Young the correct values, to within less than 1 percent, of the wavelengths of light of different colors.[8] Often cited as a model of how to perform quantitative experiments and how to analyze a difficult problem by experiment,[9] Newton's studies of light and color and his *Opticks* nevertheless did not create a revolution and were not ever considered as revolutionary in the age of Newton or afterwards. In this sense, the *Opticks* was not epochal.

From the point of view of the Newtonian revolution in science, however, there is one very significant aspect of the *Opticks*: the fact that in it Newton developed the most complete public statement he ever made of his philosophy of science or of his conception of the experimental scientific method. This methodological declaration has, in fact, been a source of some confusion ever since, because it has been read as if it applies to all of Newton's work, including the *Principia.*[10] The final paragraph of qu. 28 of the *Opticks* begins by discussing the rejection of any 'dense Fluid' supposed to fill all space, and then castigates 'Later Philosophers' (i.e., Cartesians and Leibnizians) for 'feigning Hypotheses for explaining all things mechanically, and referring other Causes to Metaphysicks'. Newton asserts, however, that 'the main Business of natural Philosophy is to argue from Phaenomena without feigning Hypotheses, and to deduce Causes from Effects, till we come to the very first Cause, which certainly is not mechanical'.[11] Not only is the main assignment 'to unfold the Mechanism of the World', but it is to 'resolve' such questions as: 'What is there in places almost empty of Matter . . . ?' 'Whence is it that Nature doth nothing in vain; and whence arises all that Order and Beauty which we see in the World?' What 'hinders the fix'd Stars from falling upon one another?' 'Was the Eye contrived without Skill in Opticks, and the Ear without Knowledge of Sounds?' or 'How do the Motions of the Body follow from the Will, and whence is the Instinct in Animals?'

In qu. 31, Newton states his general principles of analysis and synthesis, or resolution and composition, and the method of induction:

> As in Mathematicks, so in Natural Philosophy, the Investigation of difficult Things by the Method of Analysis, ought ever to precede the Method of Composition. This Analysis consists in making Experiments and Observations, and in drawing general Conclusions from them by Induction, and admitting of no Objections against the Conclusions, but such as are taken from Experiments, or other certain Truths. For Hypotheses are not to be regarded in experimental Philosophy. And although the arguing from Experiments and Observations by Induction be no Demonstration of general Conclusions; yet it is the best way of arguing which the Nature of Things admits of, and may be looked upon as so much the stronger, by how much the Induction is more general.

Analysis thus enables us to

> proceed from Compounds to Ingredients, and from Motions to the Forces producing them; and in general, from Effects to their Causes, and from particular Causes to more general ones, till the Argument end in the most general.

This method of analysis is then compared to synthesis or composition:

> And the Synthesis consists in assuming the Causes discover'd, and establish'd as Principles, and by them explaining the Phaenomena proceeding from them, and proving the Explanations.[12]

The lengthy paragraph embodying the foregoing three extracts is one of the most often quoted statements made by Newton, rivaled only by the concluding General Scholium of the **Principia,** with its noted expression: *Hypotheses non fingo.*

Newton would have us believe that he had himself followed this "scenario":[13] first, to reveal by "analysis" some simple results that were generalized by induction, thus proceeding from effects to causes and from particular causes to general causes; then, on the basis of these causes considered as principles, to explain by "synthesis" the phenomena of observation and experiment that may be derived or deduced from them, 'proving the Explanations'. Of the latter, Newton says that he has given an 'Instance . . . in the End of the first Book' where the 'Discoveries being proved [by experiment] may be assumed in the Method of Composition for explaining the Phaenomena arising from them'. An example, occurring at the end of bk. one, pt. 2, is props. 8-11, with which pt. 2 concludes. Prop. 8 reads: 'By the discovered Properties of Light to explain the Colours made by Prisms'. Props. 9-10 also begin: 'By the discovered Properties of Light to explain . . .', followed (prop. 9) by 'the Rain-bow' and (prop. 10) by 'the permanent Colours of Natural Bodies'. Then, the concluding prop. 11 reads: 'By mixing coloured Lights to compound a beam of Light of the same Colour and Nature with a beam of the Sun's direct Light'.

The formal appearance of the **Opticks** might have suggested that it was a book of synthesis, rather than analysis, since it begins (bk. one, pt. 1) with a set of eight 'definitions' followed by eight 'axioms'. But the elucidation of the propositions that follow does not make explicit reference to these axioms, and many of the individual propositions are established by a method plainly labeled 'The Proof by Experiments'. Newton himself states clearly at the end of the final qu. 31 that in bks. one and two he has 'proceeded by . . . Analysis' and that in bk. three (apart from the queries) he has 'only begun the Analysis'. The structure of the **Opticks** is superficially similar to that of the **Principia,** for the **Principia** also starts out with a set of 'definitions' (again eight in number), followed by three 'axioms' (three 'axiomata sive leges motus'), upon which the propositions of the first two books are to be constructed (as in the model of Euclid's geometry). But then, in bk. three of the **Principia,** on the system of the world, an ancillary set of so-called 'phenomena' mediate the application of the mathematical results of bks. one and two to the motions and properties of the physical universe.[14] Unlike the **Opticks,** the **Principia** does make use of the axioms and definitions.[15] The confusing aspect of Newton's stated method of analysis and synthesis (or composition) in qu. 31 of the **Opticks** is that it is introduced by the sentence 'As in Mathematicks, so in Natural Philosophy . . .', which was present when this query first appeared (as qu. 23) in the Latin *Optice* in 1706, 'Quemadmodum in Mathematica, ita etiam in Physica . . .'. A careful study, however, shows that Newton's usage in experimental natural philosophy is just the reverse of the way "analysis" and "synthesis" (or "resolution" and "composition") have been traditionally used in relation to mathematics, and hence in the **Principia**—an aspect of Newton's philosophy of science that was fully understood by Dugald Stewart a century and a half ago but that has not been grasped by present-day commentators on Newton's scientific method, who would even see in the **Opticks** the same style that is to be found in the **Principia**[16] (this point is discussed further in §3.11).

Newton's "method", as extracted from his *dicta* rather than his *opera,* has been summarized as follows: 'The main features of Newton's method, it seems, are: The rejection of hypotheses, the stress upon induction, the working sequence (induction precedes deduction), and the inclusion of metaphysical arguments in physics' (Turbayne, 1962, p. 45). Thus Colin Turbayne would have 'the deductive procedure' be a defining feature of Newton's 'mathematical way' and Descartes's *'more geometrico'* respectively: 'Descartes's "long chains of reasoning" were deductively linked. Newton's demonstrations were reduced to "the form of propositions in the mathematical way"'. He would criticize those analysts who have not recognized that the defining property of 'the Cartesian "geometrical method" or the Newtonian "mathematical way"'—paradoxical as it may seem—need be neither geometrical nor mathematical. Its defining property is demonstration, not the nature of the terms used in it'.[17] It may be observed that the phrase used here, 'the Newtonian "mathematical way"', or 'Newton's "mathematical way"', so often quoted in philosophical or methodological accounts of Newton's science, comes from the English translation of Newton's *System of the World*[18] but is not to be found in any of the manuscript versions of that tract, including the one that is still preserved among Newton's papers (see Dundon, 1969; Cohen, 1969a, 1969c).

The Newtonian revolution in the sciences, however, did not consist of his use of deductive reasoning, nor of a merely external form of argument that was presented as a series of demonstrations from first principles or axioms. Newton's outstanding achievement was to show how to introduce mathematical analysis into the study of nature in a rather new and particularly fruitful way, so as to disclose **Mathematical Principles of Natural Philosophy,** as the **Principia** was titled in full: **Philosophiae naturalis principia mathematica.** Not only did Newton exhibit a powerful means of applying mathematics to nature, he made use of a new mathematics which he himself had been forging and which may be hidden from a superficial observer by the external mask of what appears to be an example of geometry in the traditional Greek style (see n. 10 to §1.3).

In the **Principia** the science of motion is developed in a way that I have characterized as the Newtonian style. In Ch. 3 it shall be seen that this style consists of an interplay between the simplification and idealization of situations occurring in nature and their analogues in the mathematical domain. In this manner Newton was able to produce a mathematical system and mathematical principles that could then be applied to natural philosophy, that is, to the system of the world and its rules and data as determined by experience. This style permitted Newton to treat problems in the exact sciences as if they were exercises in pure mathematics and to link experiment and observation to mathematics in a notably fruitful manner. The Newtonian style also made it possible to put to one side, and to treat as an independent question, the problem of the cause of universal gravity and the manner of its action and transmission.

The Newtonian revolution in the sciences was wrought by and revealed in the **Principia.** For more than two centuries, this book set the standard against which all other science was measured; it became the goal toward which scientists in such diverse fields as paleontology, statistics, and biochemistry would strive in order to bring their own fields to a desired high estate.[19] Accordingly, I have striven in the following pages to explore and to make precise the qualities of Newton's **Principia** that made it so revolutionary. Chief among them, as I see it, is the Newtonian style, a clearly thought out procedure for combining mathematical methods with the results of experiment and observation in a way that has been more or less followed by exact scientists ever since. This study concentrates mainly on the **Principia,** because of the supreme and unique importance of that treatise in the Scientific Revolution and in the intellectual history of man. In the **Principia** the role of induction is minimal and there is hardly a trace of that analysis which Newton said should always precede synthesis.[20] Nor is there any real evidence whatever that Newton first discovered

the major propositions of the **Principia** in any way significantly different from the way in which they are published with their demonstrations.[21] Newton's studies of optical phenomena, chemistry, theory of matter, physiological and sensational psychology, and other areas of experimental philosophy did not successfully exhibit the Newtonian style. Of course, whatever Newton said about method, or induction, or analysis and synthesis, or the proper role of hypotheses, took on an added significance because of the commanding scientific position of the author. This position was attained as a result of the revolution in science that, in the age of Newton (and afterwards), was conceived to be centered in his mathematical principles of natural philosophy and his system of the world (see Ch. 2). The general philosophical issues of induction, and of analysis and synthesis, gained their importance after Newton had displayed the system of the world governed by universal gravity, but they played no significant role in the way the Newtonian style is used in the elaboration of that system or in the disclosure of that universal force.

1.3 *Mathematics in the new science (1): a world of numbers*

After modern science had emerged from the crucible of the Scientific Revolution, a characteristic expression of one aspect of it was given by Stephen Hales, often called the founder of plant physiology.[1] An Anglican clergyman and an ardent Newtonian, Hales wrote (1727) that 'we are assured that the all-wise Creator has observed the most exact proportions, of *number, weight and measure,* in the make of all things'; accordingly, 'the most likely way . . . to get any insight into the nature of those parts of the creation, which come within our observation, must in all reason be to number, weigh and measure' (Hales, 1969, p. xxxi). The two major subjects to which Hales applied this rule were plant and animal physiology: specifically the measurement of root and sap pressures in different plants under a variety of conditions and the measurement of blood pressure in animals. Hales called his method of enquiry 'statical', from the Latin version of the Greek word for weighing—in the sense that appears to have been introduced into the scientific thought of the West by Nicolaus Cusanus in the fifteenth century, in a treatise entitled *De staticis experimentis* (cf. Guerlac, 1972, p. 37; and Viets, 1922).

In the seventeenth century two famous examples of this 'statical' method were Santorio's experiments on the changes in weight that occurred in the daily life cycle of man (Grmek, 1975), and Van Helmont's experiment on the willow tree. The latter consisted of filling an earthen pot with a weighed quantity of soil that had been dried in a furnace, in which Helmont planted a previously weighed 'Trunk or Stem' of a willow tree. He 'covered the lip or mouth of the Vessel with an Iron plate covered with Tin', so that the dust flying about should not be 'co-mingled with the Earth' inside the vessel. He watered the earth regularly with rain water or distilled water for five years, and found that the original tree, weighing 5 pounds, now had grown to a weight of '169 pounds, and about three ounces' (ignoring 'the weight of the leaves that fell off in the four Automnes'). Since the earth in the vessel, when dried out at the end of the experiment, was only 'about two ounces' less in weight than the original weight of 200 pounds, Helmont concluded that 164 pounds of 'Wood, Barks, and Roots' must have been formed out of water alone.[2] Helmont did not know (or suspect) that the air itself might supply some of the weight of the tree, a discovery made by Hales, who repeated Helmont's experiment with the added precision of weighing the water added to the plant and measuring the plant's rate of 'perspiration' (Hales, 1969, Ch. 1, expts. 1-5). The original of this experiment had been proposed by Cusanus, but there is no certainty as to whether or not he may have actually performed it.

I have purposely chosen these first examples from the life (or biological) sciences, since it is usually supposed that in the Scientific Revolution, numerical reasoning was the prerogative of the physical sciences. One of the most famous uses of numerical reasoning in the Scientific Revolution occurs in Harvey's analysis of the movement of the blood. A central argument in Harvey's demonstration of the circulation is quantitative, based on an estimate of the capacity of the human heart; the left ventricle, he finds, when full may contain 'either 2, or 3, or 1½ oz.; I have found in a dead man above 4 oz.' Knowing that 'the heart in one half hour makes above a thousand pulses, yea in some, and at some times, two, three or four thousand', simple calculation shows how much blood the heart discharges into the arteries in a half hour—at least 83 pounds 4 ounces, 'which is a greater quantity than is found in the whole body'. He made similar calculations for a dog and a sheep. These numbers showed 'that more blood is continually transmitted through the heart, than either the food which we receive can furnish, or is possible in the veins'.[3] Here we may see how numerical calculation provided an argument in support of theory: an excellent example of how numbers entered theoretical discussions in the new science.

Despite the force of the foregoing examples, however, it remains true that the major use of numerical reasoning in the science of the seventeenth century occurred in the exact physical sciences: optics, statics, kinematics and dynamics, astronomy, and parts of chemistry.[4] Numerical relations of a special kind tended to become all the more prominent in seventeenth-century exact science because at that time the laws of science were not yet written in equations. Thus we today would write Galileo's laws of uniformly accelerated motion as $v = At$, and $S = ½ At^2$, but he expressed the essence

of naturally accelerated motion (free fall, for example, or motion along an inclined plane) in language that sounds much more like number theory than like algebra: 'the spaces run through in equal times by a moveable descending from rest maintain among themselves the same rule [*rationem*] as do the odd numbers following upon unity'.[5] Galileo's rule, that these first differences (or 'the progression of spaces') accord with the odd numbers, led him to another form of his rule, that the 'spaces run through in any times whatever' by a uniformly accelerated body starting from rest 'are to each other in the doubled ratio of the times [or; as the square of the times]' in which such spaces are traversed. This form of his rule, expressed in the language of ratios, comes closer to our own algebraic expression.[6] Thus while speeds increase with time according to the natural numbers, total distances or spaces traversed increase (depending on the chosen measure) according to the odd numbers or the squares[7] of the natural numbers.[8]

In the exact science of the seventeenth century, considerations of shape, or of geometry, are to be found alongside rules of numbers. In a famous statement about the mathematics of nature, Galileo said:

> Philosophy [i.e., natural philosophy, or science] is written in that vast book which stands forever open before our eyes, I mean the universe; but it cannot be read until we have learnt the language and become familiar with the characters in which it is written. It is written in mathematical language, and the letters are triangles, circles and other geometrical figures, without which means it is humanly impossible to comprehend a single word.[9]

This is not the philosophy of Newton, where mathematics suggests at once a set of equations or proportions (which may be verbal), infinite series, and the taking of limits.[10] In fact, the above-quoted statement almost sounds like Kepler, rather than Galileo. It was Kepler who found in numerical geometry a reason why the Copernican system is to be preferred to the Ptolemaic. In one of these systems—the Ptolemaic—there are seven 'planets' or wanderers (sun and moon; Mercury and Venus; and Mars, Jupiter, and Saturn), but in the other there are only six planets (Mercury and Venus; the earth; and Mars, Jupiter, and Saturn). Suppose that each planet is associated with a giant spherical shell in which it moves (or which contains its orbit). Then there would be five spaces between each pair of successive spheres. Kepler knew of Euclid's proof that there are only five regular solids that can be constructed by simple geometrical rules (cube, tetrahedron, dodecahedron, icosahedron, octahedron). By choosing them in the above order, Kepler found that they would just fit into the spaces between the spheres of the planetary orbits, the only error of any consequence occurring in the case of Jupiter. Hence number and geometry showed that there must be six planets, as in the Copernican system, and not seven, as in the Ptolemaic.[11]

Rheticus, Copernicus's first and only disciple, had proposed a purely numerical argument for the Copernican system. In the suncentered universe there are six planets, he said, and 6 is the first 'perfect' number (that is, it is the sum of its divisors, $6 = 1 + 2 + 3$).[12] Kepler, however, rejected the perfect-number argument of Rheticus, preferring to base his advocacy of the Copernican system on the five perfect solids. He said:

> I undertake to prove that God, in creating the universe and regulating the order of the cosmos, had in view the five regular bodies of geometry as known since the days of Pythagoras and Plato, and that He has fixed, according to those dimensions, the number of heavens, their proportions, and the relations of their movements.[13]

It is not without interest, accordingly, that when Kepler heard that Galileo had discovered some new "planets" by using a telescope, he was greatly concerned lest his own argument should fall to the ground (cf. Kepler, 1965, p. 10). How happy he was, he recorded, when the "planets" discovered by Galileo turned out to be secondary and not primary "planets", that is, satellites of planets.

Two reactions to Galileo's discovery of four new "planets" may show us that the use of numbers in the exact sciences in the seventeenth century was very different from what we might otherwise have imagined. Francesco Sizi, in opposition to Galileo, argued that there must be seven and only seven "planets"; hence Galileo's discovery was illusory. His assertion about the number seven was based on its occurrence in a number of physical and physiological situations, among them the number of openings in the head (two ears, two eyes, two nostrils, one mouth).[14] Kepler, who applauded Galileo, proposed that he look next for the satellites of Mars and of Saturn, since the numerical sequence of the satellites (one for the earth and four for Jupiter) seemed to demand two for Mars and eight (or possibly six) for Saturn: 1, 2, 4, 8.[15] This type of numerical reasoning had deleterious effects on astronomy in the case of at least one major scientist: Christiaan Huygens. For when Huygens had discovered a satellite of Saturn, he did not bother to look for any further ones. He was convinced, as he boldly declared in the preface to his *Systema Saturnium* (1659), that there could be no others (Huygens, 1888-1950, vol. 15, pp. 212sq). With his discovery of a new satellite, he said, the system of the universe was complete and symmetrical: one and the same "perfect" number 6 in the primary planets and in the secondary "planets" (or planetary satellites). Since his telescope could resolve the ring of Saturn and solve the mystery of its strange and inconstant shape, it could have revealed more satellites had

Huygens not concluded that God had created the universe in two sets of planetary bodies, six to a set, according to the principle of "perfect" numbers.[16] Such examples all illustrate some varieties of the association of numbers with actual observations. That we today would not accept such arguments is probably less significant than the fact that those who did included some major founders of our modern science, among them Kepler and Huygens, and Cassini.[17]

1.4 *Mathematics in the new science (2): exact laws of nature and the hierarchy of causes*

In addition to the search for special numbers (odd, prime, perfect, the number of regular solids), which did not always lead to useful results, the scientists of the seventeenth century—like scientists ever since—also sought exact relations between the numbers obtained from measurement, experiment, and observation. An example is Kepler's third (or "harmonic") law. In the Copernican system, each of the planets has a speed that seems related to its distance from the sun: the farther from the sun, the slower the speed. Both Galileo and Kepler were convinced that the speeds and distances could not be arbitrary; there must be some exact relation between these two quantities; for God, in creating the universe, must have had a plan, a law. The Keplerian scheme of the five regular solids imbedded in a nest of spheres showed an aspect of mathematical "necessity" in the distribution of the planets in space, but it did not include the data on their speeds. Thus it only partly satisfied Kepler's goal as a Copernican, expressed by him as follows: 'There were three things in particular, namely, the number, distances and motions of the heavenly bodies, as to which I [Kepler] searched zealously for reasons why they were as they were and not otherwise.'[1]

In the *Mysterium cosmographicum* (1596), in which he had used the five regular solids to show why there were five and only five planets spaced as in the Copernican system, Kepler had also tried to find 'the proportions of the motions [of the planets] to the orbits'. The orbital speed of a planet depends upon its average distance from the sun (and hence the circumference of the orbit) and its sidereal period of revolution, both values given by Copernicus in his *De revolutionibus* (1543) with a reasonably high degree of accuracy. Kepler decided that the 'anima motrix' which acts on the planets loses its strength as the distance from the sun gets greater. But rather than assuming that this force diminishes as the square of the distance (which would mean that it spreads out uniformly in all directions, as light does), Kepler thought it more likely that this force would diminish in proportion to the circle or orbit over which it spreads, directly as the increase of the distance rather than as the square of the increase of the distance. The distance from the sun, according to Kepler, 'acts twice to increase the period' of a planet;

for it acts once in slowing down the planet's motion, according to the law by which the force that moves the planet weakens in proportion as the distance increases, and again because the total path along which the planet has to move to complete a revolution increases as the distance from the sun increases. Or, 'conversely half the increase of the period is proportional to the increase of distance'.[2] This relationship comes near to the truth, Kepler observes, but he sought in vain for more than two decades for an accurate relation between the average distance (a) of the planets and their periods (T). Eventually it occurred to him to use higher powers of a and T, and on 15 May 1618 he found that the 'periodic times of any two planets are in the sesquialteral [3/2] ratio of their mean distances', that is, the ratio of the squares of the periods is the same as the ratio of the cubes of their average distances, a relationship which we express as a^3/T^2 = const. and call Kepler's third law.[3] It should be noted that Kepler's discovery apparently resulted from a purely numerical exercise and insofar differed from his discovery of the area law and of the law of elliptic orbits, both of which were presented originally (and may have been discovered) in association with a definite causal concept of solar force and a principle of force and motion.[4]

Galileo's approach to this problem was based on a kinematical law rather than on purely numerical considerations: the principle of naturally accelerated motion, which he had discovered in his studies of freely falling bodies.[5] He thought so well of his solution to the cosmic problem that he introduced it into both his *Dialogo* (1632) or the *Dialogue Concerning the Two Chief World Systems,* and his *Discorsi* (1638), or the *Two New Sciences* (Galileo, 1953, pp. 29sq; 1890-1909, vol. 4, pp. 53sq; also 1974, pp. 232-234; 1890-1909, vol. 8, pp. 283sq). He attributed the basic idea to Plato, but there is nothing even remotely resembling it in any of the Platonic works, nor has this idea been found in any known Neoplatonic composition or commentary, ancient, medieval, or modern.[6] Galileo said that there was a point out in space from which God had let fall all of the planets. When each planet arrived at its proper orbit, it would have attained its proper orbital speed and would have needed only to be turned in its path to accord with the known values of planetary distances and speeds. Galileo did not specify where that point is located, and (as an analysis by Newton revealed) the point would in fact have to be infinitely far away.[7] Galileo, furthermore, did not understand that such a descent toward the sun would require a constantly changing acceleration, which in dynamics would correspond to a constantly changing solar-planetary force that varies inversely as the square of the distance. In this example we may see that Galileo could have had no conception of a solar gravitating force. His discussion does not contain the slightest hint of a relation between force and acceleration that might be

said to have contained a germ of Newton's second law of motion.[8]

Galileo was primarily successful in applying mathematics to such areas as statics and kinematics, in both of which there is no need to take account of physical causes, such as quantifiable forces. As he himself says, in his *Two New Sciences:*

> The present does not seem to me to be an opportune time to enter into the investigation of the cause of the acceleration of natural motion, concerning which various philosophers have produced various opinions. . . . For the present, it suffices . . . that we . . . investigate and demonstrate some attributes of a motion so accelerated (whatever be the cause of its acceleration) that the momenta of its speed go increasing . . . in that simple ratio with which the continuation of time increases . . . [Galileo, 1974, pp. 158sq; 1890-1909, vol. 8, p. 202].

In part, but only in part, his procedure resembles that of the late medieval kinematicists. Like them, he defines uniform motion and then proceeds to uniformly accelerated motion. Almost at once, he reveals the mean-speed law: In uniformly accelerated motion during a time t the distance traveled is the same as if there had been uniform motion at the mean value of the changing speeds during that same time (Galileo, 1974, p. 165; 1890-1909, vol. 8, p. 208). Since the motion is uniform, the mean value is one half of the sum of the initial and final speeds. If we may somewhat anachronistically translate Galileo's verbal statements of ratios into their equivalent equations, we may show that he has proved that $s = \bar{v}t$ where $\bar{v} = (v_1 + v_2)/2$. Since $v_2 = v_1 + At$, it would follow at once that $s = v_1 t + \frac{1}{2}At^2$. In the special case of motion starting from rest, $v_1 = 0$ and $s = \frac{1}{2}At^2$.

Thus far, except for the final result (in which the relation $s = [(v_1 + v_2)/2]t$ leads to $s = vt + \frac{1}{2}At^2$), Galileo could be proceeding much like his fourteenth-century predecessors.[9] But there are significant differences of such consequence that we may easily discern in Galileo's *Two New Sciences* the beginnings of our own science of motion, whereas this feature is lacking in the medieval treatises. The major difference is that the writers of the fourteenth century were not concerned with the physics of motion, with nature as revealed by experiment and observation. Thus they constructed a generalized "latitude of forms", a mathematico-logical analysis of any quality that can be quantified, of which motion (in the sense of "local" motion, from one place to another) is but one example, along with such other quantifiable qualities as love, virtue, grace, whiteness, hotness, and so on. Even in the case of motion, they were dealing with Aristotelian "motion", defined in very general terms as the transition from actuality to potentiality. For two centuries, there is no record of any scholar ever applying the principles of uniform and accelerated motion to actual motions as observed on earth or in the heavens. Prior to Galileo, only Domingo de Soto made such an application, and he appears as a *lusus naturae* of no real importance (see §1.1, n. 13).

How different it is with Galileo! He based his very definitions on nature herself. His aim was not to study motion in the abstract, but the observed motions of bodies. The true test of his mathematical laws (as $s = \frac{1}{2}At^2$) was not their logical consistency but their conformity with the results of actual experimental tests. Thus much is said in the public record.[10] But now we know additionally, thanks to the studies of Galileo's manuscripts by Stillman Drake, that Galileo was making experiments not only to relate his discovered laws to the world of nature, but also as part of the discovery process itself.

Galileo's laws of the uniform and uniformly accelerated motion of physical bodies were derived by mathematics from sound definitions, guided to some degree by experiment, but without consideration as to the nature of gravity or the cause of motion. The concept of a physical cause did enter his analysis of projectile motion, however, but only to the limited extent of establishing that the horizontal component of the motion is not accelerated while the vertical component is. Galileo recognized that there is a force of gravity producing a downward acceleration, but that in the horizontal direction the only force that can affect the projectile's motion is the resistance of the air, which is slight (Galileo, 1974, pp. 224-227; 1890-1909, vol. 8, pp. 275-278). But he did not analyze the cause of acceleration to any degree further than being aware that acceleration requires a cause in the form of some kind of downward force. That is, he did not explore the possibility that the gravitational accelerating force may be caused by the pull of the earth on a body, or by something pushing the body toward the earth; nor whether such a cause or force is external or internal to a body; nor whether the range of this force is limited and, if so, to what distance (as far as the moon, for example); nor whether this force is constant all over the earth's surface; nor whether gravity may vary with distance from the earth's center. Galileo eschewed the search for causes, describing most causes assigned to gravity as 'fantasies' which could be 'examined and resolved' with 'little gain'. He said he would be satisfied 'if it shall be found that the events that . . . shall have been demonstrated are verified in the motion of naturally falling and accelerated heavy bodies' (Galileo, 1974, p. 159; 1890-1909, vol. 8, p. 202). In this point of view, as Stillman Drake has wisely remarked, Galileo was going against the main tradition of physics, which had been conceived as 'the study of natural motion (or more correctly, of change) in terms of its causes'. Drake would thus see 'Galileo's mature refusal to enter into debates over physical causes' as epito-

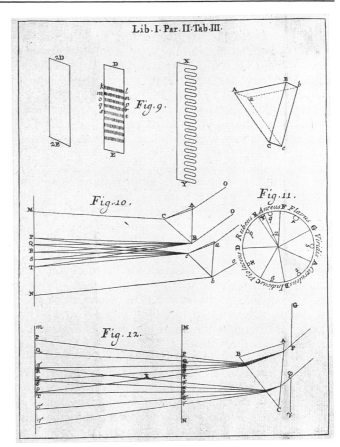

A page from Newton's Opticks *(1704).*

mizing 'his basic challenge to Aristotelian physics' (Galileo, 1974, editorial introduction, pp. xxvi-xxvii). As we shall see below, however, there is a middle ground between a study of physical or even metaphysical causes and the mathematical elucidation of their actions and properties. The recognition of this hierarchy and the exploration of the properties of gravity as a cause of phenomena (without any overt commitment to the cause of gravity) was a great advance over the physics of Galileo and may be considered a main feature of the Newtonian revolution in science (see Ch. 3).

Thus in the exact sciences of the seventeenth century we may observe a hierarchy of mathematical laws. First, there are mathematical laws deduced from certain assumptions and definitions, and which lead to experimentally testable results. If, as in Galileo's case, the assumptions and definitions are consonant with nature, then the results should be verifiable by experience. When Galileo sets forth, as a postulate, that the speed acquired in naturally accelerated motion is the same along all planes of the same heights, whatever their inclination, he declares that the 'absolute truth' of this postulate 'will be later established for us by our seeing that other conclusions, built on this hypothesis, do indeed correspond with and exactly conform to experiment'. This reads like a classic statement of the hypothetico-deductive method; but it is to be observed that it is devoid of any reference to the physical nature of the cause of the acceleration. Such a level of discourse is not essentially different in its results from another seventeenth-century way of finding mathematical laws of nature without going into causes: by the direct analysis of the data of experiment and observation. We have seen this to have been in all probability Kepler's procedure in finding his third (or "harmonic") law of planetary motion. Other examples are Boyle's law of gases and Snel's law of refraction (see Mach, 1926, pp. 32-36; Sabra, 1967; Hoppe, 1926, pp. 33sq).

The second level of the hierarchy is to go beyond the mathematical description to some sort of causes. Boyle's law, for example, is a mathematical statement of proportionality between two variables, each of which is a physical entity related to an observable or measurable quantity. Thus the volume (V) of the confined gas is measured by the mercury level according to some volumetric scale, and the pressure of the confined gas is determined by the difference between two mercury levels (h) plus the height of the mercury column in a barometer (h_1). Boyle's experiments showed that the product of V and $h + h_1$ is a constant. The sum $h + h_1$ is a height (in inches) of a mercury column equivalent to a total pressure exerted on and by the confined gas; what is measured directly in this case is not the pressure but a quantity (height of mercury) which itself is a measure of (and so can stand for) pressure. But nothing is said concerning the cause of pressure in a confined gas, nor of the reason why this pressure should increase as the gas is confined into a smaller volume, a phenomenon known to Boyle before he undertook the experiments and which he called the "spring" of the air. Now the second level of hierarchy is to explore the cause of this "spring". Boyle suggested two physical models that might serve to explain this phenomenon. One is to think of each particle being itself compressible, in the manner of a coiled spring or a piece of wood, so that the air would be 'a heap of little bodies, lying one upon another, as may be resembled to a fleece of wool'. Another is to conceive that the particles are in constant agitation, in which case 'their elastical power is not made to depend upon their shape or structure, but upon the vehement agitation'. Boyle himself, on this occasion, did not choose to decide between these explanations or to propose any other (see Cohen, 1956, p. 103; Boyle, 1772, vol. 1, pp. 11sq). But the example does show that in the exact or quantitative sciences of the seventeenth century, there was a carefully observed distinction between a purely mathematical statement of a law and a causal mechanism for explaining such a law, that is, between such a law as a mathematical

description of phenomena and the mathematical and physical exploration of its cause.

In some cases, the exploration of the cause did not require such a mechanical model, or explanation of cause, as the two mentioned by Boyle. For example, the parabolic path of projectiles is a mathematical statement of a phenomenon, with the qualifications arising from air resistance. But the mathematical conditions of a parabola are themselves suggestive of causes: for—again with the qualifications arising from air resistance—they state that there is uniform motion in the horizontal component and accelerated motion in the downward component. Since gravity acts downward and has no influence in the horizontal component, the very mathematics of the situation may lead an inquirer toward the physical causes of uniform and accelerated motion in the parabolic path of projectiles. Similarly, Newton's exploration of the physical nature and cause of universal gravity was guided by the mathematical properties of this force: that it varies inversely as the square of the distance, is proportional to the masses of the gravitating bodies and not their surfaces, extends to vast distances, is null within a uniform spherical shell, acts on a particle outside of a uniform spherical shell (or a body made up of a series of uniform spherical shells) as if the mass of that shell (or body made up of shells) were concentrated at its geometric center, has a value proportional to the distance from the center within a uniform sphere, and so on.

Such mathematical specifications of causes are different from physical explanations of the origin and mode of action of causes. This leads us to a recognition of the hierarchy of causes which it is important to keep in mind in understanding the specific qualities of the Newtonian revolution in science. For instance, Kepler found that planets move in ellipses with the sun at one focus, and that a line drawn from the sun to a planet sweeps out equal areas in equal times. Both of these laws encompass actual observations within a mathematical framework. The area law enabled Kepler to account for (or to explain) the nonuniformity of the orbital motion of planets, the speed being least at aphelion and greatest at perihelion. This is on the level of a mathematical explanation of the nonuniform motion of planets. Kepler, however, had gone well beyond such a mathematical explanation, since he had assigned a physical cause for this variation by supposing a celestial magnetic force; but he was never successful in linking this particular force mathematically to the elliptical orbits and the area law, or in finding an independent phenomenological or empirical demonstration that the sun does exert this kind of magnetic force on the planets (see Koyré, 1973, pt. 2, sect. 2, ch. 6; Aiton, 1969; Wilson, 1968).

Newton proceeded in a different manner. He did not begin with a discussion of what kind of force might act on planets. Rather he asked what are the mathematical properties of a force—whatever might be its causes or its mode of action, or whatever kind of force it might be—that can produce the law of areas. He showed that, for a body with an initial component of inertial motion, a necessary and sufficient condition for the area law is that the said force be centripetal, directed continually toward the point about which the areas are reckoned. Thus a mathematically descriptive law of motion was shown by mathematics to be equivalent to a set of causal conditions of forces and motions. Parenthetically it may be observed that the situation of a necessary and sufficient condition is rather unusual; most frequently it is the case that a force or other "cause" is but a sufficient condition for a given effect, and in fact only one of a number of such possible sufficient conditions. In the *Principia* the conditions of central forces and equal areas in equal times lead to considerations of elliptical orbits, which were shown by Newton to be a consequence of the central force varying inversely as the square of the distance (see Ch. 5).

Newton's mathematical argument does not, of course, show that in the orbital motion of planets or of planetary satellites these bodies are acted on by physical forces; Newton only shows that within the conceptual framework of forces and the law of inertia, the forces acting on planets and satellites must be directed toward a center and must as well vary inversely as the square of the distance. But in the hierarchy of causal explanation, Newton's result does finally direct us to seek out the possible physical properties and mode of action of such a centrally directed inverse-square force.[11] What is important in the Newtonian mode of analysis is that there is no need to specify at this first stage of analysis what kind of force this is, nor how it acts. Yet Newton's aim was ultimately to go on by a different mode of analysis from the mathematical to the physical properties of causes (or forces) and so he was primarily concerned with 'verae causae', causes-as he said-that are 'both true and sufficient to explain the phenomena'.[12]

This hierarchy of mathematical and physical causes may be seen also in Newton's analysis of Boyle's law, that in a confined gas (or "elastic fluid", as it was then called) the pressure is inversely proportional to the volume. We have seen that Boyle himself suggested two alternative physical explanations of the spring of the air in relation to his law, but declined to declare himself in favor of either of them. In the *Principia* (as we shall see in 3.3) Newton showed that, on the supposition that there is a special kind of force of mutual repulsion between the particles composing such an "elastic fluid", Boyle's law is both a necessary and sufficient condition that this force vary inversely as the distance. Again there is a hierarchy of mathematical and physical analyses of cause. In this second Newtonian example, it is more obvious that the phys-

ical conditions assumed as the cause of the law are themselves open to question. Newton himself concluded his discussion of this topic (*Principia,* bk. two, prop. 23) by observing that it is 'a physical question' as to 'whether elastic fluids [i.e., compressible gases] do really consist of particles so repelling one another'. He himself had been concerned only with the mathematical demonstration, so he said, in order that natural philosophers (or physical scientists) might discuss the question whether gases may be composed of particles endowed with such forces. With regard to the hierarchy of mathematical and physical causes, there is of course no real formal difference between the Newtonian analysis of Kepler's laws and of Boyle's law. In the case of Kepler's laws, however, Newton could take the law of inertia for granted, as an accepted truth of the new science, so that there would have to be some cause for the planets to depart from a rectilinear path and to trace out an elliptical orbit. If this cause is a force, then it must be directed toward a point (the sun, in the case of the planets), since otherwise there can be no area law. But in the case of compressible gases or elastic fluids, the situation is somewhat different. In the first place, in Newton's mind there was no doubt whatsoever that such 'elastic fluids do really consist of particles', since he was a firm believer in the corpuscular philosophy; but it is to be observed that there were many scientists at that time who, like the followers of Descartes, believed in neither atoms nor the void. But even if the particulate structure of gases could be taken for granted, there was the additional property attributed to such particles by Newton, that they be endowed with forces which enable them to repel one another. Many of those who believed in the "mechanical philosophy" and accepted the doctrine of particularity of matter would not necessarily go along with Newton's attribution of forces to such particles, whether atoms, molecules, or other forms of corpuscles. Furthermore, as Newton makes plain in the scholium which follows his proposal of an explanatory physical model for Boyle's law, 'All these things are to be understood of particles whose centrifugal forces terminate in those particles that are next to them, and are diffused not much further.' Accordingly, there is a great and wide gulf between the supposition of a set of mathematical conditions from which Newton derives Boyle's law and the assertion that this is a physical description of the reality of nature. As will be explained in Ch. 3, it is precisely Newton's ability to separate problems into their mathematical and physical aspects that enabled Newton to achieve such spectacular results in the *Principia.* And it is the possibility of working out the mathematical consequences of assumptions that are related to possible physical conditions, without having to discuss the physical reality of these conditions at the earliest stages, that marks the Newtonian style.

The goal of creating an exact physical science based on mathematics was hardly new in the seventeenth century. O. Neugebauer has reminded us that Ptolemy, writing in the second century A.D., had declared this very aim in the original title of his great treatise on astronomy, which we know as the *Almagest,* but which he called 'Mathematical Composition' (or 'Compilation') (Neugebauer, 1946, p. 20; cf. Neugebauer, 1948, pp. 1014-1016). But there was a fundamental difference between the old and the new mathematical physical science, which may be illustrated by an aspect of planetary theory and the theory of the moon.

It is well known that in the *Almagest* Ptolemy was concerned to produce or develop geometric models that would serve for the computation of the latitudes and longitudes of the seven "planetary bodies" (the five planets plus sun and moon) and hence would yield such special information as times of eclipses, stationary points, conjunctions and oppositions. These were quite obviously mathematical models, and were not intended to partake of physical reality. Thus there was no assumption that the true motion of these planetary bodies in the heavens necessarily is along epicycles moving around on deferents and controlled by equal angular motion about an equant. In particular, Ptolemy was perfectly aware that his order of the planets (in terms of increasing distance from the earth: moon, Mercury, Venus, sun, Mars, Jupiter, Saturn) was somewhat arbitrary for the five "planets", since their distances cannot be determined by parallaxes. In fact, Ptolemy admits that some astronomers would place Mercury and Venus beyond the sun, while others would have Mercury on one side of the sun and Venus on the other.[13] Again, in the theory of the moon, Ptolemy introduced a "crank" mechanism, which would increase the 'apparent diameter of the epicycle' so as to make the model agree with positional observations. As a result Ptolemy was able to make an accurate representation of the moon's motion in longitude, but only at the expense of introducing a fictitious variation in the distance of the moon from the earth, according to which 'the apparent diameter of the moon itself should reach almost twice its mean value, which is very definitely not the case' (Neugebauer, 1957, p. 195). This departure from reality was one of the telling points of criticism raised by Copernicus in his *De revolutionibus* (1543). Descartes also proposed hypothetical models that, according to his own system, had to be fictitious.

Newton believed that he had proved that gravity, the cause of terrestrial weight and the force producing the downward acceleration of freely falling bodies, extends as far as the moon and is the cause of the moon's motion. He gave a series of arguments that it is this same force that keeps the planets in their orbits around the sun and the satellites in their orbits about their respective planets. He showed, furthermore, how this force of gravity can account for the tides in the seas and the irregularities (as well as the regularities) in the moon's motion. He set forth the goal of explaining the

moon's motion in a new way—not by celestial geometry and models which (like Ptolemy's) obviously cannot possibly correspond to reality, but rather by 'true causes' ('verae causae') whose properties could be developed mathematically. Thus Newtonian theory would reduce the features of the moon's motion to two sources: the interactions of the earth and the moon, and the perturbing effects of the sun. It is to be remarked that this procedure does not depend on the origin, nature, or physical cause of the gravitating force but only on certain mathematically elucidated properties, as that this force varies inversely as the square of the distance, that it is null within a spherical shell (or within a homogeneous sphere or a sphere made up of homogeneous shells), that the action of a sphere on an external particle is the same as if all the mass of the sphere were concentrated at its geometric center, that within a solid sphere the force on a particle is as the distance from the center, and so on. Such investigations did not depend on whether a planet is pushed or pulled toward the center, whether gravitation arises from an aether of varying density or a shower of aether particles or is even a simple action-at-a-distance. For Newton these latter questions were far from irrelevant to a complete understanding of the system of the world, and we know that he devoted considerable energy to them. Furthermore, the mathematical analysis had revealed some of the basic properties of the force and thus made precise the analysis into its cause. But in Newton's hierarchy of causes, the elucidation of the properties of universal gravity was distinct from—that is, on a different level from—the search for the cause of gravity. He thus put forth the radical point of view in the concluding General Scholium to the *Principia*: It is enough ('satis est') that gravity exists and that it acts according to the laws he had mathematically demonstrated, and that this force of gravity suffices 'to explain all the motions of the heavenly bodies and of our sea' (see n. 12 *supra*). How revolutionary this proposal was can be seen in the number of scientists and philosophers who refused to accept it and who rejected the *Principia* together with its conclusions because they did not approve of the concept of "attraction".

1.5 Causal mathematical science in the Scientific Revolution

In the last section, an outline was given of a hierarchy in the mathematical science of nature. On the lowest or most primitive level, this phrase may mean no more than mere quantification or calculation. Numerical data may provide arguments to test or to buttress essentially nonmathematical theories such as Harvey's. On a simple level, primarily in the realms of physics and astronomy, mathematics came to signify not only the measurements of positions and apparent (observed) angular speeds, and the rather straightforward application of plane and spherical trigonometry to the solutions of problems of the celestial sphere, but also the increasing quantification of qualities ranging from temperature to speeds. The ideal was to express general laws of nature as mathematical relations between observable physical quantities, notably in relation to the science of motion: kinematics and then dynamics. Such laws expressed number-relations or geometrical properties, and they were formalized in ratios or proportions, algebraic equations (or their equivalents in words), together with geometric properties and trigonometric relations, and eventually the infinitesimal calculus and other forms of higher mathematics, notably infinite series.

Since such mathematical laws use physically observable quantities (volume, weight, position, angle, distance, time, impact, and so on), they can to a large degree be tested by further observations and direct experiment, which may limit the range in which they hold: examples are Boyle's, Snel's, and Hooke's law, and the forms of Kepler's law of refraction.[1] Or, the test may be the verification or nonverification of a prediction (as the occurrence or nonoccurrence of a lunar or solar eclipse or a particular planetary configuration), or the accurate retrodiction of past observations. Obviously, some kind of numerical data must provide the basis for applying or testing such general or specific mathematical laws or relations. In all of this, there is and there need be no concern for physical causes. Galilean science is a foremost example of the successful application of mathematics to physical events on this level. Cause enters in the argument only to the extent of an awareness that air resistance may cause a slowing down of an otherwise uniform rectilinear motion (or component of motion), and that weight may cause an acceleration downward. Thus, for Galileo, motion could continue uniformly in a straight line only if there were no air resistance and if there were an extended horizontal plane to support the mobile, on which it could move without friction.[2]

We have seen, however, that in the seventeenth century there were found to be significant quantitative laws that cannot be directly tested, such as the law of uniform motion for falling bodies that speeds acquired are as the times elapsed ($v_1:v_2 = t_1:t_2$). Galileo, as we saw, could do no more than confirm another law of falling bodies, that the distances are in the squared ratio of the times ($s_1:s_2 = (t_1:t_2)^2$); and then, since the distance law is a consequence of the speed law, he supposed that the truth (verified by experiment) of the distance law guaranteed the truth of the speed law. In our modern language, the testability of $s \propto t^2$ is the way to confirm $v \propto t$. This is a classic and simple example of what has generally come to be called the hypothetico-deductive method. Galileo tested the distance-time relation for the accelerated motion upon an inclined plane, for various angles of inclination, and showed that s does maintain a constant proportion to t^2. Since this relation

was an inference (or deduction) from an assumption (or hypothesis) that v is proportional to t, the hypothetico-deductive method assumes that experimental confirmation of the deduced result $s_1:s_2 = t_1:t_2^2$ guarantees the validity of the hypothesis $v_1:v_2 = t_1:t_2$ from which the relation of s to t^2 had been deduced (see §1.4). As Ernst Mach (1960, p. 161) put it, in his celebrated *Science of Mechanics,* 'The inference from Galileo's assumption was thus confirmed by experiment, and with it the assumption itself.' The limitations to this mode of confirmation are twofold. One is philosophical: are there any ways to be sure that only $v \propto t$ implies $s \propto t^2$? That is, granted that $v \propto t$ is a sufficient condition for $s \propto t^2$, is it also a necessary condition?[3] The second is historical as well as philosophical. That is, a scientist may make an error in logic or mathematics: This is illustrated by the fact that at one stage in his career Galileo believed that the verifiable relation $s_1:s_2 = (t_1:t_2)^2$ follows from the speeds being proportional to distances ($v_1:v_2 = s_1:s_2$) rather than the relation of speeds to times ($v_1:v_2 = t_1:t_2$) (see Galileo, 1974, pp. 159sq; 1890-1909, vol. 8, p. 203).

The Galilean science of motion embodies only one part of the revolution in the exact sciences in the seventeenth century. For, in addition to the production of exact or mathematical laws, systems, and general constructs that may or may not be like models that conform to the direct experience of nature (experiment and observation), there arose the ideal of finding the true physical causes of such laws, systems, constructs, and models, in a hierarchy of causes that began with the mathematical elucidation of the properties of forces causing motions and only then proceeded to the analysis of the nature and cause of such forces.[4] The degree to which this goal was first achieved in Newton's **Principia** set the seal on an accomplished Scientific Revolution and was in and of itself revolutionary. Lest my readers should suppose that this is an anachronistic judgment of the twentieth century superimposed upon the events of the past, let me anticipate here one aspect of the next chapter, by indicating that this was an unequivocal judgment in the Age of Newton. Clairaut, Newton's immediate intellectual successor in celestial mechanics, declared unambiguously in 1747, 'The renowned treatise of Mathematical principles of Natural Philosophy [of Isaac Newton] inaugurated a great revolution in physics', a sentiment echoed by Lagrange and others (Clairaut, 1749; see §2.2).

The program for this revolution in physical science was first clearly set forth in astronomy, in the declared goal to put aside all noncausal and nonphysical computing schemes and to discover how the sun, moon, and planets actually move in relation to the physical ("true") causes of their motions. This aspect of the revolution found its first major spokesman in Kepler, whose *Astronomia nova* (1609), or *Commentary on the Motion of Mars,* was also described by him as a 'physica coelestis', a celestial physics (see Caspar, 1959, pp. 129sqq; Koyré, 1973, pp. 166sqq, 185sqq). What made this work 'new' was that it was not merely an *Astronomia nova,* but an *Astronomia nova* ἀιτιολογητος, a 'new astronomy based on causes'; and this was the sense in which Kepler declared it to be a 'celestial physics'.[5] That is, Kepler was not content with the limited goal of previous astronomers (including Ptolemy, Copernicus, and Tycho Brahe) of choosing a fitting center of motion and then determining planetary motions by judicious combinations of circular motions that would 'save the phenomena' (cf. Duhem, 1969). He wanted to derive planetary motions from their causes, from the forces that are the causes of the motions. He thus rejected one of the basic aspects of Copernican astronomy: that planetary orbits be computed with respect to an empty point in space corresponding to the center of the earth's orbit, rather than the sun itself. Kepler reasoned that forces originate in bodies, not in points in space; hence the motion of the planets must be reckoned in relation to the center of planetary force, the central body, the sun. As a result, Kepler attempted a dynamical rather than a kinematical astronomy, based on laws of force and motion rather than on applied geometry and arithmetic (see Koyré, 1973; Cohen, 1975*a*; Beer & Beer, 1975, sect. 10). Certain of Kepler's fellow astronomers disapproved of his thus introducing into astronomy a set of physical causes and hypotheses; it were better (said his former teacher, Michael Maestlin) to stick to the traditional geometry and arithmetic (letter to Kepler, 21 Sept. 1616; Kepler, 1937-, vol. 17, p. 187). Of course, it was easier to effect this radical change in Kepler's day than it would have been earlier, since Tycho Brahe had effectively demonstrated that comets move through the solar system. As Tycho himself put it: Had there ever existed crystalline spheres to which the planets were attached, they were now shattered and existed no longer. Hence, for anyone who went along with Tycho's conclusions, there was need for a wholly new scheme for explaining how the planets can possibly move in their observed curved paths.[6]

And so we are not surprised to find that Descartes also sought for causal explanations of the celestial motions, and so did certain other astronomers of the early seventeenth century, such as Bullialdus and Borelli.[7] But others were content to confine their attention more nearly to the phenomenological level of prediction and observation, without exhibiting any concern as to physical causes, or the possible reality (or lack of reality) of geometric computational schemes. From this point of view, one of the most astonishing aspects of Galileo's *Dialogue concerning the Two Chief World Systems* is the absence of any celestial physics. Galileo, in fact, seems never to have concerned himself with any speculations on the possible forces that might be acting in the operation of a Copernican system.[8] In this sense, Galileo was not at all a pioneer in celestial

mechanics, as Kepler and Descartes were, however much his personal contributions to the science of motion influenced the course of development of theoretical dynamics at large. But he was concerned with the truth and reality of the Copernican system, and he even advanced an explanation of the tides that seemed to him to require that the earth rotate about its axis while revolving around the sun.

The enormous advance in the exact physical sciences in the seventeenth century may be gauged by the gap between both Galileo's kinematics and Kepler's faulty and unsuccessful dynamics[9] on the one hand and Newton's goal of a mathematical dynamics congruent with the phenomenological kinematical laws and disclosing their physical cause on the other. Kepler, who in so many of his precepts resembles Newton, nevertheless represents a wholly different level of scientific belief and procedure. Kepler starts out from the causes, whereas Newton concludes in causes. Kepler accepts a kind of celestial attraction, based on an analogy with terrestrial magnetism, and seeks its consequences; Newton arrives at his concept of universal gravitation only after the logic of the study of forces and motions leads him in that direction (see Ch. 5). Newton's philosophy directs him from effects to causes, and from particulars to generalities. But Kepler believed it best to proceed in the reverse direction. 'I have no hesitation', he wrote, 'in asserting that everything that Copernicus has demonstrated *a posteriori* and on the basis of observations interpreted geometrically, may be demonstrated *a priori* without any subtlety or logic'.[10]

Like Galileo's laws of falling bodies, Kepler's laws were shown by Newton to be true only in rather limited circumstances which Newton then actually specified. Newton sought to determine new forms of these laws that would be more universally true. As we shall see in Ch. 3, the revolutionary power of Newton's method came from his ability to combine new modes of mathematical analysis with the study of physical causes, controlled constantly by the rigors of experiment and observation. But an essential ingredient was Newton's clear recognition of the hierarchy of causes and his ability to separate the mathematical laws from the physical properties of forces as causes. In this process he did not produce mere mathematical constructs or abstractions that were devoid of any content of reality other than "saving the phenomena", but he did create what he conceived to be purely mathematical counterparts of simplified and idealized physical situations that could later be brought into relation with the conditions of reality as revealed by experiment and observation. It was this aspect of Newtonian science, in my opinion, that produced so outstanding a result that his ***Principia*** was conceived to have been or to have inaugurated the epoch of a revolution in science, or at least to have brought to a level of revolutionary fruition the goals of creating a mathematical science of nature that had been expressed, however imperfectly, by Galileo and by Kepler.

Notes

General note: The extracts from Newton's *Principia* and *System of the World* are either from new translations (in progress) by I. B. Cohen and Anne Whitman or are generally revisions of existing translations.

§1.1

1. The Newtonian revolution in science

[1] In recent years, much of the discussion concerning scientific revolutions has centered on Kuhn (1962). For comments on Kuhn's views, see Lakatos & Musgrave (1970). For a modified statement of Kuhn's views, see his paper, 'Second thoughts on paradigms', in Suppe (1974). The propriety of using the term "revolution" to describe scientific change is denied in Toulmin (1972), vol. 1, pp. 96-130, esp. pp. 117sq.

[2] This expression is used by historians in a generally uncritical manner that does not necessarily imply adherence to any particular concept of revolution or even to a specific and clearly formulated doctrine of historical change. On the history of this concept and name, see Ch. 2 and Cohen (1977*e*).

[3] Pierre Duhem was largely responsible for the view that many of the discoveries traditionally attributed to Galileo had been anticipated by late medieval thinkers. Duhem's thesis concerning the medieval origin of modern science has been put forth in a new way in Crombie (1953).

[4] Still valuable are such older works as Ornstein (1928), the only comprehensive work ever produced on this subject, and Brown (1934); to be supplemented by such recent works as Hahn (1971), Middleton (1971), and Purver (1967).

[5] The official name of the Royal Society is: The Royal Society of London for Improving Natural Knowledge.

[6] On the history of scientific journals, see Thornton & Tully (1971), and Knight (1975), esp. ch. 4.

[7] For Bacon's views on utility, see his *Novum organum*, bk. 1, aph. 73, aph. 124; bk. 2, aph. 3. Descartes's statements concerning the ways in which science can make us 'the masters and possessors, as it were, of nature' (chiefly 'the conservation of health' and 'the invention of . . . artifacts which would allow us the effortless enjoyment of the fruits of the earth . . .') are to be found in pt. 6 of his *Discours de la méthode* (chiefly the end of the second and the beginning of the third paragraphs, and toward the conclusion).

[8] Two now-classic statements concerning social influences on seventeenth-century science are given in Hessen (1931) and Merton (1938). A stunning example of how to investigate 'the place of science within the conceptual framework of economic, social, political and religious ideas' has been given for the period in Webster (1975), and cf. the long and thoughtful review of Webster's work by Quentin Skinner, *Times Literary Supplement* (2 July 1976), no. 3877, pp. 810-812.

[9] On Newton and ship design, see Cohen (1974*b*); on the longitude at sea, see Newton (1975), introduction, pt. 5; concerning the telescope, see Newton (1958), sect. 2, §§3-5 (§17 contains a description of another instrument, a reflecting octant for use in practical navigation, which was found among Newton's papers and which he never saw fit to make public).

[10] Descartes, in his *Discours de la méthode* (1637), says explicitly that he does not consider himself to be a man of more than average mental capacity; hence if he has done anything extraordinary, the reason must be that he had a sound method (see Descartes, 1956, p. 2).

[11] Galileo's own account occurs in the fifth paragraph of the text of his *Sidereus nuncius* (1610); Galileo (1890-1909), vol. 3, pt. 1, pp. 60sq; trans. by Drake in Galileo (1957), p. 29.

[12] Newton (1672), p. 3075; reprinted in facs. in Newton (1958), p. 47. See Newton (1959-1977), vol. 1, p. 92.

[13] The exception was Domingo de Soto (*d.* 1560), who in a commentary on Aristotle's *Physics* (1545) 'was the first to apply the expression "uniformly difform" to the motion of falling bodies, thereby indicating that they accelerate uniformly when they fall and thus adumbrating Galileo's law of falling bodies'. Quoted from William A. Wallace's (1975) account of Soto in the *Dictionary of Scientific Biography*. See Beltrán de Heredia (1961); Wallace (1968); Clagett (1959), pp. 257, 555sq, 658.

[14] *Principia,* bk. one, prop. 4, corol. 6, corol. 7. For other examples of Newton's considerations of mathematical relations that do not occur in nature, see §3.3.

[15] In the scholium following prop. 78 (bk. one) of the *Principia,* Newton refers to these two as 'major cases of attractions' and finds it 'worthy of note' that under both conditions, the attractive force of a spherical body follows the same law as that of the particles which compose it. On this topic see §3.1, n. 5.

[16] In reaction, Alexandre Koyré came to the opposite conclusion: that, far from relying on experiment (and being the founder of the modern experimental method), Galileo was not primarily an experimenter. Furthermore, Koyré even asserted that many of Galileo's

most celebrated experiments could not have been performed, at least not in the manner described. See Koyré (1943), (1950*a*), and (1960*c*); these are collected in Koyré (1968). On Galileo's thought-experiments, see Shea (1972), pp. 63-65, 156, 157sq. It is generally recognized today that Koyré's point of view was extreme and needs some modification. Some of the "unperformable" experiments cited by Koyré have since then been performed and yield the very results described by Galileo; see Settle (1961), (1967), and MacLachlan (1973). Drake has recently found that experiment very likely played a significant role in Galileo's discoveries of the principles of motion.

§1.2

[1] Leibniz and Newton both had a share in this revolution (see n. 2 to §2.2). But it must be kept in mind that Newton made a large number of discoveries or inventions in mathematics, among them the general binomial expansion of $(a + b)^n$, the fundamental theorem that finding the area under a curve and finding the tangent to a curve are inverse operations, the methods of both the differential and integral calculus, the classification of cubic curves, various properties of infinite series, both the Taylor and Maclaurin expansions, modes of calculation and methods of numerical analysis (including the methods of successive iteration, interpolation, etc.), plus other aspects of geometry, analysis, and algebra. On these topics see Whiteside's introduction to Newton (1964-1967), and Whiteside's introductions and running commentary to his edition of Newton's *Mathematical Papers* (Newton, 1967-).

[2] Newton's public positive contributions to chemistry are conveniently summed up in Partington (1961), ch. 13.
[3] The contents of these queries are conveniently summarized in Duane H. D. Roller's analytical table of contents in the Dover edition of the *Opticks* (Newton, 1952, pp. lxxix-cxvi) and in Cohen (1956), pp. 164-171, 174-177. On the development of the Queries, see Koyré (1960*c*).

[4] On this tract see Newton (1958), pp. 241-248, 256-258; also (1959-1977), vol. 3, pp. 205-214.

[5] All extracts from Newton's *Principia* are given in the text of a new translation, now in progress, by I. B. Cohen and Anne M. Whitman, or are revisions of Andrew Motte's translation.

[6] From Newton's unpublished *Conclusio,* trans. by A. R. & M. B. Hall (1962), p. 333.

[7] See Roller's analytical table of contents (Newton, 1952, pp. lxxix-cxvi).

[8] Young (1855), vol. 1, pp. 161, 183sq; see Peacock (1855), pp. 150-153. But it should not be thought that every number given in the published *Opticks* represents an exact measurement or the result of a computation based on such direct measurement.

[9] For example, Roberts & Thomas (1934) is subtitled 'A study of one of the earliest examples of scientific method' and is part of a series with the general title, Classics of Scientific Method.

[10] The strictly methodological portions of the *Opticks* are to be found in the final paragraph of qu. 28 and in the concluding pages of the lengthy qu. 31 with which the second English edition of 1717/1718 concludes; both had appeared in earlier versions in the Latin edition of 1706.

[11] Quoted from Dover ed. (Newton, 1952), pp. 369sq. This query was first published in the Latin edition (1706) as qu. 20 and then appeared in revised form in English in the second English edition (1717/1718).

[12] Quoted from Dover ed. (Newton, 1952), pp. 404sq. This query also appeared first in the Latin edition (as qu. 23) and then in revised form in the second English edition.

[13] The word "scenario" is used because Newton wrote up his initial experiments with prisms in an apparently autobiographical manner, but his MSS hint that he was trying to impose a Baconian and experimental-inductivist scenario upon what must have been the sequence of his prior beliefs, experiences, and conclusions. On this subject see Lohne (1965), (1968); Sabra (1967), pp. 245-250.

[14] See §3.6, n. 5. These "phenomena" were called "hypotheses" in the first edition of the *Principia*; see Koyré (1955*b*), Cohen (1966).

[15] This is made evident in a table I have prepared for a commentary on the *Principia* (in progress), in which I have tabulated the occurrence of every explicit reference to a definition or law, as well as to a preceding proposition or lemma, and—in the case of bk. three—the rules, phenomena, and hypotheses.

[16] The question of "analysis" and "synthesis" may cause real confusion in relation to Newton's scientific work. This pair of words (of Greek origin) and their counterparts (of Latin origin) "resolution" and "composition" are used by Newton in a general scientific sense and specifically, in qu. 31 of the *Opticks,* to describe how 'by this way of Analysis we may proceed from Compounds to Ingredients, and from Motions to the Forces producing them' and 'in general, from Effects to their Causes, and from particular Causes to more general ones, till the Argument end in the most general'. Then 'the Synthesis consists in assuming the Causes discovered, and established as Principles, and by them explaining the Phaenomena proceeding from them, and proving the Explanations'. Newton also refers to the

'Two Methods of doing things' of 'Mathematicians . . . which they call Composition & Resolution'.

Long ago Dugald Stewart showed that "analysis" and "synthesis" have different meanings in mathematics and in physics and that Newton therefore speaks with some imprecision in apparently relating the modes of investigation in physics or natural philosophy and in mathematics. Stewart even shows how in some cases "analysis" and "synthesis" may have opposing senses in the two realms. See Stewart's *Elements of the Philosophy of the Human Mind,* ch. 4 ('Logic of induction'), sect. 3 ('Of the import of the words analysis and synthesis in the language of modern philosophy'), subsect. 2 ('Critical remarks on the vague use, among modern writers, of the terms *analysis* and *synthesis*'); Stewart (1877), vol. 3, pp. 272sqq.

For a recent example of an attempt to make the method of analysis and synthesis, as expounded in qu. 31 of the *Opticks,* apply to the *Principia,* see Guerlac (1973). For Newton's published statement on analysis and synthesis in mathematics, and in the *Principia,* see n. 21 *infra.*

[17] Turbayne (1962), pp. 46, 49. On the geometric form of presentation in essentially nonmathematical books, see §3.11.

[18] The *Principia* was first written as two "books" (*De motu corporum*). Newton then expanded the end of the first "book" into a second "book" (on motion in resisting fluids, pendulum motion, wave motion, etc.), calling *these* two "books" *De motu corporum.* The subject matter of the original second "book" was wholly recast and became the third "book" of the *Principia* (called Liber tertius, *De mundi systemate*). After Newton's death, the text of the original bk. two was published in Latin and in an English version called respectively *De mundi systemate liber* (London, 1728) and *A Treatise of the System of the World* (London, 1728; London, 1731). It is in the English version of this latter work that the famous phrase, 'in a mathematical way', appears. See my introduction to Newton (1975), p. xix.

[19] Cuvier (1812), 'Discours préliminaire', p. 3. 'Sans doute les astronomes ont marché plus vite que les naturalistes, et l'époque où se trouve aujourd'hui la théorie de la terre, ressemble un peu à celle où quelques philosophes croyoient le ciel de pierres de taille, et la lune grande comme le Péloponèse:mais après les Anaxagoras, il est venu des Copernic et des Kepler, qui ont frayé la route à Newton; et pourquoi l'histoire naturelle n'auroit-elle pas aussi un jour son Newton?'

According to John T. Edsall (personal communication), Otto Warburg, in discussing the problem of biological oxidations around 1930, said: 'Heute, wie vor fünfzig Jahren, gilt das van't Hoffsche Wort: Der Newton der Chemie is noch nicht gekommen.' No doubt Warburg was referring to the general introduction ('An die Leser') to vol. 1 of the *Zeitschrift für Physikalische Chemie* (Leipzig, 1887), p. 2, where the state of chemistry is compared with the condition of astronomy in 'Kopernikus' und Kepler's Zeit', and the need is expressed for a 'Newton der Chemie'. This preface was signed jointly by Van't Hoff and Ostwald.

[20] A major exception is the general scholium, at the end of sect. 6, bk. two (which was at the end of sect. 7 in the first edition), and the scholium at the end of sect. 7 (first published in the second edition). The latter scholium describes Newton's investigations of the resistances of fluids by experiments on bodies falling in air and in water. The general scholium is devoted to Newton's experiments on the resistances of fluids, in which he studied the oscillations of pendulums under various conditions and compared the motion of pendulums in air, water, and mercury.

[21] In his later life, Newton attempted to superimpose on the history of the *Principia* a chronology in which he would have developed and used the new fluxional calculus in an algorithmic form so as to have discovered the main propositions by analysis, and then have recast them in the form of Greek geometry according to the method of synthesis. Thus he wrote: 'By the help of the new Analysis Mr. *Newton* found out most of the Propositions in his *Principia Philosophiae*: but because the Ancients for making things certain admitted nothing into Geometry before it was demonstrated synthetically, he demonstrated the Propositions synthetically, that the Systeme of the Heavens might be founded upon good Geometry. And this makes it now difficult for unskilful Men to see the Analysis by which those Propositions were found out'; quoted from Newton (1715), p. 206; cf. Cohen (1971), p. 295. There is no documentary evidence whatever to support this scenario, while abundant evidence favors the view that Newton's mode of discovery follows more or less the form of presentation in the published *Principia.*

§1.3

[1] On Hales see Guerlac (1972); Cohen (1976*b*); F. Darwin (1917), pp. 115-139.

[2] A contemporaneous English translation of Van Helmont's account of his experiment is given in Partington (1961), p. 223.

[3] *De motu cordis,* ch. 9; quoted from Harvey (1928). Cf. Kilgour (1954) and especially Pagel (1967), pp. 73sqq.

[4] Hence the quantitative method used by Harvey is at least as revolutionary as his conclusions about the cir-

culation, and possibly even more so. From a seventeenth-century point of view, such subjects as theoretical statics, kinematics, and dynamics were exact mathematical sciences which became physical sciences only when applied to physics.

[5] Galileo (1974), p. 147; (1890-1909), vol. 8, p. 190. Strictly speaking, Galileo did not ever express his physical laws as the algebraic proportions $s \propto t^2$ or $v \propto t$. As a matter of fact it is misleading even to write out his results in the form $s_1:s_2 = t_1^2:t_2^2$, much less $(S_1/S_2) = (t_1/t_2)$. On this point see n. 8 *infra*. In what follows, I shall (as a kind of shorthand) refer to relations that Galileo found as $s \propto t^2$ or $v \propto t$, but without any intended implication that these are Galileo's formulations of such laws.

[6] 'On naturally accelerated motion', third day, prop. 2; Galileo (1974), p. 166; (1890-1909), vol. 8, p. 209.

[7] In corol. 1 to prop. 2, Galileo shows that although the total distance traversed is proportional to the square of the time, the distances traversed in each successive equal interval of time are as the odd numbers starting from unity—a result that follows from number theory, since the sequence 1, 4, 9, 16, 25, . . . leads to the sequence 1(= 1 − 0), 3(= 4 − 1), 5(= 9 − 4), 7(= 16 − 9), 9(= 25 − 16), . . .

[8] Galileo did not restrict himself to such number relations. Thus (third day, prop. 2 on accelerated motion: 1974, p. 166; 1890-1909, vol. 8, p. 209): 'If a moveable descends from rest in uniformly accelerated motion, the spaces run through in any times whatever are to each other as the duplicate ratio of their times'. Galileo's proportion is thus space$_1$: space$_2$ = (time$_1$: time$_2$)^2; he does not use the functional relation s á t^2. On this point see the comments by Drake in the introduction to Galileo (1974), pp. xxi-xxiv. But in discussing quantities of the same kind (e.g., line segments), Galileo would use verbal equivalents of equations, such as "*HB est excessus NE super BL*" ($HB = NE − BL$).

[9] Quoted from *Il saggiatore* ('The assayer'), sect. 6, trans. in Crombie (1969), vol. 2, p. 151; Galileo (1890-1909), vol. 6, p. 232. This statement is omitted in Drake's version, Galileo (1957). I do not wish to enter here into discussions of Galileo's possible Platonism, for which see Koyré (1943) and a rebuttal by Clavelin (1974). Geymonat (1965), pp. 198sq, warns against reading this particular remark of Galileo's out of context.

[10] Newton's *Principia* is apt to be described, on the basis of superficial examination, as a treatise in the style of Greek geometry. Although the external form displays a geometrical style reminiscent of Euclid, a closer examination shows that Newton's method is not at all like that of the classic Greek geometers; rather,

proposition by proposition and lemma by lemma, he usually proceeds by establishing geometrical conditions and their corresponding ratios and then at once introducing some carefully defined limiting process. In sect. 1 of bk. one, Newton sets forth general principles of limits (which he calls the method of first and last ratios), so that he may apply some degree of rigor to problems using nascent or evanescent quantities (or ratios of such quantities) in the rest of the treatise. Furthermore, even in the matter of ratios and proportions, Newton is a "modern"; he does not follow the Greek style, in the sense that Galileo does and that Kepler tends to do. That is, he writes "mixed" proportions, implying a direct functional relationship, for instance stating that a force may be directly or inversely proportional to some condition of a distance. Traditionally one would have had to say that one force is to another as a condition of some distance is to that same condition of another distance. Finally, one of the distinctive features of the *Principia,* as noted by Halley in his review, was the extensive and innovative use of the method of infinite series, which shows the degree to which the *Principia* is definitely not a treatise in Greek geometry. On this topic see Cohen (1974c), pp. 65sqq, and Whiteside (1970b).

[11] Kepler's system of nested spheres is delineated in his *Mysterium cosmographicum* (1596; rev. ed. 1621). An annotated English version of this work has been completed by Eric J. Aiton and Alistair M. Duncan (Kepler, in press).

In a letter of 1595, Kepler said: 'The world of motion must be considered as made up of rectilinear [regular solids]. Of these, however, there are five. Hence if they are to be regarded as the boundaries or partitions . . . they can separate no more than six objects. Therefore six movable bodies revolve around the sun. Here is the reason for the number of planets'; quoted from Kepler (1965), p. 63. This example shows how considerations of shape and geometry were not necessarily free of numerical aspects.

[12] In the *Narratio prima* (or *First Account*), trans. in Rosen (1971), p. 147, Rheticus said, 'What is more agreeable to God's handiwork than that this first and most perfect work should be summed up in this first and most perfect number?' For a history of this problem, see Cohen (1977d).

[13] Quoted from Kepler's *Mysterium cosmographicum* (1596) in Kepler (1937-), vol. 1, p. 9; trans. in Rufus (1931), p. 10. Cf. Koyré (1973), p. 128.

[14] Sizi found other grounds for his assertion: the seven primary metals in alchemy, the time when the embryo starts to form in a mother's womb (seven hours after coitus), the date at which a human fetus is sufficiently alive to survive if born prematurely (seven months after

conception). See Drake (1958) and Ronchi's introduction to Clelia Pighetti's translation of Sizi (1964).

[15] Kepler (1965), p. 14. Since the earth has one satellite and Jupiter has four, a geometric sequence would yield two for Mars, eight for Saturn, and none for Mercury and Venus. The number 6, which Kepler suggests as an alternative for the eight satellites attributed to Saturn, is more difficult to account for. We may well understand, accordingly, why some scholars have made a "silent correction" of this 6, so as to have it be 7 or 5. This number 6 does fit the arithmetic progression 2,4,6, but in this case the earth would have no satellite, which would actually negate the basis of assigning two to Mars. Furthermore, Kepler also suggested that Venus and Mercury might have one satellite each. These two numbers would break the sequence, but there could be no other choice if each planet is to have no more satellites than the immediately superior planet.

[16] For details see Cohen (1977b), (1977d).

[17] For other examples of numerology in nineteenth- and twentieth-century science, see Cohen (1977d). An outstanding example is the so-called Bode's law (or the Titius-Bode law), which gives reasonably good values for the planetary distances (up to Uranus), including a place for the asteroids. It too fails for the first term. See, further, Nieto (1972).

§1.4

[1] Quoted from *Mysterium cosmographicum* (1596) in Kepler (1937-), vol. 1, p. 9; trans. in Rufus (1931), p. 9. Cf. Koyré (1973), p. 138. In fact, Kepler went on to say that he 'was induced to try and discover them [i.e., these three things] because of the wonderful resemblance between motionless objects, namely, the sun, the fixed stars and intermediate space, and God the Father, God the Son, and God the Holy Ghost; this analogy I shall develop further in my cosmography'.

[2] *Mysterium cosmographicum*, ch. 20. To see how this law works, note that the periods of Mercury and Venus are respectively 88^d and 224^d; hence half the increase in period is ½(224^d − 88^d) = 68^d. Kepler's rule is that 88:(88 + 68) = dist. of Mercury:dist of Venus. The results, as given by Dreyer (1906), p. 379, are Jupiter:Saturn 0.574 (0.572), Mars:Jupiter 0.274 (0.290), earth:Mars 0.694 (0.658), Venus:earth 0.762 (0.719), Mercury:Venus 0.563 (0.500); the number in parentheses in each case is the Copernican value. In an equation, Kepler's rule would read $(T_n + T_{n-1})/2T_{n-1} = A_n/A_{n-1}$; cf. Koyré (1973), pp. 153sq.

[3] See Kepler's *Harmonice mundi,* in Kepler (1937-), vol. 6, p. 302. Kepler is astonishingly silent as to how he came upon this law. Koyré (1973), p. 455, n. 27,

discusses some conjectures on this topic made by J. B. Delambre and R. Small (he gives his own opinion on p. 339). See, further, Gingerich (1977).

[4] This difference between the third law and the first two is seen in Newton's treatment of them. He admits that the third law, 'found by Kepler, is accepted by everyone' (hypoth. 6, ed. 1, phen. 4, eds. 2 and 3, *Principia,* bk. three); but he does not give Kepler credit in the *Principia* for either the area law or the law of elliptical orbits, and at least once he claimed that Kepler had only guessed planetary orbits 'to be elliptical'.

[5] Galileo's Platonic "discovery" did not embody a "causal" explanation in the sense of assigning a physical cause to the supposed accelerated motions of the planets toward the sun: for example, by supposing forces that might be operative in the celestial system to produce such accelerations.

[6] Cf. Koyré (1960b), reprinted in Koyré (1965), where (p. 218, n. 3) Koyré discusses how A. E. Taylor believed (erroneously, as it turned out) that he had found the source of this supposed cosmological doctrine of Plato.

[7] Cf. Cohen (1967c). Newton also pointed out other faults in Galileo's assumptions; see Whiteside's commentary in Newton (1967-), vol. 6, pp. 56sq, n. 73.

[8] Galileo was aware that in projectile motion there is an acceleration in the same direction as gravity or weight; whereas there is no acceleration or deceleration (save for the slight retardation caused by air resistance) at right angles to that downward direction. This is not, however, a real anticipation (however limited) of the second law, since Galileo does not specify clearly that the "impeto" is an external force acting on a body in order to produce an acceleration. And the same is true of Galileo's analysis of motion along an inclined plane, where both the "impeto" of gravity and the acceleration are diminished in the ratio of the sine of the angle of elevation. Drake has discussed Galileo's concept of cause in his introduction to Galileo (1974), pp. xxvii-xxviii; see, further, Drake (1977).

[9] For a convenient summary of the medieval physics of motion see Grant (1971), ch. 4. For texts and translations see Clagett (1959) and Grant (1974), sects. 40-51.

[10] For Galileo's description of this series of experiments, see Galileo (1974), pp. 169sq; (1890-1909), vol. 8, pp. 212sq.

[11] Whereas Kepler begins with the nature of the force, Newton concludes in the inquiry into the nature of a force with certain properties that have come to light during the antecedent investigations: as that it diminish-

es with the square of the distance, extends to great distances, and is proportional to the mass of bodies, etc.

[12] Concluding general scholium to the *Principia*: see, further, §3.2.

[13] *Almagest,* bk. 9, sect. 1.1. In his *Planetary Hypotheses,* Ptolemy developed a physical system or a physical model of astronomy in addition to the mathematical computing models of astronomy described in the *Almagest.* Cf. Hartner (1964), supplemented by Goldstein (1967).

§1.5

[1] A doctoral dissertation on Kepler's optics was completed in 1970 by Stephen Straker (Indiana University).

[2] Galileo was aware that if a moving body were to continue in motion along a horizontal path (tangent to the earth), it would in effect be getting farther and farther away from the earth's center or surface: rising up, as it were, *sponte sua.*

[3] Galileo himself fell into this trap in his arguments for the Copernican system. He developed a theory in which the tides are produced by a combination of the motions of the earth. Hence, he believed (and argued), God must have created the universe with the earth rotating on its axis and revolving in an orbit, just as Copernicus said. Pope Urban VIII argued against the "conclusiveness" of this proof of the Copernican system on the grounds that it would limit God's omnipotence. Galileo had only shown that his version of the Copernican system would imply tidal phenomena similar to those we observe; he had not demonstrated the converse. His Copernican system was a sufficient condition to explain the tides, but it was not a necessary condition. On Galileo's theory of the tides, see Aiton (1954) and Burstyn (1962); also Aiton (1963) and Burstyn (1963).

[4] Of course, as we shall see below in Ch. 4, a system, construct, or model could successively gain additional features that would bring it so nearly into harmony with experience that it would seem to be a description of reality.

[5] Koyré (1973), p. 166, says that 'the very title of Kepler's work proclaims, rather than foretells, a revolution'.

[6] Both Kepler and Newton held that the demise of the concept of crystalline spheres required a theory of planetary motions based on forces.

[7] On Borelli, see Koyré (1952*a*). There is no adequate study of the celestial system of Descartes or of Bullialdus.

[8] In Galileo's presentation of Plato's cosmological scheme (see §1.4, nn. 5 and 6, as well as Galileo, 1953, pp. 29sq; 1890-1909, vol. 4, pp. 53sq; also 1974, pp. 232-234, and 1890-1909, vol. 8, pp. 283sq), he seems to have assumed that when a planet was started off in its orbit with the proper speed, it would then move in its orbit without needing the action of any force.

[9] Unsuccessful and faulty as a system in general, Kepler's dynamics did, however, serve to establish the first two Keplerian laws of planetary motion. See Koyré (1973), pp. 185-244; Krafft (1973).

[10] *Mysterium cosmographicum* (1596), quoted in Duhem (1969), p. 101; Kepler (1937-), vol. 1, p. 16.

A. T. Winterbourne (essay date 1985)

SOURCE: "Newton's Arguments for Absolute Space," in *Archiv fur Geschichte de Philosophie,* Walter de Gruyter, 1985, pp. 80-91.

[*In the following essay, Winterbourne offers a reading of Newton's "proofs" of absolute space that supports the claim that Newton's argument has been misrepresented by modern critics. Furthermore, Winterbourne suggests that Newton's argument may be interpreted more literally than has previously been the case.*]

In this paper I shall examine Newton's 'proofs' of absolute space, and try to justify the claim that the argument has been misrepresented by recent commentators, and that it can be given a rather more literal rendering than has been the case.[1]

It is usually accepted that since Newtonian mechanics requires an absolute reference frame, Newton must defend that conception from within the framework of natural philosophy, or be compelled to present this reference frame as an epistemologically unjustified, but metaphysically necessary presupposition.[2] The orthodox view is that Newton uses the arguments of the spinning bucket, and the cord-connected spheres as evidence that 'empirically' verifies the existence of absolute space. In fact, it is not explicitly stated by Newton that these arguments prove the existence of absolute space: this conclusion is nonetheless said to follow directly from the fact that they demonstrate absolute *motion*[3]. The orthodox reading of Newton's argument is illustrated by Max Jammer, who cites this passage from *Principia*:

> The causes by which true and relative motions are distinguished one from the other, are the forces impressed upon bodies to generate motion.[4]

(I shall refer to this passage as N1, *i.e.* 'Newton's first thesis'.) What Jammer calls Newton's first argument is based on the idea that only real forces generate real motion. According to Jammer, this argument is constituted by three significant passages. The first is the one I have called N1; the second is this:

> The effects which distinguish absolute from relative motion are the forces of receding from the axis of circular motion. For there are no such forces in a circular motion purely relative, but in a true and absolute circular notion they are greater or less according to the quantity of the motion.[5]

(I shall refer to this passage as N2.) The third passage cited by Jammer as constitutive of Newton's first argument—the argument from forces—is this:

> It is indeed a matter of great difficulty to discover, and effectually to distinguish, the true motions of particular bodies from the apparent; because the parts of that immovable space, in which those motions are performed, do by no means come under the observations of our senses. *Yet the thing is not altogether desperate*; for we have some arguments to guide us, partly from the apparent motions, which are the differences of the true motions; partly from the forces, which are the causes and effects of the true motions.[6]

For reasons which will become apparent, I shall refer to this passage as N4.[7]

So much for what Jammer calls the first argument. The second argument for the existence of absolute motion is "that which proceeds from the effects that such motion produces, in particular the appearance of centrifugal forces. So we have Newton's famous pail experiment."[8] After discussing this 'experiment' Jammer says that ". . . the same inaccessibility to physical verification characterizes all the other attempts to enforce (Newton's) argument, as for example, his experiment with the two cord-connected spheres."[9] Newton's final argument—based on the distinction between absolute and relative, or apparent motion—is not, in Jammer's opinion, developed further. On this interpretation, the logical status of both 'experiments' is the same. Both are attempts to move from the existence of forces, to the existence of absolute space, via absolute motion. It is this interpretation that I intend to question. There is, in addition a tendency to change the logic of the globes thought-experiment and attribute this changed logic to Newton.[10]

To support my thesis that the orthodox reading of the relevant Scholium passages is, if not strictly wrong, then at least not Newton's view, consider Jammer's discussion. What I have referred to as N1, N2 and N4, are run together by Jammer, as representative of a single argument. Perhaps the most often cited passage of the Scholium—referring to the introduction of the two thought-experiments—in fact introduces the argument of the globes. Most commentators present this as though the passage beginning "It is indeed a matter of great difficulty to discover . . . the true motions of particular bodies from the apparent . . ."; and which includes the significant assertion, "yet the thing is not altogether desperate . . .", *preceded* the bucket experiment. But it does not. It comes after this discussion, and immediately before the introduction of the globes thought-experiment. I hope to show that this is an important and neglected aspect of Newton's reasoning, and that the Scholium passages might be taken rather more literally than has been the case.[11]

I agree with Jammer's suggestion that the bucket experiment focusses attention on the special role of certain forces and their observable effects. According to Newton, these can only be explained by postulating an absolute reference frame.[12] Newton thinks this is accomplished by pointing out that in true circular motion such forces are greater or less, and are measurable. He is trying to establish that the endeavour to recede from the axis of circular motion is due to a force that is variable and measurable. What I have called N1 is part of an argument from dynamics designed to show that true motion cannot be explained relationally. From the relational viewpoint, the translation of bodies can only be seen as a kinematic change, which means, for Newton, only by means of relative or 'sensible' measures. Since he is concerned to show that the confounding of these measures with the 'real' measures generates "vulgar prejudices" concerning space and time, Newton's task was to establish that though certain motions are kinematically equivalent, they are nonetheless dynamically distinguishable. This distinguishability is manifested by the measurable variations of certain forces. Hence the bucket experiment.[13] A dynamic explanation must be relative to a frame of reference other than the "ambient bodies".[14] Newton's argument is always from the existence of observable forces, or their effects, to absolute motion, and thence to absolute space. Although the latter cannot be observed, it can be inferred as a way of making these forces and effects intelligible.[15]

Newton advances the argument by repeating what he regards as the error of confusing sensible measures with real entities:

> Wherefore relative quantities are not the quantities themselves . . . but those sensible measures of them (either accurate or inaccurate) which are commonly used instead of the measured quantities themselves. And if the meaning of words is to be determined by their use, then by the names time, space, place and motion, their (sensible) measures are to be properly understood; and the expression will be unusual and purely mathematical, if the measured quantities themselves are meant. On this account,

those violate the accuracy of language, which ought to be kept precise, who interpret these words for the measured quantities. Nor do those less defile the purity of mathematical and philosophical truths, who cofound real quantities with their relations and sensible measures.[16]

(I shall call this passage N3.) It is after this passage that Newton asserts that it is difficult to discover and distinguish true motion from apparent, yet reassures his reader that "the thing is not altogether desperate". If we accept the conventional reading, it would clearly be an inappropriate moment for Newton to say this: that is, *after* consideration of the bucket thought-experiment, which, on the orthodox reading, establishes all Newton's purposes in the Scholium arguments. The most plausible interpretation seems to be that Newton has tried to establish that a full explanation of certain phenomena must include reference to forces differentiating real and apparent motion. And ". . . the thing is not altogether desperate; for we have some arguments to guide us, partly from the apparent motions, which are the differences of the true motions; partly from the forces, which are the causes and effects of the true motions."[17] Why should Newton, at this point, say that there are some arguments to guide us, if, as is commonly supposed, the bucket experiment constitutes the main argument? Immediately following the last quoted sentence, Newton introduces the globes thought-experiment. Perhaps Newton wishes to regard N4 as offering two separate arguments, which though related, do not aim to make precisely the same point. Suppose we assume that the bucket experiment is arguing for the special role of certain forces: we might then consider the possibility that the globes thought-experiment is the argument ". . . from the apparent motions, which are the differences of the true motions."[18]

The details of the bucket experiment are well known. It consists of suspending a bucket of water by a rope which is then twisted. A force is applied to the bucket in the direction of unwinding.[19] Newton's central point is that the resulting deformation of the water surface indicates the existence of forces acting.[20] The point is that certain kinds of forces, when applied to systems free to rotate, or to systems already rotating, give rise to centrifugal forces as their effects. The second law of motion associates accelerations with forces. With respect to what, then, is the water accelerating? Newton insists that it cannot be the bucket, since the water surface is successively plane and concave when there is relative acceleration, and since the surface may be plane or concave when there is no relative acceleration. He concludes not that the acceleration must be with respect to absolute space—this term nowhere appears in the relevant discussion in the Scholium—but that

> this endeavour (of receding from the axis of rotation) does not depend upon any translation of the water

in respect of the ambient bodies, nor can true circular motion be defined by such translation. There is only one real circular motion of any one revolving body, corresponding to only one power of endeavouring to recede from its axis of motion, as its proper and adequate effect.[21]

The fact that Newton is dealing here with a deformable body greatly complicates the issue.[22] He says that when the relative motion of the water in the vessel is greatest, it produces no endeavour to recede from the axis. The 'it' here refers to the body of water considered as *one* body, and Newton is trying to show that ". . . there is only one real circular motion of any one revolving body, corresponding to only one power of endeavouring to recede from its axis of motion, as its proper and adequate effect." However, since the water is deformable, it is not strictly true that there was *no* endeavour to recede from the axis at the beginning of the experiment. The particles of water in immediate contact with the sides of the bucket would have received an immediate centripetal force, and would have started to rotate. The vessel, says Newton, "gradually communicates" its motion to the water; the endeavour shows that the real circular motion is continually increasing, and is at rest relatively to the bucket only when the whole body of water partakes of the motion, and thus acquires its greatest quantity. The concavity of the surface is a function of the combined circular motions of the particles constituting it. The 'true' circular motion Newton is trying to demonstrate is manifest only when the centripetal force has been communicated to the whole body of water. This takes time: when the circular motion of the water—considered as one body—is at a maximum, the water is at rest with respect to the sides of the bucket.

I want to suggest three ways to analyse the globes thought-experiment. The first is the modern interpretation; the second is more firmly based on Newton, and concerns what might be called 'Clarke's embellishment'; and the third is the argument I take it that Newton offered in the Scholium itself.

The modern version, which I shall briefly outline, starts with the assumption of a universe empty except for the globes. In this case, the question of whether the globes rotate presents the problem as a matter of semantics. If one asks a relationist why we may not affirm that the globes rotate, his reply will be that the idea of circular, or any other kind of motion, is intelligible only when some other body is given as reference standard. He may simply offer a challenge to the Newtonian to say, without question-begging, what is meant by rotation in an empty universe. The relationist presupposes that motion is intelligible only relationally; the Newtonian, in trying to make sense of the globes rotation, presupposes that the relational explanation is incomplete by neglecting the facts relating forces and tension. Of course the Newtonian admits the intelligibility of relational theories of motion: for a Newtonian it is both meaningful and true—though not, of course, the whole truth.[23] This first version of the argument has the merit of recognizing that the problem can be reconstructed in terms of what it makes sense for us to affirm in certain well-understood cases of dynamics. It errs in attributing to Newton a too metaphysical cast of mind in this important argument.

The second version is, though not found in the Scholium, a recognizably Newtonian move. Consider the possibility that all objects, apart from the globes, are annihilated from the actual, non-empty universe. Does it make sense to talk about rotation and direction of motion of the globes? Newton, and Clarke (in the correspondence with Leibniz) have no hesitation in saying that it does.

> (And) yet no way is shown to avoid this absurd consequence, that the parts of a circulating body would lose the *vis centrifuga* arising from their circular motion, if all the extrinsic matter around them were annihilated.[24]

There is no doubt I think that this way of stating the problem caused Leibniz some embarrassment. It seems that he cannot agree with Newton without undermining his concept of phenomenal motion—partly because of the uneasy traffic in his system between metaphysical and phenomenal levels of reality.[25] If Leibniz denied that in the circumstances obtaining in Clarke's embellishment of Newton, there would be tension or rotation, he would commit himself to the view that an occurrence transcending the globes could have an immediate effect on the globes; he is committed, in other words, to action-at-a-distance of a quite radical kind—a thoroughly un-Leibnizian notion.

As I have said, the globes thought-experiment is not described by Newton in terms of which Sklar's account, for example, is typical. This brings me to third interpretation of the argument.[26]

> If two globes, kept at a given distance one from the other by means of a cord which connects them, were revolved about their common centre of gravity, we might, from the tension of cord, discover the endeavour of the globes to recede from the axis of their motion, and from thence we might compute the quantity of their circular motions.[27]

Evidently, at the point where Newton explains the purpose of the experiment and the results that might accrue, there is no suggestion that we should consider the globes in an otherwise empty universe. Newton is claiming only that by 'testing' the cord for tension, we could compute the amount of circular motion. He argues that variations in the application of forces to alternate faces of the globes would either add to the quantity of circular motion or diminish it.[28] It is at this point in the argument that Newton suggests for the first time that such computations would be possible ". . . even in an immense vacuum, where there was nothing external or sensible with which the globes could be compared." This extension of the conditions of the argument would not be intelligible to the relationist. The differences in the conditions given to us in various (Galilean) frames—exemplified in the argument from forces and accelerations—may be regarded either as intrinsic or as due to external influences.[29] This is Newton's only direct reference to such a possible, non-actual universe. From this point, Newton extends his reasoning by adding the fixed stars to this hypothetical universe. Even then we could not tell by means of the relative translations of the stars and the bodies, which of them was really in motion: we have to accept the kinematic equivalence of hypotheses. However,

> . . . if we observed the cord and found that its tension was that very tension which the motions of the globes required, we might conclude the motions to be in the globes, and the bodies to be at rest.[30]

What can Newton mean by ". . . that very tension which the motions of the globes required . . ."? The tension must be such as to guarantee that the globes rotate about their common centre of gravity, so we might read this as 'the tension required for orbital motion'. But what Newton seems to be referring to here is the preceding remark, where he thinks he has shown how one might come to the conclusion that variations in tension are caused by, and directly proportional to, forces variously applied to the alternate faces of the globes. This is achieved by measuring the variations of tension observed in the actual non-empty universe. Thus we could discover ". . . from the translation of the globes among the bodies" the determination of their motion. That is, once it is established that it is the globes, not the stars, that are in motion, we can compute the direction of their motion with respect to the stars considered as at rest.

Newton's last remarks in the Scholium effectively embarrass any relationist of a Leibnizian persuasion who rejects action-at-a-distance. Newton has tried to show that the addition of forces on alternate faces of the globes has a direct and measurable effect on the cord's tension, which is its "proper and adequate effect". It might be plausible to suggest that the connection between circular motion and centrifugal effects is sufficiently ambiguous, such that we could not tell if rotating the fixed stars around the globes would result in the generation of such forces on the globes: but it is a good deal less plausible to say that by addition of force on the body one effects the fixed stars.[31] It is not the existence of centrifugal effects *simpliciter* that Newton believes refutes the relationist. In this case the bucket thought-experiment would have probably been sufficient. It is the law-like connection Newton thinks he has established between the variations in the amount of tension in the cord, and the variations of applied forces. Having rejected kinematic relativity as explanations of these phenomena, the thesis must be developed mathematically and dynamically. What Newton has done thus far is indicate what is necessary to explain these causes and effects, and thus true and apparent motion. *How* this is to be done is the task of **Principia** as a whole.[32]

To summarize: the globes argument postulates the cord-connected spheres in the actual universe. Here, we may refer to impressed forces, tension *etc.* without being open to the charge that these assertions have no clear sense. It is important to keep in mind that any such assertions are based upon our *knowledge of the globes themselves,* considered in a normally inhabited universe. From this we conclude that the impressed forces and variations of tension mutually imply one another in some law-like manner. It is this that Newton believes justifies the assertion that there would be such forces even in an otherwise empty universe. To deny this would be to deny, *not* some metaphysical/theological thesis about absolute space, but the putatively established connection between forces and tension. Newton is extrapolating from the known behaviour of bodies in the actual universe to the intelligibility of the idea of force in a possible world inhabited only by the globes. In other words, in such a universe, the science of dynamics would still apply—an assumption necessary for the laws of motion.[33] The *analogical* reasoning which leads to the acceptance of the intelligibility of forces in a universe empty except for the globes, helps us to grasp the logic of the laws of motion themselves. The assertion about the existence of forces and tension in the globes system holds, for Newton, *also* in the idealized case. The whole argument is epistemological, although for Newton, and especially his contemporaries, it has metaphysical/theological consequences.

The thought-experiments are thus analogical arguments, and are less abstract and metaphysical than they are sometimes taken to be. By treating both of Newton's arguments in much the same way, commentators have missed an interesting byway in the argumentation of the Scholium.[34]

Notes

[1] I shall offer a less 'metaphysical' and more literal reading of the arguments for the existence of absolute space as given in the Scholium to Definition VIII of *Principia.* That there should be a more epistemological rendering of these famous discussions is suggested by Tamny: ". . . whereas all previous arguments drawn from Newton concerning this claim have been purely metaphysical and theological, we have seen that there may well have been epistemological considerations as well." It is my intention to take up this suggestion. See Martin Tamny, "Newton, Creation and Perception", *Isis,* 70, 1979, p. 57, footnote. I shall also suggest that Newton's original argument has been idealized, and that the logic of the globes experiment in particular has been changed. When this changed logic is attributed to Newton, important aspects of his reasoning are overlooked, and a more literal reading of these discussions obscured.

[2] For example, see A. d'Abro, *The Evolution of Scientific Thought,* Dover Books, New York, 1950, especially Ch. X, p. 106 ff., and Ch. XXXVII p. 412 ff. Also John Losee, *A Historical Introduction to the Philosophy of Science,* Oxford U.P. 1971, p. 84 ff.

[3] This view that the space-time Scholium was not intended as a proof of absolute space, has been argued recently by Laymon: see R. Laymon, "Newton's Bucket Experiment", *Journal of the History of Philosophy,* October 1978.

[4] Newton, *Principia,* p. 10. All references to *Principia* will be from the translation by Andrew Motte of 1729, revised by F. Cajori, and published as *Sir Isaac Newton's Mathematical Principles of Natural Philosophy and His System of the World*; University of California Press, 1960; hereafter cited as *Principia.* See also M. Jammer, *Concepts of Space,* Harvard U.P. 1954.

[5] *Principia,* p. 10.

[6] *Principia,* p. 12.

[7] Newton states quite clearly here that the problem is to distinguish true and relative *motion,* given the existence of absolute space. The function of the thought-experiments is to show that any relational mechanics leaves out something important in the *description* of certain kinds of motion, giving indirect support to the idea of an absolute reference frame.

[8] Jammer, p. 104.

[9] Jammer, p. 106.

[10] For example, Sklar describes the globes experiment in what has become the accepted fashion, thus idealizing Newton's original case. The orthodox manner of considering the argument is based on what are taken as the initial conditions given in the Scholium, that is, something like: ". . . consider two globes, connected by a cord, in an otherwise empty universe." See L. Sklar, *Space, Time and Space-time,* California Press, 1974, p. 183. In fact, the implications of considering a universe empty except for the globes, concerns New-

ton's extensions of his argument: this particular case, as described by Sklar (and others) is what issues from the argument, rather than being an initial condition.

[11] Here I agree with Laymon's strategy, when he says that his interpretation of Newton ". . . has the advantage of being closer to the text and of avoiding the attribution of a mistake to Newton." Laymon, *op. cit.,* p. 405.

[12] The notion of force is really what the Scholium passages are about, and it is this notion—as a fundamental reality on the phenomenal level—which most embarrasses Leibniz in the correspondence with Clarke. Once Leibniz has admitted that it is the attribution to a body of force that determines whether it is really in motion, he has made a major concession to Newton's position. Leibniz's problems are intimately related to the different levels on which force and motion are realities in his system. On the phenomenal level Leibniz adheres to a mechanical explanation: on the other hand, force is something that a body possesses as part of its intrinsic metaphysical nature.

[13] Newton expresses no doubts about this example or its results: "There are no such forces in a circular motion purely relative, but in a true and absolute circular motion, they are greather or less, according to the quantity of the motion." See *Principia,* p. 10.

[14] Laymon suggests that the proper reading of 'ambient' in this connection is one which expresses Newton's anti-Cartesianism. See Laymon, p. 404.

[15] Newton regarded it as the simplest hypothesis to explain the observed facts of mechanics. Absolute motion is motion which cannot be regarded as relative to anything observable, such as the 'ambient bodies', or matter in general.

[16] *Principia,* p. 1. McGuire has pointed out the continuity in Newton's thinking on this, from the early treatise "De gravitatione" through *Principia* and beyond. See J. E. McGuire, "Newton on Place, Time and God: An Unpublished Source", *The British Journal for the History of Science,* Vol. 11, 38, 1978, p. 124ff.

[17] This concept of "differences" is made somewhat more explicit by MacLaurin: "In general, the actions of bodies upon each other depend not upon their *absolute* but *relative* motion; which is the difference of their *absolute* motions when they have the same direction, but their sum when they are moved in opposite directions." See Colin MacLaurin, *An Account of Sir Isaac Newton's Philosophical Discoveries*: in Four Books, London, 1748, Book II, p. 128. This is what Newton seems to have in mind in the following: "But if the earth also moves, the true and absolute motion of the body will arise, partly from the true motion of the earth, in im-

movable space, partly from the relative motion of the ship on the earth." *Principia,* p. 7. McLaurin seems to use the term 'force' interchangeably with 'absolute motions of bodies'.

[18] I shall pursue this line of argument, in spite of the fact that Newton refers to the two experiments in the reverse order here. It is much harder to make sense of the Scholium argument if a distinction between the purposes of the two thought-experiments is not made. If Newton does, as I believe, intend such a distinction to be made, this seems the likeliest place in which to identify the beginning of his argument. The distinction between these two lines of argument has been confused partly by the running together of passages N1, N2 and N4, and using them as justification for the bucket experiment, without the mediation of N3.

[19] "While the cord is untwisting itself, the vessel continues for some time in this motion; the surface of the water will at first be plain, and, as before the vessel began to move; but after that, the vessel, *by gradually communicating its motion to the water,* will make it begin sensibly to revolve, and recede by little and little from the middle, and ascend to the sides of the vessel, forming itself into a concave figure . . . and the swifter the motion becomes, the higher will the water rise, till at last, performing its revolutions in the same times with the vessel, it becomes relatively at rest in it." *Principia,* p. 10, italics mine.

[20] This is not surprising, since part of the experiment specifies the application of an external force to the bucket.

[21] *Principia,* p. 11. C. D. Broad suggested that since the term 'absolute space' nowhere appears in the premises of Newton's argument, it cannot occur in the conclusion. In fact, the term occurs neither as premise nor conclusion. The argument is about *force,* both as a cause of certain kinds of motion, and as an effect of such motions. See C. D. Broad, *Scientific Thought,* Kegan Paul, 1923, p. 100ff.

[22] Cf. Laymon, *op. cit.,* p. 408.

[23] If the problem is seen in this fashion—as a semantic dispute—it could be argued that Leibniz has the most consistent position. The initial conditions of the thought-experiment, viz. 'consider an empty universe . . .' would not pass unchallenged. This would, however, be for metaphysical rather than dynamic or 'semantic' reasons. Leibniz would appeal to his metaphysical principles of 'Perfection' and 'Sufficient Reason'.

[24] *Clarke's Fifth Reply,* H. G. Alexander, *The Leibniz-Clarke Correspondence,* Manchester University Press, 1970, p. 101.

[25] This complicates Leibniz's own theory of space in turn: see my "On the Metaphysics of Leibnizian Space and Time", *Studies in History and Philosophy of Science,* 13, No. 3, 1982.

[26] Cf. also Ian Hacking: "In *Principia* we are to imagine a universe with nothing in it but a bucket of water that starts to spin. This hypothesis can make no sense to a relativist, yet we know what would happen if it were true. Although the "spin" would not be visible, the water would gradually start to rise up the side of the bucket. Hence, even if there were nothing else in the world, there would be a difference between spin and rest, and so, said Newton, relativism is refuted." In: "The Identity of Indiscernibles", *The Journal of Philosophy,* May 1975, p. 249-250. This is a considerable distortion of the argument of the Scholium: Newton nowhere suggests that we should consider the bucket in an empty universe.

[27] *Principia,* p. 12.

[28] Such computations would enable us to establish the quantity of the motion, and its direction or determination, *i.e.* its vectorial value.

[29] Newton, in his 'postulate of isolation' opts for the former. Cf. D'Abro, *op. cit.,* p. 106ff.

[30] *Principia,* p. 12.

[31] Newton anticipated this in the early treatise "De gravitatione": ". . . who will imagine that the parts of the earth endeavour to recede from its centre on account of a force impressed only upon the heavens? Or is it not more agreeable to reason that when a force imparted to the heavense makes them endeavour to recede from the centre of revolution thus caused, they are for that reason the sole bodies properly and absolutely moved." See "De gravitatione et Aequipondo Fluidorum", in *Unpublished Scientific Papers of Isaac Newton,* ed. by A. R. Hall and M. B. Hall, Cambridge University Press, 1962.

[32] "But how we are to obtain the true motions from their causes, effects and apparent differences, and *vice versa,* how from their motions either true or apparent, we may come to the knowledge of their causes and effects, shall be explained more at large in the following treatise. For to this end it was that I composed it." *Principia,* p. 12.

[33] The Laws of Motion may be taken as idealizations of the motions of observable and measurable bodies. Such observations lead to the Laws of Motion, though the latter are not merely inductive generalizations from such observations of course.

[34] I would like to thank Peter Alexander for some very helpful comments on an earlier draft of this paper. I have tried to incorporate as many of his suggestions as I felt was possible, although the responsibility for the ideas expressed here remains, of course, my own.

Betty Jo Teeter Dobbs   (essay date 1991)

SOURCE: "Isaac Newton, Philosopher by Fire," in *The Janus Faces of Genius: The Role of Alchemy in Newton's Thought,* Cambridge University Press, 1991, pp. 1-18.

[*In the following essay, Dobbs challenges critics who have doubted or suppressed the influence of alchemy on Newton's scientific thought.*]

Introduction

Isaac Newton studied alchemy from about 1668 until the second or third decade of the eighteenth century. He combed the literature of alchemy, compiling voluminous notes and even transcribing entire treatises in his own hand. Eventually he drafted treatises of his own, filled with references to the older literature. The manuscript legacy of his scholarly endeavor is very large and represents a huge commitment of his time, but to it one must add the record of experimentation. Each brief and often abruptly cryptic laboratory report hides behind itself untold hours with hand-built furnaces of brick, with crucible, with mortar and pestle, with the apparatus of distillation, and with charcoal fires: experimental sequences sometimes ran for weeks, months, or even years. As the seventeenth-century epithet "philosopher by fire" distinguished the serious, philosophical alchemist from the empiric "puffer" or the devious charlatan or the amateur "chymist," so may one use the term to characterize Isaac Newton. Surely this man earned that title if ever any did.

Since my first monograph on this subject appeared in 1975[1] Newton's alchemy has held a prominent position in historiographic debates of some centrality to the history and philosophy of science. Even though Newton's interest in alchemy had often been noted before and had indeed generated a considerable body of scholarly comment,[2] public recognition of it was forced to a new level after 1975 as the full extent of Newton's commitment to alchemical pursuits was made more and more explicit in reviews,[3] biographical works,[4] articles,[5] and definitive studies of Newton's library.[6]

Yet even so there has remained the possibility of denying the significance and importance of Newton's alchemy for his great achievements in mathematics, physics, cosmology, and methodology. I argued in 1975 that Newton's alchemy constituted one of the pillars supporting his mature scientific edifice.[7] Nevertheless, since Newton's reputation as one of the founders of modern science rests securely upon achievements in areas of thought still recognized as scientific, and since alchemy has, at least since the eighteenth century, been rejected from the canon of science as hopelessly retrograde, "occult," and false, some scholars have been reluctant to accept the validity of that notion.[8]

Newton's *Philosophiae naturalis principia mathematica,* first published in 1687 and foundational to many later developments in science, has seemed to most readers to be the epitome of austere rationality, and the writer of that remarkable work on "The Mathematical Principles of Natural Philosophy" continues to seem to some of its readers to be a very poor candidate for the epithet "philosopher by fire." Since among Newton scholars I. Bernard Cohen's knowledge of Newton's *Principia* and the manuscript remains associated with it,[9] and since Cohen has been outspoken on that point, one may take his objections as those requiring most serious response. Cohen's detailed examination of the proposition that alchemy made some difference to Newton's science came in a lengthy essay published in 1982.[10] The issue has focused on the origin of Newton's ideas on attractive forces, as Cohen pointed out. For although an attractive force of gravity appeared in the *Principia* and was fundamental to later Newtonian dynamics, ideas of attraction (operating either between small particles of matter or between gross bodies) hardly constituted orthodox mechanical philosophy in 1687. Attractive force smacked of the "occult" to the first generation of mechanical philosophers, writing thirty to forty years before Newton, and they had been careful to substitute for attraction the principles of "impact physics" in which *apparent* attractions (magnetic, electrical, gravitational) were explained by the mechanical encounter of very fine and imperceptible particles of a hypothetical aether with the larger particles of matter. Newton's reintroduction of attraction in the *Principia,* and his dismissal there of an aethereal mechanism as an explanation of gravity, had seemed to Westfall and myself a convincing argument for the influence of alchemy on Newton's thought, for much alchemical literature concerns itself with non-mechanical "active principles" that are conceptually similar to Newton's gravity. Cohen disagreed. Arguing that no documents seemed to exist in which Newton took attractive forces under consideration before 1679-80, when Robert Hooke introduced Newton to a dynamical analysis predicated upon inertia and an attractive central force, Cohen concluded that Newton's subsequent departure from orthodox mechanism derived from his own "style" of mathematical abstraction rather than from the conceptual influence of alchemical "active principles" upon him. Cohen in fact insisted that Newton was able to produce his great work of positive science only by putting aside his alchemical and Hermetic interests temporarily and rising above them.

I have challenged Cohen's argument in my review of the book in which it appeared[11] because his position seemed to be based on the a priori assumption that alchemy could never, by its very nature, make a contribution to science. To accept the premise that alchemy could not do so is to prejudge the historical question of whether it did do so in Newton's case, which is after all the point at issue. Furthermore, Newton's alchemical papers, which were not included in Cohen's analysis, document Newton's interest in alchemical "active principles" for an entire decade before his correspondence with Hooke. But while the presence of "active principles" in Newton's alchemical papers, as well as in the literature of alchemy upon which those papers were based, is hardly to be denied at this stage in the debate, it now seems rather less likely to me that Newton transferred the concept of the "active principle" directly from his alchemical studies to his new formulation of gravity, at least not at first, though he may finally have done so. Rather, as will be argued in detail in the following chapters, all issues of passivity and activity, of mechanical and nonmechanical forces, were enmeshed for Newton in a philosophical/religious complex one can only now begin to grasp. Although Newton's first encounter with attractive and "active" principles may well have been in his alchemical study, his application of such ideas to the force of gravity was almost certainly mediated by several other considerations. And because of Newton's important position in the rise of modern science, and because of the importance of the doctrine of gravity as an "active principle" within his own science, one must strive to understand them all.

My studies since 1975 have yielded hints that Newton was concerned from the first in his alchemical work to find evidence for the existence of a vegetative principle operating in the natural world, a principle that he understood to be the secret, universal, animating spirit of which the alchemists spoke. He saw analogies between the vegetable principle and light, and between the alchemical process and the work of the Deity at the time of creation. It was by the use of this active vegetative principle that God constantly molded the universe to His providential design, producing all manner of generations, resurrections, fermentations, and vegetation. In short, it was the action of the secret animating spirit of alchemy that kept the universe from being the sort of closed mechanical system for which Descartes had argued.[12] These themes will be discussed in detail in the chapters to follow as a way of searching out the relationships of alchemical modes of thought to the general concerns of Newton and his contemporaries.

Nevertheless, the primary goal here is the larger one indicated by the subtitle of this book: the role of alchemy in Newton's thought. Newton stood at the beginning of our modern scientific era and put his stamp upon it irrevocably. He may be seen as a gatekeeper, a Janus figure, for one of his faces still gazes in our direction. But only one of them. Like Janus, who symbolized the beginning of the new year but also the end of the old one, Newton looked forward in time but backward as well. It is the vision seen by the eyes of that second face that I pursue by examining the details of his alchemical labors. It is possible to grasp that vision yet not stop there.

I do not assume the irrelevancy of Newton's pursuit of an ancient, occult wisdom to those great syntheses of his that mark the foundation of modern science. The Janus-like faces of Isaac Newton were after all the production of a single mind, and their very bifurcation may be more of a modern optical illusion than an actuality. Newton's mind was equipped with a certain fundamental assumption, common to his age, from which his various lines of investigation flowed naturally: the assumption of the unity of Truth.[13] True knowledge was all in some sense a knowledge of God; Truth was one, its unity guaranteed by the unity of God. Reason and revelation were not in conflict but were supplementary. God's attributes were recorded in the written Word but were also directly reflected in the nature of nature.[14] Natural philosophy thus had immediate theological meaning for Newton and he deemed it capable of revealing to him those aspects of the divine never recorded in the Bible or the record of which had been corrupted by time and human error. By whatever route one approached Truth, the goal was the same. Experimental discovery and revelation; the productions of reason, speculation, or mathematics; the cryptic, coded messages of the ancients in myth, prophecy, or alchemical tract—all, if correctly interpreted, found their reconciliation in the infinite unity and majesty of the Deity. In Newton's conviction of the unity of Truth and its ultimate source in the divine one may find the fountainhead of all his diverse studies.

Newton's methodology

One cannot agree with Cohen's thesis, then, that an essential part of Newton's methodology was deliberately to create mathematical models as a first step.[15] Mathematics was only one avenue to Truth, and though mathematics was a powerful tool in his hands, Newton's methodology was much broader than that implied by the creation of mathematical models, and Newton's goal was incomparably more vast than the discovery of the "mathematical principles of natural philosophy." Newton wished to penetrate to the divine principles beyond the veil of nature, and beyond the veils of human record and received revelation as well. His goal was the knowledge of God, and for achieving that goal he marshaled the evidence from every source available to him: mathematics, experiment, observation, reason, revelation, historical record, myth, the tattered remnants of ancient wisdom. With the post-Newtonian diminution of interest in divinity and height-

ened interest in nature for its own sake, scholars have too often read the Newtonian method narrowly, selecting from the breadth of his studies only mathematics, experiment, observation, and reason as the essential components of his scientific method. For a science of nature, a balanced use of those approaches to knowledge suffices, or so it has come to seem since Newton's death, and one result of the restricted interests of modernity has been to look askance at Newton's biblical, chronological, and alchemical studies: to consider his pursuit of the *prisca sapientia* as irrelevant. None of those was irrelevant to Newton, for his goal was considerably more ambitious than a knowledge of nature. His goal was Truth, and for that he utilized every possible resource.

"Modeling" in the modern sense is incompatible with the pursuit of Truth in any case. To create a speculative system or to devise a mathematical scheme that will "save the phenomena" carries relativistic overtones. A modern scientist may readily admit, with a metaphorical shrug, that while we do not know whether the theoretical superstructure of our science is True, that really does not matter because our science is self-consistent and it works, accounting for known phenomena and predicting new ones. If new phenomena appear that require incorporation, or if a theory predicts falsely, our science will be adjusted, but that is a matter of no great moment. After the adjustment we will have a better science, but we will still not have Truth. As Quinn has convincingly argued, that was not Newton's attitude.[16] Newton may profitably be compared to such twentieth-century thinkers as G. E. Moore and Bertrand Russell, both intent on Truth, neither skeptical of human capacity to obtain it. In fact both expected to save humanity from skepticism and usher in a millennium. So did Newton.

To save humanity from skepticism was the ambition of many a thinker in the seventeenth century. Quinn reports a serious conversation between Descartes and John Dury in which it was agreed that the emergence of skepticism constituted the profound crisis of their period and that a way needed to be found to counter it with epistemological certainty. Descartes chose mathematics, Dury the interpretation of biblical prophecy, as the most promising response to the crisis.[17] The point, of course, is that no one knew then what would ultimately be established as effective. A modern thinker may be inclined to assume that Descartes chose the better part, but in fact the natural philosophy that he claimed to have established with mathematical certainty was soon overthrown by Newton's. Descartes's mathematico-deductive method was not adequately balanced by experiment, observation, and induction; Newton's was.

Perhaps the most important element in Newton's methodological contribution was that of balance, for no *single* approach to knowledge ever proved to be effective in settling the epistemological crisis of the Renaissance and early modern periods. Newton had perhaps been convinced of the necessity of methodological balance by Henry More, who had worked out such a procedure within the context of the interpretation of prophecy.[18] Since every single approach to knowledge was subject to error, a more certain knowledge was to be obtained by utilizing each approach to correct the other: the senses to be rectified by reason, reason to be rectified by revelation, and so forth. The self-correcting character of Newton's procedure is entirely similar to More's and constitutes the superiority of Newton's method over that of earlier natural philosophers, for others had certainly used the separate elements of reason, mathematics, experiment, and observation before him.

But Newton's method was not limited to the balancing of those approaches to knowledge that still constitute the elements of modern scientific methodology, nor has one any reason to assume that he would deliberately have limited himself to those familiar approaches even if he had been prescient enough to realize that those were all the future would consider important. Because his goal was a Truth that encompassed not only the "mathematical principles of natural philosophy" but divinity as well, Newton's balancing procedure included also the knowledge he had garnered from theology, revelation, alchemy, history, and the wise ancients. It has been difficult to establish this fact because Newton's papers largely reflect a single-minded pursuit of each and every one of his diverse studies, as if in each one of them lay the only road to knowledge. When he wrote alchemy, he wrote as an alchemist, as Sherwood Taylor long ago observed.[19] But when he wrote chemistry, his concepts conformed to those of contemporary chemists.[20] When he wrote mathematics, no one doubted him to be a pure mathematician.[21] When he adopted the mechanical philosophy, he devised hypothetical aethereal mechanisms with the best.[22] When he undertook to interpret prophecy, his attention to the meaning of the minutest symbol implied that nothing else mattered.[23] In only a few of his papers may one observe his attempt to balance one apparently isolated line of investigation with another.

The characteristic single-mindedness reflected by each set of Newton's papers has led to the modern misunderstandings of Newton's methodology, for study of any one set may lead to a limited view of Newton's interests, goals, and methods, and the papers have all too often been divided up into categories that mesh more or less well with twentieth-century academic interests. Only Westfall's recent prize-winning biography of Newton has attempted to deal with all of the papers,[24] and even there no radical reevaluation of Newton's methodology was undertaken. To Westfall, the most important part of Newton's work still seemed to be that directed toward topics that continue to be of central importance to modern science: mathematics, mathematical physics, and scientific methodology. Through the lens of the preconceptions of modern scientific culture, one still sees primarily a Newton who founded modern science.

He did do that, of course, but the historian may ask other questions and construct or reconstruct other lenses. When one sees only the Newton who founded modern science, serious historiographic problems arise, and one is left with the difficulty of explaining, or explaining away, the masses of papers Newton left behind that are focused quite otherwise. My own work on Newton began with one very questionable advantage—questionably advantageous in the opinion of most scholars, that is, because the starting point was Newton's alchemy. Newton's alchemy had almost always been considered the most peripheral of his many studies, the one furthest removed from his important work in mathematics, optics, and celestial dynamics. Most students of Newton's work preferred to ignore the alchemy, or, if not to ignore it, then to explain it away as far as possible. But one may, perhaps pardonably, remain unconvinced that a mind of the caliber of Newton's would have lavished so much attention upon any topic without a serious purpose and without a serious expectation of learning something significant from his study of it. Indeed, working one's way through Newton's alchemical papers, one becomes increasingly aware of the meticulous scholarship and the careful quantitative experimentation Newton had devoted to alchemical questions over a period of many years. Clearly, *he* thought his alchemical work was important. So one is forced to question what it meant to him: if Newton thought alchemy was an important part of his life's work, then what was that life's work? Was it possible that Newton had a unity of purpose, an overarching goal, that encompassed *all* of his various fields of study? The lens that I have attempted to reconstruct, then, is the lens through which Newton viewed himself.

In certain ways Newton's intellectual development is best understood as a product of the late Renaissance, a time when the revival of antiquity had conditioned the thinkers of Western Europe to look backward for Truth. Thanks to the revival of ancient thought, to humanism, to the Reformation, and to developments in medicine/science/natural philosophy prior to or contemporary with his period of most intense study (1660-84), Newton had access to an unusually large number of systems of thought. Each system had its own set of guiding assumptions, so in that particular historical milieu some comparative judgment between and among competing systems was perhaps inevitable. But such judgments were difficult to make without a culturally conditioned consensus on standards of evaluation, which was precisely what was lacking. The formalized skepticism of Pyrrhonism had been revived along with other aspects of antiquity, but in addition one may trace an increase in a less formal but rather generalized skepticism at least from the beginning of the sixteenth century, as competing systems laid claim to Truth and denied the claims of their rivals. As a consequence, Western Europe underwent something of an epistemological crisis in the sixteenth and seventeenth centuries. Among so many competing systems, how was one to achieve certainty? Could the human being attain Truth?[25]

But Newton was not a skeptic, and in fact his assumption of the unity of Truth constituted one answer to the problem of skepticism. Not only did Newton respect the idea that Truth was accessible to the human mind, but also he was very much inclined to accord to several systems of thought the right to claim access to some aspect of the Truth. For Newton, then, the many competing systems he encountered tended to appear complementary rather than competitive. The mechanical philosophy that has so often been seen as the necessary prelude to the Newtonian revolution probably did not hold a more privileged or dominant position in Newton's mind than did any other system. The mechanical philosophy was one system among many that Newton thought to be capable of yielding at least a partial Truth.

Blinded by the brilliance of the laws of motion, the laws of optics, the calculus, the concept of universal gravitation, the rigorous experimentation, the methodological success, we have seldom wondered whether the discovery of the laws of nature was all Newton had in mind. We have often missed the religious nature of his quest and taken the stunningly successful by-products for his primary goal. But Newton wished to look through nature to see God, and it was not false modesty when in old age he said he had been only like a boy at the seashore picking up now and again a smoother pebble or a prettier shell than usual while the great ocean of Truth lay all undiscovered before him.[26]

Newton's quest was immeasurably large; it generated questions starkly different from those of modern science. For him, the most important questions were never answered, but in reconstructing them lies our best chance of grasping the focused nature of Newton's work within the comprehensive range of his interests. His questions were not ours. They encompassed fields of knowledge that to us seem to have no relevant points of contact.

But that there was a unity and a consistency in Newton's quest will be a central theme of this book. Evidence for the unity emerges when his alchemical papers are considered in conjunction with his other literary remains, not pushed aside with an a priori assumption of irrelevance. The same may be said for the chang-

es in Newton's explanatory "mechanisms" over the long decades of his search. Although those changes have often appeared erratic and inconsistent to later scholars, from the viewpoint of Newton's primary goal the consistency appears. The consistency lies in his overwhelming religious concern to establish the relationship between Creator and creation. The pattern of change results from the slow fusion and selective disentanglement of essentially antithetical systems: Neoplatonism, Cartesian mechanical philosophy, Stoicism; chemistry, alchemy, atomism; biblical, patristic, and pagan religions. I shall argue that it was precisely where his different lines of investigation met, where he tried to synthesize their discrepancies into a more fundamental unity, when he attempted to fit partial Truth to partial Truth, that he achieved his greatest insights.

Not only was Newton's goal a unified system of God and nature, it was also his conviction that God *acted* in the world. Though Newton avoided most hints of pantheism and though his Deity remained wholly "other" and transcendental, Newton had no doubt that the world was created by divine fiat and that the Creator retained a perpetual involvement with and control over His creation. The remote and distant God of the deists, a Deity that never interacted with the world but left it to operate without divine guidance, was antithetical to Newton. Newton's God acted in time and with time, and since He was so transcendent, He required for His interaction with the created world at least one intermediary agent to put His will into effect. Just such an agent was the alchemical spirit, charged with animating and shaping the passive matter of the universe.

But was the alchemical spirit God's only agent? Newton's conviction that God acted in creating and maintaining the world never wavered, but his explanations of God's manner of acting underwent drastic and multiple revisions as he examined certain questions. Is the agent of vegetation the same as the agent of cosmogony? Is that agent light, or very similar to light? Is there a different, distinctive spirit for prophetic inspiration? How much activity does God manage by "mechanical principles" and how much requires "active principles"? Is gravity mechanical or active, and will it play a role in the final consummation of all things promised by Scripture? May not one distinguish two sorts of chemistry, the one mechanical and the other vegetative and demonstrative of God's nonmechanical powers? Will the rediscovery of the pure, potent fire that is the ultimate secret of the active alchemical principle lead to the restoration of true religion and the ushering in of the millennium?

Alchemical documentation

That alchemy played a role in Newton's thought is no longer to be denied; one can now trace its contributions with some exactitude. Any hope, however, of reconciling Newton's alchemical work with his recognized achievements in mathematics, optics, and celestial dynamics must first be launched from a firm textual framework of his own alchemical manuscripts, within which framework one may readily see the overriding importance of the alchemical spirit to him.

Newton's alchemical papers have been more widely scattered than any other set of his manuscripts.[27] Major collections of them exist at King's College, Cambridge, at Babson College, Babson Park, Massachusetts, at the Smithsonian Institution in Washington, D.C., at the Jewish National and University Library in Jerusalem, and at University Library, Cambridge. Other items have been acquired by a variety of British and American institutions: the British Library, Clifton College, St. Andrews University, Trinity College (Cambridge), the Royal Society, and the Bodleian Library; Stanford University, Yale University, Harvard University, the University of Texas, the University of Wisconsin, the Massachusetts Institute of Technology, Columbia University, and the University of Chicago. The Sotheby sale of 1936 that dispersed Newton's alchemical papers left some in the hands of private collectors; others have disappeared.

Of necessity one must be selective here in the alchemical documentation for this study, for a more extensive use of Newton's alchemical papers could swamp the book in esoteric detail without accomplishing its primary goal of relating alchemical themes to Newton's developing thought in other areas. What is needed is a series of carefully dated anchor points within the alchemical corpus from which one may survey the larger issues. For that purpose the following manuscripts will serve well.

From the decade of the 1660s I have chosen two radically different items that in themselves mark Newton's transition from exoteric to esoteric chemistry. The first,[28] a practical chemical dictionary of about 7,000 words that seems to have been completed in about 1667, offers specific definitions that sometimes tell what Newton thought about a substance or a process before he began to read alchemy. The second,[29] a brief series of alchemical propositions, was written about 1669. It represents one of Newton's earliest attempts to order the chaotic alchemical material he was encountering, and it adumbrates themes of continuing interest. Extensive selections from it appear below. The principal discovery from these two documents is of Newton's full acceptance of a living, "vegetable" chemistry, identifiable as alchemy, distinct from the more mechanical sort of chemistry. He was to make the distinction quite explicit early in the 1670s.

In the decade of the 1670s Newton wrote a treatise of about 4,500 words, **"Of Natures obvious laws & processes in vegatation."**[30] Probably completed before 1672 or during that year, this document is an invaluable conceptual source for the entire decade and beyond, and the entire English section of the treatise is transcribed in Appendix A. It tells more about vegetation, including mineral vegetation, and it leads into the closely related topics of putrefaction and fermentation. One must refer to it again and again. For the second half of the 1670s I point once more to a manuscript of about 1,200 words, the "Clavis" or "Key,"[31] in which Newton originally seemed to me to be reporting some experimental alchemical success. This document has already been published in full, with some hesitation, as Newton's own,[32] but a non-Newtonian source for it has recently been located among the papers of Robert Boyle.[33] Nevertheless, even though one now knows for certain that Newton did not compose the document, the basic alchemical process it describes continues to appear in Newton's later papers, and so the "Key" continues to provide a useful point of reference. The evidence suggests that Newton accepted, and continued to accept, the validity of the experimental report in this document, and that he used it quite literally as a "key" to unlock the secrets of other alchemical processes.[34]

A commentary by Newton on the *Emerald Tablet* of Hermes Trismegistus[35] brings one into the decade of the 1680s. About 1,000 words in length and probably written between 1680 and 1684, this manuscript shows filiation with other papers written before the **Principia** of 1687. It may be found in Appendix B and it will give some curious insights into the Newton of the early 1680s regarding alchemy and cosmogony. Themes from the pre-**Principia** period continue, however, into the latter part of the decade, as the next selection shows: "Out of La Lumiere sortant des Tenebres."[36] "Out of La Lumiere," to be found in Appendix C, consists of abstracts, translated by Newton, from a book published in 1687.[37] Since the material is abstracted, one may assume that it comprises what Newton found important in the book and in places one does find here a remarkably clear exposition of late seventeenth-century alchemical theory, especially as it delineates the themes of vegetation and divine cosmogonic action.

For the decade of the 1690s I have chosen first of all a set of papers less theoretical in orientation: **"Experiments & Observations Dec. 1692 & Jan 1692/3"**[38] When Newton's scientific papers were presented to the University of Cambridge in the nineteenth century, his chemical/alchemical notebook and a number of loose sheets were included. The present manuscript was among the loose sheets and had been precisely dated in the title by Newton himself. In fact, later entries toward the end of the manuscript, also dated by Newton, carry it forward to June 1693. The complete manuscript is reproduced in Appendix D. In it one will find the clearest sort of emphasis upon mineral fermentations, showing Newton's continued interest in that topic even after a quarter of a century. One will also find in it an experimental record of his search for the "fermental virtue" in metallic reactions that is related to the "Key" of the late 1670s and also to the experimental procedures he recommends in the next manuscript, the **"Praxis."**[39] The **"Praxis"** is a formal treatise, reproduced in Appendix E (omitting earlier drafts of the treatise that also survive with this set of papers). It was probably written about the middle of the 1690s, which would place it at or near the end of Newton's serious experimental alchemical work. Although he continued to study and to rework his papers, there is no evidence that he performed alchemical experiments after he left Cambridge for London and the Royal Mint in 1696. The final, climactic synthesis of the **"Praxis,"** however, is thoroughly demonstrative of the continuity in Newton's alchemical concerns, even ten years after the writing of the **Principia.**

These eight manuscripts then—two from each of the four decades in which Newton was most intensely involved with alchemy—provide the framework for the present study. Nevertheless, it will be necessary to draw upon other papers from Newton's alchemical hoard occasionally, either to corroborate major points or to mention specific items not contained in those selected. Such additional material will be cited as required. The interested reader is also reminded that previous publications, which inform the present work, were based on other sets of Newton's alchemical papers, and that much particular and specific information is available there: on all the pre-1680 alchemical manuscripts in the Keynes Collection, King's College, Cambridge;[40] on a series of papers and annotations on the regimens of the great work of alchemy that spans almost all of Newton's alchemical career.[41]

Prospectus

This book is predicated upon the conviction that to Newton himself all his diverse studies constituted a unified plan for obtaining Truth, and it is organized around a religious interpretation of Newton's alchemy, but more than that, a religious interpretation of all his work.[42] It is in Newton's belief in the unity of Truth, guaranteed by the unity and majesty of God, that one may find a way to reunite his many brilliant facets, which, however well polished, now remain incomplete fragments. It is my hope thus to make him again into one whole and historical human being.

Notes

[1] B. J. T. Dobbs, *The Foundations of Newton's Alchemy, or "The Hunting of the Greene Lyon"* (Cambridge University Press, 1975).

[2] The historiography of Newton's alchemy prior to 1975 is explored in ibid., pp. 6-20.

[3] See especially the following reviews of my book: P. M. Rattansi, "Newton as chymist," *Science 192* (No. 4240, 14 May 1976), 689-90; idem, "Last of the magicians," *Times Higher Education Supplement,* June 1976; Philip Morrison, *Scientific American 235* (August 1976), 113-15; Richard S. Westfall, *Journal of the History of Medicine and Allied Sciences 31* (1976), 473-4; Kathleen Ahonen, *Annals of Science 33* (1976), 615-17; Henry Guerlac, *Journal of Modern History 49* (1977), 130-3; Derek T. Whiteside, "From his claw the Greene Lyon," *Isis 68* (1977), 116-21; A. Rupert Hall, "Newton as alchemist," *Nature 266* (28 April 1977), 78; Karin Figala, "Newton as alchemist," *History of Science 15* (1977), 102-37; P. E. Spargo, *Ambix 24* (1977), 175-6; Marie Boas Hall, *British Journal for the History of Science 10* (1977), 262-4; Allen G. Debus, *Centaurus 21* (1977), 315-16; Margaret C. Jacob, *The Eighteenth Century: A Current Bibliography,* n.s. *1* (1975, published 1978), 345-7.

[4] Richard S. Westfall, *Never at Rest. A Biography of Isaac Newton* (Cambridge University Press, 1980); Gale E. Christianson, *In the Presence of the Creator. Isaac Newton and His Times* (New York: The Free Press; London: Collier Macmillan, 1984).

[5] Richard S. Westfall, "The role of alchemy in Newton's career," in *Reason, Experiment and Mysticism in the Scientific Revolution,* ed. by M. L. Righini Bonelli and William R. Shea (New York: Science History Publications, 1975), pp. 189-232; idem, "Isaac Newton's *Index Chemicus,*" *Ambix 22* (1975), 174-85; idem, "The changing world of the Newtonian industry," *Journal of the History of Ideas 37* (1976), 175-84; B. J. T. Dobbs, "Newton's copy of *Secrets Reveal'd* and the regimens of the work," *Ambix 26* (1979), 145-69; Richard S. Westfall, "The influence of alchemy on Newton," in *Science, Pseudo-Science and Society,* ed. by Marsha P. Hanen, Margaret J. Osler, and Robert G. Weyant (Waterloo, Ontario: Wilfrid Laurier University Press, 1980), pp. 145-69; B. J. T. Dobbs, "Newton's alchemy and his theory of matter," *Isis 73* (1982), 511-28; idem, "Newton's 'Clavis': new evidence on its dating and significance," *Ambix 29* (1982), 190-202; idem, "Newton's *Commentary* on *The Emerald Tablet* of Hermes Trismegistus: its scientific and theological significance," in *Hermeticism and the Renaissance. Intellectual History and the Occult in Early Modern Europe,* ed. by Ingrid Merkel and Allen G. Debus (Folger Books; Washington, D.C.: The Folger Shakespeare Library; London: Associated University Presses, 1988), pp. 182-91; idem, "Alchemische Kosmogonie und arianische Theologie bei Isaac Newton," tr. by Christoph Meinel, *Wolfenbütteler Forschungern, 32* (1986), 137-50; idem, "Newton and Stoicism," *The Southern Journal of Philosophy 23 Supplement* (1985), 109-23; idem, "Newton's alchemy and his 'active principle' of gravitation," in *Newton's Scientific and Philosophical Legacy,* ed. by P. B. Scheuer and G. Debrock

(International Archives of the History of Ideas, 123; Dordrecht: Kluwer Academic Publishers, 1988), pp. 55-80.

[6] John Harrison, *The Library of Isaac Newton* (Cambridge University Press, 1978); Richard S. Westfall, "Alchemy in Newton's library," *Ambix 31* (1984), 97-101.

[7] Richard S. Westfall, *Force in Newton's Physics. The Science of Dynamics in the Seventeenth Century* (London: Macdonald; New York: American Elsevier, 1971), esp. pp. 323-423; Dobbs, *Foundations* (1, n. 1), pp. 210-13.

[8] Whiteside, "From his claw" (1, n. 3); I. Bernard Cohen, *The Newtonian Revolution. With Illustrations of the Transformation of Scientific Ideas* (Cambridge University Press, 1980), p. 10.

[9] Isaac Newton, *Isaac Newton's Philosophiae naturalis principia mathematica. The Third Edition (1726) with Variant Readings. Assembled and Edited by Alexandre Koyré and I. Bernard Cohen with the Assistance of Anne Whitman* (2 vols.; Cambridge, MA: Harvard University Press, 1972); I. Bernard Cohen, *Introduction to Newton's "Principia"* (Cambridge, MA: Harvard University Press; Cambridge University Press, 1971); Cohen, *Newtonian Revolution* (1, n. 8).

[10] I. Bernard Cohen, "The *Principia,* universal gravitation, and the 'Newtonian style,' in relation to the Newtonian revolution in science: notes on the occasion of the 250th anniversary of Newton's death," in *Contemporary Newtonian Research,* ed. by Zev Bechler (Studies in the History of Modern Science, 9; Dordrecht: D. Reidel, 1982), pp. 21-108.

[11] Dobbs, *Isis 74* (1983), 609-10.

[12] See my articles cited earlier (1, n. 5).

[13] For a general statement on Renaissance conceptions of this problem, see Paul Oskar Kristeller, *Renaissance Thought and Its Sources,* ed. by Michael Mooney (New York: Columbia University Press, 1979), pp. 196-210; for views contemporary with Newton, see Arthur Quinn, *The Confidence of British Philosophers. An Essay in Historical Narrative* (Studies in the History of Christian Thought, Vol. 17; ed. by Heiko A. Oberman, in cooperation with Henry Chadwick, Edward A. Dowey, Jaroslav Pelikan, Brian Tierney, and E. David Willis; Leiden: E. J. Brill, 1977), esp. pp. 8-20.

[14] Here Newton stood within the mainstream of biblical tradition. See especially Psalm 19, which opens with the statement that "The heavens declare the glory of God; and the firmament sheweth his handywork," and Romans 1:20, where Paul declares, "For the invis-ible things of him [God] from the creation of the world are clearly seen, being understood by the things that are made, *even* his eternal power and Godhead. . . ." I am indebted to Mr. William Elliott for discussion and references on this point: personal communication, 1 April 1987.

[15] Cohen, *Newtonian Revolution* (1, n. 8), passim.

[16] Arthur Quinn, "On reading Newton apocalyptically," in *Millenarianism and Messianism in English Literature and Thought 1650-1800. Clark Library Lectures 1981-82,* ed. by Richard H. Popkin (Publications from the Clark Library Professorship, UCLA, No. 10; Leiden: E. J. Brill, 1988), pp. 176-92; idem, *Confidence of British Philosophers* (1, n. 13).

[17] Quinn, "On reading Newton" (1, n. 16), p. 179.

[18] Richard H. Popkin, "The third force in seventeenth-century philosophy: Scepticism, science, and biblical prophecy," *Nouvelle République des Lettres 1* (1983), 35-63.

[19] Frank Sherwood Taylor, "An alchemical work of Sir Isaac Newton," *Ambix 5* (1956), 59-84.

[20] B. J. T. Dobbs, "Conceptual problems in Newton's early chemistry: a preliminary study," in Religion, *Science, and Worldview. Essays in Honor of Richard S. Westfall,* ed. by Margaret J. Osler and Paul Lawrence Farber (Cambridge University Press, 1985), pp. 3-32.
[21] Derek T. Whiteside, "Isaac Newton: birth of a mathematician," *Notes and Records of the Royal Society of London 19* (1964), 53-62.

[22] J. E. McGuire and Martin Tamny, *Certain Philosophical Questions: Newton's Trinity Notebook* (Cambridge University Press, 1983), pp. 362-5, 426-31.

[23] See, for example, Newton's notes in his copy of Henry More, *A Plain and Continued Exposition Of the several Prophecies or Divine Visions of the Prophet Daniel, Which have or may concern the People of God, whether Jew or Christian; Whereunto is annexed a Threefold Appendage, Touching Three main Points, the First, Relating to Daniel, the other Two to the Apocalypse* (London: printed by M. F. for Walter Kettilby, at the Bishop's-Head in Saint Paul's Church-Yard, 1681); Harrison, *Library* (1, n. 6), item 1115, p. 196; now BS 1556 M 67 P 5 1681 copy 2, Bancroft Library, University of California, Berkeley.

[24] Westfall, *Never at Rest* (1, n. 4).

[25] Richard H. Popkin, *The History of Skepticism from Erasmus to Spinoza* (Berkeley: University of California Press, 1979); Charles G. Nauert, Jr., *Agrippa and the Crisis of Renaissance Thought* (Illinois Studies in

the Social Sciences, No. 55; Urbana: University of Illinois Press, 1965); Walter Pagel, *Paracelsus: An Introduction to Philosophical Medicine in the Era of the Renaissance* (Basel: Karger, 1958); idem, *Joan Baptista van Helmont. Reformer of Science and Medicine* (Cambridge University Press, 1982); Kristeller, *Renaissance Thought* (1, n. 13); Ernst Cassirer, *The Platonic Renaissance in England,* tr. by James P. Pettegrove (Austin: University of Texas Press, 1953); John Redwood, *Reason, Ridicule and Religion. The Age of Enlightenment in England 1660-1750* (London: Thames and Hudson, 1976). For this last reference, and for discussions on Arianism (to be considered in later chapters), I am indebted to Mary Louise McIntyre.

[26] Cf. David Brewster, *Memoirs of the Life, Writings, and Discoveries of Sir Isaac Newton* (2 vols.; Edinburgh: Thomas Constable and Co.; Boston: Little, Brown, and Co., 1855), vol. II, 407-8.

[27] A complete listing of chemical/alchemical papers that were retained by the family until 1936, when they were sold at auction, can be found in *Catalogue of the Newton Papers Sold by Order of the Viscount Lymington to Whom They Have descended from Catherine Conduitt, Viscountess Lymington, Great-niece of Sir Isaac Newton* (London: Sotheby and Co., 1936), pp. 1-19, and in Dobbs, *Foundations* (1, n. 1), pp. 235-48. These papers, as well as others of a chemical/alchemical nature, primarily experimental, are also listed in *A Catalogue of the Portsmouth Collection of Books and Papers written by or belonging to Sir Isaac Newton, the scientific portion of which has been presented by the Earl of Portsmouth to the University of Cambridge. Drawn up by the Syndicate appointed the 6th November, 1872* (Cambridge University Press, 1888), pp. 11-24.

[28] Sotheby lot no. 16; Bodleian Library, Oxford, MS Don. b. 15; Dobbs, "Conceptual problems" (1, n. 20).

[29] Sotheby lot. no 1; King's College, Cambridge, Keynes MS 12A.

[30] Sotheby lot no. 113; Dibner Library of the History of Science and Technology of the Smithsonian Institution Libraries, Washington, D.C., Dibner Collection MSS 1031 B (formerly Burndy MS 16). Cf. *Manuscripts of the Dibner Collection in the Dibner Library of the History of Science and Technology of the Smithsonian Institution Libraries* (Smithsonian Institution Libraries, Research Guide No. 5; Washington, D.C.: Smithsonian Institution Libraries, 1985), p. 7 (No. 80) and Plate VII (facing p. 46); B. J. T. Dobbs, "Newton manuscripts at the Smithsonian Institution," *Isis 68* (1977), 105-7. The entire manuscript is reproduced in facsimile as an appendix in B. J. T. Dobbs, *Alchemical Death & Resurrection: the Significance of Alchemy in*

the Age of Newton. A lecture sponsored by the Smithsonian Institution Libraries in conjunction with the Washington Collegium for the Humanities Lecture Series: Death and the Afterlife in Art and Literature. Presented at the Smithsonian Institution, February 16, 1988 (Washington, D.C.: Smithsonian Institution Libraries, 1990).

[31] Sotheby lot no. 11; King's College, Cambridge, Keynes MS 18.

[32] Dobbs, *Foundations* (1, n. 1), pp. 251-5.

[33] William Newman, "Newton's 'Clavis' as Starkey's 'Key,'" *Isis 78* (1987), 564-74.

[34] Cf. Dobbs, "Newton's 'Clavis'" (1, n. 5).

[35] Sotheby lot no. 31; King's College, Cambridge, Keynes MS 28; Dobbs, "Newton's *Commentary*" (1, n. 5).

[36] Sotheby lot no. 40 and lot no. 41; Jewish National and University Library, Jerusalem, Yahuda MS Var. 1, Newton MS 30, and The Sir Isaac Newton Collection, Babson College Archives, Babson Park, MA, Babson MS 414 B.

[37] *La lumière sortant par soy méme des tenebres ou veritable theorie de la Pierre des Philosophes écrite en vers Italiens, & amplifiée en Latin par un Auteur Anonyme, en forme de Commentaire; le tout traduit en Françcois par B. D. L.* (Paris: Chez Laurent D'Houry, ruë S. Jacques, devant la Fonteine S. Severin, au S. Esprit, 1687); Harrison, *Library* (1, n. 6), item 1003, p. 184; now NQ. 16. 117 in that portion of Newton's own books now returned to Trinity College, Cambridge. The book shows many signs of dog-earing, presumably by Newton himself.

[38] University Library, Cambridge, Portsmouth Collection, MS Add. 3973.8. Seventeenth-century English dating practices frequently evoke confusion for two principal reasons: (1) England adhered to the Julian calendar until 1752, whereas the Gregorian calendar had been established on the continent since 1582; (2) the English new year legally began on 25 March rather than 1 January. The first factor meant that English dates were consistently ten days behind continental dates throughout the century. The second factor entailed various ways of indicating the year for dates between 1 January and 25 March. Many Englishmen, including Newton, resolved the latter problem by utilizing a number combining the dates for both the old and new years for dates between 1 January and 25 March, as in this instance when Newton wrote "1692/3" for a date that would be January 1693 in modern notation. For further discussion, see Westfall, *Never at Rest* (1, n. 4), p. xvi.

[39] Sotheby lot no. 74; The Sir Isaac Newton Collection, Babson College Archives, Babson Park, MA, Babson MS 420 (part).

[40] Dobbs, *Foundations* (1, n. 1); idem, "Newton's 'Clavis'" (1, n. 5).

[41] Dobbs, "Newton's copy of *Secrets Reveal'd*" (1, n. 5).

[42] I owe an apology to Mary S. Churchill, who first suggested a religious interpretation of Newton's alchemy in her "*The Seven Chapters,* with explanatory notes," *Chymia* 12 (1967), 29-57. I discounted her suggestion for many years, as in Dobbs, *Foundations* (1, n. 1), pp. 14-15. However, I develop ideas similar to hers in Chapter 5 of this book.

FURTHER READING

Cohen, I. Bernard. *Introduction to Newton's 'Principia'.* Cambridge, Mass.: Harvard University Press, 1971, 380 p.

Book-length introduction to the *Principia* featuring a review of contemporary, eighteenth-, and nineteenth-century interest in the work; discussion of the problems of Newtonian scholarship; and analysis of Newton's writing, revision, and publication of the first and successive editions of *Principia.*

Hall, A. Rupert. *All Was Light: An Introduction to Newton's* Opticks. Oxford: Clarendon Press, 1993, 252 p.

Includes biographical discussion of Newton; examination of the experiments and lectures that provided the data for *Opticks*; and analysis of the development, content, and reception of *Opticks.*

Hanson, Norwood Russell. "Waves, Particles, and Newton's 'Fits'." *Journal of the History of Ideas* XXI (1960): 370-91.

Reviews the early scientific controversy between the competing wave and particle theories of light, and discusses Newton's contribution to the debate.

Harman, P. M. *The Investigation of Difficult Things: Essays on Newton and the History of the Exact Sciences.* Cambridge: Cambridge University Press, 1992, 531 p.

Collection of essays focusing on the history of mathematics and astronomy prior to Newton; analysis of several of Newton's scientific and alchemical writings, as well as the *Principia*; and the influence of Newton on eighteenth-century mathematics and physics and on the development of optics and dynamics.

McGuire, J. E. "Force, Active Principles, and Newton's Invisible Realm." *Ambix* XV, No.3 (October 1968): 154-208.

Argues that the basic tenets of Newton's natural philosophy can only be understood within the context of the larger theological framework that directed his work.

——. "Atoms and the 'Analogy of Nature': Newton's Third Rule of Philosophizing." *Studies in History and Philosophy of Science* I, No. 1 (1970): 3-38.

Analyzes Newton's "rule of philosophizing," which states that in the search for the "qualities of bodies" one must not "recede from the analogy of Nature, which uses to be simple, and always consonant to itself." McGuire maintains that this rule is not one of "induction" but "chiefly a transduction rule."

Newton-Smith, W. H. "Science, Rationality, and Newton." *Queens Quarterly* 95, No. 1 (Spring 1988): 19-35.

Examines how Newton and the *Principia* influenced the "nature of the scientific enterprise and our image of that enterprise." This discussion includes an exploration how others have used Newton within the context of the "debate concerning the rationality of science."

Peterfreund, Stuart. "Saving the Phenomenon or Saving the Hexameron?: Mosaic Self-Presentation in Newtonian Optics." *The Eighteenth Century: Theory and Interpretation* 32, No. 2 (Summer 1991): 139-65.

Studies the relationship between eighteenth-century theology and Newton's work in the field of optics.

Westfall, Richard S. "Newton's Scientific Personality." *Journal of the History of Ideas* XLVIII, No. 4 (October-December 1987): 551-70.

In examining Newton's "scientific personality," Westfall states that he refers to "the overt characteristics his career in science displayed." Westfall argues that Newton is today regarded as a scientific genius because his accomplishments coincided "with the central feature of the scientific revolution."

White, Michael. *Isaac Newton: The Last Sorcerer.* London: Fourth Estate, 1997, 402 p.

Explores the life and works of Newton to determine the influence of alchemical studies on Newton's scientific writings. Concludes that "the influence of Newton's researches in alchemy was the key to his world-changing discoveries in science."

Theology

INTRODUCTION

Newton's interest in theological matters ran broadly and deeply, extending beyond the conviction, expressed in such scientific works as his *Principia* and his *Opticks,* regarding God's role as creator and maintainer of the universe. In *The Chronology of Ancient Kingdoms Amended* (1728) and *Observations upon the Prophecies of Daniel and the Apocalypse of St. John* (1733), as well as in numerous unpublished manuscripts, Newton reveals an interest in wide-ranging aspects of biblical study. In these works he contemplates the historical accuracy of the Bible, the way in which biblical prophecies may be understood and proved, and the corruptions he believed were deliberately incorporated into the Bible in support of the doctrine of the Trinity, which Newton believed to be false. For a time, many critics ignored or disparaged Newton's theological interests; modern scholars, however, have investigated the nature and implications of his beliefs, exploring the relationship of his theological views to his scientific studies.

Major Works

The only one of his theological works that Newton authorized to have published was *The Chronology of Ancient Kingdoms Amended,* which he prepared for press prior to his death in 1727. *Observations upon the Prophecies of Daniel and the Apocalypse of St. John* was arranged and published after Newton's death by his nephew. In the *Chronology* Newton uses astronomical discoveries to construct a biblical chronology based upon the positions of the stars as described in Scripture and other ancient writings. By means of this astronomical evidence, Newton argues that the Bible is accurate as history and that it is the oldest historical record available. In *Observations* Newton focuses on the composition of the books of the Bible. Through his historical analysis, he contends that Moses did not write all parts of the Pentateuch, the first five books of the Bible. Newton also emphasizes in *Observations* that biblical prophesies have been fulfilled in history and will continue to be fulfilled; yet he does not advocate the study of such prophesies for the purpose of predicting the future. Newton's analysis of the Bible also reveals his belief that individuals such as St. Athanasius purposely corrupted the New Testament in order to support the doctrine of the Trinity, insisting that it cannot be proved from Scripture that Jesus was consubstantial with God.

Critical Reception

Many critics have looked to Newton's published and unpublished theological writings in order to flesh out the nature of his beliefs. Filled with extensive and detailed historical and Biblical scholarship, Newton's *Observations* has been the focus of study for a number of critics. Leonard Trengove outlines the scope and content of this work, examining Newton's disbelief in the Trinity and the biblical basis for this departure from the accepted tenets of the Church of England. Richard H. Popkin similarly examines *Observations* as well as various unpublished manuscripts in his survey of Newton's conclusions regarding the composition of the Pentateuch as well as the commentary of Newton's contemporaries who agreed with or took issue with his findings. Additionally, Popkin reviews the content of the *Chronology,* stressing that Newton, having analyzed biblical records, believed that God had outlined a plan for human history and natural history alike. Among other investigations of Newton's manuscripts is that of J. E. McGuire and P. M. Rattansi, which analyzesthe drafts of a Scholia to Propositions IV through IX of Book III of Newton's *Principia*. According to the critics, these drafts indicate Newton's conviction that God had revealed knowledge to the ancients, and that he, Newton, was rediscovering those truths. In his study of Newton's unpublished writings, Frank Manuel demonstrates how many of these materials indicate that Newton's religion, throughout his life, was one of "obedience to commandments in which the mercies of Christ the Redeemer played a recessive role."

Another area of critical investigation has been that of the relationship between Newton's theological interests and his scientific achievements. James E. Force points out that, while Newton's references to God in his scientific works indicate that his theology exerted some degree of influence on his scientific thinking, many critics still tend to divorce Newton's scientific interests from his theological views. Taking the reverse approach, William H. Austin attempts to ascertain the influence of Newton's science on his theology. Citing Newton's maxim that "religion and Philosophy are to be preserved distinct," Austin concludes that there is little evidence in Newton's theological writings to suggest the influence of his scientific ideas. However, the critic notes, Newton appears to have held to this maxim inconsistently, and perhaps allowed that science had some influence on his theology, possibly to avoid public controversy. Force disagrees, maintaining that Newton's conception of a "God of Dominion" integrates his scientific, theological, and political interests. In his analysis of the unity of Newton's thought, Force states that "Newton's theology, not just his religion, influences his science every bit as much as his science influences the rigorous textual scholarship of his theology."

CRITICISM

Leonard Trengove (essay date 1966)

SOURCE: "Newton's Theological Views," in *Annals of Science,* Vol. 22, No. 4, December 1966, pp. 277-94.

[*In the following essay, Trengove analyzes the content and scope of Newton's* Observations on the Prophesies of Daniel and the Apocalypse of St. John. *Trengove goes on to discuss the implications of the theological views expressed in the work, and comments on Newton's anti-Trinitarian beliefs.*]

There were three great fields to which Newton gave his mind—mechanics, chemistry, and theology—to each of which he gave almost equally intense study. Besides the *Observations on the Prophecies of Daniel and the Apocalypse of St. John* (1733) and *Two Letters from Sir Isaac Newton to Mr. Le Clerc* (1754),[1] which were published, there have survived his very extensive theological manuscripts. Professor Andrade estimated there are over 1,300,000 words in these manuscripts.[2] There are also the passages in the *Principia* and elsewhere where Newton considered God as a corollary of his system of the world. These passages have received much attention, but it is evident that Newton was not an adept in physico-theological reflection. Voltaire was right in thinking *these* were 'blindfold writings' (*Dictionnaire Philosophique,* s.v. 'Newton et Descartes'). For Newton, God was the God of revelation, the Lord of history, not the God of the philosophers, and he believed that 'religion and philosophy are to be held distinct'. Newton's biographers have dealt more or less briefly with his theological studies, but, so far as I am aware, none has treated them in their historical setting against the background of the theological trends in Newton's day. The biographers have been right, however, in thinking that a complete study of this remarkable personality and unrivalled scientific genius must include a consideration of the theology to which he devoted so much of his time and in which he displayed such astonishing learning. The present paper is derived from a much larger study I am making of Newton's theology. I am aware that the subject may not appeal to some historians of science. I have nevertheless submitted this Newtonian study for publication in a periodical concerned with the history of science in the belief that there are many historians who would wish to be better informed on this aspect of the mind of one who still remains the greatest figure in the whole history of science. For this reason I am very grateful to the editors of this journal for accepting my view on this matter and agreeing to publish this paper, in which I am mainly concerned with Newton's *Observations on the Prophecies,* a work certainly under way soon after the *Principia* was completed, if not before.[3]

In Newton's day prophecy and miracles were regarded as the two great pillars of religion,[4] but most people held that miracles had ceased since Apostolic times. The predictions of prophecy on the other hand were still being fulfilled, a *continued* witness to Christianity. In the *Observations* Newton showed how predictions of Daniel and the Apocalypse had been fulfilled in history. That prophecies of Scripture were fulfilled in history, and continued to be fulfilled, was regarded as a fact in his day and there was nothing mystical about it. There is nothing in Newton's writings to support the view that he was a mystic. In fact, what strikes one, apart from his manifest sincerity, is the lack of any sign of mystic experience, or for that matter, of any religious experience at all. To use the word 'mysticism' nowadays is to invite misunderstanding, but Newton was not even a mystic in the sense of being interested in those devices by means of which men have tried to achieve the mystical experience, such as rituals, creative powers of the letters of the alphabet, and, not least, the power of numbers.

Newton, in the introductory chapter to the *Observations,* dealt with the compilers of the books of the Old Testament. At first sight this seems out of place, but we find that it leads up to the importance of the prophecies of Daniel, who, Newton believed, was the most precise and plainest of the old prophets, and so must be made the key to the rest 'in those things which relate to the last times'.[5] It has been asserted that Newton's conclusions in this chapter are not so far from the conclusions of modern scholarship,[6] but actually his treatment is not so much that of a modern critic, as that of the Jewish commentator. This is not surprising, because, before the rise of modern literary and historical criticism, the work of the old Jewish scholars had not been superseded, and, after all, the Old Testament books were Jewish. Most of the points dealt with by Newton had been raised before, something that Young, for example, 'thought it not improper to warn his unlearned Reader of, lest he should take what Sir *Isaac* had said, from the manner of treating his subject, without any one's having considered the same things before him for a new and important Discovery.'[7] The difference was that, unlike such writers as Patrick and Prideaux who had considered these things, Newton usually came down on what might be called the more liberal side.

Newton regarded the books of the Old Testament as having been compiled at various times from books already in existence, the two great compilers being Samuel and Ezra. He thought that Samuel compiled the Pentateuch, Joshua, and Judges, and probably his own book up to the record of his death—quite a lot for one man to do. Newton was the first to assert that Samuel wrote thePentateuch, though Barrington had ascribed part of it to him.[8] He was by no means the first to doubt the Mosaic authorship. Spinoza was probably right in thinking that Ibn Ezra in the twelfth century was the first to put forward reasons for doubting that Moses wrote the Pentateuch,[9] but it was not until the seventeenth century that these doubts were openly expressed and discussed. To Spinoza himself it was clearer than the sun at noonday that the Pentateuch was not written by Moses but by someone who lived long after him. Hobbes, too, thought it sufficiently evident that the Pentateuch was written after the time of Moses, although he maintained that Moses had written all that he is *said* to have written, in particular the law itself.[10] Richard Simon also held that Moses had written the Mosaic *law*.[11]

Newton believed that the historical part of the Pentateuch was compiled from several sources such as the History of Creation by Moses (Genesis 2: 4) and the Book of the Wars of the Lord (Numbers 21: 14). Hobbes had already noted the latter as an example of a more ancient book cited by the writer of the Pentateuch, and, when dealing with Kings and Chronicles had said: 'The facts registered were always more ancient than the register; and much more ancient than such books as make mention of, and quote the register; as these books do in divers places, referring the reader to the Chronicles of the Kings of Judah, to the Chronicles of the Kings of Israel . . .'[12] Since our Book of Chronicles deals with the Kings of Judah only, Newton thought that the Book of the Chronicles of the Kings of Israel was lost—at the time when Antiochus Epiphanes ordered the sacred books of the Jews to be burnt. Afterwards Judas Maccabaeus gathered together all the writings that could be found and reduced them to order. It was at this time that certain dislocations in the text occurred.

In putting forward such conjectures Newton was, however, ahead of his time, and these views were rejected by the orthodox. Arthur Young wrote: 'I wish the inferences which *Sir Isaac Newton* has made in his first chapter, from the Interpolations in the Books of *Moses,* and what he has asserted of the Sacred Writings having been lost, were not more prejudicial to Christianity—If these things were to be granted, the *Hebrew Bible* would no longer be of any Authority.'[13]

Newton's division of the Book of Daniel into Chapters 7-12 (prophecies, written by Daniel himself) and 1-6 (a collection of historical papers written by others) has

been accepted down to modern times.[14] However, Spinoza had already maintained that Chapters 8-12 contained the undoubted writings of Daniel. His division was on the basis of language, the first seven chapters having been 'written in Chaldean'.[15]

For Newton, 'amongst the old prophets, Daniel is most distinct in order of time, and easiest to be understood: and therefore for those things which relate to the last times, he must be made the key to the rest': 'To reject his prophecies is to reject the Christian religion'.[16] Richard Amner was not far wrong when he said that for the great Isaac Newton the prophecies of Daniel were a sacred calendar, a prophetic chronology.[17]

After the introductory chapter on the compilers of the books of the Old Testament, Newton turned to the language of prophecy, which he believed to be as definite in meaning as the language of any nation. 'The curse of Babel', the nature of language, and the possibility of devising a universal language were, of course, subjects of great interest in the seventeenth century. Newton never completed the universal language he once embarked upon, but his explanation of the language ofprophecy was more complete than any that had appeared before and, one may say with confidence, more complete than any that came after. As Whiston said: 'If it could be as readily proved, as it is here distinctly *set down* [it] would be truly estimable.'[18]

Newton's idea of such a language was not new. Mede had already worked out the principles of prophetic language in his *Clavis Apocalyptica* (Cambridge, 1627), and there was some general agreement on the subject. For Newton as for Mede, 'the language [of prophecy] is taken from the analogy between the world natural, and an empire or kingdom considered as a world politic', and also, 'sacred prophecy . . . regards not single persons'.[19] But Newton aimed at giving a complete language of prophecy. Like most writers of his time, he thought the Bible was consistent from end to end, and, if a prophetic symbol could be seen to be used in a certain way in one part, one could be sure that it would be used in the same way in any part. As might be expected, the very completeness of Newton's work made the inadequacy of any such system at all the more evident. He had no occasion himself to use the greater part of it, and it was subsequently set aside. On the other hand, the belief of Mede and of Newton that the key to interpretation of prophetic symbols was to be sought in an understanding of hieroglyphics and primitive symbols in general was influential in the eighteenth century.[20] Newton did not say very much about this, although a passage in 'The Language of the Prophets' (k.ms.5) shows that he was in general agreement with this line of thought. Also influential in the eighteenth century was Newton's emphasis on the importance of Jewish history (with all the religious customs and rituals) as a fresh source of symbols.

Newton employed his knowledge of Jewish customs and rituals in his exposition of the Apocalypse, and no one before him had used such knowledge to greater advantage. His main source of information on Jewish law was the first Protestant rabbinical scholar, Johannes Buxtorf (1564-1629),[21] but his knowledge was not derived from any one writer. Further, although Newton's exposition was open to criticism in several places, subsequent work on the Apocalypse might have been done better if more attention had been paid to Newton, especially to his emphasis on the importance of the Feast of Tabernacles.[22]

Newton, in common with other seventeenth-century writers on apocalyptic, adopted the year-day theory. This theory may be stated briefly as follows. In symbolic prophecy (prophecy like that of Daniel and Revelation, which makes extensive use of symbols) a day is to be taken as meaning a year. Newton did not consider it necessary to give reasons for this, but merely stated: 'Daniel's days are years'.[23]

John Napier (the inventor of logarithms) had identified the 'time, times and half a time' of Revelation 12: 14 with the 1,260 days of Daniel and Revelation, and said that they were really 1,260 years.[24] These were the years of Antichrist's reign over Christians, which Napier associated with papal domination. This interpretation was adopted by Mede in his *Clavis Apocalyptica* and by Newton. Though they each suggested different dates for the beginning of the 1,260 years, it was generally felt that events of apocalyptic significance were taking place in the seventeenth century or would take place in the not too distant future. That seventeenth-century divines should thus be able to understand prophecies the true interpretation of which had eluded all previous scholars would not have given rise to any misgivings in those days, for these men believed themselves to be looking back beyond the cloud of errors of the Roman Church to the uncorrupted primitive church, much as the men of the Renaissance looked beyond the mists of the Dark Ages to the clear light of the ancient world. Moreover, as Bishop Andrewes pointed out at the beginning of the century, even the early Fathers of the Church, although more gifted and holier, did not know so much about prophecy as writers of his day, for these were seeing prophecy fulfilled before their very eyes—and every prophecy is an enigma until it is fulfilled.[25] It is only when it has been fulfilled and you have seen how it has come to pass that you understand it. Newton fully agreed, and said: 'The folly of interpreters hath been to foretell times and things by this prophecy, as if God designed to make them prophets. By this rashness they have not only exposed themselves, but brought this prophecy also into contempt'.

Newton helped to establish this attitude to prophecy, and his assertion that the end of prophecy is not to make us prophets was much quoted later on—often, it must be admitted, by people who wanted to discount someone else's interpretation of a particular prophecy.

It is true that Newton did not confine himself to such prophecies as he considered to have already been fulfilled. Thus in dealing with the prophecy of Daniel 8 that after 2,300 days the sanctuary would be cleansed, he said that these 2,300 *years* may be perhaps reckoned from (1) the destruction of the temple by the Romans in the reign of Vespasian, or (2) the pollution of the sanctuary by the worship of Jupiter Olympius, or (3) the desolation of Judea made at the end of the Jewish war by the banishment of all Jews out of their own country, or (4) *from some other period which time will discover.*[26] Newton, therefore, expected the fulfilment of this prophecy to take place in A. D. 2132, 2370, 2436—or, of course, some other date. Some others of this school of interpretation were less cautious. For example, William Miller, from whose movement arose the Seventh Day Adventists, assumed that the 2,300 days of Daniel 8 began at the same time as the 490 days of Daniel 9. He dated this from the decree allowing Ezra to go back to Jerusalem 457 B. C. (Ussher's date). In this way he arrived at A. D. 1843 as the date of the cleansing of the sanctuary, and also, he thought, the time of the second coming of Christ. Miller is supposed to have worked out his calculations using only Bible and concordance, but the fact that he was in the same tradition of apocalyptic interpretation as Newton was recognized even in his own day. George Bush, Professor of Hebrew and Oriental Literature in New York University, said in a letter published in the *Advent Herald* for March, 1844:

> In taking a day as the prophetical term for a year I believe you are sustained by the soundest exegesis, as well as fortified by the high names of Mede, Sir Isaac Newton, Bishop Newton, Kirby, Scott, Keith, and a host of others who have long since come to *substantially* your conclusions on this head. They all agree that the leading periods mentioned by Daniel and John do actually expire *about the age of the world,* and it would be strange logic that would convict you of heresy.[27]

After the day of 'The Great Disappointment', some of Miller's followers believed that Miller had been right in his calculations, but wrong in supposing that Christ was to come to *earth* to cleanse the sanctuary in 1843. They supposed that what had happened was that Christ had then entered the second apartment of the *heavenly* sanctuary and that this had been invisible to mortals. Newton believed that Christ would be invisible to mortals when he first returned.

After the publication of Newton's **Observations** the first event that was thought to have important apocalyptic significance was the French Revolution. The 1260 days prophecy of Daniel and Revelation was thought to refer to the fate of papal domination and the appearance of Antichrist. The French Revolution seemed to mark the beginning of the end of papal domination, and *Antichrist in the French Convention* was the title of an anonymous pamphlet published at the time. By adjusting the *terminus a quo,* it was easy to arrive at the correct date. Thus, reckoning from A. D. 533, the date of Justinian's decree conferring on the Bishop of Rome universal oversight of the Christian Church, we come after 1260 years to 1793 and the Reign of Terror. This 'fulfilment of prophecy' had a great influence on Edward Irving, the originator of the Catholic Apostolic Church, and it has been thought significant that the 1831 edition of Newton's *Observations* was dedicated to Henry Drummond, one of the founders of that church.[28]

Ironically enough, it was the rise of Newtonianism more than anything else that led to the general rejection of this kind of apocalyptic interpretation. It has not, however, been entirely abandoned even now. For example, the year-day theory is used in the teachings of the Jehovah's Witnesses.[29]

One of the chief subjects of discussion concerning the book of Daniel has been the identity of the four kingdoms represented by the image of gold, silver, bronze, and iron of Ch. 2, and also by the four beasts, the lion, the bear, the leopard, and the terrible beast with iron teeth of Ch. 7. Especially has speculation centred around the identity of the fourth kingdom. Newton said that 'in this vision of the image composed of four metals the foundation of all Daniel's prophecies is laid. It represents a body of four great nations, which should reign over the earth successively, viz. the people of Babylonia, the Persians, the Greeks and the Romans . . .'. Newton held that the Babylonian and Median empires were contemporary.[30] 'In the next vision [Dan. 7] which is of the Four Beasts, the prophecy of the four empires is repeated, with several new additions'.[31] The Greek Empire referred to is the empire of Alexander the Great. The Roman Empire dates from Caesar Augustus.

Like Mede, Newton believed that these four empires were the empires of which God's people were subjects, and that the fourth empire, the Roman, was still in existence, continuing in the ten nations into which it was supposed to have been divided. In taking the fourth beast to be the Roman Empire, Newton was in line with nearly all writers on the subject until modern times; Luther in his preface to the Book of Daniel had said that 'all the world is unanimous' in this interpretation. Newton was unique, however, in holding that not only the Roman Empire, but also he other three empires still existed—in the nations that had taken their place geographically.[32]

It is when Newton considered the meaning of the ten horns of the fourth beast that we see him especially in

his role of historian. Dr. Twiss, in his preface to the English translation of Mede's *Clavis Apocalyptica,* had pointed out that, after the prophetic terms had been interpreted, great skill in history was also required in order to apply the prophecy, and he added: 'I have found that *Master Mede's* friends, who have been acquainted with the course of his studies, would give him the bell for this as herein out-stripping all others'.[33] Mede was, however, to be surpassed by Newton in this respect. Indeed, Elliott, in his learned *Horae Apocalypticae* bracketed Newton and Gibbon as authorities on this history of the ten kingdoms that arose after the break-up of the Roman Empire.[34] There were no text-books available to Newton to provide him with an easy entry into the subject, yet he was quite at home with his sources, particularly the massive *Historia De Regno Italiae* of Sigonius.[35] True, he did not question the accuracy of his sources very much, but the techniquesrequired for this had not been developed in his day.

Of course, Newton's list of the ten kingdoms is just one among many others put forward before and after his time. Such lists had been forthcoming since the ninth century when Berengaud referred to Jerome,[36] and explained that the ten horns were the kingdoms that had already destroyed the Roman imperium. As Maitland justly remarked, if the number mentioned by Daniel had been nine or eleven, the right number would still have been found among the petty kingdoms.[37]

Tyso certainly showed this when he gave a table of twenty-nine different lists of the ten kingdoms that had been suggested at various times by various writers, containing no less than sixty-five different entries.[38] Newton's list of the Kingdoms into which the Roman Empire became divided after the attacks of the barbarians is as follows: the kingdoms of (1) Vandals and Alans in Spain and Africa, (2) Suevians in Spain, (3) Visigoths, (4) Alans in Gallia, (5) Burgundians, (6) Franks, (7) Britains, (8) Hunns, (9) Lombards, (10) Ravenna.[39] There was nothing unusual about Newton's list. What was unusual was the great learning with which he dealt with the history of these Kingdoms in the long chapter 6 of the *Observations.*

Newton dealt also with the vision of the rough goat of Dan. 8, whose horn was broken, and in place of which four others arose. He gave what would still be regarded as the most likely interpretation, taking the four horns to be the four kingdoms of the Diadochi—the kingdoms of Cassander (Macedonia), Lysimachus (Thrace and Asia Minor), Antigonus (Syria), and Ptolemy (Egypt). He recounted the history of the Greek Empire after the death of Alexander the Great, and was well aware that the empire was not simply divided into four. He said: 'the monarchy of the Greeks for want of an heir was broken into several kingdoms, *four* of which seated to the four winds of heaven, *were very eminent.* '[40] Newton's treatment here is superior to that of most of those commentators before and after him who attempted to make the history fit this prophecy. Indeed, as J. H. Todd remarked in the nineteenth century, the discrepancies and deficiencies of the original historians made it less difficult for commentators to shape their history to their peculiar interpretations of this prophecy, something which Bishop Newton, he claimed, confessed with amusing simplicity when he wrote: 'The prophecy is really more perfect than any history. No historian hath related so many circumstances, and in such exact order as the prophet hath foretold them.'[41]

On the other hand, Newton's insistence that a symbol like a horn never referred to a single person in prophecy led him astray when he dealt with the little horn that came forth from one of these four horns of the goat. He knew that this little horn was usually taken to be Antiochus Epiphanes,[42] and he was well aware of the reasons for this choice. Nevertheless, he insisted that a horn always stood for a kingdom,[43] and he argued that this horn was Macedonia, and traced the history of that kingdom from the defeat of Perseus, king of Macedonia, by the Romans in 168 B. C., to its domination by the Turks in Newton's own day.[44] No subsequent commentator adopted this exegesis.

Newton devoted two chapters to the two difficult verses, Dan. 11: 37, 38. The points at issue were the meanings of the phrase 'the desire of women' and of [a] Hebrew word. . . . Calvin, in the best commentary to come out in Reformation times, said that commentators were all over the place when dealing with these verses.[46] In the next century, however, Mede put forward the idea that 'the desire of women' meant the desire of wives or the married state, and that Mauzzims (which literally means 'strongholds') were the saints and angels in whom the Roman Church trusted for protection. The king here described would thus be opposed to marriage, and on the other hand would honour the Mauzzims.[47]

Newton interpreted these verses as referring to the rise of celibacy and to the worship of saints and relics in the Roman Church. It is perhaps a little surprising that Newton should have devoted a whole chapter to the condemnation of celibacy,[48] but celibacy was one of the most debated subjects among Protestants after the Reformation. One of the reasons for the rise of sacerdotal celibacy in the first place had doubtless been the Christian reaction against the moral laxity of the pagan world. Protestants did not want to appear more indulgent to the flesh than Catholics, but they would not enforce celibacy, believing it to be unnatural. Newton gives a remarkably good account of the use of celibacy.

Newton next turned to the growth of saint-worship in the Roman Church, and speaking of the festivals of the saints and martyrs said: 'By the pleasures of these festivals the Christians increased much in number, and decreased as much in virtue.'[49] Newton's ironic humour, although evident only occasionally, reminds us of Gibbon. His history of the worship of relics is accurate, although it provoked much opposition. Zachary Grey wrote a book of one hundred and fifty pages devoted entirely to refuting this one chapter on the Mahuzzims.[50] Arthur Young, the father of the famous agriculturist, wrote against it, adding: 'I should not have said anything against in Opposition to the Opinion of this great man, if the emissaries of Rome had not been so very busy at this time in making Converts, that we ought not to allow any of her corruptions an earlier date than in truth belongs to them.'[51] He thought, incorrectly, that Newton had put the origins of the worship of relics too early.

This particular part of Newton's ***Observations*** was praised, however, by William Whiston, although he was quite critical of the rest of it. Whiston's generally critical attitude might have been due in some measure to the difficulty of succeeding Newton as Lucasian Professor at Cambridge. His approval of the part most people criticized is easy to explain. Grey had pointed out that Newton here put much of the blame on the Athanasians 'to disparage the *Orthodox* in a covert way'—and Grey was right; this is where Newton's unorthodoxy is revealed in the ***Observations,*** and why the Arian Whiston praised this section.[52] As is well-known, Newton's belief with regard to the Trinity was not orthodox. This was not because he followed Arius, Socinus, or anyone else, and still less because he thought it was 'unscientific'. The Reformation had been followed by a period in which creeds and theological systems multiplied, as did disagreements and condemnations. In England there had been civil war. Newton and others thought that the Apostles' Creed was sufficient, a view which, as a matter of fact, had been condemned as heresy in the *consensus repetitus fidei vere Lutheranae* of Wittemberg in 1655. Newton considered himself a loyal member of the Church of England, and he held (as the sixth article of religion puts it) that all things necessary to salvation were to be found in Scripture, and anything that could not be clearly proved from Scripture was not required of anyone as an article of faith. He could not prove the doctrine of the Trinity from Scripture. There were, indeed, texts that the orthodox used as proofs, but in **'An Historical Account of Two Notable Corruptions of Scripture'** he had shown that one of the most well-known of these (1 John, 5: 7) was a corruption, and he showed also for the first time that 1 Tim. 3: 16 was a corruption by using a historical technique well-developed in his day. Further, while the orthodox in Newton's day and since have for the most part thought that the whole question had been decided once for all in the fourth century, Newton realized that the history of the period might not have been so simple as is usually supposed. After all, of the sources available for the Arian controversy, the writings of Athanasius himself, Socrates, Sozomen, and Theodoret might be expected to favour the Athanasians. It seemed to Newton that Athanasius was a ringleader in introducing unscriptural beliefs and practices into the Church, and was not above spreading lies to suit his purpose. While it is true that Athanasius does seem to have been one of those people who are to be read and not met, yet Newton certainly failed to appreciate his great ability. Thus, when he mentioned the classic *De Incarnatione Verbi,* he merely said: 'It relates to the Nestorian Heresy, and so was written by a much later writer than Athanasius.'[53] At the same time, whatever the Christology, if Newton found it in Scripture, he accepted it. Thus, speaking of worship of the beasts and elders in Rev. 7, he said that this was the worship of the primitive Church, the worship of God *and* the Lamb, worship of God for creating all things, and of the Lamb for redeeming us by his blood.[54]

Newton, in his eleventh chapter, put forward a chronology of Christ's ministry which amounted to a short harmony of the gospels. The usual form of the harmony at this time was a continuous narrative of Christ's life made up from the four evangelists and this was more or less what Newton did. It was later in the eighteenth century that the emphasis was placed on arranging the gospels in four columns for comparison.

Chronology was one of Newton's great interests, and there is no lack of originality in this section. He first noted that the dates of the Christian festivals did not come from the earliest times, but the days were fixed in the Christian calendar by mathematicians. For example, the annunciation of the Virgin Mary was kept on 25 March, the vernal equinox; the feast of John the Baptist on 24 June, the summer solstice; the feast of St. Michael on 29 September, the autumnal equinox; and the birth of Christ on 25 December, the winter solstice. Whiston said: 'This Observation I well remember I heard him [Newton] make about 22 years ago, and it is a very curious and very certain Observation,'[55]—and, it may be added, one that has been accepted since.

Newton believed that for settling the dates[56] of Christ's life 'there was nothing in tradition worth considering' and it was best to begin the investigation afresh. He held that the evangelists who were eye-witnesses, Matthew and John, unlike Mark and Luke, record the events in chronological order, and also that 'John is more distinct in the beginning and end; Matthew in the Middle: what either omits, the other supplies',[57]—a happier solution of the problem than any we have today! He maintained that we have 'in the gospels of Matthew and John compared together, the history of Christ's actions in continual order during five passovers'.[58] Most writers before Newton had reckoned that Christ's ministry lasted through four passovers. Since then there have been various estimates, but it is doubtful if anyone has followed Newton in this respect. In fact Philip Doddridge criticized Newton's scheme soon after in a kindly but very competent way.[59] It is not difficult to criticize some of Newton's arguments, but discussions of the chronology of Christ's ministry have always proceeded on somewhat similar lines.

Newton began the section on the Apocalypse by considering when it was written. It was written during persecution, and the two candidates for the role of persecuting emperor in the first century were Nero and Domitian. Like others who have favoured a date in Nero's time, Newton had to deal with the testimony of Irenæus (*Adv. Haer,* ch. 5) quoted by Eusebius (*H.E.,* iii, 18), 'For it [the Apocalypse presumably as τηνν᾽Αποκαλψιν comes in the clause immediately preceding] was seen not a long time ago, but almost in our generation, towards the end of the reign of Domitian.' He suggested that John put out *two* editions of the Apocalypse, and that it was the second edition that came out in Domitian's reign. Newton even succeeded in turning the well-known story of St. John and the highwayman[60] into support for his thesis that the Apocalypse was written in Nero's time. Further, in spite of the fact that the earliest authorities were practically unanimous in their testimony to a date in Domitian's reign, he managed to find a few ancient writers to support his view, a proof of his great learning rather than of what he was trying to prove. Nevertheless, subsequent commentators[61] had to deal with the testimony of these writers if only to show that their testimony could not be accepted. Newton also considered the style of the Apocalypse, remarking that it contained more Hebraisms than John's Gospel, inferring from this that 'it was writ when John was newly come out of Judea, where he had been used to the Syriac tongue; and that he did not write his Gospel till by long converse with the Asiatick Greeks he had left off most of the Hebraisms.'[62] Whiston criticized this novel suggestion of Newton's. He said: 'That the *Apocalypse* is fuller of Hebraisms than *John's* Gospel I never heard before. Nor does *Dionysius* of *Alexandria,* here I suppose relied on by Sir *Isaac Newton,* say any such Thing; but only that it has several Solœcisms or Expressions different from the Purity of the Greek Tongue; as has the Gospel also.'[63] Yet Dionysius, who should have known since he was talking about his own language, said that the author of the Fourth Gospel wrote Greek impeccably. . . . What is noticeable in this chapter again is Newton's rather uncritical acceptance of his authorities, in particular the untrustworthy Epiphanius, and also his tendency to assume that one writer quoted from another, without considering that it might have been the other way round, or that both might have used a common source. Here he suggested that the Apocalypse was alluded to in the epistles of Peter and in the epistle to the Hebrews.

The seventeenth century was a time of renewed interest in the Book of Revelation, and among Protestants we find a new kind of exposition. It is true that the papacy and also individual popes had been identified with Antichrist before, but the deeds of the Inquisition, and such events as the massacre of the Huguenots, the Marian persecutions, and the Gunpowder Plot seemed to make the Apocalypse specially relevant with its predictions of cruel persecution of the faithful. Moreover, a new epoch in the study of this difficult book began with Mede's *Clavis Apocalyptica.* He seemed to have provided the key to it with his 'synchronisms' by means of which it was possible to arrange the visions in the order in which the events foretold were to occur.[64] Newton adopted Mede's synchronisms, though he modified them somewhat. He also adopted Mede's division of the prophecy into events that were to take place in the Empire and events that were to take place in the Church.

Among writers who belong to this general tradition, some earlier and some later than Mede, we may note: John Napier, Arthur Dent, Jean Taffin, Richard Bernard, William Cowper, Thomas Brightman, David Pareus, John Forbes, John Cotton, John Tillinghast, William Guild, James Durham, Henry More, Pierre Jurieu, Drue Cressener, Samuel Cradock and Campegius Vitringa.

Newton followed this tradition of apocalyptic interpretation, and he thought that 'amongst the interpreters [of the Apocalypse] of the last age there is scarce one of note who hath not made some discovery worth knowing'.[65] In fact it was the success of others in this field that had prompted his own investigation. He did not mention any of the recent persecutions, but agreed with the general trend of seventeenth-century exposition in supposing the plague of locusts introduced by the fifth trumpet to refer to the Saracens. The importance of the Eastern Roman Empire had not been sufficiently recognized in the West, and even its overthrow in 1453 was not given due importance for a long time. By the seventeenth century, however, the significance of these events in the East was being seen more in its true perspective. Mede had put forward the idea that the locusts of Revelation 9 were the Saracens, and the Euphratean horsemen were the Turks.[66] Thomas Brightman applied the year-day theory to the period of five months during which the locusts were allowed to torture those men who had not the seal of God upon their foreheads. This period of one hundred and fifty prophetic days were years. Newton, without any textual grounds for doing so doubled the period, making the length of Saracen rule three hundred years.[67] This does fit the history better, but there does not seem to be any other reason for the duplication, and no one has followed Newton in this respect. On the other hand, the reason he gave for the association of the five months with locusts has been accepted ever since. It is the length of a locust's life. It must be added, however, that in all probability he owed this to the great seventeenth-century French scholar, Samuel Bochart.[68] Newton also pointed out that 'locusts often arise in Arabia Fælix, and from thence infest the neighbouring nations: and so are a very fit type of the numerous armies of Arabians invading the Romans.[69]

Calvin towards the end of his commentary on Daniel confessed: 'In numeris non sum Pythagoricus'.[70] Newton had no such limitations, and we might have expected him to make much of the numbers to be found in prophecy, particularly the famous number 666 of Rev. 13: 18. It is 'the number of a man' . . . , a cryptogram. Newton just said that the name is ΛΑΤΕΙΝΟΣ (Latin).[71] In the Keynes MS. he did explain a little more fully; he said that ΛΑΤΕΙΝΟΣ, the name of the Western Empire, was the solution given by Irenæus,[72] and he also made a suggestion regarding the way in which the number 666 had been derived.[73] But it is evident that Newton had no special love for juggling with figures. He might have employed far more complicated types of Gematria in solving this, such as using triangular numbers (taking λ, for example, not as 30 but as 465). Without doubt he would have astonished us with the possibilities of 666—had he felt so inclined. But he was no more interested in such devices than were the writers of Scripture, and he was not a mystic even in the sense of being greatly interested in mystic numbers. That could be left to Cabalistical Jews!

Newton was neither a mystic nor a heretic—at least in the sense he is usually thought to have been. He considered that his views on the Trinity accorded with the insistence of the Church of England that belief in a doctrine that could not be proved from Holy Scripture should not be required of anyone. In fact he held that certain Scriptural texts had been corrupted to support the unscriptural doctrine of the Trinity. Moreover, the Church at baptism demanded subscription to the Apostles' Creed only, and Newton believed that this should be a sufficient rule of faith. Like others in his time he was influenced by the fact that the Romish tendencies of Charles II were becoming evident, and he was one of those who wished the Church of England to be a more comprehensive Protestant church than it was. There is no doubt about Newton's great ability in Biblical and historical theology. It is true that his interpretation of the apocalyptic writings seems somewhat weird to us who no longer hold this historicist view of prophecy. There were continental commentators at the time who were more in line with the modern scientific approach to the subject, but in England Newton's approach was the usual one. His views linger on now in the beliefs of sects on the outer fringe of Christianity—a sort of 'anti-scientific' fringe. Nevertheless, to hold such views in the twentieth century is a different matter from holding them in seventeenth-century England. Brewster was right in thinking that he would have betrayed the trust committed to him if he 'had not given an account of the theological writings of a man, who was described by one Bishop as 'knowing more of the Scriptures than them all', and by another as having 'the whitest soul' he ever knew.[74]

The author wishes to express his thanks to the Librarian of King's College, Cambridge, for access to the Newtonian manuscripts.

Notes

[1] The full version was published by Horsley, *Isaaci Newtoni Opera,* London, 1779-1784, vol. v, p. 495, as 'An Historical Account of Two Notable Corruptions of Scripture'.

[2] E. N. da C. Andrade, *Isaac Newton,* London, 1950, p. 103.

[3] *Ibid.,* p. 104. *Observations upon the Prophecies . . .* published by Benjamin Smith from Newton's manuscripts, and dedicated to Peter Lord King, Baron of Ockham, Lord High Chancellor of Great Britain (and one of Newton's pall-bearers), 4to London, 1733, reprinted 8vo Dublin, 1733. A Latin version by W. Sudemann, now rare, was published in Amsterdam 1735, and this was translated into German (Leipsig and Leignitz, 1765), with notes by M. C. F. Grohmannen and A. Rosenbergen. In Horsley's *Isaaci Newtoni Opera,* vol. v, the capitals and italics of the original edition were altered to accord with later usage. In P. Borthwick's edition (London and Cambridge, 1831) the Latin quotations were translated. The last edition of the *Observations* was by Sir William Whitla, the distinguished Irish physician: *Sir Isaac Newton's Daniel and the Apocalypse with an Introductory Study of the nature and the cause of unbelief of miracles and prophecy,* London, 1922.

[4] *Cf.* W. Whiston, *The Accomplishment of Scripture Prophecies . . .* (Boyle Lectures, 1707), London, 1708.

[5] *ODA,* p. 305 (15). The quotations are from Horsley's edition of the *Observations* (referred to as *ODA*). The corresponding page-number of the 1733 edition is, however, given in brackets afterwards.

[6] F. Kenyon, *The Bible and Archaeology,* London, 1940, p. 270. n.

[7] A. Young, *An Historical Dissertation on idolatrous corruptions in religion from the beginning of the world . . .* 2 vols., London, 1734; vol. ii, p. 265.

[8] John Shute Barrington, *An Essay on the several Dispensations of God to Mankind in the order in which they lie in the Bible . . . ,* London, 1725, p. 64.

[9] *Tractatus theologico-politicus . . . ,* Hamburgi, 1670, ch. 8. Ibn Ezra (1092-1167) was a Spanish Jew.

[10] Hobbes, *Leviathan,* pt. iii, ch. 33.

[11] R. Simon, *Histoire Critique du Vieux Testament,* Amsterdam, 1685. *Cf.* Jean Le Clerc, *Sentimens de quelques théologiens de Hollande sur l'Histoire critique du Vieux Testament, composée par R. Simon,* Amsterdam, 1685, lettre 6.

[12] Hobbes, *op. cit.,* pt. iii, ch. 33.

[13] A. Young, *op. cit.,* p. 268.

[14] Newton, however, regarded the writer of Dan. 7-12 as the hero of the faith mentioned by Ezekiel, but Anthony Collins in his *Literal Scheme of Prophecy Considered* (The Hague, 1726: London, 1727) placed the Book of Daniel in the time of Antiochus Epiphanes, thus both reviving the idea of Porphyry and setting forth the modern view.

[15] Spinoza, *op. cit.,* ch. 10.

[16] *ODA,* pp. 305, 312: (15, 25). In such an appraisal of Daniel, Newton was, of course, in good company; e.g. Jerome ('Nullam prophetarum tam aperte dixisse de Christo'), Augustine ('Neminem de regni coelorum praemio in Vetere Testamento scripsisse tam diserte'), and Luther ('he above all other prophets, had this special prophecy to give, that is, his work was not only to prophesy of Christ, like the others, but also to count the times and years, determine them, and fix them with certainty').

[17] R. Amner, An *Essay towards an Interpretation of the Prophecies of Daniel,* London, 1776.

[18] Whiston, *Six Dissertations: Reflexions upon Sir Isaac Newton's Observations upon the Prophecies of Daniel,* London, 1734, p. 284.

[19] *ODA,* p. 307 (17).

[20] Cf. Hurd, *op. cit.* pp. 166 ff.

[21] Buxdorfius, *Synagoga Judaica,* Hanoviae, 1603.

[22] Dr. Austin Farrer in 1949 showed how he found that the form that expresses the intelligible progress of the sense in the Apocalypse is thoroughly Rabbinical and not a little gnostical—the last thing he wanted or expected to find: 'St. John does not see the Scriptures in what seems to be their own pattern, he sees them artificially arranged in the Jewish sacred calendar with its feasts and lessons' (A. Farrer, *A Rebirth of Images, The Making of St. John's Apocalypse,* London, 1949, p. 8).

[23] *ODA,* p. 369 (122). At the end of the twelfth century Joachim of Flora (1132-1202) in his *Expositio in Apocalypsin* (printed in Venice, 1537) said that the epoch of the Spirit would begin A. D. 1260. He did not arrive at this date by interpreting the 1,260 days of prophecy as years, but his calculation must have contributed to the rise of the theory, which was accepted by the Magdeburg Centuries in the sixteenth century.

[24] John Napier, *A Plaine Discovery of the whole Revelation of John . . . ,* 1594.

[25] 'Verissimum autem verbum est, aenigma esse prophetiam omnem cum nondum completa est' (L. Andrewes, *Tortura Torti: siue at Matthaei Torti librum responsio . . . ,* Londini, 1609, p. 186). *Cf.* Boyle, 'And though the mysterious temple and city described in *Ezekiel* as also much of the Apocalypse, and divers other passages of holy writ, do yet seem abstruse to us; yet they will not appear so to those, to whom their completion (the best expositor of dark prophecies) shall have unfolded them' (*Some considerations touching the Style of the Holy Scriptures, Works,* 1744, vol. ii, p. 100).

[26] *ODA,* p. 369 (122).

[27] James White, *Sketches of the Christian Life and Public Labors of William Miller,* Battle Creek, 1875, p. 8.

[28] *Cf.* McLachlan, *The Religious Opinions of Milton, Locke and Newton,* Manchester, 1941, p. 130. The dedication was appropriate, but Irving himself derived his views on prophecy from J. H. Frere, *A Combined view of the Prophecies of Daniel, Esdras and S. John, showing that all the prophetic writings are formed upon one plan . . . ,* London 1815.

[29] *Cf. Let God be True,* Watchtower Publication, 1952, p. 252.

[30] *ODA,* p. 312, (25). *Chronology of the Antient Kingdoms amended,* pp. 212-235. On the difficulty that Darius the Mede is not mentioned outside Scripture, Newton said: 'The last king of the Medes is by Xenophon called Cyaxeres; and by Herodotus, Astyages, the father of Mandane. But these kings were dead before; and Daniel lets us know that Darius was the true name of the last king.' He added that the Daries coined by the last king testify that his name was Darius (*ibid.,* p. 234). This is incorrect.

[31] *Ibid.,* p. 313, (28).

[32] *Ibid.,* p. 315, (21). This suggestion met with an unfavourable reception, but it seems almost as plausible as saying that the Roman Empire continues in the nations of Western Europe.

[33] Joseph Mede, *The Key to the Revelation,* translated by Richard More, London, 1643, preface (not paginated).

[34] E. B. Elliott, *Horae Apocalypticae,* 4th edn., London, 1851, vol. iii, p. 129n. Gibbon himself wrote to Joseph Warton: 'I should think myself inexcusable, if I neglected any opportunity of availing myself of the researches and reflections of Sir Isaac Newton on any subject to which he applied the powers of his understanding' (*Letters of Edward Gibbon,* ed. J. E. Norton, 3 vols., London, 1956, vol. ii, p. 244).

[35] C. Sigonii, *Historiarum de regno Italiae libri viginti . . . ,* Francofurti, 1591; *Caroli Sigonii Opera Omnia . . . ,* Mediolani, 1732, vol. ii.

[36] Jerome had written: 'In consummatione mundi, quando regnum destruendum est Romanorum decem futuros reges qui orbem Romanorum inter se dividant . . .' (Migne, *Patrologiae,* vol. xxv, p. 531). Compare, for example, the curious passage in Gibbon's *Decline and Fall:* 'The nine kings of the Latin world might disclaim their new associate [Roger, first king of Italy, A. D. 1130], unless he were consecrated by the authority of the supreme pontiff' (*op. cit.,* London, 1815, vol. x, p. 310).

[37] S. R. Maitland, *A second inquiry into the grounds on which the Prophetic period of Daniel and St. John has been supposed to consist of 1,260 years,* London, 1829, p. 35.

[38] Joseph Tyso, *An Elucidation of the Prophecies being an exposition of the Books of Daniel and the Revelation . . . ,* London, 1838, p. 100.

[39] Newton says that seven of these kingdoms are mentioned by Sigonius: 'Add the Franks Britains, and Lombards, and you have the ten, for these arose about the same time as the seven.'

[40] *ODA,* p. 400, (172).

[41] J. H. Todd, *Discourses on the Prophecies relating to antichrist in the Writings of Daniel and St. Paul,* Dublin, 1840, p. 176n (quoting T. Newton, *Dissertations on the Prophecies . . . ,* Dissert. xvi). *Cf.* Bishop Newton's dictum: 'What is Prophecy, but History anticipated; what History but Prophecy fulfilled' (*Notes on Popery and the Prophecies . . . ,* p. 47).

[42] Even Jerome, writing against Prophyry's assertion that Daniel was a Jew living in Maccabaean times and that the little horn in Dan. 7 was Antiochus Epiphanes, nevertheless thought that the horn in Dan. 8 was Antiochus (Migne, *Patrologiae,* vol. xxv . . . , p. 536f).

[43] So emphatic was Newton on this point that, when explaining Dan. 8: 21 where the rough goat is said to

represent the *king* of Graecia, he altered 'king' to 'kingdom', even although it was the angel Gabriel's interpretation he was changing!

[44] *ODA,* 368, 369 (120, 122). In A. D. 1357 it was reduced by the Sultan Bajazet, and passed into the hands of the Turks.

[45] Most of the confusion arose because the word was merely transliterated in the Septuagint . . . and Vulgate (Maozim). Newton, unlike Mede, transliterated the ayin as 'h', but, like Mede, took the word as singular in meaning although plural in form.

[46] Ioannis Calvini *Praelectiones in librum prophetiarum Danielis,* Genevae, 1591, p. 159: 'Locus ille . . . male expositus fuit. Neque enim caelum, neque terram attingunt interpretes . . .'.

[47] Mede, *Works,* p. 668. Horsley thought this prophecy of the ruler opposed to marriage was fulfilled in his own day, when in France the deputies of 1792 authorized divorce by mutual consent (*Brit. Mag.,* 1834, 5, 134: in a letter, not dated, but probably of 1797).

[48] *Cf.* Voltaire: 'Dans le cours d'une si longue vie, il [Newton] n'a eu ni passion, ni faiblesse, il n'ajamais approché d'aucune femme; c'est ce que m'a été confirmé par le medicin et le chirurgien entre les bras de qui il est mort' (*Lettres Philosophiques,* lettre 14).

[49] *ODA,* p. 419, (205).

[50] Z. Grey, *An examination of the fourteenth Chapter of Sir Isaac Newton's Observations upon the Prophecies of Daniel in which that Author's Notion of the Rise and Causes of Saint-Worship in the Christian Churches is carefully consider'd and disprov'd,* London, 1736.

[51] A. Young, *op. cit.,* vol. ii, p. 265.

[52] Whiston said: 'This is, generally speaking, a most remarkable Chapter, and discovers the true early Origin of *Popery* among the first *Athanasians,* beyond contradiction . . . *Sir Isaac Newton* . . . has fully discovered the nakedness of these pretended *Athanasian* Fathers, but really of these *Athanasian,* or rather *Antichristian* Hereticks, in the latter half of the fourth and former part of the fifth Century; which indeed he has done to the great satisfaction of such as love true Primitive *Christianity,* and to the utter confusion of those who still support Athanasianism and Popery among us' (*Six Dissertations: Reflexions upon Sir Isaac Newton's Observations upon the Prophecies of Daniel,* London, 1734, p. 320).

[53] 'An Historical Account of Two Notable Corruptions of Scripture,' Horsley, *op. cit* vol. v, p. 549.

[54] *ODA,* p. 455, (262).

[55] *Ibid.,* p. 385, (145). Whiston, *op. cit.,* p. 308.

[56] Newton used the Julian period (invented by Joseph Scaliger) for dates before Christ, As he said, Dionysius Exiguus in the sixth century invented the method of dating events A.C. (*ab Christo*). At least Dionysius popularized it in the West. Dates B. C., however, were not adopted until later in the eighteenth century.

[57] *ODA,* p. 391, (156).

[58] *Ibid.*

[59] *The Works of the Rev. P. Doddridge, D.D., in Ten Volumes,* London, 1903, vol. iv, p. 155: 'A dissertation on Sir Isaac Newton's Scheme for Reducing the several histories contained in the evangelists to their Proper Order.' Doddridge said of Newton: 'According to his usual method, he has done it [the chronology of our Lord's history] concisely, only marking out some of the outlines; and after having endeavoured to establish some of the chief principles, by arguments which he judged to be conclusive, he leaves it to his readers to apply those principles to several other particulars; which being deducible from them he did not think it necessary to enter into. Such is the method he has also taken in his chronology of the ancient kingdoms, and it was more suitable to that great genius which bore him with such amazing velocity through so vast a circle of various literature.'

[60] Clement of Alexandria, *Quis Dives Salvetur?,* ch. 42. Quoted by Eusebius, *H.E.,* iii, 23.

[61] E.g., E. B. Elliott, *op. cit.,* vol. i, p. 31ff.

[62] *ODA,* p. 441, (238).

[63] Whiston, *op. cit.,* p. 327.

[64] *Cf.* Richard Hurd, *An Introduction to the study of the Prophecies concerning the Christian Church . . . ,* London, 1839, pp. 327 ff. Mede, Newton, and others were really dealing with dislocations in the text.

[65] *ODA,* p. 450, (253).

[66] *Works,* p. 816. Brightman held that after wasting the East the locusts devoured the West, the *Western* locusts being 'the Monks, Fryars, a huge company of Religious orders, Cardinals, with the whole Popish Hierarchy' (Thomas Brightman, *The Revelation of Saint John . . . together with a most comfortable Exposition of the last and most difficult part of the Prophecy of Daniel,* Amsterdam, 1644, p. 93). Newton ignored this particular anti-Roman exegesis.

67 A. D. 637 (beginning of reign of Saracens at Damascus) to 936 (surrender of the Caliph of Baghdad to Mohomet, son of Rajici). *ODA,* p. 480, (305).

68 S. Bochart, *Hierozoicon sive de Animalibus Scripturae sanctae,* Londini, 1663, bk, iv, ch, 8: 'Ita quod [Rev. 9] versu 5 & 10 nocent hominibus per quinque menses, videtur ideo dici quia locustae vere natae sub fines aestatis obeunt, nec supra quinque menses vivere solent.' Richard Simon criticized Bochart's Biblical writings in his *Histoire Critique du Vieux Testament,* Amsterdam, 1685, p. 481, a work known to Newton, while Le Clere referred to Simon's 'injuste mepris de M. Bochart' (*Bibliothèque Universelle et Historique* 1692, 23, 273).

69 *ODA,* p. 480, (304).

70 Calvin, *op. cit.,* p. 157.

71 Using ordinary Greek alphabetic numerals we have $(30 + 1 + 300 + 5 + 10 + 50 + 70 + 100) = 666$.

72 Irenaeus, *Contra Haereses,* ch. 28, 40. Actually Irenaeus did not claim the authority of John for ΛΑΤΕΙΝΟΣ, but put it forward as his own conjecture and gave two other possible solutions.

73 K. ms. 5, p. 32.

74 D. Brewster, *Memoirs of the Life, Writings, and Discoveries of Sir Isaac Newton,* London, 1855, vol. ii, p. 525.

J. E. McGuire and P. M. Rattansi (essay date 1966)

SOURCE: "Newton and the Pipes of Pan," in *Notes and Records of the Royal Society of London,* Vol. 21, No. 2, December 1966, pp. 108-43.

[*In the following essay, McGuire and Rattansi examine unpublished drafts of a proposed Scholia to Propositions IV through IX of Newton's* Principia. *The critics argue that these papers demonstrate Newton's conviction that he was rediscovering truths once revealed to the ancients by God.*]

> What is it, by means of wch, bodies act on one another at a distance. And to what Agent did the Ancients attribute the gravity of their atoms and what did they mean by calling God an harmony and comparing him & matter (the corporeal part of the Universe) to the God Pan and his Pipe. Can any space be without something in it & what is that something in space void of matter (& what are its properties & operations on matter).
>
> Draft of Query 27 of *Opticks*[1]

Newtonian scholars have long been aware of a set of draft Scholia to Propositions IV to IX of Book III of the ***Principia.*** [2] These were composed in the 1690's, as part of an unimplemented plan for a second edition of the work. Since they describe supposed anticipations of Newton's doctrines in the thought of Graeco-Roman antiquity, they have become known as the 'classical' Scholia.[3] The analogies and parallels drawn in them are so strained, as judged by modern standards of scholarship, that it is tempting to consider them as merely literary embellishments of a scientific work.

However, the sheer bulk of the manuscripts, the number of copies and variants, their relation to Newton's other writings, and the testimony of Newton's associates together with their publication of some of the materials, all make it certain that he considered the arguments and conclusions of the Scholia an important part of his philosophy.

It would perhaps be possible to interpret the Scholia, with their discussions of legendary figures and their references to a 'mystical' philosophy, as the work of the 'magical' (and hence aberrant) Newton—as eccentric productions that possess little significance for the reconstruction of his genuinely scientific work, but merely throw light on his esoteric and occult interests. To us, however, this interpretation appears untenable. It is now amply clear that Newton's serious enquiries were not restricted to natural philosophy, investigated by an experimental-mathematical method. His studies of theology and ancient chronology were of equal importance to him, and were pursued in as rigorous a fashion as his scientific work.[4] There is sufficient evidence, even in his published writings, to show that he did not regard these different sorts of enquiry as unrelated exercises. Rather, he shared the belief, common in the seventeenth century, that natural and divine knowledge could be harmonized and shown to support each other.

We shall first describe the contents of these Scholia, and interpret them in the light of the statements of Newton's associates, and of other works by Newton. These materials will provide the basis for a re-examination of parts of the *General Scholium* and the ***Opticks.*** At that time, as is well known, Newton believed that he knew how God's agency operated in His created world, particularly in the cause of gravitation. Our analysis of the Scholia will show that Newton held (at least at the time of their composition) an equally firm belief about his own place among the *prisci theologi* who had possessed such knowledge. He believed, in brief, that God had once revealed these and other truths, but they had soon been obscured and had been partially rediscovered by certain antique sages. In this respect, Newton's work has close similarities with that of the Cambridge Platonists. These similarities may be more significant than the well-known similarity between Newton's doctrine of absolute space and that of Henry More. In re-examining Newton's relation to the Cambridge Platonists, we shall see that he did not merely borrow ideas from them, but was engaged in a private dialogue whose terms were set by a certain intellectual tradition.

The study of the 'classical' Scholia should therefore deepen our understanding of the Newton's philosophical endeavour, and make it possible to relate his work to its contemporary English natural-philosophical and theological context with greater precision.

I

The first public hint of Newton's studies of the *prisca* seems to have been contained in a letter from Fatio de Duillier to Huyghens on 5th February 1691/2. Fatio had just then begun his work of preparing a second edition of the **Principia,** the task having been entrusted to him after his return from Holland the previous September. He wrote:

> Monsieur Newton croit avoir decouvert assez clairement que les Anciens comme Pythagore, Platon &c. avoient toutes les demonstrations qu'il donne du veritable Systeme du Monde, et qui sont fondées sur la Pesanteur qui diminue reciproquement comme les quarrez des distances augmentent. Ils faisoient dit il un grand mystere de leurs connoissances. Mais il nois reste divers fragmens, pa où il paroit, à ce qu'il pretend, si on les met ensemble, qu'effectivement ils avoient les mêmes idées qui sont repandues dans les Principia Philosophiae Mathematica. Quand Monsieur Newton se seroit trompé il marque toujours beaucoup de candeur de faire un aveu comme celui la.[5]

It seems most likely that the letter was sanctioned by Newton and designed to test Huygens' reaction. Newton would hardly have countenanced the mention of these studies without his permission, and the last sentence of the quotation expressly invites Huygens' comments. Huygens' reply was courteous but negative.[6] He doubted that such ancients as the Pythagoreans could have demonstrated elliptical orbits, although he was willing to credit them with knowledge of certain general principles (like the heliocentric system and the balance of weight and centrifugal force for maintaining the moon in orbit). He used Borelli's failure to demonstrate elliptical orbits as evidence for the uniqueness of Newton's achievement, and then passed rapidly on to praise Newton's mathematical discoveries and urge their publication.

In May 1694, David Gregory visited Newton in Cambridge, and made 'Annotations Physical, Mathematical and Theological' from their conversations. Notes on the three topics follow each other in an indiscriminate sequence. Concerning the *prisca*, Gregory records:

He will spread himself in exhibiting the agreement of this philosophy with that of theancients, and principally with that of Thales. The philosophy of Epicurus and Lucretius is true and old, but was wrongly interpreted by the ancients as atheism.

It is clear from the names of the planets given by Thoth (the Egyptian Mercury)—he gave them, in fact, the names of his predecessors whom he wished to be accepted as Gods—that he was a believer in the Copernican system.[7]

There can be no doubt that Newton intended to incorporate such material into the revised version of the **Principia**; in July 1694 a memorandum of Gregory described the extensive changes planned by Newton, and mentioned:

> By far the greatest changes will be made to Book III. He will make a big change in Hypothesis III. page 402. He will show that the most ancient philosophy is in agreement with this hypothesis of his as much because the Egyptians and others taught the Copernican system, as he shows from their religion and hieroglyphics and images of the Gods, as because Plato and others—Plutarch and Galileo refer to it—observed the gravitation of all bodies towards all.[8]

Some of the materials which Newton then intended for inclusion in the revised edition of the **Principia** have survived in a reasonably complete state. The main body of text is a set of fifteen folio sheets in Newton's hand, in the Library of the Royal Society. Their contents are Scholia on Propositions IV to IX of the Third Book of the **Principia,** where the essentials of Newton's doctrine of gravitation are set out. The material includes many references to, and quotations from, the ancients on the nature of the physical world. There is not space to present the material of these 'classical' Scholia *in extenso*. We shall, however, give an indication of its character, and present important passages which he took to support these key propositions of the Third Book. Newton gave the manuscript to Gregory, probably on the visit of May 1694, either as a gift or as a loan. Gregory drew from it extensively for the preface to his *Astronomia Physicae et Geometricae Elementa,* some paragraphs being almost identical with the manuscript.[9]

The Propositions of Book III, for which the Scholia were intended, exhibit a carefully developed structure. The Book starts with six solar Phaenomena, obtained through astronomical observation and calculation. Then the first three Propositions state that the circumjovial planets, the primary planets, and the moon, are all retained in their orbits by a force which is mathematically described by the inverse-square law. The proof of this is supplied by the first four Propositions of the First Book.

So far we are at the level of the mathematical description of the phenomena. But Proposition IV states that the forces mentioned in the first three Propositions are the force of gravity. Thus it is a statement about a real force in the physical world, embodying the famous proof that the gravitational force which pulls terrestrial objects to the Earth is the same as that which pulls the moon from its inertial path. By induction and by appeal to Rules 1 and 2, Propositions V and VI extend the reasoning to cover the primary planets and then all celestial bodies. Proposition VI also introduces the proportionality of gravity to the quantity of matter in a body, which leads to a discussion of the interstitial void in the corrollaries. But more importantly, Proposition VI not only asserts the generality of the action of gravity in affecting all sensible bodies, but it implies that sub-sensibleparticles gravitate as well. This latter doctrine is explicitly treated in Proposition VII. The inverse-square law of attraction is shown, in Proposition VIII, to apply not only to celestial bodies but also to their component particles. Finally, Proposition IX asserts the law of action of the real force of gravity *within* celestial bodies. Thus, by this series of extensions, gravity is concluded to be a completely universal force.

The central purpose of the 'classical' scholia was to support the doctrine of universal gravitation as developed in these Propositions, and to enquire into its nature as a cosmic force. This doctrine is shown by Newton to be identifiable in the writings of the ancients. As will become clear, he is not using this historical evidence in a random fashion, or merely for literary ornamentation. Rather, the evidence is used in a serious and systematic fashion, as support for, and justification of, the components of Newton's theory of matter, space and gravitation. The evidence is used to establish four basic theses, which correspond to the matter of the Propositions IV to IX. These are, that there was an ancient knowledge of the truth of the following four principles: that matter is atomic in structure and moves by gravity through void space; that gravitational force acts universally; that gravity diminishes in the ratio of the inverse square of the distance between bodies; and that the true cause of gravity is the direct action of God. We shall analyse these in turn, using supporting texts from some associates of Newton, and from Newton's other writings.

It will be recalled that Propositions VI and VII are concerned with gravity as a real physical force, moving both perceptible and imperceptible bodies in a non-resisting void. In the Scholium to Proposition VI, which includes 62 lines from Lucretius, Newton says:

> Even the ancients were aware that all bodies which are round about the Earth, air and fire as well as the rest, have gravity towards the Earth, and that their gravity is proportional to the quantity of the matter

of which they consists. Lucretius thus argues in proof of the void.[10]

Newton then quotes twelve lines from Book I of *De Rerum Natura* which state that void exists, and that of any bodies which are equal in magnitude, difference in weight is explained by more or less interstitial void. This doctrine is discussed in the Corollaries to Proposition VI. Newton's comment on this passage is important:

> Lucretius here relates gravity to the function of the body, or its nature by which it is distinguished from Void, which has no gravity, and from this concludes that weight is always proportional to body. In this argument he includes all bodies, both imperceptible and perceptible. For he attributes this gravity even to those atoms of which other things consist. For he affirms that fire, and other bodies which are designated weightless, rise upwards not of their own accord but by a force which drives from below, just as wood, which is a body with gravity, rises up in water, whereas all bodies are being borne downwards through void space.[11]

Newton follows this with a passage of twenty-two lines from Book II of Lucretius, which shows his commentary to be, in part, a paraphrase. For the conclusion of this Lucretian passage states, after giving the same example of things which seem to rise upwards naturally:

> We do not doubt, but that all these things, as far as in them lies, are borne downwardsthrough the empty void.[12]

Thus it is clear from his commentary and from the passages quoted, that Newton regards Lucretius as holding in the manner of the *Principia* that all matter whatsoever gravitates in a non-resisting void. Another quotation of twenty-eight lines from Book II further supports this conclusion.

Newton then turns to the historical succession of the atomical hypothesis, which is implicit in the *Principia* and explicit in the Lucretian passages:

> This Lucretius taught from the mind of Epicurus, Epicurus from the mind of the more ancient Democritus. For certain persons, assuming the equality of the atoms, would have it that the gravity of bodies is in proportion to the number of the atoms of which they consist. Others, to whom the atoms were unequal taught that gravity is proportional not to the number of the solids but to the quality of the solid.

This distinction is supported by a quotation from Aristotle on the atomists, and by a reference to Simplicius, who places Leucippus and Democritus in the second position. For them, the 'quality' of the body is measured by the ratio of solid parts to void interstices, which together make up the body:

> But by the levity of the void these philosophers did not understand any positive quality of the void, as Aristotle's opinion is, but merely absence of gravity.

Newton concludes by bringing the 'Italic' philosophers into the succession:

> Among the philosophers therefore who have held that bodies are composed of atoms, it was a received opinion that gravity accrues both to atoms and to composite bodies, and that in individual bodies it is proportional to the quantity of matter. That bodies are compound of atoms was the view of both Ionic and Italic philosophers. *The followers of Thales and Pythagoras,* Plutarch observes, *deny that the section of those bodies which are subject to movement proceeds to infinity but ceases at those things which are individual and are called atoms.*[13]

In Proposition VII, Newton is explicitly concerned with the doctrine that the gravity of any composite body is the sum of its component parts which are held together by mutual gravitation. By analogy, he concludes that it follows that all celestial bodies mutually gravitate as the inverse square of the distance with respect to their components. Apart from the draft scholia in the Royal Society manuscript, there is another in the Portsmouth collection which is, in part, a summary of the longer set of scholia and which was probably intended as an alternative. Both documents are concerned with the absolute universality of gravitation. In the Royal Society manuscript there is a passage directly relevant to the main doctrine of Proposition VII, namely, that the quantity of matter of any body is a function of its parts:

> Therefore just as the attractive force of the whole Magnet is composed of the attractive forces of the individual particles of which the Magnet consists, even so the ancient opinion was thatGravity towards the whole Earth arises from the gravity towards its individual parts. For that reason, if the whole Earth were divided into several globes, gravity, by the mind of the ancients, would have to be extended towards each several globe, in the same way as magnetic attraction is extended towards individual fragments of the magnet. And the ratio of gravity is equally towards all bodies whatever.

> Hence Lucretius teaches that there exists no centre of the universe, and no lowest place, but that there are in infinite space worlds similar to this of ours, and in addition to this he argues for the infinity of things in these terms.[14]

Following this is another passage from Lucretius, containing an argument for the infinity of the universe:

> . . . if all the space in the universe stood contained within fixed boundaries on all sides and were limited, by this time the store of matter would by its solid weight have run together from all sides to the bottom . . .

Newton's comments on this passage are similar in the two manuscripts. The Royal Society manuscript reads:

> The force of the argument is that if the nature of things were bounded in any direction, the remotest bodies, since they would have no bodies beyond them into which to have gravity, would not stand in equilibrium but would by their own gravity make their way towards the things inside, and by flowing together from all quarters since infinite time would long ago have settled down in the midst of the whole as it were in a lowest place. Therefore, to the mind of Lucretius, each several body has gravity towards the matter situated round about it, and by virtue of overpowering gravity is carried into the region where matter is more copious, and all worlds whatsoever have mutual gravity towards one another, and by their own gravity towards worlds which are in our direction are precluded from falling on to worlds which are in another direction.[15]

An historical succession is added in the Portsmouth manuscript:

> This Lucretius records from Epicurus' philosophy, Book I line 983, and Book II lines 1064 and 1074. Now it is likely enough that Epicurus had learned all this from the mystical philosophers, seeing that Heraclides and the Pythagoreans and the followers of Orpheus said that all the stars were worlds in the infinite aether, as Plutarch has it in Book II, chapter 13, of the Beliefs of the Philosophers. This opinion also was held by Anaximander, who no doubt learned it from Thales, his teacher.[16]

In the same document, Newton dates the atomic succession back to Moschus the Phoenician.

> That all matter consists of atoms was a very ancient opinion. This was the teaching of the multitude of philosophers who preceded Aristotle, namely Epicurus, Democritus, Ecphantus, Empedocles, Zenocrates, Heraclides, Asclepiades, Diodorus, Metrodorus of Chios, Pythagoras, and previous to these Moschus the Phoenician whom Strabo declares older than the Trojan war. For I think that same opinion obtained in that mystic philosophy which flowed down to the Greeks from Egypt and Phoenicia, since atoms are sometimes found to be designated by the mystics as monads. For the mysteries of numbers equally with the rest of hieroglyphics had regard to the mystical philosophy.[17]

Newton goes on to say that such 'immutable seeds' account for the fact that 'the species of objects are conserved in perpetuity'.

It may be difficult for the modern reader to imagine Sir Isaac Newton being serious about such supposed 'anticipations' of his views. Indeed, were it not for the testimony of Fatio and Gregory, one would most naturally interpret them as adding a classical flourish to a scientific treatise. But the draft Scholium to Proposition VIII cannot be interpreted in such a fashion. For here Newton asserts unequivocally that Pythagoras discovered by experiment an inverse-square relation in the vibrations of strings (unison of two strings when tensions are reciprocally as the squares of lengths); that he extended such a relation to the weights and distances of the planets from the sun; and that this true knowledge, expressed esoterically, was lost through the misunderstanding of later generations. This is an instance of a fully developed *prisca sapientia,* and as such merits extended quotation.

> By what proportion gravity decreases by receding from the Planets the ancients have not sufficiently explained. Yet they appear to have adumbrated it by the harmony of the celestial spheres, designating the Sun and the remaining six planets, Mercury, Venus, Earth, Mars, Jupiter, Saturn, by means of Apollo with the Lyre of seven strings, and measuring the intervals of the spheres by the intervals of the tones. Thus they alleged that seven tones are brought into being, which they called the harmony diapason, and that Saturn moved by the Dorian phthong, that is, the heavy one, and the rest of the Planets by sharper ones (as Pliny, bk. 1, ch. 22 relates, by the mind of Pythagoras) and that the Sun strikes the strings. Hence Macrobius, bk. 1, ch. 19, says: 'Apollo's Lyre of seven strings provides understanding of the motions of all the celestial spheres over which nature has set the Sun as moderator.' And Proclus on Plato's Timaeus, bk. 3, page 200, 'The number seven they have dedicated to Apollo as to him who embraces all symphonies whatsoever, and therefore they used to call him the God the Hebdomagetes', that is the Prince of the number Seven. Likewise in Eusebius' Preparation of the Gospel, bk. 5, ch. 14, the Sun is called by the oracle of Apollo the King of the seven sounding harmony. But by this symbol they indicated that the Sun by his own force acts upon the planets in that harmonic ratio of distances by which the force of tension acts upon strings of different lengths, that is reciprocally in the duplicate ratio of the distances. For the force by which the same tension acts on the same string of different lengths is reciprocally as the square of the length of the string.
>
> The same tension upon a string half as long acts four times as powerfully, for it generates the Octave, and the Octave is produced by a force four times as great. For if a string of given length stretched by a given weight produces a given tone, the same tension

upon a string thrice as short acts nine times as much. For it produces the twelfth, and a string which stretched by a given weight produces a given tone needs to be stretched by nine times as much weight so as to produce the twelfth. And, in general terms, if two strings equal in thickness are stretched by weights appended, these strings will be in unison when the weights are reciprocally as the squares of the lengths of the strings. Now this argument is subtle, yet became known to the ancients. For Pythagoras, as Macrobius avows, stretched the intestines of sheep or the sinews of oxen by attaching various weights, and from this learned the ratio of the celestial harmony. Therefore, by means of such experiments he ascertained that the weights by which all tones on equal strings . . . were reciprocally as the squares of the lengths of the string by which the musical instrument emits the same tones. But the proportion discovered by these experiments, on the evidence of Macrobius, he applied to the heavens and consequently by comparing those weights with the weights of the Planets and the lengths of the strings with the distances of the Planets, he understood by means of the harmony of the heavens that the weights of the Planets towards the Sun were reciprocally as the squares of their distances from the Sun.

> But the Philosophers loved so to mitigate their mystical discourses that in the presence of the vulgar they foolishly propounded vulgar matters for the sake of ridicule, and hid the truth beneath discourses of this kind. In this sense Pythagoras numbered his musical tones from the Earth, as though from here to the Moon were a tone, and thence to Mercury a semitone, and from thence to the rest of the Planets other musical intervals. But he taught that the sounds were emitted by the motion and attrition of the solid spheres, as though a greater sphere emitted a heavier tone as happens when iron hammers are smitten. And from this, it seems, was born the Ptolemaic system of solid orbs, when meanwhile Pythagoras beneath parables of this sort was hiding his own system and the true harmony of the heavens.[18]

There is a piece of personal testimony which confirms Newton's belief in the wisdom of Pythagoras: that of Conduitt.

> Sir. I thought Pythagoras's music of the spheres was intended to typify gravity & as he makes the sounds & notes to depend on the size of the strings, so gravity depends on the density of matter.[19]

Moreover, Newton's most brilliant disciple, Maclaurin, expressed the same view, though with a slight but significant reservation:

> A musical chord gives the same notes as one double in length, while the tension or force with which the latter is stretched is quadruple: and the gravity of a planet is quadruple of the gravity of a planet at a

double distance. In general, that any musical chord may become unison to a lesser chord of the same kind, its tension must be increased in the same proportion as the square of its length is greater; and that the gravity of a planet may become equal to the gravity of another planet nearer to the sun, it must be increased in proportion as the square of its distance from the sun is greater. If therefore we should suppose musical chords extended from the sun to each planet, that all these chords might become unison, it would be requisite to increase or diminish their tensions in the same proportions as would be sufficient to render the gravities of the planets equal. And from the similitude of those proportions the celebrated doctrine of the harmony of the spheres is supposed to have been derived.[20]

He goes on to say that:

> these doctrines of the *Pythagoreans,* concerning the diurnal and annual motions of the earth, the revolutions of the comets . . . and the harmony of the spheres, are very remote from the suggestions of sense, and opposite to vulgar prejudices; so we cannot but suppose that they who first discovered them must have made a very considerable progress in astronomy and natural philosophy.

Gregory too quotes this; his description makes it clear that Pythagoras used sound Newtonian method for his discovery:

> Pythagoras afterwards applied the proposition he had thus found by experiments, to the heavens, and thus learned the harmony of the spheres.[21]

The same theme was mentioned in a draft variant to Query 23 of the Latin edition of the *Opticks* of 1706:

> By what means do bodies act on one another at a distance? The ancient Philosophers who held Atoms and Vacuum attributed gravity to atoms without telling us the means unless in figures: as by calling God Harmony representing him & matter by the God Pan and his Pipe, or by calling the Sun the prison of Jupiter because he keeps the Planets in their Orbs. Whence it seems to have been an ancient opinion that matter depends upon a Deity for its laws of motion as well as for its existence.[22]

This passage serves us as a bridge to the material of the Scholium intended for Proposition IX. We notice that at the end, Newton states the *cause* of gravity, for the ancients, was God. In this draft variant, Newton develops the idea further. After stating that matter is passive and non-active, he says:

> These are passive laws and to affirm that there are no others is to speak against experience. For we find in ourselves a power of moving our bodies by

our thought. Life and will are active principles by which we move our bodies and thence arise other laws of motion unknown to us.

> And since all matter duly formed is attended with signes of life and all things are framed with perfect art and wisdom and nature does nothing in vain; if there be an universal life and all space by the sensorium of a thinking being who by immediate presence perceives all things in it, as that which thinks in us, perceives their pictures in the brain: those laws of motion arising from life or will may be of universal extent. To some such laws the ancient Philosophers seem to have alluded when they called God Harmony and signified his actuating matter harmonically by the God Pan's playing upon a Pipe and attributing musick to the spheres made the distances and motions of the heavenly bodies to be harmonical, and represented the Planets by the seven strings of Apollo's Harp.[23]

The personal testimony of David Gregory confirms the importance of this set of ideas for Newton's philosophy. His memorandum of 21 December 1705 tells us that Newton would answer the question, 'What cause did the ancients assign to gravity?' (in the projected Latin edition of the *Opticks*) by saying that, 'they reckoned God the cause of it, nothing else, that is no body being thecause; since every body is heavy'. Thus we have in the intended Query, an expression of the Newtonian distinction between passive and active principles in an orderly universe, and the complete dependence of matter, for its existence and motion, on the will of God; and all of this expressed by the ancients through the idea of 'Harmony'.

The draft Scholium to Proposition IX develops the same theme in greater detail. It starts with Newton's customary abjuring of causal explanations, and concludes with an eloquent passage in which the ancient dieties are assimilated into the one true God.

> So far I have expounded the properties of gravity. Its cause I by no means recount. Yet I shall say what the ancients thought about this subject. Thales regarded all bodies as animate, deducing that from magnetic and electrical attractions. And by the same argument he ought to have referred the attraction of gravity to the soul of matter. Hence he taught that all things are full of Gods, understanding by Gods animate bodies. He held the sun and the Planets for Gods. And in the same sense Pythagoras, on account of its immense force of attraction, said that the sun was the prison of Zeus, that is, a body possessed of the greatest circuits. And to the mystical philosophers Pan was the supreme divinity inspiring this world with harmonic ratio like a musical instrument and handling it with modulation, according to that saying of Orpheus 'striking the harmony of the world in playful song'. Thence they named harmony God

and soul of the world composed of harmonic numbers. But they said that the Planets move in their circuits by force of their own souls, that is, by force of the gravity which takes its origin from the action of the soul. From this, it seems, arose the opinion of the Peripatetics concerning Intelligences moving solid globes. But the souls of the sun and of all the Planets the more ancient philosophers held for one and the same divinity exercising its powers in all bodies whatsoever, according to that of Orpheus in the Bowl.

> Cylennius himself is the interpreter of divinity
>   to all:
> The nymphs are water. Ceres corn, Vulcan is
>   fire.
> Neptune is the sea striking the foaming
>   shores.
> Mars is war, kindly Venus is peace, the Bull-
>   born
> Horned Bacchus frequenting gladsome feasts
> Is to mortals and to gods relief of mind from
>   care.
> Golden Themis is guardian of Justice and
>   right
> Next Apollo is the Sun, hurling his darts
> From afar, circling round, the Divines and the
>   Soothsayers
> The Epidaurian God is the expeller of
>   diseases: these things
> All are one thing, though there be many
>   names.[24]

For the material of this passage, Newton drew heavily on Macrobius, Cicero, Virgil, Porphyry, and the Orphic hymns. In it, he completes the view of nature which was developed in the earlier Scholia. In those, the universe was seen as comprising innumerable worlds, composed of immutable atoms, held together by gravity, moving in an absolute void. Now the immaterial, 'immechanical' cause of it, is seen to be God himself. Newton states this conception clearly in another manuscript intended for the same unimplemented edition of the 1690's:

> . . . those ancients who more rightly held unimpaired the mystical philosophy as Thales andthe Stoics, taught that a certain infinite spirit pervades all space *into infinity,* and contains and vivifies the entire world. And this spirit was their supreme divinity, according to the Poet cited by the Apostle. In him we live and move and have our being.[25]

Thus the more ancient philosophers, such as Orpheus, who were closer to the true philosophy, held that gravity was a direct result of the exercise of divine power. Later philosophers such as the Ionics, the Italics and Plato reveal themselves to have partial knowledge of this, if their utterances are properly interpreted. For instance, Newton says of Plato:

Hence after Plato has, by succession from Pythagorean doctrine and by the divine profundity of his own genius, shown that apart from these ratios (i.e. musical ratios) there can be no possibility of conjunction: in his Timaeus, he constitutes the soul of the world by means of the composition of those ratios, by the ineffable providence of God the craftsman. Consequently the soul of the world, which propels into movement this body of the universe visible to us, being constructed of ratios which created from themselves a musical concord, must of necessity produce musical sounds from the movement which it provides by its proper impulse having found the origin of them in the craftsmanship of its own composition.[26]

There is little doubt that Newton saw in analogy to musical harmony, the principles of law and order in the natural world. Such harmony was the profoundest expression of cosmos. But for Newton, nature operating according to these divine ratios, could scarcely be dependent on the guidance of an intermediate world soul. Rather (as we shall soon see) the exquisite structure of things immediately bespoke the providential governance of a Divine power actually present in the world.

II

It seems clear from the 'classical' Scholia, and from the testimony of his intimate friends, that Newton considered it necessary to complement his endeavours in natural philosophy by an investigation of the sources of the ancient knowledge that he believed himself to be re-discovering; and also that in that ancient tradition God was conceived as being in the most intimate relation with His creation. The draft Scholia, running parallel to the Propositions of Book III of the *Principia,* begin with classical views on matter, void, and gravity, and culminate in an affirmation of the ancient knowledge of the divine harmony by which God moved all bodies in the cosmos. Since a 'classical' edition of the *Principia,* incorporating these annotations, was never published, it may plausibly be argued that Newton considered these enquiries too speculative, or too incongruous with his inductive natural philosophy, to be made public.

Newton's thoughts on these matters were not, however, kept completely concealed. He permitted David Gregory to use the material extensively in a long historical preface to his *Astronomia physicae et geometricae elementa* (1702), if without attribution. (It was also available to Maclaurin for his much later work.) More important, the basic thesis of the Scholia is set out, more or less explicitly, in important sections of his two most important scientific works. These passages enable us to conclude that Newton was convinced of the importance of the *prisca* tradition for his philosophy, and that he believed his inductive method would yield as much certainty in historical and theologicalas in natural-philosophical studies. In both the *General Scholium* to the second edition of the **Principia** (1703) as well as the concluding pages of the **Opticks** (1704), a discussion of God's causal agency in the natural world ends with allusions to the suppressed material of the 'classical' Scholia.

In the *General Scholium,* Newton's special doctrines of the near-identification of infinite space with God and the assertion of His continuous intervention in His Creation end, not with a characteristic disclaimer, but with the affirmation:

> And thus much concerning God, to discourse of whom from the appearance of things does certainly belong to natural philosophy.[27]

This extension of the scope of natural philosophy is significant. It implies that the sequence of ever more fundamental causes in nature does not stop short of the First Cause, but includes Him as a legitimate part of a natural-philosophical inquiry. That is already implicit in the use of God's attributes to establish the properties of atoms; and it justifies the attempt to define the mode of God's causal agency, as in the 'harmony' mentioned in the *Scholium* to Proposition IX.

Newton's belief in a *prisca* tradition is expressed in the same passages. In the *General Scholium,* a lengthy discussion of the divine attributes is concluded with the remarks:

> And from his true dominion it follows that the true God is a living, intelligent, and powerful Being; and, from His other perfections, that He is supreme, or most perfect. God is the same God, always and everywhere. He is omnipresent, not *virtually* but also *substantially;* for virtue cannot subsist without substance. In Him are all things contained and moved.[28]

Newton's marginal note to the passage cites some of the main sources of the 'classical' Scholia:

> This was the opinion of the Ancients. So *Pythagoras,* in Cicer. *de Nat. Deo.* Lib. I. *Thales, Anaxagoras, Virgil* Georg. Lib. IV. Ver. 220; and the *Aeneid,* lib. VI, ver. 721. *Philo Allegor,* at the beginning of Lib. I. *Aratus,* in his *Phaenom,* at the beginning. So also the sacred writers: as *St. Paul, Acts* xvii, ver. 27, 28. *St. John*'s Gosp. Chap. xiv, ver. 2. *Moses, Deut.* iv, ver. 39; and x, ver. 14. *David, Psal.* cxxxix, ver. 7, 8, 9. *Solomon,* I *Kings,* viii, ver. 27. *Job,* xxii, ver. 12, 13, 14. *Jeremiah,* xxiii, ver. 23, 24. The Idolators supposed the sun, moon, and stars, the souls of men, and other parts of the world, to be parts of the Supreme God, and therefore to be worshipped; but erroneously.

Newton is asserting here a *prisca theologia,* an original conception of divinity from which 'the Idolators' had departed. A parallel *prisca* is described in a concluding passage of the **Opticks.** After examining the attributes of God and emphasizing His power to vary the laws of nature in different parts of the universe, he seems to pass by an abrupt transition to a review of his method of Analysis and the manner in which it was employed in the treatise. He then reverts to theological considerations, for

> . . . if Natural Philosophy in all its parts, by pursuing this method, shall at length be perfected, the bounds of Moral Philosophy will be also enlarged. For so far as we can know byNatural Philosophy what is the first cause, what power He has over us, and what benefits we receive from Him, so far our duty towards Him, as well as that towards one another, will appear to us by the Light of Nature. And no doubt, if the worship of false gods had not blinded the heathen, their Moral Philosophy would have gone farther than to the four cardinal virtues; and instead of teaching the transmigration of souls, and to worship the sun and moon and dead heroes, they would have taught us to worship our true Author and Benefactor, as their ancestors did under the government of Noah and his sons before they corrupted themselves.[29]

The *prisca sapientia* and the *prisca theologia* is implicit in the closing passage of Newton's great scientific treatise. A true natural philosophy must lead to a surer knowledge of God, and thence to a firmly-grounded moral philosophy. The curious reference to Noah and his sons can be explained only by the assumption that, if true religion follows from true natural philosophy, then the latter must have served as the foundation for the former in the pristine age before the corruption of Noah and his sons.[30] The supporting evidence from the unpublished material would appear to make that conclusion certain.

Finally, certain stylistic features of the concluding section of the **Opticks,** quoted above, make it plain that when Newton undertook to 'discourse' of God within natural philosophy, he believed that could be done by the same rigorous methods as those employed in mathematics and experimental philosophy. As mentioned above, in the last pages of the **Opticks,** a discussion of God's attributes and power is interrupted by a discussion of Newton's method of 'Analysis', consisting in a careful sequence of inductions from observations and experiment. The sequence of causes yielded by this method, could be pursued 'Till the argument end in the most general'. Newton seems to be alluding here to the First Cause or God. That interpretation is strengthened by the succeeding passage, quoted above. The perfection of natural knowledge must lead to a more perfect knowledge of God, with its attendant moral benefits.[31]

More direct evidence for Newton's confidence in his method as yielding certainty in theology, as in natural philosophy in the narrower sense, is provided by the qualifications with which he introduces his assertions. In Queries notorious for the cautions with which they are hedged, it is most significant that Newton's theological asseverations are introduced by 'must be allowed', 'nothing else but', and 'no doubt'.[32] It is inconceivable that Newton would have publicly claimed such certainty for these propositions unless they were grounded as firmly for him as the inverse-square law of gravitation and the composite nature of white light.

The published texts discussed above confirm our interpretation of the 'classical' Scholia as constituting a serious investigation for Newton. We see that Newton was prepared to make a public avowal of his belief that he believed in God's direct intervention in His creation; that theological and historical knowledge could be obtained by the sure method of inductive analysis; that there was a *prisca* in theology and philosophy which could be recovered; and that the deepest problem of natural philosophy, the cause of gravitational attraction, could only be explained within such a historical-theological framework. In the light of these assumptions, Newton would have every confidence in his interpretation of ancient sources for his 'classical' Scholia, finding there atoms, gravity and the void, the Copernican System and the inverse-square law.

In these principles, there is a direct link with Newton's immediate predecessors, the Cambridge Platonists. Newton's dialogue with the Cambridge Platonists, and his concern with the theological implications of fundamental natural philosophy, were not a passing interest of his troubled middle years. A passage from *de Gravitatione et Aequipondio Fluidorum*, written about 1670, confirms his continuing concern:

> . . . some may perhaps prefer to suppose that God imposes on the soul of the world, created by him, the task of endowing definite spaces with the properties of bodies, rather than to believe that this function is directly discharged by God. Therefore the world should not be called the creation of that soul but of God alone, who created it by constituting the soul of such a nature that the world necessarily emanates from it. But I do not see why God himself does not directly inform space with bodies; so long as we distinguish between the formal reason of bodies and the act of divine will.

Newton's Platonism was not entirely the Platonism of More and Cudworth, with their stress on such intermediaries as the Hylarchichal Principle; but it was also a Platonism in the spirit of the early Church Fathers. Still, as in More, Cudworth and the Fathers, the basic world picture of the 'classical' Scholia emerges from what Newton took to be an 'entire and genuine philosophy' which had been lost. Newton, and the Cambridge Platonists, saw as their task the unification and restoration of this philosophy. It will be one of the main tasks of the remainder of this paper to characterize further the origin and nature of this distinctively English tradition of natural philosophy.

The apparent contradiction between such a traditional Neo-Platonic philosophy, and the stern inductivism of the *Principia,* dissolves when we examine more closely how Newton modified the 'mechanical' philosophy of nature which was current earlier in the century. In one sense he expanded it, by allowing unexplained forces into his explanations of the phenomena; but in a deeper sense he restricted it, especially in its pretensions to knowledge of the natural world. A sign of this restrictive approach appeared in his early work in optics. There, he rejected the arbitrarily formulated hypotheses of such philosophers as Descartes and Hooke; for they could not from these deduce the phaenomena of nature, and their pictorial mechanisms were incompatible with the laws of such phaenomena. For Newton, the source of their error was that they did not sufficiently appreciate that the mechanical philosophy, rigorously conceived, was simply the estimation of forces in nature by geometrical calculation in terms of matter in motion. This conception was secured by the brilliant achievements of the *Principia.*

At times Newton certainly hoped that he could extend this approach to include the behaviour of the insensibly small particles of matter. But he realized that the most the 'analogy of nature' would allow was the transference of his system of quantitative laws to the motions of such invisible particles. That is, they applied only to the *atomical* part of his system, to *vis inertiae:* 'a passive Principle by which Bodies persist in their Motion or Rest, receive Motion in proportion to the Force impressing it, and resist as much as they are resisted!' But the heart of Newton's philosophy of nature, the world of forces and active principles, lay categorically beyond the systems of the *Opticks* and the *Principia.* How these principles were to be explained was a great, though hidden, problem of Newton's work. There is evidence that he tried different approaches to it at different periods; and the material of the 'classical' Scholia comes from a time when he seems to have largely abandoned earlier attempts at a quasi-material explanation of forces, and of gravity in particular. However, evenwhen in his later years he again entertained the possibility of an 'aetherial medium', this did not obviate the 'necessity of conceiving and recruiting it (motion) by active principles, such as are the cause of Gravity . . .'. Newtonian forces were never such as to be explained away by aetherial mechanisms; by nature immaterial, they required a different category of existence for their explanation.

Thus the ontological problem of causation, conceived in the classical neoplatonic framework, was central to

Newton's thought.[33] His failure to solve it is less significant than his attempt to investigate it through a unique combination of methods: a rigorously inductive philosophy, using controlled experiment and elaborate mathematics; complemented by an historical approach, reconstructing the *prisca sapientia* of the laws of God's agency in the world.

In the light of this interpretation of Newton's programme for philosophy, we may re-examine the significance of the published *Queries.* It may well be that their hints and suggestions for further experimental and theoretical work were taken by Newton's successors to be guides to the complete achievement of the new natural philosophy within the mathematical framework of the ***Principia.*** But in his private thoughts, certainly in the period of the 'classical' Scholia and probably throughout his life, Newton knew that the programme was incomparably more vast. For he saw the task of natural philosophy as the restoration of the knowledge of the complete system of the cosmos, including God as the creator and as the ever-present agent.[34]

The dream of a *science universelle* was not unique to Newton; it motivated the deepest philosophers of the seventeenth century, as Descartes and Leibniz. Where Newton stands out is in his choice of materials and methods for such a science, drawing partly on a neo-platonic tradition which flourished in England long after it had declined among leading philosophers on the Continent. That tradition will be examined in the following section.

III

The weight attached by Newton to his historical Scholia must appear curious and anachronistic in the light of the generally-accepted view of the intellectual milieu in late seventeenth- and early eighteenth-century England. The 1690's witnessed a decisive confrontation in England in a literary battle that had raged through much of the century: the 'battle of books' between those who championed and those who contested the superiority of the moderns over the ancients. In 1694 the young William Wotton published his *Reflections on Ancient and Modern Learning,* a work which gave a careful account of the scientific achievements of the century, and, while on the whole acknowledging the superiority of the ancients in literature, insisted that the moderns had far surpassed them in natural philosophy. Wotton's work was a reply to Sir William Temple's defense of the ancients in his *Essay upon the Ancient and Modern Learning* (1690). The controversy has been regarded as an indication of the extent to which the idea of progress had permeated the general intellectual consciousness by this time, as compared with Temple's circular view of history.[35] Newton's defense of his *systema mundi* by representing it as no more than a return to the views of the ancients

appears reactionary against that background, and not easily reconcilable with the idea of progress.

The discrepancy seems most glaring in Newton, since his system of the world came to be regarded as the most important argument for the superiority of the moderns over the ancients. Was Newton, in poring over the fragments of the ancients and elaborating dubious genealogies for his doctrines, reflecting a backward-looking attitude peculiar to him and his circle of intimates at Cambridge? It would be misleading to accept such a view of Newton's relations to the general intellectual currents of his time. Though a new conception of human progress had been gaining ground through the seventeenth century, there were other conceptions of the development of human knowledge whose rôle can easily be overlooked or minimized if we fix our gaze wholly on the 'idea of progress'. Through them Newton is linked to a certain Renaissance tradition, and, beyond the thinkers of the Renaissance, to the early Greek Church Fathers on whom he relied so considerably in discovering intimations of his physical doctrines among the ancients.

'Rebirth', 'rediscovery', not absolute originality but a return to truths well known to men in earlier ages, corrupted and obscured through the centuries: that is recognized as a cardinal characteristic of the Italian Renaissance. The broad similarity of Newton's scholia with that approach is immediately obvious. A more precise understanding of various *prisca* traditions and their modifications is necessary before we can place Newton's views in their historical context.

During the Renaissance, the ideal of classical antiquity aided the emergence and legitimation of a new sensibility and a new view of the world and of man. Innovation and experiment, the break with the traditional culture of the time, could be justified by a doctrine of the 'imitation' of the ancients, whose civilization typified the perfect models of conduct, arts, philosophy and polity. By the sixteenth century, the 'prisca' concept served, at least for the more critical humanists as a way of drawing attention to the undoubted superiority which classical antiquity had enjoyed over medieval Europe in civilization and refinement.[36] But there were other thinkers who interpreted the concept much more literally. They wished to demonstrate that the best of pre-Christian thought owed its excellence to the fact that it represented fragments of the only major non-Christian revelation which a Christian could acknowledge, the Mosaic one enshrined in the Old Testament. Others postulated a series of partial revelations to humanity, preceding the Christian one, through a chain of *prisci theologi.*[37] It is not surprising that the most elaborately developed Renaissance *prisca* doctrine is to be found in the works of leading thinkers of the Platonic Academy at Florence in the late fifteenth century, Marsilio Ficino (1433-1499) and Pico della

Mirandola (1463-1494), since their interest was centred upon writings and practices which the Church had traditionally regarded as heretical and diabolic: the magical works of late antiquity, and especially the newly-recovered *Corpus Hermeticum*. Through Ficino's Latin translation of the *Poemander* and *Asclepius* of Hermes Trismegistus, supposedly an Egyptian contemporary of Moses, these opinions came to be widely diffused in the sixteenth and seventeenth centuries.[38]

Tracing pagan wisdom back to Moses was far more cautious and compatible with orthodoxy than postulating a series of partial revelations, since the unique status of Old Testament was thus safeguarded. In practice, the two approaches were not kept quite distinct. Ficino, for example, had accused the Neo-Platonists of having stolen from the apostles and apostolic disciples 'anything sublime that they have said about the divine mind, angels, and other things pertaining to theology'.[39] But the tendency was pursued to such an extreme by other thinkers that every great pagan philosopher, including Plato, was placed in the debt of 'Egyptian wisdom'. The attribution was notoriginal. The cult of 'Egyptian wisdom' found many votaries at Hellenistic Alexandria in late antiquity. Jewish thinkers of the Alexandrian school sought to reconcile their own religious traditions with the Greek doctrines to which they had been exposed by attributing a Hebraic origin to Greek philosophy.[40] Even before Philo, a host of treatises had convicted the Greek philosophers of having stolen from the Hebrews, until Plato (in a famous saying attributed to Numneius) became nothing but 'an Attic Moses'. The Egyptian priests themselves began to claim an Egyptian origin for the doctrines, arts and institutions of the Greeks. Pythagoras had derived his theory of numbers, and Democritus his supposed knowledge of astronomy from the Egyptians and had transmitted these to the Hellenes.[41] The Alexandrian Christians gave the Hebraic tradition an important place in Christian apologetics.

Foremost among these was Clement of Alexandria (d. c. 213 A. D.), founder of the famous Catechetical School, whose authority was regarded as supreme by Newton in his biblical studies. Clement accepted the necessity of the heritage of Greek philosophy for Christianity. In defending Christianity and seeking the conversion of pagan intellectuals, Clement employed two basic techniques. One was allegorism. The Old Testament was represented as embodying the moral law; it was inferior to the Gospel, since it worked by fear and not by love. The rest of it revealed Christ throughout, but in riddles and symbols for those who could read it aright (the postulate adopted by Newton in his studies of the prophetical books). The other Clementine technique consisted of tracing Hellenic wisdom to borrowings from the Hebrew prophets, Plato being simply ὁ ἐς βρχίω φιλόσφος, and Clement's *Stromata* served through the centuries as he chief handbook of those

who claimed an Hebraic origin for Greek science and philosophy.[42] In Clement, as in other Christian apologists like Lactantius, Eusebius, Justin, and St. Augustine, the attribution was supported by the testimony of the mysterious Hermes Trismegistus, regarded as an Egyptian *priscus* who prefigured the Christian revelation of the future.[43]

In the sixteenth century, the many authors who adhered to these *prisca* traditions drew upon the authority of these patristic works. By a curious shift, a tactic originally employed to secure the authority of the Christian revelation against pagan philosophy was now used by Renaissance apologists for pagan philosophy. Since what was best in the philosophy of Greece and Rome was borrowed from the Mosaic revelation, Christianity had nothing to fear from the study of pagan doctrines.

The history of *prisca* doctrines in the sixteenth century is complicated by the Reformation and Counter-Reformation, and the doctrinal strife between Protestants and Catholics and among the various Protestant sects. The Protestant stress on the Bible at the expense of the mediating Church may be expected to have diminished Catholic enthusiasm for the naked text of the Scripture as the sole repository of God's revelation to mankind. It is certainly true that Catholic writers who continued to concern themselves with the *prisca* in the post-Reformation period came to be regarded with increasing suspicion by the orthodox. An over-emphasis on the *prisca* could lead to a depreciation of the uniqueness of the Christian revelation. In the closing years of the sixteenth century, two heretic south-Italian Dominicans, each in his own way, conceived it as their mission to restore the true Hermetic religion. One of these was Tommaso Campanella (1558-1639), who spent twenty-five years in the prison of the Inquisition for his part in a Calabrian revolt aiming to set up an Hermetic 'City of the Sun'.[44] The other was Giordano Bruno (1548-1600), burnt at the stakein Rome, who planned to restore the true Egyptian 'religion of the world', Christianity having been a.falling away from that true religion.[45] That is probably the reason for Francesco Patrizi's much less socially revolutionary ideas in his *Nova de universis philosophia* (1591) being placed on the Index in 1594.[46]

The *prisca* doctrines discussed so far were not without significance for natural philosophy, in as much as its adherents wished to substitute a Neo-Platonic explanation, based on secret sympathies and antipathies, stellar virtues, and the microcosm-macrocosm analogy, for the Aristotelian qualitative physics.[47] A *prisca* variant more directly concerned with natural philosophy made its appearance in the late sixteenth century. There was a growing interest in the teachings of the earliest Greek natural philosophers, the Pre-Socratics of the Ionic and Milesian schools, and ancient atomic doctrines were attracting greater attention. Even in antiquity atomism had been associated with atheism, and its assimilation into a basically religious framework raised special difficulties. The Democritean universe of jostling atoms, bereft of all qualities save the purely quantitative characteristics of size, figure and motion, needed no Creator, nor special act of creation. Becoming entangled by chance, they gave birth to bodies and universes, and served to explain all phenomena.

During the late sixteenth century, the diffusion of the works of Strabo, Sextus Empiricus, Diogenes Laertius, and Plutarch revived a certain tradition about the origins of atomism, which, in turn, suggested a *prisca* doctrine to clothe it in respectability and reconcile it with orthodoxy.[48] Relying on a now lost work of Posidonius, these authorities named a certain Moschus, a Phoenician, who lived before the Trojan war, as the first expositor of atomism. In 1598, Arcerius, a Friesian philologist, identified Moschus with Mochus, another Phoenician, whose successors Pythagoras (according to Iamblichus) had encountered and conversed with during a sojourn at Sidon. But Arcerius went much farther: he suggested that Moschus-Mochus was no other than Moses himself.[49] It was a momentous identification which proved popular and influential through the seventeenth century. Many leading Protestant scholars lent their support to it. The great Isaac Casaubon (1559-1614) confirmed that Mochus was the Tyrian name for Moses. John Selden (1584-1654) accepted the identification. Gerardus Vossius (1577-1649) discussed Strabo's account of Moschus's natural philosophy.[50]

Although Arcerius's identification of Moschus with Moses was not universally accepted, the derivation of Democritean atomism from the Hebrews is reflected in such authors as Daniel Sennert (1572-1637), the well-known German iatrochemist, in 1636,[51] Robert Boyle,[52] and Pierre Gassendi.[53]

But the most sustained attempt to develop these *prisca* doctrines into a justification for a new and revolutionary natural philosophy by tracing it to the Mosaic revelation, was undertaken in mid-seventeenth-century England by certain thinkers at Cambridge, grouped familiarly as the Cambridge Platonists. Newton was at Cambridge when their influence was considerable. He early became acquainted with their writings. There are striking similarities between their approach and his, to the relation between revelation and natural philosophy. The views of the Cambridge Platonists must therefore be discussed here in some detail.

Joseph Glanvill, who was admitted to Exeter College at Oxford in 1652, regretted having entered Oxford rather than Cambridge where he believed the 'new philosophy' was held in greater esteem.[54] It seems certain that the proponents of the 'new' (by which he

means the Cartesian) philosophy whom Glanvill had in mind were the Cambridge Platonists. At Oxford, the scientific group which came together from the late 1640's concentrated its attention on the more purely scientific aspects of the work of Descartes, Gassendi, and other Continental natural philosophers. The Cambridge Platonist approach to these philosophers was guided by different problems and preoccupations. Henry More (1614-1687) had early saluted Descartes as the prince of philosophers, but his deepest interests did not lie in Descartes' more purely technical and scientific output.[55] For him Descartes' main achievement lay in providing a rational demonstration of the existence of incorporeal substance, and in offering a grand synthesis reconciling theology and natural philosophy. More saw Descartes as making an enormous contribution towards building an 'exteriour Fortification about Theology', to repel 'gigantic batteries raised against the belief of the *existence of a God,* and of a *Reward in the World to come . . .*'.[56] More was writing during the turbulent decades of the Puritan Revolution, when these dangers were felt to have reached unprecedented heights in England. They could be refuted by resorting to the Cartesian *cogito* argument, and by showing that acceptance of the Cartesian postulate of the material world as dead and inert involved the metaphysical necessity of an immaterial principle to set it into motion and preserve its motion.

In attempting to introduce the Cartesian postulate of a dead world of matter into Neo-Platonism, the Cambridge Platonists were embarking on a formidable task, running counter to the historical tendencies of that philosophy. The hylozoistic magical philosophies of nature in the sixteenth century had drawn inspiration from late-antique Neo-Platonism, and the 'enthusiasts' in Civil-War England had urged the teaching of these philosophies of nature at English universities in place of the 'rubbish' of scholastic learning.[57] Reacting against them, as well as against Deists, Hobbists and Socinians, the Cambridge Platonists adopted a sharp distinction between matter and spirit, although the distinction lost its Cartesian clarity in their emphasis on a 'hylarchic principle', which was in effect a restatement of Neo-Platonic world-soul as intermediary between God and the universe. In order to assimilate the Cartesian natural philosophy to their Christianized Neo-Platonism, the Cambridge Platonists read Platonic innate ideas into the Cartesian *cogito* argument, the 'aetherial vehicle'[58] into his First and Second Matter, and, most important, developed an historical thesis about the origins of the Cartesian philosophy. Since the true revelation in religion as in natural philosophy had been vouchsafed to Moses, Descartes had only *rediscovered* the true natural philosophy. But that natural philosophy was to be found not in Plato, but as glimmerings in the atheistic Leucippus and Democritus. How was the paradox to be resolved? Greatly expanding Arcerius's suggestion, More proposed that the Mosaic philosophy had passed to the Greeks in two divided streams, the religious part being received by Plato, the natural philosophical part (through Pythagoras) by Leuccipus and Democritus, who had developed it in an atheistic manner. Now, after many vicissitudes, the two had again been welded into the Mosaic whole by Descartes. It is

> Therefore very evident to me, That the ancient *Pythagorick,* or Judaick Cabbala did consist of what we now call *Platonism* and *Cartesianism,* the latter being as it were the *Body,* the other the *Soul* of Cartesianism; the unhappy disjunction of which, has been a great evil to both[59] . . . *Moses* has been aforehand with *Cartesius.*[60]

Henry More's enthusiasm for Cartesianism did not last. Already by 1659 he was urging exceptions to the principle that all natural phenomena could be solved in mechanical terms,instancing gravitation as a phenomenon not susceptible of a Cartesian or Hobbist explanation.[61] Later he came to reject Cartesianism as paving the way for atheism. More faithful to Cartesianism and to More's sketch of its historical origins was Henry More's fellow-Platonist, Ralph Cudworth (1617-1688), in his influential *True Intellectual System of the Universe,* first published in 1678. Cudworth conducted his discussion on the basis of a natural philosophy 'called by some *Atomical* or *Corpuscular,* by others *Mechanical',*[62] and admitted that in driving out 'all Final and Mental Causality' from the universe, Descartes increased the danger of atheism.[63] The central weakness of Descartes' approach was that he would not accept causes other than mechanical causes; for Cudworth, over and above purely mechanical processes, there was a 'plastic nature', 'that which makes all things thus to conspire every where, and agree together into one harmony'.[64] Cudworth was no more successful than More in attempting to combine the Neo-Platonic concept of nature with the atomical and mechanical concepts of the new physics in a coherent synthesis, as shown by the fact that theological explanations were introduced by him when the phenomena in question did not easily seem to admit of a mechanical explanation. But he was convinced that the mechanical philosophy, 'if rightly understood . . . is the most effectual Engin against Atheism than can be'.[65] If matter was utterly dead and passive, and there was no motion in the world save that which resulted from contact-action ('heterokinesis'), then it was self-evident that there must be something else in the world besides body or matter. The ancients had rightly apprehended that truth, and had a 'clear and distinct' conception of two basic entities, passive matter, and active power, vigour or virtue—what they had termed 'the *Active Principle'.*[66]

Although Cudworth is primarily concerned with formulating the favourable theological and moral conse-

quences of a 'rightly understood' mechanical philosophy, it is noteworthy that throughout his treatise he relies on an historical mode of exposition, based on the fundamental presupposition that the true religious, moral and natural philosophy flowed to the Gentiles from the Hebrews, and came to be fragmented and corrupted in the course of time.

The belief in a *prisca theologia* and in the Hebraic origin of Greek learning, was not restricted to the inner circle of the Cambridge Platonists. It was widely accepted in theological discussions. A striking example is to be found in the theological writings of John Wallis (1616-1703), a distinguished scientific contemporary of Newton and Savilian Professor of Geometry at Oxford. Wallis entered the Trinitarian controversy in the last decades of the century, as a champion of the dogma. In his *Three Sermons Concerning the Sacred Trinity* (1691) he wrote:

> 'Tis well-known (to those conversant in such Studies) that much of the Heathen Learning (their Philosophy, Theology and Mythology) was borrowed from the Jews; though much Disguised, and sometimes Ridiculed by them. Which things though they are Fabulous, as disguised in a Romantick Dress: yet they are good Evidence that there was a *Truth in History,* which gave occasion to those Fables.

> None doubt but *Ovid*'s Fable of the *Chaos* (of which all things were made) took its rise from *Mose*'s of the *Creation:* And *Deucalion*'s *Flood,* from that of Noah: and the *Titan*'s fighting against the Gods, from the Builders of *Babel*'s Tower: And that of Two-faced *Janus,* from *Noah*'s looking backward and forward to the World before and since the Flood. And many the like, of which we may see in *Natalis Comes,* in *Bochartus,* and others: And of which we have a large Collection in*Theophilus Gales*'s *Court of the Gentiles.* And in Dr. *Duport*'s *Gnomologia Homerica:* wherein is a Collection of *Homer*'s Sayings, which look like Allusions to like Passages in Sacred Scripture; and seem to be borrowed (most of them) from those Books of it, which were written before Homer's time; who yet is one of the most Ancient and most Famous of Heathen Writers.

> *Plato* hath borrowed so much of his Philosophy, History, and Theology, from the *Jewish* Learning, as that he hath obtained the Title of *Moses Atticus, Moses disguised in a Greek dress . . .*

> And I am so far from thinking (as the *Socinians* would have us) that *St. John* did but *Platonize,* and borrowed his ὁ λαγος from Plato's Trinity; that I rather think, that *Plato* borrowed his *Trinity* (as he did many other things) from the *Jewish Doctrine,* though by him disguised . . .

> *Aristotle,* in the last Chapter of his Book, *De Mundo;* which is *de Dei Nominibus:* He tells us that *God, though he be but One, hath many Names:* And amongst these *many,* he reckons that of the *Tres Parcae . . .* or as we call them, the *Three Destinities*

. . . to be one of these names. Which though Numbered as *Three,* are but this *One God* . . . So that it seems that both *Plato* and *Aristotle* were of opinion, that *Three Somewhats* may be *One God.* And this, in likelihood, they derived from the Jewish Learning.

IV

Newton's earliest commonplace-book at Cambridge shows him imbibing the mechanical philosophy not only from the works of Descartes, but also from other works which presented it as part of a long historical tradition, in contradistinction to Descartes' own exposition, which acknowledged no historical debts.[67] Walter Charleton's *Physiologia Epicuro-Gassendo-Charltoniana* (1654) introduced him to the Gassendist approach, sifting the opinions of the ancients to establish their concordance with his own philosophy. At the same time, the early writings of Henry More would have acquainted him with a much more fundamentalist *prisca,* tracing the new mechanical philosophy to Moses, and making it an essential part of a new theological synthesis.

Much later, when Newton was developing his 'classical' annotations, he drew considerably on Cudworth's erudite *True Intellectual System.* His extant notes on the *System* reproduce almost verbatim Cudworth's account of Moschus and of the atomic succession from him.[68] There was a large body of shared assumptions between Newton and Cudworth. From the earliest period of his intellectual development, Newton held a view of the world as comprising both active and passive principles, with the technique later presented in the **Principia** applying only to inert matter. He believed that conceiving matter as independent of God, or endowed with self-activity, led to atheism.[69] Like Cudworth, he seems to have had the mechanical philosophies of Hobbes and of Descartes, and the 'hylozoistic atheism' of various English free-thinkers in mind.

Despite these similarities, Newton did not borrow a great deal from Cudworth's learned account in his historical annotations. Cudworth had necessarily confined himself to a very general account of the mechanical philosophy, and buttressed it with his historical learning, while Newton needed support for the details of his own system of the world; and his own classical knowledge was sufficient for the purpose. Besides such standard authorities in his own time as Diogenes Laertius's *De vita philosophorum* and the Pseudo-Plutarchian *Placita Philosophorum* (supplemented by Suidas, Pliny, Galen, the *Ecologae* of Stobaeus, and the *Academic Questions* of Cicero), he cited Plato's *Timaeus, Apology,* and *Laws,* as well as Poclus's *Commentary* on the *Timaeus.* The strongly Platonic bias in his authorities was reinforced by his extensive use of Macrobius's

Commentary on Cicero's Dream of Scipio, a work which had served virtually as a handbook of Neo-Platonism during the Christian middle ages, and discussed ancient arithmetologies in great detail.[70] Besides Macrobius, Lucretius served as the principal authority on the most ancient natural philosophy. Besides the Greek and Roman authors, the early Greek church fathers, whose works were very familiar to Newton in the course of his biblical studies, were prominently represented, including Clement, Origen, and Eusebius, as well as Cyril and Julian.[71] The only modern author cited was Natalis Conti (*c.* 1520-1582), an influential sixteenth-century mythographer, who links Newton with a Renaissance tradition attributing a hidden theological, moral, and natural-philosophical meaning to all the classical myths.[72]

Our treatment so far has stressed the similarities between the early More, Cudworth, and Newton, in order to show that Newton's historical annotations are by no means as bizarre as they may now appear, but follow a certain intellectual tradition very much alive in Newton's own day. It must also be pointed out that Newton disagrees with the two other authors on certain important points of interpretation. His notes on Cudworth show that he was not merely transcribing his conclusions, but questioned some of them, for example, his condemnation of the 'Egyptian' account of creation as atheistical.[73] A more important divergence would lie in Newton's anti-trinitarianism. *Prisca* theories, in the Renaissance as in More, Cudworth, and the industrious Theophilus Gale,[74] had generally emphasized the presence of the notion of the Trinity among the *prisci.* Since Newton was vehemently opposed to the Trinitarian dogma, which he held to be a comparatively late corruption, these arguments would be uncongenial to him.[75]

Nor would he accept More's and Cudworth's characterization of Epicurus and Lucretius as atheistic. As he had told Gregory: 'The philosophy of Epicurus and Lucretius is true and old, but was wrongly interpreted by the ancients as atheism . . .'.[76]

The most important difference between More and Cudworth on the one hand, and Newton on the other, lay in Newton's conviction that not the Cartesian philosophy (as More had once held), nor the 'mechanical philosophy' (in Cudworth's basically Cartesian interpretation), but his own system of the world represented the restoration of the true and original natural philosophy, as revealed by God even before the Flood.

In concluding this outline of the main points of agreement and disagreement between Newton and the Cambridge Platonists, attention must again be drawn to the fact that the terms of the dialogue were set by a certain theological-philosophical tradition. Only against that tradition can Newton's 'classical' endeavour be understood and explained. Newton's relation to that tradition becomes clearer if we remember that his interpretation of the texts of ancient natural philosophy was not the only 'exegetical' exercise which had engaged his attention. He had spent much time and labour on two other fields which demanded highly-developed techniques of interpretation. One was alchemy, whose practitioners wrapped up their supposed knowledge in a complex symbolism, designed to obscure it from the uninitiated. During the early seventeenth century, Michael Maier (1568-1622), whose works were deeply studied by Newton, had undertaken a survey of the entire Greek mythology to demonstrate that they represented alchemical secrets.[77] Newton's interpretation of the 'harmony of the spheres' is analogous, in that it sees it as a symbolical representation of 'physical' secrets. The other major field employing exegetical techniques was that of biblical studies, which absorbed Newton throughout his life. In interpreting the prophetical books of the Old Testament, Newton attempted to show that the prophecies had been fulfilled down to the minutest details.

Both alchemy, as well as biblical exegetics, rested on the assumption that a true body of knowledge had been available to wise men in the remotest antiquity, and that the knowledge was couched in an enigmatical, symbolical form to conceal it from the vulgar. It is evident that the same assumptions underlie Newton's exegesis of the natural philosophy of the ancients. His tortuous interpretation of the Lyre of Apollo, the Pipes of Pan, and the 'Harmony of the Spheres' rests on the belief that the true system of the world was known to the ancients, but had been turned into 'a great mystery' which only the initiates could penetrate. In his studies of the Old Testament prophecies, Newton was tracing the pristine knowledge of the historical events of future ages; in his alchemical studies, the pristine knowledge of the constitution of things; in his studies of ancient natural philosophy, the pristine knowledge of physical nature and the system of the world. The true meaning of the Old Testament prophecies would only become clear in retrospect, in the light of historical experience. In the same way, the authentic meaning of the ancient natural philosophy would only be revealed when the truths it embodied had been independently discovered by experimental investigation; it was thus that Pythagoras—and Newton—had unravelled the mystery of the most ancient 'harmony of the spheres'.

It should be quite clear that Newton's textual analysis of ancient natural philosophy was not based on a consciously *post hoc* procedure: reading into ancient texts truths arrived at in the course of his scientific work. For him, they represented a deeper penetration into the *prisca sapientia,* possible only when the preliminary work had been accomplished through experience. Besides this overriding justification, these investigations could perform a number of different functions. They could provide a pedigree for his own doctrines, to legitimate them for an audience which still widely accepted the idea of a *prisca sapientia.* He could use them as a direct defense for his own doctrines, as he does in the **Opticks,**[78] and, on one occasion, during the controversy with Leibniz.[79] Furthermore, the documents dealt with in this paper do not tell us whether his own adoption of the doctrines he ascribes to the ancients preceded his textual studies. Such basic problems as the existence of the void, the properties of matter, and the character of the divine agency lay beyond the experimental procedures he could deploy. Newton's solutions to some of these problems are explained and defended by the analogical reasoning whose patterns he defined in the *Regulae.* But the possibility that the ancient texts might have provided clues, and guided his thoughts in one direction or another, can by no means be excluded.

It is also possible to discern the function of the *prisca* arguments in Newton's more general philosophical concerns. Like Cudworth, he wished to confute 'Hobbists', Deists, and 'hylozoistick atheists', on the basis of *prisca* arguments.[80] His own variant of the history of the original natural philosophy, with its insistence on absolutely dead matter, would be his contribution to the debate. On the struggle which was taking place on another front, concerning the authenticity and reliability of the Old Testament, Newton's demonstration of a pre-Noachian *prisca sapientia* would again be a weighty argument. When we recall how deeply Newton was committed to the vindication of the Old Testament account, both in regard to the prophecies and the chronology of the ancient kingdoms,[81] it is evident that it would have been a positive act of abstention on his part to fail to extend this approach to the origins of natural philosophy.

For Newton, all the truths of God's creation were once revealed, as an interconnected whole which comprised natural, moral and divine knowledge. Though they soon became obscured, they could be recovered by a disciplined method of analysis of experience. 'Hypotheses' were not to be feigned in any of these enquiries: just as the properties of light were to be induced from experiments, so the meaning of the sacred prophecies could be ascertained from those which had already been fulfilled, and the true natural philosophy of the ancients was to be deciphered on the basis of experimental knowledge already arrived at. A sequence of inductions could therefore lead naturally from Kepler's laws and the radial acceleration of the moon, through the principle of universal gravitation, to the unveiling of the true meaning of the Pipes of Pan.

Conclusion

In the course of our analysis of the 'classical' Scholia in this paper, we have traced the intellectual ancestry of Newton's 'historical' assumptions and methods, and their development in connection with a distinctive English 'mechanical philosophy'. The analysis has shown Newton's adherence to a particular approach to theological and philosophical problems, influential among many of his contemporaries. The conclusion may be suggested, that it is not really profitable to consider Newton either as 'the last of the magicians' or 'the first of the scientists'. It is equally unhistorical to try to resolve the problem by imagining a multiplicity of Newtons, one engaging in 'science' and the others dabbling in theology, chronology, and other similar pursuits.

It is certainly difficult for us in the twentieth century to conceive one whose scientific achievements were so great, pursuing with equal interest and energy such other studies, especially when his efforts in those fields produced so little of enduring value. It is even more difficult for us to imagine the mechanics and cosmology of the **Principia** being influenced by Newton's theological views and his belief in a pristine knowledge. Sir Isaac Newton, however, was not a 'scientist' but a Philosopher of Nature. In the intellectual environment of his century, it was a legitimate task to use a wide variety of materials to reconstruct the unified wisdom of Creation.

That was the task which Newton attempted. We cannot fully understand his scientific successes, without appreciating his endeavour in problems which for him, as for many of his contemporaries, constituted the ultimate problems.

Acknowledgements

The final version of this paper owes a great deal to the generous help and criticism of Dr J. R. Ravetz. The authors would also like to thank Professor A. R. Hall for allowing them to consult his copy of Newton's notes on Cudworth from the William Andrews Clark Library, and to the Reverend Dr E. Evans for providing the basic translations of the main passages quoted from the Royal Society manuscript.

Notes

[1] University Library, Cambridge, Ad. MS. 3970.f.292^v.

[2] The first notice of the Gregory Manuscript (note 3) seems to have appeared in James Crauford Gregory's 'Notice concerning an Autograph Manuscript by Sir Isaac Newton . . .', *Trans. R. Soc. Edinb.* 12, 1834, pp. 64-76. Professor I. Bernard Cohen has announced his intention of publishing an edited version of the Newton MS. as well as Gregory's copy, '"Quantum in se est": Newton's Concept of Inertia in relation to Descartes and Lucretius', *Notes and Records Roy. Soc. Lond.* 19, 1964, p. 148.

[3] Gregory MS. 247 at the Royal Society, in Newton's hand. It is plain that both Fatio and Gregory had access to these Scholia. Gregory's notes on Newton's *Principia* contain the entire Scholia, copied in a careful hand and placed in a systematic order by Gregory. The Scholia must have been composed in the 1690's, most probably before 1694 (the year of Gregory's extended visit to Cambridge), and not later than 1697 (the date of Gregory's last note on the *Principia*). There are many alternative versions of the Newton autograph in the MSS. of the Portsmouth Collection, Ad. 3965.6 Folios 640^r-640^v and 278^r (University Library, Cambridge) contain substantially the same quotations and ideas as the R.S. autograph, although only Propositions IV, VI, VII, and VIII are dealt with. There are many other stray sheets in this section which probably represent even earlier attempts by Newton to construct his ideas. Folios 270^r 271^r and 272^r contain a long Scholium to Proposition VII, containing all of the ideas developed at greater length in the R.S. autograph, and was probably intended as another and more condensed version of it. Folio 14^a contains three paragraphs of interest. The first two embody some of the ideas of the General Scholium of 1713; the second paragraph contains ideas which only appeared in the Scholium to the last edition of the *Principia* in 1726; the last criticizes the existence of a fluid aether. It is plain therefore that the theological ideas in the *General Scholium* had been sketched by the early 1690's, and that Newton saw these being compatible with the philosophy presented in the scholia to the key propositions of Book Three. For a discussion of these passages, consult James Crauford Gregory, *loc. cit.* See also 'Fragment on the Law of Inertia', in Hall and Hall (note 23), pp. 309-311.

[4] See Frank E. Manuel, *Isaac Newton Historian,* Cambridge, 1963; H. McLachlan, *Newton: Theological Manuscripts,* Liverpool, 1950.

[5] *The Correspondence of Isaac Newton,* ed. H. W. Turnbull, Cambridge, 1961, Vol. 3, p. 193.

[6] *Ibid.* pp. 196-198, letter of 29 February 1692.

[7] *Ibid.* p. 338.

[8] *Ibid.* p. 384.

[9] That was shown by J. C. Gregory, *loc. cit.*; the *Elementa* was first published in 1702.

[10] Gregory MS. Folio 2. The quotations have been translated from the Latin.

[11] *Ibid.*

[12] *Ibid.* folio 7.

[13] *Ibid.* folio 8.

[14] *Ibid.* folio 9.

[15] *Ibid.* folio 10.

[16] U.L.C. Ad. MS. 3965.6, folio 271[r].

[17] *Ibid.* folio 270[r].

[18] Gregory MS. 247, folios 11-12; the account of Pythagoras is taken directly from *Macrobius' Commentary on the Dream of Scipio,* pp. 184-189 in W. H. Stahl's translation, New York, 1952.

[19] Keynes MS. 130, King's College Library, Cambridge.

[20] Colin MacLaurin, *An Account of Sir Isaac Newton's Philosophical Discoveries,* London, 1750, p. 34. MacLaurin is here discussing 'hints concerning the gravitation of celestial bodies in what is related of the doctrines of *Thales* and his successors: but *Pythagoras* seems to have been better acquainted with it, and is supposed to have had a view to it, in what he taught concerning the harmony of the spheres'. The authorities cited follow those given by Newton: Pliny, Macrobius (Lib. ii, cap. i), Plutarch, and Plato's *Timaeus.*

[21] *Elementa,* last page of 'Praefatio Auctoris': 'Proportionem his experimentis inventam *Pythagoras* applicuit ad Coelos, & inde didicit Harmoniam Sphaerarum'.

[22] U.L.C. Ad. 3970, folio 619[r]; the passage was written between 1704, the date of the first edition of the *Opticks,* and 1706, the date of the second.

[23] There are many other references in the draft Queries to life and will as active principles, acting harmoniously upon matter; that knowledge is clearly attributed to the ancients. The analogy between man's moving his body by volition and God's moving matter in His sensorium was developed as early as 1670 in the *De Gravitatione,* A. R. Hall and M. B. Hall, *Unpublished Scientific Papers of Isaac Newton,* Cambridge, 1962, p.141

[24] Gregory. MS 247, folio 13. Newton also cites 'On the same subject Hermesianax: Pluto Persephone, Ceres and kindly Venus and the Loves, the Tritons, Nereus, Thetis, Neptune and Mercury, Juno, Vulcan, Jupiter and Pan (,) Diana and Phoebus the dartsman are one God'.

[25] U.L.C. Ad. 3965.12, folio 269.

[26] Gregory MS. 247, folio 3.

[27] *Mathematical Principles of Natural Philosophy,* ed. F. Cajori, Berkeley, 1934, p. 545.

[28] *Ibid.* p. 545.

[29] Dover edition, based on the 4th London edition, 1952, pp. 405-406. In the first edition, the concluding passage ends with '. . . they would have taught us to worship our true Author and Benefactor'. Newton's autograph addendum to that passage, in a copy of the *Opticks* in the Babson Institute Library (No. 133, reproduced as Plate 10, in Manuel, *op. cit.*), reads: 'as their ancestors did before they corrupted themselves. For the seven Precepts of the Noachides were originally the moral Law of all nations; & the first of them was to have but one Supreme Lord God & not to alienate his worship; the second was not to profane his name; & the rest were to abstain from blood or homicide & from fornication (that is from incest adultery & all unlawful lusts), & from theft & all injuries, & to be merciful even to bruet beasts, & to set up magistrates for putting these laws in execution. Whence came the moral Philosophy of the ancient Greeks'.

[30] *Cf. The Chronology of the Ancient Kingdoms Amended,* London, 1728, pp. 186-190.

[31] *Opticks,* edition cited in note 29, p. 404.

[32] *Ibid.* p. 402, p. 403, p. 405.

[33] F. Van Steenberghen, *Aristotle in the West,* Louvain, 1955, pp. 8-22.

[34] For a different view, see H. Guerlac, 'Where the Statue Stood: Divergent Loyalties to Newton in the 18th Century', *Aspects of the Eighteenth Century,* 1965, p. 333: Newton was setting forth only the *mathematical principles* of natural philosophy, although that philosophy was still to come, 'the work of other hands, though here and there Newton offers hints and suggestions as to what it may contain'; that new natural philosophy 'must be erected . . . inside the boundaries that he (Newton) had marked out by his mathematical laws'.

[35] Wotton discuss 'the Learning of *Pythagoras,* and the most Ancient Philosophers of *Greece*' (Ch. viii), and concludes that from the reputation he enjoyed in antiquity 'one can no more conclude from thence, That *Pythagoras* knew as much as *Aristotle* or *Democritus,* than that Friar *Bacon* was as great a Mathematician as Dr. *Barrow,* or Mr. *Newton* . . . (p. 93, 3rd edition, 1705).

[36] F. A. Yates, *Giordano Bruno and the Hermetic Tradition,* London, 1964, pp. 159-166.

[37] D. P. Walker, 'The *Prisca Theologia* In France', *J. Warburg & Courtauld Insts,* 1954, 17, pp. 204-259.

[38] Yates, *op. cit.,* pp. 1-61; the standard edition and translation of the *Corpus Hermeticum* is the French one, Nock & Festugière, Paris, 3 vols., 1945-1964.

References to the *Poemander* and *Asclepius* in Ficino's edition are to be found in Newton's hand in his notes from the works of Michael Maier (about 50,000 words on 82 pages), Keynes MS. 32, at King's College, Cambridge.

[39] Walker, quoting Champier, in *op. cit.*, p. 218.

[40] C. Bigg, *The Christian Platonists of Alexandria,* new ed., Oxford, 1913; for a summary and bibliography of the vast secondary literature on this subject, see J. Quasten, *Patrology,* Vol. 2, Utrecht-Antwerp, 1953.

[41] Eduard Zeller, *A History of Greek Philosophy,* Eng. tr., London, 1889, Vol. I, pp. 27-28.

[42] Zeller, p. 28; also, C. Merk, *Clemens Alexandrianus u. seine Abhängingkeit der griechischen Philosophie,* 1879; bibliography in Quasten, pp. 12-15.

[43] Yates, *op. cit.,* pp. 7-12.

[44] *Ibid.* pp. 360-397; L. Blanchet, *Campanella,* Paris, 1920, esp. pp. 70ff.

[45] *Ibid. passim.*

[46] On Patrizi, see bibliography in P. O. Kristeller, *Eight Philosophers of the Italian Renaissance,* London, 1965, pp. 186-187.

[47] See Blanchet, esp. pp. 146-163, 193-207; Patrizi, *Nova,* 'Panarchia', Books xii and xvi. The *prisca* chains usually excluded Aristotle; those who did include him (like Pico and Steuchus) relied on pseudo-Aristotelian works like the *de mundo.*

[48] G. Aspelin, 'Cudworth's Interpretation of Greek Philosophy', *Göteborgs Högskolas Arsskrift,* 49, 1943; D. Sailor, 'Moses and Atomism', *J. Hist. Ideas,* 25, 1, 1964; H. Guerlac, *Newton et Epicure,* Paris, 1963, pp. 13-22.

[49] Arcerius, edition of Imablichus' *De vita Pythagorae,* note to p. 33.

[50] These authorities are cited by Henry More in his 'Defense of the Philosophic Cabbala', pp. 110-111, in *A Collection of Several Philosophical Writings,* 4th edition, 1711. The Selden work referred to is *De Jure Naturali juxta Hebros,* London, 1640; Vossius, *De historicis Graecis,* lib. 3, Leyden, 1624.

[51] Daniel Sennert, *Hypomnemata physica,* Francfort, 1636, p. 89.

[52] *The Sceptical Chymist* (1661), Everyman edition, 1949, p. 75.

[53] *Philosophiae Epicuri Syntagma,* 3rd edition, Lugduni, 1675, I, p. 101.

[54] Anthony à Wood, *Athenae Oxonienses,* 2nd edition, London, 1721, 2, p. 662.

[55] *A Collection,* 'Epistolae Quatuor Ad Renatum Descartes', letter of December 1648, p. 61.

[56] More, *op. cit.,* Preface General, p. vi.

[57] P. M. Rattansi, 'Paracelsus and the Puritan Revolution', *Ambix,* II, 1963, pp. 24-32.

[58] More, *op. cit.,* 'The Immortality of the Soul' (1659), Bk. II, Ch. xii, p. 124.

[59] *Ibid.* Preface General, p. xvii.

[60] *Ibid.* 'Defense of the Philosophic Cabbala', Ch. I, p. 80.

[61] *The Immortality of the Soul,* London, 1659, Preface b7v-b8v; also *Remarks upon Two late Ingenious Discourses,* London, 1676.

[62] Chapter I.

[63] *Ibid.* pp. 680-681.

[64] *Ibid.* p. 167.

[65] *Ibid.* p. 12.

[66] *Ibid.* p. 27.

[67] *Questiones quaedam Philosphicae,* U.L.C. Ad. 3996ff. 88-135; discussed by R. S. Westfall, 'The Foundations of Newton's Philosophy of Nature', *Br. J. Hist. Sci.* I, pp. 171-182, 1962. Charleton distinguished between the innovators, who 'ponder the Reasons of all, but the Reputation of none', and included Tycho, Kepler, Galileo, Scheiner, Kircher, Harvey, and 'the Epitome of all, *Des Cartes'* (p. 3); the renovators, like Ficino, Copernicus ('reviver' of Aristarchus' system), Magnenus, and 'the greatest antiquary among them, the immortal *Gassendus . . .'* (p. 4). Moschus is cited as originator of atomism on p. 87. On Gassendi's method, see F. Bernier, *Abrege de la Philosophie de Gassendi,* Paris, 1675, 'Av Lectevr', 'Car à proprement parler, Gassendi est une Biblioteque entiere; mais une Biblioteque qui en rapporant les diverses Opinions des Anciens, nou sçait toujours document insinüer la plus probable'.

[68] The notes comprise unnumbered folio pages, now at the William Andrews Clark Memorial Library of the University of California, Los Angeles. Passages from pages 16-17 of the first edition of 1678 have been

copied almost verbatim. On the origin of the atomic philosophy, he has transcribed Cudworth's opinion word for word: 'Posidonius, an ancient and learned philosopher, did (as both Strabo and Empiricus tell us) avouch it for an old tradition, that ye first inventor of the atomical philosophy was one Moschus a Phoenician, who lived before the Trojan war'. Cudworth's identification of Moschus and Moses does not seem to be accepted by Newton. On Mochus, Moschus and Moses, see J. L. Mosheim's edition of Cudworth's *System,* trans. J. Harrison, London, 1845, I, p. 21. Newton's reference to atoms being designated 'by the mystics as monads' is clarified by the note: 'The Pythagorite monads were atoms' (p. 13 of the *System*).

[69] See esp. *De Gravitatione* in Hall & Hall, *op. cit.,* pp. 142-144.

[70] See W. H. Stahl's introduction to his translation of Macrobius' work, cited in note 18 above.

[71] These sources cannot be discussed in any detail here, although the historical sketch of *prisca* doctrines in the text should help to clarify the significance of some of these citations.

[72] Conti's *Mythologiae sive explicationis fabularum libri decem,* Venice, 1551, was based on the assumption that from the earliest times, thinkers, first in Egypt and then in Greece, hid the great truths of science and philosophy under the veil of myth to secure them against vulgar profanation. Francis Bacon made extensive use of Conti in his *De sapientia veterum liber . . .* (1609). Conti is discussed by Jean Seznec, *The Survival of the Pagan Gods* (Eng. tr.), New York, 1953, Bk. 2, ch. I.

[73] See note 68 above. Commenting on Cudworth's interpretation of the Egyptian account of creation on p. 21 of the *System,* Newton says: 'By night understand invisible Deity whome the Egyptians call (blank space) & paint with an Egg in his mouth & by Love ye spirit wch moved on ye face of ye waters. Dr. Cudworth therefore is much mistaken when he represents this Philosophy as Atheistical.'

[74] Gale published *The Court of the Gentiles,* in four volumes, Oxford and London, 1669-1677, the most comprehensive seventeenth-century attempt to show that all the human arts and sciences originated in the Scriptures and the Jewish Church.

[75] Manuel, *op. cit.,* p. 156; on trinitarian controversies in 17th century England, J. Hay Colligan, *The Arian Movement in England,* Manchester, 1913.

[76] See note 7. *Cf.* Cudworth on 'the Fraud and Juggling of *Gassendus'* in praising Epicurus, *op. cit.,* p. 462.

[77] Michael Maier, *Arcana Arcanissima,* 1616, attempted to interpret the whole of Greek mythology in alchemical terms; also *Atlanta Fugiens,* 1618. J. Tollius continued the attempt in his *Fortuita &c.,* Amsterdam, 1687. See John Read, *Prelude to Chemistry,* London, 1936, pp. 228-246; W. Pagel, *Paracelsus,* Basel-New York, 1958, p. 233 and note 108.

[78] *Op. cit.,* Query 28, p. 369, 'And for rejecting such a Medium, we have the Authority of those the oldest and most celebrated Philosophers of *Greece* and *Phoenicia,* who made a *Vacuum,* and Atoms, and the Gravity of Atoms, the first Principle of their Philosophy; tacitly attributing Gravity to some other Cause than dense Matter'. The adjective 'dense' was first inserted in the 1717 English edition; see Guerlac, *Newton et Epicure,* pp. 30-31.

[79] A. Koyré and I. Bernard Cohen, 'Newton and the Leibniz-Clarke Correspondence', *Archs Int. Hist. Sci.* 15, 1962, pp. 63-126: Newton's draft letter to Conti, p. 73, complains that Leibniz 'falls foul upon my Philosophy as if I (and by consequence the ancient Phenicians & (or) Greeks) introduced Miracles & (or) occult qualities'. The final version was dated 26 February 1715/16 o.s.

[80] Hall and Hall, *op. cit.,* on Newton's view that matter conceived as independent of God or with self-activity leads to atheism, pp. 142-144.

[81] See Manuel, *op. cit.,* esp. Ch. VI.

William H. Austin (essay date 1970)

SOURCE: "Isaac Newton on Science and Religion," in *Journal of the History of Ideas,* Vol. XXXI, 1970, pp. 521-42.

[*In the following essay, Austin maintains that there is little evidence to indicate that Newton's scientific ideas significantly influenced his theological writings. In practice, however, Newton may have conceded that science had some bearing on theology, despite his "maxim" that "religion and philosophy are to be preserved distinct."*]

In his own time Isaac Newton was known as an acute and learned theologian. Conduitt reports that "Archbishop Tenison offered him, if he would take orders, the Mastership of Trinity College when it was given to Montague, and importuned him to accept any preferment in the Church; saying to him: 'Why will you not? You know more divinity than all of us put together.'" (Newton put him off with the reply that he would "be able to do you more service than if I was in orders.")[1]

His theological reputation faded, not only because theology moved on to other concerns, but also because most of his relevant writings remained unpublished, and because credence was given to Laplace's belief that Newton turned to theology only in his declining years. (This is false: there is manuscript evidence of attention to theological questions as early as 1664, and apparently his most important work was completed by 1690, though he worked it over and over thereafter, as he did with his scientific writings as well.)[2] Renewed attention to his unpublished papers, and the efforts of intellectual historians like Burtt and Koyré, have recently brought about a modest resurgence of interest in Newton's theological efforts.

In view of the continuing interest of questions about the relations between theology and science or "the scientific world view," it seems worthwhile to inquire into Newton's own views on the subject. Does he regard his scientific and theological studies as bearing on each other—and, if so, how? Or does he consider them mutually irrelevant—and, if so, why? His interpreters disagree. According to his most authoritative biographer, "Newton's philosophy and religion were two separate things, and he does not seem to have concerned himself with the problem of recounciling them."[3] But R. H. Hurlbutt finds it "clear . . . that Newton's science was intrinsic to practically all of his considerations on theology."[4] R. S. Westfall finds "a complex network of mutual influence" between Newton's religious belief and his scientific work; like all the "Christian virtuosi" of the seventeenth century, he strove for a harmony between the two, though "he went a step beyond the others in forcing Christianity into conformity with science."[5]

Moreover, Newton himself can be quoted on both sides of the dispute. He concludes a theological passage in the General Scholium to the *Principia.* "And thus much concerning God, to discourse of whom from the appearances of things does certainly belong to natural philosophy."[6] When he wrote the *Principia,* he assures Bentley, he "had an eye upon such principles as might work with considering men for the belief of a Deity."[7] On the other hand, the first of a set of seven "Statements on Religion" found among his papers reads, "That religion and Philosophy are to be preserved distinct. We are not to introduce divine revelations into Philosophy nor philosophical opinions into religion."[8] (Recall that for Newton "Philosophy" includes what we would call natural science.)

Let us call the statement about preserving religion and philosophy distinct "Newton's maxim." Since he does not explain or elaborate upon it, we must look to his practice to judge (1) how the maxim should be interpreted, and (2) whether he abides by it. My suggestions on these points are made in Part III of this paper. The basis for them is laid in two stages. In Part I, I survey his theological writings, with a view to showing what his main theological concerns were, and how he conceived of religion. Given this conception and these concerns, it is not surprising that his theological writings show very little or no trace of influence from his scientific ideas. However, it is not primarily to these writings that interpreters like Hurlbutt and Westfall appeal. Rather, it is in theological excurses in the *Principia,* the *Opticks,* and certain letters that we find Newton's so-called "scientific theism" adumbrated. In Part II, I discuss these passages and their consistency with the *content* of his theological books and papers, leaving the question of their relation to his *maxim* for Part III.

In this essay I consider only the bearing of Newton's science on his theology. Whether there were significant theological influences on his science is a subject I hope to explore in another paper.

I. *Newton's Theological Works.* None of Newton's primarily theological writings were published in his lifetime. The first to appear was the *Observations upon the Prophesies of Daniel and the Apocalypse of St. John,* edited by Benjamin Smith (Newton's half-brother's son) and published in 1773. A treatise on the Trinitarian proof texts I John 5:7f and I Timothy 3:16 appeared in 1754 in a mutilated version (passages missing at beginning and end, reconstructed skillfully by an unnamed editor), under the erroneous title. *Two Letters of Sir Isaac Newton to Mr. LeClerc.* LeClerc was the Dutch publisher to whom Locke had forwarded the manuscript in 1690, with a view to its anonymous publication in a free French translation; but Newton decided to suppress it. Bishop Horsley printed the genuine text, under the more descriptive title, *An Historical Account of Two Notable Corruptions of Scripture,* in his 1785 edition of Newton's works. Finally, in 1950, H. McLachlan edited and published a selection of manuscripts from the Portsmouth Collection of Newton's papers under the title *Sir Isaac Newton. Theological Manuscripts.*

These works provide an adequately representative basis for study of Newton's theological interests and opinions.[9] Since they are relatively unfamiliar, I will survey them in section A below. They show that Newton's main theological concerns were the promotion of ecclesiastical peace and correct biblical interpretation, and that he conceived of religion as a set of duties, all of which could be known from biblical revelation and *some* by the light of natural reason. These conclusions are defended in section B, and in section C I argue that his views should not be supposed to be affected by scientific considerations.

A. Some of the materials in McLachlan's collection have to do with the interpretation of prophetic-apocalyptic writings, others present anti-Trinitarian polemics of various kinds, and the rest consist of short schemes of true religion, connected with irenic and latitudinarian proposals as to church policy. Thus Newton's theological writings fall into three classes, and our first order of business will be to survey them briefly in turn.

The details of Newton's interpretations of Daniel and the Apocalypse are no longer of interest. What do concern us are his method and purposes.

As to method, he operated from a clearcut premise that there is a special, unique, and distinct "Mystical (i.e., allegorical) language," known to and used by all the prophets.[10]

> This language . . . was as certain and definite in its signification as is the vulgar language of any nation whatsoever, so that it is only through want of skill therein that Interpreters so frequently turn the Prophetic types and phrases to signify whatever their fancies and hypotheses lead them to.

The code is to be broken by an inductive study of the prophetic texts:

> The Rule I have followed has been to compare the several mystical places of scripture where the same prophetic phrase or type is used, and to fix such a signification to that phrase as agrees best with all the places . . . and, when I had found the necessary significations, to reject all others as the offspring of luxuriant fancy, for no more significations are to be admitted for true ones than can be proved.

The great governing principle is an analogy between the natural realm (whence the prophets draw their symbols) and the political and ecclesiastical realm (which they are really talking about). The sun stands for a King or for Kings as such, the moon for "the body of the common people considered as the King's wife," darkening of celestial luminaries for the downfall of a body politic, dens and rocks in mountains for temples in cities, etc., etc. Newton fills pages with such keys, extending an already highly developed tradition.

What does he do with his method? In the ***Observations*** he traces out, in great detail, the sequence of historical events predicted in Daniel and Revelation, insofar as they have been thus far fulfilled. He does *not* try to predict the future, and explicitly denies that that is a legitimate aim in the interpretation of prophecy. Concerning the book of Revelation he says:[11]

> The folly of Interpreters has been, to foretell times and things by this Prophecy, as if God designed to make them Prophets. By this rashness they have not only exposed themselves, but brought the Prophecy also into contempt. The design of God was much

otherwise. He gave this, and the Prophecies of the Old Testament, not to gratify men's curiosities by enabling them to foreknow things, but that after they might be interpreted by the event, and his own Providence, not the Interpreters, be then manifested thereby to the world. For the event of things predicted many ages before, will then be a convincing argument that the world is governed by providence.

Nevertheless he points out that several passages in the Apocalypse say that they will not be understood until the times of the end, and then only gradually; since great strides have been made in their interpretation in recent years, we may conclude that the end is not too far off. Had he been disposed to fix a date, one is almost forced upon him by his interpretation. He identifies the eleventh horn of the fourth beast in Daniel 7 with the whore and Beast of the Apocalypse, which stands for the Church of Rome (there is nothing novel in all this). Since he dates the emergence of the Church as a political power (in the sense fitting Daniel) in the latter half of the eighth century, and reckons its reign at 1260 years, its demise and the end of the world may be expected shortly after 2000 A. D.[12] But he does not draw the inference; he is not writing to predict; he is simply interpreting the scriptures in accordance with an inherited and elaborated-upon method and purpose, then quite customary.

Thus his primary purpose is to vindicate divine providence by showing that God revealed the future course of events to his prophets, and a subsidiary purpose is to discredit the Roman Church. Curiously, though, he does not *develop* the vindication-of-providence theme, nor does it provide a principle of organization for his book. After a rather perfunctory statement of the argument, he simply interprets the texts, indulges in long historical digressions, undertakes to calculate the year of the Passion (34 A. D.) and works in some anti-Roman polemics.

He attacked orthodox trinitarian doctrine on several fronts. The trinitarian proof texts in the Textus Receptus are neither authentic nor exegetically coherent with their contexts;[13] the doctrine was unlawfully imposed upon the church by Athanasius, who was a scoundrel, opportunist, and heretic; and it is unintelligible, an illegitimate intrusion of metaphysics into Christian belief. Woven into Newton's elaborations of all these themes is the charge that the doctrine is part and parcel of the Papist corruption of the faith.

The treatise on **"Two Notable Corruptions"** demonstrates the spuriousness of the AV readings in I John 5:7f ("For there are three that bear witness in heaven, the Father, the Word, and the Holy Ghost: and these three are one) and I Timothy 3:16 ("And without controversy, great is the mystery of godliness: God was manifest in the flesh, justified in the Spirit, seen of angels, preached unto the Gentiles, believed on in the world, received up into glory.")

The discussion of the passage in I John is the longer and more important. Newton proves that the verse as it stands in the Vulgate and the AV (along with the Greek *Textus Receptus* underlying the latter) is an outright fraud. The correct reading is: "There are three witnesses, the Spirit, the water, and the blood; and these three agree" (or "are one"). Newton carefully constructs an airtight case: the disputed reading is not in any of the ancient Greek manuscripts, nor in any of the early translations (e.g., into Syriac, Ethiopic, Egyptian Arabic, and the pre-Vulgate Latin), nor in any of the writings of the Fathers. It is particularly noteworthy, and Newton presses home the point, that none of the anti-Arian writers appeals to the text in question though they cite many passages which are much less obviously to the point. To the suggestion that the Arians may have tampered with the texts Newton responds with a burst of sarcasm:

> Yes truly, those Arrians were crafty knaves, that could conspire so cunningly and slily all the world over at once (as at the command of a Mithridates) in the latter end of the reign ofConstantius to get all men's books in their hands, and correct them without being perceived: ay, and conjurors too, without leaving any blot or chasm in their books, whereby the knavery might be suspected and discovered; and to wipe the memory of it out of all men's brains; so that neither Athanasius, nor anybody else, could afterwards remember, that they had ever seen it in their books before. . . .[14]

He also answers the objection that Cyprian read the text as in the *Textus Receptus* by pointing out that all Cyprian actually *quotes* are the words "these three are one," which occur in all texts. But the "three" in the original were Spirit, Water, and Blood. The context shows that Cyprian meant Father, Son, and Holy Ghost; but Newton establishes that Cyprian and his mentor Tertullian[15] must have interpreted "Spirit, Water, and Blood" allegorically to mean "Father, Son, and Holy Ghost," as various later writers did.

Having nailed down his case, Newton proceeds to trace how the false reading found its way into the received Greek text, through assimilation to the Vulgate and through marginal glosses with the allegorical interpretation being copied into the text by subsequent scribes. No ancient Greek manuscripts with the disputed reading have been produced; Erasmus had the correct reading in the first two editions of his text, but came under such attack that he agreed to print the Vulgate's version if one Greek codex could be found to support it. An Englishman named Lee promptly claimed to have one, and Erasmus (who had no more desire for the martyr's crown than Sir Isaac had) made no further inquiries. The only other alleged authority is that used by Cardinal Ximenes in his edition of 1515, and Newton makes a good case for supposing that the real authority there is Thomas Aquinas.

> Now to make Thomas, thus, in a few words, do all the work, was very artificial, and in Spain, where Thomas is of apostolical authority, might pass for a very judicious and substantial defense of the printed Greek. But to us, Thomas Aquinas is no Apostle. We are seeking for the authority of Greek manuscripts.[16]

We have here, then, a very effective piece of polemic, carefully researched and argued, showing a thorough acquaintance with the ancient texts and versions (or with reliable authorities on them) and the writings of the Fathers.

Another sort of antitrinitarian polemic comprises a major share of the previously unpublished material brought out in 1950 by McLachlan. Newton's papers include many drafts of a much labored-over piece called **"Paradoxical Questions Concerning the Morals and Actions of Athanasius and his Followers."** The questions are all answered in such wise as to make those morals and actions look very dubious indeed. Again we see Newton presenting an effectively researched, skillfully marshalled, pungently phrased case, in the spirit of a prosecuting attorney rather than a judicious weigher of evidence.

Without attempting to describe and assess Newton's arguments in detail, I want to call attention to two which seem particularly revealing of his own outlook. One shows how far he was from a rationalist-skeptical frame of mind: he holds that an allegedly Athanasian story, according to which a Bishop Macarius prays (successfully) for the miserable death of Arius, must be a lie, "Because theprayer of Macarius is contrary to the temper and spirit of true Christianity, and it is not likely that God would hear a wicked prayer."[17] The other revealing point is that the alleged "persecution" of the Athanasians is, according to Newton, only their due punishment for resisting the rightful authority of the State. Despite his heterodoxy, Newton was an Establishment man in that he valued ecclesiastical peace almost above all else, and thought the State had the right and duty of upholding it. He had seen enough religious strife.

Other features of Newton's outlook come out clearly in a short series of (rhetorical) **"Queries Regarding the Word 'Homoousios',"** the first of which speaks for itself:[18] "Whether Christ sent his apostles to teach metaphysics to the unlearned common people, and to their wives and children?" Trinitarian metaphysical speculations are not what religion is all about. Most of the "queries" are devoted to driving home two points: (1) that the word *homoousios* is an unscriptural innovation, which caused great uneasiness at Nicaea and thereafter, and (2) that the originators and defenders of the word were "Papists," and Rome had unlawfully usurped authority.

Besides the dubious character of its proponents, there are for Newton two main objections to the word *homoousios:* it is "contrary to the Apostles' rule of holding fast the form of sound words"[19] (i.e., introduces articles for belief that are not contained in the scriptures) and "is unintelligible. 'Twas not understood in the Council of Nice . . . nor ever since. What cannot be understood is no object of belief."[20] For Newton these are not two conflicting principles. The latter does not mean that the Bible is dispensable, and human reason and experience are an adequate autonomous source of religious knowledge. It does reflect a confidence that the Bible is intelligible (without need for any special illumination). Some parts of it are clearer than others; the clear parts are to be used to interpret the obscure. Commenting on the famous verse in I John, he says:[21]

> If it be said, that we are not to determine what is scripture, and what not by our private judgement, I confess it in places not controverted; but in disputable places, I love to take up with what I can best understand. It is the temper of the hot and superstitious part of mankind, in matters of religion, ever to be fond of misteries (*sic*), and for that reason, to like best, what they understand the least. Such men may use the Apostle St. John, as they please; but I have that honour for him, as to believe, that he wrote good sense; and therefore take that sense to be *His,* which is the best.

Here the immediate issue is which of disputed readings makes the best sense in the context; but the application to general problems of interpretation is clear.

Besides antitrinitarian polemic and apocalyptic interpretation, there is a third major class of Newton's theological writings, in which he draws up brief sets of "articles of religion," with particular attention to questions of church polity. Here Newton is seeking an end to religious strife through agreement on a common body of belief. This does not mean that he was looking for a common essence of all world religions, nor even that he proceeded by trying to find a lowest common denominator of belief among the extant Protestant communions. Rather his position was that no doctrine, or form of church government, should be regarded as binding if it is not explicitly enjoined, in a clearly understandable way, in the Bible. It is clear that he regarded all Biblical religion as fundamentally the same. In **"A Short Scheme of the True Religion"** he finds that everything "fundamental and immutable" in true religion can be set out under two headings: "our duty towards God and our duty towards man."[22] "Thou shalt love the Lord thy God . . . thou shalt love thy neighbor

as thyself": this "love" means, in fact, simply obeying the injunctions of the Decalogue. One's duty to God is to eschew atheism (which almost all men have been led to repudiate, because of such wonders of design as the eye) and idolatry (which includes trust in riches, a form of worshipping the creation instead of the Creator).

> We are therefore to acknowledge one God, infinite, eternal, omnipresent, omniscient, and omnipotent, the creator of all things, most wise, most just, most good, most holy, and to have no other gods but him. We must love him, fear him, honour him, hallow his name, obey his commandments, and set times apart for his service. . . .
>
> This always was, and always will be the religion of all God's people from the beginning to the end of the world.

There is nothing in Newton's statement about the role of Christ, nothing about sin or grace. The fundamental content of religion was known to the earliest men. When they drifted away from it, Moses gave it in the form of the Law. Prophets repeated and interpreted the Law, and now the last and greatest of the prophets has taught it still more clearly. The only new doctrine added by the New Testament is that Jesus was the Messiah. What Newton could have made of Saint Paul is hard to say. Perhaps he would regard the passages in Romans and Galatians about Law and Grace as among the hard and obscure portions of the Bible, to be interpreted by the clearer parts. In any case, the "drama of salvation" has quietly disappeared.

In other places Newton does speak of Christ in traditional sounding terms, referring to him as "God" and affirming that he "redeemed man with his blood." But such statements are given ingenious reinterpretations: the term "God" is applied in Old Testament usage to all who receive the word of God, and the atonement consists in Christ's obedience so pleasing the Father as to move him to pardon the sins of those Christ chooses as subjects in his kingdom.[23] Now the latter of these explanations, in particular, is not a simple piece of humanizing reductionism. It echoes some features of the "forensic" theories of the atonement current in certain staunchly Calvinistic circles (while, of course, differing therefrom in important ways, e.g., in eliminating, without replacing, their reason *why* Christ's obedience should be sufficient to satisfy the Father's justice). What has happened is that the Bible makes such statements about the work of Christ so Newton has to give some account of it, but it is a detail, off to the side of his thought. His understanding of what religion *is* is not affected by the theme of sin and redemption.

We have still to consider the second half of Newton's **"Short Scheme,"**—duty toward man. Be charitable and "do unto others . . ." is the gist of it. *Quod tibi fieri non vis alteri nec fieri* is

> the Ethics, or good manners, taught the first ages by Noah and his sons . . . the heathens by Socrates, Confucius and other philosophers, the Israelites by Moses and the Prophets and the Christians more fully by Christ and his Apostles. . . . Thus you see there is but one law for all nations, the law of righteousness and charity dictated to the Christians by Christ, to the Jews by Moses, and to all mankind by the light of reason, and by this law all men are to be judged in the last day. Romans ii.

Has Newton abandoned scripture as the source of religious knowledge? No, the citation from Romans is to be taken seriously, and supports what Newton says; but of course he leaves out the immediately following chapters of Romans, and the radical demands of the "fuller teaching" in Matthew 5-7. Newton acknowledges that the rationally knowable law is only part of Christianity, but it is an important part and not to be despised. He closes with a string of citations to prove the importance of righteousness and good works.

B. We have seen something of the content and tenor of Newton's religious writings. We are now in a position to answer the questions: what were his particular theological concerns?—and what was his conception of religion?

If one concern were to be singled out as the dominant one, it would have to be Newton's desire to promote ecclesiastical harmony and comprehension by isolating the true core of Christianity, the "religion of all God's people from the beginning to the end of the world." Several of the manuscripts containing various short schemes of true religion bear the title **"Irenicum."** Any attempt to impose requirements of doctrine or practice, beyond what is contained in the simple core, is unwarrantable—unbiblical, contrary to the doctrine of the primitive church, and a form of salvation by works.[24] Hence his antitrinitarian and anti-Roman polemics. Only his labors at the interpretation of apocalyptic writings seem relatively independent of the main concern, and even they tend to vindicate the authority of the Bible and destroy that of Catholic tradition. (It might be added that a great deal of effort in his *Chronology of Ancient Kingdoms,* a primarily historical work, goes into vindicating the biblical chronology.)

It is important to recognize that desire for peace and a concern for correct biblical interpretation (as clearly genuine as it was controlled by preconceptions) were the interrelated motives for his search for "the essence of true religion." Nothing in his writings suggests that acceptability to the "modern man" of his time, or harmony with a scientific world view, was an important consideration for him. To read in such motives seems

gratuitous. Locke might endeavor to demonstrate the reasonableness of Christianity, and Boyle to harmonize Christian theology with experimental science, but Newton (though he presumably sympathized with their convictions) did not address himself to either task.

Further, if the drive toward a simple religion of the two Great Commandments were an effect of a "scientific world-view" or simple common-sense rationalism, we should expect Newton to reject miracles, a Second Coming of Christ, and the resurrection of the body. In fact he accepts them all quite literally. "Miracles of good credit," he writes to Locke, "continued in the Church for about two or three hundred years."[25] And he speculates that worlds "above the clouds" may be the habitations of the blessed.[26]

As we have seen, for Newton religion is essentially a matter of duties and obligations, including the obligation to hold certain simple beliefs; the themes of sin and grace almost drop out. But it is an exaggeration to interpret Newton, as Westfall does, as "embracing natural religion as the whole of Christianity."[27] He continues:

> The original and pure religion, Newton maintained, was the moral religion which was plain to all men, love of God and love of neighbor. The natural product of human reason, it prevailedamong the uncorrupted men of the world's youth. . . . Christianity does not differ from the natural religion known to all rational men.

Newton's conception of the relation between natural and revealed religion is doubtless not very satisfactory, but he is far from wishing to dispense with revelation altogether. It is "the law" which is "dictated to all mankind by the light of reason," as well as to "the first ages by Noah . . . the heathens by Socrates, Confucius and other philosophers, the Israelites by Moses and the Prophets and the Christians more fully by Christ and his Apostles."[28] Newton's point about the "ancient religion . . . of purity and righteousness" is that

> we may lawfully proselyte heathens to it . . . and ought to value and love those who profess and practice it, even though they do not yet believe in Christ, for it is the true religion of Christians as well as heathens, *though not all of the true Christian religion.*[29]

In the paragraph just quoted from, Westfall says that Christ "added nothing to the true religion except the belief that He rose from the dead and that because of His obedience He can prevail upon God to forgive sinners." Newton would accept this characterization of his views, except that he would stress the point that Jesus was (and taught that he was) the Messiah. These are not insignificant additions. To be sure, Newton does not have much to *say* about these points in which Christianity differs from natural religion, but it does not follow that he regarded them as minor. The simple statement of these points belongs, he says, to the milk of the gospel, their elaboration and explanation to the meat.[30] But where the author of Hebrews was deploring the fact that his readers still needed milk when they should have graduated to meat, Newton's point is that only milk should be required, and meat left for those who wish and are able to receive it. He does not seem to include himself in the latter group. But that does not affect the essential point, that Newton thinks Christianity comprises more than natural religion, and for all the overlap between them, the proper basis and criterion for the whole of Christianity is revelation:

> The first principles of the Christian religion are founded, not on disputable conclusions, or human sanctions, opinions, or conjectures, but on the express words of Christ and his Apostles.[31]

C. Nowhere in his theological works does Newton discuss the relation between science and religion, save in the statement we have called "Newton's maxim." "Religion and philosophy are to be preserved distinct. We are not to introduce divine revelations into Philosophy nor philosophical opinions into religion." He does not explain why they should be "preserved distinct," though we have seen that he thinks *metaphysical* speculation has, in the case of the doctrine of the Trinity, introduced confusion and unnecessary controversy. Given his understanding of religion, and his theological interests, he had no reason to introduce natural philosophy either. The important thing is to know one's duties (including what one is duty-bound to believe), and revelation tells us all we need to know. Part of this *can* be known by natural reason, but even for this scientific discoveries are unnecessary; common knowledge is quite sufficient. In his theological papers he once or twice alludes to the design argument, but makes no appeal to scientific theories; he uses the argument as it was known in ancient times.

He had no reason to introduce natural philosophy, and he did not. Though in some respects heterodox, his theological works are traditional. They could have been written by any able unitarian-leaning theologian, innocent of scientific knowledge.

Can a more subtle influence be detected? One might claim that his drive toward simplicity in theology, his rejection of mysteries and of "enthusiasm," his insistence on intelligibility (to the plain unmetaphysical and un-"illuminated" understanding) as an essential criterion for the assessment of doctrines and biblical interpretations—all can be traced to the influence of scientific *method* on his ways of thinking or his ideal of knowledge.[32] In the nature of the case we can hardly prove that there was no such influence. But neither is there any positive evidence for it. And there is available a plausible alternative explanation of his predilection for simplicity and intelligibility in religion.

For such predilections had, independently of scientific concerns, characterized a strand of Reformation thought from the beginning. More than a century of theological strife and the construction of ever-more-elaborate confessional statements had conspicuously failed to promote peace of agreement, even among Protestants. Equally unhelpful were the "enthusiasts" with their claims of special spiritual gifts and knowledge; we have seen what Newton and his friends thought of them. As a result, by Newton's time the simplicity-and-clarity line of thought had very great support among both nonconformists and latitudinarian Anglican divines; and it is just such groups among whom he grew up, and with whom he associated at Cambridge. In short, he stands in a theological line of development which can be understood without reference to scientific influences.

It remains to take note of the one possible exception to our statement that Newton's scientific ideas did not affect his theology. In a series of twelve (unmistakably Unitarian) articles on God appears this one: "The Father is immovable, no place being capable of becoming emptier or fuller of him than it is by the eternal necessity of nature. All other beings are movable from place to place."[33] So far as I know, no previous theological tradition had seen any reason to assign just this particular attribute to God (or, if you like, to spell out this particular inference from the general doctrine of God's immutability). Newton *might* have arrived at it by arguing that an absolute, immovable space requires that the God who "constitutes" it be immovable. But even here it is hard to say which way the influence ran. Koyré has argued that Newton probably got this whole set of ideas from his friend Henry More, who developed them in the course of a controversy with Cartesianism, in which theological, metaphysical, and scientific considerations all figured.[34]

II. *Newton's "Scientific Theism."* The thesis that Newton held a "scientific theism"—i.e., that his theological views were based, in significant measure, on scientific considerations—receives no support from the writings we have considered. On the contrary, if the thesis is true, it is most remarkable that these writings show so very little evidence for it.

The *loci classici* for Newton's "scientific theism" are the General Scholium to the **Principia,** passages in Queries 28 and 31 appended to the **Opticks,** and letters to Richard Bentley and Thomas Burnet.[35] Neither the General Scholium nor the Queries in question appeared in the first editions of their respective treatises; they were added only after Newton's science had come under attack for alleged atheistic implications, and can plausibly be read as defensive in character. Moreover, the letters were written only in response to solicitations from Bentley and Burnet, and Newton could ill afford to appear uncooperative when theologians asked his help. Thus, there is a *prima facie* case for Hurlbutt's view that "Newton would rather have kept his science and his theology separate" but his desire was "dashed for the simple reason that his opponents did not wish to do so, and . . . attacked him on theological grounds."[36] If these writings are thus defensive, they may not be fully reliable as expressions of his actual theological views. However, there is manuscript evidence that their principal themes—the elaboration of a design argument from scientific evidences, the relation of God to gravity and to absolute space and time, creation and cosmogony, and the interpretation of scriptural passages which might seem to conflict with the new science—occupied Newton throughout his career.[37] Thus, while specific criticisms (e.g., by Leibniz and Berkeley) helped determine the specific content of Newton's brief and fragmentary excursions into "scientific theism," it cannot be said that without them he would not have entered upon such subjects. It *may* be, though this is difficult to judge, that he was led to discuss them by criticisms and objections that he *anticipated.*

A brief consideration of the content of Newton's "scientific theism" is now in order.

A. When Bentley inaugurated the Boyle lectures in 1692, he undertook to base a teleological argument for the existence of God on the "system of the world" recently published by Newton. He wrote to ask for Newton's comments on some lines of argument he proposed to use, and Newton responded—sometimes with approbation, sometimes with gentle discouragement, sometimes with suggested arguments—in a series of four letters.[38]

Typical of Newton's contributions is the idea that the concentric planetary orbits could not have arisen fortuitously; the excentric orbits of the comets, inclined every which way to the planetary plane, show what could be expected from chance.[39] Here he is arguing that a contrast between a perceived regularity and a perceived irregularity implies purposiveness behind the regularity—which would seem to leave him in the dubious position (for a creationist) of denying any voluntary agency behind the irregular motions. The trap is not inescapable, but the escape routes are not likely to appeal to anyone who does not hold to a purposive divine creation already.

At the end of the first letter he mentions another argument, but is unwilling to give it "till the principles on which it is grounded are better received." It is not quite clear what he had in mind, but it may have been some sort of argument from such phenomena as gravitational attraction and the coherence (which implies some strong force) of "homogeneal hard bodies."

Neither ancient atomism nor the modern (Cartesian) mechanism can explain such phenomena. These points are treated in the Queries and (in the case of gravity) in the letters to Bentley.

As to gravitation, the Cartesian medium is to be rejected as a "feigned hypothesis" (and full of difficulties anyway), and Newton is *not* willing (as he urgently impresses upon Bentley) to regard gravity as an inherent property of matter.[40] Interpreters differ as to whether Newton meant to ascribe gravitational attraction to the direct action of God, as some of his theological disciples and expositors took him to mean. No doubt, ultimately God is the cause of gravity, but is there a mediate cause? "The cause of gravity," he continues, "is what I do not know, and therefore would take more time to consider of it." In the next letter, he agrees with Bentley that "it is inconceivable that inanimate brute matter should, without the mediation of something else which is not material, operate upon and affect other matter without mutual contact," so if the void exists an immaterial agent must be involved. But he concludes, "Gravity must be caused by an agent acting constantly according to certain laws, but whether this agent be material or immaterial I have left to the consideration of my readers."[41]

Actually, Newton's opinions as to the cause of gravity seem to have wavered and shifted. At various times he seems to have inclined toward (1) an ether theory, (2) the view that God's immediate action is required, (3) attribution of gravity to low-grade spiritual agencies akin to the "plastick nature" of More and Cudworth.[42] Whichever view he favored at a given time, he was prepared to argue that it undercut atheism (at least of the Epicurean variety and the sort he thought implicit in Cartesianism, and these were the only varieties he worried about). The third view is incompatible with Epicureanism and Cartesianism, and a mechanistic ether theory would yield an argument of the familiar sort for divine contrivance. His shifting preferences seem to have been governed by scientific considerations rather than the theological utility of the various theories.

In Query 31, Newton appeals also to the powerful attractive forces that must exist to hold atoms together in homogeneous bodies (he has no patience with hooked atoms, nor with Descartes's "rest" theory),[43] and to the need for replenishment of the universe's energy: imperfectly elastic bodies lose part of their motion on contact, so some sort of active principles "such as . . . the cause of gravity . . . and the cause of fermentation" are needed to keep things from grinding to a halt.[44] He seems here to be leaning toward the third of the above theories, but he expresses himself cautiously and keeps his options open.

The notorious charge that Newton assigns God the undignified role of cosmic plumber, brought by Leibniz in his exchange with Clarke and often repeated since, is based in large part on the supposition that Newton really meant to say that God's direct action is required to replenish the universe's supply of energy. But he did not say it, and it seems wiser not to make the imputation. However, toward the end of Query 31 he concedes that the "wonderful uniformity in the planetary system" is subject to "some inconsiderable irregularities . . . which may have risen from the mutual actions of comets and planets upon one another, and which will be apt to increase until this system wants a reformation." God, being omnipresent and "very well skilled in mechanicks and geometry," is well able to do the reforming.[45] The suggestion is made only briefly and without emphasis. Contrary to what is often said, the context shows that the suggestion is made *neither* by way of invoking God to solve a scientific difficulty, *nor* in order to give God a continuing job to do in the world. Rather, Newton is trying to block any objection, based on the "inconsiderable irregularities" which might be brought against his claim that the uniformity of the system shows the contrivance of a Designer.

In the General Scholium added to the **Principia** in its second edition (1713), Newton is clearly on the defensive, and that on several fronts—scientific, theological, and metaphysical. He begins by pointing up grave difficulties in the Cartesian vortex theory. Vortices disposed of, he is free to state the design argument from the regularity of celestial motions. Then, somewhat abruptly, comes a concise but wide-ranging theological disquisition to which we must return in a moment. Newton continues with a well-known argument to the effect that his failure to establish the cause of gravity does not (as continental critics had charged) detract from the scientific achievements accomplished with the aid of that notion, and concludes with some cryptic remarks concerning the "certain mostsubtle spirit" about which he had speculated at greater length in the Queries.

Though it concludes with the affirmation that "to discourse of [God] from the appearances of things does certainly belong to natural philosophy," the aforementioned "theological disquisition" is based on the Bible and the classical theological tradition, not (with the doubtful exception of a sentence or two) on natural philosophy. Previous speculations of Newton's on the omnipresence and eternity of God as establishing absolute space and time had led to the charge that he was reviving the pantheistic doctrine of God as the "soul of the world." This doctrine he flatly rejects. Anyone who knows what the word "God" means (and for this Newton turns to the Bible) knows that it essentially connotes dominion over servants. Much of the discussion is apparently directed against Bishop Berkeley, who had complained that acceptance of absolute space forces us into the dilemma.

of thinking either that real space is God, or else that there is something beside God which is eternal, infinite, indivisible, immutable. Both of which may justly be thought pernicious and absurd notions.[46]

Newton argues that "eternity" and "infinity" as attributed to God have an entirely different force from "eternity" and "infinity" as attributed to space—simply because God is a sentient being, and the Lord of all things. I think Newton, understanding by "God" the God of the Bible, must have had some trouble getting the point of Berkeley's criticism. He does point out that space and time are divisible, as God is not. But what is striking is the way in which he simply appeals to the Bible and the classical theological tradition, and ignores (or fails to grasp?) the suggestion that his speculations might be hard to reconcile therewith.

One more Newtonian text must be considered. In 1680, Thomas Burnet published his *Sacred Theory of the Earth,* in which he outlined a speculative geological theory of the origin and early history of our planet, and tried ingeniously to harmonize it with the Genesis story. (The earth originally was nicely spherical and smooth, but geological forces, at work from the beginning, produced a catastrophic crash—precisely timed to coincide with the Fall of Adam—whence come our present mountains, ravines, and other evidences of wrack and ruin.) He asked Newton's opinion and got an interesting reply, which Newton carefully characterized as quite speculative: "I have not set down anything I have well considered or will undertake to defend."[47] He ignores Adam's Fall, and we need not concern ourselves with the details of his geological and cosmogonical suggestions. Of more interest is his approach to the problem of reconciling scientific accounts with Moses's. A full answer "would require comment upon Moses, whom I dare not pretend to understand," but the main point is that "Moses, accommodating his words to the gross conceptions of the vulgar, describes things much after the manner as one of the vulgar would have been inclined to do had he lived and seen the whole series of what Moses describes."[48] The Genesis account is neither a scientifically accurate description—that "would have made the narration tedious and confused . . . and become a philosopher more than a prophet"—nor a piece of poetry or metaphysics. Rather it is as close an approximation to a literal description of what happened as could be set out in a narrative at once succinct and comprehensible to the general run of mankind.

B. As we have seen, Newton's "scientific theism" is fragmentary and undeveloped. He nowhere attempts to integrate the theme, that from scientific evidences we can infer a Designer, with hisprimary theological concerns. We must now ask (1) why he makes no such attempt, and (2) whether his "scientific theism" *con-*

flicts with the positions taken in his primarily theological writings.

An obvious answer to the first question would be that he adhered after a fashion, to his own maxim to keep religion and philosophy distinct; he had to protect himself against attack, and against any suggestion of unwillingness to help theological apologists in their efforts, but he regarded the arguments elaborated for defensive purposes as no proper part of his theological position. This answer may be correct, and if so would support a strong interpretation of the maxim; but it is inconclusive, because another explanation is possible: Newton's theological interests were not systematic. He would pursue puzzles that intrigued him (as in the interpretation of prophetic writings), and would deal in detail with what he regarded as threats to true religion (e.g., Catholicism and antilatitudinarianism), but he had no interest in working his theological thoughts into a system. In particular, he would have seen no reason to relate his theological arguments to his other theological writings.

Except for one anomalous statement, the content of his "scientific theism" seems compatible enough with the content of his theological works, whatever we may think of its consistency with his *maxim*. Even in the case of that statement, the conflict is probably only apparent. In the General Scholium he says of God, "We know him only by his most wise and excellent contrivances of things and final causes."[49] Taken out of context, this incautiously-worded statement might well (because of the "only") suggest a stark Deism and denial of revelation. But the emphasis of the preceding discussion is on the unknowability of God's nature and manner of operation; as with any substance, we can know only his attributes. And our statement is part of a nicely-balanced rhetorical sentence:

> We know him only by his most wise and excellent contrivances of things and final causes; we admire him for his perfections, but we reverence and adore him on account of his dominion, for we adore him as his servants; and a god without dominion, providence, and final causes is nothing else but Fate and Nature.

The pleasures of rhetorical brevity may have led Newton here into a misleading overstatement. It is, however, just possible that Newton thinks we *know* of God only what the design argument permits us to infer, and revelation tells us rather what we *ought to believe*. It is also possible that by "know" he tacitly means "know naturally." But it is more likely that the "contrivances" in question include not only arrangements in nature but also the management of historical events so as to fulfill prophecy—Newton's principal ground, we recall, for confidence in the veracity of scripture.

III. *Newton's Maxim and his Practice.* As we have seen, Newton's main theological writings conform to the maxim—keep religion and philosophy (including science) distinct. But some passages about God in letters and physical treatises seem to violate it. The maxim occurs in Newton's papers without interpretation or elaboration. We are therefore free to seek interpretations of the maxim which would accord with Newton's practice. Three such "weak" interpretations will be considered in section A below: each allows some sort of bearing of science on some sort of theology. Newton's practice is compatible with two of the interpretations, but not with the third.

If we accept what I shall call the "strong" interpretation of Newton's maxim, i.e., that science properly has no bearing on theology at all, he will stand convicted of inconsistency (though perhaps with extenuating circumstances), and we will want to know why he fell into this crime. A suggestion on this point will be offered in section B.

A. The first interpretation I want to suggest is this: when Newton says "we are not to introduce . . . philosophical opinions into religion" he means merely that such opinions, and theological conclusions drawn from them, are not to be put forward as *essential articles of belief.* This interpretation assumes a sharp distinction between the essentials of religion—beliefs that can be properly required for church membership—and nonessential theological speculations. We saw in Part I that Newton was inclined to make such a distinction. While he himself was mainly interested in the essential beliefs, he did not object in principle to speculative elaborations. Thus one would be free to try to harmonize religious doctrines with scientific theories, as Newton did (cautiously) in the letter to Burnet, and one is free even to draw theological conclusions from scientific premises, as he did in the letters to Bentley and elsewhere. What one is not free to do is treat the resultant theological opinions as essentials of belief—and this Newton did not do. (The existence and providence of God are essential doctrines, of course, but they are known as such from revelation.)

The second interpretation assumes a distinction between apologetics and theology proper (i.e., the attempt to systematize and speculate upon the essential beliefs in order to gain the fullest possible understanding of them). On this interpretation, philosophical opinions are not to be introduced into theology proper; but since people invoke scientific and other philosophical arguments against religion, it is legitimate to turn their own weapons upon them. This interpretation also fits Newton's practice, though perhaps the letter to Burnet is a doubtful case. (On the face of it, it *could* have been meant as a modest contribution either to apologetics or to theology proper.)

The third interpretation involves no distinction between types or parts of theology, rather the distinction is between two senses in which science could bear on theology One might take Newton's maxim to mean that scientific theories cannot provide arguments for theological conclusions: you cannot deduce the latter from the former, nor even argue that a theologoumenon's harmony with science is a point in its favor. A scientific theory might still *suggest* a theological proposition, which perhaps would not be thought of otherwise but which would (of course) have to be evaluated on strictly theological grounds. Newton might well accept this interpretation of his maxim, but it would not save him from the charge of inconsistency, for he clearly does *argue* from scientific evidences of design to the existence of a Designer.

B. Suppose Newton meant his maxim to be taken in the strong sense, or in the third of the senses just discussed. There is still a way in which one might try to argue that his practice does not violate his admonition. Perhaps not all talk about God is theological. A metaphysician or a natural philosopher might have reason to postulate the existence of a God and ascribe properties and activities to him, without these properties and activities having any *religious* interest or relevance. I shall not discuss the general merits of this idea. It seems unpromising as a defense of Newton, because in the General Scholium and elsewhere bits of "scientific theism" are thoroughly intermingled with revelation-based statements about God and how we must conceive him.

We must conclude that, unless one of the first two interpretations of his maxim given above is correct. Newton fell into inconsistency. Or perhaps we should say he was pushed, if it is true that the offending statements were made in response (1) to charges that his "system of the world" promoted atheism, or (2) to theologians' requests for aid.

Still, why did he defend himself by advancing (albeit fragmentarily) a "scientific theism"? If he thought that science had no bearing on theology, positive or negative, why didn't he reply to his critics by saying so? The answer to this question can only be speculative. It seems likely that such an argument would have been ill-received: it would have sounded too much like what Hobbes and other skeptics had said. Moreover, it could, unless elaborated very carefully, have suggested that religious truths are of a special, mysterious, "higher" sort—just the kind of "enthusiasm" Newton deplored. Thus, had he argued for the irrelevance of natural philosophy to theology, he would very likely have been deeply embroiled in controversy. The avoidance of such embroilments was a cardinal aim of Newton's life, and in particular he had (as we have seen) good reason to want his theological views not to come under public scrutiny. On the other hand, the course he took (on the interpretation now being considered) was the standard one among the "Virtuosi" of the Royal Society, and well-received by theologians. So, in short, he took the easy way out: a little inconsistency was not too high a price to pay for peace.

Notes

[1] L. T. More, *Isaac Newton* (New York, 1962), 608.

[2] H. McLachlan, *The Religious Opinions of Milton, Locke and Newton* (Manchester, 1941), 121, 163.

[3] More, 645.

[4] R. H. Hurlbutt, *Hume, Newton, and the Design Argument* (Lincoln, Neb., 1965), 20.

[5] R. S. Westfall, *Science and Religion in Seventeenth-century England* (New Haven, 1958), 194.

[6] Sir Isaac Newton, *Mathematical Principles of Natural Philosophy,* ed. Florian Cajori (Berkeley, 1946), 546. (Hereafter cited as *Principles.*)

[7] H. W. Turnbull, ed., *The Correspondence of Isaac Newton,* III (Cambridge, 1961), 233. (Hereafter cited as *Correspondence.*)

[8] H. McLachlan, ed., *Sir Isaac Newton, Theological Manuscripts* (Liverpool, 1950), 58. (Cited hereafter as TM.)

[9] They are so regarded by the intellectual historian Frank Manuel and the theologian Klaus-Dietwardt Buchholtz, who have seen the still-unpublished manuscripts. Cf. Manuel, *Isaac Newton, Historian* (Cambridge, Mass., 1963) and Buchholtz, *Isaac Newton als Theologe* (Witten, 1965). Also, nothing in the *Catalogue of the Portsmouth Collection of Books and Papers written by or belonging to Sir Isaac Newton* (Cambridge, n.d.) suggests writings of a significantly different character.

[10] TM, 119.

[11] Isaac Newton, *Observations upon the Prophecies of Daniel, and the Apocalypse of St. John* (London, 1733), 251.

[12] *Ibid.,* 74, 113f.

[13] Buchholtz, 39.

[14] Isaac Newton, *Two Letters to Mr. LeClerc* (London, 1754), 32.

[15] Newton does not fail to take advantage of the polemical opportunity afforded him by the fact that Tertullian went over to the Montanists, a heretical sect of

ascetic rigorists and "enthusiasts" (i.e., claimers of spirit-possession and new revelations, not too different from a number of seventeenth-century English sects that so horrified Newton, the other "virtuosi" of the Royal Society, and good sound Anglicans in general). "It is most likely that so corrupt and forced an interpretation had its rise among a sect of men, accustomed to make bold with the scriptures."

[16] Newton, *Two Letters,* 59.

[17] TM, 65.

[18] *Ibid.,* 44.

[19] *Ibid.*

[20] Quoted in More, 642.

[21] Newton, *Two Letters,* 76f.

[22] TM, 48.

[23] Cf. Westfall, 210f.

[24] TM, 42.

[25] More, 369; cf. TM, 54f.

[26] Sir David Brewster, *Memoirs of the Life, Writings, and Discoveries of Sir Isaac Newton* II, (Edinburgh, 1855), 354.

[27] Westfall, 207.

[28] TM, 52.

[29] *Ibid.,* 53. Emphasis supplied.

[30] *Ibid.,* 32.

[31] *Ibid.,* 34.

[32] Cf. Buchholtz, 39.

[33] FM, 56.

[34] A. Koyré, *From the Closed World to the Infinite Universe* (New York, 1958), chs. V-VII.

[35] I shall discuss only Newton's own writings. To consider such sources as the Leibniz-Clarke correspondence would complicate the discussion without affecting my argument.

[36] Hurlbutt, 5.

[37] *Cf.* A. Rupert Hall and Marie Boas Hall (ed.), *Unpublished Scientific Papers of Isaac Newton* (Cambridge, 1962), esp. "De Gravitatione et aequipondio fluidorum." This early anti-Cartesian essay is analyzed by Alexandre Koyré, *Newtonian Studies* (Chicago, 1968), 82ff. Traces of theology have been found in the first edition of the *Principia* by I. Bernard Cohen, "Isaac Newton *Principia,* the Scriptures, and the Divine Providence," in *Philosophy, Science, and Method* (ed. Sidney Morgenbesser et al.; New York, 1969), 523-48. Also J. E. McGuire, "Body and Void and Newton's *De Mundi Systemate:* Some New Sources," *Archive for History of Exact Sciences,* 3 (1966-67), 206-48.

[38] For evidence that Newton may have had a hand in the selection of Bentley, and suggested his theme, see Henry Guerlac and M. C. Jacob, "Bentley, Newton, and Providence," this *Journal* 30 (1969), 307-18.

[39] *Correspondence,* III, 234f.

[40] *Ibid.,* 240

[41] *Ibid.,* 243f.

[42] On these matters, see Henry Guerlac, *Newton et Epicure* (Conférence donnée au Palais de la Découverte, Paris, 1963), and "Francis Hauksbee: expérimentateur au profit de Newton," *Archives internationales d'histoire des sciences,* 16 (1963), 113-28; and David Kubrin, "Newton and the Cyclical Cosmos: Providence and the Mechanical Philosophy," this *Journal* 28 (1967), 325-45.

[43] Isaac Newton, *Opticks* (New York, 1952), 388.

[44] *Ibid.,* 399.

[45] *Ibid.,* 402; cf. *Correspondence,* III, 235.

[46] George Berkeley, *The Principles of Human Knowledge,* par. 117.

[47] *Correspondence,* II, 334.

[48] *Ibid.,* 333. According to Cohen (524ff) Newton makes a similar statement (unrecognized because of Cajori's mistranslation) in the *Principia.*

[49] *Principles,* 546.

Frank E. Manuel   (essay date 1973)

SOURCE: "His Father in Heaven," in *The Religion of Isaac Newton,* Oxford at the Clarendon Press, 1974, pp. 1-24.

[*In the following essay, Manuel examines the nature of Newton's religious beliefs, as exposed through both his published and unpublished writings. Manuel contends that throughout Newton's life, Newton believed in a "religion of obedience to commandments" in which God the Father, not "Christ the Redeemer," played the dominant role.]*

That the task of searching into the religion of Isaac Newton should fall to a historian rather than a theologian may require an apology. Fortunately I discovered one among Newton's manuscripts. In a treatise on the language of Scripture he remarked on the similarity between the historian's method of periodization and the system of chapters in the books of prophecy. 'For if Historians', he wrote, 'divide their histories into Sections, Chapters, and Books at such periods of time where the less, greater, and greatest revolutions begin or end; and to do otherwise would be improper: much more ought we to suppose that the holy Ghost observes this rule accurately in his prophetick dictates since they are no other then histories of things to come.'[1] In an area where the Holy Ghost operates according to the prescribed historical canon, we historians are on familiar ground and need not fear to tread. Since it will be one of the contentions of these lectures that Newton's was a historical and a scriptural religion, that the metaphysical disputations in which he was sometimes enmeshed ranked quite low in his esteem, a historian might be as good an expositor as a philosopher or a theologian. Newton's scriptural religion was of course not a dry one; it was charged with emotion as intense as the effusions of mystics who seek direct communion with God through spiritual exercises and illumination—a path to religious knowledge that for Newton was far too facile and subjective to be true.

Newton's printed religious views have exerted no profound influence on mankind, and I doubt whether the witness of his manuscripts, upon which I hope to draw, will contribute anything to a religious revival. In the eighteenth and nineteenth centuries Newton was occasionally cited by English apologists to illustrate the compatibility of science and faith. If the greatest of all scientists was a believer, ran the argument, how could any ordinary mortal have the impudence to doubt? German theologians of the Enlightenment leaned heavily upon Newton's confession of belief in a personal God in the General Scholium to the *Principia,* and Albrecht von Haller, the paragon of science in the Germanic world of his day, reverently quoted Newton as authority to support his own reconciliation of science and religion.[2] There are even a few recorded instances of conversion inspired by Newton's *Observations upon the Prophecies of Daniel, and the Apocalypse of St. John.* Johann Georg Hamann, the great Magus of the North, who chanced upon the book in London in the 1750s, testified to his sudden enlightenment upon reading it.[3] More recently, Aleksandr Solzhenitsyn, in spiritual combat with his government, resurrected Newton

as an ally: one of the characters in the *First Circle* defends the sincerity of Newton's belief in God and refutes Marx's allegation that Newton was a covert materialist. But it must be admitted from the outset that an interest in Newton's religion can hardly be justified by its power as an instrument for the propagation of faith. His scientific discoveries and what Newtonians made of them, not his own religious utterances, helped to transform the religious outlook of the West—and in a way that would have mortified him. My dedication to the man himself and to his reputedly esoteric religious writings rests on the assumption that everything about him is worthy of study in its own right, for he remains one of those baffling prodigies of nature that arouse our curiosity and continue to intrigue us by virtue of their very existence.

Isaac the son of Isaac, a yeoman, was born prematurely on Christmas Day of 1642, and was baptized in the small ancient church of Colsterworth, Lincolnshire, on 1 January. Some eighty-five years later Sir Isaac Newton, Master of the Mint and President of the Royal Society, was borne to his grave in Westminster Abbey by great lords of the realm and eminent prelates who were his friends. The country boy's strict Church of England religion of 1661, when he first went up to Cambridge, as centred round the Bible as any Dissenter's, as repelled by Papists and enthusiasts as any young Englishman's of the Restoration, is still discernible in the latitudinarian religion of the aged autocrat of science who received French Catholic *abbés,* a notorious Socinian, High-Churchmen, and, thanks to his last illness, just missed a confrontation with Beelzebub himself in the person of an importunate visiting Frenchman named Voltaire. But between the womb and the tomb Newton underwent a great variety of religious experiences. As he strove mightily to acquire a knowledge of his God and to ward off evil, different kinds of religious concerns were successively in the forefront of his consciousness. Nor was he immune to shifting winds of theological doctrine. Over the decades the Church to which he belonged suffered many vicissitudes. In the course of a series of dynastic changes it was bereft of its head, restored, imperilled, established, and more firmly established; its prevailing temper (if not the articles of faith) was modified. In Augustan Anglicanism, undergoing a subtle movement towards a moralist and rationalistic religion, the sacrificial and redemptive quality of Christ was sometimes left by the wayside. Open theological controversies and reports of private conversations among clergymen of all ranks in the hierarchy of the Church of England convey the impression that by the early eighteenth century this Church was suffering what present day popularizers would call an identity crisis: the labels Arminian, Arian, Socinian, Unitarian were bandied about and all manner of secret heterodoxies were tolerated behind a stolid verbal façade, which often betokened indifference.

In examining the religion of the man Isaac Newton, one could investigate the measure of outward conformity of this member of the Anglican Church to those rituals minimally required by his communion. When and how often did he go to church and take the sacrament? Did he genuflect? Therecord holds no great surprises. He occasionally skipped chapel as an undergraduate in Cambridge; and during the height of his feverish creativity, his amanuensis Humphrey Newton (no relation) tells us that Newton was so absorbed with his 'indefatigable studies' that he 'scarcely knew the house of prayer'.[4] There exists an attestation of his receiving the sacrament of the Last Supper before he went up to London to become Warden of the Mint in 1696.[5] He paid for the distribution of Bibles among the poor,[6] and sharply censured any expressions of levity in matters of religion voiced in his presence. Late in life he was a member of a commission to build fifty new churches in the London area. John Conduitt, who married Newton's niece, was somewhat dismayed that Newton on his death-bed had failed to ask for the final rites, but he consoled himself with the reflection that Newton's whole life had been a preparation for another state.[7]

In one critical incident relating to the fortunes of the Anglican Communion under the Restoration, Newton took an uncompromising—one might almost say defiant—public stand. In the Father Alban Francis case, he pushed his more reluctant Cambridge colleagues to ignore an order under James II's sign-manual instructing them to admit a Benedictine monk to the degree of Master of Arts without taking the oath of loyalty to the Established Church. Newton and other members of the University ended up before the Court of High Commission for Inspecting Ecclesiastical Affairs under the redoubtable George, Lord Jeffreys, who fired the Vice-Chancellor and intimidated the rest of them with a menacing 'Go your way and sin no more lest a worse thing befall you'.[8]

To be sure, when Newton lived in London, many of his chosen disciples and most intimate friends were suspect in matters of religion. Edmond Halley and David Gregory were reputed to be unbelievers; John Locke's views on Christianity were severely censured by the orthodox; the beloved Nicolas Fatio de Duillier was condemned to stand in the pillory for acting as secretary to the Huguenot prophets from the Cévennes who were proclaiming the imminent destruction of London in a bloody holocaust; William Whiston, whom Newton had chosen as his successor to the Lucasian Chair, was ejected from Cambridge University for flagrant heresy and he continued to raise tumults in London churches; Hopton Haynes, Newton's close aid at the Mint for thirty years, was, his writings indicate, a theological humanitarian; Dr. Samuel Clarke, Newton's mouthpiece in the correspondence with Leibniz, was formally charged with spreading antitrinitarian doctrine by the lower house of the Anglican clergy, though the case was quashed by the bishops after a humiliating retraction on Clarke's part. Newton's latter-day irenics even extended far enough to embrace a wildly heterodox Balliol man: James Stirling, a Snell Exhibitioner, a brilliant mathematician and a Jacobite, who had got into trouble for refusing to take an oath to George I, was one of the last of his protégés.

Although the list of deviationists of every kind from the recognized Establishment who were Newton's sometime favourites is rather long, guilt by association was not invoked, and during Newton's lifetime nobody cast aspersions on his Anglican orthodoxy. Never did he join his friends in any public manifesto on matters of doctrine, and when Fatio became entangled in the thickets of activist millenarianism, Whiston of outright Arianism, he pushed them away. In the privacy of his chamber Newton seems to have thought that the Anglican clergymen among whom he dwelt and prospered were not a bad lot after all. While compiling notes on the gross immorality of churchmen in the age of Constantine, he digressed into a comparative study of the clergy in various ages: 'And whilst I compare these times with our own it makes me like our own the better and honour our Clergy the more, accounting them not only men of better morals but also far more judicious andknowing. Tis the nature of man to admire least what he is most acquainted with: and this makes us always think our own times the worst. Men are not sainted till their vices be forgotten.'[9]

Overt actions and private testimonials of this kind will not preoccupy us overmuch. In public Newton was a reasonable conformist and, so far as I know, it did not occur to him to break with his communion. As for the motives and feelings that underlay his conduct—that, as David Hume would say, is 'exposed to some more difficulty'.

How can one recapture the religious experience of a man who died almost 250 years ago? What can I really know about my neighbour's God?

If for the moment we narrow the horizon and play the positivist, we have two kinds of evidence about Newton's inward religion: those sentiments that he actually published during his lifetime or voiced to reliable witnesses orally and in correspondence; and those manuscripts on religion—more than a million words—that were never printed, nor even intended for publication, but that allow a historian to make inferences about Newton's religious sensibility. Direct expressions of religious emotion are sparse—he was not effusive with intimate revelations. He wrote no autobiography, no Pensées; he left no map of Christian experience with technical terms and categories such as seventeenth-century English Puritans and German Pietists drew. But there are occasional documents both public and private that record outbursts of religious passion whose authenticity is compelling. And he had a plan of salvation uniquely his own. Despite the refractory nature of the materials, with the aid of these papers one may be able to catch a reflection of his actual religious emotion.

Customarily, Newton's religion has been examined in rationalistic terms, framed propositions setting forth what he did and did not believe in matters of theological doctrine or what he thought about God's relation to the physical universe, about time and about space. In an atmosphere heavy with verbose disputation and pretensions to learning, self-aware men like Isaac Newton felt called upon to make explicit their religious position, if only for themselves, to differentiate their beliefs about Christ and the creed from those of other sects and persuasions in the Christian community of Western Europe and from dominant tendencies within their own Anglican Church. Such propositions are largely embedded in polemical writings that Newton directed against opinions he held to be dangerous to the true faith, and they serve as a form of self-definition by negation. But while these dogmatic assertions concern us, they hardly exhaust the content of his religion. And perhaps enough has already been said on the puerile question of whether or not Newton actually implied that space was the sensorium of God.

Finally, if Newton's faith be turned on every side, the relationship of his religion to his work as a scientist may be uncovered. What religious implications did he himself draw from his scientific discoveries? And then a question that is less frequently posed: What effect did his scientific method have on his mode of inquiry into matters of religion? While it is self-evident that Newton was born into a scientific world at a given stage of its development, it may sometimes be forgotten that he was also born into a European religious world which for more than half a century had been grappling with the problem of how to assimilate the growing body of scientific knowledge and that, in England at least, a fairly stable rhetoric governing the relationships between the new science and religion had been evolved. Newton could alter the rhetoric, amend it in fact while adhering to it in principle, buthe could never completely escape it.

Were we confined in our considerations of Newton's religion within the boundaries of the widely known printed documents that have been chewed and re-chewed *ad nauseam*—queries 20 and 23 in the 1706 Latin edition of the *Optics,* the prefaces and scholia to the later editions of the *Principia,* and the Clarke-Leibniz correspondence—Newton's religion might appear rather stereotyped. In 1729, shortly after his death, the rejected disciple William Whiston assembled in a little pamphlet everything that Newton had in fact published on religion under his own name, and it ran to a paltry thirty-one small pages.[10] Fortunately, there is that vast manuscript legacy that may now allow us to breathe new life into these bones.

Most of Newton's manuscripts on religion were long concealed from the world's notice. Of the major non-scientific works now in print, only one, the ***Chronology of Ancient Kingdoms Amended,*** was prepared for the press by Newton himself. The ***Observations upon the Prophecies of Daniel, and the Apocalypse of St. John*** was put together after Newton's death by his nephew Benjamin Smith, a cleric not renowned for his piety, a dilettante who had hobnobbed with artists in Paris and Rome and was not very sympathetic to this kind of literature, a man interested in making some money out of his late uncle's papers. In the plan worked out from a heap of manuscripts, the Reverend Mr. Smith favoured the blandest, most conventional, and most commonsensical materials, ignoring the more imaginative excursions. What he sent to the press in 1733 is only an insignificant selection from the vast archive at his disposal. And for two hundred years thereafter most of the manuscripts were suppressed, bowdlerized, neglected, or sequestered, lest what were believed to be shady lucubrations tarnish the image of the perfect scientific genius.

In the Sotheby sale of the Portsmouth Collection in 1936, Newton's non-scientific manuscripts were strewn about rather haphazardly. But since that date, the bulk of them have been reassembled and are now in safe keeping, thanks to the zeal of three ingenious collectors, a most improbable trio, a renowned British economist, an American stockmarket analyst, and an orientalist born in the Middle East who ended up at Yale: special collections in Cambridge, England, Wellesley, Massachusetts, and Jerusalem now bear the names of Keynes, Babson, and Yahuda respectively. Isolated papers still turn up occasionally in American universities and private collections, and there are documents from the Royal Mint (in the Public Record Office) in which accounts of the coinage are interspersed with reflections on the Gnostics and the Cabbala, but they do not materially alter conclusions based on the major repositories. For the first time since the great dispersion, virtually everything that Newton wrote on religion is freely available.

There are extant four separate commentaries on Daniel and the Apocalypse, a church history complete in multiple versions, rules for reading the language of the prophets, many drafts of an Irenicum, a treatise '**De Annis Praedictionis Christi**', and extensive notes on Christian heresies through the ages—all this in addition to hundreds of pages of excerpts from contemporary works of scholarly divinity, from Latin translations of the Talmud, and from the writings of the Church Fathers, to say nothing of a commonplace book devoted mainly to theological subjects and papers in the Cambridge University Library that appear to be related to Samuel Clarke's replies to Leibniz. If Newton was Puritan in his devotion to the text of the Bible he was Anglican in his acceptance of the witness of those Fathers of the Church who were closest to the apostolic tradition, and he spent years scrutinizing their testimony. Manuscripts that are now labelled 'chronology' and even some of those called 'philosophical alchemy' were detached from the theological manuscripts proper by nineteenth-century cataloguers. There were no such rubrics and compartmentalizations in Newton's mind, and wherever possible I shall try to reknit connections among them.

The Keynes collection in King's College includes seven autograph drafts of Newton's **'Irenicum, or Ecclesiastical Polyty tending to Peace',** a draft of **'A Short Scheme of True Religion',** a reasonably complete version of a commentary on the Apocalypse in nine chapters, and an attack on Athanasius entitled **'Paradoxical Questions Concerning the Morals and Actions of Athanasius and his Followers'**—most of these published with varying degrees of accuracy by David Brewster in 1855 and by Herbert McLachlan in 1950.[11] The Babson Institute Library in Wellesley, Massachusetts, has a text of a treatise on the Temple of Solomon complete with an architectural sketch, collections of stray notes, and sundry pieces on church history. By far the greatest part, however, of the historical-theological manuscripts, the church histories, the works on pagan religion, commentaries on prophecy, and long discussions of the nature of Christ, is in the Jewish National and University Library in Jerusalem. The manuscripts on chronology and different versions of the 'Historical Account of Two Notable Corruptions of Scripture' are largely divided between the New College manuscripts in the Bodleian Library and the Yahuda manuscripts in Jerusalem.

After Newton's death, his friend John Craig, prebendary of Salisbury, author of the indigestible *Theologiae Christianae Principia Mathematica* (1699), maintained in a letter to John Conduitt that Newton 'was much more sollicitous in his inquirys into Religion than into Natural Philosophy'. And in what appears to be the record of a confidence, Craig went on to give Newton's official explanation for not publishing these writings during his lifetime: 'They showed that his thoughts were some times different from those which are commonly received, which would ingage him in disputes, and this was a thing which he avoided as much as possible.'[12] The historian cannot of course completely silence the protesting shades of Francis Hall, Hooke, Flamsteed, Leibniz, the Bernoullis, Fréret, Conti, and other victims of Newton's thunderbolts. But Craig may have had a point. For Newton, religious controversy was a source of great anxiety, and remained in a separate category.

Whether or not to put any of his theological papers into print was a subject about which Newton vacillated throughout his life. In one famous instance in 1690, letters exposing as false the Trinitarian proof-texts in John and Timothy had been transmitted through Locke to Le Clerc for anonymous publication in Holland, but then had been withdrawn in panic. And yet, though Newton in his old age committed numerous documents to the flames, he spared these letters and scores of other theological manuscripts. Many are finished pieces that had been revised time and again; some had been recopied as if they were being readied for the press. Introductions addressed 'to the reader' in a manner that for Newton is extraordinarily ingratiating have been attached. At times these manuscripts are distinguished by a freshness and ease of expression that are rare in Newton's published works; he even lapses into colloquialisms. Many reflections scattered throughout these papers are transparently autobiographical and are among the most revealing sources for an understanding of his religion. In a history of the growth of the great apostasy within the Church, he derided the Eastern monks in terms that reveal his psychological acumen in analysing religious experience:

> I find it was general complaint among them that upon their entring into the profession of a Monastick life they found themselves more tempted in the flesh then before and those who became stricker professors thereof and on that account went by degrees further into the wilderness then others did, complained most of all of temptations. The reason they gave of it was that the devil tempted them most who were most enemies and fought most against him: but the true reason was partly that the desire was inflamed by prohibition of lawful marriage, and partly that the profession of chastity and daily fasting on that account put them perpetually in mind of what they strove against, and their idle lives gave liberty to their thoughts to follow their inclinations. The way to chastity is not to struggle with incontinent thoughts but to avert the thoughts by some imployment, or by reading, or by meditating on other things, or by convers. By immoderate fasting the body is also put out of its due temper and for want of sleep the fansy is invigorated about what ever it sets it self upon and by degrees inclines towards a delirium in so much that those Monks who fasted most arrived to a state of seeing apparitions of women and other shapes and of hearing their voices in such a lively manner as made them often think the visions true apparitions of the Devil tempting them to lust. Thus while we pray that God would not lead us into temptation these men ran themselves headlong into it.[13]

In writing about the lives of the monks, Newton did not merely copy mechanically from ecclesiastical histories or from descriptions in the Church Fathers; he relived their experience, disclosing his own personal psychotherapeutic techniques for combating temptation.

The remedy he proposed for such onslaughts of the devil as they suffered was a potion he had often mixed for himself. It was the idle, self-indulgent, day-dreaming of the monks, their neglect of the study of God's actions in the world, that led them into vice and the fabrication of superstitions. This is not a Weberian exposition of the work ethic, nor a Voltairean attack on the emptiness of contemplation, but Newton freely confessing to his own regimen for keeping the demons of lust at bay. Fighting off the threat of evil thoughts with constant labour in search of the specific knowledge of God's word and God's works was the panacea.

Even a cursory study of Newton's manuscripts excludes any bifurcation of his life into a robust youth and manhood, when he performed experiments, adhered to rigorous scientific method, and wrote the ***Principia,*** and a dotage during which he wove mystical fantasies and occupied himself with the Book of Daniel and the Apocalypse of St. John—a legend first propagated by the French astronomer Jean-Baptiste Biot in the early nineteenth century. Some of the livelier versions of Newton's commentaries on prophecy should be dated to the 1670s and 1680s, when he was in his prime. His studies of world chronology and philosophical alchemy, both linked to his theology, began early in his Cambridge University years and continued until his death. A critical edition of the whole manuscript hoard that his executor Thomas Pellet dismissed as 'loose and foul papers' must await a future generation of scholars prepared to wrestle with ten or more variations of the same text and to establish their filiation with authoritative precision; but a rough and tentative chronological order is even now possible, and what I have to say is based on that sequence.

The first intimate religious text of Newton's that has survived, written in 1662 in Shelton shorthand when he was almost twenty and at the University, is perplexing in many respects. It is a confession of his sins, forty-nine before Whit Sunday and nine afterwards. To write out one's sins in private prior to partaking of the Eucharist was common enough. But if one categorizes the sins that Newton listed, most of them turn out to be trivial acts of Sabbath-breaking, or worldly thoughts, or minor disobedience to his mother and grandmother, apparently insignificant aggressions against his schoolfellows and one against his sister, a few instances of lying and petty cheating. This profusion of peccadilloes can be likened to the snowing under of the priest in auricular confession with a barrage of venial sins in order to cover the really grievous one, or to the manner in which the associations of a psychoanalytic patient can become a veritable flood in which the most painful and crucial ones are drowned.

And there are in fact a few serious self-accusations in the mound of petty infractions that Newton assembled: a wish to burn his mother and stepfather and their house over them; a desire for self-slaughter; and unclean thoughts and dreams. But the anguish of the suicidal despair is masked by a laconic statement that takes up less room than a confession of bathing on the Sabbath or surreptitiously using his roommate's towel. As I read and re-read this document, I cannot sustain any presumption of a convulsive religious crisis at the age of twenty—nothing like Robert Boyle's vision in a Genevan thunderstorm. There are, however, a series of eight or nine sins describing Newton's fear of alienation from God in terse but moving phrases that define his religious state: 'Not turning nearer to Thee for my affections. Not living according to my belief. Not loving Thee for Thy self. Not loving Thee for Thy goodness to us. Not desiring Thy ordinances. Not long[ing] for Thee . . . Not fearing Thee so as not to offend Thee. Fearing man above Thee.'[14]

Newton's copy-books, which were not meant to serve as direct a religious purpose as the shorthand confession, are pervaded by a sense of guilt and by doubt and self-denigration. The scrupulosity, punitiveness, austerity, discipline, and industriousness of a morality that may be called puritanical for want of a better word were early stamped upon his character. He had a built-in censor and lived ever under the Taskmaster's eye. The Decalogue he had learned in childhood became an unrelenting conscience that made deadly sins of lying, coveting, Sabbath-breaking, egotistic ambition, and prohibited any expressions of hostility or any breach of control. Newton took the Biblical injunctions in deadly earnest. His God was a *dominus deus, . . . Imperator universalis,* a Master who had issued commandments, and it was his duty as a servant to obey them. From the beginning to the end of his life, Newton's was a religion of obedience to commandments, in which the mercies of Christ the Redeemer played a recessive role. By the turn of the century, the prevailing spirit in the Anglican Church was far less austere and demanding than Newton's personal religion. Sermons soothed self-satisfied parishioners with rationalist reassurances that their faith did not require too much of them, that its burdens were not oppressive. By contrast, the commandments that lie at the heart of the public confession of faith of the seventy-one-year-old Newton in the General Scholium to the ***Principia,*** composed more than half a century after his youthful confession of 1662, were exacting and had been borne with pain throughout his life. When Berkeley, Hartsoeker, and Leibniz were advertising the irreligious implications of Newton's system with an array of fancy metaphysical arguments, Newton proclaimed his belief in a personal God of commandments with plain words that harked back to the primitive source of Judaic and Christian religion. William Whiston's translation from the third edition of the ***Principia,*** incorporating phrases from the second edition, preserves the stark quality of the original far better than the more commonly quoted English versions:

This Being governs all Things, not as a *Soul of the World,* but as *Lord of the Universe;* and upon Account of his Dominion, he is stiled *Lord God,* supreme over all. For the Word *God* is arelative Term, and has Reference to Servants, and *Deity* is the Dominion of God not (*such as a Soul has*) over a Body of his own, which is the Notion of those, who make God the Soul of the World; but (*such as a Governor has*) over Servants. The supreme God is an eternal, infinite, absolutely perfect Being: But a Being, how perfect soever without Dominion is not *Lord God.* For we say, *my God, your God, the God of Israel, the God of Gods,* and *Lord of Lords.* But we do not say, *my Eternal, your Eternal, the Eternal of Israel, the Eternal of the Gods:* We do not say, *my Infinite,* (*your Infinite, the Infinite of Israel:*) We do not say, *my Perfect,* (*your Perfect, the Perfect of Israel:*) For these Terms have no Relation to Servants. The Term *God* very frequently signifies *Lord;* but every *Lord* is not *God.* The Dominion of a spiritual Being constitutes him God. True Dominion, *true God:* Supreme Dominion, *supreme God:* Imaginary Dominion, *imaginary God.* And from his having *true Dominion* it follows, that the *true God* is *living, intelligent,* and *powerful;* from his *other* Perfections it follows that he is *supreme* or *most perfect.*[15]

This is the testament of a believer who feels deeply the power of a personal, not a metaphysical, god. A *dominus* has been bearing upon him.

In patriarchal religions like Judaism and Christianity, there is a ritual identification of God and Father. Newton was a posthumous child; when he was born his father had been two months dead. The fantasy world of the posthumous has been explored in twentieth-century literature and in clinical practice. While this proves nothing about Isaac Newton in particular, it does cast light on the imagination and emotional experience of some children born after a father's death and on their search for him throughout their lives. In the folklore of many peoples there is a belief that a posthumous is endowed with curative powers. A number of years ago the minister of the little church in Colsterworth where Newton was baptized told me that country folk in the area still clung to the notion that a posthumous was destined to outstanding good fortune. A similar prognostic attaches to those born on Christmas Day, and Newton's first biographer, Dr. William Stukeley, commented on this traditional omen of his hero's future greatness.

Though all children are curious about their origins, the emotions that surround their questioning have different degrees of intensity. Leafing through the New College manuscripts in the Bodleian that trace the genealogies of pagan gods euhemeristically interpreted and of royal dynasties through the ages, and the ancestries of heroes—all of which were duly integrated into Newton's historical and chronological studies—one is overwhelmed by his preoccupation with origins. It has been suggested in recent studies that a passionate quest for the historical genesis of families and kingdoms and civilizations may be related to an anguished desire to recover lost parents; but such analogies will not convince the mockers, and are not meant to.

When Newton was being knighted, he had to present a genealogy to the College of Heralds. The number of extant copies in his own hand—in Jerusalem, in Wellesley, Massachusetts, in Cambridge, in Austin, Texas, and who knows where else—testifies to the anxiety that accompanied the preparation of this document. In the Jerusalem genealogy, he fixed his parents' marriage in 1639, when it is a matter of record that it took place in 1642, seven months before he was born. Perhaps he worried about his legitimacy. He knew neither father nor father's father, except by report; they were dead before he entered the world. Like other abandoned children—and that is the proper definition of his psychic state—he concocted strange ancestors for himself, even a remote lordly one. The mystery of the father and his origins was not dispelled by the submission of an official document to the College of Heralds, and the search continued on different psychic levels throughout his life. Newton had an especially poignant feeling about the Father who was in heaven, a longing to know Him, to be looked upon with grace by Him, to obey and to serve Him. The sense of owing to progenitors is deep-rooted in mankind, and a child has various ways of attempting to requite the debt; but the demands of a father whose face has never been seen are indefinable, insatiable. Since Newton's father was unknown to him and the child Isaac had not received the slightest sign of his affection, he could never be certain that he had pleased or appeased the Almighty Lord with whom this father was assimilated.

For Isaac Newton, theological questions were invested with personal feelings that had their roots in the earliest experiences of childhood. There was a true father and a false father, as there were true and false gods. The Reverend Barnabas Smith, whom Newton was obliged to call father and who was not his real father but his stepfather, who had carried off his mother when he was about three to live with her in a nearby parish and to sire a half-brother and two half-sisters, was the prototype of the false father and of all religious deceivers and idolaters and metaphysical falsifiers, against whom Newton inveighed with great violence. Newton would show himself to be a master of the traditional tools of scriptural exegesis as developed by the rabbis of the Talmud, Church Fathers, medieval commentators, and Protestant divines—this is the learned side of his religious studies, and I hope that I shall neither neglect nor underestimate them; but he also left behind imprints of the search for the true father who had never set eyes upon him.

That Newton was conscious of his special bond to God and that he conceived of himself as the man destined to unveil the ultimate truth about God's creation does not appear in so many words in anything he wrote. But peculiar traces of this inner conviction crop up in unexpected ways. More than once Newton used *Jeova sanctus unus* as an anagram for Isaacus Neuutonus.[16] In a manuscript interleaf in Newton's own copy of the second edition of the *Principia* a parallel between himself and God is set forth in consecutive lines: 'One and the same am I throughout life in all the organs of the senses; one and the same is God always and everywhere.'[17] (In the third edition, the *Ego* gives place to an *omnis homo.*) The downgrading of Christ in Newton's theology, which I shall discuss in a later lecture, makes room for himself as a substitute. Another Isaac had once been saved by direct divine intervention, and in patristic literature Isaac was a prefiguration of Christ. Alexander Pope may not have been aware how pithily his fluent couplet expressed Newton's own sense of his intimate relationship to God. The revelation of 'nature and nature's laws' to mankind required Providence to perform a new act of creation: '*God* said: let Newton be!' Since the fullness of knowledge had been revealed through him, his election by God had been empirically demonstrated. It is true that Newton left queries for a future scientist in the *Optics,* and in one manuscript he concedes that even his reading of prophecy is subject to some further perfection of detail.[18] But essentially there was not much left to be disclosed after Newton, either in science or in the interpretation of Scripture or in the fixing of the definitive chronological pattern of world history or in prophecy.

Perhaps for sceptics Newton's passionate yearning to know God's actions is not better understood when we translate it into a longing to know the father whom he had never seen. But that he belongs to the tribe of God-seekers who, feeling they have been appointed through a divine act for a unique mission, live ever in the presence of an exigent God to whom they owe personal service in gratefulobedience is borne out not only by the public confession in the second edition of the *Principia* in 1713, but by numerous digressions in manuscripts dealing with church history and dogma, which anticipate *almost verbatim* this more famous epilogue, especially in their attack on excessive emphasis on the abstract attributes of God, in their rejection of metaphysics, and in their exaltation of God as Master.

In defending his system of the world against Leibniz and his followers, who charged him with belittling the omniscience and omnipotence of God, I doubt whether Newton simply scurried to his pile of theological manuscripts and lifted from them religious rhetoric appropriate for the occasion. While I do not wholly exclude this possibility, I am more inclined to believe that these were formulas he had repeated to himself over and over again as all great obsessives do, and that they came to mind spontaneously when he felt obliged to write a religious apologia. And it is precisely their reiteration in so many other contexts in the manuscripts that elevates the final affirmations of the General Scholium above the level of a *pièce de circonstance* merely incident to his tragicomic battle with Leibniz. In a fragment entitled '**Of the faith which was once delivered to the Saints**', Newton wrote:

> If God be called ὁπᾳυτοκράτωρ the omnipotent, they take it in a metaphysical sense for Gods power of creating all things out of nothing whereas it is meant principally of his universal irresistible monarchical power to teach us obedience. For in the Creed after the words I believe in one God the father almighty are added the words creator of heaven and earth as not included in the former. If the father or son be called *God,* they take the name in a metaphysical sense as if it signified Gods metaphysical perfections of infinite eternal omniscient omnipotent whereas it relates only to Gods dominion to teach us obedience. The word *God* is relative and signifies the same thing with Lord and King, but in a higher degree. As we say my Lord, our Lord, your Lord, the King of Kings, and Lord of Lords, the supreme Lord, the Lord of the earth, the servants of the Lord, serve other Lords, so we say my God, our God, your God, the God of Gods, the supreme God, the God of the earth, the servants of God, serve other Gods: but we do not say my infinite, our infinite, your infinite, the infinite of infinites, the infinite of the earth, the servants of the infinite, serve other infinites. When the Apostle told the Gentiles that the Gods which they worshipped were not Gods, he did not meane that they were not infinites, (for the Gentiles did not take them to be such:) but he meant that they had no power and dominion over man. They were fals Gods; not fals infinites, but vanities falsly supposed to have power and dominion over man.[19]

A moving presentation of Newton's feeling for his God, in a totally different setting, a manuscript commentary on 2 Kings 17: 15, 16, might serve as a pendant to the emphasis in the General Scholium on God's dominion and will and on His actions, not His attributes or essence.

> To celebrate God for his eternity, immensity, omnisciency, and omnipotence is indeed very pious and the duty of every creature to do it according to capacity, but yet this part of God's glory as it almost transcends the comprehension of man so it springs not from the freedom of God's will but the necessity of his nature . . . the wisest of beings required of us to be celebrated not so much for his essence as for his actions, the creating, preserving, and governing of all things according to his good will and pleasure. The wisdom, power, goodness, and justice which he always exerts in his actions are his glory which he stands so much upon, and is so jealous of . . . even to the least title.[20]

In another passage of the manuscript church history he continued the attack on any metaphysical definitions of God:

> For the word God relates not to the metaphysical nature of God but to his dominion. It is a relative word and has relation to us as the servants of God. It is a word of the same signification with Lord and King, but in a higher degree. For as we say my Lord, our Lord, your Lord, other Lords, the King of Kings, the Lord of Lords, other Lords, the servants of the Lord, serve other Lords, so we say my God, our God, your God, other Gods, the God of Gods, the servants of God, serve other Gods.[21]

To be constantly engaged in studying and probing into God's actions was true worship and the fulfilment of the commandments of a Master. No mystical contemplation, no laying himself open to the assaults of devilish fantasies. The literature on the psychopathology of religious fanaticism was extensive in the seventeenth century and Newton accepted its basic tenets without knowing its name. Working in God's vineyard staved off evil, and work meant investigating real things in nature and in Scripture, not fabricating metaphysical systems and abstractions, not indulging in the 'vaine babblings and oppositions of science falsly so called'.[22] If God is our Master He wants servants who work and obey.

Newton could not establish relations with his God through a feeling of His love, either directly or through an intermediary. Neither love, nor grace, nor mercy plays an important role in Newton's religious writings. Only two paths are open to him in his search for knowledge of the will of God as Master: the study of His actions in the physical world, His creations, and the study of the verbal record of His commandments in Scripture, both of which have an objective historical existence. We do not know the reason why God's will manifested itself in the physical world in one way rather than in another, why He issued one commandment rather than another; all we can know is the fact that He did, and we can marvel at the consequences and study them.

The more Newton's theological and alchemical, chronological and mythological work is examined as a whole corpus, set by the side of his science, the more apparent it becomes that in his moments of grandeur he saw himself as the last of the interpreters of God's will in actions, living on the eve of the fulfilment of the times. In his generation he was the vehicle of God's eternal truth, for by using new mathematical notations and an experimental method he combined the knowledge of the priest-scientists of the earliest nations, of Israel's prophets, of the Greek mathematicians, and of the medieval alchemists. From him nothing had been withheld. Newton's frequent insistence that he was part of an ancient tradition, a rediscoverer rather than an innovator, is susceptible to a variety of interpretations.[23] In manuscript scholia to the *Principia* that date from the end of the seventeenth century he expounded his belief that a whole line of ancient philosophers had held to the atomic theory of matter, a conception of the void, the universality of gravitational force, and even the inverse square law. In part this was euhemeristic interpretation of myth—many of the Greek gods and demigods were really scientists; in historical terms, it was a survival of a major *topos* of the Renaissance tradition of knowledge and its veneration for the wisdom of antiquity. But the doctrine may also take us back to the aetiology of Newton's most profound religious emotions, with which we began. He was so terrified by the *hubris* of discovery of which he was possessed that, as if to placate God the Father, he assured his intimates and himself that he had broken no prohibitionsagainst revealing what was hidden in nature, that he had merely uttered in another language what the ancients had known before him.

To believe that one had penetrated the ultimate secrets of God's universe and to doubt it, to be the Messiah and to wonder about one's anointedness, is the fate of prophets. Newton's conviction that he was a chosen one of God, miraculously preserved, was accompanied by the terror that he would be found unworthy and would provoke the wrath of God his Father. This made one of the great geniuses of the world also one of its great sufferers.

Notes

[1] Jerusalem, Jewish National and University Library, Yahuda MS. 1. 1, fol. 16[r]. See Appendix A below, p. 122.

[2] Albrecht von Haller, *Briefe über die wichtigsten Wahrheiten der Offenbarung* (Bern, 1772), p. 6.

[3] Johann Georg Hamann, 'Betrachtungen über Newtons Abhandlung von den Weissagungen', *Sämtliche Werke,* ed. Josef Nadler, i (Vienna, 1949), 315-19, and 'Tagebuch eines Christen', op. cit. 9.

[4] David Brewster, *Memoirs of the Life, Writings and Discoveries of Sir Isaac Newton* (Edinburgh, 1855), ii. 94.

[5] Royal Commission on Historical Manuscripts, *Eighth Report,* Pt. 1 (London, 1881), 61, official certificate of the vicar and churchwarden of St. Botolph's Church, Cambridge, 18 Aug. 1695.

[6] Oxford, Bodleian Library, New College MSS. 361, II, fol. 39[r].

[7] Cambridge, King's College Library, Keynes MS. 130.

[8] T. B. Howell, compiler, *A Complete Collection of State Trials* (London, 1816), xi. 1315-40.

[9] Yahuda MS. 18. 1, fol. 3[r].

[10] William Whiston, *Sir Isaac Newton's Corollaries from his Philosophy and Chronology in his own Words* (London, 1729).

[11] Herbert McLachlan, ed., *Sir Isaac Newton: Theological Manuscripts* (Liverpool, 1950). See also A. N. L. Munby, 'The Keynes Collection of the Works of Sir Isaac Newton in King's College, Cambridge', *Notes and Records of the Royal Society of London,* x (1952), 40-50.

[12] Keynes MS. 132, letter of 7 April 1727; published in part in Sotheby and Co., *Catalogue of the Newton Papers sold by order of the Viscount Lymington* (London, 1936), pp. 56-7.

[13] Yahuda MS. 18. 1, fol. 2[v].

[14] Richard S. Westfall, 'Short-Writing and the State of Newton's Conscience, 662 (1)', *Notes and Records of the Royal Society of London,* xviii (1963), 14.

[15] Whiston, *Newton's Corollaries,* pp. 13-15.

[16] See Keynes MS. 13; *Sotheby Catalogue,* p. 2, lot 2; H. R. Luard *et al., A Catalogue of the Portsmouth Collection of Books and Papers by or belonging to Sir Isaac Newton* (Cambridge, 1888), p. 17.

[17] Newton, *Philosophiae naturalis principia mathematica,* 3rd edn. in facsimile with variant readings, ed. A. Koyré and I. B. Cohen (Cambridge, Mass., 1972), ii. 762.

[18] Yahuda MS. I. I, fol. 15[r]. See Appendix A below, p. 121.

[19] Yahuda MS. 15. 5, fols. 96[v], 97[r], 98[r].

[20] Yahuda MS. 21, fol. I[r].

[21] Yahuda MS. 15. 7, fol. 154[r].

[22] Yahuda MS. 15. 5, fol. 79[r].

[23] See J. E. McGuire and P. M. Rattansi, 'Newton and the "Pipes of Pan"', *Notes and Records of the Royal Society of London,* xxi (1966), 108-43.

Richard H. Popkin   (essay date 1984)

SOURCE: "Divine Causality: Newton, the Newtonians, and Hume," in *Greene Centennial Studies: Essays Presented to Donald Greene in the Centennial Year of the University of Southern California,* edited by Paul J. Korshin and Robert R. Allen, University Press of Virginia, 1984, pp. 40-56.

[*In the following essay, Popkin asserts that Newton, as well as other major scientists of the time (David Hartley and Joseph Priestley), conceived of divine causality in a manner that subordinated their views on natural causality and scientific achievement to their "millenarian religious views."*]

The usual picture of the development of causal theory in modern science is to portray the transformation from metaphysical to mechanistic explanations during the seventeenth century and to show that the mechanistic explanations did not account for why things happened but only constituted statements of regularities in nature. From Galileo to Hume occult qualities and necessary connections were removed from the study of nature. God as first cause dwindled in importance as Hume transformed Malebranche's denial of the efficacy of secondary causes into a commentary on the inefficacy of first causes—God's action. Father Nicolas Malebranche had shown very acutely thatsecondary agents cannot function as efficient causes. Malebranche derived this claim in part from his contention that God, the Omnipotent Being, is the sole and unique cause of everything. One kind of evidence that Malebranche offered to establish the inefficacy of secondary causes was that nothing is perceived in the alleged agent that could affect the recipient (as in the case of two billiard balls colliding).[1] Hume studied Malebranche carefully and used the French priest's ideas in his own famous analysis of the idea of necessary connection. But Hume then applied Malebranche's critique to the conception of divine causation. Hume contended that no connection is found between the idea of the Deity and any perceivable effect. He also contended that appealing to the relation of God to events added nothing to our understanding of how or why events occur as they do.[2] With Hume, we have often been told, theological and metaphysical notions of causality were exploded, clearing the way for a purely scientific theory of causality. This history of the transformation of the notion of causation to a purely scientific one may look plausible long after Hume, when most philosophers have come to adopt this view (as they only did when positivism became a major position).

However, to grasp the magnitude of the transformation that has occurred, I think that one has to appreciate fairly the views held by major scientists of the time. In this paper I shall try to show that three of the major scientists—Isaac Newton, David Hartley, and Joseph Priestley (and there were many more like them)—held a view about divine causality that overshadowed their views about natural causality and made their scientific achievements subordinate to their millenarian religious views. Natural history for these thinkers was going on within divine history and would last only as long as necessary to fulfill God's prophetic history.

I have not chosen these three because of the uniqueness of their views. Many other contemporaries of Newton and members of the Newtonian movement held the same kinds of views and often held them more blatantly (as in the case of Newton's chosen successor, William Whiston). Newton, Hartley, and Priestley were the leading figures in their fields of scientific endeavor, and in many ways their views were typical of the mainstream of intellectual activity of the time.

This sort of science seen within a religious framework continued into the nineteenth century with figures like Faraday, but the mainstream of scientists tended toward the deism, agnosticism, and atheism of the French Enlightenment, culminating in LaPlace's Newtonian cosmology without God that he presented to Napoleon.

Newton is often portrayed as the perfect empirical scientist because of his denial of hypotheses about why bodies gravitate, in favor of such a statement of the law of how gravitation goes on, and because of his rules of right reasoning, which appear to be rudimentary maxims for empirical induction. For fifty years or more a dispute has been going on among scholars as to whether Newton was such an empiricist or whether he was some kind of metaphysician believing in occult qualities and forces.[3] The vast Newtonian literature gives ammunition to both sides, but I think the evidence, especially from the Newton manuscripts, supports the contention of McGuire and Rattansi that Newton was in the Renaissance Hermetic tradition and that Newton believed in a *prisca theologia* going back to Moses and Hermes that contained all wisdom about the world.[4] Lord Keynes, who made a pretty exhaustive study of the Newton manuscripts (and saved many of them for Cambridge University before they were dispersed), claimed Newton was not the first to live in the age of reason but rather was the last of the magicians.[5] Keynes claimed that Newton "looked on the whole universe and allthat is in it *as a riddle,* as a secret which could be read by applying pure thought to certain evidence, certain mystic clues that God had laid about the world to allow a sort of philosopher's treasure hunt to the esoteric brotherhood."[6] If Newton held to a magical metaphysical view as to how things happened in nature, he also had a theological view as to why (and how) they happened. It is this view that I want to trace in this paper.

Before examining Newton's theological causal theories, let me outline what I will try to cover. Newton was *the* dominant intellectual figure in the British scientific world of the early eighteenth century. Two major figures who tried to develop the Newtonian approach

PHILOSOPHIÆ
NATURALIS
PRINCIPIA
MATHEMATICA.

Autore *JS. NEWTON,* Trin. Coll. Cantab. Soc. Matheseos Professore *Lucasiano,* & Societatis Regalis Sodali.

IMPRIMATUR·
S. PEPYS, *Reg. Soc.* PRÆSES.
Julii 5. 1686.

LONDINI,

Jussu *Societatis Regiæ* ac Typis *Josephi Streater.* Prostat apud plures Bibliopolas. *Anno* MDCLXXXVII.

Title page of Newton's Principia.

in other areas were David Hartley (in psychology) and Joseph Priestley (in electricity and in chemistry.) All three would have won the Nobel Prize if it had existed in their day. Hartley and Priestley both developed in more detail the kind of prophetic theology of Newton as the ultimate interpretation of what is going on in the world. They represented a theological tradition now ignored or forgotten, but one that was the mainstream view of the scientific community of their day. Priestley, who was the only one to live until Hume's supposed solution of the problem of the possibility of knowledge of scientific causality, sternly rebutted Hume's analysis and pointed out what he saw as its inadequacies.[7] This tradition of Newton, Hartley, and Priestley was central in eighteenth-century intellectual history. If we are to understand how we got where we are and what we have gained or lost, I believe we have to look honestly at our past and not try to ignore it or falsify it.

Having said this much, let us look at the data. Everyone knows Newton was religious. He offered a proof of the existence of God (by the argument from design) in the second edition of *Principia Mathematica.* He wrote on questions like the structure of the ancient Temple in Jerusalem. His last two published works were *The Chronology of Ancient Times,* justifying Biblical chronology, and the posthumous *Observations on the Prophecies of Daniel and the Book of Revelation* (1733). When Newton died, his followers tried to prevent the publication of the latter work, plus the voluminous religious writings, most of which are still unpublished.[8] Later explanations have claimed this suppression was (1) due to trying to save Newton's reputation as a scientist, and (2) to cover up the fruits of Newton's senility. As Frank Manuel has pointed out, however, the testimony of Newton's star disciple and later archenemy, William Whiston, shows that Newton was writing the religious material all of his life, including the period of his greatest scientific achievements.[9]

In fact, even the long delay on Newton's part in publishing his theory of gravitation seems to have been due to religious factors. In 1680 Henry More described how he and Newton were studying the Bible and "Apocalyptical Notions" together.[10] Newton drew from the passage in Daniel, which reads, "O Daniel, shut up the words and seal the book, *even* to the time of the end: Many shall run to and fro, and knowledge shall be increased," the interpretation that "tis therefore a part of this Prophecy, that it not be understood before the last age of the world; and therefore it makes for the credit of the Prophecy, that it is not yet understood. But if the last, the age of opening these things, be now approaching, as by the great successes of later interpreters it seems to be, we have more encouragement than ever to look into these things."[11] Newton believed that the text "In the time of the end the wise shall understand, but none of the wicked shall understand" applied to those of his time and that immediately following. Because of this belief, apparently, Newton told Robert Hooke that he, Newton, had "been endeavouring to bend myself from philosophy to other studies in so much that I have long grudged the time spent in that study unless it be perhaps at idle hourssometimes for a diversion."[12] Nonetheless, Newton was finally induced by Halley and others to work out and publish his *Principia Mathematica* in 1687.[13]

The suppression of Newton's religious writings seems more likely due to the fact that Newton was a heterodox Christian. Like Whiston he was an Arian *and,* in early eighteenth-century terms, a Unitarian. Whiston proclaimed and published such views and got himself fired from Newton's chair at Cambridge and from the Royal Society. Newton, who led the fight against Whiston, was a closet heretic.[14] The publication of Newton's religious writings would have ruined his reputation with the positivist-agnostic scientists of the day. (A few documents have been published by H. McLachlan. Both he and Keynes contend that Newton

was not even a Unitarian, but a "Judaic monotheist of the school of Maimonides.")[15]

(Recently I met an American mathematician. When he found out what I was working on, he asked me if it was really true that the great Isaac Newton held strange religious views. When I told him that I thought the answer was yes and that Newton believed stranger things than has been suspected, the mathematician was heartsick. How could it be possible that the discoverer of the calculus believed such nonsense?)

In Newton's theological view, God created and directs nature through intelligent design. God still intervenes in nature to keep the stars from colliding and to maintain the stability of the solar system.[16] Newton said in one of his theological papers that one should keep religion and science separate, "that religion and Philosophy are to be preserved distinct. We are not to introduce divine revelations into Philosophy nor philosophical opinions into religion."[17] However, Newton's views about the Bible would suggest this cannot be done. First, by vindicating biblical chronology, Newton made clear that he accepted Mosaic chronology *including* the creation story in Genesis 1. Frank Manuel, in his chapter "Israel Vindicated," in his *Isaac Newton, Historian,* shows that Newton was trying to deflate the claims to greater antiquity of the Greeks, the Romans, the Egyptians, the Chaldeans, the Persians, or the Chinese over the Jews. In his argument over ancient chronology Newton maintained that "the Bible [is] the most authentic history in the world."[18] Nature, therefore, starts when God commences history. Nature is part of the historical creation. In the *Observations on the Prophecies of Daniel and the Book of Revelation* Newton laid down a theory of interpreting prophetic passages that he took over principally from Joseph Mede's *Key to the Apocalypse.* Mede (1586-1638), who was professor at Cambridge early in the seventeenth century, said that he had become a complete skeptic after his university studies. He found no certainty in any of the sciences he had examined. Finally, he was saved from complete despair by discovering the key to the Apocalypse. He then became the theoretician for those trying to interpret the prophecies, especially in Daniel and Revelation. In fact, his system, with some alterations, is still being used, at least in Southern California. Mede's major work, *Clavis Apocalyptica,* became the source and model for a great many biblical interpreters, including Isaac Newton.[19]

In the theological paper **"The Language of the Prophets,"** Newton claimed that to understand the prophets one has to understand their unique mystical language.[20] In the *Observations on the Prophecies of Daniel and the Book of Revelation* he contended that "the authority of the Prophets is divine, and comprehends the sum of religion."[21] The prophecies in Daniel and Revelation describe the development of the postbiblical world until the end of time (and of history and nature). Newton did not hold that one could foretell future events this way. Rather, as events took place, one could figure out that they had been foretold in the prophecies. These are part of the clues that God has put into creation for us to find. But the whole structure of human history had been foreordained in the prophecies.[22] Newton traced how Roman and medieval history is all the fulfillment of the prophecies. However, he did not follow out further history as Hartley and Priestley did to the immediate present and the millennial future (including the end of physical creation).[23]

In the Newtonian picture God creates, directs, and has ordained a plan for history that his prophets have set forth. This plan not only involves the destruction of the mighty empires of the world but, if one takes the Book of Revelation seriously, the world itself. Newton's scientific contemporary John Ray gave a graphic picture of how the physical world will end in a fire.[24] Whiston wrote on this subject, too.[25] The result would be that Newtonian physics is an explanation of a physical universe that will last about six thousand years; it is an explanation inside a prophetic reading of the Bible. Without worrying about miracles and how they might fit in, physical science is a uniformitarian picture of an aspect of the historical creation that will be true until the prophecies about the end of the world come true.[26]

Newton did not spell out this scheme as clearly as I have painted it, though he came close to it in his *Observations on the Prophecies of Daniel and the Book of Revelation.* David Hartley (1707-1757) made the case crystal clear. Hartley, like Hume, claimed he was discovering the Newtonian laws about mental life.[27] His *Observations on Man* (1749) was more successful than Hume's *Treatise of Human Nature* and is a more scientific and systematic presentation of a mechanistic psychology. Through his influence on Coleridge and on James Mill, Hartley became the founder of modern psychology.[28] Those who know about his theory of association of ideas seem unaware that there is a second and at least coequal part of his book, devoted to explaining natural and revealed religion.[29]

Hartley began by proving God's existence principally through the argument from design. He then turned to justifying acceptance of the biblical account of how God acts in the world. Basically, Hartley followed the commonsense argument that had been developed in seventeenth-century Anglican theology, principally by William Chillingworth, Bishop Edward Stillingfleet, and Archbishop John Tillotson; namely, that it is more reasonable to accept the Mosaic account than to deny it. It is implausible that Moses and the prophets would lie. It would fly in the face of common sense to deny an account of the world that fits the facts and has been accepted by so many eminent persons. Hartley also argued that "the Genuineness of the Scriptures proves the Truth of the Facts contained in them," as well as their divine authority, and that "the Prophecies delivered in the Scriptures prove their divine Authority."[30]

If it is reasonable to accept the Bible, then a crucial part of this acceptance is recognizing the role of prophecy. That biblical prophecy is a genuine way of foretelling events is first of all established by the fact that within the Bible prophecies are made about events to come in Jewish history, and these events happened, such as the fall of the first Temple, the Babylonian captivity, the return from the exile, the fall of the second Temple. More important, prophecies principally in Isaiah foretell the coming of the Messiah. The Gospels show over and over again the way in which the arrival of Jesus of Nazareth is the fulfillment of those prophecies. Finally in Daniel, in certain lines in the Gospels, and especially in the Book of Revelation, prophecies about postbiblical history are made. Hartley claimed the same kind of success rate. The fall of the Roman Empire was predicted, and it fell. The dispersion of the Jews was predicted, and they are scattered to the four corners of the earth. And Hartley went on and on, with great detail.[31] Then he moved to the next state of things. The time for the fulfillment of the final prophecies was near. What he envisaged (though he wouldn't date when all of this would happen) was revolutions all over the world, the collapse of kingdoms, the reemergence of the Lost Tribes of Israel, the return of the Jews to Palestine, the rebuilding of the Temple, the second coming of Jesus, and the conversion of the Jews.[32] At this point developmental history would be over. Jesus would reign for one thousand years, the Millennium, and then the historical and natural world would disappear in the destruction of the world by fire (presumably a spiritual world would survive for all eternity).[33] So in Hartley's scheme prophetic history is the blueprint for what will happen in both natural and human history, and God brings about his plan through the fulfilling of prophecies in history. Hartley was more detailed than Newton (at least in his published writings). In adjoining his theological work to his psychological one, he obviously saw his scientific work as both compatible with his theology and to some extent explained by it. Hartley also made the fulfillment of the prophetic plan an immediate issue in that the specific program set forth in Revelation was about to take place though one could not tell exactly when.

Joseph Priestley (1733-1804) brought this kind of scientific theology to a climax. Priestley, unlike Newton or Hartley, was a preacher by profession, albeit a heterodox one. He was extremely influenced by Hartley's writings and was always recommending them to people. He gave Benjamin Franklin a copy of Hartley to cure him of his deism.[34] He said over and over again that Hume would not have offered so many bad arguments and would not have come to so many wrong conclusions if he had read Hartley's *Observations.*[35] Priestley put out an edition of Hartley (making his explanation of sensory processes even more materialistic and Newtonian than it was in the original).[36] And when Priestley fled to America in 1794 (when he was driven out of England for his pro-French views), he read the Bible and Hartley's religious views on the ship for comfort and solace.

Priestley made fundamental contributions to modern science in his *History of Electricity* and his work on oxygen. He also wrote dozens and dozens of religious works. He held a position similar to that of Newton and Hartley about the evidence of God's existence from the argument from design and the authenticity of the Bible as world history. In his *Discourses Relating to The Evidences of Revealed Religion,* he held that prophecy was God's exclusive province which God gave to certain Hebrews and Apostles.[37] In his *Letters to The French Philosophers,* Priestley claimed it was evident that prophecy is true from the fact that Moses predicted the fate of the Israelites to the end of the world, and his prophecies have been accurate up to the present. Also, Jesus prophesied the destruction of the Temple in Jerusalem, and it happened.[38] Since many of the prophecies have come true, it appeared to Priestley that the ultimate ones were about to be realized. In view of the fact that many of these prophecies involve the Jews, Priestley began a campaign in 1787 to convince the Jews of their role in prophetic history and to urge them to act accordingly by becoming Christians. In 1787 Priestley rejoiced at the prospects for the Jews.[39] The French Revolution increased Priestley's conviction that the millennial prophecies were about to be fulfilled.[40] (Many English theologians saw prophetic implications in the French Revolution and the Napoleonic era. There is some similar literature in France, mainly by Jansenists).[41] In his *Mémoires* there is a note that in the early 1790s he told people that the second personal appearance of Christ was very near, and he placed it at nomore than twenty years.[42]

The Jews rejected his advances. At least one Jewish writer, David Levi of London, denied in his answer to Priestley that biblical prophecies could be translated into current history.[43] Priestley, nonetheless, became more convinced by the course of events. From Philadelphia he declared in 1797 that on reading Scripture he was especially impressed by "the glorious prospects that are given us of the future state of things in the world, with respect to the great events which seem now to be approaching."[44] In 1799 Priestley tried to make clear to the Jews (and everyone else) that the great events had arrived. In *An Address to Jews on The Present State of the World and the Prophecies Relating to it,* Priestley said the Jews had been wise in not trying to fix a time of their redemption. But now "the state of the world at present is such as cannot fail to engage your particular attention."[45] The fall of various

European powers and the capture of the pope indicate that several prophecies in Daniel about the deliverance of the Jews are about to be fulfilled. Priestley dated it all within fifty years, with the Turkish Empire falling first. He presented the French Revolution as the beginning of the whole process leading to the culmination of history.[46] (Priestley was such an enthusiast for the French Revolution that he was made an honorary French citizen and a member of the National Assembly. He never took his seat.) Priestley saw that the prophetic theory advanced by Newton and Hartley was becoming reality. And in this, he, unlike them, saw immediate events as the culmination of divine history. Since he died a few years before his date for the second coming, he never knew that history just went plodding on.

What does this brief survey show? Three of the greatest mechanistic scientists in the late seventeenth and eighteenth centuries held to a picture of the natural world functioning within the divine world. The divine world was not just a general design but a prophetic plan in which nature was created when divine history began and in which nature would last only as long as divine history. They held to the view that was stated by one of Newton's greatest admirers, his namesake, Bishop Thomas Newton, who held Sir Isaac's scientific and theological work in the highest esteem. In his *Dissertation on the Prophecies* (1758), Bishop Newton declared, "In any explication of the prophecies you cannot but observe the subserviency of human learning to the study of divinity. One thing is particularly requisite, a competent knowledge of history sacred and profane, ancient and modern. Prophecy is, as I may say, history anticipated and contracted; history is prophecy accomplished and dilated; and the prophecies of scripture contain, as you can see, the fate of the most considerable nations, and the substance of the most memorable transactions in the world from the earliest to the latest time."[47]

Ultimately, the cause of everything was God acting through his prophetic plan. This picture was held to not only by Newton, Hartley, and Priestley but by most of the scientists in the United Kingdom.

Hume was a misfit in his day because he did not believe in divine causality, Scripture, or prophecy and saw events as just parts of regular sequences. In his earliest work, the *Treatise,* Hume had said that "if no impression, either of sensation or reflection, implies any force or efficacy, 'tis equally impossible to discover or even imagine any such active principle in the deity. Since philosophers, therefore, have concluded, that matter cannot be endow'd with any efficacious principle, because 'tis impossible to discover in it such a principle; the same course of reasoning shou'd determine them to exclude it from the supreme being. Or if they esteem that opinion absurd and impious, as it reallyis, I shall tell them how they may avoid it; and that is, by concluding from the very first, that they have no adequate idea of power or efficacy in any object."[48] Thus divine causal power is unknown, as is any other kind of causal power.

In his later works Hume went on to question any meaningful role that divine causation was supposed to have. In the *Enquiry,* when Hume discussed miracles, a major alleged form of divine causality, he contended that the occurrence of miracles was always extremely improbable. Also, he maintained that it was always more probable that the testimony concerning the occurrence of a miracle was false than that the supposed miraculous event had occurred. Hume applied this analysis to the Pentateuch, and declared, "I desire any one to lay his hand on his heart, and after a serious consideration declare, whether he thinks that the falsehood of such a book, supported by such a testimony, would be more extraordinary and miraculous than all of the miracles it relates; which is, however, necessary to make it be received, according to the measures of probability above established."[49] Hume followed by saying that the same point can be made about prophecies, since prophecies are supposed miracles.[50] (If they were not, they would not count as proofs of revelation.) Because human beings are not able to foretell future events by using their natural capacities, prophecies are therefore supposed to go beyond what can be known by natural means. In the next chapter, entitled "Of a Particular Providence and of a Future State," Hume insisted that "all the philosophy, therefore, in the world, and all the religion, which is nothing but a species of philosophy, will never be able to carry us beyond the usual course of experience, or give us measures of conduct and behavior different from those which are furnished by reflections on common life. No new fact can ever be inferred from the religious hypothesis; no event foreseen or foretold; no reward or punishment expected or dreaded, beyond what is already known by practice and observation."[51]

Hume's empirical theology does not allow for such speculation about what may take place in the world. In the *Dialogues concerning Natural Religion* Hume's character, Philo, asserted that it was dangerous to speculate about the two eternities "before and after the present state of things" because we have no basis for making any meaningful judgments.[52] At the close of the *Dialogues* Hume had Philo say "that the cause or causes of order in the universe probably bear some remote analogy to human intelligence."[53] From this situation no further data could be inferred. Hume, thus, had constructed a view of the world in which no providential events are likely to take place and in which there could be no prophetic knowledge of them.

On the other hand, the prophetic scientists had made great discoveries in the sciences. But their days of glory came to an end in the early nineteenth century. Two factors seem to have played a part in changing the role of the scientist from interpreter of prophecy to predicter of regularities. One is the translation of prophetic historian to interpreter of immediate events that came to a critical point in the failure of the French Revolution and the Napoleonic age to lead to the millennium. The continuation of the world after Waterloo made most see the world in secular terms. Those who continued the prophetic interpretation after 1815 (and there were and are plenty of them) were mainly outside the scientific community and became the founders of fundamentalism.[54]

The other major development was the emergence of a new scientific mentality as expressed by Pierre-Simon de La Place (1749-1827). He, unlike Newton, Hartley, or Priestley, could conceive of a Newtonian world without God. As a product of the French Enlightenment, he had been divorcedfrom the religious and theological traditions so strongly rooted in England. During the chaos of the French Revolutionary and Napoleonic periods, La Place worked out a modernized and polished version of the Newtonian world system. He believed that everything in the world could be explained by this system and that all future observations would confirm it. Unlike Newton, La Place was sure that such a perfect and beautiful system required no divine maintenance. When he explained the system to his former student, the emperor Napoleon Bonaparte, the latter asked him, according to the story, "Where does God fit in your system?" La Place is supposed to have replied, "I have no need for such an hypothesis."[55]

One reason for making such a claim was that La Place was certain that our knowledge of future events came only from our scientific knowledge of causes and effects. He said, "Being assured that nothing will interfere between these causes and their effects, we venture to extend our views into futurity, and contemplate the series of events which time alone can develop."[56] Here we have the complete separation of scientific thought from any prophetic religious view. There is no possibility in this view of prophesying the future. It can only be revealed in terms of the continuation of scientifically established causal laws. And, as a consequence of what La Place is supposed to have told Napoleon, there is no longer any need for the hypothesis that there can be prophetic clues about the future.

The failure of prophecy and the separation of science from religion created our modern scientific mentality. To appreciate what that is and what it has become, one must remember what it emerged from. And to understand the heroes of previous ages, like Newton, Hartley, and Priestley, one has to be willing to appreciate them for what they really were like, rather than what we might wish them to have been. In so doing, perhaps we will gain a richer appreciation of some of the conflicting currents of ideas that have gone into the making of our intellectual world.

Notes

Some of the research for this paper was supported by grants from the National Endowment for the Humanities (No. RO-22932-75-596), and from the Memorial Foundation for Jewish Culture. I should like to thank both foundations for their kind assistance.

[1] See, for instance, Nicolas Malebranche, *Entretiens sur la Métaphysique et sur la Religion,* in *Oeuvres complètes,* Tome XII (Paris, 1965), Entretiens VI and VII, pp. 130-72.

[2] David Hume, *A Treatise of Human Nature* (Oxford, 1951), Book I, Part III, sec. XIV, pp. 159-60.

[3] See for instance, E. A. Burtt, *The Metaphysical Foundations of Modern Physical Science* (New York, 1925), pp. 280-93; E. W. Strong, "Newton and God," *Journal of the History of Ideas,* 13 (1952), 147-67; and Alexandre Koyré, *Newtonian Studies* (Cambridge, Mass., 1965), esp. Ch. i, "The Significance of the Newtonian Synthesis," pp. 16-24.

[4] J. E. McGuire and P. M. Rattansi, "Newton and the 'Pipes of Pan,'" *Notes and Records of the Royal Society of London,* 21 (1966), 108-43; and J. E. McGuire, "Force, Active Principles, and Newton's Invisible Realm," *Ambix,* 15 (1968), 154-208.

[5] John Maynard Keynes, "Newton, the Man" in *Essays in Biography* (London, 1961), p. 311.
[6] Ibid., p. 313.

[7] See Joseph Priestley, *Letters to a Philosophical Unbeliever, Part I. Containing an Examination of the Principal Objections to the Doctrines of Religion, and especially those contained in the Writings of Mr. Hume* (Bath, 1780). Priestley criticized Hume in many of his works, and especially in this work attacked Hume's causal analysis. See R. H. Popkin, "Joseph Priestley's Criticisms of David Hume's Philosophy," *Journal of the History of Philosophy,* 15 (1977), 437-47.

[8] On what happened to the manuscripts, see H. McLachlan, Introduction, *Sir Isaac Newton's Theological Manuscripts* (Liverpool, 1950). See also Keynes, p. 323. On the struggle about the *Observations on the Prophecies of Daniel and the Book of Revelation,* see Frank E. Manuel, *Isaac Newton Historian* (Cambridge, Mass., 1963), Ch. x. The greater part of Newton's theological papers are in the National Library of Israel, Jersusalem, forming Yahuda MSS Var.1. Out of this vast collection, only one item has been published, as an appendix to Frank Manuel's *The Religion of Isaac Newton* (Oxford, 1974). Professors B. J. Dobbs, Richard S. Westfall, and myself are preparing an edition of all of Newton's theological and alchemical papers, which Cambridge University Press will publish.

[9] Manuel, p. 171. Keynes states that Newton's writings on esoteric subjects and on theological matters "were nearly all composed during the same twenty-five years of his mathematical studies" (p. 316).

[10] Arthur Quinn, *The Confidence of British Philosophers, an Essay in Historical Narrative* (Leiden, 1977), p. 31, drawn from Henry More, *A Plain and Continued Exposition of the several Prophecies or Divine Visions of the Prophet Daniel* (London, 1681).

[11] Ibid., p. 32. Cited from Isaac Newton, *Observations upon the Prophecies of Daniel and the Apocalypse of St. John* (London, 1733).

[12] Quinn, pp. 32-33.

[13] Ibid., pp. 33-34.

[14] Cf. McLachlan, Ch. ii, "Newton's Theology," in *Newton's Theological Writings,* esp. pp. 12-16; Manuel, p. 143; and Keynes, pp. 316-18. James Force has done an excellent study of Whiston as a dissertation under my direction. He is presently preparing it for publication.

[15] McLachlan, p. 13, and Keynes, p. 316.

[16] Dudley Shapere, "Isaac Newton," in *Encyclopedia of Philosophy,* V, 490.

[17] Isaac Newton, "Seven Statements on Religion," in McLachlan, p. 58.

[18] Manuel, Ch. vi. The quotation is on p. 89.

[19] On Joseph Mede, see "The Author's Life," in *The Works of the Pious and Profoundly Learned Joseph Mede, B. C.* (London 1672), pp. I-XXXIV; Ernest Tuveson, *Millennium and Utopia* (Gloucester, Mass., 1972), pp. 76-85; Quinn, pp. 11-12; and Peter Toon, *Puritans, the Millennium and the Future of Israel: Puritan Eschatology, 1600-1660* (Cambridge and London, 1970), pp. 56-65.

[20] McLachlan, pp. 119-20.

[21] Isaac Newton, *Observations upon the Prophecies of Daniel and the Apocalypse of St. John,* p. 14.

[22] Ibid., p. 251.

[23] In the *Observations* Newton covered events in prophetic terms up to the fall of Constantinople in 1453.

[24] John Ray (Fellow of the Royal Society), *Three Physio-Theological Discourses concerning, I. The Primitive Chaos, and Creation of the World. II. The General Deluge, its Causes and Effects. III. The Dissolution of the World and Future Conflagration* (London, 1713).

[25] William Whiston, *A New Theory of the Earth from its Original, to the Consummation of all Things, wherein the Creation of the World in six Days, The Universal Deluge, and the Great Conflagration, as laid down in the Holy Scripture, are shown to be perfectly agreeable to Reason and Phylosophy With a Discourse concerning the Mosaick History of the Creation* (London, 1696). This is the work of Whiston's that first brought him to Newton's attention.

[26] There was some dispute about whether the natural world had proceeded by uniform laws, or whether the Flood had altered the laws.

[27] In his opening chapter, Hartley indicated that both his methods and his subject matter derived from Newton. David Hartley, *Observations on Man, his Fame, his Duty and his Expectations* (London, 1749), facs. ed. (Gainesville, Fla., 1966), introd. by Theodore L. Huguelet. Hume, in the *Treatise*, claimed he was introducing the Newtonian method of reasoning into moral subjects (title page), and later on that he, Hume, had discovered the law of attraction for the mental world (Book I, Part I, section iv).

[28] Coleridge even named his son Hartley. T. L. Huguelet traces Hartley's influence in the development of psychology. See his introduction to the Scholars' Facsimile ed. of Hartley.

[29] One of the few studies of the relation of the two parts is Robert Marsh, "The Second Part of Hartley's System," *Journal of the History of Ideas*, 20 (1959), 264-73.

[30] Hartley, *Observations*, Part II, Chs. i and ii.

[31] Ibid., Ch. ii.

[32] Ibid., Ch. iv, sec. ii, propositions 81-84. While making it appear that signs point to the rather imminent fulfillment of these prophecies, Hartley cautiously said, "How near the Dissolution of the present Governments, generally or particularly, may be, would be great Rashness to affirm" (p. 368).

[33] See proposition 85, *"It is not probable, that there will be any pure or complete Happiness, before the Destruction of this World by Fire,"* p. 380. Sect. iii, which follows this proposition, deals with *"Of a Future State after the Expiration of this Life."*

[34] Joseph Priestley, *Observations on the Increase of Infidelity*, 3d ed. (Philadelphia, 1797), p. 110, and *The Memoires of Dr. Joseph Priestley*, ed. and abr. John T. Boyer (Washington, D.C., 1964), p. 77.

[35] Hartley was brought up throughout Priestley's answer to Hume in the *Letter to a Philosophical Unbeliever*. At one point Priestley declared, "Mr. Hume had not even a glimpse of what was at the same time executing by Dr. Hartley, who, in an immence work, of wonderful comprehension and accuracy, has demonstrated" (p. 20).

[36] Priestley's edition was entitled *Hartley's Theory of the Human Mind, on the Principle of the Association of Ideas; with Essays Relating to the Subject of It* (London, 1775).

[37] Joseph Priestley, *Discourses relating to the Evidences of Revealed Religion, Delivered in the Church of the Universalists at Philadelphia* (Philadelphia, 1796).

[38] Joseph Priestley, *Letters to the Philosophers and Politicians of France*, in *Theological and Miscellaneous Works* (London, 1817-32), XXI, 122.

[39] Joseph Priestley, *Letter to the Jews* (Birmingham, 1787) in *Theological and Miscellaneous Works*, XXI, 231.

[40] Priestley's strongest statement on the role of the French Revolution in fulfilling prophecies is his *The Present State of Europe Compared with Ancient Prophecies* (London, 1794). Newton is used as a source.

[41] Two leading English prophetic interpreters of the French events were the Reverend James Bicheno with his *The Signs of the Times; or the Overthrow of the Papal Tyranny in France, The Prelude of Destruction to Popery and Despotism* (London, 1793), and *The Restoration of the Jews, The Crisis of All Nations to which is now prefixed, A Brief History of the Jews from their first Dispersion to the Calling of their Grand Sanhedrin at Paris, October 6, 1806*, 2d ed. (London, 1807); and the Reverend George Stanley Faber, *A General and Connected View of the Prophecies relative to the Conversion, Restoration, Union, and Future Glory, of the Houses of Judah and Israel; The Progress and Final Overthrow of the Antichristian Confederacy in the Land Palestine*, 2 vols. (London, 1809).

For a survey of prophetic interpretations of French events from 1789 to Waterloo, see Leroy E. Froom, *The Prophetic Faith of our Fathers*, Vol. II (Washington, 1948), pp. 744-82, and Mayir Vereté, "The Restoration of the Jews in English Protestant Thought," *Middle Eastern Studies*, 8 (1972), 3-50.

There is a French Millenarian literature that has hardly been studied. There are works like *Dissertation sur l'époque du Rappel des Juifs, et sur l'heureuse révolution qu'il doit opérer dans l'Eglise* (Paris, 1779); and *Avis aux Catholiques sur le caractère et les signes du temps où nous vivons; ou de la Conversion des Juifs, de l'Avènement intermédiaire de Jesus-Christ et de son Règne visible sur la terre* (N.p., 1795). A small portion of French millennial thought is treated in R. H. Popkin, "La Peyrère, the Abbé Grégoire and the Jewish Question in the Eighteenth Century," *Studies in Eighteenth-Century Culture,* 4 (1975), 209-22. See also Clarke Garrett, *Respectable Folly* (Baltimore, 1975).

[42] Priestley, *Memoires* (London, 1831-82) II, 119.

[43] David Levi, *Letters to Dr. Priestley in answer to his Letters to the Jews* (London, 1787).

[44] Priestley, *Observations on The Increase of Infidelity,* 3d ed. (Philadelphia, 1797), p. vi.

[45] Priestley, *An Address to the Jews on the Present State of The World and the Prophecies Relating to it* (Northumberland, 1799) in *Theological and Miscellaneous Works,* XX, 283.

[46] Ibid., pp. 286-89.

[47] Thomas Newton, *Dissertation on the Prophecies,* 2d ed. (London, 1760), III, 439.

[48] Hume, *Treatise,* p. 160.

[49] Hume, "Of Miracles," in *An Enquiry concerning Human Understanding,* ed. Selby-Bigge (Oxford, 1966), p. 130.

[50] Ibid., pp. 130-31.

[51] Hume, *Enquiry,* p. 146. See also R. H. Popkin, "Hume: Philosophical versus Prophetic Historian," in K. R. Merrill and R. W. Shahan, eds., *David Hume, Many-Sided Genius* (Norman, Okla., 1976), pp. 83-95.

[52] Hume, *Dialogues concerning Natural Religion,* ed. Norman Kemp Smith (London, 1947), pp. 134-35.

[53] Ibid., p. 227.

[54] Ernest R. Sandeen, *The Roots of Fundamentalism, British and American Millenarianism, 1800-1930* (Chicago, 1970).

[55] R. Harre, "Pierre Simon de LaPlace," *Encyclopedia of Philosophy,* IV, 291-92.

[56] Ibid., p. 393.

Robert Markley (essay date 1989)

SOURCE: "Isaac Newton's Theological Writings: Problems and Prospects," in *Restoration: Studies in English Literary Culture, 1660-1700,* Vol. 13, No. 1, Spring 1989, pp. 35-48.

[*In the following essay, Markley offers an overview of how Newton's theological writings have been treated by critics. After presenting possibilities for future inquiry, Markley outlines the difficulties confronting scholars who wish to study Newton's religious works.*]

Over the past fifteen years, studies by Frank Manuel, Richard S. Westfall, and other scholars on the problems posed by Isaac Newton's religious and theological writings have finally put to rest at least some of the hoary myths that had, for over two hundred years, effectively severed Newton the scientist from Newton the alchemist and Newton the supposedly doddering writer on biblical history and prophecy.[1] If the dispersal of Newton's unpublished manuscripts in the 1936 sale to Jerusalem, Wellesley (Massachusetts), and Cambridge (England) has created logistical problems for scholars interested in Newton's "non-scientific" work, the fact that this vast body of material is now more-or-less accessible has allowed Manuel and Westfall to offer preliminary accounts of what Newton's theological manuscripts contain. I say "preliminary" because both of these noted historians have stopped after a few steps of what promises to be a long journey; they have surveyed the manuscripts, reprinted some, discussed the significance of others, and offered plausible accounts of the basics of Newton's religious beliefs, but they have not investigated in detail the ideological and ideational implications of his theology for our understanding of the scientific work. Although it is now customary for historians of science (and even literary historians) to acknowledge the "significance" of Newton's religious writings, if for no other reason than their sheer bulk, there is still no consensus about what we are supposed to do with this mass of manuscripts: ignore them? study them? edit them? Westfall, who has read through all the available manuscripts, voices a prevalent opinion when he states that if the stuff were not Newton's we would not bother to read it.[2] But a different point of view can be found in James Force's argument that the study of biblical prophecy constitutes an important part of eighteenth-century Newtonianism and, more radically, in the eccentric but at times fascinating account of David Castillejo, who argues that all of Newton's work—theological, alchemical, and mathematical—represents a unified inquiry into God's creation, shot through with numerological symbolism and structured around the dominant symbol of Solomon's Temple.[3]

Admittedly, anyone who has skimmed Newton's posthumously published historical and theological works,

The Chronology of the Ancient Kingdoms Amended
(1728) and *Observations upon the Prophecies of Daniel and the Apocalypse of St. John* (1733), may decide
that the problems of Newton's religion are best left to
dedicated historians like Manuel and Westfall or confined to "see also" footnotes. But the more scholars
plow through the material in Cambridge and Jerusalem, the less likely the questions posed by Newton's
theology are to go away. The most obvious of these
questions concerns the relation of Newton's theological to his scientific work, but there are others that
might provide a necessary—indeed crucial—impetus
to our ongoing reinterpretations of Restoration and early
eighteenth-century culture.[4] The most basic of these
might be for us to ask how "marginal" Newton's theological works really are, and lead us to explore epistemological and methodological relationships between
Newton's scientific and theological writing. Another
set of questions might seek, like Force's study and the
essays recently collected by Richard Popkin,[5] to reexamine the myths of a progressive "secularization" of
science and society in the late seventeenth and early
eighteenth centuries. Yet another might encourage us
to look more closely at Newton's habits of self-censorship and the resulting differences between public conceptions of his work and his antitrinitarian religious
beliefs. In this respect, a short-hand way of reassessing
the significance of the specifically literary images of
Newtonianism might be to ask what Blake would have
made of Newton's legacy had he had access to his
predecessor's attacks on the apostasy of trinitarianism.
And, to extend the valuable work by M. C. Jacob on
Newtonians and radicals in the eighteenth century, we
might ask how the sociopolitical and literary implications of Newton's religious views relate to the seemingly contradictory impulses of Newtonian ideology—
its justifications of an hierarchically-ordered physical
and political universe on the one hand and its insistent,
if often muted, questioning of received doctrines and
interpretations in both theology and natural philosophy
on the other. If nothing else, pondering these kinds of
questions might suggest new ways to explain to sceptical audiences of scientists and philosophers why the
bulk of the extended correspondence between Newton
and Locke concerned alchemical secrets and thinly
veiled attacks, particularly by the former, on Athanasius, Jerome, and the doctrine of the Trinity.

Obviously, in a brief overview such as this, I do not
have time to suggest answers to all or even a few of
these questions. My purpose, though, is not to offer a
definitive critique of everything written on Newton's
religion in the last fifty years but to take stock of where
we are and, as my previous questions suggest, to outline some of the ways in which historians of science,
intellectual historians, and even literary scholars might
go about identifying and tackling the problems posed
by the volume and complexity of Newton's non-scientific writing. In my mind, this process also has a heuristic value because it may force us to consider redrawing some of the disciplinary boundaries that have
traditionally made the problems of Newton's theology
seem trivial or tangential to accounts of his scientific
thought.

Any assessment of the problems confronting would-be
scholars of Newton's religion must begin with the logistical difficulties of finding the time and money to
read his theological manuscripts. Westfall appends a
checklist of Newton's known theological manuscripts
to his 1982 article: the bulk of these, the Yahuda papers, are in the Jewish National and University Library
in Jerusalem; twelve manuscripts (some reprinted by
McLachlan) are in the Keynes Collection at Cambridge;
and still others are in the Bodleian Library, Oxford,
the Clark Library in Los Angeles, the Babson College
Library in Wellesley, Massachusetts, the Humanities
Research Center at the University of Texas, Austin,
and the Bodmer Library in Geneva. And we cannot be
certain that more manuscripts will not surface in the
future; Newton apparently completed a history of the
early Church which was extant in the eighteenth century but is now lost. Westfall's list includes one-line
descriptions of the contents of each manuscript; however brief, they indicate something of the enormous
difficulties facing a scholar who, presumably having
piled grant upon grant to travel from Israel to Austin,
wishes to analyze Newton's thoughts on even relatively narrow topics. Given Newton's penchant for revision and for drafting new versions of old material,
there exist as many as five or six drafts of "treatises"
or observations on the same subject. For example, the
Clark Library manuscript and Keynes MS.10 (reprinted in McLachlan) are both devoted to Newton's villifying of Athanasius. But the relationship between the
two versions is complex: some passages have been
reshaped, others added, and others cut. Although the
Keynes manuscript is quite clean, neither it nor the
Clark manuscript can be said to represent a final, copytext version of Newton's "intentions." And there are
also manuscript notes on Athanasius (Babson MS. 436,
in Latin, and Yahuda MS. 5.3 which Westfall describes
as "notes on Athanasius [late 1670s]") that have not
been examined, as far as I know, in detail.

Westfall makes a similar point about the difficulty of
trying to sort out the various manuscript states of
Newton's unpublished treatise, *Theologiae gentilis
origines philosophicae (The Philosophical* [that is,
scientific] *Origins of Gentile Theology)*, which exists,
as he says, "only as a chaos of notes and drafts." To
complicate matters, large chunks of various versions
of the *Origines* find their way into *The Chronology of
Antient Kingdoms Amended,* which Westfall calls a
"sanitized rendition [of Newton's antitrinitarian views]
. . . suitable for public consumption."[6] But what Westfall sees as a pallid version of Newton's earlier and
more forceful antitrinitarian rhetoric, Kenneth Knoespel

argues represents a further refinement—and significant conjunction—of Newton's late scientific and theological thought.[7] To accept either view would require one to formulate, at least embryonically, an account of Newton's habits of composition and an accompanying portrait of him as either a meticulous, even obsessive reviser of his work (Knoespel) or an aging member of the establishment who, late in life, produced an "emasculated embodiment" of his earlier heretical work (Westfall). Regardless of which alternative we choose, we are forced to ask a number of historically and theoretically difficult questions about the processes by which Newton composed, revised, and abandoned the drafts of his work on ancient chronology.

In this regard, Newton's manuscripts seem likely to resist the kind of editorial practice familiar to literary scholars: the establishment of a copytext, the search for variants, the concern with determining the author's intentions. In short, there may not be any easy way to edit Newton, to provide a "clean" version of the *Origines* which might then be compared to the *Chronology.* Although I think it is plausible to assume that the basic tenets of Newton's antitrinitarian theology did not change over the course of his adult life, it seems much more difficult to follow the different transmutations of and tensions within his thought that are represented by the various drafts of his treatises on ancient theology, biblical prophecy, and the politics of the early Church. Westfall argues that when the *Origines* "was composed [in the 1680s], it still only hinted at its own implications," that is, at a far-reaching attack on the basic tenets of Christianity ("*Origines,*" p. 30). This aspect of self-censorship, Newton's compulsive habit of proffering, withdrawing, and recasting interpretations of theological material, underscores the problems inherent in assuming, let alone finding, a definitive "intention" in his work.

The sorts of editorial and ideational problems that I have been discussing point up one of the basic problems for scholars who seek to interpret Newton's work. The disciplinary boundaries of our post-Kantian academic world work against anyone's acquiring the combinations of expertise that would be necessary to navigate the complex currents of his thought. The questions asked by historians of religion generally are not those asked by historians or philosophers of science; nor, for that matter, are the kinds of questions asked by intellectual historians those that trouble literary critics seeking to analyze concepts of language and representation in Newton's England. The efforts by Westfall and Betty Jo Dobbs to demonstrate the importance of alchemy in Newton's thought suggest something of the diligence required to cross disciplinary boundaries.[8] Their studies suggest that when we divide Newton's work among our highly specialized, post-Enlightenment disciplines, we are projecting our ways of seeing, our habits of cultural

perception, onto seventeenth-century practices. In effect, when we try to understand what Newton had in mind in his theological writings, we must consciously undo or demystify the conceptions of "science" and "theology" that we have inherited from the eighteenth century. To a great extent the seeming intractability of the *Chronology* and *Observations upon Daniel* results from our lack of a sense of the context in which they were written, although, in this regard, the works of Manuel, Westfall, Force, and Knoespel have made important contributions to our understanding of the place of Newton's non-scientific work in its seventeenth- and eighteenth-century intellectual contexts.

The recent studies of Newton's theological manuscripts have also, then, necessarily complicated our understanding of the relationships between science and religion both in his work and in that of many of his contemporaries. Given the work of Westfall, Castillejo, and Knoespel, we are now in the difficult position of being able neither to assume nor to discount a fundamental coherence among Newton's writings in theology, history, alchemy, and science. We are caught between what scientists would call "weak" and "strong" views of the relationship between Newton's science and his theology. For example, Westfall, while acknowledging the importance of the *Origines* to Newton's thought, downplays its influence on his scientific and mathematical work; at the other extreme, Castillejo maintains that the *Principia* and the *Opticks* reveal myriad mystical connections to the theological manuscripts and semi-direct invocations of the Mosaic science that provides the rationale for all of Newton's scientific, historical, alchemical, and theological projects. Twenty years ago it would have been easy—indeed expected—to dismiss Castillejo as a crackpot who understands nothing about Newton or the history of science. But, as the recent interest among historians in probing the connections between scientific and occult practices in the seventeenth century suggests,[9] the more scholarly work that is done on Newton's theological writings, the less far-fetched Castillejo's admittedly quirky book may seem. Manuel and Westfall, for example, both acknowledge that Newton's scientific projects should be seen within the context of statements like the one that Newton originally intended for the final book of the *Principia* but that remained unpublished until after his death:

> It was the ancient opinion of not a few in the earliest ages of Philosophy, That the fixed Stars stood immoveable in the highest parts of the world; that under the Fixed Stars the Planets were carried about the Sun, that the Earth, as one of the Planets, described an annual course about the Sun, while by a diurnal motion it was in the mean time revolved about its own axe; and that the Sun, as the common Fire which served to warm the Whole, was fixed in the center of the Universe.

This was the philosophy taught of old by *Philolaus, Aristarchus* of *Samos, Plato* in his riper years, and the whole sect of the *Pythagoreans*. And this was the judgment of *Anaximander,* more ancient than any of them, and that wise king of the *Romans Numa Pompilius*. . . .

The *Egyptians* were the earliest observers of the heavens. And from them probably this philosophy was spread abroad. For from them it was, and from the nations about them, that the *Greeks,* a people of themselves more addicted to the study of philology than of nature, derived their first as well as their soundest notions of philosophy. And in the vestal ceremonies we may yet trace the spirit of the *Egyptians.* For it was their way to deliver their mysteries, that is, their philosophy of things above the vulgar way of thinking under the veil of religious rites and hieroglyphick symbols.[10]

Given our improved knowledge of Newton's fascination with these ancient "mysteries," it is now orthodox, internalist historians of science who are on the defensive in maintaining that his religion and science can and should remain separate areas of scholarly investigation. The traditional spectrum of views on Newton—with, say, Bernard Cohen at one end, Westfall in the middle, and Castillejo at the other, distant extreme—could easily be reimagined as a slippery slope. Once one acknowledges, as Westfall and many others have done, that Newton's theological and scientific writings do interpenetrate, it becomes difficult to indicate where one set of interests ends and the other begins, to apply the brakes, in other words, short of endorsing the broad outlines of Castillejo's thesis, if not all of his readings. To try to find a middle ground between, say, Westfall and Castillejo is to risk maintaining that Newton's work is "somewhat" unified or that it gestures towards a quasi-mystical coherence but stops short of a conscious effort to develop a unified, theocentric theory to account for all physical phenomena. In her work on alchemy, Dobbs argues persuasively that Newton was actively seeking in the 1670s and 1680s microcosmic principles in what we would call the atomic world to complete his work on the macrocosmic system set forth in the *Principia.* For Newton scholars of the 1990s, then, the surprise might be to find evidence of major ideational ruptures among his theological, historical, experimental, and mathematical writings.

I am not, I should emphasize, arguing for a view of Newton as a latter-day Paracelsian magus. Because his theological manuscripts are not generally accessible, because our understanding of the intellectual substance as well as contexts of seventeenth-century prophetic and mystical writings is still relatively incomplete, any attempts to pigeonhole Newton the historian of religions will, in my mind, prove no more successful than efforts to describe in simple terms his mathematical and experimental achievements. But, at the very least, I would maintain that the mass of his historical, chro-

nological, prophetical, and exegetical writings can neither be dismissed nor, what seems more likely, shunted aside as someone else's domain. Although it might well prove a lifetime's undertaking, the ideal for the Newton scholar of, say, the twenty-first century would be to immerse himself or herself in patristic commentaries, Renaissance interpretations of the Old Testament Prophecies and the Book of Revelation, Renaissance histories of the ancient world, commentaries on the Arian heresies of the third and fourth centuries, sixteenth- and seventeenth-century scholarship on the textual disseminations of various biblical manuscripts in the middle ages and Renaissance, sixteenth- and seventeenth-century work on chronology and astronomy, and various contemporary accounts of Egyptian hieroglyphics. In short, the task facing the next generation of Newton scholars may prove to be, in one respect, pulling together the kind of work that is usually done in relative isolation.

This synthesizing process will, by its very nature, cross disciplinary boundaries and require a reassessment of the traditional interpretive languages—historical, theological, philosophical, and scientific—by which Newton has been understood.[11] The need for scholars to develop (or appropriate) new critical vocabularies to analyze Newton's "non-canonical" works will, I believe, make the impact of new-historicist and postmodern approaches to his scientific, alchemical, theological, and historical writings a crucial issue in Newton studies. In this regard, I would venture the guess that we are at the threshold of an upcoming era of interdisciplinary, theoretical, and metacritical commentary on Newton. Although this prospect may initially seem threatening to "internalist" historians of science, it offers the possibility that Newton's scientific and non-scientific works will be read and reread from new and potentially valuable perspectives—for scientists as well as new-wave historians and theorists. Without claiming to offer even a modest blueprint for future studies, I would like to suggest some of the ways in which contemporary literary and psychoanalytical theory might be used to investigate a complex range of issues in Newton's writing. For brevity's sake, I shall confine my discussion to two related areas of cross-disciplinary interest—Newton's antitrinitarian theology and its implications for familiar psychological interpretations of his character.

Many, if not most, literary scholars and historians of science have shied away from the problems posed by Newton's religious beliefs because they have traditionally been cast in the uncongenial rhetoric of controversies about the substance of the Son, the nature of the Holy Spirit, and so on. For many critics, the more detailed the theological archaeology becomes, the less relevant and interesting it seems. A more profitable way to explore Newton's theology, however, might be through an analysis of his tortuous, often contradictory attempts to characterize Christ. My use of the literary term "characterize" here is deliberate; what Newton attempts in many of his theological writings is, in effect, to develop a narrative strategy for dealing with a "Son of Man" who is neither divine nor merely superfluous to God's ends. At different points in Newton's theological writings, Jesus becomes the last great prophet, the active agent in God's creation, an earthly intermediary for human prayers, a representative of human hope for progress, and an historically-constrained agent whose power extends only so far as the finite creation of this earth which, Newton believed, was but one of an infinite number of possible or potential worlds.[12] Newton's obsession with the status of Jesus is evident in his many tirades against the doctrine of the Trinity, from his "Letter to a Friend" on the corruption of Biblical texts (which was almost published in the early 1690s through Locke's agency) to his de facto trials of Athanasius for a variety of historical and historically-embellished crimes, specifically his championing of the doctrine of the Trinity.

As Manuel and Gale Christianson, among others, have demonstrated, Newton's antitrinitarianism cannot be easily divorced from the problems we confront when we try to assess his "character"; the details of Newton's biography at times seem to have been concocted by a conspiratorial clique of orthodox Freudians.[13] Although psychoanalytic interpretations of Newton may tell us more about the ingenuity of his twentieth-century interpreters than about his psychological makeup, they do raise important questions about what we define as constituting historical "evidence," about what we accept as "legitimate" vocabularies of historical investigation and representation. Psychoanalytic interpretations of Newton can easily suspend us between sceptical distrust of their holistic claims and admiration for their narrative consistency and symbolic virtuosity.

Born on Christmas day in 1642, Newton was a posthumous son; his mother remarried when he was three and moved to her new husband's house a mile away, leaving Newton to be raised primarily by his grandmother. It is, then, relatively easy to read in Newton's career a series of attempts to please an always and already absent father; the remoteness of Newton's God may be seen as Manuel argues, as the reinscription of a Freudian conflict in theological terms. But, in this case, his relationship to the Son becomes extremely complicated as the interpretive vocabularies of theology and psychoanalysis are superimposed. In one sense, Newton may see Jesus as a rival for the Father's affection; he may see himself as necessarily having to displace Jesus to (re)gain his Father's approval. In this regard, it is relevant that Newton consistently associates his scientific endeavors with the rediscovery of Mosaic, literally pre-Christian, ancient knowledge.

To displace Jesus, in other words, he must establish his anterior claim to knowledge, to worthiness, to the special status of Son. Jesus also, then, functions as a father-figure who must be displaced to regain the love of the mother who "abandoned" him. Devoted to his mother throughout his adult life, Newton provides a textbook example, at least for Manuel, of a man suffering from repressed homosexual desires; his obsession with Jesus can be interpreted as a form of displaced desire. One might also note, in this regard, how his attacks on Athanasius, the trinitarian villain of much of Newton's theological writing, often slip into fulminations about the lust and depravity of monkish defenders of the Trinity. For Newton, trinitarianism and corruption go hand in hand.

It is easy enough to turn Newton's psychobiography into a caricature of Freudian analysis done at a three-hundred years remove. But my synopsis is not intended to argue for a single, definitive interpretation of Newton's character but to suggest that the implication of Newton's theological beliefs in this psychological history requires a more subtle and flexible vocabulary than the rigorous and nearly self-parodic Oedipal terminology that has so far been applied. Dobbs, for example, in her explication of Newton's alchemy relies on Jung's thesis that alchemy provided a way for would-be adepts to integrate disparate elements of their personalities; alchemy, therefore, becomes a means of psychic healing. But Jung's vocabulary, like that of orthodox Freudians, has been called into question by the re-examination of both psychoanalysis and its analytic vocabularies by a variety of analysts and theorists, including Lacan, Kristeva, Cixous, Bakhtin, and a number of others.[14] Rather than simply imposing prefabricated psychological models on Newton, it seems more worthwhile to ask what kind of psychological assumptions might underlie, inform, or help us account for his theological and historical writings.

The postmodern rereading of psychoanalysis has important implications for how we approach what Derrida calls "the scene of writing." Those critics and theorists who have called into question conventional notions of historical and psychological "truth" and writerly "intention" have also suggested new epistemological approaches to the kinds of difficult questions posed by the intersections of writing, psychology, and, I would argue, even seventeenth-century theological controversies. In their important work on the nature of language, Lev Vygotsky and Mikhail Bakhtin, for example, argue that no difference exists between "inner" psychological "speech" and "outer" sociohistorical discourse; the "internal" language of the individual is itself ideologically constrained because it exists only in the dialogic interaction of the individual word or utterance with the words and utterances of others. For Vygotsky and Bakhtin, there is no pre-existent, pre-linguistic, coherent "self" for us to analyze; there are only the dialogic or double-voiced utterances of the individual that are set against competing utterances within his or her socioeconomic environment. Consequently, a pre-existent, individual "psychology" no longer becomes the primary determinant of behavior; instead, the "self" is historically, ideologically, and materially constituted by and among "internal" and "external" discourses. To develop provisional notions of "style" and "self" along Bahktinian lines, then, is to go beyond narrowly deterministic pyschoanalytic accounts of Newton's "character." In this respect, there is no "Newton" who can be authoritatively analyzed as suffering from this or that neurosis, only the writer for whom no clear distinction exists between the external languages of theology and history and the inner discourse of psychological desire and repression. A postmodern reading of Newton would privilege neither psychoanalytic nor theological—nor for that matter scientific—readings of his religious writings. What it would explore is the interplay—the dialogic tension—among the competing discourses that shape his writing.

A postmodern re-envisioning of Newton's theology and psychology would also have important implications for future studies of his prose style and, more broadly, of scientific writing in the seventeenth and eighteenth centuries. In recent years, several critics have challenged simplistic accounts of the "rise" of an objective, scientific prose style under the auspices of the Royal Society in the 1660s and 1670s.[15] However, these much needed efforts to explode the "myth" of a late seventeenth-century change in stylistic practice have stopped short of questioning Newton's status as the pre-eminent figure in the eighteenth century's progress toward a modern, dispassionate, and utilitarian prose style capable of accurately describing natural phenomena. Arakelian, for example, literally makes Newton the hero of this account of stylistic change, arguing that his prose, particularly in the *Opticks,* exhibits the values of orderliness and clarity to a greater extent than the styles of either Addison or Pope. But the more literary critics read Newton's historical, prophetical, and theological writings, the less tenable this traditional view becomes. So, too, I would argue, do assumptions based on schematic views of decorum that suggest Newton wrote one way for scientific audiences and another when he was scribbling about alchemy and hieroglyphics. The privileging of his scientific works over his non-scientific manuscripts ultimately depends on theoretical assumptions about language and on specific assumptions about Newton's style that are, at best, suspect.

At times, particularly in his attacks on Athanasius and the doctrine of the Trinity, Newton's prose is forceful, even strident, and as tightly structured as a legal brief. Each piece of historical or textual evidence is introduced and examined from several vantage points; an interpretation is offered, alternatives considered, and

conclusions reached. Allowing for Newton's polemical intentions, this method of investigation is structured in ways that recall his strategies of presentation in his early optical papers presented to the Royal Society. But as Knoespel has demonstrated, the "style" of Newton's *Chronology,* like that of his other theological and historical works, is more complicated and more problematically structured. Also significant is the evidence of Newton's interest over morethan half a century in problems of style and representation.[16] These are crucial, I believe, to even a preliminary understanding of his fascination with biblical prophecy.

Newton devotes the second chapter of his *Observations on Daniel* to an "authoritative" account "Of the Prophetic Language"; this chapter is a shortened redaction of a longer manuscript, **"The First Book Concerning the Language of the Prophets"** (partially reprinted in McLachlan). The relation between the two versions could itself be the subject of an extended study; in brief, however, it seems that the issues that Newton felt compelled to explore at length in the 1680s are reduced to a series of statements about the exact correspondences of prophetic images to historical and political events. His thesis is that all of the Old Testament prophets "write in one and the same mystical language" that is "certain and definite in its signification" (McLachlan, p. 119). Newton, therefore, sees his work as an attempt to "fix such a signification as agrees best" with all figurative or "mystical" usages in "all the places" in the Bible. This ideal of a stable scheme of representation—an authoritative key to interpreting the scriptures—is founded on his belief that "the language of the Prophets, being Hieroglyphical, had affinity with that of the Egyptian priests and Eastern wise men" and that it operates "by the analogy between the world natural and the world politic" (p. 120).[17] What follows in both the manuscript and published versions is Newton's attempt to "fix" significations by a precise, analogical method: "the heavens and things therein signify thrones and dignities, and those who enjoy them; and the earth, with the things thereon, the inferior people; and the lowest parts of the earth, called *Hades* or Hell, the lowest or most miserable part of them" (*Daniel,* p. 16; and with some changes in the phrasing, McLachlan, pp. 120-21). It does not take a skilled biblical scholar to realize that if one accepts this method of one-to-one correspondence in interpreting the books of prophecy, the analogies of heaven, earth, and hell to the social order of seventeenth- and eighteenth-century England produce a fixed "signification" that equates moral good with the maintenance of the status quo and evil with threats from "below." Yet this sort of schematic structure turns extremely complex, even within the relatively short span of seven pages of the chapter in *Daniel:*[18]

If the world politic, considered in prophecy, consists of many kingdoms, they are represented by as many parts of the world natural; as the noblest by the celestial frame, and then the Moon and Clouds are put for the common people; the less noble, by the earth, sea, and rivers, and by the animals or vegetables, or buildings therein; and then the greater and more powerful animals and taller trees, are put for Kings, Princes, and Nobles. And because the whole kingdom is the body politic of the King, therefore the Sun, or a Tree, or a Beast, or Bird, or a Man, whereby the King is represented, is put in a large signification for the whole kingdom; and several animals, as a Lion, a Bear, a Leopard, a Goat, according to their qualities, are put for several kingdoms and bodies politic; and sacrificing of beasts, for slaughtering and conquering of kingdoms; and friendship between beasts, for peace between kingdoms. Yet sometimes vegetables and animals are, by certain epithets or circumstances, extended to other significations; as a Tree, when called *the tree of life* or *of knowledge;* and a Beast, when called *the old serpent,* or worshipped. (p. 20)

What Newton ends up describing are interpretive rules that must be applied contextually, that depend on what are ultimately arbitrary systems of assigning value. In this regard, his efforts to "fix" meanings for the language of prophecy meet a fate reminiscent of the grandiose schemes for "real characters" and "universal languages" proposed by Dalgarno, Wilkins, and others in the 1650s and1660s. The "certain epithets and circumstances" of the prophetic style force Newton to describe his "system" of fixing meanings relationally. Regardless of his attempts to articulate an ideal scheme of interpretation, the practice of prophetic interpretation becomes, as anyone who has read *Daniel* can testify, increasingly and bewilderingly convoluted.

In an important sense, then, it is ultimately misleading to speak of Newton's "style" of writing. His works display a variety of styles that work against traditional notions of what constitutes "scientific" or "literary" styles. At best, one could offer a few generalizations that might be explored further: Newton's writing is often fragmented into discrete elements conjoined by "and" or ampersands; there is comparatively little logical or rhetorical subordination; and often the complexities of his epistemology depend on what we make of the "ands" and periods that separate clauses and sentences. More radically, however, Newton's "style"— in, for example, the *Chronology*—depends on a complex intersection of different semiotic systems and representational schemes: the historical "narrative" of that work is penetrated by and interacts dialogically with mathematical calculations, genealogical lists, and etymological flights of fancy as Newton seeks to demonstrate that various names for ancient gods and heroes refer to the same historical individual. It is not that Newton's combination of these various epistemological styles is merely idiosyncratic but that his interweaving of them calls into question the very common-

places about the relationship of style to individuality that figure in most discussions of eighteenth-century literature.[19] The complexities of semiotic systems impinging on each other suggests that we need new sorts of interpretive vocabularies to understand and describe Newton's stylistic experiments as well as his complex theological and polemical agendas.

The advantage of a broadly postmodern approach to Newton's writings is that it can allow us to deploy new interpretive strategies without sacrificing our detailed historical knowledge of his life and scientific works. In fact, I am tempted to claim that it is only through a sophisticated theoretical awareness of the problems of language, narrativity, and referentiality that we can begin to explore the relationships that may exist among Newton's works in science, theology, and history. To take only one example, we might consider the only antitrinitarian tracts that he came close to publishing during his lifetime. In 1690, Newton wrote a third letter to (presumably) Locke, continuing his attacks on the doctrine of the Trinity begun in **"An Historical Account of Two Notable Corruptions of Scripture."**[20] Ostensibly a discussion of the corruption of 1 John 5.20 (transferring the epithet "true" from God to Jesus) and other "trinitarian" biblical texts, this letter, like its longer predecessor, is concerned to discover the "true," pristine, authoritative, and antitrinitarian text of the Bible. As he does in his other theological manuscripts, Newton demonstrates a vast knowledge of patristic writing and a good deal of rhetorical effectiveness in using his readers' (presumed) anti-Catholic sentiments to undermine their acceptance of the doctrine of the Trinity. Having meticulously detailed specific problems of the transmission of the New Testament text, Newton concludes that there is no scriptural authority for the belief that the Son and the Father are of the same substance:

> By these instances it's manifest that ye scriptures have been very much corrupted in ye first ages & chiefly in the fourth Century in the times of the Arian Controversy. And to ye shame of Christians be it spoken ye Catholicks are here found much more guilty of these corruptions then the hereticks. In ye earliest ages the Gnosticks were much accused of this crime & seem to have beenguilty & yet the catholicks were not then wholy innocent. But in the fourth fift & sixt Centuries when the Arians Macedonians Nestorians & Eutychians were much exclaimed against for this crime I cannot find any one instance wherein they were justly accused. The Catholicks ever made ye corruptions (so far as I can yet find) & then to justify & propagate them exclaimed against the Hereticks & old Interpreters, as if the ancient genuine readings & translations had been corrupted. Whoever was the author of the Latin Version wch did insert ye testimony of the three in heaven, he charges the Authors of ye ancient Latin versions with infidelity for leaving it out. . . . And if [the Catholics] have taken this liberty wth ye

scriptures, its to be feared they have not spared other authors: So Ruffin (if we may believe Jerome) corrupted Origen's works & pretended that he only purged them from ye corruptions of ye Arians. And such was the liberty of that age that learned men blushed not in translating Authors to correct them at their pleasure & confess openly yt that they did so as if it were a crime to translate them faithfully. All wch I mention out of the great hatred I have to pious frauds, & to shame Christians out of these practices. (III, 138-139)

Newton's "great hatred," his zeal in attacking the trinitarian corrupters of the Bible, sets his theological works apart from both the scepticism of the deists and from, say, the less passionate defense of religious principles that one finds in Dryden's *Religio Laici*.[21] Newton is, at once, meticulous in documenting his case and ruthless in prosecuting it. The dominant metaphor in Newton's "Letters" on scriptural corruption is legal: the author becomes investigator, prosecutor, and judge determined to eradicate the "crimes" of the "corrupters" and to unveil their false accusations against the Arians. But "corruption" for Newton takes on a complex double meaning: technically, "corruption" refers to those passages that he methodically demonstrates were changed to comply with trinitarian doctrine; morally, it becomes a measure of the depravity of his enemies and the enormities of their "crimes." Newton's claim in his first Letter that his subject is "no article of faith, no point of discipline, nothing but a criticism concerning a text of scripture" (III, 83) belies his sweeping indictment of the "pious frauds of ye Roman Church" and his efforts to "make it part of our religion to detect & renounce all" vestiges of Catholic—and by implication trinitarian—doctrine: "we must acknowledge it," he continues, "a greater crime in us to favor such practices, then in the Papists we so much blame on that account" (III, 83). In this respect, Newton's criticism of the corruption of biblical texts reveals a network of interests: his fervent desire to set aright Church history; his polemical campaign to deny trinitarian doctrines and, in effect, to reconstitute "our religion" along unitarian lines; his obsessive efforts to uncover the origins of the authoritative word of primitive Christianity; and his desire to apply the same kinds of consistent methodological principles to theological controversy that he applies to the investigation and description of natural phenomena. This passage, then, recovered from the manuscript draft of an unpublished treatise, has a great deal to tell us about Newton's habits of thinking, his theological and psychological interests, that would be difficult to glean from his published, self-censored scientific works.

Although any general comments about what we can or will learn by studying Newton's theological writings are necessarily provisional, some tentative claims are probably worth making, if only to serve as targets for others to refute or as initial points from which others

may depart. The mass of material that Newton left in incomplete or half-complete form suggests that his writings—scientific, theological, alchemical, and historical—never achieved a grand synthesis or offered a unified theory of nature and that, to the contrary, Newton himself was aware that his was a necessarily incomplete quest to establish an incontrovertible basis for a metaphysical order. His works, in this regard, donot provide the kind of psychological integration that Jung saw as the rationale for alchemical experiments but testify to Newton's struggle to make his own voice heard against a host of competing voices—religious and scientific—that claimed an unquestioning patriarchal and psychopolitical authority. In fact, his theological writings suggest that he saw himself displacing traditional forms of authority—the "voices" of the trinitarian Church, St. Jerome's Bible, and the Athanasian Creed—in his efforts to restore the true, pristine authority of God's word. Newton, then, is not—or not only—the "autocrat of science" attacked by Blake and the Romantics but a dialogician in search of an authorizing Logos.

In this respect, the study of Newton's theological manuscripts may ultimately lead us to reread and revise our understanding of Newtonian science. The allegation that Newton's religion is not important to our understanding of his science because—paradoxically—it tells us the "same" information about the universe may have to be replaced by a recognition that Newton's scientific, alchemical, theological, and historical investigations offer a complex interweaving of different semiotic systems, different "languages," none of which in and of itself is adequate to the exposition of the complexities of the universe. In this regard, Newton's writings on the prophecies that posit a remote God and a millenarian revelation deferred far into the future, may send us back to Query 31 of the *Opticks* to puzzle out the implications of Newton's questions about the physical nature of creation. A "postmodern" reading of Newton will necessarily transgress the disciplinary boundaries in which his scientific works have been enclosed; if it does nothing else, it will allow for a good deal of debate about what we mean by terms like "Newtonian" and "science." Although such simplifications are risky, it seems worth considering the notion that, for Newton, natural philosophy, like prophecy, can be described only in deliberately heuristic and provisional terms. What Newtonian science would then offer us is not a vision of a coherent system and watertight theories but "systems" and "theories" that resist precisely those definitive formulations which Newton's followers in the early eighteenth century—Whiston, Desaguliers, Martin, 'sGravesande, Derham, Pemberton, and others—abstracted from his work. To conclude, we might find that the piles of scattered theological manuscripts that Newton left behind stand metonymically for the scientific and psychological quests that he undertook but could never complete.

Notes

[1] Manuel, *Isaac Newton, Historian* (Cambridge, Mass.: Harvard UP, 1963); *A Portrait of Isaac Newton* (Cambridge, Mass.: Harvard UP, 1968); and *The Religion of Isaac Newton* (Oxford; Clarendon, 1974); Richard S. Westfall, *Never at Rest: A Biography of Isaac Newton* (Cambridge: Cambridge UP, 1980); "Newton's Theological Manuscripts," in *Contemporary Newtonian Research,* ed. Zev Bechler (Dordrecht: Reidel, 1982), pp. 129-43); and "Isaac Newton's *Theologiae Gentilis Origines Philosophicae,*" in *The Secular Mind: Transformations of Faith in Modern Europe,* ed. W. Warren Wagar (New York: Holmes & Meier, 1982), pp. 15-34. All of these works contain generous quotations from Newton's unpublished manuscripts that are not otherwise available. H. McLachlan has edited a short collection, *Sir Isaac Newton: Theological Manuscripts* (Liverpool: Liverpool UP, 1950), but as Westfall notes, McLachlan took a number of liberties in his editing and his versions of the manuscripts must be used with caution. Wherever possible, I have cited published versions of Newton's theological writings.

[2] "Newton's Theological Manuscripts," p. 139. On the same page Westfall makes an important distinction between religious and theological "influences" on Newton's science, although I ultimately disagree with Westfall's claim that "it is difficult if not impossible to demonstrate [a theological] influence on some concrete element of his science" (p. 140). As Westfall argued thirty years ago, invocations of a Supreme Being are legion in seventeenth- and early eighteenth-century scientific texts (*Science and Religion in Seventeenth-Century England* (New Haven: Yale UP, 1958); "natural philosophy" virtually presupposes the existence of a Judeo-Christian God. But the common vocabulary of religious belief in the period masks profound *theological* disagreements among scientists and allowed men like Newton and Whiston, who were virtual heretics, to conceal their heterodox beliefs within a generalized rhetoric of religious belief. In emphasizing the significance of Newton's theological manuscripts, I am, in effect, arguing that we need to pay more attention to the ways in which ideational tensions and problems within Newton's "non-scientific" writings shaped and were shaped by his scientific work.

[3] Force, *William Whiston, Honest Newtonian* (Cambridge; Cambridge UP, 1985); Castillejo, *The Expanding Force in Newton's Cosmos* (Madrid; Ediciones de Arte y Bibliofilia, 1981).

[4] There have been a number of important reinterpretations of Restoration literary culture in recent years. See, for example, Michael McKeon, *Politics and Poetry in Restoration England: Dryden's "Annus Mirabilis"* (Cambridge: Harvard UP, 1975) and "Marxist Criticism and Marriage à la Mode," *The Eighteenth Century: Theory and Interpretation,* 24 (1983), 141-62; Laura Brown, "The Ideology of Restoration Poetic Form: John Dryden," *PMLA,* 97 (1982), 395-407; J. Douglas Canfield, "The Ideology of Restoration Tragicomedy," *ELH,* 51 (1984), 447-64; J. R. Jacob, *Henry Stubbe: Radical Protestantism and the Early Enlightenment in England* (Cambridge: Cambridge UP, 1983); Nicholas Jose, *Ideas of the Restoration in English Literature 1660-71* (Cambridge, Mass.: Harvard UP, 1984); and Susan Staves, *Players' Scepters: Fictions of Authority in the Restoration* (Lincoln: U of Nebraska P, 1979).

[5] *Millenarianism and Messianism in Enlightenment Culture,* ed. Richard Popkin (Berkeley: U of California P, 1987).

[6] Westfall, "Newton's *Origines,*" p. 16. Subsequent quotations will be indicated parenthetically in the text.

[7] Knoespel, "Newton and the School of Time: *The Chronology of Ancient Kingdoms Amended* and the Crisis in Late Seventeenth-Century Historiography," *The Eighteenth Century: Theory and Interpretation,* 29 (1988), forthcoming.

[8] Dobbs, *The Foundations of Newton's Alchemy* (Cambridge: Cambridge UP, 1975), and "Newton's Copy of *Secrets Reveal'd* and the Regimen of the Work, "*Ambix,* 26 (1979), 145-69; Westfall, "The Role of Alchemy in Newton's Career," in *Reason, Experiment, and Mysticism in the Scientific Revolution,* ed. M. L. Righini Bonelli and William R. Shea (New York: Science History Publications, 1975), pp. 189-232, and "Newton and Alchemy," in *Occult and Scientific Mentalities in the Renaissance,* ed. Brian Vickers (Cambridge; Cambridge UP, 1984), pp. 315-35.

[9] On the relationships among the occult, science, and politics see D. P. Walker, *The Decline of Hell* (Chicago: U of Chicago P, 1964); Frances Yates, *The Rosicrucian Enlightenment* (1972; rpt. New York: Routledge and Kegan Paul, 1986); Keith Thomas, *Religion and the Decline of Magic* (London: Weidenfeld, 1971); Margaret C. Jacob, *The Newtonians and the English Revolution, 1689-1720* (Ithaca: Cornell UP, 1976); Christopher Hill, *The World Turned Upside Down: Radical Ideas during the English Revolution* (1971; rpt. Harmondsworth: Penguin, 1975); Brian Easlea, *Witch-Hunting, Magic and the New Philosophy: An Introduction to the Debates of the Scientific Revolution 1450-1750* (Brighton, Sussex: Harvester, 1980); and *Occult and Scientific Mentalities,* ed. Vickers.

[10] Newton, *The System of the World* (London, 1728), pp. 1-2.

[11] For a polemical defense of a "dialogic" analytical language in literary criticism see Don H. Bialostosky,

"Dialogics as an Art of Discourse in Literary Criticism," *PMLA,* 101 (1986), 788-97.

[12] Westfall, "Newton's Theological Manuscripts," pp. 137-38.

[13] Christianson, *In the Presence of the Creator: Isaac Newton and His Time* (New York: Free Press, 1984).

[14] See Jacques Lacan, *Ecrits: A Selection,* trans. Alan Sheridan (New York: Norton, 1977); Jane Gallop, *Reading Lacan* (Ithaca: Cornell UP, 1985); Julia Kristeva, *Desire in Language: A Semiotic Approach to Literature and Art,* ed. Leon Roudiez; trans. Alice Jardine, Thomas Gora, and Leon Roudiez (New York: Columbia UP, 1980); Mikhail Bakhtin, *The Dialogic Imagination,* ed. Michael Holquist; trans. Caryl Emerson and Michael Holquist (Austin: U of Texas P, 1981); V. N. Voloshinov [Bakhtin], *Marxism and the Philosophy of Language,* trans. Ladislav Matejka and I. R. Titunik (1973; rpt. Cambridge, Mass.: Harvard UP, 1986); Lev Vygotsky, *Thought and Language,* trans. Alex Kozulin, rev. ed. (Cambridge, Mass.: MIT P, 1986); and the recent special issue of *Critical Inquiry,* edited by Francoise Meltzer, *The Trial(s) of Psychoanalysis,* 13 (1987).

[15] Brian Vickers, "The Royal Society and English Prose Style: A Reassessment," *Rhetoric and the Pursuit of Truth: Language Change in the Seventeenth and Eighteenth Centuries* (Los Angeles: Clark Library, 1985), pp. 1-76; Paul Arakelian, "The Myth of a Restoration Style Shift," *The Eighteenth Century: Theory and Interpretation,* 20 (1979), 227-45.

[16] See Ralph W. V. Elliott, "Isaac Newton's 'Of an Universall Language,'" *MLR,* 52 (1957), 1-18.

[17] Significantly, in *Daniel,* Newton cut all the references to Egyptians, "Eastern expositors," and hieroglyphics, bringing his account of biblical language more in line with traditional interpretations of the prophecies of the sort practiced by Joseph Mede, Henry More, and others in the seventeenth century.

[18] The "First Book" in manuscript runs to over 150 pages; see McLachlan, p. 119.

[19] Drawing on the work of Bakhtin and seventeenth-century writers on language, I have made thisargument at greater length in chapters one and two of *Two-Edg'd Weapons: Style and Ideology in the Comedies of Etherege, Wycherley, and Congreve* (Oxford: Clarendon, 1988).

[20] *The Correspondence of Isaac Newton,* seven volumes, ed. H. W. Turnball, et. al (Cambridge: Cambridge UP, 1957-1976), III, 83-128; 129-44. For Newton's plans to publish the "Letter to a Friend," see pp. 123-24.

[21] See Westfall, *"Origines,"* p. 31 and, on Dryden, Phillip Harth, *Contexts of Dryden's Thought* (Chicago: U of Chicago P., 1968), especially pp. 115-48.

James E. Force (essay date 1990)

SOURCE: "Newton's God of Dominion: The Unity of Newton's Theological Scientific, and Political Thought," in *Essays on the Context, Nature, and Influence of Isaac Newton's Theology,* by James E. Force and Richard H. Popkin, Kluwer Academic Publishers, 1990, pp. 75-102.

[*In the following essay, Force argues that Newton's conception of a "God of Dominion" is the key factor that unites and informs all aspects of Newton's studies.*]

Introduction: The Hues and Shades of Newton's Genius (or Torturing a Metaphor)

Today, when we consider Newton and his work, there is a tendency among both popularizers and scholars to see Newton through a prism, so to speak, and to study Newton in refraction just as Newton studies light by passing it through a prism and breaking it down into its primary colors. Newton is seen, at different times, as a heretical theologian, a scientific genius, or a politically connected man of affairs. There often seem to be as many Newtons as there are primary colors and we study Newton by studying the many manifestations of his multi-hued genius independently. Failing to appreciate the synthetic unity in Newton's thought is the inevitable result of overemphasizing one or another of its integrated components.

Primarily, of course, Newton is for us the father of modern, i.e., of *our,* physics. We mean it as a compliment to Newton when we induct him into our Pantheon of scientific heroes whose work has culminated in our scientific world-view and our splendid technological achievements. In his recent trashing of American universities and American university students, Allan Bloom unhesitatingly enlists Newton in his personal cult of the custodians of our civilization. Bloom explains that the differences between ancients and moderns

> is not like the differences between Moses and Socrates, or Jesus and Lucretius, where there is no common universe of discourse but more like the differences between Newton and Einstein. It is a struggle for the possession of rationalism by the rationalists.[1]

In Bloom's view, Newton and Einstein share a "common universe of discourse" which is rational and, therefore, scientific. Newton is one of the intellectually respectable elite because of hisrationality; he certainly would have hated rock and roll.

The three-hundredth anniversary of the publication of Newton's **Principia** on July 5, 1987, has provided the occasion for a number of conferences and lectures celebrating that "watershed work" with its rigorous experimental method in alliance with an elegant mathematical description of the natural forces at work in the frame of nature. To quote one elegy commemorating this tricentenary:

> In short, Newton opened up one of the main avenues of modern scientific research and showed how to follow it. No other figure in the history of science has done as much except Charles Darwin, whose 19th-century work with evolution established an equally rigorous strategy for the scientific study of the development of organic life. This is why even the greatest scientists today hold Newton in awe.

Earlier, the same writer states:

> The next time you're flying, you might give a thought to Sir Isaac Newton. Engineers need modern quantum theory to design the aircraft's electronics. But Newton's classical mechanics still accounts for the jet engine's thrust, the aerodynamic forces that hold the craft up, and gravity's tug, which tries to pull it down. Furthermore, were your plane forced down in the wilderness or at sea, the satellite that would relay its search and rescue signal travels on an orbit that Newton showed how to calculate 300 years ago.[2]

Color the right stuff of Newton's steely-eyed, essentially modern, scientific rationalism the blue of the wild blue yonder or the jet black of deep space. One refracted image of Newton as seen through the prism of anachronism, then, is Newton the heroic scientist who has, with other scientific hall-of-famers (Darwin, Einstein) "charted the course" of modern thought. An intermediate shade is, of course, the blue-black of Newton the mathematician.[3]

There is a second Newton: the heretical theologian who disbelieves in the Holy Trinity and believes in the literal fulfillment of the apocalyptic scenario in the book of Revelation. The pioneers in revealing this second Newton have been Frank E. Manuel and Richard S. Westfall. Westfall's work has been particularly valuable both in its gargantuan scope and in its absolutely meticulous precision. Westfall's glorious biography of Newton, *Never At Rest,*[4] establishes a new paradigm of excellence and comprehensiveness in the study of Newton. Westfall is the only writer in the world today who knows intimately all the hues and shades in Newton's rainbow: the blues of his scientific rationalism, the reds of his theological concerns ("reds," perhaps, because of the apocalyptic destruction of the

earth by fire [Rev. 20:9] or, perhaps, because of Newton's identification of the woman arrayed in purple and scarlet [Rev. 17:4] as the Church of Rome), the greens of a former member of parliament who perhaps owes his job at the Mint to his political connections among influential Court Whigs.

But, in considering the relationship between Newton's theology and Newton's science, for example, Westfall holds to studying each hue separately. It is highly significant when a scholar of Westfall's attainments and stature writes:

> Having studied the entire corpus of his theological papers, I remain unconvinced that it isvalid to speak of a theological influence on Newton's science. I say specifically "theological influences," not "religious influence." The second can, I believe, be readily shown and is generally admitted. A theological influence, by which I mean the influence of Newton's central Arian position and his allied view of the prophecies, is another matter. As I indicated earlier, perhaps we can find the source of the God of the General Scholium in his Arianism. It is not clear which came first, however, his view of God or his Arianism; and even if we grant the influence we remain still on a plane of high generality from which it is difficult if not impossible to demonstrate an influence on some concrete element of his science.

Westfall concludes that he is

> inclined to examine the relation [between Newton's "theology" and his science] from the other side. At the end of the 17th century, theology was the study with a firmly established, long dominant role of [sic] European civilization, a role then beginning to be challenged by the early success of modern science. It appears to me that we are more likely to find the flow of influence moving from science, the rising enterprise, toward theology, the old and (as we know from hindsight) fading one.[5]

Westfall's view on this point issues from his complete mastery of all the sources, manuscript and printed, primary and secondary. It is not a view to be lightly challenged. On Westfall's view, Newton probably must remain permanently refracted into scientist and theologian. If there is any lcakagc across wavelengths, it is Newton's science which colors his theology and not vice-versa.

Refracted, finally, through the prism of our 20th-century perspective is a third Newton who is a political appointee (Master of the Mint) in his nation's capital. In his biography, Westfall has detailed Newton's political life and involvements: his efforts to obstruct James II's Catholic candidates for positions in the university, his service as a member of parliament, his interest in the success of the Revolution, and his (and his niece's) relationship—whatever it may have been—with the Whig minister, Baron Halifax of Halifax (Charles Montague).

Regarding the case of Newton and Halifax, Westfall recounts Voltaire's story of his London visit in the 1720's (first published by Voltaire in 1757) in which Voltaire writes:

> I thought in my youth that Newton made his fortune by his merit. I supposed that the Court and the City of London named him Master of the Mint by acclamation. No such thing. Isaac Newton has a very charming niece, Madame Conduitt, who made a conquest of the minister Halifax. Fluxions and gravitation would have been of no use without a pretty niece.[6]

Westfall examines the tangled skein of evidence surrounding this allegation and concludes that it seems to be dubious but that we lack the necessary data to pass final judgement. The important point for Westfall is that "The **Principia** remains the **Principia** for us whatever the relation of Catherine Barton to Halifax and whatever Newton's role in the affair."[7] Newton's science remains as uncolored by his politics as his theology.

By way of contrast, Margaret C. Jacob has shown how Newton's science, in the hands of latitudinarian churchmen between 1689 and 1721, becomes the basis for a political argument to support the status quo and, consequently, their own position, together with their Whig sponsors, in the ruling elite. From the orderly and law-abiding behavior of matter in Newton's frame of nature, these latitudinarian churchmen argue by analogy to the fittingness of order and law-abiding behavior in the socio-political fabric. As above in the "world natural," so below in the "world politic."[8] Jacob is the first writer to have emphasized the connection between Newtonian science and the political theorizing of his day and to have treated the subject in depth. Nevertheless, Jacob's focus is on the latitudinarians and their use of Newtonian science to bolster the established church and state and not on any connection which Newton may have held between his theology or his science and his political viewpoint.

Having briefly traced how Newton has been refracted into various shades and hues, my project in this essay is to take these shades of Newton and to send them back through the lens of Newton's incandescent genius. As Newton himself demonstrates, the whiteness of the sun's light is compounded of all the primary colors[9] and so, too, is the blinding white light of Newton's intellect.

I want to argue that Newton's theology, not just his religion, influences his science every bit as much as his science influences the rigorous textual scholarship of his theology. The key to understanding the integrated nature of Newton's thought is to appreciate fully his view about the nature of God. His God is the Lord God of Dominion. Westfall is quite right to observe that it is possible to find the "source" for Newton's God of Dominion, articulated so clearly in the General Scholium, in Newton's Arianism. But, if that is the case, then one must acknowledge a true influence of theology upon all aspects of Newton's thought *if* it can be demonstrated that Newton's God of Dominion finally comes to be seen by Newton as underlying his various other theories in science, metaphysics, epistemology, and politics. At least a sketch of the possible role of Newton's Lord God as the metaphysical underpinning for his theology, science, and politics is the purpose of this paper. I maintain that Newton's God of Dominion is the key to understanding how he finally integrates his world and his theories in whatever field into a synthetic unity of a startling coherence. I do not claim that this voluntaristic theory of the nature of God develops first in any historical sense although it seems clear that Newton comes to this view early in his career at the time when he becomes a committed Arian in the early 1670's. I claim only that Newton's view concerning God's dominion—a theory in which Newton emphasizes God's totally free will in conjunction with his absolute power—finally becomes the common denominator in all his intellectual work of whatever shade or hue and so provides the key to understanding the systematic unity and coherence of all of his thought. It doesn't matter whether Newton's science or his mathematics precede, in any temporal sense, his theory of the nature of God. Once he comes to that metaphysical view—and he comes to it quite early—it provides the background for all his other work and provides the key to seeing how Newton's true genius is greater in the aggregate whole than it is in any of its refracted parts.

Theology: Newton's God of Dominion

Westfall rightly argues that it is impossible to determine whether Newton's philosophical conception of the nature of God precedes his Christological doctrine of Arianism.[10] It probably is the case that they develop in Newton's thought simultaneously because they are two sides to the same coin.

The doctrines of Arius began to emerge following the year 318 A. .D., when Arius, Presbyter of Alexandria (260-336 A. D.), first challenged the eternity of Christ thus precipitating the "Arian Crisis" in the early church which culminated, in one sense, with the rejection of Arius' doctrines and the adoption of the Trinitarian Athanasian creed in 325 A. D. at the Council of Nicaea. In fact, this controversy continued to rage throughout the fourth century.

For Arius, there is a fundamental distinction between God, the Creator, and *all* his creation. Jesus is one of

God's creatures, he is a "work" of God, who is neither co-eternal nor co-substantial with God the Father. Jesus *is* sinful mankind's redeemer, the divine son of God, but only because of the power and will of the Lord God.

The diminution of Christ's nature and powers in the Arian doctrine involves necessarily the augmentation of the powers and nature of God the Father. All God's creatures, even Jesus Christ, are under the dominion of God the Father, the true Lord God.

But whether Newton's theological doctrine of Arianism precedes or follows Newton's voluntaristic theory of the dominion of God (again, I think it more likely that they are logically connected and, hence, emerge together) both emerge early. Faced with the necessity of entering the Anglican priesthood to retain his fellowship at Trinity College, in the early 1670's Newton began an intensive study of theology and of the history of the early church. From the period between 1672 and 1675 there is a sheet summarizing Newton's conclusions about both the nature of Christ *and* the nature of God and Father. Proposition 5, for example, proclaims that "The Son in several places confesseth his dependance on the will of the father."[11] Proposition 10 is even more instructive:

> It is a proper epithete of ye father to be called almighty. For by God almighty we always understand ye Father. Yet this is not to limit the power of ye Son, for he doth what soever he seeth ye Father do; but to acknowledge y^t all power is originally in ye Father & that ye son hath no power in him but w^t derives from ye father for he professes that of himself he can do nothing.[12]

Forty years later, we find Newton repeating this combined Arian Christology and voluntaristic metaphysical theory emphasizing the ultimate will and power of the Lord God of Dominion. And we find it both in his manuscripts and in his General Scholium to the second edition of the ***Principia*** published in 1713. No more clear statement of Newton's view of the nature of God's dominion exists than the General Scholium:

> The Supreme God is a Being eternal, infinite, absolutely perfect; but a being, however perfect, without dominion, cannot be said to be Lord God; for we say, my God, your God, the God of *Israel,* the God of Gods, and Lord of Lords; but we do not say, my Eternal, your Eternal, the Eternal of *Israel,* the Eternal of God; we do not say, my Infinite, or my Perfect: these are titles which have no respect to servants. The word God usually signifies *Lord;* but every lord is not a God. It is the dominion of a spiritual being which constitutes a God: a true, supreme, or imaginary dominion makes a true, supreme, or imaginary God.[13]

For Newton, only a God of true and supreme dominion is a supreme and true God. A manuscript note from 1710 reaffirms the Christological consequences of this metaphysical voluntarism regarding the deity. Newton still, forty years after his intensive theological researches of the early 70's, views Jesus as deriving from God a

> unity of dominion, the Son receiving all things from the Father, being subject to him executing his will, sitting in his throne and calling him his God, and so is but one God with the Father as a King and viceroy are but one King. For the word God relates not to the metaphysical nature of God but to dominion.[14]

Ordinary mortals are no less under the dominion of God than Jesus Christ. In an entry to his theological notebook from the 1670's there is a tantalizing hint that Newton is much impressed by St. Paul's comparison of the relation between God and man to that between a potter and his clay. In an entry entitled simply "Predestinatio," Newton quotes the famous ninth chapter of Romans where St. Paul places the eternal fate of men under the dominion of their supreme Lord God:

> What shall we say then? Is there unrighteousness with God? God forbid. For he saith to Moses, I will have mercy on whom I will have mercy, & I will have compassion on whom I will have compassion. So than it is not of him that willeth, or of him y^t runneth, but of God that sheweth merch. For ye scripture saith unto Pharoh Even for this same purpose have I raised thee up that I might shew my power in thee, & that my name might be declared throughout all ye Earth. Therefore he hath mercy on whom he will have mercy, & whom he will he hardeneth. Thou wilt say then unto me; why doth he yet find fault? For who hath resisted his will? Nay but O man, who art thou that repliest against God? Shall ye thing formed say to him y^t formed it why hast thou made me thus? Hath not the potter power over the clay of ye same lump to make one vessel unto honour and another unto dishonour?[15]

God's very "deitas" results, on Newton's view, from his "dominium" over the whole of his creation. For Newton, the nature of God's "dominium" is his infinite will and omnipotent power over everything else that there is. Everything that God created in the world of physical nature such as drops of dew (Job 38:28), the world of natural inconstant creatures (Deut. 32:18), the human world including inconstant sons (Isa. 1:2), even Jesus Christ, falls under the dominion of God. All his creatures are consequently his servants and all the rest of his physical creation, the fabric of nature itself, is likewise owned, possessed, and used in accord with the dictates of God's will and power.

Newton's theory about the dominion of God is central to all the other aspects of his theology in particular and to the rest of his thought in general. For example, one of his central theological concerns throughout his life is to combat what he calls idolatry. Worshipping anything but the Lord God of true and supreme dominion lessens the absolute nature of God's dominion and constitutes idolatry. The Roman Church is his chief target beginning with his theological notebook of the early 70's owing to its Trinitarian creed which lessens the Father's dominion by promoting the co-eternality and co-substantiality of the Son. "Never," he writes, "was Pagan Idolatry so bad as the Roman."[16]

Newton's studies in the early 70's render him incapable of submitting to ordination in the Church of England which would have required him to subscribe to the 39 Articles (including its loathsomely idolatrous Trinitarian creed.) Yet, in Newton's day, most fellowships required ordination. By early 1675, as his deadline for taking orders approached, Newton fully expected to have to leave Cambridge and vacate his fellowship. At the eleventh hour, by nothing less than a Royal dispensation exempting in perpetuity holders of the Lucasian Chair of Mathematics from the necessity of entering the church, Newton, who had held the Lucasian Chair since 1669, was enabled to remain in the university as a very low-profile, i.e., silent, Arian heretic and not as a public, if insincere, subscriber to an idolatrous creed.[17]

Even more importantly, Newton's voluntaristic God of Dominion, with his concomitant Arian Christology, directly influences his views on Biblical prophecy. Newton begins an intensive study of prophetic language in the very early 1680's and returns to it between 1705 and 1710. Newton is vitally concerned with what the language of the prophets means because the prophecies, properly interpreted, illustrate the extent of God's dominion over his creation. Westfall is absolutely right that all the theological manuscripts on the interpretation of prophecy, with Newton's emphasis on "methodising" the prophetic language, reveal the rigor and orderliness of a great scientific mind. But the most important aspect of the prophetic prediction of events to come and the cataloging of the historical fulfillment of them is that it is Newton's favorite method for demonstrating God's providential dominion. In the famous reply to Bentley of December 10, 1692, when Newton rejoices in Bentley's adaptation of his *Principia* for the purposes of developing a design argument, he goes on to say that, in addition to the design argument of natural religion,

> There is yet another argument for a Deity wch I take to be a very strong one, but till ye principles on wch tis grounded be better received I think it advisable to let it sleep.[18]

It seems clear to me that behind this passing reference are the many years of disciplined and historical

work revealed only in the many manuscripts on the interpretation of fulfilled prophecies. Newton permitted their argument to continue sleeping for political reasons.

For Newton, the central point in studying the prophecies in such detail over so many years is just because they illustrate the dominion of God over nature and man. As Westfall rightly puts it:

> To Newton, the correspondence of prophecy with fact demonstrated the dominion of God, a dominion exercised over human history even as it is exercised over the natural world.[19]

In addition to prophetic predictions regarding natural and political events already fulfilled and of which we have testimony from the sacred prophets, there are those prophecies regarding natural and political events predicted for the future but which remain unfulfilled. It is within this context that one must understand Newton's keen interest in the millennial prophecies. By the 1670's he regards the future prophecies recorded in Revelation to be especially preserved by God for mankind's instruction: "There [is] no book in all the scriptures so much recommended & guarded by providence as this."[20]

In the 80's, Newton begins to spell out his differences with the standard interpretation of the Apocalypse of St. John. In the standard view of the Puritans in the preceding generation, the opening of the seventh and final seal (Rev. 8:1-5) is often identified with the diplomatic and political triumph of the Catholic Church at the Council of Constantinople in 381 A. D. To this date is often added 1260 years, the "time, two times, and half a time" of Daniel 8:25 when, it is hoped, the messianic kingdom will commence.

The equation of this obscure text from Daniel with the figure of 1260 years results from interpreting one "time" to equal one year. "Time, two times, and half a time," therefore, equals 3 and ½ years. Assuming a year to equal 360 days, 3 and ½ such years equals 1260 days. This figure corresponds to Rev. 12:6 according to which:

> And the woman [identified as God's persecuted apostolic church] fled into the wilderness, where she hath a place prepared of God, that they should feed her there a thousand two hundred and threescore days.

One obtains 1260 years from the figure of 1260 days by the simple and widespread expedient among Biblical interpreters in Newton's day of assuming that one day equals one year. This dating places the advent of Christ's messianic kingdom at 1641 A. D. (381 A. D. + 1260 years.) As the decades slip by the date is adjusted forward by dating the opening of the seventh seal forward from the year 381 A. D.

By Newton's day, scholars try to preserve the framework of the Book of Revelation by accommodating it to a new date for the opening of the seventh seal. William Whiston, Newton's hand-picked successor in the Lucasian Chair at Cambridge, dates the opening of the seventh seal from 476 A. D. when Odoacer and his Goths capture the last Emperor of the West, Romulus Augustulus and relegate him to a Campenian villa on a pension. By 1736, consequently (476 A. D. + 1260 years), Whiston expects momentous events at least to begin which will lead subsequently to the millennial reign of Christ on earth and the rest of the apocalyptic scenario described in Revelation. Up to and after that date, Whiston is busily engaged in illustrating how the penultimate events in Revelation have come to pass in the events of contemporary history, a current history project which he states is first suggested to him by Isaac Newton and which results in Whiston's set of Boyle Lectures *The Accomplishment of Scripture Prophecy* (London, 1708).[21]

In the early 70's, Newton spells out his own differences with other millennial interpreters. Newton dates the beginning of the 1260 year period to begin with the year 607 A. D. (an event he correlates with the blowing of the fourth trumpet in Rev. 8:12-3) when the idolatrous Trinitarianism of the Roman Church triumphs. Because of his intensive historical research into the barbarian invasions of the fifth and sixth centuries, Newton reckons that by 607 A. D. the invading barbarians—all of whom were Arian Christians when they began despoiling the empire—had been converted to the idolatrous trinitarian apostasy of the conquered empire.[22] In the 80's at least, Newton does not expect the second coming and the subsequent messianic kingdom to begin until the middle of the nineteenth century (607 A. D. + 1260 years).

The central point behind this recounting of Newton's basic view of prophecies is to show that the scriptural histories of these prophesied events, predicted by God and then—through his will and power—brought to pass, illustrate God's dominion and providential control over creation. Scriptural history reveals a continuously present God, not simply a God who observes events. His will and power direct both the "world politic" and, as we shall see in the next section, the "world natural." One extremely important consequence of this view is that God has permitted the spread of apostasy, with its eternally damning consequences, through his dominion. Just as God permits the apostasies of the scribes and pharisees in Christ's day and those of the Trinitarian Catholic Church in the 4th century (a virulent apostasy which continues down to his own day), so he permits those of any Trinitarian Protestant sect in Newton's time. Newton writes of his contemporary learned apostates:

Are not these men like the Scribes and Pharisees who would not attend to the law and the prophets but required a signe of Christ? Wherefore if Christ thought it just to deny a signe to that wicked and adultcratc generation notwithstanding that they were God's own people, [even] and the Catholique Church; much more may God think it just that this generation should be permitted to dy in their sins, who do not onely like the Scribes neglect but trample upon the law and the Prophets . . .

And from this consideration may also appear the vanity of those men who regard splendor of churches and measure them by the external form and constitution. Whereas it is more agreeable to God's designe that his church appear contemptible and scandalous to the world of men. For this end doubtless he suffered the many revoltings of the Jewish Church under the Law, and for the same end was the grand Apostasy to happen under the Gospel. Rev. [sic].[23]

Newton is convinced that God possesses dominion over the wise who will understand as well as over the wicked who, through vanity and idolatry, will not. Newton does not cite which text he has in mind from Revelation in the above quotation, but I would suggest the following from Chap. 17, verses 17-8, which suggests Newton's point that the forces of iniquity fulfill the purposes of the Lord God because God chooses them for that purpose and enables them to succeed in their iniquities. Of the success of the harlot sitting astride the beast, St. John writes:

God has put it into their hearts to carry out his purpose by being of one mind and giving over their royal power to the beast, until the words of God be fulfilled. And the woman that you saw is the great city which has dominion over the kings of the earth.

But, so what? So what if Newton is an extreme metaphysical voluntarist who emphasizes the absolute primacy of God's will and power over creation (even at the expense of God's love and, apparently, God's intellect), who therefore simultaneously adopts an Arian Christology, and who is also, consequently, keenly interested in understanding historically fulfilled events in prophetic history and prophetically predicted future acts of God as testimony to God's dominion? Is not the *Principia* still the *Principia*? What has Newton's science really got to do, beyond the superficial level of the Newtonian design argument, with Newton's voluntaristic theory of the absolute dominion of the Lord God?

The short answer is that, *for us,* Newton's theology is not necessarily related to his science in any way. The longer, less anachronistically refracting, answer is that, *for Newton,* God's real and absolute dominion profoundly affects his metaphysical view of nature and of how we can know nature.

Newton's God of Dominion, Matter, and Knowledge

It is perhaps Hume who first systematically undertakes to sever Newton's physics from Newton's theology in the middle of the 18th century. By the end of the 18th century, a confident natural philosopher of the Enlightenment such as Laplace remarks that he has no need of the "hypothesis" of God in his physical system. Since then generations of critics have celebrated Newton's "gift" to the modern world of a pre-eminently rational material order which mechanically flies along obedient to necessary natural laws and to nothing else. A recent writer exults that

> Newton's universe, when stripped of metaphysical considerations, as stripped it would be, is an infinite void of which only an infinitesimal part is occupied by unattached material bodies moving freely through the boundless and bottomless abyss, a colossal machine made up of components whose only attributes are position, extension, and mass. Life and the sensate world have no effect upon it and are banished, à la Descartes, from its rigorously mechanical operations. And yet, for all its lack of feeling, Newton's universe is a precise, harmonious, and rationally ordered whole. Mathematical law binds each particle of matter to every other particle, barring the gate to chaos and disunity. By flinging gravity across the infinite void, he was able to unite physics and astronomy in a single science of matter in motion, fulfilling the dream of Pythagoras. . . . And even though Newton was unable to discover a demonstrable principle with which actually to explain the phenomenon of gravitation, the laws he formulated provided convincing proof that man inhabits a preeminently orderly world. We remember and honor him today not for providing us with ultimate answers to the most profound scientific questions but because, in apprehending the Pythagorean power by which number holds sway above the flux, Isaac Newton contributed more than any other individual of the modern age to the establishment and acceptance of a rational world view.[24]

Hume first argues that metaphysics is a "shelter to superstition" and finally urges the burning of any volume "of divinity or school metaphysics."[25] On the above interpretation, given in citation 24, Newton is part of Hume's brave new positivistic world in which superstitious metaphysics is banished and replaced by the mathematical study of the principles of natural philosophy.

I will argue that the above reading is a misunderstanding of the role of metaphysics and, consequently, of epistemology in the natural philosophy of Isaac Newton. It has been time honored tradition since Hume to banish metaphysics from natural philosophy, but it has nothing to do with Newton's position. What the impact of theology and metaphysics is upon Newton's conception of matter and upon how we can gain knowl-

edge about the laws governing matter we shall see. Newton's thought is a seamless unity of theology, metaphysics, and natural science. Newton's view of God's Dominion, i.e., the total supremacy of God's power and will over every aspect of creation, colors every aspect of his views about how matter (and the laws regulating the ordinary operation of matter) is created, preserved, reformed, and, occasionally, interdicted by a voluntary and direct act of God's sovereign will and power. Newton's commitment to the Lord God of Dominion issues necessarily in the dependence of nature upon God's will. He creates it and (at the same time) he creates it to operate by the ordinary concourse of the laws of nature. He preserves it, he reforms it, from time to time he directly suspends its ordinary operation through a specially provident act of will, and he has promised in prophecy to destroy it as the wise have good reason to understand and to believe. Hume's universe is stripped of metaphysical considerations, not Newton's.

Matter does not move, as it generally does, in accord with mathematically precise laws of naturesuch as those described in the **Principia** because of any Neoplatonic overflow of God's being into the world or because of any Hobbist, Cartesian, or Leibnizian notion of necessary rational order intrinsically immanent within matter or imposed once and for all long ago by a deity who long since has absented himself from the daily operations of creation. Such metaphysical views dilute the total subordination of matter to the will of God and are the metaphysical equivalent of theological idolatry. Rather, matter exists and ordinarily operates in accord with natural law for one reason: God wills it so by divine *fiat.* Both matter and natural law originate in the will and power of God. God's dominion is the fundamental first metaphysical principle underlying Newtonian mechanics. Newton writes (in Query 31), therefore, that because

> Matter is not necessarily in all places, it may be also allow'd that God is able to create Particles of Matter of several Sizes and Figures, and in several Proportions to Space, and perhaps of difference Densities and Forces, and thereby to vary the Laws of Nature, and make Worlds of several Sorts in several Parts of the Universe.[26]

God is the Lord God, the "Pantocrator," as Newton styles him in the General Scholium, of creation. God, exercising the dominion which makes him to be God, chooses one material system by an act of his will. That is the system which we study through mathematical empiricism for the time being. In future, it might be that God chooses to reorder his "new heaven and new earth," predicted in prophecy (Rev. 21:1), into a physical system totally beyond the current grasp of our limited human reason. The mathematically demonstrable, necessary, "universal" laws of nature operate as they ordinarily do only in this particular creation and, even then, as we shall see, there are specially provident exceptions. Truly, there are more things possible in Newton's philosophy, on heaven and on earth, than are dreamed of in Hume's philosophy.

Having chosen matter of particular densities and forces of particular sorts (chiefly, gravity) this time around, God's ordained frame of nature has since been wheeling routinely along betraying in almost every motion the generally provident dominion of the Lord God of creation. God's will and power are detectable in the routine, everyday operation of secondary causes as described in the laws of nature. At the heart of this view is the medieval distinction between God's "potentia ordinata" and "potentia absoluta." These terms have been happily translated by J. E. McGuire, the most philosophically sophisticated of all of Newton's many commentators, as "ordinary concourse" and "extraordinary concourse," respectively.[27]

One measure of God's dominion, then, is the regularity, persistence, and mathematically describable and predictable recurrence of natural phenomena in accordance with the laws of nature established at the creation by the Lord God of Dominion. God's Dominion over the material world which he chose to create is further demonstrated by the nearly continuous operation of the forces governing matter since that time. Preserving this order in being is one more aspect of the Lord God's dominion. In his sermon on 2 Kings 17:15-6, which Westfall dates from the 80's, Newton foreshadows the General Scholium while pointing out the preserving role which the Lord God of Dominion continuously has exercised over physical nature. God requires us, writes Newton, to worship him not because we can fathom his innermost essence. Rather, God,

> the wisest of beings require[s] of us to be celebrated not so much for his essences as for hisactions, the *creating, preserving, and governing* of all things according to his good will and pleasure.[28]

God's preservation of the created order is necessary owing to the original forces he created. Because of gravity, he writes, "a continual miracle is needed to prevent the sun and fixed stars from rushing together through gravity."[29] The most important use of Divine Will since the creation is God's usual maintenance, in continuous routine operation, of the laws governing the forces and densities of matter which he created. As William Whiston, Newton's successor in the Lucasian Chair of Mathematics at Cambridge writes:

> 'Tis now evident, that *Gravity* the most mechanical affection of Bodies, and which seems most natural, depends entirely on the constant and efficacious, and, if you will, the supernatural and miraculous Influence of Almighty God.[30]

The physical world of creation, with all its demonstrable regularity and its nearly continuous operation since the creation, betokens God's voluntary dominion. A more lengthy quote from Whiston drives home the Newtonian view of God's will and power as *both* "potentia ordinata" and "potentia absoluta" while simultaneously dispelling the myth that Newtonian voluntarism emphasizes God's power at the expense of God's intellect. Whiston notes how even the most religious and philosophical persons are perplexed about the interaction between God's special, direct, interventionist providence (his "potentia absoluta") and God's ordinary providence displayed in the lawful operations of secondary causes (his "potentia ordinata"):

> . . . while the Philosopher was in Danger of doubting of the Success, and so ready to grow cold in his Devotions; and the more unthinking, yet more religious Man rejected the Consideration of the Manner, or the Operation of second Causes, and more wisely look'd up only to God, and imagin'd him immediately concern'd in every Occurrence, and on that Principle doubted not the Effect of his Prayers. But 'tis, methinks, evident that neither of these were exactly in the Right . . . 'Tis true that Natural Causes will operate as usual. 'Tis also true that Miracles are not ordinarily to be expected: But withal 'tis as true that the same all-wise Creator, who appointed that constant Course of Nature, foresaw at the same time all those Dispositions of Men, and in particular those Devotions of his Worshippers, to which suitable Rewards were to be provided, and suitable Answers returned.[31]

In short,

> God's Prescience enables him to *act* after a more sublime manner, and by a constant Course of Nature, and Chain of Mechanical Causes, to do everything so, as it shall not be distinguishable from a particular Interposition of his Power. . . .[32]

The nearly continuous, daily, routine operation of the secondary mechanical causes mathematically described by natural laws, such as that of gravity, reveal God's dominion in "a more sublime manner" than the extraordinary concourse of God's will interposing itself in a miraculous fashion involving the breaking or suspending of the ordinary concourse of the laws of nature. Nevertheless, when pressed (as in the case of Leibniz who chides Newton and his followers forreducing God to the status of an inferior clock-maker/repairman), Newton and his closest followers such as Clarke and Whiston agree that God's will is supreme: real miracles have occurred in the past and, because of God's unlimited power and dominion, such miracles may occur in the future. Newton's clearest statement of his insistence upon the possibility of God's specially provident disruption of the mechanics he originally created is found in a manuscript draft of his views on

God's power (a text first revealed by McGuire), and which dates from the early 90's:

> That God is an entity in the highest degree perfect, all agree. But the highest idea of perfection of an entity is that it should be one substance, simple, indivisible, living and lifegiving, always everywhere of necessity existing, in the highest degree understanding all things, freely willing good things; by his will effecting things possible; communicating as far as it possible his own similitude to the more noble effects; containing all things in himself as their principle and location; decreeing and ruling all things by means of his substantial presence (as the thinking part of man perceives the appearances of things brought into the brain and thence its own body); and constantly cooperating with all things according to accurate laws, as being the foundation and cause of the whole of nature, *except where it is good to act otherwise.*[33]

Of course, Newton and Whiston prefer *not* to demonstrate the specially provident aspect of God's dominion over nature by recourse to miracles, if at all possible. Most "miracles," observes Newton, are not really examples of voluntary acts of God's will in which he first suspends the ordinary concourse of nature and then supplants them with an extraordinary, specially provident, miracle. Most miracles "are not so called because they are the works of God, but because they happened seldom and for that reason excite wonder."[34] In his manuscript concerning the various crimes, lies, and forgeries perpetrated by Athanasius, Newton devotes much time to showing how "that crafty Politician" almost single handedly, foists the idolatrous Trinitarian doctrine upon the heathen through the use of "monstrous Legends, fals miracles, veneration of reliques, charmes, yᵉ doctrine of Ghosts or Demons, & their intercession & worship. . . ."[35]

Apart from the creation and the continued overseeing of the survival of that creation, Newton's preferred argument for illustrating the specially provident aspect of God's dominion is the record of fulfilled scripture prophecy. Prophecies are uniquely suited to demonstrating the dominion of God in the historical events predicted and then brought to pass in both the "world natural" and the "world politic." Owing to God's omniscience and power to effect his will, he is able to synchronize most natural and political events (predicted through the mouths of his chosen prophets) with the ordinary concourse of natural law while always reserving his sovereign right directly to interpose his will. As the historical events of the natural and political past have illustrated God's dominion, the signs of Newton's own times will continue progressively to unfold the true state of God's dominion over creation:

> For the event of things predicted many ages before, will then be a convincing argument that the world

is governed by providence. For as few and obscure prophecies concerning *Christ's* first coming were for setting up the *Christian* religion, which all nations have since corrupted; so the many and clear Prophecies concerning the things to be done at *Christ's* second coming, are not only for predicting but also for effecting a recovery and re-establishment of the long-lost truth, and setting up a Kingdom wherein dwells righteousness.

Furthermore, writes Newton:

> But if the last age, the age of opening these things, be now approaching, as by the successes of late Interpreters it seems to be, we have more encouragement than ever to look into these things.[36]

Behind the mechanical framework of the *Principia* is Newton's God of Dominion creating and then preserving creation. The Lord God exercises dominion either through secondary, mechanical causes (which is the usual case) or through extraordinary, direct, voluntary interpositions of his will (which are very unusual but, owing to God's power, are still possible at any time.)

The metaphysics of the *Principia* is absolutely pervaded by Newton's God. But, one might ask, what has metaphysics to do with mathematics? Is not Newton's raw mechanism of a world devoid of metaphysics? Is not at least the mathematical aspect of the method of the *Principia* sacrosanct from any sort of metaphysical "sideshow."[37]

The dominion of God over his creation is just as important to Newton's epistemology as it is to his metaphysics. They are clearly inseparable in Newton's integrated system of thought. Newton is most famous for combining mathematics with empirical observations but both these elements of his scientific method are intrinsically related to his voluntaristic conception of God's dominion.

Without the metaphysically justified conception of the perseverance of the ordinary concourse of natural laws, which Newton derives from the will and power of the Lord God of Dominion, there could be no mathematical demonstration of the "necessary" forces of nature within this particular order of material creation chosen so long ago by the deity. Without God first creating and then sustaining the generally regular operations of nature, there could be no ordinary concourse of natural law to describe with mathematical principles.

Beyond this point, but closely allied to it, is Newton's best known contribution to mathematics, his famous method of fluxions which dates from 1665. Newton's method of fluxions is inevitably connected with his theory of the continuous dominion of God since the creation; fluxions are a method which view geometrical quantities as arising from a continuous motion as if they were computer-generated. Any line or curve can be seen as the result of the continuous flowing motion of a point. The rate of flow Newton calls a "fluxion." The flowing line itself is called a "fluent." Newton's early mathematical work is given over to demonstrating, their corresponding fluxion given any particular relationship between two fluents. Inversely, Newton demonstrates how to determine the necessary relationship between two fluents given two related fluxions.

Newton's calculus is based on the continuity of flow as supervised by the God of Dominion operating in his generally provident mode of creator and preserver of the current state of natural law. A. Rupert Hall, in his exacting treatise on the "war" of priority in the discovery of the calculus waged between Leibniz and the followers of Newton, has pointed out that Newton's method is conceived in an entirely different metaphysical framework than that of Leibniz's differential calculus which is rooted in the relative discontinuity and individual freedom of monads created by an absconding deity long ago.[38]

But perhaps the most important reason for regarding Newton's theology as part of his scientific methodology is his empiricism. Why, for example, does not Newton go along with Leibniz's necessitarian and rationalist view that experiments and empirical observations are completely unnecessary? Newton, after all, begins with observations of the phenomena of nature before seeking to describe the covering law behind those phenomena in necessary mathematical terms.

While mathematically necessary descriptions will hold as "universally" true, for the most part, owing to the ordinary concourse of God's dominion, ultimately God suffers no restraint upon his absolute will and power. Because God is so powerful that he can alter the course of nature at will, scientific knowledge of nature must necessarily be based upon *repeated* empirical observations just because we humans do not know when or where he might exercise his specially provident power of miraculous will and suspend or reverse what we have been pleased to call the "laws" of nature generally operative in this creation until now. Our knowledge of whether scientific "laws" of nature imposed by the Lord God of Dominion at the time of creation will continue to be "laws" in the future, and to express then the same relationships previously discovered to hold between forces, can ultimately be only very highly probable owing to the contingent aspect of our knowledge of nature which results from Newton's conception of the unlimited power and will of the Lord God of Dominion.

Newton's experimentalism is inextricable from his theology and his voluntaristic metaphysics because of the contingency which it introduces into human knowledge of nature. In the 1713 Preface to the second edition of the **Principia,** Roger Cotes explains how the Newtonian God of Dominion forces us to be experimentalists:

> Without all doubt this world, so diversified with that variety of forms and motions we find in it, could arise from nothing but the perfectly free will of God directing and presiding over all.
>
> From this fountain it is that those laws, which we call the laws of Nature, have flowed, in which there appear many traces indeed of the most wise contrivance, but not the least shadow of necessity. These therefore we must not seek from uncertain conjectures, but learn them from observations and experiments.[39]

Newton, in his Fourth Rule of Reasoning first added in 1723 to the third edition of the **Principia,** underscores Cotes' concern to refute the God of the rationalists who, once finished with creating matter and the laws governing it, absents himself from further involvement. Newton notes the methodological impact for human knowledge of a physical nature subservient either to God's ordinary or to his extraordinary acts of will:

> Rule IV *In experimental philosophy we are to look upon propositions inferred by general induction from phenomena as accurately or very nearly true, notwithstanding any contrary hypothesis that may be imagined, till such time as other phenomena occur, by which they may either be made more accurate, or liable to exception.*

> This rule we must follow that the argument of induction may not be evaded by hypotheses.[40]

Newton's universe is in one sense necessary and in another contingent. For God, the universe is always necessarily dependent upon his will. As the generally provident author of the physical laws which ordinarily govern motion in the current structure of the material realm or as the specially provident interventionist, Newton's God rules on earth and in heaven. But the absolute nature of God's dominion over creation makes human knowledge of the usually lawful structure of the material world necessarily contingent upon the will of God. Human knowledge is contingent upon whether God is exercising his will through the ordinary concourse of nature (as has ordinarily been the case in the past) or through the very rare instances of an extraordinary direct interposition of his will. Mathematically demonstrable laws of nature which apply to a great many observed phenomena are "necessary" only while God sustains and preserves them in their ordinary concourse. As Whiston puts it, "'Tis true that Natural Causes will operate as usual," but only if God wills them to continue doing so in the future as they have in the past.

Because of the basic Newtonian view about the voluntaristic nature of God's dominion which underlies any attempt to seek knowledge—whether in the interpretation of prophecies or the understanding of the laws of nature—finally what matters most is a cautious empiricism. Newton writes, for example, of the "design" of God in giving men prophetic predictions. It is not to enable interpreters to gratify

> men's curiosities by enabling them to foreknow things, but that after they were fulfilled they might be interpreted by the Event, and his [God's] own Providence, not the Interpreters be manifested thereby to the world.[41]

So, too, in natural philosophy Whiston, echoing the fourth Rule, explains why empiricism is the only path to follow:

> Our imperfection is such, that we can only act *pro re nata,* can never know beforehand the Behaviours of Actions of Men; neither can we forsee what Circumstances and Conjectures will happen at any certain time hereafter. . . .[42]

The contingent nature of our knowledge, which is the direct result of the nature of God's power and will to change the ordinary concourse of events, results for Newton and the Newtonians in a characteristic note of caution in both theological speculations about future prophecies and scientific "predictions" about the course of future events.

Nevertheless and however reluctantly, Newton accepts the possibility that God may choose to suspend or overturn the ordinary course of nature by a specially provident act of his sovereign will. Though such acts are possible, Whiston says that they "are not ordinarily to be expected." The contingent feature which God's will and power introduce into what humans may know about the fabric of God's creation limits human knowledge of the natural laws ordinarily governing mechanical causes to probabilistic inductions based upon repeated observations. To the question of whether "there be a continual immediate Government of the Universe; or whether god so disposed all things *at first,* as not to interpose by a *continual actual Operation* upon them," Clarke gives the characteristically Newtonian response that God "preserves and governs, disposes and directs continually all the Motions and Powers of Things in the natural world."[43]

For Newton, there are real consequences in his science for his theological view that the whole of nature is subordinate to God "and subservient to his Will"[44] just as it is no doubt the case, as Westfall has persuasively argued, that there are real consequences introduced into Newton's method of studying theology which result from his rigorously trained scientific

intellect. They are mutually influential. Newton would have been astonished to learn that some of his interpreters, following Hume's lead, have claimed that theology, metaphysics and epistemology have no necessary, integrated, synthetic relationship in themselves, much less that he has himself been placed into this school. Newton's own thought is in fact a seamless unity composed of theology, metaphysics, and epistemology all mixed together simply because, at their base, is the Lord God of supreme dominion. It is permissible, of course, to refract Newton's thought into its various hues and shades and to study them independently so long as we remember not to take any one element as logically prior to any other element. Refracting Newton into shades and hues may be a reasonable learning aid but we miss the blinding incandescent light of his true genius if we forget finally to recombine his many parts into the integrated whole which is the totality of his genius.

Newton's God and Newton's Politics

Many writers, in Newton's day and in ours, have been convinced that science and politics are woven tightly together in Newtonian thought. Nick Herbert, in his fine book *Quantum Reality,* has correctly pointed out that

> For better or for worse, humans have tended to pattern their domestic, social, and political arrangements according to the dominant vision of physical reality. Inevitably the cosmic view trickles down to the most mundane details of everyday life.[45]

In Newton's case, Herbert states baldly that Newton's conception of passive, inert matter gliding through space, like the giant spaceship in *2001: A Space Odyssey,* in accord with the forces of nature as computed by the HAL-9000 computer, overturns the medieval metaphysics of hierarchical gradations of celestial matter arranged in successive spheres. This metaphysical revolution occurs "coincidentally" with a profound political revolution. Just at the time when Newton substitutes, in his **Principia,** a universe "of ordinary matter governed by mathematical laws" for a Dantean (medieval) universe of hierarchical quintessences presided over by the direct command of God, society moves from a feudal monarchy (which mirrors the metaphysics of the medievals) to democracies where individual parts, composed of Newtonian matter, are both equal and equally under the rule of law. Herbert writes:

> Coincident with the rise of Newtonian physics was the ascent of the modern democracy which stresses "rules of laws rather than men" and which posits a theoretical equality between the parts of the social machinery. The Declaration of Independence, for example, [sic] "We hold these truths to be self-

evident" reads more like a mathematical theorem than a political document. As above, so below. The egalitarian mechanism that Newton discovered in the heavens has insinuated itself into every aspect of ordinary life. For better or worse, we live today in a largely mechanistic world.[46]

It is reasonable to expect such a viewpoint to be expressed in passing in the Introduction toa book devoted primarily to describing the development of modern quantum mechanics. One is quite surprised to encounter such an anachronism in a scholarly treatment of Newton, however. Nevertheless, of the law of gravity, Gale E. Christianson writes:

> With this single law of physics Isaac Newton "democratized" the universe, as it were, by laying permanently to rest the concept of a hierarchical dominance among the celestial bodies. . . . In the seemingly infinite universe envisioned by Newton, no one body is more important than any other.[47]

There is, certainly, a relationship between the metaphysics of scientific world-views. And one may even wish to read an embryonic declaration of political independence back into Newton's view of matter. But to do so loses sight of the fact that Newton's God creates that matter, installs the laws which regulate it, continually supervises the maintenance and repair of those laws, and occasionally suspends them. A God without such dominion, writes Newton, "is nothing else but Fate and nature."[48] Newton simplifies the hierarchy, but he strengthens the basic ontology of hierarchical dependency by his emphasis upon the Lord God of Dominion. Newton rails against the atheistic tendencies of Descartes precisely for forgetting the nature of this relationship:

> Indeed however we cast about we find almost no other reason for atheism than this notion of bodies having as it were, a complete, absolute and independent reality in themselves.[49]

But there is a much more sophisticated position which relates Newton's physical theories to the developing Whig ideology of his day. Newton's thought emphasizes order and simplicity in both the rules of reasoning and in his theological notebooks. This methodological preference for order and simplicity is echoed in Newton's many manuscripts "methodizing" the interpretation of prophecies: God is "the god of order not confusion," writes Newton.[50] In the "Rules of Reasoning in Philosophy," this attitude is expressed in Rule I, the principle of the simplicity of nature, according to which "Nature is pleased with simplicity, and affects not the pomp of superfluous causes."[51] As Margaret C. Jacob and others have argued, latitudinarian low churchmen are quick to seize upon this aspect of Newton's thought and to make the orderliness of the Newtonian

heavens the political and social ectype for the rising Whig ideology of the first decades of the eighteenth century.[52] In his *The Newtonian System of the World, The Best Model of Government,* J. T. Desaguliers makes this analogy crystal clear:

> ATTRACTION now in all the Realm is seen, To bless the Reign of George and Caroline.[53]

Jacob's point is well taken, but one may still inquire whether such a use of Newton's science is one which Newton himself makes or would have sanctioned. Does Newton wish to make the same connection between the orderliness of the heavens and the political theory of the moderate Whigs and their latitudinarian apologists? Within the context of the high and low church parties and the Whig-Tory struggle for power which is central in England from the 1690's onward,[54] it is tempting to argue that Newton is himself a latitudinarian Whig, albeit a silent one. He owes his job to the rising Whig tide and his arguments and positions are quickly adapted by latitudinarian churchmen to support the Whig party.[55]

But William Whiston records a conversation which indicates that Newton's distance from the politicians of his day is more than just another manifestation of his shyness to engage in controversy and which also suggests that there is a real intellectual difference between Newton and his Whig patrons. Whiston writes that he

> early asked him [Newton], why he did not at first draw such Consequences from his Principles, as Dr. *Bentley* soon did in his excellent Sermons at Mr. *Boyle's Lectures;* and as I soon did in my *New Theory;* and more largely afterward in my *Astronomical Principles of Religion;* and as that Great Mathematician Mr. *Cotes* did in his excellent *Preface* to the later Editions of Sir I. N.'s **Principia**: I mean for the advantage of Natural Religion, and the Interposition of the Divine Power and Providence in the Constitution of the World; His answer was, that He saw those Consequences; but thought it better to let his Readers draw them first of themselves: Which Consequences however, He did in great measure draw himself long afterwards in the later Editions of his **Principia,** in that admirable *Genera* [sic] *Scholium* at its conclusion; and elsewhere, in his **Opticks**. . . . Nor can I dispence with myself to omit the Declaration of his Opinion to me, Of the Wicked Behavior of most modern Courtiers, and the Cause of it, which he took to be their having *laughed themselves out of Religion;* or, to use my own usual phrase to express both our Notions, because *they have not the fear of God before their Eyes,* Which Characters being, I doubt, full as applicable to our present Courtiers, as they were to those of whom he apply'd them long ago, is a Cause of Lamentation.

Whiston concludes that his own experience has led him to distrust all politicians and courtiers. When even honest Christians go to court his experience has shown them rarely "to amend those Courts, but to be almost always greatly and fatally corrupted by them."[56]

Amidst the raging tumult of party, sectarian, and intellectual strife which characterizes his society before and after the Glorious Revolution of 1688, Newton calmly goes about the business of illustrating the true nature and extent of God's dominion in theology, in science, and in politics for those who have eyes to see and ears to hear. He is secure in his view that in the latter days such knowledge will increase even while "many will run to and fro." (Daniel 12:4) While Newton is in fact very much interested in eradicating any Roman Catholic influence, once the Catholic menace evaporates his job reverts to illustrating the dominion of God to all remaining idolaters whether Whig or Tory, high church or low church, deist or Anglican who have the ears to hear and eyes to see. In London increasingly in the 1690's where he is seeking an appointed public office, he seeks to accomplish this goal through his role as one of those who helps to select the Boyle Lecturers, through his revisions to the **Principia** which he works on in the early 90's and which remains in a most important manuscript in which he anticipates the Lord God of the 1713 General Scholium,[57] and through such controversies as the debate with Leibniz which begins over the question of the priority of the discovery of the method of fluxions but, by 1710, enlarges beyond the priority dispute into a debate concerning the dominion of God.

In the realm of politics, there is no reason to read Newton as a kind of latitudinarian moderate Whig just because he owes his political appointments at the Mint to the political ascendancy of that party. As the above text suggests, he may have mistrusted "most Courtiers." Certainly, the retention of the Trinitarian idolatry in the established Anglican church, high or low, idolatrously continued to mock the power and will of the Lord God of Dominion as illustrated in fulfilled prophetic predictions andalso demonstrated in the Newtonian fabric of the heavens.

Herbert is correct that for better or for worse there is a linkage between metaphysics and politics. In Newton's case, this linkage simply does not produce a latitudinarian, low church, moderate Whig. Rather, the one-way dependency of created mankind upon God the creator underpins a political philosophy in which God's dominion is the central feature in explaining man's moral and political duties both to God and to other men.

God voluntarily creates the world and preserves it through acts of will. God's act of will in making the world is exactly analogous to the way a human being wills his body to move. Newton writes that "God . . . created the World solely by an act of the will, just as we move our bodies by an act of the will."[58] We un-

derstand God's will and power to act over the whole of creation to be analogous, in a limited way, to our will and power to act over our bodies. We remotely understand God's infinite dominion over the totality of his creation by analogy with our finite dominion over our bodies.

And this understanding of the extent and nature of God's dominion is the key to Newton's political and moral views about the duties and obligations of man. Newton writes that

> so far as we can know by natural philosophy the first cause, *what power He has over us,* and what benefits we receive from Him, *so far our duty towards Him, as well as that towards one another,* will appear to us by the light of nature.[59]

A clear statement of the sorts of duties owed to the Lord God of Dominion and to our fellow men is found in the first paragraph of Newton's brief manuscript note entitled "Religion":

> Our Religion to God: God made the world and governs it invisibly, and hath commanded us to love, honour and worship him and no other God but him and to do it without making any image of him, and not to name him idly and without reverence, and *to honour our parents, masters and governors,* and love our neighbors as ourselves, and to be temperate, moderate, just and peaceable, and to be merciful even to brute beasts.[60]

Because man and God both have will and the power to create, the analogy may be extended from God's dominion over us, his creations, to our dominion over property, our creation. The implications of this voluntaristic theory of God's dominion for human property are largely drawn out by John Locke in both his *Essay Concerning Human Understanding* and in his *Two Treatises of Civil Government* where Locke discusses the ability of human beings to understand God's dominion by analogy with how the human will operates to move our bodies.[61] In a footnote which Pierre Coste writes for the third French edition of Locke's *Essay* (1734), Coste reports a discussion that Coste had with Newton long after Locke had died. Coste records that Newton then informed him that he, Newton, had suggested this theory to Locke when he once met with Locke at the Earl of Pembroke's house.[62]

Newton's God of dominion causes him to spurn as idolatrous anyone who dilutes the dominion of God whether through deistic mockery of God's power or through misguidedly worshipping false images of God or false metaphysical conceptions of God. This includes deistic radical Whigs wholaugh at the story of Moses and the flood as well as moderate low churchmen who subscribe to the Trinitarian heresy and the moderate

Whig political establishment which supports that false creed. But he does so in an enigmatic way through the metaphysical statements in the General Scholium which are designed only for the illumination of the wise. Newton's religion is at the root of Newton's political activity. His view of God's dominion keeps him steady in the swirling eddies of his contemporary political surroundings. It is a fact that he gets along with all sides. He wins Royal release by the Stuart king from ordination in the Church of England as a condition for maintaining his Cambridge Fellowship in 1675 and is appointed Warden of the Mint in 1696, with the help of the Whig minister Halifax, and Master of the Mint in 1700, this time without the intercession of Halifax who was no longer in office.

There *is* one possible way to interpret Newton as a member of the moderate Whig party and that is the fact that he does support the will of the people over the will of the king at the time of the Glorious Revolution. This doctrine is a defining characteristic of the moderate Whigs who displace the king in spite of the Tory argument that the king's dominion over his kingdom derives directly from God. To find Newton supporting the will of the people would seem to make him some sort of Whig. So, one might argue, yet again, that here is a good example of how Newton's religion is separated from his political theorizing and activity. But, it seems to me that here, too, Newton's guiding intellectual principle of the dominion of God is central and probably places him in the moderate Whig camp for reasons which have more to do with his metaphysical view of the nature of God's dominion rather than with any republican allegiance to the sovereign will of the people. William Whiston has outlined how this is possible and while I am fully aware of the dangers involved in taking Whiston's position to be isomorphic with that of Newton on this (or any other) point, Whiston's "compromise" seems to me at least suggestive of how it is possible for a committed Arian, who despises idolatry and emphasizes God's dominion, might support the Parliament over the king in a revolution. Whiston develops a moderate position midway between the radical republican Whigs—according to whom the will of the people is absolutely sovereign—and the Tories—according to whom the people always owe passive obedience to their monarch by virtue of his divinely ordained right to rule, a right which is transferred by hereditary succession. Whiston modifies the notion of divine right to show that God still providentially directs the political affairs of his creatures by guiding the will of the people in their choice of a new king. God's dominion is completely preserved by this new mechanism in which the choice of the people, and not the institution of primogeniture, is divinely guided. The analogy is complete because such an extraordinary act of God operating directly through the will of the people does not happen always or even often. Ordinarily, God does confer his dominion to his chosen kings through the ordinary concourse of the mechanism of heredity. But his power is such that he can choose to alter this means of succession by an act of extraordinary concourse. Whiston combs the Bible for examples to show that God has operated in just such a fashion in the prophetic histories.[63] And what if the new monarch supports a false and idolatrous doctrine such as the Trinity? Well, God works in mysterious ways his wonders to perform. It may be his way of effecting his plan for the end of times, we'll just have to wait and see. But his dominion is never in doubt for Whiston or for Newton.

Conclusion

It is certainly possible to study Newton's many various theories over the wide range of his thought separately but we do less than full justice to the range and scope of his genius if we neglect his emphatic regulative principle concerning the dominion of the Lord God of creation which underlies all his work. Newton's conception of a voluntaristic deity, a supremely powerful, absolute sovereign who is the Lord God of creation directly influences his theology, his natural philosophy, and his politics and provides the key to understanding the synthetic unity in his thought which constitutes the true incandescence of his genius. To overemphasize any one aspect of Newton's philosophy by neglecting the implications of his underlying view of the God of Dominion is to run the risk of completely misunderstanding him in his own terms even though we may thereby anachronistically induct him into the modern Pantheon of heroes who have created our present culture. He is neither a scientist, nor a theologian, nor a political theorist in any recognizably individuated, modern sense.[64]

Notes

[1] Allan Bloom, *The Closing of the American Mind* (New York: Simon and Schuster, 1987), p. 264. Consider the sort of modern Valhalla into which modern scientific rationalists seek to enshrine Newton. In the Introduction by Zev Bechler to a collection of essays entitled *Contemporary Newtonian Research* (Dordrecht: D. Reidel, 1982), Bechler writes that "This belief in the overall rationality of the scientist is the unbreakable tie that unifies historians of scientific ideas into one big loving family in which disputes can't really be fundamental. Here everyone works for the common good and deviations are negligible, and the common good is an exhibition of true rationality silently throbbing wherever science exists." (p. 2)

[2] Robert C. Cowen, "Sir Isaac Newton: Charting the Course of Modern Thought," *The Christian Science Monitor* (July 17, 1987), p. 16. Other journalists have helped to define Newton as the positivistic father of all

that is "good," i.e., rational, and, therefore, serious and "objective," in modern science. But journalists tend to write their stories based on what the people they interview tell them. Writing in *The New York Times* (March 31, 1987), Malcolm W. Browne "pegs" his story of the three-hundredth anniversary of the publication of Newton's *Principia* to the many events celebrating this anniversary, from specially issued postage stamps to symposia and conferences. His story features a long interview with Dr. Subrahmanyan Chandrasekhar, one of the "leading physicists participating in the current symposiums on Newton's Principia. . . ." In answering Browne's question about how Newton would have felt about the course of science since his death, Dr. Chandrasekhar replies, "I think he would have been troubled by the development of quantum theory since so much in quantum physics is indeterminate and acausal. But he would have been far less surprised by today's science than would any of his contemporaries. He would have been much more disturbed, I think, by today's religious evangelism." (p. 21)

[3] D. T. Whiteside, "Newton the Mathematician," in *Contemporary Newtonian Research,* ed. Zev Bechler (Dordrecht: D. Reidel, 1987), pp. 109-27.

[4] Richard S. Westfall, *Never at Rest: A Biography of Isaac Newton* (Cambridge: Cambridge University Press, 1980.)

[5] Richard S. Westfall, "Newton's Theological Manuscripts," in *Contemporary Newtonian Research,* pp. 139-40.

[6] Westfall, *Never At Rest,* p. 596.

[7] *Ibid.,* p. 597.

[8] Margaret C. Jacob, *The Newtonians and the English Revolution, 1689-1720* (Ithaca: Cornell University Press, 1976), passim, but especially, p. 175.

[9] Sir Isaac Newton, *Opticks or A Treatise of the Reflections, Refractions, Inflections & Colours of Light.* Based on the fourth edition, London, 1730. With a Foreword by Albert Einstein, and Introduction by Sir Edmund Whittaker, a Preface by I. Bernard Cohen, and an Analytical Table of Contents prepared by Duane H. D. Roller (New York: Dover Publications, 1952), Book One, Part II, Prop. v, Theor, iv, p. 134.

[10] Westfall, "Newton's Theological Manuscripts," p. 130.

[11] Newton, Yahuda MS 14, f. 25, Hebrew University, Jerusalem.

[12] *Ibid.* Frank E. Manuel, in his book *The Religion of Isaac Newton* (Oxford: Clarendon Press, 1974), dis-

cusses a fragment from Yahuda MS 15.5 (dated by Westfall as from the period around 1710) on p. 21. Manuel argues that the Lord God of the General Scholium must not be seen as merely the result of the great dispute with Leibniz. It is a view reiterated too many times in too many other contexts. The text pointed to by Manuel reads:

> If the father or son be called *God,* they take the name in a metaphysical sense as if it signified Gods metaphysical perfections of infinite eternal omniscient omnipotent whereas it relates only Gods dominion to teach us obedience. The word *God* is relative and signifies the same thing with Lord and King, but in a higher degree. As we say my Lord, our Lord, your Lord, the King of Kings, and Lord of Lords, the supreme Lord, so we say my God, our God, your God, the God of Gods, the supreme God, the God of the earth, the servants of God, serve other Gods; but we do not say my infinite, our infinite, your infinite, the infinite of infinities, the infinite of the earth, the servants of the infinite, serve other infinities. When the Apostle told the Gentiles that the Gods which they wor-shipped were not Gods, he did not meane that they were not infinities, (for the Gentiles did not take them to be such:) but he meant that they had no power and dominion over man. They were fals Gods; not fals infinities, but vanities falsely sup-posed to have power and dominion over man. (Yahuda MS 15.5, folios 96 verso, 97 recto, and 98 recto.)

[13] *Sir Isaac Newton's Mathematical Principles of Natural Philosophy and His System of the World.* Translated into English by Andrew Motte in 1729. The translations revised, and supplied with an historical and explanatory appendix by Florian Cajori. 2 vols. (Berkeley and Los Angeles: University of California Press, 1962), 2:544. In a footnote to this text, Newton states that, according to Dr. Edward Pococke (the Biblical scholar and orientalist who had introduced the study of Arabic into Oxford and then become the first Professor of Arabic there), the Latin word *Deus* derives from the (transliteration of) *du* in the Arabic which means *lord.*

[14] Newton, Yahuda MS 15.1, Hebrew University, Jerusalem. Newton's conception of the nature of God's dominion and its necessary consequence that Jesus is not divine in his metaphysical nature is adopted by his disciples Samuel Clarke and William Whiston. The following text from Clarke, for example, resoundingly echoes the quotation cited above from Newton's General Scholium. In his *The Scripture-Doctrine of the Trinity. In Three Parts. Wherein All the "Texts" in the New Testament relating to that Doctrine, and the principal Passages in the Liturgy of the Church of England, are collected, compared, and explained* (London, 1712), Clarke writes:

> The reason why the Scripture, though it stiles the *Father* God, and also stiles the *Son* God, yet at the

same time always declares there is but *One God;* is because in the *Monarchy* of the Universe, there is but *One Authority,* original in the *Father,* derivative in the *Son:* The *Power of the Son* being, not *Another* Power *opposite* to That of the *Father,* nor *Another* Power *coordinate* to That of the *Father;* but it self *The Power and Authority of the Father,* communicated *to,* manifested *in,* and exercised *by* the *Son.* (pp. 332-3)

One author, the low church Whig, William Stephens, clearly recognizes the heterodoxy of Clarke's position in this text, which Stephens quotes, and then controverts, in his sermon entitled *The Divine Persons One God by an Unity of Nature: Or, That Our Saviour is One God with his Father, by an Eternal Generation from his Substance, Asserted from Scripture, and the Ante-Nicene Fathers* (Oxford, 1722.) Stephens quotes the entire text of Clarke cited immediately above and then writes:

In this Proposition, the Unity of the Godhead is plainly resolv'd into an Unity, not of *Nature* and *Essence,* but of *Dominion* and *Authority:* And, if this be the *Scripture-Doctrine,* as this Author would perswade us, Our Saviour is no otherwise God, than as his Father has been pleas'd to associate him with Himself in the Government of the Universe.

This Artifice of *speciously* continuing to our Saviour the Name and Title of god, (and yet in reality of denying it him,) by supposing him to be God only by *Authority* and *Power,* and not by *Nature,* is not a novel or late-invented Scheme. The *Arians* of the *fourth* Century pleaded the same thing: And hence it came to pass, that in the Great Defenders of the *Nicene* Faith in that Century we find so much Labour expended in shewing that the Word *God* is not a Name of *Office* and *Authority,* but of *Being* and *Substance;* that it does not denote *Ruler, Governour,* and the *like;* but a *Nature* and *Essence, Infinite, Eternal,* and *Divine,* in that Person of whom it is praedicated. When the Followers of *Socinus* reviv'd the same Plea, they met with no better Success than their Predecessors in the Evasion: and, the Godhead has been by *many* Hands so accurately shewn to be a *Substance,* not an *Office,* that it would be Superfluous and Unnecessary to attempt a further Proof of it. (pp. 4-5)

[15] Newton, "Commonplace Book," s.v. "Predestinatio," Keynes MS 2, King's College Library, Cambridge.

[16] Newton, Yahuda MS 14, f. 9 verso. Cited in Westfall, *Never At Rest,* p. 315.

[17] See Westfall, *Never At Rest,* pp. 330-4.

[18] Newton to Bentley, December 10, 1962, in *The Correspondence of Isaac Newton,* 7 vols., ed. H. W.

Turnbull, J. F. Scott, A. R. Hall, and Laura Tilling (Cambridge: Cambridge University Press,1963), 3: 233.

[19] Westfall, *Never At Rest,* p. 329.

[20] Newton, Yahuda MS 7.2, f. 4. Cited in Westfall, *Never At Rest,* p. 319.

[21] See James E. Force, *William Whiston, Honest Newtonian* (Cambridge: Cambridge University Press, 1985), p. 76.

[22] Newton, Yahuda MS 1.2, ff. 60-1; Yahuda MS 1.3; ff. 40-8. Cited in Westfall, *Never At Rest,* p. 325.

[23] Manuel reproduces Newton's "Fragments from a Treatise of Revelation," Yahuda MS. 1, as Appendix A in his *The Religion of Isaac Newton.* The citation is from p. 124 of Manuel's book. Westfall dates this work from the early 70's.

[24] Gale E. Christianson, *In the Presence of the Creator. Isaac Newton and His Times* (New York: The Free Press, 1984), pp. 312-3. Christianson also reminds us that "we remember Newton and honor him today not for providing us with ultimate answers to the most profound scientific questions but because, in apprehending the Pythagorean power by which number holds sway above the flux, Isaac Newton contributed more than any other individual to a rational world view." These statements must be juxtaposed with the following quotation from Christianson's Preface:

Historians have tended increasingly to interpret Newton and his intellectual achievements not in seventeenth-century terms but in the light of our times. In doing so we have been made ever more conscious of his limitations and ever less appreciative of the revolutionary nature of his many accomplishments. Moreover, the twentieth century has made out of Newton something that he was not—an Enlightenment figure whose dedication to the principle of a mechanical universe became his reason for being and his single most important legacy to posterity. That Newton did adhere to a philosophy of mechanistic causation in the physical world is undeniable; but to argue, as did Voltaire, that this is the whole Newton, or even the essential Newton, is erroneous. Isaac Newton held tight the conviction that science (or natural philosophy, as it was known in his day) must be employed to demonstrate the continuing presence of the Creator in the world of nature.

Christianson, like Westfall, feels that what influence there is between Newton's theology and Newton's science runs from Newton's science to Newton's theology. As Christianson points out, for Newton and the Newtonians, science is used to reveal a God with "continuing presence," but it also reveals, in conjunction with the argument from prophecy, a God of supreme dominion, a Lord God whose will and power are sovereign. Another way to put this point is to argue that, for Newton, natural philosophy is something beyond what we today would call science and that it contains a heavily metaphysical approach to nature which, in Newton's case especially, is necessarily related to theology. Newton does not strip his universe of metaphysical considerations simply because in his voluntaristic theory of God's nature, God is always supervising nature, whether directly or indirectly.

[25] David Hume, *An Enquiry Concerning Human Understanding* in *Enquiries Concerning Human Understandings and Concerning the Principles of Morals,* ed. L.A. Selby-Bigge, third edition with text revised and notes by P. H. Nidditch (Oxford: Clarendon Press, 1975) pp. 16 and 165.

[26] Newton, *Opticks,* pp. 403-4.

[27] The line of interpretation which I am adopting in this paper was first established nearly thirty years ago by Alexandre Koyré in his *From the Closed World to the Infinite Universe* (Baltimore: The Johns Hopkins Press, 1957), Chap. XI. Koyré is not always given the respect which is his just due. In the mid-fifties, he clearly saw the connection between empiricism and a priorism in physics and a *deus artifex* and a *dieu fainéant* in theology. Twenty years ago, J. E. McGuire wrote a fundamental article based on first rate and highly original research in manuscript sources which further established beyond doubt that Newton's theology is inextricably and mutually bound up with his metaphysics and his natural philosophy. See J. E. McGuire, "Force, Active Principles, and Newton's Invisible Realm," *Ambix* 15, No. 3 (1968), esp. pp. 187-94. The writer who has done the most to link Newton's conception of God with such medieval metaphysical theologians as Ockham and Suarez has been Francis Oakley. See his *The Political Thought of Pierre d'Ailly: The Voluntarist Tradition* (New Haven: Yale University Press, 1964); his "Medieval Theories of Natural Law: William of Ockham and the Significance of the Voluntarist Tradition," *Natural Law Forum* 6 (1961), pp. 65-83; and his "Christian Theology and the Newtonian Science: The Rise of the Concept of the Laws of Nature," *Church History* 30, No. 4 (1961), pp. 433-57.

[28] Newton, Yahuda MS 21, fol. 1 recto. In the General Scholium, Newton writes, "We know [God] only by his most wise and excellent contrivances of things, and final causes; we admire him for his perfections; but we reverence and adore him on account of his dominion: for we adore him as his servants; and a god without dominion, providence, and final causes, is nothing else but Fate and Nature." *Sir Isaac Newton's Mathematical Principles of Natural Philosophy,* 2:546. The point is that what makes a king to be a king is his dominion, i.e., his ability to exert his will and power. One worships God because of his power over us unless one is wickedly vain and thus caught up in idolatry. The text of 2 Kings 17:15-6, which is the text for this sermon, is most significant. After journeying to Damascus where he met the King of Assyria, Tiglath-Pileser, the King of Judah saw a bronze altar. He sent the details of the construction of the altar home to "Uriah the Priest" ordering him to build a copy for use in the temple at Jerusalem. Ahaz is regarded as one of the worst kings in the history of Judah because of his reinstitution of human sacrifice. The text for Newton's sermon is preceded in verse 14 by the remark that the people of Israel and Judah "were stubborn, as their fathers had been, who did not believe in the LORD their God." Newton's text then reads:

> They despised his statutes, and his covenant that he made with their fathers, and the warnings which he gave them. They went after false idols, and became false, and they followed the nations that were around them, concerning whom the LORD had commanded them that they should not do like them. And they forsook all the commandments of the LORD their god, and made for themselves molten images of two calves; and they made an Ashe'rah, and wor-shipped all the host of heaven, and served Ba'al.

[29] Memoranda by David Gregory, 5, 6, 7 May 1694, in *The Correspondence of Isaac Newton,* 3:336.

[30] William Whiston, *A New Theory of the Earth,* second ed. (London, 1708, p. 284. In this text, Whiston cites as corroboration for this point Dr. Bentley's seventh sermon from his Boyle Lectures delivered in 1692 under the title *A Confutation of Atheism From the Origin and Frame of the World* (London, 1693.)

[31] Whiston, *A New Theory,* pp. 435-6.

[32] *Ibid.,* pp. 432-3. I have emphasized the term "act."

[33] David Gregory MS.245, fol. 14a, Library of the Royal Society, London. This translation is found in the seminal article by J. E. McGuire, "Force, Active Principles, and Newton's Invisible Realm," p. 190. As an example of how this distinction works in the writing of one of Newton's followers, consider William Whiston. Whiston accepts some events to be genuine transgressions of natural law by a special, voluntary interposition of God's power: the Creation of the matter of the Universe out of nothing; the changing of a chaotic comet's orbit into that of a planet; the formation of the seeds of animals, especially "our First Parents," and vegetables. And

The Natures, Conditions, Rules and Quantities, of those several Motions and Powers according to which all Bodies, (of the same general nature in themselves,) are specifi'd, distinguish'd, and fitted for their several uses, were no otherwise determin'd than by the immediate *Fiat,* Command, Power, and Efficiency of Almighty God (*New Theory of the Earth,* pp. 287-95.)

As for Clarke, he, too, makes a place for real miracles in the ordinary coursing of nature. In his 1705 Boyle Lectures, he writes that a miracle

is a work effected in a manner unusual or different from the common and regular method of Providence by the interposition either of God Himself, or some intelligent agent superior to man, in the proof or evidence of some particular doctrine or in attestation to the authority of some particular person. [*A Discourse Concerning the Unchangeable Obligations of Natural Religion, and the Truth and Certainty of the Christian Revelation, Being Eight Sermons Preached at the Cathedral Church of St. Paul in the Year 1705 in A Defense of Natural and Revealed Religion,* 2 vols. (London, 1707), 2:165.]

[34] Quoted in *Sir Isaac Newton's Theological Manuscripts,* ed. H. McLachlan (Liverpool, University Press, 1930.), p. 17. Like Whiston who wrote a book on when miraculous acts ceased in the early church, Newton believed that true miracles ceased being performed by God early in the church's history. See Newton to Locke, 16 February 1691-2, *The Correspondence of Isaac Newton,* 3:195.

[35] Newton, "Paradoxical Questions concerning ye morals & actions of Athanasius & his followers," Clark Library Manuscript. Cited by Westfall, *Never At Rest,* p. 345.

[36] Newton, *Observations Upon the Prophecies of Daniel and the Apocalypse of St. John. In TwoParts* (London, 1733), pp. 251-2.

[37] The term is Frank E. Manuel's and comes in the context of Manuel's reluctance to entertain any metaphysical significance beyond the debate over who discovered calculus first in the dispute between Newton and Leibniz. See his *A Portrait of Isaac Newton* (Cambridge: Harvard University Press, 1968), p. 333.

[38] A. Rupert Hall, *Philosophers at War. The Quarrel Between Newton and Leibniz* (Cambridge: Cambridge University Press, 1980), p. 258. To Hall, the relationship between metaphysics and mathematics is a "Pandora's box" which he mentions in passing:

Let me release from this Pandora's box no more than the simplistic affirmation that Leibniz's was a calculus of discontinuity, of monads, while Newton's

was concerned with the continuity of flow, with time; or, one might say, differentials belong to the relative, fluxions to the absolute. Does not this involve seeing different things?" (p. 258.)

The irony of finding this position stated in a book in which the author has already stated his general position that the path of the argument from the priority dispute into the realm of metaphysics was "a largely regrettable and pointless diversification" is pointed out by Steven Shapin, "Licking Leibniz," *History of Science* 19 (1981), p. 302.

Another famous scholar who argues for the complete autonomy of Newton's scientific mechanics from any taint of metaphysics, is Edward W. Strong. He believes that Clarke departs from Newton's own line of thinking

by taking the religious addendum to be fundamental to his science, for therein [Clarke does] violence to the autonomy of science in methods and results upon which Newton had clearly and vigorously insisted. [Strong, "Newton and God," *Journal of the History of Ideas* 7, No. 2 (April, 1952), p. 167.]

[39] *Sir Isaac Newton's Mathematical Principles of Natural Philosophy,* "Cotes's Preface to the Second Edition," 1:xxxii. Just as Strong has argued that Clarke departs from Newton's position so, too, he argues that Cotes in this Preface "might have prompted Newton to relax his caution as a scientist." ("Newton and God," p. 167.)

[40] *Sir Isaac Newton's Mathematical Principles of Natural Philosophy,* Book III. 2:400. Newton's view about the contingency of human knowledge in the light of God's total dominion over nature parallels that of Robert Boyle who puts

this point most clearly when he observes that in this very phenomenal world of partial regularity, at any moment all our science may be upset by the elimination, or change of regularity through the operation of Him who is the guider of its concourse. For the most optimistic investigator must acknowledge that if God be the author of the universe, and the free establisher of the laws of motion, whose general concourse is necessary to the conservation and efficacy of every particular physical agent, God can certainly invalidate all experimentalism by withholding His concourse, orchanging these laws of motion, which depend perfectly upon His will, and could thus vitiate the value of most, if not all the axioms and theorems of natural philosophy. Therefore reason operating in the mechanical world is constantly limited by the possibility that there is not final regularity in that world, and that existential regularity may readily be destroyed at any moment by the God upon whom it depends. [Mitchell Salem Fisher, *Robert Boyle: Devout Naturalist. A Study in Science and Religion in the Seventeenth Century*

(Philadelphia: Oshiver Studio Press, 1945), pp. 127-8, citing *Reconcileableness of Reason and Religion,* in *The Works of the Honourable Robert Boyle,* 6 vols, ed. Thomas Birch (London, 1772), 4:161.]

This text is cited by Mitchell Salem Fisher in *Robert Boyle: Devout Naturalist. A Study in Science and Religion in the Seventeenth Century* (Philadelphia: Oshiver Studio Press, 1945), pp. 127-8. Fisher goes on to note that Newton agrees with Boyle's view about God's power over creation: "[Boyle's] God, like that of Newton's was an absolute, free, and omniscient being who governed all the phenomena of nature not at all as any indwelling soul of the world, but as the mechanical master and lord of the universe." (p. 160)

[41] Newton, *Observations Upon the Prophecies,* p. 251.

[42] Whiston, *A New Theory of the Earth,* p. 432.

[43] A. A. Sykes, "The Elogium of the late . . . Samuel Clarke," *The Present State of the Republic of Letters* 4 (1729), pp. 54-6.

[44] Newton, *Opticks,* Query 31, p. 403.

[45] Nick Herbert, *Quantum Reality. Beyond the New Physics* (Garden City: Anchor Press/Doubleday, 1987), p. xi.

[46] *Ibid.,* pp. xi-xii.

[47] Gale E. Christianson, *In the Presence of the Creator,* p. 307. A. J. Meadows has also found in the American Constitution the "logical culmination" of Newton's "mechanical" frame of nature. See his *The High Firmament* (Leicester: Leicester University Press, 1969), p. 148. It may very well be the logical culmination of the frame of nature once that framework is ripped out of the dominion of God. But it is not the logical culmination for Newton just because he cannot imagine eliminating God from the structure of the heavens. This logical consequence is first arrived at by Hume who starts from vastly different metaphysical suppositions.

[48] *Sir Isaac Newton's Mathematical Principles of Natural Philosophy,* 2:546.

[49] *Unpublished Scientific Papers of Isaac Newton,* ed. A. Rupert Hall and Marie Boas (Cambridge: Cambridge University Press, 1962), p. 144.

[50] Newton, Yahuda MS 1, bundle 1, folio 14r.

[51] *Sir Isaac Newton's Mathematical Principles of Natural Philosophy,* 2:398.

[52] Margaret C. Jacob's book, *The Newtonians and the English Revolution, 1689-1720,* will remain the standard work on how Newton's work is taken up for the purpose of low church latitudinarian apologetics. Another approach is found in Steven Shapin, "Of Gods and Kings: Natural Philosophy and Politics in the Leibniz-Clarke Disputes," *Isis* 72 (June, 1981), pp. 187-215. Shapin is concerned to cast the Leibniz-Clarke dispute over the dominion of God into the context of the Whig-Tory, low church-high church, dynastic politics of the day. On the whole, he is quite successful; certainly he is correct in emphasizing the centrality of the metaphysical issue of the debate. Like Jacob he is primarily concerned with the uses others make of Newton's work and not about inquiring "Whether or not Newton . . . intended that his philosophy of nature should be put to specific political uses. . . ." (p. 189).

[53] J. T. Desaguliers, *The Newtonian System of the World, The Best Model of Government* (London, 1728), lines 191-2, p. 34.

[54] Geoffrey Holmes, "Science, Reason, and Religion in the Age of Newton," *British Journal for the History of Science* II, Part 2, No. 38 (July, 1978), p. 168.

[55] Perhaps the strongest statement of the contention by both Margaret C. Jacob and James R. Jacob that the latitudinarian churchmen who utilize Newton's science for the defense of religion do so in behalf of low church orthodoxy and against the crypto-Republican forces of Radical Enlightenment is found in their joint article entitled "The Anglican Origins of Modern Science: The Metaphysical Foundations of the Whig Constitution," *Isis* 71, No. 257 (June, 1980), pp. 251-67. I take no issue with the general conclusion that Newtonian scientific arguments are used by others to give vital ideological support to the Protestant monarchy.

[56] William Whiston, *A Collection of Authentick Records Belonging to the Old and New Testament,* 2 vols. (London, 1728), 2:1073-4.

[57] See J. E. McGuire, "Newton on Place, Time, and God: An Unpublished Source," *British Journal of the History of Science* 11, No. 38 (1978), pp. 115-29.

[58] Newton, *Unpublished Scientific Papers,* p. 107. Cf. Henry Guerlac, "Theological Voluntarism and Biological Analogies in Newton's Physical Thought," *Journal of the History of Ideas* 44, No. 2 (April-June, 1983), pp. 219-29.

[59] Newton, *Opticks,* p. 182.

[60] Newton, "Irenicum," Keynes MS 3.

[61] See James Tully, *A Discourse on Property. John Locke and His Adversaries* (Cambridge: Cambridge University Press, 1980), pp. 35-50.

[62] John Locke, *An Essay Concerning Human Understanding.* Collated and annotated by AlexanderCampbell Fraser, 2 vols. (New York: Dover Publications, 1959), 2:321-2. See also Alexandre Koyré, *Newtonian Studies* (Chicago: The University of Chicago Press, 1965), p. 92.

[63] See Force, *William Whiston,* p. 103.

[64] This paper is being printed for the first time in this volume. An earlier version of it was presented by the author as part of a public lecture series devoted to the topic of "Science, Politics, and Religion in 17th Century England" on December 1, 1987. This lecture series was sponsored by The Claremont Colleges Program in Critical Studies of Science and Technology and The Humanities and Social Sciences Department of Harvey Mudd College through the generosity of the Garrett Fund.

Richard H. Popkin (essay date 1990)

SOURCE: "Newton as Bible Scholar," in *Essays on the Context, Nature and Influence of Isaac Newton's Theology,* by James E. Force and Richard H. Popkin, Kluwer Academic Publishers, 1990, pp. 103-118.

[*In the following essay, Popkin reviews Newton's writings on the Bible, demonstrating how Newton analyzed the composition and nature of the Bible's books. Popkin maintains that Newton sought to present the Bible as historically accurate, and that Newton also believed the Bible contained corruptions deliberately placed there to encourage a false Trinitarian doctrine.*]

In his views about the text and import of the Bible, Sir Isaac Newton combined a most interesting mixture of modern Bible scholarship *with* an application, to the understanding of the Bible, of some of the findings of modern science *and* a firm conviction that, in the proper reading of the scriptural text, one could discover God's plan for human and world history. Newton wrote much about the Bible as a historical document, about the accuracy of Biblical chronology, and about the message of the Bible. All of these topics were burning issues during the 17th century. Newton wrote on these subjects from his early student years at Cambridge until his death. For many years, including the central ones in his intellectual career, he was composing manuscripts on these issues.[1]

He published none of his writings on the Bible during his lifetime. But after his death four items appeared in print, **The Chronology of Ancient Kingdoms Amended** (1728),[2] the **Observations upon the Prophecies of Daniel, and the Apocalypse of St. John** (1733),[3] an essay on the sacred cubit of the Hebrews (1737),[4] and

two letters written to John Locke concerning doubts abut the textual basis for the Doctrine of the Trinity.[5] (A third letter to Locke on this subject was only published in 1961.)[6] In addition to the material that has been published in the two and one-half centuries since Newton's death, an enormous amount of unpublished manuscript writings are still unpublished. They are in libraries from California to Jerusalem.[7] The largest amount of the unpublished work is in the Yahuda collection at the National and University Library of Israel.[8]

Newton's writings on the Bible seem to have been penned over a sixty-year period. Because most of the manuscripts have not been published, it is not yet possible to give a succinct statement of hisviews on the subject. Newton's views changed and developed over the years. Early in his career, Newton composed a paper on how to interpret scripture. He wrote this around 1671. It is the first item in the vast Yahuda collection (Yahuda MS 1.1) Part of the text was published by Frank Manuel in *The Religion of Isaac Newton* in 1974.[9] (This is the only item of the Yahuda collection so far published.) In this manuscript, Newton presented a view close to the Calvinist literalism of the mid-17th century. Newton writes that he prefers to choose "those interpretations which are most according to the litterall meaning of the scriptures unles where the tenour and circumstances of the place plainly require an Allegory."[10] A few pages later on, just after the portion of the text published by Manuel, Newton says that it "is ye wisdom of God that he hath so framed ye scriptures as to distinguish between ye good & ye bad, that they should be demonstrative to ye one & foolishness to the other,"[11] a view similar to that stated by Pascal whose *Pensées* were just becoming known.

In subsequent writings, Newton, influenced probably by the Biblical researches of Father Richard Simon and possibly by Spinoza's work on the subject as well as by interchanges with John Locke, developed a rather critical view about the accuracy of existing texts of the Old and New Testaments. Newton owned several of Simon's works,[12] which.were causing quite a stir in England in the 1680's.[13] Spinoza's views were discussed in some detail by Simon.[14] Three of Newton's Cambridge colleagues, Isaac Barrow, Ralph Cudworth, and Henry More, had access to copies of Spinoza's *Tractatus Theologico-Politicus.* Newton had catalogued Barrow's library and so must have catalogued this work by Spinoza.[15] Cudworth and More were very concerned about Spinoza's critical views about the Bible and published critical replies in the 1670's, which Newton probably read.[16] At that point in his career Newton was involved with Henry More in working out Biblical exegeses and was consulting Cudworth, the Regius Professor of Hebrew, on various textual matters.

In various manuscripts at Oxford and Jerusalem (e.g., New College, Oxford, MS II, fol. 192, and Yahuda

MSS 1.7 and 1.9) as well as in the published version of the **Observations** on Daniel and Revelation, Newton set forth a picture of how the text of the Old Testament got into its present state. He presented a theory of how the Biblical texts were composed and how they became mixed up and corrupted over time. Newton sought to describe in some detail how various texts became confused. On the basis of his researches, he concluded that no text of the Old Testament dated before Talmudic times.[17]

Newton based his historical theory of the development of the Biblical text on internal evidence in scripture and on historical events mentioned in the books. A brief version of his results appears in the first chapter of the **Observations.** Much more detail is given in some of the Yahuda manuscripts. The opening chapter in the **Observations** is entitled, "Introduction concerning the Compilers of the books of the Old Testament."[18] After going over some of the details in the Biblical narrative, Newton says, concerning a passage in Genesis, "therefore that book was not written entirely in the form now extant, before the reign of *Saul.*"[19] If this were so, Moses could not be the author of that part of the text. The first five books of the Old Testament, the Pentateuch, are called the Books of Moses. But, on Newton's account, the historical part about God's people was put together from several earlier books. These were, according to Newton, a history of the Creation composed by Moses, a book of the generations after Adam, and a book of the wars of the Lord, each of which is mentioned in the present text.[20] The book of the wars of the Lord, Newton claimed, was begun by Moses and was continued by Joshua. Samuel, writing during the reign of Saul, put them in their present form.[21] Thelater historical material in the Pentateuch, Joshua, and Judges contained one continuous history from Creation to the death of Samson. Examining the history therein, Newton declares, "Therefore all these books have been composed out of the writings of *Moses, Joshua* and other records, by one and the same hand,"[22] during the reign of Saul or early in David's kingship. Newton's guess was that Samuel was the author.[23] After the battles with the Philistines, Newton states that Samuel might have had time to collect "the scattered writings of *Moses* and *Joshua,* and the records of the Patriarchs and Judges, and compose them in the form now extant."[24] Newton also ascribed to Samuel the book of Ruth and the beginning of Samuel. Other books had later authors and "were therefore collected out of the historical writings of the antient Seers and Prophets."[25] Ezra, Newton said, was the compiler of the book of Kings and Chronicles. The prophecies of Isaiah were written at several times, as were the other prophetic writings.[26] The book of Daniel, which is all important in Newton's interpretation of the Bible, "is a collection of papers written at several times. The six last chapters contain Prophecies written at several times by *Daniel* himself: the six first are a collection of histor-

ical papers written by others. . . . The first chapter was written after *Daniel's* death . . . ," as were the fifth and sixth chapters.[27] Newton surmises that some of the verses were added by the collector of the papers, "whom I take to be *Ezra.*"[28] Newton says, too, that the Psalms, which were composed by Moses, David, and others, "seem to have been also collected by *Ezra* into one volume."[29]

Newton offered some textual evidence for his theory of the various authors of the books. By and large, Newton offered more or less the same picture which Spinoza and Father Richard Simon had offered about how the present text got put together. For Spinoza, this messy and somewhat confused picture was a basic reason for doubting that scripture was anything more than a collection of ancient Hebrew writings. For both Simon and Newton, the fact that there were multiple authors, even of the Books of Moses, did not detract from the revelatory nature of the text.

Spinoza, after presenting his version of how the text got put together, says, "We may, therefore, conclude that all the books we have considered hitherto are compilations, and that the events therein are recorded as having happened in old time."[30] The books "are compilations made many generations after the events they relate had taken place" and are written by a single historian, probably Ezra.[31] Going over the Pentateuch, Spinoza comes to the sad conclusion that:

> If anyone pays attention to the way in which all the histories and precepts in these five books are set down promiscuously and without order, with no regard for dates; and further, how the same story is often repeated, sometimes in a different version, he will easily, I say, discern that all the materials were promiscuously collected and heaped together, in order that they might at some subsequent time be more readily examined and reduced to order. Not only these five books, but also the narratives contained in the remaining seven, going down to the destruction of the city, are compiled in the same way.[32]

Spinoza followed Isaac La Peyrère's view that the text which now exists is nothing but copies of copies of confused compilations.[33] Understanding what a mess the text is in and how it got this way during its compilation was enough for Spinoza to be dubious that there could be any divine message in scripture *except* for its teaching of the moral law.[34] Simon and Newton offered much the same account of how Ezra put together various strands and fragments without giving up confidence in scripture as the crucial source of God's revelation to mankind.[35] Until the beginning of modernBible criticism with Thomas Hobbes and Isaac La Peyrère, the usually accepted guarantee of the connection of the Biblical text with God was that Moses wrote what God revealed to him. Aben Ezra, around 1100 A. D., had pointed out that there were lines in the Pentateuch that were not written by Moses, including those telling of the death of Moses. Aben Ezra just indicated that these non-Mosaic verses had some different status but did not try to specify what that was.

Hobbes said that he accepted canonical Scripture, as recognized by the Church of England, as Divine Revelation and just wanted to consider the historical question of who wrote the various parts. Hobbes supposedly shocked his contemporaries with the news that Moses could not have written all of Deuteronomy because of the verses about his death. So, for Hobbes there had to have been two or more authors. La Peyrère went further and suggested that Moses was not the author at all and that a diary of Moses was used by later authors, along with a lot of other materials.[36] Spinoza then worked out a general theory of how the work grew. Unlike his predecessors, who still at least gave lip-service to the claim that the Bible was a special book of Divine Revelation, Spinoza presented it as a human production which gave a confused picture of ancient Israelite history.[37]

Father Simon, who said that he followed the method of Spinoza but that he disagreed with Spinoza's radical conclusions, made a much more intensive study of the text. He concluded, much as Spinoza had, that various narratives had been put together by Ezra. But, Simon insisted, the text began with a Mosaic core which had the privileged status of recording a Divine communication. And, Simon said, in answer to Spinoza, that additional parts by later authors did not reduce the value of the Mosaic part. The additional parts could also be divinely inspired text.[38]

Newton, having looked at the evidence, at least in the form that Simon had presented it, accepted a revelatory core in the documents. For Newton, this consisted of the prophetic parts, especially in Daniel and Revelation.[39]

Before describing Newton's interpretation of these divinely revealed prophecies, another, second-order problem must be considered. Given the Spinoza-Simon-Newton theory that Ezra compiled the basic narrative we now have in scripture, mostly out of preexisting materials, is there any accurate copy of the Ezra compilation? From information in scripture, in the story of the Maccabees in the Apocrypha, in Josephus' *History of the Jews,* and in Jewish accounts in the Talmud, we learn that the historical, legal, and prophetic writings compiled by Ezra were partially destroyed by Antiochus Epiphanes who "caused the sacred books to be burnt wherever they could be found."[40] After the successful Maccabaean revolt, "*Judas Maccabaeus* gathered together all those writings that were to be met with. . . ."[41] At this time, some books were entirely lost and others got jumbled together. In the

manuscripts, Newton offered a detailed theory of how pages from Samuel got mixed with pages of Nehemiah, among other disorders.[42]

Newton then said that the reconstructed Maccabaean text was further confused by copyists. Spinoza and Simon had supplied lots of data about how glosses, errors, etc., got into the text. Newton then points out that it was only after the Romans captured Judaea that the Jews sought to preserve their traditions, putting them in writing in the Talmud, "and for preserving their scriptures, agreed upon an Edition, and pointed it [that is, put in the vowel markers], and counted the letters of every sort in every book."[43] This edition was the only one which had been preserved. All earlier versions werelost, except for those in the Greek Septuagint Version. As a result, "such marginal notes, or other corruptions, as by the errors of the transcribers, before this Edition was made, had crept into the text, are now scarce to be corrected."[44] Spinoza took all of this to mean that one could never get back to an accurate text. Simon offered a program for reconstructing the right text that would unfortunately involve an endless amount of research.

Newton accepted this general conclusion, namely that what survives is a corrupt text which is probably truncated from what the original looked like. Thus, Newton does not accept the contention of the Westminster Confession of the mid-17th century according to which "The Old Testament in Hebrew (which was the Native Language of the People of GOD of old), and the New Testament in Greek . . . being immediately inspired by God, and by his singular care and Providence kept pure in all Ages, are therefore Authentical".[45] Instead, Newton was about as avant-garde as Spinoza and Simon in his view about how the Biblical text got to be what it is.[46] Nonetheless, Newton adamantly insists that a divinely revealed prophetic message is contained in scripture, as we have it and that, as Daniel says (xii. 9-10), in the latter days, *the wise may understand, but the wicked shall do wickedly, and none of the wicked shall understand."*

For Newton, "The authority of the Prophets is divine, and comprehends the sum of religion. . . . Their writings contain the covenant between God and his people, with instructions for keeping this covenant; instances of God's judgments upon them that break it: and predictions of things to come."[47] Of the prophets of the Old Testament, Daniel is the most distinct and the easiest to understand—"and therefore in those things which relate to the last times, he must be made the key to the rest."[48] And so, regardless of the history of the text and the vagaries of how our current copies have come down to us, it is all important to try to figure out what is being said by the prophet. Newton devoted a great deal of time and energy to trying to decipher the symbolism in Daniel's prophecies.

When Newton turned to the New Testament, he was much more critical about the reliability of the texts. His chief concern was to argue for the primacy of the book of Revelation and to point out the deliberate alteration of New Testament texts by wicked characters such as Saint Athanasius.[49] With regard to the Old Testament, Newton never claimed that any of the extant texts had been deliberately falsified. But, since he was an Arian and was convinced that the doctrine of the Trinity was *not* stated in the true revealed text, he had to hold that the lines in John and Timothy, which appear to state a Trinitarian position, were deliberately forged attempts to deceive the faithful.

From the time of the 2nd and 3rd centuries, Christian Church authorities claimed that Revelation was a late work and unconnected with Jesus's life on earth, and, therefore, not to be taken seriously. In opposition to this view, Newton contended that Revelation was the earliest work in the New Testament and that it was written before the destruction of the Temple in Jerusalem in 70 A. D. and the expulsion of the Jews from the city. Its author, John the Evangelist, received the revelation he recorded directly from Jesus and wrote it down in a style that contains many more Hebraisms than the Gospel of John (which Newton thought was written by the same person.) Therefore, Newton argued, Revelation was written when John "was newly come out of *Judea,* where he had been used to the *Syriac* tongue; and that he did not write his Gospel, till by long converse with the *Asiatick* Greeks he had left off most of the *Hebraisms.*"[50]

Newton offered a wide range of scholarly historical details to support his claim that Revelation was written in the very earliest days of Christianity. This was an old Christian view, going back before the early Church Fathers. According to the Syriac version of Revelation, it was written in the time of Nero. In the extant text itself, there are allusions to the Temple and the Holy City as still standing. Next, Newton pointed out that many false books of the Apocalypse, attributed variously to Peter, Paul, Thomas, Stephen, Elias, and Cerinthus, had appeared in ancient times in imitation of the Revelation of John. This constituted evidence that there was a true Apostolic work on the Apocalypse in the earliest days of Christianity for the others to imitate. From the possible dates of the false ones, Newton tried to date when St. John's Revelation was written.[51]

He added to these considerations some evidence that Revelation is alluded to in the Epistles to Peter and the Hebrews. Newton offered evidence showing that the same metaphors are used in each.[52] Newton did not consider the reverse possibility, namely, that their appearance in Revelation may indicate borrowings by a later author. Rather, he insisted that the text of Revelation had to precede the text of those Epistles and, hence, that it had to be a very early Christian work.[53]

Scouring materials in early Christian writings, Newton came to the conclusion that John and Peter stayed with their churches in Judaea and Syria until the Romans made war in the twelfth year of Nero's reign. John was then banished to the Greek island of Patmos. "It seems also probable to me that the *Apocalypse* was there composed, and that soon after the Epistle to the *Hebrews* and those of *Peter* were written. . . ."[54] Many writings of the Church Fathers confirmed this. As Newton says, "This account of things agrees best with history when duly rectified."[55]

If one accepts Newton's rectification, then the next question becomes, is the book of Revelation true? For Newton, the answer is yes, "since it was in such request with the first ages, that many endeavoured to imitate it",[56] and because of certain phrases in it. Christ was not called the Word of God in any book of the New Testament written before the Apocalypse.[57] All true Christians in the early days of Christianity accepted Revelation as genuine and true. Every one who believed that there would be a millennium accepted Revelation "as the foundation for their opinion."[58] The early Christian Millenarians accepted the text as genuine and most important. "I do not indeed find any other book of the New Testament so strongly attested, or commented upon so early as this."[59] Later on, for bad reasons, Christians became prejudiced against the work, in part because of the Hebraisms in it that Greek Christians did not like. So they began, in the fourth century, to doubt the genuineness or significance of the book.[60]

Newton goes on to point out that, according to Daniel 10.21 and 12.4-9, Daniel is commanded to shut up and seal the ultimate prophecy until the end of time:

> 'Tis therefore a part of this Prophecy, that it should not be understood before the last age of the world; and therefore it makes for the credit of the Prophecy, that it is not yet understood. But if the last age, the age of opening these things, be now approaching, as by the great successes of late Interpreters it seems to be, we have more encouragement than ever to look into these things.[61]

This was the context for Daniel's cryptic observation that, in the time of the end, the wise shall understand, but none of the wicked shall understand.

Newton then went on to condemn those who wanted to predict exactly when the great events forecast in Daniel and Revelation would take place. But from this text—"Amongst the Interpreters of the last age there is scarce one of note who hath not made some discovery worth knowing; and thence I seem to gather that God is about opening these mysteries"[62]—there seems to have been no doubt in Newton's mind that Revelation is the book which Daniel is commanded to shut up and seal and that it is true.

In his discussions of the state of the text of the New Testament, Newton made quite clear that he thought that there were not only normal errors in the historical transmission of the documents, but that there were also deliberate corruptions and falsifications in texts stating the doctrine of the Trinity. In sharp contrast to the corruptions of much of the New Testament, Newton believed that special protection had been given to the conservation of the text of Revelation. And, it may be of some interest that, in this view, Newton seems to hold a reverse view from that of Spinoza who declares that "the books of both Testaments were not written by express command at one place for all ages, but are a fortuitous collection of the works of men, writing each as his period and disposition dictated."[63] (Both Father Simon and Newton agreed and yet insisted that this did not preclude the writings from containing divine messages.) For Spinoza, the so-called Word of God "is faulty, mutilated, tampered with, and inconsistent; . . . we possess it only in fragments."[64] But, nonetheless what is important in both Testaments is the statement, which has "come down to us uncorrupted," of the Divine Law which is:

> To love God above all things, and one's neighbour as one's self. This cannot be a spurious passage, nor due to a hasty and mistaken scribe, for if the Bible had ever put forth a different doctrine it would have had to change the whole of its teachings, for this is the corner-stone of religion, without which the whole fabric would fall headlong to the ground.[65]

For Spinoza, the moral message of both Testaments was what was crucial. This moral message had not been changed by the history of the transmission of the texts. Spinoza's interest in the New Testament was only in the statement of the moral principle in the Gospels. He showed no interest in the book of Revelation, although it was probably the most widely interpreted Biblical book of his time.

Newton, in contrast, concentrated on the prophetic message. And in the one place where I could find an explanation of the guarantee of the accuracy of Revelation, in an unpublished note still in private hands (which is actually written by Newton on the back of an envelope and around the text of a letter to him when he was Director of the Mint), Newton explained that God was so concerned that John get the text right that he sent Jesus, the messenger of God, to watch over John as he wrote down the prophecies.[66]

Further, for Newton, it was Divine action ever since that had enabled various scholars to understand parts of the prophecies and it will be Divine action at the end of history which will make the whole of Daniel and Revelation intelligible to the wise. For Spinoza, it was solely by the use of human reason that one understood the Divine message. No matter what language it

was written in, no matter what corruptions had occurred, the Bible would contain the Divine message if it contained only the moral law which was capable of being understood by reason. And, because this moral law wasknowable by reason, it was also by reason that we could tell whether the text had become too corrupt. Spinoza writes that:

> We remain then unshaken in our belief that this has always been the doctrine of Scripture, and, consequently, that no error sufficient to vitiate it can have crept in without being instantly observed by all; nor can anyone have succeeded in tampering with it and escaped the discovery of his malice.[67]

According to Newton, some crucial texts of the New Testament had been changed deliberately and the Church had kept people from realizing this. Newton was an Arian, a denier of the doctrine of the Trinity and of the divinity of Jesus. The New Testament authorized by the Church of England contained passages in the revelation of St. John and in the letter to Timothy which appeared to justify the doctrine of the Trinity. Newton insisted that these passages were false and, furthermore, that they had been deliberately falsified. In one of the manuscripts in the Yahuda collection, he listed pages and pages of the variant readings of these texts in as many manuscripts as he could examine.[68] Here he made no effort to try to decide which of these readings was the accurate one. But, in 1690, he sent two letters to John Locke detailing his case that the doctrine of the Trinity was not in the original or early texts of the New Testament and was not the view held by the early Christians. These letters, which apparently grew out of a conversation between Newton and Locke about Trinitarianism, were intended for anonymous publication in Jean Le Clerc's *Bibliothèque universelle.* After sending them to Locke who forwarded them to Le Clerc, Newton panicked and directed Locke to withdraw them from publication, fearing that people would recognize his authorship of these heretical letters and the subsequent loss of his post at Cambridge. The letters were only published in 1754, eleven years after Le Clerc's death.[69] A more accurate text of them appeared in the fifth volume of the 1785 edition of Newton's ***Opera Omnia,*** edited by Bishop Samuel Horsley, who utilized a holograph manuscript of the letters for his edition.[70] Newton showed immense historical erudition in making out his case. In a third letter to Locke, not published until the 1961 edition of Newton's correspondence, Newton says that he has been looking over his earlier two letters and is "so far satisfied in the discoveries that it has put me upon the curiosity of enquiring whether the like corruptions may not have happened in other places, & upon search I find reason to suspect a great many more places of this kind then I expected."[71] He then gave a list of these corruptions. Newton compared all sorts of versions of the Bible, including the Ethiopic one, looking for corruptions in the text. He relied on both his own researches and those of other Bible scholars such as Grotius, Richard Simon, and Gilbert Burnet.[72]

One of the questions which Newton was most interested in was who was responsible for the changes in the Biblical text. On the basis of his study of early Church history, Newton came to the conclusion that it was primarily through the efforts of Saint Athanasius and his Trinitarian followers that the Church became corrupt and that these corrupters had altered Biblical texts and Church council records to support their anti-Christian views. There are three unpublished manuscript variants of the **"Paradoxical Questions concerning yᵉ morals & actions of Athanasius & his followers."** In all of them, Newton set forth his indictment of Saint Athanasius.[73]

In the longest unpublished manuscript on this topic, at the Bodmer Library in Geneva, Newton presented his grandiose theory of how the Church became corrupt and how it falsified the truedoctrines of Christianity, in part by tinkering with the texts of the New Testament.[74]

To pull together various threads of Newton's Bible scholarship, one can say that, with regard to the scriptural text that has come down to us, Newton, with Spinoza and Father Simon, accepted the Hebrew Text as corrupted because of various historical events. But, unlike Spinoza, and like Simon, he insisted that the text was usable. Simon says that:

> We may by this same principle easily answer all the false and pernicious consequences drawn by *Spinoza* from these alterations or additions for the running down the Authority of the Holy Scripture, as if these corrections had been purely of humane Authority; whereas he ought to have consider'd that the Authors of these alterations having had the Power of writing Holy Scripture, had also the Power of correcting them.[75]

Through careful research and evaluation, one could work out an acceptable text of the Old Testament. With regard to the New Testament, Newton insisted the text had to be rescued from the Trinitarians and restored to its pristine doctrine according to which Jesus was the Lamb of God, but was not co-substantial. Because Newton, unlike Spinoza, was convinced that the essential prophetic message of the Bible survived in the texts of Daniel and Revelation, he did not become a sceptic about religious knowledge. Newton, on the other hand, with Spinoza, thought that much of the Old Testament could be studied as an early historical document and could be evaluated in terms of our other historical data. In this way its accuracy could be determined.

The first of Newton's writings about the Bible to be published, *The Chronology of Ancient Kingdoms Amended* (London, 1728), is a most interesting effort to employ newly discovered scientific findings to evaluate the historical status of the Bible. In the mid-17th century, Archbishop James Ussher of Ireland had carefully worked out the chronology of Biblical events and had dated them from the Creation, in 4004 B. C., onward.[76] Newton, using astronomical discoveries, constructed a chronology based upon the positions of the stars described in scripture and in other ancient writings which superceded Ussher's effort. Using his astronomical method of dating, Newton came to the conclusion that the Bible was historically accurate and was the oldest historical record that we have. Scriptural history is more accurate than Greek, Phoenician, Babylonian, or Egyptian records. The earliest chronologists, Manetho and Eratosthenes, contradicted both scripture and 17th-century astronomy. In view of the fact that we do not have any records older than the Bible, there are good reasons to question the claims to great antiquity in some of the early pagan authors. We should begin, Newton said, where we can have reasonable confidence in the available data. This, he thought, involved accepting the history and chronology in the Bible up to the books of Ezra and Nehemiah, as well as accepting the astronomical records mentioned by Thucydides and Ptolemy. From the description of the stars in the constellations in the zodiac presented in accounts of the mission of Jason and the Argonauts and the events in the Trojan War, we could calculate when these events took place. The procession of various stars in these constellations was measurable and followed a uniform law. From present observations, we could calculate backward to where these stars were historically described as being and date when the stars were in the positions described in early Greek history.[77]

For Newton, the dramatic result of using this astronomical method to calculate the date of previousevents was that it showed that the earliest events described in the Bible took place *before* the earliest events in Greek history. Newton calculated that Jason's voyage took place in 937 B. C. The earliest known events in Egyptian history also postdated the earliest Biblical events. Therefore, our earliest historical knowledge came from the Bible. The ancient Israelites were the first civilization and had the first monarchy. All other cultures and kingdoms, Newton declared, were derivative from the original Hebrew one.[78]

Newton's elaborate astronomical argument and his debunking of pagan chronological and historical claims aimed to show that the Bible was accurate as history, no matter how corrupted the text had become over the years. And, assumed Newton, the message in the Bible was still of the greatest importance to mankind. The fact that the Bible was accurate historically meant that God had presented His message from the very beginning of the world through the history of the Hebrews and through the prophetic insights given to them. (This, of course, was another major difference between Newton and Spinoza. Spinoza contended from the beginning of the *Tractatus Theologico-Politicus* that the prophets did not have any special information, only very vivid imaginations.[79] For Newton, in contrast, the prophetic material was the most important element in the Bible and definitely contained divinely revealed information if only it could be understood.)

As I have discussed in "Newton and Fundamentalism, II" (infra), A. S. Yahuda, the renowned Arabist who purchased the majority of Newton's unpublished writings on religion and theology when they were auctioned off at Sotheby's in 1936, did so in part because he had his own "proof" of the accuracy of the Bible about which he was lecturing and writing in England at the time. Yahuda contended that the story of the Exodus had to have been written by an eyewitness because so many Egyptian terms appear in it. Israelites of subsequent generations would no longer have known Egyptian. (Various Egyptologists immediately challenged Yahuda's theory.)[80] Apparently, one of the motives for Yahuda's purchase of the Newton material was to see if Newton had other evidence to establish the accuracy of the Bible. Yahuda's notes, written on Newton's manuscripts, and his own unfinished essay on Newton's religious views showed that Yahuda, a 20th-century scholar trained in the world of German Higher Criticism of the Bible and in the best methods of historical scholarship, felt a strong affinity with Newton in trying to establish some meaningful sense in which it could be said that the Bible was accurate.[81] (I have been told by an eyewitness that Yahuda's close friend, Albert Einstein, was present when Yahuda first advanced his theory and that Einstein wept with joy when he heard that one could establish the accuracy of the Bible on the basis of historical and philological research.)

For Newton, once one accepted that the Bible was accurate in a significant sense, then one could use materials contained in it to explain the origins of mankind, of human institutions, and of human social and cultural abilities, for example, writing. Newton left a lot of manuscripts on these subjects. He was also convinced that one could find some basic understanding of the universe in the plans God laid down for building Solomon's Temple, a microcosm of the macrocosm. Newton's essay on the sacred cubit of the Hebrews and his analysis of the construction of the Temple show that he was sure that there was a mystical architecture in its dimensions that explained God's total dominion over all of creation.

But the most important idea to be gleaned from an analysis of the Biblical records, for Newton, was that God laid down a plan of human history, as well as a plan for natural history. One studied the latter primarily in terms of studying the Book of Nature through scientific researches. The former, the plan of human history, must be studied in the central prophetic statements about the course of human history put forth in Daniel and Revelation. No matter what the textual problems about these texts may be, these two works were continuous and united and presented in cryptic form a blueprint of what would happen to mankind up to the apocalyptic end of human history.

To those who question whether Daniel and Revelation contain the core of God's message, Newton replies: why would God have provided so many clues to mankind, in the form of prophetic symbols, if we are not supposed to figure them out?[82] To repeat, Daniel tells us that the wise will understand and that the wicked will not near the end of time. So, if one could not find a message, this indicated one's own moral deficiencies or, perhaps, that the end was not quite yet, rather than the absence of a message.[83]

The message contained in the prophetic writings, Newton contended, was confirmed by carefully examining human history from the time of the writing of Daniel onward. And, Newton insisted, much of what had happened was an exact fulfillment of the prophecies set forth in these works. All during his adult life, Newton was writing definitive explications of Daniel and Revelation, building upon what scholars such as Joseph Mede, Isaac Barrow, and Henry More had written. (Newton came to a bitter disagreement with More around 1680 about how to interpret the opening passage in Revelation.)

Newton did a great deal of original historical research to discern the events in world history which constituted the fulfillment of the prophecies. Some of his interpretations have been accepted by later Bible interpreters, especially among the fundamentalists. Newton studied the history of the Roman Empire, the European Middle Ages, and the rise of Islam in the Middle East in order to identify what actually happened in history with what was predicted in prophecy.

Newton differed from many of those who had worked on the interpretation of prophecies in denying that we could or should figure out exactly when the climactic events in world history would occur, when Jesus would return, when the Jews would return to Palestine and rebuild Jerusalem, etc. Newton, in a famous passage, declared that God had not intended people to be prophets. What people *could* do was recognize after the fact that events which had occurred were in fact those previously predicted in the prophecies. This post facto reading of history would demonstrate that the course of historical events was divinely providential. God had laid out the whole sequence. We, in studying history, could realize that this was the case as we recognized that each major event which happened had already been forecast in the prophetic writings.[84] When we realized this, we should be in awe of God's dominion over our history, as well as over nature, and we should realize that, in studying the scriptural text, we were also learning what events remained to be fulfilled before the end of human and natural history.

Newton opposed the prophetic seers of his day who were continually announcing the exact moment of the end of the world. In contrast, Newton offered a theory of the progressive development of our understanding of the prophecies. As we approach the end of history, "Then, saith Daniel, many shall run to and fro, and knowledge shall be increased." But, Newton continues, "'Tis therefore a part of this Prophecy that it should not be understood before the last age of the world; and therefore it makes for the credit of the Prophecy, that it is not yet understood."[85] Newton took the progress made in the 17th century in interpreting Biblical prophecies by Joseph Mede and his followers (including Newton himself), as a clear sign that we might be approaching the time of the end. It is at this point in his **Observations** that Newton condemns those who predict the end with precision, as if they are themselves prophets, and says, "The folly of Interpreters has been, to foretel times and things by this Prophecy, as if God designed to make them Prophets. By this rashness they not only exposed themselves, but brought Prophecy also into contempt."[86] So, people should restrain themselves and devote themselves to *post facto* interpretations of events in terms of the prophecies. In so doing, we would realize the on-going fulfillment of the prophecies and might be able to say, with Newton, "I seem to gather that God is about opening these mysteries."[87] The world to come prophesied in the Bible was near fruition.

Newton's conception of the Bible was that it was a historical document and a cryptogram containing God's historical plan. The historical document was as open to critical examination as any other historical document. Critical investigations of the sort offered by Spinoza and Simon helped us to realize the defects in the documents and enabled us to assess them. Using historical standards and modern scientific information about the movements of the stars in history enabled us to determine that the Bible was the oldest historical document which we possessed. And, except for parts of the New Testament, it had been preserved fairly well. The Bible was the most accurate account we possessed about early human history.

But, for Newton, in contrast to Spinoza, the Bible was more than just a historical document. It was the way in which God had communicated to us in the Book of Words and was analogous to the way God had communicated to us in the Book of Nature. Tremendous effort, insight, and pious attention were needed to understand the natural and verbal messages. Science and the study of Biblical prophecy went hand in hand as ways of comprehending God's message. Progress in science and progress in deciphering Daniel and Revelation indicated that God was opening the seals, thereby gradually and progressively unfolding to us the nature and destiny of man. Newton's role in this process of progressive understanding was to be in the forefront of those decoding both Nature and scripture.

Newton as a Bible scholar used the techniques of Spinoza and Simon and accepted a similar view about how the surviving text developed. But, he did not accept Spinoza's doubts about the Divine character of the Bible, regardless of its fortunes in human history as a document. Newton broke new interpretive ground both in the application of modern scientific techniques to the understanding of the Bible and in the historical interpretation of prophecies. Newton attempted to provide a better basis for dating ancient literature through astronomical events. Of course, his method has been superceded by archaeological and anthropological techniques. Those dating the events in the Bible, and dating events in other cultures by these means, would no longer support Newton's conclusion that the Biblical world is the most ancient part of human history.

Newton's historical research into the interpretation of historically fulfilled prophecies was taken over by many 19th-century fundamentalists who regarded him as one of the very best in this field. When the various components of Newton's Bible scholarship are examined and evaluated, he can indeed be seen to be in the forefront of the critical scholarship of his time, in the forefront in applying modern science to understanding the Bible, and in the forefront of those offering new historical data for interpreting prophecies. Because many of those who devoted themselves to the first two ventures became sceptical of traditional religions in the manner of Spinoza, it is at first hard to fathom how Newton managed to be so serious about the third venture. Perhaps if he is seen in terms of *both* 17th-century Biblical criticism *and* 17th-century Millenarianism, we can better appreciate the nature of his theological position and his contribution to theology. Perhaps, when his theological manuscripts have been published, we will be able to assess more accurately his entire theory and see his originality and his stature as a commentator on the scriptures. We will then be able to see if he was as great a thinker in this area as he was in the sciences.

Notes

[1] For the biographical details about Newton's intellectual life, see Richard S. Westfall, *Never at Rest. A Biography of Isaac Newton* (Cambridge: Cambridge University Press, 1980.)

[2] Isaac Newton, *The Chronology of Ancient Kingdoms Amended* (London, 1728.)

[3] Newton, *Observations upon the Prophecies of Daniel, and the Apocalypse of St. John* (London, 1733.)

[4] Newton, "A Dissertation upon the Sacred *Cubit* of the Jews and the *Cubits* of the several Nations; in which from the Dimensions of the Greatest Pyramid, as taken by Mr John Greaves, the Antient Cubit of Memphis is Determined," in *Miscellaneous Works of John Greaves,* ed. Thomas Birch (London, 1737), Vol. II, pp. 405-33.

[5] Newton, *Two Letters of Sir Isaac Newton to Mr Le Clerc* (London, 1754.)

[6] In *The Correspondence of Isaac Newton,* ed. H. W. Turnbull (Cambridge: Cambridge University Press, 1961), Vol. 3, pp. 83-146.

[7] No complete list exists. Richard Westfall has prepared an unpublished inventory covering almost all of what is known to exist, though some items are still in private hands. I have found a few items not in Westfall's inventory. The unpublished papers were auctioned off at Sotheby's in 1936. These are listed in the *Catalogue of the Newton Papers Sold by Order of the Viscount Lymington to whom they have descended from Catherine Conduitt, Viscountess Lymington, Great-Niece of Sir Isaac Newton. Which will be Sold by Auction by Messrs. Sotheby and Co. . . . At their Large Galleries, 34 & 35 New Bond Street W.1. On Monday, July 13th, 1936, and Following Day, at One O'clock Precisely* (London, 1936.)

[8] The majority of Newton's theological manuscripts belonged to the collection of Abraham Shalom Yahuda, a wealthy Palestinian Jew, who became a professor of medieval Judaism and of Arabic in Spain and Germany. He moved to England when Hitler came to power. He had an enormous collection of manuscripts, including his purchases of most of Newton's theological writings. In 1940, he moved to the United States, where he lived until his death in 1951. He and his friend, AlbertEinstein, tried to get Harvard, Yale, or Princeton to take the Newton papers. All of them refused. On his death-bed, although he was a strong anti-Zionist, he decided to leave the papers to the National Library of Israel. Due to legal disputes about his will, the Yahuda papers only got sent to Jerusalem in 1969, where they are now available for public examination by scholars.

[9] Frank E. Manuel, *The Religion of Isaac Newton* (Oxford: Clarendon Press, 1974), Appendix A, "Fragments from a Treatise on Revelation," pp. 107-25.

[10] *Ibid.,* p. 118.

[11] Yahuda MS 1.1, f. 19v.

[12] Among other works by Richard Simon, Newton possessed in his library a copy of Simon's *A Critical History of the Old Testament . . . Translated into English, by a person of quality* (London, 1682.) He also owned some of the works of the time whose authors were critical of Simon's position.

[13] See, for example, the discussion of Simon's impact in England in Louis I. Bredvold, *The Intellectual Milieu of John Dryden* (Ann Arbor: University of Michigan Press, 1959), esp. pp. 98-107.

[14] See "The Author's Preface," in Simon, *A Critical History of the Old Testament.*

[15] Cf. Manuel, *The Religion of Isaac Newton,* p. 84.

[16] Cudworth offered his criticism of Spinoza in Part V of *The True Intellectual System of the Universe,* which was completed in 1671 and published in London in 1678. More wrote two essays against Spinoza, one a letter to Lady Anne Conway, the other, some demonstrations against Spinoza's atheism. These are published in Henry More, *Opera Omnia* (London, 1679), Vol. 1, pp. 565-614 and 615-35. More's letter to Robert Boyle, written soon after Spinoza's *Tractatus* appeared, shows that More was very upset by the work. See *The Works of the Honourable Robert Boyle* (London, 1772), Vol. 6, p. 514.

[17] Newton, *Observations,* Part I, chap. 1.

[18] *Ibid.,* pp. 1-15.

[19] *Ibid.,* p. 4.

[20] *Ibid.,* p. 5.

[21] *Ibid.*

[22] *Ibid.,* p. 6.

[23] *Ibid.,* p. 6.

[24] *Ibid.,* p. 7.

[25] *Ibid.,* p. 9.

[26] *Ibid.,* pp. 9-10.

[27] *Ibid.,* p. 10.

[28] *Ibid.*

[29] *Ibid.,* p. 11.

[30] Benedict de Spinoza, *Theologico-Political Treatise,* chap. 8, in *The Chief Works of Benedict de Spinoza,* trans. R. H. M. Elwes, 2 vols. (New York: Dover, 1965), p. 125. (This English translation of Spinoza's work is

cited hereafter as *Treatise.*) Cf. Spinoza, *Tractatus Theologico-Politicus,* ed. Carl Gebhardt, 4 vols. (Heidelberg: Carl Winter, 1926), 2:125. (This Latin edition of Spinoza's work is cited hereafter as *Tractatus.*)

[31] Spinoza, *Treatise,* chap. 8, pp. 129-30. Cf. *Tractatus,* p. 126.

[32] Spinoza, *Treatise,* chap. 9, p. 135. Cf. *Tractatus,* p. 135.

[33] Isaac La Peyrère, *Men Before Adam* (London, 1656), Book IV, p. 208.

[34] Spinoza, *Treatise,* chap. 12, pp. 165-6; Cf. *Tractatus,* pp. 158-9.

[35] For Simon's account, see his *A Critical History of the Old Testament,* Book I, chaps. 1-8.

[36] See Richard H. Popkin, *Isaac La Peyrère (1596-1676). His Life, Work and Influence* (Leiden: Brill, 1987), chap. 4.

[37] Spinoza, *Treatise,* chaps. 5-10.

[38] Richard Simon, "The Author's Preface" and Book I, chap. 5, pp. 249-50, in *A Critical History of the Old Testament.*

[39] Newton, *Observations,* pp. 13-5.

[40] *Ibid.,* p. 11.

[41] *Ibid.*

[42] Yahuda MS 7.3 and 10B.

[43] Newton, *Observations,* p. 11.

[44] *Ibid.,* p. 12.

[45] *The Confession of Faith . . . composed by the Reverend Assembly of Divines sitting at Westminster* (London, 1658), chap. 1, p. 6.

[46] Bishop Gilbert Burnet also rejected the claim in the Westminster Confession and offered a view much like that of Newton. In Burnet's *An Exposition of the Thirty-Nine Articles of the Church of England* (London, 1699), he explained how the Biblical text could have become corrupted through the copying process. All sorts of mistakes, additions, and deletions may have occurred: "There is no reason to think that every Copier was so divinely guided, that no small Error might surprize him. In Fact, we know that there are many various Readings, which might have arisen from the haste and carelessness of Copiers, from their guessing wrong that which which appeared doubtful or imperfect in the Copy, and from superstitious adhering to some apparent Faults, when they found them in Copies of a Venerable Antiquity." Nonetheless, Burnet also says that the texts "are preserved pure down to us, as to all those thing for which they were written; that is, in every thing that is either an Object of Faith, or a Rule of Life." (p. 86) So all of the corruptions and errors in various manuscripts do not matter.

[47] Newton, *Observations,* p. 14.

[48] *Ibid.,* p. 15.

[49] Three unpublished manuscripts by Newton deal with his charges against St. Athanasius. See note 73.

[50] Newton, *Observations,* Part II, chap. 1, p. 238.

[51] *Ibid.,* pp. 238-9.
[52] *Ibid.,* pp. 239-40.

[53] *Ibid.,* p. 244.

[54] *Ibid.*

[55] *Ibid.,* p. 245.

[56] *Ibid.,* p. 246.

[57] *Ibid.,* p. 247.

[58] *Ibid.,* p. 248.

[59] *Ibid.,* p. 249.

[60] *Ibid.*

[61] *Ibid.,* pp. 250-1.

[62] *Ibid.,* p. 253.

[63] Spinoza, *Treatise,* chap. 12, p. 170. Cf. *Tractatus,* p. 163.

[64] *Treatise,* chap. 12, p. 165. Cf. *Tractatus,* pp. 158-9.

[65] *Treatise,* chap. 12, p. 172. Cf. *Tractatus,* pp. 164-5.

[66] In this manuscript, written in the early 18th century, Newton said that the historical parts of scripture were written with the ordinary assistance of the Spirit, which the prophets had at all times. The prophetic sections involved special impulses of the Spirit, which the prophets only had on certain occasions. St. John wrote "his Apocalyps when Christ sent his messenger to him with that prophecy. He had y[t] spirit at all times, but not in that extraordinary manner w[ch] made him say that he was in the spirit of the Lord."

[67] Spinoza, *Treatise,* chap. 12, p. 172. Cf. *Tractatus,* p. 165.

[68] Yahuda MS 1.4

[69] On the history of the publication of *Two Letters of Sir Isaac Newton to Mr Le Clerc,* see Westfall, *Never at Rest,* pp. 489-91.

[70] *Isaaci Newton opera quae existant omnia,* 5 vols. (London, 1779-85), vol. 5.

[71] Newton, *Correspondence,* 3:144-5.

[72] *Ibid.,* pp. 145-6. Discussing the manuscripts that did not contain the vital text from John, Newton adds in his letters to John Locke that "Dr. Gilb. Burnett has lately in the first letters of his Travelles noted it wanting in five other ancient ones kept at Strasburg, Zurich & Basil, one of wch MSS he reccons about 1000 years old & ye other about 800." Newton, *Correspondence,* 3:94. Newton's reference to Gilbert's "Travelles" is to Burnet's *Some Letters concerning an Account of what seemed most remarkable in Switzerland, Italy, etc.,* first published in Rotterdam by Abraham Archer in 1687. Burnet begins his discussion of manuscripts he has examined by noting that "I have taken some Pains in my Travels to examine all the most ancient Manuscripts of the New Testament, concerning that doubted Passage of St. John's Epistles." (p. 49) Burnet then discussed manuscripts he had examined in Zurich, Venice, Florence, Basel, Strasbourg, Rome, and London which did not have the passage in question. (pp. 49-51)

Newton says "And by the best enquiry y^t I have been able to make [i.e., regarding the Trinitarian passage in John] it is wanting in the manuscripts of all Languages but the Latine." Newton says that it is not the in the Ethiopic, Syriac, Arabic, Armenian, or Slavonic versions and that he has been toldthat "it is not in the Greek mss in Turkey." *correspondence,* 3:94. Newton's evidence is all second hand from Erasmus, Burnet, Simon, and others. He apparently did not even check the London manuscript at St. James's that Burnet mentioned.

[73] There are three variant manuscripts relating to the "Paradoxical questions concerning ye morals & actions of Athanasius & his followers." One is located in the William Andrews Clark Memorial Library, Los Angeles. One (Keynes 10) is in the King's College Library, Cambridge. And one Yahuda MS 14) is in the Yahuda Collection, Jerusalem. Bishop Burnet, who, as we have seen, checked various manuscripts and reported that the crucial Trinitarian text was missing in the gospel of John, did not draw Newton's anti-Trinitarian conclusion. In his *Exposition of the Thirty-Nine Articles,* he says that, with regard to Article One about the

Trinity, "I do not insist on that contested Passage of *St. John's* Epistle. There are great doubtings made about it: The main ground for doubting being the Silence of the Fathers, who never made use of it in the Disputes with the *Arrians* and *Macedonians.* There are very considerable things urged on the other hand, to support the Authority of that Passage; yet I think it is safer to build upon sure and undisputable grounds. So I leave it to be maintained by others who are more fully persuaded of its being Authentical. There is no need of it. This matter is capable of a very full Proof, whether that Passage is believed to be a part of the Canon, or not." (p. 40)

Burnet's "proof" was that the Trinitarian view was accepted by the Church long before the Council of Nicaea. All that the Nicene Council did was make official what was already the Faith of the Church "with the addition only of the Word *Consubstantial.*" (p. 40) This particular word was, of course, the heart of what was in dispute between Arians and the Trinitarians.

Burnet was immediately accused of Arianism when his "Travelles" appeared in 1687 with his account of what he had found, or rather had not found, in his examination of ancient manuscripts throughout Europe. Antonie Varillas asks, in his *Reflexions on Dr. Gilbert Burnet's Travels into Swizerland, Italy, and certain parts of Germany and France* (London, 1688), "Were so many Copiers therefore exact in every thing else, and did they, through negligence, fail in the Translation of this onely Passage; or did they commit an errour by joint consent? Nevertheless I do not say this much to defend Arrianism, which is not indeed my sentiment, but to shew the cunningness and malignity of our Author, who (as many others have done) seem to oppose that Sect with such weak Arguments, on purpose to establish it the better." (p. 48)

In answer to Varillas, Burnet, in his *Dr. Burnet's Vindication of Himself from the Calumnies with which he is aspersed,* in *A Second Collection of Several Tracts and Discourses written in the Years 1686, 1687, 1688, 1689* (London, 1689), replies that his opponent "represents me as an Enemy to the Divinity of *Jesus Christ,* because of the various readings of a verse in St. *John's Epistle,* that I gave from some Ancient *Manuscripts,* which I saw in my *Travels.*" (p. 186) Burnet points out that all the Church Fathers who write against the Arians accept the doctrine of the Trinity, but do *not* cite the passage in question from John, "from which it was reasonable to conclude, that it was not in their Bibles; otherwise it is not to be imagined, that such men as St. *Athanase* and St. *Austin,* should not have mentioned it." Burnet says he believes in the *"Divinity of the Saviour of the World,"* whether the passage be legitimate or not. Over the years, Burnet went on, he had continued to check Bible manuscripts he had come across to see if the passage turned up. It had not. Even so, writes Gilbert, he has "given the account of what I saw sincerely. . . . For I have learned from *Job, not to lye for God,* since truth needs no support from falshood." (p. 187) Burnet, in contrast to Newton, claimed that he held the view that the Divine Savior was equal with God the Father. Further examination of Burnet's theology may show that he was closer to Newton's view than he admitted in public.

[74] This manuscript is a history of the development of the Christian religion and the institutional church.

[75] Simon, "The Author's Preface," in *A Critical History of the Old Testament,* p. (a)2.

[76] On Ussher's achievement, see Hugh Trevor-Roper, "James Ussher, Archbishop of Armagh," in *Catholics, Anglicans and Puritans. Seventeenth Century Essays,* chap. 3.

[77] Newton's method and his achievements with it are described and analyzed in Frank E. Manuel, *Isaac Newton, Historian* (Cambridge, Mass.: Harvard University Press, 1963), esp. chap. 4.

[78] Manuel, *Isaac Newton, Historian,* chaps. 5-6.

[79] Spinoza, *Treatise,* chaps. 1-2.

[80] Yahuda's theories were criticized by such leading Egyptologists as Professor Wilhelm Speigelberg, the father of Herbert Speigelberg.

[81] See Richard H. Popkin, "Newton and Fundamentalism, II," infra.

[82] Newton, *Observations,* pp. 252-3.

[83] Newton, Yahuda MS 1.1, f. 19v.

[84] Newton, *Observations,* pp. 251-2.

[85] *Ibid.,* pp. 250-1.

[86] *Ibid.,* p. 251.

[87] *Ibid.,* p. 253.

J. E. McGuire (essay date 1990)

SOURCE: "Predicates of Pure Existence: Newton on God's Space and Time," in *Philosophical Perspectives on Newtonian Science,* edited by Phillip Bricker and R. I. G. Hugues, MIT Press, 1990.

[*In the following essay, McGuire examines the relation of time and space to divine existence, as discussed by Newton in his theological writings.*]

Some years ago I argued that Newton's doctrine of absolute space and time is motivated by his view of the existence of a divine being.[1] In the course of this study I advance the opinion that Newton attempts "to distance" space and time from divine essence. In effect, I argue that Newton links the infinity of space and time to divine existence, which he then associates with the actuality of God and not directly with his essence. Here I wish to return to this view in the light of further thinking and in response to some of John Carriero's observations on my earlier views. Also, I want to reconsider my claim that Newton's conception of how space and time relate to God's existence is not an instance of causal dependence. I think now with Carriero that the dependence may be taken as causal, but, if this is so, the distinction between ontic (my earlier view) and causal dependence is extremely attenuated indeed. If I spell out my agreements and disagreements with Carriero's commentary, I do so not to have the last word but to advance the dialogue.

The first part of this study deals with the nature of Newton's religious sentiment and its associated theological framework. The second considers the metaphysical position that these views engender and its implication.

i. God and Worship: The Theology of a Living God

An obvious fact about Newton is the pious and biblical nature of his religious experience. To follow the Christian dispensation is to give unwavering obedience to the commandments of God. Moreover, it is our duty to seek knowledge of God from the evidence of his works: in this way we give him honor for the glory and design of creation. It is true, as Manuel claims, that Newton distrusts the conceits of abstract metaphysical theology.[2] It is wrong, however, to suppose that he avoids altogether the theological implications of his religious views. In a manuscript of the early 1690s, which I entitle "Tempus et Locus," this "theological turn" is made abundantly clear.[3] The manuscript indicates Newton's particular theological approach to questions concerning the religious experience of God. It shows, moreover, that a close relationship obtains for Newton between his view of the existence of God and his conception of absolute space and time. Furthermore, the manuscript provides understanding of the motives that inform Newton's conception of God's existence. In turn, these motives help to clarify the implications of his conception of divine presence in relation to his views on the nature of space, time, and creation.

Even a casual reading of the manuscript indicates that Newton conceives God as a real person and not as an abstract metaphysical being. God is a living, intelligent, and powerful agent who always and everywhere exists. He is likened to an absolute king who freely decrees the law to all created things. To think of God as existing beyond space and time is an unduly abstract conception. It is not easily comprehended by the mind and fails to promote suitable attitudes of worship (pp. 121-123). In the first draft of the manuscript Newton in fact characterizes abstract conceptions of God as arising "ex Scholasticorum disputationibus." The reference is of course meant to be pejorative. And in fact the metaphysical views of God found in the writings of many Scholastics do indeed differ from Newton's. Newton's God is a biblical God of dominion whose immediate presence in nature purposively enacts the destiny of all created things. Thus providence is directly grounded in divineuniquity and omnipresence. And God, in virtue of his actual presence in space and time, is "able to act in all times & places for creating and governing the Universe."[4]

In developing the details of his theological position in "Tempus et Locus," Newton rhetorically juxtaposes eight contrasting opinions concerning divine nature. In each case it is the second opinion that he supports, and for which he urges acceptance. They constitute an interesting set and go beyond anything he had previously written.

First, Newton rejects the view that God's existence is "all at once," as expressed by the phrase *totum simul.* That is, he affirms that God's existence can be characterized by successiveness and the temporality of earlier and later. Indeed he calls God's life by the name "He that was and is and is to come" (p. 121). Thus in Newton's conception God's existence is sempiternal; for there is no time past, present, or future at which God does not exist. This view is also expressed in the **Principia** (1687): "Since every particle of space is *always,* and every indivisible moment of duration is *everywhere,* certainly the Maker and Lord of all things cannot be *never* and *nowhere.*"[5] Accordingly, God does not exist in a timeless present; he endures in unending time, his living existence devoid of beginning and end.

That Newton does not conceive God's existence as timeless is supported by two further passages. In a draft variant to the General Scholium he states: "His duration is not a *nunc stans* without duration, nor is his presence nowhere." He writes to Des Maizeaux in a similar vein in 1717: "The Schoolmen made a *Nunc stans* to be eternity & by consequence an attribute of God & eternal duration hath a better title to that name, though it be but a mode of his existence. For a *nunc stans* is a moment wch always is & yet never was nor will be; which is a contradiction in terms."[6] Thus, for Newton, God's living existence is irreducibly durational. To think of him as existing in a *nunc stans*—a stationary and timeless now—is to deny that he exists. For Newton the actuality of anything that exists must be successive and involve time: "What is never and nowhere, it is not in *rerum natura*" ("Tempus et

Locus," p. 117). Furthermore, the conception of a "stationary and timeless now" is for Newton contradictory. What would it be like, Newton seems to ask, to exist in a timeless moment? Can anything be said actually to exist in an unchanging and indivisible moment? Do we have a coherent conception of an unchanging "now" which always is? For Newton this sort of talk is parasitic on the tense structure of language. It has significance only if it is contrasted with what was and what will be. Thus, those who use the phrase *nunc stans* to refer to the mode of God's existence, are covertly employing tensed forms of *is* while pretending that tensed expressions are inappropriate to the manner of divine being. According to Newton, then, although the phrase is meant to capture a timeless mode of existence, it in fact implies temporal devices. For Newton it is best to conceive God's existence as sempiternal, since the mind can grasp this notion. Moreover, it is a coherent notion, and accords better with the biblical conception of divine existence, where divine presence is not unambiguously debarred from temporality. An apologist is hard-pressed (as Newton well knew) to find biblical passages that straightforwardly support a conception of God's existence in terms of the phrases *totum simul* and *nunc stans.*

The conception of eternity that Newton rejects has its first systematic articulation in Plotinus' *Ennead* III.7.[7] In the West, the doctrine of eternity as the eternal "now," which derives from Plotinus' treatise on eternity and time, appears in the writings of Augustine and Boethius, and through themthe *nunc stans* and *totum simul* of eternity pass into medieval and subsequent thought. To any thinker of Plotinus' sensibility the notion of an eternal life apart from duration and change is neither self-contradictory nor incoherent, nor does the use of temporal language imply any duration or temporalization of eternity. Plotinus himself makes use of Aristotle's conception of ἐνεργείᾳ in articulating his notion of the durationess and eternal life of νοῦς. At *Metaphysics* θ. 1048b. 21-23, Aristotle distinguishes between two sorts of actuality (which he calls κίνησις and πρᾶξις) the first sort *has* an end or τέλος, while the second sort *is* an end. Seeing, for example, is an activity of the latter sort. As such, it cannot be analyzed into stages leading to its actualization, since it is by its nature complete at every point. Hence, in a complete activity like seeing, which is itself an end, there is no distinction between coming to activate a potential for seeing and the completion of this activation. Hence no duration need be involved in such an activity: its actualization is instantaneous. This Aristotelian notion of ἐνεργείᾳ is clearly the model for Plotinus' conception of the eternal life of νοῦς, and he seems right to suggest that there need be nothing intrinsically durational or temporal about it.

This Plotinian view of the eternal ζωή is deeply antithetical to Newton's anthropomorphic conception of divine nature. In Newton's view a deity worthy of human worship must exist in the world actually, substantially, and intimately. God must therefore be able to exist at all times and in all places and possess an intelligent life that literally exists through unending duration. For Newton this view cannot be captured by the atemporal notion of duration implied by the *nunc stans* doctrine, nor, of course, by the view that God exists supratemporally. In Newton's eyes his conception alone provides proper motivation for Christian belief and worship, and coheres with the biblical view of God as an individual person who is able to act intentionally and purposively in nature, and providentially through history. In the second section I return to Newton's anthropomorphic account of God, in particular to his attempt to envision God according to the same composition of essence and existence that holds of finite things. There is a clear connection between this view and Newton's conception of how space and time relate to divine existence.

Newton also believes that God exists literally in infinite space. This means two things. Considered from the perspective of his living existence, God is said to exist necessarily in every place at all times whatsoever: but considered by virtue of his individual nature, God's immensity and omnipresence have reference to space itself. Of God's existence in all places whatsoever, Newton says in his Twelve Articles of faith: "The Father is immovable, no place being capable of becoming emptier or fuller of him than it is by the eternal necessity of nature. All other beings are movable from place to place."[8] Essentially the same is said in the Yahuda manuscript: "For God is alike in all places, He is substantially omnipresent, and as much present in the lowest Hell as in the highest heaven."[9] God's existence is thus without limitation in every place of space, for space itself is in fact infinite.

But God does not merely exist sempiternally in infinite space. According to Newton, it is appropriate to his supreme perfections that he is always active. Thus, God can and does act in space and through time. In a draft fragment to the first version of the "Tempus et Locus" manuscript Newton asks approvingly "whether the Prophets more correctly say that God is present absolutely in all places, and constantly sets in motion the bodies contained in them acording to mathematical laws, except where it is to the good to violate those laws."[10] A related view appears in a late draft version of the scholium on space and time of the ***Principia*** (1687). After remarking (in a passage that later appears in print) on the difficulty of distinguishing true from apparent motions with respect to the parts of absolute space, Newton begins but does not finish the following sentence: "Solus enim Deus, qui singulis immobiliter et insensibiliter." Following Cohen's interpretation, and the context of the passage, the sentence may reasonably be completed as follows: "For

God alone, who [gives motion to] individual [bodies] without moving and without being perceived, [can truly distinguish true motions from apparent]."[11] Thus, not only does God exist in infinite space, and not only is he immediately present in all created things, but he can act directly on things that exist in the vast receptacle of space; for "all spaces are and always have been equally capacious of containing things" ("Tempus et Locus," p. 121). In Newton's view, God's creative power is clearly unrestricted in scope. He is not limited to creating the present world, so long as logical impossibilities are not in question. For God cannot do what is impossible (undo what is done), any more than he can do anything that implies an imperfection (for example, lie or deceive).

Given these commitments, it is not surprising that Newton claims God "is omnipresent not *virtually* only, but also *substantially;* for power cannot subsist without substance. In him are all things contained and moved; yet neither affects the other: God suffers nothing from the motion of bodies; bodies find no resistance from the omnipresence of God."[12] This is a characteristic expression of Newton's conception of divine omnipresence. In "Tempus et Locus" he states unambiguously that the infinity of God's space is the expression of his "eternal omnipresence" (p. 121). Because he actually and substantially exists in infinite space, God can act in and at every place. The Cartesian conception of a God who is everywhere according to power, but nowhere as to essence and substance, is for Newton a nonbiblical God who is beyond nature (p. 121). To Newton's mind this view implies that God is present in his creation only as its ultimate and remote causal ground. But for Newton, God's power, substance, and essence are inseparable, and he acts where he is, namely, everywhere.

Newton also conceives God's immensity in a literal sense. In **"De Gravitatione"** he speaks of God's "quantity of existence" as infinite with respect to absolute space. This is clearly a conception of divine immensity.[13] By virtue of this notion Newton conceives the immensity of divine existence as unlimited, for it implies that if God should fail (*per impossibile*) to exist in any particular place, his quantity of existence would be diminished, and his individual presence thus limited. Newton attempts to preclude this consequence by denying the possibility "that a dwarf-god should fill only a tiny part of infinite space with this visible world created by him" (p. 121). In Newton's mind there is a close conceptual link between divine omnipresence and the conception of spiritual immensity. God is actually everywhere by virtue of his existence in infinite space, and in every place he wills everything that he thinks fit to choose. The immensity of God's omnipresence is manifested through his real presence in this created world and in the fact that he exists beyond it.

To distinguish God from space, Newton uses the Hebrew term *makom* in "Tempus et Locus" in speaking of divine omnipresence. The term is also used in the same context and for the same purpose in Newton's *Advertissement au lecteur,* which he sent to Des Maizeaux: "So when the Hebrews called God *MAKOM* place, the place in wch we live & move & have our being [they] did not mean that space is God in a literal sense."[14] Newton's use of *makom* is meant to convey the point that God dwells *in* space, not that space itself is a property of God's nature. This view is also conveyed in another passage. In the "classical scholia" intended for the unimplemented edition of the *Principia* (which was in preparation in the early 1690s—the same period as the present manuscript), Newton copies from Macrobius the sentence "The entire universe was rightly designated the Temple of God." He comments: "This one God they [the ancients] would have it dwelt in all bodies whatsoever as in his own temple, and hence they shaped ancient temples in the manner of the heavens."[15] It is clear that these figures are meant to invoke a sense of God's direct omnipresence throughout the created world. In Newton's use, *makom* is to some extent detached from its contexts in Jewish mystical and Cabalistic thinking. Moreover, his manner of using it differs in certain respects from that of Henry Moore, Samual Clarke, and Joseph Raphson.[16]

Newton's conception of God as an in-dwelling spirit omnipresent in the world is not pantheistic. That this is his view is clear in a manuscript intended for an unimplemented second edition of the *Principia* in the 1690s. Newton writes: "Those ancients who more rightly held unimpaired the mystical philosophy as Thales and the Stoics, taught that a certain infinite spirit pervades all space *into infinity,* and contains and vivifies the entire world. And this spirit was their supreme divinity, according to the Poet cited by the Apostle. In him we live and move and have our being."[17] Also a footnote in the General Scholium to the phrase "in him are all things contained and moved" refers to Cicero, Virgil, Philo, Aratus, and to "the sacred writers" from both the New and the Old Testaments.[18] The citations to their writings that Newton gives in each case reveal commitment to the notion of a divine mind, spirit, or life permeating and interpenetrating the cosmos, but in no way identified with space, time, or creation.

I have covered this material in detail to give as clear a picture as possible of Newton's theological conception of the nature and existence of God. "Tempus et Locus" also deals with the traditional attributes of divinity. God is said to be a necessary being, necessarily existing in all times and places. Moreover, Newton mentions three central attributes: eternity, omniscience, and omnipotence. It is not these characteristics that he is concerned to stress, however. God's nature is, of course, simple and indivisible. But more important in Newton's mind is the conception of God as an agent who is preeminently free to act in accordance with the perfections of his nature; he is truly alive, the maker and sustainer of life; he is an intelligent being who brings about "all things that are best and accord most with reason"; he has an immediate understanding and control of all things "just as the cognitive part of man perceives the form of things brought into the brain"; he is directly in contact with things that exist together with him in omnipresent space. It is these characteristics that make God a "most perfect being," and an agent best able to produce the great variety and design of creation (p. 123). In other words, it is God's actions in the real world that command our respect and demand true worship. This is the powerful Lord and God of the General Scholium, who exercises direct dominion over the constitution and governance of his creation. For a being "however perfect, without dominion, cannot be said to be Lord God."[19] Only a being that in fact has dominion over heaven and earth and all its creatures can signify the title of Lord or King, and thus command attitudes of obedience analogous to those of servants toward their earthly master, though in a much higher degree.

This conception of God's nature is further clarified by the Yahuda manuscript:

> To celebrate God for his eternity, immensity, omnisciency, and omnipotence is indeed very pious and the duty of every creature to do it according to his capacity, but yet this part of God's glory as it almost transcends the comprehension of man so it springs not from the freedom of God's will but the necessity of his nature—the wisest of beings required of us to be celebrated not so much for his essence as for his actions, the creating, preserving, and governing of all things according to his good will and pleasure.[20]

It is God's actions, then, emanating from his free and omnipresent will, that are manifest in his works, not the transcendent perfections of his essential nature. If the mind concentrates on the abstract features of God's infinite nature, it will lose its drift, according to Newton. It will fail to honor God for his direct and purposive dominion over the natural world. This is not to say, of course, that Newton rejects a metaphysical approach to God's nature. We must, however, guard lest such musings mask the significant aspect of God's nature—that he is a lordly master who is worthy of servants in virtue of the goodness and wisdom of his intelligent actions.

From all these considerations it is clear that Newton's primary motive is to make God comprehensible to the mind and worthy of attitudes of worship. Strictly conceived, God ought not "to be worshipped under the representation of any corporeal thing"; nevertheless "all our notions of God are taken from the ways of mankind by a certain similitude, which, though not perfect, has some likeness" to us. Accordingly, in the General Scholium, as in the manuscript under discussion, Newton insists that we know God best from the design of his creation, which reveals intrinsically his intentions and actions. By virtue of these characteristics "we reverence and adore him on account of his dominion" while "we admire him for his perfections."[21]

ii. Divine Existence and the Doctrines of Infinite Space and Time

The theological picture that emerges from Newton's religious sensibility is this: God is a being who always has existed and always will exist. His essential nature remains the same: he still is what he was and will continue to be what he is. On this view it is natural enough to think of God's existence as uncaused, such that there is never a time at which his being is preceded by anything else. For Newton this also means that God's nature is causally independent of any conditions, states of affairs, and circumstances external to his nature. Divine existence is explained solely by reference to God's previous existence, since existing omnitemporally is an essential fact pertaining to God's unending and permanent duration.

Furthermore, Newton does not hold that God is identical with Wisdom, Power, and Goodness, conceived as intrinsic attributes of his essential nature.[22] According to Newton's theory of perfection, characteristics such as being wise, powerful, and good are attributes that divine nature instantiates in the highest and most complete manner, namely, infinitely, where infinity is understood as a transcendental characterization not subsumable under the Aristotelian categories. Thus, to say that God is infinitely wise is to characterize the view that he cannot but act wisely. Nor can anything prevent God from acting in any way that is appropriate in this respect to his nature. For God can never change, nor be changed, with respect to the attribute of omniscience.[23]

On the assumption, therefore, that God possesses his perfections infinitely, nothing can prevent him from exercising his essential abilities. For all created things, including the uncreated natures of infinite space and time, are inferior to God's intrinsic perfections, since "by reason of its eternity andinfinity space will neither be God nor wise nor powerful nor alive, but will merely be increased in duration and magnitude, whereas God by reason of the eternity and infinity of his space (that is, by reason of his eternal omnipresence) will be rendered the most perfect being."[24] The same line of reasoning applies to divine immutability. Unlike Spinoza, who is able uniquely to specify divine immutability *in alio,* or by virtue of God's intrinsic nature alone, Newton adopts a position that obliges him to consider the condition of God's existence in relation to the nature of other existents.[25] On this view, God is an immutable

being in that there is nothing whatsoever that can *causally* change or in any way affect his defining nature and attributes. Thus, God is fully able to be identically one and the same person by virtue of his defining attributes at all possible and actual times; for there is nothing whatsoever by virtue of which he can be caused to be otherwise than he is. And Newton concludes in the light of his theory of perfection and infinity that "not everything eternal and infinite will be God, nor will God be prevented from the eternal and infinite exercise of his omnipotence in the creating and governing of things, by the imperfect nature of created things."[26]

For Newton infinity is a character that can be predicated of different sorts of things. It is a way of characterizing the mode of instantiation of first-level properties insofar as they allow something to be the highest exemplification of its kind. In itself infinity is neither a perfection nor an imperfection, nor is it defining of anything's nature. For "infinity is not a perfection except when it is attributed to perfections. Infinity of intellect, power, happiness, and so forth, is the height of perfection; but infinity of ignorance, impotence, wretchedness, and so on, is the height of imperfection; and infinity of extension is so far perfect as that which is extended." Accordingly, to conceive spatial extension as infinite is not to conceive space as constituting "God because of the perfection of infinity."[27]

Newton's reasoning turns on the notion that things exemplify the nature that specifies the class or kind to which they belong. Furthermore, things can be conceived as either perfect or imperfect in accordance with the nature that they exemplify. In Newton's view there are levels of reality, and difference in level is defined in terms of the specific nature of the kind to which things belong, whether the reality in question is a perfection or an imperfection. A thing is infinite of the kind if it manifests in an exemplary manner the nature of that kind, but "no thing is by eternity and infinity made better or of a more perfect nature" ("Tempus et Locus," p. 120).

So, according to Newton's scheme of predication, a thing can instantiate one and the same nature infinitely (that is, completely which another thing possesses deficiently. Thus, both God and we can be said to possess one and the same type of a given ability, except God possesses it infinitely, whereas we, in comparison, possess it deficiently. There are serious difficulties in this position. Standardly in theological thinking the notion that God has absolutely every perfection, such that he is uniquely one and the same being, is justified by arguing that the possession of every perfection implies supremacy and that supremacy implies uniqueness; otherwise there can be more than one supreme being. But Newton's account of the infinity of God's perfections (the notion that he possesses to the highest possible degree what other beings instantiate deficiently) provides no basis for ruling out the possibility that other beings might equally well exemplify the same perfections. Nor does his view that God transcends causal change help; for again it does not show necessarily that only *one* unique individual satisfies the claim. Here then is another example of Newton's anthropomorphic conception in which he holds that the same ontological principles apply to God that apply to finite things. And it raises the same difficulty that is present in his view that the composition of essence and existence that holds of God holds also of finite things.

The difficulty is this: How can Newton defend the unity and the uniqueness of divine being? I want to approach the larger framework of this issue by first considering if and how the dependence of space and time on God is causal. This question in turn is closely related to Newton's association of space and time with God's existence and also to the extent to which he "distances" existence from God's essence and substance.

Now, in my earlier study I argue that space, time, and existence function in Newton's divine ontology as "transcendental" predicates. In draft sheets intended for Des Maizeaux he tells us this about these special predicates:

> The Reader is desired to observe, that whenever in the following papers through unavoidable narrowness of language, infinite space or Immensity & endless duration or Eternity, are spoken of as *Qualities* or *Properties* of the substance such is Immense or Eternal, the terms *Quality & Property* are not taken in that sense wherein they are vulgarly, by the writers of *Logick & Metaphysicks* applied to matter; but in such a sense as only implies them to be modes of existence in all beings, & unbounded *modes* & consequences of the existence of a substance which is really necessarily & substantially Omnipresent & Eternal; which existence is neither substance nor a quality, but the existence of a substance with all its attributes, properties & qualities, & yet is so modified by place & duration that those modes cannot be rejected without rejecting the existence.[28]

Of this and cognate drafts I observed three things. First, that Newton is claiming that existence is not a real attribute or quality of the defining nature of substance. Second, that he connects space and time with the concept of actuality, that is, with the actuality of existence. And last, that Newton conceives these two doctrines as applying to divine existence itself.

Now, in order to secure this interpretation I argued that Newton was committed to the following basic perspectives:

(1) Newton tells us that "infinite space or Immensity" and "endless duration or Eternity" are not *Qualities or Properties*" of God's defining nature, because they do not inhere in divine substance in the manner of the properties or accidents of matter. In other words, these phrases denote transcendental features because they fall under none of the ten Aristotelian categories nor under the fifth of Porphyry's predicables, accident. In another of the draft variants for Des Maizeaux he says that these phrases should be taken "in such a sense as if the Predicaments of *Ubi & Quando* should be called qualities or properties when applied to the existence of a being which is omnipresent & eternal." That is, when God is declared immense, or everywhere with respect to space, and eternal, or of unending duration in time, these are not properties, let alone specific properties, that are ascribed to divine nature. The phrases refer, rather, to the manner of God's existence. "*Ubi & Quando*" answer two general questions: Where does God exist? "Everywhere" in respect to space. When does God exist? "Always" in respect to time. *Ubi & Quando* are therefore "transcendental" predicates in the precise sense that they refer to conditions of existence that every actually existing thing, God included, must satisfy. This line of reasoning is present in the thought of many thinkers, including Tommaso Campanella, Francesco Patrizi, Pierre Gassendi, and Walter Charleton, each of whom argues that space and time are infinite and presupposed by the items in Aristotle's categories, and are thus the general conditions through which the actuality of any existing thing, God included, must be understood.[29]

(2) I was struck by the fact that Newton is at pains to stress that "existence is neither a substance nor a quality," but rather an irreducible feature of all individuals insofar as they are actual, where to refer to a thing's actuality is not at all like speaking of the properties of its defining nature. I was also struck by the fact that Newton goes on to say that anything's existence "is so modified by place & duration that these modes cannot be rejected without rejecting the existence." Thus, to exist is to exist in the general order of the nexus of space and time in a manner appropriate to the nature of the thing in question. So in speaking of God's existence, "the existence of a substance which is . . . substantially Omnipresent & Eternal," we refer to God's state of being actual with respect to the infinity of space and time. Thus, to be an actual being with respect to infinite space and time is an inseparable fact about divine existence. And when Newton speaks of space and time as "unbounded *modes* & consequences" of God's existence, he means that they are irreducibly associated with the necessary existence of God's eternal and omnipresent being.

Now, these perspectives on space, time, and existence seem to me to inform Newton's opening statement in "Tempus et Locus": "Time and Place are common affections of all things without which nothing whatsoever can exist. All things are in time as regards duration of existence, and in place as regards amplitude of presence. And what is never and nowhere is not in *rerum natura*" (p. 116). Here Newton makes a distinction between affections that characterize all the sorts of physical things and, by implication, those that are specific to various sorts and kinds. But there is another distinction that Newton has in mind. Common affections of course apply universally to all things, but time and place for Newton are special sorts of common affections. Notice that he stresses the phrases "duration of existence" and "amplitude of presence" in characterizing the association of time and place with the actuality of anything's existence. This implies that time and place specify anything's actual existence, in contrast to properties that inhere in a thing's specific nature. Thus, Newton probably has in mind a traditional distinction among affections: those that characterize things by virtue of their nature, and those that pertain universally to their sheer existence alone. Moreover, common affections of this latter sort are often categorized as external affections, again on the ground that they are not specific to any particular sort or kind. Thus, individual things not only endure in time; they are present in the same or different places through time. In **"De Gravitatione"** (c1668) the same line of reasoning is applied explicitly to God's "quantity of existence." Newton tells us that the "quantity of existence of each individual [being] is denominated as regards its amplitude of presence and its perseverance in existence. So the quantity of existence of God is eternal in relation to duration, and infinite in relation to the space in which he is present."[30] It is clear that Newton thinks of space and time as "common affections" of God's "quantity of existence." But in saying that space and time are "affections of being in so far as it is being," he is not saying that being in itself entails duration and extension in space (that is, that to be is to be extended and to endure). Again, he invokes a distinction between affections that characterize natures as natures and those that pertain to the fact that a natured individual exists. Of the latter kind are space and time.

Carriero is not happy with this account of why Newton associates space and time with God's existence rather than with his substance. Nor is he happy with reading Newton's claim in the GeneralScholium that God is not eternity and infinity but only eternal and infinite to mean that Newton is breaking with the traditional view of God as strictly identical with all his attributes, existence included. I am not happy with the implications of this reading either. It raises in acute form the problem of the unity of divine being.

I will come to this issue and the implications for my interpretation shortly. In order to approach the problem of unity, let me briefly consider Carriero's alter-native interpretation. He concentrates on a passage from Newton's defender Clarke in which Clarke says that to claim God exists in space and in time means only that God is "*Omnipresent* and *Eternal,* that is, that *Boundless Space and Time* are necessary *Consequences* of his Existence.*" Carriero interprets the last phrase on space and time as being in apposition with the claim that God "is *Omnipotent* and *Eternal.*" To Carriero this suggests two things: (1) that Clarke and Newton believe that an omnipresent existent is one whose existence necessarily produces boundless space, and an eternal existent is one whose existence necessarily produces boundless time; and (2) when Clarke and Newton claim that God is not identical with boundless space and time, they are not denying that he is identical with his attributes *omnipresent* and *eternal.* Their claim means, rather, that God is "not identical with the necessary causal consequences of those two attributes, boundless space and time." Thus, for Carriero infinite space and time are necessary emanations from a necessary being, and are therefore causally dependent on God.

There are two points, then, on which Carriero and I disagree. (1) Contrary to my view he believes Newton holds that God *is* omnipresence and eternity, the traditional view that God is *one* with his defining characteristics. (2) Given this conception, Carriero goes on to suggest that space and time are necessary *causal* productions of an eternal and omnipresent being. Accordingly, what God is *not* identical with on this view is the necessary *causal* consequences of these two attributes, namely, boundless space and endless time.

As to the first point of disagreement, I find it difficult to square Carriero's view with Newton's theory of divine predication. The evidence I adduce seems to indicate that Newton views God's omnipresence in relation to the "infinity of his space" and his existence in terms of the omnitemporality of his duration. On this view God's existence differs from finite existence in that it is infinite with respect to space and unending with respect to time. Thus God is not to be understood Platonically either as infinity itself or as eternity itself. The point is put succinctly in the General Scholium: As God "is not eternity and infinity, but eternal and infinite" so "he is not duration or space, but endures and is present."[31] Closely related to this is Newton's conception of space and time as items outside the categories; indeed, they are the invariant conditions necessary for the *actual* existence of anything, God included.

This brings me to the second point. When Newton says that space and time are consequences of God's existence, Carriero reads this claim as stating a *causal* relation between God's being and what that being produces necessarily. It is not clear, however, how Carriero understands the relation; for example, is it efficient or formal causation? It will be useful, then, to explore this issue briefly as it bears on the question of the ground of divine unity.

In my earlier study I argued that the relation between divine being and the infinity of space and time is one of ontic dependence. I now think it can be seen (in a curious sense) as a causal dependency, and, moreover, one that has a legacy in theological and philosophical thought. Noticing that Newton claims that space "is, as it were, an emanative effect of God," and also an affection of being qua being, I suggest that a possible influence is Henry More, who views space as an "effectus emanativus" of divine being and also an attribute of "ens quatanus ens." More defines "an emanative effect" as "coexistent with the very substance of that which is said to be the cause thereof." And "an emanative cause" is understood as "such a cause as merely by Being, no other activity or causality interposed, produces an effect."[32] Noting also that More denies that any action or active causal efficacy obtains between an emanative cause and its effect, I argued that the relationship for More is ontic rather than causal, and that Newton also views the matter in this way.

Interestingly enough, there is medieval background for reading this relationship under the rubric of *efficient* causation. In the writings of Duns Scotus and Robert Grosseteste we find the idea that divine power is causally prior to its acts.[33] Moreover, this type of causal priority holds between things existing at the same time, or, in the case of God and his acts, together in eternity. This view of course involves the commonplace medieval conception that causes need not precede their effects. Indeed, not only need they not necessarily precede their effects, but they need not exist in time at all. The cause, however, is naturally prior to its effects both temporally and eternally since the effect has no being without its cause. But causal priority among eternal things does not require the *creation* or *production* of the effect by the cause. The effect has being just because the cause *is simpliciter,* but the converse does not hold. Augustine's foot eternally embedded in dust, and thus eternally causing its footprint, is an example of this relationship.

There is medieval precedent, then, for speaking of eternal *and* efficient causes. And something of this sensibility may be reflected in More's notion of an "emanative cause," and similarly in Newton's view of the relationship between divine existence and the reality of space and time. But since the notion of an eternal and efficient cause does not involve any activity, production, creation, or active efficacy between it and its effect, it is difficult to distinguish natural or ontic dependence in these contexts from the notion of causal dependence between eternal things.

Now, both Carriero and I want to argue that Newton associates space and time with God's existence in an attempt to distance them from divine essence. For Carriero, Newton makes this maneuver because he thinks the association of space and time with divine existence best fits his conception of space and time as necessary emanations from a necessary being. For me it is because infinite space and time characterize best Newton's view of the nature and manner of divine existence as such, as well as his belief that God is continuously present to creation in a dynamic and providential way. Carriero's interpretation has the difficulty that there is no compelling reason why a necessary being (one who *is* both eternity itself and infinite presence itself) must necessarily generate space and time from the necessity of its being. This is an emanationist model of creation which holds that a necessary being necessarily creates by emanation from its being. But why should Newton's Christian and voluntarist God necessarily create anything, let alone externalize space and time as necessary emanations from its essential attributes?

But my position also harbors a difficulty. To claim that Newton believes space and time to be essential conditions for the *actuality* of all existing things, God included, has the consequence that the unity of God's essence and existence is threatened. Newton can hold that the existence of a finite thing is grounded in its nature because God has actualized the concrete existence of that nature. It is thus unified by God's creation act. But what unifies God's existence and essence? The claim that God exists eternally, in the sense that there is no time at which his existence can fail, does not ground the necessity of his existence. The modal notion that God can at no time fail to exist cannot itself be grounded in the claim that God exists omnitemporally. From the temporal "exists at all the times there are" one cannot derive the modal "cannot not exist at any time." That God cannot not exist is a claim about his nature as such, not a claim about sheer omnitemporal existence. Thus the conception that God's existence is eternal and omnitemporal still allows that a contingent relation obtains between divine essence and existence. It seems, then, that to preserve divine unity, Newton must fall back on the traditional view that God's existence is a necessary perfection of his nature if God is to be conceived as a necessary being. But then why should that necessary nature need to externalize space and time as necessary consequences of its essential attributes, and why should its actuality demand existence with respect to the infinity of space and time?

Notes

[1] J. E. McGuire, "Existence, Actuality, and Necessity: Newton on Space and Time," *Annals of Science* 35 (1978), 463-508.

[2] Frank E. Manuel, *The Religion of Isaac Newton* (Oxford: Clarendon Press, 1974), chap. 2.

[3] J.E. McGuire, "Newton on Place, Time, and God: An Unpublished Source," *British Journal for the History of Science* 11 (1978), 114-129. Page references to this article will be given in the text.

[4] Alexandre Koyré and I. Bernard Cohen, "Newton and the Leibniz-Clarke Correspondence," *Archives internationales d'histoire des sciences,* nos: 58-59 (1962), 101.

[5] Isaac Newton, *Mathematical Principles of Natural Philosophy,* ed. Florian Cajori (Berkeley: University of California Press, 1960), p. 545. *Isaac Newton's Philosophiae Naturalis Principia Mathematica: The Third Edition (1726),* assembled and edited by Alexandre Koyré and I. Bernard Cohen, 2 vols. (Cambridge, Mass.: Harvard University Press, 1972), II, 759.

[6] A. Rupert Hall and Marie Boas Hall, *Unpublished Papers of Isaac Newton* (Cambridge: Cambridge University Press, 1962), p. 357. Koyré and Cohen, op. cit., p. 97.

[7] See J. E. McGuire and Steven K. Strange, "An Annotated Translation of Plotinus, *Ennead* 111.7 on Eternity and Time," *Ancient Philosophy* 8 (1989), 251-271.

[8] H. McLachlan, *Sir Isaac Newton: The Theological Manuscripts* (Liverpool: The University Press, 1950), p. 56.

[9] Op. cit. (n. 2), p. 101.

[10] University Library, Cambridge, Add. 3965, sec. 13, folio *542*[r].

[11] I. Bernard Cohen, "Isaac Newton's *Principia,* the Scriptures, and the Divine Providence," in *Philosophy, Science, and Method,* ed. Sidney Morgenbesser, Patrick Suppes, and Morton White (New York: St. Martin's, 1969), p. 528.

[12] Op. cit. (n. 5), p. 545.

[13] Op. cit. (n. 6), p. 104.

[14] Op. cit. (n. 4), p. 101.

[15] Gregory MS, 247, Library of the Royal Society. See J. E. McGuire and P. M. Rattansi, "Newton and the 'Pipes of Pan,'" *Notes and Records of the Royal Society of London* 21 (1966), 108-143.

[16] See A. Koyré, *From the Closed World to the Infinite Universe* (New York: Harper & Row, 1958), chaps. 6 and 8; and op. cit. (n. 4), for the view that Cabala has little real influence on Newton. For a careful and comprehensive discussion of *makom* and *simsum* in the writings of More and Raphson and the relation of these writers to Newton, see Brian P. Copenhaver, "Jewish Theologies of Space in the Scientific Revolution: Henry More, Joseph Raphson, Isaac Newton, and Their Predecessors," *Annals of Science* 37 (1980), 489-548.

[17] Portsmouth Collection MS, Add. 3965, 12, f.269 VLC. See also McGuire and Rattansi, op. cit. (n. 15), p. 120.

[18] Op. cit. (n. 5), pp. 545, 759.

[19] Ibid., pp. 544, 759.

[20] Op. cit. (n. 2), pp. 21-22.

[21] Op. cit. (n. 5), pp. 545-546, 759-760.

[22] Ibid., p. 545.

[23] See McGuire, op. cit. (n. 1), for a discussion of this conception.

[24] Op. cit. (n. 3), p. 118.

[25] See op. cit. (n. 1), for a discussion.

[26] Op. cit. (n. 3), p. 120. See also "De Gravitatione" in Hall and Hall, op. cit.

[27] See "De Gravitatione," pp. 102-103.

[28] Op. cit. (n. 4), p. 101.

[29] See McGuire, op. cit. (n. 1), for discussion of these thinkers.

[30] Op. cit. (n. 6), p. 103.

[31] Op. cit. (n. 5), pp. 545, 759.

[32] See McGuire, op. cit. (n. 1), for a discussion of More's views.

[33] John Duns Scotus, *God and Creatures: The Quadlibetal Questions,* trans. Felix Alluntis and Allan B. Wolter (Princeton: Princeton University Press, 1975), question 19, art. 11, 19.27, 19.28, 19.29. John Duns Scotus, *De Primo Principia,* trans. Allan B. Wolter (Chicago: Franciscan Herald Press, 1966), 2.29, 2.31, 2.32, 2.33. Robert Grosseteste, *Commentarius in VIII Libros Physicorum Aristotelis,* ed. Richard C. Dales (Boulder: University of Colorado Press, 1963), Liber Quartus, 96-97.

FURTHER READING

Faur, José. "Newton, Maimonides, and Esoteric Knowledge." *Cross Currents: Religion and Intellectual Life* 40, No. 4 (Winter 1990-91): 526-38.

Examines Newton's interest in the fundamental Rabbinic views on religion and the relation between Newton's views on the harmony between science and religion and those views held by Maimonides, "the most successful thinker to emerge from the Jewish Golden Age."

Ferrone, Vincenzo. "Enlightened Catholics and Newtonian Natural Theology." In *The Intellectual Roots of the Italian Enlightenment: Newtonian Science, Religion, and Politics in the Early Eighteenth Century,* translated by Sue Brotherton, pp. 63-88. New Jersey: Humanities Press, 1995.

Traces the flow of Newton's writings to Italy and discusses the appeal to "enlightened Catholics" of Newton's conception of a universe in which God directly and regularly intervened "through active and immaterial principles."

Hall, Rupert A. *Philosophers at War: The Quarrel Between Newton and Leibniz.* Cambridge: Cambridge University Press, 1980, 338 p.

Investigates the nature and development of the ongoing debate between Newton and Leibniz concerning mathematics, science, and theology.

Kubrin, David. "Newton and the Cyclical Cosmos: Providence and the Mechanical Philosophy." *Journal of the History of Ideas* XXVIII, No. 3 (July-September 1967): 325-46.

Analyzes Newton's belief in a cosmos that was "unwinding" in such a way that intervention from its Creator would be necessary.

How to Use This Index

The main references

Calvino, Italo
1923–1985 .... CLC 5, 8, 11, 22, 33, 39,
73; SSC 3

list all author entries in the following Gale Literary Criticism series:

BLC = *Black Literature Criticism*
CLC = *Contemporary Literary Criticism*
CLR = *Children's Literature Review*
CMLC = *Classical and Medieval Literature Criticism*
DA = *DISCovering Authors*
DAB = *DISCovering Authors: British*
DAC = *DISCovering Authors: Canadian*
DAM = *DISCovering Authors: Modules*
  DRAM: *Dramatists Module;* *MST*: *Most-Studied Authors Module;*
  MULT: *Multicultural Authors Module;* *NOV*: *Novelists Module;*
  POET: *Poets Module;* *POP*: *Popular Fiction and Genre Authors Module*
DC = *Drama Criticism*
HLC = *Hispanic Literature Criticism*
LC = *Literature Criticism from 1400 to 1800*
NCLC = *Nineteenth-Century Literature Criticism*
PC = *Poetry Criticism*
SSC = *Short Story Criticism*
TCLC = *Twentieth-Century Literary Criticism*
WLC = *World Literature Criticism, 1500 to the Present*

The cross-references

See also CANR 23; CA 85-88;
 obituary CA116

list all author entries in the following Gale biographical and literary sources:

AAYA = *Authors & Artists for Young Adults*
AITN = *Authors in the News*
BEST = *Bestsellers*
BW = *Black Writers*
CA = *Contemporary Authors*
CAAS = *Contemporary Authors Autobiography Series*
CABS = *Contemporary Authors Bibliographical Series*
CANR = *Contemporary Authors New Revision Series*
CAP = *Contemporary Authors Permanent Series*
CDALB = *Concise Dictionary of American Literary Biography*
CDBLB = *Concise Dictionary of British Literary Biography*
DLB = *Dictionary of Literary Biography*
DLBD = *Dictionary of Literary Biography Documentary Series*
DLBY = *Dictionary of Literary Biography Yearbook*
HW = *Hispanic Writers*
JRDA = *Junior DISCovering Authors*
MAICYA = *Major Authors and Illustrators for Children and Young Adults*
MTCW = *Major 20th-Century Writers*
NNAL = *Native North American Literature*
SAAS = *Something about the Author Autobiography Series*
SATA = *Something about the Author*
YABC = *Yesterday's Authors of Books for Children*

Literary Criticism Series
Cumulative Author Index

7

Anderson, Sherwood 1876-1941 **TCLC 1, 10, 24; DA; DAB; DAC; DAM MST, NOV; SSC 1; WLC**
See also AAYA 30; CA 104; 121; CANR 61; CDALB 1917-1929; DA3; DLB 4, 9, 86; DLBD 1; MTCW 1, 2

Andier, Pierre
See Desnos, Robert

Andouard
See Giraudoux, (Hippolyte) Jean

Andrade, Carlos Drummond de **CLC 18**
See also Drummond de Andrade, Carlos

Andrade, Mario de 1893-1945 **TCLC 43**

Andreae, Johann V(alentin) 1586-1654 **LC 32**
See also DLB 164

Andreas-Salome, Lou 1861-1937 **TCLC 56**
See also CA 178; DLB 66

Andress, Lesley
See Sanders, Lawrence

Andrewes, Lancelot 1555-1626 **LC 5**
See also DLB 151, 172

Andrews, Cicily Fairfield
See West, Rebecca

Andrews, Elton V.
See Pohl, Frederik

Andreyev, Leonid (Nikolaevich) 1871-1919 **TCLC 3**
See also CA 104

Andric, Ivo 1892-1975 **CLC 8; SSC 36**
See also CA 81-84; 57-60; CANR 43, 60; DLB 147; MTCW 1

Androvar
See Prado (Calvo), Pedro

Angelique, Pierre
See Bataille, Georges

Angell, Roger 1920- **CLC 26**
See also CA 57-60; CANR 13, 44, 70; DLB 171, 185

Angelou, Maya 1928- **CLC 12, 35, 64, 77; BLC 1; DA; DAB; DAC; DAM MST, MULT, POET, POP; WLCS**
See also AAYA 7, 20; BW 2, 3; CA 65-68; CANR 19, 42, 65; CDALBS; CLR 53; DA3; DLB 38; MTCW 1, 2; SATA 49

Anna Comnena 1083-1153 **CMLC 25**

Annensky, Innokenty (Fyodorovich) 1856-1909 **TCLC 14**
See also CA 110; 155

Annunzio, Gabriele d'
See D'Annunzio, Gabriele

Anodos
See Coleridge, Mary E(lizabeth)

Anon, Charles Robert
See Pessoa, Fernando (Antonio Nogueira)

Anouilh, Jean (Marie Lucien Pierre) 1910-1987 **CLC 1, 3, 8, 13, 40, 50; DAM DRAM; DC 8**
See also CA 17-20R; 123; CANR 32; MTCW 1, 2

Anthony, Florence
See Ai

Anthony, John
See Ciardi, John (Anthony)

Anthony, Peter
See Shaffer, Anthony (Joshua); Shaffer, Peter (Levin)

Anthony, Piers 1934- **CLC 35; DAM POP**
See also AAYA 11; CA 21-24R; CANR 28, 56, 73; DLB 8; MTCW 1, 2; SAAS 22; SATA 84

Anthony, Susan B(rownell) 1916-1991 **T C L C 84**
See also CA 89-92; 134

Antoine, Marc
See Proust, (Valentin-Louis-George-Eugene-) Marcel

Antoninus, Brother
See Everson, William (Oliver)

Antonioni, Michelangelo 1912- **CLC 20**
See also CA 73-76; CANR 45, 77

Antschel, Paul 1920-1970
See Celan, Paul
See also CA 85-88; CANR 33, 61; MTCW 1

Anwar, Chairil 1922-1949 **TCLC 22**
See also CA 121

Anzaldua, Gloria 1942-
See also CA 175; DLB 122; HLCS 1

Apess, William 1798-1839(?) **NCLC 73; DAM MULT**
See also DLB 175; NNAL

Apollinaire, Guillaume 1880-1918 **TCLC 3, 8, 51; DAM POET; PC 7**
See also Kostrowitzki, Wilhelm Apollinaris de
See also CA 152; MTCW 1

Appelfeld, Aharon 1932- **CLC 23, 47**
See also CA 112; 133

Apple, Max (Isaac) 1941- **CLC 9, 33**
See also CA 81-84; CANR 19, 54; DLB 130

Appleman, Philip (Dean) 1926- **CLC 51**
See also CA 13-16R; CAAS 18; CANR 6, 29, 56

Appleton, Lawrence
See Lovecraft, H(oward) P(hillips)

Apteryx
See Eliot, T(homas) S(tearns)

Apuleius, (Lucius Madaurensis) 125(?)-175(?) **CMLC 1**
See also DLB 211

Aquin, Hubert 1929-1977 **CLC 15**
See also CA 105; DLB 53

Aquinas, Thomas 1224(?)-1274 **CMLC 33**
See also DLB 115

Aragon, Louis 1897-1982 **CLC 3, 22; DAM NOV, POET**
See also CA 69-72; 108; CANR 28, 71; DLB 72; MTCW 1, 2

Arany, Janos 1817-1882 **NCLC 34**

Aranyos, Kakay
See Mikszath, Kalman

Arbuthnot, John 1667-1735 **LC 1**
See also DLB 101

Archer, Herbert Winslow
See Mencken, H(enry) L(ouis)

Archer, Jeffrey (Howard) 1940- **CLC 28; DAM POP**
See also AAYA 16; BEST 89:3; CA 77-80; CANR 22, 52; DA3; INT CANR-22

Archer, Jules 1915- **CLC 12**
See also CA 9-12R; CANR 6, 69; SAAS 5; SATA 4, 85

Archer, Lee
See Ellison, Harlan (Jay)

Arden, John 1930- **CLC 6, 13, 15; DAM DRAM**
See also CA 13-16R; CAAS 4; CANR 31, 65, 67; DLB 13; MTCW 1

Arenas, Reinaldo 1943-1990 **CLC 41; DAM MULT; HLC 1**
See also CA 124; 128; 133; CANR 73; DLB 145; HW 1; MTCW 1

Arendt, Hannah 1906-1975 **CLC 66, 98**
See also CA 17-20R; 61-64; CANR 26, 60; MTCW 1, 2

Aretino, Pietro 1492-1556 **LC 12**

Arghezi, Tudor 1880-1967 **CLC 80**
See also Theodorescu, Ion N.
See also CA 167

Arguedas, Jose Maria 1911-1969 **CLC 10, 18; HLCS 1**
See also CA 89-92; CANR 73; DLB 113; HW 1

Argueta, Manlio 1936- **CLC 31**
See also CA 131; CANR 73; DLB 145; HW 1

Arias, Ron(ald Francis) 1941-
See also CA 131; CANR 81; DAM MULT; DLB 82; HLC 1; HW 1, 2; MTCW 2

Ariosto, Ludovico 1474-1533 **LC 6**

Aristides
See Epstein, Joseph

Aristophanes 450B.C.-385B.C. **CMLC 4; DA; DAB; DAC; DAM DRAM, MST; DC 2; WLCS**
See also DA3; DLB 176

Aristotle 384B.C.-322B.C. **CMLC 31; DA; DAB; DAC; DAM MST; WLCS**
See also DA3; DLB 176

Arlt, Roberto (Godofredo Christophersen) 1900-1942 **TCLC 29; DAM MULT; HLC 1**
See also CA 123; 131; CANR 67; HW 1, 2

Armah, Ayi Kwei 1939- **CLC 5, 33; BLC 1; DAM MULT, POET**
See also BW 1; CA 61-64; CANR 21, 64; DLB 117; MTCW 1

Armatrading, Joan 1950- **CLC 17**
See also CA 114

Arnette, Robert
See Silverberg, Robert

Arnim, Achim von (Ludwig Joachim von Arnim) 1781-1831 **NCLC 5; SSC 29**
See also DLB 90

Arnim, Bettina von 1785-1859 **NCLC 38**
See also DLB 90

Arnold, Matthew 1822-1888 **NCLC 6, 29; DA; DAB; DAC; DAM MST, POET; PC 5; WLC**
See also CDBLB 1832-1890; DLB 32, 57

Arnold, Thomas 1795-1842 **NCLC 18**
See also DLB 55

Arnow, Harriette (Louisa) Simpson 1908-1986 **CLC 2, 7, 18**
See also CA 9-12R; 118; CANR 14; DLB 6; MTCW 1, 2; SATA 42; SATA-Obit 47

Arouet, Francois-Marie
See Voltaire

Arp, Hans
See Arp, Jean

Arp, Jean 1887-1966 **CLC 5**
See also CA 81-84; 25-28R; CANR 42, 77

Arrabal
See Arrabal, Fernando

Arrabal, Fernando 1932- **CLC 2, 9, 18, 58**
See also CA 9-12R; CANR 15

Arreola, Juan Jose 1918-
See also CA 113; 131; CANR 81; DAM MULT; DLB 113; HLC 1; HW 1, 2

Arrick, Fran **CLC 30**
See also Gaberman, Judie Angell

Artaud, Antonin (Marie Joseph) 1896-1948 **TCLC 3, 36; DAM DRAM**
See also CA 104; 149; DA3; MTCW 1

Arthur, Ruth M(abel) 1905-1979 **CLC 12**
See also CA 9-12R; 85-88; CANR 4; SATA 7, 26

Artsybashev, Mikhail (Petrovich) 1878-1927 **TCLC 31**
See also CA 170

Arundel, Honor (Morfydd) 1919-1973 **CLC 17**
See also CA 21-22; 41-44R; CAP 2; CLR 35; SATA 4; SATA-Obit 24

Arzner, Dorothy 1897-1979 **CLC 98**

Asch, Sholem 1880-1957 **TCLC 3**

See also CA 105

Ash, Shalom
See Asch, Sholem

Ashbery, John (Lawrence) 1927-**CLC 2, 3, 4, 6, 9, 13, 15, 25, 41, 77; DAM POET; PC 26**
See also CA 5-8R; CANR 9, 37, 66; DA3; DLB 5, 165; DLBY 81; INT CANR-9; MTCW 1, 2

Ashdown, Clifford
See Freeman, R(ichard) Austin

Ashe, Gordon
See Creasey, John

Ashton-Warner, Sylvia (Constance) 1908-1984 **CLC 19**
See also CA 69-72; 112; CANR 29; MTCW 1, 2

Asimov, Isaac 1920-1992 **CLC 1, 3, 9, 19, 26, 76, 92; DAM POP**
See also AAYA 13; BEST 90:2; CA 1-4R; 137; CANR 2, 19, 36, 60; CLR 12; DA3; DLB 8; DLBY 92; INT CANR-19; JRDA; MAICYA; MTCW 1, 2; SATA 1, 26, 74

Assis, Joaquim Maria Machado de
See Machado de Assis, Joaquim Maria

Astley, Thea (Beatrice May) 1925-   **CLC 41**
See also CA 65-68; CANR 11, 43, 78

Aston, James
See White, T(erence) H(anbury)

Asturias, Miguel Angel 1899-1974 **CLC 3, 8, 13; DAM MULT, NOV; HLC 1**
See also CA 25-28; 49-52; CANR 32; CAP 2; DA3; DLB 113; HW 1; MTCW 1, 2

Atares, Carlos Saura
See Saura (Atares), Carlos

Atheling, William
See Pound, Ezra (Weston Loomis)

Atheling, William, Jr.
See Blish, James (Benjamin)

Atherton, Gertrude (Franklin Horn) 1857-1948 **TCLC 2**
See also CA 104; 155; DLB 9, 78, 186

Atherton, Lucius
See Masters, Edgar Lee

Atkins, Jack
See Harris, Mark

Atkinson, Kate   CLC 99
See also CA 166

Attaway, William (Alexander) 1911-1986**CLC 92; BLC 1; DAM MULT**
See also BW 2, 3; CA 143; CANR 82; DLB 76

Atticus
See Fleming, Ian (Lancaster); Wilson, (Thomas) Woodrow

Atwood, Margaret (Eleanor) 1939-**CLC 2, 3, 4, 8, 13, 15, 25, 44, 84; DA; DAB; DAC; DAM MST, NOV, POET; PC 8; SSC 2; WLC**
See also AAYA 12; BEST 89:2; CA 49-52; CANR 3, 24, 33, 59; DA3; DLB 53; INT CANR-24; MTCW 1, 2; SATA 50

Aubigny, Pierre d'
See Mencken, H(enry) L(ouis)

Aubin, Penelope 1685-1731(?)   **LC 9**
See also DLB 39

Auchincloss, Louis (Stanton) 1917-**CLC 4, 6, 9, 18, 45; DAM NOV; SSC 22**
See also CA 1-4R; CANR 6, 29, 55; DLB 2; DLBY 80; INT CANR-29; MTCW 1

Auden, W(ystan) H(ugh) 1907-1973**CLC 1, 2, 3, 4, 6, 9, 11, 14, 43; DA; DAB; DAC; DAM DRAM, MST, POET; PC 1; WLC**
See also AAYA 18; CA 9-12R; 45-48; CANR 5, 61; CDBLB 1914-1945; DA3; DLB 10,

20; MTCW 1, 2

Audiberti, Jacques 1900-1965 **CLC 38; DAM DRAM**
See also CA 25-28R

Audubon, John James 1785-1851   **NCLC 47**

Auel, Jean M(arie) 1936-**CLC 31, 107; DAM POP**
See also AAYA 7; BEST 90:4; CA 103; CANR 21, 64; DA3; INT CANR-21; SATA 91

Auerbach, Erich 1892-1957   **TCLC 43**
See also CA 118; 155

Augier, Emile 1820-1889   **NCLC 31**
See also DLB 192

August, John
See De Voto, Bernard (Augustine)

Augustine 354-430**CMLC 6; DA; DAB; DAC; DAM MST; WLCS**
See also DA3; DLB 115

Aurelius
See Bourne, Randolph S(illiman)

Aurobindo, Sri
See Ghose, Aurabinda

Austen, Jane 1775-1817**NCLC 1, 13, 19, 33, 51, 81; DA; DAB; DAC; DAM MST, NOV; WLC**
See also AAYA 19; CDBLB 1789-1832; DA3; DLB 116

Auster, Paul 1947-   **CLC 47**
See also CA 69-72; CANR 23, 52, 75; DA3; MTCW 1

Austin, Frank
See Faust, Frederick (Schiller)

Austin, Mary (Hunter) 1868-1934 **TCLC 25**
See also CA 109; 178; DLB 9, 78, 206

Averroes 1126-1198   **CMLC 7**
See also DLB 115

Avicenna 980-1037   **CMLC 16**
See also DLB 115

Avison, Margaret 1918- **CLC 2, 4, 97; DAC; DAM POET**
See also CA 17-20R; DLB 53; MTCW 1

Axton, David
See Koontz, Dean R(ay)

Ayckbourn, Alan 1939- **CLC 5, 8, 18, 33, 74; DAB; DAM DRAM**
See also CA 21-24R; CANR 31, 59; DLB 13; MTCW 1, 2

Aydy, Catherine
See Tennant, Emma (Christina)

Ayme, Marcel (Andre) 1902-1967   **CLC 11**
See also CA 89-92; CANR 67; CLR 25; DLB 72; SATA 91

Ayrton, Michael 1921-1975   **CLC 7**
See also CA 5-8R; 61-64; CANR 9, 21

Azorin   CLC 11
See also Martinez Ruiz, Jose

Azuela, Mariano 1873-1952 **TCLC 3; DAM MULT; HLC 1**
See also CA 104; 131; CANR 81; HW 1, 2; MTCW 1, 2

Baastad, Babbis Friis
See Friis-Baastad, Babbis Ellinor

Bab
See Gilbert, W(illiam) S(chwenck)

Babbis, Eleanor
See Friis-Baastad, Babbis Ellinor

Babel, Isaac
See Babel, Isaak (Emmanuilovich)

Babel, Isaak (Emmanuilovich) 1894-1941(?)
- **TCLC 2, 13; SSC 16**
See also CA 104; 155; MTCW 1

Babits, Mihaly 1883-1941   **TCLC 14**
See also CA 114

Babur 1483-1530   **LC 18**

Baca, Jimmy Santiago 1952-
See also CA 131; CANR 81; DAM MULT; DLB 122; HLC 1; HW 1, 2

Bacchelli, Riccardo 1891-1985   **CLC 19**
See also CA 29-32R; 117

Bach, Richard (David) 1936- **CLC 14; DAM NOV, POP**
See also AITN 1; BEST 89:2; CA 9-12R; CANR 18; MTCW 1; SATA 13

Bachman, Richard
See King, Stephen (Edwin)

Bachmann, Ingeborg 1926-1973   **CLC 69**
See also CA 93-96; 45-48; CANR 69; DLB 85

Bacon, Francis 1561-1626   **LC 18, 32**
See also CDBLB Before 1660; DLB 151

Bacon, Roger 1214(?)-1292   **CMLC 14**
See also DLB 115

Bacovia, George   TCLC 24
See also Vasiliu, Gheorghe

Badanes, Jerome 1937-   **CLC 59**

Bagehot, Walter 1826-1877   **NCLC 10**
See also DLB 55

Bagnold, Enid 1889-1981   **CLC 25; DAM DRAM**
See also CA 5-8R; 103; CANR 5, 40; DLB 13, 160, 191; MAICYA; SATA 1, 25

Bagritsky, Eduard 1895-1934   **TCLC 60**

Bagrjana, Elisaveta
See Belcheva, Elisaveta

Bagryana, Elisaveta 1893-1991   **CLC 10**
See also Belcheva, Elisaveta
See also CA 178; DLB 147

Bailey, Paul 1937-   **CLC 45**
See also CA 21-24R; CANR 16, 62; DLB 14

Baillie, Joanna 1762-1851   **NCLC 71**
See also DLB 93

Bainbridge, Beryl (Margaret) 1933-**CLC 4, 5, 8, 10, 14, 18, 22, 62; DAM NOV**
See also CA 21-24R; CANR 24, 55, 75; DLB 14; MTCW 1, 2

Baker, Elliott 1922-   **CLC 8**
See also CA 45-48; CANR 2, 63

Baker, Jean H.   TCLC 3, 10
See also Russell, George William

Baker, Nicholson 1957- **CLC 61; DAM POP**
See also CA 135; CANR 63; DA3

Baker, Ray Stannard 1870-1946   **TCLC 47**
See also CA 118

Baker, Russell (Wayne) 1925-   **CLC 31**
See also BEST 89:4; CA 57-60; CANR 11, 41, 59; MTCW 1, 2

Bakhtin, M.
See Bakhtin, Mikhail Mikhailovich

Bakhtin, M. M.
See Bakhtin, Mikhail Mikhailovich

Bakhtin, Mikhail
See Bakhtin, Mikhail Mikhailovich

Bakhtin, Mikhail Mikhailovich 1895-1975
CLC 83
See also CA 128; 113

Bakshi, Ralph 1938(?)-   **CLC 26**
See also CA 112; 138

Bakunin, Mikhail (Alexandrovich) 1814-1876
NCLC 25, 58

Baldwin, James (Arthur) 1924-1987**CLC 1, 2, 3, 4, 5, 8, 13, 15, 17, 42, 50, 67, 90; BLC 1; DA; DAB; DAC; DAM MST, MULT, NOV, POP; DC 1; SSC 10, 33; WLC**
See also AAYA 4; BW 1; CA 1-4R; 124; CABS 1; CANR 3, 24; CDALB 1941-1968; DA3; DLB 2, 7, 33; DLBY 87; MTCW 1, 2; SATA 9; SATA-Obit 54

Ballard, J(ames) G(raham) 1930-**CLC 3, 6, 14, 36; DAM NOV, POP; SSC 1**
See also AAYA 3; CA 5-8R; CANR 15, 39, 65; DA3; DLB 14, 207; MTCW 1, 2; SATA 93

Balmont, Konstantin (Dmitriyevich) 1867-1943 **TCLC 11**
See also CA 109; 155

Baltausis, Vincas
See Mikszath, Kalman

Balzac, Honore de 1799-1850**NCLC 5, 35, 53; DA; DAB; DAC; DAM MST, NOV; SSC 5; WLC**
See also DA3; DLB 119

Bambara, Toni Cade 1939-1995 **CLC 19, 88; BLC 1; DA; DAC; DAM MST, MULT; SSC 35; WLCS**
See also AAYA 5; BW 2, 3; CA 29-32R; 150; CANR 24, 49, 81; CDALBS; DA3; DLB 38; MTCW 1, 2

Bamdad, A.
See Shamlu, Ahmad

Banat, D. R.
See Bradbury, Ray (Douglas)

Bancroft, Laura
See Baum, L(yman) Frank

Banim, John 1798-1842 **NCLC 13**
See also DLB 116, 158, 159

Banim, Michael 1796-1874 **NCLC 13**
See also DLB 158, 159

Banjo, The
See Paterson, A(ndrew) B(arton)

Banks, Iain
See Banks, Iain M(enzies)

Banks, Iain M(enzies) 1954- **CLC 34**
See also CA 123; 128; CANR 61; DLB 194; INT 128

Banks, Lynne Reid **CLC 23**
See also Reid Banks, Lynne
See also AAYA 6

Banks, Russell 1940- **CLC 37, 72**
See also CA 65-68; CAAS 15; CANR 19, 52, 73; DLB 130

Banville, John 1945- **CLC 46, 118**
See also CA 117; 128; DLB 14; INT 128

Banville, Theodore (Faullain) de 1832-1891 **NCLC 9**

Baraka, Amiri 1934-**CLC 1, 2, 3, 5, 10, 14, 33, 115; BLC 1; DA; DAC; DAM MST, MULT, POET, POP; DC 6; PC 4; WLCS**
See also Jones, LeRoi
See also BW 2, 3; CA 21-24R; CABS 3; CANR 27, 38, 61; CDALB 1941-1968; DA3; DLB 5, 7, 16, 38; DLBD 8; MTCW 1, 2

Barbauld, Anna Laetitia 1743-1825**NCLC 50**
See also DLB 107, 109, 142, 158

Barbellion, W. N. P. **TCLC 24**
See also Cummings, Bruce F(rederick)

Barbera, Jack (Vincent) 1945- **CLC 44**
See also CA 110; CANR 45

Barbey d'Aurevilly, Jules Amedee 1808-1889 **NCLC 1; SSC 17**
See also DLB 119

Barbour, John c. 1316-1395 **CMLC 33**
See also DLB 146

Barbusse, Henri 1873-1935 **TCLC 5**
See also CA 105; 154; DLB 65

Barclay, Bill
See Moorcock, Michael (John)

Barclay, William Ewert
See Moorcock, Michael (John)

Barea, Arturo 1897-1957 **TCLC 14**
See also CA 111

Barfoot, Joan 1946- **CLC 18**

See also CA 105

Barham, Richard Harris 1788-1845**NCLC 77**
See also DLB 159

Baring, Maurice 1874-1945 **TCLC 8**
See also CA 105; 168; DLB 34

Baring-Gould, Sabine 1834-1924 **TCLC 88**
See also DLB 156, 190

Barker, Clive 1952- **CLC 52; DAM POP**
See also AAYA 10; BEST 90:3; CA 121; 129; CANR 71; DA3; INT 129; MTCW 1, 2

Barker, George Granville 1913-1991 **CLC 8, 48; DAM POET**
See also CA 9-12R; 135; CANR 7, 38; DLB 20; MTCW 1

Barker, Harley Granville
See Granville-Barker, Harley
See also DLB 10

Barker, Howard 1946- **CLC 37**
See also CA 102; DLB 13

Barker, Jane 1652-1732 **LC 42**

Barker, Pat(ricia) 1943- **CLC 32, 94**
See also CA 117; 122; CANR 50; INT 122

Barlach, Ernst 1870-1938 **TCLC 84**
See also CA 178; DLB 56, 118

Barlow, Joel 1754-1812 **NCLC 23**
See also DLB 37

Barnard, Mary (Ethel) 1909- **CLC 48**
See also CA 21-22; CAP 2

Barnes, Djuna 1892-1982**CLC 3, 4, 8, 11, 29; SSC 3**
See also CA 9-12R; 107; CANR 16, 55; DLB 4, 9, 45; MTCW 1, 2

Barnes, Julian (Patrick) 1946- **CLC 42; DAB**
See also CA 102; CANR 19, 54; DLB 194; DLBY 93; MTCW 1

Barnes, Peter 1931- **CLC 5, 56**
See also CA 65-68; CAAS 12; CANR 33, 34, 64; DLB 13; MTCW 1

Barnes, William 1801-1886 **NCLC 75**
See also DLB 32

Baroja (y Nessi), Pio 1872-1956**TCLC 8; HLC 1**
See also CA 104

Baron, David
See Pinter, Harold

Baron Corvo
See Rolfe, Frederick (William Serafino Austin Lewis Mary)

Barondess, Sue K(aufman) 1926-1977 **CLC 8**
See also Kaufman, Sue
See also CA 1-4R; 69-72; CANR 1

Baron de Teive
See Pessoa, Fernando (Antonio Nogueira)

Baroness Von S.
See Zangwill, Israel

Barres, (Auguste-) Maurice 1862-1923**TCLC 47**
See also CA 164; DLB 123

Barreto, Afonso Henrique de Lima
See Lima Barreto, Afonso Henrique de

Barrett, (Roger) Syd 1946- **CLC 35**

Barrett, William (Christopher) 1913-1992 **CLC 27**
See also CA 13-16R; 139; CANR 11, 67; INT CANR-11

Barrie, J(ames) M(atthew) 1860-1937 **TCLC 2; DAB; DAM DRAM**
See also CA 104; 136; CANR 77; CDBLB 1890-1914; CLR 16; DA3; DLB 10, 141, 156; MAICYA; MTCW 1; SATA 100; YABC 1

Barrington, Michael
See Moorcock, Michael (John)

Barrol, Grady
See Bograd, Larry

Barry, Mike
See Malzberg, Barry N(athaniel)

Barry, Philip 1896-1949 **TCLC 11**
See also CA 109; DLB 7

Bart, Andre Schwarz
See Schwarz-Bart, Andre

Barth, John (Simmons) 1930-**CLC 1, 2, 3, 5, 7, 9, 10, 14, 27, 51, 89; DAM NOV; SSC 10**
See also AITN 1, 2; CA 1-4R; CABS 1; CANR 5, 23, 49, 64; DLB 2; MTCW 1

Barthelme, Donald 1931-1989**CLC 1, 2, 3, 5, 6, 8, 13, 23, 46, 59, 115; DAM NOV; SSC 2**
See also CA 21-24R; 129; CANR 20, 58; DA3; DLB 2; DLBY 80, 89; MTCW 1, 2; SATA 7; SATA-Obit 62

Barthelme, Frederick 1943- **CLC 36, 117**
See also CA 114; 122; CANR 77; DLBY 85; INT 122

Barthes, Roland (Gerard) 1915-1980**CLC 24, 83**
See also CA 130; 97-100; CANR 66; MTCW 1, 2

Barzun, Jacques (Martin) 1907- **CLC 51**
See also CA 61-64; CANR 22

Bashevis, Isaac
See Singer, Isaac Bashevis

Bashkirtseff, Marie 1859-1884 **NCLC 27**

Basho
See Matsuo Basho

Basil of Caesaria c. 330-379 **CMLC 35**

Bass, Kingsley B., Jr.
See Bullins, Ed

Bass, Rick 1958- **CLC 79**
See also CA 126; CANR 53; DLB 212

Bassani, Giorgio 1916- **CLC 9**
See also CA 65-68; CANR 33; DLB 128, 177; MTCW 1

Bastos, Augusto (Antonio) Roa
See Roa Bastos, Augusto (Antonio)

Bataille, Georges 1897-1962 **CLC 29**
See also CA 101; 89-92

Bates, H(erbert) E(rnest) 1905-1974**CLC 46; DAB; DAM POP; SSC 10**
See also CA 93-96; 45-48; CANR 34; DA3; DLB 162, 191; MTCW 1, 2

Bauchart
See Camus, Albert

Baudelaire, Charles 1821-1867 **NCLC 6, 29, 55; DA; DAB; DAC; DAM MST, POET; PC 1; SSC 18; WLC**
See also DA3

Baudrillard, Jean 1929- **CLC 60**

Baum, L(yman) Frank 1856-1919 **TCLC 7**
See also CA 108; 133; CLR 15; DLB 22; JRDA; MAICYA; MTCW 1, 2; SATA 18, 100

Baum, Louis F.
See Baum, L(yman) Frank

Baumbach, Jonathan 1933- **CLC 6, 23**
See also CA 13-16R; CAAS 5; CANR 12, 66; DLBY 80; INT CANR-12; MTCW 1

Bausch, Richard (Carl) 1945- **CLC 51**
See also CA 101; CAAS 14; CANR 43, 61; DLB 130

Baxter, Charles (Morley) 1947- **CLC 45, 78; DAM POP**
See also CA 57-60; CANR 40, 64; DLB 130; MTCW 2

Baxter, George Owen
See Faust, Frederick (Schiller)

Baxter, James K(eir) 1926-1972 **CLC 14**
See also CA 77-80

79; JRDA; SAAS 4; SATA 41, 87; SATA-Brief 27

Bennett, Louise (Simone) 1919- **CLC 28; BLC 1; DAM MULT**
See also BW 2, 3; CA 151; DLB 117

Benson, E(dward) F(rederic) 1867-1940 **TCLC 27**
See also CA 114; 157; DLB 135, 153

Benson, Jackson J. 1930- **CLC 34**
See also CA 25-28R; DLB 111

Benson, Sally 1900-1972 **CLC 17**
See also CA 19-20; 37-40R; CAP 1; SATA 1, 35; SATA-Obit 27

Benson, Stella 1892-1933 **TCLC 17**
See also CA 117; 155; DLB 36, 162

Bentham, Jeremy 1748-1832 **NCLC 38**
See also DLB 107, 158

Bentley, E(dmund) C(lerihew) 1875-1956 **TCLC 12**
See also CA 108; DLB 70

Bentley, Eric (Russell) 1916- **CLC 24**
See also CA 5-8R; CANR 6, 67; INT CANR-6

Beranger, Pierre Jean de 1780-1857 **NCLC 34**

Berdyaev, Nicolas
See Berdyaev, Nikolai (Aleksandrovich)

Berdyaev, Nikolai (Aleksandrovich) 1874-1948 **TCLC 67**
See also CA 120; 157

Berdyayev, Nikolai (Aleksandrovich)
See Berdyaev, Nikolai (Aleksandrovich)

Berendt, John (Lawrence) 1939- **CLC 86**
See also CA 146; CANR 75; DA3; MTCW 1

Beresford, J(ohn) D(avys) 1873-1947 **TCLC 81**
See also CA 112; 155; DLB 162, 178, 197

Bergelson, David 1884-1952 **TCLC 81**

Berger, Colonel
See Malraux, (Georges-)Andre

Berger, John (Peter) 1926- **CLC 2, 19**
See also CA 81-84; CANR 51, 78; DLB 14, 207

Berger, Melvin H. 1927- **CLC 12**
See also CA 5-8R; CANR 4; CLR 32; SAAS 2; SATA 5, 88

Berger, Thomas (Louis) 1924- **CLC 3, 5, 8, 11, 18, 38; DAM NOV**
See also CA 1-4R; CANR 5, 28, 51; DLB 2; DLBY 80; INT CANR-28; MTCW 1, 2

Bergman, (Ernst) Ingmar 1918- **CLC 16, 72**
See also CA 81-84; CANR 33, 70; MTCW 2

Bergson, Henri(-Louis) 1859-1941 **TCLC 32**
See also CA 164

Bergstein, Eleanor 1938- **CLC 4**
See also CA 53-56; CANR 5

Berkoff, Steven 1937- **CLC 56**
See also CA 104; CANR 72

Bermant, Chaim (Icyk) 1929- **CLC 40**
See also CA 57-60; CANR 6, 31, 57

Bern, Victoria
See Fisher, M(ary) F(rances) K(ennedy)

Bernanos, (Paul Louis) Georges 1888-1948 **TCLC 3**
See also CA 104; 130; DLB 72

Bernard, April 1956- **CLC 59**
See also CA 131

Berne, Victoria
See Fisher, M(ary) F(rances) K(ennedy)

Bernhard, Thomas 1931-1989 **CLC 3, 32, 61**
See also CA 85-88; 127; CANR 32, 57; DLB 85, 124; MTCW 1

Bernhardt, Sarah (Henriette Rosine) 1844-1923 **TCLC 75**
See also CA 157

Berriault, Gina 1926- **CLC 54, 109; SSC 30**

See also CA 116; 129; CANR 66; DLB 130

Berrigan, Daniel 1921- **CLC 4**
See also CA 33-36R; CAAS 1; CANR 11, 43, 78; DLB 5

Berrigan, Edmund Joseph Michael, Jr. 1934-1983
See Berrigan, Ted
See also CA 61-64; 110; CANR 14

Berrigan, Ted **CLC 37**
See also Berrigan, Edmund Joseph Michael, Jr.
See also DLB 5, 169

Berry, Charles Edward Anderson 1931-
See Berry, Chuck
See also CA 115

Berry, Chuck **CLC 17**
See also Berry, Charles Edward Anderson

Berry, Jonas
See Ashbery, John (Lawrence)

Berry, Wendell (Erdman) 1934- **CLC 4, 6, 8, 27, 46; DAM POET; PC 28**
See also AITN 1; CA 73-76; CANR 50, 73; DLB 5, 6; MTCW 1

Berryman, John 1914-1972 **CLC 1, 2, 3, 4, 6, 8, 10, 13, 25, 62; DAM POET**
See also CA 13-16; 33-36R; CABS 2; CANR 35; CAP 1; CDALB 1941-1968; DLB 48; MTCW 1, 2

Bertolucci, Bernardo 1940- **CLC 16**
See also CA 106

Berton, Pierre (Francis Demarigny) 1920- **CLC 104**
See also CA 1-4R; CANR 2, 56; DLB 68; SATA 99

Bertrand, Aloysius 1807-1841 **NCLC 31**

Bertran de Born c. 1140-1215 **CMLC 5**

Besant, Annie (Wood) 1847-1933 **TCLC 9**
See also CA 105

Bessie, Alvah 1904-1985 **CLC 23**
See also CA 5-8R; 116; CANR 2, 80; DLB 26

Bethlen, T. D.
See Silverberg, Robert

Beti, Mongo **CLC 27; BLC 1; DAM MULT**
See also Biyidi, Alexandre
See also CANR 79

Betjeman, John 1906-1984 **CLC 2, 6, 10, 34, 43; DAB; DAM MST, POET**
See also CA 9-12R; 112; CANR 33, 56; CDBLB 1945-1960; DA3; DLB 20; DLBY 84; MTCW 1, 2

Bettelheim, Bruno 1903-1990 **CLC 79**
See also CA 81-84; 131; CANR 23, 61; DA3; MTCW 1, 2

Betti, Ugo 1892-1953 **TCLC 5**
See also CA 104; 155

Betts, Doris (Waugh) 1932- **CLC 3, 6, 28**
See also CA 13-16R; CANR 9, 66, 77; DLBY 82; INT CANR-9

Bevan, Alistair
See Roberts, Keith (John Kingston)

Bey, Pilaff
See Douglas, (George) Norman

Bialik, Chaim Nachman 1873-1934 **TCLC 25**
See also CA 170

Bickerstaff, Isaac
See Swift, Jonathan

Bidart, Frank 1939- **CLC 33**
See also CA 140

Bienek, Horst 1930- **CLC 7, 11**
See also CA 73-76; DLB 75

Bierce, Ambrose (Gwinett) 1842-1914(?) **TCLC 1, 7, 44; DA; DAC; DAM MST; SSC 9; WLC**
See also CA 104; 139; CANR 78; CDALB

1865-1917; DA3; DLB 11, 12, 23, 71, 74, 186

Biggers, Earl Derr 1884-1933 **TCLC 65**
See also CA 108; 153

Billings, Josh
See Shaw, Henry Wheeler

Billington, (Lady) Rachel (Mary) 1942- **CLC 43**
See also AITN 2; CA 33-36R; CANR 44

Binyon, T(imothy) J(ohn) 1936- **CLC 34**
See also CA 111; CANR 28

Bioy Casares, Adolfo 1914-1999 **CLC 4, 8, 13, 88; DAM MULT; HLC 1; SSC 17**
See also CA 29-32R; 177; CANR 19, 43, 66; DLB 113; HW 1, 2; MTCW 1, 2

Bird, Cordwainer
See Ellison, Harlan (Jay)

Bird, Robert Montgomery 1806-1854 **NCLC 1**
See also DLB 202

Birkerts, Sven 1951- **CLC 116**
See also CA 128; 133; 176; CAAE 176; CAAS 29; INT 133

Birney, (Alfred) Earle 1904-1995 **CLC 1, 4, 6, 11; DAC; DAM MST, POET**
See also CA 1-4R; CANR 5, 20; DLB 88; MTCW 1

Biruni, al 973-1048(?) **CMLC 28**

Bishop, Elizabeth 1911-1979 **CLC 1, 4, 9, 13, 15, 32; DA; DAC; DAM MST, POET; PC 3**
See also CA 5-8R; 89-92; CABS 2; CANR 26, 61; CDALB 1968-1988; DA3; DLB 5, 169; MTCW 1, 2; SATA-Obit 24

Bishop, John 1935- **CLC 10**
See also CA 105

Bissett, Bill 1939- **CLC 18; PC 14**
See also CA 69-72; CAAS 19; CANR 15; DLB 53; MTCW 1

Bissoondath, Neil (Devindra) 1955- **CLC 120; DAC**
See also CA 136

Bitov, Andrei (Georgievich) 1937- **CLC 57**
See also CA 142

Biyidi, Alexandre 1932-
See Beti, Mongo
See also BW 1, 3; CA 114; 124; CANR 81; DA3; MTCW 1, 2

Bjarme, Brynjolf
See Ibsen, Henrik (Johan)

Bjoernson, Bjoernstjerne (Martinius) 1832-1910 **TCLC 7, 37**
See also CA 104

Black, Robert
See Holdstock, Robert P.

Blackburn, Paul 1926-1971 **CLC 9, 43**
See also CA 81-84; 33-36R; CANR 34; DLB 16; DLBY 81

Black Elk 1863-1950 **TCLC 33; DAM MULT**
See also CA 144; MTCW 1; NNAL

Black Hobart
See Sanders, (James) Ed(ward)

Blacklin, Malcolm
See Chambers, Aidan

Blackmore, R(ichard) D(oddridge) 1825-1900 **TCLC 27**
See also CA 120; DLB 18

Blackmur, R(ichard) P(almer) 1904-1965 **CLC 2, 24**
See also CA 11-12; 25-28R; CANR 71; CAP 1; DLB 63

Black Tarantula
See Acker, Kathy

Blackwood, Algernon (Henry) 1869-1951

TCLC 5
See also CA 105; 150; DLB 153, 156, 178
Blackwood, Caroline 1931-1996 **CLC 6, 9, 100**
See also CA 85-88; 151; CANR 32, 61, 65; DLB
14, 207; MTCW 1
Blade, Alexander
See Hamilton, Edmond; Silverberg, Robert
Blaga, Lucian 1895-1961 **CLC 75**
See also CA 157
Blair, Eric (Arthur) 1903-1950
See Orwell, George
See also CA 104; 132; DA; DAB; DAC; DAM
MST, NOV; DA3; MTCW 1, 2; SATA 29
Blair, Hugh 1718-1800 **NCLC 75**
Blais, Marie-Claire 1939- **CLC 2, 4, 6, 13, 22;**
DAC; DAM MST
See also CA 21-24R; CAAS 4; CANR 38, 75;
DLB 53; MTCW 1, 2
Blaise, Clark 1940- **CLC 29**
See also AITN 2; CA 53-56; CAAS 3; CANR
5, 66; DLB 53
Blake, Fairley
See De Voto, Bernard (Augustine)
Blake, Nicholas
See Day Lewis, C(ecil)
See also DLB 77
Blake, William 1757-1827 **NCLC 13, 37, 57;**
DA; DAB; DAC; DAM MST, POET; PC
12; WLC
See also CDBLB 1789-1832; CLR 52; DA3;
DLB 93, 163; MAICYA; SATA 30
Blasco Ibanez, Vicente 1867-1928 **TCLC 12;**
DAM NOV
See also CA 110; 131; CANR 81; DA3; HW 1,
2; MTCW 1
Blatty, William Peter 1928- **CLC 2; DAM POP**
See also CA 5-8R; CANR 9
Bleeck, Oliver
See Thomas, Ross (Elmore)
Blessing, Lee 1949- **CLC 54**
Blish, James (Benjamin) 1921-1975 **CLC 14**
See also CA 1-4R; 57-60; CANR 3; DLB 8;
MTCW 1; SATA 66
Bliss, Reginald
See Wells, H(erbert) G(eorge)
Blixen, Karen (Christentze Dinesen) 1885-1962
See Dinesen, Isak
See also CA 25-28; CANR 22, 50; CAP 2; DA3;
MTCW 1, 2; SATA 44
Bloch, Robert (Albert) 1917-1994 **CLC 33**
See also AAYA 29; CA 5-8R, 179; 146; CAAE
179; CAAS 20; CANR 5, 78; DA3; DLB 44;
INT CANR-5; MTCW 1; SATA 12; SATA-
Obit 82
Blok, Alexander (Alexandrovich) 1880-1921
TCLC 5; PC 21
See also CA 104
Blom, Jan
See Breytenbach, Breyten
Bloom, Harold 1930- **CLC 24, 103**
See also CA 13-16R; CANR 39, 75; DLB 67;
MTCW 1
Bloomfield, Aurelius
See Bourne, Randolph S(illiman)
Blount, Roy (Alton), Jr. 1941- **CLC 38**
See also CA 53-56; CANR 10, 28, 61; INT
CANR-28; MTCW 1, 2
Bloy, Leon 1846-1917 **TCLC 22**
See also CA 121; DLB 123
Blume, Judy (Sussman) 1938- **CLC 12, 30;**
DAM NOV, POP
See also AAYA 3, 26; CA 29-32R; CANR 13,
37, 66; CLR 2, 15; DA3; DLB 52; JRDA;

MAICYA; MTCW 1, 2; SATA 2, 31, 79
Blunden, Edmund (Charles) 1896-1974 **C L C**
2, 56
See also CA 17-18; 45-48; CANR 54; CAP 2;
DLB 20, 100, 155; MTCW 1
Bly, Robert (Elwood) 1926- **CLC 1, 2, 5, 10, 15,**
38; DAM POET
See also CA 5-8R; CANR 41, 73; DA3; DLB
5; MTCW 1, 2
Boas, Franz 1858-1942 **TCLC 56**
See also CA 115
Bobette
See Simenon, Georges (Jacques Christian)
Boccaccio, Giovanni 1313-1375 **CMLC 13;**
SSC 10
Bochco, Steven 1943- **CLC 35**
See also AAYA 11; CA 124; 138
Bodel, Jean 1167(?)-1210 **CMLC 28**
Bodenheim, Maxwell 1892-1954 **TCLC 44**
See also CA 110; DLB 9, 45
Bodker, Cecil 1927- **CLC 21**
See also CA 73-76; CANR 13, 44; CLR 23;
MAICYA; SATA 14
Boell, Heinrich (Theodor) 1917-1985 **CLC 2,**
3, 6, 9, 11, 15, 27, 32, 72; DA; DAB; DAC;
DAM MST, NOV; SSC 23; WLC
See also CA 21-24R; 116; CANR 24; DA3;
DLB 69; DLBY 85; MTCW 1, 2
Boerne, Alfred
See Doeblin, Alfred
Boethius 480(?)-524(?) **CMLC 15**
See also DLB 115
Boff, Leonardo (Genezio Darci) 1938-
See also CA 150; DAM MULT; HLC 1; HW 2
Bogan, Louise 1897-1970 **CLC 4, 39, 46, 93;**
DAM POET; PC 12
See also CA 73-76; 25-28R; CANR 33, 82; DLB
45, 169; MTCW 1, 2
Bogarde, Dirk 1921-1999 **CLC 19**
See also Van Den Bogarde, Derek Jules Gaspard
Ulric Niven
See also DLB 14
Bogosian, Eric 1953- **CLC 45**
See also CA 138
Bograd, Larry 1953- **CLC 35**
See also CA 93-96; CANR 57; SAAS 21; SATA
33, 89
Boiardo, Matteo Maria 1441-1494 **LC 6**
Boileau-Despreaux, Nicolas 1636-1711 **LC 3**
Bojer, Johan 1872-1959 **TCLC 64**
Boland, Eavan (Aisling) 1944- **CLC 40, 67,**
113; DAM POET
See also CA 143; CANR 61; DLB 40; MTCW
2
Boll, Heinrich
See Boell, Heinrich (Theodor)
Bolt, Lee
See Faust, Frederick (Schiller)
Bolt, Robert (Oxton) 1924-1995 **CLC 14; DAM**
DRAM
See also CA 17-20R; 147; CANR 35, 67; DLB
13; MTCW 1
Bombal, Maria Luisa 1910-1980
See also CA 127; CANR 72; HLCS 1; HW 1
Bombet, Louis-Alexandre-Cesar
See Stendhal
Bomkauf
See Kaufman, Bob (Garnell)
Bonaventura **NCLC 35**
See also DLB 90
Bond, Edward 1934- **CLC 4, 6, 13, 23; DAM**
DRAM
See also CA 25-28R; CANR 38, 67; DLB 13;

MTCW 1
Bonham, Frank 1914-1989 **CLC 12**
See also AAYA 1; CA 9-12R; CANR 4, 36;
JRDA; MAICYA; SAAS 3; SATA 1, 49;
SATA-Obit 62
Bonnefoy, Yves 1923- **CLC 9, 15, 58; DAM**
MST, POET
See also CA 85-88; CANR 33, 75; MTCW 1, 2
Bontemps, Arna(ud Wendell) 1902-1973 **C L C**
1, 18; BLC 1; DAM MULT, NOV, POET
See also BW 1; CA 1-4R; 41-44R; CANR 4,
35; CLR 6; DA3; DLB 48, 51; JRDA;
MAICYA; MTCW 1, 2; SATA 2, 44; SATA-
Obit 24
Booth, Martin 1944- **CLC 13**
See also CA 93-96; CAAS 2
Booth, Philip 1925- **CLC 23**
See also CA 5-8R; CANR 5; DLBY 82
Booth, Wayne C(layson) 1921- **CLC 24**
See also CA 1-4R; CAAS 5; CANR 3, 43; DLB
67
Borchert, Wolfgang 1921-1947 **TCLC 5**
See also CA 104; DLB 69, 124
Borel, Petrus 1809-1859 **NCLC 41**
Borges, Jorge Luis 1899-1986 **CLC 1, 2, 3, 4, 6,**
8, 9, 10, 13, 19, 44, 48, 83; DA; DAB; DAC;
DAM MST, MULT; HLC 1; PC 22; SSC
4; WLC
See also AAYA 26; CA 21-24R; CANR 19, 33,
75; DA3; DLB 113; DLBY 86; HW 1, 2;
MTCW 1, 2
Borowski, Tadeusz 1922-1951 **TCLC 9**
See also CA 106; 154
Borrow, George (Henry) 1803-1881 **NCLC 9**
See also DLB 21, 55, 166
Bosch (Gavino), Juan 1909-
See also CA 151; DAM MST, MULT; DLB 145;
HLCS 1; HW 1, 2
Bosman, Herman Charles 1905-1951 **T C L C**
49
See also Malan, Herman
See also CA 160
Bosschere, Jean de 1878(?)-1953 **TCLC 19**
See also CA 115
Boswell, James 1740-1795 **LC 4, 50; DA; DAB;**
DAC; DAM MST; WLC
See also CDBLB 1660-1789; DLB 104, 142
Bottoms, David 1949- **CLC 53**
See also CA 105; CANR 22; DLB 120; DLBY
83
Boucicault, Dion 1820-1890 **NCLC 41**
Boucolon, Maryse 1937(?)-
See Conde, Maryse
See also BW 3; CA 110; CANR 30, 53, 76
Bourget, Paul (Charles Joseph) 1852-1935
TCLC 12
See also CA 107; DLB 123
Bourjaily, Vance (Nye) 1922- **CLC 8, 62**
See also CA 1-4R; CAAS 1; CANR 2, 72; DLB
2, 143
Bourne, Randolph S(illiman) 1886-1918
TCLC 16
See also CA 117; 155; DLB 63
Bova, Ben(jamin William) 1932- **CLC 45**
See also AAYA 16; CA 5-8R; CAAS 18; CANR
11, 56; CLR 3; DLBY 81; INT CANR-11;
MAICYA; MTCW 1; SATA 6, 68
Bowen, Elizabeth (Dorothea Cole) 1899-1973
CLC 1, 3, 6, 11, 15, 22, 118; DAM NOV;
SSC 3, 28
See also CA 17-18; 41-44R; CANR 35; CAP 2;
CDBLB 1945-1960; DA3; DLB 15, 162;
MTCW 1, 2

Bowering, George 1935- **CLC 15, 47**
See also CA 21-24R; CAAS 16; CANR 10; DLB 53

Bowering, Marilyn R(uthe) 1949- **CLC 32**
See also CA 101; CANR 49

Bowers, Edgar 1924- **CLC 9**
See also CA 5-8R; CANR 24; DLB 5

Bowie, David **CLC 17**
See also Jones, David Robert

Bowles, Jane (Sydney) 1917-1973 **CLC 3, 68**
See also CA 19-20; 41-44R; CAP 2

Bowles, Paul (Frederick) 1910- **CLC 1, 2, 19, 53; SSC 3**
See also CA 1-4R; CAAS 1; CANR 1, 19, 50, 75; DA3; DLB 5, 6; MTCW 1, 2

Box, Edgar
See Vidal, Gore

Boyd, Nancy
See Millay, Edna St. Vincent

Boyd, William 1952- **CLC 28, 53, 70**
See also CA 114; 120; CANR 51, 71

Boyle, Kay 1902-1992 **CLC 1, 5, 19, 58, 121; SSC 5**
See also CA 13-16R; 140; CAAS 1; CANR 29, 61; DLB 4, 9, 48, 86; DLBY 93; MTCW 1, 2

Boyle, Mark
See Kienzle, William X(avier)

Boyle, Patrick 1905-1982 **CLC 19**
See also CA 127

Boyle, T. C. 1948-
See Boyle, T(homas) Coraghessan

Boyle, T(homas) Coraghessan 1948- **CLC 36, 55, 90; DAM POP; SSC 16**
See also BEST 90:4; CA 120; CANR 44, 76; DA3; DLBY 86; MTCW 2

Boz
See Dickens, Charles (John Huffam)

Brackenridge, Hugh Henry 1748-1816 **NCLC 7**
See also DLB 11, 37

Bradbury, Edward P.
See Moorcock, Michael (John)
See also MTCW 2

Bradbury, Malcolm (Stanley) 1932- **CLC 32, 61; DAM NOV**
See also CA 1-4R; CANR 1, 33; DA3; DLB 14, 207; MTCW 1, 2

Bradbury, Ray (Douglas) 1920- **CLC 1, 3, 10, 15, 42, 98; DA; DAB; DAC; DAM MST, NOV, POP; SSC 29; WLC**
See also AAYA 15; AITN 1, 2; CA 1-4R; CANR 2, 30, 75; CDALB 1968-1988; DA3; DLB 2, 8; MTCW 1, 2; SATA 11, 64

Bradford, Gamaliel 1863-1932 **TCLC 36**
See also CA 160; DLB 17

Bradley, David (Henry), Jr. 1950- **CLC 23, 118; BLC 1; DAM MULT**
See also BW 1, 3; CA 104; CANR 26, 81; DLB 33

Bradley, John Ed(mund, Jr.) 1958- **CLC 55**
See also CA 139

Bradley, Marion Zimmer 1930- **CLC 30; DAM POP**
See also AAYA 9; CA 57-60; CAAS 10; CANR 7, 31, 51, 75; DA3; DLB 8; MTCW 1, 2; SATA 90

Bradstreet, Anne 1612(?)-1672 **LC 4, 30; DA; DAC; DAM MST, POET; PC 10**
See also CDALB 1640-1865; DA3; DLB 24

Brady, Joan 1939- **CLC 86**
See also CA 141

Bragg, Melvyn 1939- **CLC 10**

See also BEST 89:3; CA 57-60; CANR 10, 48; DLB 14

Brahe, Tycho 1546-1601 **LC 45**

Braine, John (Gerard) 1922-1986 **CLC 1, 3, 41**
See also CA 1-4R; 120; CANR 1, 33; CDBLB 1945-1960; DLB 15; DLBY 86; MTCW 1

Bramah, Ernest 1868-1942 **TCLC 72**
See also CA 156; DLB 70

Brammer, William 1930(?)-1978 **CLC 31**
See also CA 77-80

Brancati, Vitaliano 1907-1954 **TCLC 12**
See also CA 109

Brancato, Robin F(idler) 1936- **CLC 35**
See also AAYA 9; CA 69-72; CANR 11, 45; CLR 32; JRDA; SAAS 9; SATA 97

Brand, Max
See Faust, Frederick (Schiller)

Brand, Millen 1906-1980 **CLC 7**
See also CA 21-24R; 97-100; CANR 72

Branden, Barbara **CLC 44**
See also CA 148

Brandes, Georg (Morris Cohen) 1842-1927 **TCLC 10**
See also CA 105

Brandys, Kazimierz 1916- **CLC 62**

Branley, Franklyn M(ansfield) 1915- **CLC 21**
See also CA 33-36R; CANR 14, 39; CLR 13; MAICYA; SAAS 16; SATA 4, 68

Brathwaite, Edward (Kamau) 1930- **CLC 11; BLCS; DAM POET**
See also BW 2, 3; CA 25-28R; CANR 11, 26, 47; DLB 125

Brautigan, Richard (Gary) 1935-1984 **CLC 1, 3, 5, 9, 12, 34, 42; DAM NOV**
See also CA 53-56; 113; CANR 34; DA3; DLB 2, 5, 206; DLBY 80, 84; MTCW 1; SATA 56

Brave Bird, Mary 1953-
See Crow Dog, Mary (Ellen)
See also NNAL

Braverman, Kate 1950- **CLC 67**
See also CA 89-92

Brecht, (Eugen) Bertolt (Friedrich) 1898-1956 **TCLC 1, 6, 13, 35; DA; DAB; DAC; DAM DRAM, MST; DC 3; WLC**
See also CA 104; 133; CANR 62; DA3; DLB 56, 124; MTCW 1, 2

Brecht, Eugen Berthold Friedrich
See Brecht, (Eugen) Bertolt (Friedrich)

Bremer, Fredrika 1801-1865 **NCLC 11**

Brennan, Christopher John 1870-1932 **TCLC 17**
See also CA 117

Brennan, Maeve 1917-1993 **CLC 5**
See also CA 81-84; CANR 72

Brent, Linda
See Jacobs, Harriet A(nn)

Brentano, Clemens (Maria) 1778-1842 **NCLC 1**
See also DLB 90

Brent of Bin Bin
See Franklin, (Stella Maria Sarah) Miles (Lampe)

Brenton, Howard 1942- **CLC 31**
See also CA 69-72; CANR 33, 67; DLB 13; MTCW 1

Breslin, James 1930-1996
See Breslin, Jimmy
See also CA 73-76; CANR 31, 75; DAM NOV; MTCW 1, 2

Breslin, Jimmy **CLC 4, 43**
See also Breslin, James
See also AITN 1; DLB 185; MTCW 2

Bresson, Robert 1901- **CLC 16**

See also CA 110; CANR 49

Breton, Andre 1896-1966 **CLC 2, 9, 15, 54; PC 15**
See also CA 19-20; 25-28R; CANR 40, 60; CAP 2; DLB 65; MTCW 1, 2

Breytenbach, Breyten 1939(?)- **CLC 23, 37; DAM POET**
See also CA 113; 129; CANR 61

Bridgers, Sue Ellen 1942- **CLC 26**
See also AAYA 8; CA 65-68; CANR 11, 36; CLR 18; DLB 52; JRDA; MAICYA; SAAS 1; SATA 22, 90; SATA-Essay 109

Bridges, Robert (Seymour) 1844-1930 **TCLC 1; DAM POET; PC 28**
See also CA 104; 152; CDBLB 1890-1914; DLB 19, 98

Bridie, James **TCLC 3**
See also Mavor, Osborne Henry
See also DLB 10

Brin, David 1950- **CLC 34**
See also AAYA 21; CA 102; CANR 24, 70; INT CANR-24; SATA 65

Brink, Andre (Philippus) 1935- **CLC 18, 36, 106**
See also CA 104; CANR 39, 62; INT 103; MTCW 1, 2

Brinsmead, H(esba) F(ay) 1922- **CLC 21**
See also CA 21-24R; CANR 10; CLR 47; MAICYA; SAAS 5; SATA 18, 78

Brittain, Vera (Mary) 1893(?)-1970 **CLC 23**
See also CA 13-16; 25-28R; CANR 58; CAP 1; DLB 191; MTCW 1, 2

Broch, Hermann 1886-1951 **TCLC 20**
See also CA 117; DLB 85, 124

Brock, Rose
See Hansen, Joseph

Brodkey, Harold (Roy) 1930-1996 **CLC 56**
See also CA 111; 151; CANR 71; DLB 130

Brodskii, Iosif
See Brodsky, Joseph

Brodsky, Iosif Alexandrovich 1940-1996
See Brodsky, Joseph
See also AITN 1; CA 41-44R; 151; CANR 37; DAM POET; DA3; MTCW 1, 2

Brodsky, Joseph 1940-1996 **CLC 4, 6, 13, 36, 100; PC 9**
See also Brodskii, Iosif; Brodsky, Iosif Alexandrovich
See also MTCW 1

Brodsky, Michael (Mark) 1948- **CLC 19**
See also CA 102; CANR 18, 41, 58

Bromell, Henry 1947- **CLC 5**
See also CA 53-56; CANR 9

Bromfield, Louis (Brucker) 1896-1956 **TCLC 11**
See also CA 107; 155; DLB 4, 9, 86

Broner, E(sther) M(asserman) 1930- **CLC 19**
See also CA 17-20R; CANR 8, 25, 72; DLB 28

Bronk, William (M.) 1918-1999 **CLC 10**
See also CA 89-92; 177; CANR 23; DLB 165

Bronstein, Lev Davidovich
See Trotsky, Leon

Bronte, Anne 1820-1849 **NCLC 71**
See also DA3; DLB 21, 199

Bronte, Charlotte 1816-1855 **NCLC 3, 8, 33, 58; DA; DAB; DAC; DAM MST, NOV; WLC**
See also AAYA 17; CDBLB 1832-1890; DA3; DLB 21, 159, 199

Bronte, Emily (Jane) 1818-1848 **NCLC 16, 35; DA; DAB; DAC; DAM MST, NOV, POET; PC 8; WLC**
See also AAYA 17; CDBLB 1832-1890; DA3;

Bunyan, John 1628-1688   **LC 4; DA; DAB; DAC; DAM MST; WLC**
See also CDBLB 1660-1789; DLB 39

Burckhardt, Jacob (Christoph) 1818-1897
NCLC 49

Burford, Eleanor
See Hibbert, Eleanor Alice Burford

Burgess, Anthony **CLC 1, 2, 4, 5, 8, 10, 13, 15, 22, 40, 62, 81, 94; DAB**
See also Wilson, John (Anthony) Burgess
See also AAYA 25; AITN 1; CDBLB 1960 to Present; DLB 14, 194; DLBY 98, MTCW 1

Burke, Edmund 1729(?)-1797 **LC 7, 36; DA; DAB; DAC; DAM MST; WLC**
See also DA3; DLB 104

Burke, Kenneth (Duva) 1897-1993 **CLC 2, 24**
See also CA 5-8R; 143; CANR 39, 74; DLB 45, 63; MTCW 1, 2

Burke, Leda
See Garnett, David

Burke, Ralph
See Silverberg, Robert

Burke, Thomas 1886-1945   **TCLC 63**
See also CA 113; 155; DLB 197

Burney, Fanny 1752-1840   **NCLC 12, 54**
See also DLB 39

Burns, Robert 1759-1796   **LC 3, 29, 40; DA; DAB; DAC; DAM MST, POET; PC 6; WLC**
See also CDBLB 1789-1832; DA3; DLB 109

Burns, Tex
See L'Amour, Louis (Dearborn)

Burnshaw, Stanley 1906-   **CLC 3, 13, 44**
See also CA 9-12R; DLB 48; DLBY 97

Burr, Anne 1937-   **CLC 6**
See also CA 25-28R

Burroughs, Edgar Rice 1875-1950 **TCLC 2, 32; DAM NOV**
See also AAYA 11; CA 104; 132; DA3; DLB 8; MTCW 1, 2; SATA 41

Burroughs, William S(eward) 1914-1997 **CLC 1, 2, 5, 15, 22, 42, 75, 109; DA; DAB; DAC; DAM MST, NOV, POP; WLC**
See also AITN 2; CA 9-12R; 160; CANR 20, 52; DA3; DLB 2, 8, 16, 152; DLBY 81, 97; MTCW 1, 2

Burton, Sir Richard F(rancis) 1821-1890
NCLC 42
See also DLB 55, 166, 184

Busch, Frederick 1941-   **CLC 7, 10, 18, 47**
See also CA 33-36R; CAAS 1; CANR 45, 73; DLB 6

Bush, Ronald 1946-   **CLC 34**
See also CA 136

Bustos, F(rancisco)
See Borges, Jorge Luis

Bustos Domecq, H(onorio)
See Bioy Casares, Adolfo; Borges, Jorge Luis

Butler, Octavia E(stelle) 1947- **CLC 38, 121; BLCS; DAM MULT, POP**
See also AAYA 18; BW 2, 3; CA 73-76; CANR 12, 24, 38, 73; DA3; DLB 33; MTCW 1, 2; SATA 84

Butler, Robert Olen (Jr.) 1945- **CLC 81; DAM POP**
See also CA 112; CANR 66; DLB 173; INT 112; MTCW 1

Butler, Samuel 1612-1680   **LC 16, 43**
See also DLB 101, 126

Butler, Samuel 1835-1902 **TCLC 1, 33; DA; DAB; DAC; DAM MST, NOV; WLC**
See also CA 143; CDBLB 1890-1914; DA3; DLB 18, 57, 174

Butler, Walter C.
See Faust, Frederick (Schiller)

Butor, Michel (Marie Francois) 1926- **CLC 1, 3, 8, 11, 15**
See also CA 9-12R; CANR 33, 66; DLB 83; MTCW 1, 2

Butts, Mary 1892(?)-1937   **TCLC 77**
See also CA 148

Buzo, Alexander (John) 1944-   **CLC 61**
See also CA 97-100; CANR 17, 39, 69

Buzzati, Dino 1906-1972   **CLC 36**
See also CA 160; 33-36R; DLB 177

Byars, Betsy (Cromer) 1928-   **CLC 35**
See also AAYA 19; CA 33-36R; CANR 18, 36, 57; CLR 1, 16; DLB 52; INT CANR-18; JRDA; MAICYA; MTCW 1; SAAS 1; SATA 4, 46, 80; SATA-Essay 108

Byatt, A(ntonia) S(usan Drabble) 1936- **CLC 19, 65; DAM NOV, POP**
See also CA 13-16R; CANR 13, 33, 50, 75; DA3; DLB 14, 194; MTCW 1, 2

Byrne, David 1952-   **CLC 26**
See also CA 127

Byrne, John Keyes 1926-
See Leonard, Hugh
See also CA 102; CANR 78; INT 102

Byron, George Gordon (Noel) 1788-1824 **NCLC 2, 12; DA; DAB; DAC; DAM MST, POET; PC 16; WLC**
See also CDBLB 1789-1832; DA3; DLB 96, 110

Byron, Robert 1905-1941   **TCLC 67**
See also CA 160; DLB 195

C. 3. 3.
See Wilde, Oscar

Caballero, Fernan 1796-1877   **NCLC 10**

Cabell, Branch
See Cabell, James Branch

Cabell, James Branch 1879-1958   **TCLC 6**
See also CA 105; 152; DLB 9, 78; MTCW 1

Cable, George Washington 1844-1925 **TCLC 4; SSC 4**
See also CA 104; 155; DLB 12, 74; DLBD 13

Cabral de Melo Neto, Joao 1920-   **CLC 76; DAM MULT**
See also CA 151

Cabrera Infante, G(uillermo) 1929- **CLC 5, 25, 45, 120; DAM MULT; HLC 1**
See also CA 85-88; CANR 29, 65; DA3; DLB 113; HW 1, 2; MTCW 1, 2

Cade, Toni
See Bambara, Toni Cade

Cadmus and Harmonia
See Buchan, John

Caedmon fl. 658-680   **CMLC 7**
See also DLB 146

Caeiro, Alberto
See Pessoa, Fernando (Antonio Nogueira)

Cage, John (Milton, Jr.) 1912-1992   **CLC 41**
See also CA 13-16R; 169; CANR 9, 78; DLB 193; INT CANR-9

Cahan, Abraham 1860-1951   **TCLC 71**
See also CA 108; 154; DLB 9, 25, 28

Cain, G.
See Cabrera Infante, G(uillermo)

Cain, Guillermo
See Cabrera Infante, G(uillermo)

Cain, James M(allahan) 1892-1977 **CLC 3, 11, 28**
See also AITN 1; CA 17-20R; 73-76; CANR 8, 34, 61; MTCW 1

Caine, Mark
See Raphael, Frederic (Michael)

Calasso, Roberto 1941-   **CLC 81**
See also CA 143

Calderon de la Barca, Pedro 1600-1681 **LC 23; DC 3; HLCS 1**

Caldwell, Erskine (Preston) 1903-1987 **CLC 1, 8, 14, 50, 60; DAM NOV; SSC 19**
See also AITN 1; CA 1-4R; 121; CAAS 1; CANR 2, 33; DA3; DLB 9, 86; MTCW 1, 2

Caldwell, (Janet Miriam) Taylor (Holland) 1900-1985 **CLC 2, 28, 39; DAM NOV, POP**
See also CA 5-8R; 116; CANR 5; DA3; DLBD 17

Calhoun, John Caldwell 1782-1850 **NCLC 15**
See also DLB 3

Calisher, Hortense 1911- **CLC 2, 4, 8, 38; DAM NOV; SSC 15**
See also CA 1-4R; CANR 1, 22, 67; DA3; DLB 2; INT CANR-22; MTCW 1, 2

Callaghan, Morley Edward 1903-1990 **CLC 3, 14, 41, 65; DAC; DAM MST**
See also CA 9-12R; 132; CANR 33, 73; DLB 68; MTCW 1, 2

Callimachus c. 305B.C.-c. 240B.C. **CMLC 18**
See also DLB 176

Calvin, John 1509-1564   **LC 37**

Calvino, Italo 1923-1985 **CLC 5, 8, 11, 22, 33, 39, 73; DAM NOV; SSC 3**
See also CA 85-88; 116; CANR 23, 61; DLB 196; MTCW 1, 2

Cameron, Carey 1952-   **CLC 59**
See also CA 135

Cameron, Peter 1959-   **CLC 44**
See also CA 125; CANR 50

Camoens, Luis Vaz de 1524(?)-1580
See also HLCS 1

Camoes, Luis de 1524(?)-1580
See also HLCS 1

Campana, Dino 1885-1932   **TCLC 20**
See also CA 117; DLB 114

Campanella, Tommaso 1568-1639   **LC 32**

Campbell, John W(ood, Jr.) 1910-1971 **CLC 32**
See also CA 21-22; 29-32R; CANR 34; CAP 2; DLB 8; MTCW 1

Campbell, Joseph 1904-1987   **CLC 69**
See also AAYA 3; BEST 89:2; CA 1-4R; 124; CANR 3, 28, 61; DA3; MTCW 1, 2

Campbell, Maria 1940-   **CLC 85; DAC**
See also CA 102; CANR 54; NNAL

Campbell, (John) Ramsey 1946- **CLC 42; SSC 19**
See also CA 57-60; CANR 7; INT CANR-7

Campbell, (Ignatius) Roy (Dunnachie) 1901-1957   **TCLC 5**
See also CA 104; 155; DLB 20; MTCW 2

Campbell, Thomas 1777-1844   **NCLC 19**
See also DLB 93; 144

Campbell, Wilfred   **TCLC 9**
See also Campbell, William

Campbell, William 1858(?)-1918
See Campbell, Wilfred
See also CA 106; DLB 92

Campion, Jane   **CLC 95**
See also CA 138

Campos, Alvaro de
See Pessoa, Fernando (Antonio Nogueira)

Camus, Albert 1913-1960 **CLC 1, 2, 4, 9, 11, 14, 32, 63, 69, 124; DA; DAB; DAC; DAM DRAM, MST, NOV; DC 2; SSC 9; WLC**
See also CA 89-92; DA3; DLB 72; MTCW 1, 2

Canby, Vincent 1924-   **CLC 13**
See also CA 81-84

Cancale

See Desnos, Robert

Canetti, Elias 1905-1994 **CLC 3, 14, 25, 75, 86**
See also CA 21-24R; 146; CANR 23, 61, 79;
DA3; DLB 85, 124; MTCW 1, 2

Canfield, Dorothea F.
See Fisher, Dorothy (Frances) Canfield

Canfield, Dorothea Frances
See Fisher, Dorothy (Frances) Canfield

Canfield, Dorothy
See Fisher, Dorothy (Frances) Canfield

Canin, Ethan 1960- **CLC 55**
See also CA 131; 135

Cannon, Curt
See Hunter, Evan

Cao, Lan 1961- **CLC 109**
See also CA 165

Cape, Judith
See Page, P(atricia) K(athleen)

Capek, Karel 1890-1938 **TCLC 6, 37; DA;
DAB; DAC; DAM DRAM, MST, NOV; DC
1; SSC 36; WLC**
See also CA 104; 140; DA3; MTCW 1

Capote, Truman 1924-1984 **CLC 1, 3, 8, 13, 19,
34, 38, 58; DA; DAB; DAC; DAM MST,
NOV, POP; SSC 2; WLC**
See also CA 5-8R; 113; CANR 18, 62; CDALB
1941-1968; DA3; DLB 2, 185; DLBY 80,
84; MTCW 1, 2; SATA 91

Capra, Frank 1897-1991 **CLC 16**
See also CA 61-64; 135

Caputo, Philip 1941- **CLC 32**
See also CA 73-76; CANR 40

Caragiale, Ion Luca 1852-1912 **TCLC 76**
See also CA 157

Card, Orson Scott 1951- **CLC 44, 47, 50; DAM
POP**
See also AAYA 11; CA 102; CANR 27, 47, 73;
DA3; INT CANR-27; MTCW 1, 2; SATA 83

Cardenal, Ernesto 1925- **CLC 31; DAM
MULT, POET; HLC 1; PC 22**
See also CA 49-52; CANR 2, 32, 66; HW 1, 2;
MTCW 1, 2

Cardozo, Benjamin N(athan) 1870-1938
TCLC 65
See also CA 117; 164

Carducci, Giosue (Alessandro Giuseppe) 1835-
1907 **TCLC 32**
See also CA 163

Carew, Thomas 1595(?)-1640 **LC 13**
See also DLB 126

Carey, Ernestine Gilbreth 1908- **CLC 17**
See also CA 5-8R; CANR 71; SATA 2

Carey, Peter 1943- **CLC 40, 55, 96**
See also CA 123; 127; CANR 53, 76; INT 127;
MTCW 1, 2; SATA 94

Carleton, William 1794-1869 **NCLC 3**
See also DLB 159

Carlisle, Henry (Coffin) 1926- **CLC 33**
See also CA 13-16R; CANR 15

Carlsen, Chris
See Holdstock, Robert P.

Carlson, Ron(ald F.) 1947- **CLC 54**
See also CA 105; CANR 27

Carlyle, Thomas 1795-1881 **NCLC 70; DA;
DAB; DAC; DAM MST**
See also CDBLB 1789-1832; DLB 55; 144

Carman, (William) Bliss 1861-1929 **TCLC 7;
DAC**
See also CA 104; 152; DLB 92

Carnegie, Dale 1888-1955 **TCLC 53**

Carossa, Hans 1878-1956 **TCLC 48**
See also CA 170; DLB 66

Carpenter, Don(ald Richard) 1931-1995 **C L C**

41
See also CA 45-48; 149; CANR 1, 71

Carpenter, Edward 1844-1929 **TCLC 88**
See also CA 163

Carpentier (y Valmont), Alejo 1904-1980 **CLC
8, 11, 38, 110; DAM MULT; HLC 1; SSC
35**
See also CA 65-68; 97-100; CANR 11, 70; DLB
113; HW 1, 2

Carr, Caleb 1955(?)- **CLC 86**
See also CA 147; CANR 73; DA3

Carr, Emily 1871-1945 **TCLC 32**
See also CA 159; DLB 68

Carr, John Dickson 1906-1977 **CLC 3**
See also Fairbairn, Roger
See also CA 49-52; 69-72; CANR 3, 33, 60;
MTCW 1, 2

Carr, Philippa
See Hibbert, Eleanor Alice Burford

Carr, Virginia Spencer 1929- **CLC 34**
See also CA 61-64; DLB 111

Carrere, Emmanuel 1957- **CLC 89**

Carrier, Roch 1937- **CLC 13, 78; DAC; DAM
MST**
See also CA 130; CANR 61; DLB 53; SATA
105

Carroll, James P. 1943(?)- **CLC 38**
See also CA 81-84; CANR 73; MTCW 1

Carroll, Jim 1951- **CLC 35**
See also AAYA 17; CA 45-48; CANR 42

Carroll, Lewis **NCLC 2, 53; PC 18; WLC**
See also Dodgson, Charles Lutwidge
See also CDBLB 1832-1890; CLR 2, 18; DLB
18, 163, 178; DLBY 98; JRDA

Carroll, Paul Vincent 1900-1968 **CLC 10**
See also CA 9-12R; 25-28R; DLB 10

Carruth, Hayden 1921- **CLC 4, 7, 10, 18, 84;
PC 10**
See also CA 9-12R; CANR 4, 38, 59; DLB 5,
165; INT CANR-4; MTCW 1, 2; SATA 47

Carson, Rachel Louise 1907-1964 **CLC 71;
DAM POP**
See also CA 77-80; CANR 35; DA3; MTCW 1,
2; SATA 23

Carter, Angela (Olive) 1940-1992 **CLC 5, 41,
76; SSC 13**
See also CA 53-56; 136; CANR 12, 36, 61;
DA3; DLB 14, 207; MTCW 1, 2; SATA 66;
SATA-Obit 70

Carter, Nick
See Smith, Martin Cruz

Carver, Raymond 1938-1988 **CLC 22, 36, 53,
55; DAM NOV; SSC 8**
See also CA 33-36R; 126; CANR 17, 34, 61;
DA3; DLB 130; DLBY 84, 88; MTCW 1, 2

Cary, Elizabeth, Lady Falkland 1585-1639
LC 30

Cary, (Arthur) Joyce (Lunel) 1888-1957
TCLC 1, 29
See also CA 104; 164; CDBLB 1914-1945;
DLB 15, 100; MTCW 2

Casanova de Seingalt, Giovanni Jacopo 1725-
1798 **LC 13**

Casares, Adolfo Bioy
See Bioy Casares, Adolfo

Casely-Hayford, J(oseph) E(phraim) 1866-1930
TCLC 24; BLC 1; DAM MULT
See also BW 2; CA 123; 152

Casey, John (Dudley) 1939- **CLC 59**
See also BEST 90:2; CA 69-72; CANR 23

Casey, Michael 1947- **CLC 2**
See also CA 65-68; DLB 5

Casey, Patrick

See Thurman, Wallace (Henry)

Casey, Warren (Peter) 1935-1988 **CLC 12**
See also CA 101; 127; INT 101

Casona, Alejandro **CLC 49**
See also Alvarez, Alejandro Rodriguez

Cassavetes, John 1929-1989 **CLC 20**
See also CA 85-88; 127; CANR 82

Cassian, Nina 1924- **PC 17**

Cassill, R(onald) V(erlin) 1919- **CLC 4, 23**
See also CA 9-12R; CAAS 1; CANR 7, 45; DLB
6

Cassirer, Ernst 1874-1945 **TCLC 61**
See also CA 157

Cassity, (Allen) Turner 1929- **CLC 6, 42**
See also CA 17-20R; CAAS 8; CANR 11; DLB
105

Castaneda, Carlos (Cesar Aranha) 1931(?)-
1998 **CLC 12, 119**
See also CA 25-28R; CANR 32, 66; HW 1;
MTCW 1

Castedo, Elena 1937- **CLC 65**
See also CA 132

Castedo-Ellerman, Elena
See Castedo, Elena

Castellanos, Rosario 1925-1974 **CLC 66; DAM
MULT; HLC 1**
See also CA 131; 53-56; CANR 58; DLB 113;
HW 1; MTCW 1

Castelvetro, Lodovico 1505-1571 **LC 12**

Castiglione, Baldassare 1478-1529 **LC 12**

Castle, Robert
See Hamilton, Edmond

Castro (Ruz), Fidel 1926(?)-
See also CA 110; 129; CANR 81; DAM MULT;
HLC 1; HW 2

Castro, Guillen de 1569-1631 **LC 19**

Castro, Rosalia de 1837-1885 **NCLC 3, 78;
DAM MULT**

Cather, Willa
See Cather, Willa Sibert

Cather, Willa Sibert 1873-1947 **TCLC 1, 11,
31; DA; DAB; DAC; DAM MST, NOV;
SSC 2; WLC**
See also AAYA 24; CA 104; 128; CDALB 1865-
1917; DA3; DLB 9, 54, 78; DLBD 1; MTCW
1, 2; SATA 30

Catherine, Saint 1347-1380 **CMLC 27**

Cato, Marcus Porcius 234B.C.-149B.C.
CMLC 21
See also DLB 211

Catton, (Charles) Bruce 1899-1978 **CLC 35**
See also AITN 1; CA 5-8R; 81-84; CANR 7,
74; DLB 17; SATA 2; SATA-Obit 24

Catullus c. 84B.C.-c. 54B.C. **CMLC 18**
See also DLB 211

Cauldwell, Frank
See King, Francis (Henry)

Caunitz, William J. 1933-1996 **CLC 34**
See also BEST 89:3; CA 125; 130; 152; CANR
73; INT 130

Causley, Charles (Stanley) 1917- **CLC 7**
See also CA 9-12R; CANR 5, 35; CLR 30; DLB
27; MTCW 1; SATA 3, 66

Caute, (John) David 1936- **CLC 29; DAM
NOV**
See also CA 1-4R; CAAS 4; CANR 1, 33, 64;
DLB 14

Cavafy, C(onstantine) P(eter) 1863-1933
TCLC 2, 7; DAM POET
See also Kavafis, Konstantinos Petrou
See also CA 148; DA3; MTCW 1

Cavallo, Evelyn
See Spark, Muriel (Sarah)

Chitty, Thomas Willes 1926-   CLC 11
    See also Hinde, Thomas
    See also CA 5-8R
Chivers, Thomas Holley 1809-1858 NCLC 49
    See also DLB 3
Choi, Susan   CLC 119
Chomette, Rene Lucien 1898-1981
    See Clair, Rene
    See also CA 103
Chopin, Kate TCLC 5, 14; DA; DAB; SSC 8;
    WLCS
    See also Chopin, Katherine
    See also CDALB 1865-1917; DLB 12, 78
Chopin, Katherine 1851-1904
    See Chopin, Kate
    See also CA 104; 122; DAC; DAM MST, NOV;
    DA3
Chretien de Troyes c. 12th cent. -   CMLC 10
    See also DLB 208
Christie
    See Ichikawa, Kon
Christie, Agatha (Mary Clarissa) 1890-1976
    CLC 1, 6, 8, 12, 39, 48, 110; DAB; DAC;
    DAM NOV
    See also AAYA 9; AITN 1, 2; CA 17-20R; 61-
    64; CANR 10, 37; CDBLB 1914-1945; DA3;
    DLB 13, 77; MTCW 1, 2; SATA 36
Christie, (Ann) Philippa
    See Pearce, Philippa
    See also CA 5-8R; CANR 4
Christine de Pizan 1365(?)-1431(?)   LC 9
    See also DLB 208
Chubb, Elmer
    See Masters, Edgar Lee
Chulkov, Mikhail Dmitrievich 1743-1792 LC 2
    See also DLB 150
Churchill, Caryl 1938-   CLC 31, 55; DC 5
    See also CA 102; CANR 22, 46; DLB 13;
    MTCW 1
Churchill, Charles 1731-1764   LC 3
    See also DLB 109
Chute, Carolyn 1947-   CLC 39
    See also CA 123
Ciardi, John (Anthony) 1916-1986   CLC 10,
    40, 44; DAM POET
    See also CA 5-8R; 118; CAAS 2; CANR 5, 33;
    CLR 19; DLB 5; DLBY 86; INT CANR-5;
    MAICYA; MTCW 1, 2; SAAS 26; SATA 1,
    65; SATA-Obit 46
Cicero, Marcus Tullius 106B.C.-43B.C.
    CMLC 3
    See also DLB 211
Cimino, Michael 1943-   CLC 16
    See also CA 105
Cioran, E(mil) M. 1911-1995   CLC 64
    See also CA 25-28R; 149
Cisneros, Sandra 1954- CLC 69, 118; DAM
    MULT; HLC 1; SSC 32
    See also AAYA 9; CA 131; CANR 64; DA3;
    DLB 122, 152; HW 1, 2; MTCW 2
Cixous, Helene 1937-   CLC 92
    See also CA 126; CANR 55; DLB 83; MTCW
    1, 2
Clair, Rene   CLC 20
    See also Chomette, Rene Lucien
Clampitt, Amy 1920-1994   CLC 32; PC 19
    See also CA 110; 146; CANR 29, 79; DLB 105
Clancy, Thomas L., Jr. 1947-
    See Clancy, Tom
    See also CA 125; 131; CANR 62; DA3; INT
    131; MTCW 1, 2
Clancy, Tom   CLC 45, 112; DAM NOV, POP
    See also Clancy, Thomas L., Jr.

See also AAYA 9; BEST 89:1, 90:1; MTCW 2
Clare, John 1793-1864 NCLC 9; DAB; DAM
    POET; PC 23
    See also DLB 55, 96
Clarin
    See Alas (y Urena), Leopoldo (Enrique Garcia)
Clark, Al C.
    See Goines, Donald
Clark, (Robert) Brian 1932-   CLC 29
    See also CA 41-44R; CANR 67
Clark, Curt
    See Westlake, Donald E(dwin)
Clark, Eleanor 1913-1996   CLC 5, 19
    See also CA 9-12R; 151; CANR 41; DLB 6
Clark, J. P.
    See Clark, John Pepper
    See also DLB 117
Clark, John Pepper 1935- CLC 38; BLC 1;
    DAM DRAM, MULT; DC 5
    See also Clark, J. P.
    See also BW 1; CA 65-68; CANR 16, 72;
    MTCW 1
Clark, M. R.
    See Clark, Mavis Thorpe
Clark, Mavis Thorpe 1909-   CLC 12
    See also CA 57-60; CANR 8, 37; CLR 30;
    MAICYA; SAAS 5; SATA 8, 74
Clark, Walter Van Tilburg 1909-1971 CLC 28
    See also CA 9-12R; 33-36R; CANR 63; DLB
    9, 206; SATA 8
Clark Bekederemo, J(ohnson) P(epper)
    See Clark, John Pepper
Clarke, Arthur C(harles) 1917- CLC 1, 4, 13,
    18, 35; DAM POP; SSC 3
    See also AAYA 4; CA 1-4R; CANR 2, 28, 55,
    74; DA3; JRDA; MAICYA; MTCW 1, 2;
    SATA 13, 70
Clarke, Austin 1896-1974   CLC 6, 9; DAM
    POET
    See also CA 29-32; 49-52; CAP 2; DLB 10, 20
Clarke, Austin C(hesterfield) 1934- CLC 8, 53;
    BLC 1; DAC; DAM MULT
    See also BW 1; CA 25-28R; CAAS 16; CANR
    14, 32, 68; DLB 53, 125
Clarke, Gillian 1937-   CLC 61
    See also CA 106; DLB 40
Clarke, Marcus (Andrew Hislop) 1846-1881
    NCLC 19
Clarke, Shirley 1925-   CLC 16
Clash, The
    See Headon, (Nicky) Topper; Jones, Mick;
    Simonon, Paul; Strummer, Joe
Claudel, Paul (Louis Charles Marie) 1868-1955
    TCLC 2, 10
    See also CA 104; 165; DLB 192
Claudius, Matthias 1740-1815   NCLC 75
    See also DLB 97
Clavell, James (duMaresq) 1925-1994 CLC 6,
    25, 87; DAM NOV, POP
    See also CA 25-28R; 146; CANR 26, 48; DA3;
    MTCW 1, 2
Cleaver, (Leroy) Eldridge 1935-1998 CLC 30,
    119; BLC 1; DAM MULT
    See also BW 1, 3; CA 21-24R; 167; CANR 16,
    75; DA3; MTCW 2
Cleese, John (Marwood) 1939-   CLC 21
    See also Monty Python
    See also CA 112; 116; CANR 35; MTCW 1
Cleishbotham, Jebediah
    See Scott, Walter
Cleland, John 1710-1789   LC 2, 48
    See also DLB 39
Clemens, Samuel Langhorne 1835-1910

See Twain, Mark
    See also CA 104; 135; CDALB 1865-1917; DA;
    DAB; DAC; DAM MST, NOV; DA3; DLB
    11, 12, 23, 64, 74, 186, 189; JRDA;
    MAICYA; SATA 100; YABC 2
Cleophil
    See Congreve, William
Clerihew, E.
    See Bentley, E(dmund) C(lerihew)
Clerk, N. W.
    See Lewis, C(live) S(taples)
Cliff, Jimmy   CLC 21
    See also Chambers, James
Cliff, Michelle 1946-   CLC 120; BLCS
    See also BW 2; CA 116; CANR 39, 72; DLB
    157
Clifton, (Thelma) Lucille 1936- CLC 19, 66;
    BLC 1; DAM MULT, POET; PC 17
    See also BW 2, 3; CA 49-52; CANR 2, 24, 42,
    76; CLR 5; DA3; DLB 5, 41; MAICYA;
    MTCW 1, 2; SATA 20, 69
Clinton, Dirk
    See Silverberg, Robert
Clough, Arthur Hugh 1819-1861   NCLC 27
    See also DLB 32
Clutha, Janet Paterson Frame 1924-
    See Frame, Janet
    See also CA 1-4R; CANR 2, 36, 76; MTCW 1,
    2
Clyne, Terence
    See Blatty, William Peter
Cobalt, Martin
    See Mayne, William (James Carter)
Cobb, Irvin S(hrewsbury) 1876-1944 T C L C
    77
    See also CA 175; DLB 11, 25, 86
Cobbett, William 1763-1835   NCLC 49
    See also DLB 43, 107, 158
Coburn, D(onald) L(ee) 1938-   CLC 10
    See also CA 89-92
Cocteau, Jean (Maurice Eugene Clement) 1889-
    1963 CLC 1, 8, 15, 16, 43; DA; DAB; DAC;
    DAM DRAM, MST, NOV; WLC
    See also CA 25-28; CANR 40; CAP 2; DA3;
    DLB 65; MTCW 1, 2
Codrescu, Andrei 1946- CLC 46, 121; DAM
    POET
    See also CA 33-36R; CAAS 19; CANR 13, 34,
    53, 76; DA3; MTCW 2
Coe, Max
    See Bourne, Randolph S(illiman)
Coe, Tucker
    See Westlake, Donald E(dwin)
Coen, Ethan 1958-   CLC 108
    See also CA 126
Coen, Joel 1955-   CLC 108
    See also CA 126
The Coen Brothers
    See Coen, Ethan; Coen, Joel
Coetzee, J(ohn) M(ichael) 1940- CLC 23, 33,
    66, 117; DAM NOV
    See also CA 77-80; CANR 41, 54, 74; DA3;
    MTCW 1, 2
Coffey, Brian
    See Koontz, Dean R(ay)
Coffin, Robert P(eter) Tristram 1892-1955
    TCLC 95
    See also CA 123; 169; DLB 45
Cohan, George M(ichael) 1878-1942 TCLC 60
    See also CA 157
Cohen, Arthur A(llen) 1928-1986   CLC 7, 31
    See also CA 1-4R; 120; CANR 1, 17, 42; DLB
    28

Cohen, Leonard (Norman) 1934- **CLC 3, 38; DAC; DAM MST**
  See also CA 21-24R; CANR 14, 69; DLB 53; MTCW 1
Cohen, Matt 1942-   **CLC 19; DAC**
  See also CA 61-64; CAAS 18; CANR 40; DLB 53
Cohen-Solal, Annie 19(?)-   **CLC 50**
Colegate, Isabel 1931-   **CLC 36**
  See also CA 17-20R; CANR 8, 22, 74; DLB 14; INT CANR-22; MTCW 1
Coleman, Emmett
  See Reed, Ishmael
Coleridge, M. E.
  See Coleridge, Mary E(lizabeth)
Coleridge, Mary E(lizabeth) 1861-1907**TCLC 73**
  See also CA 116; 166; DLB 19, 98
Coleridge, Samuel Taylor 1772-1834**NCLC 9, 54; DA; DAB; DAC; DAM MST, POET; PC 11; WLC**
  See also CDBLB 1789-1832; DA3; DLB 93, 107
Coleridge, Sara 1802-1852   **NCLC 31**
  See also DLB 199
Coles, Don 1928-   **CLC 46**
  See also CA 115; CANR 38
Coles, Robert (Martin) 1929-   **CLC 108**
  See also CA 45-48; CANR 3, 32, 66, 70; INT CANR-32; SATA 23
Colette, (Sidonie-Gabrielle) 1873-1954**T C L C 1, 5, 16; DAM NOV; SSC 10**
  See also CA 104; 131; DA3; DLB 65; MTCW 1, 2
Collett, (Jacobine) Camilla (Wergeland) 1813-1895   **NCLC 22**
Collier, Christopher 1930-   **CLC 30**
  See also AAYA 13; CA 33-36R; CANR 13, 33; JRDA; MAICYA; SATA 16, 70
Collier, James L(incoln) 1928-**CLC 30; DAM POP**
  See also AAYA 13; CA 9-12R; CANR 4, 33, 60; CLR 3; JRDA; MAICYA; SAAS 21; SATA 8, 70
Collier, Jeremy 1650-1726   **LC 6**
Collier, John 1901-1980   **SSC 19**
  See also CA 65-68; 97-100; CANR 10; DLB 77
Collingwood, R(obin) G(eorge) 1889(?)-1943
  TCLC 67
  See also CA 117; 155
Collins, Hunt
  See Hunter, Evan
Collins, Linda 1931-   **CLC 44**
  See also CA 125
Collins, (William) Wilkie 1824-1889**NCLC 1, 18**
  See also CDBLB 1832-1890; DLB 18, 70, 159
Collins, William 1721-1759   **LC 4, 40; DAM POET**
  See also DLB 109
Collodi, Carlo 1826-1890   **NCLC 54**
  See also Lorenzini, Carlo
  See also CLR 5
Colman, George 1732-1794
  See Glassco, John
Colt, Winchester Remington
  See Hubbard, L(afayette) Ron(ald)
Colter, Cyrus 1910-   **CLC 58**
  See also BW 1; CA 65-68; CANR 10, 66; DLB 33
Colton, James
  See Hansen, Joseph

Colum, Padraic 1881-1972   **CLC 28**
  See also CA 73-76; 33-36R; CANR 35; CLR 36; MAICYA; MTCW 1; SATA 15
Colvin, James
  See Moorcock, Michael (John)
Colwin, Laurie (E.) 1944-1992**CLC 5, 13, 23, 84**
  See also CA 89-92; 139; CANR 20, 46; DLBY 80; MTCW 1
Comfort, Alex(ander) 1920-**CLC 7; DAM POP**
  See also CA 1-4R; CANR 1, 45; MTCW 1
Comfort, Montgomery
  See Campbell, (John) Ramsey
Compton-Burnett, I(vy) 1884(?)-1969**CLC 1, 3, 10, 15, 34; DAM NOV**
  See also CA 1-4R; 25-28R; CANR 4; DLB 36; MTCW 1
Comstock, Anthony 1844-1915   **TCLC 13**
  See also CA 110; 169
Comte, Auguste 1798-1857   **NCLC 54**
Conan Doyle, Arthur
  See Doyle, Arthur Conan
Conde (Abellan), Carmen 1901-
  See also CA 177; DLB 108; HLCS 1; HW 2
Conde, Maryse 1937-   **CLC 52, 92; BLCS; DAM MULT**
  See also Boucolon, Maryse
  See also BW 2; MTCW 1
Condillac, Etienne Bonnot de 1714-1780   **L C 26**
Condon, Richard (Thomas) 1915-1996**CLC 4, 6, 8, 10, 45, 100; DAM NOV**
  See also BEST 90:3; CA 1-4R; 151; CAAS 1; CANR 2, 23; INT CANR-23; MTCW 1, 2
Confucius 551B.C.-479B.C.   **CMLC 19; DA; DAB; DAC; DAM MST; WLCS**
  See also DA3
Congreve, William 1670-1729 **LC 5, 21; DA; DAB; DAC; DAM DRAM, MST, POET; DC 2; WLC**
  See also CDBLB 1660-1789; DLB 39, 84
Connell, Evan S(helby), Jr. 1924-**CLC 4, 6, 45; DAM NOV**
  See also AAYA 7; CA 1-4R; CAAS 2; CANR 2, 39, 76; DLB 2; DLBY 81; MTCW 1, 2
Connelly, Marc(us Cook) 1890-1980   **CLC 7**
  See also CA 85-88; 102; CANR 30; DLB 7; DLBY 80; SATA-Obit 25
Connor, Ralph   **TCLC 31**
  See also Gordon, Charles William
  See also DLB 92
Conrad, Joseph 1857-1924**TCLC 1, 6, 13, 25, 43, 57; DA; DAB; DAC; DAM MST, NOV; SSC 9; WLC**
  See also AAYA 26; CA 104; 131; CANR 60; CDBLB 1890-1914; DA3; DLB 10, 34, 98, 156; MTCW 1, 2; SATA 27
Conrad, Robert Arnold
  See Hart, Moss
Conroy, Pat
  See Conroy, (Donald) Pat(rick)
  See also MTCW 2
Conroy, (Donald) Pat(rick) 1945-**CLC 30, 74; DAM NOV, POP**
  See also Conroy, Pat
  See also AAYA 8; AITN 1; CA 85-88; CANR 24, 53; DA3; DLB 6; MTCW 1
Constant (de Rebecque), (Henri) Benjamin 1767-1830   **NCLC 6**
  See also DLB 119
Conybeare, Charles Augustus
  See Eliot, T(homas) S(tearns)
Cook, Michael 1933-   **CLC 58**

See also CA 93-96; CANR 68; DLB 53
Cook, Robin 1940-   **CLC 14; DAM POP**
  See also AAYA 32; BEST 90:2; CA 108; 111; CANR 41; DA3; INT 111
Cook, Roy
  See Silverberg, Robert
Cooke, Elizabeth 1948-   **CLC 55**
  See also CA 129
Cooke, John Esten 1830-1886   **NCLC 5**
  See also DLB 3
Cooke, John Estes
  See Baum, L(yman) Frank
Cooke, M. E.
  See Creasey, John
Cooke, Margaret
  See Creasey, John
Cook-Lynn, Elizabeth 1930- **CLC 93; DAM MULT**
  See also CA 133; DLB 175; NNAL
Cooney, Ray   **CLC 62**
Cooper, Douglas 1960-   **CLC 86**
Cooper, Henry St. John
  See Creasey, John
Cooper, J(oan) California (?)-**CLC 56; DAM MULT**
  See also AAYA 12; BW 1; CA 125; CANR 55; DLB 212
Cooper, James Fenimore 1789-1851**NCLC 1, 27, 54**
  See also AAYA 22; CDALB 1640-1865; DA3; DLB 3; SATA 19
Coover, Robert (Lowell) 1932- **CLC 3, 7, 15, 32, 46, 87; DAM NOV; SSC 15**
  See also CA 45-48; CANR 3, 37, 58; DLB 2; DLBY 81; MTCW 1, 2
Copeland, Stewart (Armstrong) 1952-**CLC 26**
Copernicus, Nicolaus 1473-1543   **LC 45**
Coppard, A(lfred) E(dgar) 1878-1957 **T C L C 5; SSC 21**
  See also CA 114; 167; DLB 162; YABC 1
Coppee, Francois 1842-1908   **TCLC 25**
  See also CA 170
Coppola, Francis Ford 1939-   **CLC 16**
  See also CA 77-80; CANR 40, 78; DLB 44
Corbiere, Tristan 1845-1875   **NCLC 43**
Corcoran, Barbara 1911-   **CLC 17**
  See also AAYA 14; CA 21-24R; CAAS 2; CANR 11, 28, 48; CLR 50; DLB 52; JRDA; SAAS 20; SATA 3, 77
Cordelier, Maurice
  See Giraudoux, (Hippolyte) Jean
Corelli, Marie 1855-1924   **TCLC 51**
  See also Mackay, Mary
  See also DLB 34, 156
Corman, Cid 1924-   **CLC 9**
  See also Corman, Sidney
  See also CAAS 2; DLB 5, 193
Corman, Sidney 1924-
  See Corman, Cid
  See also CA 85-88; CANR 44; DAM POET
Cormier, Robert (Edmund) 1925-**CLC 12, 30; DA; DAB; DAC; DAM MST, NOV**
  See also AAYA 3, 19; CA 1-4R; CANR 5, 23, 76; CDALB 1968-1988; CLR 12, 55; DLB 52; INT CANR-23; JRDA; MAICYA; MTCW 1, 2; SATA 10, 45, 83
Corn, Alfred (DeWitt III) 1943-   **CLC 33**
  See also CA 179; CAAE 179; CAAS 25; CANR 44; DLB 120; DLBY 80
Corneille, Pierre 1606-1684   **LC 28; DAB; DAM MST**
Cornwell, David (John Moore) 1931- **CLC 9, 15; DAM POP**

See also le Carre, John
See also CA 5-8R; CANR 13, 33, 59; DA3;
  MTCW 1, 2
Corso, (Nunzio) Gregory 1930-　　**CLC 1, 11**
See also CA 5-8R; CANR 41, 76; DA3; DLB 5,
  16; MTCW 1, 2
Cortazar, Julio 1914-1984**CLC 2, 3, 5, 10, 13,
  15, 33, 34, 92; DAM MULT, NOV; HLC 1;
  SSC 7**
See also CA 21-24R; CANR 12, 32, 81; DA3;
  DLB 113; HW 1, 2; MTCW 1, 2
CORTES, HERNAN 1484-1547　　**LC 31**
Corvinus, Jakob
See Raabe, Wilhelm (Karl)
Corwin, Cecil
See Kornbluth, C(yril) M.
Cosic, Dobrica 1921-　　　　　**CLC 14**
See also CA 122; 138; DLB 181
Costain, Thomas B(ertram) 1885-1965　**C L C
  30**
See also CA 5-8R; 25-28R; DLB 9
Costantini, Humberto 1924(?)-1987　**CLC 49**
See also CA 131; 122; HW 1
Costello, Elvis 1955-　　　　　**CLC 21**
Costenoble, Philostene
See Ghelderode, Michel de
Cotes, Cecil V.
See Duncan, Sara Jeannette
Cotter, Joseph Seamon Sr. 1861-1949　**T C L C
  28; BLC 1; DAM MULT**
See also BW 1; CA 124; DLB 50
Couch, Arthur Thomas Quiller
See Quiller-Couch, SirArthur (Thomas)
Coulton, James
See Hansen, Joseph
Couperus, Louis (Marie Anne) 1863-1923
  TCLC 15
See also CA 115
Coupland, Douglas 1961-**CLC 85; DAC; DAM
  POP**
See also CA 142; CANR 57
Court, Wesli
See Turco, Lewis (Putnam)
Courtenay, Bryce 1933-　　·　　**CLC 59**
See also CA 138
Courtney, Robert
See Ellison, Harlan (Jay)
Cousteau, Jacques-Yves 1910-1997　**CLC 30**
See also CA 65-68; 159; CANR 15, 67; MTCW
  1; SATA 38, 98
Coventry, Francis 1725-1754　　　**LC 46**
Cowan, Peter (Walkinshaw) 1914-　**SSC 28**
See also CA 21-24R; CANR 9, 25, 50, 83
Coward, Noel (Peirce) 1899-1973**CLC 1, 9, 29,
  51; DAM DRAM**
See also AITN 1; CA 17-18; 41-44R; CANR
  35; CAP 2; CDBLB 1914-1945; DA3; DLB
  10; MTCW 1, 2
Cowley, Abraham 1618-1667　　　**LC 43**
See also DLB 131, 151
Cowley, Malcolm 1898-1989　　　**CLC 39**
See also CA 5-8R; 128; CANR 3, 55; DLB 4,
  48; DLBY 81, 89; MTCW 1, 2
Cowper, William 1731-1800　**NCLC 8; DAM
  POET**
See also DA3; DLB 104, 109
Cox, William Trevor 1928-　　**CLC 9, 14, 71;
  DAM NOV**
See also Trevor, William
See also CA 9-12R; CANR 4, 37, 55, 76; DLB
  14; INT CANR-37; MTCW 1, 2
Coyne, P. J.
See Masters, Hilary

Cozzens, James Gould 1903-1978**CLC 1, 4, 11,
  92**
See also CA 9-12R; 81-84; CANR 19; CDALB
  1941-1968; DLB 9; DLBD 2; DLBY 84, 97;
  MTCW 1, 2
Crabbe, George 1754-1832　　　　**NCLC 26**
See also DLB 93
Craddock, Charles Egbert
See Murfree, Mary Noailles
Craig, A. A.
See Anderson, Poul (William)
Craik, Dinah Maria (Mulock) 1826-1887
  NCLC 38
See also DLB 35, 163; MAICYA; SATA 34
Cram, Ralph Adams 1863-1942　　**TCLC 45**
See also CA 160
Crane, (Harold) Hart 1899-1932　**TCLC 2, 5,
  80; DA; DAB; DAC; DAM MST, POET;
  PC 3; WLC**
See also CA 104; 127; CDALB 1917-1929;
  DA3; DLB 4, 48; MTCW 1, 2
Crane, R(onald) S(almon) 1886-1967**CLC 27**
See also CA 85-88; DLB 63
Crane, Stephen (Townley) 1871-1900　**T C L C
  11, 17, 32; DA; DAB; DAC; DAM MST,
  NOV, POET; SSC 7; WLC**
See also AAYA 21; CA 109; 140; CANR 84;
  CDALB 1865-1917; DA3; DLB 12, 54, 78;
  YABC 2
Cranshaw, Stanley
See Fisher, Dorothy (Frances) Canfield
Crase, Douglas 1944-　　　　　　**CLC 58**
See also CA 106
Crashaw, Richard 1612(?)-1649　　　**LC 24**
See also DLB 126
Craven, Margaret 1901-1980　**CLC 17; DAC**
See also CA 103
Crawford, F(rancis) Marion 1854-1909**TCLC
  10**
See also CA 107; 168; DLB 71
Crawford, Isabella Valancy 1850-1887**N C L C
  12**
See also DLB 92
Crayon, Geoffrey
See Irving, Washington
Creasey, John 1908-1973　　　　　**CLC 11**
See also CA 5-8R; 41-44R; CANR 8, 59; DLB
  77; MTCW 1
Crebillon, Claude Prosper Jolyot de (fils) 1707-
  1777　　　　　　　　　　　**LC 1, 28**
Credo
See Creasey, John
Credo, Alvaro J. de
See Prado (Calvo), Pedro
Creeley, Robert (White) 1926-**CLC 1, 2, 4, 8,
  11, 15, 36, 78; DAM POET**
See also CA 1-4R; CAAS 10; CANR 23, 43;
  DA3; DLB 5, 16, 169; DLBD 17; MTCW 1,
  2
Crews, Harry (Eugene) 1935-　**CLC 6, 23, 49**
See also AITN 1; CA 25-28R; CANR 20, 57;
  DA3; DLB 6, 143, 185; MTCW 1, 2
Crichton, (John) Michael 1942-**CLC 2, 6, 54,
  90; DAM NOV, POP**
See also AAYA 10; AITN 2; CA 25-28R; CANR
  13, 40, 54, 76; DA3; DLBY 81; INT CANR-
  13; JRDA; MTCW 1, 2; SATA 9, 88
Crispin, Edmund　　　　　　　　**CLC 22**
See also Montgomery, (Robert) Bruce
See also DLB 87
Cristofer, Michael 1945(?)-　　**CLC 28; DAM
  DRAM**
See also CA 110; 152; DLB 7

Croce, Benedetto 1866-1952　　　**TCLC 37**
See also CA 120; 155
Crockett, David 1786-1836　　　　**NCLC 8**
See also DLB 3, 11
Crockett, Davy
See Crockett, David
Crofts, Freeman Wills 1879-1957　**TCLC 55**
See also CA 115; DLB 77
Croker, John Wilson 1780-1857　　**NCLC 10**
See also DLB 110
Crommelynck, Fernand 1885-1970　**CLC 75**
See also CA 89-92
Cromwell, Oliver 1599-1658　　　　**LC 43**
Cronin, A(rchibald) J(oseph) 1896-1981**C L C
  32**
See also CA 1-4R; 102; CANR 5; DLB 191;
  SATA 47; SATA-Obit 25
Cross, Amanda
See Heilbrun, Carolyn G(old)
Crothers, Rachel 1878(?)-1958　　**TCLC 19**
See also CA 113; DLB 7
Croves, Hal
See Traven, B.
Crow Dog, Mary (Ellen) (?)-　　　**CLC 93**
See also Brave Bird, Mary
See also CA 154
Crowfield, Christopher
See Stowe, Harriet (Elizabeth) Beecher
Crowley, Aleister　　　　　　　　**TCLC 7**
See also Crowley, Edward Alexander
Crowley, Edward Alexander 1875-1947
See Crowley, Aleister
See also CA 104
Crowley, John 1942-　　　　　　　**CLC 57**
See also CA 61-64; CANR 43; DLBY 82; SATA
  65
Crud
See Crumb, R(obert)
Crumarums
See Crumb, R(obert)
Crumb, R(obert) 1943-　　　　　　**CLC 17**
See also CA 106
Crumbum
See Crumb, R(obert)
Crumski
See Crumb, R(obert)
Crum the Bum
See Crumb, R(obert)
Crunk
See Crumb, R(obert)
Crustt
See Crumb, R(obert)
Cruz, Victor Hernandez 1949-
See also BW 2; CA 65-68; CAAS 17; CANR
  14, 32, 74; DAM MULT, POET; DLB 41;
  HLC 1; HW 1, 2; MTCW 1
Cryer, Gretchen (Kiger) 1935-　　**CLC 21**
See also CA 114; 123
Csath, Geza 1887-1919　　　　　　**TCLC 13**
See also CA 111
Cudlip, David R(ockwell) 1933-　　**CLC 34**
See also CA 177
Cullen, Countee 1903-1946**TCLC 4, 37; BLC
  1; DA; DAC; DAM MST, MULT, POET;
  PC 20; WLCS**
See also BW 1; CA 108; 124; CDALB 1917-
  1929; DA3; DLB 4, 48, 51; MTCW 1, 2;
  SATA 18
Cum, R.
See Crumb, R(obert)
Cummings, Bruce F(rederick) 1889-1919
See Barbellion, W. N. P.
See also CA 123

Defoe, Daniel 1660(?)-1731 **LC 1, 42; DA;**
DAB; DAC; DAM MST, NOV; WLC
See also AAYA 27; CDBLB 1660-1789; DA3;
DLB 39, 95, 101; JRDA; MAICYA; SATA
22
de Gourmont, Remy(-Marie-Charles)
See Gourmont, Remy (-Marie-Charles) de
de Hartog, Jan 1914- **CLC 19**
See also CA 1-4R; CANR 1
de Hostos, E. M.
See Hostos (y Bonilla), Eugenio Maria de
de Hostos, Eugenio M.
See Hostos (y Bonilla), Eugenio Maria de
Deighton, Len **CLC 4, 7, 22, 46**
See also Deighton, Leonard Cyril
See also AAYA 6; BEST 89:2; CDBLB 1960 to
Present; DLB 87
Deighton, Leonard Cyril 1929-
See Deighton, Len
See also CA 9-12R; CANR 19, 33, 68; DAM
NOV, POP; DA3; MTCW 1, 2
Dekker, Thomas 1572(?)-1632 **LC 22; DAM**
DRAM
See also CDBLB Before 1660; DLB 62, 172
Delafield, E. M. 1890-1943 **TCLC 61**
See also Dashwood, Edmee Elizabeth Monica
de la Pasture
See also DLB 34
de la Mare, Walter (John) 1873-1956TCLC 4,
53; DAB; DAC; DAM MST, POET; SSC
14; WLC
See also CA 163; CDBLB 1914-1945; CLR 23;
DA3; DLB 162; MTCW 1; SATA 16
Delaney, Franey
See O'Hara, John (Henry)
Delaney, Shelagh 1939-CLC 29; DAM DRAM
See also CA 17-20R; CANR 30, 67; CDBLB
1960 to Present; DLB 13; MTCW 1
Delany, Mary (Granville Pendarves) 1700-1788
LC 12
Delany, Samuel R(ay, Jr.) 1942-CLC 8, 14, 38;
BLC 1; DAM MULT
See also AAYA 24; BW 2, 3; CA 81-84; CANR
27, 43; DLB 8, 33; MTCW 1, 2
De La Ramee, (Marie) Louise 1839-1908
See Ouida
See also SATA 20
de la Roche, Mazo 1879-1961 **CLC 14**
See also CA 85-88; CANR 30; DLB 68; SATA
64
De La Salle, Innocent
See Hartmann, Sadakichi
Delbanco, Nicholas (Franklin) 1942- **CLC 6,**
13
See also CA 17-20R; CAAS 2; CANR 29, 55;
DLB 6
del Castillo, Michel 1933- **CLC 38**
See also CA 109; CANR 77
Deledda, Grazia (Cosima) 1875(?)-1936
TCLC 23
See also CA 123
Delgado, Abelardo B(arrientos) 1931-
See also CA 131; CAAS 15; DAM MST, MULT;
DLB 82; HLC 1; HW 1, 2
Delibes, Miguel **CLC 8, 18**
See also Delibes Setien, Miguel
Delibes Setien, Miguel 1920-
See Delibes, Miguel
See also CA 45-48; CANR 1, 32; HW 1; MTCW
1
DeLillo, Don 1936- CLC 8, 10, 13, 27, 39, 54,
76; DAM NOV, POP
See also BEST 89:1; CA 81-84; CANR 21, 76;

DA3; DLB 6, 173; MTCW 1, 2
de Lisser, H. G.
See De Lisser, H(erbert) G(eorge)
See also DLB 117
De Lisser, H(erbert) G(eorge) 1878-1944
TCLC 12
See also de Lisser, H. G.
See also BW 2; CA 109; 152
Deloney, Thomas 1560(?)-1600 **LC 41**
See also DLB 167
Deloria, Vine (Victor), Jr. 1933-CLC 21, 122;
DAM MULT
See also CA 53-56; CANR 5, 20, 48; DLB 175;
MTCW 1; NNAL; SATA 21
Del Vecchio, John M(ichael) 1947- **CLC 29**
See also CA 110; DLBD 9
de Man, Paul (Adolph Michel) 1919-1983
CLC 55
See also CA 128; 111; CANR 61; DLB 67;
MTCW 1, 2
De Marinis, Rick 1934- **CLC 54**
See also CA 57-60; CAAS 24; CANR 9, 25, 50
Dembry, R. Emmet
See Murfree, Mary Noailles
Demby, William 1922-CLC 53; BLC 1; DAM
MULT
See also BW 1, 3; CA 81-84; CANR 81; DLB
33
de Menton, Francisco
See Chin, Frank (Chew, Jr.)
Demetrius of Phalerum c. 307B.C.-CMLC 34
Demijohn, Thom
See Disch, Thomas M(ichael)
de Molina, Tirso 1580-1648
See also HLCS 2
de Montherlant, Henry (Milon)
See Montherlant, Henry (Milon) de
Demosthenes 384B.C.-322B.C. **CMLC 13**
See also DLB 176
de Natale, Francine
See Malzberg, Barry N(athaniel)
Denby, Edwin (Orr) 1903-1983 **CLC 48**
See also CA 138; 110
Denis, Julio
See Cortazar, Julio
Denmark, Harrison
See Zelazny, Roger (Joseph)
Dennis, John 1658-1734 **LC 11**
See also DLB 101
Dennis, Nigel (Forbes) 1912-1989 **CLC 8**
See also CA 25-28R; 129; DLB 13, 15; MTCW
1
Dent, Lester 1904(?)-1959 **TCLC 72**
See also CA 112; 161
De Palma, Brian (Russell) 1940- **CLC 20**
See also CA 109
De Quincey, Thomas 1785-1859 **NCLC 4**
See also CDBLB 1789-1832; DLB 110; 144
Deren, Eleanora 1908(?)-1961
See Deren, Maya
See also CA 111
Deren, Maya 1917-1961 **CLC 16, 102**
See also Deren, Eleanora
Derleth, August (William) 1909-1971CLC 31
See also CA 1-4R; 29-32R; CANR 4; DLB 9;
DLBD 17; SATA 5
Der Nister 1884-1950 **TCLC 56**
de Routisie, Albert
See Aragon, Louis
Derrida, Jacques 1930- **CLC 24, 87**
See also CA 124; 127; CANR 76; MTCW 1
Derry Down Derry
See Lear, Edward

Dersonnes, Jacques
See Simenon, Georges (Jacques Christian)
Desai, Anita 1937-CLC 19, 37, 97; DAB; DAM
NOV
See also CA 81-84; CANR 33, 53; DA3; MTCW
1, 2; SATA 63
Desai, Kiran 1971- **CLC 119**
See also CA 171
de Saint-Luc, Jean
See Glassco, John
de Saint Roman, Arnaud
See Aragon, Louis
Descartes, Rene 1596-1650 **LC 20, 35**
De Sica, Vittorio 1901(?)-1974 **CLC 20**
See also CA 117
Desnos, Robert 1900-1945 **TCLC 22**
See also CA 121; 151
Destouches, Louis-Ferdinand 1894-1961C L C
9, 15
See also Celine, Louis-Ferdinand
See also CA 85-88; CANR 28; MTCW 1
de Tolignac, Gaston
See Griffith, D(avid Lewelyn) W(ark)
Deutsch, Babette 1895-1982 **CLC 18**
See also CA 1-4R; 108; CANR 4, 79; DLB 45;
SATA 1; SATA-Obit 33
Devenant, William 1606-1649 **LC 13**
Devkota, Laxmiprasad 1909-1959 **TCLC 23**
See also CA 123
De Voto, Bernard (Augustine) 1897-1955
TCLC 29
See also CA 113; 160; DLB 9
De Vries, Peter 1910-1993 CLC 1, 2, 3, 7, 10,
28, 46; DAM NOV
See also CA 17-20R; 142; CANR 41; DLB 6;
DLBY 82; MTCW 1, 2
Dewey, John 1859-1952 **TCLC 95**
See also CA 114; 170
Dexter, John
See Bradley, Marion Zimmer
Dexter, Martin
See Faust, Frederick (Schiller)
Dexter, Pete 1943- **CLC 34, 55; DAM POP**
See also BEST 89:2; CA 127; 131; INT 131;
MTCW 1
Diamano, Silmang
See Senghor, Leopold Sedar
Diamond, Neil 1941- **CLC 30**
See also CA 108
Diaz del Castillo, Bernal 1496-1584 **LC 31;**
HLCS 1
di Bassetto, Corno
See Shaw, George Bernard
Dick, Philip K(indred) 1928-1982CLC 10, 30,
72; DAM NOV, POP
See also AAYA 24; CA 49-52; 106; CANR 2,
16; DA3; DLB 8; MTCW 1, 2
Dickens, Charles (John Huffam) 1812-1870
NCLC 3, 8, 18, 26, 37, 50; DA; DAB; DAC;
DAM MST, NOV; SSC 17; WLC
See also AAYA 23; CDBLB 1832-1890; DA3;
DLB 21, 55, 70, 159, 166; JRDA; MAICYA;
SATA 15
Dickey, James (Lafayette) 1923-1997 CLC 1,
2, 4, 7, 10, 15, 47, 109; DAM NOV, POET,
POP
See also AITN 1, 2; CA 9-12R; 156; CABS 2;
CANR 10, 48, 61; CDALB 1968-1988; DA3;
DLB 5, 193; DLBD 7; DLBY 82, 93, 96, 97,
98; INT CANR-10; MTCW 1, 2
Dickey, William 1928-1994 **CLC 3, 28**
See also CA 9-12R; 145; CANR 24, 79; DLB 5
Dickinson, Charles 1951- **CLC 49**

Doyle, Conan
See Doyle, Arthur Conan
Doyle, John
See Graves, Robert (von Ranke)
Doyle, Roddy 1958(?)-   **CLC 81**
See also AAYA 14; CA 143; CANR 73; DA3;
DLB 194
Doyle, Sir A. Conan
See Doyle, Arthur Conan
Doyle, Sir Arthur Conan
See Doyle, Arthur Conan
Dr. A
See Asimov, Isaac; Silverstein, Alvin
Drabble, Margaret 1939-CLC **2, 3, 5, 8, 10, 22,
53; DAB; DAC; DAM MST, NOV, POP**
See also CA 13-16R; CANR 18, 35, 63; CDBLB
1960 to Present; DA3; DLB 14, 155; MTCW
1, 2; SATA 48
Drapier, M. B.
See Swift, Jonathan
Drayham, James
See Mencken, H(enry) L(ouis)
Drayton, Michael 1563-1631   **LC 8; DAM
POET**
See also DLB 121
Dreadstone, Carl
See Campbell, (John) Ramsey
Dreiser, Theodore (Herman Albert) 1871-1945
**TCLC 10, 18, 35, 83; DA; DAC; DAM
MST, NOV; SSC 30; WLC**
See also CA 106; 132; CDALB 1865-1917;
DA3; DLB 9, 12, 102, 137; DLBD 1; MTCW
1, 2
Drexler, Rosalyn 1926-   **CLC 2, 6**
See also CA 81-84; CANR 68
Dreyer, Carl Theodor 1889-1968   **CLC 16**
See also CA 116
Drieu la Rochelle, Pierre(-Eugene) 1893-1945
TCLC 21
See also CA 117; DLB 72
Drinkwater, John 1882-1937   **TCLC 57**
See also CA 109; 149; DLB 10, 19, 149
Drop Shot
See Cable, George Washington
Droste-Hulshoff, Annette Freiin von 1797-1848
NCLC 3
See also DLB 133
Drummond, Walter
See Silverberg, Robert
Drummond, William Henry 1854-1907**T C L C
25**
See also CA 160; DLB 92
Drummond de Andrade, Carlos 1902-1987
CLC 18
See also Andrade, Carlos Drummond de
See also CA 132; 123
Drury, Allen (Stuart) 1918-1998   **CLC 37**
See also CA 57-60; 170; CANR 18, 52; INT
CANR-18
Dryden, John 1631-1700LC **3, 21; DA; DAB;
DAC; DAM DRAM, MST, POET; DC 3;
PC 25; WLC**
See also CDBLB 1660-1789; DLB 80, 101, 131
Duberman, Martin (Bauml) 1930-   **CLC 8**
See also CA 1-4R; CANR 2, 63
Dubie, Norman (Evans) 1945-   **CLC 36**
See also CA 69-72; CANR 12; DLB 120
Du Bois, W(illiam) E(dward) B(urghardt) 1868-
1963   **CLC 1, 2, 13, 64, 96; BLC 1; DA;
DAC; DAM MST, MULT, NOV; WLC**
See also BW 1, 3; CA 85-88; CANR 34, 82;
CDALB 1865-1917; DA3; DLB 47, 50, 91;
MTCW 1, 2; SATA 42

Dubus, Andre 1936-1999CLC **13, 36, 97; SSC
15**
See also CA 21-24R; 177; CANR 17; DLB 130;
INT CANR-17
Duca Minimo
See D'Annunzio, Gabriele
Ducharme, Rejean 1941-   **CLC 74**
See also CA 165; DLB 60
Duclos, Charles Pinot 1704-1772   **LC 1**
Dudek, Louis 1918-   **CLC 11, 19**
See also CA 45-48; CAAS 14; CANR 1; DLB
88
Duerrenmatt, Friedrich 1921-1990 CLC **1, 4,
8, 11, 15, 43, 102; DAM DRAM**
See also CA 17-20R; CANR 33; DLB 69, 124;
MTCW 1, 2
Duffy, Bruce 1953(?)-   **CLC 50**
See also CA 172
Duffy, Maureen 1933-   **CLC 37**
See also CA 25-28R; CANR 33, 68; DLB 14;
MTCW 1
Dugan, Alan 1923-   **CLC 2, 6**
See also CA 81-84; DLB 5
du Gard, Roger Martin
See Martin du Gard, Roger
Duhamel, Georges 1884-1966   **CLC 8**
See also CA 81-84; 25-28R; CANR 35; DLB
65; MTCW 1
Dujardin, Edouard (Emile Louis) 1861-1949
TCLC 13
See also CA 109; DLB 123
Dulles, John Foster 1888-1959   **TCLC 72**
See also CA 115; 149
Dumas, Alexandre (pere)
See Dumas, Alexandre (Davy de la Pailleterie)
Dumas, Alexandre (Davy de la Pailleterie)
1802-1870   **NCLC 11; DA; DAB; DAC;
DAM MST, NOV; WLC**
See also DA3; DLB 119, 192; SATA 18
Dumas, Alexandre (fils) 1824-1895NCLC **71;
DC 1**
See also AAYA 22; DLB 192
Dumas, Claudine
See Malzberg, Barry N(athaniel)
Dumas, Henry L. 1934-1968   **CLC 6, 62**
See also BW 1; CA 85-88; DLB 41
du Maurier, Daphne 1907-1989CLC **6, 11, 59;
DAB; DAC; DAM MST, POP; SSC 18**
See also CA 5-8R; 128; CANR 6, 55; DA3; DLB
191; MTCW 1, 2; SATA 27; SATA-Obit 60
Dunbar, Paul Laurence 1872-1906 **TCLC 2,
12; BLC 1; DA; DAC; DAM MST, MULT,
POET; PC 5; SSC 8; WLC**
See also BW 1, 3; CA 104; 124; CANR 79;
CDALB 1865-1917; DA3; DLB 50, 54, 78;
SATA 34
Dunbar, William 1460(?)-1530(?)   **LC 20**
See also DLB 132, 146
Duncan, Dora Angela
See Duncan, Isadora
Duncan, Isadora 1877(?)-1927   **TCLC 68**
See also CA 118; 149
Duncan, Lois 1934-   **CLC 26**
See also AAYA 4; CA 1-4R; CANR 2, 23, 36;
CLR 29; JRDA; MAICYA; SAAS 2; SATA
1, 36, 75
Duncan, Robert (Edward) 1919-1988 CLC **1,
2, 4, 7, 15, 41, 55; DAM POET; PC 2**
See also CA 9-12R; 124; CANR 28, 62; DLB
5, 16, 193; MTCW 1, 2
Duncan, Sara Jeannette 1861-1922 TCLC **60**
See also CA 157; DLB 92
Dunlap, William 1766-1839   **NCLC 2**

See also DLB 30, 37, 59
Dunn, Douglas (Eaglesham) 1942- CLC **6, 40**
See also CA 45-48; CANR 2, 33; DLB 40;
MTCW 1
Dunn, Katherine (Karen) 1945-   **CLC 71**
See also CA 33-36R; CANR 72; MTCW 1
Dunn, Stephen 1939-   **CLC 36**
See also CA 33-36R; CANR 12, 48, 53; DLB
105
Dunne, Finley Peter 1867-1936   **TCLC 28**
See also CA 108; 178; DLB 11, 23
Dunne, John Gregory 1932-   **CLC 28**
See also CA 25-28R; CANR 14, 50; DLBY 80
Dunsany, Edward John Moreton Drax Plunkett
1878-1957
See Dunsany, Lord
See also CA 104; 148; DLB 10; MTCW 1
Dunsany, Lord   **TCLC 2, 59**
See also Dunsany, Edward John Moreton Drax
Plunkett
See also DLB 77, 153, 156
du Perry, Jean
See Simenon, Georges (Jacques Christian)
Durang, Christopher (Ferdinand) 1949-C L C
27, 38
See also CA 105; CANR 50, 76; MTCW 1
Duras, Marguerite 1914-1996CLC **3, 6, 11, 20,
34, 40, 68, 100**
See also CA 25-28R; 151; CANR 50; DLB 83;
MTCW 1, 2
Durban, (Rosa) Pam 1947-   **CLC 39**
See also CA 123
Durcan, Paul 1944-CLC **43, 70; DAM POET**
See also CA 134
Durkheim, Emile 1858-1917   **TCLC 55**
Durrell, Lawrence (George) 1912-1990 C L C
1, 4, 6, 8, 13, 27, 41; DAM NOV
See also CA 9-12R; 132; CANR 40, 77; CDBLB
1945-1960; DLB 15, 27, 204; DLBY 90;
MTCW 1, 2
Durrenmatt, Friedrich
See Duerrenmatt, Friedrich
Dutt, Toru 1856-1877   **NCLC 29**
Dwight, Timothy 1752-1817   **NCLC 13**
See also DLB 37
Dworkin, Andrea 1946-   **CLC 43**
See also CA 77-80; CAAS 21; CANR 16, 39,
76; INT CANR-16; MTCW 1, 2
Dwyer, Deanna
See Koontz, Dean R(ay)
Dwyer, K. R.
See Koontz, Dean R(ay)
Dwyer, Thomas A. 1923-   **CLC 114**
See also CA 115
Dye, Richard
See De Voto, Bernard (Augustine)
Dylan, Bob 1941-   **CLC 3, 4, 6, 12, 77**
See also CA 41-44R; DLB 16
E. V. L.
See Lucas, E(dward) V(errall)
Eagleton, Terence (Francis) 1943-
See Eagleton, Terry
See also CA 57-60; CANR 7, 23, 68; MTCW 1,
2
Eagleton, Terry   **CLC 63**
See also Eagleton, Terence (Francis)
See also MTCW 1
Early, Jack
See Scoppettone, Sandra
East, Michael
See West, Morris L(anglo)
Eastaway, Edward
See Thomas, (Philip) Edward

Eastlake, William (Derry) 1917-1997 **CLC 8**
See also CA 5-8R; 158; CAAS 1; CANR 5, 63;
DLB 6, 206; INT CANR-5

Eastman, Charles A(lexander) 1858-1939
TCLC 55; DAM MULT
See also CA 179; DLB 175; NNAL; YABC 1

Eberhart, Richard (Ghormley) 1904- **CLC 3,
11, 19, 56; DAM POET**
See also CA 1-4R; CANR 2; CDALB 1941-
1968; DLB 48; MTCW 1

Eberstadt, Fernanda 1960- **CLC 39**
See also CA 136; CANR 69

Echegaray (y Eizaguirre), Jose (Maria Waldo)
1832-1916 **TCLC 4; HLCS 1**
See also CA 104; CANR 32; HW 1; MTCW 1

Echeverria, (Jose) Esteban (Antonino) 1805-
1851 **NCLC 18**

Echo
See Proust, (Valentin-Louis-George-Eugene-)
Marcel

Eckert, Allan W. 1931- **CLC 17**
See also AAYA 18; CA 13-16R; CANR 14, 45;
INT CANR-14; SAAS 21; SATA 29, 91;
SATA-Brief 27

Eckhart, Meister 1260(?)-1328(?) **CMLC 9**
See also DLB 115

Eckmar, F. R.
See de Hartog, Jan

Eco, Umberto 1932- **CLC 28, 60; DAM NOV,
POP**
See also BEST 90:1; CA 77-80; CANR 12, 33,
55; DA3; DLB 196; MTCW 1, 2

Eddison, E(ric) R(ucker) 1882-1945 **TCLC 15**
See also CA 109; 156

Eddy, Mary (Ann Morse) Baker 1821-1910
TCLC 71
See also CA 113; 174

Edel, (Joseph) Leon 1907-1997 **CLC 29, 34**
See also CA 1-4R; 161; CANR 1, 22; DLB 103;
INT CANR-22

Eden, Emily 1797-1869 **NCLC 10**

Edgar, David 1948- **CLC 42; DAM DRAM**
See also CA 57-60; CANR 12, 61; DLB 13;
MTCW 1

Edgerton, Clyde (Carlyle) 1944- **CLC 39**
See also AAYA 17; CA 118; 134; CANR 64;
INT 134

Edgeworth, Maria 1768-1849 **NCLC 1, 51**
See also DLB 116, 159, 163; SATA 21

Edison, Thomas 1847-1931 **TCLC 96**

Edmonds, Paul
See Kuttner, Henry

Edmonds, Walter D(umaux) 1903-1998 **C L C
35**
See also CA 5-8R; CANR 2; DLB 9; MAICYA;
SAAS 4; SATA 1, 27; SATA-Obit 99

Edmondson, Wallace
See Ellison, Harlan (Jay)

Edson, Russell **CLC 13**
See also CA 33-36R

Edwards, Bronwen Elizabeth
See Rose, Wendy

Edwards, G(erald) B(asil) 1899-1976 **CLC 25**
See also CA 110

Edwards, Gus 1939- **CLC 43**
See also CA 108; INT 108

Edwards, Jonathan 1703-1758 **LC 7; DA;
DAC; DAM MST**
See also DLB 24

Efron, Marina Ivanovna Tsvetaeva
See Tsvetaeva (Efron), Marina (Ivanovna)

Ehle, John (Marsden, Jr.) 1925- **CLC 27**
See also CA 9-12R

Ehrenbourg, Ilya (Grigoryevich)
See Ehrenburg, Ilya (Grigoryevich)

Ehrenburg, Ilya (Grigoryevich) 1891-1967
CLC 18, 34, 62
See also CA 102; 25-28R

Ehrenburg, Ilyo (Grigoryevich)
See Ehrenburg, Ilya (Grigoryevich)

Ehrenreich, Barbara 1941- **CLC 110**
See also BEST 90:4; CA 73-76; CANR 16, 37,
62; MTCW 1, 2

Eich, Guenter 1907-1972 **CLC 15**
See also CA 111; 93-96; DLB 69, 124

Eichendorff, Joseph Freiherr von 1788-1857
NCLC 8
See also DLB 90

Eigner, Larry **CLC 9**
See also Eigner, Laurence (Joel)
See also CAAS 23; DLB 5

Eigner, Laurence (Joel) 1927-1996
See Eigner, Larry
See also CA 9-12R; 151; CANR 6, 84; DLB
193

Einstein, Albert 1879-1955 **TCLC 65**
See also CA 121; 133; MTCW 1, 2

Eiseley, Loren Corey 1907-1977 **CLC 7**
See also AAYA 5; CA 1-4R; 73-76; CANR 6;
DLBD 17

Eisenstadt, Jill 1963- **CLC 50**
See also CA 140

Eisenstein, Sergei (Mikhailovich) 1898-1948
TCLC 57
See also CA 114; 149

Eisner, Simon
See Kornbluth, C(yril) M.

Ekeloef, (Bengt) Gunnar 1907-1968 **CLC 27;
DAM POET; PC 23**
See also CA 123; 25-28R

Ekelof, (Bengt) Gunnar
See Ekeloef, (Bengt) Gunnar

Ekelund, Vilhelm 1880-1949 **TCLC 75**

Ekwensi, C. O. D.
See Ekwensi, Cyprian (Odiatu Duaka)

Ekwensi, Cyprian (Odiatu Duaka) 1921- **C L C
4; BLC 1; DAM MULT**
See also BW 2, 3; CA 29-32R; CANR 18, 42,
74; DLB 117; MTCW 1, 2; SATA 66

Elaine **TCLC 18**
See also Leverson, Ada

El Crummo
See Crumb, R(obert)

Elder, Lonne III 1931-1996 **DC 8**
See also BLC 1; BW 1, 3; CA 81-84; 152;
CANR 25; DAM MULT; DLB 7, 38, 44

Elia
See Lamb, Charles

Eliade, Mircea 1907-1986 **CLC 19**
See also CA 65-68; 119; CANR 30, 62; MTCW
1

Eliot, A. D.
See Jewett, (Theodora) Sarah Orne

Eliot, Alice
See Jewett, (Theodora) Sarah Orne

Eliot, Dan
See Silverberg, Robert

Eliot, George 1819-1880 **NCLC 4, 13, 23, 41,
49; DA; DAB; DAC; DAM MST, NOV; PC
20; WLC**
See also CDBLB 1832-1890; DA3; DLB 21,
35, 55

Eliot, John 1604-1690 **LC 5**
See also DLB 24

Eliot, T(homas) S(tearns) 1888-1965 **CLC 1, 2,
3, 6, 9, 10, 13, 15, 24, 34, 41, 55, 57, 113;**
**DA; DAB; DAC; DAM DRAM, MST,
POET; PC 5; WLC**
See also AAYA 28; CA 5-8R; 25-28R; CANR
41; CDALB 1929-1941; DA3; DLB 7, 10,
45, 63; DLBY 88; MTCW 1, 2

Elizabeth 1866-1941 **TCLC 41**

Elkin, Stanley L(awrence) 1930-1995 **CLC 4,
6, 9, 14, 27, 51, 91; DAM NOV, POP; SSC
12**
See also CA 9-12R; 148; CANR 8, 46; DLB 2,
28; DLBY 80; INT CANR-8; MTCW 1, 2

Elledge, Scott **CLC 34**

Elliot, Don
See Silverberg, Robert

Elliott, Don
See Silverberg, Robert

Elliott, George P(aul) 1918-1980 **CLC 2**
See also CA 1-4R; 97-100; CANR 2

Elliott, Janice 1931- **CLC 47**
See also CA 13-16R; CANR 8, 29, 84; DLB 14

Elliott, Sumner Locke 1917-1991 **CLC 38**
See also CA 5-8R; 134; CANR 2, 21

Elliott, William
See Bradbury, Ray (Douglas)

Ellis, A. E. **CLC 7**

Ellis, Alice Thomas **CLC 40**
See also Haycraft, Anna
See also DLB 194; MTCW 1

Ellis, Bret Easton 1964- **CLC 39, 71, 117; DAM
POP**
See also AAYA 2; CA 118; 123; CANR 51, 74;
DA3; INT 123; MTCW 1

Ellis, (Henry) Havelock 1859-1939 **TCLC 14**
See also CA 109; 169; DLB 190

Ellis, Landon
See Ellison, Harlan (Jay)

Ellis, Trey 1962- **CLC 55**
See also CA 146

Ellison, Harlan (Jay) 1934- **CLC 1, 13, 42;
DAM POP; SSC 14**
See also AAYA 29; CA 5-8R; CANR 5, 46; DLB
8; INT CANR-5; MTCW 1, 2

Ellison, Ralph (Waldo) 1914-1994 **CLC 1, 3,
11, 54, 86, 114; BLC 1; DA; DAB; DAC;
DAM MST, MULT, NOV; SSC 26; WLC**
See also AAYA 19; BW 1, 3; CA 9-12R; 145;
CANR 24, 53; CDALB 1941-1968; DA3;
DLB 2, 76; DLBY 94; MTCW 1, 2

Ellmann, Lucy (Elizabeth) 1956- **CLC 61**
See also CA 128

Ellmann, Richard (David) 1918-1987 **CLC 50**
See also BEST 89:2; CA 1-4R; 122; CANR 2,
28, 61; DLB 103; DLBY 87; MTCW 1, 2

Elman, Richard (Martin) 1934-1997 **CLC 19**
See also CA 17-20R; 163; CAAS 3; CANR 47

Elron
See Hubbard, L(afayette) Ron(ald)

Eluard, Paul **TCLC 7, 41**
See also Grindel, Eugene

Elyot, Sir Thomas 1490(?)-1546 **LC 11**

Elytis, Odysseus 1911-1996 **CLC 15, 49, 100;
DAM POET; PC 21**
See also CA 102; 151; MTCW 1, 2

Emecheta, (Florence Onye) Buchi 1944- **C L C
14, 48; BLC 2; DAM MULT**
See also BW 2, 3; CA 81-84; CANR 27, 81;
DA3; DLB 117; MTCW 1, 2; SATA 66

Emerson, Mary Moody 1774-1863 **NCLC 66**

Emerson, Ralph Waldo 1803-1882 **NCLC 1,
38; DA; DAB; DAC; DAM MST, POET;
PC 18; WLC**
See also CDALB 1640-1865; DA3; DLB 1, 59,
73

Eminescu, Mihail 1850-1889   NCLC 33

Empson, William 1906-1984CLC 3, 8, 19, 33,
    34
    See also CA 17-20R; 112; CANR 31, 61; DLB
    20; MTCW 1, 2

Enchi, Fumiko (Ueda) 1905-1986   CLC 31
    See also CA 129; 121; DLB 182

Ende, Michael (Andreas Helmuth) 1929-1995
    CLC 31
    See also CA 118; 124; 149; CANR 36; CLR
    14; DLB 75; MAICYA; SATA 61; SATA-
    Brief 42; SATA-Obit 86

Endo, Shusaku 1923-1996 CLC 7, 14, 19, 54,
    99; DAM NOV
    See also CA 29-32R; 153; CANR 21, 54; DA3;
    DLB 182; MTCW 1, 2

Engel, Marian 1933-1985   CLC 36
    See also CA 25-28R; CANR 12; DLB 53; INT
    CANR-12

Engelhardt, Frederick
    See Hubbard, L(afayette) Ron(ald)

Enright, D(ennis) J(oseph) 1920-CLC 4, 8, 31
    See also CA 1-4R; CANR 1, 42, 83; DLB 27;
    SATA 25

Enzensberger, Hans Magnus 1929- CLC 43;
    PC 28
    See also CA 116; 119

Ephron, Nora 1941-   CLC 17, 31
    See also AITN 2; CA 65-68; CANR 12, 39, 83

Epicurus 341B.C.-270B.C.   CMLC 21
    See also DLB 176

Epsilon
    See Betjeman, John

Epstein, Daniel Mark 1948-   CLC 7
    See also CA 49-52; CANR 2, 53

Epstein, Jacob 1956-   CLC 19
    See also CA 114

Epstein, Jean 1897-1953   TCLC 92

Epstein, Joseph 1937-   CLC 39
    See also CA 112; 119; CANR 50, 65

Epstein, Leslie 1938-   CLC 27
    See also CA 73-76; CAAS 12; CANR 23, 69

Equiano, Olaudah 1745(?)-1797 LC 16; BLC
    2; DAM MULT
    See also DLB 37, 50

ER   TCLC 33
    See also CA 160; DLB 85

Erasmus, Desiderius 1469(?)-1536   LC 16

Erdman, Paul E(mil) 1932-   CLC 25
    See also AITN 1; CA 61-64; CANR 13, 43, 84

Erdrich, Louise 1954-CLC 39, 54, 120; DAM
    MULT, NOV, POP
    See also AAYA 10; BEST 89:1; CA 114; CANR
    41, 62; CDALBS; DA3; DLB 152, 175, 206;
    MTCW 1; NNAL; SATA 94

Erenburg, Ilya (Grigoryevich)
    See Ehrenburg, Ilya (Grigoryevich)

Erickson, Stephen Michael 1950-
    See Erickson, Steve
    See also CA 129

Erickson, Steve 1950-   CLC 64
    See also Erickson, Stephen Michael
    See also CANR 60, 68

Ericson, Walter
    See Fast, Howard (Melvin)

Eriksson, Buntel
    See Bergman, (Ernst) Ingmar

Ernaux, Annie 1940-   CLC 88
    See also CA 147

Erskine, John 1879-1951   TCLC 84
    See also CA 112; 159; DLB 9, 102

Eschenbach, Wolfram von
    See Wolfram von Eschenbach

Eseki, Bruno
    See Mphahlele, Ezekiel

Esenin, Sergei (Alexandrovich) 1895-1925
    TCLC 4
    See also CA 104

Eshleman, Clayton 1935-   CLC 7
    See also CA 33-36R; CAAS 6; DLB 5

Espriella, Don Manuel Alvarez
    See Southey, Robert

Espriu, Salvador 1913-1985   CLC 9
    See also CA 154; 115; DLB 134

Espronceda, Jose de 1808-1842   NCLC 39

Esquivel, Laura 1951(?)-
    See also AAYA 29; CA 143; CANR 68; DA3;
    HLCS 1; MTCW 1

Esse, James
    See Stephens, James

Esterbrook, Tom
    See Hubbard, L(afayette) Ron(ald)

Estleman, Loren D. 1952-CLC 48; DAM NOV,
    POP
    See also AAYA 27; CA 85-88; CANR 27, 74;
    DA3; INT CANR-27; MTCW 1, 2

Euclid 306B.C.-283B.C.   CMLC 25

Eugenides, Jeffrey 1960(?)-   CLC 81
    See also CA 144

Euripides c. 485B.C.-406B.C.CMLC 23; DA;
    DAB; DAC; DAM DRAM, MST; DC 4;
    WLCS
    See also DA3; DLB 176

Evan, Evin
    See Faust, Frederick (Schiller)

Evans, Caradoc 1878-1945   TCLC 85

Evans, Evan
    See Faust, Frederick (Schiller)

Evans, Marian
    See Eliot, George

Evans, Mary Ann
    See Eliot, George

Evarts, Esther
    See Benson, Sally

Everett, Percival L. 1956-   CLC 57
    See also BW 2; CA 129

Everson, R(onald) G(ilmour) 1903- CLC 27
    See also CA 17-20R; DLB 88

Everson, William (Oliver) 1912-1994 CLC 1,
    5, 14
    See also CA 9-12R; 145; CANR 20; DLB 212;
    MTCW 1

Evtushenko, Evgenii Aleksandrovich
    See Yevtushenko, Yevgeny (Alexandrovich)

Ewart, Gavin (Buchanan) 1916-1995CLC 13,
    46
    See also CA 89-92; 150; CANR 17, 46; DLB
    40; MTCW 1

Ewers, Hanns Heinz 1871-1943   TCLC 12
    See also CA 109; 149

Ewing, Frederick R.
    See Sturgeon, Theodore (Hamilton)

Exley, Frederick (Earl) 1929-1992 CLC 6, 11
    See also AITN 2; CA 81-84; 138; DLB 143;
    DLBY 81

Eynhardt, Guillermo
    See Quiroga, Horacio (Sylvestre)

Ezekiel, Nissim 1924-   CLC 61
    See also CA 61-64

Ezekiel, Tish O'Dowd 1943-   CLC 34
    See also CA 129

Fadeyev, A.
    See Bulgya, Alexander Alexandrovich

Fadeyev, Alexander   TCLC 53
    See also Bulgya, Alexander Alexandrovich

Fagen, Donald 1948-   CLC 26

Fainzilberg, Ilya Arnoldovich 1897-1937
    See Ilf, Ilya
    See also CA 120; 165

Fair, Ronald L. 1932-   CLC 18
    See also BW 1; CA 69-72; CANR 25; DLB 33

Fairbairn, Roger
    See Carr, John Dickson

Fairbairns, Zoe (Ann) 1948-   CLC 32
    See also CA 103; CANR 21

Falco, Gian
    See Papini, Giovanni

Falconer, James
    See Kirkup, James

Falconer, Kenneth
    See Kornbluth, C(yril) M.

Falkland, Samuel
    See Heijermans, Herman

Fallaci, Oriana 1930-   CLC 11, 110
    See also CA 77-80; CANR 15, 58; MTCW 1

Faludy, George 1913-   CLC 42
    See also CA 21-24R

Faludy, Gyoergy
    See Faludy, George

Fanon, Frantz 1925-1961   CLC 74; BLC 2;
    DAM MULT
    See also BW 1; CA 116; 89-92

Fanshawe, Ann 1625-1680   LC 11

Fante, John (Thomas) 1911-1983   CLC 60
    See also CA 69-72; 109; CANR 23; DLB 130;
    DLBY 83

Farah, Nuruddin 1945-CLC 53; BLC 2; DAM
    MULT
    See also BW 2, 3; CA 106; CANR 81; DLB
    125

Fargue, Leon-Paul 1876(?)-1947   TCLC 11
    See also CA 109

Farigoule, Louis
    See Romains, Jules

Farina, Richard 1936(?)-1966   CLC 9
    See also CA 81-84; 25-28R

Farley, Walter (Lorimer) 1915-1989 CLC 17
    See also CA 17-20R; CANR 8, 29, 84; DLB
    22; JRDA; MAICYA; SATA 2, 43

Farmer, Philip Jose 1918-   CLC 1, 19
    See also AAYA 28; CA 1-4R; CANR 4, 35; DLB
    8; MTCW 1; SATA 93

Farquhar, George 1677-1707   LC 21; DAM
    DRAM
    See also DLB 84

Farrell, J(ames) G(ordon) 1935-1979 CLC 6
    See also CA 73-76; 89-92; CANR 36; DLB 14;
    MTCW 1

Farrell, James T(homas) 1904-1979CLC 1, 4,
    8, 11, 66; SSC 28
    See also CA 5-8R; 89-92; CANR 9, 61; DLB 4,
    9, 86; DLBD 2; MTCW 1, 2

Farren, Richard J.
    See Betjeman, John

Farren, Richard M.
    See Betjeman, John

Fassbinder, Rainer Werner 1946-1982CLC 20
    See also CA 93-96; 106; CANR 31

Fast, Howard (Melvin) 1914- CLC 23; DAM
    NOV
    See also AAYA 16; CA 1-4R; CAAS 18; CANR
    1, 33, 54, 75; DLB 9; INT CANR-33; MTCW
    1; SATA 7; SATA-Essay 107

Faulcon, Robert
    See Holdstock, Robert P.

Faulkner, William (Cuthbert) 1897-1962CLC
    1, 3, 6, 8, 9, 11, 14, 18, 28, 52, 68; DA; DAB;
    DAC; DAM MST, NOV; SSC 1, 35; WLC
    See also AAYA 7; CA 81-84; CANR 33;

Fontane, Theodor 1819-1898 **NCLC 26**
See also DLB 129
Foote, Horton 1916-**CLC 51, 91; DAM DRAM**
See also CA 73-76; CANR 34, 51; DA3; DLB 26; INT CANR-34
Foote, Shelby 1916-**CLC 75; DAM NOV, POP**
See also CA 5-8R; CANR 3, 45, 74; DA3; DLB 2, 17; MTCW 2
Forbes, Esther 1891-1967 **CLC 12**
See also AAYA 17; CA 13-14; 25-28R; CAP 1; CLR 27; DLB 22; JRDA; MAICYA; SATA 2, 100
Forche, Carolyn (Louise) 1950- **CLC 25, 83, 86; DAM POET; PC 10**
See also CA 109; 117; CANR 50, 74; DA3; DLB 5, 193; INT 117; MTCW 1
Ford, Elbur
See Hibbert, Eleanor Alice Burford
Ford, Ford Madox 1873-1939**TCLC 1, 15, 39, 57; DAM NOV**
See also CA 104; 132; CANR 74; CDBLB 1914-1945; DA3; DLB 162; MTCW 1, 2
Ford, Henry 1863-1947 **TCLC 73**
See also CA 115; 148
Ford, John 1586-(?) **DC 8**
See also CDBLB Before 1660; DAM DRAM; DA3; DLB 58
Ford, John 1895-1973 **CLC 16**
See also CA 45-48
Ford, Richard 1944- **CLC 46, 99**
See also CA 69-72; CANR 11, 47; MTCW 1
Ford, Webster
See Masters, Edgar Lee
Foreman, Richard 1937- **CLC 50**
See also CA 65-68; CANR 32, 63
Forester, C(ecil) S(cott) 1899-1966 **CLC 35**
See also CA 73-76; 25-28R; CANR 83; DLB 191; SATA 13
Forez
See Mauriac, Francois (Charles)
Forman, James Douglas 1932- **CLC 21**
See also AAYA 17; CA 9-12R; CANR 4, 19, 42; JRDA; MAICYA; SATA 8, 70
Fornes, Maria Irene 1930-**CLC 39, 61; DC 10; HLCS 1**
See also CA 25-28R; CANR 28, 81; DLB 7; HW 1, 2; INT CANR-28; MTCW 1
Forrest, Leon (Richard) 1937-1997 **CLC 4; BLCS**
See also BW 2; CA 89-92; 162; CAAS 7; CANR 25, 52; DLB 33
Forster, E(dward) M(organ) 1879-1970 **C L C 1, 2, 3, 4, 9, 10, 13, 15, 22, 45, 77; DA; DAB; DAC; DAM MST, NOV; SSC 27; WLC**
See also AAYA 2; CA 13-14; 25-28R; CANR 45; CAP 1; CDBLB 1914-1945; DA3; DLB 34, 98, 162, 178, 195; DLBD 10; MTCW 1, 2; SATA 57
Forster, John 1812-1876 **NCLC 11**
See also DLB 144, 184
Forsyth, Frederick 1938-**CLC 2, 5, 36; DAM NOV, POP**
See also BEST 89:4; CA 85-88; CANR 38, 62; DLB 87; MTCW 1, 2
Forten, Charlotte L. **TCLC 16; BLC 2**
See also Grimke, Charlotte L(ottie) Forten
See also DLB 50
Foscolo, Ugo 1778-1827 **NCLC 8**
Fosse, Bob **CLC 20**
See also Fosse, Robert Louis
Fosse, Robert Louis 1927-1987
See Fosse, Bob
See also CA 110; 123

Foster, Stephen Collins 1826-1864 **NCLC 26**
Foucault, Michel 1926-1984 **CLC 31, 34, 69**
See also CA 105; 113; CANR 34; MTCW 1, 2
Fouque, Friedrich (Heinrich Karl) de la Motte 1777-1843 **NCLC 2**
See also DLB 90
Fourier, Charles 1772-1837 **NCLC 51**
Fournier, Pierre 1916- **CLC 11**
See Gascar, Pierre
See also CA 89-92; CANR 16, 40
Fowles, John (Philip) 1926- CLC **1, 2, 3, 4, 6, 9, 10, 15, 33, 87; DAB; DAC; DAM MST; SSC 33**
See also CA 5-8R; CANR 25, 71; CDBLB 1960 to Present; DA3; DLB 14, 139, 207; MTCW 1, 2; SATA 22
Fox, Paula 1923- **CLC 2, 8, 121**
See also AAYA 3; CA 73-76; CANR 20, 36, 62; CLR 1, 44; DLB 52; JRDA; MAICYA; MTCW 1; SATA 17, 60
Fox, William Price (Jr.) 1926- **CLC 22**
See also CA 17-20R; CAAS 19; CANR 11; DLB 2; DLBY 81
Foxe, John 1516(?)-1587 **LC 14**
See also DLB 132
Frame, Janet 1924-CLC **2, 3, 6, 22, 66, 96; SSC 29**
See also Clutha, Janet Paterson Frame
France, Anatole **TCLC 9**
See also Thibault, Jacques Anatole Francois
See also DLB 123; MTCW 1
Francis, Claude 19(?)- **CLC 50**
Francis, Dick 1920-CLC **2, 22, 42, 102; DAM POP**
See also AAYA 5, 21; BEST 89:3; CA 5-8R; CANR 9, 42, 68; CDBLB 1960 to Present; DA3; DLB 87; INT CANR-9; MTCW 1, 2
Francis, Robert (Churchill) 1901-1987 **C L C 15**
See also CA 1-4R; 123; CANR 1
Frank, Anne(lies Marie) 1929-1945TCLC **17; DA; DAB; DAC; DAM MST; WLC**
See also AAYA 12; CA 113; 133; CANR 68; DA3; MTCW 1, 2; SATA 87; SATA-Brief 42
Frank, Bruno 1887-1945 **TCLC 81**
See also DLB 118
Frank, Elizabeth 1945- **CLC 39**
See also CA 121; 126; CANR 78; INT 126
Frankl, Viktor E(mil) 1905-1997 **CLC 93**
See also CA 65-68; 161
Franklin, Benjamin
See Hasek, Jaroslav (Matej Frantisek)
Franklin, Benjamin 1706-1790 **LC 25; DA; DAB; DAC; DAM MST; WLCS**
See also CDALB 1640-1865; DA3; DLB 24, 43, 73
Franklin, (Stella Maria Sarah) Miles (Lampe) 1879-1954 **TCLC 7**
See also CA 104; 164
Fraser, (Lady) Antonia (Pakenham) 1932- **CLC 32, 107**
See also CA 85-88; CANR 44, 65; MTCW 1, 2; SATA-Brief 32
Fraser, George MacDonald 1925- **CLC 7**
See also CA 45-48, 180; CAAE 180; CANR 2, 48, 74; MTCW 1
Fraser, Sylvia 1935- **CLC 64**
See also CA 45-48; CANR 1, 16, 60
Frayn, Michael 1933-CLC **3, 7, 31, 47; DAM DRAM, NOV**
See also CA 5-8R; CANR 30, 69; DLB 13, 14, 194; MTCW 1, 2
Fraze, Candida (Merrill) 1945- **CLC 50**

See also CA 126
Frazer, J(ames) G(eorge) 1854-1941TCLC **32**
See also CA 118
Frazer, Robert Caine
See Creasey, John
Frazer, Sir James George
See Frazer, J(ames) G(eorge)
Frazier, Charles 1950- **CLC 109**
See also CA 161
Frazier, Ian 1951- **CLC 46**
See also CA 130; CANR 54
Frederic, Harold 1856-1898 **NCLC 10**
See also DLB 12, 23; DLBD 13
Frederick, John
See Faust, Frederick (Schiller)
Frederick the Great 1712-1786 **LC 14**
Fredro, Aleksander 1793-1876 **NCLC 8**
Freeling, Nicolas 1927- **CLC 38**
See also CA 49-52; CAAS 12; CANR 1, 17, 50, 84; DLB 87
Freeman, Douglas Southall 1886-1953 **T C L C 11**
See also CA 109; DLB 17; DLBD 17
Freeman, Judith 1946- **CLC 55**
See also CA 148
Freeman, Mary Eleanor Wilkins 1852-1930 **TCLC 9; SSC 1**
See also CA 106; 177; DLB 12, 78
Freeman, R(ichard) Austin 1862-1943 **T C L C 21**
See also CA 113; CANR 84; DLB 70
French, Albert 1943- **CLC 86**
See also BW 3; CA 167
French, Marilyn 1929-CLC **10, 18, 60; DAM DRAM, NOV, POP**
See also CA 69-72; CANR 3, 31; INT CANR-31; MTCW 1, 2
French, Paul
See Asimov, Isaac
Freneau, Philip Morin 1752-1832 **NCLC 1**
See also DLB 37, 43
Freud, Sigmund 1856-1939 **TCLC 52**
See also CA 115; 133; CANR 69; MTCW 1, 2
Friedan, Betty (Naomi) 1921- **CLC 74**
See also CA 65-68; CANR 18, 45, 74; MTCW 1, 2
Friedlander, Saul 1932- **CLC 90**
See also CA 117; 130; CANR 72
Friedman, B(ernard) H(arper) 1926- **CLC 7**
See also CA 1-4R; CANR 3, 48
Friedman, Bruce Jay 1930- **CLC 3, 5, 56**
See also CA 9-12R; CANR 25, 52; DLB 2, 28; INT CANR-25
Friel, Brian 1929- **CLC 5, 42, 59, 115; DC 8**
See also CA 21-24R; CANR 33, 69; DLB 13; MTCW 1
Friis-Baastad, Babbis Ellinor 1921-1970**CLC 12**
See also CA 17-20R; 134; SATA 7
Frisch, Max (Rudolf) 1911-1991**CLC 3, 9, 14, 18, 32, 44; DAM DRAM, NOV**
See also CA 85-88; 134; CANR 32, 74; DLB 69, 124; MTCW 1, 2
Fromentin, Eugene (Samuel Auguste) 1820-1876 **NCLC 10**
See also DLB 123
Frost, Frederick
See Faust, Frederick (Schiller)
Frost, Robert (Lee) 1874-1963**CLC 1, 3, 4, 9, 10, 13, 15, 26, 34, 44; DA; DAB; DAC; DAM MST, POET; PC 1; WLC**
See also AAYA 21; CA 89-92; CANR 33; CDALB 1917-1929; DA3; DLB 54; DLBD

7; MTCW 1, 2; SATA 14

Froude, James Anthony 1818-1894 **NCLC 43**
See also DLB 18, 57, 144

Froy, Herald
See Waterhouse, Keith (Spencer)

Fry, Christopher 1907- **CLC 2, 10, 14; DAM DRAM**
See also CA 17-20R; CAAS 23; CANR 9, 30, 74; DLB 13; MTCW 1, 2; SATA 66

Frye, (Herman) Northrop 1912-1991 **CLC 24, 70**
See also CA 5-8R; 133; CANR 8, 37; DLB 67, 68; MTCW 1, 2

Fuchs, Daniel 1909-1993 **CLC 8, 22**
See also CA 81-84; 142; CAAS 5; CANR 40; DLB 9, 26, 28; DLBY 93

Fuchs, Daniel 1934- **CLC 34**
See also CA 37-40R; CANR 14, 48

Fuentes, Carlos 1928- **CLC 3, 8, 10, 13, 22, 41, 60, 113; DA; DAB; DAC; DAM MST, MULT, NOV; HLC 1; SSC 24; WLC**
See also AAYA 4; AITN 2; CA 69-72; CANR 10, 32, 68; DA3; DLB 113; HW 1, 2; MTCW 1, 2

Fuentes, Gregorio Lopez y
See Lopez y Fuentes, Gregorio

Fuertes, Gloria 1918- **PC 27**
See also CA 178, 180; DLB 108; HW 2

Fugard, (Harold) Athol 1932- **CLC 5, 9, 14, 25, 40, 80; DAM DRAM; DC 3**
See also AAYA 17; CA 85-88; CANR 32, 54; MTCW 1

Fugard, Sheila 1932- **CLC 48**
See also CA 125

Fuller, Charles (H., Jr.) 1939- **CLC 25; BLC 2; DAM DRAM, MULT; DC 1**
See also BW 2; CA 108; 112; DLB 38; INT 112; MTCW 1

Fuller, John (Leopold) 1937- **CLC 62**
See also CA 21-24R; CANR 9, 44; DLB 40

Fuller, Margaret **NCLC 5, 50**
See also Ossoli, Sarah Margaret (Fuller marchesa d')

Fuller, Roy (Broadbent) 1912-1991 **CLC 4, 28**
See also CA 5-8R; 135; CAAS 10; CANR 53, 83; DLB 15, 20; SATA 87

Fulton, Alice 1952- **CLC 52**
See also CA 116; CANR 57; DLB 193

Furphy, Joseph 1843-1912 **TCLC 25**
See also CA 163

Fussell, Paul 1924- **CLC 74**
See also BEST 90:1; CA 17-20R; CANR 8, 21, 35, 69; INT CANR-21; MTCW 1, 2

Futabatei, Shimei 1864-1909 **TCLC 44**
See also CA 162; DLB 180

Futrelle, Jacques 1875-1912 **TCLC 19**
See also CA 113; 155

Gaboriau, Emile 1835-1873 **NCLC 14**

Gadda, Carlo Emilio 1893-1973 **CLC 11**
See also CA 89-92; DLB 177

Gaddis, William 1922-1998 **CLC 1, 3, 6, 8, 10, 19, 43, 86**
See also CA 17-20R; 172; CANR 21, 48; DLB 2; MTCW 1, 2

Gage, Walter
See Inge, William (Motter)

Gaines, Ernest J(ames) 1933- **CLC 3, 11, 18, 86; BLC 2; DAM MULT**
See also AAYA 18; AITN 1; BW 2, 3; CA 9-12R; CANR 6, 24, 42, 75; CDALB 1968-1988; DA3; DLB 2, 33, 152; DLBY 80; MTCW 1, 2; SATA 86

Gaitskill, Mary 1954- **CLC 69**

See also CA 128; CANR 61

Galdos, Benito Perez
See Perez Galdos, Benito

Gale, Zona 1874-1938 **TCLC 7; DAM DRAM**
See also CA 105; 153; CANR 84; DLB 9, 78

Galeano, Eduardo (Hughes) 1940- **CLC 72; HLCS 1**
See also CA 29-32R; CANR 13, 32; HW 1

Galiano, Juan Valera y Alcala
See Valera y Alcala-Galiano, Juan

Galilei, Galileo 1546-1642 **LC 45**

Gallagher, Tess 1943- **CLC 18, 63; DAM POET; PC 9**
See also CA 106; DLB 212

Gallant, Mavis 1922- **CLC 7, 18, 38; DAC; DAM MST; SSC 5**
See also CA 69-72; CANR 29, 69; DLB 53; MTCW 1, 2

Gallant, Roy A(rthur) 1924- **CLC 17**
See also CA 5-8R; CANR 4, 29, 54; CLR 30; MAICYA; SATA 4, 68, 110

Gallico, Paul (William) 1897-1976 **CLC 2**
See also AITN 1; CA 5-8R; 69-72; CANR 23; DLB 9, 171; MAICYA; SATA 13

Gallo, Max Louis 1932- **CLC 95**
See also CA 85-88

Gallois, Lucien
See Desnos, Robert

Gallup, Ralph
See Whitemore, Hugh (John)

Galsworthy, John 1867-1933 **TCLC 1, 45; DA; DAB; DAC; DAM DRAM, MST, NOV; SSC 22; WLC**
See also CA 104; 141; CANR 75; CDBLB 1890-1914; DA3; DLB 10, 34, 98, 162; DLBD 16; MTCW 1

Galt, John 1779-1839 **NCLC 1**
See also DLB 99, 116, 159

Galvin, James 1951- **CLC 38**
See also CA 108; CANR 26

Gamboa, Federico 1864-1939 **TCLC 36**
See also CA 167; HW 2

Gandhi, M. K.
See Gandhi, Mohandas Karamchand

Gandhi, Mahatma
See Gandhi, Mohandas Karamchand

Gandhi, Mohandas Karamchand 1869-1948 **TCLC 59; DAM MULT**
See also CA 121; 132; DA3; MTCW 1, 2

Gann, Ernest Kellogg 1910-1991 **CLC 23**
See also AITN 1; CA 1-4R; 136; CANR 1, 83

Garcia, Cristina 1958- **CLC 76**
See also CA 141; CANR 73; HW 2

Garcia Lorca, Federico 1898-1936 **TCLC 1, 7, 49; DA; DAB; DAC; DAM DRAM, MST, MULT, POET; DC 2; HLC 2; PC 3; WLC**
See also CA 104; 131; CANR 81; DA3; DLB 108; HW 1, 2; MTCW 1, 2

Garcia Marquez, Gabriel (Jose) 1928- **CLC 2, 3, 8, 10, 15, 27, 47, 55, 68; DA; DAB; DAC; DAM MST, MULT, NOV, POP; HLC 1; SSC 8; WLC**
See also AAYA 3; BEST 89:1, 90:4; CA 33-36R; CANR 10, 28, 50, 75, 82; DA3; DLB 113; HW 1, 2; MTCW 1, 2

Garcilaso de la Vega, El Inca 1503-1536
See also HLCS 1

Gard, Janice
See Latham, Jean Lee

Gard, Roger Martin du
See Martin du Gard, Roger

Gardam, Jane 1928- **CLC 43**
See also CA 49-52; CANR 2, 18, 33, 54; CLR

12; DLB 14, 161; MAICYA; MTCW 1; SAAS 9; SATA 39, 76; SATA-Brief 28

Gardner, Herb(ert) 1934- **CLC 44**
See also CA 149

Gardner, John (Champlin), Jr. 1933-1982 **CLC 2, 3, 5, 7, 8, 10, 18, 28, 34; DAM NOV, POP; SSC 7**
See also AITN 1; CA 65-68; 107; CANR 33, 73; CDALBS; DA3; DLB 2; DLBY 82; MTCW 1; SATA 40; SATA-Obit 31

Gardner, John (Edmund) 1926- **CLC 30; DAM POP**
See also CA 103; CANR 15, 69; MTCW 1

Gardner, Miriam
See Bradley, Marion Zimmer

Gardner, Noel
See Kuttner, Henry

Gardons, S. S.
See Snodgrass, W(illiam) D(e Witt)

Garfield, Leon 1921-1996 **CLC 12**
See also AAYA 8; CA 17-20R; 152; CANR 38, 41, 78; CLR 21; DLB 161; JRDA; MAICYA; SATA 1, 32, 76; SATA-Obit 90

Garland, (Hannibal) Hamlin 1860-1940 **TCLC 3; SSC 18**
See also CA 104; DLB 12, 71, 78, 186

Garneau, (Hector de) Saint-Denys 1912-1943 **TCLC 13**
See also CA 111; DLB 88

Garner, Alan 1934- **CLC 17; DAB; DAM POP**
See also AAYA 18; CA 73-76, 178; CAAE 178; CANR 15, 64; CLR 20; DLB 161; MAICYA; MTCW 1, 2; SATA 18, 69; SATA-Essay 108

Garner, Hugh 1913-1979 **CLC 13**
See also CA 69-72; CANR 31; DLB 68

Garnett, David 1892-1981 **CLC 3**
See also CA 5-8R; 103; CANR 17, 79; DLB 34; MTCW 2

Garos, Stephanie
See Katz, Steve

Garrett, George (Palmer) 1929- **CLC 3, 11, 51; SSC 30**
See also CA 1-4R; CAAS 5; CANR 1, 42, 67; DLB 2, 5, 130, 152; DLBY 83

Garrick, David 1717-1779 **LC 15; DAM DRAM**
See also DLB 84

Garrigue, Jean 1914-1972 **CLC 2, 8**
See also CA 5-8R; 37-40R; CANR 20

Garrison, Frederick
See Sinclair, Upton (Beall)

Garro, Elena 1920(?)-1998
See also CA 131; 169; DLB 145; HLCS 1; HW 1

Garth, Will
See Hamilton, Edmond; Kuttner, Henry

Garvey, Marcus (Moziah, Jr.) 1887-1940 **TCLC 41; BLC 2; DAM MULT**
See also BW 1; CA 120; 124; CANR 79

Gary, Romain **CLC 25**
See also Kacew, Romain
See also DLB 83

Gascar, Pierre **CLC 11**
See also Fournier, Pierre

Gascoyne, David (Emery) 1916- **CLC 45**
See also CA 65-68; CANR 10, 28, 54; DLB 20; MTCW 1

Gaskell, Elizabeth Cleghorn 1810-1865 **NCLC 70; DAB; DAM MST; SSC 25**
See also CDBLB 1832-1890; DLB 21, 144, 159

Gass, William H(oward) 1924- **CLC 1, 2, 8, 11, 15, 39; SSC 12**
See also CA 17-20R; CANR 30, 71; DLB 2;

MTCW 1, 2

Gasset, Jose Ortega y
See Ortega y Gasset, Jose

Gates, Henry Louis, Jr. 1950-**CLC 65; BLCS; DAM MULT**
See also BW 2, 3; CA 109; CANR 25, 53, 75; DA3; DLB 67; MTCW 1

Gautier, Theophile 1811-1872 **NCLC 1, 59; DAM POET; PC 18; SSC 20**
See also DLB 119

Gawsworth, John
See Bates, H(erbert) E(rnest)

Gay, John 1685-1732 **LC 49; DAM DRAM**
See also DLB 84, 95

Gay, Oliver
See Gogarty, Oliver St. John

Gaye, Marvin (Penze) 1939-1984 **CLC 26**
See also CA 112

Gebler, Carlo (Ernest) 1954- **CLC 39**
See also CA 119; 133

Gee, Maggie (Mary) 1948- **CLC 57**
See also CA 130; DLB 207

Gee, Maurice (Gough) 1931- **CLC 29**
See also CA 97-100; CANR 67; CLR 56; SATA 46, 101

Gelbart, Larry (Simon) 1923- **CLC 21, 61**
See also CA 73-76; CANR 45

Gelber, Jack 1932- **CLC 1, 6, 14, 79**
See also CA 1-4R; CANR 2; DLB 7

Gellhorn, Martha (Ellis) 1908-1998 **CLC 14, 60**
See also CA 77-80; 164; CANR 44; DLBY 82, 98

Genet, Jean 1910-1986**CLC 1, 2, 5, 10, 14, 44, 46; DAM DRAM**
See also CA 13-16R; CANR 18; DA3; DLB 72; DLBY 86; MTCW 1, 2

Gent, Peter 1942- **CLC 29**
See also AITN 1; CA 89-92; DLBY 82

Gentile, Giovanni 1875-1944 **TCLC 96**
See also CA 119

Gentlewoman in New England, A
See Bradstreet, Anne

Gentlewoman in Those Parts, A
See Bradstreet, Anne

George, Jean Craighead 1919- **CLC 35**
See also AAYA 8; CA 5-8R; CANR 25; CLR 1; DLB 52; JRDA; MAICYA; SATA 2, 68

George, Stefan (Anton) 1868-1933**TCLC 2, 14**
See also CA 104

Georges, Georges Martin
See Simenon, Georges (Jacques Christian)

Gerhardi, William Alexander
See Gerhardie, William Alexander

Gerhardie, William Alexander 1895-1977 **CLC 5**
See also CA 25-28R; 73-76; CANR 18; DLB 36

Gerstler, Amy 1956- **CLC 70**
See also CA 146

Gertler, T. **CLC 34**
See also CA 116; 121; INT 121

Ghalib **NCLC 39, 78**
See also Ghalib, Hsadullah Khan

Ghalib, Hsadullah Khan 1797-1869
See Ghalib
See also DAM POET

Ghelderode, Michel de 1898-1962 **CLC 6, 11; DAM DRAM**
See also CA 85-88; CANR 40, 77

Ghiselin, Brewster 1903- **CLC 23**
See also CA 13-16R; CAAS 10; CANR 13

Ghose, Aurabinda 1872-1950 **TCLC 63**

See also CA 163

Ghose, Zulfikar 1935- **CLC 42**
See also CA 65-68; CANR 67

Ghosh, Amitav 1956- **CLC 44**
See also CA 147; CANR 80

Giacosa, Giuseppe 1847-1906 **TCLC 7**
See also CA 104

Gibb, Lee
See Waterhouse, Keith (Spencer)

Gibbon, Lewis Grassic **TCLC 4**
See also Mitchell, James Leslie

Gibbons, Kaye 1960-**CLC 50, 88; DAM POP**
See also CA 151; CANR 75; DA3; MTCW 1

Gibran, Kahlil 1883-1931 **TCLC 1, 9; DAM POET, POP; PC 9**
See also CA 104; 150; DA3; MTCW 2

Gibran, Khalil
See Gibran, Kahlil

Gibson, William 1914- **CLC 23; DA; DAB; DAC; DAM DRAM, MST**
See also CA 9-12R; CANR 9, 42, 75; DLB 7; MTCW 1; SATA 66

Gibson, William (Ford) 1948- **CLC 39, 63; DAM POP**
See also AAYA 12; CA 126; 133; CANR 52; DA3; MTCW 1

Gide, Andre (Paul Guillaume) 1869-1951 **TCLC 5, 12, 36; DA; DAB; DAC; DAM MST, NOV; SSC 13; WLC**
See also CA 104; 124; DA3; DLB 65; MTCW 1, 2

Gifford, Barry (Colby) 1946- **CLC 34**
See also CA 65-68; CANR 9, 30, 40

Gilbert, Frank
See De Voto, Bernard (Augustine)

Gilbert, W(illiam) S(chwenck) 1836-1911 **TCLC 3; DAM DRAM, POET**
See also CA 104; 173; SATA 36

Gilbreth, Frank B., Jr. 1911- **CLC 17**
See also CA 9-12R; SATA 2

Gilchrist, Ellen 1935-**CLC 34, 48; DAM POP; SSC 14**
See also CA 113; 116; CANR 41, 61; DLB 130; MTCW 1, 2

Giles, Molly 1942- **CLC 39**
See also CA 126

Gill, Eric 1882-1940 **TCLC 85**

Gill, Patrick
See Creasey, John

Gilliam, Terry (Vance) 1940- **CLC 21**
See also Monty Python
See also AAYA 19; CA 108; 113; CANR 35; INT 113

Gillian, Jerry
See Gilliam, Terry (Vance)

Gilliatt, Penelope (Ann Douglass) 1932-1993 **CLC 2, 10, 13, 53**
See also AITN 2; CA 13-16R; 141; CANR 49; DLB 14

Gilman, Charlotte (Anna) Perkins (Stetson) 1860-1935 **TCLC 9, 37; SSC 13**
See also CA 106; 150; MTCW 1

Gilmour, David 1949- **CLC 35**
See also CA 138, 147

Gilpin, William 1724-1804 **NCLC 30**

Gilray, J. D.
See Mencken, H(enry) L(ouis)

Gilroy, Frank D(aniel) 1925- **CLC 2**
See also CA 81-84; CANR 32, 64; DLB 7

Gilstrap, John 1957(?)- **CLC 99**
See also CA 160

Ginsberg, Allen 1926-1997**CLC 1, 2, 3, 4, 6, 13, 36, 69, 109; DA; DAB; DAC; DAM MST,**

POET; PC 4; WLC
See also AITN 1; CA 1-4R; 157; CANR 2, 41, 63; CDALB 1941-1968; DA3; DLB 5, 16, 169; MTCW 1, 2

Ginzburg, Natalia 1916-1991**CLC 5, 11, 54, 70**
See also CA 85-88; 135; CANR 33; DLB 177; MTCW 1, 2

Giono, Jean 1895-1970 **CLC 4, 11**
See also CA 45-48; 29-32R; CANR 2, 35; DLB 72; MTCW 1

Giovanni, Nikki 1943- **CLC 2, 4, 19, 64, 117; BLC 2; DA; DAB; DAC; DAM MST, MULT, POET; PC 19; WLCS**
See also AAYA 22; AITN 1; BW 2, 3; CA 29-32R; CAAS 6; CANR 18, 41, 60; CDALBS; CLR 6; DA3; DLB 5, 41; INT CANR-18; MAICYA; MTCW 1, 2; SATA 24, 107

Giovene, Andrea 1904- **CLC 7**
See also CA 85-88

Gippius, Zinaida (Nikolayevna) 1869-1945
See Hippius, Zinaida
See also CA 106

Giraudoux, (Hippolyte) Jean 1882-1944 **TCLC 2, 7; DAM DRAM**
See also CA 104; DLB 65

Gironella, Jose Maria 1917- **CLC 11**
See also CA 101

Gissing, George (Robert) 1857-1903**TCLC 3, 24, 47**
See also CA 105; 167; DLB 18, 135, 184

Giurlani, Aldo
See Palazzeschi, Aldo

Gladkov, Fyodor (Vasilyevich) 1883-1958 **TCLC 27**
See also CA 170

Glanville, Brian (Lester) 1931- **CLC 6**
See also CA 5-8R; CAAS 9; CANR 3, 70; DLB 15, 139; SATA 42

Glasgow, Ellen (Anderson Gholson) 1873-1945 **TCLC 2, 7; SSC 34**
See also CA 104; 164; DLB 9, 12; MTCW 2

Glaspell, Susan 1882(?)-1948**TCLC 55; DC 10**
See also CA 110; 154; DLB 7, 9, 78; YABC 2

Glassco, John 1909-1981 **CLC 9**
See also CA 13-16R; 102; CANR 15; DLB 68

Glasscock, Amnesia
See Steinbeck, John (Ernst)

Glasser, Ronald J. 1940(?)- **CLC 37**

Glassman, Joyce
See Johnson, Joyce

Glendinning, Victoria 1937- **CLC 50**
See also CA 120; 127; CANR 59; DLB 155

Glissant, Edouard 1928- **CLC 10, 68; DAM MULT**
See also CA 153

Gloag, Julian 1930- **CLC 40**
See also AITN 1; CA 65-68; CANR 10, 70

Glowacki, Aleksander
See Prus, Boleslaw

Gluck, Louise (Elisabeth) 1943-**CLC 7, 22, 44, 81; DAM POET; PC 16**
See also CA 33-36R; CANR 40, 69; DA3; DLB 5; MTCW 2

Glyn, Elinor 1864-1943 **TCLC 72**
See also DLB 153

Gobineau, Joseph Arthur (Comte) de 1816-1882 **NCLC 17**
See also DLB 123

Godard, Jean-Luc 1930- **CLC 20**
See also CA 93-96

Godden, (Margaret) Rumer 1907-1998 **CLC 53**
See also AAYA 6; CA 5-8R; 172; CANR 4, 27,

36, 55, 80; CLR 20; DLB 161; MAICYA;
SAAS 12; SATA 3, 36; SATA-Obit 109
Godoy Alcayaga, Lucila 1889-1957
See Mistral, Gabriela
See also BW 2; CA 104; 131; CANR 81; DAM
MULT; HW 1, 2; MTCW 1, 2
Godwin, Gail (Kathleen) 1937- **CLC 5, 8, 22,
31, 69; DAM POP**
See also CA 29-32R; CANR 15, 43, 69; DA3;
DLB 6; INT CANR-15; MTCW 1, 2
Godwin, William 1756-1836   **NCLC 14**
See also CDBLB 1789-1832; DLB 39, 104, 142,
158, 163
Goebbels, Josef
See Goebbels, (Paul) Joseph
Goebbels, (Paul) Joseph 1897-1945 **TCLC 68**
See also CA 115; 148
Goebbels, Joseph Paul
See Goebbels, (Paul) Joseph
Goethe, Johann Wolfgang von 1749-1832
**NCLC 4, 22, 34; DA; DAB; DAC; DAM
DRAM, MST, POET; PC 5; WLC**
See also DA3; DLB 94
Gogarty, Oliver St. John 1878-1957**TCLC 15**
See also CA 109; 150; DLB 15, 19
Gogol, Nikolai (Vasilyevich) 1809-1852**NCLC
5, 15, 31; DA; DAB; DAC; DAM DRAM,
MST; DC 1; SSC 4, 29; WLC**
See also DLB 198
Goines, Donald 1937(?)-1974**CLC 80; BLC 2;
DAM MULT, POP**
See also AITN 1; BW 1, 3; CA 124; 114; CANR
82; DA3; DLB 33
Gold, Herbert 1924-   **CLC 4, 7, 14, 42**
See also CA 9-12R; CANR 17, 45; DLB 2;
DLBY 81
Goldbarth, Albert 1948-   **CLC 5, 38**
See also CA 53-56; CANR 6, 40; DLB 120
Goldberg, Anatol 1910-1982   **CLC 34**
See also CA 131; 117
Goldemberg, Isaac 1945-   **CLC 52**
See also CA 69-72; CAAS 12; CANR 11, 32;
HW 1
Golding, William (Gerald) 1911-1993**CLC 1,
2, 3, 8, 10, 17, 27, 58, 81; DA; DAB; DAC;
DAM MST, NOV; WLC**
See also AAYA 5; CA 5-8R; 141; CANR 13,
33, 54; CDBLB 1945-1960; DA3; DLB 15,
100; MTCW 1, 2
Goldman, Emma 1869-1940   **TCLC 13**
See also CA 110; 150
Goldman, Francisco 1954-   **CLC 76**
See also CA 162
Goldman, William (W.) 1931-   **CLC 1, 48**
See also CA 9-12R; CANR 29, 69; DLB 44
Goldmann, Lucien 1913-1970   **CLC 24**
See also CA 25-28; CAP 2
Goldoni, Carlo 1707-1793**LC 4; DAM DRAM**
Goldsberry, Steven 1949-   **CLC 34**
See also CA 131
Goldsmith, Oliver 1728-1774 **LC 2, 48; DA;
DAB; DAC; DAM DRAM, MST, NOV,
POET; DC 8; WLC**
See also CDBLB 1660-1789; DLB 39, 89, 104,
109, 142; SATA 26
Goldsmith, Peter
See Priestley, J(ohn) B(oynton)
Gombrowicz, Witold 1904-1969**CLC 4, 7, 11,
49; DAM DRAM**
See also CA 19-20; 25-28R; CAP 2
Gomez de la Serna, Ramon 1888-1963**CLC 9**
See also CA 153; 116; CANR 79; HW 1, 2
Goncharov, Ivan Alexandrovich 1812-1891

NCLC 1, 63
Goncourt, Edmond (Louis Antoine Huot) de
1822-1896   **NCLC 7**
See also DLB 123
Goncourt, Jules (Alfred Huot) de 1830-1870
NCLC 7
See also DLB 123
Gontier, Fernande 19(?)-   **CLC 50**
Gonzalez Martinez, Enrique 1871-1952
TCLC 72
See also CA 166; CANR 81; HW 1, 2
Goodman, Paul 1911-1972   **CLC 1, 2, 4, 7**
See also CA 19-20; 37-40R; CANR 34; CAP 2;
DLB 130; MTCW 1
Gordimer, Nadine 1923-**CLC 3, 5, 7, 10, 18, 33,
51, 70; DA; DAB; DAC; DAM MST, NOV;
SSC 17; WLCS**
See also CA 5-8R; CANR 3, 28, 56; DA3; INT
CANR-28; MTCW 1, 2
Gordon, Adam Lindsay 1833-1870 **NCLC 21**
Gordon, Caroline 1895-1981**CLC 6, 13, 29, 83;
SSC 15**
See also CA 11-12; 103; CANR 36; CAP 1;
DLB 4, 9, 102; DLBD 17; DLBY 81; MTCW
1, 2
Gordon, Charles William 1860-1937
See Connor, Ralph
See also CA 109
Gordon, Mary (Catherine) 1949- **CLC 13, 22**
See also CA 102; CANR 44; DLB 6; DLBY
81; INT 102; MTCW 1
Gordon, N. J.
See Bosman, Herman Charles
Gordon, Sol 1923-   **CLC 26**
See also CA 53-56; CANR 4; SATA 11
Gordone, Charles 1925-1995**CLC 1, 4; DAM
DRAM; DC 8**
See also BW 1, 3; CA 93-96; 180; 150; CAAE
180; CANR 55; DLB 7; INT 93-96; MTCW
1
Gore, Catherine 1800-1861   **NCLC 65**
See also DLB 116
Gorenko, Anna Andreevna
See Akhmatova, Anna
Gorky, Maxim 1868-1936**TCLC 8; DAB; SSC
28; WLC**
See also Peshkov, Alexei Maximovich
See also MTCW 2
Goryan, Sirak
See Saroyan, William
Gosse, Edmund (William) 1849-1928**TCLC 28**
See also CA 117; DLB 57, 144, 184
Gotlieb, Phyllis Fay (Bloom) 1926-   **CLC 18**
See also CA 13-16R; CANR 7; DLB 88
Gottesman, S. D.
See Kornbluth, C(yril) M.; Pohl, Frederik
Gottfried von Strassburg fl. c. 1210- **CMLC
10**
See also DLB 138
Gould, Lois   **CLC 4, 10**
See also CA 77-80; CANR 29; MTCW 1
Gourmont, Remy (-Marie-Charles) de 1858-
1915   **TCLC 17**
See also CA 109; 150; MTCW 2
Govier, Katherine 1948-   **CLC 51**
See also CA 101; CANR 18, 40
Goyen, (Charles) William 1915-1983**CLC 5, 8,
14, 40**
See also AITN 2; CA 5-8R; 110; CANR 6, 71;
DLB 2; DLBY 83; INT CANR-6
Goytisolo, Juan 1931-   **CLC 5, 10, 23; DAM
MULT; HLC 1**
See also CA 85-88; CANR 32, 61; HW 1, 2;

MTCW 1, 2
Gozzano, Guido 1883-1916   **PC 10**
See also CA 154; DLB 114
Gozzi, (Conte) Carlo 1720-1806   **NCLC 23**
Grabbe, Christian Dietrich 1801-1836**NCLC
2**
See also DLB 133
Grace, Patricia Frances 1937-   **CLC 56**
See also CA 176
Gracian y Morales, Baltasar 1601-1658**LC 15**
Gracq, Julien   **CLC 11, 48**
See also Poirier, Louis
See also DLB 83
Grade, Chaim 1910-1982   **CLC 10**
See also CA 93-96; 107
Graduate of Oxford, A
See Ruskin, John
Grafton, Garth
See Duncan, Sara Jeannette
Graham, John
See Phillips, David Graham
Graham, Jorie 1951-   **CLC 48, 118**
See also CA 111; CANR 63; DLB 120
Graham, R(obert) B(ontine) Cunninghame
See Cunninghame Graham, R(obert) B(ontine)
See also DLB 98, 135, 174
Graham, Robert
See Haldeman, Joe (William)
Graham, Tom
See Lewis, (Harry) Sinclair
Graham, W(illiam) S(ydney) 1918-1986 **CLC
29**
See also CA 73-76; 118; DLB 20
Graham, Winston (Mawdsley) 1910- **CLC 23**
See also CA 49-52; CANR 2, 22, 45, 66; DLB
77
Grahame, Kenneth 1859-1932**TCLC 64; DAB**
See also CA 108; 136; CANR 80; CLR 5; DA3;
DLB 34, 141, 178; MAICYA; MTCW 2;
SATA 100; YABC 1
Granovsky, Timofei Nikolaevich 1813-1855
NCLC 75
See also DLB 198
Grant, Skeeter
See Spiegelman, Art
Granville-Barker, Harley 1877-1946**TCLC 2;
DAM DRAM**
See also Barker, Harley Granville
See also CA 104
Grass, Guenter (Wilhelm) 1927-**CLC 1, 2, 4, 6,
11, 15, 22, 32, 49, 88; DA; DAB; DAC;
DAM MST, NOV; WLC**
See also CA 13-16R; CANR 20, 75; DA3; DLB
75, 124; MTCW 1, 2
Gratton, Thomas
See Hulme, T(homas) E(rnest)
Grau, Shirley Ann 1929-   **CLC 4, 9; SSC 15**
See also CA 89-92; CANR 22, 69; DLB 2; INT
CANR-22; MTCW 1
Gravel, Fern
See Hall, James Norman
Graver, Elizabeth 1964-   **CLC 70**
See also CA 135; CANR 71
Graves, Richard Perceval 1945-   **CLC 44**
See also CA 65-68; CANR 9, 26, 51
Graves, Robert (von Ranke) 1895-1985 **CLC
1, 2, 6, 11, 39, 44, 45; DAB; DAC; DAM
MST, POET; PC 6**
See also CA 5-8R; 117; CANR 5, 36; CDBLB
1914-1945; DA3; DLB 20, 100, 191; DLBD
18; DLBY 85; MTCW 1, 2; SATA 45
Graves, Valerie
See Bradley, Marion Zimmer

Gray, Alasdair (James) 1934-   CLC 41
    See also CA 126; CANR 47, 69; DLB 194; INT
    126; MTCW 1, 2
Gray, Amlin 1946-   CLC 29
    See also CA 138
Gray, Francine du Plessix 1930-   CLC 22;
    DAM NOV
    See also BEST 90:3; CA 61-64; CAAS 2;
    CANR 11, 33, 75, 81; INT CANR-11;
    MTCW 1, 2
Gray, John (Henry) 1866-1934   TCLC 19
    See also CA 119; 162
Gray, Simon (James Holliday) 1936- CLC 9,
    14, 36
    See also AITN 1; CA 21-24R; CAAS 3; CANR
    32, 69; DLB 13; MTCW 1
Gray, Spalding 1941-CLC 49, 112; DAM POP;
    DC 7
    See also CA 128; CANR 74; MTCW 2
Gray, Thomas 1716-1771LC 4, 40; DA; DAB;
    DAC; DAM MST; PC 2; WLC
    See also CDBLB 1660-1789; DA3; DLB 109
Grayson, David
    See Baker, Ray Stannard
Grayson, Richard (A.) 1951-   CLC 38
    See also CA 85-88; CANR 14, 31, 57
Greeley, Andrew M(oran) 1928-   CLC 28;
    DAM POP
    See also CA 5-8R; CAAS 7; CANR 7, 43, 69;
    DA3; MTCW 1, 2
Green, Anna Katharine 1846-1935 TCLC 63
    See also CA 112; 159; DLB 202
Green, Brian
    See Card, Orson Scott
Green, Hannah
    See Greenberg, Joanne (Goldenberg)
Green, Hannah 1927(?)-1996   CLC 3
    See also CA 73-76; CANR 59
Green, Henry 1905-1973   CLC 2, 13, 97
    See also Yorke, Henry Vincent
    See also CA 175; DLB 15
Green, Julian (Hartridge) 1900-1998
    See Green, Julien
    See also CA 21-24R; 169; CANR 33; DLB 4,
    72; MTCW 1
Green, Julien   CLC 3, 11, 77
    See also Green, Julian (Hartridge)
    See also MTCW 2
Green, Paul (Eliot) 1894-1981CLC 25; DAM
    DRAM
    See also AITN 1; CA 5-8R; 103; CANR 3; DLB
    7, 9; DLBY 81
Greenberg, Ivan 1908-1973
    See Rahv, Philip
    See also CA 85-88
Greenberg, Joanne (Goldenberg) 1932- C L C
    7, 30
    See also AAYA 12; CA 5-8R; CANR 14, 32,
    69; SATA 25
Greenberg, Richard 1959(?)-   CLC 57
    See also CA 138
Greene, Bette 1934-   CLC 30
    See also AAYA 7; CA 53-56; CANR 4; CLR 2;
    JRDA; MAICYA; SAAS 16; SATA 8, 102
Greene, Gael   CLC 8
    See also CA 13-16R; CANR 10
Greene, Graham (Henry) 1904-1991CLC 1, 3,
    6, 9, 14, 18, 27, 37, 70, 72; DA; DAB; DAC;
    DAM MST, NOV; SSC 29; WLC
    See also AITN 2; CA 13-16R; 133; CANR 35,
    61; CDBLB 1945-1960; DA3; DLB 13, 15,
    77, 100, 162, 201, 204; DLBY 91; MTCW
    1, 2; SATA 20

Greene, Robert 1558-1592   LC 41
    See also DLB 62, 167
Greer, Richard
    See Silverberg, Robert
Gregor, Arthur 1923-   CLC 9
    See also CA 25-28R; CAAS 10; CANR 11;
    SATA 36
Gregor, Lee
    See Pohl, Frederik
Gregory, Isabella Augusta (Persse) 1852-1932
    TCLC 1
    See also CA 104; DLB 10
Gregory, J. Dennis
    See Williams, John A(lfred)
Grendon, Stephen
    See Derleth, August (William)
Grenville, Kate 1950-   CLC 61
    See also CA 118; CANR 53
Grenville, Pelham
    See Wodehouse, P(elham) G(renville)
Greve, Felix Paul (Berthold Friedrich) 1879-
    1948
    See Grove, Frederick Philip
    See also CA 104; 141, 175; CANR 79; DAC;
    DAM MST
Grey, Zane 1872-1939   TCLC 6; DAM POP
    See also CA 104; 132; DA3; DLB 212; MTCW
    1, 2
Grieg, (Johan) Nordahl (Brun) 1902-1943
    TCLC 10
    See also CA 107
Grieve, C(hristopher) M(urray) 1892-1978
    CLC 11, 19; DAM POET
    See also MacDiarmid, Hugh; Pteleon
    See also CA 5-8R; 85-88; CANR 33; MTCW 1
Griffin, Gerald 1803-1840   NCLC 7
    See also DLB 159
Griffin, John Howard 1920-1980   CLC 68
    See also AITN 1; CA 1-4R; 101; CANR 2
Griffin, Peter 1942-   CLC 39
    See also CA 136
Griffith, D(avid Lewelyn) W(ark) 1875(?)-1948
    TCLC 68
    See also CA 119; 150; CANR 80
Griffith, Lawrence
    See Griffith, D(avid Lewelyn) W(ark)
Griffiths, Trevor 1935-   CLC 13, 52
    See also CA 97-100; CANR 45; DLB 13
Griggs, Sutton Elbert 1872-1930(?) TCLC 77
    See also CA 123; DLB 50
Grigson, Geoffrey (Edward Harvey) 1905-1985
    CLC 7, 39
    See also CA 25-28R; 118; CANR 20, 33; DLB
    27; MTCW 1, 2
Grillparzer, Franz 1791-1872   NCLC 1
    See also DLB 133
Grimble, Reverend Charles James
    See Eliot, T(homas) S(tearns)
Grimke, Charlotte L(ottie) Forten 1837(?)-1914
    See Forten, Charlotte L.
    See also BW 1; CA 117; 124; DAM MULT,
    POET
Grimm, Jacob Ludwig Karl 1785-1863NCLC
    3, 77; SSC 36
    See also DLB 90; MAICYA; SATA 22
Grimm, Wilhelm Karl 1786-1859NCLC 3, 77;
    SSC 36
    See also DLB 90; MAICYA; SATA 22
Grimmelshausen, Johann Jakob Christoffel von
    1621-1676   LC 6
    See also DLB 168
Grindel, Eugene 1895-1952
    See Eluard, Paul

See also CA 104
Grisham, John 1955-   CLC 84; DAM POP
    See also AAYA 14; CA 138; CANR 47, 69;
    DA3; MTCW 2
Grossman, David 1954-   CLC 67
    See also CA 138
Grossman, Vasily (Semenovich) 1905-1964
    CLC 41
    See also CA 124; 130; MTCW 1
Grove, Frederick Philip   TCLC 4
    See also Greve, Felix Paul (Berthold Friedrich)
    See also DLB 92
Grubb
    See Crumb, R(obert)
Grumbach, Doris (Isaac) 1918-CLC 13, 22, 64
    See also CA 5-8R; CAAS 2; CANR 9, 42, 70;
    INT CANR-9; MTCW 2
Grundtvig, Nicolai Frederik Severin 1783-1872
    NCLC 1
Grunge
    See Crumb, R(obert)
Grunwald, Lisa 1959-   CLC 44
    See also CA 120
Guare, John 1938-   CLC 8, 14, 29, 67; DAM
    DRAM
    See also CA 73-76; CANR 21, 69; DLB 7;
    MTCW 1, 2
Gudjonsson, Halldor Kiljan 1902-1998
    See Laxness, Halldor
    See also CA 103; 164
Guenter, Erich
    See Eich, Guenter
Guest, Barbara 1920-   CLC 34
    See also CA 25-28R; CANR 11, 44, 84; DLB
    5, 193
Guest, Edgar A(lbert) 1881-1959   TCLC 95
    See also CA 112; 168
Guest, Judith (Ann) 1936- CLC 8, 30; DAM
    NOV, POP
    See also AAYA 7; CA 77-80; CANR 15, 75;
    DA3; INT CANR-15; MTCW 1, 2
Guevara, Che   CLC 87; HLC 1
    See also Guevara (Serna), Ernesto
Guevara (Serna), Ernesto 1928-1967CLC 87;
    DAM MULT; HLC 1
    See also Guevara, Che
    See also CA 127; 111; CANR 56; HW 1
Guicciardini, Francesco 1483-1540   LC 49
Guild, Nicholas M. 1944-   CLC 33
    See also CA 93-96
Guillemin, Jacques
    See Sartre, Jean-Paul
Guillen, Jorge 1893-1984   CLC 11; DAM
    MULT, POET; HLCS 1
    See also CA 89-92; 112; DLB 108; HW 1
Guillen, Nicolas (Cristobal) 1902-1989 C L C
    48, 79; BLC 2; DAM MST, MULT, POET;
    HLC 1; PC 23
    See also BW 2; CA 116; 125; 129; CANR 84;
    HW 1
Guillevic, (Eugene) 1907-   CLC 33
    See also CA 93-96
Guillois
    See Desnos, Robert
Guillois, Valentin
    See Desnos, Robert
Guimaraes Rosa, Joao 1908-1967
    See also CA 175; HLCS 2
Guiney, Louise Imogen 1861-1920 TCLC 41
    See also CA 160; DLB 54
Guiraldes, Ricardo (Guillermo) 1886-1927
    TCLC 39
    See also CA 131; HW 1; MTCW 1

48, 53, 72; DA; DAB; DAC; DAM MST, NOV, POET; PC 8; SSC 2; WLC
See also CA 104; 123; CDBLB 1890-1914; DA3; DLB 18, 19, 135; MTCW 1, 2

Hare, David 1947-   **CLC 29, 58**
See also CA 97-100; CANR 39; DLB 13; MTCW 1

Harewood, John
See Van Druten, John (William)

Harford, Henry
See Hudson, W(illiam) H(enry)

Hargrave, Leonie
See Disch, Thomas M(ichael)

Harjo, Joy 1951- **CLC 83; DAM MULT; PC 27**
See also CA 114; CANR 35, 67; DLB 120, 175; MTCW 2; NNAL

Harlan, Louis R(udolph) 1922-   **CLC 34**
See also CA 21-24R; CANR 25, 55, 80

Harling, Robert 1951(?)-   **CLC 53**
See also CA 147

Harmon, William (Ruth) 1938-   **CLC 38**
See also CA 33-36R; CANR 14, 32, 35; SATA 65

Harper, F. E. W.
See Harper, Frances Ellen Watkins

Harper, Frances E. W.
See Harper, Frances Ellen Watkins

Harper, Frances E. Watkins
See Harper, Frances Ellen Watkins

Harper, Frances Ellen
See Harper, Frances Ellen Watkins

Harper, Frances Ellen Watkins 1825-1911
   TCLC 14; BLC 2; DAM MULT, POET; PC 21
See also BW 1, 3; CA 111; 125; CANR 79; DLB 50

Harper, Michael S(teven) 1938-   **CLC 7, 22**
See also BW 1; CA 33-36R; CANR 24; DLB 41

Harper, Mrs. F. E. W.
See Harper, Frances Ellen Watkins

Harris, Christie (Lucy) Irwin 1907- **CLC 12**
See also CA 5-8R; CANR 6, 83; CLR 47; DLB 88; JRDA; MAICYA; SAAS 10; SATA 6, 74

Harris, Frank 1856-1931   **TCLC 24**
See also CA 109; 150; CANR 80; DLB 156, 197

Harris, George Washington 1814-1869 **NCLC 23**
See also DLB 3, 11

Harris, Joel Chandler 1848-1908   **TCLC 2; SSC 19**
See also CA 104; 137; CANR 80; CLR 49; DLB 11, 23, 42, 78, 91; MAICYA; SATA 100; YABC 1

Harris, John (Wyndham Parkes Lucas) Beynon 1903-1969
See Wyndham, John
See also CA 102; 89-92; CANR 84

Harris, MacDonald   **CLC 9**
See also Heiney, Donald (William)

Harris, Mark 1922-   **CLC 19**
See also CA 5-8R; CAAS 3; CANR 2, 55, 83; DLB 2; DLBY 80

Harris, (Theodore) Wilson 1921-   **CLC 25**
See also BW 2, 3; CA 65-68; CAAS 16; CANR 11, 27, 69; DLB 117; MTCW 1

Harrison, Elizabeth Cavanna 1909-
See Cavanna, Betty
See also CA 9-12R; CANR 6, 27

Harrison, Harry (Max) 1925-   **CLC 42**
See also CA 1-4R; CANR 5, 21, 84; DLB 8; SATA 4

Harrison, James (Thomas) 1937- **CLC 6, 14, 33, 66; SSC 19**
See also CA 13-16R; CANR 8, 51, 79; DLBY 82; INT CANR-8

Harrison, Jim
See Harrison, James (Thomas)

Harrison, Kathryn 1961-   **CLC 70**
See also CA 144; CANR 68

Harrison, Tony 1937-   **CLC 43**
See also CA 65-68; CANR 44; DLB 40; MTCW 1

Harriss, Will(ard Irvin) 1922-   **CLC 34**
See also CA 111

Harson, Sley
See Ellison, Harlan (Jay)

Hart, Ellis
See Ellison, Harlan (Jay)

Hart, Josephine 1942(?)- **CLC 70; DAM POP**
See also CA 138; CANR 70

Hart, Moss 1904-1961 **CLC 66; DAM DRAM**
See also CA 109; 89-92; CANR 84; DLB 7

Harte, (Francis) Bret(t) 1836(?)-1902 **TCLC 1, 25; DA; DAC; DAM MST; SSC 8; WLC**
See also CA 104; 140; CANR 80; CDALB 1865-1917; DA3; DLB 12, 64, 74, 79, 186; SATA 26

Hartley, L(eslie) P(oles) 1895-1972 **CLC 2, 22**
See also CA 45-48; 37-40R; CANR 33; DLB 15, 139; MTCW 1, 2

Hartmann, Geoffrey H. 1929-   **CLC 27**
See also CA 117; 125; CANR 79; DLB 67

Hartmann, Eduard von 1842-1906 **TCLC 97**

Hartmann, Sadakichi 1867-1944   **TCLC 73**
See also CA 157; DLB 54

Hartmann von Aue c. 1160-c. 1205 **CMLC 15**
See also DLB 138

Hartmann von Aue 1170-1210   **CMLC 15**

Haruf, Kent 1943-   **CLC 34**
See also CA 149

Harwood, Ronald 1934-   **CLC 32; DAM DRAM, MST**
See also CA 1-4R; CANR 4, 55; DLB 13

Hasegawa Tatsunosuke
See Futabatei, Shimei

Hasek, Jaroslav (Matej Frantisek) 1883-1923 **TCLC 4**
See also CA 104; 129; MTCW 1, 2

Hass, Robert 1941-   **CLC 18, 39, 99; PC 16**
See also CA 111; CANR 30, 50, 71; DLB 105, 206; SATA 94

Hastings, Hudson
See Kuttner, Henry

Hastings, Selina   **CLC 44**

Hathorne, John 1641-1717   **LC 38**

Hatteras, Amelia
See Mencken, H(enry) L(ouis)

Hatteras, Owen   **TCLC 18**
See also Mencken, H(enry) L(ouis); Nathan, George Jean

Hauptmann, Gerhart (Johann Robert) 1862-1946 **TCLC 4; DAM DRAM**
See also CA 104; 153; DLB 66, 118

Havel, Vaclav 1936-   **CLC 25, 58, 65; DAM DRAM; DC 6**
See also CA 104; CANR 36, 63; DA3; MTCW 1, 2

Haviaras, Stratis   **CLC 33**
See also Chaviaras, Strates

Hawes, Stephen 1475(?)-1523(?)   **LC 17**
See also DLB 132

Hawkes, John (Clendennin Burne, Jr.) 1925-1998 **CLC 1, 2, 3, 4, 7, 9, 14, 15, 27, 49**
See also CA 1-4R; 167; CANR 2, 47, 64; DLB 2, 7; DLBY 80, 98; MTCW 1, 2

Hawking, S. W.
See Hawking, Stephen W(illiam)

Hawking, Stephen W(illiam) 1942- **CLC 63, 105**
See also AAYA 13; BEST 89:1; CA 126; 129; CANR 48; DA3; MTCW 2

Hawkins, Anthony Hope
See Hope, Anthony

Hawthorne, Julian 1846-1934   **TCLC 25**
See also CA 165

Hawthorne, Nathaniel 1804-1864 **NCLC 39; DA; DAB; DAC; DAM MST, NOV; SSC 3, 29; WLC**
See also AAYA 18; CDALB 1640-1865; DA3; DLB 1, 74; YABC 2

Haxton, Josephine Ayres 1921-
See Douglas, Ellen
See also CA 115; CANR 41, 83

Hayaseca y Eizaguirre, Jorge
See Echegaray (y Eizaguirre), Jose (Maria Waldo)

Hayashi, Fumiko 1904-1951   **TCLC 27**
See also CA 161; DLB 180

Haycraft, Anna
See Ellis, Alice Thomas
See also CA 122; MTCW 2

Hayden, Robert E(arl) 1913-1980 **CLC 5, 9, 14, 37; BLC 2; DA; DAC; DAM MST, MULT, POET; PC 6**
See also BW 1, 3; CA 69-72; 97-100; CABS 2; CANR 24, 75, 82; CDALB 1941-1968; DLB 5, 76; MTCW 1, 2; SATA 19; SATA-Obit 26

Hayford, J(oseph) E(phraim) Casely
See Casely-Hayford, J(oseph) E(phraim)

Hayman, Ronald 1932-   **CLC 44**
See also CA 25-28R; CANR 18, 50; DLB 155

Haywood, Eliza (Fowler) 1693(?)-1756 **LC 1, 44**
See also DLB 39

Hazlitt, William 1778-1830   **NCLC 29**
See also DLB 110, 158

Hazzard, Shirley 1931-   **CLC 18**
See also CA 9-12R; CANR 4, 70; DLBY 82; MTCW 1

Head, Bessie 1937-1986 **CLC 25, 67; BLC 2; DAM MULT**
See also BW 2, 3; CA 29-32R; 119; CANR 25, 82; DA3; DLB 117; MTCW 1, 2

Headon, (Nicky) Topper 1956(?)-   **CLC 30**

Heaney, Seamus (Justin) 1939- **CLC 5, 7, 14, 25, 37, 74, 91; DAB; DAM POET; PC 18; WLCS**
See also CA 85-88; CANR 25, 48, 75; CDBLB 1960 to Present; DA3; DLB 40; DLBY 95; MTCW 1, 2

Hearn, (Patricio) Lafcadio (Tessima Carlos) 1850-1904 **TCLC 9**
See also CA 105; 166; DLB 12, 78, 189

Hearne, Vicki 1946-   **CLC 56**
See also CA 139

Hearon, Shelby 1931-   **CLC 63**
See also AITN 2; CA 25-28R; CANR 18, 48

Heat-Moon, William Least   **CLC 29**
See also Trogdon, William (Lewis)
See also AAYA 9

Hebbel, Friedrich 1813-1863 **NCLC 43; DAM DRAM**
See also DLB 129

Hebert, Anne 1916- **CLC 4, 13, 29; DAC; DAM MST, POET**
See also CA 85-88; CANR 69; DA3; DLB 68; MTCW 1, 2

Hecht, Anthony (Evan) 1923- **CLC 8, 13, 19;**
DAM POET
See also CA 9-12R; CANR 6; DLB 5, 169

Hecht, Ben 1894-1964 **CLC 8**
See also CA 85-88; DLB 7, 9, 25, 26, 28, 86

Hedayat, Sadeq 1903-1951 **TCLC 21**
See also CA 120

Hegel, Georg Wilhelm Friedrich 1770-1831
NCLC 46
See also DLB 90

Heidegger, Martin 1889-1976 **CLC 24**
See also CA 81-84; 65-68; CANR 34; MTCW
1, 2

Heidenstam, (Carl Gustaf) Verner von 1859-
1940 **TCLC 5**
See also CA 104

Heifner, Jack 1946- **CLC 11**
See also CA 105; CANR 47

Heijermans, Herman 1864-1924 **TCLC 24**
See also CA 123

Heilbrun, Carolyn G(old) 1926- **CLC 25**
See also CA 45-48; CANR 1, 28, 58

Heine, Heinrich 1797-1856**NCLC 4, 54; PC 25**
See also DLB 90

Heinemann, Larry (Curtiss) 1944- **CLC 50**
See also CA 110; CAAS 21; CANR 31, 81;
DLBD 9; INT CANR-31

Heiney, Donald (William) 1921-1993
See Harris, MacDonald
See also CA 1-4R; 142; CANR 3, 58

Heinlein, Robert A(nson) 1907-1988**CLC 1, 3,**
8, 14, 26, 55; DAM POP
See also AAYA 17; CA 1-4R; 125; CANR 1,
20, 53; DA3; DLB 8; JRDA; MAICYA;
MTCW 1, 2; SATA 9, 69; SATA-Obit 56

Helforth, John
See Doolittle, Hilda

Hellenhofferu, Vojtech Kapristian z
See Hasek, Jaroslav (Matej Frantisek)

Heller, Joseph 1923-**CLC 1, 3, 5, 8, 11, 36, 63;**
DA; DAB; DAC; DAM MST, NOV, POP;
WLC
See also AAYA 24; AITN 1; CA 5-8R; CABS
1; CANR 8, 42, 66; DA3; DLB 2, 28; DLBY
80; INT CANR-8; MTCW 1, 2

Hellman, Lillian (Florence) 1906-1984**CLC 2,**
4, 8, 14, 18, 34, 44, 52; DAM DRAM; DC 1
See also AITN 1, 2; CA 13-16R; 112; CANR
33; DA3; DLB 7; DLBY 84; MTCW 1, 2

Helprin, Mark 1947-**CLC 7, 10, 22, 32; DAM**
NOV, POP
See also CA 81-84; CANR 47, 64; CDALBS;
DA3; DLBY 85; MTCW 1, 2

Helvetius, Claude-Adrien 1715-1771 **LC 26**

Helyar, Jane Penelope Josephine 1933-
See Poole, Josephine
See also CA 21-24R; CANR 10, 26; SATA 82

Hemans, Felicia 1793-1835 **NCLC 71**
See also DLB 96

Hemingway, Ernest (Miller) 1899-1961 **C L C**
1, 3, 6, 8, 10, 13, 19, 30, 34, 39, 41, 44, 50,
61, 80; DA; DAB; DAC; DAM MST, NOV;
SSC 1, 25, 36; WLC
See also AAYA 19; CA 77-80; CANR 34;
CDALB 1917-1929; DA3; DLB 4, 9, 102,
210; DLBD 1, 15, 16; DLBY 81, 87, 96, 98;
MTCW 1, 2

Hempel, Amy 1951- **CLC 39**
See also CA 118; 137; CANR 70; DA3; MTCW
2

Henderson, F. C.
See Mencken, H(enry) L(ouis)

Henderson, Sylvia

See Ashton-Warner, Sylvia (Constance)

Henderson, Zenna (Chlarson) 1917-1983**S S C**
29
See also CA 1-4R; 133; CANR 1, 84; DLB 8;
SATA 5

Henkin, Joshua **CLC 119**
See also CA 161

Henley, Beth **CLC 23; DC 6**
See also Henley, Elizabeth Becker
See also CABS 3; DLBY 86

Henley, Elizabeth Becker 1952-
See Henley, Beth
See also CA 107; CANR 32, 73; DAM DRAM,
MST; DA3; MTCW 1, 2

Henley, William Ernest 1849-1903 **TCLC 8**
See also CA 105; DLB 19

Hennissart, Martha
See Lathen, Emma
See also CA 85-88; CANR 64

Henry, O. **TCLC 1, 19; SSC 5; WLC**
See also Porter, William Sydney

Henry, Patrick 1736-1799 **LC 25**

Henryson, Robert 1430(?)-1506(?) **LC 20**
See also DLB 146

Henry VIII 1491-1547 **LC 10**
See also DLB 132

Henschke, Alfred
See Klabund

Hentoff, Nat(han Irving) 1925- **CLC 26**
See also AAYA 4; CA 1-4R; CAAS 6; CANR
5, 25, 77; CLR 1, 52; INT CANR-25; JRDA;
MAICYA; SATA 42, 69; SATA-Brief 27

Heppenstall, (John) Rayner 1911-1981 **C L C**
10
See also CA 1-4R; 103; CANR 29

Heraclitus c. 540B.C.-c. 450B.C. **CMLC 22**
See also DLB 176

Herbert, Frank (Patrick) 1920-1986**CLC 12,**
23, 35, 44, 85; DAM POP
See also AAYA 21; CA 53-56; 118; CANR 5,
43; CDALBS; DLB 8; INT CANR-5; MTCW
1, 2; SATA 9, 37; SATA-Obit 47

Herbert, George 1593-1633 **LC 24; DAB;**
DAM POET; PC 4
See also CDBLB Before 1660; DLB 126

Herbert, Zbigniew 1924-1998 **CLC 9, 43;**
DAM POET
See also CA 89-92; 169; CANR 36, 74; MTCW
1

Herbst, Josephine (Frey) 1897-1969 **CLC 34**
See also CA 5-8R; 25-28R; DLB 9

Heredia, Jose Maria 1803-1839
See also HLCS 2

Hergesheimer, Joseph 1880-1954 **TCLC 11**
See also CA 109; DLB 102, 9

Herlihy, James Leo 1927-1993 **CLC 6**
See also CA 1-4R; 143; CANR 2

Hermogenes fl. c. 175- **CMLC 6**

Hernandez, Jose 1834-1886 **NCLC 17**

Herodotus c. 484B.C.-429B.C. **CMLC 17**
See also DLB 176

Herrick, Robert 1591-1674**LC 13; DA; DAB;**
DAC; DAM MST, POP; PC 9
See also DLB 126

Herring, Guilles
See Somerville, Edith

Herriot, James 1916-1995**CLC 12; DAM POP**
See also Wight, James Alfred
See also AAYA 1; CA 148; CANR 40; MTCW
2; SATA 86

Herrmann, Dorothy 1941- **CLC 44**
See also CA 107

Herrmann, Taffy

See Herrmann, Dorothy

Hersey, John (Richard) 1914-1993**CLC 1, 2, 7,**
9, 40, 81, 97; DAM POP
See also AAYA 29; CA 17-20R; 140; CANR
33; CDALBS; DLB 6, 185; MTCW 1, 2;
SATA 25; SATA-Obit 76

Herzen, Aleksandr Ivanovich 1812-1870
NCLC 10, 61

Herzl, Theodor 1860-1904 **TCLC 36**
See also CA 168

Herzog, Werner 1942- **CLC 16**
See also CA 89-92

Hesiod c. 8th cent. B.C.- **CMLC 5**
See also DLB 176

Hesse, Hermann 1877-1962**CLC 1, 2, 3, 6, 11,**
17, 25, 69; DA; DAB; DAC; DAM MST,
NOV; SSC 9; WLC
See also CA 17-18; CAP 2; DA3; DLB 66;
MTCW 1, 2; SATA 50

Hewes, Cady
See De Voto, Bernard (Augustine)

Heyen, William 1940- **CLC 13, 18**
See also CA 33-36R; CAAS 9; DLB 5

Heyerdahl, Thor 1914- **CLC 26**
See also CA 5-8R; CANR 5, 22, 66, 73; MTCW
1, 2; SATA 2, 52

Heym, Georg (Theodor Franz Arthur) 1887-
1912 **TCLC 9**
See also CA 106

Heym, Stefan 1913- **CLC 41**
See also CA 9-12R; CANR 4; DLB 69

Heyse, Paul (Johann Ludwig von) 1830-1914
TCLC 8
See also CA 104; DLB 129

Heyward, (Edwin) DuBose 1885-1940 **T C L C**
59
See also CA 108; 157; DLB 7, 9, 45; SATA 21

Hibbert, Eleanor Alice Burford 1906-1993
CLC 7; DAM POP
See also BEST 90:4; CA 17-20R; 140; CANR
9, 28, 59; MTCW 2; SATA 2; SATA-Obit 74

Hichens, Robert (Smythe) 1864-1950 **T C L C**
64
See also CA 162; DLB 153

Higgins, George V(incent) 1939-**CLC 4, 7, 10,**
18
See also CA 77-80; CAAS 5; CANR 17, 51;
DLB 2; DLBY 81, 98; INT CANR-17;
MTCW 1

Higginson, Thomas Wentworth 1823-1911
TCLC 36
See also CA 162; DLB 1, 64

Highet, Helen
See MacInnes, Helen (Clark)

Highsmith, (Mary) Patricia 1921-1995**CLC 2,**
4, 14, 42, 102; DAM NOV, POP
See also CA 1-4R; 147; CANR 1, 20, 48, 62;
DA3; MTCW 1, 2

Highwater, Jamake (Mamake) 1942(?)- **C L C**
12
See also AAYA 7; CA 65-68; CAAS 7; CANR
10, 34, 84; CLR 17; DLB 52; DLBY 85;
JRDA; MAICYA; SATA 32, 69; SATA-Brief
30

Highway, Tomson 1951-**CLC 92; DAC; DAM**
MULT
See also CA 151; CANR 75; MTCW 2; NNAL

Higuchi, Ichiyo 1872-1896 **NCLC 49**

Hijuelos, Oscar 1951- **CLC 65; DAM MULT,**
POP; HLC 1
See also AAYA 25; BEST 90:1; CA 123; CANR
50, 75; DA3; DLB 145; HW 1, 2; MTCW 2

Hikmet, Nazim 1902(?)-1963 **CLC 40**

See Woolrich, Cornell
See also CA 13-14; CANR 58; CAP 1; MTCW 2

Horatio
See Proust, (Valentin-Louis-George-Eugene-) Marcel

Horgan, Paul (George Vincent O'Shaughnessy) 1903-1995 **CLC 9, 53; DAM NOV**
See also CA 13-16R; 147; CANR 9, 35; DLB 212; DLBY 85; INT CANR-9; MTCW 1, 2; SATA 13; SATA-Obit 84

Horn, Peter
See Kuttner, Henry

Hornem, Horace Esq.
See Byron, George Gordon (Noel)

Horney, Karen (Clementine Theodore Danielsen) 1885-1952 **TCLC 71**
See also CA 114; 165

Hornung, E(rnest) W(illiam) 1866-1921 **TCLC 59**
See also CA 108; 160; DLB 70

Horovitz, Israel (Arthur) 1939- **CLC 56; DAM DRAM**
See also CA 33-36R; CANR 46, 59; DLB 7

Horvath, Odon von
See Horvath, Oedoen von
See also DLB 85, 124

Horvath, Oedoen von 1901-1938 **TCLC 45**
See also Horvath, Odon von
See also CA 118

Horwitz, Julius 1920-1986 **CLC 14**
See also CA 9-12R; 119; CANR 12

Hospital, Janette Turner 1942- **CLC 42**
See also CA 108; CANR 48

Hostos, E. M. de
See Hostos (y Bonilla), Eugenio Maria de

Hostos, Eugenio M. de
See Hostos (y Bonilla), Eugenio Maria de

Hostos, Eugenio Maria
See Hostos (y Bonilla), Eugenio Maria de

Hostos (y Bonilla), Eugenio Maria de 1839-1903 **TCLC 24**
See also CA 123; 131; HW 1

Houdini
See Lovecraft, H(oward) P(hillips)

Hougan, Carolyn 1943- **CLC 34**
See also CA 139

Household, Geoffrey (Edward West) 1900-1988 **CLC 11**
See also CA 77-80; 126; CANR 58; DLB 87; SATA 14; SATA-Obit 59

Housman, A(lfred) E(dward) 1859-1936 **TCLC 1, 10; DA; DAB; DAC; DAM MST, POET; PC 2; WLCS**
See also CA 104; 125; DA3; DLB 19; MTCW 1, 2

Housman, Laurence 1865-1959 **TCLC 7**
See also CA 106; 155; DLB 10; SATA 25

Howard, Elizabeth Jane 1923- **CLC 7, 29**
See also CA 5-8R; CANR 8, 62

Howard, Maureen 1930- **CLC 5, 14, 46**
See also CA 53-56; CANR 31, 75; DLBY 83; INT CANR-31; MTCW 1, 2

Howard, Richard 1929- **CLC 7, 10, 47**
See also AITN 1; CA 85-88; CANR 25, 80; DLB 5; INT CANR-25

Howard, Robert E(rvin) 1906-1936 **TCLC 8**
See also CA 105; 157

Howard, Warren F.
See Pohl, Frederik

Howe, Fanny (Quincy) 1940- **CLC 47**
See also CA 117; CAAS 27; CANR 70; SATA-Brief 52

Howe, Irving 1920-1993 **CLC 85**
See also CA 9-12R; 141; CANR 21, 50; DLB 67; MTCW 1, 2

Howe, Julia Ward 1819-1910 **TCLC 21**
See also CA 117; DLB 1, 189

Howe, Susan 1937- **CLC 72**
See also CA 160; DLB 120

Howe, Tina 1937- **CLC 48**
See also CA 109

Howell, James 1594(?)-1666 **LC 13**
See also DLB 151

Howells, W. D.
See Howells, William Dean

Howells, William D.
See Howells, William Dean

Howells, William Dean 1837-1920 **TCLC 7, 17, 41; SSC 36**
See also CA 104; 134; CDALB 1865-1917; DLB 12, 64, 74, 79, 189; MTCW 2

Howes, Barbara 1914-1996 **CLC 15**
See also CA 9-12R; 151; CAAS 3; CANR 53; SATA 5

Hrabal, Bohumil 1914-1997 **CLC 13, 67**
See also CA 106; 156; CAAS 12; CANR 57

Hroswitha of Gandersheim c. 935-c. 1002 **CMLC 29**
See also DLB 148

Hsun, Lu
See Lu Hsun

Hubbard, L(afayette) Ron(ald) 1911-1986 **CLC 43; DAM POP**
See also CA 77-80; 118; CANR 52; DA3; MTCW 2

Huch, Ricarda (Octavia) 1864-1947 **TCLC 13**
See also CA 111; DLB 66

Huddle, David 1942- **CLC 49**
See also CA 57-60; CAAS 20; DLB 130

Hudson, Jeffrey
See Crichton, (John) Michael

Hudson, W(illiam) H(enry) 1841-1922 **TCLC 29**
See also CA 115; DLB 98, 153, 174; SATA 35

Hueffer, Ford Madox
See Ford, Ford Madox

Hughart, Barry 1934- **CLC 39**
See also CA 137

Hughes, Colin
See Creasey, John

Hughes, David (John) 1930- **CLC 48**
See also CA 116; 129; DLB 14

Hughes, Edward James
See Hughes, Ted
See also DAM MST, POET; DA3

Hughes, (James) Langston 1902-1967 **CLC 1, 5, 10, 15, 35, 44, 108; BLC 2; DA; DAB; DAC; DAM DRAM, MST, MULT, POET; DC 3; PC 1; SSC 6; WLC**
See also AAYA 12; BW 1, 3; CA 1-4R; 25-28R; CANR 1, 34, 82; CDALB 1929-1941; CLR 17; DA3; DLB 4, 7, 48, 51, 86; JRDA; MAICYA; MTCW 1, 2; SATA 4, 33

Hughes, Richard (Arthur Warren) 1900-1976 **CLC 1, 11; DAM NOV**
See also CA 5-8R; 65-68; CANR 4; DLB 15, 161; MTCW 1; SATA 8; SATA-Obit 25

Hughes, Ted 1930-1998 **CLC 2, 4, 9, 14, 37, 119; DAB; DAC; PC 7**
See also Hughes, Edward James
See also CA 1-4R; 171; CANR 1, 33, 66; CLR 3; DLB 40, 161; MAICYA; MTCW 1, 2; SATA 49; SATA-Brief 27; SATA-Obit 107

Hugo, Richard F(ranklin) 1923-1982 **CLC 6, 18, 32; DAM POET**

See also CA 49-52; 108; CANR 3; DLB 5, 206

Hugo, Victor (Marie) 1802-1885 **NCLC 3, 10, 21; DA; DAB; DAC; DAM DRAM, MST, NOV, POET; PC 17; WLC**
See also AAYA 28; DA3; DLB 119, 192; SATA 47

Huidobro, Vicente
See Huidobro Fernandez, Vicente Garcia

Huidobro Fernandez, Vicente Garcia 1893-1948 **TCLC 31**
See also CA 131; HW 1

Hulme, Keri 1947- **CLC 39**
See also CA 125; CANR 69; INT 125

Hulme, T(homas) E(rnest) 1883-1917 **TCLC 21**
See also CA 117; DLB 19

Hume, David 1711-1776 **LC 7**
See also DLB 104

Humphrey, William 1924-1997 **CLC 45**
See also CA 77-80; 160; CANR 68; DLB 212

Humphreys, Emyr Owen 1919- **CLC 47**
See also CA 5-8R; CANR 3, 24; DLB 15

Humphreys, Josephine 1945- **CLC 34, 57**
See also CA 121; 127; INT 127

Huneker, James Gibbons 1857-1921 **TCLC 65**
See also DLB 71

Hungerford, Pixie
See Brinsmead, H(esba) F(ay)

Hunt, E(verette) Howard, (Jr.) 1918- **CLC 3**
See also AITN 1; CA 45-48; CANR 2, 47

Hunt, Kyle
See Creasey, John

Hunt, (James Henry) Leigh 1784-1859 **NCLC 1, 70; DAM POET**
See also DLB 96, 110, 144

Hunt, Marsha 1946- **CLC 70**
See also BW 2, 3; CA 143; CANR 79

Hunt, Violet 1866(?)-1942 **TCLC 53**
See also DLB 162, 197

Hunter, E. Waldo
See Sturgeon, Theodore (Hamilton)

Hunter, Evan 1926- **CLC 11, 31; DAM POP**
See also CA 5-8R; CANR 5, 38, 62; DLBY 82; INT CANR-5; MTCW 1; SATA 25

Hunter, Kristin (Eggleston) 1931- **CLC 35**
See also AITN 1; BW 1; CA 13-16R; CANR 13; CLR 3; DLB 33; INT CANR-13; MAICYA; SAAS 10; SATA 12

Hunter, Mary
See Austin, Mary (Hunter)

Hunter, Mollie 1922- **CLC 21**
See also McIlwraith, Maureen Mollie Hunter
See also AAYA 13; CANR 37, 78; CLR 25; DLB 161; JRDA; MAICYA; SAAS 7; SATA 54, 106

Hunter, Robert (?)-1734 **LC 7**

Hurston, Zora Neale 1903-1960 **CLC 7, 30, 61; BLC 2; DA; DAC; DAM MST, MULT, NOV; SSC 4; WLCS**
See also AAYA 15; BW 1, 3; CA 85-88; CANR 61; CDALBS; DA3; DLB 51, 86; MTCW 1, 2

Huston, John (Marcellus) 1906-1987 **CLC 20**
See also CA 73-76; 123; CANR 34; DLB 26

Hustvedt, Siri 1955- **CLC 76**
See also CA 137

Hutten, Ulrich von 1488-1523 **LC 16**
See also DLB 179

Huxley, Aldous (Leonard) 1894-1963 **CLC 1, 3, 4, 5, 8, 11, 18, 35, 79; DA; DAB; DAC; DAM MST, NOV; WLC**
See also AAYA 11; CA 85-88; CANR 44; CDBLB 1914-1945; DA3; DLB 36, 100,

162, 195; MTCW 1, 2; SATA 63
Huxley, T(homas) H(enry) 1825-1895 **N C L C 67**
See also DLB 57
Huysmans, Joris-Karl 1848-1907**TCLC 7, 69**
See also CA 104; 165; DLB 123
Hwang, David Henry 1957- **CLC 55; DAM DRAM; DC 4**
See also CA 127; 132; CANR 76; DA3; DLB 212; INT 132; MTCW 2
Hyde, Anthony 1946- **CLC 42**
See also CA 136
Hyde, Margaret O(ldroyd) 1917- **CLC 21**
See also CA 1-4R; CANR 1, 36; CLR 23; JRDA; MAICYA; SAAS 8; SATA 1, 42, 76
Hynes, James 1956(?)- **CLC 65**
See also CA 164
Hypatia c. 370-415 **CMLC 35**
Ian, Janis 1951- **CLC 21**
See also CA 105
Ibanez, Vicente Blasco
See Blasco Ibanez, Vicente
Ibarbourou, Juana de 1895-1979
See also HLCS 2; HW 1
Ibarguengoitia, Jorge 1928-1983 **CLC 37**
See also CA 124; 113; HW 1
Ibsen, Henrik (Johan) 1828-1906 **TCLC 2, 8, 16, 37, 52; DA; DAB; DAC; DAM DRAM, MST; DC 2; WLC**
See also CA 104; 141; DA3
Ibuse, Masuji 1898-1993 **CLC 22**
See also CA 127; 141; DLB 180
Ichikawa, Kon 1915- **CLC 20**
See also CA 121
Idle, Eric 1943- **CLC 21**
See also Monty Python
See also CA 116; CANR 35
Ignatow, David 1914-1997 **CLC 4, 7, 14, 40**
See also CA 9-12R; 162; CAAS 3; CANR 31, 57; DLB 5
Ignotus
See Strachey, (Giles) Lytton
Ihimaera, Witi 1944- **CLC 46**
See also CA 77-80
Ilf, Ilya **TCLC 21**
See also Fainzilberg, Ilya Arnoldovich
Illyes, Gyula 1902-1983 **PC 16**
See also CA 114; 109
Immermann, Karl (Lebrecht) 1796-1840 **NCLC 4, 49**
See also DLB 133
Ince, Thomas H. 1882-1924 **TCLC 89**
Inchbald, Elizabeth 1753-1821 **NCLC 62**
See also DLB 39, 89
Inclan, Ramon (Maria) del Valle
See Valle-Inclan, Ramon (Maria) del
Infante, G(uillermo) Cabrera
See Cabrera Infante, G(uillermo)
Ingalls, Rachel (Holmes) 1940- **CLC 42**
See also CA 123; 127
Ingamells, Reginald Charles
See Ingamells, Rex
Ingamells, Rex 1913-1955 **TCLC 35**
See also CA 167
Inge, William (Motter) 1913-1973 **CLC 1, 8, 19; DAM DRAM**
See also CA 9-12R; CDALB 1941-1968; DA3; DLB 7; MTCW 1, 2
Ingelow, Jean 1820-1897 **NCLC 39**
See also DLB 35, 163; SATA 33
Ingram, Willis J.
See Harris, Mark
Innaurato, Albert (F.) 1948(?)- **CLC 21, 60**

See also CA 115; 122; CANR 78; INT 122
Innes, Michael
See Stewart, J(ohn) I(nnes) M(ackintosh)
Innis, Harold Adams 1894-1952 **TCLC 77**
See also DLB 88
Ionesco, Eugene 1909-1994**CLC 1, 4, 6, 9, 11, 15, 41, 86; DA; DAB; DAC; DAM DRAM, MST; WLC**
See also CA 9-12R; 144; CANR 55; DA3; MTCW 1, 2; SATA 7; SATA-Obit 79
Iqbal, Muhammad 1873-1938 **TCLC 28**
Ireland, Patrick
See O'Doherty, Brian
Iron, Ralph
See Schreiner, Olive (Emilie Albertina)
Irving, John (Winslow) 1942-**CLC 13, 23, 38, 112; DAM NOV, POP**
See also AAYA 8; BEST 89:3; CA 25-28R; CANR 28, 73; DA3; DLB 6; DLBY 82; MTCW 1, 2
Irving, Washington 1783-1859 **NCLC 2, 19; DA; DAB; DAC; DAM MST; SSC 2; WLC**
See also CDALB 1640-1865; DA3; DLB 3, 11, 30, 59, 73, 74, 186; YABC 2
Irwin, P. K.
See Page, P(atricia) K(athleen)
Isaacs, Jorge Ricardo 1837-1895 **NCLC 70**
Isaacs, Susan 1943- **CLC 32; DAM POP**
See also BEST 89:1; CA 89-92; CANR 20, 41, 65; DA3; INT CANR-20; MTCW 1, 2
Isherwood, Christopher (William Bradshaw) 1904-1986 **CLC 1, 9, 11, 14, 44; DAM DRAM, NOV**
See also CA 13-16R; 117; CANR 35; DA3; DLB 15, 195; DLBY 86; MTCW 1, 2
Ishiguro, Kazuo 1954- **CLC 27, 56, 59, 110; DAM NOV**
See also BEST 90:2; CA 120; CANR 49; DA3; DLB 194; MTCW 1, 2
Ishikawa, Hakuhin
See Ishikawa, Takuboku
Ishikawa, Takuboku 1886(?)-1912 **TCLC 15; DAM POET; PC 10**
See also CA 113; 153
Iskander, Fazil 1929- **CLC 47**
See also CA 102
Isler, Alan (David) 1934- **CLC 91**
See also CA 156
Ivan IV 1530-1584 **LC 17**
Ivanov, Vyacheslav Ivanovich 1866-1949 **TCLC 33**
See also CA 122
Ivask, Ivar Vidrik 1927-1992 **CLC 14**
See also CA 37-40R; 139; CANR 24
Ives, Morgan
See Bradley, Marion Zimmer
Izumi Shikibu c. 973-c. 1034 **CMLC 33**
J. R. S.
See Gogarty, Oliver St. John
Jabran, Kahlil
See Gibran, Kahlil
Jabran, Khalil
See Gibran, Kahlil
Jackson, Daniel
See Wingrove, David (John)
Jackson, Jesse 1908-1983 **CLC 12**
See also BW 1; CA 25-28R; 109; CANR 27; CLR 28; MAICYA; SATA 2, 29; SATA-Obit 48
Jackson, Laura (Riding) 1901-1991
See Riding, Laura
See also CA 65-68; 135; CANR 28; DLB 48
Jackson, Sam

See Trumbo, Dalton
Jackson, Sara
See Wingrove, David (John)
Jackson, Shirley 1919-1965 **CLC 11, 60, 87; DA; DAC; DAM MST; SSC 9; WLC**
See also AAYA 9; CA 1-4R; 25-28R; CANR 4, 52; CDALB 1941-1968; DA3; DLB 6; MTCW 2; SATA 2
Jacob, (Cyprien-)Max 1876-1944 **TCLC 6**
See also CA 104
Jacobs, Harriet A(nn) 1813(?)-1897**NCLC 67**
Jacobs, Jim 1942- **CLC 12**
See also CA 97-100; INT 97-100
Jacobs, W(illiam) W(ymark) 1863-1943 **TCLC 22**
See also CA 121; 167; DLB 135
Jacobsen, Jens Peter 1847-1885 **NCLC 34**
Jacobsen, Josephine 1908- **CLC 48, 102**
See also CA 33-36R; CAAS 18; CANR 23, 48
Jacobson, Dan 1929- **CLC 4, 14**
See also CA 1-4R; CANR 2, 25, 66; DLB 14, 207; MTCW 1
Jacqueline
See Carpentier (y Valmont), Alejo
Jagger, Mick 1944- **CLC 17**
Jahiz, al- c. 780-c. 869 **CMLC 25**
Jakes, John (William) 1932- **CLC 29; DAM NOV, POP**
See also AAYA 32; BEST 89:4; CA 57-60; CANR 10, 43, 66; DA3; DLBY 83; INT CANR-10; MTCW 1, 2; SATA 62
James, Andrew
See Kirkup, James
James, C(yril) L(ionel) R(obert) 1901-1989 **CLC 33; BLCS**
See also BW 2; CA 117; 125; 128; CANR 62; DLB 125; MTCW 1
James, Daniel (Lewis) 1911-1988
See Santiago, Danny
See also CA 174; 125
James, Dynely
See Mayne, William (James Carter)
James, Henry Sr. 1811-1882 **NCLC 53**
James, Henry 1843-1916 **TCLC 2, 11, 24, 40, 47, 64; DA; DAB; DAC; DAM MST, NOV; SSC 8, 32; WLC**
See also CA 104; 132; CDALB 1865-1917; DA3; DLB 12, 71, 74, 189; DLBD 13; MTCW 1, 2
James, M. R.
See James, Montague (Rhodes)
See also DLB 156
James, Montague (Rhodes) 1862-1936 **T C L C 6; SSC 16**
See also CA 104; DLB 201
James, P. D. 1920- **CLC 18, 46, 122**
See also White, Phyllis Dorothy James
See also BEST 90:2; CDBLB 1960 to Present; DLB 87; DLBD 17
James, Philip
See Moorcock, Michael (John)
James, William 1842-1910 **TCLC 15, 32**
See also CA 109
James I 1394-1437 **LC 20**
Jameson, Anna 1794-1860 **NCLC 43**
See also DLB 99, 166
Jami, Nur al-Din 'Abd al-Rahman 1414-1492 **LC 9**
Jammes, Francis 1868-1938 **TCLC 75**
Jandl, Ernst 1925- **CLC 34**
Janowitz, Tama 1957- **CLC 43; DAM POP**
See also CA 106; CANR 52
Japrisot, Sebastien 1931- **CLC 90**

Jarrell, Randall 1914-1965**CLC 1, 2, 6, 9, 13, 49; DAM POET**
See also CA 5-8R; 25-28R; CABS 2; CANR 6, 34; CDALB 1941-1968; CLR 6; DLB 48, 52; MAICYA; MTCW 1, 2; SATA 7

Jarry, Alfred 1873-1907 **TCLC 2, 14; DAM DRAM; SSC 20**
See also CA 104; 153; DA3; DLB 192

Jeake, Samuel, Jr.
See Aiken, Conrad (Potter)

Jean Paul 1763-1825 **NCLC 7**

Jefferies, (John) Richard 1848-1887**NCLC 47**
See also DLB 98, 141; SATA 16

Jeffers, (John) Robinson 1887-1962**CLC 2, 3, 11, 15, 54; DA; DAC; DAM MST, POET; PC 17; WLC**
See also CA 85-88; CANR 35; CDALB 1917-1929; DLB 45, 212; MTCW 1, 2

Jefferson, Janet
See Mencken, H(enry) L(ouis)

Jefferson, Thomas 1743-1826 **NCLC 11**
See also CDALB 1640-1865; DA3; DLB 31

Jeffrey, Francis 1773-1850 **NCLC 33**
See also DLB 107

Jelakowitch, Ivan
See Heijermans, Herman

Jellicoe, (Patricia) Ann 1927- **CLC 27**
See also CA 85-88; DLB 13

Jen, Gish **CLC 70**
See also Jen, Lillian

Jen, Lillian 1956(?)-
See Jen, Gish
See also CA 135

Jenkins, (John) Robin 1912- **CLC 52**
See also CA 1-4R; CANR 1; DLB 14

Jennings, Elizabeth (Joan) 1926- **CLC 5, 14**
See also CA 61-64; CAAS 5; CANR 8, 39, 66; DLB 27; MTCW 1; SATA 66

Jennings, Waylon 1937- **CLC 21**

Jensen, Johannes V. 1873-1950 **TCLC 41**
See also CA 170

Jensen, Laura (Linnea) 1948- **CLC 37**
See also CA 103

Jerome, Jerome K(lapka) 1859-1927**TCLC 23**
See also CA 119; 177; DLB 10, 34, 135

Jerrold, Douglas William 1803-1857**NCLC 2**
See also DLB 158, 159

Jewett, (Theodora) Sarah Orne 1849-1909 **TCLC 1, 22; SSC 6**
See also CA 108; 127; CANR 71; DLB 12, 74; SATA 15

Jewsbury, Geraldine (Endsor) 1812-1880 **NCLC 22**
See also DLB 21

Jhabvala, Ruth Prawer 1927-**CLC 4, 8, 29, 94; DAB; DAM NOV**
See also CA 1-4R; CANR 2, 29, 51, 74; DLB 139, 194; INT CANR-29; MTCW 1, 2

Jibran, Kahlil
See Gibran, Kahlil

Jibran, Khalil
See Gibran, Kahlil

Jiles, Paulette 1943- **CLC 13, 58**
See also CA 101; CANR 70

Jimenez (Mantecon), Juan Ramon 1881-1958 **TCLC 4; DAM MULT, POET; HLC 1; PC 7**
See also CA 104; 131; CANR 74; DLB 134; HW 1; MTCW 1, 2

Jimenez, Ramon
See Jimenez (Mantecon), Juan Ramon

Jimenez Mantecon, Juan
See Jimenez (Mantecon), Juan Ramon

Jin, Ha 1956- **CLC 109**
See also CA 152

Joel, Billy **CLC 26**
See also Joel, William Martin

Joel, William Martin 1949-
See Joel, Billy
See also CA 108

John, Saint 7th cent. - **CMLC 27**

John of the Cross, St. 1542-1591 **LC 18**

Johnson, B(ryan) S(tanley William) 1933-1973 **CLC 6, 9**
See also CA 9-12R; 53-56; CANR 9; DLB 14, 40

Johnson, Benj. F. of Boo
See Riley, James Whitcomb

Johnson, Benjamin F. of Boo
See Riley, James Whitcomb

Johnson, Charles (Richard) 1948-**CLC 7, 51, 65; BLC 2; DAM MULT**
See also BW 2, 3; CA 116; CAAS 18; CANR 42, 66, 82; DLB 33; MTCW 2

Johnson, Denis 1949- **CLC 52**
See also CA 117; 121; CANR 71; DLB 120

Johnson, Diane 1934- **CLC 5, 13, 48**
See also CA 41-44R; CANR 17, 40, 62; DLBY 80; INT CANR-17; MTCW 1

Johnson, Eyvind (Olof Verner) 1900-1976 **CLC 14**
See also CA 73-76; 69-72; CANR 34

Johnson, J. R.
See James, C(yril) L(ionel) R(obert)

Johnson, James Weldon 1871-1938 **TCLC 3, 19; BLC 2; DAM MULT, POET; PC 24**
See also BW 1, 3; CA 104; 125; CANR 82; CDALB 1917-1929; CLR 32; DA3; DLB 51; MTCW 1, 2; SATA 31

Johnson, Joyce 1935- **CLC 58**
See also CA 125; 129

Johnson, Judith (Emlyn) 1936- **CLC 7, 15**
See also CA 25-28R; 153; CANR 34

Johnson, Lionel (Pigot) 1867-1902 **TCLC 19**
See also CA 117; DLB 19

Johnson, Marguerite (Annie)
See Angelou, Maya

Johnson, Mel
See Malzberg, Barry N(athaniel)

Johnson, Pamela Hansford 1912-1981**CLC 1, 7, 27**
See also CA 1-4R; 104; CANR 2, 28; DLB 15; MTCW 1, 2

Johnson, Robert 1911(?)-1938 **TCLC 69**
See also BW 3; CA 174

Johnson, Samuel 1709-1784 **LC 15, 52; DA; DAB; DAC; DAM MST; WLC**
See also CDBLB 1660-1789; DLB 39, 95, 104, 142

Johnson, Uwe 1934-1984 **CLC 5, 10, 15, 40**
See also CA 1-4R; 112; CANR 1, 39; DLB 75; MTCW 1

Johnston, George (Benson) 1913- **CLC 51**
See also CA 1-4R; CANR 5, 20; DLB 88

Johnston, Jennifer 1930- **CLC 7**
See also CA 85-88; DLB 14

Jolley, (Monica) Elizabeth 1923-**CLC 46; SSC 19**
See also CA 127; CAAS 13; CANR 59

Jones, Arthur Llewellyn 1863-1947
See Machen, Arthur
See also CA 104; 179

Jones, D(ouglas) G(ordon) 1929- **CLC 10**
See also CA 29-32R; CANR 13; DLB 53

Jones, David (Michael) 1895-1974**CLC 2, 4, 7, 13, 42**
See also CA 9-12R; 53-56; CANR 28; CDBLB 1945-1960; DLB 20, 100; MTCW 1

Jones, David Robert 1947-
See Bowie, David
See also CA 103

Jones, Diana Wynne 1934- **CLC 26**
See also AAYA 12; CA 49-52; CANR 4, 26, 56; CLR 23; DLB 161; JRDA; MAICYA; SAAS 7; SATA 9, 70, 108

Jones, Edward P. 1950- **CLC 76**
See also BW 2, 3; CA 142; CANR 79

Jones, Gayl 1949- **CLC 6, 9; BLC 2; DAM MULT**
See also BW 2, 3; CA 77-80; CANR 27, 66; DA3; DLB 33; MTCW 1, 2

Jones, James 1921-1977 **CLC 1, 3, 10, 39**
See also AITN 1, 2; CA 1-4R; 69-72; CANR 6; DLB 2, 143; DLBD 17; DLBY 98; MTCW 1

Jones, John J.
See Lovecraft, H(oward) P(hillips)

Jones, LeRoi **CLC 1, 2, 3, 5, 10, 14**
See also Baraka, Amiri
See also MTCW 2

Jones, Louis B. 1953- **CLC 65**
See also CA 141; CANR 73

Jones, Madison (Percy, Jr.) 1925- **CLC 4**
See also CA 13-16R; CAAS 11; CANR 7, 54, 83; DLB 152

Jones, Mervyn 1922- **CLC 10, 52**
See also CA 45-48; CAAS 5; CANR 1; MTCW 1

Jones, Mick 1956(?)- **CLC 30**

Jones, Nettie (Pearl) 1941- **CLC 34**
See also BW 2; CA 137; CAAS 20

Jones, Preston 1936-1979 **CLC 10**
See also CA 73-76; 89-92; DLB 7

Jones, Robert F(rancis) 1934- **CLC 7**
See also CA 49-52; CANR 2, 61

Jones, Rod 1953- **CLC 50**
See also CA 128

Jones, Terence Graham Parry 1942- **CLC 21**
See also Jones, Terry; Monty Python
See also CA 112; 116; CANR 35; INT 116

Jones, Terry
See Jones, Terence Graham Parry
See also SATA 67; SATA-Brief 51

Jones, Thom 1945(?)- **CLC 81**
See also CA 157

Jong, Erica 1942- **CLC 4, 6, 8, 18, 83; DAM NOV, POP**
See also AITN 1; BEST 90:2; CA 73-76; CANR 26, 52, 75; DA3; DLB 2, 5, 28, 152; INT CANR-26; MTCW 1, 2

Jonson, Ben(jamin) 1572(?)-1637 **LC 6, 33; DA; DAB; DAC; DAM DRAM, MST, POET; DC 4; PC 17; WLC**
See also CDBLB Before 1660; DLB 62, 121

Jordan, June 1936-**CLC 5, 11, 23, 114; BLCS; DAM MULT, POET**
See also AAYA 2; BW 2, 3; CA 33-36R; CANR 25, 70; CLR 10; DLB 38; MAICYA; MTCW 1; SATA 4

Jordan, Neil (Patrick) 1950- **CLC 110**
See also CA 124; 130; CANR 54; INT 130

Jordan, Pat(rick M.) 1941- **CLC 37**
See also CA 33-36R

Jorgensen, Ivar
See Ellison, Harlan (Jay)

Jorgenson, Ivar
See Silverberg, Robert

Josephus, Flavius c. 37-100 **CMLC 13**

Josipovici, Gabriel 1940- **CLC 6, 43**
See also CA 37-40R; CAAS 8; CANR 47, 84;

Author Index

See also BW 1, 3; CA 21-24R; 133; CANR 23, 82; DLB 41; MTCW 2

Knight, Sarah Kemble 1666-1727   **LC 7**
See also DLB 24, 200

Knister, Raymond 1899-1932   **TCLC 56**
See also DLB 68

Knowles, John 1926-   **CLC 1, 4, 10, 26; DA; DAC; DAM MST, NOV**
See also AAYA 10; CA 17-20R; CANR 40, 74, 76; CDALB 1968-1988; DLB 6; MTCW 1, 2; SATA 8, 89

Knox, Calvin M.
See Silverberg, Robert

Knox, John c. 1505-1572   **LC 37**
See also DLB 132

Knye, Cassandra
See Disch, Thomas M(ichael)

Koch, C(hristopher) J(ohn) 1932-   **CLC 42**
See also CA 127; CANR 84

Koch, Christopher
See Koch, C(hristopher) J(ohn)

Koch, Kenneth 1925-   **CLC 5, 8, 44; DAM POET**
See also CA 1-4R; CANR 6, 36, 57; DLB 5; INT CANR-36; MTCW 2; SATA 65

Kochanowski, Jan 1530-1584   **LC 10**

Kock, Charles Paul de 1794-1871   **NCLC 16**

Koda Shigeyuki 1867-1947
See Rohan, Koda
See also CA 121

Koestler, Arthur 1905-1983 **CLC 1, 3, 6, 8, 15, 33**
See also CA 1-4R; 109; CANR 1, 33; CDBLB 1945-1960; DLBY 83; MTCW 1, 2

Kogawa, Joy Nozomi 1935-   **CLC 78; DAC; DAM MST, MULT**
See also CA 101; CANR 19, 62; MTCW 2; SATA 99

Kohout, Pavel 1928-   **CLC 13**
See also CA 45-48; CANR 3

Koizumi, Yakumo
See Hearn, (Patricio) Lafcadio (Tessima Carlos)

Kolmar, Gertrud 1894-1943   **TCLC 40**
See also CA 167

Komunyakaa, Yusef 1947- **CLC 86, 94; BLCS**
See also CA 147; CANR 83; DLB 120

Konrad, George
See Konrad, Gyoergy

Konrad, Gyoergy 1933-   **CLC 4, 10, 73**
See also CA 85-88

Konwicki, Tadeusz 1926- **CLC 8, 28, 54, 117**
See also CA 101; CAAS 9; CANR 39, 59; MTCW 1

Koontz, Dean R(ay) 1945-   **CLC 78; DAM NOV, POP**
See also AAYA 9, 31; BEST 89:3, 90:2; CA 108; CANR 19, 36, 52; DA3; MTCW 1; SATA 92

Kopernik, Mikolaj
See Copernicus, Nicolaus

Kopit, Arthur (Lee) 1937- **CLC 1, 18, 33; DAM DRAM**
See also AITN 1; CA 81-84; CABS 3; DLB 7; MTCW 1

Kops, Bernard 1926-   **CLC 4**
See also CA 5-8R; CANR 84; DLB 13

Kornbluth, C(yril) M. 1923-1958   **TCLC 8**
See also CA 105; 160; DLB 8

Korolenko, V. G.
See Korolenko, Vladimir Galaktionovich

Korolenko, Vladimir
See Korolenko, Vladimir Galaktionovich

Korolenko, Vladimir G.
See Korolenko, Vladimir Galaktionovich

Korolenko, Vladimir Galaktionovich 1853-1921   **TCLC 22**
See also CA 121

Korzybski, Alfred (Habdank Skarbek) 1879-1950   **TCLC 61**
See also CA 123; 160

Kosinski, Jerzy (Nikodem) 1933-1991 **CLC 1, 2, 3, 6, 10, 15, 53, 70; DAM NOV**
See also CA 17-20R; 134; CANR 9, 46; DA3; DLB 2; DLBY 82; MTCW 1, 2

Kostelanetz, Richard (Cory) 1940-   **CLC 28**
See also CA 13-16R; CAAS 8; CANR 38, 77

Kostrowitzki, Wilhelm Apollinaris de 1880-1918
See Apollinaire, Guillaume
See also CA 104

Kotlowitz, Robert 1924-   **CLC 4**
See also CA 33-36R; CANR 36

Kotzebue, August (Friedrich Ferdinand) von 1761-1819   **NCLC 25**
See also DLB 94

Kotzwinkle, William 1938-   **CLC 5, 14, 35**
See also CA 45-48; CANR 3, 44, 84; CLR 6; DLB 173; MAICYA; SATA 24, 70

Kowna, Stancy
See Szymborska, Wislawa

Kozol, Jonathan 1936-   **CLC 17**
See also CA 61-64; CANR 16, 45

Kozoll, Michael 1940(?)-   **CLC 35**

Kramer, Kathryn 19(?)-   **CLC 34**

Kramer, Larry 1935- **CLC 42; DAM POP; DC 8**
See also CA 124; 126; CANR 60

Krasicki, Ignacy 1735-1801   **NCLC 8**

Krasinski, Zygmunt 1812-1859   **NCLC 4**

Kraus, Karl 1874-1936   **TCLC 5**
See also CA 104; DLB 118

Kreve (Mickevicius), Vincas 1882-1954 **TCLC 27**
See also CA 170

Kristeva, Julia 1941-   **CLC 77**
See also CA 154

Kristofferson, Kris 1936-   **CLC 26**
See also CA 104

Krizanc, John 1956-   **CLC 57**

Krleza, Miroslav 1893-1981   **CLC 8, 114**
See also CA 97-100; 105; CANR 50; DLB 147

Kroetsch, Robert 1927- **CLC 5, 23, 57; DAC; DAM POET**
See also CA 17-20R; CANR 8, 38; DLB 53; MTCW 1

Kroetz, Franz
See Kroetz, Franz Xaver

Kroetz, Franz Xaver 1946-   **CLC 41**
See also CA 130

Kroker, Arthur (W.) 1945-   **CLC 77**
See also CA 161

Kropotkin, Peter (Aleksieevich) 1842-1921   **TCLC 36**
See also CA 119

Krotkov, Yuri 1917-   **CLC 19**
See also CA 102

Krumb
See Crumb, R(obert)

Krumgold, Joseph (Quincy) 1908-1980   **CLC 12**
See also CA 9-12R; 101; CANR 7; MAICYA; SATA 1, 48; SATA-Obit 23

Krumwitz
See Crumb, R(obert)

Krutch, Joseph Wood 1893-1970   **CLC 24**
See also CA 1-4R; 25-28R; CANR 4; DLB 63, 206

Krutzch, Gus
See Eliot, T(homas) S(tearns)

Krylov, Ivan Andreevich 1768(?)-1844 **NCLC 1**
See also DLB 150

Kubin, Alfred (Leopold Isidor) 1877-1959   **TCLC 23**
See also CA 112; 149; DLB 81

Kubrick, Stanley 1928-1999   **CLC 16**
See also AAYA 30; CA 81-84; 177; CANR 33; DLB 26

Kumin, Maxine (Winokur) 1925- **CLC 5, 13, 28; DAM POET; PC 15**
See also AITN 2; CA 1-4R; CAAS 8; CANR 1, 21, 69; DA3; DLB 5; MTCW 1, 2; SATA 12

Kundera, Milan 1929- **CLC 4, 9, 19, 32, 68, 115; DAM NOV; SSC 24**
See also AAYA 2; CA 85-88; CANR 19, 52, 74; DA3; MTCW 1, 2

Kunene, Mazisi (Raymond) 1930-   **CLC 85**
See also BW 1, 3; CA 125; CANR 81; DLB 117

Kunitz, Stanley (Jasspon) 1905- **CLC 6, 11, 14; PC 19**
See also CA 41-44R; CANR 26, 57; DA3; DLB 48; INT CANR-26; MTCW 1, 2

Kunze, Reiner 1933-   **CLC 10**
See also CA 93-96; DLB 75

Kuprin, Aleksandr Ivanovich 1870-1938   **TCLC 5**
See also CA 104

Kureishi, Hanif 1954(?)-   **CLC 64**
See also CA 139; DLB 194

Kurosawa, Akira 1910-1998   **CLC 16, 119; DAM MULT**
See also AAYA 11; CA 101; 170; CANR 46

Kushner, Tony 1957(?)- **CLC 81; DAM DRAM; DC 10**
See also CA 144; CANR 74; DA3; MTCW 2

Küttner, Henry 1915-1958   **TCLC 10**
See also Vance, Jack
See also CA 107; 157; DLB 8

Kuzma, Greg 1944-   **CLC 7**
See also CA 33-36R; CANR 70

Kuzmin, Mikhail 1872(?)-1936   **TCLC 40**
See also CA 170

Kyd, Thomas 1558-1594 **LC 22; DAM DRAM; DC 3**
See also DLB 62

Kyprianos, Iossif
See Samarakis, Antonis

La Bruyere, Jean de 1645-1696   **LC 17**

Lacan, Jacques (Marie Emile) 1901-1981   **CLC 75**
See also CA 121; 104

Laclos, Pierre Ambroise Francois Choderlos de 1741-1803   **NCLC 4**

La Colere, Francois
See Aragon, Louis

Lacolere, Francois
See Aragon, Louis

La Deshabilleuse
See Simenon, Georges (Jacques Christian)

Lady Gregory
See Gregory, Isabella Augusta (Persse)

Lady of Quality, A
See Bagnold, Enid

La Fayette, Marie (Madelaine Pioche de la Vergne Comtes 1634-1693   **LC 2**

Lafayette, Rene
See Hubbard, L(afayette) Ron(ald)

Laforgue, Jules 1860-1887 **NCLC 5, 53; PC 14; SSC 20**

Leavis, F(rank) R(aymond) 1895-1978CLC 24
See also CA 21-24R; 77-80; CANR 44; MTCW
1, 2
Leavitt, David 1961-   CLC 34; DAM POP
See also CA 116; 122; CANR 50, 62; DA3; DLB
130; INT 122; MTCW 2
Leblanc, Maurice (Marie Emile) 1864-1941
TCLC 49
See also CA 110
Lebowitz, Fran(ces Ann) 1951(?)-CLC 11, 36
See also CA 81-84; CANR 14, 60, 70; INT
CANR-14; MTCW 1
Lebrecht, Peter
See Tieck, (Johann) Ludwig
le Carre, John   CLC 3, 5, 9, 15, 28
See also Cornwell, David (John Moore)
See also BEST 89:4; CDBLB 1960 to Present;
DLB 87; MTCW 2
Le Clezio, J(ean) M(arie) G(ustave) 1940-
CLC 31
See also CA 116; 128; DLB 83
Leconte de Lisle, Charles-Marie-Rene 1818-
1894   NCLC 29
Le Coq, Monsieur
See Simenon, Georges (Jacques Christian)
Leduc, Violette 1907-1972   CLC 22
See also CA 13-14; 33-36R; CANR 69; CAP 1
Ledwidge, Francis 1887(?)-1917   TCLC 23
See also CA 123; DLB 20
Lee, Andrea 1953-   CLC 36; BLC 2; DAM
MULT
See also BW 1, 3; CA 125; CANR 82
Lee, Andrew
See Auchincloss, Louis (Stanton)
Lee, Chang-rae 1965-   CLC 91
See also CA 148
Lee, Don L.   CLC 2
See also Madhubuti, Haki R.
Lee, George W(ashington) 1894-1976CLC 52;
BLC 2; DAM MULT
See also BW 1; CA 125; CANR 83; DLB 51
Lee, (Nelle) Harper 1926-   CLC 12, 60; DA;
DAB; DAC; DAM MST, NOV; WLC
See also AAYA 13; CA 13-16R; CANR 51;
CDALB 1941-1968; DA3; DLB 6; MTCW
1, 2; SATA 11
Lee, Helen Elaine 1959(?)-   CLC 86
See also CA 148
Lee, Julian
See Latham, Jean Lee
Lee, Larry
See Lee, Lawrence
Lee, Laurie 1914-1997   CLC 90; DAB; DAM
POP
See also CA 77-80; 158; CANR 33, 73; DLB
27; MTCW 1
Lee, Lawrence 1941-1990   CLC 34
See also CA 131; CANR 43
Lee, Li-Young 1957-   PC 24
See also CA 153; DLB 165
Lee, Manfred B(ennington) 1905-1971CLC 11
See also Queen, Ellery
See also CA 1-4R; 29-32R; CANR 2; DLB 137
Lee, Shelton Jackson 1957(?)-   CLC 105;
BLCS; DAM MULT
See also Lee, Spike
See also BW 2, 3; CA 125; CANR 42
Lee, Spike
See Lee, Shelton Jackson
See also AAYA 4, 29
Lee, Stan 1922-   CLC 17
See also AAYA 5; CA 108; 111; INT 111
Lee, Tanith 1947-   CLC 46

See also AAYA 15; CA 37-40R; CANR 53;
SATA 8, 88
Lee, Vernon   TCLC 5; SSC 33
See also Paget, Violet
See also DLB 57, 153, 156, 174, 178
Lee, William
See Burroughs, William S(eward)
Lee, Willy
See Burroughs, William S(eward)
Lee-Hamilton, Eugene (Jacob) 1845-1907
TCLC 22
See also CA 117
Leet, Judith 1935-   CLC 11
Le Fanu, Joseph Sheridan 1814-1873NCLC 9,
58; DAM POP; SSC 14
See also DA3; DLB 21, 70, 159, 178
Leffland, Ella 1931-   CLC 19
See also CA 29-32R; CANR 35, 78, 82; DLBY
84; INT CANR-35; SATA 65
Leger, Alexis
See Leger, (Marie-Rene Auguste) Alexis Saint-
Leger
Leger, (Marie-Rene Auguste) Alexis Saint-
Leger 1887-1975   CLC 4, 11, 46; DAM
POET; PC 23
See also CA 13-16R; 61-64; CANR 43; MTCW
1
Leger, Saintleger
See Leger, (Marie-Rene Auguste) Alexis Saint-
Leger
Le Guin, Ursula K(roeber) 1929- CLC 8, 13,
22, 45, 71; DAB; DAC; DAM MST, POP;
SSC 12
See also AAYA 9, 27; AITN 1; CA 21-24R;
CANR 9, 32, 52, 74; CDALB 1968-1988;
CLR 3, 28; DA3; DLB 8, 52; INT CANR-
32; JRDA; MAICYA; MTCW 1, 2; SATA 4,
52, 99
Lehmann, Rosamond (Nina) 1901-1990CLC 5
See also CA 77-80; 131; CANR 8, 73; DLB 15;
MTCW 2
Leiber, Fritz (Reuter, Jr.) 1910-1992 CLC 25
See also CA 45-48; 139; CANR 2, 40; DLB 8;
MTCW 1, 2; SATA 45; SATA-Obit 73
Leibniz, Gottfried Wilhelm von 1646-1716LC
35
See also DLB 168
Leimbach, Martha 1963-
See Leimbach, Marti
See also CA 130
Leimbach, Marti   CLC 65
See also Leimbach, Martha
Leino, Eino   TCLC 24
See also Loennbohm, Armas Eino Leopold
Leiris, Michel (Julien) 1901-1990   CLC 61
See also CA 119; 128; 132
Leithauser, Brad 1953-   CLC 27
See also CA 107; CANR 27, 81; DLB 120
Lelchuk, Alan 1938-   CLC 5
See also CA 45-48; CAAS 20; CANR 1, 70
Lem, Stanislaw 1921-   CLC 8, 15, 40
See also CA 105; CAAS 1; CANR 32; MTCW
1
Lemann, Nancy 1956-   CLC 39
See also CA 118; 136
Lemonnier, (Antoine Louis) Camille 1844-1913
TCLC 22
See also CA 121
Lenau, Nikolaus 1802-1850   NCLC 16
L'Engle, Madeleine (Camp Franklin) 1918-
CLC 12; DAM POP
See also AAYA 28; AITN 2; CA 1-4R; CANR
3, 21, 39, 66; CLR 1, 14, 57; DA3; DLB 52;

JRDA; MAICYA; MTCW 1, 2; SAAS 15;
SATA 1, 27, 75
Lengyel, Jozsef 1896-1975   CLC 7
See also CA 85-88; 57-60; CANR 71
Lenin 1870-1924
See Lenin, V. I.
See also CA 121; 168
Lenin, V. I.   TCLC 67
See also Lenin
Lennon, John (Ono) 1940-1980   CLC 12, 35
See also CA 102
Lennox, Charlotte Ramsay 1729(?)-1804
NCLC 23
See also DLB 39
Lentricchia, Frank (Jr.) 1940-   CLC 34
See also CA 25-28R; CANR 19
Lenz, Siegfried 1926-   CLC 27; SSC 33
See also CA 89-92; CANR 80; DLB 75
Leonard, Elmore (John, Jr.) 1925-CLC 28, 34,
71, 120; DAM POP
See also AAYA 22; AITN 1; BEST 89:1, 90:4;
CA 81-84; CANR 12, 28, 53, 76; DA3; DLB
173; INT CANR-28; MTCW 1, 2
Leonard, Hugh   CLC 19
See also Byrne, John Keyes
See also DLB 13
Leonov, Leonid (Maximovich) 1899-1994
CLC 92; DAM NOV
See also CA 129; CANR 74, 76; MTCW 1, 2
Leopardi, (Conte) Giacomo 1798-1837N C L C
22
Le Reveler
See Artaud, Antonin (Marie Joseph)
Lerman, Eleanor 1952-   CLC 9
See also CA 85-88; CANR 69
Lerman, Rhoda 1936-   CLC 56
See also CA 49-52; CANR 70
Lermontov, Mikhail Yuryevich 1814-1841
NCLC 47; PC 18
See also DLB 205
Leroux, Gaston 1868-1927   TCLC 25
See also CA 108; 136; CANR 69; SATA 65
Lesage, Alain-Rene 1668-1747   LC 2, 28
Leskov, Nikolai (Semyonovich) 1831-1895
NCLC 25; SSC 34
Lessing, Doris (May) 1919-CLC 1, 2, 3, 6, 10,
15, 22, 40, 94; DA; DAB; DAC; DAM MST,
NOV; SSC 6; WLCS
See also CA 9-12R; CAAS 14; CANR 33, 54,
76; CDBLB 1960 to Present; DA3; DLB 15,
139; DLBY 85; MTCW 1, 2
Lessing, Gotthold Ephraim 1729-1781   LC 8
See also DLB 97
Lester, Richard 1932-   CLC 20
Lever, Charles (James) 1806-1872 NCLC 23
See also DLB 21
Leverson, Ada 1865(?)-1936(?)   TCLC 18
See also Elaine
See also CA 117; DLB 153
Levertov, Denise 1923-1997 CLC 1, 2, 3, 5, 8,
15, 28, 66; DAM POET; PC 11
See also CA 1-4R, 178; 163; CAAE 178; CAAS
19; CANR 3, 29, 50; CDALBS; DLB 5, 165;
INT CANR-29; MTCW 1, 2
Levi, Jonathan   CLC 76
Levi, Peter (Chad Tigar) 1931-   CLC 41
See also CA 5-8R; CANR 34, 80; DLB 40
Levi, Primo 1919-1987 CLC 37, 50; SSC 12
See also CA 13-16R; 122; CANR 12, 33, 61,
70; DLB 177; MTCW 1, 2
Levin, Ira 1929-   CLC 3, 6; DAM POP
See also CA 21-24R; CANR 17, 44, 74; DA3;
MTCW 1, 2; SATA 66

Levin, Meyer 1905-1981 **CLC 7; DAM POP**
See also AITN 1; CA 9-12R; 104; CANR 15;
DLB 9, 28; DLBY 81; SATA 21; SATA-Obit
27

Levine, Norman 1924- **CLC 54**
See also CA 73-76; CAAS 23; CANR 14, 70;
DLB 88

Levine, Philip 1928-**CLC 2, 4, 5, 9, 14, 33, 118;**
DAM POET; PC 22
See also CA 9-12R; CANR 9, 37, 52; DLB 5

Levinson, Deirdre 1931- **CLC 49**
See also CA 73-76; CANR 70

Levi-Strauss, Claude 1908- **CLC 38**
See also CA 1-4R; CANR 6, 32, 57; MTCW 1,
2

Levitin, Sonia (Wolff) 1934- **CLC 17**
See also AAYA 13; CA 29-32R; CANR 14, 32,
79; CLR 53; JRDA; MAICYA; SAAS 2;
SATA 4, 68

Levon, O. U.
See Kesey, Ken (Elton)

Levy, Amy 1861-1889 **NCLC 59**
See also DLB 156

Lewes, George Henry 1817-1878 **NCLC 25**
See also DLB 55, 144

Lewis, Alun 1915-1944 **TCLC 3**
See also CA 104; DLB 20, 162

Lewis, C. Day
See Day Lewis, C(ecil)

Lewis, C(live) S(taples) 1898-1963**CLC 1, 3, 6,**
14, 27, 124; DA; DAB; DAC; DAM MST,
NOV, POP; WLC
See also AAYA 3; CA 81-84; CANR 33, 71;
CDBLB 1945-1960; CLR 3, 27; DA3; DLB
15, 100, 160; JRDA; MAICYA; MTCW 1,
2; SATA 13, 100

Lewis, Janet 1899-1998 **CLC 41**
See also Winters, Janet Lewis
See also CA 9-12R; 172; CANR 29, 63; CAP
1; DLBY 87

Lewis, Matthew Gregory 1775-1818**NCLC 11,**
62
See also DLB 39, 158, 178

Lewis, (Harry) Sinclair 1885-1951 **TCLC 4,**
13, 23, 39; DA; DAB; DAC; DAM MST,
NOV; WLC
See also CA 104; 133; CDALB 1917-1929;
DA3; DLB 9, 102; DLBD 1; MTCW 1, 2

Lewis, (Percy) Wyndham 1882(?)-1957**TCLC**
2, 9; SSC 34
See also CA 104; 157; DLB 15; MTCW 2

Lewisohn, Ludwig 1883-1955 **TCLC 19**
See also CA 107; DLB 4, 9, 28, 102

Lewton, Val 1904-1951 **TCLC 76**

Leyner, Mark 1956- **CLC 92**
See also CA 110; CANR 28, 53; DA3; MTCW
2

Lezama Lima, Jose 1910-1976**CLC 4, 10, 101;**
DAM MULT; HLCS 2
See also CA 77-80; CANR 71; DLB 113; HW
1, 2

L'Heureux, John (Clarke) 1934- **CLC 52**
See also CA 13-16R; CANR 23, 45

Liddell, C. H.
See Kuttner, Henry

Lie, Jonas (Lauritz Idemil) 1833-1908(?)
TCLC 5
See also CA 115

Lieber, Joel 1937-1971 **CLC 6**
See also CA 73-76; 29-32R

Lieber, Stanley Martin
See Lee, Stan

Lieberman, Laurence (James) 1935- **CLC 4,**
36
See also CA 17-20R; CANR 8, 36

Lieh Tzu fl. 7th cent. B.C.-5th cent. B.C.
CMLC 27

Lieksman, Anders
See Haavikko, Paavo Juhani

Li Fei-kan 1904-
See Pa Chin
See also CA 105

Lifton, Robert Jay 1926- **CLC 67**
See also CA 17-20R; CANR 27, 78; INT
CANR-27; SATA 66

Lightfoot, Gordon 1938- **CLC 26**
See also CA 109

Lightman, Alan P(aige) 1948- **CLC 81**
See also CA 141; CANR 63

Ligotti, Thomas (Robert) 1953-**CLC 44; SSC**
16
See also CA 123; CANR 49

Li Ho 791-817 **PC 13**

Liliencron, (Friedrich Adolf Axel) Detlev von
1844-1909 **TCLC 18**
See also CA 117

Lilly, William 1602-1681 **LC 27**

Lima, Jose Lezama
See Lezama Lima, Jose

Lima Barreto, Afonso Henrique de 1881-1922
TCLC 23
See also CA 117

Limonov, Edward 1944- **CLC 67**
See also CA 137

Lin, Frank
See Atherton, Gertrude (Franklin Horn)

Lincoln, Abraham 1809-1865 **NCLC 18**

Lind, Jakov **CLC 1, 2, 4, 27, 82**
See also Landwirth, Heinz
See also CAAS 4

Lindbergh, Anne (Spencer) Morrow 1906-
CLC 82; DAM NOV
See also CA 17-20R; CANR 16, 73; MTCW 1,
2; SATA 33

Lindsay, David 1878-1945 **TCLC 15**
See also CA 113

Lindsay, (Nicholas) Vachel 1879-1931 **T C L C**
17; DA; DAC; DAM MST, POET; PC 23;
WLC
See also CA 114; 135; CANR 79; CDALB
1865-1917; DA3; DLB 54; SATA 40

Linke-Poot
See Doeblin, Alfred

Linney, Romulus 1930- **CLC 51**
See also CA 1-4R; CANR 40, 44, 79

Linton, Eliza Lynn 1822-1898 **NCLC 41**
See also DLB 18

Li Po 701-763 **CMLC 2**

Lipsius, Justus 1547-1606 **LC 16**

Lipsyte, Robert (Michael) 1938-**CLC 21; DA;**
DAC; DAM MST, NOV
See also AAYA 7; CA 17-20R; CANR 8, 57;
CLR 23; JRDA; MAICYA; SATA 5, 68

Lish, Gordon (Jay) 1934- **CLC 45; SSC 18**
See also CA 113; 117; CANR 79; DLB 130;
INT 117

Lispector, Clarice 1925(?)-1977 **CLC 43;**
HLCS 2; SSC 34
See also CA 139; 116; CANR 71; DLB 113;
HW 2

Littell, Robert 1935(?)- **CLC 42**
See also CA 109; 112; CANR 64

Little, Malcolm 1925-1965
See Malcolm X
See also BW 1, 3; CA 125; 111; CANR 82; DA;
DAB; DAC; DAM MST, MULT; DA3;

MTCW 1, 2

Littlewit, Humphrey Gent.
See Lovecraft, H(oward) P(hillips)

Litwos
See Sienkiewicz, Henryk (Adam Alexander
Pius)

Liu, E 1857-1909 **TCLC 15**
See also CA 115

Lively, Penelope (Margaret) 1933- **CLC 32,**
50; DAM NOV
See also CA 41-44R; CANR 29, 67, 79; CLR
7; DLB 14, 161, 207; JRDA; MAICYA;
MTCW 1, 2; SATA 7, 60, 101

Livesay, Dorothy (Kathleen) 1909-**CLC 4, 15,**
79; DAC; DAM MST, POET
See also AITN 2; CA 25-28R; CAAS 8; CANR
36, 67; DLB 68; MTCW 1

Livy c. 59B.C.-c. 17 **CMLC 11**
See also DLB 211

Lizardi, Jose Joaquin Fernandez de 1776-1827
NCLC 30

Llewellyn, Richard
See Llewellyn Lloyd, Richard Dafydd Vivian
See also DLB 15

Llewellyn Lloyd, Richard Dafydd Vivian 1906-
1983 **CLC 7, 80**
See also Llewellyn, Richard
See also CA 53-56; 111; CANR 7, 71; SATA
11; SATA-Obit 37

Llosa, (Jorge) Mario (Pedro) Vargas
See Vargas Llosa, (Jorge) Mario (Pedro)

Lloyd, Manda
See Mander, (Mary) Jane

Lloyd Webber, Andrew 1948-
See Webber, Andrew Lloyd
See also AAYA 1; CA 116; 149; DAM DRAM;
SATA 56

Llull, Ramon c. 1235-c. 1316 **CMLC 12**

Lobb, Ebenezer
See Upward, Allen

Locke, Alain (Le Roy) 1886-1954 **TCLC 43;**
BLCS
See also BW 1, 3; CA 106; 124; CANR 79; DLB
51

Locke, John 1632-1704 **LC 7, 35**
See also DLB 101

Locke-Elliott, Sumner
See Elliott, Sumner Locke

Lockhart, John Gibson 1794-1854 **NCLC 6**
See also DLB 110, 116, 144

Lodge, David (John) 1935-**CLC 36; DAM POP**
See also BEST 90:1; CA 17-20R; CANR 19,
53; DLB 14, 194; INT CANR-19; MTCW 1,
2

Lodge, Thomas 1558-1625 **LC 41**
Lodge, Thomas 1558-1625 **LC 41**
See also DLB 172

Loennbohm, Armas Eino Leopold 1878-1926
See Leino, Eino
See also CA 123

Loewinsohn, Ron(ald William) 1937-**CLC 52**
See also CA 25-28R; CANR 71

Logan, Jake
See Smith, Martin Cruz

Logan, John (Burton) 1923-1987 **CLC 5**
See also CA 77-80; 124; CANR 45; DLB 5

Lo Kuan-chung 1330(?)-1400(?) **LC 12**

Lombard, Nap
See Johnson, Pamela Hansford

London, Jack **TCLC 9, 15, 39; SSC 4; WLC**
See also London, John Griffith
See also AAYA 13; AITN 2; CDALB 1865-
1917; DLB 8, 12, 78, 212; SATA 18

See also Millar, Kenneth
See also DLBD 6
MacDougal, John
See Blish, James (Benjamin)
MacEwen, Gwendolyn (Margaret) 1941-1987
CLC 13, 55
See also CA 9-12R; 124; CANR 7, 22; DLB
53; SATA 50; SATA-Obit 55
Macha, Karel Hynek 1810-1846 **NCLC 46**
Machado (y Ruiz), Antonio 1875-1939 **TCLC
3**
See also CA 104; 174; DLB 108; HW 2
Machado de Assis, Joaquim Maria 1839-1908
TCLC 10; BLC 2; HLCS 2; SSC 24
See also CA 107; 153
Machen, Arthur **TCLC 4; SSC 20**
See also Jones, Arthur Llewellyn
See also CA 179; DLB 36, 156, 178
Machiavelli, Niccolo 1469-1527 **LC 8, 36; DA;
DAB; DAC; DAM MST; WLCS**
MacInnes, Colin 1914-1976 **CLC 4, 23**
See also CA 69-72; 65-68; CANR 21; DLB 14;
MTCW 1, 2
MacInnes, Helen (Clark) 1907-1985 **CLC 27,
39; DAM POP**
See also CA 1-4R; 117; CANR 1, 28, 58; DLB
87; MTCW 1, 2; SATA 22; SATA-Obit 44
Mackenzie, Compton (Edward Montague)
1883-1972 **CLC 18**
See also CA 21-22; 37-40R; CAP 2; DLB 34,
100
Mackenzie, Henry 1745-1831 **NCLC 41**
See also DLB 39
Mackintosh, Elizabeth 1896(?)-1952
See Tey, Josephine
See also CA 110
MacLaren, James
See Grieve, C(hristopher) M(urray)
Mac Laverty, Bernard 1942- **CLC 31**
See also CA 116; 118; CANR 43; INT 118
MacLean, Alistair (Stuart) 1922(?)-1987 **CLC
3, 13, 50, 63; DAM POP**
See also CA 57-60; 121; CANR 28, 61; MTCW
1; SATA 23; SATA-Obit 50
Maclean, Norman (Fitzroy) 1902-1990 **CLC
78; DAM POP; SSC 13**
See also CA 102; 132; CANR 49; DLB 206
MacLeish, Archibald 1892-1982 **CLC 3, 8, 14,
68; DAM POET**
See also CA 9-12R; 106; CANR 33, 63;
CDALBS; DLB 4, 7, 45; DLBY 82; MTCW
1, 2
MacLennan, (John) Hugh 1907-1990 **CLC 2,
14, 92; DAC; DAM MST**
See also CA 5-8R; 142; CANR 33; DLB 68;
MTCW 1, 2
MacLeod, Alistair 1936- **CLC 56; DAC; DAM
MST**
See also CA 123; DLB 60; MTCW 2
Macleod, Fiona
See Sharp, William
MacNeice, (Frederick) Louis 1907-1963 **CLC
1, 4, 10, 53; DAB; DAM POET**
See also CA 85-88; CANR 61; DLB 10, 20;
MTCW 1, 2
MacNeill, Dand
See Fraser, George MacDonald
Macpherson, James 1736-1796 **LC 29**
See also Ossian
See also DLB 109
Macpherson, (Jean) Jay 1931- **CLC 14**
See also CA 5-8R; DLB 53
MacShane, Frank 1927- **CLC 39**

See also CA 9-12R; CANR 3, 33; DLB 111
Macumber, Mari
See Sandoz, Mari(e Susette)
Madach, Imre 1823-1864 **NCLC 19**
Madden, (Jerry) David 1933- **CLC 5, 15**
See also CA 1-4R; CAAS 3; CANR 4, 45; DLB
6; MTCW 1
Maddern, Al(an)
See Ellison, Harlan (Jay)
Madhubuti, Haki R. 1942- **CLC 6, 73; BLC 2;
DAM MULT, POET; PC 5**
See also Lee, Don L.
See also BW 2, 3; CA 73-76; CANR 24, 51,
73; DLB 5, 41; DLBD 8; MTCW 2
Maepenn, Hugh
See Kuttner, Henry
Maepenn, K. H.
See Kuttner, Henry
Maeterlinck, Maurice 1862-1949 **TCLC 3;
DAM DRAM**
See also CA 104; 136; CANR 80; DLB 192;
SATA 66
Maginn, William 1794-1842 **NCLC 8**
See also DLB 110, 159
Mahapatra, Jayanta 1928- **CLC 33; DAM
MULT**
See also CA 73-76; CAAS 9; CANR 15, 33, 66
Mahfouz, Naguib (Abdel Aziz Al-Sabilgi)
1911(?)-
See Mahfuz, Najib
See also BEST 89:2; CA 128; CANR 55; DAM
NOV; DA3; MTCW 1, 2
Mahfuz, Najib **CLC 52, 55**
See also Mahfouz, Naguib (Abdel Aziz Al-
Sabilgi)
See also DLBY 88
Mahon, Derek 1941- **CLC 27**
See also CA 113; 128; DLB 40
Mailer, Norman 1923- **CLC 1, 2, 3, 4, 5, 8, 11,
14, 28, 39, 74, 111; DA; DAB; DAC; DAM
MST, NOV, POP**
See also AAYA 31; AITN 2; CA 9-12R; CABS
1; CANR 28, 74, 77; CDALB 1968-1988;
DA3; DLB 2, 16, 28, 185; DLBD 3; DLBY
80, 83; MTCW 1, 2
Maillet, Antonine 1929- **CLC 54, 118; DAC**
See also CA 115; 120; CANR 46, 74, 77; DLB
60; INT 120; MTCW 2
Mais, Roger 1905-1955 **TCLC 8**
See also BW 1, 3; CA 105; 124; CANR 82; DLB
125; MTCW 1
Maistre, Joseph de 1753-1821 **NCLC 37**
Maitland, Frederic 1850-1906 **TCLC 65**
Maitland, Sara (Louise) 1950- **CLC 49**
See also CA 69-72; CANR 13, 59
Major, Clarence 1936- **CLC 3, 19, 48; BLC 2;
DAM MULT**
See also BW 2, 3; CA 21-24R; CAAS 6; CANR
13, 25, 53, 82; DLB 33
Major, Kevin (Gerald) 1949- **CLC 26; DAC**
See also AAYA 16; CA 97-100; CANR 21, 38;
CLR 11; DLB 60; INT CANR-21; JRDA;
MAICYA; SATA 32, 82
Maki, James
See Ozu, Yasujiro
Malabaila, Damiano
See Levi, Primo
Malamud, Bernard 1914-1986 **CLC 1, 2, 3, 5,
8, 9, 11, 18, 27, 44, 78, 85; DA; DAB; DAC;
DAM MST, NOV, POP; SSC 15; WLC**
See also AAYA 16; CA 5-8R; 118; CABS 1;
CANR 28, 62; CDALB 1941-1968; DA3;
DLB 2, 28, 152; DLBY 80, 86; MTCW 1, 2

Malan, Herman
See Bosman, Herman Charles; Bosman, Herman
Charles
Malaparte, Curzio 1898-1957 **TCLC 52**
Malcolm, Dan
See Silverberg, Robert
Malcolm X **CLC 82, 117; BLC 2; WLCS**
See also Little, Malcolm
Malherbe, Francois de 1555-1628 **LC 5**
Mallarme, Stephane 1842-1898 **NCLC 4, 41;
DAM POET; PC 4**
Mallet-Joris, Francoise 1930- **CLC 11**
See also CA 65-68; CANR 17; DLB 83
Malley, Ern
See McAuley, James Phillip
Mallowan, Agatha Christie
See Christie, Agatha (Mary Clarissa)
Maloff, Saul 1922- **CLC 5**
See also CA 33-36R
Malone, Louis
See MacNeice, (Frederick) Louis
Malone, Michael (Christopher) 1942- **CLC 43**
See also CA 77-80; CANR 14, 32, 57
Malory, (Sir) Thomas 1410(?)-1471(?) **LC 11;
DA; DAB; DAC; DAM MST; WLCS**
See also CDBLB Before 1660; DLB 146; SATA
59; SATA-Brief 33
Malouf, (George Joseph) David 1934- **CLC 28,
86**
See also CA 124; CANR 50, 76; MTCW 2
Malraux, (Georges-)Andre 1901-1976 **CLC 1,
4, 9, 13, 15, 57; DAM NOV**
See also CA 21-22; 69-72; CANR 34, 58; CAP
2; DA3; DLB 72; MTCW 1, 2
Malzberg, Barry N(athaniel) 1939- **CLC 7**
See also CA 61-64; CAAS 4; CANR 16; DLB 8
Mamet, David (Alan) 1947- **CLC 9, 15, 34, 46,
91; DAM DRAM; DC 4**
See also AAYA 3; CA 81-84; CABS 3; CANR
15, 41, 67, 72; DA3; DLB 7; MTCW 1, 2
Mamoulian, Rouben (Zachary) 1897-1987
CLC 16
See also CA 25-28R; 124
Mandelstam, Osip (Emilievich) 1891(?)-1938(?)
TCLC 2, 6; PC 14
See also CA 104; 150; MTCW 2
Mander, (Mary) Jane 1877-1949 **TCLC 31**
See also CA 162
Mandeville, John fl. 1350- **CMLC 19**
See also DLB 146
Mandiargues, Andre Pieyre de **CLC 41**
See also Pieyre de Mandiargues, Andre
See also DLB 83
Mandrake, Ethel Belle
See Thurman, Wallace (Henry)
Mangan, James Clarence 1803-1849 **NCLC 27**
Maniere, J.-E.
See Giraudoux, (Hippolyte) Jean
Mankiewicz, Herman (Jacob) 1897-1953
TCLC 85
See also CA 120; 169; DLB 26
Manley, (Mary) Delariviere 1672(?)-1724 **LC
1, 42**
See also DLB 39, 80
Mann, Abel
See Creasey, John
Mann, Emily 1952- **DC 7**
See also CA 130; CANR 55
Mann, (Luiz) Heinrich 1871-1950 **TCLC 9**
See also CA 106; 164; DLB 66, 118
Mann, (Paul) Thomas 1875-1955 **TCLC 2, 8,
14, 21, 35, 44, 60; DA; DAB; DAC; DAM
MST, NOV; SSC 5; WLC**

See also CA 104; 128; DA3; DLB 66; MTCW 1, 2

Mannheim, Karl 1893-1947   TCLC 65

Manning, David
   See Faust, Frederick (Schiller)

Manning, Frederic 1887(?)-1935   TCLC 25
   See also CA 124

Manning, Olivia 1915-1980   CLC 5, 19
   See also CA 5-8R; 101; CANR 29; MTCW 1

Mano, D. Keith 1942-   CLC 2, 10
   See also CA 25-28R; CAAS 6; CANR 26, 57; DLB 6

Mansfield, Katherine TCLC 2, 8, 39; DAB; SSC 9, 23; WLC
   See also Beauchamp, Kathleen Mansfield
   See also DLB 162

Manso, Peter 1940-   CLC 39
   See also CA 29-32R; CANR 44

Mantecon, Juan Jimenez
   See Jimenez (Mantecon), Juan Ramon

Manton, Peter
   See Creasey, John

Man Without a Spleen, A
   See Chekhov, Anton (Pavlovich)

Manzoni, Alessandro 1785-1873   NCLC 29

Map, Walter 1140-1209   CMLC 32

Mapu, Abraham (ben Jekutiel) 1808-1867
   NCLC 18

Mara, Sally
   See Queneau, Raymond

Marat, Jean Paul 1743-1793   LC 10

Marcel, Gabriel Honore 1889-1973   CLC 15
   See also CA 102; 45-48; MTCW 1, 2

March, William 1893-1954   TCLC 96

Marchbanks, Samuel
   See Davies, (William) Robertson

Marchi, Giacomo
   See Bassani, Giorgio

Margulies, Donald   CLC 76

Marie de France c. 12th cent. -   CMLC 8; PC 22
   See also DLB 208

Marie de l'Incarnation 1599-1672   LC 10

Marier, Captain Victor
   See Griffith, D(avid Lewelyn) W(ark)

Mariner, Scott
   See Pohl, Frederik

Marinetti, Filippo Tommaso 1876-1944 TCLC 10
   See also CA 107; DLB 114

Marivaux, Pierre Carlet de Chamblain de 1688-1763   LC 4; DC 7

Markandaya, Kamala   CLC 8, 38
   See also Taylor, Kamala (Purnaiya)

Markfield, Wallace 1926-   CLC 8
   See also CA 69-72; CAAS 3; DLB 2, 28

Markham, Edwin 1852-1940   TCLC 47
   See also CA 160; DLB 54, 186

Markham, Robert
   See Amis, Kingsley (William)

Marks, J
   See Highwater, Jamake (Mamake)

Marks-Highwater, J
   See Highwater, Jamake (Mamake)

Markson, David M(errill) 1927-   CLC 67
   See also CA 49-52; CANR 1

Marley, Bob   CLC 17
   See also Marley, Robert Nesta

Marley, Robert Nesta 1945-1981
   See Marley, Bob
   See also CA 107; 103

Marlowe, Christopher 1564-1593   LC 22, 47; DA; DAB; DAC; DAM DRAM, MST; DC

1; WLC
   See also CDBLB Before 1660; DA3; DLB 62

Marlowe, Stephen 1928-
   See Queen, Ellery
   See also CA 13-16R; CANR 6, 55

Marmontel, Jean-Francois 1723-1799 LC 2

Marquand, John P(hillips) 1893-1960 CLC 2, 10
   See also CA 85-88; CANR 73; DLB 9, 102; MTCW 2

Marques, Rene 1919-1979   CLC 96; DAM MULT; HLC 2
   See also CA 97-100; 85-88; CANR 78; DLB 113; HW 1, 2

Marquez, Gabriel (Jose) Garcia
   See Garcia Marquez, Gabriel (Jose)

Marquis, Don(ald Robert Perry) 1878-1937 TCLC 7
   See also CA 104; 166; DLB 11, 25

Marric, J. J.
   See Creasey, John

Marryat, Frederick 1792-1848   NCLC 3
   See also DLB 21, 163

Marsden, James
   See Creasey, John

Marsh, (Edith) Ngaio 1899-1982   CLC 7, 53; DAM POP
   See also CA 9-12R; CANR 6, 58; DLB 77; MTCW 1, 2

Marshall, Garry 1934-   CLC 17
   See also AAYA 3; CA 111; SATA 60

Marshall, Paule 1929-   CLC 27, 72; BLC 3; DAM MULT; SSC 3
   See also BW 2, 3; CA 77-80; CANR 25, 73; DA3; DLB 157; MTCW 1, 2

Marshallik
   See Zangwill, Israel

Marsten, Richard
   See Hunter, Evan

Marston, John 1576-1634 LC 33; DAM DRAM
   See also DLB 58, 172

Martha, Henry
   See Harris, Mark

Marti (y Perez), Jose (Julian) 1853-1895
   NCLC 63; DAM MULT; HLC 2
   See also HW 2

Martial c. 40-c. 104   CMLC 35; PC 10
   See also DLB 211

Martin, Ken
   See Hubbard, L(afayette) Ron(ald)

Martin, Richard
   See Creasey, John

Martin, Steve 1945-   CLC 30
   See also CA 97-100; CANR 30; MTCW 1

Martin, Valerie 1948-   CLC 89
   See also BEST 90:2; CA 85-88; CANR 49

Martin, Violet Florence 1862-1915 TCLC 51

Martin, Webber
   See Silverberg, Robert

Martindale, Patrick Victor
   See White, Patrick (Victor Martindale)

Martin du Gard, Roger 1881-1958   TCLC 24
   See also CA 118; DLB 65

Martineau, Harriet 1802-1876   NCLC 26
   See also DLB 21, 55, 159, 163, 166, 190; YABC 2

Martines, Julia
   See O'Faolain, Julia

Martinez, Enrique Gonzalez
   See Gonzalez Martinez, Enrique

Martinez, Jacinto Benavente y
   See Benavente (y Martinez), Jacinto

Martinez Ruiz, Jose 1873-1967

See Azorin; Ruiz, Jose Martinez
   See also CA 93-96; HW 1

Martinez Sierra, Gregorio 1881-1947 TCLC 6
   See also CA 115

Martinez Sierra, Maria (de la O'LeJarraga) 1874-1974   TCLC 6
   See also CA 115

Martinsen, Martin
   See Follett, Ken(neth Martin)

Martinson, Harry (Edmund) 1904-1978 C L C 14
   See also CA 77-80; CANR 34

Marut, Ret
   See Traven, B.

Marut, Robert
   See Traven, B.

Marvell, Andrew 1621-1678   LC 4, 43; DA; DAB; DAC; DAM MST, POET; PC 10; WLC
   See also CDBLB 1660-1789; DLB 131

Marx, Karl (Heinrich) 1818-1883   NCLC 17
   See also DLB 129

Masaoka Shiki   TCLC 18
   See also Masaoka Tsunenori

Masaoka Tsunenori 1867-1902
   See Masaoka Shiki
   See also CA 117

Masefield, John (Edward) 1878-1967 CLC 11, 47; DAM POET
   See also CA 19-20; 25-28R; CANR 33; CAP 2; CDBLB 1890-1914; DLB 10, 19, 153, 160; MTCW 1, 2; SATA 19

Maso, Carole 19(?)-   CLC 44
   See also CA 170

Mason, Bobbie Ann 1940- CLC 28, 43, 82; SSC 4
   See also AAYA 5; CA 53-56; CANR 11, 31, 58, 83; CDALBS; DA3; DLB 173; DLBY 87; INT CANR-31; MTCW 1, 2

Mason, Ernst
   See Pohl, Frederik

Mason, Lee W.
   See Malzberg, Barry N(athaniel)

Mason, Nick 1945-   CLC 35

Mason, Tally
   See Derleth, August (William)

Mass, William
   See Gibson, William

Master Lao
   See Lao Tzu

Masters, Edgar Lee 1868-1950   TCLC 2, 25; DA; DAC; DAM MST, POET; PC 1; WLCS
   See also CA 104; 133; CDALB 1865-1917; DLB 54; MTCW 1, 2

Masters, Hilary 1928-   CLC 48
   See also CA 25-28R; CANR 13, 47

Mastrosimone, William 19(?)-   CLC 36

Mathe, Albert
   See Camus, Albert

Mather, Cotton 1663-1728   LC 38
   See also CDALB 1640-1865; DLB 24, 30, 140

Mather, Increase 1639-1723   LC 38
   See also DLB 24

Matheson, Richard Burton 1926-   CLC 37
   See also AAYA 31; CA 97-100; DLB 8, 44; INT 97-100

Mathews, Harry 1930-   CLC 6, 52
   See also CA 21-24R; CAAS 6; CANR 18, 40

Mathews, John Joseph 1894-1979   CLC 84; DAM MULT
   See also CA 19-20; 142; CANR 45; CAP 2; DLB 175; NNAL

Author Index

Mathias, Roland (Glyn) 1915-   **CLC 45**
  See also CA 97-100; CANR 19, 41; DLB 27
Matsuo Basho 1644-1694   **PC 3**
  See also DAM POET
Mattheson, Rodney
  See Creasey, John
Matthews, Brander 1852-1929   **TCLC 95**
  See also DLB 71, 78; DLBD 13
Matthews, Greg 1949-   **CLC 45**
  See also CA 135
Matthews, William (Procter, III) 1942-1997
  CLC 40
  See also CA 29-32R; 162; CAAS 18; CANR
    12, 57; DLB 5
Matthias, John (Edward) 1941-   **CLC 9**
  See also CA 33-36R; CANR 56
Matthiessen, Peter 1927-**CLC 5, 7, 11, 32, 64;**
  DAM NOV
  See also AAYA 6; BEST 90:4; CA 9-12R;
    CANR 21, 50, 73; DA3; DLB 6, 173; MTCW
    1, 2; SATA 27
Maturin, Charles Robert 1780(?)-1824**N C L C**
  6
  See also DLB 178
Matute (Ausejo), Ana Maria 1925-   **CLC 11**
  See also CA 89-92; MTCW 1
Maugham, W. S.
  See Maugham, W(illiam) Somerset
Maugham, W(illiam) Somerset 1874-1965
  CLC 1, 11, 15, 67, 93; DA; DAB; DAC;
  DAM DRAM, MST, NOV; SSC 8; WLC
  See also CA 5-8R; 25-28R; CANR 40; CDBLB
    1914-1945; DA3; DLB 10, 36, 77, 100, 162,
    195; MTCW 1, 2; SATA 54
Maugham, William Somerset
  See Maugham, W(illiam) Somerset
Maupassant, (Henri Rene Albert) Guy de 1850-
  1893**NCLC 1, 42; DA; DAB; DAC; DAM**
  MST; SSC 1; WLC
  See also DA3; DLB 123
Maupin, Armistead 1944-**CLC 95; DAM POP**
  See also CA 125; 130; CANR 58; DA3; INT
    130; MTCW 2
Maurhut, Richard
  See Traven, B.
Mauriac, Claude 1914-1996   **CLC 9**
  See also CA 89-92; 152; DLB 83
Mauriac, Francois (Charles) 1885-1970 **C L C**
  4, 9, 56; SSC 24
  See also CA 25-28; CAP 2; DLB 65; MTCW 1,
    2
Mavor, Osborne Henry 1888-1951
  See Bridie, James
  See also CA 104
Maxwell, William (Keepers, Jr.) 1908-**CLC 19**
  See also CA 93-96; CANR 54; DLBY 80; INT
    93-96
May, Elaine 1932-   **CLC 16**
  See also CA 124; 142; DLB 44
Mayakovski, Vladimir (Vladimirovich) 1893-
  1930   **TCLC 4, 18**
  See also CA 104; 158; MTCW 2
Mayhew, Henry 1812-1887   **NCLC 31**
  See also DLB 18, 55, 190
Mayle, Peter 1939(?)-   **CLC 89**
  See also CA 139; CANR 64
Maynard, Joyce 1953-   **CLC 23**
  See also CA 111; 129; CANR 64
Mayne, William (James Carter) 1928-**CLC 12**
  See also AAYA 20; CA 9-12R; CANR 37, 80;
    CLR 25; JRDA; MAICYA; SAAS 11; SATA
    6, 68
Mayo, Jim

  See L'Amour, Louis (Dearborn)
Maysles, Albert 1926-   **CLC 16**
  See also CA 29-32R
Maysles, David 1932-   **CLC 16**
Mazer, Norma Fox 1931-   **CLC 26**
  See also AAYA 5; CA 69-72; CANR 12, 32,
    66; CLR 23; JRDA; MAICYA; SAAS 1;
    SATA 24, 67, 105
Mazzini, Guiseppe 1805-1872   **NCLC 34**
McAlmon, Robert (Menzies) 1895-1956**TCLC**
  97
  See also CA 107; 168; DLB 4, 45; DLBD 15
McAuley, James Phillip 1917-1976   **CLC 45**
  See also CA 97-100
McBain, Ed
  See Hunter, Evan
McBrien, William Augustine 1930-   **CLC 44**
  See also CA 107
McCaffrey, Anne (Inez) 1926-**CLC 17; DAM**
  NOV, POP
  See also AAYA 6; AITN 2; BEST 89:2; CA 25-
    28R; CANR 15, 35, 55; CLR 49; DA3; DLB
    8; JRDA; MAICYA; MTCW 1, 2; SAAS 11;
    SATA 8, 70
McCall, Nathan 1955(?)-   **CLC 86**
  See also BW 3; CA 146
McCann, Arthur
  See Campbell, John W(ood, Jr.)
McCann, Edson
  See Pohl, Frederik
McCarthy, Charles, Jr. 1933-
  See McCarthy, Cormac
  See also CANR 42, 69; DAM POP; DA3;
    MTCW 2
McCarthy, Cormac 1933- **CLC 4, 57, 59, 101**
  See also McCarthy, Charles, Jr.
  See also DLB 6, 143; MTCW 2
McCarthy, Mary (Therese) 1912-1989**CLC 1,**
  3, 5, 14, 24, 39, 59; SSC 24
  See also CA 5-8R; 129; CANR 16, 50, 64; DA3;
    DLB 2; DLBY 81; INT CANR-16; MTCW
    1, 2
McCartney, (James) Paul 1942- **CLC 12, 35**
  See also CA 146
McCauley, Stephen (D.) 1955-   **CLC 50**
  See also CA 141
McClure, Michael (Thomas) 1932-**CLC 6, 10**
  See also CA 21-24R; CANR 17, 46, 77; DLB
    16
McCorkle, Jill (Collins) 1958-   **CLC 51**
  See also CA 121; DLBY 87
McCourt, Frank 1930-   **CLC 109**
  See also CA 157
McCourt, James 1941-   **CLC 5**
  See also CA 57-60
McCourt, Malachy 1932-   **CLC 119**
McCoy, Horace (Stanley) 1897-1955**TCLC 28**
  See also CA 108; 155; DLB 9
McCrae, John 1872-1918   **TCLC 12**
  See also CA 109; DLB 92
McCreigh, James
  See Pohl, Frederik
McCullers, (Lula) Carson (Smith) 1917-1967
  CLC 1, 4, 10, 12, 48, 100; DA; DAB; DAC;
  DAM MST, NOV; SSC 9, 24; WLC
  See also AAYA 21; CA 5-8R; 25-28R; CABS
    1, 3; CANR 18; CDALB 1941-1968; DA3;
    DLB 2, 7, 173; MTCW 1, 2; SATA 27
McCulloch, John Tyler
  See Burroughs, Edgar Rice
McCullough, Colleen 1938(?)- **CLC 27, 107;**
  DAM NOV, POP
  See also CA 81-84; CANR 17, 46, 67; DA3;

  MTCW 1, 2
McDermott, Alice 1953-   **CLC 90**
  See also CA 109; CANR 40
McElroy, Joseph 1930-   **CLC 5, 47**
  See also CA 17-20R
McEwan, Ian (Russell) 1948-   **CLC 13, 66;**
  DAM NOV
  See also BEST 90:4; CA 61-64; CANR 14, 41,
    69; DLB 14, 194; MTCW 1, 2
McFadden, David 1940-   **CLC 48**
  See also CA 104; DLB 60; INT 104
McFarland, Dennis 1950-   **CLC 65**
  See also CA 165
McGahern, John 1934- **CLC 5, 9, 48; SSC 17**
  See also CA 17-20R; CANR 29, 68; DLB 14;
    MTCW 1
McGinley, Patrick (Anthony) 1937- **CLC 41**
  See also CA 120; 127; CANR 56; INT 127
McGinley, Phyllis 1905-1978   **CLC 14**
  See also CA 9-12R; 77-80; CANR 19; DLB 11,
    48; SATA 2, 44; SATA-Obit 24
McGinniss, Joe 1942-   **CLC 32**
  See also AITN 2; BEST 89:2; CA 25-28R;
    CANR 26, 70; DLB 185; INT CANR-26
McGivern, Maureen Daly
  See Daly, Maureen
McGrath, Patrick 1950-   **CLC 55**
  See also CA 136; CANR 65
McGrath, Thomas (Matthew) 1916-1990**CLC**
  28, 59; DAM POET
  See also CA 9-12R; 132; CANR 6, 33; MTCW
    1; SATA 41; SATA-Obit 66
McGuane, Thomas (Francis III) 1939-**CLC 3,**
  7, 18, 45
  See also AITN 2; CA 49-52; CANR 5, 24, 49;
    DLB 2, 212; DLBY 80; INT CANR-24;
    MTCW 1
McGuckian, Medbh 1950-   **CLC 48; DAM**
  POET; PC 27
  See also CA 143; DLB 40
McHale, Tom 1942(?)-1982   **CLC 3, 5**
  See also AITN 1; CA 77-80; 106
McIlvanney, William 1936-   **CLC 42**
  See also CA 25-28R; CANR 61; DLB 14, 207
McIlwraith, Maureen Mollie Hunter
  See Hunter, Mollie
  See also SATA 2
McInerney, Jay 1955-**CLC 34, 112; DAM POP**
  See also AAYA 18; CA 116; 123; CANR 45,
    68; DA3; INT 123; MTCW 2
McIntyre, Vonda N(eel) 1948-   **CLC 18**
  See also CA 81-84; CANR 17, 34, 69; MTCW
    1
McKay, Claude **TCLC 7, 41; BLC 3; DAB; PC**
  2
  See also McKay, Festus Claudius
  See also DLB 4, 45, 51, 117
McKay, Festus Claudius 1889-1948
  See McKay, Claude
  See also BW 1, 3; CA 104; 124; CANR 73; DA;
    DAC; DAM MST, MULT, NOV, POET;
    MTCW 1, 2; WLC
McKuen, Rod 1933-   **CLC 1, 3**
  See also AITN 1; CA 41-44R; CANR 40
McLoughlin, R. B.
  See Mencken, H(enry) L(ouis)
McLuhan, (Herbert) Marshall 1911-1980
  CLC 37, 83
  See also CA 9-12R; 102; CANR 12, 34, 61;
    DLB 88; INT CANR-12; MTCW 1, 2
McMillan, Terry (L.) 1951- **CLC 50, 61, 112;**
  BLCS; DAM MULT, NOV, POP
  See also AAYA 21; BW 2, 3; CA 140; CANR

60; DA3; MTCW 2

McMurtry, Larry (Jeff) 1936-**CLC 2, 3, 7, 11, 27, 44; DAM NOV, POP**
See also AAYA 15; AITN 2; BEST 89:2; CA 5-8R; CANR 19, 43, 64; CDALB 1968-1988; DA3; DLB 2, 143; DLBY 80, 87; MTCW 1, 2

McNally, T. M. 1961- **CLC 82**

McNally, Terrence 1939- **CLC 4, 7, 41, 91; DAM DRAM**
See also CA 45-48; CANR 2, 56; DA3; DLB 7; MTCW 2

McNamer, Deirdre 1950- **CLC 70**

McNeal, Tom **CLC 119**

McNeile, Herman Cyril 1888-1937
See Sapper
See also DLB 77

McNickle, (William) D'Arcy 1904-1977 **C L C 89; DAM MULT**
See also CA 9-12R; 85-88; CANR 5, 45; DLB 175, 212; NNAL; SATA-Obit 22

McPhee, John (Angus) 1931- **CLC 36**
See also BEST 90:1; CA 65-68; CANR 20, 46, 64, 69; DLB 185; MTCW 1, 2

McPherson, James Alan 1943- **CLC 19, 77; BLCS**
See also BW 1, 3; CA 25-28R; CAAS 17; CANR 24, 74; DLB 38; MTCW 1, 2

McPherson, William (Alexander) 1933- **C L C 34**
See also CA 69-72; CANR 28; INT CANR-28

Mead, George Herbert 1873-1958 **TCLC 89**

Mead, Margaret 1901-1978 **CLC 37**
See also AITN 1; CA 1-4R; 81-84; CANR 4; DA3; MTCW 1, 2; SATA-Obit 20

Meaker, Marijane (Agnes) 1927-
See Kerr, M. E.
See also CA 107; CANR 37, 63; INT 107; JRDA; MAICYA; MTCW 1; SATA 20, 61, 99; SATA-Essay 111

Medoff, Mark (Howard) 1940- **CLC 6, 23; DAM DRAM**
See also AITN 1; CA 53-56; CANR 5; DLB 7; INT CANR-5

Medvedev, P. N.
See Bakhtin, Mikhail Mikhailovich

Meged, Aharon
See Megged, Aharon

Meged, Aron
See Megged, Aharon

Megged, Aharon 1920- **CLC 9**
See also CA 49-52; CAAS 13; CANR 1

Mehta, Ved (Parkash) 1934- **CLC 37**
See also CA 1-4R; CANR 2, 23, 69; MTCW 1

Melanter
See Blackmore, R(ichard) D(oddridge)

Melies, Georges 1861-1938 **TCLC 81**

Melikow, Loris
See Hofmannsthal, Hugo von

Melmoth, Sebastian
See Wilde, Oscar

Meltzer, Milton 1915- **CLC 26**
See also AAYA 8; CA 13-16R; CANR 38; CLR 13; DLB 61; JRDA; MAICYA; SAAS 1; SATA 1, 50, 80

Melville, Herman 1819-1891 **NCLC 3, 12, 29, 45, 49; DA; DAB; DAC; DAM MST, NOV; SSC 1, 17; WLC**
See also AAYA 25; CDALB 1640-1865; DA3; DLB 3, 74; SATA 59

Menander c. 342B.C.-c. 292B.C. **CMLC 9; DAM DRAM; DC 3**
See also DLB 176

Menchu, Rigoberta 1959-
See also HLCS 2

Menchu, Rigoberta 1959-
See also CA 175; HLCS 2

Mencken, H(enry) L(ouis) 1880-1956 **T C L C 13**
See also CA 105; 125; CDALB 1917-1929; DLB 11, 29, 63, 137; MTCW 1, 2

Mendelsohn, Jane 1965(?)- **CLC 99**
See also CA 154

Mercer, David 1928-1980**CLC 5; DAM DRAM**
See also CA 9-12R; 102; CANR 23; DLB 13; MTCW 1

Merchant, Paul
See Ellison, Harlan (Jay)

Meredith, George 1828-1909 **TCLC 17, 43; DAM POET**
See also CA 117; 153; CANR 80; CDBLB 1832-1890; DLB 18, 35, 57, 159

Meredith, William (Morris) 1919-**CLC 4, 13, 22, 55; DAM POET; PC 28**
See also CA 9-12R; CAAS 14; CANR 6, 40; DLB 5

Merezhkovsky, Dmitry Sergeyevich 1865-1941 **TCLC 29**
See also CA 169

Merimee, Prosper 1803-1870**NCLC 6, 65; SSC 7**
See also DLB 119, 192

Merkin, Daphne 1954- **CLC 44**
See also CA 123

Merlin, Arthur
See Blish, James (Benjamin)

Merrill, James (Ingram) 1926-1995**CLC 2, 3, 6, 8, 13, 18, 34, 91; DAM POET; PC 28**
See also CA 13-16R; 147; CANR 10, 49, 63; DA3; DLB 5, 165; DLBY 85; INT CANR-10; MTCW 1, 2

Merriman, Alex
See Silverberg, Robert

Merriman, Brian 1747-1805 **NCLC 70**

Merritt, E. B.
See Waddington, Miriam

Merton, Thomas 1915-1968 **CLC 1, 3, 11, 34, 83; PC 10**
See also CA 5-8R; 25-28R; CANR 22, 53; DA3; DLB 48; DLBY 81; MTCW 1, 2

Merwin, W(illiam) S(tanley) 1927- **CLC 1, 2, 3, 5, 8, 13, 18, 45, 88; DAM POET**
See also CA 13-16R; CANR 15, 51; DA3; DLB 5, 169; INT CANR-15; MTCW 1, 2

Metcalf, John 1938- **CLC 37**
See also CA 113; DLB 60

Metcalf, Suzanne
See Baum, L(yman) Frank

Mew, Charlotte (Mary) 1870-1928 **TCLC 8**
See also CA 105; DLB 19, 135

Mewshaw, Michael 1943- **CLC 9**
See also CA 53-56; CANR 7, 47; DLBY 80

Meyer, Conrad Ferdinand 1825-1905 **N C L C 81**
See also DLB 129

Meyer, June
See Jordan, June

Meyer, Lynn
See Slavitt, David R(ytman)

Meyer-Meyrink, Gustav 1868-1932
See Meyrink, Gustav
See also CA 117

Meyers, Jeffrey 1939- **CLC 39**
See also CA 73-76; CANR 54; DLB 111

Meynell, Alice (Christina Gertrude Thompson) 1847-1922 **TCLC 6**

See also CA 104; 177; DLB 19, 98

Meyrink, Gustav **TCLC 21**
See also Meyer-Meyrink, Gustav
See also DLB 81

Michaels, Leonard 1933- **CLC 6, 25; SSC 16**
See also CA 61-64; CANR 21, 62; DLB 130; MTCW 1

Michaux, Henri 1899-1984 **CLC 8, 19**
See also CA 85-88; 114

Micheaux, Oscar (Devereaux) 1884-1951 **TCLC 76**
See also BW 3; CA 174; DLB 50

Michelangelo 1475-1564 **LC 12**

Michelet, Jules 1798-1874 **NCLC 31**

Michels, Robert 1876-1936 **TCLC 88**

Michener, James A(lbert) 1907(?)-1997 **C L C 1, 5, 11, 29, 60, 109; DAM NOV, POP**
See also AAYA 27; AITN 1; BEST 90:1; CA 5-8R; 161; CANR 21, 45, 68; DA3; DLB 6; MTCW 1, 2

Mickiewicz, Adam 1798-1855 **NCLC 3**

Middleton, Christopher 1926- **CLC 13**
See also CA 13-16R; CANR 29, 54; DLB 40

Middleton, Richard (Barham) 1882-1911 **TCLC 56**
See also DLB 156

Middleton, Stanley 1919- **CLC 7, 38**
See also CA 25-28R; CAAS 23; CANR 21, 46, 81; DLB 14

Middleton, Thomas 1580-1627 **LC 33; DAM DRAM, MST; DC 5**
See also DLB 58

Migueis, Jose Rodrigues 1901- **CLC 10**

Mikszath, Kalman 1847-1910 **TCLC 31**
See also CA 170

Miles, Jack **CLC 100**

Miles, Josephine (Louise) 1911-1985**CLC 1, 2, 14, 34, 39; DAM POET**
See also CA 1-4R; 116; CANR 2, 55; DLB 48

Militant
See Sandburg, Carl (August)

Mill, John Stuart 1806-1873 **NCLC 11, 58**
See also CDBLB 1832-1890; DLB 55, 190

Millar, Kenneth 1915-1983 **CLC 14; DAM POP**
See also Macdonald, Ross
See also CA 9-12R; 110; CANR 16, 63; DA3; DLB 2; DLBD 6; DLBY 83; MTCW 1, 2

Millay, E. Vincent
See Millay, Edna St. Vincent

Millay, Edna St. Vincent 1892-1950 **TCLC 4, 49; DA; DAB; DAC; DAM MST, POET; PC 6; WLCS**
See also CA 104; 130; CDALB 1917-1929; DA3; DLB 45; MTCW 1, 2

Miller, Arthur 1915-**CLC 1, 2, 6, 10, 15, 26, 47, 78; DA; DAB; DAC; DAM DRAM, MST; DC 1; WLC**
See also AAYA 15; AITN 1; CA 1-4R; CABS 3; CANR 2, 30, 54, 76; CDALB 1941-1968; DA3; DLB 7; MTCW 1, 2

Miller, Henry (Valentine) 1891-1980**CLC 1, 2, 4, 9, 14, 43, 84; DA; DAB; DAC; DAM MST, NOV; WLC**
See also CA 9-12R; 97-100; CANR 33, 64; CDALB 1929-1941; DA3; DLB 4, 9; DLBY 80; MTCW 1, 2

Miller, Jason 1939(?)- **CLC 2**
See also AITN 1; CA 73-76; DLB 7

Miller, Sue 1943- **CLC 44; DAM POP**
See also BEST 90:3; CA 139; CANR 59; DA3; DLB 143

Miller, Walter M(ichael, Jr.) 1923-**CLC 4, 30**

See also CA 85-88; DLB 8

Millett, Kate 1934- **CLC 67**
See also AITN 1; CA 73-76; CANR 32, 53, 76; DA3; MTCW 1, 2

Millhauser, Steven (Lewis) 1943-**CLC 21, 54, 109**
See also CA 110; 111; CANR 63; DA3; DLB 2; INT 111; MTCW 2

Millin, Sarah Gertrude 1889-1968 **CLC 49**
See also CA 102; 93-96

Milne, A(lan) A(lexander) 1882-1956**TCLC 6, 88; DAB; DAC; DAM MST**
See also CA 104; 133; CLR 1, 26; DA3; DLB 10, 77, 100, 160; MAICYA; MTCW 1, 2; SATA 100; YABC 1

Milner, Ron(ald) 1938-**CLC 56; BLC 3; DAM MULT**
See also AITN 1; BW 1; CA 73-76; CANR 24, 81; DLB 38; MTCW 1

Milnes, Richard Monckton 1809-1885 **N C L C 61**
See also DLB 32, 184

Milosz, Czeslaw 1911- **CLC 5, 11, 22, 31, 56, 82; DAM MST, POET; PC 8; WLCS**
See also CA 81-84; CANR 23, 51; DA3; MTCW 1, 2

Milton, John 1608-1674 **LC 9, 43; DA; DAB; DAC; DAM MST, POET; PC 19; WLC**
See also CDBLB 1660-1789; DA3; DLB 131, 151

Min, Anchee 1957- **CLC 86**
See also CA 146

Minehaha, Cornelius
See Wedekind, (Benjamin) Frank(lin)

Miner, Valerie 1947- **CLC 40**
See also CA 97-100; CANR 59

Minimo, Duca
See D'Annunzio, Gabriele

Minot, Susan 1956- **CLC 44**
See also CA 134

Minus, Ed 1938- **CLC 39**

Miranda, Javier
See Bioy Casares, Adolfo

Miranda, Javier
See Bioy Casares, Adolfo

Mirbeau, Octave 1848-1917 **TCLC 55**
See also DLB 123, 192

Miro (Ferrer), Gabriel (Francisco Victor) 1879-1930 **TCLC 5**
See also CA 104

Mishima, Yukio 1925-1970**CLC 2, 4, 6, 9, 27; DC 1; SSC 4**
See also Hiraoka, Kimitake
See also DLB 182; MTCW 2

Mistral, Frederic 1830-1914 **TCLC 51**
See also CA 122

Mistral, Gabriela **TCLC 2; HLC 2**
See also Godoy Alcayaga, Lucila
See also MTCW 2

Mistry, Rohinton 1952- **CLC 71; DAC**
See also CA 141

Mitchell, Clyde
See Ellison, Harlan (Jay); Silverberg, Robert

Mitchell, James Leslie 1901-1935
See Gibbon, Lewis Grassic
See also CA 104; DLB 15

Mitchell, Joni 1943- **CLC 12**
See also CA 112

Mitchell, Joseph (Quincy) 1908-1996**CLC 98**
See also CA 77-80; 152; CANR 69; DLB 185; DLBY 96

Mitchell, Margaret (Munnerlyn) 1900-1949 **TCLC 11; DAM NOV, POP**

See also AAYA 23; CA 109; 125; CANR 55; CDALBS; DA3; DLB 9; MTCW 1, 2

Mitchell, Peggy
See Mitchell, Margaret (Munnerlyn)

Mitchell, S(ilas) Weir 1829-1914 **TCLC 36**
See also CA 165; DLB 202

Mitchell, W(illiam) O(rmond) 1914-1998**CLC 25; DAC; DAM MST**
See also CA 77-80; 165; CANR 15, 43; DLB 88

Mitchell, William 1879-1936 **TCLC 81**

Mitford, Mary Russell 1787-1855 **NCLC 4**
See also DLB 110, 116

Mitford, Nancy 1904-1973 **CLC 44**
See also CA 9-12R; DLB 191

Miyamoto, (Chujo) Yuriko 1899-1951 **T C L C 37**
See also CA 170, 174; DLB 180

Miyazawa, Kenji 1896-1933 **TCLC 76**
See also CA 157

Mizoguchi, Kenji 1898-1956 **TCLC 72**
See also CA 167

Mo, Timothy (Peter) 1950(?)- **CLC 46**
See also CA 117; DLB 194; MTCW 1

Modarressi, Taghi (M.) 1931- **CLC 44**
See also CA 121; 134; INT 134

Modiano, Patrick (Jean) 1945- **CLC 18**
See also CA 85-88; CANR 17, 40; DLB 83

Moerck, Paal
See Roelvaag, O(le) E(dvart)

Mofolo, Thomas (Mokopu) 1875(?)-1948 **TCLC 22; BLC 3; DAM MULT**
See also CA 121; 153; CANR 83; MTCW 2

Mohr, Nicholasa 1938-**CLC 12; DAM MULT; HLC 2**
See also AAYA 8; CA 49-52; CANR 1, 32, 64; CLR 22; DLB 145; HW 1, 2; JRDA; SAAS 8; SATA 8, 97

Mojtabai, A(nn) G(race) 1938- **CLC 5, 9, 15, 29**
See also CA 85-88

Moliere 1622-1673**LC 10, 28; DA; DAB; DAC; DAM DRAM, MST; WLC**
See also DA3

Molin, Charles
See Mayne, William (James Carter)

Molnar, Ferenc 1878-1952 **TCLC 20; DAM DRAM**
See also CA 109; 153; CANR 83

Momaday, N(avarre) Scott 1934- **CLC 2, 19, 85, 95; DA; DAB; DAC; DAM MST, MULT, NOV, POP; PC 25; WLCS**
See also AAYA 11; CA 25-28R; CANR 14, 34, 68; CDALBS; DA3; DLB 143, 175; INT CANR-14; MTCW 1, 2; NNAL; SATA 48; SATA-Brief 30

Monette, Paul 1945-1995 **CLC 82**
See also CA 139; 147

Monroe, Harriet 1860-1936 **TCLC 12**
See also CA 109; DLB 54, 91

Monroe, Lyle
See Heinlein, Robert A(nson)

Montagu, Elizabeth 1720-1800 **NCLC 7**

Montagu, Mary (Pierrepont) Wortley 1689-1762 **LC 9; PC 16**
See also DLB 95, 101

Montagu, W. H.
See Coleridge, Samuel Taylor

Montague, John (Patrick) 1929- **CLC 13, 46**
See also CA 9-12R; CANR 9, 69; DLB 40; MTCW 1

Montaigne, Michel (Eyquem) de 1533-1592 **LC 8; DA; DAB; DAC; DAM MST; WLC**

Montale, Eugenio 1896-1981**CLC 7, 9, 18; PC 13**
See also CA 17-20R; 104; CANR 30; DLB 114; MTCW 1

Montesquieu, Charles-Louis de Secondat 1689-1755 **LC 7**

Montgomery, (Robert) Bruce 1921(?)-1978
See Crispin, Edmund
See also CA 179; 104

Montgomery, L(ucy) M(aud) 1874-1942 **TCLC 51; DAC; DAM MST**
See also AAYA 12; CA 108; 137; CLR 8; DA3; DLB 92; DLBD 14; JRDA; MAICYA; MTCW 2; SATA 100; YABC 1

Montgomery, Marion H., Jr. 1925- **CLC 7**
See also AITN 1; CA 1-4R; CANR 3, 48; DLB 6

Montgomery, Max
See Davenport, Guy (Mattison, Jr.)

Montherlant, Henry (Milon) de 1896-1972 **CLC 8, 19; DAM DRAM**
See also CA 85-88; 37-40R; DLB 72; MTCW 1

Monty Python
See Chapman, Graham; Cleese, John (Marwood); Gilliam, Terry (Vance); Idle, Eric; Jones, Terence Graham Parry; Palin, Michael (Edward)
See also AAYA 7

Moodie, Susanna (Strickland) 1803-1885 **NCLC 14**
See also DLB 99

Mooney, Edward 1951-
See Mooney, Ted
See also CA 130

Mooney, Ted **CLC 25**
See also Mooney, Edward

Moorcock, Michael (John) 1939-**CLC 5, 27, 58**
See also Bradbury, Edward P.
See also AAYA 26; CA 45-48; CAAS 5; CANR 2, 17, 38, 64; DLB 14; MTCW 1, 2; SATA 93

Moore, Brian 1921-1999**CLC 1, 3, 5, 7, 8, 19, 32, 90; DAB; DAC; DAM MST**
See also CA 1-4R; 174; CANR 1, 25, 42, 63; MTCW 1, 2

Moore, Edward
See Muir, Edwin

Moore, G. E. 1873-1958 **TCLC 89**

Moore, George Augustus 1852-1933**TCLC 7; SSC 19**
See also CA 104; 177; DLB 10, 18, 57, 135

Moore, Lorrie **CLC 39, 45, 68**
See also Moore, Marie Lorena

Moore, Marianne (Craig) 1887-1972**CLC 1, 2, 4, 8, 10, 13, 19, 47; DA; DAB; DAC; DAM MST, POET; PC 4; WLCS**
See also CA 1-4R; 33-36R; CANR 3, 61; CDALB 1929-1941; DA3; DLB 45; DLBD 7; MTCW 1, 2; SATA 20

Moore, Marie Lorena 1957-
See Moore, Lorrie
See also CA 116; CANR 39, 83

Moore, Thomas 1779-1852 **NCLC 6**
See also DLB 96, 144

Mora, Pat(ricia) 1942-
See also CA 129; CANR 57, 81; CLR 58; DAM MULT; DLB 209; HLC 2; HW 1, 2; SATA 92

Morand, Paul 1888-1976 **CLC 41; SSC 22**
See also CA 69-72; DLB 65

Morante, Elsa 1918-1985 **CLC 8, 47**
See also CA 85-88; 117; CANR 35; DLB 177;

MTCW 1, 2

Moravia, Alberto 1907-1990 **CLC 2, 7, 11, 27, 46; SSC 26**
See also Pincherle, Alberto
See also DLB 177; MTCW 2

More, Hannah 1745-1833 **NCLC 27**
See also DLB 107, 109, 116, 158

More, Henry 1614-1687 **LC 9**
See also DLB 126

More, Sir Thomas 1478-1535 **LC 10, 32**

Moreas, Jean **TCLC 18**
See also Papadiamantopoulos, Johannes

Morgan, Berry 1919- **CLC 6**
See also CA 49-52; DLB 6

Morgan, Claire
See Highsmith, (Mary) Patricia

Morgan, Edwin (George) 1920- **CLC 31**
See also CA 5-8R; CANR 3, 43; DLB 27

Morgan, (George) Frederick 1922- **CLC 23**
See also CA 17-20R; CANR 21

Morgan, Harriet
See Mencken, H(enry) L(ouis)

Morgan, Jane
See Cooper, James Fenimore

Morgan, Janet 1945- **CLC 39**
See also CA 65-68

Morgan, Lady 1776(?)-1859 **NCLC 29**
See also DLB 116, 158

Morgan, Robin (Evonne) 1941- **CLC 2**
See also CA 69-72; CANR 29, 68; MTCW 1; SATA 80

Morgan, Scott
See Kuttner, Henry

Morgan, Seth 1949(?)-1990 **CLC 65**
See also CA 132

Morgenstern, Christian 1871-1914 **TCLC 8**
See also CA 105

Morgenstern, S.
See Goldman, William (W.)

Moricz, Zsigmond 1879-1942 **TCLC 33**
See also CA 165

Morike, Eduard (Friedrich) 1804-1875 **NCLC 10**
See also DLB 133

Moritz, Karl Philipp 1756-1793 **LC 2**
See also DLB 94

Morland, Peter Henry
See Faust, Frederick (Schiller)

Morley, Christopher (Darlington) 1890-1957 **TCLC 87**
See also CA 112; DLB 9

Morren, Theophil
See Hofmannsthal, Hugo von

Morris, Bill 1952- **CLC 76**

Morris, Julian
See West, Morris L(anglo)

Morris, Steveland Judkins 1950(?)-
See Wonder, Stevie
See also CA 111

Morris, William 1834-1896 **NCLC 4**
See also CDBLB 1832-1890; DLB 18, 35, 57, 156, 178, 184

Morris, Wright 1910-1998 **CLC 1, 3, 7, 18, 37**
See also CA 9-12R; 167; CANR 21, 81; DLB 2, 206; DLBY 81; MTCW 1, 2

Morrison, Arthur 1863-1945 **TCLC 72**
See also CA 120; 157; DLB 70, 135, 197

Morrison, Chloe Anthony Wofford
See Morrison, Toni

Morrison, James Douglas 1943-1971
See Morrison, Jim
See also CA 73-76; CANR 40

Morrison, Jim **CLC 17**

See also Morrison, James Douglas

Morrison, Toni 1931- **CLC 4, 10, 22, 55, 81, 87; BLC 3; DA; DAB; DAC; DAM MST, MULT, NOV, POP**
See also AAYA 1, 22; BW 2, 3; CA 29-32R; CANR 27, 42, 67; CDALB 1968-1988; DA3; DLB 6, 33, 143; DLBY 81; MTCW 1, 2; SATA 57

Morrison, Van 1945- **CLC 21**
See also CA 116; 168

Morrissy, Mary 1958- **CLC 99**

Mortimer, John (Clifford) 1923- **CLC 28, 43; DAM DRAM, POP**
See also CA 13-16R; CANR 21, 69; CDBLB 1960 to Present; DA3; DLB 13; INT CANR-21; MTCW 1, 2

Mortimer, Penelope (Ruth) 1918- **CLC 5**
See also CA 57-60; CANR 45

Morton, Anthony
See Creasey, John

Mosca, Gaetano 1858-1941 **TCLC 75**

Mosher, Howard Frank 1943- **CLC 62**
See also CA 139; CANR 65

Mosley, Nicholas 1923- **CLC 43, 70**
See also CA 69-72; CANR 41, 60; DLB 14, 207

Mosley, Walter 1952- **CLC 97; BLCS; DAM MULT, POP**
See also AAYA 17; BW 2; CA 142; CANR 57; DA3; MTCW 2

Moss, Howard 1922-1987 **CLC 7, 14, 45, 50; DAM POET**
See also CA 1-4R; 123; CANR 1, 44; DLB 5

Mossgiel, Rab
See Burns, Robert

Motion, Andrew (Peter) 1952- **CLC 47**
See also CA 146; DLB 40

Motley, Willard (Francis) 1909-1965 **CLC 18**
See also BW 1; CA 117; 106; DLB 76, 143

Motoori, Norinaga 1730-1801 **NCLC 45**

Mott, Michael (Charles Alston) 1930- **CLC 15, 34**
See also CA 5-8R; CAAS 7; CANR 7, 29

Mountain Wolf Woman 1884-1960 **CLC 92**
See also CA 144; NNAL

Moure, Erin 1955- **CLC 88**
See also CA 113; DLB 60

Mowat, Farley (McGill) 1921- **CLC 26; DAC; DAM MST**
See also AAYA 1; CA 1-4R; CANR 4, 24, 42, 68; CLR 20; DLB 68; INT CANR-24; JRDA; MAICYA; MTCW 1, 2; SATA 3, 55

Mowatt, Anna Cora 1819-1870 **NCLC 74**

Moyers, Bill 1934- **CLC 74**
See also AITN 2; CA 61-64; CANR 31, 52

Mphahlele, Es'kia
See Mphahlele, Ezekiel
See also DLB 125

Mphahlele, Ezekiel 1919- **CLC 25; BLC 3; DAM MULT**
See also Mphahlele, Es'kia
See also BW 2, 3; CA 81-84; CANR 26, 76; DA3; MTCW 2

Mqhayi, S(amuel) E(dward) K(rune Loliwe) 1875-1945 **TCLC 25; BLC 3; DAM MULT**
See also CA 153

Mrs. Belloc-Lowndes
See Lowndes, Marie Adelaide (Belloc)

Mtwa, Percy (?)- **CLC 47**

Mueller, Lisel 1924- **CLC 13, 51**
See also CA 93-96; DLB 105

Muir, Edwin 1887-1959 **TCLC 2, 87**
See also CA 104; DLB 20, 100, 191

Muir, John 1838-1914 **TCLC 28**
See also CA 165; DLB 186

Mujica Lainez, Manuel 1910-1984 **CLC 31**
See also Lainez, Manuel Mujica
See also CA 81-84; 112; CANR 32; HW 1

Mukherjee, Bharati 1940- **CLC 53, 115; DAM NOV**
See also BEST 89:2; CA 107; CANR 45, 72; DLB 60; MTCW 1, 2

Muldoon, Paul 1951- **CLC 32, 72; DAM POET**
See also CA 113; 129; CANR 52; DLB 40; INT 129

Mulisch, Harry 1927- **CLC 42**
See also CA 9-12R; CANR 6, 26, 56

Mull, Martin 1943- **CLC 17**
See also CA 105

Muller, Wilhelm **NCLC 73**

Mulock, Dinah Maria
See Craik, Dinah Maria (Mulock)

Munford, Robert 1737(?)-1783 **LC 5**
See also DLB 31

Mungo, Raymond 1946- **CLC 72**
See also CA 49-52; CANR 2

Munro, Alice 1931- **CLC 6, 10, 19, 50, 95; DAC; DAM MST, NOV; SSC 3; WLCS**
See also AITN 2; CA 33-36R; CANR 33, 53, 75; DA3; DLB 53; MTCW 1, 2; SATA 29

Munro, H(ector) H(ugh) 1870-1916
See Saki
See also CA 104; 130; CDBLB 1890-1914; DA; DAB; DAC; DAM MST, NOV; DA3; DLB 34, 162; MTCW 1, 2; WLC

Murdoch, (Jean) Iris 1919-1999 **CLC 1, 2, 3, 4, 6, 8, 11, 15, 22, 31, 51; DAB; DAC; DAM MST, NOV**
See also CA 13-16R; 179; CANR 8, 43, 68; CDBLB 1960 to Present; DA3; DLB 14, 194; INT CANR-8; MTCW 1, 2

Murfree, Mary Noailles 1850-1922 **SSC 22**
See also CA 122; 176; DLB 12, 74

Murnau, Friedrich Wilhelm
See Plumpe, Friedrich Wilhelm

Murphy, Richard 1927- **CLC 41**
See also CA 29-32R; DLB 40

Murphy, Sylvia 1937- **CLC 34**
See also CA 121

Murphy, Thomas (Bernard) 1935- **CLC 51**
See also CA 101

Murray, Albert L. 1916- **CLC 73**
See also BW 2; CA 49-52; CANR 26, 52, 78; DLB 38

Murray, Judith Sargent 1751-1820 **NCLC 63**
See also DLB 37, 200

Murray, Les(lie) A(llan) 1938- **CLC 40; DAM POET**
See also CA 21-24R; CANR 11, 27, 56

Murry, J. Middleton
See Murry, John Middleton

Murry, John Middleton 1889-1957 **TCLC 16**
See also CA 118; DLB 149

Musgrave, Susan 1951- **CLC 13, 54**
See also CA 69-72; CANR 45, 84

Musil, Robert (Edler von) 1880-1942 **TCLC 12, 68; SSC 18**
See also CA 109; CANR 55, 84; DLB 81, 124; MTCW 2

Muske, Carol 1945- **CLC 90**
See also Muske-Dukes, Carol (Anne)

Muske-Dukes, Carol (Anne) 1945-
See Muske, Carol
See also CA 65-68; CANR 32, 70

Musset, (Louis Charles) Alfred de 1810-1857
NCLC **7**
See also DLB 192

Mussolini, Benito (Amilcare Andrea) 1883-1945
TCLC **96**
See also CA 116

My Brother's Brother
See Chekhov, Anton (Pavlovich)

Myers, L(eopold) H(amilton) 1881-1944
TCLC **59**
See also CA 157; DLB 15

Myers, Walter Dean 1937- CLC **35; BLC 3;
DAM MULT, NOV**
See also AAYA 4, 23; BW 2; CA 33-36R;
CANR 20, 42, 67; CLR 4, 16, 35; DLB 33;
INT CANR-20; JRDA; MAICYA; MTCW 2;
SAAS 2; SATA 41, 71, 109; SATA-Brief 27

Myers, Walter M.
See Myers, Walter Dean

Myles, Symon
See Follett, Ken(neth Martin)

Nabokov, Vladimir (Vladimirovich) 1899-1977
CLC **1, 2, 3, 6, 8, 11, 15, 23, 44, 46, 64;
DA; DAB; DAC; DAM MST, NOV; SSC
11; WLC**
See also CA 5-8R; 69-72; CANR 20; CDALB
1941-1968; DA3; DLB 2; DLBD 3; DLBY
80, 91; MTCW 1, 2

Nagai Kafu 1879-1959 TCLC **51**
See also Nagai Sokichi
See also DLB 180

Nagai Sokichi 1879-1959
See Nagai Kafu
See also CA 117

Nagy, Laszlo 1925-1978 CLC **7**
See also CA 129; 112

Naidu, Sarojini 1879-1943 TCLC **80**

Naipaul, Shiva(dhar Srinivasa) 1945-1985
CLC **32, 39; DAM NOV**
See also CA 110; 112; 116; CANR 33; DA3;
DLB 157; DLBY 85; MTCW 1, 2

Naipaul, V(idiadhar) S(urajprasad) 1932-
CLC **4, 7, 9, 13, 18, 37, 105; DAB; DAC;
DAM MST, NOV**
See also CA 1-4R; CANR 1, 33, 51; CDBLB
1960 to Present; DA3; DLB 125, 204, 206;
DLBY 85; MTCW 1, 2

Nakos, Lilika 1899(?)- CLC **29**

Narayan, R(asipuram) K(rishnaswami) 1906-
CLC **7, 28, 47, 121; DAM NOV; SSC 25**
See also CA 81-84; CANR 33, 61; DA3; MTCW
1, 2; SATA 62

Nash, (Frediric) Ogden 1902-1971 CLC **23;
DAM POET; PC 21**
See also CA 13-14; 29-32R; CANR 34, 61; CAP
1; DLB 11; MAICYA; MTCW 1, 2; SATA 2,
46

Nashe, Thomas 1567-1601(?) LC **41**
See also DLB 167

Nashe, Thomas 1567-1601 LC **41**

Nathan, Daniel
See Dannay, Frederic

Nathan, George Jean 1882-1958 TCLC **18**
See also Hatteras, Owen
See also CA 114; 169; DLB 137

Natsume, Kinnosuke 1867-1916
See Natsume, Soseki
See also CA 104

Natsume, Soseki 1867-1916 TCLC **2, 10**
See also Natsume, Kinnosuke
See also DLB 180

Natti, (Mary) Lee 1919-
See Kingman, Lee

See also CA 5-8R; CANR 2

Naylor, Gloria 1950-CLC **28, 52; BLC 3; DA;
DAC; DAM MST, MULT, NOV, POP;
WLCS**
See also AAYA 6; BW 2, 3; CA 107; CANR 27,
51, 74; DA3; DLB 173; MTCW 1, 2

Neihardt, John Gneisenau 1881-1973CLC **32**
See also CA 13-14; CANR 65; CAP 1; DLB 9,
54

Nekrasov, Nikolai Alekseevich 1821-1878
NCLC **11**

Nelligan, Emile 1879-1941 TCLC **14**
See also CA 114; DLB 92

Nelson, Willie 1933- CLC **17**
See also CA 107

Nemerov, Howard (Stanley) 1920-1991CLC **2,
6, 9, 36; DAM POET; PC 24**
See also CA 1-4R; 134; CABS 2; CANR 1, 27,
53; DLB 5, 6; DLBY 83; INT CANR-27;
MTCW 1, 2

Neruda, Pablo 1904-1973CLC **1, 2, 5, 7, 9, 28,
62; DA; DAB; DAC; DAM MST, MULT,
POET; HLC 2; PC 4; WLC**
See also CA 19-20; 45-48; CAP 2; DA3; HW
1; MTCW 1, 2

Nerval, Gerard de 1808-1855NCLC **1, 67; PC
13; SSC 18**

Nervo, (Jose) Amado (Ruiz de) 1870-1919
TCLC **11; HLCS 2**
See also CA 109; 131; HW 1

Nessi, Pio Baroja y
See Baroja (y Nessi), Pio

Nestroy, Johann 1801-1862 NCLC **42**
See also DLB 133

Netterville, Luke
See O'Grady, Standish (James)

Neufeld, John (Arthur) 1938- CLC **17**
See also AAYA 11; CA 25-28R; CANR 11, 37,
56; CLR 52; MAICYA; SAAS 3; SATA 6,
81

Neville, Emily Cheney 1919- CLC **12**
See also CA 5-8R; CANR 3, 37; JRDA;
MAICYA; SAAS 2; SATA 1

Newbound, Bernard Slade 1930-
See Slade, Bernard
See also CA 81-84; CANR 49; DAM DRAM

Newby, P(ercy) H(oward) 1918-1997 CLC **2,
13; DAM NOV**
See also CA 5-8R; 161; CANR 32, 67; DLB
15; MTCW 1

Newlove, Donald 1928- CLC **6**
See also CA 29-32R; CANR 25

Newlove, John (Herbert) 1938- CLC **14**
See also CA 21-24R; CANR 9, 25

Newman, Charles 1938- CLC **2, 8**
See also CA 21-24R; CANR 84

Newman, Edwin (Harold) 1919- CLC **14**
See also AITN 1; CA 69-72; CANR 5

Newman, John Henry 1801-1890 NCLC **38**
See also DLB 18, 32, 55

Newton, (Sir)Isaac 1642-1727 LC **35, 53**

Newton, Suzanne 1936- CLC **35**
See also CA 41-44R; CANR 14; JRDA; SATA
5, 77

Nexo, Martin Andersen 1869-1954 TCLC **43**

Nezval, Vitezslav 1900-1958 TCLC **44**
See also CA 123

Ng, Fae Myenne 1957(?)- CLC **81**
See also CA 146

Ngema, Mbongeni 1955- CLC **57**
See also BW 2; CA 143; CANR 84

Ngugi, James T(hiong'o) CLC **3, 7, 13**
See also Ngugi wa Thiong'o

Ngugi wa Thiong'o 1938- CLC **36; BLC 3;
DAM MULT, NOV**
See also Ngugi, James T(hiong'o)
See also BW 2; CA 81-84; CANR 27, 58; DLB
125; MTCW 1, 2

Nichol, B(arrie) P(hillip) 1944-1988 CLC **18**
See also CA 53-56; DLB 53; SATA 66

Nichols, John (Treadwell) 1940- CLC **38**
See also CA 9-12R; CAAS 2; CANR 6, 70;
DLBY 82

Nichols, Leigh
See Koontz, Dean R(ay)

Nichols, Peter (Richard) 1927- CLC **5, 36, 65**
See also CA 104; CANR 33; DLB 13; MTCW
1

Nicolas, F. R. E.
See Freeling, Nicolas

Niedecker, Lorine 1903-1970 CLC **10, 42;
DAM POET**
See also CA 25-28; CAP 2; DLB 48

Nietzsche, Friedrich (Wilhelm) 1844-1900
TCLC **10, 18, 55**
See also CA 107; 121; DLB 129

Nievo, Ippolito 1831-1861 NCLC **22**

Nightingale, Anne Redmon 1943-
See Redmon, Anne
See also CA 103

Nightingale, Florence 1820-1910 TCLC **85**
See also DLB 166

Nik. T. O.
See Annensky, Innokenty (Fyodorovich)

Nin, Anais 1903-1977 CLC **1, 4, 8, 11, 14, 60;
DAM NOV, POP; SSC 10**
See also AITN 2; CA 13-16R; 69-72; CANR
22, 53; DLB 2, 4, 152; MTCW 1, 2

Nishida, Kitaro 1870-1945 TCLC **83**

Nishiwaki, Junzaburo 1894-1982 PC **15**
See also CA 107

Nissenson, Hugh 1933- CLC **4, 9**
See also CA 17-20R; CANR 27; DLB 28

Niven, Larry CLC **8**
See also Niven, Laurence Van Cott
See also AAYA 27; DLB 8

Niven, Laurence Van Cott 1938-
See Niven, Larry
See also CA 21-24R; CAAS 12; CANR 14, 44,
66; DAM POP; MTCW 1, 2; SATA 95

Nixon, Agnes Eckhardt 1927- CLC **21**
See also CA 110

Nizan, Paul 1905-1940 TCLC **40**
See also CA 161; DLB 72

Nkosi, Lewis 1936- CLC **45; BLC 3; DAM
MULT**
See also BW 1, 3; CA 65-68; CANR 27, 81;
DLB 157

Nodier, (Jean) Charles (Emmanuel) 1780-1844
NCLC **19**
See also DLB 119

Noguchi, Yone 1875-1947 TCLC **80**

Nolan, Christopher 1965- CLC **58**
See also CA 111

Noon, Jeff 1957- CLC **91**
See also CA 148; CANR 83

Norden, Charles
See Durrell, Lawrence (George)

Nordhoff, Charles (Bernard) 1887-1947
TCLC **23**
See also CA 108; DLB 9; SATA 23

Norfolk, Lawrence 1963- CLC **76**
See also CA 144

Norman, Marsha 1947-CLC **28; DAM DRAM;
DC 8**
See also CA 105; CABS 3; CANR 41; DLBY

84
Normyx
 See Douglas, (George) Norman
Norris, Frank 1870-1902   **SSC 28**
 See also Norris, (Benjamin) Frank(lin, Jr.)
 See also CDALB 1865-1917; DLB 12, 71, 186
Norris, (Benjamin) Frank(lin, Jr.) 1870-1902
    TCLC 24
 See also Norris, Frank
 See also CA 110; 160
Norris, Leslie 1921-   **CLC 14**
 See also CA 11-12; CANR 14; CAP 1; DLB 27
North, Andrew
 See Norton, Andre
North, Anthony
 See Koontz, Dean R(ay)
North, Captain George
 See Stevenson, Robert Louis (Balfour)
North, Milou
 See Erdrich, Louise
Northrup, B. A.
 See Hubbard, L(afayette) Ron(ald)
North Staffs
 See Hulme, T(homas) E(rnest)
Norton, Alice Mary
 See Norton, Andre
 See also MAICYA; SATA 1, 43
Norton, Andre 1912-   **CLC 12**
 See also Norton, Alice Mary
 See also AAYA 14; CA 1-4R; CANR 68; CLR
 50; DLB 8, 52; JRDA; MTCW 1; SATA 91
Norton, Caroline 1808-1877   **NCLC 47**
 See also DLB 21, 159, 199
Norway, Nevil Shute 1899-1960
 See Shute, Nevil
 See also CA 102; 93-96; MTCW 2
Norwid, Cyprian Kamil 1821-1883 **NCLC 17**
Nosille, Nabrah
 See Ellison, Harlan (Jay)
Nossack, Hans Erich 1901-1978   **CLC 6**
 See also CA 93-96; 85-88; DLB 69
Nostradamus 1503-1566   **LC 27**
Nosu, Chuji
 See Ozu, Yasujiro
Notenburg, Eleanora (Genrikhovna) von
 See Guro, Elena
Nova, Craig 1945-   **CLC 7, 31**
 See also CA 45-48; CANR 2, 53
Novak, Joseph
 See Kosinski, Jerzy (Nikodem)
Novalis 1772-1801   **NCLC 13**
 See also DLB 90
Novis, Emile
 See Weil, Simone (Adolphine)
Nowlan, Alden (Albert) 1933-1983   **CLC 15;
 DAC; DAM MST**
 See also CA 9-12R; CANR 5; DLB 53
Noyes, Alfred 1880-1958   **TCLC 7; PC 27**
 See also CA 104; DLB 20
Nunn, Kem   **CLC 34**
 See also CA 159
Nye, Robert 1939- **CLC 13, 42; DAM NOV**
 See also CA 33-36R; CANR 29, 67; DLB 14;
 MTCW 1; SATA 6
Nyro, Laura 1947-   **CLC 17**
Oates, Joyce Carol 1938-**CLC 1, 2, 3, 6, 9, 11,
 15, 19, 33, 52, 108; DA; DAB; DAC; DAM
 MST, NOV, POP; SSC 6; WLC**
 See also AAYA 15; AITN 1; BEST 89:2; CA 5-
 8R; CANR 25, 45, 74; CDALB 1968-1988;
 DA3; DLB 2, 5, 130; DLBY 81; INT CANR-
 25; MTCW 1, 2
O'Brien, Darcy 1939-1998   **CLC 11**

 See also CA 21-24R; 167; CANR 8, 59
O'Brien, E. G.
 See Clarke, Arthur C(harles)
O'Brien, Edna 1936- **CLC 3, 5, 8, 13, 36, 65,
 116; DAM NOV; SSC 10**
 See also CA 1-4R; CANR 6, 41, 65; CDBLB
 1960 to Present; DA3; DLB 14; MTCW 1, 2
O'Brien, Fitz-James 1828-1862   **NCLC 21**
 See also DLB 74
O'Brien, Flann   **CLC 1, 4, 5, 7, 10, 47**
 See also O Nuallain, Brian
O'Brien, Richard 1942-   **CLC 17**
 See also CA 124
O'Brien, (William) Tim(othy) 1946- **CLC 7,
 19, 40, 103; DAM POP**
 See also AAYA 16; CA 85-88; CANR 40, 58;
 CDALBS; DA3; DLB 152; DLBD 9; DLBY
 80; MTCW 2
Obstfelder, Sigbjoern 1866-1900   **TCLC 23**
 See also CA 123
O'Casey, Sean 1880-1964**CLC 1, 5, 9, 11, 15,
 88; DAB; DAC; DAM DRAM, MST;
 WLCS**
 See also CA 89-92; CANR 62; CDBLB 1914-
 1945; DA3; DLB 10; MTCW 1, 2
O'Cathasaigh, Sean
 See O'Casey, Sean
Ochs, Phil 1940-1976   **CLC 17**
 See also CA 65-68
O'Connor, Edwin (Greene) 1918-1968**CLC 14**
 See also CA 93-96; 25-28R
O'Connor, (Mary) Flannery 1925-1964 **C L C
 1, 2, 3, 6, 10, 13, 15, 21, 66, 104; DA; DAB;
 DAC; DAM MST, NOV; SSC 1, 23; WLC**
 See also AAYA 7; CA 1-4R; CANR 3, 41;
 CDALB 1941-1968; DA3; DLB 2, 152;
 DLBD 12; DLBY 80; MTCW 1, 2
O'Connor, Frank   **CLC 23; SSC 5**
 See also O'Donovan, Michael John
 See also DLB 162
O'Dell, Scott 1898-1989   **CLC 30**
 See also AAYA 3; CA 61-64; 129; CANR 12,
 30; CLR 1, 16; DLB 52; JRDA; MAICYA;
 SATA 12, 60
Odets, Clifford 1906-1963**CLC 2, 28, 98; DAM
 DRAM; DC 6**
 See also CA 85-88; CANR 62; DLB 7, 26;
 MTCW 1, 2
O'Doherty, Brian 1934-   **CLC 76**
 See also CA 105
O'Donnell, K. M.
 See Malzberg, Barry N(athaniel)
O'Donnell, Lawrence
 See Kuttner, Henry
O'Donovan, Michael John 1903-1966**CLC 14**
 See also O'Connor, Frank
 See also CA 93-96; CANR 84
Oe, Kenzaburo 1935- **CLC 10, 36, 86; DAM
 NOV; SSC 20**
 See also CA 97-100; CANR 36, 50, 74; DA3;
 DLB 182; DLBY 94; MTCW 1, 2
O'Faolain, Julia 1932-   **CLC 6, 19, 47, 108**
 See also CA 81-84; CAAS 2; CANR 12, 61;
 DLB 14; MTCW 1
O'Faolain, Sean 1900-1991 **CLC 1, 7, 14, 32,
 70; SSC 13**
 See also CA 61-64; 134; CANR 12, 66; DLB
 15, 162; MTCW 1, 2
O'Flaherty, Liam 1896-1984**CLC 5, 34; SSC 6**
 See also CA 101; 113; CANR 35; DLB 36, 162;
 DLBY 84; MTCW 1, 2
Ogilvy, Gavin
 See Barrie, J(ames) M(atthew)

O'Grady, Standish (James) 1846-1928 **T C L C
 5**
 See also CA 104; 157
O'Grady, Timothy 1951-   **CLC 59**
 See also CA 138
O'Hara, Frank 1926-1966 **CLC 2, 5, 13, 78;
 DAM POET**
 See also CA 9-12R; 25-28R; CANR 33; DA3;
 DLB 5, 16, 193; MTCW 1, 2
O'Hara, John (Henry) 1905-1970**CLC 1, 2, 3,
 6, 11, 42; DAM NOV; SSC 15**
 See also CA 5-8R; 25-28R; CANR 31, 60;
 CDALB 1929-1941; DLB 9, 86; DLBD 2;
 MTCW 1, 2
O Hehir, Diana 1922-   **CLC 41**
 See also CA 93-96
Ohiyesa
 See Eastman, Charles A(lexander)
Okigbo, Christopher (Ifenayichukwu) 1932-
 1967   **CLC 25, 84; BLC 3; DAM MULT,
 POET; PC 7**
 See also BW 1, 3; CA 77-80; CANR 74; DLB
 125; MTCW 1, 2
Okri, Ben 1959-   **CLC 87**
 See also BW 2, 3; CA 130; 138; CANR 65; DLB
 157; INT 138; MTCW 2
Olds, Sharon 1942-   **CLC 32, 39, 85; DAM
 POET; PC 22**
 See also CA 101; CANR 18, 41, 66; DLB 120;
 MTCW 2
Oldstyle, Jonathan
 See Irving, Washington
Olesha, Yuri (Karlovich) 1899-1960   **CLC 8**
 See also CA 85-88
Oliphant, Laurence 1829(?)-1888   **NCLC 47**
 See also DLB 18, 166
Oliphant, Margaret (Oliphant Wilson) 1828-
 1897   **NCLC 11, 61; SSC 25**
 See also DLB 18, 159, 190
Oliver, Mary 1935-   **CLC 19, 34, 98**
 See also CA 21-24R; CANR 9, 43, 84; DLB 5,
 193
Olivier, Laurence (Kerr) 1907-1989 **CLC 20**
 See also CA 111; 150; 129
Olsen, Tillie 1912-**CLC 4, 13, 114; DA; DAB;
 DAC; DAM MST; SSC 11**
 See also CA 1-4R; CANR 1, 43, 74; CDALBS;
 DA3; DLB 28, 206; DLBY 80; MTCW 1, 2
Olson, Charles (John) 1910-1970**CLC 1, 2, 5,
 6, 9, 11, 29; DAM POET; PC 19**
 See also CA 13-16; 25-28R; CABS 2; CANR
 35, 61; CAP 1; DLB 5, 16, 193; MTCW 1, 2
Olson, Toby 1937-   **CLC 28**
 See also CA 65-68; CANR 9, 31, 84
Olyesha, Yuri
 See Olesha, Yuri (Karlovich)
Ondaatje, (Philip) Michael 1943-**CLC 14, 29,
 51, 76; DAB; DAC; DAM MST; PC 28**
 See also CA 77-80; CANR 42, 74; DA3; DLB
 60; MTCW 2
Oneal, Elizabeth 1934-
 See Oneal, Zibby
 See also CA 106; CANR 28, 84; MAICYA;
 SATA 30, 82
Oneal, Zibby   **CLC 30**
 See also Oneal, Elizabeth
 See also AAYA 5; CLR 13; JRDA
O'Neill, Eugene (Gladstone) 1888-1953**TCLC
 1, 6, 27, 49; DA; DAB; DAC; DAM DRAM,
 MST; WLC**
 See also AITN 1; CA 110; 132; CDALB 1929-
 1941; DA3; DLB 7; MTCW 1, 2
Onetti, Juan Carlos 1909-1994   **CLC 7, 10;**

Author Index

Parson Lot
See Kingsley, Charles
Partridge, Anthony
See Oppenheim, E(dward) Phillips
Pascal, Blaise 1623-1662   **LC 35**
Pascoli, Giovanni 1855-1912   **TCLC 45**
See also CA 170
Pasolini, Pier Paolo 1922-1975   **CLC 20, 37, 106; PC 17**
See also CA 93-96; 61-64; CANR 63; DLB 128, 177; MTCW 1
Pasquini
See Silone, Ignazio
Pastan, Linda (Olenik) 1932- **CLC 27; DAM POET**
See also CA 61-64; CANR 18, 40, 61; DLB 5
Pasternak, Boris (Leonidovich) 1890-1960
    CLC 7, 10, 18, 63; DA; DAB; DAC; DAM MST, NOV, POET; PC 6; SSC 31; WLC
See also CA 127; 116; DA3; MTCW 1, 2
Patchen, Kenneth 1911-1972   **CLC 1, 2, 18; DAM POET**
See also CA 1-4R; 33-36R; CANR 3, 35; DLB 16, 48; MTCW 1
Pater, Walter (Horatio) 1839-1894   **NCLC 7**
See also CDBLB 1832-1890; DLB 57, 156
Paterson, A(ndrew) B(arton) 1864-1941
    TCLC 32
See also CA 155; SATA 97
Paterson, Katherine (Womeldorf) 1932-**C L C 12, 30**
See also AAYA 1, 31; CA 21-24R; CANR 28, 59; CLR 7, 50; DLB 52; JRDA; MAICYA; MTCW 1; SATA 13, 53, 92
Patmore, Coventry Kersey Dighton 1823-1896
    NCLC 9
See also DLB 35, 98
Paton, Alan (Stewart) 1903-1988 **CLC 4, 10, 25, 55, 106; DA; DAB; DAC; DAM MST, NOV; WLC**
See also AAYA 26; CA 13-16; 125; CANR 22; CAP 1; DA3; DLBD 17; MTCW 1, 2; SATA 11; SATA-Obit 56
Paton Walsh, Gillian 1937-
See Walsh, Jill Paton
See also CANR 38, 83; JRDA; MAICYA; SAAS 3; SATA 4, 72, 109
Patton, George S. 1885-1945   **TCLC 79**
Paulding, James Kirke 1778-1860   **NCLC 2**
See also DLB 3, 59, 74
Paulin, Thomas Neilson 1949-
See Paulin, Tom
See also CA 123; 128
Paulin, Tom   **CLC 37**
See also Paulin, Thomas Neilson
See also DLB 40
Paustovsky, Konstantin (Georgievich) 1892-1968   **CLC 40**
See also CA 93-96; 25-28R
Pavese, Cesare 1908-1950   **TCLC 3; PC 13; SSC 19**
See also CA 104; 169; DLB 128, 177
Pavic, Milorad 1929-   **CLC 60**
See also CA 136; DLB 181
Pavlov, Ivan Petrovich 1849-1936 **TCLC 91**
See also CA 118; 180
Payne, Alan
See Jakes, John (William)
Paz, Gil
See Lugones, Leopoldo
Paz, Octavio 1914-1998**CLC 3, 4, 6, 10, 19, 51, 65, 119; DA; DAB; DAC; DAM MST, MULT, POET; HLC 2; PC 1; WLC**

See also CA 73-76; 165; CANR 32, 65; DA3; DLBY 90, 98; HW 1, 2; MTCW 1, 2
p'Bitek, Okot 1931-1982   **CLC 96; BLC 3; DAM MULT**
See also BW 2, 3; CA 124; 107; CANR 82; DLB 125; MTCW 1, 2
Peacock, Molly 1947-   **CLC 60**
See also CA 103; CAAS 21; CANR 52, 84; DLB 120
Peacock, Thomas Love 1785-1866   **NCLC 22**
See also DLB 96, 116
Peake, Mervyn 1911-1968   **CLC 7, 54**
See also CA 5-8R; 25-28R; CANR 3; DLB 15, 160; MTCW 1; SATA 23
Pearce, Philippa   **CLC 21**
See Christie, (Ann) Philippa
See also CLR 9; DLB 161; MAICYA; SATA 1, 67
Pearl, Eric
See Elman, Richard (Martin)
Pearson, T(homas) R(eid) 1956-   **CLC 39**
See also CA 120; 130; INT 130
Peck, Dale 1967-   **CLC 81**
See also CA 146; CANR 72
Peck, John 1941-   **CLC 3**
See also CA 49-52; CANR 3
Peck, Richard (Wayne) 1934-   **CLC 21**
See also AAYA 1, 24; CA 85-88; CANR 19, 38; CLR 15; INT CANR-19; JRDA; MAICYA; SAAS 2; SATA 18, 55, 97; SATA-Essay 110
Peck, Robert Newton 1928-   **CLC 17; DA; DAC; DAM MST**
See also AAYA 3; CA 81-84; CANR 31, 63; CLR 45; JRDA; MAICYA; SAAS 1; SATA 21, 62, 111; SATA-Essay 108
Peckinpah, (David) Sam(uel) 1925-1984 **C L C 20**
See also CA 109; 114; CANR 82
Pedersen, Knut 1859-1952
See Hamsun, Knut
See also CA 104; 119; CANR 63; MTCW 1, 2
Peeslake, Gaffer
See Durrell, Lawrence (George)
Peguy, Charles Pierre 1873-1914   **TCLC 10**
See also CA 107
Peirce, Charles Sanders 1839-1914 **TCLC 81**
Pellicer, Carlos 1900(?)-1977
See also CA 153; 69-72; HLCS 2; HW 1
Pena, Ramon del Valle y
See Valle-Inclan, Ramon (Maria) del
Pendennis, Arthur Esquir
See Thackeray, William Makepeace
Penn, William 1644-1718   **LC 25**
See also DLB 24
PEPECE
See Prado (Calvo), Pedro
Pepys, Samuel 1633-1703 **LC 11; DA; DAB; DAC; DAM MST; WLC**
See also CDBLB 1660-1789; DA3; DLB 101
Percy, Walker 1916-1990**CLC 2, 3, 6, 8, 14, 18, 47, 65; DAM NOV, POP**
See also CA 1-4R; 131; CANR 1, 23, 64; DA3; DLB 2; DLBY 80, 90; MTCW 1, 2
Percy, William Alexander 1885-1942**TCLC 84**
See also CA 163; MTCW 2
Perec, Georges 1936-1982   **CLC 56, 116**
See also CA 141; DLB 83
Pereda (y Sanchez de Porrua), Jose Maria de 1833-1906   **TCLC 16**
See also CA 117
Pereda y Porrua, Jose Maria de
See Pereda (y Sanchez de Porrua), Jose Maria

de
Peregoy, George Weems
See Mencken, H(enry) L(ouis)
Perelman, S(idney) J(oseph) 1904-1979 **C L C 3, 5, 9, 15, 23, 44, 49; DAM DRAM; SSC 32**
See also AITN 1, 2; CA 73-76; 89-92; CANR 18; DLB 11, 44; MTCW 1, 2
Peret, Benjamin 1899-1959   **TCLC 20**
See also CA 117
Peretz, Isaac Loeb 1851(?)-1915   **TCLC 16; SSC 26**
See also CA 109
Peretz, Yitzkhok Leibush
See Peretz, Isaac Loeb
Perez Galdos, Benito 1843-1920   **TCLC 27; HLCS 2**
See also CA 125; 153; HW 1
Peri Rossi, Cristina 1941-
See also CA 131; CANR 59, 81; DLB 145; HLCS 2; HW 1, 2
Perrault, Charles 1628-1703   **LC 3, 52**
See also MAICYA; SATA 25
Perry, Brighton
See Sherwood, Robert E(mmet)
Perse, St.-John
See Leger, (Marie-Rene Auguste) Alexis Saint-Leger
Perutz, Leo(pold) 1882-1957   **TCLC 60**
See also CA 147; DLB 81
Peseenz, Tulio F.
See Lopez y Fuentes, Gregorio
Pesetsky, Bette 1932-   **CLC 28**
See also CA 133; DLB 130
Peshkov, Alexei Maximovich 1868-1936
See Gorky, Maxim
See also CA 105; 141; CANR 83; DA; DAC; DAM DRAM, MST, NOV; MTCW 2
Pessoa, Fernando (Antonio Nogueira) 1888-1935**TCLC 27; DAM MULT; HLC 2; PC 20**
See also CA 125
Peterkin, Julia Mood 1880-1961   **CLC 31**
See also CA 102; DLB 9
Peters, Joan K(aren) 1945-   **CLC 39**
See also CA 158
Peters, Robert L(ouis) 1924-   **CLC 7**
See also CA 13-16R; CAAS 8; DLB 105
Petofi, Sandor 1823-1849   **NCLC 21**
Petrakis, Harry Mark 1923-   **CLC 3**
See also CA 9-12R; CANR 4, 30
Petrarch 1304-1374 **CMLC 20; DAM POET; PC 8**
See also DA3
Petronius c. 20-66   **CMLC 34**
See also DLB 211
Petrov, Evgeny   **TCLC 21**
See also Kataev, Evgeny Petrovich
Petry, Ann (Lane) 1908-1997   **CLC 1, 7, 18**
See also BW 1, 3; CA 5-8R; 157; CAAS 6; CANR 4, 46; CLR 12; DLB 76; JRDA; MAICYA; MTCW 1; SATA 5; SATA-Obit 94
Petursson, Halligrimur 1614-1674 **LC 8**
Peychinovich
See Vazov, Ivan (Minchov)
Phaedrus c. 18B.C.-c. 50   **CMLC 25**
See also DLB 211
Philips, Katherine 1632-1664   **LC 30**
See also DLB 131
Philipson, Morris H. 1926-   **CLC 53**
See also CA 1-4R; CANR 4
Phillips, Caryl 1958- **CLC 96; BLCS; DAM MULT**

See also BW 2; CA 141; CANR 63; DA3; DLB 157; MTCW 2
Phillips, David Graham 1867-1911 **TCLC 44**
See also CA 108; 176; DLB 9, 12
Phillips, Jack
See Sandburg, Carl (August)
Phillips, Jayne Anne 1952-**CLC 15, 33; SSC 16**
See also CA 101; CANR 24, 50; DLBY 80; INT CANR-24; MTCW 1, 2
Phillips, Richard
See Dick, Philip K(indred)
Phillips, Robert (Schaeffer) 1938-   **CLC 28**
See also CA 17-20R; CAAS 13; CANR 8; DLB 105
Phillips, Ward
See Lovecraft, H(oward) P(hillips)
Piccolo, Lucio 1901-1969   **CLC 13**
See also CA 97-100; DLB 114
Pickthall, Marjorie L(owry) C(hristie) 1883-1922   **TCLC 21**
See also CA 107; DLB 92
Pico della Mirandola, Giovanni 1463-1494**LC 15**
Piercy, Marge 1936- **CLC 3, 6, 14, 18, 27, 62**
See also CA 21-24R; CAAS 1; CANR 13, 43, 66; DLB 120; MTCW 1, 2
Piers, Robert
See Anthony, Piers
Pieyre de Mandiargues, Andre 1909-1991
See Mandiargues, Andre Pieyre de
See also CA 103; 136; CANR 22, 82
Pilnyak, Boris   **TCLC 23**
See also Vogau, Boris Andreyevich
Pincherle, Alberto 1907-1990   **CLC 11, 18; DAM NOV**
See also Moravia, Alberto
See also CA 25-28R; 132; CANR 33, 63; MTCW 1
Pinckney, Darryl 1953-   **CLC 76**
See also BW 2, 3; CA 143; CANR 79
Pindar 518B.C.-446B.C.   **CMLC 12; PC 19**
See also DLB 176
Pineda, Cecile 1942-   **CLC 39**
See also CA 118
Pinero, Arthur Wing 1855-1934   **TCLC 32; DAM DRAM**
See also CA 110; 153; DLB 10
Pinero, Miguel (Antonio Gomez) 1946-1988 **CLC 4, 55**
See also CA 61-64; 125; CANR 29; HW 1
Pinget, Robert 1919-1997   **CLC 7, 13, 37**
See also CA 85-88; 160; DLB 83
Pink Floyd
See Barrett, (Roger) Syd; Gilmour, David; Mason, Nick; Waters, Roger; Wright, Rick
Pinkney, Edward 1802-1828   **NCLC 31**
Pinkwater, Daniel Manus 1941-   **CLC 35**
See also Pinkwater, Manus
See also AAYA 1; CA 29-32R; CANR 12, 38; CLR 4; JRDA; MAICYA; SAAS 3; SATA 46, 76
Pinkwater, Manus
See Pinkwater, Daniel Manus
See also SATA 8
Pinsky, Robert 1940- **CLC 9, 19, 38, 94, 121; DAM POET; PC 27**
See also CA 29-32R; CAAS 4; CANR 58; DA3; DLBY 82, 98; MTCW 2
Pinta, Harold
See Pinter, Harold
Pinter, Harold 1930-**CLC 1, 3, 6, 9, 11, 15, 27, 58, 73; DA; DAB; DAC; DAM DRAM, MST; WLC**

See also CA 5-8R; CANR 33, 65; CDBLB 1960 to Present; DA3; DLB 13; MTCW 1, 2
Piozzi, Hester Lynch (Thrale) 1741-1821 **NCLC 57**
See also DLB 104, 142
Pirandello, Luigi 1867-1936**TCLC 4, 29; DA; DAB; DAC; DAM DRAM, MST; DC 5; SSC 22; WLC**
See also CA 104; 153; DA3; MTCW 2
Pirsig, Robert M(aynard) 1928-**CLC 4, 6, 73; DAM POP**
See also CA 53-56; CANR 42, 74; DA3; MTCW 1, 2; SATA 39
Pisarev, Dmitry Ivanovich 1840-1868 **NCLC 25**
Pix, Mary (Griffith) 1666-1709   **LC 8**
See also DLB 80
Pixerecourt, (Rene Charles) Guilbert de 1773-1844   **NCLC 39**
See also DLB 192
Plaatje, Sol(omon) T(shekisho) 1876-1932 **TCLC 73; BLCS**
See also BW 2, 3; CA 141; CANR 79
Plaidy, Jean
See Hibbert, Eleanor Alice Burford
Planche, James Robinson 1796-1880**NCLC 42**
Plant, Robert 1948-   **CLC 12**
Plante, David (Robert) 1940- **CLC 7, 23, 38; DAM NOV**
See also CA 37-40R; CANR 12, 36, 58, 82; DLBY 83; INT CANR-12; MTCW 1
Plath, Sylvia 1932-1963 **CLC 1, 2, 3, 5, 9, 11, 14, 17, 50, 51, 62, 111; DA; DAB; DAC; DAM MST, POET; PC 1; WLC**
See also AAYA 13; CA 19-20; CANR 34; CAP 2; CDALB 1941-1968; DA3; DLB 5, 6, 152; MTCW 1, 2; SATA 96
Plato 428(?)B.C.-348(?)B.C.   **CMLC 8; DA; DAB; DAC; DAM MST; WLCS**
See also DA3; DLB 176
Platonov, Andrei   **TCLC 14**
See also Klimentov, Andrei Platonovich
Platt, Kin 1911-   **CLC 26**
See also AAYA 11; CA 17-20R; CANR 11; JRDA; SAAS 17; SATA 21, 86
Plautus c. 251B.C.-184B.C. **CMLC 24; DC 6**
See also DLB 211
Plick et Plock
See Simenon, Georges (Jacques Christian)
Plimpton, George (Ames) 1927-   **CLC 36**
See also AITN 1; CA 21-24R; CANR 32, 70; DLB 185; MTCW 1, 2; SATA 10
Pliny the Elder c. 23-79   **CMLC 23**
See also DLB 211
Plomer, William Charles Franklin 1903-1973 **CLC 4, 8**
See also CA 21-22; CANR 34; CAP 2; DLB 20, 162, 191; MTCW 1; SATA 24
Plowman, Piers
See Kavanagh, Patrick (Joseph)
Plum, J.
See Wodehouse, P(elham) G(renville)
Plumly, Stanley (Ross) 1939-   **CLC 33**
See also CA 108; 110; DLB 5, 193; INT 110
Plumpe, Friedrich Wilhelm 1888-1931**TCLC 53**
See also CA 112
Po Chu-i 772-846   **CMLC 24**
Poe, Edgar Allan 1809-1849 **NCLC 1, 16, 55, 78; DA; DAB; DAC; DAM MST, POET; PC 1; SSC 34; WLC**
See also AAYA 14; CDALB 1640-1865; DA3; DLB 3, 59, 73, 74; SATA 23

Poet of Titchfield Street, The
See Pound, Ezra (Weston Loomis)
Pohl, Frederik 1919-   **CLC 18; SSC 25**
See also AAYA 24; CA 61-64; CAAS 1; CANR 11, 37, 81; DLB 8; INT CANR-11; MTCW 1, 2; SATA 24
Poirier, Louis 1910-
See Gracq, Julien
See also CA 122; 126
Poitier, Sidney 1927-   **CLC 26**
See also BW 1; CA 117
Polanski, Roman 1933-   **CLC 16**
See also CA 77-80
Poliakoff, Stephen 1952-   **CLC 38**
See also CA 106; DLB 13
Police, The
See Copeland, Stewart (Armstrong); Summers, Andrew James; Sumner, Gordon Matthew
Polidori, John William 1795-1821 **NCLC 51**
See also DLB 116
Pollitt, Katha 1949-   **CLC 28, 122**
See also CA 120; 122; CANR 66; MTCW 1, 2
Pollock, (Mary) Sharon 1936-**CLC 50; DAC; DAM DRAM, MST**
See also CA 141; DLB 60
Polo, Marco 1254-1324   **CMLC 15**
Polonsky, Abraham (Lincoln) 1910- **CLC 92**
See also CA 104; DLB 26; INT 104
Polybius c. 200B.C.-c. 118B.C.   **CMLC 17**
See also DLB 176
Pomerance, Bernard 1940-   **CLC 13; DAM DRAM**
See also CA 101; CANR 49
Ponge, Francis (Jean Gaston Alfred) 1899-1988 **CLC 6, 18; DAM POET**
See also CA 85-88; 126; CANR 40
Poniatowska, Elena 1933-
See also CA 101; CANR 32, 66; DAM MULT; DLB 113; HLC 2; HW 1, 2
Pontoppidan, Henrik 1857-1943   **TCLC 29**
See also CA 170
Poole, Josephine   **CLC 17**
See also Helyar, Jane Penelope Josephine
See also SAAS 2; SATA 5
Popa, Vasko 1922-1991   **CLC 19**
See also CA 112; 148; DLB 181
Pope, Alexander 1688-1744 **LC 3; DA; DAB; DAC; DAM MST, POET; PC 26; WLC**
See also CDBLB 1660-1789; DA3; DLB 95, 101
Porter, Connie (Rose) 1959(?)-   **CLC 70**
See also BW 2, 3; CA 142; SATA 81
Porter, Gene(va Grace) Stratton 1863(?)-1924 **TCLC 21**
See also CA 112
Porter, Katherine Anne 1890-1980**CLC 1, 3, 7, 10, 13, 15, 27, 101; DA; DAB; DAC; DAM MST, NOV; SSC 4, 31**
See also AITN 2; CA 1-4R; 101; CANR 1, 65; CDALBS; DA3; DLB 4, 9, 102; DLBD 12; DLBY 80; MTCW 1, 2; SATA 39; SATA-Obit 23
Porter, Peter (Neville Frederick) 1929-**CLC 5, 13, 33**
See also CA 85-88; DLB 40
Porter, William Sydney 1862-1910
See Henry, O.
See also CA 104; 131; CDALB 1865-1917; DA; DAB; DAC; DAM MST; DA3; DLB 12, 78, 79; MTCW 1, 2; YABC 2
Portillo (y Pacheco), Jose Lopez
See Lopez Portillo (y Pacheco), Jose
Portillo Trambley, Estela 1927-1998

See also CANR 32; DAM MULT; DLB 209;
HLC 2; HW 1
Post, Melville Davisson 1869-1930 **TCLC 39**
See also CA 110
Potok, Chaim 1929- **CLC 2, 7, 14, 26, 112;**
DAM NOV
See also AAYA 15; AITN 1, 2; CA 17-20R;
CANR 19, 35, 64; DA3; DLB 28, 152; INT
CANR-19; MTCW 1, 2; SATA 33, 106
Potter, (Helen) Beatrix 1866-1943
See Webb, (Martha) Beatrice (Potter)
See also MAICYA; MTCW 2
Potter, Dennis (Christopher George) 1935-1994
CLC 58, 86
See also CA 107; 145; CANR 33, 61; MTCW 1
Pound, Ezra (Weston Loomis) 1885-1972**CLC**
1, 2, 3, 4, 5, 7, 10, 13, 18, 34, 48, 50, 112;
DA; DAB; DAC; DAM MST, POET; PC
4; WLC
See also CA 5-8R; 37-40R; CANR 40; CDALB
1917-1929; DA3; DLB 4, 45, 63; DLBD 15;
MTCW 1, 2
Povod, Reinaldo 1959-1994 **CLC 44**
See also CA 136; 146; CANR 83
Powell, Adam Clayton, Jr. 1908-1972**CLC 89;**
BLC 3; DAM MULT
See also BW 1, 3; CA 102; 33-36R
Powell, Anthony (Dymoke) 1905-**CLC 1, 3, 7,**
9, 10, 31
See also CA 1-4R; CANR 1, 32, 62; CDBLB
1945-1960; DLB 15; MTCW 1, 2
Powell, Dawn 1897-1965 **CLC 66**
See also CA 5-8R; DLBY 97
Powell, Padgett 1952- **CLC 34**
See also CA 126; CANR 63
Power, Susan 1961- **CLC 91**
Powers, J(ames) F(arl) 1917-**CLC 1, 4, 8, 57;**
SSC 4
See also CA 1-4R; CANR 2, 61; DLB 130;
MTCW 1
Powers, John J(ames) 1945-
See Powers, John R.
See also CA 69-72
Powers, John R. **CLC 66**
See also Powers, John J(ames)
Powers, Richard (S.) 1957- **CLC 93**
See also CA 148; CANR 80
Pownall, David 1938- **CLC 10**
See also CA 89-92, 180; CAAS 18; CANR 49;
DLB 14
Powys, John Cowper 1872-1963**CLC 7, 9, 15,**
46
See also CA 85-88; DLB 15; MTCW 1, 2
Powys, T(heodore) F(rancis) 1875-1953
TCLC 9
See also CA 106; DLB 36, 162
Prado (Calvo), Pedro 1886-1952 **TCLC 75**
See also CA 131; HW 1
Prager, Emily 1952- **CLC 56**
Pratt, E(dwin) J(ohn) 1883(?)-1964 **CLC 19;**
DAC; DAM POET
See also CA 141; 93-96; CANR 77; DLB 92
Premchand **TCLC 21**
See also Srivastava, Dhanpat Rai
Preussler, Otfried 1923- **CLC 17**
See also CA 77-80; SATA 24
Prevert, Jacques (Henri Marie) 1900-1977
CLC 15
See also CA 77-80; 69-72; CANR 29, 61;
MTCW 1; SATA-Obit 30
Prevost, Abbe (Antoine Francois) 1697-1763
LC 1
Price, (Edward) Reynolds 1933-**CLC 3, 6, 13,**

43, 50, 63; **DAM NOV; SSC 22**
See also CA 1-4R; CANR 1, 37, 57; DLB 2;
INT CANR-37
Price, Richard 1949- **CLC 6, 12**
See also CA 49-52; CANR 3; DLBY 81
Prichard, Katharine Susannah 1883-1969
CLC 46
See also CA 11-12; CANR 33; CAP 1; MTCW
1; SATA 66
Priestley, J(ohn) B(oynton) 1894-1984**CLC 2,**
5, 9, 34; DAM DRAM, NOV
See also CA 9-12R; 113; CANR 33; CDBLB
1914-1945; DA3; DLB 10, 34, 77, 100, 139;
DLBY 84; MTCW 1, 2
Prince 1958(?)- **CLC 35**
Prince, F(rank) T(empleton) 1912- **CLC 22**
See also CA 101; CANR 43, 79; DLB 20
Prince Kropotkin
See Kropotkin, Peter (Alekseievich)
Prior, Matthew 1664-1721 **LC 4**
See also DLB 95
Prishvin, Mikhail 1873-1954 **TCLC 75**
Pritchard, William H(arrison) 1932- **CLC 34**
See also CA 65-68; CANR 23; DLB 111
Pritchett, V(ictor) S(awdon) 1900-1997 **C L C**
5, 13, 15, 41; DAM NOV; SSC 14
See also CA 61-64; 157; CANR 31, 63; DA3;
DLB 15, 139; MTCW 1, 2
Private 19022
See Manning, Frederic
Probst, Mark 1925- **CLC 59**
See also CA 130
Prokosch, Frederic 1908-1989 **CLC 4, 48**
See also CA 73-76; 128; CANR 82; DLB 48;
MTCW 2
Propertius, Sextus c. 50B.C.-c. 16B.C.**C M L C**
32
See also DLB 211
Prophet, The
See Dreiser, Theodore (Herman Albert)
Prose, Francine 1947- **CLC 45**
See also CA 109; 112; CANR 46; SATA 101
Proudhon
See Cunha, Euclides (Rodrigues Pimenta) da
Proulx, Annie
See Proulx, E(dna) Annie
Proulx, E(dna) Annie 1935- **CLC 81; DAM**
POP
See also CA 145; CANR 65; DA3; MTCW 2
Proust, (Valentin-Louis-George-Eugene-)
Marcel 1871-1922 **TCLC 7, 13, 33; DA;**
DAB; DAC; DAM MST, NOV; WLC
See also CA 104; 120; DA3; DLB 65; MTCW
1, 2
Prowler, Harley
See Masters, Edgar Lee
Prus, Boleslaw 1845-1912 **TCLC 48**
Pryor, Richard (Franklin Lenox Thomas) 1940-
CLC 26
See also CA 122; 152
Przybyszewski, Stanislaw 1868-1927**TCLC 36**
See also CA 160; DLB 66
Pteleon
See Grieve, C(hristopher) M(urray)
See also DAM POET
Puckett, Lute
See Masters, Edgar Lee
Puig, Manuel 1932-1990**CLC 3, 5, 10, 28, 65;**
DAM MULT; HLC 2
See also CA 45-48; CANR 2, 32, 63; DA3; DLB
113; HW 1, 2; MTCW 1, 2
Pulitzer, Joseph 1847-1911 **TCLC 76**
See also CA 114; DLB 23

Purdy, A(lfred) W(ellington) 1918-**CLC 3, 6,**
14, 50; DAC; DAM MST, POET
See also CA 81-84; CAAS 17; CANR 42, 66;
DLB 88
Purdy, James (Amos) 1923-**CLC 2, 4, 10, 28,**
52
See also CA 33-36R; CAAS 1; CANR 19, 51;
DLB 2; INT CANR-19; MTCW 1
Pure, Simon
See Swinnerton, Frank Arthur
Pushkin, Alexander (Sergeyevich) 1799-1837
NCLC 3, 27; DA; DAB; DAC; DAM
DRAM, MST, POET; PC 10; SSC 27;
WLC
See also DA3; DLB 205; SATA 61
P'u Sung-ling 1640-1715 **LC 49; SSC 31**
Putnam, Arthur Lee
See Alger, Horatio, Jr.
Puzo, Mario 1920-1999 **CLC 1, 2, 6, 36, 107;**
DAM NOV, POP
See also CA 65-68; CANR 4, 42, 65; DA3; DLB
6; MTCW 1, 2
Pygge, Edward
See Barnes, Julian (Patrick)
Pyle, Ernest Taylor 1900-1945
See Pyle, Ernie
See also CA 115; 160
Pyle, Ernie 1900-1945 **TCLC 75**
See also Pyle, Ernest Taylor
See also DLB 29; MTCW 2
Pyle, Howard 1853-1911 **TCLC 81**
See also CA 109; 137; CLR 22; DLB 42, 188;
DLBD 13; MAICYA; SATA 16, 100
Pym, Barbara (Mary Crampton) 1913-1980
CLC 13, 19, 37, 111
See also CA 13-14; 97-100; CANR 13, 34; CAP
1; DLB 14, 207; DLBY 87; MTCW 1, 2
Pynchon, Thomas (Ruggles, Jr.) 1937-**CLC 2,**
3, 6, 9, 11, 18, 33, 62, 72; DA; DAB; DAC;
DAM MST, NOV, POP; SSC 14; WLC
See also BEST 90:2; CA 17-20R; CANR 22,
46, 73; DA3; DLB 2, 173; MTCW 1, 2
Pythagoras c. 570B.C.-c. 500B.C. **CMLC 22**
See also DLB 176
Q
See Quiller-Couch, SirArthur (Thomas)
Qian Zhongshu
See Ch'ien Chung-shu
Qroll
See Dagerman, Stig (Halvard)
Quarrington, Paul (Lewis) 1953- **CLC 65**
See also CA 129; CANR 62
Quasimodo, Salvatore 1901-1968 **CLC 10**
See also CA 13-16; 25-28R; CAP 1; DLB 114;
MTCW 1
Quay, Stephen 1947- **CLC 95**
Quay, Timothy 1947- **CLC 95**
Queen, Ellery **CLC 3, 11**
See also Dannay, Frederic; Davidson, Avram
(James); Lee, Manfred B(ennington);
Marlowe, Stephen; Sturgeon, Theodore
(Hamilton); Vance, John Holbrook
Queen, Ellery, Jr.
See Dannay, Frederic; Lee, Manfred
B(ennington)
Queneau, Raymond 1903-1976 **CLC 2, 5, 10,**
42
See also CA 77-80; 69-72; CANR 32; DLB 72;
MTCW 1, 2
Quevedo, Francisco de 1580-1645 **LC 23**
Quiller-Couch, SirArthur (Thomas) 1863-1944
TCLC 53
See also CA 118; 166; DLB 135, 153, 190

Renoir, Jean 1894-1979　　　　**CLC 20**
　See also CA 129; 85-88
Resnais, Alain 1922-　　　　　**CLC 16**
Reverdy, Pierre 1889-1960　　　**CLC 53**
　See also CA 97-100; 89-92
Rexroth, Kenneth 1905-1982 **CLC 1, 2, 6, 11,**
　　22, 49, 112; DAM POET; PC 20
　See also CA 5-8R; 107; CANR 14, 34, 63;
　　CDALB 1941-1968; DLB 16, 48, 165, 212;
　　DLBY 82; INT CANR-14; MTCW 1, 2
Reyes, Alfonso 1889-1959**TCLC 33; HLCS 2**
　See also CA 131; HW 1
Reyes y Basoalto, Ricardo Eliecer Neftali
　See Neruda, Pablo
Reymont, Wladyslaw (Stanislaw) 1868(?)-1925
　　TCLC 5
　See also CA 104
Reynolds, Jonathan 1942-　　　**CLC 6, 38**
　See also CA 65-68; CANR 28
Reynolds, Joshua 1723-1792　　　**LC 15**
　See also DLB 104
Reynolds, Michael Shane 1937-　　**CLC 44**
　See also CA 65-68; CANR 9
Reznikoff, Charles 1894-1976　　　**CLC 9**
　See also CA 33-36; 61-64; CAP 2; DLB 28, 45
Rezzori (d'Arezzo), Gregor von 1914-1998
　　CLC 25
　See also CA 122; 136; 167
Rhine, Richard
　See Silverstein, Alvin
Rhodes, Eugene Manlove 1869-1934**TCLC 53**
Rhodius, Apollonius c. 3rd cent. B.C.- **C M L C
　　28**
　See also DLB 176
R'hoone
　See Balzac, Honore de
Rhys, Jean 1890(?)-1979**CLC 2, 4, 6, 14, 19, 51,
　　124; DAM NOV; SSC 21**
　See also CA 25-28R; 85-88; CANR 35, 62;
　　CDBLB 1945-1960; DA3; DLB 36, 117,
　　162; MTCW 1, 2
Ribeiro, Darcy 1922-1997　　　　**CLC 34**
　See also CA 33-36R; 156
Ribeiro, Joao Ubaldo (Osorio Pimentel) 1941-
　　CLC 10, 67
　See also CA 81-84
Ribman, Ronald (Burt) 1932-　　　**CLC 7**
　See also CA 21-24R; CANR 46, 80
Ricci, Nino 1959-　　　　　　**CLC 70**
　See also CA 137
Rice, Anne 1941-　　　**CLC 41; DAM POP**
　See also AAYA 9; BEST 89:2; CA 65-68; CANR
　　12, 36, 53, 74; DA3; MTCW 2
Rice, Elmer (Leopold) 1892-1967 **CLC 7, 49;
　　DAM DRAM**
　See also CA 21-22; 25-28R; CAP 2; DLB 4, 7;
　　MTCW 1, 2
Rice, Tim(othy Miles Bindon) 1944- **CLC 21**
　See also CA 103; CANR 46
Rich, Adrienne (Cecile) 1929-**CLC 3, 6, 7, 11,
　　18, 36, 73, 76; DAM POET; PC 5**
　See also CA 9-12R; CANR 20, 53, 74;
　　CDALBS; DA3; DLB 5, 67; MTCW 1, 2
Rich, Barbara
　See Graves, Robert (von Ranke)
Rich, Robert
　See Trumbo, Dalton
Richard, Keith　　　　　　　　**CLC 17**
　See also Richards, Keith
Richards, David Adams 1950- **CLC 59; DAC**
　See also CA 93-96; CANR 60; DLB 53
Richards, I(vor) A(rmstrong) 1893-1979**C L C
　　14, 24**

　See also CA 41-44R; 89-92; CANR 34, 74; DLB
　　27; MTCW 2
Richards, Keith 1943-
　See Richard, Keith
　See also CA 107; CANR 77
Richardson, Anne
　See Roiphe, Anne (Richardson)
Richardson, Dorothy Miller 1873-1957**TCLC
　　3**
　See also CA 104; DLB 36
Richardson, Ethel Florence (Lindesay) 1870-
　　1946
　See Richardson, Henry Handel
　See also CA 105
Richardson, Henry Handel　　　**TCLC 4**
　See also Richardson, Ethel Florence (Lindesay)
　See also DLB 197
Richardson, John 1796-1852 **NCLC 55; DAC**
　See also DLB 99
Richardson, Samuel 1689-1761**LC 1, 44; DA;
　　DAB; DAC; DAM MST, NOV; WLC**
　See also CDBLB 1660-1789; DLB 39
Richler, Mordecai 1931-**CLC 3, 5, 9, 13, 18, 46,
　　70; DAC; DAM MST, NOV**
　See also AITN 1; CA 65-68; CANR 31, 62; CLR
　　17; DLB 53; MAICYA; MTCW 1, 2; SATA
　　44, 98; SATA-Brief 27
Richter, Conrad (Michael) 1890-1968**CLC 30**
　See also AAYA 21; CA 5-8R; 25-28R; CANR
　　23; DLB 9, 212; MTCW 1, 2; SATA 3
Ricostranza, Tom
　See Ellis, Trey
Riddell, Charlotte 1832-1906　　　**TCLC 40**
　See also CA 165; DLB 156
Ridgway, Keith 1965-　　　　　**CLC 119**
　See also CA 172
Riding, Laura　　　　　　　　**CLC 3, 7**
　See also Jackson, Laura (Riding)
Riefenstahl, Berta Helene Amalia 1902-
　See Riefenstahl, Leni
　See also CA 108
Riefenstahl, Leni　　　　　　　**CLC 16**
　See also Riefenstahl, Berta Helene Amalia
Riffe, Ernest
　See Bergman, (Ernst) Ingmar
Riggs, (Rolla) Lynn 1899-1954　　**TCLC 56;
　　DAM MULT**
　See also CA 144; DLB 175; NNAL
Riis, Jacob A(ugust) 1849-1914　　**TCLC 80**
　See also CA 113; 168; DLB 23
Riley, James Whitcomb 1849-1916**TCLC 51;
　　DAM POET**
　See also CA 118; 137; MAICYA; SATA 17
Riley, Tex
　See Creasey, John
Rilke, Rainer Maria 1875-1926**TCLC 1, 6, 19;
　　DAM POET; PC 2**
　See also CA 104; 132; CANR 62; DA3; DLB
　　81; MTCW 1, 2
Rimbaud, (Jean Nicolas) Arthur 1854-1891
　　**NCLC 4, 35; DA; DAB; DAC; DAM MST,
　　POET; PC 3; WLC**
　See also DA3
Rinehart, Mary Roberts 1876-1958 **TCLC 52**
　See also CA 108; 166
Ringmaster, The
　See Mencken, H(enry) L(ouis)
Ringwood, Gwen(dolyn Margaret) Pharis
　　1910-1984　　　　　　　　**CLC 48**
　See also CA 148; 112; DLB 88
Rio, Michel 19(?)-　　　　　　**CLC 43**
Ritsos, Giannes
　See Ritsos, Yannis

Ritsos, Yannis 1909-1990　　**CLC 6, 13, 31**
　See also CA 77-80; 133; CANR 39, 61; MTCW
　　1
Ritter, Erika 1948(?)-　　　　　**CLC 52**
Rivera, Jose Eustasio 1889-1928　**TCLC 35**
　See also CA 162; HW 1, 2
Rivera, Tomas 1935-1984
　See also CA 49-52; CANR 32; DLB 82; HLCS
　　2; HW 1
Rivers, Conrad Kent 1933-1968　　　**CLC 1**
　See also BW 1; CA 85-88; DLB 41
Rivers, Elfrida
　See Bradley, Marion Zimmer
Riverside, John
　See Heinlein, Robert A(nson)
Rizal, Jose 1861-1896　　　　　**NCLC 27**
Roa Bastos, Augusto (Antonio) 1917-**CLC 45;
　　DAM MULT; HLC 2**
　See also CA 131; DLB 113; HW 1
Robbe-Grillet, Alain 1922-**CLC 1, 2, 4, 6, 8, 10,
　　14, 43**
　See also CA 9-12R; CANR 33, 65; DLB 83;
　　MTCW 1, 2
Robbins, Harold 1916-1997　　**CLC 5; DAM
　　NOV**
　See also CA 73-76; 162; CANR 26, 54; DA3;
　　MTCW 1, 2
Robbins, Thomas Eugene 1936-
　See Robbins, Tom
　See also CA 81-84; CANR 29, 59; DAM NOV,
　　POP; DA3; MTCW 1, 2
Robbins, Tom　　　　　　**CLC 9, 32, 64**
　See also Robbins, Thomas Eugene
　See also AAYA 32; BEST 90:3; DLBY 80;
　　MTCW 2
Robbins, Trina 1938-　　　　　**CLC 21**
　See also CA 128
Roberts, Charles G(eorge) D(ouglas) 1860-1943
　　TCLC 8
　See also CA 105; CLR 33; DLB 92; SATA 88;
　　SATA-Brief 29
Roberts, Elizabeth Madox 1886-1941 **T C L C
　　68**
　See also CA 111; 166; DLB 9, 54, 102; SATA
　　33; SATA-Brief 27
Roberts, Kate 1891-1985　　　　**CLC 15**
　See also CA 107; 116
Roberts, Keith (John Kingston) 1935-**CLC 14**
　See also CA 25-28R; CANR 46
Roberts, Kenneth (Lewis) 1885-1957**TCLC 23**
　See also CA 109; DLB 9
Roberts, Michele (B.) 1949-　　　**CLC 48**
　See also CA 115; CANR 58
Robertson, Ellis
　See Ellison, Harlan (Jay); Silverberg, Robert
Robertson, Thomas William 1829-1871**NCLC
　　35; DAM DRAM**
Robeson, Kenneth
　See Dent, Lester
Robinson, Edwin Arlington 1869-1935**T C L C
　　5; DA; DAC; DAM MST, POET; PC 1**
　See also CA 104; 133; CDALB 1865-1917;
　　DLB 54; MTCW 1, 2
Robinson, Henry Crabb 1775-1867**NCLC 15**
　See also DLB 107
Robinson, Jill 1936-　　　　　**CLC 10**
　See also CA 102; INT 102
Robinson, Kim Stanley 1952-　　　**CLC 34**
　See also AAYA 26; CA 126; SATA 109
Robinson, Lloyd
　See Silverberg, Robert
Robinson, Marilynne 1944-　　　**CLC 25**
　See also CA 116; CANR 80; DLB 206

Santoka, Taneda 1882-1940 **TCLC 72**

Santos, Bienvenido N(uqui) 1911-1996 **C L C 22; DAM MULT**
See also CA 101; 151; CANR 19, 46

Sapper **TCLC 44**
See also McNeile, Herman Cyril

Sapphire
See Sapphire, Brenda

Sapphire, Brenda 1950- **CLC 99**

Sappho fl. 6th cent. B.C.- **CMLC 3; DAM POET; PC 5**
See also DA3; DLB 176

Saramago, Jose 1922- **CLC 119; HLCS 1**
See also CA 153

Sarduy, Severo 1937-1993**CLC 6, 97; HLCS 1**
See also CA 89-92; 142; CANR 58, 81; DLB 113; HW 1, 2

Sargeson, Frank 1903-1982 **CLC 31**
See also CA 25-28R; 106; CANR 38, 79

Sarmiento, Domingo Faustino 1811-1888
See also HLCS 2

Sarmiento, Felix Ruben Garcia
See Dario, Ruben

Saro-Wiwa, Ken(ule Beeson) 1941-1995**C L C 114**
See also BW 2; CA 142; 150; CANR 60; DLB 157

Saroyan, William 1908-1981**CLC 1, 8, 10, 29, 34, 56; DA; DAB; DAC; DAM DRAM, MST, NOV; SSC 21; WLC**
See also CA 5-8R; 103; CANR 30; CDALBS; DA3; DLB 7, 9, 86; DLBY 81; MTCW 1, 2; SATA 23; SATA-Obit 24

Sarraute, Nathalie 1900-**CLC 1, 2, 4, 8, 10, 31, 80**
See also CA 9-12R; CANR 23, 66; DLB 83; MTCW 1, 2

Sarton, (Eleanor) May 1912-1995 **CLC 4, 14, 49, 91; DAM POET**
See also CA 1-4R; 149; CANR 1, 34, 55; DLB 48; DLBY 81; INT CANR-34; MTCW 1, 2; SATA 36; SATA-Obit 86

Sartre, Jean-Paul 1905-1980**CLC 1, 4, 7, 9, 13, 18, 24, 44, 50, 52; DA; DAB; DAC; DAM DRAM, MST, NOV; DC 3; SSC 32; WLC**
See also CA 9-12R; 97-100; CANR 21; DA3; DLB 72; MTCW 1, 2

Sassoon, Siegfried (Lorraine) 1886-1967**C L C 36; DAB; DAM MST, NOV, POET; PC 12**
See also CA 104; 25-28R; CANR 36; DLB 20, 191; DLBD 18; MTCW 1, 2

Satterfield, Charles
See Pohl, Frederik

Saul, John (W. III) 1942-**CLC 46; DAM NOV, POP**
See also AAYA 10; BEST 90:4; CA 81-84; CANR 16, 40, 81; SATA 98

Saunders, Caleb
See Heinlein, Robert A(nson)

Saura (Atares), Carlos 1932- **CLC 20**
See also CA 114; 131; CANR 79; HW 1

Sauser-Hall, Frederic 1887-1961 **CLC 18**
See also Cendrars, Blaise
See also CA 102; 93-96; CANR 36, 62; MTCW 1

Saussure, Ferdinand de 1857-1913 **TCLC 49**

Savage, Catharine
See Brosman, Catharine Savage

Savage, Thomas 1915- **CLC 40**
See also CA 126; 132; CAAS 15; INT 132

Savan, Glenn 19(?)- **CLC 50**

Sayers, Dorothy L(eigh) 1893-1957 **TCLC 2, 15; DAM POP**

See also CA 104; 119; CANR 60; CDBLB 1914-1945; DLB 10, 36, 77, 100; MTCW 1, 2

Sayers, Valerie 1952- **CLC 50, 122**
See also CA 134; CANR 61

Sayles, John (Thomas) 1950- **CLC 7, 10, 14**
See also CA 57-60; CANR 41, 84; DLB 44

Scammell, Michael 1935- **CLC 34**
See also CA 156

Scannell, Vernon 1922- **CLC 49**
See also CA 5-8R; CANR 8, 24, 57; DLB 27; SATA 59

Scarlett, Susan
See Streatfeild, (Mary) Noel

Scarron
See Mikszath, Kalman

Schaeffer, Susan Fromberg 1941- **CLC 6, 11, 22**
See also CA 49-52; CANR 18, 65; DLB 28; MTCW 1, 2; SATA 22

Schary, Jill
See Robinson, Jill

Schell, Jonathan 1943- **CLC 35**
See also CA 73-76; CANR 12

Schelling, Friedrich Wilhelm Joseph von 1775-1854 **NCLC 30**
See also DLB 90

Schendel, Arthur van 1874-1946 **TCLC 56**

Scherer, Jean-Marie Maurice 1920-
See Rohmer, Eric
See also CA 110

Schevill, James (Erwin) 1920- **CLC 7**
See also CA 5-8R; CAAS 12

Schiller, Friedrich 1759-1805 **NCLC 39, 69; DAM DRAM**
See also DLB 94

Schisgal, Murray (Joseph) 1926- **CLC 6**
See also CA 21-24R; CANR 48

Schlee, Ann 1934- **CLC 35**
See also CA 101; CANR 29; SATA 44; SATA-Brief 36

Schlegel, August Wilhelm von 1767-1845 **NCLC 15**
See also DLB 94

Schlegel, Friedrich 1772-1829 **NCLC 45**
See also DLB 90

Schlegel, Johann Elias (von) 1719(?)-1749**L C 5**

Schlesinger, Arthur M(eier), Jr. 1917-**CLC 84**
See also AITN 1; CA 1-4R; CANR 1, 28, 58; DLB 17; INT CANR-28; MTCW 1, 2; SATA 61

Schmidt, Arno (Otto) 1914-1979 **CLC 56**
See also CA 128; 109; DLB 69

Schmitz, Aron Hector 1861-1928
See Svevo, Italo
See also CA 104; 122; MTCW 1

Schnackenberg, Gjertrud 1953- **CLC 40**
See also CA 116; DLB 120

Schneider, Leonard Alfred 1925-1966
See Bruce, Lenny
See also CA 89-92

Schnitzler, Arthur 1862-1931**TCLC 4; SSC 15**
See also CA 104; DLB 81, 118

Schoenberg, Arnold 1874-1951 **TCLC 75**
See also CA 109

Schonberg, Arnold
See Schoenberg, Arnold

Schopenhauer, Arthur 1788-1860 **NCLC 51**
See also DLB 90

Schor, Sandra (M.) 1932(?)-1990 **CLC 65**
See also CA 132

Schorer, Mark 1908-1977 **CLC 9**
See also CA 5-8R; 73-76; CANR 7; DLB 103

Schrader, Paul (Joseph) 1946- **CLC 26**
See also CA 37-40R; CANR 41; DLB 44

Schreiner, Olive (Emilie Albertina) 1855-1920 **TCLC 9**
See also CA 105; 154; DLB 18, 156, 190

Schulberg, Budd (Wilson) 1914- **CLC 7, 48**
See also CA 25-28R; CANR 19; DLB 6, 26, 28; DLBY 81

Schulz, Bruno 1892-1942**TCLC 5, 51; SSC 13**
See also CA 115; 123; MTCW 2

Schulz, Charles M(onroe) 1922- **CLC 12**
See also CA 9-12R; CANR 6; INT CANR-6; SATA 10

Schumacher, E(rnst) F(riedrich) 1911-1977 **CLC 80**
See also CA 81-84; 73-76; CANR 34

Schuyler, James Marcus 1923-1991**CLC 5, 23; DAM POET**
See also CA 101; 134; DLB 5, 169; INT 101

Schwartz, Delmore (David) 1913-1966**CLC 2, 4, 10, 45, 87; PC 8**
See also CA 17-18; 25-28R; CANR 35; CAP 2; DLB 28, 48; MTCW 1, 2

Schwartz, Ernst
See Ozu, Yasujiro

Schwartz, John Burnham 1965- **CLC 59**
See also CA 132

Schwartz, Lynne Sharon 1939- **CLC 31**
See also CA 103; CANR 44; MTCW 2

Schwartz, Muriel A.
See Eliot, T(homas) S(tearns)

Schwarz-Bart, Andre 1928- **CLC 2, 4**
See also CA 89-92

Schwarz-Bart, Simone 1938- **CLC 7; BLCS**
See also BW 2; CA 97-100

Schwitters, Kurt (Hermann Edward Karl Julius) 1887-1948 **TCLC 95**
See also CA 158

Schwob, Marcel (Mayer Andre) 1867-1905 **TCLC 20**
See also CA 117; 168; DLB 123

Sciascia, Leonardo 1921-1989 **CLC 8, 9, 41**
See also CA 85-88; 130; CANR 35; DLB 177; MTCW 1

Scoppettone, Sandra 1936- **CLC 26**
See also AAYA 11; CA 5-8R; CANR 41, 73; SATA 9, 92

Scorsese, Martin 1942- **CLC 20, 89**
See also CA 110; 114; CANR 46

Scotland, Jay
See Jakes, John (William)

Scott, Duncan Campbell 1862-1947 **TCLC 6; DAC**
See also CA 104; 153; DLB 92

Scott, Evelyn 1893-1963 **CLC 43**
See also CA 104; 112; CANR 64; DLB 9, 48

Scott, F(rancis) R(eginald) 1899-1985**CLC 22**
See also CA 101; 114; DLB 88; INT 101

Scott, Frank
See Scott, F(rancis) R(eginald)

Scott, Joanna 1960- **CLC 50**
See also CA 126; CANR 53

Scott, Paul (Mark) 1920-1978 **CLC 9, 60**
See also CA 81-84; 77-80; CANR 33; DLB 14, 207; MTCW 1

Scott, Sarah 1723-1795 **LC 44**
See also DLB 39

Scott, Walter 1771-1832 **NCLC 15, 69; DA; DAB; DAC; DAM MST, NOV, POET; PC 13; SSC 32; WLC**
See also AAYA 22; CDBLB 1789-1832; DLB 93, 107, 116, 144, 159; YABC 2

Scribe, (Augustin) Eugene 1791-1861 **N C L C**

22; DA3; DLB 7, 212; MTCW 1, 2
Shepherd, Michael
See Ludlum, Robert
Sherburne, Zoa (Lillian Morin) 1912-1995
CLC 30
See also AAYA 13; CA 1-4R; 176; CANR 3,
37; MAICYA; SAAS 18; SATA 3
Sheridan, Frances 1724-1766   **LC 7**
See also DLB 39, 84
Sheridan, Richard Brinsley 1751-1816**N C L C
5; DA; DAB; DAC; DAM DRAM, MST;
DC 1; WLC**
See also CDBLB 1660-1789; DLB 89
Sherman, Jonathan Marc   **CLC 55**
Sherman, Martin 1941(?)-   **CLC 19**
See also CA 116; 123
Sherwin, Judith Johnson
See Johnson, Judith (Emlyn)
Sherwood, Frances 1940-   **CLC 81**
See also CA 146
Sherwood, Robert E(mmet) 1896-1955**T C L C
3; DAM DRAM**
See also CA 104; 153; DLB 7, 26
Shestov, Lev 1866-1938   **TCLC 56**
Shevchenko, Taras 1814-1861   **NCLC 54**
Shiel, M(atthew) P(hipps) 1865-1947**TCLC 8**
See also Holmes, Gordon
See also CA 106; 160; DLB 153; MTCW 2
Shields, Carol 1935-   **CLC 91, 113; DAC**
See also CA 81-84; CANR 51, 74; DA3; MTCW
2
Shields, David 1956-   **CLC 97**
See also CA 124; CANR 48
Shiga, Naoya 1883-1971   **CLC 33; SSC 23**
See also CA 101; 33-36R; DLB 180
Shikibu, Murasaki c. 978-c. 1014   **CMLC 1**
Shilts, Randy 1951-1994   **CLC 85**
See also AAYA 19; CA 115; 127; 144; CANR
45; DA3; INT 127; MTCW 2
Shimazaki, Haruki 1872-1943
See Shimazaki Toson
See also CA 105; 134; CANR 84
Shimazaki Toson 1872-1943   **TCLC 5**
See also Shimazaki, Haruki
See also DLB 180
Sholokhov, Mikhail (Aleksandrovich) 1905-
1984   **CLC 7, 15**
See also CA 101; 112; MTCW 1, 2; SATA-Obit
36
Shone, Patric
See Hanley, James
Shreve, Susan Richards 1939-   **CLC 23**
See also CA 49-52; CAAS 5; CANR 5, 38, 69;
MAICYA; SATA 46, 95; SATA-Brief 41
Shue, Larry 1946-1985**CLC 52; DAM DRAM**
See also CA 145; 117
Shu-Jen, Chou 1881-1936
See Lu Hsun
See also CA 104
Shulman, Alix Kates 1932-   **CLC 2, 10**
See also CA 29-32R; CANR 43; SATA 7
Shuster, Joe 1914-   **CLC 21**
Shute, Nevil   **CLC 30**
See also Norway, Nevil Shute
See also MTCW 2
Shuttle, Penelope (Diane) 1947-   **CLC 7**
See also CA 93-96; CANR 39, 84; DLB 14, 40
Sidney, Mary 1561-1621   **LC 19, 39**
Sidney, Sir Philip 1554-1586 **LC 19, 39; DA;
DAB; DAC; DAM MST, POET**
See also CDBLB Before 1660; DA3; DLB 167
Siegel, Jerome 1914-1996   **CLC 21**
See also CA 116; 169; 151

Siegel, Jerry
See Siegel, Jerome
Sienkiewicz, Henryk (Adam Alexander Pius)
1846-1916   **TCLC 3**
See also CA 104; 134; CANR 84
Sierra, Gregorio Martinez
See Martinez Sierra, Gregorio
Sierra, Maria (de la O'LeJarraga) Martinez
See Martinez Sierra, Maria (de la O'LeJarraga)
Sigal, Clancy 1926-   **CLC 7**
See also CA 1-4R
Sigourney, Lydia Howard (Huntley) 1791-1865
NCLC 21
See also DLB 1, 42, 73
Siguenza y Gongora, Carlos de 1645-1700**L C
8; HLCS 2**
Sigurjonsson, Johann 1880-1919   **TCLC 27**
See also CA 170
Sikelianos, Angelos 1884-1951   **TCLC 39**
Silkin, Jon 1930-   **CLC 2, 6, 43**
See also CA 5-8R; CAAS 5; DLB 27
Silko, Leslie (Marmon) 1948-**CLC 23, 74, 114;
DA; DAC; DAM MST, MULT, POP;
WLCS**
See also AAYA 14; CA 115; 122; CANR 45,
65; DA3; DLB 143, 175; MTCW 2; NNAL
Sillanpaa, Frans Eemil 1888-1964   **CLC 19**
See also CA 129; 93-96; MTCW 1
Sillitoe, Alan 1928-   **CLC 1, 3, 6, 10, 19, 57**
See also AITN 1; CA 9-12R; CAAS 2; CANR
8, 26, 55; CDBLB 1960 to Present; DLB 14,
139; MTCW 1, 2; SATA 61
Silone, Ignazio 1900-1978   **CLC 4**
See also CA 25-28; 81-84; CANR 34; CAP 2;
MTCW 1
Silver, Joan Micklin 1935-   **CLC 20**
See also CA 114; 121; INT 121
Silver, Nicholas
See Faust, Frederick (Schiller)
Silverberg, Robert 1935- **CLC 7; DAM POP**
See also AAYA 24; CA 1-4R; CAAS 3; CANR
1, 20, 36; CLR 59; DLB 8; INT CANR-20;
MAICYA; MTCW 1, 2; SATA 13, 91; SATA-
Essay 104
Silverstein, Alvin 1933-   **CLC 17**
See also CA 49-52; CANR 2; CLR 25; JRDA;
MAICYA; SATA 8, 69
Silverstein, Virginia B(arbara Opshelor) 1937-
CLC 17
See also CA 49-52; CANR 2; CLR 25; JRDA;
MAICYA; SATA 8, 69
Sim, Georges
See Simenon, Georges (Jacques Christian)
Simak, Clifford D(onald) 1904-1988**CLC 1, 55**
See also CA 1-4R; 125; CANR 1, 35; DLB 8;
MTCW 1; SATA-Obit 56
Simenon, Georges (Jacques Christian) 1903-
1989   **CLC 1, 2, 3, 8, 18, 47; DAM POP**
See also CA 85-88; 129; CANR 35; DA3; DLB
72; DLBY 89; MTCW 1, 2
Simic, Charles 1938-   **CLC 6, 9, 22, 49, 68;
DAM POET**
See also CA 29-32R; CAAS 4; CANR 12, 33,
52, 61; DA3; DLB 105; MTCW 2
Simmel, Georg 1858-1918   **TCLC 64**
See also CA 157
Simmons, Charles (Paul) 1924-   **CLC 57**
See also CA 89-92; INT 89-92
Simmons, Dan 1948-   **CLC 44; DAM POP**
See also AAYA 16; CA 138; CANR 53, 81
Simmons, James (Stewart Alexander) 1933-
CLC 43
See also CA 105; CAAS 21; DLB 40

Simms, William Gilmore 1806-1870 **NCLC 3**
See also DLB 3, 30, 59, 73
Simon, Carly 1945-   **CLC 26**
See also CA 105
Simon, Claude 1913-1984   **CLC 4, 9, 15, 39;
DAM NOV**
See also CA 89-92; CANR 33; DLB 83; MTCW
1
Simon, (Marvin) Neil 1927-**CLC 6, 11, 31, 39,
70; DAM DRAM**
See also AAYA 32; AITN 1; CA 21-24R; CANR
26, 54; DA3; DLB 7; MTCW 1, 2
Simon, Paul (Frederick) 1941(?)-   **CLC 17**
See also CA 116; 153
Simonon, Paul 1956(?)-   **CLC 30**
Simpson, Harriette
See Arnow, Harriette (Louisa) Simpson
Simpson, Louis (Aston Marantz) 1923-**CLC 4,
7, 9, 32; DAM POET**
See also CA 1-4R; CAAS 4; CANR 1, 61; DLB
5; MTCW 1, 2
Simpson, Mona (Elizabeth) 1957-   **CLC 44**
See also CA 122; 135; CANR 68
Simpson, N(orman) F(rederick) 1919-**CLC 29**
See also CA 13-16R; DLB 13
Sinclair, Andrew (Annandale) 1935- **CLC 2,
14**
See also CA 9-12R; CAAS 5; CANR 14, 38;
DLB 14; MTCW 1
Sinclair, Emil
See Hesse, Hermann
Sinclair, Iain 1943-   **CLC 76**
See also CA 132; CANR 81
Sinclair, Iain MacGregor
See Sinclair, Iain
Sinclair, Irene
See Griffith, D(avid Lewelyn) W(ark)
Sinclair, Mary Amelia St. Clair 1865(?)-1946
See Sinclair, May
See also CA 104
Sinclair, May 1863-1946   **TCLC 3, 11**
See also Sinclair, Mary Amelia St. Clair
See also CA 166; DLB 36, 135
Sinclair, Roy
See Griffith, D(avid Lewelyn) W(ark)
Sinclair, Upton (Beall) 1878-1968 **CLC 1, 11,
15, 63; DA; DAB; DAC; DAM MST, NOV;
WLC**
See also CA 5-8R; 25-28R; CANR 7; CDALB
1929-1941; DA3; DLB 9; INT CANR-7;
MTCW 1, 2; SATA 9
Singer, Isaac
See Singer, Isaac Bashevis
Singer, Isaac Bashevis 1904-1991**CLC 1, 3, 6,
9, 11, 15, 23, 38, 69, 111; DA; DAB; DAC;
DAM MST, NOV; SSC 3; WLC**
See also AAYA 32; AITN 1, 2; CA 1-4R; 134;
CANR 1, 39; CDALB 1941-1968; CLR 1;
DA3; DLB 6, 28, 52; DLBY 91; JRDA;
MAICYA; MTCW 1, 2; SATA 3, 27; SATA-
Obit 68
Singer, Israel Joshua 1893-1944   **TCLC 33**
See also CA 169
Singh, Khushwant 1915-   **CLC 11**
See also CA 9-12R; CAAS 9; CANR 6, 84
Singleton, Ann
See Benedict, Ruth (Fulton)
Sinjohn, John
See Galsworthy, John
Sinyavsky, Andrei (Donatevich) 1925-1997
CLC 8
See also CA 85-88; 159
Sirin, V.

See Nabokov, Vladimir (Vladimirovich)
Sissman, L(ouis) E(dward) 1928-1976 **CLC 9, 18**
See also CA 21-24R; 65-68; CANR 13; DLB 5
Sisson, C(harles) H(ubert) 1914- **CLC 8**
See also CA 1-4R; CAAS 3; CANR 3, 48, 84; DLB 27
Sitwell, Dame Edith 1887-1964 **CLC 2, 9, 67; DAM POET; PC 3**
See also CA 9-12R; CANR 35; CDBLB 1945-1960; DLB 20; MTCW 1, 2
Siwaarmill, H. P.
See Sharp, William
Sjoewall, Maj 1935- **CLC 7**
See also CA 65-68; CANR 73
Sjowall, Maj
See Sjoewall, Maj
Skelton, John 1463-1529 **PC 25**
Skelton, Robin 1925-1997 **CLC 13**
See also AITN 2; CA 5-8R; 160; CAAS 5; CANR 28; DLB 27, 53
Skolimowski, Jerzy 1938- **CLC 20**
See also CA 128
Skram, Amalie (Bertha) 1847-1905 **TCLC 25**
See also CA 165
Skvorecky, Josef (Vaclav) 1924- **CLC 15, 39, 69; DAC; DAM NOV**
See also CA 61-64; CAAS 1; CANR 10, 34, 63; DA3; MTCW 1, 2
Slade, Bernard **CLC 11, 46**
See also Newbound, Bernard Slade
See also CAAS 9; DLB 53
Slaughter, Carolyn 1946- **CLC 56**
See also CA 85-88
Slaughter, Frank G(ill) 1908- **CLC 29**
See also AITN 2; CA 5-8R; CANR 5; INT CANR-5
Slavitt, David R(ytman) 1935- **CLC 5, 14**
See also CA 21-24R; CAAS 3; CANR 41, 83; DLB 5, 6
Slesinger, Tess 1905-1945 **TCLC 10**
See also CA 107; DLB 102
Slessor, Kenneth 1901-1971 **CLC 14**
See also CA 102; 89-92
Slowacki, Juliusz 1809-1849 **NCLC 15**
Smart, Christopher 1722-1771 **LC 3; DAM POET; PC 13**
See also DLB 109
Smart, Elizabeth 1913-1986 **CLC 54**
See also CA 81-84; 118; DLB 88
Smiley, Jane (Graves) 1949- **CLC 53, 76; DAM POP**
See also CA 104; CANR 30, 50, 74; DA3; INT CANR-30
Smith, A(rthur) J(ames) M(arshall) 1902-1980 **CLC 15; DAC**
See also CA 1-4R; 102; CANR 4; DLB 88
Smith, Adam 1723-1790 **LC 36**
See also DLB 104
Smith, Alexander 1829-1867 **NCLC 59**
See also DLB 32, 55
Smith, Anna Deavere 1950- **CLC 86**
See also CA 133
Smith, Betty (Wehner) 1896-1972 **CLC 19**
See also CA 5-8R; 33-36R; DLBY 82; SATA 6
Smith, Charlotte (Turner) 1749-1806 **NCLC 23**
See also DLB 39, 109
Smith, Clark Ashton 1893-1961 **CLC 43**
See also CA 143; CANR 81; MTCW 2
Smith, Dave **CLC 22, 42**
See also Smith, David (Jeddie)
See also CAAS 7; DLB 5

Smith, David (Jeddie) 1942-
See Smith, Dave
See also CA 49-52; CANR 1, 59; DAM POET
Smith, Florence Margaret 1902-1971
See Smith, Stevie
See also CA 17-18; 29-32R; CANR 35; CAP 2; DAM POET; MTCW 1, 2
Smith, Iain Crichton 1928-1998 **CLC 64**
See also CA 21-24R; 171; DLB 40, 139
Smith, John 1580(?)-1631 **LC 9**
See also DLB 24, 30
Smith, Johnston
See Crane, Stephen (Townley)
Smith, Joseph, Jr. 1805-1844 **NCLC 53**
Smith, Lee 1944- **CLC 25, 73**
See also CA 114; 119; CANR 46; DLB 143; DLBY 83; INT 119
Smith, Martin
See Smith, Martin Cruz
Smith, Martin Cruz 1942- **CLC 25; DAM MULT, POP**
See also BEST 89:4; CA 85-88; CANR 6, 23, 43, 65; INT CANR-23; MTCW 2; NNAL
Smith, Mary-Ann Tirone 1944- **CLC 39**
See also CA 118; 136
Smith, Patti 1946- **CLC 12**
See also CA 93-96; CANR 63
Smith, Pauline (Urmson) 1882-1959 **TCLC 25**
Smith, Rosamond
See Oates, Joyce Carol
Smith, Sheila Kaye
See Kaye-Smith, Sheila
Smith, Stevie **CLC 3, 8, 25, 44; PC 12**
See also Smith, Florence Margaret
See also DLB 20; MTCW 2
Smith, Wilbur (Addison) 1933- **CLC 33**
See also CA 13-16R; CANR 7, 46, 66; MTCW 1, 2
Smith, William Jay 1918- **CLC 6**
See also CA 5-8R; CANR 44; DLB 5; MAICYA; SAAS 22; SATA 2, 68
Smith, Woodrow Wilson
See Kuttner, Henry
Smolenskin, Peretz 1842-1885 **NCLC 30**
Smollett, Tobias (George) 1721-1771 **LC 2, 46**
See also CDBLB 1660-1789; DLB 39, 104
Snodgrass, W(illiam) D(e Witt) 1926- **CLC 2, 6, 10, 18, 68; DAM POET**
See also CA 1-4R; CANR 6, 36, 65; DLB 5; MTCW 1, 2
Snow, C(harles) P(ercy) 1905-1980 **CLC 1, 4, 6, 9, 13, 19; DAM NOV**
See also CA 5-8R; 101; CANR 28; CDBLB 1945-1960; DLB 15, 77; DLBD 17; MTCW 1, 2
Snow, Frances Compton
See Adams, Henry (Brooks)
Snyder, Gary (Sherman) 1930- **CLC 1, 2, 5, 9, 32, 120; DAM POET; PC 21**
See also CA 17-20R; CANR 30, 60; DA3; DLB 5, 16, 165, 212; MTCW 2
Snyder, Zilpha Keatley 1927- **CLC 17**
See also AAYA 15; CA 9-12R; CANR 38; CLR 31; JRDA; MAICYA; SAAS 2; SATA 1, 28, 75, 110
Soares, Bernardo
See Pessoa, Fernando (Antonio Nogueira)
Sobh, A.
See Shamlu, Ahmad
Sobol, Joshua **CLC 60**
Socrates 469B.C.-399B.C. **CMLC 27**
Soderberg, Hjalmar 1869-1941 **TCLC 39**
Sodergran, Edith (Irene)

See Soedergran, Edith (Irene)
Soedergran, Edith (Irene) 1892-1923 **TCLC 31**
Softly, Edgar
See Lovecraft, H(oward) P(hillips)
Softly, Edward
See Lovecraft, H(oward) P(hillips)
Sokolov, Raymond 1941- **CLC 7**
See also CA 85-88
Solo, Jay
See Ellison, Harlan (Jay)
Sologub, Fyodor **TCLC 9**
See also Teternikov, Fyodor Kuzmich
Solomons, Ikey Esquir
See Thackeray, William Makepeace
Solomos, Dionysios 1798-1857 **NCLC 15**
Solwoska, Mara
See French, Marilyn
Solzhenitsyn, Aleksandr I(sayevich) 1918- **CLC 1, 2, 4, 7, 9, 10, 18, 26, 34, 78; DA; DAB; DAC; DAM MST, NOV; SSC 32; WLC**
See also AITN 1; CA 69-72; CANR 40, 65; DA3; MTCW 1, 2
Somers, Jane
See Lessing, Doris (May)
Somerville, Edith 1858-1949 **TCLC 51**
See also DLB 135
Somerville & Ross
See Martin, Violet Florence; Somerville, Edith
Sommer, Scott 1951- **CLC 25**
See also CA 106
Sondheim, Stephen (Joshua) 1930- **CLC 30, 39; DAM DRAM**
See also AAYA 11; CA 103; CANR 47, 68
Song, Cathy 1955- **PC 21**
See also CA 154; DLB 169
Sontag, Susan 1933- **CLC 1, 2, 10, 13, 31, 105; DAM POP**
See also CA 17-20R; CANR 25, 51, 74; DA3; DLB 2, 67; MTCW 1, 2
Sophocles 496(?)B.C.-406(?)B.C. **CMLC 2; DA; DAB; DAC; DAM DRAM, MST; DC 1; WLCS**
See also DA3; DLB 176
Sordello 1189-1269 **CMLC 15**
Sorel, Georges 1847-1922 **TCLC 91**
See also CA 118
Sorel, Julia
See Drexler, Rosalyn
Sorrentino, Gilbert 1929- **CLC 3, 7, 14, 22, 40**
See also CA 77-80; CANR 14, 33; DLB 5, 173; DLBY 80; INT CANR-14
Soto, Gary 1952- **CLC 32, 80; DAM MULT; HLC 2; PC 28**
See also AAYA 10; CA 119; 125; CANR 50, 74; CLR 38; DLB 82; HW 1, 2; INT 125; JRDA; MTCW 2; SATA 80
Soupault, Philippe 1897-1990 **CLC 68**
See also CA 116; 147; 131
Souster, (Holmes) Raymond 1921- **CLC 5, 14; DAC; DAM POET**
See also CA 13-16R; CAAS 14; CANR 13, 29, 53; DA3; DLB 88; SATA 63
Southern, Terry 1924(?)-1995 **CLC 7**
See also CA 1-4R; 150; CANR 1, 55; DLB 2
Southey, Robert 1774-1843 **NCLC 8**
See also DLB 93, 107, 142; SATA 54
Southworth, Emma Dorothy Eliza Nevitte 1819-1899 **NCLC 26**
Souza, Ernest
See Scott, Evelyn
Soyinka, Wole 1934- **CLC 3, 5, 14, 36, 44; BLC**

3; DA; DAB; DAC; DAM DRAM, MST, MULT; DC 2; WLC
See also BW 2, 3; CA 13-16R; CANR 27, 39, 82; DA3; DLB 125; MTCW 1, 2

Spackman, W(illiam) M(ode) 1905-1990 **C L C 46**
See also CA 81-84; 132

Spacks, Barry (Bernard) 1931- **CLC 14**
See also CA 154; CANR 33; DLB 105

Spanidou, Irini 1946- **CLC 44**

Spark, Muriel (Sarah) 1918- **CLC 2, 3, 5, 8, 13, 18, 40, 94; DAB; DAC; DAM MST, NOV; SSC 10**
See also CA 5-8R; CANR 12, 36, 76; CDBLB 1945-1960; DA3; DLB 15, 139; INT CANR-12; MTCW 1, 2

Spaulding, Douglas
See Bradbury, Ray (Douglas)

Spaulding, Leonard
See Bradbury, Ray (Douglas)

Spence, J. A. D.
See Eliot, T(homas) S(tearns)

Spencer, Elizabeth 1921- **CLC 22**
See also CA 13-16R; CANR 32, 65; DLB 6; MTCW 1; SATA 14

Spencer, Leonard G.
See Silverberg, Robert

Spencer, Scott 1945- **CLC 30**
See also CA 113; CANR 51; DLBY 86

Spender, Stephen (Harold) 1909-1995 **CLC 1, 2, 5, 10, 41, 91; DAM POET**
See also CA 9-12R; 149; CANR 31, 54; CDBLB 1945-1960; DA3; DLB 20; MTCW 1, 2

Spengler, Oswald (Arnold Gottfried) 1880-1936 **TCLC 25**
See also CA 118

Spenser, Edmund 1552(?)-1599 **LC 5, 39; DA; DAB; DAC; DAM MST, POET; PC 8; WLC**
See also CDBLB Before 1660; DA3; DLB 167

Spicer, Jack 1925-1965 **CLC 8, 18, 72; DAM POET**
See also CA 85-88; DLB 5, 16, 193

Spiegelman, Art 1948- **CLC 76**
See also AAYA 10; CA 125; CANR 41, 55, 74; MTCW 2; SATA 109

Spielberg, Peter 1929- **CLC 6**
See also CA 5-8R; CANR 4, 48; DLBY 81

Spielberg, Steven 1947- **CLC 20**
See also AAYA 8, 24; CA 77-80; CANR 32; SATA 32

Spillane, Frank Morrison 1918-
See Spillane, Mickey
See also CA 25-28R; CANR 28, 63; DA3; MTCW 1, 2; SATA 66

Spillane, Mickey **CLC 3, 13**
See also Spillane, Frank Morrison
See also MTCW 2

Spinoza, Benedictus de 1632-1677 **LC 9**

Spinrad, Norman (Richard) 1940- **CLC 46**
See also CA 37-40R; CAAS 19; CANR 20; DLB 8; INT CANR-20

Spitteler, Carl (Friedrich Georg) 1845-1924 **TCLC 12**
See also CA 109; DLB 129

Spivack, Kathleen (Romola Drucker) 1938- **CLC 6**
See also CA 49-52

Spoto, Donald 1941- **CLC 39**
See also CA 65-68; CANR 11, 57

Springsteen, Bruce (F.) 1949- **CLC 17**
See also CA 111

Spurling, Hilary 1940- **CLC 34**

See also CA 104; CANR 25, 52

Spyker, John Howland
See Elman, Richard (Martin)

Squires, (James) Radcliffe 1917-1993 **CLC 51**
See also CA 1-4R; 140; CANR 6, 21

Srivastava, Dhanpat Rai 1880(?)-1936
See Premchand
See also CA 118

Stacy, Donald
See Pohl, Frederik

Stael, Germaine de 1766-1817
See Stael-Holstein, Anne Louise Germaine Necker Baronn
See also DLB 119

Stael-Holstein, Anne Louise Germaine Necker Baronn 1766-1817 **NCLC 3**
See also Stael, Germaine de
See also DLB 192

Stafford, Jean 1915-1979 **CLC 4, 7, 19, 68; SSC 26**
See also CA 1-4R; 85-88; CANR 3, 65; DLB 2, 173; MTCW 1, 2; SATA-Obit 22

Stafford, William (Edgar) 1914-1993 **CLC 4, 7, 29; DAM POET**
See also CA 5-8R; 142; CAAS 3; CANR 5, 22; DLB 5, 206; INT CANR-22

Stagnelius, Eric Johan 1793-1823 **NCLC 61**

Staines, Trevor
See Brunner, John (Kilian Houston)

Stairs, Gordon
See Austin, Mary (Hunter)

Stairs, Gordon
See Austin, Mary (Hunter)

Stalin, Joseph 1879-1953 **TCLC 92**

Stannard, Martin 1947- **CLC 44**
See also CA 142; DLB 155

Stanton, Elizabeth Cady 1815-1902 **TCLC 73**
See also CA 171; DLB 79

Stanton, Maura 1946- **CLC 9**
See also CA 89-92; CANR 15; DLB 120

Stanton, Schuyler
See Baum, L(yman) Frank

Stapledon, (William) Olaf 1886-1950 **T C L C 22**
See also CA 111; 162; DLB 15

Starbuck, George (Edwin) 1931-1996 **CLC 53; DAM POET**
See also CA 21-24R; 153; CANR 23

Stark, Richard
See Westlake, Donald E(dwin)

Staunton, Schuyler
See Baum, L(yman) Frank

Stead, Christina (Ellen) 1902-1983 **CLC 2, 5, 8, 32, 80**
See also CA 13-16R; 109; CANR 33, 40; MTCW 1, 2

Stead, William Thomas 1849-1912 **TCLC 48**
See also CA 167

Steele, Richard 1672-1729 **LC 18**
See also CDBLB 1660-1789; DLB 84, 101

Steele, Timothy (Reid) 1948- **CLC 45**
See also CA 93-96; CANR 16, 50; DLB 120

Steffens, (Joseph) Lincoln 1866-1936 **T C L C 20**
See also CA 117

Stegner, Wallace (Earle) 1909-1993 **CLC 9, 49, 81; DAM NOV; SSC 27**
See also AITN 1; BEST 90:3; CA 1-4R; 141; CAAS 9; CANR 1, 21, 46; DLB 9, 206; DLBY 93; MTCW 1, 2

Stein, Gertrude 1874-1946 **TCLC 1, 6, 28, 48; DA; DAB; DAC; DAM MST, NOV, POET; PC 18; WLC**

See also CA 104; 132; CDALB 1917-1929; DA3; DLB 4, 54, 86; DLBD 15; MTCW 1, 2

Steinbeck, John (Ernst) 1902-1968 **CLC 1, 5, 9, 13, 21, 34, 45, 75, 124; DA; DAB; DAC; DAM DRAM, MST, NOV; SSC 11; WLC**
See also AAYA 12; CA 1-4R; 25-28R; CANR 1, 35; CDALB 1929-1941; DA3; DLB 7, 9, 212; DLBD 2; MTCW 1, 2; SATA 9

Steinem, Gloria 1934- **CLC 63**
See also CA 53-56; CANR 28, 51; MTCW 1, 2

Steiner, George 1929- **CLC 24; DAM NOV**
See also CA 73-76; CANR 31, 67; DLB 67; MTCW 1, 2; SATA 62

Steiner, K. Leslie
See Delany, Samuel R(ay, Jr.)

Steiner, Rudolf 1861-1925 **TCLC 13**
See also CA 107

Stendhal 1783-1842 **NCLC 23, 46; DA; DAB; DAC; DAM MST, NOV; SSC 27; WLC**
See also DA3; DLB 119

Stephen, Adeline Virginia
See Woolf, (Adeline) Virginia

Stephen, Sir Leslie 1832-1904 **TCLC 23**
See also CA 123; DLB 57, 144, 190

Stephen, Sir Leslie
See Stephen, Sir Leslie

Stephen, Virginia
See Woolf, (Adeline) Virginia

Stephens, James 1882(?)-1950 **TCLC 4**
See also CA 104; DLB 19, 153, 162

Stephens, Reed
See Donaldson, Stephen R.

Steptoe, Lydia
See Barnes, Djuna

Sterchi, Beat 1949- **CLC 65**

Sterling, Brett
See Bradbury, Ray (Douglas); Hamilton, Edmond

Sterling, Bruce 1954- **CLC 72**
See also CA 119; CANR 44

Sterling, George 1869-1926 **TCLC 20**
See also CA 117; 165; DLB 54

Stern, Gerald 1925- **CLC 40, 100**
See also CA 81-84; CANR 28; DLB 105

Stern, Richard (Gustave) 1928- **CLC 4, 39**
See also CA 1-4R; CANR 1, 25, 52; DLBY 87; INT CANR-25

Sternberg, Josef von 1894-1969 **CLC 20**
See also CA 81-84

Sterne, Laurence 1713-1768 **LC 2, 48; DA; DAB; DAC; DAM MST, NOV; WLC**
See also CDBLB 1660-1789; DLB 39

Sternheim, (William Adolf) Carl 1878-1942 **TCLC 8**
See also CA 105; DLB 56, 118

Stevens, Mark 1951- **CLC 34**
See also CA 122

Stevens, Wallace 1879-1955 **TCLC 3, 12, 45; DA; DAB; DAC; DAM MST, POET; PC 6; WLC**
See also CA 104; 124; CDALB 1929-1941; DA3; DLB 54; MTCW 1, 2

Stevenson, Anne (Katharine) 1933- **CLC 7, 33**
See also CA 17-20R; CAAS 9; CANR 9, 33; DLB 40; MTCW 1

Stevenson, Robert Louis (Balfour) 1850-1894 **NCLC 5, 14, 63; DA; DAB; DAC; DAM MST, NOV; SSC 11; WLC**
See also AAYA 24; CDBLB 1890-1914; CLR 10, 11; DA3; DLB 18, 57, 141, 156, 174; DLBD 13; JRDA; MAICYA; SATA 100; YABC 2

Stewart, J(ohn) I(nnes) M(ackintosh) 1906-

Swift, Graham (Colin) 1949-   **CLC 41, 88**
  See also CA 117; 122; CANR 46, 71; DLB 194;
  MTCW 2
Swift, Jonathan 1667-1745   **LC 1, 42; DA;
  DAB; DAC; DAM MST, NOV, POET; PC
  9; WLC**
  See also CDBLB 1660-1789; CLR 53; DA3;
  DLB 39, 95, 101; SATA 19
Swinburne, Algernon Charles 1837-1909
  **TCLC 8, 36; DA; DAB; DAC; DAM MST,
  POET; PC 24; WLC**
  See also CA 105; 140; CDBLB 1832-1890;
  DA3; DLB 35, 57
Swinfen, Ann   **CLC 34**
Swinnerton, Frank Arthur 1884-1982 **CLC 31**
  See also CA 108; DLB 34
Swithen, John
  See King, Stephen (Edwin)
Sylvia
  See Ashton-Warner, Sylvia (Constance)
Symmes, Robert Edward
  See Duncan, Robert (Edward)
Symonds, John Addington 1840-1893 **NCLC
  34**
  See also DLB 57, 144
Symons, Arthur 1865-1945   **TCLC 11**
  See also CA 107; DLB 19, 57, 149
Symons, Julian (Gustave) 1912-1994 **CLC 2,
  14, 32**
  See also CA 49-52; 147; CAAS 3; CANR 3,
  33, 59; DLB 87, 155; DLBY 92; MTCW 1
Synge, (Edmund) J(ohn) M(illington) 1871-
  1909   **TCLC 6, 37; DAM DRAM; DC 2**
  See also CA 104; 141; CDBLB 1890-1914;
  DLB 10, 19
Syruc, J.
  See Milosz, Czeslaw
Szirtes, George 1948-   **CLC 46**
  See also CA 109; CANR 27, 61
Szymborska, Wislawa 1923-   **CLC 99**
  See also CA 154; DA3; DLBY 96; MTCW 2
T. O., Nik
  See Annensky, Innokenty (Fyodorovich)
Tabori, George 1914-   **CLC 19**
  See also CA 49-52; CANR 4, 69
Tagore, Rabindranath 1861-1941 **TCLC 3, 53;
  DAM DRAM, POET; PC 8**
  See also CA 104; 120; DA3; MTCW 1, 2
Taine, Hippolyte Adolphe 1828-1893 **NCLC
  15**
Talese, Gay 1932-   **CLC 37**
  See also AITN 1; CA 1-4R; CANR 9, 58; DLB
  185; INT CANR-9; MTCW 1, 2
Tallent, Elizabeth (Ann) 1954-   **CLC 45**
  See also CA 117; CANR 72; DLB 130
Tally, Ted 1952-   **CLC 42**
  See also CA 120; 124; INT 124
Talvik, Heiti 1904-1947   **TCLC 87**
Tamayo y Baus, Manuel 1829-1898 **NCLC 1**
Tammsaare, A(nton) H(ansen) 1878-1940
  TCLC 27
  See also CA 164
Tam'si, Tchicaya U
  See Tchicaya, Gerald Felix
Tan, Amy (Ruth) 1952- **CLC 59, 120; DAM
  MULT, NOV, POP**
  See also AAYA 9; BEST 89:3; CA 136; CANR
  54; CDALBS; DA3; DLB 173; MTCW 2;
  SATA 75
Tandem, Felix
  See Spitteler, Carl (Friedrich Georg)
Tanizaki, Jun'ichiro 1886-1965 **CLC 8, 14, 28;
  SSC 21**

See also CA 93-96; 25-28R; DLB 180; MTCW
  2
Tanner, William
  See Amis, Kingsley (William)
Tao Lao
  See Storni, Alfonsina
Tarassoff, Lev
  See Troyat, Henri
Tarbell, Ida M(inerva) 1857-1944   **TCLC 40**
  See also CA 122; DLB 47
Tarkington, (Newton) Booth 1869-1946 **TCLC
  9**
  See also CA 110; 143; DLB 9, 102; MTCW 2;
  SATA 17
Tarkovsky, Andrei (Arsenyevich) 1932-1986
  CLC 75
  See also CA 127
Tartt, Donna 1964(?)-   **CLC 76**
  See also CA 142
Tasso, Torquato 1544-1595   **LC 5**
Tate, (John Orley) Allen 1899-1979 **CLC 2, 4,
  6, 9, 11, 14, 24**
  See also CA 5-8R; 85-88; CANR 32; DLB 4,
  45, 63; DLBD 17; MTCW 1, 2
Tate, Ellalice
  See Hibbert, Eleanor Alice Burford
Tate, James (Vincent) 1943-   **CLC 2, 6, 25**
  See also CA 21-24R; CANR 29, 57; DLB 5,
  169
Tavel, Ronald 1940-   **CLC 6**
  See also CA 21-24R; CANR 33
Taylor, C(ecil) P(hilip) 1929-1981   **CLC 27**
  See also CA 25-28R; 105; CANR 47
Taylor, Edward 1642(?)-1729   **LC 11; DA;
  DAB; DAC; DAM MST, POET**
  See also DLB 24
Taylor, Eleanor Ross 1920-   **CLC 5**
  See also CA 81-84; CANR 70
Taylor, Elizabeth 1912-1975   **CLC 2, 4, 29**
  See also CA 13-16R; CANR 9, 70; DLB 139;
  MTCW 1; SATA 13
Taylor, Frederick Winslow 1856-1915 **TCLC
  76**
Taylor, Henry (Splawn) 1942-   **CLC 44**
  See also CA 33-36R; CAAS 7; CANR 31; DLB
  5
Taylor, Kamala (Purnaiya) 1924-
  See Markandaya, Kamala
  See also CA 77-80
Taylor, Mildred D.   **CLC 21**
  See also AAYA 10; BW 1; CA 85-88; CANR
  25; CLR 9, 59; DLB 52; JRDA; MAICYA;
  SAAS 5; SATA 15, 70
Taylor, Peter (Hillsman) 1917-1994 **CLC 1, 4,
  18, 37, 44, 50, 71; SSC 10**
  See also CA 13-16R; 147; CANR 9, 50; DLBY
  81, 94; INT CANR-9; MTCW 1, 2
Taylor, Robert Lewis 1912-1998   **CLC 14**
  See also CA 1-4R; 170; CANR 3, 64; SATA 10
Tchekhov, Anton
  See Chekhov, Anton (Pavlovich)
Tchicaya, Gerald Felix 1931-1988   **CLC 101**
  See also CA 129; 125; CANR 81
Tchicaya U Tam'si
  See Tchicaya, Gerald Felix
Teasdale, Sara 1884-1933   **TCLC 4**
  See also CA 104; 163; DLB 45; SATA 32
Tegner, Esaias 1782-1846   **NCLC 2**
Teilhard de Chardin, (Marie Joseph) Pierre
  1881-1955   **TCLC 9**
  See also CA 105
Temple, Ann
  See Mortimer, Penelope (Ruth)

Tennant, Emma (Christina) 1937- **CLC 13, 52**
  See also CA 65-68; CAAS 9; CANR 10, 38,
  59; DLB 14
Tenneshaw, S. M.
  See Silverberg, Robert
Tennyson, Alfred 1809-1892   **NCLC 30, 65;
  DA; DAB; DAC; DAM MST, POET; PC
  6; WLC**
  See also CDBLB 1832-1890; DA3; DLB 32
Teran, Lisa St. Aubin de   **CLC 36**
  See St. Aubin de Teran, Lisa
Terence c. 184B.C.-c. 159B.C. **CMLC 14; DC 7**
  See also DLB 211
Teresa de Jesus, St. 1515-1582   **LC 18**
Terkel, Louis 1912-
  See Terkel, Studs
  See also CA 57-60; CANR 18, 45, 67; DA3;
  MTCW 1, 2
Terkel, Studs   **CLC 38**
  See also Terkel, Louis
  See also AAYA 32; AITN 1; MTCW 2
Terry, C. V.
  See Slaughter, Frank G(ill)
Terry, Megan 1932-   **CLC 19**
  See also CA 77-80; CABS 3; CANR 43; DLB 7
Tertullian c. 155-c. 245   **CMLC 29**
Tertz, Abram
  See Sinyavsky, Andrei (Donatevich)
Tesich, Steve 1943(?)-1996   **CLC 40, 69**
  See also CA 105; 152; DLBY 83
Tesla, Nikola 1856-1943   **TCLC 88**
Teternikov, Fyodor Kuzmich 1863-1927
  See Sologub, Fyodor
  See also CA 104
Tevis, Walter 1928-1984   **CLC 42**
  See also CA 113
Tey, Josephine   **TCLC 14**
  See also Mackintosh, Elizabeth
  See also DLB 77
Thackeray, William Makepeace 1811-1863
  **NCLC 5, 14, 22, 43; DA; DAB; DAC; DAM
  MST, NOV; WLC**
  See also CDBLB 1832-1890; DA3; DLB 21,
  55, 159, 163; SATA 23
Thakura, Ravindranatha
  See Tagore, Rabindranath
Tharoor, Shashi 1956-   **CLC 70**
  See also CA 141
Thelwell, Michael Miles 1939-   **CLC 22**
  See also BW 2; CA 101
Theobald, Lewis, Jr.
  See Lovecraft, H(oward) P(hillips)
Theodorescu, Ion N. 1880-1967
  See Arghezi, Tudor
  See also CA 116
Theriault, Yves 1915-1983   **CLC 79; DAC;
  DAM MST**
  See also CA 102; DLB 88
Theroux, Alexander (Louis) 1939- **CLC 2, 25**
  See also CA 85-88; CANR 20, 63
Theroux, Paul (Edward) 1941- **CLC 5, 8, 11,
  15, 28, 46; DAM POP**
  See also AAYA 28; BEST 89:4; CA 33-36R;
  CANR 20, 45, 74; CDALBS; DA3; DLB 2;
  MTCW 1, 2; SATA 44, 109
Thesen, Sharon 1946-   **CLC 56**
  See also CA 163
Thevenin, Denis
  See Duhamel, Georges
Thibault, Jacques Anatole Francois 1844-1924
  See France, Anatole
  See also CA 106; 127; DAM NOV; DA3;
  MTCW 1, 2

Thiele, Colin (Milton) 1920- **CLC 17**
    See also CA 29-32R; CANR 12, 28, 53; CLR
    27; MAICYA; SAAS 2; SATA 14, 72
Thomas, Audrey (Callahan) 1935-**CLC 7, 13,
    37, 107; SSC 20**
    See also AITN 2; CA 21-24R; CAAS 19; CANR
    36, 58; DLB 60; MTCW 1
Thomas, Augustus 1857-1934 **TCLC 97**
Thomas, D(onald) M(ichael) 1935- **CLC 13,
    22, 31**
    See also CA 61-64; CAAS 11; CANR 17, 45,
    75; CDBLB 1960 to Present; DA3; DLB 40,
    207; INT CANR-17; MTCW 1, 2
Thomas, Dylan (Marlais) 1914-1953**TCLC 1,
    8, 45; DA; DAB; DAC; DAM DRAM,
    MST, POET; PC 2; SSC 3; WLC**
    See also CA 104; 120; CANR 65; CDBLB
    1945-1960; DA3; DLB 13, 20, 139; MTCW
    1, 2; SATA 60
Thomas, (Philip) Edward 1878-1917 **TCLC
    10; DAM POET**
    See also CA 106; 153; DLB 98
Thomas, Joyce Carol 1938- **CLC 35**
    See also AAYA 12; BW 2, 3; CA 113; 116;
    CANR 48; CLR 19; DLB 33; INT 116;
    JRDA; MAICYA; MTCW 1, 2; SAAS 7;
    SATA 40, 78
Thomas, Lewis 1913-1993 **CLC 35**
    See also CA 85-88; 143; CANR 38, 60; MTCW
    1, 2
Thomas, M. Carey 1857-1935 **TCLC 89**
Thomas, Paul
    See Mann, (Paul) Thomas
Thomas, Piri 1928- **CLC 17; HLCS 2**
    See also CA 73-76; HW 1
Thomas, R(onald) S(tuart) 1913- **CLC 6, 13,
    48; DAB; DAM POET**
    See also CA 89-92; CAAS 4; CANR 30;
    CDBLB 1960 to Present; DLB 27; MTCW 1
Thomas, Ross (Elmore) 1926-1995 **CLC 39**
    See also CA 33-36R; 150; CANR 22, 63
Thompson, Francis Clegg
    See Mencken, H(enry) L(ouis)
Thompson, Francis Joseph 1859-1907**TCLC 4**
    See also CA 104; CDBLB 1890-1914; DLB 19
Thompson, Hunter S(tockton) 1939- **CLC 9,
    17, 40, 104; DAM POP**
    See also BEST 89:1; CA 17-20R; CANR 23,
    46, 74, 77; DA3; DLB 185; MTCW 1, 2
Thompson, James Myers
    See Thompson, Jim (Myers)
Thompson, Jim (Myers) 1906-1977(?)**CLC 69**
    See also CA 140
Thompson, Judith **CLC 39**
Thomson, James 1700-1748 **LC 16, 29, 40;
    DAM POET**
    See also DLB 95
Thomson, James 1834-1882 **NCLC 18; DAM
    POET**
    See also DLB 35
Thoreau, Henry David 1817-1862**NCLC 7, 21,
    61; DA; DAB; DAC; DAM MST; WLC**
    See also CDALB 1640-1865; DA3; DLB 1
Thornton, Hall
    See Silverberg, Robert
Thucydides c. 455B.C.-399B.C. **CMLC 17**
    See also DLB 176
Thurber, James (Grover) 1894-1961 **CLC 5,
    11, 25; DA; DAB; DAC; DAM DRAM,
    MST, NOV; SSC 1**
    See also CA 73-76; CANR 17, 39; CDALB
    1929-1941; DA3; DLB 4, 11, 22, 102;
    MAICYA; MTCW 1, 2; SATA 13

Thurman, Wallace (Henry) 1902-1934**TCLC
    6; BLC 3; DAM MULT**
    See also BW 1, 3; CA 104; 124; CANR 81; DLB
    51
Ticheburn, Cheviot
    See Ainsworth, William Harrison
Tieck, (Johann) Ludwig 1773-1853 **NCLC 5,
    46; SSC 31**
    See also DLB 90
Tiger, Derry
    See Ellison, Harlan (Jay)
Tilghman, Christopher 1948(?)- **CLC 65**
    See also CA 159
Tillinghast, Richard (Williford) 1940-**CLC 29**
    See also CA 29-32R; CAAS 23; CANR 26, 51
Timrod, Henry 1828-1867 **NCLC 25**
    See also DLB 3
Tindall, Gillian (Elizabeth) 1938- **CLC 7**
    See also CA 21-24R; CANR 11, 65
Tiptree, James, Jr. **CLC 48, 50**
    See also Sheldon, Alice Hastings Bradley
    See also DLB 8
Titmarsh, Michael Angelo
    See Thackeray, William Makepeace
**Tocqueville, Alexis (Charles Henri Maurice
    Clerel, Comte) de** 1805-1859**NCLC 7, 63**
Tolkien, J(ohn) R(onald) R(euel) 1892-1973
    **CLC 1, 2, 3, 8, 12, 38; DA; DAB; DAC;
    DAM MST, NOV, POP; WLC**
    See also AAYA 10; AITN 1; CA 17-18; 45-48;
    CANR 36; CAP 2; CDBLB 1914-1945; CLR
    56; DA3; DLB 15, 160; JRDA; MAICYA;
    MTCW 1, 2; SATA 2, 32, 100; SATA-Obit
    24
Toller, Ernst 1893-1939 **TCLC 10**
    See also CA 107; DLB 124
Tolson, M. B.
    See Tolson, Melvin B(eaunorus)
Tolson, Melvin B(eaunorus) 1898(?)-1966
    CLC 36, 105; BLC 3; DAM MULT, POET
    See also BW 1, 3; CA 124; 89-92; CANR 80;
    DLB 48, 76
Tolstoi, Aleksei Nikolaevich
    See Tolstoy, Alexey Nikolaevich
Tolstoy, Alexey Nikolaevich 1882-1945**TCLC
    18**
    See also CA 107; 158
Tolstoy, Count Leo
    See Tolstoy, Leo (Nikolaevich)
Tolstoy, Leo (Nikolaevich) 1828-1910**TCLC 4,
    11, 17, 28, 44, 79; DA; DAB; DAC; DAM
    MST, NOV; SSC 9, 30; WLC**
    See also CA 104; 123; DA3; SATA 26
Tomasi di Lampedusa, Giuseppe 1896-1957
    See Lampedusa, Giuseppe (Tomasi) di
    See also CA 111
Tomlin, Lily **CLC 17**
    See also Tomlin, Mary Jean
Tomlin, Mary Jean 1939(?)-
    See Tomlin, Lily
    See also CA 117
Tomlinson, (Alfred) Charles 1927-**CLC 2, 4, 6,
    13, 45; DAM POET; PC 17**
    See also CA 5-8R; CANR 33; DLB 40
Tomlinson, H(enry) M(ajor) 1873-1958**TCLC
    71**
    See also CA 118; 161; DLB 36, 100, 195
Tonson, Jacob
    See Bennett, (Enoch) Arnold
Toole, John Kennedy 1937-1969 **CLC 19, 64**
    See also CA 104; DLBY 81; MTCW 2
Toomer, Jean 1894-1967**CLC 1, 4, 13, 22; BLC
    3; DAM MULT; PC 7; SSC 1; WLCS**

    See also BW 1; CA 85-88; CDALB 1917-1929;
    DA3; DLB 45, 51; MTCW 1, 2
Torley, Luke
    See Blish, James (Benjamin)
Tornimparte, Alessandra
    See Ginzburg, Natalia
Torre, Raoul della
    See Mencken, H(enry) L(ouis)
Torrence, Ridgely 1874-1950 **TCLC 97**
    See also DLB 54
Torrey, E(dwin) Fuller 1937- **CLC 34**
    See also CA 119; CANR 71
Torsvan, Ben Traven
    See Traven, B.
Torsvan, Benno Traven
    See Traven, B.
Torsvan, Berick Traven
    See Traven, B.
Torsvan, Berwick Traven
    See Traven, B.
Torsvan, Bruno Traven
    See Traven, B.
Torsvan, Traven
    See Traven, B.
Tournier, Michel (Edouard) 1924-**CLC 6, 23,
    36, 95**
    See also CA 49-52; CANR 3, 36, 74; DLB 83;
    MTCW 1, 2; SATA 23
Tournimparte, Alessandra
    See Ginzburg, Natalia
Towers, Ivar
    See Kornbluth, C(yril) M.
Towne, Robert (Burton) 1936(?)- **CLC 87**
    See also CA 108; DLB 44
Townsend, Sue **CLC 61**
    See also Townsend, Susan Elaine
    See also AAYA 28; SATA 55, 93; SATA-Brief
    48
Townsend, Susan Elaine 1946-
    See Townsend, Sue
    See also CA 119; 127; CANR 65; DAB; DAC;
    DAM MST
Townshend, Peter (Dennis Blandford) 1945-
    CLC 17, 42
    See also CA 107
Tozzi, Federigo 1883-1920 **TCLC 31**
    See also CA 160
Traill, Catharine Parr 1802-1899 **NCLC 31**
    See also DLB 99
Trakl, Georg 1887-1914 **TCLC 5; PC 20**
    See also CA 104; 165; MTCW 2
Transtroemer, Tomas (Goesta) 1931-**CLC 52,
    65; DAM POET**
    See also CA 117; 129; CAAS 17
Transtromer, Tomas Gosta
    See Transtroemer, Tomas (Goesta)
Traven, B. (?)-1969 **CLC 8, 11**
    See also CA 19-20; 25-28R; CAP 2; DLB 9,
    56; MTCW 1
Treitel, Jonathan 1959- **CLC 70**
Tremain, Rose 1943- **CLC 42**
    See also CA 97-100; CANR 44; DLB 14
Tremblay, Michel 1942- **CLC 29, 102; DAC;
    DAM MST**
    See also CA 116; 128; DLB 60; MTCW 1, 2
Trevanian **CLC 29**
    See also Whitaker, Rod(ney)
Trevor, Glen
    See Hilton, James
Trevor, William 1928-**CLC 7, 9, 14, 25, 71, 116;
    SSC 21**
    See also Cox, William Trevor
    See also DLB 14, 139; MTCW 2

Trifonov, Yuri (Valentinovich) 1925-1981
CLC 45
See also CA 126; 103; MTCW 1
Trilling, Lionel 1905-1975   CLC 9, 11, 24
See also CA 9-12R; 61-64; CANR 10; DLB 28,
63; INT CANR-10; MTCW 1, 2
Trimball, W. H.
See Mencken, H(enry) L(ouis)
Tristan
See Gomez de la Serna, Ramon
Tristram
See Housman, A(lfred) E(dward)
Trogdon, William (Lewis) 1939-
See Heat-Moon, William Least
See also CA 115; 119; CANR 47; INT 119
Trollope, Anthony 1815-1882 NCLC 6, 33; DA;
DAB; DAC; DAM MST, NOV; SSC 28;
WLC
See also CDBLB 1832-1890; DA3; DLB 21,
57, 159; SATA 22
Trollope, Frances 1779-1863   NCLC 30
See also DLB 21, 166
Trotsky, Leon 1879-1940   TCLC 22
See also CA 118; 167
Trotter (Cockburn), Catharine 1679-1749 LC
8
See also DLB 84
Trout, Kilgore
See Farmer, Philip Jose
Trow, George W. S. 1943-   CLC 52
See also CA 126
Troyat, Henri 1911-   CLC 23
See also CA 45-48; CANR 2, 33, 67; MTCW 1
Trudeau, G(arretson) B(eekman) 1948-
See Trudeau, Garry B.
See also CA 81-84; CANR 31; SATA 35
Trudeau, Garry B.   CLC 12
See also Trudeau, G(arretson) B(eekman)
See also AAYA 10; AITN 2
Truffaut, Francois 1932-1984   CLC 20, 101
See also CA 81-84; 113; CANR 34
Trumbo, Dalton 1905-1976   CLC 19
See also CA 21-24R; 69-72; CANR 10; DLB
26
Trumbull, John 1750-1831   NCLC 30
See also DLB 31
Trundlett, Helen B.
See Eliot, T(homas) S(tearns)
Tryon, Thomas 1926-1991 CLC 3, 11; DAM
POP
See also AITN 1; CA 29-32R; 135; CANR 32,
77; DA3; MTCW 1
Tryon, Tom
See Tryon, Thomas
Ts'ao Hsueh-ch'in 1715(?)-1763   LC 1
Tsushima, Shuji 1909-1948
See Dazai Osamu
See also CA 107
Tsvetaeva (Efron), Marina (Ivanovna) 1892-
1941   TCLC 7, 35; PC 14
See also CA 104; 128; CANR 73; MTCW 1, 2
Tuck, Lily 1938-   CLC 70
See also CA 139
Tu Fu 712-770   PC 9
See also DAM MULT
Tunis, John R(oberts) 1889-1975   CLC 12
See also CA 61-64; CANR 62; DLB 22, 171;
JRDA; MAICYA; SATA 37; SATA-Brief 30
Tuohy, Frank   CLC 37
See also Tuohy, John Francis
See also DLB 14, 139
Tuohy, John Francis 1925-1999
See Tuohy, Frank

See also CA 5-8R; 178; CANR 3, 47
Turco, Lewis (Putnam) 1934-   CLC 11, 63
See also CA 13-16R; CAAS 22; CANR 24, 51;
DLBY 84
Turgenev, Ivan 1818-1883   NCLC 21; DA;
DAB; DAC; DAM MST, NOV; DC 7; SSC
7; WLC
Turgot, Anne-Robert-Jacques 1727-1781 L C
26
Turner, Frederick 1943-   CLC 48
See also CA 73-76; CAAS 10; CANR 12, 30,
56; DLB 40
Tutu, Desmond M(pilo) 1931- CLC 80; BLC 3;
DAM MULT
See also BW 1, 3; CA 125; CANR 67, 81
Tutuola, Amos 1920-1997 CLC 5, 14, 29; BLC
3; DAM MULT
See also BW 2, 3; CA 9-12R; 159; CANR 27,
66; DA3; DLB 125; MTCW 1, 2
Twain, Mark TCLC 6, 12, 19, 36, 48, 59; SSC
34; WLC
See also Clemens, Samuel Langhorne
See also AAYA 20; CLR 58, 60; DLB 11, 12,
23, 64, 74
Tyler, Anne 1941- CLC 7, 11, 18, 28, 44, 59,
103; DAM NOV, POP
See also AAYA 18; BEST 89:1; CA 9-12R;
CANR 11, 33, 53; CDALBS; DLB 6, 143;
DLBY 82; MTCW 1, 2; SATA 7, 90
Tyler, Royall 1757-1826   NCLC 3
See also DLB 37
Tynan, Katharine 1861-1931   TCLC 3
See also CA 104; 167; DLB 153
Tyutchev, Fyodor 1803-1873   NCLC 34
Tzara, Tristan 1896-1963   CLC 47; DAM
POET; PC 27
See also CA 153; 89-92; MTCW 2
Uhry, Alfred 1936-   CLC 55; DAM DRAM,
POP
See also CA 127; 133; DA3; INT 133
Ulf, Haerved
See Strindberg, (Johan) August
Ulf, Harved
See Strindberg, (Johan) August
Ulibarri, Sabine R(eyes) 1919- CLC 83; DAM
MULT; HLCS 2
See also CA 131; CANR 81; DLB 82; HW 1, 2
Unamuno (y Jugo), Miguel de 1864-1936
TCLC 2, 9; DAM MULT, NOV; HLC 2;
SSC 11
See also CA 104; 131; CANR 81; DLB 108;
HW 1, 2; MTCW 1, 2
Undercliffe, Errol
See Campbell, (John) Ramsey
Underwood, Miles
See Glassco, John
Undset, Sigrid 1882-1949 TCLC 3; DA; DAB;
DAC; DAM MST, NOV; WLC
See also CA 104; 129; DA3; MTCW 1, 2
Ungaretti, Giuseppe 1888-1970 CLC 7, 11, 15
See also CA 19-20; 25-28R; CAP 2; DLB 114
Unger, Douglas 1952-   CLC 34
See also CA 130
Unsworth, Barry (Forster) 1930-   CLC 76
See also CA 25-28R; CANR 30, 54; DLB 194
Updike, John (Hoyer) 1932-CLC 1, 2, 3, 5, 7,
9, 13, 15, 23, 34, 43, 70; DA; DAB; DAC;
DAM MST, NOV, POET, POP; SSC 13, 27;
WLC
See also CA 1-4R; CABS 1; CANR 4, 33, 51;
CDALB 1968-1988; DA3; DLB 2, 5, 143;
DLBD 3; DLBY 80, 82, 97; MTCW 1, 2
Upshaw, Margaret Mitchell

See Mitchell, Margaret (Munnerlyn)
Upton, Mark
See Sanders, Lawrence
Upward, Allen 1863-1926   TCLC 85
See also CA 117; DLB 36
Urdang, Constance (Henriette) 1922-CLC 47
See also CA 21-24R; CANR 9, 24
Uriel, Henry
See Faust, Frederick (Schiller)
Uris, Leon (Marcus) 1924- CLC 7, 32; DAM
NOV, POP
See also AITN 1, 2; BEST 89:2; CA 1-4R;
CANR 1, 40, 65; DA3; MTCW 1, 2; SATA
49
Urista, Alberto H. 1947-
See Alurista
See also CA 45-48; CANR 2, 32; HLCS 1; HW
1
Urmuz
See Codrescu, Andrei
Urquhart, Guy
See McAlmon, Robert (Menzies)
Urquhart, Jane 1949-   CLC 90; DAC
See also CA 113; CANR 32, 68
Usigli, Rodolfo 1905-1979
See also CA 131; HLCS 1; HW 1
Ustinov, Peter (Alexander) 1921-   CLC 1
See also AITN 1; CA 13-16R; CANR 25, 51;
DLB 13; MTCW 2
U Tam'si, Gerald Felix Tchicaya
See Tchicaya, Gerald Felix
U Tam'si, Tchicaya
See Tchicaya, Gerald Felix
Vachss, Andrew (Henry) 1942-   CLC 106
See also CA 118; CANR 44
Vachss, Andrew H.
See Vachss, Andrew (Henry)
Vaculik, Ludvik 1926-   CLC 7
See also CA 53-56; CANR 72
Vaihinger, Hans 1852-1933   TCLC 71
See also CA 116; 166
Valdez, Luis (Miguel) 1940- CLC 84; DAM
MULT; DC 10; HLC 2
See also CA 101; CANR 32, 81; DLB 122; HW
1
Valenzuela, Luisa 1938- CLC 31, 104; DAM
MULT; HLCS 2; SSC 14
See also CA 101; CANR 32, 65; DLB 113; HW
1, 2
Valera y Alcala-Galiano, Juan 1824-1905
TCLC 10
See also CA 106
Valery, (Ambroise) Paul (Toussaint Jules) 1871-
1945   TCLC 4, 15; DAM POET; PC 9
See also CA 104; 122; DA3; MTCW 1, 2
Valle-Inclan, Ramon (Maria) del 1866-1936
TCLC 5; DAM MULT; HLC 2
See also CA 106; 153; CANR 80; DLB 134;
HW 2
Vallejo, Antonio Buero
See Buero Vallejo, Antonio
Vallejo, Cesar (Abraham) 1892-1938 TCLC 3,
56; DAM MULT; HLC 2
See also CA 105; 153; HW 1
Valles, Jules 1832-1885   NCLC 71
See also DLB 123
Vallette, Marguerite Eymery
See Rachilde
Valle Y Pena, Ramon del
See Valle-Inclan, Ramon (Maria) del
Van Ash, Cay 1918-   CLC 34
Vanbrugh, Sir John 1664-1726 LC 21; DAM
DRAM

See also DLB 80

Van Campen, Karl
See Campbell, John W(ood, Jr.)

Vance, Gerald
See Silverberg, Robert

Vance, Jack   **CLC 35**
See also Kuttner, Henry; Vance, John Holbrook
See also DLB 8

Vance, John Holbrook 1916-
See Queen, Ellery; Vance, Jack
See also CA 29-32R; CANR 17, 65; MTCW 1

Van Den Bogarde, Derek Jules Gaspard Ulric Niven 1921-1999
See Bogarde, Dirk
See also CA 77-80; 179

Vandenburgh, Jane   **CLC 59**
See also CA 168

Vanderhaeghe, Guy 1951-   **CLC 41**
See also CA 113; CANR 72

van der Post, Laurens (Jan) 1906-1996 **CLC 5**
See also CA 5-8R; 155; CANR 35; DLB 204

van de Wetering, Janwillem 1931-   **CLC 47**
See also CA 49-52; CANR 4, 62

Van Dine, S. S.   **TCLC 23**
See also Wright, Willard Huntington

Van Doren, Carl (Clinton) 1885-1950   **TCLC 18**
See also CA 111; 168

Van Doren, Mark 1894-1972   **CLC 6, 10**
See also CA 1-4R; 37-40R; CANR 3; DLB 45; MTCW 1, 2

Van Druten, John (William) 1901-1957 **TCLC 2**
See also CA 104; 161; DLB 10

Van Duyn, Mona (Jane) 1921-   **CLC 3, 7, 63, 116; DAM POET**
See also CA 9-12R; CANR 7, 38, 60; DLB 5

Van Dyne, Edith
See Baum, L(yman) Frank

van Itallie, Jean-Claude 1936-   **CLC 3**
See also CA 45-48; CAAS 2; CANR 1, 48; DLB 7

van Ostaijen, Paul 1896-1928   **TCLC 33**
See also CA 163

Van Peebles, Melvin 1932- **CLC 2, 20; DAM MULT**
See also BW 2, 3; CA 85-88; CANR 27, 67, 82

Vansittart, Peter 1920-   **CLC 42**
See also CA 1-4R; CANR 3, 49

Van Vechten, Carl 1880-1964   **CLC 33**
See also CA 89-92; DLB 4, 9, 51

Van Vogt, A(lfred) E(lton) 1912-   **CLC 1**
See also CA 21-24R; CANR 28; DLB 8; SATA 14

Varda, Agnes 1928-   **CLC 16**
See also CA 116; 122

Vargas Llosa, (Jorge) Mario (Pedro) 1936-
    CLC 3, 6, 9, 10, 15, 31, 42, 85; DA; DAB; DAC; DAM MST, MULT, NOV; HLC 2
See also CA 73-76; CANR 18, 32, 42, 67; DA3; DLB 145; HW 1, 2; MTCW 1, 2

Vasiliu, Gheorghe 1881-1957
See Bacovia, George
See also CA 123

Vassa, Gustavus
See Equiano, Olaudah

Vassilikos, Vassilis 1933-   **CLC 4, 8**
See also CA 81-84; CANR 75

Vaughan, Henry 1621-1695   **LC 27**
See also DLB 131

Vaughn, Stephanie   **CLC 62**

Vazov, Ivan (Minchov) 1850-1921 **TCLC 25**
See also CA 121; 167; DLB 147

Veblen, Thorstein B(unde) 1857-1929 **TCLC 31**
See also CA 115; 165

Vega, Lope de 1562-1635   **LC 23; HLCS 2**

Venison, Alfred
See Pound, Ezra (Weston Loomis)

Verdi, Marie de
See Mencken, H(enry) L(ouis)

Verdu, Matilde
See Cela, Camilo Jose

Verga, Giovanni (Carmelo) 1840-1922 **TCLC 3; SSC 21**
See also CA 104; 123

Vergil 70B.C.-19B.C.   **CMLC 9; DA; DAB; DAC; DAM MST, POET; PC 12; WLCS**
See also Virgil
See also DA3

Verhaeren, Emile (Adolphe Gustave) 1855-1916 **TCLC 12**
See also CA 109

Verlaine, Paul (Marie) 1844-1896 **NCLC 2, 51; DAM POET; PC 2**

Verne, Jules (Gabriel) 1828-1905 **TCLC 6, 52**
See also AAYA 16; CA 110; 131; DA3; DLB 123; JRDA; MAICYA; SATA 21

Very, Jones 1813-1880   **NCLC 9**
See also DLB 1

Vesaas, Tarjei 1897-1970   **CLC 48**
See also CA 29-32R

Vialis, Gaston
See Simenon, Georges (Jacques Christian)

Vian, Boris 1920-1959   **TCLC 9**
See also CA 106; 164; DLB 72; MTCW 2

Viaud, (Louis Marie) Julien 1850-1923
See Loti, Pierre
See also CA 107

Vicar, Henry
See Felsen, Henry Gregor

Vicker, Angus
See Felsen, Henry Gregor

Vidal, Gore 1925- **CLC 2, 4, 6, 8, 10, 22, 33, 72; DAM NOV, POP**
See also AITN 1; BEST 90:2; CA 5-8R; CANR 13, 45, 65; CDALBS; DA3; DLB 6, 152; INT CANR-13; MTCW 1, 2

Viereck, Peter (Robert Edwin) 1916- **CLC 4; PC 27**
See also CA 1-4R; CANR 1, 47; DLB 5

Vigny, Alfred (Victor) de 1797-1863 **NCLC 7; DAM POET; PC 26**
See also DLB 119, 192

Vilakazi, Benedict Wallet 1906-1947 **TCLC 37**
See also CA 168

Villa, Jose Garcia 1904-1997   **PC 22**
See also CA 25-28R; CANR 12

Villarreal, Jose Antonio 1924-
See also CA 133; DAM MULT; DLB 82; HLC 2; HW 1

Villaurrutia, Xavier 1903-1950   **TCLC 80**
See also HW 1

Villiers de l'Isle Adam, Jean Marie Mathias Philippe Auguste, Comte de 1838-1889 **NCLC 3; SSC 14**
See also DLB 123

Villon, Francois 1431-1463(?)   **PC 13**
See also DLB 208

Vinci, Leonardo da 1452-1519   **LC 12**

Vine, Barbara   **CLC 50**
See also Rendell, Ruth (Barbara)
See also BEST 90:4

Vinge, Joan (Carol) D(ennison) 1948- **CLC 30; SSC 24**
See also AAYA 32; CA 93-96; CANR 72; SATA

36

Violis, G.
See Simenon, Georges (Jacques Christian)

Viramontes, Helena Maria 1954-
See also CA 159; DLB 122; HLCS 2; HW 2

Virgil 70B.C.-19B.C.
See Vergil
See also DLB 211

Visconti, Luchino 1906-1976   **CLC 16**
See also CA 81-84; 65-68; CANR 39

Vittorini, Elio 1908-1966   **CLC 6, 9, 14**
See also CA 133; 25-28R

Vivekananda, Swami 1863-1902   **TCLC 88**

Vizenor, Gerald Robert 1934- **CLC 103; DAM MULT**
See also CA 13-16R; CAAS 22; CANR 5, 21, 44, 67; DLB 175; MTCW 2; NNAL

Vizinczey, Stephen 1933-   **CLC 40**
See also CA 128; INT 128

Vliet, R(ussell) G(ordon) 1929-1984 **CLC 22**
See also CA 37-40R; 112; CANR 18

Vogau, Boris Andreyevich 1894-1937(?)
See Pilnyak, Boris
See also CA 123

Vogel, Paula A(nne) 1951-   **CLC 76**
See also CA 108

Voigt, Cynthia 1942-   **CLC 30**
See also AAYA 3, 30; CA 106; CANR 18, 37, 40; CLR 13, 48; INT CANR-18; JRDA; MAICYA; SATA 48, 79; SATA-Brief 33

Voigt, Ellen Bryant 1943-   **CLC 54**
See also CA 69-72; CANR 11, 29, 55; DLB 120

Voinovich, Vladimir (Nikolaevich) 1932- **CLC 10, 49**
See also CA 81-84; CAAS 12; CANR 33, 67; MTCW 1

Vollmann, William T. 1959-   **CLC 89; DAM NOV, POP**
See also CA 134; CANR 67; DA3; MTCW 2

Voloshinov, V. N.
See Bakhtin, Mikhail Mikhailovich

Voltaire 1694-1778 **LC 14; DA; DAB; DAC; DAM DRAM, MST; SSC 12; WLC**
See also DA3

von Aschendrof, Baron Ignatz
See Ford, Ford Madox

von Daeniken, Erich 1935-   **CLC 30**
See also AITN 1; CA 37-40R; CANR 17, 44

von Daniken, Erich
See von Daeniken, Erich

von Heidenstam, (Carl Gustaf) Verner
See Heidenstam, (Carl Gustaf) Verner von

von Heyse, Paul (Johann Ludwig)
See Heyse, Paul (Johann Ludwig von)

von Hofmannsthal, Hugo
See Hofmannsthal, Hugo von

von Horvath, Odon
See Horvath, Oedoen von

von Horvath, Oedoen
See Horvath, Oedoen von

von Liliencron, (Friedrich Adolf Axel) Detlev
See Liliencron, (Friedrich Adolf Axel) Detlev von

Vonnegut, Kurt, Jr. 1922- **CLC 1, 2, 3, 4, 5, 8, 12, 22, 40, 60, 111; DA; DAB; DAC; DAM MST, NOV, POP; SSC 8; WLC**
See also AAYA 6; AITN 1; BEST 90:4; CA 1-4R; CANR 1, 25, 49, 75; CDALB 1968-1988; DA3; DLB 2, 8, 152; DLBD 3; DLBY 80; MTCW 1, 2

Von Rachen, Kurt
See Hubbard, L(afayette) Ron(ald)

von Rezzori (d'Arezzo), Gregor

See Rezzori (d'Arezzo), Gregor von

von Sternberg, Josef
See Sternberg, Josef von

Vorster, Gordon 1924- **CLC 34**
See also CA 133

Vosce, Trudie
See Ozick, Cynthia

Voznesensky, Andrei (Andreievich) 1933-
CLC 1, 15, 57; DAM POET
See also CA 89-92; CANR 37; MTCW 1

Waddington, Miriam 1917- **CLC 28**
See also CA 21-24R; CANR 12, 30; DLB 68

Wagman, Fredrica 1937- **CLC 7**
See also CA 97-100; INT 97-100

Wagner, Linda W.
See Wagner-Martin, Linda (C.)

Wagner, Linda Welshimer
See Wagner-Martin, Linda (C.)

Wagner, Richard 1813-1883 **NCLC 9**
See also DLB 129

Wagner-Martin, Linda (C.) 1936- **CLC 50**
See also CA 159

Wagoner, David (Russell) 1926- **CLC 3, 5, 15**
See also CA 1-4R; CAAS 3; CANR 2, 71; DLB 5; SATA 14

Wah, Fred(erick James) 1939- **CLC 44**
See also CA 107; 141; DLB 60

Wahloo, Per 1926-1975 **CLC 7**
See also CA 61-64; CANR 73

Wahloo, Peter
See Wahloo, Per

Wain, John (Barrington) 1925-1994 **CLC 2, 11, 15, 46**
See also CA 5-8R; 145; CAAS 4; CANR 23, 54; CDBLB 1960 to Present; DLB 15, 27, 139, 155; MTCW 1, 2

Wajda, Andrzej 1926- **CLC 16**
See also CA 102

Wakefield, Dan 1932- **CLC 7**
See also CA 21-24R; CAAS 7

Wakoski, Diane 1937- **CLC 2, 4, 7, 9, 11, 40; DAM POET; PC 15**
See also CA 13-16R; CAAS 1; CANR 9, 60; DLB 5; INT CANR-9; MTCW 2

Wakoski-Sherbell, Diane
See Wakoski, Diane

Walcott, Derek (Alton) 1930- **CLC 2, 4, 9, 14, 25, 42, 67, 76; BLC 3; DAB; DAC; DAM MST, MULT, POET; DC 7**
See also BW 2; CA 89-92; CANR 26, 47, 75, 80; DA3; DLB 117; DLBY 81; MTCW 1, 2

Waldman, Anne (Lesley) 1945- **CLC 7**
See also CA 37-40R; CAAS 17; CANR 34, 69; DLB 16

Waldo, E. Hunter
See Sturgeon, Theodore (Hamilton)

Waldo, Edward Hamilton
See Sturgeon, Theodore (Hamilton)

Walker, Alice (Malsenior) 1944- **CLC 5, 6, 9, 19, 27, 46, 58, 103; BLC 3; DA; DAB; DAC; DAM MST, MULT, NOV, POET, POP; SSC 5; WLCS**
See also AAYA 3; BEST 89:4; BW 2, 3; CA 37-40R; CANR 9, 27, 49, 66, 82; CDALB 1968-1988; DA3; DLB 6, 33, 143; INT CANR-27; MTCW 1, 2; SATA 31

Walker, David Harry 1911-1992 **CLC 14**
See also CA 1-4R; 137; CANR 1; SATA 8; SATA-Obit 71

Walker, Edward Joseph 1934-
See Walker, Ted
See also CA 21-24R; CANR 12, 28, 53

Walker, George F. 1947- **CLC 44, 61; DAB; DAC; DAM MST**
See also CA 103; CANR 21, 43, 59; DLB 60

Walker, Joseph A. 1935- **CLC 19; DAM DRAM, MST**
See also BW 1, 3; CA 89-92; CANR 26; DLB 38

Walker, Margaret (Abigail) 1915-1998 **CLC 1, 6; BLC; DAM MULT; PC 20**
See also BW 2, 3; CA 73-76; 172; CANR 26, 54, 76; DLB 76, 152; MTCW 1, 2

Walker, Ted **CLC 13**
See also Walker, Edward Joseph
See also DLB 40

Wallace, David Foster 1962- **CLC 50, 114**
See also CA 132; CANR 59; DA3; MTCW 2

Wallace, Dexter
See Masters, Edgar Lee

Wallace, (Richard Horatio) Edgar 1875-1932 **TCLC 57**
See also CA 115; DLB 70

Wallace, Irving 1916-1990 **CLC 7, 13; DAM NOV, POP**
See also AITN 1; CA 1-4R; 132; CAAS 1; CANR 1, 27; INT CANR-27; MTCW 1, 2

Wallant, Edward Lewis 1926-1962 **CLC 5, 10**
See also CA 1-4R; CANR 22; DLB 2, 28, 143; MTCW 1, 2

Wallas, Graham 1858-1932 **TCLC 91**

Walley, Byron
See Card, Orson Scott

Walpole, Horace 1717-1797 **LC 49**
See also DLB 39, 104

Walpole, Hugh (Seymour) 1884-1941 **TCLC 5**
See also CA 104; 165; DLB 34; MTCW 2

Walser, Martin 1927- **CLC 27**
See also CA 57-60; CANR 8, 46; DLB 75, 124

Walser, Robert 1878-1956 **TCLC 18; SSC 20**
See also CA 118; 165; DLB 66

Walsh, Jill Paton **CLC 35**
See also Paton Walsh, Gillian
See also AAYA 11; CLR 2; DLB 161; SAAS 3

Walter, Villiam Christian
See Andersen, Hans Christian

Wambaugh, Joseph (Aloysius, Jr.) 1937- **CLC 3, 18; DAM NOV, POP**
See also AITN 1; BEST 89:3; CA 33-36R; CANR 42, 65; DA3; DLB 6; DLBY 83; MTCW 1, 2

Wang Wei 699(?)-761(?) **PC 18**

Ward, Arthur Henry Sarsfield 1883-1959
See Rohmer, Sax
See also CA 108; 173

Ward, Douglas Turner 1930- **CLC 19**
See also BW 1; CA 81-84; CANR 27; DLB 7, 38

Ward, E. D.
See Lucas, E(dward) V(errall)

Ward, Mary Augusta
See Ward, Mrs. Humphry

Ward, Mrs. Humphry 1851-1920 **TCLC 55**
See also DLB 18

Ward, Peter
See Faust, Frederick (Schiller)

Warhol, Andy 1928(?)-1987 **CLC 20**
See also AAYA 12; BEST 89:4; CA 89-92; 121; CANR 34

Warner, Francis (Robert le Plastrier) 1937- **CLC 14**
See also CA 53-56; CANR 11

Warner, Marina 1946- **CLC 59**
See also CA 65-68; CANR 21, 55; DLB 194

Warner, Rex (Ernest) 1905-1986 **CLC 45**
See also CA 89-92; 119; DLB 15

Warner, Susan (Bogert) 1819-1885 **NCLC 31**
See also DLB 3, 42

Warner, Sylvia (Constance) Ashton
See Ashton-Warner, Sylvia (Constance)

Warner, Sylvia Townsend 1893-1978 **CLC 7, 19; SSC 23**
See also CA 61-64; 77-80; CANR 16, 60; DLB 34, 139; MTCW 1, 2

Warren, Mercy Otis 1728-1814 **NCLC 13**
See also DLB 31, 200

Warren, Robert Penn 1905-1989 **CLC 1, 4, 6, 8, 10, 13, 18, 39, 53, 59; DA; DAB; DAC; DAM MST, NOV, POET; SSC 4; WLC**
See also AITN 1; CA 13-16R; 129; CANR 10, 47; CDALB 1968-1988; DA3; DLB 2, 48, 152; DLBY 80, 89; INT CANR-10; MTCW 1, 2; SATA 46; SATA-Obit 63

Warshofsky, Isaac
See Singer, Isaac Bashevis

Warton, Thomas 1728-1790 **LC 15; DAM POET**
See also DLB 104, 109

Waruk, Kona
See Harris, (Theodore) Wilson

Warung, Price 1855-1911 **TCLC 45**

Warwick, Jarvis
See Garner, Hugh

Washington, Alex
See Harris, Mark

Washington, Booker T(aliaferro) 1856-1915 **TCLC 10; BLC 3; DAM MULT**
See also BW 1; CA 114; 125; DA3; SATA 28

Washington, George 1732-1799 **LC 25**
See also DLB 31

Wassermann, (Karl) Jakob 1873-1934 **TCLC 6**
See also CA 104; 163; DLB 66

Wasserstein, Wendy 1950- **CLC 32, 59, 90; DAM DRAM; DC 4**
See also CA 121; 129; CABS 3; CANR 53, 75; DA3; INT 129; MTCW 2; SATA 94

Waterhouse, Keith (Spencer) 1929- **CLC 47**
See also CA 5-8R; CANR 38, 67; DLB 13, 15; MTCW 1, 2

Waters, Frank (Joseph) 1902-1995 **CLC 88**
See also CA 5-8R; 149; CAAS 13; CANR 3, 18, 63; DLB 212; DLBY 86

Waters, Roger 1944- **CLC 35**

Watkins, Frances Ellen
See Harper, Frances Ellen Watkins

Watkins, Gerrold
See Malzberg, Barry N(athaniel)

Watkins, Gloria 1955(?)-
See hooks, bell
See also BW 2; CA 143; MTCW 2

Watkins, Paul 1964- **CLC 55**
See also CA 132; CANR 62

Watkins, Vernon Phillips 1906-1967 **CLC 43**
See also CA 9-10; 25-28R; CAP 1; DLB 20

Watson, Irving S.
See Mencken, H(enry) L(ouis)

Watson, John H.
See Farmer, Philip Jose

Watson, Richard F.
See Silverberg, Robert

Waugh, Auberon (Alexander) 1939- **CLC 7**
See also CA 45-48; CANR 6, 22; DLB 14, 194

Waugh, Evelyn (Arthur St. John) 1903-1966 **CLC 1, 3, 8, 13, 19, 27, 44, 107; DA; DAB; DAC; DAM MST, NOV, POP; WLC**
See also CA 85-88; 25-28R; CANR 22; CDBLB 1914-1945; DA3; DLB 15, 162, 195; MTCW 1, 2

See also White, Walter
See also BW 1; CA 115; 124; DLB 51
White, William Hale 1831-1913
See Rutherford, Mark
See also CA 121
Whitehead, Alfred North 1861-1947**TCLC 97**
See also CA 117; 165; DLB 100
Whitehead, E(dward) A(nthony) 1933-**CLC 5**
See also CA 65-68; CANR 58
Whitemore, Hugh (John) 1936-   **CLC 37**
See also CA 132; CANR 77; INT 132
Whitman, Sarah Helen (Power) 1803-1878
NCLC 19
See also DLB 1
Whitman, Walt(er) 1819-1892**NCLC 4, 31, 81;**
DA; DAB; DAC; DAM MST, POET; PC
3; WLC
See also CDALB 1640-1865; DA3; DLB 3, 64;
SATA 20
Whitney, Phyllis A(yame) 1903-   **CLC 42;**
DAM POP
See also AITN 2; BEST 90:3; CA 1-4R; CANR
3, 25, 38, 60; CLR 59; DA3; JRDA;
MAICYA; MTCW 2; SATA 1, 30
Whittemore, (Edward) Reed (Jr.) 1919-**CLC 4**
See also CA 9-12R; CAAS 8; CANR 4; DLB 5
Whittier, John Greenleaf 1807-1892**NCLC 8,**
59
See also DLB 1
Whittlebot, Hernia
See Coward, Noel (Peirce)
Wicker, Thomas Grey 1926-
See Wicker, Tom
See also CA 65-68; CANR 21, 46
Wicker, Tom   **CLC 7**
See also Wicker, Thomas Grey
Wideman, John Edgar 1941-**CLC 5, 34, 36, 67,**
122; BLC 3; DAM MULT
See also BW 2, 3; CA 85-88; CANR 14, 42,
67; DLB 33, 143; MTCW 2
Wiebe, Rudy (Henry) 1934-   **CLC 6, 11, 14;**
DAC; DAM MST
See also CA 37-40R; CANR 42, 67; DLB 60
Wieland, Christoph Martin 1733-1813**NCLC**
17
See also DLB 97
Wiene, Robert 1881-1938   **TCLC 56**
Wieners, John 1934-   **CLC 7**
See also CA 13-16R; DLB 16
Wiesel, Elie(zer) 1928- **CLC 3, 5, 11, 37; DA;**
DAB; DAC; DAM MST, NOV; WLCS
See also AAYA 7; AITN 1; CA 5-8R; CAAS 4;
CANR 8, 40, 65; CDALBS; DA3; DLB 83;
DLBY 87; INT CANR-8; MTCW 1, 2; SATA
56
Wiggins, Marianne 1947-   **CLC 57**
See also BEST 89:3; CA 130; CANR 60
Wight, James Alfred 1916-1995
See Herriot, James
See also CA 77-80; SATA 55; SATA-Brief 44
Wilbur, Richard (Purdy) 1921-**CLC 3, 6, 9, 14,**
53, 110; DA; DAB; DAC; DAM MST,
POET
See also CA 1-4R; CABS 2; CANR 2, 29, 76;
CDALBS; DLB 5, 169; INT CANR-29;
MTCW 1, 2; SATA 9, 108
Wild, Peter 1940-   **CLC 14**
See also CA 37-40R; DLB 5
Wilde, Oscar 1854(?)-1900**TCLC 1, 8, 23, 41;**
DA; DAB; DAC; DAM DRAM, MST,
NOV; SSC 11; WLC
See also CA 104; 119; CDBLB 1890-1914;
DA3; DLB 10, 19, 34, 57, 141, 156, 190;

SATA 24
Wilder, Billy   **CLC 20**
See also Wilder, Samuel
See also DLB 26
Wilder, Samuel 1906-
See Wilder, Billy
See also CA 89-92
Wilder, Thornton (Niven) 1897-1975**CLC 1, 5,**
6, 10, 15, 35, 82; DA; DAB; DAC; DAM
DRAM, MST, NOV; DC 1; WLC
See also AAYA 29; AITN 2; CA 13-16R; 61-
64; CANR 40; CDALBS; DA3; DLB 4, 7, 9;
DLBY 97; MTCW 1, 2
Wilding, Michael 1942-   **CLC 73**
See also CA 104; CANR 24, 49
Wiley, Richard 1944-   **CLC 44**
See also CA 121; 129; CANR 71
Wilhelm, Kate   **CLC 7**
See also Wilhelm, Katie Gertrude
See also AAYA 20; CAAS 5; DLB 8; INT
CANR-17
Wilhelm, Katie Gertrude 1928-
See Wilhelm, Kate
See also CA 37-40R; CANR 17, 36, 60; MTCW
1
Wilkins, Mary
See Freeman, Mary Eleanor Wilkins
Willard, Nancy 1936-   **CLC 7, 37**
See also CA 89-92; CANR 10, 39, 68; CLR 5;
DLB 5, 52; MAICYA; MTCW 1; SATA 37,
71; SATA-Brief 30
William of Ockham 1285-1347   **CMLC 32**
Williams, Ben Ames 1889-1953   **TCLC 89**
See also DLB 102
Williams, C(harles) K(enneth) 1936-**CLC 33,**
56; DAM POET
See also CA 37-40R; CAAS 26; CANR 57; DLB
5
Williams, Charles
See Collier, James L(incoln)
Williams, Charles (Walter Stansby) 1886-1945
TCLC 1, 11
See also CA 104; 163; DLB 100, 153
Williams, (George) Emlyn 1905-1987**CLC 15;**
DAM DRAM
See also CA 104; 123; CANR 36; DLB 10, 77;
MTCW 1
Williams, Hank 1923-1953   **TCLC 81**
Williams, Hugo 1942-   **CLC 42**
See also CA 17-20R; CANR 45; DLB 40
Williams, J. Walker
See Wodehouse, P(elham) G(renville)
Williams, John A(lfred) 1925-**CLC 5, 13; BLC**
3; DAM MULT
See also BW 2, 3; CA 53-56; CAAS 3; CANR
6, 26, 51; DLB 2, 33; INT CANR-6
Williams, Jonathan (Chamberlain) 1929-
CLC 13
See also CA 9-12R; CAAS 12; CANR 8; DLB
5
Williams, Joy 1944-   **CLC 31**
See also CA 41-44R; CANR 22, 48
Williams, Norman 1952-   **CLC 39**
See also CA 118
Williams, Sherley Anne 1944-**CLC 89; BLC 3;**
DAM MULT, POET
See also BW 2, 3; CA 73-76; CANR 25, 82;
DLB 41; INT CANR-25; SATA 78
Williams, Shirley
See Williams, Sherley Anne
Williams, Tennessee 1911-1983**CLC 1, 2, 5, 7,**
8, 11, 15, 19, 30, 39, 45, 71, 111; DA; DAB;
DAC; DAM DRAM, MST; DC 4; WLC

See also AAYA 31; AITN 1, 2; CA 5-8R; 108;
CABS 3; CANR 31; CDALB 1941-1968;
DA3; DLB 7; DLBD 4; DLBY 83; MTCW
1, 2
Williams, Thomas (Alonzo) 1926-1990**CLC 14**
See also CA 1-4R; 132; CANR 2
Williams, William C.
See Williams, William Carlos
Williams, William Carlos 1883-1963**CLC 1, 2,**
5, 9, 13, 22, 42, 67; DA; DAB; DAC; DAM
MST, POET; PC 7; SSC 31
See also CA 89-92; CANR 34; CDALB 1917-
1929; DA3; DLB 4, 16, 54, 86; MTCW 1, 2
Williamson, David (Keith) 1942-   **CLC 56**
See also CA 103; CANR 41
Williamson, Ellen Douglas 1905-1984
See Douglas, Ellen
See also CA 17-20R; 114; CANR 39
Williamson, Jack   **CLC 29**
See also Williamson, John Stewart
See also CAAS 8; DLB 8
Williamson, John Stewart 1908-
See Williamson, Jack
See also CA 17-20R; CANR 23, 70
Willie, Frederick
See Lovecraft, H(oward) P(hillips)
Willingham, Calder (Baynard, Jr.) 1922-1995
CLC 5, 51
See also CA 5-8R; 147; CANR 3; DLB 2, 44;
MTCW 1
Willis, Charles
See Clarke, Arthur C(harles)
Willis, Fingal O'Flahertie
See Wilde, Oscar
Willy
See Colette, (Sidonie-Gabrielle)
Willy, Colette
See Colette, (Sidonie-Gabrielle)
Wilson, A(ndrew) N(orman) 1950-   **CLC 33**
See also CA 112; 122; DLB 14, 155, 194;
MTCW 2
Wilson, Angus (Frank Johnstone) 1913-1991
CLC 2, 3, 5, 25, 34; SSC 21
See also CA 5-8R; 134; CANR 21; DLB 15,
139, 155; MTCW 1, 2
Wilson, August 1945-   **CLC 39, 50, 63, 118;**
BLC 3; DA; DAB; DAC; DAM DRAM,
MST, MULT; DC 2; WLCS
See also AAYA 16; BW 2, 3; CA 115; 122;
CANR 42, 54, 76; DA3; MTCW 1, 2
Wilson, Brian 1942-   **CLC 12**
Wilson, Colin 1931-   **CLC 3, 14**
See also CA 1-4R; CAAS 5; CANR 1, 22, 33,
77; DLB 14, 194; MTCW 1
Wilson, Dirk
See Pohl, Frederik
Wilson, Edmund 1895-1972**CLC 1, 2, 3, 8, 24**
See also CA 1-4R; 37-40R; CANR 1, 46; DLB
63; MTCW 1, 2
Wilson, Ethel Davis (Bryant) 1888(?)-1980
CLC 13; DAC; DAM POET
See also CA 102; DLB 68; MTCW 1
Wilson, John 1785-1854   **NCLC 5**
Wilson, John (Anthony) Burgess 1917-1993
See Burgess, Anthony
See also CA 1-4R; 143; CANR 2, 46; DAC;
DAM NOV; DA3; MTCW 1, 2
Wilson, Lanford 1937- **CLC 7, 14, 36; DAM**
DRAM
See also CA 17-20R; CABS 3; CANR 45; DLB
7
Wilson, Robert M. 1944-   **CLC 7, 9**
See also CA 49-52; CANR 2, 41; MTCW 1

Literary Criticism Series
Cumulative Topic Index

This index lists all topic entries in Gale's *Classical and Medieval Literature Criticism, Contemporary Literary Criticism, Literature Criticism from 1400 to 1800, Nineteenth-Century Literature Criticism,* and *Twentieth-Century Literary Criticism*

Topic Index

Topic Index

LC Cumulative Nationality Index

LC Cumulative Title Index

Title Index

Title Index

Title Index

Title Index

Title Index

Title Index

Title Index

Title Index

Title Index

Title Index

Title Index

Title Index

Title Index

Title Index

Title Index

ISBN 0-7876-3268-6

90000

9 780787 632687